FINANCIAL REPORTS

CASH FLOW ANALYSIS
CHAPTERS 4, 6, & 17

SUSTAINABLE EARNINGS & CASH FLOW FORECASTS
CHAPTERS 5, 6, & 7

DECISIONS:

- **DESIGNING FINANCIAL CONTRACTS**
- **VALUATION & INVESTMENT**
- **EVALUATING AUDIT RISKS**
- **CREDIT ANALYSIS & RISK ASSESSMENT**

www.prenhall.com/revsine

THIRD EDITION

Financial Reporting and Analysis

Lawrence Revsine

*John and Norma Darling
Distinguished Professor of Financial Accounting
Kellogg Graduate School of Management, Northwestern University*

Daniel W. Collins

*Henry B. Tippie Research Chair in Accounting
Tippie College of Business
The University of Iowa*

W. Bruce Johnson

*Arthur Andersen Professor of Accounting
Tippie College of Business
The University of Iowa*

PEARSON

Prentice Hall

Prentice Hall
Upper Saddle River, NJ 07458

Library of Congress Cataloging-in-Publication Data
Revsine, Lawrence.
    Financial reporting & analysis / Lawrence Revsine, Daniel W. Collins, W. Bruce
Johnson—3rd ed.
      p. cm.
    Includes bibliographical references and index.
    ISBN 0-13-143021-1
    1. Financial statements. 2. Financial statements—Case studies. 3. Corporations—
Accounting. I. Title: Financial reporting and analysis. II. Collins, Daniel W. III. Johnson,
W. Bruce. IV. Title.

HF5681.B2R398 2004
657'.3—dc22   2004046655

Acquisitions Editor: Bill Larkin
VP/Editorial Director: Jeff Shelstad
Assistant Editor: Sam Goffinett
Senior Editorial Assistant: Jane Avery
Development Editors: Mike Elia and Amy Ray
Senior Media Project Manager: Nancy Welcher
Executive Marketing Manager: Beth Toland
Marketing Assistant: Melissa Owens
Managing Editor (Production): Cynthia Regan
Production Assistant: Joe DeProspero
Production Manager: Arnold Vila
Design Director: Maria Lange
Art Director: Blair Brown
Interior/Cover Design: Blair Brown
Illustrator (Interior): ElectraGraphics, Inc.
Print Production Liaison: Ashley Scattergood
Composition/Full-Service Project Management: GGS Book Services, Atlantic Highlands
Printer/Binder: R.R. Donnelley/Willard
Typeface: 10/13.5 Minion

Credits and acknowledgments borrowed from other sources and reproduced, with permission, in this textbook appear on appropriate page within the text. Where indicated, chapter-end problems and exercises were adapted from various CPA and CMA exams. Copyright © by the American Institute of Certified Public Accountants, Inc. Adapted by permission. Adapted with permission of the Institute of Certified Management Accountants (ICMA). CFA problems were also adapted.

The information contained in this publication is of broad general usefulness to the accounting student and to those with an interest in accounting practices. However, it is sold with the understanding that the Publisher and the Authors are not engaged in rendering legal, accounting, investment, or other professional services or advice. The examples used in this publication, and the references to or opinions expressed about financial reporting practices or companies identified in this book, are intended to serve educational purposes, including encouraging classroom discussion, and are not intended to serve as examples of effective or ineffective, or good or poor management practices.

Pearson Education LTD.
Pearson Education Singapore, Pte. Ltd
Pearson Education, Canada, Ltd
Pearson Education–Japan

Pearson Education Australia PTY, Limited
Pearson Education North Asia Ltd
Pearson Educación de Mexico, S.A. de C.V.
Pearson Education Malaysia, Pte. Ltd

10 9 8 7 6 5 4 3 2 1
ISBN 0-13-143021-1

Dedicated to our Families

Barbara, Pamela, David, Michele, and Meredith (LR)

In memory of my late wife, Mary, and my daughters Melissa, and Theresa (DC)

Diane, Cory Elizabeth, Mason, and Mia (WBJ)

About the Authors

Lawrence Revsine

John and Norma Darling Distinguished Professor of Financial Accounting. Kellogg Graduate School of Management, Northwestern University, BS 1963, MBA 1965, Ph.D. 1968, Northwestern University; CPA 1963

Lawrence Revsine joined the Kellogg faculty in 1971 and served as chair of the Accounting Information and Management Department for eight years.

The author of several books on various financial reporting issues, he has had approximately 50 articles published in leading academic journals.

His academic recognitions include participation in three American Accounting Association Doctoral Consortia. He has received both Ford Foundation and Peat Marwick Mitchell Foundation research grants. He was selected the American Accounting Association's Distinguished Overseas Lecturer, and the AAA named him the 1992 Outstanding Educator. The Illinois CPA Society designated Revsine its 1993 Outstanding Educator. Professor Revsine received the Alumni Choice Faculty Award from the 1995 Reunion Classes; this award is given to the Kellogg faculty member who has had the greatest impact on their professional and personal lives.

Professor Revsine has been a consultant to the American Institute of Certified Public Accountants, the Securities and Exchange Commission, and the Financial Accounting Standards Board and served on the Financial Accounting Standards Advisory Council.

He is a consultant to industry on external reporting issues and regulatory cases and has taught extensively in management development and continuing executive education programs in the United States and abroad. Professor Revsine has received numerous commendations for teaching excellence, including Teacher of the Year from the Kellogg Graduate Management Association student group, and the Sidney J. Levy Teaching Award, presented by the Kellogg Dean's Office.

Daniel W. Collins

Henry B. Tippie Research Chair in Accounting, Tippie College of Business, The University of Iowa. BBA 1968, Ph.D. 1973, The University of Iowa

Winner of the University of Iowa Board of Regents Award for Faculty Excellence in 2000 and the American Accounting Association's Outstanding Educator Award in 2001, Professor Collins' research focuses on the role of accounting numbers in equity valuation, earnings management and the relation between firms' corporate governance mechanisms and cost of equity and debt financing. A prolific writer and frequent contributor to the top academic accounting journals, Collins has been recognized as one of the top ten most highly cited authors in the accounting literature over the last 20 years.

Professor Collins is on the editorial review boards of the Journal of Accounting Research and the Journal of Accounting and Economics. He has also served as Associate Editor of The Accounting Review and as Director of Publications for the American Accounting Association (AAA). Professor Collins has served on numerous AAA committees including the Financial Accounting Standards Committee and has chaired the Publications Committee, the National Program Committee, and the Doctoral Consortium Committee. He also served on the Financial Accounting Standards Advisory Council from 1994–1997.

A member of the American Accounting Association and an invited member of Accounting Researchers International Association, Collins is a frequent presenter at research colloquia, conferences, and doctoral consortia. He has also received outstanding teaching awards at both Michigan State University and The University of Iowa.

W. Bruce Johnson

Arthur Andersen Professor of Accounting, Tippie College of Business, The University of Iowa. BS 1970, University of Oregon, MS 1973, Ph.D. 1975, The Ohio State University.

W. Bruce Johnson joined the University of Iowa faculty in 1988 and has served as director of its McGladrey Institute for Accounting Education and Research, accounting group chairman, and associate dean for graduate programs, where he was responsible for Iowa's MBA and Executive MBA programs.

Professor Johnson has previously held faculty appointments at the University of Wisconsin, Northwestern University, and the University of Chicago.

His teaching and research interests include corporate financial reporting, financial analysis, value-driven management systems and investment strategies, and executive compensation practices. He has received the Gilbert P. Maynard Award for Excellence in Accounting Instruction, and the Chester A. Phillips Outstanding Professor Award.

A well-respected author, Professor Johnson's articles have appeared in numerous scholarly publications and in academic and professional journals. He has served on editorial boards of more than a dozen academic journals. Professor Johnson has also served as a research consultant to the Financial Accounting Standards Board, and on the Research Advisory, Professional Practice Quality and Outstanding Educator committees of the American Accounting Association. He is a member of the American Accounting Association, the Financial Executives Institute, and was formerly Senior Vice President for Equity Strategy at SCI Capital Management, a money management firm.

Brief Contents

End-of-Chapter material includes Exercises, Problems/Discussion Questions, and Cases

Contents

Chapter 12 Financial Reporting
for Leases   631

Chapter 13 Income Tax Reporting   687

Chapter 14 Pensions and Postretirement
Benefits   749

Preface

Consistent with the mandates of the Accounting Education Change Commission (AECC), our objective in writing *Financial Reporting and Analysis*, Third Edition, is to change the way the second-level course in financial accounting is taught, both to graduate and undergraduate students. Typically this course—often called Intermediate Accounting—focuses on the details of GAAP with little emphasis on understanding the economics of transactions or how statement readers use the resultant numbers for decision making. Traditional intermediate texts are encyclopedic in nature and approach, emphasizing the accounting process and the myriad of arcane accounting rules and procedures that comprise GAAP.

In contrast, the goal of our book is to develop a "critical thinking" approach to financial accounting and reporting. We seek to develop students' understanding of the environment in which financial reporting choices are made, what the options are, how these data are used for various types of decisions, and—most importantly—how to avoid misusing financial statement data. We convey the exciting nature of financial reporting in two stages. First, we provide a framework for understanding management's accounting choices and how the accounting affects reported financial numbers. Business contracts—like loan agreements and management compensation agreements—are usually linked to accounting numbers. We show how this often creates incentives for managers to exploit the flexibility in GAAP to "manage" reported accounting numbers to benefit themselves as well as shareholders. Second, we use real-world financial reports and events to illustrate vividly how GAAP alternatives and subjective accounting estimates give managers discretion in the timing of earnings and in reporting the components of financial position.

The approach adopted in this book integrates the perspectives of accounting, corporate finance, economics, and critical analysis to help students grasp how business transactions get reported and understand their decision implications. In this approach, we cover all of the core topics of intermediate accounting by first describing the business transactions that affect various accounts, the technical details of GAAP, how these rules are applied in practice, and what the financial statements look like. Then we go a step further and ask: What do the reported numbers mean? Does the accounting process yield numbers that accurately reflect the underlying economic situation of a company? And, if not, what can statement users do to overcome this limitation in order to make more informed decisions?

Our book is aimed not only at those charged with the responsibility for preparing financial statements, but also at those who will use financial statements for making decisions. Our definition of "users" is broad and includes lenders, equity analysts, investment bankers, boards of directors, and others charged with monitoring corporate performance and the behavior of management. As such, it includes auditors who establish audit scope and conduct analytical review procedures to spot problem areas in external financial statements. Statement on Auditing Standards (SAS) 99, "Consideration of Fraud in a Financial Statement Audit," stresses that auditors must act as "financial detectives" to uncover financial reporting irregularities. It further states that "the auditor should conduct the engagement with a mindset that recognizes the possibility that a material misstatement due to fraud could be present . . . " (p. 10). To do this effectively requires an understanding of the incentives of managers, how the flexibility of GAAP can sometimes be exploited to conceal rather than reveal financial truth, and the potential danger signals that should be investigated. Our intent is to help readers learn how to perform better audits, improve cash flow forecasts, undertake realistic valuations, conduct better comparative analyses, and make more informed judgments about the performance of management.

Financial Reporting and Analysis, Third Edition, provides instructors with the teaching/learning approach for achieving many of the goals stressed by the Accounting Education Change Commission. Specifically, our book is designed to instill capacities for: 1) thinking in an abstract, logical manner, 2) solving unstructured problems, 3) understanding the determining forces behind management's accounting choices, and 4) encouraging an integrated, cross-disciplinary view of financial reporting. Text discussions were written, and exercises, problems, and cases were carefully chosen to help achieve these objectives. **But the book achieves these AECC goals without sacrificing technical underpinnings.** Throughout, we explain in detail where the numbers come from, what measurement rules are used, and how they are entered into the accounting records. We have strived to provide a comprehensive user-oriented focus while simultaneously helping students build a strong technical foundation.

Key Changes from the Second Edition

The first two editions of our book have been widely adopted in accounting departments at business schools throughout the United States, Canada, Europe, and the Pacific Rim. Our book has been used successfully at both the graduate and undergraduate levels as well as in investment banking, commercial lending, and other corporate training programs. Many of our colleagues who used the first two editions have provided us with valuable feedback. Based on their input, we have made a number of changes in this edition of the book to achieve more effectively the objectives outlined above. Key changes include the following:

■ Expanded end-of-chapter problem material spanning a wider range of difficulty. Accessible "stepping stone" exercises and problems have been added at the end of each chapter to reinforce basic concepts.

International

Analysis

Valuation

Contracting

■ More international examples and discussion of International Financial Reporting Standards (IFRS) are interspersed throughout the book.

■ Special "Getting Behind the Numbers" icons are used to highlight and link discussions in later chapters back to the analysis, valuation, and contracting framework set forth in Chapters 5, 6, and 7.

■ New, rich, in-text examples provide students with insights about the Sarbanes-Oxley Act and recent accounting scandals including Adelphia Communications, Enron, Worldcom, Sunbeam, and Xerox. The financial reporting practices of scores of other real companies are illustrated throughout the text and are used extensively in end-of-chapter material.

■ Expanded use of charts, decision diagrams, and data displays serve to enhance student understanding.

Chapter Highlights:

■ Chapter 1, "Economic and Institutional Setting," opens with a Worldcom vignette that highlights the importance of understanding accounting rules and analyzing financial statement figures. The major provisions of the Sarbanes-Oxley Act are discussed along with the responsibilities of the Public Company Accounting Oversight Board.

■ Chapter 2, "Accrual Accounting and Income Determination," contains a revised discussion and illustration of accounting for discontinued operations to reflect the new reporting requirements of *SFAS No. 144*. There is an expanded discussion of "Extraordinary Items," the reporting of gains and losses on early debt retirement under *SFAS No. 145*, and illustrations of earnings per share disclosures.

■ Chapter 3, "Additional Topics in Income Determination" includes a new discussion and illustration of accounting for franchise sales, sales with right of return, and bundled (software) sales. Also added is an overview of accounting errors, earnings restatements, and prior period adjustments.

- Chapter 4, "Structure of the Balance Sheet and Statement of Cash Flows," contains an expanded discussion and illustration of the cash flow statement.

- Chapter 5, "Essentials of Financial Statement Analysis," contains an expanded discussion of credit analysis and default risk, including an appendix on bankruptcy prediction. This chapter also presents a more extensive treatment of earnings quality and financial statement analysis.

- Chapter 6, "The Role of Financial Information in Valuation," incorporates new material on valuation that has been made more accessible by use of simple examples. A new section describes how accountants and auditors use valuation models in estimating goodwill impairment as required by *SFAS No. 142*. A new appendix describes how financial statement forecasts are formed.

- Chapter 7, "The Role of Financial Information in Contracting," has been rewritten to make the material more accessible for students. The chapter provides an expanded discussion of executive pay at a real company—Computer Associates.

- Chapter 8, "Receivables," now includes an example that illustrates the ratio effects of securitizations. There is also a new appendix on the time value of money.

- Chapter 9, "Inventories," contains an expanded example infused throughout the chapter to tie concepts related to inventory accounting together. A short Intel example showing the potential time-series distortions of absorption cost accounting has been added.

- Chapter 10, "Long-Lived Assets and Depreciation," has an expanded discussion of the financial statement effects of interest capitalization using a real company example. New examples are provided illustrating the *SFAS No. 144* reporting rules for "Accounting for the Impairment or Disposal of Long-lived Assets." A new section has been added on accounting for exchanges of assets that incorporates the December 2003 FASB Exposure Draft.

- Chapter 11, "Financial Instruments as Liabilities," has an expanded discussion of current liabilities and balance sheet classifications issues using Oracle Corporation. A new section has been added on "imputed interest" and installment notes and there is an expanded discussion of contingent liabilities.

- Chapter 12, "Financial Reporting for Leases," contains an expanded discussion of guaranteed versus unguaranteed residual values and sale/leaseback accounting. The financial statement distortions arising from telecom line capacity swaps are also covered.

- Chapter 13, "Income Tax Reporting," has been updated with new tax footnote disclosures from actual company reports, and we have expanded the discussion of analytical insights that can be gleaned from tax footnote disclosures.

- Chapter 14, "Pensions and Postretirement Benefits," contains an expanded discussion of the minimum pension liability disclosures using AMR Corporation's pension footnotes. The chapter also contains a new self-study problem illustrating how pension obligations and the elements of pension expense are computed.

- Chapter 15, "Financial Reporting for Owners' Equity," describes the ongoing debate about employee stock options and the likely new GAAP rules requiring that they be expensed. The chapter also contains an expanded discussion of convertible debt and pending changes to GAAP rules for convertible securities.

- Chapter 16, "Intercorporate Equity Investments," contains a new discussion of accounting for business combinations under *SFAS No. 141* and new discussion and illustration of accounting for goodwill impairment under *SFAS No. 142*. A new section has been added on special purpose or variable interest entities.

- Chapter 17, "Statement of Cash Flows," contains a simplified discussion of why changes in working capital balance sheet accounts do not correspond to adjustments to accrual earnings to arrive at operating cash flows shown on the cash flow statement. It also contains a new Analytical Insights section that discusses "cash burn rates" and "time to burnout" measures for Internet and start-up companies.

- Chapter 18, "Overview of International Financial Reporting Differences and Inflation," contains a totally new discussion of international financial reporting standards and the increasingly important role of the International Accounting Standards Board (IASB). This chapter also contains an expanded discussion of the SEC's conditions for accepting international financial reporting standards in filings with the commission.

Acknowledgments

Colleagues at Iowa and Northwestern have shared insights and provided many helpful comments. These individuals are Mark Finn, Robert Magee, Morton Pincus, Robert Hartman, and Shyam V. Sunder. Former colleagues and doctoral students who provided feedback are Rachel Hayes (University of Chicago), Elizabeth Keating (Harvard) Reuven Lehavy (University of Michigan), Kin Lo (University of British Columbia), K. Ramesh (Michigan State University), Srinivasan Rangan (University of Colorado, Boulder), Leonard Soffer (University of Illinois, Chicago), Ramu Thiagarajan (Mellon Capital Management Corporation), and Charles Wasley (University of Rochester). We also wish to thank Daniel Cohen, Emre Karaoglu, Meredith Maher, and the thousands of other former M.B.A. and Ph.D. students who patiently raised issues and helped us communicate more straightforwardly.

Several colleagues at other universities have served as a sounding board on a wide range of issues over the past years and their input has helped us improve this book. In particular we thank Norman Bartczak (Columbia University), James Boatsman (Arizona State University), Thomas Linsmeier (Michigan State), and Stephen Zeff (Rice University). We also greatly appreciate the insight we received from the late Michael J. Murphy (First Chicago Bank) and Stephen Scheetz (Bank of America), which helped shape the financial-analytical focus of this book.

We are grateful to many users of prior editions of our book whose constructive comments and suggestions have contributed to an improved and expanded third edition. In particular, we wish to thank the following people for their valuable input:

Mark P. Bauman *University of Illinois-Chicago*	Florence R. Kirk *SUNY-Oswego*	Robert Magee *Northwestern University*
Frank J. Beil *University of Minnesota*	Andrew J. Leone *University of Rochester*	Eric Press *Temple University*
Mahendra R. Gujarathi *Bentley College*	Brian Leventhal *University of Illinois-Chicago*	Thomas L. Stober *University of Notre Dame*
Robert Hartman *University of Iowa*	Thomas Linsmeier *Michigan State University*	Gary Taylor *University of Alabama*
Rachel Hayes *University of Chicago*	Robert Lipe *University of Oklahoma*	John Twombly *Illinois Institute of Technology*
Ole-Kristian Hope *University of Toronto*	Kin Lo *University of British Columbia*	Paul Zarowin *New York University*
Elizabeth Keating *Harvard University*	The late Arijit Mukherji *University of Minnesota*	Stephen A. Zeff *Rice University*

We appreciate the contributions to the exercises, problems and cases made by Hollis Ashbaugh (University of Wisconsin), James Boatsman (Arizona State University), Kevin Den Adel (Central College), Mark Finn (Northwestern University), Robert Hartman (University of Iowa), Sheila Handy (Lafayette College), Robert Magee (Northwestern University), Barbara Muller (Arizona State–West), K. Ramesh (Michigan State University), Lynn Stallworth (Southeastern Louisiana University), Charles Wasley (University of Rochester) and Stephen D. Willits (Bucknell University).

We thank Daniel Cohen and Bei Huang whose diligence and care in preparing various aspects of the book were most helpful. We also wish to thank Bonnie Lee, whose help and unfailing good humor kept the book on schedule.

Finally, we thank Cynthia Regan, our Pearson-Prentice Hall managing editor for her help in making the third edition of this book a reality.

Our goal in writing this book was to improve the way financial reporting is taught and mastered. We would appreciate receiving your comments and suggestions.

—*Lawrence Revsine*   —*Daniel W. Collins*   —*W. Bruce Johnson*

The Textbook's Accessories

This edition offers instructors a greatly expanded and improved package of supplements. To learn more about these supplements, visit the Revsine/Collins/Johnson Accounting website at **www.prenhall.com/revsine**, contact your Prentice Hall sales representative, or call the Accounting and Tax Hotline at 1-800-227-1816.

Instructor Resources

Instructor's Resource Center ◆ Conveniently located at **www.prenhall.com/revsine**, instructors can easily download all faculty supplements directly from the prenhall.com catalog page.

IRC on CD ◆ Containing all ancillaries on one disk, the IRC on CD provides a wealth of information and resources for instructors looking to streamline classroom presentations. With features such as a search function and 'on-the-fly' resource silos.

Teaching Transparencies ◆ Available on the IRC and IRC on CD, a complete, full-color set of every figure and exhibit in the text.

Solutions Manual ◆ Prepared by the text authors, this extensive ancillary provides detailed solutions for every end-of-chapter assignment. The manual is designed in large font for easy conversion to overheads that can be used in the classroom.

Instructor's Resource Manual ◆ Written by Michael Gallagher of Defiance College, this manual contains chapter overviews, outlines, and questions and answers. It also includes teaching tips and suggested readings to enhance your lectures and discussion groups.

Test Item File ◆ Completely revised by Fred Mittelstaedt of The University of Notre Dame, Benjamin Segal of The University of California at Davis, and Charles Fazzi of St. Vincent College, this new test bank includes a variety of examination questions to test students' grasp of chapter-by-chapter concepts and applications.

TestGen Testing Software ◆ This is the computerized version of the Test Item File that enables you to create your own exams, as well as evaluate and track student results.
 Sample syllabi are also available on the website at **www.prenhall.com/revsine**.

Student Resources

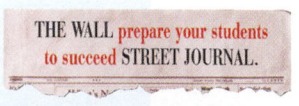

NEW! ◆ Give your students 10 weeks of both the print AND online editions of the Wall Street Journal for only $12.00 net when they purchase a special version of the text (new texts only) with subscription card. All faculty requiring this version of the text for adoption receive complimentary print and online subscriptions. Or, students can receive 15 weeks of the Financial Times for only $12.00 net.

Study Guide ◆ Written by Charles Fazzi of St. Vincent College, this guide serves as the students' principal reality check. Do they really know the material? It provides detailed chapter summaries, a glossary of terms, and demonstration problems and solutions that will reinforce key principles and concepts and help students master the core material.

Technology Resources

Companion Website—www.prenhall.com/revsine ◆ A convenient, one-stop site for students looking to enhance their understanding of book material. The Online Study Guide, written by David Baglia of Grove City College, includes multiple-choice, true/false, and essay questions so students can quiz themselves. Grading is done on the spot!

PowerPoint Slide Presentations ◆ These slides, prepared by Bruce Johnson, include key lecture points as well as a variety of exhibits and graphics from the text. You can download these files from the text website at no charge.

Spreadsheet Transparencies ◆ Prepared by Bruce Johnson, these templates provide students with text data in Excel format. These are also available at no charge from the website.

The Economic and Institutional Setting for Financial Reporting

"No one ever said accounting was an exact science."

Learning Objectives

After studying this chapter, you will understand:

1. Why financial statements are a valuable source of information about companies, their current health, and their prospects for the future.

2. How investors, creditors, securities analysts, and auditors use financial statements.

3. How accounting rules are established, and why management can shape the financial information communicated to outsiders and still be within those rules.

4. How the demand for financial information comes from its ability to improve decision making and monitor managers' activities.

5. How the supply of financial information is influenced by the costs of producing and disseminating it and by the benefits it provides.

It's the middle of May 2002.[1] An e-mail from your brother arrived late yesterday. He just bought 10,000 shares of WorldCom stock and he thinks you should buy some too. A favorable research report on the company from a highly regarded Wall Street analyst is attached to the e-mail. According to that report, WorldCom is a global leader in the telecommunications industry, providing a complete package of communications services (voice, data, and Internet) to businesses and consumers. The company grew fast, very fast—an average of 58% each year from 1996 through 2000—as a result of a robust economy and a near insatiable demand for wireless communication and high-speed Internet access. Then, in March 2001, the dot.com bubble burst and Internet spending came to a halt. Companies like WorldCom suddenly faced excess capacity and shrinking demand for their communications and Internet services.

According to the stock analyst, WorldCom is doing surprisingly well despite tough times throughout the industry. The company's 2002 first-quarter results, announced just two weeks ago, indicate sales of $8,120 million and $843 million in pre-tax operating profits. That's a 16% decline in sales and a 34% decline in profits but other firms in the industry, including giants like AT&T, are reporting even steeper sales and earnings decreases. And the stock looks incredibly cheap at its current price of $2 per share! As your brother points out: "The company has $2.3 billion in cash. That's nearly $0.78 per share. It has $104 billion in assets and only $44 billion in debt, which translates into a $20.50 book value per share. And you have to pay only $2 a share for this gem! You cannot find a more attractive investment opportunity in the market."

Your brother's enthusiasm for WorldCom gets you thinking about it. World-Com stock has dropped from a high of $64.50 in June 1999. It's hard to believe the

---

[1] This publication is designed to provide accurate and authoritative information in regard to the subject matter. It is sold with the understanding that the Publishers and the Authors are not engaged in rendering legal, accounting, investment, or other professional services. If legal advice or other expert assistance is required, the services of a competent professional person should be sought.

share price could fall even further below $2. After all, WorldCom still dominates its segment of the telecommunications industry and it continues to report solid sales and profits. Perhaps investors have overreacted to the current slump in Internet spending and WorldCom's stock price suffered as a result. If so, now may be the ideal time to buy. This investment possibility intrigues you, so you decide to take a closer look at the company's business model, its past financial performance, and its prospects for the future.

WorldCom's financial statements confirm what your brother and the analyst are saying. Sales and earnings look solid and outpace the competition by a wide margin. Operating cash flows are positive and exceed the cash being spent for capacity expansion. And the balance sheet remains healthy. Overall the company seems to be on a solid footing.

But what's this? An article in this morning's newspaper raises a new concern. The article says that WorldCom's "line costs"—the rent WorldCom pays other companies for the use of their telecommunications networks—are holding steady at about 42% of sales. That's odd because line costs as a percentage of sales are rising at AT&T and other companies in the industry. WorldCom decided several years ago to lease large amounts of network capacity instead of building its own global communications network. These leases call for fixed rental payments each month without regard to message volume ("traffic"). This means that WorldCom must still pay the same amount of rent even though its customers are not sending much traffic through the network these days. What seems odd to the news reporter is that the same rental payment each month combined with lower traffic revenue should produce an increase in line costs as a percent of sales. That appears to be what's happening at other companies in the industry, but at WorldCom line costs have not increased. Perhaps WorldCom is particularly adept at managing this aspect of its business.

You call your broker who confirms that WorldCom's stock is available at $1.75 per share in early trading. Should you take advantage of this investment opportunity and buy 10,000 shares? Should you call your brother and tell him to sell his shares because WorldCom's income statement may contain a torpedo that could potentially sink the stock? Or should you take a closer look at company fundamentals—traffic volume, line costs, and other aspects of the business—before deciding whether to buy or sell WorldCom shares? The unusual trend in line costs could indicate that WorldCom is successfully managing its excess capacity problems during a period of slack demand or it could be a warning signal of problems at the company.

What do you do?

Why Financial Statements Are Important

This dilemma illustrates a fundamental point: Without adequate information, investors cannot properly judge the opportunities and risks of investment alternatives. To make informed decisions, investors use information about the economy, various industries, specific companies, and the products or services those companies sell. Complete information provided by reliable sources enhances the probability that the best decisions will be made. Of course, only later will you be able to tell whether your investment decision was a good one. What we can tell you now is that *if you want to know more about a company, its past performance, its current health, and its prospects for the future, the best source of information is the company's own financial statements.*

Why? Because the economic events and activities that affect a company and that can be translated into accounting numbers are reflected in the company's financial statements. Some financial statements provide a picture of the company at a moment in time; others describe changes that took place over a period of time. Both provide a basis for *evaluating* what happened in the past and for *projecting* what might occur in the future. For example, what is the annual rate of sales growth? Are accounts receivable increasing at an even greater rate than sales? How do sales and receivable growth rates compare to those of competitors? What rates of growth can be expected next year? These trends and relationships provide insights into a company's economic opportunities and risks, including growth and market acceptance, costs, productivity, profitability, and liquidity. Consequently, *a company's financial statements can be used for various purposes*:

- *as an analytical tool,*
- *as a management report card,*
- *as an early warning signal,*
- *as a basis for prediction, and*
- *as a measure of accountability.*

As our prospective WorldCom stockholder knows, financial statements contain information that investors need to know to decide whether to invest in the company. Others need financial statement information to decide whether to extend credit, negotiate contract terms, or do business with the company. Financial statements serve a crucial role in allocating capital to the most productive and deserving firms. Doing so promotes the efficient use of resources, encourages innovation, and provides a liquid market for buying and selling securities and for obtaining and granting credit.

However, published financial statements do not always contain the most up-to-date information about a company's changing economic fortunes. To ensure that important financial news reaches interested parties as soon as possible, companies send press releases or hold meetings with analysts. Press releases typically announce things like contract awards, new product introductions, capital spending plans, or anticipated acquisitions or divestitures.

Although not as timely as press releases, periodic financial statements do provide an economic history that is comprehensive and quantitative, and therefore can be used to gauge company performance. **For this reason financial statements are indispensable for developing an accurate profile of ongoing performance and prospects**. Financial reports also help in assessing the company's viability as changes occur in input and output markets, in production technologies, among competitors, or in general economic conditions.

Our WorldCom prospective stockholder will learn an even more important lesson: Financial statements sometimes conceal more than they reveal.

Epilogue to WorldCom

In late June 2002, WorldCom stunned investors by announcing that it intended to restate its financial statements for 2001 and the first quarter of 2002. According to the press release, an internal audit of the company's capital expenditures had uncovered $3.8 billion in improper transfers from line cost expense to the balance sheet. Without those transfers, the company would have reported a loss for 2001 and the first quarter of 2002 (see Figure 1.1). The company's chief financial officer was fired and its controller resigned. A special committee was formed by the company's board of directors to look further into the matter. Trading in the company's stock was immediately halted on the exchange. When trading resumed a few days later, the stock was worth only 6 cents per share having lost more than 90% of its value.

Figure 1.1

WORLDCOM'S DISAPPEARING PROFITS
WorldCom transferred a total of $3.8 billion in line cost expenses from the income statement to the balance sheet. This chart shows the company's profits (in millions) by quarter as reported originally and as later restated.

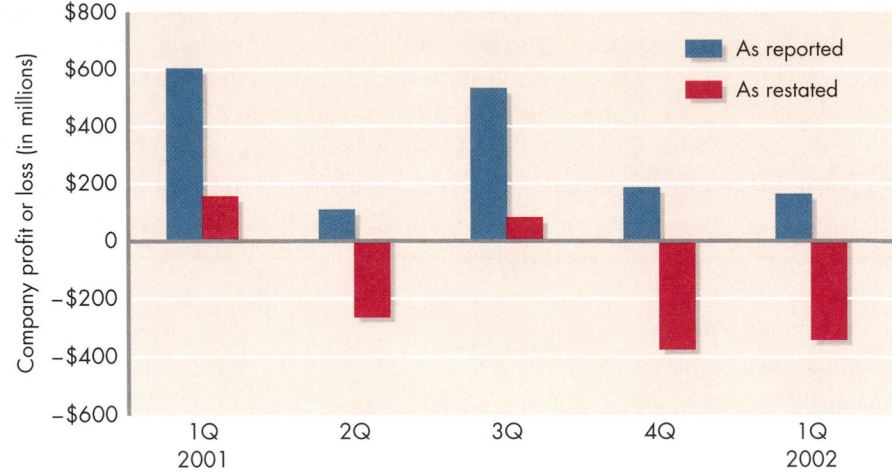

The accounting rule that WorldCom violated is easy to understand. It says that when expenditures (think "money spent") provide a future benefit to the company, then and only then can the expenditures be recorded as balance sheet assets (Chapter 2 provides the details). This means that if the company spends a dollar today buying equipment that will be used for the next five years (the "future benefit"), the dollar spent should be shown as a balance sheet asset. But what if the dollar spent doesn't buy a *future* benefit? Then it cannot be shown as a balance sheet asset but instead must be shown on the income statement as a current period expense. That's the rule!

What did this accounting rule mean for the money WorldCom spent on line costs? Recall that these line costs were just the monthly rent WorldCom paid to other companies for the use of their communications networks. Because the rent had to be paid each month, the money WorldCom spent wasn't buying a *future* benefit. So, all line costs should have been shown on the income statement as a current expense. Instead, WorldCom improperly "transferred" $3.8 billion of these costs from the income statement back to the balance sheet where they were shown as an asset. This transfer violated the accounting rule and allowed WorldCom to appear more profitable than was actually the case.

Over the next few weeks, the situation at WorldCom grew far worse:

- Shareholder class-action lawsuits were filed against the company and its management.
- The Securities and Exchange Commission (SEC) sued the company for accounting fraud and launched its own investigation.
- Five former executives of the company were indicted on criminal charges, and four of them pleaded guilty.
- The company defaulted on a $4.25 billion credit line and was negotiating new payment terms with more than 30 banks.
- In mid-July 2002, WorldCom filed for bankruptcy. The company was saddled with over $40 billion in debt and had less than $10 billion in assets that could be readily converted into cash.
- In August, the company acknowledged more than $7 billion in accounting errors over the previous several years.

The special committee and its audit team would eventually uncover more than $11 billion in improper transfers and other accounting improprieties at the company. At least two dozen employees of WorldCom were dismissed or resigned over the fraud. WorldCom—which now calls itself MCI—reached a settlement with the SEC to pay $750 million in penalties, the largest fine ever levied against one company by the SEC. Although a number of civil and criminal lawsuits are still pending, most experts agree that WorldCom's accounting improprieties were designed to meet the financial targets of Wall Street analysts.

ACCOUNTING'S PERFECT STORM

WorldCom's revelation in June 2002 that it improperly hid $3.8 billion in expenses during the previous five quarters, or longer, set a low-water mark in a tide of accounting scandals among many firms. One out of every 10 companies listed on the stock exchanges (or 845 companies in total) found flaws in past financial statements and restated earnings between 1997 and June 2002. Investors in those companies lost over $100 billion when the restatements were announced. By comparison, only three companies restated earnings in 1981.

According to some observers, a confluence of events during the late 1990s created a climate in which accounting fraud wasn't just possible, it was likely! This was accounting's perfect storm: the conjunction of unprecedented economic growth with inordinate incentive compensation, an extremely aggressive management culture, investors preoccupied with quarterly profits, and lax auditors. At companies that didn't make the Wall Street earnings number by even as little as a penny, the stock price tanked and put top management jobs at risk. Individually, some of these forces may have been good news. But when they all came together, it was a disaster waiting to happen.

Congress responded to the almost daily onslaught of accounting scandals by passing the **Sarbanes-Oxley Act** in late July 2002. This legislation was hailed as the most groundbreaking corporate reform since the 1934 Securities Act that, among other things, established the Securities and Exchange Commission. Key provisions of the Sarbanes-Oxley Act are intended to strengthen auditor independence and improve financial statement transparency by:

- Creating the Public Companies Accounting Oversight Board (PCAOB) charged with establishing audit, independence, and ethical standards for auditors; investigating auditor conduct; and imposing penalties.
- Requiring the chief executive officer (CEO) and chief financial officer (CFO) to certify in writing that the numbers in their company's financial reports are correct. Executives face potential civil charges of fraud or criminal charges of lying to the government if their company's numbers turn out to be bogus.
- Banning outside auditors from providing certain non-audit services—bookkeeping, financial-system work, appraisals, actuarial work, internal audits, management and human resource consulting, investment-advisory work, and other advocacy-related services—to their audit clients so that independence is not compromised. Fees paid to auditors for services must now be disclosed in the client's annual report.
- Requiring public companies to disclose if the audit committee—comprised of outside directors and charged with oversight of the annual audit—has a financial expert and if not, why not. Companies must also now reveal their off-balance-sheet arrangements (see Chapter 11)) and reconcile "pro forma" earnings (see Chapter 5) with the audited earnings number.

In the words of one observer, "Our free market system does not depend on executives being saintly or altruistic. But markets do rely on institutional mechanisms, such as auditing and independent boards, to offset opportunistic, not to mention illegal, behavior."* The Sarbanes-Oxley Act strengthens those important institutional mechanisms and, in so doing, calms the accounting storm.

*Robert Simmons as quoted in *CFO Magazine* (August 2002).

Financial statement fraud is rare.[2] Most managers are honest and responsible, and their financial statements are free from the kind of distortions that occurred at WorldCom. However, this example underscores the fact that investors and others should not simply accept the numbers in financial statements at face value. Instead, they must analyze the numbers in sufficient detail to assess the degree to which the financial statements faithfully represent the economic events and activities affecting the company.

Company data used by investors and analysts come primarily from published financial statements and from the company's willingness to provide additional financial and operating data voluntarily. Management has some latitude in deciding what financial information will be made available and when it will be released. For example, even though financial statements must conform to accepted guidelines and standards, management has considerable discretion over the particular accounting procedures used in the statements and over the details contained in supplemental footnotes and related disclosures. To further complicate matters, *accounting is not an exact science*. Some financial statement items are measured with a high degree of precision and reliability, such as the amount of cash on deposit in a company bank account. Other items are more judgmental and uncertain in their measurement because they are derived from estimates of future events, such as product warranty liabilities.

[2] See *Fraudulent Financial Reporting: 1987–1997* (Washington, DC: Committee of Sponsoring Organizations of the Treadway Commission, 1999) and *1998 Fraud Survey* (New York: KPMG LLP, 1999).

Statement readers must:

- understand current financial reporting standards and guidelines,
- recognize that management can shape the financial information communicated to outside parties, and
- distinguish between financial statement information that is highly reliable and information that is judgmental.

All three considerations weigh heavily in determining the quality of the information in financial statements—and thus the extent to which it should be relied on for decision-making purposes. By quality of information, we mean the degree to which the financial statements are grounded in facts and sound judgments, and thus are free from distortion. The analytical tools and perspectives in this and later chapters will enable you to understand and better interpret the information in financial statements and accompanying disclosures, as well as to appreciate fully the limitations of that information.

Economics of Accounting Information

> Managers have a **stewardship** responsibility to investors and creditors. The company's resources belong to investors and creditors, but managers are "stewards" of those resources and thus responsible for their efficient use and for protecting them from adversity.

The role of financial accounting information is to facilitate economic transactions and to foster the efficient allocation of resources among businesses and individuals.[3] Perhaps the most familiar transactions involve raising financial capital; in these cases a company seeks to attract additional financial resources by issuing common stock or debt securities. Here, financial reports provide information that can reduce investors' uncertainty about the company's opportunities and risks, thereby lowering the company's cost of capital. If you think about this, you can see demand and supply at work. Investors **demand** information regarding the company's opportunities and risks. Because companies need to raise capital at the lowest possible cost, they have an economic incentive to **supply** the information investors want. In this section you will see that the amount and type of financial accounting information provided by companies depend on demand and supply forces much like the demand and supply forces affecting any economic commodity.

Financial statements are demanded because of their value as a source of information about the company's performance, financial condition, and stewardship of its resources. People demand financial statements because the data reported in them improve decision making.

The supply of financial information is guided by the costs of producing and disseminating it and the benefits it will provide to the company. Firms weigh the benefits they may gain from financial disclosures against the costs they incur in making those disclosures.

Of course, regulatory groups such as the Securities and Exchange Commission (SEC), the Financial Accounting Standards Board (FASB), and the International Accounting Standards Board (IASB) influence the amount and type of financial information companies disclose as well as when it is disclosed.

Demand for Financial Statements

A company's financial statements are demanded by:

1. Shareholders and investors
2. Managers and employees
3. Lenders and suppliers
4. Customers
5. Government and regulatory agencies

---

[3] The company may participate directly in the transaction as, for example, when it issues debt or equity securities, or when it negotiates a loan or acquires equipment on credit. However, financial statement information also facilitates transactions in secondary markets—like the New York Stock Exchange (NYSE)—where the company's debt and equity securities are subsequently traded.

Shareholders and Investors Shareholders and investors, including investment advisors and securities analysts, use financial information to help decide on a portfolio of securities that meets their preferences for risk, return, dividend yield, and liquidity.

Financial statements are crucial in investment decisions that use **fundamental analysis** to identify mispriced securities—a stock or bond selling for substantially more or less than it seems to be worth. Fundamental analysis uses financial statement information—including footnotes in those statements—along with industry and macroeconomic data to forecast future stock price movements. Investors who use this approach consider past sales, earnings, cash flow, product acceptance and management performance to predict future trends in these financial drivers of a company's economic success or failure. Then they assess whether a particular stock or group of stocks is undervalued or overvalued at the current market price.

Investors who believe in the **efficient markets hypothesis**—and who thus presume they have no insights about company value beyond the current security price—also find financial statement data useful. To efficient markets investors, financial statement data provide a basis for assessing risk, dividend yield, or other firm attributes that are important to portfolio selection decisions.

Of course, investment analysis can be performed by shareholders and investors themselves—or by professional securities analysts who may possess specialized expertise or some comparative advantage in the acquisition, interpretation, and analysis of financial statements.

Shareholders and investors also use financial statement information when evaluating the performance of the company's top executives. When earnings and share price performance fall below acceptable levels, disgruntled shareholders will voice their complaints in letters and phone calls to management and outside directors. If this approach doesn't work, dissident shareholders may launch a campaign, referred to as a **proxy contest**, to elect their own slate of directors at the next annual meeting. New investors often see this as a buying opportunity. By purchasing shares of the underperforming company at a bargain price, these investors hope to gain by joining forces with existing shareholders, replacing top management, and "turning the company around."

Such a company's performance as described in its recent financial statements often becomes the focal point of the proxy contest. Management defends its record of past accomplishments while perhaps acknowledging a need for improvement in some areas of the business. Dissident shareholders point to management's past failures and the need to hire a new executive team. Of course, both sides are pointing to the same financial statements. Where one side sees success, the other sees only failure—and undecided shareholders must be capable of forming their own opinion on the matter.

> The **efficient markets hypothesis** says a stock's current market price reflects the knowledge and expectations of all investors. Those who adhere to this theory consider it futile to search for undervalued or overvalued stocks or to forecast stock price movements using financial statements or other public data, because any new development is quickly reflected in a firm's stock price. This perspective does not entirely preclude the use of financial statements for investment decisions, however, because financial information about a firm can still have value for predicting the stock's systematic risk (or Beta). Systematic risk—the degree to which a company's stock price moves up or down with marketwise stock price movements—remains important to the investment decision even if markets are efficient. One commercial service, BARRA, provides fundamental estimates of systematic risk to investment professionals worldwide. See T. D. Coqqin and F. J. Fabozzi, *Applied Equity Valuation* (New Hope, PA: Frank J. Fabozzi Associates, 1999).

Managers and Employees Although managers regularly make operating and financing decisions based on information that is much more detailed and timely than the information found in financial statements, they also need—and therefore demand—financial statement data. Their demand arises from contracts (such as executive compensation agreements) that are linked to financial statement variables.

Executive compensation contracts usually contain annual bonus and longer term pay components tied to financial statement results. Using accounting data in this manner increases the efficiency of executive compensation contracts. Rather than trying to determine first-hand whether a manager has performed capably during the year (and whether the manager deserves a bonus), the board of directors' compensation committee only needs to look at reported profitability or some other accounting measure that functions as a summary of the company's (and thus the manager's) performance.

Employees demand financial statement information for several reasons:

- the increasing popularity of employee profit sharing and employee stock ownership plans (ESOPs, discussed in Chapter 15);
- to monitor the health of company-sponsored pension plans and to gauge the likelihood that promised benefits will be provided upon retirement;
- union contracts may link negotiated wage increases to the company's financial performance;
- and more generally, to help employees gauge their company's current and potential future profitability and solvency.

Lenders and Suppliers   Financial statements play several roles in the relationship between the company and those who supply financial capital. Commercial lenders (banks, insurance companies, and pension funds) use financial statement information to help decide the loan amount, the interest rate, and the security (called **collateral**) needed for a business loan. Loan agreements contain contractual provisions (called **covenants**) that require the borrower to maintain minimum levels of working capital, debt-to-assets, or other key accounting variables that provide a safety net to the lender. Violation of these loan provisions can result in technical default and allow the lender to accelerate repayment, to request additional security, or to raise interest rates. So lenders monitor financial statement data to ascertain whether the covenants are being adhered to or violated.

Suppliers demand financial statements for many reasons. A steel company may sell millions of dollars of rolled steel to an appliance manufacturer on credit. Before extending credit, careful suppliers scrutinize the buyer's financial position in much the same way that a commercial bank does—and for essentially the same reason. That is, suppliers assess the financial strength of their customers to determine whether they will be paid for goods shipped. Suppliers continuously monitor the financial health of companies with whom they have a significant business relationship.

Customers   Repeat purchases and product guarantees or warranties create continuing relationships between a company and its customers. A buyer needs to know if its supplier has the financial strength to deliver a high-quality product on an agreed-upon schedule and if the supplier will be able to provide replacement parts and technical support after the sale. You wouldn't buy a personal computer from a door-to-door vendor without first checking out the product and the company that stands behind it. Financial statement information can help current and potential customers monitor a supplier's financial health and thus decide whether to purchase that supplier's goods and services.

In most industrialized countries, the accounting rules that businesses use for external financial reporting purposes differ from the accounting rules required for taxation purposes. Only in a few countries—notably France—are firms compelled to use external financial reporting methods that conform to taxation rules. The United States allows divergence between the rules used to compute taxable income and rules used for shareholder reports. As a consequence, corporate financial reporting choices are seldom influenced by the U.S. Internal Revenue Code. See Chapter 13 for details.

Government and Regulatory Agencies   Government and regulatory agencies demand financial statement information for various reasons. For example, the Securities and Exchange Commission (SEC) requires publicly traded companies to compile annual financial reports (called 10-Ks) and quarterly financial reports (called 10-Qs). These reports are deposited with the Commission, and then made available to investors and other interested parties. This process of **mandatory reporting** allows the SEC to monitor compliance with the securities laws and to ensure that investors have a "level playing field" with timely access to financial statement information.

Taxing authorities sometimes use financial statement information as a basis for establishing tax policies designed to enhance social welfare. For example, the U.S. Congress could point to widespread financial statement losses as justification for instituting a tax reduction during economic downturns.

Government agencies are often customers of businesses. For example, the U.S. Army purchases weapons from suppliers whose contracts guarantee that they are reimbursed for costs and that they get an agreed-upon profit margin. So, financial statement information is essential to resolving contractual disputes between the Army and its suppliers, and for monitoring whether companies engaged in government business are earning profits beyond what the contracts allow.

Financial statement information is used to regulate businesses—especially public utilities, such as gas and electric companies. To achieve economies of scale in the production and distribution of natural gas and electricity, local governments have historically granted exclusive franchises to individual gas and electric companies serving a specified geographical area. In exchange for this monopoly privilege, the rates these companies are permitted to charge consumers are closely regulated. Accounting measures of profit and of asset value are essential because the accounting **rate of return**—reported profit divided by asset book value—is a key factor that regulators use in setting allowable charges.[4] If a utility company earns a rate of return that seems too high, regulators can decrease the allowable charge to consumers and thereby reduce the company's profitability.

Banks, insurance companies, and savings and loan associations are also subject to regulation aimed at protecting individual customers and society from insolvency losses—for example, the inability of a bank to honor deposit withdrawal requests or the failure of an insurance company to provide compensation for covered damages as promised. Financial statements aid regulators in monitoring the health of these companies so that corrective action can be taken when needed.

Regulatory intervention (in the form of antitrust litigation, protection from foreign imports, government loan guarantees, price controls, and so on) by government agencies and legislators constitutes another source of demand for financial statement information.

> **RECAP**
>
> Financial statement information has value either because it reduces uncertainty about a company's future profitability or economic health or because it provides evidence about the quality of its management, about its ability to fulfill its obligations under supply agreements or labor contracts, or about other facets of the company's business activities. Financial statements are demanded because they provide information that helps improve decision making or makes it possible to monitor managers' activities.

Disclosure Incentives and the Supply of Financial Information

Investment bankers and commercial lenders sometimes possess enough bargaining power to allow them to compel companies to deliver the financial information they need for analysis. For example, a cash-starved company applying for a bank loan has a strong incentive to provide all the data the lender requests. But most financial statement users are less fortunate. They must rely on mandated reporting (for example, SEC 10-K filings), voluntary company disclosures that go beyond the minimum required reporting (for example, corporate "fact" books), and sources outside the company (for example, analysts and reporters) for the financial information needed to make decisions.

What forces induce managers to supply information? Browse through several corporate financial reports and you will notice substantial differences across companies—and perhaps over time—in the quality and quantity of the information provided.

---

[4] This regulation process is intended to enhance economic efficiency by precluding the construction of duplicate facilities that might otherwise occur in a competitive environment. Eliminating redundancies presumably lowers the ultimate service cost to consumers. Regulatory agencies specify the accounting practices and disclosure policies that must be followed by companies under their jurisdiction. As a consequence, the accounting practices that utility companies use in preparing financial statements for regulatory agencies sometimes differ from those used in their shareholder reports.

Some companies routinely disclose operating profits, production levels, and order backlogs by major product category so analysts and investors can quickly spot changes in product costs and market acceptance. Other companies provide detailed descriptions of their outstanding debt and their efforts to hedge interest rate risk or foreign currency risk. Still other companies seem to disclose only the bare minimum required. What explains this diversity in the quality and quantity of financial information?

If the financial reporting environment were unregulated, disclosure would occur *voluntarily* as long as the incremental benefits to the company and its management from supplying financial information exceeded the incremental costs of providing that information. In other words, management's decisions about the scope, timing, and content of the company's financial statements and notes would be guided solely by the same cost and benefit considerations that influence the supply of any commodity. Managers would assess the benefits created by voluntary disclosures and weigh those benefits against the costs of making the information available. Any differences in financial disclosures across companies and over time would then be due to differences in the benefits or costs of voluntarily supplying financial information.

But, in fact, financial reporting in the United States and in many other developed countries is regulated by public agencies such as the SEC and by private agencies such as the FASB. The various public and private sector regulatory agencies establish and enforce financial reporting requirements ***designed to ensure that companies meet certain minimum levels of financial disclosure.***[5] Nevertheless, companies frequently communicate financial information that exceeds these minimum levels. They apparently believe that the benefits of the "extra" disclosures outweigh the costs. What are the potential benefits from voluntary disclosures that exceed minimum requirements?

Disclosure Benefits Companies compete with one another in capital, labor, and product markets. This competition creates incentives for management to reveal "good news" financial information about the firm. The news itself may be about a successful new product introduction, increased consumer demand for an existing product, an effective quality improvement, or other matters favorable to the financial perception of the company. By voluntarily disclosing otherwise unknown good news, the company may be able to obtain capital more cheaply or get better terms from suppliers.

To see how these incentives work, consider the market for raising financial capital. Companies seek capital at the lowest possible cost. They compete with one another both in terms of the return they promise to capital suppliers and in terms of the characteristics of the financial instrument offered. The capital market has two important features:

1. Investors are uncertain about the quality (that is, the riskiness) of each company's debt or equity offerings because the ultimate return from the security depends on future events.
2. It is costly for a company to be mistakenly perceived as offering investors a low-quality ("high-risk") stock or debt instrument—a "lemon."[6]

This lemon cost has various forms. It could be lower proceeds received from issuing stock, a higher interest rate that will have to be paid on a commercial loan, or more stringent conditions—such as borrowing restrictions—placed on that loan.

---

[5] Corporate financial reporting in the United States has been regulated by the Securities and Exchange Commission (SEC) since its creation by an act of Congress in 1934. The SEC has historically relied on private sector organizations such as the American Institute of Certified Public Accountants (AICPA) and the Financial Accounting Standards Board (FASB) to formulate financial accounting and reporting standards. Another example involves the financial accounting and disclosure standards in Germany; those standards are prescribed by law in the Commercial Code (*Handelsgesetz*), the Corporation Act (*Aktiengesetz*), the Cooperatives Act (*Genossenschaftsgesetz*), and other laws related to specific types of business.

[6] "Lemon," a term commonly associated with automobiles, refers to an auto with hidden defects. In financial capital markets, lemon refers to a financial instrument (for example, stock or debt) with hidden risks. See G. Akerlof, "The Market for 'Lemons': Quality Uncertainty and the Market Mechanism," *Quarterly Journal of Economics* (August 1970), pp. 488–500.

These market forces mean that owners and managers have an economic incentive to supply the amount and type of financial information that will enable them to raise capital most cheaply. A company offering attractive, low-risk securities can avoid the lemon penalty by voluntarily supplying financial information that enables investors and lenders to gauge the risk and expected return of each instrument accurately. Of course, companies offering higher risk securities have incentives to mask their true condition by supplying overly optimistic financial information. However, other forces partially offset this tendency. Examples include requirements for audited financial statements and legal penalties associated with issuing false or misleading financial statements. Managers also want to maintain access to capital markets and establish a reputation for supplying credible financial information to investors and analysts.

Financial statement disclosures can convey economic benefits to firms—and thus to their owners and managers. But, firms cannot obtain these benefits at zero cost.

Disclosure Costs Four costs can arise from informative financial disclosures:

1. Information collection, processing, and dissemination costs
2. Competitive disadvantage costs
3. Litigation costs
4. Political costs

The costs associated with **financial information collection, processing, and dissemination** can be large. Determining the company's obligation for postretirement employee health-care benefits provides an example. This disclosure requires numerous complicated actuarial computations as well as future healthcare cost projections for existing or anticipated medical treatments. Whether companies compile the data themselves or hire employee benefit consultants to do it, the cost of generating a reasonable estimate of the company's postretirement obligation can be considerable. The costs of developing and presenting financial information also include the cost incurred to audit the accounting statement item (if the information is audited). Owners—that's the shareholders—ultimately pay all of these costs, just as they ultimately bear all other company costs.

> Many firms promise to pay some of the healthcare costs employees incur after retirement. See Chapter 14 for details.

Another financial disclosure cost is the possibility that competitors may use the information to harm the company providing the disclosure. Several disclosures—financial and nonfinancial—might create a **competitive disadvantage**:

- Details about the company's strategies, plans, and tactics, such as new products, pricing strategies, or new customer markets.
- Information about the company's technological and managerial innovations, such as new manufacturing and distribution systems, successful process redesign and continuous quality improvement methods, or uniquely effective marketing approaches.
- Detailed information about company operations, such as sales and cost figures for individual product lines or narrow geographical markets.[7]

Disclosing sales and profits by product line or geographical area may highlight opportunities previously unknown to competitors, thereby undermining a company's competitive advantage. For example, Uniroyal Inc., an automobile tire manufacturer, objected to disclosing its financial data by geographical area because:

> . . . this type of data would be more beneficial to our competition than to the general users of financial data. This is especially true in those countries or geographical areas where we might not be as diversified as we are in the United States. In these cases, the data disclosed could be quite specific, thereby jeopardizing our competitive situation.[8]

---

[7] R. B. Stevenson, Jr., *Corporations and Information: Secrecy, Access, and Disclosure* (Baltimore, MD: Johns Hopkins University Press, 1980), pp. 9–11.

[8] Uniroyal Inc. correspondence as reported in G. Foster, *Financial Statement Analysis* (Upper Saddle River, NJ: Prentice Hall, 1986), p. 185.

Labor unions or suppliers may also use the company's financial information to improve their bargaining power, which would increase the company's costs and possibly weaken its competitive advantage.

Litigation costs result when shareholders, creditors, and other financial statement users initiate court actions against the company and its management for alleged financial misrepresentations. For example, it's common for shareholders to initiate litigation when there's a sudden drop in stock price. If the price falls soon after the company has released new financial information, shareholders may sue the company and claim damages based on the disclosure. These shareholders argue they would not have committed financial capital to the company if they had known then (back when they bought the stock) what they know now (after the company's disclosure).

The costs of defending against suits, even those without merit, can be substantial. Beyond legal fees and settlement costs, there is the damage to corporate and personal reputations and the distraction of executives from productive activities that would otherwise add value to the company.

There are potential **political costs** of financial reporting, especially for companies in highly visible industries like oil or pharmaceuticals. Politically vulnerable firms with high earnings are often attacked in the financial and popular press, which alleges that those earnings constitute evidence of anticompetitive business practices. Politicians sometimes respond to (or exploit) heightened public opinion. They propose solutions to the "crisis" that is causing high earnings, thereby gaining media exposure for themselves and improving their chances for reelection or reappointment. These "solutions" are often political initiatives designed to impose taxes on unpopular companies or industries. The windfall profits tax levied on U.S. oil companies in the late 1970s is one example. This tax was prompted, in part, by the large profit increases that oil companies reported during several years prior to enactment of the legislation.

Antitrust litigation, environmental regulations, and the elimination of protective import quotas are other examples of the costs politicians and government bureaucrats can impose on unpopular companies and industries. Financial reports are one source of information that politicians and bureaucrats can use to identify target firms or industries. For this reason, astute managers carefully weigh political considerations when choosing what financial information to report and how best to report it. As a result, some highly profitable—but politically vulnerable—firms may make themselves appear less profitable than they really are.[9]

RECAP | A company's financial reporting decisions are driven by economic considerations— and thus by cost-benefit trade-offs. Companies that confront distinctly different competitive pressures in the marketplace and that face different financial reporting costs and benefits are likely to choose different accounting and reporting practices. A clear understanding of the economic factors that influence a company's financial reporting choices can help you to assess more keenly the quality of the provided information. That's what we'll help you do in this textbook.

A Closer Look at Professional Analysts

Financial statements that help users make informed decisions also help allocate capital efficiently. Different types of users—investors, lenders, customers, suppliers, managers, employees, and so on—find corporate financial statements helpful in making decisions. *Financial*

---

[9] There is another side to this "excessive profits" story. Politicians sometimes respond to public concern over record losses at highly visible companies by providing subsidies in the form of government loan guarantees (for example, Chrysler Corporation), import tariffs (for example, Harley Davidson), and restrictions on the activities of competitors.

statement users have diverse information needs because they face different decisions or may use different approaches to making the same kind of decision. For example, a retail customer deciding which brand of automobile to purchase needs far less financial information about each automotive manufacturer than does a long-term equity investor who is planning to purchase stock in one of those companies. Similarly, a commercial banker engaged in asset-based lending—meaning the borrower's inventory or receivables are pledged to repay the loan—needs far different financial information about the business than does a banker who lends solely on the basis of the borrower's projected future cash flows.

> "To perform good audits, we need more skills than just forensic accounting . . . general accounting skills, tax planning, risk management, and securities analysis are all vital competencies for auditors to possess." Samuel DiPiazza, Jr., global CEO of PricewaterhouseCoopers.

It would be difficult (maybe impossible!) to frame our examination of corporate financial reporting and analysis around the diverse information needs of all potential users and the varied decisions they might possibly confront. Instead, we focus attention on professional analysts. But we define **analyst** broadly to include investors, creditors, financial advisors, and auditors—anyone who uses financial statements to make decisions as part of their job. Let's see what professional analysts do.

Analysts' Decisions

The task confronting **equity investors** is first to form an educated opinion about the value of the company and its equity securities—common and preferred stock—and then to make investment decisions based on that opinion. Investors who follow a *fundamental analysis approach* estimate the value of a security by assessing the amount, timing, and uncertainty of future cash flows that will accrue to the company issuing the security. The company's financial statements and other data are used to develop projections of its future cash flows. These cash flow estimates are then discounted for risk and the time value of money.

> Chapter 6 shows how to estimate a company's *fundamental* value and describes the role financial statement information plays in the valuation process.

The discounted cash flow estimate or **fundamental value** (say, $25 per share) is then compared to the current price of the company's stock (say, $18 per share). This comparison allows the investor to make decisions about whether to buy, hold, or sell the stock.

Other valuation approaches are used by investors. One is to estimate a company's **liquidation value**. Here the investor tries to determine the value the company's assets would yield if sold individually, and then subtracts any debt the company owes. Another is to compute the price-to-earnings (or price-to-cash flow) ratio for other companies in the industry and then to apply that ratio to the company's current or projected earnings. Still other approaches rely on projections of the company's quarterly earnings, changes in earnings, and changes in trends of earnings to identify possible short-term changes in share prices.

Financial statement information is essential, in one way or another, to all these equity investment strategies.

Creditors' decisions require an assessment of the company's ability to meet its debt-related financial obligations through the timely payment of interest and principal, or through asset liquidation in the event interest and principal cannot be repaid. Creditors include commercial banks, insurance companies and other lenders, suppliers who sell to the company on credit, and those who invest in the company's publicly traded debt securities. Creditors form educated opinions about the company's **credit risk** by comparing required principal and interest payments to estimates of the company's current and future cash flows. Companies that are good credit risks have projected operating cash flows that are more than sufficient to meet these debt payments. Credit risk assessments are also influenced by the company's **financial flexibility**—the ability to raise additional cash by selling assets, issuing stock, or borrowing more.

> Chapter 5 explains how to assess a company's credit risk.

"Consideration of Fraud in a Financial Statement Audit," *Statement of Auditing Standards No. 99* (New York: AICPA, 2002) provides examples of **fraud risk factors** that auditors must be aware of in designing audit procedures. These examples include rapid growth or unusual profitability compared to other firms in the same industry, unduly aggressive financial targets, a significant portion of management pay tied to accounting numbers, an excessive interest by management in maintaining or increasing the firm's stock price or earnings trend and ineffective board of directors or audit committee oversight of the financial reporting process. These factors provide a motivation for managers to engage in fraudulent financial reporting.

Companies judged to be high credit risks are charged higher rates of interest and may have more stringent conditions—referred to as covenants—placed on their loan agreements. These loan covenants may restrict the company from paying dividends, selling assets, buying other companies, forming joint ventures, or borrowing additional funds without prior approval by the lender. Other types of covenants, particularly those based on reported accounting figures, protect the lender from deterioration in the borrower's credit risk. This is why creditors must monitor the company's ongoing ability to comply with lending agreement covenants.

Financial advisors include securities analysts, brokers, credit rating agencies, portfolio managers, industry consultants, and others who provide information and advice to investors and creditors. They are often able to gather, process, and evaluate financial information more economically and accurately than individual investors and creditors can, because they possess specialized skills or knowledge (for example, industry expertise) or because they have access to specialized resources provided by their organizations. As a consequence, financial advisors can play a crucial role in the decision-making process of investors and creditors. Securities analysts, in particular, are among the most important and influential users of financial statements.

Independent auditors carefully examine financial statements prepared by the company prior to conducting an audit of those statements. An understanding of management's reporting incentives coupled with detailed knowledge of reporting rules enables auditors to recognize vulnerable areas where financial reporting abuses are likely to occur. Astute auditors choose audit procedures designed to ensure that major improprieties can be detected.

But the Treadway Commission believes that independent auditors can (and should) do more:

The potential of analytical review procedures for detecting fraudulent financial reporting has not been realized fully. Unusual year-end transactions, deliberate manipulations of estimates or reserves, and misstatements of revenues and assets often introduce aberrations in otherwise predictable amounts, ratios, or trends that will stand out to a skeptical auditor.[10]

Analytical review procedures are the tools auditors use to illuminate relationships among the data. These procedures range from simple ratio and trend analysis to complex statistical techniques—a tool kit not unlike that used by any financial analyst. The auditor's goal is to assess the general reasonableness of the reported numbers in relation to the company's activities, industry conditions, and business climate. Astute auditors are careful to "look behind the numbers" when the reported figures seem unusual.

Current auditing standards require independent auditors to use analytical review procedures on each engagement. Why? Because they can help auditors avoid the embarrassment and economic loss from accounting "surprises," such as the one that occurred at WorldCom.

Independent auditors need to be well versed in the techniques of financial analysis to design effective audits. That's why auditors are included among those people we call analysts. Current auditing standards echo the lessons of past audit failures: ***You can't build a bulletproof audit unless you know how the game is played.*** That means understanding the incentives of managers and being a skilled financial analyst.

Analysts' Information Needs

What specific information about a company do professional analysts want? What types of information are most useful in predicting a company's earnings and cash flows when valuing its equity securities, assessing its debt repayment prospects, and evaluating audit vulnerabilities? Professional analysts say three types of financial information are needed:

---

[10] *Report of the National Commission of Fraudulent Financial Reporting* (Washington, DC: 1987), p. 48. The "Treadway Commission"—officially the National Commission on Fraudulent Financial Reporting—was formed in 1985 to study the causal factors that can lead to fraudulent financial reporting and to develop recommendations for public companies and their independent auditors, for the SEC and other regulators, and for educational institutions.

1. Quarterly and annual financial statements along with nonfinancial operating and performance data like order backlogs, customer retention rates, and so on.
2. Management's analysis of financial and nonfinancial data (including reasons for changes) along with key trends and a discussion of the past effect of those trends.
3. Information that makes it possible both to identify the future opportunities and risks confronting each of the company's businesses and to evaluate management's plans for the future.[11]

A company's financial statements provide professional investors, creditors, financial advisors, and auditors with information that heavily influences their decisions. Published financial statements of public companies also contain a **management's discussion and analysis (MD&A)** section. This section describes in considerable detail the company's business risks, its financial condition, and the results of its operations. MD&A is one of the ways management communicates the reasons for changes in financial condition and performance. Because management presumably understands the business, MD&A disclosures are an important information source for analysts. MD&A is the starting point professional analysts use in forming their own assessment of the company's profitability and health, and the reasons for changes in financial condition or performance. This is especially true when the MD&A also contains forward-looking information about changing business opportunities and risks, and about management's plans for the company.

> The Securities Exchange Act of 1934 requires that corporations solicit shareholders' votes since many shareholders will not be physically present at meetings to vote on corporate matters. This solicitation is called a **proxy**, and the information that accompanies it is called the **proxy statement**. Annual meetings are required by state corporation laws. The proxy statement will—among other things—provide information about nominees for directors, the recommended auditor for the ensuing year, the compensation of the five highest paid executives, proposed changes in compensation plans, and other matters that periodically arise (such as shareholder proposals of various kinds).

Some of the information needed by professional analysts is contained in documents other than the financial statements. For example, annual proxy statements furnished to shareholders contain information about the credentials of senior corporate executives and directors, about management compensation and ownership, and about the identity of major stockholders. Trade journals, industry surveys, and various other sources contain information about current and potential competitors, changing technologies and markets, threats from substitute products or services, and the bargaining power of customers and suppliers. Such information is essential to those who want to form a complete picture of a company's opportunities and risks—and its prospects for the future.

RECAP

Financial statement information helps investors assess the value of a firm's debt and equity securities; it helps creditors assess the company's ability both to meet its debt payments and to abide by loan terms; it helps financial advisors and securities analysts to do their job of providing information and advice to investors and creditors; and it helps auditors both to recognize potential financial reporting abuses and to choose audit procedures to detect them.

The Rules of the Financial Reporting Game

"There's virtually no standard that the FASB has ever written that is free from judgment in its application."

—D. R. Beresford, chairman of the FASB (1987–1997)[12]

Professional analysts are forward-looking. Their goal is to predict what will happen in the future to the value of a company and its ability to repay debt. Financial statements and footnotes depict the past—an economic history of transactions and other events that affected the company. These past data provide analysts with a jumping-off point for forecasting future events, especially future earnings and cash flows.

---

[11] These findings are based on a comprehensive study of professional analysts' information needs conducted by the American Institute of Certified Public Accountants (AICPA). Further details can be found in *Improving Business Reporting—A Customer Focus: Meeting the Information Needs of Investors and Creditors* (New York: AICPA, 1994).
[12] As quoted by F. Norris, "From the Chief Accountant, a Farewell Ledger," *New York Times* (June 1, 1997).

To extrapolate into the future from financial statement data, investors, creditors, and their financial advisors must first understand the accounting measurement rules used to produce the data. Financial statements present a picture of the company at a point in time, a picture that translates many (but not all) of the economic events affecting the business into financial terms. For example, the act of providing goods and services to customers in exchange for promised future cash payments is translated by the company's accounting system into financial statement amounts known as "sales revenue" and "accounts receivable." This linkage between economic events and how those events are depicted in a financial statement can sometimes seem mysterious or confusing to the analyst. For example, some companies record sales revenue *before* goods are actually delivered to customers. Other companies record revenue at the date of delivery to customers. And still others record revenue only when payment for the goods is received from the customer, which can be long *after* delivery. We'll now look more closely at the rules that govern accounting and financial reporting practices.

Generally Accepted Accounting Principles

Over time, the accounting profession has developed a network of conventions, rules, guidelines, and procedures, collectively referred to as **generally accepted accounting principles (GAAP)**. The principles and rules that govern financial reporting continue to develop and evolve in response to changing business conditions. Consider, for example, the lease of retail store space at a shopping mall. As people moved from the city to the suburbs, shopping malls emerged as convenient and accessible alternatives to traditional urban retail stores. Leasing became a popular alternative to ownership because it enabled retailing companies to gain access to store space without having to bear the burden of the large dollar outlay necessary to buy or build the store. Leasing was also attractive because it shared risks—like the risk of competition from a new mall opening nearby—between the retailer and shopping mall owner. As leasing increased in popularity, the accounting profession developed guidelines—some are complex—that are followed when accounting for leases. The guidelines that evolved are now part of GAAP and are discussed in detail in Chapter 12.

> This "reflect economic condition and performance" philosophy of financial reporting describes GAAP in Canada, Mexico, the United Kingdom, the United States, and many other countries. But GAAP financial reports in a few other countries are required to conform to tax law and/or commercial law. Chapter 18 provides details.

The goal of GAAP is to ensure that financial statements clearly represent the economic condition and performance of the company. To achieve this goal, financial statements should possess certain qualitative characteristics (summarized in Figure 1.2) that are important to the needs of professional analysts:[13]

- **Relevance:** Financial information capable of making a difference in a decision. Relevant information helps users form more accurate predictions about the future, or it allows them to better understand how past economic events have affected the business. Relevant information is timely and has both predictive and feedback value.

  Timeliness: Information that is available to decision makers while it is "fresh" and capable of influencing their decisions. For example, sales to customers made during the current quarter as opposed to sales made several quarters ago.

  Predictive value: Information that improves the decision maker's ability to forecast the outcome of past or present events. For example, suppose a company's balance sheet lists accounts receivable of $200,000 and an allowance for uncollectible accounts of $15,000. The information has predictive value with regard to future cash collections; that is, management is saying that only $185,000 ($200,000 − $15,000) of the accounts receivable will be collected.

---

[13] A detailed discussion of these qualitative characteristics and related issues is contained in "Qualitative Characteristics of Accounting Information," *Statement of Financial Accounting Concepts No. 2* (Stamford, CT: FASB, 1980).

Figure 1.2 DESIRABLE CHARACTERISTICS OF ACCOUNTING INFORMATION

Source: "Qualitative Characteristics of Accounting Information," *Statement of Financial Concepts No. 2* (Stamford, CT: FASB, 1980).

Feedback value: Information that confirms or alters the decision maker's earlier expectations. For example, suppose we learn next year that the company mentioned above collected $190,000 of its accounts receivable instead of the $185,000 originally forecasted. This information has feedback value and indicates that management's original estimate of uncollectible accounts was too high.

- **Reliability:** Financial information that is reasonably free of error and bias, and faithfully represents what it purports to represent. Reliable financial information is factual, truthful, and unbiased. Reliability can be further described using three characteristics:

    Verifiability: Independent measurers should get similar results when using the same accounting measurement method. For example, the 2002 net sales of $4,171 million reported by Gateway Computer is verifiable to the extent that knowledgeable accountants and auditors would agree on this amount after examining the company's sales transactions for the year. So verifiability refers to the degree of consensus among measurers.

    Representational faithfulness: The degree to which the accounting actually represents the underlying economic event. If a company's balance sheet reports trade accounts payable of $254.3 million when the company actually owes suppliers $266.2 million, then the reported figure is not a faithful representation.

    Neutrality: Information cannot be selected to favor one set of interested parties over another. For example, accountants cannot allow a company to reduce an estimated expense just so the company can evade a bank loan covenant.

- **Comparability:** Financial information must be measured and reported in a similar manner across companies. Comparability allows analysts to identify real economic similarities and differences among diverse companies, because those differences and similarities are not obscured by accounting methods or disclosure practices.

- **Consistency:** The same accounting methods are used to describe similar events from period to period. Consistency allows analysts to identify trends—and turning points—in the economic condition and performance of a company over time, because the trends are not obscured by changes in accounting methods or disclosure practices.

> Companies can change accounting methods, but the changes are restricted to situations where it can be persuasively argued that the newly adopted accounting method is "preferable" to the old one. Companies that change accounting methods must disclose the nature and effect of the accounting change—as well as the justification for it—in the financial statements for the period in which the change is made. Common justifications include "to conform to industry practice" (that is, improved comparability) and "to more accurately represent the company's activities" (that is, greater representational faithfulness).

No single accounting method has all of these characteristics all of the time. In fact, GAAP frequently requires financial statement users to accept a compromise that favors some qualitative characteristics over others. For example, GAAP financial statements would show a real estate company's office building investment at its historical cost (original purchase price) minus accumulated depreciation. The most *relevant* measure of the office building is often the discounted present value of its expected future rental revenues. But this measure is not as *reliable* or *verifiable* as historical cost because future vacancy rates are unpredictable. GAAP's use of historical cost trades off increased reliability and verifiability for decreased relevance. Qualitative trade-offs such as this arise frequently and make it difficult to identify what are the "best" accounting methods and disclosure practices.

In evaluating whether financial reports are complete, understandable, and helpful to readers, accounting professionals use two additional conventions—**materiality** and **conservatism**.

Materiality plays a critical role, first in the judgments of management in preparing the financial statements and then in the judgments of independent accountants who audit them. Suppose management unintentionally fails to record a $100,000 expense and the bookkeeping error is discovered shortly after the end of the quarter. Unless this error is corrected, quarterly earnings will be overstated by, say, 2.4% but the overstatement will reverse out next quarter when the expense is eventually recorded. Is the misstatement material? Should the quarterly financial statements be corrected now? Or, is the self-correcting misstatement immaterial and unimportant?

According to both the FASB and the SEC, the answer depends on both *quantitative* (the amount of the misstatement) and *qualitative* (the possible impact of the misstatement) considerations. Financial statements are materially misstated when they contain omissions or misstatements that would alter the judgment of a reasonable person.[14] Quantitative materiality thresholds—such as "an item is material if it exceeds 5% of pre-tax income"—are inadequate because they fail to recognize how even small misstatements can impact users' perceptions. For example, a small percentage misstatement can be material if it allows the company to avoid a loan covenant violation, reverses an earnings trend, or transforms a loss into a profit.

Conservatism in accounting strives to ensure that business risks and uncertainties are adequately reflected in the financial reports. For example, it is prudent to record possible losses from product liability litigation as soon as those losses become probable and measurable. Doing so helps statement readers assess the potential cash flow implications of the litigation even though an exact dollar amount has not yet been determined. Unfortunately, conservatism is sometimes used to defend poor accounting judgments like overstated provisions for "big bath" restructuring costs or "cookie-jar" reserves discussed in Chapter 3.

Who Determines the Rules?

GAAP comes from two main sources:

1. Written pronouncements by designated organizations like the FASB for U.S. companies or the International Accounting Standards Board (IASB) for many non-U.S. companies.
2. Accounting practices that have evolved over time.

The U.S. federal government, through the SEC, has the ultimate authority to determine the rules to be followed in preparing financial statements by companies whose securities are sold to the general public in the United States. This authority was given to the SEC when it was established in 1934 by Congress in response to the severe stock market decline of 1929. The SEC requires companies to file both annual *and* quarterly financial statements as well as other types of reports. In 1990 alone, the 11,000 or so companies subject to SEC filing requirements submitted

[14] Material misstatements can result either from errors, which are unintentional, or fraud, which is intentional and meant to deceive financial statement users. See "Materiality," *SEC Staff Accounting Bulletin No. 99* (Washington, DC: SEC, August 12, 1999).

more than 280,000 documents to the Commission. By 1998, the SEC's electronic document retrieval system (EDGAR) had 650,000 connections and 25 gigabytes of downloads each day.

Although the SEC has the ultimate legal authority to set accounting principles, it has looked to private-sector organizations to establish these principles. The FASB, or simply "the Board," is the organization that currently sets accounting standards in the United States. The FASB's activities are monitored by the SEC, and the SEC works closely with the FASB in formulating reporting rules. Although the FASB receives funding from various sources, it exists as an independent group with seven full-time members and a large staff. Board members are appointed to five-year terms and are required to sever all ties with the companies and institutions they served prior to joining the Board. The FASB has issued more than 150 financial accounting standards since it was created in the early 1970s. The Board has also issued seven statements of financial accounting concepts, which serve to guide the Board in setting accounting standards.

> Statements of Financial Accounting *Standards* establish new standards—such as how to value investment securities—or amend standards previously issued by the FASB and its predecessors. Statements of Financial Accounting *Concepts* establish the fundamentals—such as what qualitative characteristics accounting reports should possess. Financial accounting and reporting standards are based on the concepts.

Prior to the establishment of the FASB, the **American Institute of Certified Public Accountants (AICPA)** had the primary responsibility for setting accounting standards in the United States through its Accounting Principles Board.[15] The AICPA continues to take an active role in establishing GAAP through its participation in the FASB's deliberation process. Until recently, the AICPA was also solely responsible for setting the *auditing* standards to be followed by public accounting firms. Auditing standards are now set by the **Public Company Accounting Oversight Board (PCAOB)**, a private-sector, nonprofit corporation created by the Sarbanes-Oxley Act of 2002.

Chapter 18 describes how financial reporting standards are determined outside the United States. In some countries it's by professional accounting organizations akin to the FASB and in other countries it's by commercial law and/or tax law requirements. The growth of global investing has spurred the development of worldwide accounting standards. These standards are written by the **International Accounting Standards Board (IASB)**, an organization established in 1973 following an agreement by professional accounting organizations in Australia, Canada, France, West Germany, Japan, Mexico, the Netherlands, the United Kingdom, and the United States. The IASB works to formulate accounting standards, promote their worldwide acceptance, and achieve greater convergence of financial reporting regulations, standards, and procedures across countries. The IASB has issued 43 International Financial Reporting Standards and 33 Interpretations of existing standards. Compared to U.S. GAAP, existing IASB standards allow firms much more latitude; this is a natural result of the organization's diverse constituency.

International

> Prior to April 2001, this group was called the International Accounting Standards Committee (IASC).

Adversarial Nature of Financial Reporting

GAAP permits alternatives (such as, LIFO versus FIFO for inventory valuation), requires estimates (for example, the useful life of depreciable assets), and incorporates management judgments (are assets impaired?). Managers have a degree of flexibility in choosing specific accounting techniques and reporting procedures—and the resulting financial statements are sometimes open to interpretation.

Managers have reasons to exploit this flexibility. Their interests may conflict with the interests of shareholders, lenders, and others who rely on financial statement information. Some companies adopt exemplary reporting standards, while others tend to be less forthright. Analysts who understand these conflicting incentives as well as the flexibility available under GAAP will see

---

[15] Before the Accounting Principles Board was formed in 1959, accounting rules were issued by a predecessor organization known as the Committee on Accounting Procedure. The evolution of U.S. GAAP is discussed in more detail in the appendix to this chapter.

that a decision based on uncritical acceptance of financial statement data may turn out to be naïve—and financially dangerous.

The flexibility of GAAP financial reporting standards provides opportunities to use accounting tricks that make the company seem less risky than it really is. For instance, some real liabilities like equipment leases can be transformed into off-balance sheet (and thus less visible) items. The company would then appear, from the balance sheet data alone, to have less debt and more borrowing capacity than is really the case. Commercial lenders who fail to spot off-balance sheet liabilities of this sort can underestimate the credit risk lurking in their loan portfolios.

Companies can also **smooth** reported earnings by strategically timing the recognition of revenues and expenses to dampen the normal ups and downs of business activity. This strategy projects an image of a stable company that can easily service its debt, even in a severe business downturn. The benefits of such deceptions can be large if lenders are fooled.[16] Furthermore, once the loan is granted, the company has additional incentives to report its financial results in ways that avoid default on loan covenants tied to accounting numbers.

> Manville Corporation's 1982 bankruptcy changed the way analysts view legal contingencies. Although some people had been asking questions about the company's exposure to asbestos-related litigation for quite some time, Manville's bankruptcy announcement on August 26, 1982 caught most analysts and investors by surprise. That's because the company's last quarterly report prior to bankruptcy estimated the total cost of settling asbestos-related claims at about $350 million, less than half of Manville's $830 million of shareholders' equity. On August 26, Manville put the potential damages at no less than $2 billion—and the company's stock plunged by 35% the next day.

Self-interest sometimes drives managers to manipulate the reported financial statement numbers to earn bonuses linked to sales or earnings targets. For example, if earnings are down late in the fiscal year, product deliveries may be accelerated to increase recognized revenues and income before year's end. Or managers can delay until next year discretionary expenses like building repairs and maintenance if earnings this year are expected to be too low. On the other hand, if earnings are comfortably above the bonus goal, managers may write off obsolete equipment and inventory or increase reserves for uncollectible trade receivables, whereas those same accounting adjustments may be postponed if earnings are inadequate.

Another way in which financial reporting practices can be molded to suit management's interests is to downplay the significance of contingent liabilities—such as unresolved product liability lawsuits—that may affect the value of the firm. There are many reasons why management is likely to understate the true significance of a major legal contingency. In a lawsuit, candid disclosure could compromise the company's case. Similarly, public disclosure of impending financial hardships may harm the company if creditors respond by accelerating loan repayment schedules, by curtailing trade credit, or by seeking to liquidate the business.

This discussion states the case boldly and may portray the motives underlying financial reporting practices in an unflattering light. In reality, most companies strive to provide fair and reasonable disclosure of their financial affairs. Some of these companies are undoubtedly motivated as much by honor and integrity as by the knowledge that they will be rewarded for being forthright. Nevertheless, there are companies that take full advantage of the leeway available under GAAP.

The SEC and the FASB provide constraints that limit the range of financial statement discretion. Auditors and the courts further counterbalance opportunistic financial reporting practices. Nevertheless, the analyst should recognize the adversarial nature of financial reporting, maintain a healthy skepticism, and understand that financial disclosures sometimes conceal more than they reveal. The flexibility inherent in GAAP can have dire consequences for those caught unaware.

---

[16] Lenders are fooled when they mistakenly assign too little risk (thus charging too low an interest rate) to the borrowing. An interest-cost savings of one half of a percentage point on $1 billion of borrowings equates to $5 million (pre-tax) per year. If the company is in a 34% tax bracket and its stock trades at 15 times earnings, the payoff for concealing risk on financial statements is $49.5 million in share value. This value increase represents a wealth transfer to shareholders from creditors.

Aggressive Financial Reporting: A Case Study

America Online (AOL) was a leader in the expanding global market for online services and internet access. AOL offered its subscribers many services including electronic mail, conferencing, software, computing support, interactive magazines and newspapers, as well as easy access to the Internet. Since its founding in 1985, it had become the world's most popular Internet online service, with over 26 million members in the United States alone. But things have not always been rosy at AOL.

> In 2001, America Online bought Time Warner, Inc. The combined company, now called Time Warner, is one of the world's leading media and entertainment companies whose businesses include interactive services, cable systems, filmed entertainment, television networks, music, and publishing.

In 1996, the company faced stiff competition on several fronts. Other commercial online service providers like Prodigy and CompuServ were capturing market share through aggressive pricing. The advent of the World Wide Web meant that potential subscribers who wanted just a Web ramp with no additional services could now buy that service from access companies like PSINet more cheaply than from AOL. Looming on the horizon was the Microsoft Network (MSN). Despite these competitive forces, 1996 was a record year for AOL. Revenues grew to over $1 billion from $51 million in 1993. Net income was just under $30 million, compared to $1.5 million in 1993. Despite this strong performance, AOL's share price suffered. From its November 1995 peak of $82 per share, the company's stock price had fallen to $29 amid concerns about subscriber growth and aggressive accounting for marketing costs. Some Wall Street analysts were uneasy about the quality of AOL's earnings, citing the company's unorthodox accounting for certain marketing costs: AOL showed those marketing costs as balance sheet assets rather than as operating expenses.

Then AOL abandoned the aggressive accounting. The announcement to do so was part of a press release that described several strategy changes at the company.

We have italicized the accounting change in the company's press release below. To put the change in perspective, the $385 million write-off represented 35% of AOL's 1996 revenues and 1,283% of its 1996 earnings. The write-off was more than five times as large as the total pre-tax earnings that AOL had reported for the previous five fiscal years combined.

DULLES, VA—America Online, Inc. (NYSE: AOL) announced today a series of initiatives to fully leverage its global assets in consumer networks, content, and access by more closely aligning its business structure with emerging opportunities in the interactive market, and to further distinguish its flagship online brand as the leader in value, content, and service.

Steve Case, Chairman and Chief Executive Officer of America Online, Inc., stated, "America Online has grown rapidly in recent years, and is now the global leader in interactive services. The steps we're announcing today build on that leadership by fully leveraging our assets in consumer networks, content, and access as separate business opportunities. At the same time, through new competitive 'unlimited' pricing and a superior consumer offering enhanced by new programming and design advances, we are further strengthening the position of our flagship America Online brand as the undisputed leader in value and service and the clear choice for millions of consumers worldwide." . . .

The company also announced that effective immediately it will expense all marketing costs as they are incurred. Previously, the company has deferred the cost of certain of its marketing activities, such as the costs of mailing diskettes to prospective customers, and then amortized those costs over a period of time. To reflect the changes to its evolving business model as it reduces reliance on subscriber fees by growing new revenue streams, and as a result of changing market dynamics, the company will take a charge, as of September 30, 1996, of approximately $385 million, representing the balance of deferred subscriber acquisition costs, as of that date. [Italics added for emphasis.] The company also plans to take a one-time charge in the December 1996 quarter of up to $75 million, representing costs the company expects to incur as it aligns the organization with emerging opportunities in the interactive market.

"The creation of these three new operating divisions, the rollout of new pricing and features, and this shift toward a simpler approach to financial reporting positions AOL for a business model reflecting sustained, controllable growth based on clearly establishing AOL as the best service for the widest range of consumers," Case said. "AOL is making the necessary moves to position itself as the global leader in interactive services well into the next century." . . .

Source: From *PR Newswire* (October 29, 1996). Reprinted with permission of *PR Newswire*.

What Was the Issue? The accounting controversy at AOL was when to expense "subscriber acquisition" costs such as cash outlays for subscriber starter kits, direct marketing mailers, and purchased customer lists. Should they be shown on the balance sheet as an asset with future benefit, or should they be listed on the income statement as an operating expense?

Under its initial accounting method, if AOL spent $24 million on advertising and free trials to lure newcomers in June of a given year, the company would not recognize an immediate expense to income. Instead, AOL would create a balance sheet asset called "deferred subscriber acquisition costs." The $24 million asset would then be gradually reduced by a monthly charge to earnings, effectively spreading the cost over the average life of a subscription (about 24 months). Because AOL uses a June fiscal year end, only $1 million would be expensed the first year. The remaining $23 million would be expensed over the next 23 months. This practice [Figure 1.3(a)] was viewed by some accounting experts as unorthodox and aggressive. But it was not prohibited by GAAP! The criticism may have prompted AOL to announce in October 1996 that it would adopt the standard industry practice of recording the entire subscriber acquisition expense immediately [Figure 1.3(b)].

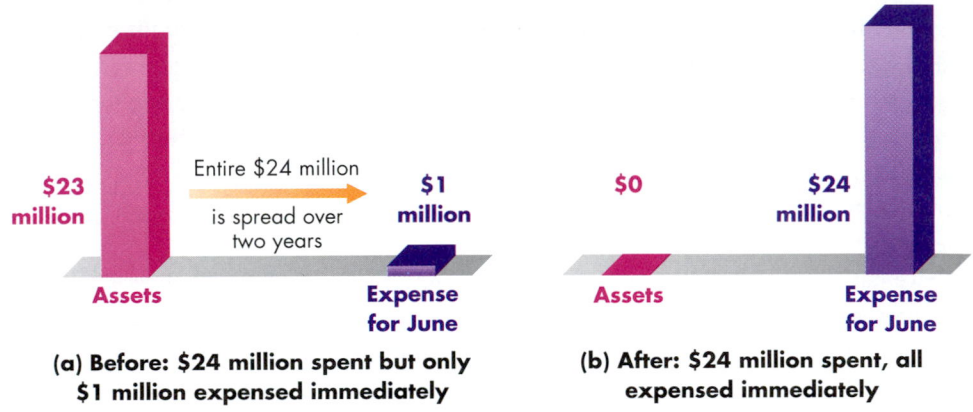

(a) **Before: $24 million spent but only $1 million expensed immediately**

(b) **After: $24 million spent, all expensed immediately**

Figure 1.3 AMERICA ONLINE'S ACCOUNTING CHANGE:

(*a*) Before the Accounting Change: Capitalize and Then Expense Some Each Year; (*b*) After the Accounting Change: Expense It All When Spent

AOL has a June fiscal year end. Using its initial accounting method (part a), the $24 million spent in June would produce a $1 million expense for the year. The remaining $23 million would be charged to income over the next 23 months, or $12 million the following year and $11 million the year after.

This accounting change had a major financial statement effect. In fiscal 1996 the company spent $363 million—one third of its revenue—on subscription promotions but recorded only $126 million of that amount as an expense. The company's one-time $385 million write-off to change accounting methods exceeded total revenues for the quarter and produced a net loss of $354 million. Instead of that $354 million loss, AOL said it would have reported quarterly earnings of $19 million under the old accounting method. The company's operating cash flows were not affected by the accounting adjustment, however, because the $385 million charge to earnings represented amounts that had already been spent.

How Did Wall Street Respond? Shareholder reaction was difficult to gauge because news of the accounting change was buried in a flurry of other announcements made by the company. But the investment community clearly favored the new, more conservative accounting method. As one Merrill Lynch analyst put it, "While the earnings impact is certainly negative, we think it is more than overshadowed by the positive reaction the change in accounting should engender."[17] AOL shares closed up $1 on the day of the announcement.

Every Wall Street analyst was presumably aware that AOL was deferring its subscriber acquisition costs rather than expensing them as incurred. But analysts who favored the stock had dismissed the accounting issue while enthusiastically trumpeting AOL's reported (but now vaporized) "profits." By calling them profits, these analysts overlooked or minimized the fact that AOL was in a price war with Internet access providers and was spending more cash than it was taking in. As one *Wall Street Journal* reporter observed:

> It [the accounting change] underscores just how massive the company's marketing efforts have been—and how illusory its profits may have been. The change raises the question of whether AOL will be able to report much profit at all in future quarters.[18]

Steve Case, the company's CEO, said scrapping the controversial deferred-cost method was aimed at stemming Wall Street concerns that had dogged the company for years.

> We've decided it's best not to spend all our time in this debate over accounting practices. There will be no argument over the quality of earnings.[19]

This scenario raises several intriguing questions about corporate financial reporting practices, managerial behavior, and the influence of accounting information on the decisions of investors, creditors, and others:

- How flexible is GAAP, and how much latitude is available to managers in the choice of "acceptable" accounting practices?
- What factors influence the accounting methods managers use? Why do firms change accounting methods? Does a change in accounting imply that previously reported figures (that is, those produced using the old method) were incorrect?
- Do company disclosures make clear what accounting methods are used? Do those disclosures enable analysts to adjust reported figures when a company's accounting method either deviates from industry norms or changes through time?
- Why were analysts not surprised by AOL's decision to alter its accounting practices and by the company's $354 million loss for the quarter?
- Why didn't AOL's stock price fall when five years' worth of profits were eliminated by the accounting change?
- How do shareholders use reported earnings and asset book values when valuing a firm's common stock?
- How does an accounting change alter creditors' opinions about a company's future cash flows and credit risk?

> In May 2000, AOL agreed to pay a $3.5 million penalty to settle SEC allegations that the company's deferred-cost accounting for subscriber acquisition costs in 1995 and 1996 violated GAAP. The SEC argued that accounting rules generally don't allow companies to record advertising costs as assets unless past performance indicates revenue from new customers will exceed the costs. At the time, AOL didn't have enough of a track record to demonstrate they could recover advertising costs, the SEC said. See M. Schroeder and N. Wingfield, "AOL Settles SEC Charges Over Its Costs," *Wall Street Journal* (May 16, 2000). Questionable accounting has continued to plague the company. In October 2002, AOL Time Warner restated its financial results for the past two years, reducing revenues by $190 million, after it uncovered faulty accounting for advertising transactions. See M. Peers and J. Angwin, "AOL to Restate Two Years of Results," *Wall Street Journal* (October 24, 2002).

Perhaps the most provocative question, however, centers on the allegations raised by an SEC investigation launched shortly after AOL announced its decision to change accounting methods. Did the company violate GAAP and mislead investors by using accounting procedures that failed to provide an accurate and timely portrayal of the company's historical profit performance, current financial condition, and future prospects? Subsequent chapters of this book help you formulate answers to these and related questions about financial reporting practices in the United States and other countries.

---

[17] "America Online Changes Accounting Method," *Dow Jones News Service* (October 29, 1996).

[18] J. Sandberg, "America Online Plans $385 Million Charge," *Wall Street Journal* (October 30, 1996).

[19] R. Lowenstein, "Did AOL Succeed in Spinning the Street?" *Wall Street Journal* (November 7, 1996).

An International Perspective

Because financial reporting practices vary widely in countries outside the United States, and because international business transactions are now more frequent and complex, the professional life of an analyst—in any country—has become more difficult. Multinational companies are regularly shifting resources throughout the world. These shifts cannot be accomplished efficiently without reliable financial information that permits careful analysis of investment opportunities and continuous control over how resources are deployed. Multinational companies must also resolve differences in national currencies and accounting rules when combining the financial statements of all their foreign and domestic businesses into consolidated reports.

The Coca-Cola Company, for example, generates only about 20% of its operating income from sales inside the United States. The company conducts business in more than 200 countries, hedges foreign currency cash flows, and uses foreign loans to finance investments outside the United States. Exhibit 1.1 indicates the scope of Coca-Cola's worldwide operating activities from 2000 through 2002. Sales in North America (Canada and U.S.) represented 32.0% of 2002 worldwide revenues and generated 27.4% of worldwide operating income. By contrast, Latin America sales were only 10.7% of 2002 operating revenues but this region produced 19.0% of Coca-Cola's worldwide operating income.

EXHIBIT 1.1	Coca-Cola Company					

Operating Revenue and Income by Geographical Area

	2000		2001		2002	
	Revenue	Income	Revenue	Income	Revenue	Income
North America	32.7%	38.2%	32.7%	27.7%	32.0%	27.4%
Africa	3.6	4.4	3.6	5.2	3.5	4.1
Europe, Eurasia & Middle East	22.6	35.5	22.6	27.3	26.9	29.5
Latin America	11.7	24.6	12.4	20.4	10.7	19.0
Asia	28.5	25.9	27.7	32.9	25.8	33.3
Corporate	0.9	(28.6)	1.0	(13.5)	1.1	(13.3)

Source: Coca-Cola Company 2002 Annual Report.

Understanding the economic, political, and cultural factors that contribute to regional differences in operating performance is daunting even for the most experienced financial analyst. Yet, assessing a multinational company's current performance and future prospects requires experience, knowledge, and skill with these factors.

Global competition is prevalent in most industries today, as companies facing mature domestic markets look outside their home borders for new customers and growth. Exhibit 1.2 presents 2001 sales, net income, and assets for three wireless phone manufacturers that compete on a worldwide basis. Ericsson, a Swedish firm, reports financial statement amounts in Swedish kronor; Motorola uses U.S. dollars; and Nokia, a Finnish company, uses the Euro for financial reporting purposes. Which company was the least profitable in 2001?

In the upper part of Exhibit 1.2, the financial statement amounts reported by these three companies are not directly comparable because each firm uses a different currency. For example, Ericsson had sales of 238,839 million kronor and a net loss of 21,264 million kronor for 2001, but the krona/dollar exchange rate averaged 10.799 for the year. That means each U.S. dollar was worth about 10.799 kronor during 2001. Similarly, the Euro/dollar exchange rate averaged 1.122 for the year. The lower part of the exhibit shows each company's sales, net income, and assets

---

| **EXHIBIT 1.2** | **Ericsson, Motorola, and Nokia** |

Revenue, Net Income, and Assets for 2001

	Ericsson (Sweden)	Motorola (United States)	Nokia (Finland)
As reported in local currency:			
Revenue	238,839	30,004	31,191
Net income	(21,264)	(3,937)	2,200
Assets	250,056	33,398	22,427
U.S. dollar equivalents:			
Revenue	22,117	30,004	27,801
Net income	(2,029)	(3,937)	1,961
Assets	23,855	33,398	19,989
Local currency	Swedish kronor	U.S. dollars	Euros
Accounting methods	Swedish GAAP	U.S. GAAP	IFRS

Note: Sales and net income in the lower part of the table are restated into U.S. dollars using the average exchange rate for 2001 because the flows occurred throughout the year. *Year-end* assets are restated into U.S. dollars using the exchange rate as of the end of 2001.

Source: Company reports.

---

expressed in U.S. dollars. Here, you can see that Motorola has the largest sales ($30,004 million) but the lowest net income (a $3,937 million loss) on the largest asset base ($33,398 million). Nokia has sales of $27,801 million, the largest net income ($1,961 million) and the smallest asset base ($19,989 million).

There is another factor that complicates our analysis. Financial statement comparisons of this sort become less meaningful when accounting standards and measurement rules vary from one country to another. Ericsson uses Swedish GAAP, Motorola uses U.S. GAAP, and Nokia prepares its financial statements using International Financial Reporting Standards (IFRS). As a result, Motorola's lower *reported* profitability might not be attributable to economic factors if U.S. GAAP income recognition rules are more conservative than Swedish or IFRS rules.

In some countries there must be conformity between the accounting methods used in shareholder financial statements and the rules used in computing taxable income. So the legislative branch of the government sets acceptable accounting principles for shareholder reporting purposes. In other countries the accounting profession, through its various committees, sets accounting principles. And these financial reporting rules differ from taxation rules.

The differing objectives of these standard-setting organizations (for example, taxation, versus fair reporting to investors) result in diverse sets of accounting principles across countries. Analysts must be aware of this diversity and guard against the tendency to assume financial statements are readily comparable across national borders. These issues are examined in Chapter 18).

In the United States, the SEC permits foreign businesses to list their securities on a U.S. stock exchange as long as certain procedures are followed. Foreign businesses that do not use U.S. GAAP to prepare financial statements must file a Form 20-F each year with the SEC. This form transforms the foreign GAAP financial statements into U.S. GAAP. Form 20-F filings are public information, and thus they can be of considerable value to the analyst.

The financial reporting requirements for foreign companies listed on the London Stock Exchange permit greater flexibility than those that currently exist in the United States. Foreign business listed there can file financial statements that conform to any one of three accounting standards: U.K. GAAP, U.S. GAAP, or the accounting principles of the International Accounting Standards Board (IASB). Reconciliation to a common

> DaimlerChrysler's Form 20-F filing for 2001 says the company had net income of $733 million according to German GAAP, but a loss of $589 million under U.S. GAAP.

set of accounting principles is not required. The London Stock Exchange also must allow all European Union (EU) countries to use their national GAAP—for instance, German companies can use German GAAP—under the well-established principle of mutual recognition.

RECAP

> Diversity is a fact of life in international accounting practice. Readers of financial statements must never lose sight of this diversity.

Challenges Confronting the Analyst

During the last three decades, financial statements have become increasingly complex and more accessible.

Corporate financial reports are more complicated today simply because the business world has become more dynamic and complex. Global competition and the spread of free enterprise throughout the world prompted firms to rely increasingly on foreign countries as a market for products and services, and as a source of capital and customers. Competitive pressures have also contributed to a fundamental change in the way firms organize and finance their activities. Corporate restructurings abound. New types of financial instruments are now used by companies to raise capital and manage risk. Service firms and e-commerce companies now comprise a major portion of business activity. These and other features of the changing business landscape pose difficult challenges for contemporary financial reporting practices—and for an accounting model originally developed to fit companies engaged in local manufacturing and merchandising.

There has also been explosive growth in the use of electronic means to assemble and examine financial information in the last three decades. The accessibility of computers and analytical software continues to rise as their costs fall. Quantitative methods for analyzing financial data have become increasingly popular, which in turn has meant increasing demand for and use of electronic databases containing financial information. Corporate press releases, analysts' research reports, historical financial data, and complete annual and quarterly financial reports are now readily available in electronic form through commercial vendors. Documents filed with the SEC can now be obtained from the agency's electronic data gathering and retrieval system (EDGAR, available at www. sec. gov).

These developments place new burdens on analysts. On the one hand, there is a wealth of financial statement data and related information available to the analyst at relatively low cost. On the other hand, firms today operate in a dynamic environment that has made the task of analyzing financial statements even more complex. The financial reporting practices of business firms are continually challenged on many fronts, and the astute analyst must remain vigilant to the possibility that financial reports sometimes do not capture underlying economic realities.

SUMMARY

Financial statements are an extremely important source of information about a company, its economic health, and its prospects. They help improve decision making and make it possible to monitor managers' activities.

- Equity investors use financial statements to form opinions about the value of a company and its stock.
- Creditors use statement information to gauge a company's ability to repay its debt and to check if the company is complying with loan covenants.
- Stock analysts, brokers, and portfolio managers use financial statements as the basis for their recommendations to investors and creditors.
- Auditors use financial statements to help design more effective audits by spotting areas of potential reporting abuses.

But what governs the supply of financial information?

- Mandatory reporting is a partial answer. Most companies in the United States and other developed countries are required to compile and distribute financial statements to shareholders as well as to file a copy with a government agency—in the United States, that agency is the SEC; this requirement allows all interested parties to view the statements.
- The advantages of voluntary disclosure is the rest of the answer. Financial information that goes beyond the minimum requirements can benefit the company, its managers, and owners. For example, voluntary financial disclosures can help the company obtain capital more cheaply or negotiate better terms from suppliers. But benefits like these come with potential costs: information collection, processing, and dissemination costs; competitive disadvantage costs; litigation costs; and political costs. This means that two companies with different financial reporting benefits and costs are likely to choose different accounting policies and reporting strategies.

Different companies choose different accounting policies and reporting strategies because financial reporting standards are often imprecise and open to interpretation. This imprecision gives managers an opportunity to shape financial statements in ways that allow them to achieve specific reporting goals.

- Most managers use their accounting flexibility to paint a truthful economic picture of the company.
- Other managers mold the financial statements to mask weaknesses and to hide problems.
- Analysts who understand financial reporting, managers' incentives, as well as the accounting flexibility available to managers, will maintain a healthy skepticism about the numbers and recognize that financial statements sometimes conceal more than they reveal.

APPENDIX

GAAP IN THE UNITED STATES

This is a brief, historical overview of the public and private-sector organizations that have influenced the development of financial accounting practices in the United States. As you shall see, some organizations have explicit legal authority to decide what constitutes U.S. GAAP. Other organizations lack that authority but remain influential.

Early Developments

Corporate financial reporting practices in the United States prior to 1900 were primarily intended to provide accounting information for management's use. Financial statements were rarely made available to shareholders, creditors, or other interested external parties. The **New York Stock Exchange (NYSE)**, established in 1792, was the primary mechanism for trading ownership in corporations. As such, it could establish specific requirements for the disclosure of financial information, and thereby dictate accounting standards for corporations whose shares it listed. Beginning in 1869, the NYSE attempted to persuade listed companies to make their financial statements public. Few companies complied. The prevailing view of corporate management was that financial information was a private concern of the company and that public disclosure would harm the company's competitive advantage.

Passage of the Sixteenth Amendment to the U.S. Constitution in 1913 and subsequent legislation allowing the federal government to tax corporate profits set the stage for expanded corporate financial disclosure. This legislation required companies to maintain accurate financial recordkeeping systems; the goal of this legislation was to ensure proper tax accounting and to facilitate collection. However, corporate financial disclosures to outsiders were still limited.

The stock market crash of 1929 and the Great Depression that followed provoked widespread concern about financial disclosure. Some observers alleged that the collapse of the stock market was due largely to the lack of meaningful requirements for reporting corporate financial information to investors and creditors.[20] Moreover, many felt that economic conditions would not improve until

---

[20] See E. R. Willet, *Fundamentals of Securities Markets* (New York: Appleton-Century-Crofts, 1968), pp. 208–14.

investors regained confidence in the financial markets. Responding to this concern in January 1933, the NYSE began to require all companies seeking exchange listing to submit independently audited financial statements and to agree to audits of all future reports.

When Franklin D. Roosevelt was sworn in as president in March 1933, the economy was paralyzed, unemployment was rampant, and the nation's banking system was on the verge of collapse. In the Senate, public hearings exposed a pattern of financial abuse by such distinguished banking institutions as J. P. Morgan, National City Bank, and Chase National Bank that included insider trading, market manipulation, reckless speculation, and special favors to influential friends.

In an effort to bolster public confidence and restore order to the securities market, Congress enacted the Securities Act of 1933, which required companies selling capital stock or debt in interstate commerce to provide financial information pertinent to establishing the value and risk associated with those securities. One year later, the Act was amended to establish the SEC as an independent agency of the government, an agency whose function was to regulate both the securities sold to the public and the exchanges where those securities were traded. Companies issuing stock or debt listed on organized exchanges were required to file annual audited reports with the SEC.[21] The SEC was also empowered to establish and enforce the accounting policies and practices followed by registered companies.

These powers are given to the SEC in Section 19(a) of the Securities Act of 1933 as amended:

> . . . the Commission shall have authority, for the purposes of this title, to prescribe the form or forms in which required information shall be set forth, the items or details to be shown in the balance sheet and earning statement, and the methods to be followed in the preparation of accounts, in the appraisal or valuation of assets and liabilities, in the determination of depreciation and depletion, in the differentiation of recurring and nonrecurring income, in the differentiation of investment and operating income, and in the preparation, where the Commission deems it necessary or desirable, of consolidated balance sheets or income accounts of any person directly or indirectly controlling or controlled by the issuer, or any person under direct or indirect common control with the issuer. The rules and regulations of the Commission shall be effective upon publication in the manner which the Commission shall prescribe.

In addition to its primary pronouncement—*Regulation S-X*, which describes the principal formal financial disclosure requirements for companies—the SEC issues *Financial Reporting Releases* and other publications stating its position on accounting and auditing matters.

Accounting Series Release No. 4, issued in April 1938, first expressed the SEC's position that generally accepted accounting principles for which there is "substantial authoritative support" constitute the SEC standard for financial reporting and disclosure. The release further indicated that a company filing financial statements reflecting an accounting principle that had been formally disapproved by the SEC—or for which there was no substantial authoritative support—would be presumed to be filing misleading financial statements even though there was full disclosure of the accounting principles applied. However, the release did not provide guidance as to what the SEC meant by *substantial authoritative support*. This void was later filled.

Emergence of GAAP

The Securities Exchange Act of 1934 required the financial statements of all publicly traded firms to be audited by independent accountants. This requirement elevated the role of the independent accountants' professional organizations. These organizations were active in influencing accounting policy prior to the 1930s, but the securities acts accentuated the need for more formal accounting standards and for systematic public announcement of those standards.

During the years immediately following passage of the 1933 and 1934 securities acts, the SEC relied primarily on the American Institute of Certified Public Accountants (AICPA)—the national professional organization of certified public accountants—to develop and enforce accounting stan-

---

[21] Security registration statements and other reports filed under the 1934 amendments to the Securities Act are public information and are available for inspection at the SEC and at the securities exchange where the company's securities are listed.

dards.[22] In response to the SEC and to the growing need to report reliable financial information, the AICPA created the Committee on Accounting Procedure in 1939 to establish, review, and evaluate accepted accounting procedures. This committee began the practice of developing U.S. financial accounting and reporting standards in the private sector.

Between 1938 and 1959, the AICPA's Committee on Accounting Procedure was responsible for narrowing the differences and inconsistencies in accounting practice. The committee issued 51 Accounting Research Bulletins (ARBs) and four Accounting Terminology Bulletins that set forth what the committee believed GAAP should be. These pronouncements were not binding on corporations or their auditors.

In 1959, the AICPA established the Accounting Principles Board (APB) to replace the Committee on Accounting Procedure. The APB's basic charge was to develop a statement of accounting concepts— that is, a conceptual foundation for accounting—and to issue pronouncements resolving current accounting controversies. During its existence from 1959 to 1973, the APB issued 31 Opinions and four Statements designed to improve external financial accounting and disclosure. At the outset, the force of these pronouncements, as with earlier ARBs, depended on general acceptance and persuasion. The APB sought compliance with financial reporting standards by attempting to persuade corporations and independent auditors that the standards improved the quality of financial reporting. By 1964 many accounting professionals and business leaders were convinced that persuasion alone could neither reduce the tremendous latitude available under then-existing accounting and reporting practices nor eliminate inconsistencies in the application of those practices. Critics cited instances in which identical transactions could be accounted for by any one of several different methods—and net income could be manipulated by selecting a particular accounting approach from among several considered to be "generally accepted."

A turning point in the development of corporate financial reporting standards occurred in October 1964 when the Council (or governing body) of the AICPA adopted a requirement that was incorporated into the rules of ethics for independent CPAs:

> **Rule 203—Accounting Principles:**
>
> A member shall not (1) express an opinion or state affirmatively that the financial statements or other financial data of any entity are presented in conformity with generally accepted accounting principles or (2) state that he or she is not aware of any material modifications that should be made to such statements or data in order for them to be in conformity with generally accepted accounting principles, if such statements or data contain any departure from an accounting principle promulgated by bodies designated by Council to establish such principles that has a material effect on the statements or data taken as a whole. If, however, the statements or data contain such a departure and the member can demonstrate that due to unusual circumstances the financial statements or data would otherwise have been misleading, the member can comply with the rule by describing the departure, its approximate effects, if practicable, and the reasons why compliance with the principle would result in a misleading statement. [As amended.][23]

This compliance requirement forced corporations and their auditors to implement the accounting standards prescribed in APB opinions and in earlier pronouncements not superseded by these opinions. This in turn caused greater attention to be focused on the activities of the APB.

Complaints about the process used to develop financial reporting and accounting standards surfaced in the 1960s and early 1970s. Corporate management, government regulators, and other interested external parties voiced concern about the lack of participation by organizations other than the AICPA, about the quality of the opinions issued, about the failure of the APB to develop a coherent conceptual foundation for external financial reporting, about the insufficient output by the APB, and about the APB's failure to act promptly to correct alleged accounting and reporting abuses.

---

[22] The American Association of Public Accountants was established in 1887 and represented the core of the accounting profession in the United States. The name of the organization was changed to the American Institute of Accountants in 1917, and it became the AICPA in 1957.

[23] The GAAP "override" provision described in the last sentence of Rule 203 is rarely seen these days in the financial statements of companies subject to SEC oversight, and most observers believe the SEC will not accept departures from GAAP.

The APB was not immune to criticism from politicians, government regulators, and the business community. One example occurred in the early 1960s when the APB attempted to resolve the question of accounting for the **investment tax credit**. The APB initially required the tax credit to be treated as a balance sheet item—a reduction in the asset's cost—rather than as an immediate increase to earnings. This decision met with strong resistance from business and several major accounting firms. After the SEC said it would allow both methods in filings with the Commission, the APB had no alternative but to rescind its earlier pronouncement (*Opinion No. 2*) and to permit the earnings increase (*Opinion No. 4*).[24] This change in the accounting standard enabled firms to use the accounting methods they preferred for the investment tax credit.

During the transition period between the APB and FASB, the SEC seemed to take on a more active and aggressive role in policy making. During its last nine months of operation (October 1972 through June 1973), the APB issued seven opinions in an attempt to complete its agenda of in-process accounting policy considerations. The SEC issued eight releases on accounting matters during this same period and another nine during the first year of the FASB.

The 1971 Study Group on Establishment of Accounting Principles (or "Wheat Committee") was formed to review and evaluate the private-sector standard-setting process as well as to recommend improvements where possible. This committee was created because of growing concern among accounting professionals over the APB's ability to withstand pressure from the business community. The committee recommended that a new and more independent, full-time standard-setting organization be established in the private sector to replace the APB. This recommendation, which was approved by the AICPA and which became effective in July 1973, created the Financial Accounting Standards Board (FASB). The FASB differed from its predecessors in several ways:

1. Board membership consisted of seven voting members, in contrast to the 18 members on the APB.
2. Autonomy and independence were enhanced by requiring members to sever all ties with their prior employers and by dictating that member salaries were paid directly by the FASB.
3. Broader representation was achieved by not requiring board members to hold a CPA license.
4. Staff and advisory support was increased substantially.

Accounting Series Release No. 150, issued by the SEC in December 1973, formally acknowledged that financial accounting pronouncements of the FASB (and its predecessor organizations) are ordinarily considered by the SEC as having "substantial authoritative support" and thus are the SEC standards for financial reporting and disclosure. Accounting practices that are contrary to FASB pronouncements are considered to not have such support. This release also reaffirmed the SEC's private-sector approach to standard setting. It said,

> . . . the Commission intends to continue its policy of looking to the private sector for leadership in establishing and improving accounting principles and standards through the FASB with the expectation that the body's conclusions will promote the interests of investors.

Current Institutional Structure in the United States

The SEC still retains broad statutory powers to define accounting terms, to prescribe the methods to be followed in preparing financial reports, and to specify the details to be presented in financial statements. Under the Securities Act of 1933, companies wanting to issue securities interstate must file a prospectus with the SEC. The prospectus is a public document—prepared for each new security offering—containing information about the company, its officers, and its financial affairs. The financial section of the prospectus must be audited by an independent CPA who is registered to practice before the SEC. Once securities have been sold to the public, the company is required to file publicly accessible, audited financial statements with the SEC each year. These annual statements are known as the 10-K filing. In addition, unaudited quar-

[24] In fact, Congress later passed legislation permitting the investment tax credit to "flow through" to reported earnings in the year the credit was taken against the company's federal tax obligation. This situation illustrates the ultimate power of the Congress over the establishment of financial reporting and accounting standards in the United States. See "Accounting for the Investment Credit," *APB Opinion No. 2* (New York: AICPA, 1962); "Accounting for the Investment Credit," *APB Opinion No. 4* (New York: AICPA, 1964).

terly financial reports (called 10-Q filings) are required. The annual 10-K disclosure requirements closely overlap the information in the company's published financial statements, but are more extensive.[25]

Although the SEC has wide statutory authority to impose financial reporting rules, it continues to rely on the accounting profession to set and enforce accounting standards and to regulate the profession. The SEC has occasionally forced the accounting profession to tackle critical problems, and it once rejected an accounting standard issued by the FASB.[26] Such situations occur rarely.

Since July 1973, the FASB has been responsible for establishing accounting standards in the United States. The FASB has issued over 150 Statements of Financial Accounting Standards, seven Statements of Financial Accounting Concepts, and numerous technical bulletins. The FASB has neither the authority nor the responsibility to enforce compliance with GAAP. That responsibility rests with company management, the accounting profession, the SEC, and the courts. Some observers believe that compliance is the weak link in the private-sector standard-setting chain. These critics point to frequent litigation on financial reporting matters in the courts, the escalating cost of liability insurance premiums paid by audit firms, and criticism by the SEC's chief accountant regarding the independence of external auditors.[27]

The FASB follows a "due process" procedure in developing accounting standards. This process is designed to ensure public input in the decision process. Most accounting standards issued by the FASB go through three steps:

1. *Discussion-memorandum stage:* After the Board and its staff have considered a topic on its agenda—and perhaps consulted with experts and other interested parties—a discussion memorandum is issued. This memorandum outlines the key issues involved and the Board's preliminary views on those issues. The public is invited to comment in writing on the memorandum, and public hearings are sometimes held to permit interested individuals to express their views in person.
2. *Exposure-draft stage:* After further deliberation and modification by the Board and its staff, an exposure draft of the standard is issued. During this stage, a period of not less than 30 days, further public comment is requested and evaluated.
3. *Voting stage:* Finally, the Board votes on whether to issue the standard as contained in the exposure draft or to revise it and reissue a new exposure draft. For a proposed standard to become official and a part of generally accepted accounting principles, five of the seven Board members must approve it.

Influential groups and organizations use the due process of the FASB to plead for alternative solutions. The arguments often include cost-benefit considerations; claims that the proposed accounting treatment is not theoretically sound or will not be understood by users; implementation issues; and concerns that the proposed standard will be economically harmful to specific companies, industries, or the country.[28] Government agencies, preparer organizations such as the Business

---

[25] The financial reporting and accounting requirements pertaining to SEC registrants are described in the following publications: Regulation S-X, the original and comprehensive document issued by the commission that prescribes financial reporting rules and the forms to be filed with the SEC; Accounting Series Releases, which are amendments, extensions, and additions to Regulation S-X; Special SEC Releases that relate to current issues as they arise; Accounting and Auditing Enforcement Releases (AAERs), which document the SEC response to accounting and auditing irregularities; and Financial Reporting Releases (FRRs). The FRRs, together with AAERs, are the successors to Accounting Series Releases. Staff Accounting Bulletins are issued by Office of the Chief Accountant and serve as interpretations of Regulation S-X and its amendments, extensions, and additions; they do not carry the legal weight of Commission releases.

[26] "Financial Accounting and Reporting by Oil and Gas Producing Companies," *Statement of Financial Accounting Standards (SFAS) NO. 19* (Stamford, CT: FASB, 1977). This statement was issued after protracted deliberation, and it identified a single method of accounting that was to be followed by all affected companies. In August 1978 the SEC ruled that a new method of accounting for oil and gas reserves needed to be developed and that in the meantime companies could use any method that had been generally accepted prior to *SFAS No. 19*. This directly contradicted the FASB and required the issuance of both a statement suspending *SFAS No. 19* and a second FASB statement finally bringing the SEC and FASB into conformity with one another. SEC involvement was, in part, due to enactment of a public law requiring an investigation into, and action on, the state of oil and gas accounting rules by December 25, 1977. Such legal deadlines in connection with the accounting standard setting process are rare. Aspects of this controversy are discussed in Chapter 10.

[27] W. P. Schuetze, "A Mountain or a Molehill?" *Accounting Horizons* (March 1994), pp. 69–75.

[28] For example, SEC reversal of *SFAS No. 19* was justified on the grounds that implementation of the proposed accounting standard would sharply inhibit petroleum exploration and development activities.

Roundtable, and industry trade organizations such as the Financial Executives Institute create substantial pressures on the Board. Some contend that the interests of investors, creditors, and other financial statement users are not always well represented in this political forum. Others disagree.

Public Company Accounting Oversight Board

When Congress gave the task of setting accounting standards to the newly created SEC in 1934, it left the job of overseeing auditing standards and individual audit firms to the accounting profession. For nearly seven decades, the job has been performed by the AICPA and its predecessor organization through a group called the Public Oversight Board. The Board was established to monitor the conduct of auditors and was funded by industry, but it had little power to enforce auditing standards or discipline wayward audit firms.

The successor to the old Board, the Public Company Accounting Oversight Board (PCAOB) is funded by mandatory fees from public companies and operates under the oversight of the SEC. The new Board was created by the Sarbanes-Oxley Act of 2002. The Board is empowered to establish auditing standards, including standards for independence and ethics, and to conduct periodic quality reviews ("inspections") of auditors' work. The Board can also investigate alleged audit failures and impose penalties on auditors and their firms. The PCAOB can fine, censure, suspend, or bar from practice auditors and audit firms for wrongdoing.

International Accounting Standards

International

When looking to register securities in U.S. markets, a major impediment foreign companies encounter is the significant differences between U.S. and foreign accounting standards. Several groups have long worked to achieve "convergence" of worldwide accounting and reporting standards. At the center of this effort are the International Accounting Standards Board (IASB), which sets international accounting rules, and the International Organization of Securities Commissions (IOSCO), of which the SEC is a member. The International Accounting Standards Committee (IASC) was the predecessor body of the IASB. As part of an agreement with the IOSCO, the IASC developed a core set of International Accounting Standards (IAS), completed in 1999. The IOSCO endorsed these accounting standards for cross-border capital raising and stock exchange listing purposes in May 2000.

Formed in 1973, the IASC was the result of an agreement by accountancy bodies in Australia, Canada, France, West Germany, Japan, Mexico, the Netherlands, the United Kingdom, and the United States. The IASC was restructured in 2001 and the IASB assumed its duties. The IASB now has a membership that includes 153 professional accounting organizations from more than 112 countries around the world. The standard-setting function is performed by a board made up of 14 members. The IASB has issued 43 standards and 33 interpretations of existing standards. Existing IASB standards typically allow firms greater latitude in their accounting and reporting practices than does U.S. GAAP.

Founded in 1974, the IOSCO seeks member cooperation to improve domestic and international financial markets, to promote the development of domestic markets through information exchange, to establish standards and effective surveillance of international securities transactions, and to ensure the integrity of markets by rigorous application of standards and enforcement. In 1998, the IOSCO adopted disclosure standards that enable multinational companies to prepare a single nonfinancial-statement disclosure document (including, for example, a description of the company's history, business, risks, and ownership) for cross-border securities offerings and stock exchange listings. In addition to greatly simplifying preparation, investors benefit from the comprehensive required disclosures and enhanced comparability of information. The SEC adopted these IOSCO disclosure standards in 1999.

The SEC continues to make it clear that U.S. financial reporting standards will not be lowered for domestic public companies. The SEC will consider international accounting standards for use by foreign companies, without reconciliation to U.S. GAAP, but only when the standards meet certain criteria:

> The IASB was originally named the International Accounting Standards Committee (IASC) and its pronouncements were called International Accounting Standards (IAS). Pronouncements issued by the IASB are known as International Financial Reporting Standards (IFRS).

- They include a core set of accounting pronouncements constituting a comprehensive, generally accepted basis of accounting.
- They are high quality—that is, they result in comparability and transparency, and provide for full disclosure.
- They can and will be rigorously interpreted and applied.

It remains to be seen to what extent the SEC will fully embrace international accounting standards for financial statement filings.

PROBLEMS/DISCUSSION QUESTIONS

P1 – 1

Demand for accounting information

Required:

1. Explain why each of the following groups might want financial accounting information. What type of financial information would each group find most useful?

   a. the company's existing shareholders
   b. prospective investors
   c. financial analysts who follow the company
   d. company managers
   e. current employees
   f. commercial lenders who have loaned money to the company
   g. current suppliers
   h. debt rating agencies like Moody's or Standard and Poor's
   i. regulatory agencies like the Federal Trade Commission

2. Identify at least one other group that might want financial accounting information about the company, and describe how the information would be used.

P1 – 2

Incentives for voluntary disclosure

Required:

1. Describe how the following market forces influence the supply of financial accounting information:

   a. debt and equity financial markets
   b. managerial labor markets
   c. the market for corporate control (for example, mergers, takeovers, and divestitures)

2. What other forces might cause managers to voluntarily release financial information about the company?
3. Identify five ways managers can voluntarily provide information about the company to outsiders. What advantages do these voluntary approaches have over the required financial disclosures contained in annual and quarterly reports to shareholders?

P1 – 3

Costs of disclosure

Required:

1. Define each of the following disclosure costs associated with financial accounting information, and provide an example of each cost:

   a. information collection, processing, dissemination costs
   b. competitive disadvantage costs
   c. litigation costs
   d. political costs

2. Identify at least one other potential disclosure cost.

P1 – 4

Proxy statement disclosures

A company's proxy statement contains information about major shareholders, management compensation (salary, bonus, stock options, etc.), composition of the board of directors, and shares owned by top managers and members of the board of directors.

Required:

Explain why this information might be useful to a financial analyst following the firm.

P1 – 5

Relevant and reliable information

You have decided to buy a new automobile, and have been gathering information about the purchase price. The manufacturer's website shows a "list price" of $24,500, which includes all of your preferred options—leather trim, CD player, and so on. You have also consulted the "Blue Book" guide to car prices and found that the average price paid for a similar vehicle is $19,500. However, the guide also indicates that recent selling prices have ranged from $18,000 up to $22,000.

Required:

1. Which price quote—the "list price" or the "Blue Book" average price—is the most relevant for your decision? Why?
2. Which price quote is the most reliable? Why?

P1 – 6

Relevant and reliable
accounting information

Farmers State Bank is considering a $500,000 loan to Willard Manufacturing. Three items appearing on the balance sheet of Willard Manufacturing are:
a. Cash on hand and in the bank, $20,000
b. Accounts receivable of $60,000, less an allowance for uncollectibles of $15,000
c. Accumulated depreciation of $36,000

Required:

1. Which of the balance sheet items—cash, net accounts receivable, or accumulated depreciation—is the most relevant for the bank's loan decision? Why?
2. Which of the balance sheet items is the most reliable? Why?

P1 – 7

Accounting conservatism

Suppose your company purchased land and a warehouse for $5 million. The price was steep, but you were told that a new interstate highway was going to be built nearby. Two months later, the highway project is cancelled and your property is now worth only $3 million.

Required:

1. How does the concept of accounting conservatism apply to this situation?
2. Suppose instead that you paid $3 million and later learned that the property is worth $5 million because a new highway is going to be built nearby. How does the conservatism concept apply to this new situation? Why?

P1 – 8

Your position on the issues

Provide a two- or three-sentence response that argues for or against (indicate which) each of these statements:
a. Accounting is an exact science.
b. Managers choose accounting procedures that produce the most accurate picture of the company's operating performance and financial condition.
c. Accounting standards in the United States are influenced more by politics than by science or economics.
d. If the FASB and SEC were not around to require and enforce minimum levels of financial disclosure, most companies would provide little (if any) information to outsiders.
e. When managers possess good news about the company (that is, information that will increase the stock price), they have an incentive to disclose the information as soon as possible.
f. When managers possess bad news about the company (that is, information that will decrease the stock price), they have an incentive to delay disclosure as long as possible.
g. An investor who uses fundamental analysis for investment decisions has little need for financial statement information.
h. An investor who believes that capital markets are efficient has little need for financial statement information.
i. Managers who disclose only the minimum information required to meet FASB and SEC requirements may be doing a disservice to shareholders.
j. Financial statements are the only source of information analysts use when forecasting the company's future profitability and financial condition.

P1 – 9

How managers and
professional investors
rate information

A wide variety of financial and nonfinancial information is used in managing a company and in making decisions about whether or not to invest in a company. A survey of senior corporate managers and professional investors asked each group to rank the following items according to their relative importance ("1" being the most important and "14" being the least important). How do you think each item was ranked?

	Importance Ranking	
	Corporate Managers	Professional Investors
Business segment results	_____	_____
Capital expenditures	_____	_____
Cash flow	_____	_____
Cost control	_____	_____
Customer satisfaction	_____	_____
Earnings	_____	_____
Market growth	_____	_____
Market share	_____	_____
Measures of strategic achievement	_____	_____
New product development	_____	_____
Product and process quality	_____	_____
Research and development (R & D)	_____	_____
R & D productivity	_____	_____
Strategic goals	_____	_____

P1 – 10

Economic consequences of accounting standards

In the early 1990s, the Financial Accounting Standards Board issued new rules that dramatically altered the way in which many companies recorded their obligations for postretirement healthcare benefits. The Board found that most companies used "cash basis" accounting and waited until expenditures for benefits were actually made before recording any expense. This meant that no liability to pay future benefits appeared on the companies' balance sheets even though an obligation to pay future healthcare benefits clearly existed. The FASB concluded that this approach was inappropriate, and instead required companies to record the cost of future healthcare benefits as incurred.

The affected companies and their trade organizations argued that having to record a liability and an expense equal to the extremely large dollar amounts of these healthcare benefit commitments would cause employers to substantially reduce their promised benefits to employees, and perhaps curtail the benefits entirely.

Required:

1. Why were companies concerned about suddenly reporting a large liability (and corresponding expense) for postretirement healthcare benefits? What economic consequences might this accounting change have on the affected companies?
2. Some affected companies said they would reduce or eliminate promised benefits in order to avoid recording the liability and expense. This action harms employees who will then have to bear the burden of future healthcare costs. Should the FASB take economic consequences of this sort into consideration when setting accounting standards? Why or why not?

P1 – 11

Two sets of books

"It's time for the government to stop enabling accounting fraud. The Internal Revenue Service and the SEC let companies keep two sets of books, one for tax reporting and the other for financial reporting. There should be no difference in the figures corporations report to the IRS and the SEC. The combined surveillance and enforcement by these agencies of one set of books and identical tax and financial reports should give the investing public a clearer picture of corporate performance." Letter to the Editor, *BusinessWeek* (August 12, 2002).

Required:

1. Why do companies keep two sets of accounting books, one for tax reporting and the other for shareholder financial reports?
2. Why might it *not* be a good idea to force companies to issue the same financial statements for both IRS and SEC purposes?

P1 – 12

Accounting quality and the audit committee

The New York Stock Exchange (NYSE), the National Association of Securities Dealers (NASD), and the American Stock Exchange (AMEX) require that listed firms have audit committees comprised of independent (that is, outside) company directors. Audit committees review the firm's audited financial statements with management and with the outside auditor, and recommend to the full board of directors that the statements be included in the company's annual report. As a committee member, you might ask management about the following:

1. What are the key business and financial risks the company has to deal with in its financial reporting?
2. What financial reporting areas involved subjective judgments or estimates?
3. Are there significant areas where the company's accounting policies were difficult to determine?
4. How do the company's accounting practices compare with those of others in the industry?
5. How are significant accounting judgments made and estimates determined?
6. Are the financial statements and underlying accounting methods consistent with those used last year?
7. What major business transactions or events required significant accounting or disclosure judgments?
8. Are alternative accounting practices being proposed or considered that should be brought to the committee's attention?
9. Were there serious problems in preparing the financial statements?
10. Have outside parties—including the SEC, major investors, analysts, and the news media—voiced concern about the company's accounting practices?
11. Were there disagreements between management and the auditor regarding accounting practices and, if so, how were they resolved?

Source: Audit Committee Update 2000, PricewaterhouseCoopers LLP.

Required:

Explain for each question why the audit committee and investors might be interested in the answer.

CASES

C1 – 1

AST Research: Restating quarter results

AST Research Inc., a personal computer manufacturer, announced an accounting change that in many ways parallels the one made at America Online: Costs previously deferred were to be expensed immediately, and the change had no direct impact on current or future cash flows. A copy of the *Wall Street Journal* article announcing AST's accounting change follows:

AST Research said it is restating results for its fiscal 1994 fourth quarter as a result of a disagreement with the Securities and Exchange Commission over accounting rules.

The restatement will cause AST to report a loss of $8.1 million, or 25 cents a share, for the fourth quarter ended July 2, instead of the previously reported net income of $14.1 million, or 41 cents a share. The dispute arose out of an SEC review of AST's proxy statement for a $377.5 million investment in the company by Samsung Electronics Company.

The SEC staff concluded that $33.6 million of the expenses related to AST's 1993 acquisition of the computer manufacturing operations of Tandy Corporation should be charged to sales during the fourth quarter, rather than amortized over future quarters as goodwill.

AST said that the SEC didn't force it to restate the results, and that AST had agreed to the restatement to avoid delays in approval of the proxy and the Samsung investment. The redesignation of income has no material effect on AST. It's a noncash loss and will be offset by increases in net income in subsequent quarters, because of the lack of goodwill amortization.

In Nasdaq Stock Market trading yesterday, AST closed at $17.625, up 25 cents.

"They [the SEC] had a different interpretation on a piece of the accounting for the acquisition," said Bruce Edwards, AST's chief financial officer. "We decided to do the restatement to move forward on the transaction" with Samsung.

An SEC official acknowledged that the agency's corporation finance division had been in talks with AST about its fourth-quarter earnings report but wouldn't say whether the SEC pressured AST to revise the report.

It isn't unusual for the agency to question a company's account of its own earnings, the official said. Only in rare cases does such a review spell bigger problems for the company, such as when the SEC thinks executives intentionally misstated earnings to hype a stock price. But there isn't any indication that AST did that in this case, the official added.

AST also agreed to issue additional shares to Samsung if AST incurs any uninsured losses, in excess of a certain threshold, as a result of being sued by shareholders. AST said it has now received all necessary approvals for Samsung's investment.

The company scheduled a special meeting of shareholders for June 30 to vote on the transaction.

Source: "AST Research," *Wall Street Journal* (June 8, 1995); Republished with permission of Dow Jones & Co.

Required:

Why was the stock market so forgiving in evaluating the accounting method change made by AST Research?

As your first week at Henley Manufacturing Inc. draws to a close, you find a memorandum on your desk from the company's CEO. The memo outlines sales and earnings goals for next year: Sales are expected to increase 15% with net income growing by 20%.

The memo says that these goals are ambitious in light of the company's performance over the past two years—ambitious, but attainable if "everyone remains focused and committed to our business strategy."

As you finish the memo, your boss, the vice president of finance, steps into your office. She asks you what you think about the memo. You reply that it is important to have clear financial goals but that you would need to know more before making any comments on whether the goals will be easy or difficult to achieve. As she leaves your office, you ask if the CEO will be announcing these goals at next week's annual shareholders' meeting. Your boss answers, "We've never disclosed our sales and earning goals in the past." When you ask why, she says, "We aren't required to under U.S. securities regulations."

Two days later, your boss stops by again and tells you that she raised the issue of disclosing to shareholders the firm's net income and sales goals at this morning's executive committee meeting. The CEO was intrigued but requested that someone identify the costs and benefits of doing so. As she leaves your office, your boss asks you to prepare a briefing document for presentation at the next executive committee meeting.

C1 – 2

Henley Manufacturing Inc. (CW): Announcing sales and earnings goals

Required A:

1. What are the potential costs and benefits to Henley Manufacturing of announcing its sales and earnings goals at the shareholders' meeting?
2. Would you recommend that the CEO announce both, one, or neither goal? Why?
3. If the company's sales and earnings goals covered three years rather than just next year, would your recommendation change? Why or why not?

Required B:

Suppose the memo was more detailed and described the following financial goals for next year: annual sales growth of 15%; annual earnings growth of 20%; a return on net tangible assets of 16%; a return on common equity of 20%; a minimum current ratio of 2.4; a minimum interest coverage ratio of 7.0; a minimum profit margin of 5%; a dividend payout ratio (dividends/net income) of 35% to 40%; a maximum long-term debt to common equity ratio of 40% to 45%; a minimum increase of 15% in annual capital expenditures; and a minimum inventory turnover ratio of 4.5.

Would you recommend that the CEO disclose all, some, or none of these goals at the shareholders' meeting? Which ones and why?

The following excerpt is from Whirlpool Corporation's 2002 10-K report filed with the SEC and is a required disclosure:

> The company has been the principal supplier of home laundry appliances to Sears, Roebuck and Co. ("Sears") for over 80 years. The company is also the principal supplier to Sears of residential trash compactors and a major supplier to Sears of dishwashers, free-standing ranges, home refrigerators and freezers, and microwave-hood combinations. The company supplies products to Sears for sale under Sears' Kenmore brand name. Sears has also been a major outlet for the company's Whirlpool and KitchenAid brand products since 1989. In 2002 approximately 21% of the company's net sales were attributable to sales to Sears.

C1 – 3

Whirlpool (CW): Disclosing major customers

Required:

1. Why does the SEC require companies like Whirlpool to alert financial statement readers to the existence of major customers?
2. How might this information be of use to a financial analyst?
3. Why might Sears want to monitor the financial performance and health of Whirlpool? What specific information about Whirlpool would be of most interest to Sears?
4. Why might Whirlpool want to monitor the financial performance and health of Sears? What information about Sears would be of most interest to Whirlpool?

C1 – 4

The gap in GAAP (CW)

It is often alleged that the value of financial statement information is compromised by the latitude that GAAP gives to management. Companies can use different accounting methods to summarize and report the outcome of otherwise similar transactions. Inventory valuation and depreciation are examples in which GAAP allows several alternative accounting methods.

At one extreme the FASB and the SEC could limit accounting flexibility by establishing a single set of accounting methods and procedures that all companies would apply. At the other extreme, the FASB and the SEC could simply require companies to provide relevant and reliable financial information to outsiders, without placing any restrictions on the accounting methods used.

Required:

1. Why should managers be allowed some flexibility in their financial accounting and reporting choices?
2. Of the two approaches to accounting standard-setting that are mentioned above, which best describes the current financial reporting environment in the United States?
3. Describe the advantages and disadvantages of these two approaches to accounting standard-setting, and tell how these advantages and disadvantages vary across different groups of financial statement users.

C1 – 5

IES Industries: Voting on a merger

In early 1996 IES Industries signed a definitive merger agreement with two other neighboring utilities—Wisconsin Power and Light (WPL) and Interstate Power Company (IPC). This was the first "three-way" merger in the rapidly consolidating electrical utility industry.

The merger seemed to make good economic sense. Predictions indicated that deregulation of the industry would create intense price competition. All three companies had low-cost generating capacity when compared to other utilities in the Midwest. By forming a single company, the merger partners could become even more price competitive by eliminating redundancies in energy distribution, maintenance, customer service, and corporate staffs. They could then expand their combined geographical reach to lucrative metropolitan markets in the region.

Wall Street was ambivalent about the merger. The merger announcement resulted in a 10% share price increase for IPC, but IES and WPL share prices remained flat. Part of the market's ambivalence was due to the fact that the merger required state and federal regulatory approval. Analysts predicted a lengthy approval process and voiced uncertainty about the eventual outcome.

In July 1996 MidAmerican Energy launched a hostile takeover of IES Industries. MidAmerican offered to pay $35 per share for IES stock, a $5 per-share premium over the closing price that prevailed before the takeover announcement. The board of directors at IES rejected the buyout offer and told shareholders that the company was worth more than $35 per share when combined with WPL and IPC. Shares of IES common stock closed at $33.50 following MidAmerican Energy's hostile offer, and this price was unchanged after the IES rejection.

MidAmerican's tender offer could not have been better timed. IES shareholders were scheduled to vote on the three-way merger agreement in mid-August. With MidAmerican's offer on the table, IES shareholders could vote either to approve the WPL and IPC merger or to reject the merger in favor of MidAmerican's cash bid. IES and MidAmerican launched intense advertising and public relations campaigns to sway IES shareholders. This contest for proxies (shareholder votes) cost the two companies in excess of $10 million.

Required:

1. As an employee of IES Industries and the owner of 100 shares of the company's common stock, what questions would you like answered at the August shareholders' meeting just prior to submitting your vote? How might the company's financial reports help answer those questions?
2. As an institutional investor with 5% of your portfolio invested in IES shares, what questions would you like answered at the August shareholders' meeting just prior to submitting your vote? How might the company's financial reports help answer those questions?

C1 – 6

Trans World Airlines' (TWA) earnings announcement (CW)

Returning home from your job as a financial analyst covering the airline industry, you find a message from your father, a veteran pilot for TWA. He will be in town this evening and would like you to join him for dinner. He needs your investment advice. Having been with TWA during the company's two trips to bankruptcy court, he is ecstatic over an article in today's issue of the *Wall Street Journal*.

TWA announced net income of $623.8 million for the year, compared to a loss of $317.7 million in the prior year. At last the company seems to have recovered from its financial difficulty.

As a stockholder of TWA, your father is wondering if he should purchase more of the company's stock and if TWA might start paying dividends again now that it is profitable. He thinks the pilots' union might recover some of the wage concessions that it made during the bankruptcy process. Given the age of TWA's fleet (about 18 years), he hopes that some of the profits might be used to buy new airliners.

As you finish reading the news article, you realize that dinner is less than two hours away. What advice do you have for your father?

ST. LOUIS—Trans World Airlines, helped by a big gain from retiring debt, posted 1993 net income of $623.8 million compared with a year-earlier loss of $317.7 million.

Before the $1.08 billion gain, TWA's 1993 loss widened to $451.8 million from $317.7 million in 1992. TWA, which emerged from bankruptcy-law proceedings last November, said the gain reflected a debt-for-equity swap that was part of its reorganization plan. Creditors received a 55% stake in TWA for forgiving about $1 billion in debt.

The airline's operating losses, before taxes and credits and charges, were $281.3 million in 1993 and $404.6 million in 1992. TWA's revenue fell 13% to $3.16 billion from $3.63 billion, as the company reduced its airline operations about 15% beginning in the fall of 1992.

The carrier didn't break out fourth-quarter results, saying there is 'no meaningful comparison' with the year-earlier figures. Because of its emergence from Chapter 11 protection from creditors, TWA said its financial statements were prepared on both a pre- and post-reorganization basis for different parts of the fourth quarter.

The company's load factor, or percentage of seats filled, slipped to 63.5% during 1993 from 64.7%. TWA's yield, or revenue per passenger mile, increased to 11.35 cents in 1993 from 10.22 cents the year before.

Source: "St. Louis: Trans World Airlines," *Wall Street Journal* (April 1, 1994); Republished with permission of Dow Jones & Co.

COLLABORATIVE LEARNING CASE

C1 – 7

Landfil's Accounting Change

You have been asked to attend a hastily called meeting of Landfil's senior executives. The meeting was called to formulate a strategy for responding to questions from shareholders, analysts, and the media about Landfil's accounting for site development costs. A major competitor, Chambers Development, announced yesterday that it would no longer capitalize site development costs but instead would expense those costs as they were incurred. Stock market reaction to the Chambers' announcement was swift and negative, with the stock down 57% at this morning's opening of the NYSE.

Landfil Inc. acquires, operates, and develops nonhazardous solid waste disposal facilities. Landfil is the third largest waste management company of its type in the United States, with 37 disposal sites. Sales have been growing at the rate of 30% annually for the last five years, and the company has established a solid record of earnings and operating cash flow performance.

Accounting Policy

Landfil capitalizes site development costs in much the same way that Chambers Development did prior to its announcement yesterday. Under the old accounting method at Chambers Development, when the firm spent $20 million on landfill site development, it would book the entire amount as a deferred asset. Then Chambers would spread the cost over 10 years by charging $2 million to earnings each year. Under the new accounting method, all $20 million is expensed in the first year.

Landfil has included the following description of its site development accounting in all annual reports issued during the last five years:

> The Company capitalizes landfill acquisition costs, including out-of-pocket incremental expenses incurred in connection with the preacquisition phase of a specific project (for example, engineering, legal, and accounting due-diligence fees); the acquisition purchase price, including future

guaranteed payments to sellers; and commissions. If an acquisition is not consummated, or a development project is abandoned, all of such costs are expensed. Salaries, office expenses, and similar administrative costs are not capitalized. Landfill development and permitting costs, including the cost of property, engineering, legal, and other professional fees, and interest are capitalized and amortized over the estimated useful life of the property upon commencement of operations.

The Meeting

Discussion at the meeting became rather heated as several different points of view emerged. Some members of the executive team argued that Landfil should do nothing but reaffirm its capitalization policy, informing shareholders and others who contacted the company that this policy was consistent with GAAP and disclosed fully in the annual report. Other members of the team argued for a more proactive response involving both direct communication with shareholders and analysts as well as press releases to the media. These communications would also reaffirm the company's capitalization policy but in a more strident manner. Still other members of the executive team argued that Landfil should immediately announce that it too was discontinuing capitalization in favor of immediate expensing. No clear consensus emerged as the meeting progressed, and the group decided to take a 10-minute break before resuming discussion.

As the meeting was about to reconvene, the CEO stopped by your chair and said, "I've been handed a phone message indicating that our largest shareholder has just called. She wants to know our reaction to the events at Chambers Development. I have to call her back in 15 minutes with an answer. When the meeting starts, I'd like you to summarize the major issues we face and to state how you think we should proceed."

C1 – 8

AstroText Company: Questions for the stockholders' meeting

Yesterday, AstroText announced its friendly acquisition of TextTools Inc. AstroText intends to pay $20 per share for all the outstanding common stock of TextTools. At this price TextTools stockholders will be receiving a per share premium of $7 over the company's closing stock price just two days ago. There are 3 million shares outstanding, so the $7 per share premium represents $21 million in total.

AstroText and TextTools are both relatively young software development companies with similar product lines. Both companies have developed leading edge document creation software for the Internet. AstroText has focused its product line on individuals, on small businesses, and on academic markets. TextTools has targeted the corporate market, where security and encryption are extremely important. To maintain their technological edge, both companies must continue to invest heavily in software research and development. Frequent product updates are the norm for companies like AstroText and TextTools. In addition, both companies have historically spent considerable resources on product marketing and advertising.

AstroText is hosting a stockholders' meeting later today to discuss details of the acquisition. So far, the company has said very little about why it's willing to pay a $7 per share premium for TextTools, about how the all-cash deal will be financed, or about why the two companies will be worth more together than they are separately.

Required:

1. Suppose you are an employee of AstroText who owns 100 shares of the company's stock. You have also received a substantial number of long-term stock options as part of your compensation package. What questions do you want answered at the stockholders' meeting? What information (if any) in the company's financial reports might help answer those questions?
2. Assume you are the lead banker for AstroText. You were quite surprised to learn of the TextTools acquisition, in part because your loan to AstroText contains a provision that prohibits the company from making cash acquisitions without your approval. What questions do you want answered at the stockholders' meeting? What information (if any) in the company's financial reports might help answer those questions?

Remember to check the book's Companion Website for additional problem and case material.

Accrual Accounting and Income Determination

This chapter describes the key concepts and practices that govern the measurement of annual or quarterly income (or earnings) for financial reporting purposes. Income is the difference between **revenues** and **expenses**. The cornerstone of income measurement is **accrual accounting**. Under accrual accounting *revenues are recorded in the period when they are "earned" and become "measurable"—* that is, when the seller has performed a service or conveyed an asset to a buyer and the value to be received for that service or asset is reasonably assured and can be measured with a high degree of reliability.[1] *Expenses are the expired costs or assets "used up" in producing those revenues, and they are recorded in the same accounting period in which the revenues are recognized using the "matching principle."*

A natural consequence of accrual accounting is the decoupling of measured earnings from operating cash inflows and outflows. Reported revenues under accrual accounting generally do not correspond to cash receipts for the period; also, reported expenses do not always correspond to cash outlays of the period. In fact, *accrual accounting can produce large discrepancies between the firm's reported profit performance and the amount of cash generated from operations. Frequently, however, accrual accounting earnings provide a more accurate measure of the economic value added during the period than do operating cash flows.*[2]

This point is illustrated by the following example, which highlights the basic distinction between cash and accrual accounting measures of performance.

---

[1] In "Elements of Financial Statements," *Statement of Financial Accounting Concepts No. 6*, the Financial Accounting Standards Board (FASB) defines revenues as ". . . inflows or other enhancements of assets of an entity or settlements of its liabilities (or a combination of both) from delivering or producing goods, rendering services, or other activities that constitute the entity's ongoing major or central operations" (para. 78). Expenses are defined as ". . . outflows or other using up of assets or incurrences of liabilities (or a combination of both) from delivering or producing goods, rendering services, or carrying out other activities that constitute the entity's ongoing major or central operations" (para. 80).

[2] *Economic value added* represents the increase in the value of a product or service as a consequence of operating activities. To illustrate, the value of an assembled automobile far exceeds the value of its separate steel, glass, plastic, rubber, and electronics components. The difference between the aggregate cost of the various parts utilized in manufacturing the automobile and the price at which the car is sold to the dealer represents economic value added (or lost) by production.

Learning Objectives
After studying this chapter, you will understand:

1. The distinction between cash-basis versus accrual income, and why accrual income generally is a better measure of operating performance.

2. The criteria for revenue recognition under accrual accounting, and how they are used in selected industries.

3. The matching principle, and how it is applied to recognize expenses under accrual accounting.

4. The difference between product and period costs.

5. The format and classifications for a multiple-step income statement, and how the statement format is designed to differentiate earnings components that are more sustainable from those that are more transitory.

6. The distinction between special and unusual items, discontinued operations, extraordinary items, and the cumulative effect of accounting changes.

7. The distinction between basic and diluted earnings per share (EPS) and required EPS disclosures for certain income statement components.

8. What comprises comprehensive income and alternative formats for displaying this amount in the financial statements.

9. The basic procedures for preparing financial statements and how to conduct T-account analysis.

Example: Cash versus Accrual Income Measurement

> The entries to record the initial borrowing and repayment of the loan principal are ignored since they are financing activities that do not affect the determination of cash-basis income.

In January 2005 Canterbury Publishing sells a three-year subscription to its quarterly publication, *Windy City Living*, to 1,000 subscribers. The subscription plan requires prepayment by the customers, so the full subscription price of $300 (12 issues × $25 per issue) was received by Canterbury from each of the subscribers ($300 × 1,000 = $300,000) at the beginning of 2005. To help finance the purchase of newsprint and other printing supplies, Canterbury takes out a $100,000 three-year loan from a local bank on January 1, 2005. The loan calls for interest of 10% of the face amount of the loan each year (10% × $100,000 = $10,000), but the interest is not payable until the loan matures on December 31, 2007. The cost of publishing and distributing the magazine amounts to $60,000 each year ($60 per subscriber), which is paid in cash at the time of publication. The entries to record the **cash-basis** revenues and expenses for each year would be as follows:

> Throughout this book **DR** represents the debit side and **CR** represents the credit side of the accounting entry to record the transaction being discussed. See the appendix to this chapter for a review of how these transactions are recorded.

Cash-basis entries for 2005

DR Cash	$300,000	
CR Subscriptions revenue		$300,000

To record collection of 1,000 three-year subscriptions at $300 each for *Windy City Living.*

DR Publishing and distribution expense	$ 60,000	
CR Cash		$ 60,000

To record publishing and distribution expenses paid in cash.

Cash-basis entries for 2006

DR Publishing and distribution expense	$ 60,000	
CR Cash		$ 60,000

To record publishing and distribution expenses paid in cash.

Cash-basis entries for 2007

DR Publishing and distribution expense	$ 60,000	
CR Cash		$ 60,000

To record publishing and distribution expenses paid in cash.

DR Interest expense	$ 30,000	
CR Cash		$ 30,000

To record interest expense paid on the three-year loan ($100,000 × .10 × 3 years = $30,000).

A schedule of operating cash inflows and outflows and cash-basis income would look as follows:

Cash-Basis Income Determination			
($000 omitted)	2005	2006	2007
Cash inflows	$300	$—	$—
Cash outflows for production and distribution	(60)	(60)	(60)
Cash outflow for interest on loan	—	—	(30)
Net income (loss)—Cash basis	$240	$(60)	$(90)

Publishing the magazine and servicing the subscriptions requires economic effort in each of the years 2005 through 2007, as indicated by the $60,000 of operating cash outflows each period.

However, under cash-basis accounting, the entire $300,000 of cash inflow from subscription receipts would be treated as revenue in 2005, the year in which the subscriptions are sold and cash is collected, with no revenue recognized in the remaining two years of the subscription period. Likewise, the $30,000 of interest ($10,000 per year × 3 years) paid on December 31, 2007 would be recorded as an expense in year 2007 under the cash basis of accounting, with no interest expense recognized in the first two years. Consequently, on a cash basis, Canterbury Publishing would report a relatively high "profit" of $240,000 in 2005 when the subscriptions are sold and collected, and this 2005 profit would be followed by operating "losses" of $60,000 in 2006 and $90,000 in 2007 when the costs associated with publishing the remaining issues and financing the operations are paid.

Clearly, cash-basis accounting distorts our view of the operating performance of Canterbury on a year-by-year basis. Moreover, none of the annual cash-basis profit figures provide a reliable benchmark for predicting future operating results. This distortion is due to differences in the timing of when cash inflows and outflows occur. Recognizing cash inflows as revenue and cash outflows as expenses results in a cash-basis income number that fails to properly match effort and accomplishment.

The principles that govern revenue and expense recognition under accrual accounting are designed to alleviate the mismatching problems that exist under cash-basis accounting, making accrual earnings a more useful measure of firm performance. Accrual accounting allocates $100,000 of subscription revenue to each of the years 2005, 2006, and 2007 as the magazine is delivered to subscribers and the revenues are "earned." Likewise, accrual accounting recognizes $10,000 of interest expense in each year the bank loan is outstanding, not just in year 2007 when the interest is paid. These modifications to the cash-basis results to obtain accrual earnings are accomplished by means of the following series of "deferral" and "accrual" **adjusting entries**, which are made at the end of each year under accrual accounting (see the appendix for details).

> Revenues are "earned" as a consequence of publishing magazines and servicing subscriptions—economic activities that span a three-year period. Canterbury's obligation to subscribers is fulfilled gradually over these three years as each issue is delivered, not just in 2005 when cash is collected.

Adjusting entries on December 31, 2005

DR Subscriptions revenue	$200,000	
CR Deferred subscriptions revenue		$200,000

To adjust the subscriptions revenue account for subscriptions received but not yet earned. ($300,000 was initially credited to subscriptions revenue. Only $100,000 was earned in 2005. Therefore, subscriptions revenue must be debited for $200,000.) Deferred subscriptions revenue is a liability account reflecting Canterbury's obligation to provide subscribers with future issues of *Windy City Living*.

DR Interest expense	$ 10,000	
CR Accrued interest payable		$ 10,000

To adjust for interest expense incurred but not yet paid, and to set up a liability for interest accrued during the period that will be paid on December 31, 2007.

Adjusting entries on December 31, 2006

DR Deferred subscriptions revenue	$100,000	
CR Subscriptions revenue		$100,000

To adjust deferred subscriptions revenue and recognize revenue for subscriptions earned during the year by providing customers with four issues of *Windy City Living*.

DR Interest expense	$ 10,000	
CR Accrued interest payable		$ 10,000

To adjust for interest expense incurred but not yet paid, and to set up a liability for interest accrued during the period that will be paid on December 31, 2007.

On December 31, 2007 the accrued interest is paid and the following entry would be made:

DR Accrued interest
  payable $30,000
CR Cash $30,000

Adjusting entries on December 31, 2007

DR Deferred subscriptions revenue $100,000
  CR Subscriptions revenue $100,000
To adjust deferred subscriptions revenue and recognize revenue for subscriptions earned during the year by providing customers with four issues of *Windy City Living.*

DR Interest expense $ 10,000
  CR Accrued interest payable $ 10,000
To adjust for interest expense incurred during the year. After this adjusting entry, the Accrued interest payable account will have a balance of $30,000.

After these adjustments, the diagram of accrual-basis income looks like this:

Accrual-Basis Income Determination

($000 omitted)	2005	2006	2007	
Cash received	$300			
Deferred to future years	−$200			
Revenues recognized as "earned" each year	$100	$100	$100	
Expenses				
Publication and distribution (paid in cash)	(60)	(60)	(60)	
			(30)	Interest paid in cash
Interest accrued	(10)	(10)	20	Add: Amounts accrued in prior years
Net income—accrual basis	$ 30	$ 30	$ 30	

From this example, note that accrual accounting revenues for a period do not correspond to cash receipts for the same period ($100,000 of accrual-basis revenue in 2005 does not correspond to the $300,000 of cash received in that year; nor does the $100,000 of recorded accrual revenue in 2006 and 2007 correspond to $0 cash received in those years). Likewise, the reported accrual-basis expenses in a period do not correspond to cash outflows in that period ($10,000 of interest expense recorded under accrual accounting in 2005 and 2006 does not correspond to the $0 of interest paid in those periods; and the $10,000 of interest expense in 2007 does not correspond to the $30,000 of interest paid in cash in that year). As you can see, *a consequence of accrual accounting is the decoupling of measured earnings from operating cash flows.* Indeed, accrual accounting can result in large discrepancies between the firm's reported accrual-basis earnings and the amount of cash generated from operations (cash-basis earnings) year by year, as shown in Figure 2.1.

As this example illustrates, *accrual accounting better matches economic benefit* (revenues from subscriptions) *with economic effort* (magazine publication and distribution expenses and interest costs), *thereby producing a measure of operating performance—accrual earnings—that provides a more realistic picture of past economic activities.* Many believe that accrual accounting numbers also provide a better basis for predicting future performance of an enterprise.

The view that accrual earnings dominate cash flow measures of performance is asserted in *Statement of Financial Accounting Concepts No. 1,* which was issued by the Financial Accounting Standards Board (FASB) in 1978. It stated:

> "... [I]nformation about enterprise earnings and its components measured by accrual accounting generally provides a better indication of enterprise performance than does information about current cash receipts and payments."[3]

---

[3] "Objectives of Financial Reporting by Business Enterprises," *Statement of Financial Accounting Concepts No. 1* (Stamford, CT: FASB, 1978), para. 44.

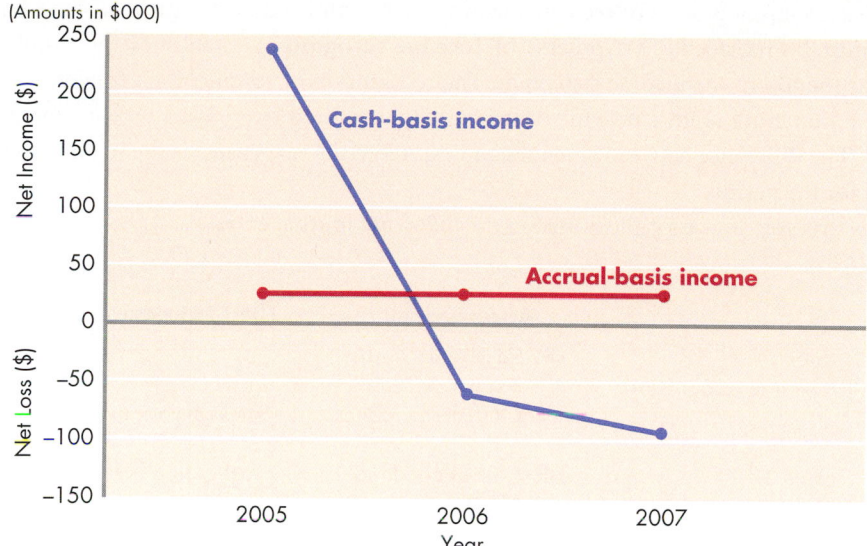

Figure 2.1

CANTERBURY PUBLISHING
Comparison of Accrual-
and Cash-Basis Income

Despite the assertions of the FASB and others regarding the superiority of accrual earnings relative to net cash flows as a measure of a firm's performance, it is important to recognize that reported accrual accounting income for a given period may not always provide an accurate picture of underlying economic performance for that period. One of our objectives is to help you, as a user of accounting information, understand not only the benefits of accrual accounting numbers but also their limitations. Throughout the book we will contrast accounting measurements and their earnings impact with the underlying economic circumstances, highlighting those situations in which the two may diverge.

Measuring Profit Performance: Revenues and Expenses

We have introduced the concept of accrual accounting income and contrasted it with cash-basis earnings in a simplified setting. Now, in more realistic (and complex) settings, we will review some of the mechanics associated with measuring accrual accounting revenues and expenses.

For virtually all firms, income is not earned as a result of just one activity. A manufacturing firm, for example, earns income as a result of these separate and diverse activities:

1. Marketing the product
2. Receiving customers' orders
3. Negotiating and signing production contracts
4. Ordering materials
5. Manufacturing the product
6. Delivering the product
7. Collecting the cash from customers.

The sequence of activities comprising the **operating cycle** of a firm that is presented here is only one of several possible sequences. The activities comprising the operating cycle can vary across firms—or even across products for a given firm. Some companies manufacture the product for inventory prior to identifying a particular purchaser and perhaps even in advance of launching a marketing campaign intended to stimulate product demand (for example, IBM manufacturing a new model of laptop computer). In other cases the product is manufactured to customer order (for example, Boeing manufacturing a new airplane for one of the airlines).

Since income is earned as a result of complex, multiple-stage processes, some guidelines are needed to determine at which stage income is to be recognized in the financial statements. The key issue is the *timing* of income recognition: *When*, under generally accepted accounting principles (GAAP), are revenues and expenses—and thus income—to be recognized?

The accounting process of recognizing income is comprised of two distinct steps. First, revenues must be recorded. This process of **revenue recognition** establishes the numbers that appear at the top of the income statement. The recognition of revenue then triggers the second step—the **matching** against revenue of the costs that expired (were used up) in generating the revenue. The difference between revenues and expired costs (expenses) is the **income** that is recognized for the period.

This two-step process is illustrated in the following journal entries:

	Accounting Entry	Effect on Income (+ or −)
(Step 1) **Revenue recognition**	**DR** Cash or accounts receivable	
	CR Sales revenues	Sales revenues (+)
(Step 2) **Matching of expense**	**DR** Cost of goods sold	Cost of goods sold (−)
	CR Inventory	
Income recognition		Net Income

Income recognition is a by-product of revenue recognition and expense matching. It is not a separate step that is independent of the other two steps. Once revenues are recognized and expenses are matched against the revenue, net income is simply the net difference that results.

The process of revenue recognition and matching expenses against revenue has an obvious effect on the income statement—the bottom-line net income number is increased by the excess of recognized revenues over expired costs. But accrual accounting affects more than income statement accounts. Due to the double-entry, self-balancing nature of accounting, important changes also occur in **net assets** (that is, assets minus liabilities) on the balance sheet. To understand the effect that accrual accounting has on net assets, consider the following example.

ABC Company has only one asset—inventory—with a cost of $100. Its balance sheet appears as:

ABC Company

Initial Balance Sheet

Assets		Liabilities + Owners' Equity	
Inventory	$100	Initial equity	$100

Assume that all of the inventory is sold for $130, which is immediately received in cash. Clearly, income should be recognized as a result of this transaction. We will focus on the balance sheet effects and analyze the transaction using the basic accounting equation:

Assets	=	Liabilities	+	Owners' equity

First, we record the inflow of the asset (cash) and the source of the inflow (sales revenues):

Step 1: **Revenue Recognition**

Assets	=	Liabilities	+	Owners' equity
+$130 Cash				+$130 Sales revenue

Next, we record the outflow of the asset (inventory) and match this expired cost against recognized revenues:

Step 2: **Expense Matching**

Assets	=	Liabilities	+	Owners' equity
−$100 Inventory				−$100 Cost of goods sold

After recording these transactions, the balance sheet shows:

ABC COMPANY

Subsequent Balance Sheet

Assets		Liabilities + Owners' Equity	
Cash	$130	Liabilities	$—
Inventory	—	Initial equity	$100
		+ increase in equity:	
		Income (+$130 − $100)	30
	$130		$130

Comparing the initial and subsequent balance sheets shows that equity has increased by $30, the amount of income recognized from the transaction. Equally important, net assets have also increased by $30 (that is, $130 of cash inflow minus $100 of inventory outflow = net asset increase of $30). The point of this example is that when income is recognized in the financial statements, two things happen:

1. Owners' equity is increased by the amount of the income.
2. Net assets (that is, gross assets minus gross liabilities) are increased by an identical amount.

Thus, there are two equivalent ways of thinking about the financial statement effects of income recognition. One perspective is that when income is recognized, the bottom-line income number (and thus, owners' equity) increases. The other is that when income is recognized, net assets are increased.

The two approaches to thinking about income recognition merely focus on different aspects of the same transaction. The approach that focuses on the net asset effect on the balance sheet provides a means for understanding the *total* financial statement effects of income recognition. This approach reminds us that income recognition simultaneously triggers an increase in the book value (carrying value) of net assets—*that is, net asset valuation and income determination are inextricably intertwined.* When income is recognized in the financial statements, the accountant is acknowledging that the company's net assets have increased in value.[4] The real issue in income recognition is this: At what point in the cycle of operating activities is it appropriate to recognize that a firm's net assets have increased in value? The next section addresses this.

As noted, income recognition comprises two separate steps:

1. Revenue recognition
2. Expense matching.

Let's consider each step separately.

> **Book value** or **carrying value** refers to the amount at which an account (or set of related accounts) is reported on a company's financial statements. For example, the cost of "Property, plant and equipment" may be reported at $1,000,000 with accumulated depreciation of $300,000. The net book value or carrying value of "Property, plant and equipment" would be the cost minus accumulated depreciation, or $700,000.

---

[4] Notice that the accounting concept of income recognition is really a specific application of the economic concept of value added.

Criteria for Revenue Recognition

According to generally accepted accounting principles, revenue is recognized at the *earliest* moment in time that *both* of the following conditions are satisfied:

Condition 1.   The **critical event** in the process of earning the revenue has taken place.

Condition 2.   The amount of revenue that will be collected is reasonably assured and is **measurable** with a reasonable degree of reliability.

U.S. GAAP uses different words to describe these two revenue recognition conditions. Condition 1, rephrased using the FASB's terminology, says revenues are not recognized until **earned**. The Board defined "earned" as:*

"... [R]evenues are considered to have been earned when the entity has substantially accomplished what it must do to be entitled to the benefits represented by the revenues."

The FASB's terminology for Condition 2 says revenues must also be **realizable**. The Board defined "realizable" as (para. 83):

"Revenues and gains are realizable when related assets received or held are readily convertible to known amounts of cash or claims to cash. Readily convertible assets have (i) interchangeable (fungible) units and (ii) quoted prices available in an active market that can rapidly absorb the quantity held by the entity without significantly affecting the price."

While the concepts embodied in "earned" and "realizable" are identical to "critical event" and "measurable," we believe that the latter terms are more easily understood and accordingly use them throughout this book.

*"Recognition and Measurement in Financial Statements of Business Enterprises," *Statement of Financial Accounting Concepts No. 5* (Stamford, CT: FASB, 1984), para. 83.

The International Accounting Standard Board (IASB)—formerly called the International Accounting Standards Committee (IASC)—uses the following criteria to determine when an entity should recognize revenue:*

1. Significant risks and rewards of ownership have been transferred from the seller to the buyer.
2. Managerial involvement and control over the asset being transferred has passed from the seller to the buyer.
3. The seller can reliably measure the amount of revenue or consideration received in the exchange.
4. It is probable that the seller will receive economic benefits.
5. The seller can reliably measure the costs (both past and future) of the transaction.

*"Revenue," *IASC Statement No. 18*, 1984, Revised and Reissued 1995 (London: International Accounting Standards Committee [IASC], 1995).

 International

Condition 1: The Critical Event While the earnings process is the result of many separate activities, it is generally acknowledged that there is usually one critical event or key stage considered to be absolutely essential to the ultimate increase in net asset value of the firm. The exact nature of this critical event varies from industry to industry, as we will show in subsequent examples. Unless the critical event takes place, no increase in value is added to the firm's net assets. Thus, the occurrence of the critical event is a first step that must be satisfied before revenue can be recognized. It is a "necessary," but not "sufficient," condition for revenue to be recognized.

Condition 2: Measurability Accountants do not immediately recognize revenue just because the critical event has taken place. There must be something else: It must be possible to measure the amount of revenue that has been earned with a reasonable degree of assurance. Condition 2 indicates that revenue cannot be recognized merely on the basis of an intuitive "feel" that certain events have added value to the firm's assets. There must be objective, verifiable evidence as to the amount of value that has been added. Unless the amount of value added can be reliably quantified, GAAP does not allow an increase in asset values to be recorded. Generally, this translates into having a readily determinable price for the goods or service, a price established in the marketplace where buyers and sellers are free to negotiate the terms of trade. So-called "list prices" assigned to the good or service by the seller often do not satisfy the measurability condition, because they can deviate from the market-clearing price paid by the buyer.

Only after Conditions 1 and 2 are *both* met can revenue be recognized under generally accepted accounting principles. To illustrate how these revenue recognition conditions are applied, let's return to the example of the three-year subscriptions sold by Canterbury Publishing in January 2005. Recall that accrual accounting would not recognize the $300,000 as revenue when the cash is received because the subscriptions revenue will be "earned" only as each magazine issue is published and delivered to the customers. If the publisher were to discontinue the magazine before all 12 issues were published, a refund would be owed to the subscribers. ***In this magazine example, the critical event in earning subscription revenue is actually providing the product to the customers.*** Thus, $100,000 of revenue will be recorded in each of the three years, as the magazine is published and sent to subscribers. Stated somewhat differently, while revenue recognition Condition 2 is met in this example on initial receipt of the subscription order (that is, the amount of ultimate revenue—$300,000—is measurable with a high degree of assurance and reliability), Condition 1 is not met at that time and, therefore, no revenue is recognized because the critical event has not yet occurred. That is, Canterbury has not *earned* the revenue that has been collected because the company has not delivered the magazines promised to the customer.

To further illustrate how the revenue recognition conditions are applied, let us consider another example. On January 2, 2005 Gigantic Motors Corporation assembles 1,000 automobiles, each with a sticker price of $18,000. Since these cars have not yet been sold to dealers, they are parked in a lot adjacent to the plant. Let's examine how revenue recognition Conditions 1 and 2 operate in this setting.

Most observers would agree that the critical event in adding value in automobile manufacturing is production itself.[5] Accordingly, the critical event occurred as the automobiles rolled off the production line. However, no revenue would be recognized at that time. Although revenue recognition Condition 1 is satisfied, Condition 2 is *not* satisfied merely on completion of production. ***This revenue recognition condition is not satisfied because the ultimate sale price of the automobiles is still unknown.*** While Gigantic Motors has established a suggested list price of $18,000 per vehicle, the ultimate amount of cash that will actually be received in the future will depend upon general economic conditions, consumer tastes and preferences, as well as the availability and asking price of competing automobile models. Thus, the specific amount of value that has been added by production is not yet measurable with a reasonable degree of assurance. Revenue will be recognized only when the cars are sold to dealers at a known price. Only then is revenue recognition Condition 2 satisfied.

The magazine subscription and automobile production examples illustrate that revenue recognition only takes place when revenue recognition Conditions 1 and 2 are *both* met. When the cash subscriptions to the magazine are received by Canterbury Publishing, Condition 2 (measurability) is satisfied but not Condition 1—no revenue is recognized until Canterbury provides the magazines to the customers and earns the revenue. When automobile production takes place at Gigantic Motors, Condition 1 (critical event) is satisfied but not Condition 2—no revenue is recognized until the sale takes place, which determines with reasonable assurance the amount that Gigantic will receive from the customer.

The financial reporting rules governing revenue recognition are often misunderstood. Because revenue is usually recognized at the time of sale in most industries, some observers erroneously conclude that the sale is itself the sole criterion for recognizing revenue. But this is not correct. The financial reporting rule for recognizing revenue is more complicated and subtle. Specifically, revenue is recognized as soon as Condition 1 (critical event) *and* Condition 2 (measurability) are *both* satisfied. ***In most instances the time of sale turns out to be the earliest moment at which both Conditions 1 and 2 are satisfied, which is why revenue is most frequently recognized at the time of sale of the product or service.***

But Conditions 1 and 2 are occasionally satisfied even before a legal sale (that is, transfer of title) occurs. The following example illustrates where revenue can be recognized prior to sale:

Weld Shipyards has been building ocean-going oil tankers since 1951. In January 2005 Weld signs a contract to build a standard-design tanker for Humco Oil. The contract price is $60 million, and construction costs are estimated to total approximately $45 million. The tanker is expected to be completed by December 31, 2006. Weld intends to account for the project using the **percentage-of-completion** method.

---

[5] Automobile manufacturers eventually sell all units produced, although not always immediately following production or always at the sticker price.

Under the percentage-of-completion method (discussed in Chapter 3), revenues and expenses are recognized as production takes place rather than at the time of completion (the sale). For example, if the tanker is 40% complete at the end of 2005 and finished in 2006, revenues and expenses would be recognized according to the following percentage-of-completion schedule:

($ in millions)	2005	2006	Two-Year Total
Percentage	40%	60%	100%
Revenue	$24	$36	$60
Expense	(18)	(27)	(45)
Income	$ 6	$ 9	$15

This method is permitted under GAAP when certain conditions—as in the Weld Shipyards example—are met. Condition 1 (critical event) is satisfied over time as the tanker is built—just as it was in the Gigantic automotive production example. But unlike the Gigantic Motors example, *revenue recognition Condition 2 is satisfied* for Weld Shipyards, since a firm contract with a known buyer at a set price of $60 million exists. Thus, the tanker example satisfies *both* of the two conditions necessary for revenue to be recognized. Additionally, expenses are also measurable with a reasonable degree of assurance since the tanker is of a standard design that Weld has built repeatedly in past years. This example provides an overview of why the percentage-of-completion method, when used properly, meets revenue recognition Conditions 1 and 2.

In other circumstances Conditions 1 and 2 may not both be satisfied until *after* the time of sale—for instance, until the cash is collected. In these cases it would be inappropriate to recognize income when the sale is made; instead, income recognition is deferred and is ultimately recognized in proportion to cash collections. Chapter 3 discusses the **installment sales method**, an example in which revenue and expense are recognized at the time of cash collection rather than at the time of sale.

Figure 2.2 is a time-line diagram depicting the activities comprising the revenue recognition process for some selected industries.

Figure 2.2

THE REVENUE RECOGNITION PROCESS

Industries Recognizing Revenue at Indicated Phases

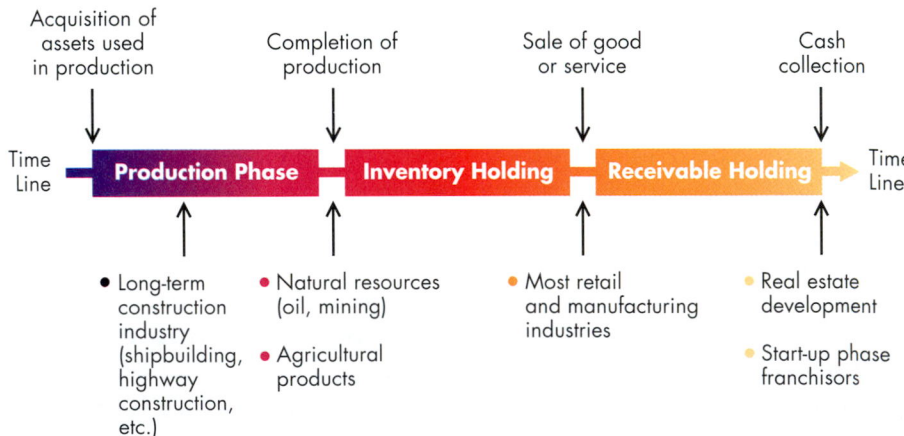

To justify recognizing revenue during the **production phase**, the following conditions must be met:

1. A specific customer must be identified and an exchange price agreed on. In most cases a formal contract must be signed.
2. A significant portion of the services to be performed has been performed, and the expected costs of future services can be reliably estimated.
3. An assessment of the customer's credit standing permits a reasonably accurate estimate of the amount of cash that will be collected.

Situations where these conditions may be satisfied include long-term contracts for the construction of ships, bridges, and office buildings—as well as, for example, special-order government contracts for the production of military equipment.

As depicted in Figure 2.2, in some industries revenue may be recognized on **completion of production**. This is justified under the following conditions:

1. The product is immediately saleable at quoted market prices.
2. Units are homogeneous.
3. No significant uncertainty exists regarding the costs of distributing the product.

Examples where these circumstances exist include mining of natural resources and harvesting agricultural crops. These commodities are traded in active, organized markets, and thus a reliable market price can be determined at production even though the eventual buyer's identity is unknown at that time. Although GAAP permits mining and other natural resource companies to recognize revenue at completion of production, few actually do so. Instead, most delay revenue recognition until the time of sale.

Revenue recognition *at the time of sale* is the dominant practice in most retail and manufacturing industries. Occasionally, revenue is not recognized until *after the time of sale*. To justify postponing recognition of revenues, one or more of the following conditions must generally be present:

1. Extreme uncertainty exists regarding the amount of cash to be collected from customers. This uncertainty may be attributable to various factors:

   - The customer's precarious financial condition
   - Contingencies in the sales agreement that allow the buyer or seller to terminate the exchange
   - The customer having the right to return the product and this right being frequently exercised

2. Future services to be provided are substantial, and their costs cannot be estimated with reasonable precision.

These conditions exist in circumstances like real estate sales, where collection of the sale price occurs in protracted installments, and in sales of franchises for new or unproved concepts or products.

Regardless of which basis of revenue recognition is used, the recognition of expenses must always adhere to the matching principle—all costs incurred in generating the revenue must be recorded as expenses in the same period the related revenue is recognized. Matching expenses with revenues is the second step of the income recognition process and is discussed next.

Matching Expenses with Revenues

Once gross revenues for the period are determined, the next step in determining income is to accumulate and record the costs associated with generating those revenues. Some costs are easily traced to the revenues themselves. These **traceable costs**—also called **product costs**—are described as being **matched** with revenues. Other costs are clearly also important in generating revenue, but their contribution to a specific sale or to revenues of a particular period is more difficult to quantify. Such costs are expensed in the *time periods benefited*, which is why they are called **period costs**. Let's see how the matching principle is applied to traceable or product costs—as well as to period costs.

Traceable or Product Costs This next example illustrates how product costs are matched with revenue under GAAP income measurement rules.

> Cory TV and Appliance, a retailer, sells one 24-inch color television set on the last day of February for $500 cash. The TV set was purchased from the manufacturer for $240 cash in January of that same year. Cory provides a 60-day "parts and labor" warranty to the customer. A typical 24-inch color TV requires $10 of warranty service during the first month following the sale and another $15 of service in the second month.

The expected (as well as the actually experienced) cash flows associated with this single transaction are depicted in Figure 2.3.

Figure 2.3

CASH FLOW DIAGRAM

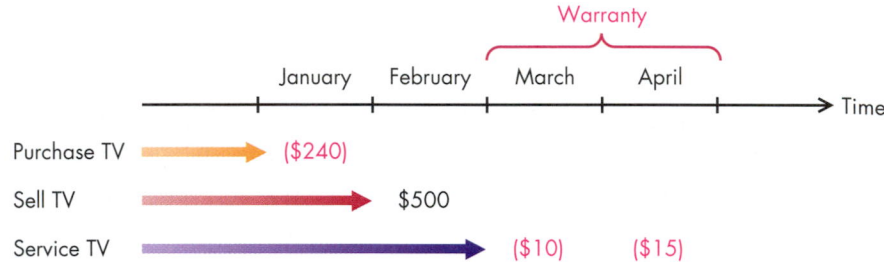

GAAP revenue recognition criteria are satisfied by the cash sale in February, so $500 of revenue is recorded in that month. The current and expected future costs of generating that revenue are $265 ($240 + $10 + $15), and these costs are recorded as expenses in the same month (February) that the revenue is recognized. Thus, accrual accounting transforms the cash flow diagram of Figure 2.3 into the revenue recognition and expense matching diagram shown in Figure 2.4.

Figure 2.4

REVENUE RECOGNITION AND
EXPENSE MATCHING

Period Costs Cory TV and Appliance incurs other types of costs that also are crucial in generating revenues. However, the linkage between these costs and individual sales is difficult to establish. One example of costs of this nature is advertising expenditures.

Assume Cory TV buys five minutes of advertising time on a local radio station each month for a monthly cost of $700. Obviously, the purpose of advertising is to generate sales. However, it is virtually impossible to associate any month's advertising expenditure with any specific sale, since consumer behavior is the result of diverse influences and repeated advertising exposure. Consequently, GAAP does not try to match advertising expenditures with specific sales. Instead, the cost of advertising is charged as an expense in the period in which the ads run. Such costs are called period costs. No effort is made to link any particular advertising campaign with particular sales, since no objective means for establishing this linkage exists.

The distinction between traceable (product) costs and period costs is discussed further in Chapter 9. At this point it is important to understand that in applying the matching concept, some costs are directly matched against revenues while others are associated with time periods.

Matching associates expired costs (expenses) with the revenues recognized in a period or with the passage of time. Costs directly matched against revenues are called product costs; costs matched with the passage of time are called period costs.

RE*CAP*

Income Statement Format and Classification

Virtually all decision models in modern corporate finance are based on future cash flows. Recognizing this, the FASB stated:

> "Thus, financial reporting should provide information to help investors, creditors, and others assess the amounts, timing, and uncertainty of prospective net cash inflows to the related enterprise."[6]

One way to provide users with information regarding prospective future cash flows would be to present them with cash flow forecasts prepared by management. Traditional financial reporting rejects presenting forecasted cash flow information because such numbers are considered to be too "soft"—too speculative or manipulatable.

Another way to satisfy users' needs for assessing future cash flows is to provide financial information based on past and current events in a format that gives statement users reliable and representative baseline numbers for generating *their own* forecasts of future cash flows. To accomplish this, an income statement format that segregates components of income has evolved. The intent of this format is to classify separately income components that are "transitory" and to clearly differentiate them from income components believed to be "sustainable" or likely to be repeated in future reporting periods.

As we survey the existing format and classification rules, you will see that the rationale behind the rules for multiple-step income statements is intended to subdivide income in a manner that facilitates forecasting. Most of the disclosure formats reviewed in this section were written into GAAP by the standard setting organization that preceded the FASB, the current private-sector standard-setting group.[7] Our discussion is based on the comparative income statements of Mythical Corporation for 2003–2005, presented in Exhibit 2.1 on the next page. This exhibit illustrates how existing disclosure rules are designed to help users predict future events.

The income statement isolates a key figure called **Income from continuing operations**. (See ① in Exhibit 2.1.) This component of income should include only *the normal, recurring, (presumably) more sustainable, ongoing economic activities* of the organization. As we'll discuss shortly, this intermediate income number can sometimes include gains and losses that occur infrequently—called **"Special or unusual items"** (item ② in Exhibit 2.1)—but nevertheless arise

Valuation

---

[6] "Objectives of Financial Reporting by Business Enterprises," *Statement of Financial Accounting Concepts No. 1* (Stamford, CT: FASB, 1978), para. 37.

[7] The opinions of the predecessor group—the Accounting Principles Board (APB)—continue in effect until they are either rescinded or altered by the FASB. The disclosure formats discussed in this section were developed in three separate APB opinions. These are: "Reporting the Results of Operations," *APB Opinion No. 9* (New York: AICPA, 1966); "Accounting Changes," *APB Opinion No. 20* (New York: AICPA, 1971); and "Reporting the Results of Operations—Reporting the Effects of Disposal of a Segment of a Business, and Extraordinary, Unusual and Infrequently Occurring Events and Transactions," *APB Opinion No. 30* (New York: AICPA, 1973). More recently, the FASB issued two statements that amend or supersede certain provisions of APB Opinion No 30: "Accounting for the Impairment or Disposal of Long-Lived Assets," *Statement of Financial Accounting Standards No. 144* (Norwalk, CT: FASB, 2001), and "Rescission of FASB Statements No. 4, 44, and 64, Amendment of FASB Statement No. 13, and Technical Corrections," *Statement of Financial Accounting Standards No. 145* (Norwalk, CT: FASB 2002).

EXHIBIT 2.1	Mythical Corporation

Income Statements For the Years Ended December 31, 2003–2005

($ in millions)	2005	2004	2003
Net sales	$3,957	$3,478	$3,241
Costs of goods sold	(1,364)	(1,189)	(1,096)
Gross profit	$2,593	$2,289	$2,145
Selling, general and administrative	(1,093)	(949)	(922)
② Special or unusual charges (Note 1)	(251)	—	—
Income from continuing operations before income taxes	1,249	1,340	1,223
Income tax expense	(406)	(436)	(411)
① Income from continuing operations	$843	$904	$812
③ Discontinued operations (Note 2):			
Income from operation of discontinued business division, net of tax	203	393	528
Gain on disposal of discontinued business division, net of tax	98	—	—
Income before extraordinary item and change in accounting principle	$1,144	$1,297	$1,340
④ Extraordinary loss, net of income tax effect (Note 3)	—	(170)	—
⑤ Cumulative effect of change in accounting principle, net of income tax effect (Note 4)	(118)	—	—
Net income	$1,026	$1,127	$1,340
Pro forma amounts assuming the change in accounting principle had been applied retroactively			
Income from continuing operations	$843	$871	$774
Income from continuing operations per share	$9.25	$9.55	$8.49

Note 1: Special or Unusual Charges—A strike closed operations in the Pleasant Grove manufacturing facility for five months in mid-2005. The fixed costs incurred at the idle plant totaled $251,000,000.

Note 2: Discontinued Operations—The Company discontinued a business segment in 2005. The 2005 operating income and gain on disposal for this segment, net of tax, were $203 million and $98 million, respectively.

Note 3: Extraordinary Loss—The extraordinary loss arose as a consequence of a fire that partially destroyed the chemical plant in River City. The Company had no insurance coverage for such losses due to its long-standing policy of self-insurance.

Note 4: Change in Accounting Principle—Effective January 1, 2005 the Company changed its method of depreciation for property, plant, and equipment from the straight-line method to the sum-of-years digits method. The Company believes the sum-of-years digits method is preferable since the new method corresponds to the depreciation methods used by most companies in the industry, thereby improving comparability of financial reporting. This change decreased 2005 income from continuing operations by $31 million ($0.34 per share).

from a firm's ongoing, continuing operations. With the possible exception of some of these special or unusual items, "Income from continuing operations" summarizes the wealth effects of recurring transactions or activities that are expected to continue into the future. Therefore, this figure is intended to serve as the anchor or jumping-off point for forecasting future profits.

There are other components of income that are not recurring—and, hence, do not form a good basis for projecting future income. These other, more transitory components of income are isolated and disclosed separately so that statement users can place less weight on these earnings components when forecasting the future profitability of an enterprise (see discussion in Ch. 6). These transitory earnings components fall into four categories:

- Special or unusual items (item ②)
- Discontinued operations (item ③)
- Extraordinary items (item ④)
- Cumulative effect of accounting changes (item ⑤)

The rules governing the classification and placement of these four categories of transitory items within the income statement are discussed in the following sections. These classification rules provide detailed guidance regarding what qualifies for inclusion in each statement category. As you will see, the rules standardize the format of disclosures as well as prevent certain "abuses" or distortions that might occur if firms were allowed to commingle these nonrecurring components of earnings with more sustainable, recurring revenue and expense items.

Special or Unusual Items (Item ②)

Material events that arise from a firm's ongoing, continuing activities but that are either unusual in nature or infrequent in occurrence—but not both—must be disclosed as a separate line item as part of income from continuing operations (or in footnotes to the financial statements). For example, the Mythical Corporation income statement presented in Exhibit 2.1 includes "Special or unusual charges" for losses incurred in conjunction with a labor strike, which is disclosed as a separate line item and discussed in a statement note (see item ② and Note 1 in Exhibit 2.1).

> As used in the authoritative accounting literature, an item is considered material if it is of sufficient magnitude or importance to make a difference in a statement user's decision.

Other examples of special or unusual items include:[8]

1. Write-downs or write-offs of receivables, inventories, equipment leased to others, and intangibles.
2. Gains or losses from the exchange or translation of foreign currencies.
3. Gains or losses from the sale or abandonment of property, plant or equipment.
4. Special one-time charges resulting from corporate restructurings.
5. Gains or losses from the sale of investments.

Including special or unusual items as a component of income from continuing operations complicates financial forecasting and analysis. These special items are treated as a part of income from continuing operations because collectively they represent events that arise repeatedly as a normal part of ongoing business activities.[9] However, some special items occur often while others recur sporadically. For example, some firms are continuously selling or disposing of obsolete manufacturing assets as well as taking write-downs on inventory or selling investment securities. However, other special items—like strikes and reorganizations—occur less frequently. Consequently, the persistence of special or unusual items is likely to vary from period to period and from item to item. As a result, separate disclosure is provided for these items to assist users in forecasting future results. Since these items are included as part of income from continuing operations before tax (sometimes referred to as being reported "above the line"), they are not disclosed net of tax effects.

> Some companies tend to report special, nonrecurring items on a regular basis, perhaps hoping that investors will discount or ignore what are frequently large charges to earnings. For example, Motorola was recently cited for reporting special, nonrecurring items for *fifteen* consecutive quarters.*
>
> *J. Drucker, "Motorola's Profit: 'Special' Again?" *Wall Street Journal* (October 15, 2002).

Discontinued Operations (Item ③)

Since a primary objective of financial reporting is to assist users in generating estimates of future cash flows, transactions related to operations that the firm intends to discontinue or has already discontinued must be separated from other income items.[10] The reason is straightforward since, by definition, discontinued operations will not generate *future* operating cash flows.

In Exhibit 2.1 Mythical Corporation discontinued a component of its business in 2005 (item ③). Notice that the operating results of this recently discontinued business component are not included in income from continuing operations in the current period (2005) when the decision to discontinue was made; nor are they included in any of the prior years (2004 and 2003) for

---

[8] *APB Opinion No. 30*, para. 23.
[9] Evidence that special items are likely to recur in the aggregate is provided by P. M. Fairfield, R. J. Sweeney, and T. L. Yohn, "Accounting Classification and the Predictive Content of Earnings," *The Accounting Review* (July 1996), pp. 337–55.
[10] *SFAS No. 144*, op. cit., para. 43.

which comparative data are provided.[11] That is, the revenues and expenses of this component of Mythical Corporation that was disposed of in 2005 are removed from the corresponding numbers reflecting 2004 and 2003 results (highlighted). This makes the "Income from continuing operations" number of $843 million in 2005, the year of the discontinued operations, truly comparable with the "Income from continuing operations" numbers of $904 million and $812 million in 2004 and 2003, respectively. Restating the 2004 and 2003 results to make them comparable to the 2005 results means that all the numbers from the "Net sales" line through the "Income from continuing operations" line reported in the 2004 and 2003 columns of the 2005 annual report will be different from the corresponding numbers originally reported in the 2004 and 2003 statements. While initially confusing to analysts who wish to review the past sequence of earnings numbers to detect trends in a company's financial performance (often referred to as **time-series analysis**), this adjustment to the numbers is essential for valid year-to-year comparisons.

> A component of an entity may be a reportable segment or operating segment, a reporting unit, a subsidiary, or an asset group. An asset group represents the lowest level for which identifiable cash flows are largely independent of the cash flows of other groups of assets and liabilities within the entity. [Op. cit., para. 4].

Prior to 2001, the authoritative guidance for reporting discontinued operations was provided by *APB Opinion No. 30*.[12] This standard defined a discontinued operation as a separate line of business or a separate class of customer. *SFAS No. 144*, issued in August 2001, broadened the scope of operations that qualify for separate disclosure as discontinued operations by introducing the notion of a **component of an entity**.[13] A component of an entity comprises operations and cash flows that can be clearly distinguished, operationally and for financial reporting purposes, from the rest of the entity.[14]

To illustrate the broadened scope of operations that qualify for discontinued operations treatment under *SFAS No. 144* versus *APB Opinion No. 30*, consider Quaker Oats' 1997 sale of its Snapple beverage business to Triarc Companies. Under *APB Opinion No. 30* guidance, Quaker reported the $1.4 billion loss on the Snapple sale *above the line* as a special item adjustment to income from continuing operations. This treatment was deemed appropriate since Quaker continued in the beverage business by producing and marketing Gatorade. Therefore, it did not sell its entire beverage drink product line. Under *SFAS No. 144* guidelines, the Snapple sale would likely qualify for separate disclosure as a discontinued operation (with associated restatement of prior year sales and expense figures as illustrated for Mythical Corporation) since the operations and cash flows from Snapple, a wholly owned subsidiary of Quaker, were clearly distinguishable from the Gatorade operations.

> *SFAS No. 144*, para. 30, sets forth six conditions for an asset group to be considered "held for sale." The most important of these are:
> - Management has adopted a formal plan to sell the asset group.
> - An active program to locate a buyer has been initiated.
> - The sale of the asset group is probable and the sale is expected to be completed within one year.

If a component of an entity has either been sold during the period or is classified as **held for sale**, its results of operations are to be reported as discontinued operations ("below the line") if the following two conditions are met:

- The operations and cash flows of the component have been (or will be) eliminated from the firm's ongoing operations.
- The firm will not have any significant continuing involvement in the operations of the component after the disposal transaction.

---

[11] Securities and Exchange Commission (SEC) rules (Regulation S-X, Article 3) require that comparative income statement data for at least three years and comparative balance sheet data for two years be provided in filings with the Commission. For this reason, most publicly held corporations provide these comparative income statement and balance sheet data in their annual report to shareholders.

[12] *APB Opinion No. 30*, op. cit.

[13] *SFAS No. 144*, op. cit., para. 41.

[14] *IAS 35:* "Discontinuing Operations" provides authoritative accounting and disclosure guidance for those firms following international accounting standards for operations that are to be discontinued. The standard defines "discontinuing operations" as a business or geographical segment that an enterprise either is disposing of entirely or is terminating through abandonment or piecemeal sale. Among other things, entities are required to disclose (1) the amounts of revenues, expenses, and pre-tax profit or loss attributable to the discontinuing operation and related tax expense (benefit), and (2) the amount of any gain or loss that is recognized on the disposal of the discontinuing operation, net of related tax effects. [See "Discontinuing Operations," *IAS 35* (London, UK: International Accounting Standards Committee [IASC], 1998.)]

International

If either of these two conditions is not met, then the component's operating results will be reported as part of income from continuing operations and prior years' results will not be restated for comparative purposes.

Amounts reported when assets (disposal group) have been sold When the discontinued component is sold before the end of the reporting period, companies are required to report two elements as part of discontinued operations:

1. Operating income or loss (that is, revenues minus expenses) from operating the component from the beginning of the reporting period to the disposal date, net of related tax effects.
2. Gain or loss on disposal computed as the net sale price minus book value of net assets disposed of, net of related tax effects.

Panel (a) of Exhibit 2.2 illustrates a typical income statement disclosure for this situation where the disposal date is September 5, 2005.

Amounts reported when assets (disposal group) are considered "held for sale" If a company has decided to discontinue a component of its business but the component has not sold by the end of the reporting period, then the income effects of the discontinued operations are reported in two elements as follows:

1. Operating income or loss (that is, revenues minus expenses) from operating the component from the beginning of the reporting period to the end of the reporting period, net of tax effects.
2. An "impairment loss" (net of tax effects) if the book value of the net assets in the disposal group is more than the fair value minus cost to sell.

Panel (b) of Exhibit 2.2 illustrates a typical income statement disclosure for this situation where there is an after-tax impairment loss on assets "held for sale" of $32,500.

See Chapter 10 for further details on determining whether an asset (disposal group) has become impaired and, if so, the amount of the loss.

APB Opinion No. 30 allowed companies to estimate profits (losses) from operating a discontinued segment in future periods and to include these estimated amounts as part of "Gain (loss) on disposal of discontinued operations." This flexibility invited income shifting and/or income smoothing behavior by management. *SFAS No. 144* effectively eliminates this potential for opportunistic behavior.

EXHIBIT 2.2	Alternative Disclosure for Discontinued Operations

Partial Income Statement Format for Discontinued Operations

Panel (a)

When Assets Have Been Sold:

Income from continuing operations	$800,000
Income tax expense	(280,000)
Income from continuing operations after tax	520,000
Discontinued operations:	
Operating income (net of taxes of $35,000) from	
January 1, 2005 through September 5, 2005	65,000
Loss on disposal of discontinued operation	
(net of $21,000 tax benefit)	(39,000)
Net Income	$546,000

Panel (b)

When Assets are "Held for sale":

Income from continuing operations	$800,000
Income tax expense	(280,000)
Income from continuing operations after tax	520,000
Discontinued operations:	
Operating income (net of taxes of $42,000) from	
January 1, 2005 through December 31, 2005	78,000
Impairment loss (net of $17,500 tax benefit)	
on assets "held for sale"	(32,500)
Net Income	$565,500

It is important to notice that both the income (loss) from operating the discontinued component and any gain (loss) from sale (or impairment loss) are reported net of tax effects. This "net of tax" treatment is called **intraperiod income tax allocation**. The reason for this net of tax treatment is the belief that the income tax burden or benefit should be matched with the item giving rise to it. The allocation of the tax burden or benefit across components of income is believed to make the income figures more informative to users.

Here's why: If income tax were not matched with the item giving rise to it, then total reported income tax expense would combine taxes arising both from items that were transitory as well as from other items that were more sustainable. Mixing together the tax effect of continuing activities with the tax effect of single occurrence events would make it difficult for statement readers to forecast future tax outflows arising from ongoing events. Under intraperiod income tax allocation, the income tax associated with the (presumably) transitory items ③, ④, and ⑤ are not included in Mythical's $406 million income tax expense figure for 2005 (Exhibit 2.1, p. 54) related to income from continuing operations, thus facilitating forecasts of expected future flows after tax.

Extraordinary Items (Item ④)

Another category of transitory items reported separately on the income statement is extraordinary items (item ④ in Exhibit 2.1). To be treated as an extraordinary item, the event or transaction must meet *both* of the following criteria:[15]

1. *Unusual nature:* The underlying event or transaction possesses a high degree of abnormality, and taking into account the environment in which the company operates, that event or transaction is unrelated to the ordinary activities of the business.
2. *Infrequent occurrence:* The underlying event or transaction is a type that would not reasonably be expected to recur in the foreseeable future, again taking into account the environment in which the business operates.

The business environment in which an enterprise operates is a primary consideration in determining whether an underlying event or transaction is unusual in nature and infrequent in occurrence. The environment of an enterprise includes such factors as the characteristics of the industry or industries in which it operates, the geographical location of its operations, and the nature and extent of government regulation. For example, a plant explosion that results in uninsured losses would be considered an extraordinary loss by most businesses. But for a company that manufactures explosive materials (for example, dynamite), losses from such an event may not be considered unusual in nature or infrequent in occurrence, given the environment in which the entity conducts its operations.

The justification for defining extraordinary items so precisely and for requiring separate disclosure of special or potentially nonrecurring items is to prevent statement manipulation. Without such requirements management might, in a "down" earnings year, be tempted to treat nonrecurring gains as part of income from continuing operations and nonrecurring losses as extraordinary. Precise guidelines preclude this.

Like discontinued operations, extraordinary items are reported net of tax. Given the stringency of the criteria, few events qualify as extraordinary items. Examples of qualifying items include losses resulting from natural disasters (for example, tornadoes) or losses arising from new laws or edicts (for example, an expropriation by a foreign government), and, in some cases, gains and losses on early debt retirement.

Income statement reporting of gains and losses resulting from the retirement of debt prior to its scheduled maturity is covered in *SFAS No. 145*.[16] *SFAS No. 145* calls for gains and losses from early debt retirement to be classified as extraordinary only if they meet the criteria in *APB Opinion No. 30*. Accordingly, firms that use early debt retirement on a recurring basis as part of their ongoing risk management practices will report the associated gains and losses as part of income from continuing operations with separate line-item disclosure. Other firms, for which early debt retirement is an unusual and infrequent occurrence, are required to report associated gains and losses as an extraordinary item.

Another event that presented difficult reporting issues with respect to extraordinary item treatment was the terrorist attacks on the World Trade Center and the Pentagon on September

---

[15] *APB Opinion No. 30*, para. 20.
[16] *SFAS No. 145*, op. cit., paras. 1, 6a, A4–A6.

11, 2001. Clearly, the events of 9–11 were both unusual in nature and infrequent in occurrence. However, the Emerging Issues Task Force (EITF) of the FASB concluded that reporting the associated losses as extraordinary would not be an effective way of communicating the financial effects of these events since it would be virtually impossible to isolate the financial effects of the extraordinary terrorist attacks from the generally poor ongoing economic conditions leading up to and following the attacks.[17] The EITF reasoned that the economic effects of the terrorists' attacks themselves and the subsequent disruption of economic activity were so extensive and pervasive that it would be impossible to capture their impact in any one financial statement line item. Accordingly, they encouraged companies to report these losses "above the line" as a special charge and to provide sufficient disclosure and discussion to help statement users understand how the events of 9–11 impacted the reporting entity.

Exhibit 2.3 provides excerpts from UAL's (parent company for United Airlines) 2001 annual report related to the impact of 9–11 on its operations. Note that UAL reported on its 2001 income

EXHIBIT 2.3	UAL Corporation and Subsidiary Companies

Condensed Statements of Consolidated Operations

Panel (a)

	Years Ended December 31		
($ in millions)	2001	2000	1999
Operating revenues	$16,138	$19,352	$18,027
Operating expenses:			
Salaries and related costs	7,080	6,877	6,426
Aircraft fuel	2,476	2,511	1,776
Commissions, rent, and aircraft maintenance	2,238	2,611	2,704
Purchased services, landing fees, other rent	2,659	2,670	2,524
Depreciation and amortization	1,026	988	850
Cost of sales	1,280	1,061	602
Other operating expenses	1,722	1,841	1,737
Special charges ($1,313 related to 9–11 plus $115 of other charges)	1,428	139	17
	19,909	18,698	16,636
Earnings (loss) from operations	(3,771)	654	1,391
Other income (expense):			
Interest (net of amounts capitalized)	(341)	(224)	(219)
Equity in earnings (losses) of affiliates	(23)	(12)	37
Gain on sale of investments	261	109	731
Non-operating special charges	(49)	(61)	—
Airline stabilization grant	652		
Miscellaneous, net	(86)	(35)	2
	414	(223)	551
Earnings (loss) before income taxes,	(3,357)	431	1,942
Provision for income taxes	(1,226)	160	699
Earnings (loss) before distributions on preferred securities, extraordinary item and cumulative effect	(2,131)	271	1,243
Distributions on preferred securities, net of tax	(6)	(6)	(5)
Earnings (loss) before extraordinary item and cumulative effect	(2,137)	265	1,238
Extraordinary loss on early extinguishment of debt, net of tax	—	(6)	(3)
Cumulative effect of accounting change, net of tax	(8)	(209)	—
Net earnings (loss)	$(2,145)	$ 50	$ 1,235

[17] "Accounting for the Impact of the Terrorist Attacks of September 11, 2001," *Issue No. 11-10*, Emerging Issues Task Force (Norwalk, CT: FASB, 2001).

statement [panel (a)] losses related to the terrorists' attack as both an operating special charge and a non-operating special charge along with the airline stabilization grant received from the federal government (see highlighted numbers). Additional details on the effects of the terrorists' attacks on UAL's operations are provided in footnote (2), shown in panel (b) of Exhibit 2.3 and in the Management's Discussion and Analysis section of UAL's 2001 annual report (not shown).

RECAP

To be categorized as extraordinary and to appear below the "Income from continuing operations" line, an item must be unusual in nature *and* occur infrequently. Special or unusual items that do not meet both criteria, but are considered material, must be disclosed separately as part of pre-tax income from continuing operations.

EXHIBIT 2.3 **UAL Footnote on 9-11 Attacks**

Panel (b)

(2) Special Charges Related to the September 11 Terrorist Attacks

On September 11, 2001, two United aircraft were hijacked and destroyed in terrorist attacks on the World Trade Center in New York City and in a crash near Johnstown, Pennsylvania. On the same day, two American Airlines aircraft were also hijacked and used in terrorist attacks on the World Trade Center and the Pentagon. In addition to the loss of all passengers and crew on board the aircraft, these attacks resulted in numerous deaths and injuries to persons on the ground and massive property damage. In the immediate aftermath of the attacks, the FAA ordered all aircraft operating in the U.S. grounded immediately. This grounding effectively lasted for three days, and the Company was able to operate only a portion of its scheduled flights for several days thereafter. When flights were permitted to resume, passenger traffic and yields were significantly lower than prior to the attacks. In a direct response to the adverse impact on air travel as a result of the September 11 terrorist attacks, United reduced capacity by as much as 23%, which allowed for the retirement of the entire B727-200 and B737-200 fleets. In addition, on September 19, United announced that it would begin the process of furloughing approximately 20,000 employees. Since that time, however, due to slightly increased customer demand, and an increase to the April 2002 schedule, Untied plans to recall 1,200 flight attendants to active status on April 1, 2002 and to furlough fewer pilots than previously planned.

During the third quarter, United recorded a special charge of $1.3 billion in operating expense and $49 million in non-operating expense for amounts relating to the September 11 terrorist attacks and the resulting impact on the Company's schedule and operations. In addition, as of December 31, 2001, United had received $652 million in compensation under the Air Transportation Safety and System Stabilization Act (the "Act"). For further information, see "September 11 Terrorist Attacks" in Management's Discussion and Analysis of financial Condition and Results of Operations.

The Special charge is made up of the following:

($ in millions)	Amount	Amount (net of tax)
Special charges:		
Aircraft groundings and impairment	$ 788	
Reduction in force	217	
Early termination fees	181	
Discontinued capital projects	107	
Miscellaneous	20	
Total operating special charges	$1,313	$834
Non-operating special charges	49	31
Airline stabilization grant	(652)	(414)
Special charges, net of grant	$ 710	$451

Frequency and Magnitude of Various Categories of Transitory Income Statement Items

As Exhibit 2.1 illustrates, financial reporting rules for presenting operating results are designed to isolate transitory and nonsustainable components of earnings in order to assist users in predicting future earnings and cash flows. Research evidence confirms that the GAAP income statement classification framework we have discussed is useful to statement users. Specifically, subdividing earnings into three transitory components—special or unusual items, discontinued operations, and extraordinary items—and disclosing these amounts separately so that they are distinguished from the income that comes from continuing operations improves forecasts of future earnings.[18]

Figure 2.5(a) reveals that the proportion of firms reporting one or more of the kinds of transitory earnings components highlighted in the previous discussion has generally increased over time. In 1992 roughly 54% of firms listed on either the New York Stock Exchange (NYSE) or

Panel (a)

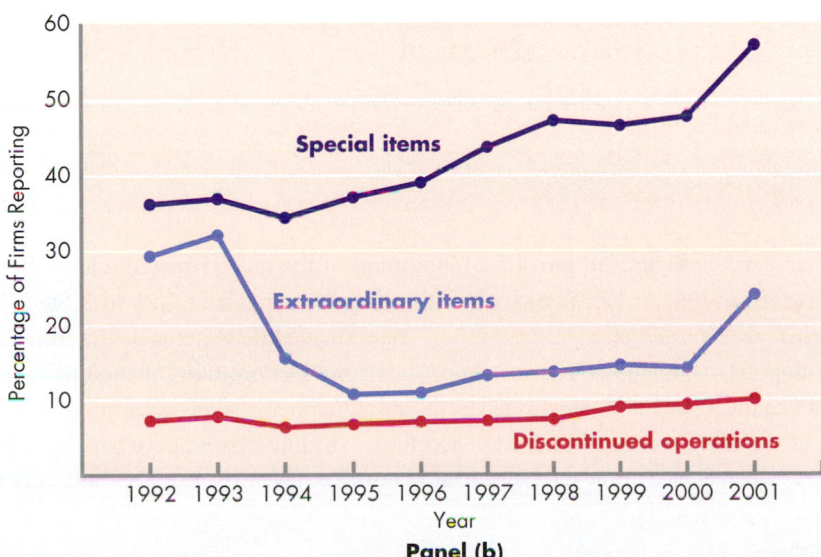

Panel (b)

Figure 2.5

PROPORTION OF NYSE/ AMEX FIRMS REPORTING NONRECURRING ITEMS (1992–2001)

Source: Standard and Poor's Compustat® Annual Industrial File as data source; methodology not verified or controlled by Standard & Poor's.

[18] Evidence that special items are likely to recur in the aggregate is provided by P. M. Fairfield, R. J. Sweeney, and T. L. Yohn, "Accounting Classification and the Predictive Content of Earnings," *The Accounting Review* (July 1996), pp. 337–55.

American Stock Exchange (AMEX) reported at least one of the transitory earnings components on their income statement. Ten years later, in 2001, that proportion had risen to nearly 69%. Clearly, material, separately disclosed gains and losses have become increasingly common elements of firms' earnings statements in recent years.

Figure 2.5(b) displays the proportion of NYSE and AMEX firms reporting (1) "Special or unusual items," (2) "Discontinued operations," or (3) "Extraordinary items" on their income statement from 1992–2001. The most common category of separately disclosed earnings components is for special or unusual items reported as part of income from continuing operations. Slightly more than 57% of the sample firms reported such items in 2001, compared to 36% in 1992. "Extraordinary items" are the next most common separately disclosed item, appearing on approximately 24% of the earnings statements of firms in 2001 compared to 29% in 1992. The proportion of firms disclosing gains or losses from discontinued operations didn't change much—roughly 6% to 10%—over the 1992–2001 period.

Exhibit 2.4 shows that over the 1992–2001 period, the majority of "special or unusual" items, "discontinued operations," and "extraordinary items" were losses (for example, 81.5% of special items in 2001—see highlight). The preponderance of losses for special or unusual items reflects the following two things:

1. The conservative bias of accrual accounting rules encourages early recognition of declines in asset values below cost or book value but tends to delay recognition of increases in value until the asset is sold.
2. Firms have an incentive to separately disclose and clearly label losses more than gains. To merge such (presumably) nonrecurring losses undisclosed as part of the "income from continuing operations" line would cause statement users to underestimate future income. Hence, firms opt for separate line-item disclosure of losses.

EXHIBIT 2.4	Percentage of Nonrecurring Items Resulting in Losses (1992–2001)									
	1992	1993	1994	1995	1996	1997	1998	1999	2000	2001
Special or unusual items	69.4%	70.1%	66.5%	70.6%	69.0%	70.6%	74.2%	69.4%	70.3%	81.5%
Discontinued operations	66.5	60.2	53.0	51.7	49.8	36.7	47.3	47.1	48.9	57.4
Extraordinary items	61.4	57.9	67.8	77.8	82.7	85.3	85.2	78.6	71.7	72.1
Any nonrecurring item (net)	62.1	61.3	63.1	68.8	68.0	69.6	73.5	67.6	66.7	77.9

Source: Compustat Annual Industrial File, Standard and Poor's Compustat® Services, Inc., Englewood, CO.

The bar charts in Figure 2.6 provide an indication of the relative magnitude of the gains and losses reported from 1992 to 2001 in each of the three nonrecurring item categories. Since "Special or unusual items" are reported on a pre-tax basis, we have divided these items by the absolute value of pre-tax earnings from operations. The gains and losses from "Discontinued operations" and "Extraordinary items" in the figure have been divided by the absolute value of after-tax earnings, since these latter two categories of items are reported net of tax effects. The line crossing each bar shows the median gain or loss as a percentage of the relevant earnings number. The top of each bar indicates the 75th[19]

[19] "The 75th percentile value means that of the firms reporting one of the three types of nonrecurring items in the indicated year, one-quarter of the firms reported items that *equaled or exceeded* the indicated percentage of income. The 25th percentile value means that one-quarter of the reported gains or losses were *equal to or below* the indicated percentage of income. The median value means that 50% were above (below) this amount.

Figure 2.6 MAGNITUDES OF NONRECURRING ITEMS (1992–2001)

Source: Standard and Poor's Compustat® Annual Industrial File as data source; methodology not verified or controlled by Standard & Poor's.

percentile value, while the bottom of each bar shows the 25th percentile value for each category of nonrecurring items.

Three features stand out from these diagrams.

First, the median value of the items disclosed in each of these categories tends to be a significant component of income, ranging approximately between 10% and 40% of the relevant earnings number.

Second, for both "Special or unusual items" and "Discontinued operations," the median value of the losses tends to be larger than the median value of the gains. Median losses reported in these two categories range between 17% and 44% of the relevant earnings number, while median gains range between 10% and 35% of earnings.

And third, for Discontinued operations, the upper quartile of firms reported gains in excess of 100% of adjusted after-tax earnings for a significant proportion of the sample years. The large percentage effect on earnings exists because the after-tax earnings number (before considering the effects of the gain) is close to zero. Thus, it appears that some firms try to cover up poor performance by triggering transactions that resulted in gains when their earnings were low or slightly negative.

> To improve comparability, all earnings numbers have been adjusted for the nonrecurring gain or loss being reported—that is, gains have been subtracted and losses have been added to the reported earnings to arrive at an adjusted earnings number used in computing the percentages.

To users of financial statements, the point of these exhibits and graphs is that transitory (nonrecurring) gains and losses occur relatively frequently. Moreover, these items tend to have a material effect on earnings. Since they may be less sustainable than other earnings components, the weight assigned to these items when predicting future profitability and cash flows must be assessed on a case-by-case basis. (In Chapter 6 we discuss assigning weights to various earnings components for equity valuation purposes.)

ANALYSIS

Changes in Accounting Principles

Let's return to the Mythical Corporation income statement in Exhibit 2.1. The last separately disclosed item just above the bottom-line income number is the "Cumulative effect of change in accounting principle." When a firm changes from one accounting method to another, the income number for both current and past periods is usually affected. How these income effects are reported varies, depending on the nature of the principle change.

Reporting Most Accounting Changes

Under current GAAP, prior periods' income statements generally are *not* restated to reflect the income effect of changing to a new principle. Instead, the new principle is first used to compute income from continuing operations in the year of the change. For Mythical Corporation this means that depreciation expense on the 2005 income statement will be computed using the new method—that is, sum-of-the-years' digits—rather than the old straight-line method.

The FASB has recently issued a new Exposure Draft* that would require firms to restate prior period financial statements that are presented for comparative purposes for changes in accounting principles (both voluntary and mandatory) unless it is impracticable to determine either the cumulative effect or the period-specific effects of the change. The proposed statement would also require that a change in depreciation method be accounted for as a change in accounting estimate (see discussion on this page) and not as a change in accounting principle.

*"Accounting Changes and Error Corrections—A Replacement of APB Opinion No. 20 and FASB Statement No. 3," *FASB Exposure Draft* (Stamford, CT: FASB, 2003).

Next, the **cumulative effect** of the change (net of income tax effects) on all prior years' income is shown as a separate line item at the bottom of the income statement for the year of the change. The cumulative effect is measured as the after-tax difference between prior periods' income under the old method and what would have been reported if the new method had been used in those prior years. This cumulative effect treatment is illustrated in the Mythical Corporation income statement by item ⑤, where a $118 million after-tax earnings reduction appears in 2005 for the switch from the straight-line to the sum-of-the-years' digits method for computing depreciation expense. In other words, if Mythical had been using the sum-of-the-years' digits rather than the straight-line method to compute depreciation in the years *prior* to 2005, the cumulative after-tax earnings would have been $118 million lower.

Because prior years' income is not restated, it is impossible to compare the figures in both the 2005 "Income from continuing operations" line and the total 2005 "Net income" bottom line with previous years' income figures. The income from continuing operations numbers are not comparable with the corresponding numbers in 2004 and 2003 because 2005 operating income of $843 million was determined using the new accounting principle, whereas the 2004 and 2003 income figures were computed using the old accounting principle. The 2005 net income number ($1,026 million) is not comparable with the 2004 net income of $1,127 million and the 2003 net income of $1,340 million because the full cumulative impact of the principle change on all prior years ($118 million in Exhibit 2.1) is deducted from 2005 income.

To provide comparable income numbers, existing disclosure standards require companies to provide a **pro forma** income figure computed "as if" the new accounting principle had been applied during all past periods that are presented. These pro forma income figures are shown immediately below "Net income" on the Mythical Corporation income statement in Exhibit 2.1.

In the year a change from one accounting principle to another is made, firms are compelled to highlight—as a separate line item on the income statement—the cumulative effect of the change on all prior periods' income. Retroactive restatement of prior periods' income is *not* permitted. To illustrate why, we will use the situation described in Note 4 of the Mythical Corporation statements (in Exhibit 2.1).

Mythical Corporation switched from straight-line to the sum-of-the-years' digits depreciation method, effective January 1, 2005. This change in accounting principle increased prior years' depreciation expense as follows:

Year	Gross Increase in Depreciation Expense	Net Increase After Tax Effect Is Considered
2004	$ 49	$ 33
2003	56	38
2002 and earlier	70	47
Total increase	$175	$118

In addition, the switch to the sum-of-the-years' digits depreciation method increased 2005 depreciation expense by $46 ($31 after tax effect).

In implementing the change in principle, Mythical would make the following entry:

DR Cumulative effect of change in accounting
      principle, net of income tax effect $118

DR Deferred income tax payable   57

    CR Accumulated depreciation $175

The credit adjusts the balance sheet accumulated depreciation account to reflect the higher total amounts under the sum-of-the-years' digits method. The debit of $118 represents the decrease in after-tax net income. The difference between the credit of $175 and the income statement debit of $118 arises because of deferred income taxes, which are discussed in detail in Chapter 13.

This example will help you understand why GAAP compels firms to highlight the cumulative effect of accounting principles changes in the income statement. If firms were allowed to change accounting principles and retroactively restate prior periods' income, it would be possible for them to manipulate earnings and mislead investors.

To illustrate how this might happen if retroactive restatements were permitted, let's suppose that Mythical Corporation's management had initially chosen straight-line depreciation for fixed assets even though it knew that this method overstated income in Mythical's particular economic circumstances. The motive for this overstatement might be to mislead the securities market and to allow the firm to raise capital more cheaply. Later, once it became apparent that accelerated depreciation should have been used all along, the firm would then change the accounting depreciation principle and unobtrusively adjust prior periods' income. However, ***by forcing the cumulative effect of $118 million through the income statement, all such changes must take place "in the sunshine"—and in that case the type of opportunistic accounting principle choice just discussed is made transparent.***

Figure 2.7 provides data on the frequency and magnitude of the cumulative effect of accounting changes (net of tax effects) reported on the income statements of NYSE and AMEX firms from 1992 to 2001. Panel (a) shows that with the exception of 1992–1993, the percentage of firms reporting accounting change cumulative effects was generally less than 10%. During 1992–1993 the percentage of firms reporting this item on their income statements rose to 19% and 21%, respectively. The vast majority of the accounting changes reported in these two years related to the adoption of a new FASB standard (*SFAS No. 106*) on accounting for other postemployment (for example, healthcare) benefits, which is discussed further in Chapter 14. Figure 2.7(b) shows that the median gain from cumulative effect of accounting changes ranged from roughly 2% of adjusted after-tax earnings in 2001 to slightly over 34% in 1995. The median losses from cumulative effect accounting changes were generally larger and more variable, ranging from approximately 3% in 2001 to 42% in 1992.

Applying Changes Retroactively There are, however, some circumstances in which GAAP requires the prior years' income effect of a newly adopted accounting principle to be applied retroactively. When this is done in the comparative income statements, there is no need for a pro

We believe the recent FASB Exposure Draft* calling for retroactively restating prior periods' income for accounting principle changes makes the effects of accounting changes less transparent and potentially invites the kind of opportunistic management behavior described in this paragraph.

*"Accounting Changes and Error Corrections—A Replacement of APB Opinion No. 20 and FASB Statement No. 3," *FASB Exposure Draft* (Stamford, CT: FASB, 2003).

Figure 2.7

FREQUENCY AND
MAGNITUDE OF CUMULATIVE
EFFECTS OF ACCOUNTING
CHANGES (1992–2001)

*Source: Standard and Poor's
Compustat® Annual Industrial File
as data source; methodology not
verified or controlled by Standard
& Poor's.*

**(a) Percentages of NYSE/AMEX Firms Reporting
Cumulative Effects of Accounting Changes (1992–2001)**

(b) Magnitudes of Accounting Changes

forma footnote, since the retroactively adjusted income numbers will be comparable to the current period's income.

The retroactive adjustment approach has been allowed by the FASB when new accounting principles are mandated by a newly issued standard. Examples include the capitalization of leases, changes in foreign currency accounting rules, and new deferred income tax reporting requirements.[20] In circumstances such as these, the cumulative effect of the mandated change in the accounting principle is often exceedingly large relative to income from continuing operations. If, say, income from continuing operations was $400 million and if the cumulative effect of the change on prior years' income was $4.5 billion, the cumulative effect would so swamp the continuing income number that adding the two together would make the $4.9 billion net income unrepresentative of the firm's long-run sustainable earnings prospects. Under these circumstances, forcing the cumulative effect through the current period's income statement may hinder informed analysis. Furthermore, since the accounting principle change was mandated by standard setters—not made voluntarily by firms themselves—the fear of opportunistic management behavior is reduced. Accordingly, retroactive adjustment in these circumstances is allowed.

Retroactive adjustment is also required for a very small number of changes among previously existing (rather than newly mandated) accounting principles. Examples include a switch from Last-In, First-Out (LIFO) to some other inventory accounting method and a change in accounting for long-term construction projects (for example, from the completed-contract method to the

---

[20] "Accounting for Leases," *Statement of Financial Accounting Standards (SFAS) No. 13* (Stamford, CT: FASB 1976), para. 48; "Foreign Currency Translation," *SFAS No. 52* (Stamford, CT: FASB, 1981), para. 33; "Accounting for Income Taxes," *SFAS No. 109* (Norwalk, CT: FASB, 1992), para. 50.

percentage-of-completion method, or vice versa). Typically, changes of these sorts will also generate cumulative effects that swamp the income from continuing operations number. This appears to be the reason why standard setters require such changes to be adjusted retroactively.

Retroactive Effect Indeterminable The LIFO inventory accounting method requires that firms keep track of when inventory is increased as well as the cost of these new inventory layers. Therefore, LIFO entails more detailed inventory recordkeeping than either the FIFO or weighted average methods. A firm that switches to LIFO would have had no reason to have kept detailed inventory data on new layers of inventory costs prior to LIFO adoption. Accordingly, computing what income *would have been* for previous years on LIFO could be difficult or even impossible. For this reason the LIFO adoption disclosure is limited to reporting what income *would have been* under the old inventory method in the year of the change. The cumulative effect on prior years is deemed to be indeterminable and is therefore not disclosed. Exhibit 2.5 illustrates the 2002 disclosure arising from LIFO adoption by Salton Inc., a leading domestic distributor of branded small appliances including George Foreman™ grills.

EXHIBIT 2.5	Salton Inc.

Accounting Change—Retroactive Effect Indeterminable
Inventories at June 30 consisted of the following:

($ in thousands)	2002	2001
Raw materials	$ 4,545	$ 5,986
Work-in-process	3,391	1,293
Finished goods	236,224	185,223
Total	$244,160	$192,502

During the fourth quarter of fiscal year 2002, the Company changed its method of accounting for certain inventories (principally Salton branded products) from the first-in, first-out method ("FIFO") to the last-in, first-out ("LIFO") method, retroactively effective as of July 1, 2001. The Company believes the new method is preferable because the LIFO method of valuing inventories more closely matches current costs and revenues in periods of price level changes. This change was also made to apply a consistent method of inventory valuation for all U.S. inventories.

The net effect of this change was to decrease net income by $0.4 million, or $.03 per diluted share. It is not possible to determine the cumulative effect of the change on retained earnings at July 1, 2002 or the pro forma effect of retroactive application of the change for prior periods. The impact on quarterly financial results during fiscal year 2002 was de minimis (minimal).

Source: Salton Inc. 2002 annual Report.

Changes in Accounting Estimates The useful life of a depreciable asset or the percentage of accounts receivable deemed uncollectible constitutes what are called **accounting estimates**. When the economic circumstances underlying an accounting estimate change, GAAP requires that the estimate also be changed. For instance, when unforeseen technological advances shorten the service life of an asset, the period over which the asset is depreciated must be similarly shortened.

When accounting estimates are changed, past income is never adjusted; instead, the income effects of the changed estimate are accounted for in the period of the change—and in future periods, if the change affects both. If the change in estimate has a material effect on current and future income, the dollar amount of the effect must be disclosed. Exhibit 2.6 shows the disclosure of the effect of a change in accounting estimate for Hanover Compressor, one that increased the useful lives of some of its compression equipment.

EXHIBIT 2.6 — Hanover Compressor

Excerpt from Footnotes to 2001 Annual Report

Effective July 1, 2001, the Company changed its estimate of the useful life of certain compression equipment to range from 15 to 30 years instead of a 15 year life. The Company's new estimated lives are based on different types of compressors presently in the Company's rental fleet rather than a blanket life applied to all compressors and more accurately reflects the economic lives of the compressors. The effect of this change in estimate on the year ended December 31, 2001 was a decrease in depreciation expense of approximately $5,000,000 and an increase in net income of approximately $3,100,000 ($0.04 per share).

Source: Hanover Compressor, Co., 2001 Annual Report.

We'll use another example to illustrate how current and future period numbers are adjusted when a change in an accounting estimate is made. Miles Corporation purchases a production machine on January 1, 2003 for $6 million. The machine has no salvage value, an expected useful life of ten years, and it is being depreciated on a straight-line basis. On January 1, 2005 the book value of the machine is $4.8 million (that is, $6 million of original cost minus two years of accumulated depreciation at $0.6 million per year). At that date, it becomes evident that due to changes in demand for the machine's output, its *remaining* useful life is six years, not eight years. If Miles Corporation had perfect foresight, the annual depreciation charge should have been $0.75 million ($6 million divided by eight years), amounting to $1.5 million over the first two years. Consequently, there is $0.3 million too little accumulated depreciation ($1.5 million minus $1.2 million) on January 1, 2005, and pre-tax income for the previous two years is overstated by $0.3 million. Rather than forcing Miles to retroactively adjust reported past income, the GAAP disclosure rules require the change in estimate to be reflected in higher depreciation charges over the new remaining life of the asset—in this case, from 2005 to 2010.[21] Depreciation in those years will be $0.8 million per year (that is, the remaining book value of $4.8 million divided by the remaining useful life of six years). Over the eight-year life of the asset, depreciation will appear as follows:

2003–2004	2 years × $0.6 million per year	=	$1.2 million
2005–2010	6 years × $0.8 million per year	=	$4.8 million
Total cost of the asset			$6.0 million

From the perspective of perfect foresight, in which depreciation would have been $0.75 million per year, depreciation in the first two years is understated by $0.15 million annually, and in each of the last six years it is overstated by $0.05 million annually. Obviously, over the eight-year life of the asset, depreciation totals $6.0 million.

---

[21] *APB Opinion No. 20*, paras. 31–33.

Why are changes in estimates "corrected" in this peculiar fashion? The reason is that accrual accounting requires many estimates; since the future is highly uncertain, a high proportion of these estimates turn out to be incorrect. If past income were corrected for each misestimate, income statements would be cluttered with numerous retroactive adjustments. The approach illustrated by this example provides an expedient way to deal with the uncertainty in financial statements without generating burdensome corrections.

Change in Reporting Entity Another type of accounting change can arise when a company acquires another company. In such circumstances the newly combined entity presents consolidated financial statements in place of the previously separate statements of each party to the merger. Such combinations result in what is called a **change in reporting entity**.

When a change in a reporting entity occurs, comparative financial statements for prior years must be restated for comparative purposes to reflect the new reporting entity as if it had been in existence during all the years presented. The disclosure rule states:

> . . . [A]ccounting changes which result in financial statements that are in effect the statements of a different reporting entity . . . should be reported by restating the financial statements of all prior periods presented in order to show financial information for the new reporting entity for all periods.[22]

Comparative financial statements represent an important resource for analysts, since they provide potentially valuable data for assessing trends and turning points. However, under current GAAP not all business combinations or spin-offs result in a change in the reporting entity. Consequently, analysts must understand the circumstances under which retroactive restatement takes place (and when it does not) in order to ensure that the data being used are indeed comparable. These matters are discussed in more detail in Chapter 16.

Accounting changes can dramatically affect reported earnings and distort year-to-year comparisons. For these reasons, GAAP requires special disclosures to improve interperiod comparability and to help the statement user understand what effect the accounting change has had on the current period's reported profits. The three basic types of accounting changes are:

1. change in accounting principles;
2. change in accounting estimates; and
3. change in reporting entity.

Earnings per Share

One of the most commonly reported measures of a company's operating performance is **earnings per share (EPS)**. All publicly traded companies must report EPS numbers on the face of their income statement. Exhibit 2.7 illustrates the EPS disclosures for Hewlett Packard Company. Note that two sets of numbers are reported—one set for **basic EPS** and another set for **diluted EPS**. Basic EPS is computed by dividing income available to common shareholders (that is, net income minus dividends to preferred shareholders) by the weighted average common shares outstanding for the period. Diluted EPS reflects the EPS that would result if all potentially dilutive securities were converted into common shares. It is reported for firms with complex capital structures—that is, firms with convertible debt, convertible preferred stock, options or warrants outstanding. The calculations involved for diluted EPS are complex and are covered in detail in Chapter 15. Here we simply illustrate the financial statement presentation of EPS.

---

[22] *APB Opinion No. 20*, para. 34.

EXHIBIT 2.7	Hewlett Packard Company

Condensed Income Statements

	Years Ended October 31		
($ in millions, except per share amounts)	2002	2001	2000
Net revenue	$56,588	$45,226	$48,870
Total costs and expenses	57,600	43,787	44,845
(Loss) earnings from operations	(1,012)	1,439	4,025
Total interest and other income, net	(40)	(737)	600
(Loss) earnings from continuing operations before extraordinary item, cumulative effect of change in accounting principle and taxes	(1,052)	702	4,625
(Benefit from) provision for taxes	(129)	78	1,064
Net (loss) earnings from continuing operations before extraordinary item, cumulative effect of change in accounting principle	(923)	624	3,561
Net earnings from discontinued operations	—	—	136
Extraordinary item gain on early extinguishment of debt, net of taxes	20	56	—
Cumulative effect of change in accounting principle, net of taxes	—	(272)	—
Net (loss) earnings	$ (903)	$ 408	$ 3,697
Earnings (loss) per share:			
Basic:			
Continuing operations	$ (0.37)	$ 0.32	$ 1.80
Discontinued operations	—	—	0.07
Extraordinary item gain on early extinguishment of debt, net of taxes	0.01	0.03	—
Cumulative effect of change in accounting principle, net of taxes	—	(0.14)	—
Net (loss) earnings	$ (0.36)	$ 0.21	$ 1.87
Diluted:			
Continuing operations	$ (0.37)	$ 0.32	$ 1.73
Discontinued operations	—	—	0.07
Extraordinary item gain on early extinguishment of debt, net of taxes	0.01	0.03	—
Cumulative effect of change in accounting principle, net of taxes	—	(0.14)	—
Net (loss) earnings	$ (0.36)	$ 0.21	$ 1.80
Weighted average shares used to compute net (loss) earnings per share:			
Basic	2,499	1,936	1,979
Diluted	2,499	1,974	2,077

Thompson Financial (First Call) is a leading provider of analyst EPS forecasts in the United States. The EPS forecasts reported by Thompson are typically basic EPS for income from continuing operations excluding the effects of special, nonrecurring gains or losses and certain other non-cash charges (for example, depreciation and goodwill amortization). Such earnings are frequently referred to as pro forma or "Street" earnings. See Chapter 5 for further discussion.

Note that each set of EPS numbers includes separately reported numbers for income from continuing operations, discontinued operations, extraordinary items, cumulative effect of a change in accounting principle, and bottom-line net income. Therefore, it is important for the statement user to be aware of how the number being reported in companies' earnings announcements is defined. This caution applies both to announcements in the financial press and to analysts' forecasts of firms' performance.

Comprehensive Income

Generally, items included in net income are considered to be **closed transactions**. A closed transaction is one whose ultimate "payoff" results from events (1) that have already occurred and (2) whose dollar flows can be predicted fairly accurately. Recollect that income recognition automatically triggers a corresponding change in the carrying amount (book value) of net assets.

Sometimes balance sheet carrying amounts change even though the transaction is not yet closed. Let's consider a specific example, such as a bank or other financial institution that has investments in stocks or other financial instruments with readily determinable market values.

Assume that these securities are held in the firm's "available-for-sale" portfolio and that their current market values exceed original purchase prices. In 1993 the FASB decided that the fair market value of the securities—rather than invested historical cost (the amount originally invested in them)—should appear on the balance sheet. To recognize a market value increase, the following accounting entry must be made:

> A market value decrease would be debited to "Owners' equity—unrealized holding loss on investment securities" account with an offsetting credit to the "Marketable securities" accounts.

DR Marketable securities	XXX	
CR Owners' equity—unrealized holding gain on investment securities		XXX

Obviously, the credit to offset the increase in the marketable securities account must be made to some sort of equity account. Notice, however, that this is not a closed transaction, since the securities have not been sold. Because such transactions are still *open*, the FASB does not require the credit to run through the income statement. Instead, the owners' equity increase is reported directly as a separate component of stockholders' equity in the balance sheet.[23] Thus, selected unrealized gains (or losses) arising from incomplete (or open) transactions sometimes bypass the income statement and are reported as direct adjustments to stockholders' equity. Such items are called **other comprehensive income** components and fall into one of the four following categories:[24]

1. Unrealized gains (losses) on marketable securities held in firms' "available-for-sale" portfolios (discussed more fully in Chapter 16).
2. Unrealized gains (losses) resulting from translating foreign currency financial statements of majority-owned subsidiaries into U.S. dollar amounts for the purpose of preparing consolidated financial statements (discussed in Chapter 16).
3. In certain cases, unrealized losses resulting from recognition of minimum pension obligations under *SFAS No. 87* (discussed in Chapter 14).
4. Unrealized gains (losses) on derivatives used to hedge certain risks (discussed in Chapter 11).

SFAS No. 130 requires firms to report comprehensive income in a statement that is displayed with the same prominence as other financial statements. Firms are permitted to display the components of other comprehensive income in one of several alternative formats:

1. In a single-statement format, one in which net income and other comprehensive income are added together to disclose (total) comprehensive income.
2. In a two-statement approach, one in which net income comprises one statement and a second, which presents a separate statement of comprehensive income.
3. As part of the statement of changes in stockholders' equity.

> In "Elements of Financial Statements," *Statement of Financial Accounting Concepts Statement No. 6* (Stamford, CT: FASB, 1985), para. 70, comprehensive income is defined as "the change in equity (net assets) of a business enterprise during a period from transactions and other events and circumstances from nonowner sources. It includes all changes in equity during a period except those resulting from investments by owners and distributions to owners."

Exhibit 2.8 (on the next page) from Arden Group's 2002 annual report illustrates the first approach, Exhibit 2.9 (on page 72) shows the two-statement approach for Merck & Company and Exhibit 2.10 (on page 73) demonstrates the disclosure of other comprehensive income components as part of Deere & Company's 2002 Statement of Changes in Stockholders' Equity.

---

[23] "Accounting for Certain Investments in Debt and Equity Securities," *SFAS No. 115* (Norwalk, CT: FASB, 1993), para. 13.
[24] "Reporting Comprehensive Income," *SFAS No. 130* (Norwalk, CT: FASB, 1997).

EXHIBIT 2.8	Arden Group, Incorporated and Consolidated Subsidiary

Consolidated Statements of Operations and Comprehensive Income

	Years Ended December 31		
($ in thousands)	2002	2001	2000
Sales	$401,378	$391,880	$359,994
Cost of sales	226,916	226,302	210,884
Gross profit	174,462	165,578	149,110
Delivery, selling, general and administrative expenses	152,119	145,466	129,272
Operating income	22,343	20,112	19,838
Interest and dividend income	1,867	2,166	2,265
Other income (expense), net	98	356	(464)
Interest expense	(321)	(596)	(782)
Income before income taxes	23,987	22,038	20,857
Income tax provision	9,641	8,731	8,498
Net income	$ 14,346	$ 13,307	$ 12,359
Other comprehensive income (loss), net of tax:			
Unrealized gain (loss) from investments:			
Unrealized holding gains (losses) arising during the period	732	(680)	184
Reclassification adjustment for realized losses included in net income	153	28	261
Net unrealized gain (loss), net of income tax expense (benefits) of $608 for 2002, ($449) for 2001 and $306 for 2000	885	(652)	445
Comprehensive income	$ 15,231	$ 12,655	$ 12,804

EXHIBIT 2.9	Merck & Company, Incorporated and Subsidiaries

Consolidated Statement of Income

	Years Ended December 31		
($ in millions)	2002	2001	2000
Sales	$51,790.3	$47,715.7	$40,363.2
Costs, Expenses and Other			
Materials and production	33,053.6	28,976.5	22,443.5
Marketing and administrative	6,186.8	6,224.4	6,167.7
Research and development	2,677.2	2,456.4	2,343.8
Equity income from affiliates	(644.7)	(685.9)	(764.9)
Other (income) expense, net	303.8	341.7	349.0
	41,576.7	37,313.1	30,539.1
Income Before Taxes	10,213.6	10,402.6	9,824.1
Taxes on income	3,064.1	3,120.8	3,002.4
Net Income	$ 7,149.5	$ 7,281.8	$ 6,821.7
Other Comprehensive Income (Loss)			
Net unrealized (loss) gain on derivatives, net of tax and net income realization	(20.0)	7.3	—
Net unrealized gain on investments, net of tax and net income realization	7.31	11.1	24.3
Minimum pension liability, net of tax	(162.5)	(38.6)	(1.6)
	(175.19)	(20.2)	22.7
Comprehensive Income	$ 6,974.31	$ 7,261.6	$ 6,844.4

EXHIBIT 2.10	Deere & Company

Statement of Changes in Consolidated Stockholders' Equity

Year Ended October 31, 2002 ($ in millions)	Total Equity	Common Stock	Treasury Stock	Unamortized Restricted Stock*	Retained Earnings	Other Comprehensive Income (Loss)
Balance October 31, 2001	$3,992.2	$1,948.6	$(1,405.5)	$(16.8)	$3,834.8	$(368.9)
Comprehensive income (loss)						
Net income	319.2				319.2	
Other comprehensive income (loss)						
Minimum pension liability adjustment	(1,015.9)					(1,015.9)
Cumulative translation adjustment	(7.6)					(7.6)
Unrealized gain on derivatives	25.0					25.0
Unrealized gain on investments	1.0					1.0
Total comprehensive income	(678.3)					
Repurchases of common stock	(1.2)		(1.2)			
Treasury shares reissued	84.5		84.5			
Dividends declared	(209.3)				(209.3)	
Other stockholder transactions	(24.7)	8.4		(1.0)	(32.1)	
Balance October 31, 2002	$3,163.2	$1,957.0	$(1,322.2)	$(17.8)	$3,912.6	$(1,366.4)

*Unamortized restricted stock includes restricted stock issued at market price net of amortization to compensation expense.

RECAP

Comprehensive income measures the change in equity (net assets) of a company that results from all nonowner transactions and events. It is comprised of both bottom-line accrual income that is reported on the income statement and other comprehensive income components. Other comprehensive income is comprised of selected unrealized gains and losses on incomplete (or open) transactions that bypass the income statement and that are reported as direct credits or debits to stockholders' equity. Firms are required to report comprehensive income in a statement that is displayed with the same prominence as other financial statements. But firms are free to choose the format of presentation—either as a separate statement or as part of a statement that is combined with the income statement or a statement of changes in stockholders' equity.

SUMMARY

- This chapter highlights the key differences between cash and accrual income measurement.
- In most instances accrual-basis revenues do not equal cash receipts, and accrual expenses do not equal cash disbursements.
- The principles that govern revenue and expense recognition under accrual accounting are designed to alleviate the mismatching of effort and accomplishment that occurs under cash-basis accounting.
- Revenue is recognized when *both* the "critical event" and "measurability" conditions are satisfied.
- The critical event establishes when the entity has done something to "earn" the asset being received, and measurability is established when the revenue can be measured with a reasonable degree of assurance.
- The critical event and measurability conditions may be satisfied before or after the point of sale.
- The matching principle determines how and when the assets that are "used up" in generating the revenue—or that expire with the passage of time—are expensed.

- Relative to current operating cash flows, accrual earnings generally provide a more useful measure of firm performance, and serve as a more useful benchmark for predicting future cash flows.
- Predicting future cash flows and earnings is critical to assessing the value of a firm's shares and its creditworthiness.
- Multiple-step income statements are designed to facilitate this forecasting process by isolating the more recurring or sustainable components of earnings from the nonrecurring or transitory earnings components.
- GAAP disclosure requirements for various types of accounting changes also facilitate the analysis of company performance over time.
- All publicly traded companies must report earnings per share (EPS) numbers on the face of their income statement. All firms are required to report basic EPS based on the weighted average number of shares actually outstanding during the period.
- In addition to basic EPS, firms with complex capital structures—that include convertible debt, convertible preferred stock, options or warrants—are required to disclose diluted EPS, which reflects the EPS that would result if all potentially dilutive securities were converted into common shares.
- Occasionally, changes in assets and liabilities resulting from incomplete or "open" transactions bypass the income statement and are reported as direct adjustments to stockholders' equity. These direct adjustments are called "other comprehensive income components."
- Comprehensive income provides a measure of all changes in equity of an enterprise that result from transactions with nonowners.
- When used with related disclosures in the financial statements, comprehensive income and its components can provide valuable information to investors and creditors for assessing the magnitude and timing of an entity's future cash flows.

APPENDIX

REVIEW OF ACCOUNTING PROCEDURES AND T-ACCOUNT ANALYSIS

The basic accounting equation is the foundation of financial reporting:

$$A = L + OE$$

The basic accounting equation says that at all times, the dollar sum of a firm's assets (A) must be equal to the dollar sum of the firm's liabilities (L) plus its owners' equity (OE). To understand why this equality must always hold, keep two things in mind:

1. Assets don't materialize out of thin air—they have to be financed from somewhere.
2. There are only two parties that can provide financing for a firm's assets:

   a. Creditors of the company—for example, when a supplier ships inventory to a firm on credit (an asset—inventory—is received).
   b. Owners of the company—for example, when owners buy newly issued shares directly from the firm (an asset—cash—is received).

Putting these two things together explains why the two sides of the basic accounting equation must be equal. The equation says the total resources a firm owns or controls (its assets) must, by definition, be equal to the total of the financial claims against those assets held by either creditors or owners.

We'll now use the basic accounting equation to show how various transactions affect its components. Notice, each transaction maintains the basic equality; for example, any increase in an asset must be offset by (1) a corresponding increase in a liability or owners' equity account or (2) a decrease in some other asset.

For simplicity, we ignore nuances of the par value of the stock, etc., and simply treat the entire amount as "common stock." The details of stock transactions are explored further in Chapter 15.

Assume that Chicago Corporation sells office furniture and provides office design consulting services. It is incorporated on January 1, 2005 and issues $1,000,000 of stock to investors for cash. Here's how the basic accounting equation will be affected by this and subsequent transactions:

Transaction 1:

Assets	=	Liabilities	+	Owners' equity
+$1,000,000 Cash				+$1,000,000 Common stock

On the next day, Chicago Corporation buys a combination office building and warehouse for $330,000, paying $30,000 in cash and taking out a $300,000 loan at 8% interest per year.

Transaction 2:

Assets	=	Liabilities	+	Owners' equity
− $30,000 Cash		+$300,000 Loan payable		
+$330,000 Building				

Suppliers ship a wide assortment of inventory costing $97,000 to the firm on credit on January 11.

Transaction 3:

Assets	=	Liabilities	+	Owners' equity
+$97,000 Inventory		+$97,000 Accounts payable		

On January 15, Chicago corporation sells a portion of its inventory costing $50,000 to several customers for $76,000.

Transaction 4:

Assets	=	Liabilities	+	Owners' equity
+$76,000 Accounts receivable				+$76,000 Sales revenue
−$50,000 Inventory				−$50,000 Cost of goods sold

A sale causes assets to flow into the company. Who benefits from this inflow of assets? The owners do. That's why owners' equity is increased by $76,000 in Transaction 4. The source of this increase is labeled—in this case, the source of the increase is sales revenue. But in making a sale, the firm must relinquish an asset, inventory. Whose claims are reduced as a result of this outflow of assets? The owners'. That's why owners' equity is decreased by $50,000 in the second part of Transaction 4. Again, the reason for the decrease in owners' equity is labeled—in this case, the need to deliver inventory to the customer reduces owners' equity claims on the firm's assets by $50,000—the cost of goods sold.

In addition to the balance sheet (which follows the "balancing" format of the basic accounting equation), there is another financial statement called the income statement. Recollect that "Sales revenue" is the top line of the income statement and that "Cost of goods sold" is deducted from revenues. So Transaction 4, which was illustrated in a basic accounting equation (that is, balance sheet) format, really includes income statement accounts. ***Another way of saying the same thing is that the revenue and expense accounts that appear on the income statement are really owners' equity accounts. Revenues are owners' equity increases; expenses are owners' equity decreases.*** (Later in this appendix, we'll show how these accounts are "closed" into retained earnings—a component of owners' equity—as part of the adjusting and closing process.)

Understanding Debits and Credits

Keeping track of transactions using the basic accounting equation—as we did in Transactions 1 through 4—is cumbersome. For this reason, a streamlined approach is used for recording how transactions either increase or decrease financial statement accounts. Increases and decreases in accounts are based on the convention of "debits" and "credits." Debit (abbreviated DR) means "left-side" of accounts and credit (abbreviated CR) means "right-side" of accounts.

We now depict the basic accounting equation in T-account form and show the rules for how debits and credits operate to reflect increases or decreases to various accounts.

Asset Accounts		=	Liability Accounts		+	Owners' Equity Accounts	
Debits	Credits		Debits	Credits		Debits	Credits
(DR)	(CR)		(DR)	(CR)		(DR)	(CR)
increase the account balance	decrease the account balance		decrease the account balance	increase the account balance		decrease the account balance	increase the account balance

Since Transaction 4 showed us that revenue accounts increase owners' equity and expense accounts decrease it, the DR and CR rules treat revenue and expense accounts just like any other owners' equity accounts. The rules can be summarized as follows:

Revenues (that is, OE increases)		Expenses (that is, OE decreases)	
Debits	Credits	Debits	Credits
(DR)	(CR)	(DR)	(CR)
decrease the account balance	increase the account balance	increase the account balance	decrease the account balance

Let's elaborate on the debit/credit rules for expense accounts. Expense accounts are increased by debits. An increase in an expense *decreases* owners' equity. Owners' equity is decreased by debits. That's why increases in an expense account (which decrease owners' equity) are debits.

The basic accounting equation must always be "in balance"—the total of the assets must always equal the total of the liabilities plus owners' equity. ***Similarly, for each transaction, the dollar total of the debits must equal the dollar total of the credits.*** Adherence to the debit and credit rules for each transaction automatically keeps the basic accounting equation "in balance." To help you visualize how this happens, we will redo Transactions 1–4 in debit/credit format and show (in brackets to the right of the account) what happens to the basic accounting equation:

Transaction 1: Stock issued for cash

DR Cash [+A]		$1,000,000	
CR Common stock [+OE]			$1,000,000

Transaction 2: Purchase of building

DR Building [+A]		$330,000	
CR Cash [−A]			$30,000
CR Loan payable [+L]			300,000

Transaction 3: Purchase of inventory on credit

DR Inventory [+A]		$97,000	
CR Accounts payable [+L]			$97,000

Transaction 4: Sale of inventory on account

DR Accounts receivable [+A]		$76,000	
DR Cost of goods sold [−OE]		50,000	
CR Sales revenue [+OE]			$76,000
CR Inventory [−A]			50,000

As the pluses and minuses to the right of the debits and credits show, adherence to the DR/CR rules automatically maintains the balance of the basic accounting equation.

We next introduce four additional transactions for Chicago Corporation. Assume that Chicago purchases a one-year fire and theft insurance policy on the building and its contents on January 15, 2005 for $6,000. They make the following journal entry upon purchasing the policy:

Transaction 5: **Purchase of prepaid insurance**

DR Prepaid insurance [+A]	$6,000	
CR Cash [−A]		$6,000

Prepaid insurance is an asset account because the policy provides a valuable benefit to the company—insurance coverage for the ensuing 12 months.

Next, assume the company receives a $10,000 fee, in advance, from a law firm to help the firm design their new office space. The fee is received on January 17, and the consulting/design services are to be provided over the next month. The following journal entry is made by Chicago Corporation:

Transaction 6: **Receipt of consulting fees in advance**

DR Cash [+A]	$10,000	
CR Fee received in advance [+L]		$10,000

The credit is to a liability account "Fee received in advance" because the firm has an obligation to provide the consulting services (or return the fee).

Further assume, Chicago Corporation pays certain suppliers $37,000 for inventory recorded in Transaction 3. Other suppliers will be paid in ensuing periods.

Transaction 7: **Payment on account**

DR Accounts payable [−L]	$37,000	
CR Cash [−A]		$37,000

Finally, $30,000 is received from one of the customers to whom inventory was sold in Transaction 4.

Transaction 8: **Collections on account**

DR Cash [+A]	$30,000	
CR Accounts receivable [−A]		$30,000

Adjusting Entries

Before financial statements are prepared (either monthly, quarterly, or annually), a firm's financial accounts must be reviewed to determine whether all economic events that have occurred are reflected in the accounts. It is usually the case that certain readily identifiable types of events will *not* be reflected in the accounts. To include these events in the accounts, **adjusting entries** must be made. These adjusting entries fall into four categories:

1. Adjustments for prepayments
2. Adjustments for unearned revenues
3. Adjustments for accrued expenses
4. Adjustments for accrued revenues

We now assume that Chicago Corporation is preparing financial statements for the month ended January 31, 2005. Adjusting entries in each of the four categories are necessary and discussed next.

Adjustments for Prepayments

The insurance policy acquired for $6,000 on January 15 in Transaction 5 has partially expired. One-half of one-month's coverage has now elapsed; consequently, 1/24 of the original *annual* premium payment is no longer an asset. The passage of time means that *past* insurance coverage has no future value. So the following adjusting entry is made:

> **Adjusting Entry A1:**
> **DR** Insurance expense [−OE] $250
>   **CR** Prepaid insurance [−A] $250
>   ($6,000 ÷ 12 = $500; $500 × 1/2 mo. = $250)

After this entry is made, the balance in the Prepaid insurance account will be $5,750; this is the original $6,000 balance minus the $250 credit in "Adjusting Entry A1." The $5,750 represents the remaining asset—insurance coverage for the ensuing 11 1/2 months. The adjusting entry has *simultaneously* accomplished two things:

1. The DR recognizes that portion of the premium that has "expired"—that is, the portion that is an expense of January. This is the matching principle in action, since the expense is matched against revenues of January.
2. The CR reduces the carrying amount in the asset account by $250. As a result of this reduction, the prepaid insurance account is shown at $5,750; this is the portion of the original $6,000 insurance premium that has not yet expired.

The building acquired in Transaction 2 also represents a prepayment. Chicago Corporation paid for the building in early January 2005 but this building is expected to be used in operations over a series of *future* years. As the building is used, a portion of its future service potential declines. This decline in service potential value is an expense of the period called **depreciation**. Assume Chicago Corporation estimates building depreciation for January totaled $1,250. The following adjusting entry will then be made:

> We will discuss the various methods for estimating depreciation in Chapter 10.

> **Adjusting Entry A2:**
> **DR** Depreciation expense [−OE] $1,250
>   **CR** Accumulated depreciation [−A] $1,250

(The accumulated depreciation account represents a "contra-asset" account that is deducted from the cost of the building, as we shall see later.)

Adjustments for Unearned Revenues

By the end of January, let's assume 60% of the design work for the law firm has been completed. Consequently, the following adjusting entry is made:

> A **contra** account is an account that is *subtracted* from another account to which it relates. Contra-asset accounts carry credit balances because they are subtracted from asset accounts that carry debit balances.

> **Adjusting Entry A3:**
> **DR** Fee received in advance [−L] $6,000
>   **CR** Consulting fees revenue [+OE] $6,000

Notice this entry also accomplishes two things. One, the debit lowers the balance in the liability account "Fee received in advance" to $4,000 (that is, the original $10,000 minus the $6,000 liability reduction arising from the debit). Two, the credit properly recognizes that 60% of the $10,000 advance has been earned in January and thereby increases owners' equity.

Adjustments for Accrued Expenses

Salaries and wages for the month of January totaled $16,000. The paychecks will not be issued to employees until Monday, February 3. Because the expense arose in January and a liability exists for money owed to the employees, the following entry must be made:

> **Adjusting Entry A4:**
> **DR** Salary and wages expense [−OE] $16,000
>   **CR** Salary and wages payable [+L] $16,000

Adjusting entries like this one must be made for a wide range of expenses that *accrue* over the reporting period. ***Accrual accounting recognizes expenses as the underlying real economic event occurs, not necessarily when the cash flows out.*** Consequently, adjusting entries for accrued expenses must be made not only for accrued wages payable, but also for items like heat, light and power that were used during the month and interest that has accumulated during the period but has not yet been paid. Assume the utility bill arrives on January 31 but will not be paid until February 9, the due date of the bill. If the utility bill for January totaled $9,000, the following additional adjusting entry is necessary:

Adjusting Entry A5:
DR	Heat, light and power expense [−OE]	$9,000	
CR	Accounts payable [+L]		$9,000

Furthermore, interest of $2,000 has accrued on the loan principal that was used to buy the building. (The accrued interest is determined as follows: $300,000 \times 8\% = \$24,000 \times 1/12$ of year $= \$2,000$.) The following entry is made:

Adjusting Entry A6:
DR	Interest expense [−OE]	$2,000	
CR	Accrued interest payable [+L]		$2,000

Adjustments for Accrued Revenues

During the last week in January, Chicago Corporation provides design consulting services to a physician who is remodeling her office. The physician is billed for the $2,100 due. The adjusting entry is:

Adjusting Entry A7:
DR	Accounts receivable [+A]	$2,100	
CR	Consulting fees revenue [+OE]		$2,100

Again, the adjusting entry simultaneously accomplishes two things:

1. The DR reflects the asset that the firm expects to collect as a result of consulting services rendered in January.
2. The CR shows the corresponding increase in owners' equity that arises when the asset write-up is recognized.

Posting Journal Entries to Accounts and Preparing Financial Statements

Throughout this book, we will use journal entries as a streamlined mechanism for showing you how economic events affect financial statement accounts. In this section of the appendix we provide a terse overview of how professional accountants use journal entries as the building blocks for preparing financial statements. We will use T-accounts to demonstrate this. We will also show how analysis of T-accounts can be used to infer what transactions (and dollar amounts) a firm entered into between two balance sheet dates.

The DRs and CRs in each journal entry that is made are posted to T-accounts. **Posting** means the DR or CR is entered in the appropriate left (or right) side of the affected T-account. A separate T-account is maintained for each asset, liability and owners' equity account. (Remember: Revenue and expense accounts are effectively owners' equity accounts, too. The balances accumulated in these accounts for a particular reporting period will be "closed out" or transferred to owners' equity at the end of the period.) Exhibit 2.11 shows all the T-accounts that arise from the transactions of Chicago Corporation during January 2005. The journal entry DR or CR that gave rise to the amount posted in the T-account is indicated by a number to the left of each item. For example, in the cash T-account, the (1) to the left of the DR of $1,000,000 indicates that this item arose from the $1,000,000 DR in transaction 1. The (1) to the left of the $1,000,000 credit to common stock indicates that this item resulted from the balancing CR in Transaction 1. Posting *both* the DR and CR to the T-accounts reflected in the original entry maintains the equality of the basic accounting equation.

EXHIBIT 2.11	Posting to T-Accounts

	Assets	=	Liabilities	+		Owners' Equity	

Cash

(1)	$1,000,000	(2)	$30,000
(6)	10,000	(5)	6,000
(8)	30,000	(7)	37,000

Bal. $967,000

Accounts Payable

| (7) | $37,000 | (3) | $97,000 |
| | | (A5) | 9,000 |

Bal. $69,000

Common Stock

| | | (1) | $1,000,000 |

Bal. $1,000,000

Retained Earnings

(Revenue and expense account balances will be closed out to this account at end of the accounting period.)

Accounts Receivable

| (4) | $76,000 | (8) | $30,000 |
| (A7) | 2,100 | | |

Bal. $48,100

Salary and Wages Payable

| | | (A4) | $16,000 |

Bal. $16,000

Consulting Fees Revenue

| | | (A3) | $6,000 |
| | | (A7) | 2,100 |

Bal. $8,100

Sales Revenue

| | | (4) | $76,000 |

Bal. $76,000

Inventory

| (3) | $97,000 | (4) | $50,000 |

Bal. $47,000

Accrued Interest Payable

| | | (A6) | $2,000 |

Bal. $2,000

Cost of Goods Sold

| (4) | $50,000 | |

Bal. $50,000

Insurance Expense

| (A1) | $250 | |

Bal. $250

Prepaid Insurance

| (5) | $6,000 | (A1) | $250 |

Bal. $5,750

Loan Payable

| | | (2) | $300,000 |

Bal. $300,000

Depreciation Expense

| (A2) | $1,250 | |

Bal. $1,250

Salary and Wages Expense

| (A4) | $16,000 | |

Bal. $16,000

Building

| (2) | $330,000 | |

Bal. $330,000

Fee Received in Advance

| (A3) | $6,000 | (6) | $10,000 |

Bal. $4,000

Heat, Light and Power Expense

| (A5) | $9,000 | |

Bal. $9,000

Interest Expense

| (A6) | $2,000 | |

Bal. $2,000

Accumulated Depreciation

| | | (A2) | $1,250 |

Bal. $1,250

The adjusting entries are also posted to the T-accounts shown in those entries. For example, in Exhibit 2.11, the (A1) to the left of the $250 DR to the "Insurance expense" T-account tells us that this item arose from adjusting entry A1. (Notice the CR from that entry was posted as a credit to the "Prepaid insurance" account, with the A1 designation to the left of the posting.)

The accountant preparing the financial statements would use the balances in the revenue and expense accounts (entered in black in Exhibit 2.11) to prepare the January 2005 income statement. As shown in Exhibit 2.12, income for January (ignoring taxes) is $5,600. This amount represents the **net** increase in owners' equity for the month arising from operations. Consequently, the $5,600 appears again *in the balance sheet* as an owners' equity increase labeled "retained earnings" (shown by the arrows). The asset, liability, and common stock T-accounts (entered in black) comprise the other balance sheet accounts. (Notice, the credit balance in accumulated depreciation is deducted from the building account. That's why this is a "contra-asset" account.)

> This is true because revenues increase owners' equity and expenses decrease owners' equity (review Transaction 4). So, the excess of revenues over expenses represents the *net* increase in owners' equity.

Closing Entries

After the income statement for the month of January 2005 is prepared, the revenue and expense accounts have served their purpose. So balances in these accounts are "zeroed out" (or closed) to get them ready to reflect February transactions. To get the revenue and expense account balances to zero, a **closing journal entry** is made. All revenue account balances (which are credits) are *debited* (to get

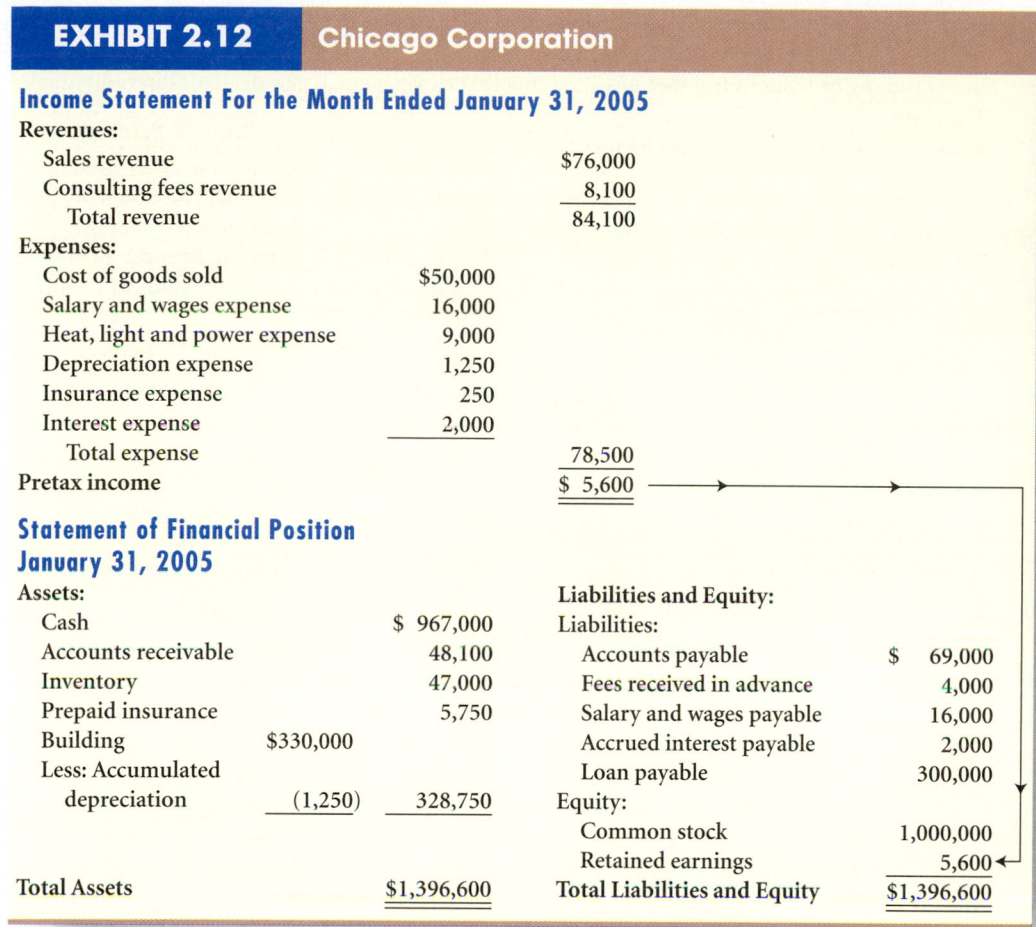

EXHIBIT 2.12   **Chicago Corporation**

Income Statement For the Month Ended January 31, 2005

Revenues:		
Sales revenue		$76,000
Consulting fees revenue		8,100
Total revenue		84,100
Expenses:		
Cost of goods sold	$50,000	
Salary and wages expense	16,000	
Heat, light and power expense	9,000	
Depreciation expense	1,250	
Insurance expense	250	
Interest expense	2,000	
Total expense		78,500
Pretax income		$ 5,600

Statement of Financial Position
January 31, 2005

Assets:			Liabilities and Equity:	
Cash		$ 967,000	Liabilities:	
Accounts receivable		48,100	Accounts payable	$ 69,000
Inventory		47,000	Fees received in advance	4,000
Prepaid insurance		5,750	Salary and wages payable	16,000
Building	$330,000		Accrued interest payable	2,000
Less: Accumulated			Loan payable	300,000
depreciation	(1,250)	328,750	Equity:	
			Common stock	1,000,000
			Retained earnings	5,600
Total Assets		**$1,396,600**	**Total Liabilities and Equity**	**$1,396,600**

them to zero); all expense account balances (which are debits) are *credited* (to get them to zero). The difference between the closing entry debits and credits—in this case, a credit of $5,600—is made to retained earnings. Here's the entry:

DR	Sales revenue	$76,000	
DR	Consulting fees revenue	8,100	
	CR Cost of goods sold		$50,000
	CR Salary and wages expense		16,000
	CR Heat, light and power expense		9,000
	CR Depreciation expense		1,250
	CR Insurance expense		250
	CR Interest expense		2,000
	CR Retained earnings		5,600

After this entry is posted to the accounts, all of the revenue and expense accounts will have zero balances. The accounts are now clear to receive February income statement transactions.

T-accounts Analysis as an Analytical Technique

Understanding the various events or transactions that affect individual account balances is critical to analyzing financial statements. Users of financial statements can't "see" the individual transactions that underlie various account balances and changes in account balances in comparative balance sheets. Nevertheless, it's often possible to deduce the aggregate amount of certain common events or transactions that have taken place during the reporting period. Armed with the following knowledge, one can reconstruct transactions that have occurred during a given reporting period.

A comparative balance sheet reflects the asset, liability, and owners' equity account balances as of the end of the current reporting period (typically a quarter or year) and for one or more previous reporting periods. Firms are required to show ending account balances for at least two years in annual reports issued to shareholders.

- Start with beginning and ending balances in various balance sheet T-accounts (which are always available from comparative balance sheets).
- Know the major types of transactions or events that cause increases or decreases in individual T-accounts.
- Know how various accounts and financial statement items articulate with one another.

T-account analysis also can be used to gain insights into why accrual-basis earnings and cash-basis earnings (that is, cash flows from operations) differ.

Let's use a new example, Trevian corporation, to illustrate how T-account analysis can be used to infer or deduce unknown or unobservable transactions. Consider the following analysis of Accounts receivable (net of the Allowance for doubtful accounts):

Accounts Receivable—Net			
Beginning Balance	$1,000,000		
		Collections on account	(B)
Sales on account	(A)		
Ending Balance	$1,200,000		

Note that the major transaction that increases accounts receivable (debits to this account) is sales on account, while the major transaction causing a decrease in accounts receivable (credits to this account) is the collections on account. Assuming these are the only events that affected Accounts receivable during the period, we can infer from the $200,000 increase in Trevian's Accounts receivable that sales on account exceeded collections on account during the period by $200,000. But can we go a step further and deduce the aggregate amounts of the debits (A) and credits (B) to this account? Yes, we can. However, to do so we need to understand how parts of the income statement and balance sheet articulate with one another.

Recall that the first line of the income statements of most companies is sales revenue. Typically, when one business sells a product or service to another company the sale is a credit sale, meaning that the sale is "on account" and will be collected within 30, 60, or 90 days depending upon industry credit terms. Suppose sales revenue for Trevian was $3,500,000 and all sales were credit sales. We can recreate the following entry that summarizes the credit sales for the period and shows directly how income statement and balance sheet accounts reflect opposite sides of the same transaction and, thus, articulate with one another.

> Other transactions that can affect the Accounts receivable account include write-offs of specific accounts determined to be uncollectible, sales returns and allowances, and customers that take advantage of sales discounts by paying off their account balance within the discount period. Typically, these events have a minimal effect on the Accounts receivable balance for the period.

DR Accounts receivable	$3,500,000	
CR Sales revenue		$3,500,000

Knowing that all sales on account are reflected in an offsetting debit to Accounts receivable allows us to deduce the amount (A) = $3,500,000 in the Accounts receivable T-account presented above. Next, we can combine this information with the fact that the net increase in Accounts receivable was $200,000 to deduce that the collections on account during the period—unknown amount (B)—must have been $3,300,000. In other words,

Beginning accounts receivable balance	$1,000,000
+ Sales on account	3,500,000
− Collections on account	(3,300,000) ← (Plug to balance = B)
= Ending accounts receivable balance	$1,200,000

Analysis of the Accounts receivable T-account also provides information for understanding differences between accrual-basis income and cash from operations. The important insight from the analysis of the Accounts receivable T-account is that sales on account (reflected as revenue in accrual-basis income) is recorded on the debit side of this account, while collections on account (reflected as revenue in cash-basis income measurement—that is, cash flow from operations) is recorded on the credit side of this account. Knowing that Trevian's Accounts receivable has increased by $200,000 tells us that accrual-basis revenue exceeded cash-basis revenue for the period by $200,000. Therefore, we would need to *subtract* this increase in Accounts receivable from the accrual-basis income number to convert accrual earnings to cash flow from operations. Conversely, if collections on account had exceeded sales on account by $200,000, this *decrease* in Accounts receivable would have to be *added* to accrual-basis net income to arrive at cash flow from operations.

Analogous reasoning can be used to gain insights into transactions that affect Accounts payable and the differences between accrual-basis expenses and cash-basis expenses. The following T-account summarizes the key events that cause changes in Trevian's Accounts payable for a period:

Accounts Payable			
		Beginning balance	$2,000,000
Payments on account	(B)		
		Purchases of inventory on account	(A)
		Ending balance	$1,500,000

Here we can see that payments on account exceeded purchases of inventory on account by $500,000, resulting in a decrease in the Accounts payable T-account for the period. We can deduce the amount of purchases on account by again referring to the income statement and recalling the components that comprise the cost of goods sold computation for a merchandising firm. For purposes of this illustration, assume Trevian's cost of goods sold is $2,100,000, and the beginning and ending inventory from its comparative balance sheets are $1,500,000 and $1,800,000, respectively. Purchases of inventory for the period can be deduced as follows:

Beginning inventory	$1,500,000
+ Purchases of inventory	2,400,000 ← (Plug to balance = A)
− Ending inventory	(1,800,000)
Cost of goods sold	$2,100,000

Assuming that all purchases of merchandise inventory was purchased on credit (generally the case for most businesses), we can determine through T-account analysis that payments on account must have been $2,900,000 determined as follows:

Beginning accounts payable balance	$2,000,000
+ Purchases on account (see above)	2,400,000
− Payments on account	(2,900,000) ← (Plug to balance = B)
= Ending accounts payable balance	$1,500,000

Changes in the Accounts payable and Inventory T-accounts help us understand the differences between accrual accounting's cost of goods sold expense and the cash-basis expense for inventory purchases. We'll use the schedules above for Trevian's cost of goods sold and Accounts payable to demonstrate this point:

Accrual accounting cost of goods sold deduction included in determining income	$2,100,000
Add: Inventory increase	300,000
Equals: Total inventory purchases in 2005	2,400,000
Add: Accounts payable decrease	500,000
Equals: Cash basis expense for inventory purchases	$2,900,000

As shown, two adjustments are required to convert accrual-basis cost of goods sold ($2,100,000) to cash-basis expense for inventory purchases ($2,900,000). The first adjustment for the inventory increase is because beginning inventory is a *non-cash addition* to cost of goods sold, while ending inventory is a *non-cash deduction* in arriving at cost of goods sold (see cost of goods sold schedule on page 83). Therefore, to remove the net non-cash effects of beginning and ending inventory from cost of goods sold, we must add the increase in inventory. (If inventory had declined, we would subtract the decrease.) Making this adjustment to cost of goods sold gives us the total inventory purchased in 2005. (We've assumed that all inventory purchases are on account. Consequently, all inventory purchases during the year would be credited to Accounts payable.)

The second adjustment—for the decrease in Accounts payable—is because Trevian's cash *payments* for inventory purchased on account exceeded new inventory *purchases* on account in the current period (see Accounts payable schedule on page 83). Thus, Trevian's cash payments for inventory actually exceeded the credit purchases of inventory that's included in the accrual-basis cost of goods sold number. Accordingly, to convert the accrual-basis cost of goods sold expense to a cash-basis expense, the decrease in accounts payable must be added. (If Accounts payable had increased, this change would have been subtracted.)

Note that in the previous discussion the adjustments made are to convert accrual-basis *expense* to cash-basis *expense*. To adjust accrual-basis *income* to obtain cash-basis *income* (cash flow from operations), the adjustment for the changes in Inventory and Accounts payable would be in the opposite direction. That is, the increase in Inventory and the decrease in Accounts payable would be *subtracted* from accrual income to obtain cash flow from operations. This is because adjustments to expense have the opposite effect on income.

In general, analyses similar to that used for Accounts receivable and Accounts payable can be carried out for Accrued revenue, Accrued expense, Deferred (unearned) revenue, and Deferred (prepaid) expense accounts to deduce other differences between accrual-basis income and cash-basis income. Understanding that differences between accrual-basis and cash-basis income can be gleaned from most working capital accounts (that is, current asset and current liability accounts reported on the balance sheet) is one of the key lessons in financial statement analysis that we will return to repeatedly throughout later chapters in this book.

EXERCISES

E2 – 1

Determining accrual- and cash-basis revenue

In November and December 2005 Gee Company, a newly organized magazine publisher, received $36,000 for 1,000 three-year subscriptions at $12 per year, starting with the January 2006 issue of the magazine.

Required:

How much should Gee report in its 2005 income statement for subscriptions revenue on an accrual basis? How much revenue would be reported in 2005 on a cash basis?

E2 – 2

Determining unearned subscription revenue

Aneen's Video Mart sells one- and two-year mail-order subscriptions for its video-of-the-month business. Subscriptions are collected in advance and credited to sales. An analysis of the recorded sales activity revealed the following:

	2004	2005
Sales	$420,000	$500,000
Less cancellations	(20,000)	(30,000)
Net sales	$400,000	$470,000
Subscription expirations		
2004	$120,000	
2005	155,000	$130,000
2006	125,000	200,000
2007		140,000
	$400,000	$470,000

Required:

What amount of unearned subscription revenue should Aneen report on its December 31, 2005 balance sheet?

Regal Department Store sells gift certificates, redeemable for store merchandise, that expire one year after their issuance. Regal has the following information pertaining to its gift certificates sales and redemptions:

E2 – 3

Determining unearned revenue

AICPA
ADAPTED

Unredeemed at 12/31/05	$75,000
2006 sales	250,000
2006 redemptions of prior year sales	25,000
2006 redemptions of current year sales	175,000

Regal's experience indicates that 10% of gift certificates sold will not be redeemed.

Required:

In its December 31, 2006 balance sheet, what amount should Regal report as unearned revenue?

On October 1, 2005, Hawkeye Company sold 100,000 gallons of heating oil to Johnson Co. at $3 per gallon. Fifty thousand gallons were delivered on December 15, 2005, and the remaining 50,000 gallons were delivered on January 15, 2006. Payment terms were: 50% due on October 1, 2005, 25% due on first delivery, and the remaining 25% due on second delivery.

E2 – 4

Determining when to recognize revenue

AICPA
ADAPTED

Required:

What amount of revenue should Hawkeye recognize from this sale during 2005 on an accrual basis?

In its accrual-basis income statement for the year ended December 31, 2005, Dart Company reported revenue of $1,750,000. Additional information was as follows:

E2 – 5

Converting from accrual- to cash-basis revenue

AICPA
ADAPTED

Accounts receivable 12/31/04	$375,000
Uncollectible accounts written off during 2005	20,000
Accounts receivable 12/31/05	505,000

Required:

Under the cash basis of income determination, how much should Dart report as revenue for 2005?

Tara Company reported accrual-basis revenue of $1,980,000 in its income statement for the year ended December 31, 2005. Additional information was as follows:

E2 – 6

Converting from accrual- to cash-basis revenue

AICPA
ADAPTED

	2004	2005
Accounts receivable	$415,000	$550,000
Allowance for doubtful accounts	25,000	40,000

No uncollectible accounts were written off during 2005.

Required:

Had the cash basis of accounting been used instead, how much revenue would Tara Company have recognized for 2005?

John Tracey, M.D., keeps his accounting records on the cash basis. During 2005 Dr. Tracey collected $150,000 in fees from his patients. At December 31, 2004 Dr. Tracey had accounts receivable of $20,000. At December 31, 2005 Dr. Tracey had accounts receivable of $35,000 and unearned fees of $5,000.

E2 – 7

Converting from cash- to accrual-basis revenue

AICPA
ADAPTED

Required:

On the accrual basis, what was Dr. Tracey's patient service revenue for 2005?

E2 – 8

Converting from cash- to accrual-basis revenue

AICPA
ADAPTED

Marr Corporation reported rental revenue of $2,210,000 in its cash-basis income statement for the year ended November 30, 2005. Additional information is as follows:

Rents receivable—November 30, 2005	$1,060,000
Rents receivable—November 30, 2004	800,000
Uncollectible rents written off during the fiscal year	30,000

Required:

On the accrual basis, how much gross rental revenue should Marr report in 2005?

E2 – 9

Converting from accrual- to cash-basis expense

AICPA
ADAPTED

Under Hart Company's accounting system, all insurance premiums paid are debited to prepaid insurance. For interim financial reports, Hart makes monthly estimated charges to insurance expense with credits to prepaid insurance. Additional information for the year ended December 31, 2005 is as follows:

Prepaid insurance at December 31, 2004	$210,000
Charges to insurance expense during 2005, including a year-end adjustment of $35,000	875,000
Unexpired insurance premiums at December 31, 2005	245,000

Required:

What was the total amount of insurance premiums paid by Hart during 2005?

E2 – 10

Determining accrued liabilities

AICPA
ADAPTED

Dix Company operates a retail store and must determine the proper December 31, 2005 year-end accrual for the following expenses:

- The store lease calls for fixed rent payments of $1,200 per month, payable at the beginning of the month, and additional rent equal to 6% of net sales over $250,000 per calendar year, payable on January 31 of the following year. Net sales for 2005 are $450,000.
- An electric bill of $850 covering the period December 16, 2005 through January 15, 2006 was received January 22, 2006.
- A $400 telephone bill was received January 7, 2006 covering:

Service in advance for January 2006	$150
Local and toll calls for December 2005	250

Required:

What amount should Dix Company report as accrued liabilities on its December 31, 2005 balance sheet?

E2 – 11

Determining gain (loss) from discontinued operations

AICPA
ADAPTED

Munn Corporation's income statements for the years ended December 31, 2006 and 2005 included the following information before adjustments:

	2006	2005
Operating income	$ 800,000	$600,000
Gain on sale of division	450,000	—
	1,250,000	600,000
Provision for income taxes	375,000	180,000
Net income	$ 875,000	$420,000

On January 1, 2006 Munn Corporation agreed to sell the assets and product line of one of its operating divisions for $1,600,000. The sale was consummated on December 31, 2006, and it resulted in a gain on disposition of $450,000. This division's pre-tax net losses were $320,000 in 2006 and $250,000 in 2005. The income tax rate for both years was 30%.

Required:

Starting with operating income (before tax), prepare revised comparative income statements for 2006 and 2005 showing appropriate details for gain (loss) from discontinued operations.

On September 1, 2005, Revsine Co. approved a plan to dispose of a segment of its business. Revsine expected that the sale would occur on March 31, 2006, at an estimated gain of $350,000. The segment had actual and estimated operating profits (losses) as follows:

Realized loss from 1/1/05 to 8/31/05	$(300,000)
Realized loss from 9/1/05 to 12/31/05	(200,000)
Expected profit from 1/1/06 to 3/30/06	400,000

Assume the marginal tax rate is 30%.

E2 – 12

Determining loss on discontinued operations

Required:

In its 2005 income statement, what should Revsine report as profit or loss from discontinued operations (net of tax effects)?

Effective January 1, 2005 Younger Company adopted the accounting principle of expensing incurred advertising and promotion costs. Previously, advertising and promotion costs applicable to future periods were recorded in prepaid expenses. Younger can justify the change, which was made for both financial statement and income tax purposes. Younger's prepaid advertising and promotion costs totaled $500,000 at December 31, 2004. Assume that the income tax rate is 40% for 2004 and 2005.

E2 – 13

Determining cumulative effect of accounting change

AICPA
ADAPTED

Required:

The adjustment for the effect of this change in accounting principle should result in a net charge against income in the 2005 income statement of how much?

On January 1, 2005 Roem Corporation changed its inventory method to FIFO from LIFO for both financial and income tax reporting purposes. The change resulted in a $500,000 increase in the January 1, 2005 inventory. Assume that the income tax rate for all years is 30%.

E2 – 14

Determining cumulative effect of accounting change

AICPA
ADAPTED

Required:

Determine the cumulative effect of the accounting change that Roem should report in its 2005 income statement.

Required:

Classify the following costs as period or product costs. If a product cost, indicate which will be matched with sales as part of cost of goods sold, and which will be shown as a direct deduction from sales.

E2 – 15

Determining period versus product costs

Depreciation on office building	Depreciation on factory
Insurance expense for factory building	Bonus to factory workers
Product liability insurance premium	Salary to marketing staff
Transportation charges for raw materials	Administrative expenses
Factory repairs and maintenance	Bad debt expense
Rent for inventory warehouse	Advertising expenses
Cost of raw materials	Research and development
Factory wages	Warranty expense
Salary to chief executive officer	Electricity for plant

The following information is provided for Kelly Plumbing Supply.

Cash received from customers during December 2005	$387,000
Cash paid to suppliers for inventory during December 2005	$131,000

Cash received from customers includes November accounts receivables of $139,000. Sales totaling $141,000 were made on account during December and are expected to be collected in January 2006. Cash paid to suppliers in December included payments of $19,000 for inventory purchased and used in November. All inventory purchased in December and $39,000 of inventory purchased in November was used in December.

E2 – 16

Converting from cash to accrual basis

Required:

What is gross profit for the month of December under accrual accounting?

E2 – 17

Accrual basis revenue recognition

Runway Care, Inc. provides contract-mowing services for private airfields with grass runways. Some clients prepay for their mowing services early in the spring and their payment is credited to unearned revenue. The following information was taken from Runway's 2005 financial statements.

	Balance at	
	June 30	July 31
Accounts receivable	$30,000	$29,000
Unearned revenue	5,000	3,000

Runway received $73,000 of payments on accounts receivable during July.

Required:

How much revenue should Runway report for the month of July?

E2 – 18

Determining effect of omitting year-end adjusting entries

Hentzel Landscaping commenced its business on January 1, 2005.

1. During the first year of its operations, Hentzel purchased supplies in the amount of $12,000 (debited to "Supplies inventory"), and of this amount, $3,000 were unused as of December 31, 2005.
2. On March 1, 2005 Hentzel Landscaping received $18,000 for landscaping services to be rendered for 18 months (beginning July 1, 2005). This amount was credited to "Unearned landscaping revenue."
3. The company's gasoline bill for $2,500 for the month of December 2005 was not received until January 15, 2006.
4. The company had borrowed $50,000 from HomeTown Financing on April 1, 2005 at an interest rate of 12% per annum. The principal, along with all the interest, is due on April 1, 2006.
5. On January 1, 2005 the company purchased 10 lawnmowers at $3,000 per unit. The lawnmowers are expected to last for three years with no salvage value.

On December 31, 2005 Hentzel Landscaping did not record any adjusting entries with respect to these transactions.

Required:

Using the table format below, show the effect of the *omission* of each year-end adjusting entry on the following: (Indicate both the amount and the direction of the effect.) Use "OS" for overstated, "US" for understated, and "NE" for no effect.

Item Number	Assets	Liabilities	Net Income
Direction of effect			
Dollar amount of effect			

E2 – 19

Preparation of a multiple-step income statement

Presented below is a combined single-step income and retained earnings statement for Amalgamated Steel Co. for 2005.

Amalgamated Steel Co.

Income Statement
Year Ended December 31, 2005
($ in 000)

Net sales	$4,801,776
Costs and expenses:	
Cost of products sold	4,332,277
Marketing, administrative and other expenses	175,588
Interest expense	14,286
Other, net	49,572
Total expenses before taxes	4,571,723
Earnings before income taxes	230,053
Provision for income taxes	69,016
Net income	161,037
Retained earnings at 1/1/05	2,538,883
Dividends on common stock	(59,383)
Retained earnings at 12/31/05	$2,640,537

Additional facts gleaned from Amalgamated's financial statement footnotes are as follows:
1. "Other, net" for 2005 included a corporate restructuring charge of $9,753,000 and a gain of $11,000,000 resulting from compensation paid by the U.S. government for company property taken under the right of "eminent domain." The remainder of the caption is comprised of investment losses.
2. "Marketing, administrative and other expenses" for 2005 included a loss on currency translation of $50,000.
3. All of the above transactions were subject to Amalgamated's income tax rate of 30%.
4. Amalgamated disclosed earnings per share data only in the notes to the financial statements. The company had 10,000,000 shares of common stock outstanding throughout 2005.

Required:

Recast this single-step combined income statement and retained earnings statement as a multi-step income statement in appropriate form. Include appropriate per share amounts.

KEW Corp. has 500,000 shares of common stock outstanding. In 2005, KEW reports income from continuing operations before taxes of $4,350,000. Additional transactions from 2005—and not considered in the $4,350,000—are as follows:
1. The company reviewed its notes receivable and discovered that a note carried at $16,000 was 18 months past due. The note was not likely to be collected.
2. KEW sold machinery for $85,000 that originally cost $300,000. Accumulated depreciation at the time of the sale amounted to $225,000. KEW sells unneeded machinery occasionally when retooling one of its production processes.
3. KEW sold a division during 2005 resulting in a pre-tax loss of $890,000. The operating loss incurred by the discontinued division prior to its sale was $650,000; the loss from its disposal was $240,000. This transaction meets the *SFAS No. 144* criteria for discontinued operations.
4. KEW lost $395,000 (pre-tax) when a plant it operated in a third-world country was expropriated following a revolution. The company had no other foreign operations.

E2 – 20

Preparation of income statement with irregular items

Required:

Based on the above information, prepare an income statement for the year ended December 31, 2005, starting with income from continuing operations before income taxes; include proper earnings per share disclosures. KEW's total effective tax rate on all items was 35%.

During 2005, various events (consider each to be independent and "material") occurred at several of your CPA firm's clients.
1. Martin Manufacturing's production facility is located near Miami, Florida. Two hurricanes (one was considered major) struck southern Florida in 2005. One of the storms caused extensive damage to Martin's plant.
2. ACF, Inc. manufactures railroad tank cars and has been doing so since the 1860s. Because some of ACF's production equipment had become obsolete, the equipment was sold at a loss and new equipment acquired.
3. Furman Foods produces canned and frozen foods that are "private labeled" for various supermarket chains. Because profit margins on the frozen food operation were disappointing, Furman sold it to a competitor, taking a loss on the sale.
4. *SFAS No. 142*—issued in June 2001—altered accounting for goodwill. Annual amortization of goodwill is no longer required; instead, goodwill must be periodically evaluated for impairment. If no impairment has occurred, goodwill should not be amortized. Unfortunately, the controller at Jensen Company overlooked this mandated change in accounting principles and continued to amortize goodwill in keeping with past practices. This fact was discovered only this year. (Assume Jensen's goodwill is not impaired.)
5. Smithfield Corporation restructured its operations. The company consolidated its five regional offices into three operating districts, thus enabling two "regional headquarters" facilities to be closed and staff to be reassigned or terminated. Although Smithfield believes this restructuring will save money in the long term, a loss was incurred when these facilities were closed.

E2 – 21

Income statement presentation

6. Magnum Motors changed its method of inventory valuation. As the only "FIFO company" in the industry, Magnum's management believed that readers of the company's financial statements would find them more useful if Magnum used LIFO like its competitors.

7. Andy's Colors, a paint manufacturer, decided to discontinue the manufacture of latex paints. The company's line of oil-based paints will be continued. These two paint lines are separable both operationally and financially. Andy's management found a buyer for the latex paint manufacturing facilities. Unfortunately, some "environmental problems" were discovered during the buyer's examination of these facilities and the sale is on hold pending a resolution of this matter. Andy's management believes this problem can be satisfactorily dealt with, but that it may take a few years to do so.

Required:

Briefly discuss the 2005 financial statement presentation of each of the events listed above. Ignore earnings per share disclosures.

E2 – 22

Income statement presentation

Krewatch, Inc. is a vertically integrated manufacturer and retailer of golf clubs and accessories (gloves, shoes, bags, etc.). Krewatch, Inc. maintains separate financial reporting systems for each of its facilities. The company experienced the following events in 2005:

1. After several years of production problems at the accessories manufacturing plant, Krewatch sold the plant to an investor group headed by a former manager at the plant. Krewatch plans to continue to carry the accessory line in its retail stores and is committed to purchase the entire annual output of the plant.

2. Krewatch incurred restructuring costs of $12,562,990 when it eliminated a layer of middle management.

3. Krewatch extinguished $200 million in 30-year bonds that were issued 18 years ago. These bonds were the only ones issued in the company's history. Krewatch recognized a gain on this transaction.

4. Krewatch changed its method of accounting for inventory from FIFO to the average cost method.

5. Due to technological advances in golf club manufacturing, management determined that production equipment would need to be upgraded more frequently than in the past. Consequently, the useful lives of equipment for depreciation purposes were reduced.

6. The company wrote off inventory that was not salable at the insistence of its auditors.

7. Equipment was sold at a loss.

Required:

For each event, (1) identify the appropriate reporting treatment from the list below (consider each event to be material), and (2) indicate whether it would be included in income from continuing operations, or would appear on the income statement below that subtotal.

a. Change in accounting estimate.
b. Change in accounting principle.
c. Discontinued operation.
d. Special or unusual item.
e. Extraordinary item.

E2 – 23

Comprehensive income

Joanna Danielle Corporation reported the following for 2005: net sales $3,255,000; cost of goods sold $1,985,550; selling and administrative expenses $651,000; and an unrealized holding loss on available-for-sale securities $18,000. Joanna Danielle's tax rate was 35%.

Required:

Prepare a multiple-step income statement and a statement of comprehensive income, using the two-income statement format. Ignore earnings per share.

E2 – 24

Comprehensive income

Andrew's Extreme Sports reported the following information for 2005: net sales $1,680,000; cost of goods sold $1,041,600; selling and administrative expenses $369,600; and an unrealized holding gain from foreign currency translations of $4,900. Andrew's Extreme Sports issued common stock for $500,000 and paid a dividend of $0.10 per share on the weighted average number of shares outstanding for the year (250,000 shares). The company has January 1, 2005 balances in common stock $1,500,000; retained earnings $985,100; and other comprehensive income $(14,800).

Required:

Prepare a multiple-step income statement and a statement of stockholders' equity that includes comparative income effects for Andrew's Extreme Sports. Assume a 35% income tax rate.

An analyst gathered the following information about a company whose fiscal year end is December 31:

- Net income for the year was $10.5 million.
- Preferred stock dividends for $2 million were paid for the year.
- Common stock dividends of $3.5 million were paid for the year.
- There were 20 million shares of common stock outstanding on January 1, 2005.
- The company issued 6 million new shares of common stock on April 1, 2005.
- The capital structure does not include any potentially dilutive convertible securities, options, warrants, or other contingent securities.

E2 – 25

EPS calculation

Required:

What would the company's basic earnings per share be for 2005?

PROBLEMS/DISCUSSION QUESTIONS

Seldin Company owns a royalty interest in an oil well. The contract stipulates that Seldin will receive royalty payments semiannually on January 31 and July 31. The January 31 payment will be for 20% of the oil sold to jobbers between the previous June 1 and November 30, and the July 31 payment will be for oil sold between the previous December 1 and May 31. Royalty receipts for 2006 amounted to $80,000 and $100,000 on January 31 and July 31, respectively. On December 31, 2005, accrued royalty revenue receivable amounted to $15,000. Production reports show the following oil sales:

P2 – 1

Determining royalty revenue

AICPA
ADAPTED

June 1, 2005–November 30, 2005	$400,000
December 1, 2005–May 31, 2006	500,000
June 1, 2006–November 30, 2006	425,000
December 1, 2006–December 31, 2006	70,000

Required:

What amount should Seldin report as royalty revenue for 2006?

- On January 1, 2005 Frances Corporation started doing business and the owners contributed $200,000 capital in cash.
- The company paid $24,000 to cover the rent for the office space for the 24-month period from January 1, 2005 to December 31, 2006.
- On March 1, 2005 MSK Inc. entered into a consulting contract under which Frances Corporation promised to provide consulting to MSK Inc. for the ten-month period from March 1, 2005 to December 31, 2005. In return MSK promised to pay a monthly consulting fee of $15,000, which was to be paid in January 2006. Frances Corporation fulfilled its contractual obligation during 2005.
- On July 1, 2005 Frances Corporation purchased office equipment for $100,000 cash. The equipment has an estimated useful life of five years and no salvage value. The equipment was immediately placed into use. Frances Corporation uses the straight-line method of depreciation. Frances Corporation records depreciation expense in proportion to the number of months' usage.
- Through November 30, 2005, the company had paid $66,000 to its employees for 11 months of salaries. Accrued salaries on December 31, 2005 were $6,000.
- On December 31, 2005, Norbert Corporation advanced $20,000 to Frances Corporation for consulting services to be provided during 2006.

P2 – 2

Journal entries and statement preparation

Required:

1. Provide journal entries for each of these transactions.
2. Provide adjusting entries at the end of the year.
3. Prepare an income statement for the year ended December 31, 2005.
4. Prepare a balance sheet as of December 31, 2005.

P2 – 3

Converting accounting records from cash basis to accrual basis

www.prenhall.com/revsine

● Student Resources

☑ Template for solution

The following information pertains to Baron Flowers, a calendar-year sole proprietorship, which maintained its books on the cash basis during the year.

Baron Flowers

Trial Balance December 31, 2005

	DR	CR
Cash	$ 25,600	
Accounts receivable 12/31/04	16,200	
Inventory 12/31/04	62,000	
Furniture and fixtures	118,200	
Land improvements	45,000	
Accumulated depreciation 12/31/04		$ 32,400
Accounts payable 12/31/04		17,000
Baron, drawings		–0–
Baron, capital 12/31/04		124,600
Sales		653,000
Purchases	305,100	
Salaries	174,000	
Payroll taxes	12,400	
Insurance	8,700	
Rent	34,200	
Utilities	12,600	
Living expenses	13,000	
	$827,000	$827,000

The "Baron, drawings" account is used to record any distributions to Mr. Baron. The "Baron, capital" account is used to record any capital contributions that Mr. Baron makes to the business and any profits or losses retained in the business.

Baron has developed plans to expand into the wholesale flower market and is in the process of negotiating a bank loan to finance the expansion. The bank is requesting 2005 financial statements prepared on the accrual basis of accounting from Baron. During the course of a review engagement, Mr. Muir, Baron's accountant, obtained the following additional information:

1. Amounts due from customers totaled $32,000 at December 31, 2005.
2. An analysis of the receivables revealed that an allowance for uncollectible accounts of $3,800 should be provided.
3. Unpaid invoices for flower purchases totaled $30,500 and $17,000 at December 31, 2005 and December 31, 2004, respectively.
4. A physical count of the goods at December 31, 2005 determined that the inventory totaled $72,800. The inventory was priced at cost, which approximates market value.
5. On May 1, 2005 Baron paid $8,700 to renew its comprehensive insurance coverage for one year. The premium on the previous policy, which expired on April 30, 2005, was $7,800.
6. On January 2, 2005 Baron entered into a 25-year operating lease for the vacant lot adjacent to Baron's retail store, which was to be used as a parking lot. As agreed to in the lease, Baron paved and fenced in the lot at a cost of $45,000. The improvements were completed on April 1, 2005, and they have an estimated useful life of 15 years. No provision for depreciation or amortization has been recorded. Depreciation on furniture and fixtures was $12,000 for 2005.

7. Accrued expenses at December 31, 2004 and 2005 were as follows:

	2004	2005
Utilities	$ 900	$1,500
Payroll taxes	1,100	1,600
	$2,000	$3,100

8. Baron was notified late in the year of a lawsuit filed against his business for an injury to a customer. Baron's attorney believes that the unfavorable outcome is probable and that a reasonable estimate of the settlement exclusive of amounts covered by insurance is $50,000.

9. The salaries account includes $4,000 per month paid to the proprietor. Baron also receives $250 per week for living expenses. These amounts should have been charged to Baron's drawing account.

Required:

1. Determine the adjustments that are required to convert the trial balance of Baron Flowers to the accrual basis of accounting for the year ended December 31, 2005. Prepare formal journal entries to support your adjustments.

2. Write a brief memo to Baron explaining why the bank would require financial statements prepared on the accrual basis instead of the cash basis.

The following is the preclosing trial balance of Antonia Retailers, Inc.:

P2 – 4

Adjusting entries and statement preparation

www.prenhall.com/revsine

● Student Resources

☑ Template for solution

Antonia Retailers, Inc.

Preclosing Trial Balance as of December 31, 2005

	DR	CR
Cash	$ 42,000	
Accounts receivable	67,500	
Prepaid rent	15,000	
Inventory	100,000	
Equipment	60,000	
Building	90,000	
Allowance for doubtful accounts		$ 5,000
Accumulated depreciation—equipment		30,000
Accumulated depreciation—building		9,000
Advance from customers		25,000
Accounts payable		18,000
Salaries payable		4,000
Capital stock		70,000
Retained earnings 1/1/05		187,500
Sales revenue		350,000
Cost of goods sold	185,000	
Salaries expense	50,000	
Bad debt expense	10,500	
Rent expense	30,000	
Insurance expense	18,000	
Depreciation expense—building	5,000	
Depreciation expense—equipment	2,000	
Dividends	23,500	
Totals	$698,500	$698,500

The following additional information is provided to you:

1. The company paid a salary advance of $10,000 to one of its employees, a total that was debited to the salaries expense account. This was an advance against the employee's salary for the year 2006.

2. On January 1, 2005 the company paid an insurance premium of $18,000, which was debited to the insurance expense account. The premium provided insurance coverage for 18 months beginning on January 1, 2005.

3. The company decided to revise its estimate of bad debts expense by calculating it at 10% of its sales revenue.
4. On January 1, 2006 the board of directors of the company declared an additional dividend of $10,000 for the year 2005.

Required:

1. Prepare the necessary adjusting entries for the year ended December 31, 2005.
2. Prepare an income statement for the year ended December 31, 2005.
3. Prepare a balance sheet as of December 31, 2005.

P2 – 5

Understanding the accounting equation

Following is selected information from the balance sheet for Flaps Inc. Solve for the missing amounts for each of the five years.

	Year				
	2004	2005	2006	2007	2008
Total liabilities and stockholders' equity	$13,765	F	K	P	U
Current liabilities	A	3,420	3,467	3,517	V
Common stock	138	139	L	142	144
Contributed capital	2,340	G	2,387	2,422	W
Non-current assets	8,667	8,721	M	8,968	X
Retained earnings	2,795	2,813	2,851	Q	Y
Total assets	B	H	14,040	R	14,351
Non-current liabilities	5,231	I	5,335	S	5,454
Additional paid-in capital	C	2,216	2,247	T	2,296
Current assets	D	J	5,200	5,275	5,315
Total liabilities	8,630	8,683	N	8,929	Z
Total stockholders' equity	E	5,168	O	5,314	5,354

P2 – 6

Understanding the accounting equation

The following is selected information from Flightscape Adventures' financial statements. Solve for the missing amounts for each of the five years. You may have to use some numbers from the year before or the year after to solve for certain current year numbers. (NA = not available.)

	Year				
	2004	2005	2006	2007	2008
Current assets (CA)	A	$2,285	L	$2,150	X
Non-current assets	3,665	F	3,604	R	3,732
Total assets	5,821	G	M	5,805	Y
Current liabilities (CL)	1,437	H	N	S	1,463
Non-current liabilities	B	2,345	O	2,206	2,252
Contributed capital	990	I	P	1,049	Z
Retained earnings (ending)	1,182	J	1,087	T	1,204
Total stockholder's equity	C	2,302	2,136	U	AA
Total liabilities and stockholders' equity	D	K	5,724	5,805	BB
Working capital (CA–CL)	E	762	707	V	732
Net income (loss)	NA	85	Q	40	99
Dividends	NA	14	9	W	12

P2 – 7

Converting from cash to accrual basis

During August 2005, Packer Manufacturing had the following cash receipts and disbursements:

Cash received from customers	$319,000
Cash received from selling equipment	11,200
Cash paid for salaries	47,000
Cash paid to suppliers for inventory purchases	130,000

In addition, the following balance sheet account balances were shown on Packer's books:

	July 31	August 31
Accounts receivable	$128,000	$135,000
Inventory	33,000	25,000
Accounts payable	21,000	25,000
Salaries payable	8,000	5,000

Assume all sales and purchases are on account.

Required:

1. Determine sales for August 2005.
2. Determine salary expense for August 2005.
3. Determine cost of goods sold for August 2005.

During the month of October 2005, HAWK-I Rentals had the following cash receipts and payments:

P2 – 8

Converting from cash to accrual basis

Rental receipts (cash) received	$43,000
Cash paid for insurance	5,000
Cash paid for taxes	6,000
Cash received from sale of used equipment	11,000

Of the rental receipts collected, $2,000 was reported as rent receivable at September 30, and $3,500 was a prepayment of November's rent. An insurance premium of $1,000 was owed at the end of October. Taxes of $1,000 and $700 were owed at October 1 and October 31, respectively. Equipment sold in October had a book value (cost minus accumulated depreciation) of $12,200 at the time of sale.

Required:

1. Determine rental income for October 2005.
2. Determine insurance expense for October 2005.
3. Determine tax expense for October 2005.
4. Assuming the accumulated depreciation on the equipment sold was $1,300, what is the appropriate journal entry to record the sale of the used equipment?

Bob's Chocolate Chips and More, a bakery specializing in gourmet pizza and chocolate chip cookies, started business October 1, 2005. The following transactions occurred during the month.

P2 – 9

Journal entries and statement preparation

a. Common stock of $90,000 was sold to start the business.
b. Equipment consisting of mixers and ovens were acquired October 1 for $30,000 cash. The equipment is expected to last five years and can be sold, at that time, for $5,000. Management uses the straight-line method to calculate depreciation expense.
c. Ingredients costing $15,000 were purchased on account during the month and all but $5,000 was paid for by the end of the month.
d. Rent is $500 a month. October, November and December's rent were paid October 5.
e. A payment of $800 for utilities was made during the month.
f. Sixty percent of the ingredients purchased in (c) were prepared and sold for $35,000 on account; $26,000 was collected on account receivable during the month.
g. Wages of $5,200 were paid during the month. Moreover, wages for the last three days of the month amounted to $400 and will be paid during the first week of November.
h. $12,000 was borrowed from the bank for additional working capital requirements, and $3,000 was repaid by month-end. Interest on the unpaid loan balance amounted to $450 at the end of October and was paid on November 5.

Required:

Prepare the required journal entries and adjustments as well as an income statement and balance sheet, in good form, for Bob's Chocolate Chips and More as of October 31, 2005. (*Hint:* You may want to consider using T-accounts to classify and accumulate the above transactions prior to preparing the statements.)

P2 – 10

Journal entries and
statement preparation

The following is the pre-adjusted trial balance of JetCo Fuel Services as of December 31, 2005.

JetCo Fuel Services

Pre-Adjusted Trial Balance
December 31, 2005

	Debits	Credits
Cash	$ 39,800	
Accounts receivable, net	70,700	
Fuel inventory	42,600	
Equipment	30,000	
Fuel tanker	75,000	
Accumulated depreciation		$ 3,000
Accounts payable		35,100
Accrued expenses		12,500
Customer deposits		2,400
Notes payable		75,000
JetCo capital stock		75,000
Retained earnings		15,300
Fuel sales		840,000
Fuel expense	641,200	
Salary expense	75,000	
Insurance expense	72,000	
Rent expense	12,000	
	$1,058,300	$1,058,300

Additional Information:

a. A fuel tanker was purchased July 1, 2005 by issuing a three-year 10% interest-bearing note payable for $75,000. The tanker is expected to last ten years and then be scrapped. JetCo uses the straight-line depreciation method.

b. After taking a physical inventory, it was discovered that fuel inventories were overstated by $6,100.

c. Equipment on the balance sheet was acquired January 1, 2004 and has a ten-year life.

d. A search of unrecorded liabilities reveals unrecorded fuel expenses of $4,800.

e. A 36-month insurance policy was acquired for $72,000 on August 31, 2005 and charged to insurance expense.

f. On June 1, 2005 one-year's rent ($12,000) was paid and charged to rent expense.

g. The balance in the Customer deposits account was earned in 2005.

h. During 2005, JetCo paid a dividend of $75,000, which was subtracted from retained earnings.

Required:

1. Prepare any required adjustments as of December 31, 2005.
2. Prepare JetCo's income statement for the year ending 2005 and its balance sheet.

P2 – 11

IVAX Corporation
Determining missing
amounts on income
statement

The following information was taken from a recent income statement of IVAX Corporation. IVAX is a holding company with subsidiaries providing research, development, manufacturing and marketing of brand-name pharmaceutical products.

	($ in 000)
Amortization of intangible assets	$?
Cost of goods sold	?
Cumulative effect of change in accounting principle, net of taxes (debit)	(3,048)
Extraordinary gain on extinguishment of debt, net of taxes	1,121
General and administrative expenses	88,434
Gross profit	241,171
Income before cumulative effect of change in accounting principle	74,642
Income before extraordinary item and cumulative effect of change in accounting principle	?

	($ in 000)
Income from continuing operations	?
Income from continuing operations before income taxes	34,664
Income from discontinued operations, net of taxes	48,904
Interest expense	?
Interest income	11,972
Net income	?
Net revenues	?
Operating income	?
Other income, net	20,830
Provision for income taxes	(10,047)
Research and development	48,615
Restructuring costs and asset write-downs	12,222
Selling expenses	79,508
Gross profit as percent of sales	37.81%
Total operating expenses	$232,452

Required:

1. Recast IVAX's income statement and present it in good form. Fill in the missing data.
2. Consider the item "Restructuring costs and asset write-downs." What impact did this charge have on IVAX's cash flows?
3. IVAX's income statements over the last three years report Research and development expenses averaging $51.3 million per year. These expenses are incurred by IVAX to enhance current products and to develop new products in the hope of generating higher future sales. Generally accepted accounting principles require that all such costs be expensed in the year incurred. Consider the following statement:

   Research and development expenditures are really assets because they will benefit the future operations of the firm (that is, lead to higher sales).

   If you agree, suggest an alternative way to account for research and development expenditures rather than expensing them in the year incurred. If you disagree, what are your reasons?
4. Assume that you are a financial analyst for IVAX Corporation. Your boss has asked you to project next year's net earnings. What earnings number from the information provided above would you use as the basis for your projection? Why?

The following condensed statement of income of Helen Corporation, a diversified company, is presented for the two years ended December 31, 2006 and 2005:

	2006	2005
Net sales	$10,000,000	$9,600,000
Cost of sales	(6,200,000)	(6,000,000)
Gross profit	3,800,000	3,600,000
Operating expenses	(2,200,000)	(2,400,000)
Operating income	1,600,000	1,200,000
Gain on sale of division	900,000	—
Net income before taxes	2,500,000	1,200,000
Provision for income taxes	(1,250,000)	(600,000)
Net income	$ 1,250,000	$ 600,000

P2 – 12

Determining income from continuing operations and gain (loss) from discontinued operations

AICPA
ADAPTED

On January 1, 2006 Helen entered into an agreement to sell for $3,200,000 the assets and product line of one of its separate operating divisions. The sale was consummated on December 31, 2006 and resulted in a gain on disposition of $900,000. This division's contribution to Helen's reported income before taxes for each year was as follows:

2006	$640,000 loss
2005	$500,000 loss

Assume an income tax rate of 50%.

Required:

1. In the preparation of a revised comparative statement of income, Helen should report income from continuing operations after income taxes for 2006 and 2005, respectively, amounting to how much?
2. Starting with the revised income from continuing operations numbers you obtained in part 1, prepare the revised comparative income statements for 2006 and 2005 showing appropriate details for gain (loss) from discontinued operations.

P2 – 13

Income statement preparation with irregular items

Wing, Inc., a sporting goods retailer, began operations on January 2, 2003. The corporation reported net income during 2005 of $3,091,660. Additional information about transactions occurring in 2005 is as follows:

1. The corporation realized a $175,000 gain from settling a trademark infringement lawsuit. While this is an infrequent event for Wing, trademark lawsuits are fairly common in Wing's industry.
2. The corporation disposed of its catalog sales component at a pre-tax loss of $345,000. This transaction meets the criteria for discontinued operations specified in *SFAS No. 144.*
3. Sale of 10,000 shares of Xerox stock held as a short-term investment resulted in a gain of $23,450.
4. The corporation changed its method of depreciating fixed assets from the straight-line method to the declining balance method, which was used to determine income in 2005. Had the declining balance method been used in prior years, pre-tax income would have been decreased by $100,000 and $89,000 in 2003 and 2004, respectively.
5. The corporation suffered a $23,000 impairment loss on fixed assets in 2005. This impairment loss was not related to discontinued operations.
6. The corporation experienced an (extraordinary) uninsured tornado loss in the amount of $83,500 before tax.

Required:

Prepare an income statement for the year ended December 31, 2005 starting with income from continuing operations before taxes; include proper earnings per share disclosures. Wing, Inc. had 150,000 common shares outstanding for the year. Assume a 35% tax rate on all items.

P2 – 14

Discontinued operations components held for sale

For 2005, Silvertip Construction, Inc. reported income from continuing operations (after tax) of $1,650,000 before considering the following information. On November 15, 2005 the company adopted a plan to dispose of a component of the business. This component qualifies for discontinued operations treatment under *SFAS No. 144.* During 2005, the component had pre-tax operating losses of $95,000. The component's assets have a book value on December 31, 2005 of $760,000. A recent market value analysis of these assets placed their estimated selling price at $735,000, less a 6% brokerage commission. Management appropriately determines that these assets are impaired, and expects to find a buyer for the component and complete the sale early in 2006.

Required:

Prepare a partial income statement for Silvertip—including EPS disclosures—for the year ended December 31, 2005. Begin at income from continuing operations. Assume a 35% income tax rate and 1,000,000 shares of outstanding common stock.

P2 – 15

Preparing a multiple-step income statement

The preliminary 2005 income statement of Athletic Footwear, Inc. is presented below:

Athletic Footwear, Inc.

Income Statement
For the Year Ended December 31, 2005
($ in 000, except earnings per share)

Revenues and gains:	
Net sales	$257,348
Other income	26,533
Interest	790
Total revenue and gains	$284,671

Expenses and losses:	
Cost of goods sold	$159,556
Selling and administrative	48,896
Discontinued operations	30,882
Income taxes	17,228
Total expenses	$256,562
Net income	$ 28,109
Earnings per share	$ 0.56

Additional facts pertaining to the company's 2005 operations:

1. "Selling and administrative" expenses included $6,231,000 in restructuring costs.
2. "Other income" represents a gain on the early extinguishment of debt.
3. Early debt extinguishment is part of Athletic Footwear's risk management strategy.
4. A tax rate of 38% applies to all items.
5. Athletic Footwear had 50,000,000 shares of common stock outstanding throughout 2005.
6. Discontinued operations, as reported, resulted from the sale of Athletic Footwear's manufacturing facility (in addition to selling brand name shoes, the company sold shoes of its own manufacture under the "AFRules" brand). In the future, Athletic Footwear will only carry brand name footwear in its stores. Included in the reported loss was a loss of $19,402,000 attributable to the sale of the manufacturing division's assets; the remainder of the loss stems from the division's pre-sale operations.

Required:

Prepare a revised multiple-step income statement reflecting the additional facts in the above information (include required EPS data).

The following information was taken from the records of Liz's Theatrical Supplies for 2005. In addition to selling theatrical supplies, Liz owned and operated a theater until October 15, 2005 when this component of the business was sold. All listed amounts are pre-tax, but are subject to a 38% income tax rate.

P2 – 16

Combined single-step and comprehensive income statement

Cost of goods sold	$490,823
Extraordinary loss	50,000
Income from discontinued operations	70,000
Interest income	4,650
Loss from disposal of discontinued component	95,000
Loss on write-off of obsolete inventory	23,500
Net sales	791,650
Rent revenue	16,000
Selling and administrative expenses	158,330
Unrealized holding loss on available-for-sale securities	15,000

Required:

Prepare a single-step income statement and statement of comprehensive income for 2005 using a single-statement format.

Smithfield Beverage, Inc.

P2 – 17

Early extinguishment of debt

Income Statement for the Year Ended December 31, 2005

Sales	$3,512,000
Cost of goods sold	(2,177,440)
Gross profit	1,334,560
Selling and administrative expenses	(772,640)
Income from operations, before income taxes	561,920
Income taxes	(196,672)
Net income	$ 365,248
Earnings per share	$ 1.46

The income statement of Smithfield Beverage, Inc. that follows does not include any required reporting related to a $62,000 pre-tax gain that was realized in 2005 when Smithfield repurchased and retired

$1,000,000 of its 8% term bonds (scheduled to mature in 2012). Smithfield's income tax rate is 35%; 250,000 shares of common stock were outstanding during 2005.

Required:

Discuss any modifications to Smithfield's Income Statement necessitated by this gain under each of the following independent assumptions (do not produce "corrected" income statements):
1. Such early debt retirements are part of Smithfield's risk management strategy.
2. Smithfield has been in business for 65 years. The company occasionally issues term bonds, but has not previously retired bonds prior to normal maturity.

P2 – 18

Discontinued operations

Roger's Plumbing, Inc. operates two segments: (1) a division that installs residential and commercial plumbing in buildings being constructed, and (2) a service division that has both residential and commercial components. A recent construction boom has kept Roger's Plumbing so busy that the company has been unable to handle all of the service work on a timely basis. Growing tired of phone messages from irritated customers who wanted their leak fixed yesterday (and unable to hire additional qualified employees), in October management decides to sell the service business, begins to advertise its availability, and has the division's assets appraised. Roger (CEO) believes the service business will be easier to sell if it is split into residential and commercial components. The appraisal results in the following information. "Goodwill" is the appraiser's estimate of the value of the company's customer base as Roger's Plumbing plans to forward all service calls for a period of three years to whomever buys each component of the service business. Roger's Plumbing has income before taxes of $2,756,000 for 2005 (the year management decides to sell the service division). This amount includes $185,400 residential service income and $215,000 commercial service income. Roger's Plumbing is subject to an income tax rate of 35%.

Assets	Book Value	Fair Market Value
Residential service component:		
Service vehicles	$ 40,000	$ 45,000
Repair parts inventory	25,000	22,000
Tool and equipment	9,500	8,000
Goodwill	—	20,000
Total—Residential service	$ 74,500	$ 95,000
Commercial service component:		
Service vehicles	55,000	53,500
Repair parts inventory	21,000	21,000
Tool and equipment	14,500	12,000
Goodwill	—	25,000
Total—Commercial service	$ 90,500	$111,500
Total for service division	$165,000	$206,500

Required:

Assume that Roger's Plumbing sells the residential service component on December 5, 2005 for $99,500 (less disposal costs of $2,000). By year's end, the company has received three firm offers for the commercial service component that ranged from $82,500 to $87,000. Management is still actively seeking a better offer, but if none is obtained plans to sell the component to the highest bidder before the end of January 2006. The company's auditors tell management that the consistency of the bids to date indicates an error in the appraisal and that an impairment loss should be recognized to comply with *SFAS No. 144*. Assume estimated costs of $2,500 to sell the commercial service component. Prepare an income statement for Roger's Plumbing, Inc. (for 2005) beginning with income from continuing operations. For purposes of working this problem, report the various components of the gains/losses for discontinued operations separately for actual sales versus assets held for sale. Ignore per share disclosures.

The Mohegan Tribe is a federally recognized Native American tribe with an approximately 405-acre reservation located in southeastern Connecticut. Under the Indian Gaming Regulatory Act of 1988, or IGRA, federally recognized Native American tribes are permitted to conduct full-scale casino gaming operations on tribal land.

In October 1996, the tribe opened a gaming and entertainment complex known as Mohegan Sun. Recently, the tribe substantially completed a major expansion of Mohegan Sun known as Project Sunburst. The first phase of Project Sunburst, the Casino of the Sky, which included increased gaming, restaurant and retail space, and an entertainment arena, opened on September 25, 2001. The remaining components, including the majority of a 1,200-room luxury hotel and approximately 100,000 square feet of convention space, opened in April 2002, with substantial completion of construction occurring in June 2002. Gambling operations include slot machines, table games, off-track wagering, and (until recently) bingo.

Loss from "discontinued operations" for a recent fiscal year was $591,000. The loss was the result of the Tribe's decision to cease bingo operations in order to convert the floor space into the 637-unit Hall of the Lost Tribes smoke-free slot machine venue. The loss related to severance pay and disposal of bingo inventory.

Required:

1. Review *SFAS No. 144*, "Accounting for the Impairment or Disposal of Long-Lived Assets," using the FASB's Financial Accounting Research System (FARS), Pricewaterhouse Cooper's Comperio® authoritative financial reporting database or other reference sources in your local library. Does the loss referenced above qualify as a loss from discontinued operations? Explain your answer citing relevant paragraphs from *SFAS No. 144*.

2. Would the loss qualify as a loss from discontinued operations if the Tribe turned the bingo operation over to the Mohawks? The Mohawks do not currently have a casino on their tribal lands, but are considering getting into the business. To gain experience with casino operations, the Mohawks have arranged with the Mohegan Tribe to take over the bingo operation at Mohegan Sun for an indefinite period. While the bingo profits will go to the Mohawks, facilities rent and a "training fee" of 10% of gaming revenues will be paid to the Mohegan Tribe. Again, explain your answer citing relevant paragraphs from *SFAS No. 144*.

Corrpro Companies, Inc., founded in 1984, provides corrosion control related services, systems, equipment and materials to the infrastructure, environmental, and energy markets. Corrpro's products and services include (a) corrosion control engineering services, systems and equipment, (b) coatings services, and (c) pipeline integrity and risk assessment services. The following information was abridged from the company's March 31, 2003 Form 10-K.

ASSETS AND LIABILITIES HELD FOR SALE

In July 2002, the Company's Board of Directors approved a formal business restructuring plan. The multi-year plan includes a series of initiatives to improve operating income and reduce debt. The Company intends to sell non-core business units and use the proceeds to reduce debt. The Company has engaged outside professionals to assist in the disposition of the domestic and international non-core business units. Prior to the quarter ended September 30, 2002, the Company's non-core domestic and international units were reported as the Other Operations and International Operations reporting segments. Effective for the quarter ended September 30, 2002, the Other Operations and the International Operations reporting segments have been eliminated and the non-core domestic and international units are reported as Discontinued operations. Prior-year financial statements have been reclassified to reflect these non-core units as Discontinued operations, which are also referred to as "assets and liabilities held for sale."

Corrpro, Inc.

Consolidated Statements of Operations
For the years ended March 31,

($ in 000s)	2003	2002	2001
Revenues	$104,220	$123,058	$120,489
Operating costs and expenses:			
Cost of sales	71,607	87,326	85,325
Selling, general, and administrative	29,788	32,327	35,535
Operating income (loss)	2,825	3,405	(371)
Interest expense	5,907	5,055	4,401
Loss from continuing operations before income taxes	(3,082)	(1,650)	(4,772)
Provision (benefit) for income taxes	(331)	10,669	(934)
Loss from continuing operations	(2,751)	(12,319)	(3,838)
Discontinued operations:			
Loss from operations, net of taxes	(9,931)	(5,898)	(4,443)
Gain on disposals, net of taxes	2,095	—	—
Loss before cumulative effect of change in accounting principle	(10,587)	(18,217)	(8,281)
Cumulative effect of change in accounting principle	(18,238)	—	—
Net loss	$(28,825)	$(18,217)	$(8,281)

Required:

Refer to *SFAS No. 144*, "Accounting for the Impairment or Disposal of Long-Lived Assets," when answering the following questions about Corrpro's discontinued operations.

1. What criteria must be met to warrant reclassifying the non-core business units as discontinued operations effective with the quarter ending September 30, 2002?
2. Suppose that in March 2003 a buyer signed a purchase commitment for Corrpro's Rohrback Cosasco Systems division. This sale requires regulatory approval that is expected to take at least 18 months to obtain. Should Corrpro's 2003 financial statements include this division in "assets and liabilities held for sale"? Explain.
3. Assume that in February 2003 a potential buyer of another of the domestic non-core business units insisted on a site assessment prior to signing a purchase commitment. The purpose of the assessment was to determine if the site was environmentally impaired. Unfortunately for Corrpro, trace amounts of a suspected carcinogen were discovered, causing the buyer to terminate the purchase. The buyer is willing to reconsider its decision if the site is remediated. While the site can be remediated using existing technology, doing so will be costly enough to negate the purpose of the sale—to raise funds to reduce debt. Management believes that employing new remediation methods currently being tested will make this sale economically feasible and thus places the sale of this business unit on hold. Should Corrpro's 2003 financial statements include this division in "assets and liabilities held for sale"?
4. Is there any reason for management to prefer discontinued operations treatment for these non-core business units?

C2 – 3

Baldwin Piano and Organ I (KR): Identifying critical events for revenue recognition

The following information is based on the annual report and 10-K statement of Baldwin Piano and Organ Company.

The company is the largest domestic manufacturer of keyboard musical instruments, and it manufactures or distributes all major product classes of pianos and electronic organs. The company believes that the breadth and quality of its line of keyboard musical instruments, its large and well-established dealer distribution networks, and its efficient and low-cost manufacturing capabilities have enabled it to maintain its strong market share in the keyboard musical instrument market.

Over the company's 131-year history, its principal products have been pianos and organs. The company significantly expanded its principal business lines through its 1988 acquisition of the keyboard operations of The Wurlitzer Company, which now operates as a wholly owned subsidiary of the company. Over the years, the company has also expanded and diversified its product line in order to utilize excess capacity and its woodworking, electronics, and technical expertise. The company manufactures printed circuit boards, electronic assemblies, grandfather and other quality clocks, and wooden cabinets.

The company ships keyboard instruments and clocks to its dealer network on a consignment basis. Accordingly, revenue is recognized at the time the dealer sells the instrument to a third party. The company charges a monthly display fee on all consigned inventory held by dealers longer than 90 days. This display fee, on an annual basis, ranges from 12% to 16% of the selling price of such inventory to the dealer. Display fee income is included under the component "Other operating income, net."

The company distributes its Baldwin keyboard musical instruments in the United States through approximately 500 independent dealers (600 outlets) and 11 company-owned stores operating in six major metropolitan areas. Most of the independent dealers carry Baldwin products as their principal line—and often their exclusive one.

The company has been engaged in financing the retail purchase of its products for over 80 years. In the current year approximately 35% of the company's domestic sales were financed by the company in retail installment programs offered through the company's dealers. Installment contract receivables are recorded at the principal amount of the contracts. Interest on the contracts is recorded as income over the life of the contracts. The company has entered into agreements with an independent financial institution to sell substantially all its installment receivable contracts. The company continues to service (collect cash and perform other administrative services) all installment receivables sold. Over the lives of the contracts, the difference between the original interest earned on the contracts and the interest paid to the independent financial institution is recognized as the component labeled "Income on the sale of installment receivables." The installment contracts are written generally at fixed rates ranging from 12% to 16% with terms extending over three to five years. The interest paid to the independent financial institution is around 5%. Under the agreement with the independent financial institution, the company is required to repurchase either installment receivables that become more than 120 days past due or accounts that are deemed uncollectible.

Wurlitzer and the electronic contract business transfer title and recognize revenue at the time of shipment to their dealers and customers, respectively.

The company distributes its Wurlitzer products through approximately 400 independent dealers. The company's networks of Baldwin dealers and Wurlitzer dealers are separate and distinct, with no significant overlap. Certain Wurlitzer dealers finance their inventory from an independent bank. Dealers can borrow money from the bank based upon the value of the inventory purchased from Wurlitzer, with the musical instruments pledged as collateral. The dealers are required to pay the bank monthly interest payments and pay the principal balance after inventory is sold or if it is held longer than twelve months. The bank may request Wurlitzer to repurchase notes due from delinquent dealers. The company believes that its financial statements contain adequate provisions for any loss that may be incurred as a result of this commitment.

The electronic contract business consists of manufacturing printed circuit boards and electro-mechanical assemblies for manufacturers outside the music industry. These products were a natural extension of the company's production and those research and development capabilities developed in connection with its electronic keyboard musical instrument business. The company currently produces printed circuit boards and other electronic assemblies for a diverse group of original equipment manufacturers, which sell to the medical electronics, telecommunications, computer peripheral, specialty consumer, data communications, and industrial control markets.

Required:

1. Baldwin uses different critical events to recognize revenue from the sale of inventory for its different business segments. Identify the critical events and rank them from the most to the least conservative policy based on your judgment of the circumstances. For each source of revenue, does

the chosen revenue recognition method satisfy both the critical event and the measurability criteria? If you don't have enough information, discuss what additional information is needed to form a judgment on this issue.

2. In addition to income from the sale of inventory, Baldwin also earns income from financing the sale of some of its inventories. Identify the critical event used by Baldwin to record the financing income. Discuss whether the revenue recognition method for the financing income satisfies the critical event and measurability criteria. Total financing income includes gain or loss on sale of installment receivables and interest income.

COLLABORATIVE LEARNING CASE

C2 – 4

Baldwin Piano and Organ II (KR): Analysis and interpretation of income statement

COLLABORATIVE

In addition to the information provided in Baldwin Piano I, consider the following information we've provided along with information from the annual report and 10-K statement of Baldwin Piano and Organ company.

Baldwin Piano and Organ Company

Income Statements for the Years Ended December 31

	Year 3	Year 2	Year 1
Net sales	$120,657,455	$110,076,904	$103,230,431
Cost of goods sold	(89,970,702)	(79,637,060)	(74,038,724)
Gross profit	30,686,753	30,439,844	29,191,707
Income on the sale of installment receivables	5,746,125	5,256,583	4,023,525
Interest income on installment receivables	443,431	308,220	350,058
Other operating income, net	3,530,761	3,803,228	3,768,760
	40,407,070	39,807,875	37,334,050
Operating expenses			
Selling, general, and administrative expense	(26,187,629)	(25,118,465)	(23,970,568)
Provision for doubtful accounts	(1,702,234)	(2,053,189)	(2,131,644)
Operating profit	12,517,207	12,636,221	11,231,838
Interest expense	(2,232,258)	(2,610,521)	(3,932,830)
Income before income taxes	10,284,949	10,025,700	7,299,008
Income taxes	(4,120,000)	(4,090,000)	(2,884,000)
Income before cumulative effects of change in accounting principles	6,164,949	5,935,700	4,415,008
Cumulative effect of changes in postretirement and postemployment benefits	(1,604,000)	—	—
Net income	$ 4,560,949	$ 5,935,700	$ 4,415,008

Interest income on installment receivables represents interest on receivables not sold to the independent financial institution.

The following summary table was prepared on the basis of the business segment data reported by Baldwin:

Business	Segment Revenue as a Percentage of Total Revenue		Segment Profit as a Percentage of Segment Revenue	
	Year 3	Year 2	Year 3	Year 2
Musical products	72.70%	81.50%	5.00%	7.60%
Electronic	22.20	13.30	14.80	13.90
Financing services	5.20	5.10	52.80	49.20

The cash flow statement indicates that the company has repaid long-term debt of about $8.6 million, $5.6 million, and $8.3 million during Year 1, Year 2, and Year 3, respectively. The balance sheet indicates that the book value of the company's finished goods inventory decreased by about 8% from Year 2 to Year 3.

In March Year 3 the contents of one of the company's finished goods warehouses were damaged by exposure to smoke from a fire adjacent to the warehouse. The company has received insurance proceeds equal to the wholesale value of the destroyed inventory. Accordingly, a gain of approximately $1,412,000 on the insurance settlement is included in the Year 3 Consolidated Statements of Earnings in the component labeled "Other operating income, net."

On January 27, Year 3 the company entered into an agreement in principle whereby Peridot Associates, Inc. (Peridot) would acquire all outstanding shares of the company's common stock at a per-share price of $18.25, subject to certain contingencies. The agreement expired on May 16, Year 3. Under the agreement, the company was obligated to reimburse Peridot $800,000 for certain expenses incurred by Peridot. Additionally, the company incurred other expenses of approximately $305,000 related to the proposed acquisition. These combined expenses are included in the Year 3 Consolidated Statements of Earnings as the component labeled "Other operating income, net."

Required:

Identify and explain the sources of the change in Baldwin's profitability from Year 2 to Year 3 with a view to evaluating its current earnings quality and future prospects. To what extent can this change be attributed to changes in the management's estimates?

Hint: Preparing a common-size income statement and/or year-to-year percentage change analysis of income statement items will help you formulate your response. Additional information regarding Baldwin Piano can be found in case C2–3.

Remember to check the book's Companion Website for additional problem and case material.

www.prenhall.com/revsine

CHAPTER **3**

Additional Topics in Income Determination

This chapter covers special topics in income determination. The first part of the chapter outlines the conditions and describes the accounting procedures for recognizing revenue and profit either before a sale occurs or after a sale occurs. We also discuss selected transactions or circumstances where the timing and amount of revenue recognition presents significant challenges. The second part of the chapter looks at earnings management and how firms can sometimes exploit the flexibility in GAAP to manage annual earnings up or down. We conclude with a discussion of accounting errors and irregularities and how these errors are corrected and reported once they are discovered.

Because revenue is usually recognized at the time of sale in most industries, some people erroneously conclude that the sale is itself the *sole* criterion in recognizing revenue. This is not correct! The correct rule for recognizing revenue is more complicated and subtle. As noted in Chapter 2, revenue is recognized at the earliest moment in time that Condition 1 (the "critical event") *and* Condition 2 ("measurability") are *both* satisfied. That is, at what point in the earnings process is the revenue "earned" and when do the benefits received become realized or realizable? *The earliest moment at which Conditions 1 and 2 are both satisfied is usually the time of sale.* That is why revenue is usually recognized when the sale is made.

But there are cases in which Conditions 1 and 2 are satisfied *before* the sale—for example, as production takes place on a long-term construction contract. When this happens and when expenses are *also* measurable with a reasonable degree of assurance, GAAP allows income to be recognized before the sale.

In other circumstances Conditions 1 and 2 may not both be satisfied until *after* the time of sale—for instance, not until the cash is received on installment sales where there is considerable uncertainty regarding ultimate collection. In these cases GAAP disallows revenue recognition when the sale occurs; instead, revenue recognition is deferred until cash is received.

Revenue Recognition Prior to Sale
Percentage-of-Completion Method

Long-term construction projects—such as roads and bridges, military hardware, and costly items such as oil tankers—frequently satisfy both revenue recognition conditions prior to the time of sale.

These types of projects are usually begun only after a formal contract with a purchaser has been signed. Since a buyer for the completed project is assured, the critical event in the earning of revenue is the actual construction—that is, revenue recognition Condition 1 is satisfied as construction progresses. Furthermore, since the contract price is specified, the amount of the revenue that has been earned is measurable with a reasonable degree of assurance, thus satisfying revenue recognition Condition 2.

In many construction projects it is also possible to estimate with reasonable accuracy the cost of the project and to measure its stage of completion. Furthermore, construction contracts usually require purchasers to make progress payments to the contractor as construction progresses. These interim payment requirements help ensure that the contractor will receive payment for the work performed.

When long-term construction contracts possess all these attributes, revenue recognition Conditions 1 and 2 are both satisfied as construction progresses, and expenses can be matched against revenues to determine income. This is called the **percentage-of-completion method**. Here's how it works.

Solid Construction Corporation signs a contract with the City of Springfield on January 1, 2005 to build a highway bridge over Stony Creek. The contract price is $1,000,000; construction costs are estimated to be $800,000; and the project is scheduled to be completed by December 31, 2007. Periodic cash payments are to be made by the City of Springfield as construction progresses.

	Actual Experience on the Project as of December 31		
	2005	**2006**	**2007**
Costs incurred to date	$240,000	$544,000	$ 850,000
Estimated future costs	560,000	306,000	—
Billings to date	280,000	650,000	1,000,000
Cash collections to date	210,000	600,000	1,000,000

Under the percentage-of-completion method, the profit to be recognized in any year is based on the ratio of incurred contract costs divided by estimated total contract costs. Using the data in the example, we compute the profit for 2005 using the following steps:

Step 1: **Compute the percentage-of-completion ratio by dividing costs incurred to date by estimated total costs.**

This is done to estimate the percentage of completion at any given point during the project. At the end of 2005 estimated total costs on the project are $800,000—comprising $240,000 of costs incurred in 2005 plus $560,000 of estimated future costs. The cost ratio is:

$$\frac{\$240,000}{\$800,000} = 0.30 \text{ or } 30\%$$

Step 2: **Determine the estimated total profit on the contract by comparing the contract price with the estimated total costs.**

At the end of 2005 the estimated profit on the contract is still $200,000—that is, the difference between the contract price of $1,000,000 and estimated total costs of $800,000.

Step 3: **Compute the estimated profit earned to date.**

The estimated profit earned to date is the cost ratio (or percentage-of-completion) computed in Step 1 multiplied by the estimated profit computed in Step 2—that is, .30 × $200,000 = $60,000.

Notice that 30% of the total estimated costs of $800,000 have been incurred by the end of 2005, so 30% of the total estimated profit of $200,000 can be recognized in that same year—that is, profit is recognized in proportion to costs incurred. Since no profit has been recognized prior to 2005, all the $60,000 is recognizable in 2005.

Because cost estimates and completion stages change, these computations must be repeated in each subsequent year. Furthermore, the profit computation for each subsequent contract year must incorporate an additional step. The computation for 2006 illustrates this.

Step 1: Compute the percentage-of-completion ratio, determined by dividing incurred costs to date by estimated total costs.

At the end of 2006 estimated total costs on this contract have risen to $850,000— $544,000 of costs incurred through 2006 plus $306,000 of estimated future costs. The cost ratio (or percentage-of-completion) is:

$$\frac{\$544,000}{\$850,000} = 0.64 \text{ or } 64\%$$

Step 2: Determine the estimated profit on the contract.

The estimated profit on the contract has now dropped to $150,000—the difference between the contract price of $1,000,000 and the newly estimated total costs of $850,000 as of the end of 2006.

Step 3: Compute the estimated profit earned to date.

Since 64% of the total estimated costs have already been incurred (Step 1), 64% of the revised estimated profit of $150,000 (Step 2), or $96,000, has been earned through December 31, 2006.

Be sure to notice that a portion of the profit on this contract—$60,000—has already been recognized in 2005. Therefore, only the *incremental profit* earned in 2006 should be recognized. This requires an additional computation.

Step 4: Compute the incremental profit earned in the current year.

The estimated total profit earned through December 31, 2006 is $96,000 (Step 3). Since $60,000 of the estimated profit was recognized on this contract in 2005, only $36,000 ($96,000 − $60,000) of additional profit can be recognized in 2006.

These four steps can be expressed succinctly using the following profit computation formula:

$$\underbrace{\left[\frac{\text{Costs incurred to date}}{\text{Estimated total costs}} \times \frac{\text{Estimated}}{\text{total profit}}\right]}_{\text{Profit earned to date}} - \underbrace{\frac{\text{Profit recognized}}{\text{in previous years}}}_{\substack{\text{Previously recognized} \\ \text{profit}}} = \frac{\text{Profit recognized}}{\text{in current year}} \qquad (3.1)$$

The previously recognized profit is the sum of all profits (or losses) recognized on the contract in prior years—that is, the sum of all profits (or losses) that were determined by multiplying the cost-completion ratio by the total profit estimated at those earlier dates. Again, the reason for subtracting this amount from the profit-earned-to-date figure is to avoid double-counting profits recognized in prior years.

Repeating the computations for 2005 and 2006 using the formula in equation (3.1) gives the following results:

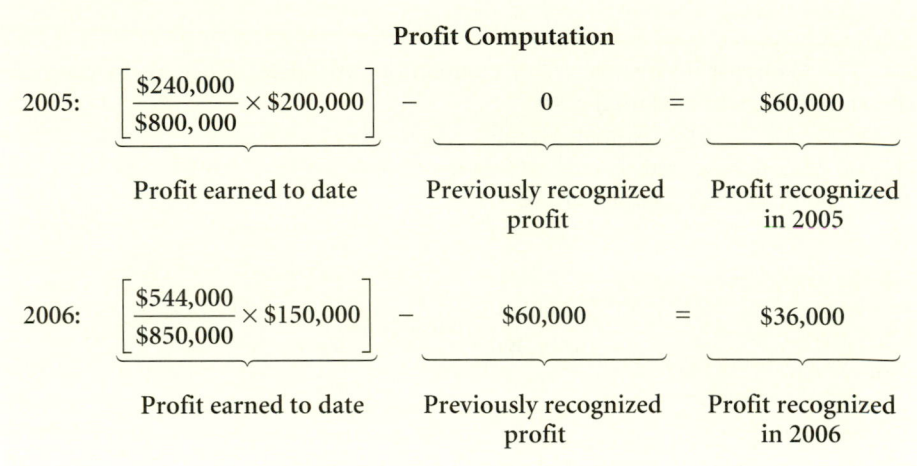

Of course, these results are identical to those derived using the multiple-step approach illustrated previously. The computation for 2003 would be:

$$2007: \quad \left[\frac{\$850,000}{\$850,000} \times \$150,000\right] \underbrace{} - \underbrace{\$96,000}_{} = \underbrace{\$54,000}_{}$$

Profit earned to date   Previously recognized profit   Profit recognized in 2007

Using percentage-of-completion, the cumulative profit recognized over the three years totals $150,000 ($60,000 + $36,000 + $54,000). This total equals the difference between the contract price of $1,000,000 and the actual costs of $850,000.

The journal entries shown in Exhibit 3.1 would be used to record these events on the books of Solid Construction Corporation.

Entries (2) and (3) of Exhibit 3.1 require elaboration. Income is recognized in entry (2) using the income recognition formula of equation (3.1). An alternative to entry (2), which provides more detailed information, is to separately record the construction expense as shown in Exhibit 3.1. The amount debited to "Construction expense" each period is the actual construction costs incurred in that period. The credit to "Construction revenue" is determined by multiplying the total contract price by the completion percentage and then subtracting any revenue recognized in prior periods. For example, the revenue recognized in 2006 is determined by multiplying the contract price of $1,000,000 times the completion percentage as of the end of 2006 (64%) giving total revenue earned to date of $640,000. Subtracting the $300,000 of revenue recognized in 2005 yields "Construction revenue" of $340,000 recognized in 2006.

EXHIBIT 3.1	Solid Construction Corporation

Journal Entries
Percentage-of-Completion Method

	2005		2006		2007	
(1) To record costs incurred						
DR Inventory: Construction						
in progress	$240,000		$304,000		$ 306,000	
CR Accounts payable,						
cash, etc.		$240,000		$304,000		$ 306,000
(2) To record income recognized						
DR Inventory: Construction						
in progress	$ 60,000		$ 36,000		$ 54,000	
CR Income on long-term						
construction contract		$ 60,000		$ 36,000		$ 54,000
Alternative entry						
DR Inventory: Construction						
in progress	$ 60,000[a]		$ 36,000[a]		$ 54,000[a]	
DR Construction expense	240,000[b]		304,000[b]		306,000[b]	
CR Construction						
revenue		$300,000[c]		$340,000[c]		$ 360,000[c]
(3) To record customer billings						
DR Accounts receivable	$280,000		$370,000		$ 350,000	
CR Billings on construction						
in progress		$280,000		$370,000		$ 350,000
(4) To record cash received						
DR Cash	$210,000		$390,000		$ 400,000	
CR Accounts receivable		$210,000		$390,000		$ 400,000
(5) To record completion and						
acceptance of the project						
DR Billings on construction						
in progress					$1,000,000	
CR Construction in						
progress						$1,000,000

	2005	2006	2007
[a]Gross profit earned in current period	30% × ($1,000,000 − $800,000)	64% × ($1,000,000 − $850,000) − $60,000	($1,000,000 − $850,000) − $96,000
[b]Actual construction costs incurred in current period	$240,000	$544,000 − $240,000	$850,000 − $544,000
[c]Revenues earned in current period	30% × $1,000,000	(64% × $1,000,000) − $300,000	$1,000,000 − $300,000 − $340,000

Consistent with asset valuation and income determination being linked together, as discussed in Chapter 2, the carrying value of net assets is also increased as income is recognized. This is why the entry (2) debit increases the "Construction in progress" account, which is a part of inventory. Thus, entry (2) reflects the dual financial statement impact of income recognition: *both net assets and income increase*.

In entry (3) the account labeled "Billings on construction in progress" is a contra-account (reduction) to the inventory subcomponent labeled "Construction in progress." The net of these two accounts is shown as a current asset (if there is a debit balance) or as a current liability (if there is a credit balance). In our example, the balance sheet presentation for Solid Construction Corporation would be as follows for 2005 and 2006:

2005		
Current Assets		
Accounts receivable		$70,000
Inventory: Construction in progress	$300,000	
Less: Billings on construction in progress	(280,000)	
Inventory in excess of contract billings		$20,000
2006		
Current Assets		
Accounts receivable		$50,000
Current Liabilities		
Inventory: Construction in progress	$(640,000)	
Less: Billings on construction in progress	650,000	
Contract billings in excess of inventory		$10,000

The component "Billings on construction in progress" must be treated as a contra-inventory account (that is, shown as a deduction from inventory) to avoid balance sheet double-counting. Here's why. Typically, a sale results in an asset (Accounts receivable) being increased for the selling price of the goods with a simultaneous decrease in another asset, inventory, for the cost of goods sold. However, inventory is not reduced at the time the receivable is recorded under long-term construction accounting. Rather, the "Inventory: Construction in progress" account remains on the company's books until the project is complete and the sale is finalized. Treating the "Billings on construction in progress" account as an off-set (contra) to the construction inventory account avoids including certain costs and profits twice on the balance sheet—once in inventory (Inventory: Construction in progress) and a second time in the Accounts receivable account.

Finally, although profits are recognized proportionately to percentage-of-completion as construction progresses, *estimated losses on a contract are recognized in their entirety as soon as it becomes known that a contract loss will ensue.*

In our example, cumulative income to date is determined by using the ratio of incurred costs to date divided by estimated total costs. This cost ratio is widely used since it provides a simple index of progress toward completion—that is, work done to date. However, there are situations in which this cost ratio may not accurately reflect construction progress. For example, consider a case in which raw materials to be used in construction are stockpiled in advance of use. In such situations costs are being incurred as the raw materials are received and recorded on the books. Yet these costs do not increase the stage of completion until the raw materials are actually *used*. In projects in which this stockpiling is significant, some other means for measuring progress toward completion would be preferable. Possibilities include labor hours worked or various output measures (such as miles of roadway completed).

Completed-Contract Method

There are cases in which it is not possible to determine expected costs with a high degree of reliability under long-term construction contracts (for example, building underground street tunnels in Boston), making the use of the percentage-of-completion method inappropriate. In these situations, the **completed-contract method** is used instead.

The completed-contract method defers recognition of income until the project is completed. Journal entries under the completed-contract method are identical to the journal entries illustrated previously for the percentage-of-completion method except that entry (2) in Exhibit 3.1, which records income as construction progresses, is omitted. Instead, all the income on the contract is recognized when the contract is completed. The entry for recognizing income under the completed-contract method in 2007 is shown at the top of the next page.

DR Billings on construction in progress	$1,000,000	
CR Construction in progress		$850,000
CR Income on long-term construction contract		150,000

Although income is recognized only on completion, losses are recognized in their entirety as soon as their probable existence is known.

Exhibit 3.2 illustrates that total income for the three years is the same under both the completed-contract method and the percentage-of-completion method ($150,000). However, the timing of income recognition differs considerably.

EXHIBIT 3.2	**Yearly Income Comparison of Two Long-Term Contract Accounting Methods**

Year	Completed-Contract Method	Percentage-of-Completion Method
2005	-0-	$ 60,000
2006	-0-	36,000
2007	$150,000	54,000
Total income	$150,000	$150,000

The net asset balance at intermediate construction stages will also differ between the two methods. As shown in column (g) of Exhibit 3.3, *the amount of this net asset balance difference in any year is precisely equal to the difference in cumulative profit recognized on each basis.* This difference in net asset balances exists because the recognition of income has a corresponding effect on net asset balances.

EXHIBIT 3.3	**Comparative Account Balances**

Percentage-of-Completion versus Completed-Contract Method
December 31, Year-End Account Balances

	Completed-Contract Method			Percentage-of-Completion Method			
	(a) Construction in Progress	(b) Billings	(c) Net Asset Balance Col. (a) – Col. (b)	(d) Construction in Progress	(e) Billings	(f) Net Asset Balance Col. (d) – Col. (e)	(g) Difference in Net Asset Balances Between Methods Col. (f) – Col. (c)
2005	$240,000	$280,000	$−40,000	$300,000	$280,000	$+20,000	$+60,000[*]
2006	544,000	650,000	−106,000	640,000	650,000	−10,000	+96,000[**]
2007	-0-	-0-	-0-	-0-	-0-	-0-	-0-

[*]Also equals difference between cumulative profit on percentage-of-completion method ($60,000) and the completed-contract method ($0) from Exhibit 3.2.
[**]Also equals difference between cumulative profit on percentage-of-completion method ($60,000 + $36,000 = $96,000) and the completed-contract method ($0 + $0) from Exhibit 3.2.

Revenue Recognition on Commodities

The timing of revenue recognition for producers of agricultural and mining commodities raises some interesting issues. There is general agreement that in both mining and farming, the critical event in adding value usually comes *before* the actual sale. The critical event in mining is extracting the resource from the ground. In agriculture the critical event is harvest. (The critical event is harvest, since prior to harvest the crop may still be lost because of drought, hail, insects, or disease. Only after the crop is safely out of the field have these income threatening possibilities been avoided.) Thus, revenue recognition Condition 1 is satisfied prior to the sale itself.

However, the precise time at which revenue recognition Condition 2 ("measurability") is satisfied for commodities producers is open to some dispute. The following example explores the issues.

> A farmer harvests 110,000 bushels of corn on September 30, 2005. On this date the posted market price per bushel was $3.50. The total cost of growing the crop was $220,000, or $2.00 per bushel. The farmer decides to sell 100,000 bushels for cash on September 30 at the posted price of $3.50 and stores the remaining 10,000 bushels. On January 2, 2006 the market price drops to $3.00. Fearing further price declines, the farmer immediately sells the bushels in storage at a price of $3.00 per bushel.

Completed-Transaction (Sales) Method The timing of revenue recognition on the 100,000 bushels of corn that were sold on September 30 is straightforward. Revenue recognition Conditions 1 and 2 are both satisfied at September 30, and income would be recognized at the time of sale. The income statement would show:

2005 Income Statement

Revenues (sale of 100,000 bushels at a market price of $3.50 per bushel)	$350,000
Expenses (costs of $2.00 per bushel for 100,000 bushels sold)	(200,000)
Income from sale	$150,000

As costs are incurred during the year, the direct costs of crop production—things like seed, fertilizer, fuel, and depreciation on machinery—are charged to a "Production in process" or "Crop inventory" account with offsetting credits to Cash, Accounts payable, or Accumulated depreciation.

Under the traditional view, which we call the **completed-transaction (sales) method**, no income would be recognized at September 30 on the 10,000 bushels that were harvested but not sold. For these 10,000 bushels, revenue recognition Condition 2 is considered not to have been met since the eventual selling price is unknown—that is, the sale transaction is not yet completed. The bushels in storage would be reflected on the farmer's balance sheet at their *cost* of $20,000 ($2.00 per bushel × 10,000 bushels).

When the bushels in storage are sold in 2006, the income statement would show the profit on the sale of the 10,000 bushels:

2006 Income Statement

Revenues (sale of 10,000 bushels at a market price of $3.00 per bushel)	$30,000
Expenses (costs of $2.00 per bushel for 10,000 bushels sold)	(20,000)
Income from sale	$10,000

Note the traditional approach avoids recognizing any income on the 10,000 unsold bushels until the sales transaction is completed in 2006.

Market Price (Production) Method There is another way for measuring income in the previous example. This alternative recognizes that well-organized markets exist for most agricultural and many mining commodities. In addition, the quantities offered for sale by any individual producer are usually very small in relation to the total size of the market. Producers face an established price for as many units as they choose to sell. These factors mean that a readily determinable market price at which output *could be sold* is continuously available. In this view, revenue recognition Condition 2 ("measurability") is satisfied prior to the actual sale of actively traded commodities.

> International Accounting Standards Board (IASB) requires that agricultural produce harvested by an enterprise should be measured at its fair value less estimated point-of-sale cost at point of harvest. Any gain or loss arising from initial recognition of harvested assets and from the change in fair value less estimated point-of-sale costs of harvested assets are to be included in net profit or loss for the period in which it arises. See "Agriculture," *IAS 41* (London: International Accounting Standards Board [IASB], 2002)

Since revenue recognition Condition 1 ("critical event") occurs at harvest, both conditions necessary to recognize revenue are satisfied as soon as the crop is safely out of the field (that is, at the point of production or harvest). Thus, farming income on all 110,000 bushels is recognized under this approach on September 30 (when grain is harvested):

International

Revenues (100,000 bushels sold at a market price of $3.50)	$350,000
Expenses (costs of $2.00 per bushel for 100,000 bushels sold)	(200,000)
Market gain on unsold inventory (10,000 bushels times the difference between the $3.50 market price at the date of harvest and the $2.00 cost per bushel)	15,000
Total income from farming activities	$165,000

This **market price (or production) method** recognizes farming income on the 10,000 unsold bushels as well as on the 100,000 bushels sold. This view emphasizes the fact that the farmer *could have sold* these 10,000 bushels at the time of harvest for a readily determinable price of $3.50 per bushel. Since the critical event in farming is harvest and since the potential sales price at the time of harvest is known, both revenue

> The market price used in this calculation is the net realizable value—that is, the market price at point of delivery less any delivery costs. Thus, if it costs the farmer $0.10 per bushel to transport the grain from the farm to the local elevator, the net realizable value would be $3.40 ($3.50 − $0.10). This would be the price used to compute the gain on the unsold inventory.

recognition conditions relating to farming are deemed to be satisfied on September 30. Therefore, farming income of $165,000 is immediately determinable.

Under the market price method, the bushels in storage are reflected on the farmer's balance sheet at $35,000 ($3.50 market price at harvest times 10,000 bushels). If the corn was initially carried at its *cost* of $20,000 ($2.00 per bushel times 10,000 bushels), the entry necessary to reflect the value added by farming is:

DR Crop inventory	$15,000	
CR Market gain on unsold inventory		$15,000

The credit would appear as shown on the income statement for 2005.

After the corn is harvested, the activity called farming has ended. However, this farmer is actually engaged in another business in addition to farming. By withholding 10,000 bushels from the market, the farmer is also pursuing a separate (nonfarming) activity called **speculation**. This speculation is undertaken in the hope that prices will rise above their September 30 level of $3.50 per bushel. Subsequent changes in the market price of corn will thus give rise to speculative gains or losses—also called **inventory holding gains and losses**.

To illustrate, recollect that at the start of 2006, the market price of corn drops from $3.50 to $3.00 per bushel. This decline in price gives rise to a speculative (holding) loss in 2006 of $5,000 (a decline of $0.50 per bushel times 10,000 bushels). The inventory is marked-to-market, and the journal entry to reflect the loss is:

DR Inventory (holding) loss on speculation	$5,000	
CR Crop inventory		$5,000

After this entry is posted, the carrying value of the inventory is now reduced to $30,000 (10,000 bushels times $3.00 per bushel).

Fearing further price declines, the farmer immediately sells the remaining 10,000 bushels at $3.00 on January 2. The entry is:

DR Cost of goods sold	$30,000	
CR Crop inventory		$30,000
DR Cash	$30,000	
CR Crop revenue		$30,000

Comparison: Completed-Transaction (Sales) and Market Price (Production) Methods

Although total income over the two periods is the same under each approach, the income recognized in each period is not the same, and the activities to which the income is attributed also differ:

Completed-Transaction (Sales) Method			Market Price (Production) Method	
Income from sales	$150,000	2005	Income from farming activities	$165,000
Income from sales	10,000	2006	Holding loss on speculation	(5,000)
Total income	$160,000		Total income	$160,000

The completed-transaction (sales) method avoids recognizing any income on the 10,000 unsold bushels until the transaction is completed (when the grain is sold). However, in emphasizing completed transactions, this traditional approach—the completed-transaction method—merges the results of the farmer's speculative and farming activities and does not reflect the separate results of either.

This example illustrates why income recognition can be controversial—should market price changes on agricultural commodities be recognized by the farmer prior to sale? In practice the completed-transaction method is far more prevalent. However, the market price method is deemed to be in conformity with generally accepted accounting principles when readily determinable market values are continuously available. The market price method has the dual advantages of:

1. explicitly recognizing the separate results arising from the farming and speculative activities that the farmer is engaged in, and
2. conforming more closely to the income recognition conditions introduced in Chapter 2.

RECAP   For long-term construction contracts and commodities (natural resources and agricultural products), the two conditions for revenue recognition—"critical event" and "measurability"—are frequently satisfied prior to sale. The percentage-of-completion method recognizes revenue and profits (losses) on long-term construction contracts as work progresses. The market price (production) method recognizes the difference between the cost of the natural resource or agricultural commodity and its prevailing market price as income at the time of production or harvest. In both cases an inventory account—"Construction in progress" for long-term construction contracts and "Crop inventory" for commodities—is debited to reflect the increase in value that is recognized on the income statement, thereby maintaining the linkage between income determination and asset valuation.

Revenue Recognition Subsequent to Sale
Installment Sales Method

Sometimes revenue is not recognized at the point of sale even though a valid sale has taken place. This accounting treatment is acceptable only under highly unusual circumstances. One instance in which revenue recognition might be delayed beyond the point of sale is when sales are made under very extended cash collection terms. Examples include installment sales of consumer durables and retail land sales of vacation or retirement property. A lengthy collection period considerably increases the risk of nonpayment. *Where the risk of noncollection is unusually high and where there is no reasonable basis for estimating the proportion of installment accounts likely to prove uncollectible, then revenue recognition may be deferred.*

When these extreme risk situations exist, neither of the two revenue recognition conditions is satisfied. Specifically, when it's highly uncertain whether customers will make the cash payments called for in the contract, then the sale itself is not the critical event in creating value. In such circumstances the actual cash collection is the critical event, and revenue recognition Condition 1 is satisfied only as the amounts due from customers are received. Similarly, revenue recognition Condition 2 is not satisfied because the amount ultimately collectible from customers is not measurable with a reasonable degree of assurance at the time of sale.

Since Conditions 1 and 2 are both satisfied only over time as cash collections take place, a revenue recognition method tied to cash collections has been devised to deal with such situations. This revenue recognition approach is called the **installment sales method**.

Installment Sales Method Illustrated The installment sales method recognizes revenue and income proportionately as cash is collected. The amount recognized in any period is based on two factors:

1. The installment-sales gross-profit percentage (gross profit/sales).
2. The amount of cash collected on installment accounts receivable.

Here's an example of revenue and income recognition under the installment sales method:

	2005	2006
Installment sales	$1,200,000	$1,300,000
Cost of installment goods sold	840,000	884,000
Gross profit	$ 360,000	$ 416,000
Gross-profit percentage	30%	32%
Cash collections		
On 2005 installment sales	$ 300,000	$ 600,000
On 2006 installment sales		340,000

During 2005 installment sales of $1,200,000 were made. The potential gross profit on these sales was $360,000. The installment contracts call for cash payments over each of the next four years. Because of the extreme uncertainties regarding ultimate collectibility, this gross profit will be recognized only as customers pay on their accounts. Since $300,000 of cash was collected in 2005, the gross profit recognized in 2005 will be $90,000—that is, $300,000 multiplied by 30%, the gross-profit percentage (gross profit/sales) on 2005 installment sales. This $90,000 is shown on the 2005 income statement as 2005 income from installment sales. The difference between the total potential gross profit of $360,000 and the $90,000 of recognized income—or $270,000—is deferred gross profit (see entries [4] and [5] in Exhibit 3.4 on the following page).

EXHIBIT 3.4	**Installment Sales Method**			

Journal Entries

	2005		2006	
(1) **To record installment sales**				
DR Accounts receivable—2005 installment sales	$1,200,000			
DR Accounts receivable—2006 installment sales			$1,300,000	
CR Installment sales revenue		$1,200,000		$1,300,000
(2) **To record cost of goods sold**				
DR Cost of installment goods sold	$ 840,000		$ 884,000	
CR Inventory		$ 840,000		$ 884,000
(3) **To record cash collections**				
DR Cash	$ 300,000		$ 940,000	
CR Accounts receivable—2005 installment sales		$ 300,000		$ 600,000
CR Accounts receivable—2006 installment sales				340,000
(4) **To defer gross profit on portion of current-period sales that are not yet collected**				
DR Deferred gross profit (income statement)	$ 270,000		$ 307,200	
CR Deferred gross profit—Adjustment to accounts receivable		$ 270,000		$ 307,200
(5) **To recognize realized gross profit on installment sales of prior periods**				
DR Deferred gross profit—Adjustment to accounts receivable			$ 180,000	
CR Recognized gross profit on installment sales—prior year				$ 180,000

Income recognized in 2006 from installment sales comprises two components:

1. A component relating to 2006 cash collections on 2005 installment sales.
2. A component relating to 2006 cash collections on 2006 installment sales.

The computation for installment sales income recognized in 2006 is:

Total 2006 Installment Sales Income

	Gross Profit Recognized
Component relating to 2005 sales	
Cash collections in year 2006 from 2005 sales	$600,000
Multiplied by year 2005 gross-profit percentage	30%
	$180,000
Component relating to year 2006 sales	
Cash collections in year 2006 from 2006 sales	$340,000
Multiplied by year 2006 gross-profit percentage	32%
	$108,800
Total installment sales income recognized in year 2006	$288,800

Journal entries to record these facts for years 2005 and 2006 are shown in Exhibit 3.4.

The income statement would appear as follows:

	2005	2006
Installment sales	$1,200,000	$1,300,000
Cost of installment goods sold	(840,000)	(884,000)
Gross profit	360,000	416,000
Less: Deferred gross profit on installment sales of current year	(270,000)	(307,200)
Gross profit recognized on current year's sales	90,000	108,800
Plus: Gross profit recognized on installment sales of prior years	—	180,000
Total gross profit recognized this year	$ 90,000	$ 288,800

Some additional internal recordkeeping is necessary when applying the installment sales method. Installment sales and the related cost of goods sold must be tracked by individual year in order to compute the gross-profit percentage that applies to each year. In addition, the accounting system must match cash collections with the specific sales year to which the cash collections relate. This matching is needed to apply the correct gross-profit percentage to cash receipts.

On the balance sheet, the "Accounts receivable—installment sales" components are classified as current assets if they are due within 12 months of the balance sheet date. Amounts not expected to be collected within the next year may also be classified as current assets if installment sales are a normal part of the company's operations, since the company's operating cycle would include the installment collection period. Existing practice typically classifies the deferred gross-profit account as a contra-asset, which is shown as a reduction to accounts receivable.

Selling, general, and administrative expenses relating to installment sales are treated as period costs—that is, as costs that are expensed in the period in which they are incurred—because they provide no future benefits. This treatment is consistent with the manner in which period costs are handled for normal (non-installment) sales.

Interest on Installment Contracts The essence of an installment sales contract is that the cash payments arising from the sale are spread over multiple periods. Because of this delay in receiving the sales proceeds, sellers charge interest on installment sales contracts. Consequently, the required monthly or quarterly installment payments include both interest and principal. This complication was omitted from the example we just illustrated. GAAP requires that the interest component of the periodic cash proceeds must be recorded separately. This means that interest payments are not considered when computing the recognized gross profit on installment sales. Chapter 8 outlines the procedures for differentiating between principal and interest payments on customer receivables.

Cost Recovery Method

When collections on installment sales occur over an extended period and there is no reasonable basis for estimating collectibility, GAAP allows companies to use the **cost recovery method** for recognizing profits on such sales.[1] This method is commonly used where there is a high degree of uncertainty regarding the collection of receivables (for example, for retail land development sales). Under this method, no profit is recognized until cash payments received from the buyer exceed the seller's cost of goods sold. After the cost of the merchandise has been recovered, any cash collected in excess of this amount is recorded as recognized gross profit on the seller's income statement.

---

[1] "Omnibus Opinion—1966," *Accounting Principles Board Opinion No. 10* (New York: AICPA, 1969).

The following example illustrates the accounting treatment under the cost recovery method.

In 2005, Florida Swamp Land Development Company sells 100 one-acre lots for $12,000 each. One-third of the sales price, $4,000 per lot, or $400,000 total, is collected when the contract is signed and the remainder is to be collected in two equal installments in the following two years. The cost of acquiring and developing the land was $600,000. Because most of the sales are made to individuals who reside outside the state of Florida, there tends to be a high rate of default on collections, which is difficult to estimate. If the cost recovery method is applied to these sales and the cash is collected on schedule, the accounting entries would be as follows.

2005

DR Installment receivables	$1,200,000	
CR Land inventory		$600,000
CR Deferred gross profit		600,000

To record sale of 100 lots at $12,000 each.

DR Cash	$ 400,000	
CR Installment receivables		$400,000

To record collections on account.

2006

DR Cash	$ 400,000	
CR Installment receivables		$400,000

To record collections on account.

DR Deferred gross profit	$ 200,000	
CR Realized gross profit		$200,000

To record realized gross profit equal to cumulative cash collections in excess of cost of land sold = $800,000 − $600,000 = $200,000.

2007

DR Cash	$ 400,000	
CR Installment receivables		$400,000

To record collections on account.

DR Deferred gross profit	$ 400,000	
CR Realized gross profit		$400,000[a]

[a]To record realized gross profit determined as follows:

Cumulative cash collections	$1,200,000
Cost of land sold	−600,000
Gross profit recognized in prior periods	−200,000
Amount recognized in 2007	$ 400,000

Note that the cost recovery method is more conservative than the regular installment sales method because the regular installment method recognizes gross profit on each dollar collected, while the cost recovery method only recognizes profit when the cumulative cash collections exceed the total cost of land sold.

RECAP | The installment sales method of revenue recognition is used when the risk of non-collection is high or when it is impractical to estimate the amount of uncollectibles. Under the installment sales method, the gross profit on sales is deferred and recognized in income in subsequent periods—that is, when the installment receivables are collected in cash. The linkage between income determination and asset valuation is maintained by showing deferred gross profit as a contra-account (reduction) to installment accounts receivable.

Revenue Recognition for Specialized Sales Transactions

In this section, we briefly review accounting requirements for industries or transactions where there are specialized applications of revenue recognition principles. Specifically, we consider the unique revenue recognition issues for the following areas:

- Franchise sales
- Sales with right of return
- Bundled sales (Software sales)

Franchise Sales

Franchising is a popular way of expanding sales of products and services in a variety of industries. In 2000, franchise operations accounted for over $1 trillion of sales in the United States. Exhibit 3.5 identifies the ten fastest growing franchise operations for 2003 and the industries in which they operate.

EXHIBIT 3.5	Ten Fastest Growing Franchise Operations for 2003

Curves for Women—Service (Weight loss)
Subway—Restaurants/Fast food
7-Eleven—Retail food
Taco Bell Corporation—Fast food
Jani-King—Commercial cleaning (Service)
McDonald's—Fast food
Jan Pro Franchising International, Inc.—Commercial cleaning (Service)
Baskin-Robbins USA, Inc.—Specialty food
Quizno's Franchise Company, Inc.—Fast food
KFC Corporation—Fast food

Source: Entrepreneur Magazine's Fastest-Growing Franchises.html

In franchise arrangements, the franchisor (seller) gives the franchisee (buyer) the exclusive right to sell a product or service in a given locale or area and use the franchisor's name for a specified period of time. Typically, franchise agreements call for both of the following two types of payments:

1. an initial franchise fee, all or part of which is paid to the franchisor at the time the franchise agreement is signed with the remainder due in installments (with interest) over a specified period; and
2. continuing or periodic fees that are generally based on a percentage of sales generated by the franchisee.

Accounting for continuing periodic fees received by the franchisor poses little difficulty. These fees are recorded as revenue in the period they are received and earned. Accounting for the initial franchise fee, however, raises some challenging revenue recognition issues as you will see.

The initial franchise fee typically is comprised of two elements:

1. Payment for the right to operate a franchise in a given area.
2. Payment for services to be performed by the franchisor.

Examples of initial services include:

- Finding and securing a site for the franchise
- Overseeing construction of the facilities
- Training employees
- Setting up and maintaining a recordkeeping system
- Sales promotion and advertising

Occasionally, initial franchise fees may also include payment for tangible property such as signs, equipment, inventory, land, and buildings. Fees received for tangible assets are recognized when title to the property passes to the franchisee.

The key issue in franchise fee accounting centers on when and how much of the initial franchise fee should be recognized by the franchisor. *SFAS No. 45* specifies that revenue from initial franchise fees should be recognized when all material services or conditions relating to the sale have been substantially performed or satisfied by the franchisor.[2] Essentially the question is—when are the initial franchise fees earned by the franchisor? The answer to this question is not always easily discernable—opening the way for possible abuses from recognizing revenue before it is earned.

The following example illustrates the key measurement and recognition issues related to franchise fee revenue.

On January 1, 2005 Diet Right sells a dieting/weight loss franchise for an initial fee of $25,000 with $10,000 due at the signing of the franchise agreement and the remainder due in three annual installments (due December 31) of $5,000 each plus interest at 8% on the unpaid balance. The $10,000 up-front payment gives the franchisee the right to use Diet Right's name and sell pre-packaged health conscious meals prepared at Diet Right's corporate headquarters. In return for the initial franchise fee, Diet Right agrees to train employees, set up a recordkeeping system, maintain a website with online dietary counseling by a registered dietician and provide advertising and various promotional materials. In addition to the initial franchise fee, Diet Right will receive 2% of the franchise's annual sales for allowing the franchisee to purchase prepackaged meals at below market prices.

Recording Initial Franchise Fees Assuming that the deferred payments under the franchise agreement are for services not yet performed (for example, training of employees, maintaining website and advertising), Diet Right would record the following entry for the initial franchise fee when the franchise agreement is signed.

January 1, 2005:

DR	Cash	$10,000	
DR	Note receivable	15,000[a]	
CR	Earned franchise fee revenue		$10,000[b]
CR	Unearned franchise fees		15,000

[a]Initial fee of $25,000 minus $10,000 received at signing of franchise agreement
[b]Amount received for right to use Diet Right name and to sell Diet Right's prepackaged meals

The unearned franchise fees will be recognized as earned when the initial services are performed. These services could be performed evenly over time or at one point in time.

Assuming that half of the deferred payment ($7,500) is for employee training and recordkeeping system installation that is completed by Diet Right before the franchise opens, the follow-

---

2 "Accounting for Franchise Fee Revenue," *Statement of Financial Accounting Standards No. 45* (Stamford, CT: FASB, 1981).

ing entry would be made on Diet Right's books when the franchise commences operations on March 1, 2005.

> **March 1, 2005:**
> **DR** Unearned franchise fees $7,500
>   **CR** Earned franchise fees $7,500

Note that this portion of the initial franchise fee is recognized even though the amount has not been received in cash. This treatment is appropriate assuming that the collectibility of the note receivable from the franchisee is reasonably assured.

If the remaining $7,500 of the initial franchise fee is for services provided by Diet Right on an ongoing basis over the term of the note (for example, maintenance of website and advertising), then the following adjusting entry would be made at the end of each year to record franchise fee revenue earned during the period.

> Recall from Chapter 2 that the second condition that must be satisfied before revenue can be recognized is that it must be "measurable" or "realizable." Having a promissory note from a creditworthy customer is deemed to satisfy this condition.

> **December 31, 2005 (2006 and 2007):**
> **DR** Unearned franchise fees $2,500
>   **CR** Earned franchise fee revenue $2,500

In addition, the entry to record the receipt of payment on the note receivable and interest earned at 8% on the outstanding note balance would be as follows at December 31:

	2005		2006		2007	
DR Cash	$5,000		$5,000		$5,000	
CR Notes receivable		$5,000		$5,000		$5,000
DR Cash	$1,200[a]		$ 800[b]		$ 400[c]	
CR Interest revenue		$1,200		$ 800		$ 400

[a]$0.08 \times \$15,000 = \$1,200$ [b]$0.08 \times \$10,000 = \$800$ [c]$0.08 \times \$5,000 = \$400$

Recording Continuing Franchise Fees If the franchisee sales were $100,000 in 2005, the entry for the continuing or periodic fee ($0.02 \times \$100,000 = \$2,000$) would be:

> **DR** Cash $2,000
>   **CR** Earned franchise fee revenue $2,000

Costs incurred by the franchisor to provide for initial and continuing services (for example, counseling by a registered dietician or advertising) are expensed and recognized in the same periods as the franchise revenue following the matching principle.

Sales with Right of Return

> These returns may be made by the ultimate customer or by a party who resells the product to the final customer (that is, a distributor).

Due to the nature of their products, certain companies like book publishers, record and tape recording companies, and semiconductor manufacturers experience high rates of return of their products. For example, it is common for book publishers to have rates of return in excess of 25% for hardcover books. Because of rapid obsolescence of their product, semiconductor manufacturers like Motorola and Intel grant distributors the right to return semiconductors they are unable to sell.

When the frequency and magnitude of returns are high, a question arises as to whether an entity should recognize revenue at the time of sale or defer recognition until the uncertainty regarding product returns is resolved. *SFAS No. 45* specifies that for a seller to record revenue at time of sale when **right of return** exists the following criteria must be met:[3]

- The seller's price to the buyer is substantially fixed or determinable at the date of sale.
- The buyer has paid the seller, or the buyer is obligated to pay the seller and the obligation is not contingent on the resale of the product.
- The buyer's obligation to the seller does not change in the event of theft or physical destruction or damage of the product.
- The buyer acquiring the product for resale has economic substance and exists separate and distinct from the seller. That is, the buyer cannot be an entity established by the seller for the purpose of allowing the seller to recognize sales to that entity. For example, the buyer cannot be a **special purpose entity** established by the seller for the sole purpose of buying and reselling the seller's product.
- The seller does not have significant obligations for future performance to directly bring about resale of the product to the buyer.
- The amount of future returns can be reasonably estimated.

This is perhaps the most important of these criteria, and the one subject to greatest uncertainty. Because estimation of future product returns entails considerable judgment, it can lead to manipulation and revenue overstatement. Statement users need to be particularly wary of unusual patterns in return provisions for those entities that operate in industries with high levels and variability of product returns.

When all six of these conditions are met, an entity will debit Sales returns & allowances and credit Allowance for sales returns & allowances for the estimated returns from sales made during the period. Sales returns & allowances is netted against (shown contra to) the gross sales figure for the period to avoid overstatement of sales revenue and the allowance account is shown contra to Accounts receivable to avoid overstatement of this asset account.

When any of these conditions are not met, then sales revenue and the related cost of sales are deferred and recognized either when the return privilege has substantially expired or when the conditions set forth above are met, whichever comes first.

Statement of Position (SOPs) on accounting issues present the conclusions of at least two-thirds of the Accounting Standards Executive Committee (AcSEC) of the American Institute of CPAs. AcSEC is the senior technical body of the Institute authorized to speak for the Institute on financial accounting and reporting matters. AICPA SOPs that have been cleared by the FASB are deemed to be part of GAAP.

Bundled Sales

Software vendors like Microsoft and Oracle often package their products in "bundles" of more than one product or service ("multiple deliverables") that are sold for a lump-sum contract price. Besides the software itself (or the license to use the software), other deliverables include such things as training in the use of the software, upgrades and enhancements, post-contract customer support and other services. The key accounting issue related to bundled sales transactions is the timing of revenue recognition. That is, how much of the lump-sum contract price should be recognized up front when the product is delivered to the customer, and how much should be deferred and recognized as the seller satisfies its commitment for other deliverables specified in the contract?

Authoritative guidance on this issue is provided in *Statement of Position (SOP) 97-2* issued in 1997.[4] *SOP 97-2* states that if a software sales arrangement includes multiple, distinct elements, then the revenue from the arrangement should be allocated to the various elements based on vendor-specific objective evidence of the elements' relative fair value. As a practical matter, vendor-specific objective evidence is obtained from observed prices charged when the elements are sold separately.

[3] "Revenue Recognition When Right of Return Exists," *Statement of Financial Accounting Standards (SFAS) No. 48* (Stamford, CT: FASB 1981).
[4] "Software Revenue Recognition," *Statement of Position 97-2* (New York: AICPA, 1997).

To illustrate how revenue is allocated with multiple deliverables, assume that Oracle sells its database management software system to a corporate client for $1 million. The contract stipulates that in addition to the software, Oracle will provide staff training on the use of the software, a free upgrade on a when-and-if-available basis and customer support over the five years of the licensing agreement. Objective evidence of relative fair market values, based on what Oracle would charge for these individual elements if sold separately, is as follows:

	Fair Value	% of Total Fair Value
Database management software	$ 600,000	40%
Training	450,000	30
Upgrades	300,000	20
Customer support	150,000	10
Total estimated fair values	$1,500,000	100%

In this example, Oracle would recognize $400,000 (0.40 × $1 million) of revenue when the software is delivered and installed for the client, $300,000 (0.30 × $1 million) when the training is complete, $200,000 (0.20 × $1 million) when upgrades are installed and $100,000 (0.10 × $1 million) recognized evenly over the five years of the contract as the customer service is provided.

Exhibit 3.6 contains an excerpt from Oracle's footnote on significant accounting policies that explains its revenue recognition policies for software licensing revenues and service revenues. The amount of sales revenue that Oracle deferred and reported as unearned revenue amounted to $1.276 billion as of May 31, 2002.

EXHIBIT 3.6 **Oracle Corporation**
Excerpts from Significant Accounting
Policies on Revenue Recognition

We derive revenues from two primary sources: (1) software license revenues and (2) services revenues, which include support, consulting, education and outsourcing revenues. While the basis for software license revenue recognition is substantially governed by the provisions of Statement of Position No. 97-2, "*Software Revenue Recognition,*" issued by the American Institute of Certified Public Accountants ("SOP 97-2"), we exercise judgment and use estimates in connection with the determination of the amount of software license and services revenues to be recognized in each accounting period.

For arrangements with multiple elements, we allocate revenue to each element of a transaction based upon its fair value as determined in reliance on "vendor specific objective evidence." Vendor specific objective evidence of fair value for all elements of an arrangement is based upon the normal pricing and discounting practices for those products and services when sold separately and, for support services, is additionally measured by the renewal rate. If we cannot objectively determine the fair value of any undelivered element included in bundled software and service arrangements, we defer revenue until all elements are delivered, services have been performed, or until fair value can objectively be determined. When the fair value of a license element has not been established, we use the residual method to record license revenue if the fair value of all undelivered elements is determinable. Under the residual method, the fair value of the undelivered elements is deferred and the remaining portion of the arrangement fee is allocated to the delivered elements and is recognized as revenue.

Source: 2001 Oracle Annual Report.

Because the determination of relative fair values of multiple deliverables requires considerable judgment on the part of companies' management, there is potential for premature revenue recognition and/or arbitrary income shifting from period to period. Accordingly, statement users need to be particularly vigilant when assessing revenue and profits of companies with significant amounts of bundled sales.

Earnings Management

"Executives rarely have to violate the law to put a gloss on dreary earnings. Accepted accounting principles leave ample room for those who want to fudge the numbers."[5]

The criteria for revenue and expense recognition outlined in Chapter 2 provide general guidelines for accrual accounting income determination. But applying these rules in specific settings still leaves room for considerable latitude and judgment. For example, determining when revenue has been earned (critical event) and is realizable (measurability)—the two conditions for revenue recognition—are often judgment calls. Managers can sometimes exploit the flexibility in GAAP to manipulate reported earnings in ways that mask the underlying performance of the company. Some managers have even resorted to outright financial fraud to inflate reported earnings, but this is relatively rare.

The growing propensity of managers to bolster earnings by exploiting the flexibility in GAAP or by resorting to financial fraud led former SEC Chairman Arthur Levitt to warn:

> "Increasingly, I have become concerned that the motivation to meet Wall Street earnings expectations may be overriding common sense business practices. Too many corporate managers, auditors, and analysts are participating in a game of nods and winks. In the zeal to satisfy consensus earnings estimates and project a smooth earnings path, wishful thinking may be winning the day over faithful representation. As a result, I fear that we are witnessing an erosion in the quality of earnings, and therefore, the quality of financial reporting. Managing may be giving way to manipulation; integrity may be losing to illusion."[6]

Earnings management is not new. But the perception is that it has become increasingly common in today's marketplace because of pressure to meet analysts' earnings forecasts. Companies that miss analysts' earnings per share estimates by even a few pennies frequently experience significant stock price declines. Several highly publicized examples of alleged accounting "irregularities"[7] and recent research studies[8] lend support to Chairman Levitt's concerns about earnings management.

One way to avoid a decline in stock price for reporting a loss is to make sure to report an accounting profit. Ideally, this should be accomplished through real economic events that are correctly accounted for. But when all else fails, managers sometimes resort to various sorts of

---

[5] F. S. Worthy. "Manipulating Profits: How It's Done," *Fortune* (June 25, 1984), pp. 50–54.

[6] Statements made by Arthur Levitt, Chairman of the Securities and Exchange Commission, in a speech entitled, "The Numbers Game," delivered at the New York University Center for Law and Business, September 28, 1998.

[7] D. Bank, "Informix Says Accounting Problems Were More Serious Than First Disclosed," *Wall Street Journal* (September 23, 1997); T. O'Brien, "KnowledgeWare Accounting Practices Are Questioned," *Wall Street Journal* (September 7, 1994); M. Maremont, "Anatomy of a Fraud: How Kurzweil's Straight-Arrow CEO Went Awry," *Business Week* (September 16, 1996), pp. 90–93; S. Lipin, "How Telxon Corp. Came to Restate Earnings," *Wall Street Journal* (December 23, 1998); J. Laing, "Dangerous Games: Did 'Chainsaw Al' Dunlap Manufacture Sunbeam's Earnings Last Year?" *Barron's Online* (June 8, 1998), pp. 1–8; E. Nelson and J. Lublin, "Whistle-Blowers Set Off Cendant Probe," *Wall Street Journal* (August 13, 1998).

[8] D. Burgstahler and I. Dichev, "Earnings Management to Avoid Earnings Decreases and Losses," *Journal of Accounting and Economics* (December 1997), pp. 99–126; F. Degeorge, J. Patel, and R. Zeckhauser, "Earnings Management to Exceed Thresholds," *Journal of Business* (January, 1999), pp. 1–33; P. Dechow, S. Richardson, and A. Tuna, "Are Benchmark Beaters Doing Anything Wrong?" Working Paper, University of Michigan Business School, April 2000.

accounting "tricks" (described more fully below) to artificially inflate earnings. Results from a recent research study suggest that artificially inflating earnings is a common occurrence, especially for firms that would otherwise report small losses.[9] Figure 3.1(a) shows a frequency distribution of annual reported earnings for a large number of firms over a 20-year period. The horizontal axis represents groupings of individual firms' reported earnings stated as a percentage of their beginning-of-year market value of equity. The interval width of each grouping (that is, the interval width for each bar on the graph) is 0.5% or half of one percent. Thus, the grouping labeled −1 includes firms whose earnings stated as a percentage of beginning-of-year market value of equity falls in the range from −0.5% to just less than the negative side of 0.00%. Grouping 0 contains values from 0.00% to just less than +0.5% while grouping +1 contains values from +0.5% to just less than 1.0%. The vertical axis measures the number of firms whose reported earnings fall into the various categories.

> Let's use a number example for clarity. Assume Hong Company reports 2005 earnings of $500,000 and the market value of its equity on January 1, 2005 was $62,500,000. Thus, $500,000 ÷ $62,500,000 = .008 or .8%. Since .8% is within the interval of .5% to 1.0%, Hong Company would appear in interval +1.

*Earnings intervals are based on annual net income stated as a percentage of beginning of year market value of equity. The interval width is 0.5% (one half percent), e.g., interval −1 includes values from −0.5% to just less than 0.0%, while interval +1 includes values from +0.5% to just less than +1.0%.

Panel (a)

Figure 3.1(a) DISTRIBUTION OF ANNUAL NET INCOME

Source: P. Dechow, S. Richardson, and A. Tuna (see footnote 8).

The striking feature of this graph is the discontinuity in the number of firms reporting slightly negative earnings versus slightly positive earnings. Substantially fewer firms fall just below zero (grouping −1) while a substantially higher number of firms report earnings at or just above zero (groupings 0 and +1). What appears to be happening is that managers of firms that would otherwise report small losses (group −1) are finding ways to prop up earnings in order to move the firm's reported profits into the group 0 or group 1 range (that is, slightly positive range). One way of doing so, even in troubled times, is to exploit the flexibility in GAAP or to resort to a variety of accounting gimmicks to push earnings into the positive range.

As noted above, investors often penalize companies that fail to meet analysts' earnings expectations. Figure 3.1(b) provides indirect evidence on the strong incentive managers have to meet or beat analysts' earnings estimates. This graph shows the distribution of analysts' annual earnings per share (EPS) forecast errors—that is, actual EPS minus analysts' consensus EPS estimate. The interval width of each bar is one cent. Thus, forecast error bar labeled −1 cent (+1 cent) reflects the number of firm-years where actual earnings per share falls below (above) the analysts' consensus forecasts by 1 cent. Note the large number of observations clustered in the

> The analysts' consensus EPS estimates come from I/B/E/S. This acronym stands for Institutional Brokers Estimate System and provides institutional analyst earnings per share forecasts (both annual and quarterly) for over 18,000 companies in over 50 countries.

---

[9] Dechow et al., ibid.

"For years, Wall Street has known that companies manage earnings. Academic studies have found that actual earnings do not fall randomly around the consensus estimate. Instead, they tend to come in at or above the forecast. Some companies, like General Electric, almost always seem to beat estimates by a penny or two a share, no matter what the economic conditions. . . . Managements try to give investors what they want, and companies whose earnings are predictable are prized on Wall Street, which does not like unhappy surprises." A. Berenson, "Tweaking Numbers to Meet Goals Comes Back to Haunt Executives," *New York Times* (June 29, 2002).

zero forecast error interval where actual EPS equals the consensus estimate. Also, note the much smaller number of forecast errors that fall in the bar just below zero (−1 cent) compared to the number that fall just above zero (+1 cent). One explanation of this result is that some companies are managing earnings upward to "meet or beat" analysts' earnings projections.

*Consensus EPS forecasts of analysts as reported by Institutional Brokers Estimate System (IBES). The interval width is 1 cent, e.g., interval -1 includes all firm-years where actual EPS fell below the consensus forecast by 1 cent, while interval +1 includes cases where actual EPS exceeded the consensus forecast by 1 cent.

Panel (b)

Figure 3.1(b) DISTRIBUTION OF ANNUAL FORECAST ERRORS (IN CENTS) AS REPORTED BY I/B/E/S

Source: P. Dechow, S. Richardson, and A. Tuna (see footnote 8).

Popular Earnings Management Devices

What are some of the more popular techniques firms use to manage earnings? Former Chairman Levitt singles out five areas that the SEC finds particularly troublesome and pervasive.[10]

- *"Big Bath" restructuring charges:* The 1990s was the decade of **restructuring** in corporate America. To remain competitive and become more efficient, hundreds of companies closed plants, consolidated operations, reduced their labor force and sold off non-core business units. Once a decision to restructure is made, GAAP requires companies to estimate the future costs they expect to incur to carry out the restructuring—for such things as employee severance payments and plant closings. These estimated restructuring costs are then charged to an expense account with an offsetting credit to a liability account ("Restructuring reserve") in the current period. In an effort to "clean up" company balance sheets, managers have often taken excessive restructuring write-offs and overstated estimated charges for future expenditures. Examples of questionable items that the SEC has found in restructuring charges include services to be provided in some future period by lawyers, accountants and investment bankers; special bonuses for officers; and expenses for retraining and relocating people. Amazingly, some companies even took charges for training people not yet hired!

---

[10] Levitt, op. cit.

Why are companies tempted to overstate restructuring charges? The conventional wisdom is that investors look beyond one-time special charges and write-offs and, instead, value a company's stock based on sustainable operating earnings (see Chapter 6). So, many believe that taking "big bath" charges does not adversely affect stock price.[11] Moreover, these restructuring charges and associated liability reserves are sometimes reversed in future years when earnings fall short of targets, thereby providing a boost to the bottom line at opportune times.

- *Creative acquisition accounting and purchased R&D:* When one company buys another company and uses the **purchase method** of accounting for the combination (see Chapter 16), the buyer must allocate a portion of the purchase price to the acquired firm's identifiable net assets, including intangibles like in-process (incomplete) research and development (R&D) activities (that is, **in-process R&D**). *Statement of Financial Standards (SFAS) No. 2* states that "while future benefits from a particular research and development project may be foreseen, they generally cannot be measured with a reasonable degree of certainty."[12] Accordingly, values assigned to R&D projects that have no alternative future use are immediately expensed (that is, in the period in which the acquisition occurs). This treatment results in an economic asset (potential benefits from in-process R&D) that never appears on the balance sheet. If and when revenues from these R&D investments materialize, there are no offsetting charges to expense because the cost of the purchased R&D was written off in the period acquired. This is a classic example of mismatching revenues and expenses that gives the appearance of excessive profitability in later years.

The fair value of in-process R&D is difficult to measure and, therefore, difficult to verify. This creates considerable opportunity to manage post-acquisition earnings by allocating a disproportionate share of the initial purchase price to in-process R&D. This problem has been particularly acute for acquisitions of technology and software development companies where a major portion of the purchase price has been allocated to in-process R&D activities that are then immediately written off.

- *Miscellaneous "cookie jar reserves":* Accrual accounting allows companies to estimate and accrue for obligations that will be paid in *future periods* as a result of transactions or events in the *current period*. Similar reserves are allowed for estimated declines in asset values. Examples include provisions for bad debts and loan losses, warranty costs, sales returns, and reserves for various future expenditures related to corporate restructuring. Some companies use unrealistic assumptions to arrive at these estimated charges. They over-reserve in good times and cut back on estimated charges, or even reverse previous charges, in bad times. As a result, these "cookie jar reserves" become a convenient income smoothing device.

> A recent report prepared by outside investigators for the Board of Freddie Mac, a big mortgage financier, highlights how management used a variety of cookie jar reserves to artificially smooth earnings.
>
> "Freddie Mac, which for most of the last few years has faced the uncommon problem of having profits that substantially exceeded Wall Street forecasts, did not want to deviate too much from those expectations, the report said. So it used techniques to make its underlying business of insuring and buying mortgages seem less profitable and to create a reserve of earnings for later years. . . . Freddie Mac said it had understated its pretax profits by as much as $6.9 billion in 2002 and previous years as a result of serious accounting problems, and the company ousted its three top executives. The report offers more evidence of what regulators and many investors say is a culture of earnings management in corporate America. Like many other big publicly traded companies, Freddie Mac put a premium on meeting analysts' forecasts of its profits and providing consistent growth in reported earnings." [A. Berenson, "Report Says Freddie Mac Misled Investors," *New York Times* (July 24, 2003).]

---

[11] J. Elliott and D. Hanna, "Repeated Accounting Write-Offs and the Information Content of Earnings," *Journal of Accounting Research, Supplement* (1996), pp. 135–155.

[12] "Accounting for Research and Development Costs," *Statement of Financial Accounting Standards (SFAS) No. 2* (Stamford, CT: Financial Accounting Standards Board [FASB], 1974), para. 45.

- *Intentional errors deemed to be "immaterial" and intentional bias in estimates:* Materiality thresholds are another way of using financial reporting flexibility to inflate earnings. Sometimes, companies intentionally misapply GAAP—for example, capitalizing an expenditure that should be expensed. If this incorrect treatment is subsequently caught by the auditor, management might justify the error by arguing that the earnings effect is "immaterial" and, therefore, not worth correcting. The problem, of course, is that a series of these "immaterial" errors spread across several accounts can, in the aggregate, have a material effect on bottom-line earnings.

  Intentional misstatement of estimates is another area of abuse. Estimates abound in accrual accounting. Examples include estimated useful lives and salvage values for fixed assets, estimates of bad debts, and the amount of write-down for obsolete inventory. Management can often shade these estimates in one direction or the other to achieve a desired earnings target. As long as these estimates fall within "acceptable" ranges, the biased estimate is unlikely to draw attention from the external auditor.

- *Premature or aggressive revenue recognition:* Another common abuse is to recognize revenues before they have been "earned" (the critical event criterion) or become "realized" (the measurability criterion). This important earnings management device is discussed in the next section.

Revenue Recognition Abuses   The SEC says that revenue is earned (critical event) and is realized or realizable (measurability)—and, therefore, can be recognized—when all of the following criteria are met:

1. Persuasive evidence of an exchange arrangement exists,
2. Delivery has occurred or services have been rendered,
3. The seller's price to the buyer is fixed or determinable, and
4. Collectibility is reasonably assured.

The following scenarios taken from *SEC Staff Accounting Bulletin (SAB) No. 104* illustrate some troublesome areas of revenue recognition as well as the SEC's recommendation regarding the appropriate treatment.[13]

> "Arrangement" means there is a final understanding between the parties as to the specific nature and terms of the agreed-upon transaction.

- *Scenario 1—Goods shipped on consignment:* A software manufacturer (seller) ships 100,000 copies of a new video game to distributors, charging $50 per copy. Under terms of the signed agreement, distributors have the right (a) to return unsold copies of the video game, and (b) not to pay the seller until they resell the product to final customers through their retail outlets. The software manufacturer wants to recognize $5,000,000 of revenue upon delivery of the video games to the distributors. Can the company do this?

  SEC interpretive response: No revenue can be recognized on delivery. The reason is the seller retains the risks and rewards of ownership of the product. Title does not pass to the distributor when the goods are shipped. Also, under criterion 4 above, there is considerable uncertainty as to ultimate collectibility of the sales price on the goods shipped.

- *Scenario 2—Sales with delayed delivery:* Prior to the close of its September 30 fiscal quarter, a manufacturer (seller) completes production of 50,000 specialized gas valves. The valves sell for $60 each and were ordered by customers that assemble and sell gas fireplaces. The customers are unable to take delivery by September 30 for reasons that include: (1) lack of available storage space, (2) having ample inventory on hand to cover production for the next month, and (3) delayed production schedules. The seller segregates the valves awaiting shipment from other unsold products in its own warehouse and wishes to recognize $3,000,000 of revenue in the current quarter from these goods produced, but not shipped.

  SEC interpretive response: Without evidence of an exchange being spelled out in the sales agreement (criterion 1), the seller cannot recognize revenue until delivery has taken

---

[13] "Revenue Recognition," *Staff Accounting Bulletin No. 104* (Washington, DC: Securities and Exchange Commission, December 17, 2003).

place (criterion 2). Generally, delivery is *not* considered to have occurred unless the customer (a) takes title, and (b) assumes the risks and rewards of ownership of the products. Typically, these conditions are met when a product is received at the customer's place of business or when the product is shipped to the customer and the customer assumes responsibility for the product once it leaves the seller's premises. If the buyer requests in the sales agreement that the transaction be on a "bill and hold" basis, and has a substantial business purpose for doing so, then the seller may recognize revenue when the production of the goods is complete.

- *Scenario 3—Goods sold on layaway:* Company R, a retailer, offers layaway sales to its customers. Company R collects an initial cash deposit from the customer but retains the merchandise and sets it aside in its inventory. Although a date may be specified within which the customer must finalize the purchase, Company R does not require the customer to sign a fixed payment agreement. The merchandise is not released to the customer until full payment is received. Company R wants to recognize revenue equal to a pro-rata portion of the merchandise sales price as cash is collected.

   SEC interpretive response: Company R should postpone recognizing revenue until merchandise is delivered to the customer (criterion 2, delivery, has not occurred). Until then, the cash received to date should be recognized as a liability such as "Deposits from layaway customers." Because Company R retains the risks of ownership, receives only deposits, and does not have an enforceable right to the remainder of the purchase price, it is not entitled to recognize revenue until the sales price is received in full.

- *Scenario 4—Nonrefundable up-front fees:* Increasingly, service providers negotiate agreements with customers that require the customer to pay a nonrefundable up-front "initiation" or service "activation" fee. For example, companies that provide telecommunications services typically charge each new customer a nonrefundable activation fee. Once enrolled for service, customers then pay monthly usage fees that just cover the company's operating costs. The costs to activate the telecommunications service are minimal. Thus, the up-front fee customers pay more than covers these costs. The key question here is when should revenue from nonrefundable up-front activation fees be recognized?

   SEC interpretive response: Unless the up-front fee is in exchange for products delivered or services performed that represent the culmination of a separate earnings process, deferral of revenue is appropriate because service has not been rendered (criterion 2, delivery). In such circumstances the up-front fees, even if nonrefundable, are deemed to be earned as the services are delivered over the full term of the service agreement. This means that the up-front fees should be deferred and recognized pro-rata over the periods when services are provided because that's when the fees are earned.

- *Scenario 5—Gross versus net basis for Internet resellers:* Another troublesome area is the method used to record sales by certain Internet companies that simply act as an agent or broker in a transaction. For example, assume Dot.com Company operates an Internet site from which it sells airline tickets. Customers place orders by selecting a specific flight from Dot.com's Web site and providing a credit card number for payment. Dot.com receives the order and credit card authorization and passes this information along to the airline. The airline sends the tickets directly to the customer. Dot.com does not take title to the tickets and, therefore, has no ownership risk or other responsibility for the tickets. The airline is fully responsible for all returned tickets and disputed credit card charges. (So, Dot.com is just an agent or broker that facilitates the transaction between the customer and the airline.) The average ticket price is $500 of which Dot.com receives a $25 commission. In the event a credit card sale is rejected, Dot.com loses its $25 commission on sale. Because the management of Dot.com believes that revenue growth is what drives its share price, it seeks to report the revenue from this transaction on a "gross" basis at $500, along with cost of sales of $475.

   SEC interpretive response: Dot.com should report the revenue from this transaction on a "net" basis—$25 as commission revenue and $0 for cost of sales. In determining whether revenue should be reported gross (with separate display of cost of sales) or on a net basis, the SEC stipulates that the following factors be considered:

1. Is Dot.com acting as a principal or as an agent/broker in the transaction?
2. Does Dot.com take title to the ticket?
3. Does Dot.com assume the risks of ownership such as possible losses from bad debts or returns?

If Dot.com acts as a principal in the transaction, takes title to the tickets or assumes the ownership risks, then the gross method is deemed appropriate. Otherwise, the net method must be used.

- *Scenario 6—Capacity Swaps:* Over the past decade, revenue growth has been a major factor that affects the value of telecommunications companies. In an effort to bolster quarter-over-quarter revenue growth and build capacity for future expected customer demand, several telecommunication companies entered into a series of **"capacity swap"** transactions in which access to each other's networks was exchanged. As an example, assume that on January 1, 2005 San Francisco Telecom agrees to exchange $150 million worth of capacity over its fiber optic network between San Francisco and Asia for $175 million of capacity on Boston Telecom's communications network between New York and Europe. Company engineers estimate that current customer demand would have to increase fivefold (not a likely outcome for the foreseeable future) before the capacity being acquired would be needed. On signing the agreement, each company seeks to book revenue equal to the capacity rights being sold while booking the capacity bought as a capital expense that will be written off on a straight-line basis over the ten-year term of the swap agreement. As a consequence, San Francisco Telecom plans to book $150 million of revenue and $17.5 million per year ($175 million ÷ 10 years) of expenses resulting in increased pre-tax profits of $132.5 million in the year the swap agreement is signed. Boston Telecom would book $175 million of revenue, $15 million of expenses and $160 million in pre-tax profits. Thus, both companies stand to report substantially higher revenues and profits in the current period despite the fact that none, or very little, of the capacity exchanged is likely to be used by paying customers in the current period.

  SEC interpretive response:[14] The SEC position is that rather than recognizing the entire amount of the swapped capacity as revenue up front when the contract is signed, revenues should be deferred and recognized over the term of the swap agreement as the capacity is brought on line and used by the acquiring firm's customers. Capacity acquired is to be charged against earnings over the life of the swap agreement as indicated above.

It is important to note that *SAB 101* was not meant to change GAAP. Instead, it is intended to close some loopholes and eliminate gray areas in how GAAP is being applied in practice. A recent survey of annual reports indicates that the SEC guidelines have diminished abuses.[15] However, aggressive revenue recognition still occurs. So analysts must be vigilant for firms that overstate true earnings performance by bending revenue recognition rules.

RECAP   The criteria for revenue and expense recognition are intended to provide general guidance for accrual accounting income determination. However, these general criteria leave ample room for judgment and interpretation that creates flexibility in GAAP. Analysts and investors must be alert for management's attempts to exploit this flexibility in ways that push the boundaries of acceptable revenue and expense recognition.

---

[14] This interpretative response was issued subsequent to *SAB 101* as part of enforcement actions brought against companies deemed to have violated GAAP. The SEC publishes details of major enforcement actions against firms with accounting irregularities in a series called Accounting and Auditing Enforcement Releases.

[15] P. McConnell, J. Pegg, and D. Zion, "Revenue Recognition 101," *Accounting Issues* (New York: Bear, Stearns & Co. Inc., March 10, 2000).

Accounting Errors, Earnings Restatements and Prior Period Adjustments

Accounting errors or irregularities[16] can occur for a variety of reasons. Sometimes they occur because of simple oversight. For example, a buyer may fail to include in its ending inventory the cost of merchandise in transit for which title transfers at the time goods are shipped by the seller (see Chapter 9). Errors can also occur because different parties disagree on how to account for a given transaction, resulting in misapplication of GAAP. For example, practicing accountants, looking at a given set of facts, can sometimes disagree on when the "critical event" and "measurability" conditions have been satisfied for revenue recognition. Finally, errors sometimes occur because management attempts to exploit the flexibility in GAAP or commits outright financial fraud to inflate earnings and overstate net assets. The Enron and Worldcom restatements in 2001 and 2002 that led to the largest corporate failures in U.S. history provide recent examples.

Several different parties are charged with the responsibility of discovering accounting errors and irregularities:

- The company's internal audit staff and audit committee of the board of directors are charged with the responsibility of evaluating internal controls, overseeing the preparation of the financial statements and ensuring that their content fully and accurately depicts the company's financial condition and results of operations. As part of their ongoing review of control systems and financial reporting process, the audit committee and the company's internal audit staff provide the first-line defense against accounting errors/irregularities.
- External auditors provide an additional safeguard in identifying and correcting accounting errors and irregularities. Although the company's management is responsible for the preparation and content of the published financial statements, the independent external auditor is charged with the responsibility of auditing the financial statements to ensure that they are fairly presented in all material respects in accordance with GAAP. As part of their interim review and year-end audit, the external auditor will occasionally uncover accounting errors and irregularities that require correction of current period results or restatement of prior period financial statements.
- As noted in Chapter 1, the Securities Act of 1933 and the Securities Exchange Act of 1934 require companies that sell securities in the United States to register with the SEC and make periodic financial filings with the Commission. As part of its oversight of the registration and filing process, the SEC staff reviews selected issuer's filings to ensure compliance with SEC accounting and disclosure requirements. Through this process, the SEC staff sometimes identifies accounting irregularities that require correction.

A recent report issued by the United States General Accounting Office (GAO) demonstrates a dramatic increase in the incidence of accounting irregularities leading to earnings restatements from 1997 through 2002.[17] Figure 3.2 summarizes the major findings from this study. Panel (a) shows that the number of restatements due to accounting errors and irregularities among firms listed on the AMEX, NYSE and Nasdaq exchanges rose from 92 in 1997 to a projected 250 restatements in 2002—an increase of nearly 270%. From January 1997 through June 2002, approximately 10 percent of all listed companies announced at least one restatement.

---

[16] Some characterize an accounting error as an unintentional mistake in applying GAAP, while an accounting irregularity is an accounting choice that is knowingly made by management that is subsequently determined to have gone beyond the boundaries of acceptable GAAP. In this section, we use the terms "accounting error" and "irregularity" interchangeably since they both have the same reporting consequence in terms of required restatements.

[17] "Financial Statement Restatements: Trends, Market Impacts, Regulatory Responses, and Remaining Challenges," Report to the Chairman, Committee on Banking, Housing, and Urban Affairs, U.S. Senate (Washington, DC: U.S. General Accounting Office, 2002).

Figure 3.2(a)

TOTAL NUMBER
OF RESTATEMENT
ANNOUNCEMENTS
IDENTIFIED, 1997–2002

Source: United States General
Accounting Office: *Financial State-
ment Restatements: Trends, Market
Impacts, Regulatory Responses,
and Remaining Challenges*
(October 2002).

Panel (a)

Worldcom provides a recent example of this type
of accounting irregularity. During 2001 and the
first quarter of 2002, Worldcom improperly capitalized over $3.8 billion of operating line costs.
After announcing this improper accounting treatment, Worldcom's market value plummeted
nearly $29 billion and the company was forced
into bankruptcy.

Panel (b) of Figure 3.2 summarizes the major reasons for the restatements. Revenue recognition irregularities constitute the most frequently
cited reason for restating—accounting for 38% of the 919 announced
restatements during the sample period. Restatements due to revenue
recognition irregularities include recognizing revenue sooner or later than
is allowed under GAAP, or recognizing questionable or fictitious revenue.
Cost or expense-related issues were the next most common reason for
restatement constituting nearly 16% of the restatements during the
1997–2002 period. This category includes improper recognition of costs
or expenses, improperly capitalizing as assets expenditures that should be expensed on the
income statement, and improper treatment of tax liabilities, income tax reserves and other tax-
related items. Other reasons for restatements include improper restructuring charges and asset
write-offs, improper accounting for acquisitions and mergers including under or overstatement
of gains/losses related to acquisitions, and improper valuations of in-process R&D at acquisition.

Figure 3.2(b)

REASONS FOR EARNINGS
RESTATEMENTS: JANUARY
1997–JUNE 2002

Source: United States General
Accounting Office: *Financial State-
ment Restatements: Trends, Market
Impacts, Regulatory Responses,
and Remaining Challenges*
(October 2002).

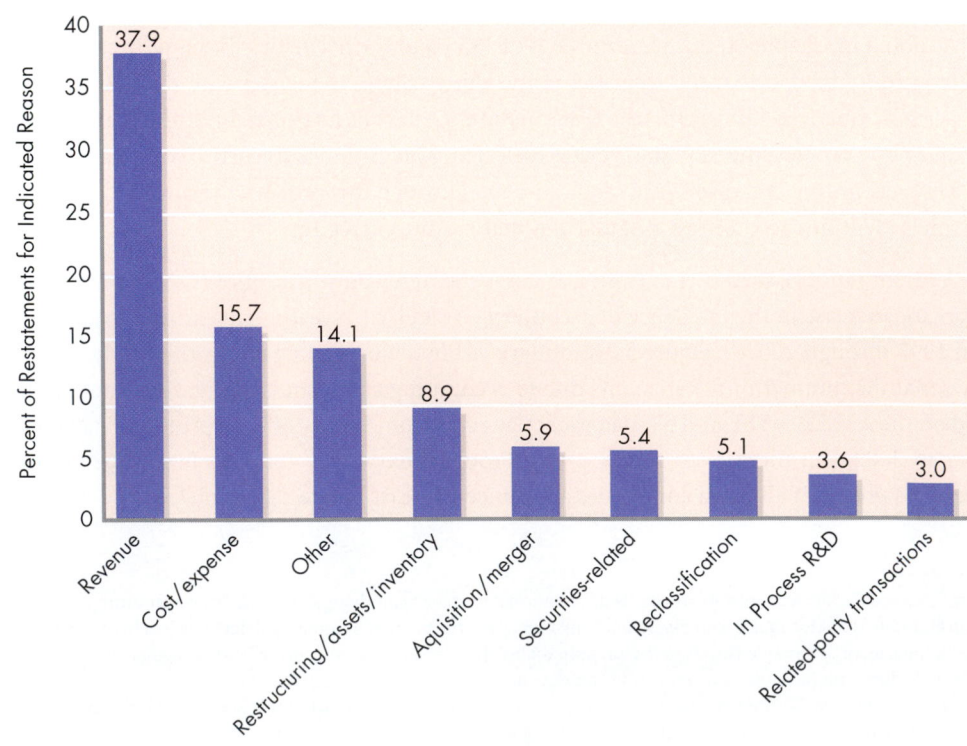

Panel (b)

Once discovered, accounting errors and irregularities must be corrected and disclosed. Material errors discovered after the year in which the error is made are corrected through a **prior period adjustment**. A prior period adjustment results in an addition to, or subtraction from, the company's beginning retained earnings balance (for the year the error is detected) and correction of related asset or liability balances. In addition to making the prior period adjustment to retained earnings, previous years' financial statements that are presented for comparative purposes are retroactively restated to reflect the specific accounts that are corrected and the impact of the error on current and prior period reported net income is disclosed in the footnotes to the financial statements.

A recent study finds that firms forced to restate earnings suffer a dramatic decline in stock prices.[18] Figure 3.3 plots the average cumulative abnormal daily stock returns of firms that announced earnings restatements from 1971 to 2000. Day 0 in the plot is the day that the restatement is announced in the financial press. The figure shows the returns from 120 days before to 120 days after the announcement. The striking feature of this graph is that restatement firms lose, on average, 25% of their market value over the time period examined, with most of the decline occurring in the narrow window surrounding the announcement of the restatement. Clearly, earnings restatements are important events that are viewed very negatively by the market. Firms that are caught manipulating their accounting numbers suffer a significant loss in market value, and law suits against firms' management and their auditors often ensue. That's why it's so important you understand the rules for proper revenue and expense recognition, and the various methods that are sometimes used by management to circumvent these rules in order to manipulate earnings.

Figure 3.3 CUMULATIVE ABNORMAL RETURNS FOR FIRMS RESTATING EARNINGS 1971–2000

Exhibit 3.7 provides an example of a restatement disclosure for Xerox Corporation from its 2001 revised 10-K report (issued on 6/28/02). Xerox restated financial statements for fiscal years 1997 through 2000 due to a series of accounting irregularities related primarily to

---

[18] S. Richardson, I. Tuna and M. Wu, "Predicting Earnings Management: The Case of Earnings Restatements," working paper, University of Pennsylvania, 2002.

accounting for sales-type leases for copy machines with bundled service and supplies agreements that were uncovered during an SEC investigation. Under sales-type lease arrangements, Xerox customers are charged a single monthly fee that covers the value of the copy machine, financing charges for the amount being financed, supplies, and servicing fees. The SEC claimed that by shifting assumptions about the value assigned to various lease components, Xerox improperly booked more income up front when the lease was signed instead of over time.

Panel (a) provides excerpts from Note 2 of Xerox's 2001 revised 10-K that describe the accounting treatments that were challenged by the SEC. Panel (b) shows the restatements to various revenue and expense accounts on Xerox's income statements for 2000 and 1999 and adjustments to retained earnings as of January 1, 1999. Finally, Panel (c) shows the adjustments to various balance sheet accounts at December 31, 2000.

Further details of this major restatement can be found in Case 12-5 of this book.

EXHIBIT 3.7	Xerox Corporation Excerpts from Revised 2001 10-K report

Panel (a)

Note 2: Restatement

On April 11, 2002, we reached a settlement with the Securities and Exchange Commission (SEC) relating to matters that had been under investigation by the SEC since June 2000. In connection with the settlement, we agreed to restate our financial statements as of and for the years ended December 31, 1997 through 2000 as well as undertake a review of our material internal controls and accounting policies. In addition, as a result of the re-audit of our 2000 and 1999 consolidated financial statements, additional adjustments were recorded. The restatement reflects adjustments which are corrections of errors made in the application of U.S. generally accepted accounting principles (GAAP) and includes (i) adjustments related to the application of the provisions of Statement of Financial Accounting Standards No. 13 "Accounting for Leases" (SFAS No. 13) and (ii) adjustments that arose as a result of other errors in the application of GAAP. The principal adjustments are discussed below.

Application of SFAS No. 13

Revenue allocations in bundled arrangements: We sell most of our products and services under bundled arrangements which contain multiple deliverable elements. These multiple element arrangements typically include separate equipment, service, supplies and financing components for which a customer pays a single fixed negotiated price on a monthly basis as well as a variable amount for page volumes in excess of stated minimums. The restatement primarily reflects adjustments related to the allocation of revenue and the resultant timing of revenue recognition for sales-type leases under bundled lease arrangements.

Source: Xerox Corporation 2001 Restated 10-K Report (Issued 6/28/02).

EXHIBIT 3.7	Xerox Restatements for Years Ended December 31, 1997 through December 31, 2000 (Condensed)

Panel (b)

The following table presents the effects of the aforementioned adjustments on pre-tax income (loss):

Increase (decrease) to pre-tax (loss) income:

	Years Ended December 31	
($ in millions)	2000	1999
Pre-tax (loss) income, previously reported	$(384)	$1,908
Revenue restatement adjustments (net)	48	(443)
Other restatement adjustments (net)	(31)	(177)
Pre-tax (loss) income, restated	$(367)	$1,288

These adjustments resulted in a cumulative net reduction of Common Shareholders' Equity of $1,692 as of December 31, 2000. The following table presents the impact of the restatement adjustments on Common Shareholders' Equity as of January 1, 1999:

Increase (decrease) in Common Shareholders' Equity:

Common Shareholders Equity balance, January 1, 1999, previously reported	$ 4,633
Net decrease in Common Shareholders' Equity from restatements	(1,607)
Common Shareholders Equity balance, January 1, 1999, restated	3,026

EXHIBIT 3.7	Xerox Corporation Balance Sheet Restatements as of December 31, 2000 (Condensed)

Panel (c)

The following schedule presents the impact of the restatements on selected balance sheet accounts:

($ in millions)	As Previously Reported	As Restated
Balance Sheet:		
Total current assets	12,298	11,472
Total non-current assets	17,177	16,781
Total Assets	$29,475	$28,253
Total current liabilities	6,268	6,544
Total non-current liabilities	18,477	18,679
Total Liabilities	24,745	25,223
Common Shareholders' Equity	3,493	1,801
Other Shareholders' Equity[1]	1,237	1,229
Total Liabilities and Equity	$29,475	$28,253

[1] Added by author. Not in original schedule provided by Xerox.

SUMMARY

- This chapter outlines the special accounting procedures used when revenue recognition doesn't occur at the point of sale.
- The "critical event" and "measurability" conditions for revenue recognition are typically satisfied at point of sale.
- There are circumstances—long-term construction contracts, production of natural resources, and agricultural commodities—where it is appropriate to recognize revenue prior to sale.
- Revenue recognition may also be delayed until after the sale—specifically, when cash is collected. The installment sales method or cost recovery method are used when there is considerable uncertainty about the collectibility of the sales price or where there are significant costs that will be incurred after the sale that are difficult to predict.
- Franchise sales, sales with right of return, and bundled sales (software sales) pose particularly challenging revenue recognition issues that statement users need to be aware of.
- The broad criteria for revenue and expense recognition leave room for considerable latitude and judgment. This flexibility in GAAP can sometimes be exploited by management to hide or misrepresent the underlying economic performance of a company.
- This chapter outlines some of the more common ways of managing earnings that have come under SEC scrutiny. Later chapters provide further examples of how earnings can be manipulated.
- Auditors and financial statement users must be aware of management's incentives to manage earnings, and the ways in which this is accomplished. Armed with this knowledge, you will be in a much better position to spot "accounting irregularities" and to avoid their unpleasant consequences.
- Once discovered, accounting errors or irregularities must be corrected and disclosed. Errors discovered after the year in which they occur are corrected through a prior period adjustment to retained earnings.

EXERCISES

E3 – 1

Long-term construction contract accounting

AICPA
ADAPTED

The following data pertain to Pell Company's construction jobs, which commenced during 2005:

	Project 1	Project 2
Contract price	$420,000	$300,000
Costs incurred during 2005	240,000	280,000
Estimated cost to complete	120,000	40,000
Billed to customers during 2005	150,000	270,000
Received from customers during 2005	90,000	250,000

Required:

1. If Pell used the completed-contract method, what amount of gross profit (loss) would be reported in its 2005 income statement?
2. If Pell used the percentage-of-completion method, what amount of gross profit (loss) would be reported in the 2005 income statement?

E3 – 2

Determining gross profit under percentage-of-completion

AICPA
ADAPTED

Haft Construction Company has consistently applied the percentage-of-completion method. On January 10, 2005, Haft began work on a $3,000,000 construction contract. At the inception date, the estimated cost of construction was $2,250,000. The following data relate to the progress of the contract:

Income recognized at 12/31/05	$ 300,000
Costs incurred 1/10/06 through 12/31/06	1,800,000
Estimated cost to complete at 12/31/06	600,000

Required:

In its income statement for the year ended December 31, 2006, what amount of gross profit should Haft report?

Lang Company uses the installment method of revenue recognition. The following data pertain to Lang's installment sales for the years ended December 31, 2005 and 2006:

	2005	2006
Installment receivables at year-end on 2005 sales	$60,000	$30,000
Installment receivables at year-end on 2006 sales	—	69,000
Installment sales	80,000	90,000
Cost of sales	40,000	60,000

E3 – 3

Determining gross profit using installment sales

AICPA
ADAPTED

Required:

What amount should Lang report as deferred gross profit in its December 31, 2005 and 2006 balance sheets?

Since there is no reasonable basis for estimating the degree of collectibility, Astor Company uses the installment method of revenue recognition for the following sales:

	2005	2004
Sales	$900,000	$600,000
Collections from:		
2004 sales	100,000	200,000
2005 sales	300,000	—
Accounts written off:		
2004 sales	150,000	50,000
2005 sales	50,000	—
Gross profit percentage	40%	30%

E3 – 4

Determining gross profit using the installment sales method

AICPA
ADAPTED

Required:

What amount should Astor report as deferred gross profit in its December 31, 2005 balance sheet for the 2004 and 2005 sales?

On January 2, 2005, Yardley Company sold a plant to Ivory Inc. for $1,500,000. On that date, the plant's carrying cost was $1,000,000. Ivory gave Yardley $300,000 cash and a $1,200,000 note, payable in four annual installments of $300,000 cash plus 12% interest. Ivory made the first principal and interest payment of $444,000 on December 31, 2005. Yardley uses the installment method of revenue recognition.

E3 – 5

Determining realized gross profit using the installment method

AICPA
ADAPTED

Required:

In its 2005 income statement, what amount of realized gross profit should Yardley report?

Taft Corporation, which began business on January 1, 2005, appropriately uses the installment sales method of accounting. The following data are available for December 31, 2005 and 2006:

	2005	2006
Balance of deferred gross profit on sales on account for:		
2005	$300,000	$120,000
2006		440,000
Gross profit on sales	30%	40%

E3 – 6

Determining installment accounts receivable

AICPA
ADAPTED

Required:

The installment accounts receivable balances at December 31, 2005 and 2006 would be how much?

Kul Company, which began operations on January 1, 2005, appropriately uses the installment sales method of accounting. The following information is available for 2005:

Installment accounts receivable, December 31, 2005	$400,000
Deferred gross profit, December 31, 2005 (before recognition of realized gross profit for 2005)	280,000
Gross profit on sales	40%

E3 – 7

Determining realized gross profit on installment sales

AICPA
ADAPTED

Required:

For the year ended December 31, 2005, cash collections and realized gross profit on installment sales should be how much?

E3 – 8

Determining deferred franchise fee revenue

AICPA
ADAPTED

On December 31, 2005, Rice, Inc. authorized Graf to operate as a franchise for an initial franchise fee of $150,000. Of this amount, $60,000 was received upon signing the agreement and the balance, represented by a note, is due in three annual payments of $30,000 each, beginning December 31, 2006. The present value on December 31, 2005 of the three annual payments appropriately discounted is $72,000. According to the agreement, the nonrefundable down payment represents a fair measure of the services already performed by Rice; however, substantial future services are required of Rice. Collectibility of the note is reasonably certain.

Required:

In Rice's December 31, 2005 balance sheet, unearned franchise fees from Graf's franchise should be reported as how much?

E3 – 9

Determining revenue recognized with advanced fees

AICPA
ADAPTED

For $50 a month, Rawl Company visits its customers' premises and performs insect control services. If customers experience problems between regularly scheduled visits, Rawl makes service calls at no additional charge. Instead of paying monthly, customers may pay an annual fee of $540 in advance.

Required:

For a customer who pays the annual fee in advance, Rawl should recognize the related revenue in what amounts and when?

E3 – 10

Determining deferred service contract revenue

AICPA
ADAPTED

Dunne Company sells equipment service contracts that cover a two-year period. The sales price of each contract is $600. Dunne's past experience is that, of the total dollars spent for repairs on service contracts, 40% is incurred evenly during the first contract year and 60% evenly during the second contract year. Dunne sold 1,000 contracts evenly throughout 2005.

Required:

In its December 31, 2005 balance sheet, what amount should Dunne report as deferred service contract revenue?

E3 – 11

Determining account balances under installment sales method

AICPA
ADAPTED

Bear Company, which began operations on January 2, 2005, appropriately uses the installment sales method of accounting. The following information is available for 2005:

Installment sales	$1,400,000
Realized gross profit on installment sales	240,000
Gross profit percentage on sales	40%

Required:

For the year ended December 31, 2005, what amounts should Bear report as accounts receivable and deferred gross profit?

E3 – 12

Determining gross profit and deferred gross profit under the installment method

AICPA
ADAPTED

Baker Company is a real estate developer that began operations on January 2, 2005. Baker appropriately uses the installment method of revenue recognition. Baker's sales are made on the basis of a 10% down payment, with the balance payable over 30 years. Baker's gross profit percentage is 40%. Relevant information for Baker's first two years of operations is as follows:

	2006	2005
Sales	$16,000,000	$14,000,000
Cash collections	2,020,000	1,400,000

Required:

1. At December 31, 2005, Baker's deferred gross profit was how much?
2. Baker's realized gross profit for 2006 was how much?

Each of Potter Pie Co.'s 21 new franchisees contracted to pay an initial franchise fee of $30,000. By December 31, 2005, each franchisee had paid a nonrefundable $10,000 fee and signed a note to pay $10,000 principal plus the market rate of interest on December 31, 2006, and December 31, 2007. Experience indicates that one franchisee will default on the additional payments. Services for the initial fee will be performed in 2006.

E3 – 13

Determining unearned franchise fees

AICPA
ADAPTED

Required:

What amount of net unearned franchise fees would Potter report at December 31, 2005?

Several of Fox, Inc.'s customers are having cash flow problems. Information pertaining to these customers for the year ended March 31, 2004 and 2005 follows:

	3/31/04	3/31/05
Sales	$10,000	$15,000
Cost of sales	8,000	9,000
Cash collections		
on 2004 sales	7,000	3,000
on 2005 sales	—	12,000

E3 – 14

Cost recovery method

AICPA
ADAPTED

Required:

If the cost recovery method is used, what amount would Fox report as gross profit from sales for the year ended March 31, 2005?

On August 19, 2005, the Lewisburg Steel Company sold building materials to Coyne Construction for $600,000, collecting $200,000 upon delivery of the materials. The $400,000 balance due—plus interest at a market rate on the unpaid balance—will be repaid as follows:

Payment Date	Payment Amount
August 19, 2006	$150,000
August 19, 2007	150,000
August 19, 2008	100,000

E3 – 15

Journal entries: Point-of-sale, cost recovery, and installment sales methods

The building materials cost Lewisburg Steel $390,000. The company uses a perpetual inventory system (that is, cost of the goods is subtracted from inventory when the sale occurs).

Required:

1. Prepare the required journal entries for 2005, 2006, and 2007 using point-of-sale revenue recognition (ignore interest revenue).
2. Repeat requirement 1 using the cost recovery method.
3. Repeat requirement 1 using the installment sales method.

On August 1, 2005, the Flintstone Company sold inventory to the Rubble Company for $400,000. The original cost of this inventory was $100,000. The sales contract stipulates that Rubble make a 10% down payment followed by four annual installments on each August 1, beginning August 1, 2006. Flintstone employs a perpetual inventory system under which inventory is decreased by the cost of merchandise sold at time of sale.

E3 – 16

Journal entries: point-of-sale, installment sales, and cost recovery methods

Required:

1. Prepare the necessary journal entries for 2005 and 2006 using point-of-sale revenue recognition.
2. Repeat requirement 1 using the installment sales method.
3. Repeat requirement 1 using the cost recovery method.
4. Typically, interest charges are also included in financing arrangements like this one between Flintstone and Rubble. How would the consideration of interest impact your answer to requirement 1?

On April 1, 2005, the Oversized Burrito Company entered into a 10-year franchise agreement with a group of individuals. The company receives an initial franchise fee of $300,000 and agrees to assist in the design of the building, help secure financing, and provide management advice over the first half of the franchise agreement. A down payment of 20% of the franchise fee is due on April 1, 2005. The remaining 80% is to be payable in eight equal installments beginning on April 1, 2006.

E3 – 17

Franchise sales: revenue recognition

Assume that services to be performed by Oversized Burrito between April 1, 2005 and August 15, 2005, the date that the franchise opened, are substantial and that the installment receivable is reasonably collectible. Also assume that substantial performance of the initial services has occurred as of August 15, 2005.

Required:

1. Prepare the necessary journal entries for Oversized Burrito for April 1, 2005 (ignore interest).
2. Prepare the necessary journal entries for August 15, 2005 (ignore interest).

E3 – 18

Franchise sales

The Healthy & Tasty Food Company entered into an agreement with a franchisee on July 1, 2005. The agreement specified that Healthy & Tasty receive an initial franchise fee of $150,000 (20% due at signing; the balance to be paid in equal annual installments plus interest at 9% of the unpaid balance beginning July 1, 2006). The franchise fee is comprised of (1) consideration for the right to operate the franchise, and (2) payment for services to be performed by Healthy & Tasty that include: site selection and building design, employee training, and management training. Substantial performance of these services is deemed to have occurred when the franchise opens for business in March 2006. Healthy & Tasty allocates the fee equally between the two elements.

Required:

1. Prepare the entry to record the signing of the franchise agreement and receipt of the payment due at that time.
2. Prepare any adjusting journal entries necessitated by this agreement at December 31, 2005.
3. Prepare the entry Healthy & Tasty should make when the franchise opens in March 2006.

E3 – 19

Revenue recognition: Bundled sales

Megabyte Software Developers shipped its tax return preparation product to a customer on September 15, 2005. In addition to the software, Megabyte's contract requires the company to provide: (1) training to the customer's accounting staff during October of 2005, (2) technical product support for one year starting October 1, 2005, and (3) an upgrade early in 2006 to the software that reflects last-minute changes in tax laws affecting tax returns for 2005. The customer paid the total contract price of $85,000 prior to product shipment. Megabyte would charge the following if these individual contract elements were sold separately:

	Fair Value
Tax return preparation software	$ 70,000
Training customer's staff	10,000
Customer support	15,000
Software upgrade	5,000
Total fair value	$100,000

Required:

1. Prepare a journal entry to record receipt of the cash payment.
2. Determine the amount of revenue to be recognized in 2005 and prepare the necessary journal entry.

E3 – 20

Installment sales and cost recovery methods

York's Rustic Furniture began operations on January 1, 2005. As a means of building its customer base, the company permitted customers—regardless of their credit history—to pay in installments when they made a major purchase. Installment sales amounted to $750,000 in 2005; these items cost York's Rustic Furniture $400,000. Given the questionable credit histories of many of York's customers, and York's inability to use past history to estimate collection rates, the company adopted the cost recovery method and accordingly recognized $75,000 in gross profit.

Required:

1. How much cash did the company collect on installment sales in 2005?
2. Assume that York's Rustic Furniture had instead used the installment sales method. What amount of gross profit would they have deferred in 2005?

Terry, Inc. is a calendar year corporation whose financial statements for 2003 and 2004 included errors as follows:

Year	Ending Inventory	Depreciation Expense
2003	$15,000 overstated	$12,500 overstated
2004	5,000 understated	4,000 understated

Assume that purchases were recorded correctly and that no correcting entries were made at December 31, 2003 or at December 31, 2004.

Required:

1. Ignoring income taxes, what amount should Terry report as a prior period adjustment to the beginning retained earnings in its statement of retained earnings at January 1, 2005?
2. Give the journal entries that Terry would make in 2005 to correct the errors.

Tack, Inc. reported a retained earnings balance of $150,000 at December 31, 2004. In June 2005, Tack's internal audit staff discovered two errors that were made in preparing the 2004 financial statements that are considered material:

1. Merchandise costing $40,000 was mistakenly omitted from the 2004 ending inventory.
2. Equipment purchased on July 1, 2004 for $70,000 was mistakenly charged to a repairs expense account. The equipment should have been capitalized and depreciated using straight-line depreciation, a 10-year useful life, and $10,000 salvage value.

Required:

1. What amount should Tack report as a prior period adjustment to beginning retained earnings at January 1, 2005? (Ignore taxes)
2. Give the journal entries that Tack would make in June 2005 to correct the errors made in 2004. Assume that depreciation for 2005 is made as a year-end adjusting entry. (Ignore taxes)

Krafty Kris, Inc. discovered the following errors after the 2005 financial statements were issued:

1. A major supplier shipped inventory valued at $8,550 to Krafty Kris, Inc. on consignment. This merchandise was mistakenly included in the inventory taken by Krafty Kris on December 31, 2004. (Goods shipped on consignment are the property of the consignor and should be included in its inventory.)
2. Krafty Kris renewed its liability insurance policy on October 1, 2004, paying a $36,000 premium and debiting "insurance expense." No further entries have been made. The premium purchased insurance coverage for a period of 36 months.
3. "Repair expense" was debited at the time equipment was purchased for $100,000 on January 8, 2005. The equipment has a life of five years; its salvage value is considered immaterial. Krafty uses straight-line depreciation method.

Required:

1. Prepare journal entries to correct these errors. Ignore income taxes.
2. Assuming that these errors remain uncorrected, explain their effects on the 2006 financial statements issued by Krafty Kris, Inc.

PROBLEMS/DISCUSSION QUESTIONS

Ms. Fuji started a business on January 1, 2005. Key operating statistics for 2005 were as follows:

Beginning inventory	0
Number of units produced	20,000
Number of units sold (delivery basis)	16,000
Number of units sold for which cash has been received by December 31, 2005	14,000

Direct production costs were $12 per unit. There were no fixed costs or selling/delivery expenses. The selling price per unit was $16.00.

On January 1, 2006, Ms. Fuji decided to liquidate the business. She sold the remaining inventory at $13.00 per unit for cash. By January 15, 2006, she collected the amount due from customers for sales made during 2005.

Required:

Based on the above information, compute the net income of Ms. Fuji for the years 2005 and 2006 under:
1. Production basis
2. Sales (or delivery) basis
3. Cash collection basis.

P3 – 2

Income determination under alternative bases of revenue recognition

Agri Pro, a farm corporation, produced 15,000 bushels of wheat in its first year of operations. During the year, Agri Pro sold 10,000 bushels of the grain produced for $2.40 per bushel and collected three-fourths of the selling price on the grain sold; the balance is to be collected in equal amounts during each of the two following years. The local grain elevator is quoting a year-end market price of $3.00 per bushel. Additional data for the first year are as follows:

Depreciation on equipment	$ 3,000
Other production costs (cash)—per bushel	0.50
Miscellaneous administrative costs (cash)	4,000
Selling and delivery costs (incurred and paid at time of sale), per bushel	0.10
Dividends paid to stockholders during year	10,000
Interest on borrowed money (1/2 paid in cash)	5,000

Agri Pro is enthusiastic about the accountant's concept of matching product costs with revenues.

Required:

Compute net income under each of the methods indicated below and determine the carrying (book) value of inventory and accounts receivable at the end of the first year of operation for each of these methods.
1. Recognize revenue when production is complete.
2. Recognize revenue at point of sale.
3. Recognize revenue on an installment (cash collection) basis.

P3 – 3

Determining pre-tax income and accounts receivable using the installment method

Lowery, Inc., an Arizona land speculator, started business on May 1, 2005. Lowery sold 700 acres of desert sand to a local developer for $960 an acre. Lowery is paid 60% of the selling price at the time the contract is signed, with the balance due in 24 months; however, collection is not assured. Lowery's property acquisition costs were $350 per acre and property taxes of $75,000 were paid during the year.

Required:

Compute Lowery's 2005 pre-tax income and determine its accounts receivable balance at December 31, 2005 using the installment sales method.

P3 – 4

Determining pre-tax income, inventory carrying value, and accounts receivable under sales and production basis

Howe, Inc., a Texas crude oil producer, started business on May 1, 2005. Howe sells all its production, f.o.b. shipping point, to a single customer at the current spot price for West Texas crude. The customer pays Howe 60% of the selling price at the time of delivery with the remaining to be paid in 10 months. Throughout 2005 the spot market price for the oil was $28.00 per barrel; however, on December 31, 2005 the market price jumped to $31.00 per barrel, where it is expected to remain. Howe's direct production costs are $12.00 per barrel, drilling equipment depreciation expense totaled $180,000 for the eight-month period ending December 31, and property taxes of $75,000 were paid during the year. Howe produced 30,000 barrels of oil of which 6,000 barrels were included in January 1, 2006 opening inventory.

Required:

Compute Howe's 2005 pre-tax income and determine its inventory carrying value and accounts receivable balance at December 31, 2005 under the following:
1. Production basis
2. Sales (completed transaction) basis
3. Installment (cash collection) basis

In 2005, Long Construction began work under a three-year contract. The contract price is $800,000. Long uses the percentage-of-completion method for financial accounting purposes. The income to be recognized each year is based on the proportion of cost incurred to total estimated costs for completing the contract. The financial-statement presentations relating to this contract at December 31, 2005 follow:

P3 – 5

Percentage of completion accounting

Balance Sheet

Accounts receivable—construction contract billings	$15,000
Construction in progress	$50,000
Less contract billings	(47,000)
Construction in progress less billings	$ 3,000

Income Statement

Income (before tax) on the contract recognized in 2001	$10,000

Required:

1. How much cash was collected in 2005 on this contract?
2. What was the initial estimated total cost on this project?
3. What is the estimated total income (before tax) on this contract?

MSK Construction Company contracted to construct a factory building for $525,000. Construction started during 2005 and was completed in 2006. Information relating to the contract is provided below:

P3 – 6

Long-term construction contract accounting

	2005	2006
Costs incurred during the year	$290,000	$150,000
Estimated additional cost to complete	145,000	—
Billings during the year	260,000	265,000
Cash collections during the year	240,000	285,000

Required:

Record the above transactions in the books of MSK Construction Company under the completed-contract and the percentage-of-completion methods. Determine amounts that will be reported on the balance sheet at the end of 2005.

The Maple Corporation sells farm machinery on the installment plan. On July 1, 2005, Maple entered into an installment sale contract with Agriculture, Inc., for an eight-year period. Equal annual payments under the installment sale are $100,000 and are due on July 1. The first payment was made on July 1, 2005. Additional information is as follows:

P3 – 7

Determining income under installment sales method

AICPA ADAPTED

- The amount that would be realized on an outright sale of similar farm machinery is $556,000.
- The cost of the farm machinery sold to Agriculture is $417,000.
- The finance charges relating to the installment period are $244,000 based on a stated interest rate of 12%, which is appropriate.
- Circumstances are such that the collection of the installments due under the contract is reasonably assured.

Required:

What income or loss before income taxes should Maple record for the year ended December 31, 2005 as a result of the above transaction? Show supporting computations in good form.

Englewood Marine is a builder of 30-foot fiberglass fishing boats. The boats are marketed through a network of third-party dealers on a consignment basis. The consignment agreement stipulates that Englewood retains title to the boats until final sale to the customer. Dealers can return unsold boats to Englewood by paying shipping expenses and a financing fee for the time held. Each boat's cost to dealers is fixed at $28,000. Englewood's gross profit margin per boat is 30%.

P3 – 8

Revenue recognition for goods on consignment

Englewood shipped 41 boats to dealers during the six months ending October 31. Shipments were:

Monthly Boat Shipments to Dealers

May—3	August—9
June—6	September—8
July—8	October—7

Dealers had three Englewood boats on hand for the quarter ended July 31 and two boats on hand at October 31.

Required:

1. Prepare a schedule showing Englewood Marine's revenues, cost of goods sold and gross profit for the quarters ending July 31 and October 31.
2. Indicate how Englewood Marine would report the unsold boats and for how much at July 31 and October 31.

P3 – 9

Revenue recognition based on delivery performance

Composite, Inc. is a manufacturer of modular homes. Due to lack of storage space for raw material inventories, Composite implemented a just-in-time inventory process in early 2003. Composite contracts with qualified vendors to be sole suppliers for a given raw material. In return, the vendors guarantee performance in accordance with Composite's purchase order.

On Friday, November 2, 2005, Composite placed a purchase order with Mogul Chemical Company for plastic resins. Composite's purchase order specifically states that all material is shipped so that Composite takes title to the goods when they are received. Delivery is to be made at 6:00 A.M. on the designated delivery date. Designated delivery date, pounds, and selling price per pound are:

Delivery Date	Pounds	Selling Price per Pound
Friday, November 30, 2005	75,000	$1.00
Friday, December 7, 2005	80,000	1.00
Friday, December 14, 2005	60,000	1.10
Friday, December 21, 2005	50,000	1.20
Friday, January 4, 2006	50,000	1.20

In December, Mogul Chemical was experiencing a slowdown in sales and decided to produce Composite's January 2006 order over the Christmas holidays. After completing the production on December 29, the material was promptly loaded on a staged trailer, which was immediately locked and sealed. An invoice and a bill of lading were prepared. The invoice was then sent to Composite on a "bill and hold" basis.

Upon receiving the invoice, Composite contacted Mogul and was told that the material was invoiced because Mogul wanted to include the sale in the quarter ended December 31, 2005. However, actual delivery would take place according to the purchase order terms. Composite accepted the explanation.

Required:

1. Determine the sales revenue that Mogul should recognize on transactions with Composite for the quarter ended December 31, 2005.
2. What would Mogul's justification be for including the production on December 29 in its December sales?
3. Should Mogul include the December 29 production in its December sales? Why or why not?

P3 – 10

Revenue recognition on layaways

DW Hooks is a customer-oriented retailer of high-definition televisions and other similar electronic and computer equipment. Hooks will accept layaway sales provided the customer makes a minimum down payment of 20% of the retail price and pays the balance off within 90 days. After the customer makes the initial deposit, Hooks transfers the merchandise from a "Retail Inventory" account to a "Layaway—Merchandise Inventory" account. Inventory is valued at approximately 80% of the retail-selling price. When the layaway sale is paid in full, Hooks will deliver the merchandise to the customer.

At January 31, 2005 Hooks had $72,000 of merchandise on layaway, for which customers have made cash deposits totaling $55,000. For the quarter ending April 30, 2005 Hooks had the following layaway transactions:

Month	Amounts Added to Layaway Inventory	Deposits Made During Month	Deliveries	
			Cost	Retail
February	$49,000	$45,000	$24,000	$30,000
March	50,000	67,000	56,000	70,000
April	40,000	51,000	48,000	60,000

Required:

1. Prepare the journal entries required to record these transactions.
2. Prepare a schedule showing sales revenue earned for the period, and reconcile the balances in lay-away and customer deposits at January 31, 2005 to April 30, 2005.
3. How should Hook report the customer deposits in its financial statements?

On July 1, 2005, the Quincy Company sold a piece of industrial equipment to the Tana Company for $200,000. The equipment cost Quincy $80,000 to manufacture. Per the sales agreement, Tana made a down payment of 20% and paid the remaining balance in four equal quarterly installments, plus 10% on the unpaid balance, starting October 1, 2005.

P3 – 11

Alternative bases of revenue recognition

Required:

1. Identify and explain three alternative methods for revenue and cost recognition available to Quincy in the above scenario.
2. Calculate the amount of gross profit recognized in 2005 under each of the alternatives identified in requirement 1.
3. Elaborate on what circumstances would have to exist for each alternative to be employed.

Founded in 1989, Brio Software, Inc. helps Global 3000 companies improve business performance by creating new value from existing information systems and, ultimately, aligning everyone in the enter-prise with key corporate goals. Brio's business intelligence software lets companies access, analyze, and share information, offering users relevant, accurate, and timely insight into the variables that impact their business. With this insight, companies can make superior business decisions.

P3 – 12

Bundled services

The following information appears in Brio Software's March 31, 2003 10-K report regarding its revenue recognition policies:

Revenue Recognition

Brio derives revenues from two sources, perpetual license fees and services. Services include soft-ware maintenance and support, training and consulting and system implementation services. Maintenance and support consists of technical support and software upgrades and enhancements. Significant management judgments and estimates are made and used to determine the revenue rec-ognized in any accounting period. Material differences may result in the amount and timing of Brio's revenue for any period if different conditions were to prevail.

Brio applies the provisions of Statement of Position (SOP) 97-2, "Software Revenue Recogni-tion," as amended by SOP 98-9 "Modification of SOP 97-2, Software Revenue Recognition, With Respect to Certain Transactions" and related technical practice aids to all transactions involving the sale of software products.

Brio recognizes product revenue when persuasive evidence of an arrangement exists, the prod-uct has been delivered, the fee is fixed or determinable and collection of the resulting receivable is probable. In software arrangements that include rights to multiple elements, such as software prod-ucts and services, Brio uses the residual method under which revenue is allocated to the undelivered elements based on vendor-specific objective evidence (VSOE) of the fair value of such undelivered elements. VSOE of the undelivered elements is determined based on the price charged when such ele-ments are sold separately. The residual amount of revenue is allocated to the delivered elements and recognized as revenue. Such undelivered elements in these arrangements typically consist of services.

Brio uses a purchase order or a signed contract as persuasive evidence of an arrangement for sales of software, maintenance renewals and training. Sales through Brio's value added resellers, private label partners, resellers, system integrators and distributors (collectively "resellers") are evi-denced by a master agreement governing the relationship together with binding purchase orders on a transaction-by-transaction basis. Brio uses a signed statement of work to evidence an arrangement for consulting and system implementation services.

Software is delivered to customers electronically or on a CD-ROM. Brio assesses whether the fee is fixed or determinable based on the payment terms associated with the transaction. Brio's standard payment terms are generally less than 90 days. In instances where payments are subject to extended payment terms, revenue is deferred until payments become due, which is generally when the payment is received. Brio assesses collectibility based on a number of factors, including the customer's past payment history and its current creditworthiness. If Brio determines that collection of a fee is not probable, Brio defers the revenue and recognizes it at the time collection becomes probable, which is generally upon receipt of cash payment. If an acceptance period is other than in accordance with standard user documentation, revenue is recognized upon the earlier of customer acceptance or the expiration of the acceptance period.

When licenses are sold together with consulting and system implementation services, license fees are recognized upon shipment, provided that (1) the above criteria have been met, (2) payment of the license fees is not dependent upon the performance of the consulting and system implementation services, (3) the services are not essential to the functionality of the software and (4) VSOE exists for the undelivered elements. For arrangements that do not meet the above criteria, both the product license revenues and services revenues are recognized in accordance with the provisions of SOP 81-1, "Accounting for Performance of Construction Type and Certain Production Type Contracts." Brio accounts for the arrangements under the completed-contract method pursuant to SOP 81-1 as reliable estimates are typically not available for the costs and efforts necessary to complete the consulting and system implementation services.

The majority of Brio's consulting and system implementation services qualify for separate accounting. Brio uses VSOE of fair value for the services and maintenance to account for the arrangement using the residual method, regardless of any separate prices stated within the contract for each element. Brio's consulting and system implementation service contracts are bid either on a fixed-fee basis or on a time-and-materials basis. For a fixed-fee contract, Brio recognizes revenue using the completed-contract method. For time-and-materials contracts, Brio recognizes revenue as services are performed.

Maintenance and support revenue is recognized ratably over the term of the maintenance contract, which is typically one year. Training revenue is recognized when the training is provided.

Assume that Brio enters into a contract with a customer for deliverable software and services as follows. The prices listed are those quoted in the contract.

Perpetual license fee	$650,000
Elements undelivered at contract signing:	
Technical support	120,000
Training	80,000
System implementation services	100,000
Software upgrades and enhancements	50,000
Total contract price	$1,000,000

The above contract elements, if purchased separately, would be priced as follows:

Perpetual license fee	$840,000
Elements undelivered at contract signing:	
Technical support	120,000
Training	72,000
System implementation services	108,000
Software upgrades and enhancements	60,000
Total contract price	$1,200,000

Required:

1. Following Brio's stated revenue recognition policies, how much revenue would be recognized on this contract?
2. Prepare the journal entry to record receipt of the signed contract and electronic delivery of the software. Assume the sale conforms to Brio's normal billing terms and that collectibility is not an issue.
3. How much revenue would Brio recognize on this contract if the various elements included in the contract were not sold separately?

Roxio, Inc. is a leading provider of digital media software and services for the consumer market. The company provides software that enables individuals to record digital content onto CDs and DVDs and offers photo and video editing products. Roxio's Form 10-K for the year ended March 31, 2003 reported the following information:

Roxio, Inc.

($ in 000s)	Selected Financial Data for the Years Ended March 31		
	2001	2002	2003
Net revenues	$121,908	$142,521	$120,408
Net income	3,570	2,349	(9,944)
Allowance for sales returns and certain sales incentives:			
Balance at beginning of period	2,186	4,602	5,492
Additions	8,351	16,286	18,333
Deductions	5,935	15,396	16,749
Balance at the end of period	4,602	5,492	7,076

BUSINESS RISKS:

We rely on distributors and retailers to sell our products. If our distributors attempt to reduce their levels of inventory or if they do not maintain sufficient levels to meet customer demand, our sales could be negatively impacted. If we reduce the prices of our products to our distributors, we may have to compensate them for the difference between the higher price they paid to buy their inventory and the new lower prices. In addition, we are exposed to the risk of product returns from distributors through their exercise of contractual return rights.

REVENUE RECOGNITION:

For software product sales to distributors, revenues are recognized upon product shipment to the distributors or receipt of the products by the distributor, depending on the shipping terms, provided that all fees are fixed or determinable, evidence of an arrangement exists and collectibility is probable. Our distributor arrangements provide distributors with certain product rotation rights. Additionally, we permit our distributors to return products in certain circumstances, generally during periods of product transition. End users additionally have the right to return their product within 30 days of the purchase. We establish allowances for expected product returns in accordance with *SFAS No. 48*, "Revenue Recognition When Right of Return Exists," and *SAB 101*. These allowances are recorded as a direct reduction of revenues and accounts receivable. Management applies significant judgment and relies on historical experience in establishing these allowances. If future return patterns differ from past return patterns, due to reduced demand for our product or other factors beyond our control, we may be required to increase these allowances in the future and may be required to reduce future revenues. If at any point in the future we become unable to estimate returns reliably, we could be required to defer recognizing revenues until the distributor notifies us that the product has been sold to an end user. We provide for estimated product returns and pricing adjustments in the period in which the revenues are recognized.

Required:

1. Re-create (in summary form) the journal entries Roxio made in the "Allowance for sales returns and certain sales incentives" account for fiscal years 2001–2003. Explain the rising balance in this account.
2. Are opportunities for "earnings management" present in Roxio's stated accounting policies for expected product returns? Is there any evidence in the data presented that Roxio's management has availed themselves of any of the opportunities you identify?
3. Determine Roxio's gross revenues for fiscal years 2001–2003.

Holman Electronics manufactures audio equipment, selling it through various distributors. Holman's days sales outstanding (Accounts receivable / average daily credit sales) figures increased steadily in 2005 and then spiked dramatically in 2006, peaking at 120 days in the second quarter. In the third quarter of 2006, Holman's days sales outstanding figure dropped to 90 days. Holman's chief financial officer engineered this drop by artificially reducing the amount of outstanding accounts receivable. Channel partners with large outstanding receivables were pressured into signing notes for those amounts. Once sales personnel secured the notes, the CFO directed a reclassification entry to the general ledger converting over $30 million in trade receivables into notes receivable, which are not included in the days sales outstanding calculation. This reclassification was not disclosed in the Form 10-Q that Holman filed for that quarter.

Required:

What might be the motive for the CFO's actions? Explain your answer.

Correction of errors and worksheet preparation

GWH Enterprises began operations in January 2003 to manufacturing a cleaning solution that promised to be more effective and less toxic than existing products. Family members, one of whom was delegated to be the office manager and bookkeeper, staffed the company. Although conscientious, the office manager lacked formal accounting training, which became apparent when the growing company was forced in March 2006 to hire a CPA as controller. Although ostensibly brought in to relieve some of the office manager's stress, management made it clear to the new controller that they had some concerns about the quality of information they were receiving. Accordingly, the controller made it a priority to review the records of prior years, looking for ways to improve the accounting system. From this review, the following errors were uncovered.

1. The office manager expensed rent on equipment and facilities when paid. Amounts paid in 2003, 2004, and 2005 that represent prepaid rent are $3,000, $3,500, and $4,600, respectively.
2. No adjusting entries were ever made to reflect accrued salaries. The amounts $7,000, $9,500 and $6,200 should have been accrued in each of the three prior years, respectively.
3. Errors occurred in the depreciation calculations that resulted in depreciation expense being understated by $2,500 in 2003, understated by $5,000 in 2004, and overstated by $4,000 in 2005.
4. In February 2006 some surplus production equipment was sold for $2,000 that originally had cost $7,000 and $6,000 in depreciation had correctly been taken on this equipment. The office manager made this entry to record the sale:

   To record sale of surplus equipment

DR Cash	$2,000	
DR Accumulated depreciation	5,000	
CR Equipment		$7,000

5. Utility expenses in the amount of $1,800 were incorrectly classified as selling expenses in 2005.

Required:

Complete the worksheet shown below to assist in preparing the correcting entry. (By way of example, the first required entry on the worksheet has been made.)

Error Corrections Worksheet

Description	2003	2004	2005	2006	Dr.	Cr.
	\<Effect on Income>				\<Accounts to be Adjusted>	
Reported income	$(18,000)	$27,000	$25,000	N/A		
1 Prepaid rent—2003 Prepaid rent—2004 Prepaid rent—2005	3,000	(3,000)				Counterbalancing error
2 Accrued wages—2003 Accrued wages—2004 Accrued wages—2005						
3 Depreciation						
4 Gain on machinery						
5 Classification						
Adjusted income	–	–	–			

In 2005, the new CEO of Watsontown Electric Supply grew concerned about the company's apparently deteriorating financial position. Wishing to make certain that the grim monthly reports he was receiving from the company's bookkeeper were accurate, the CEO engaged a CPA firm to examine the company's financial records. The CPA firm discovered the following facts during the course of the engagement, which was completed prior to any adjusting or closing entries being prepared for 2005.

P3 – 16

Correcting errors/Prior period adjustment

1. A new digital imaging system was acquired on January 5, 2004 at a cost of $5,000. Although this asset was expected to be in use for the next four years, the purchase was inadvertently charged to office expense. Per the company's accounting manual, office equipment of this type should be depreciated using the straight-line method with no salvage value assumed.

2. A used truck, purchased on November 18, 2005, was recorded with this entry:

    To record truck expenditure:

DR Vehicle expense	$18,000	
CR Cash		$18,000

    Management plans to use this truck for three years and then trade it on a new one. Salvage is estimated at $3,000. Watsontown Electric Supply has always used straight-line depreciation for fixed assets, recording a half-year of depreciation in the year the asset is acquired.

3. On July 1, 2005 the company rented a warehouse for three years. The lease agreement specified that each year's rent be paid in advance, so a check for the first year's rent in the amount of $18,000 was issued and recorded as an addition to the "buildings" account.

4. Late in 2004, Watsontown Electric Supply collected $23,500 from a customer in full payment of his account. The cash receipt was credited to revenue. Two months before the audit, Watsontown's bookkeeper was reviewing outstanding receivables and noticed the outstanding balance. Knowing the customer in question had recently died, she wrote off the account. Because Watsontown Electric Supply seldom has bad debts, the company uses the direct write-off method whereby it charges bad debts expense and credits accounts receivable when an account is deemed uncollectible.

5. A three-year property and casualty insurance policy was purchased in January 2004 for $30,000. The entire amount was recorded as an insurance expense at the time.

6. On October 1, 2004 Watsontown Electric Supply borrowed $100,000 from a local bank. The loan terms specified annual interest payments of $8,000 on the anniversary date of the loan. The first interest payment was made on October 1, 2005 and expensed in its entirety.

Required:

Prepare any journal entry necessary to correct each error as well as any year-end adjusting entry for 2005 related to the described situation. Ignore income tax effects.

CASES

Thomas Smith owns and operates a farm in Kansas. During 2005, he produced and harvested 40,000 bushels of wheat. Smith had no inventory of wheat at the start of the year. Immediately after harvesting the wheat in the late summer of 2005, Smith sold 30,000 bushels to a local grain elevator operator. As of December 31, 2005, Smith had received payment for 20,000 bushels. Additional information relating to the farm follows:

C3 – 1

Smith's Farm: Alternative bases of income determination

Price:	
Market price per bushel at the time of harvest and sale to the grain elevator operator	$ 3.60
Market price per bushel at December 31, 2005	3.60
Costs:	
Variable production costs per bushel	0.50
Delivery costs per bushel	0.20
Annual fixed cost of operating the farm that are unrelated to the volume of production	$25,000

Required:

1. Prepare a 2005 income statement for Smith's Farm under each of the following assumptions regarding what constitutes the "critical event" in the process of recognizing income:

   a. Assuming that production is the critical event
   b. Assuming that the sale is the critical event
   c. Assuming that cash collection is the critical event
   (For simplicity, treat the fixed operating costs as period—rather than product—costs.)

2. Determine the December 31, 2005 balances for wheat inventory and accounts receivable under each of the three income recognition methods in requirement 1.
3. Assume that the farm is left idle during 2006. Since there is no harvest, Smith's only transaction consists of an October 2006 sale of the 10,000 bushels in inventory at a price of $2.80 per bushel. Further assume that no fixed costs are incurred while the farm is idle.

   Compute 2006 income on both the sale and production basis. Discuss the causes for any profit or loss reported under each income determination alternative.

C3 – 2

London, Inc.: Determining gross profit under the percentage-of-completion method

AICPA
ADAPTED

London, Inc. began operation of its construction division on October 1, 2005 and entered into contracts for two separate projects. The Beta project contract price was $600,000 and provided for penalties of $10,000 per week for late completion. Although during 2006 the Beta project had been on schedule for timely completion, it was completed four weeks late in August 2007. The Gamma project's original contract price was $800,000. Change orders during 2007 added $40,000 to the original contract price. The following data pertains to the separate long-term construction projects in progress:

	Beta	Gamma
As of September 30, 2006:		
Costs incurred to date	$360,000	$410,000
Estimated costs to complete	40,000	410,000
Billings	315,000	440,000
Cash collections	275,000	365,000
As of September 30, 2007:		
Cost incurred to date	450,000	720,000
Estimated costs to complete	—	180,000
Billings	560,000	710,000
Cash collections	560,000	625,000

Additional Information:

London accounts for its long-term construction contracts using the percentage-of-completion method for financial reporting purposes and the completed-contract method for income tax purposes.

Required:

1. Prepare a schedule showing London's gross profit (loss) recognized for the years ended September 30, 2006 and 2007 under the percentage-of-completion method.
2. Prepare a schedule showing London's balances in the following accounts at September 30, 2006 under the percentage-of-completion method:

   • Accounts receivable
   • Costs and estimated earnings in excess of billings
   • (Billings in excess of costs and estimated earnings)

3. Determine how much income would be recognized if London, Inc. used the completed-contract method for the 2006 and 2007 fiscal years.

Stewart & Stevenson Services, Inc. manufactures motors and generators. The following is extracted from the Year 2 financial statements of Stewart & Stevenson Services, Inc.

C3 – 3

Stewart & Stevenson Services, Inc. (KR): Understanding accounts used for long-term construction contract accounting

Stewart & Stevenson Services, Inc.

	Year 2	Year 1
Balance Sheet Items		
Accounts receivable	$143,166	$121,030
Costs incurred on uncompleted contracts	190,670	70,766
Accrued profits	13,117	9,857
Cost incurred + accrued profits	203,787	80,623
Less: Customer progress payments	(164,078)	(55,258)
Cost in excess of billings (net)	$ 39,709	$ 25,365
Income Statement Items		
Sales revenue	$812,526	$686,363
Cost of sales	685,879	569,695
Gross margin	$126,647	$116,668
Gross margin rate	15.6%	17.0%

Assumption: All sales revenue are from long-term construction contracts.

Required:

1. Using the information provided above, reconstruct the following T-accounts, showing how the accounts changed from their beginning to ending balances in Year 2.

Stewart & Stevenson Services, Inc.

Construction in Process Inventory

Beginning balance $ 80,623	
Ending balance 203,787	

Billings on Contract (Progress Payments)

	$ 55,258 Beginning balance
	164,078 Ending balance

Accounts Receivable

Beginning balance $121,030	
Ending balance 143,166	

2. Compute sales revenue, cost of goods sold, and gross margin assuming the company was using the completed-contract method during Year 2.
3. Assuming a tax effect rate of 40% and further assuming that the company switched from the percentage-of-completion method to the completed-contract method at the end of Year 2, provide the effect of this change of accounting principle on the accounting equation at the end of Year 2.
4. Assuming the information on accrued profits is not available, estimate the gross margin assuming the company was using the completed-contract method during Year 2.
5. Explain the difference in the gross margins obtained from requirements 2 and 4.
6. Assuming the information on accrued profits is not available, estimate the gross margin if revenue were recognized on a cash-collection basis.

Uncle Mike's is a discount club retailer that generates revenues through membership fees and from selling products at discounted prices to its club members. To shop at its stores, the customer must purchase a $40 annual membership, which expires on December 31. The cost of the membership is prorated over the remaining months of the year; for example, the cost of a membership purchased in July would be $20 ($40 × 6 months/12 months). However, the customer has the right to cancel the membership at any time during the year and receive a full refund, at the end of the respective calendar quarter, of the membership fee originally paid.

C3 – 4

Revenue recognition—Membership fees

Based on historical data and industry averages, Uncle Mike's estimates that 30% of its members will request a refund before the end of their membership period. Uncle Mike's data for the past ten years indicates that significant variations between actual and estimated cancellations have not occurred. Furthermore, Uncle Mike's does not expect significant variations to occur in the foreseeable future.

During the calendar year ended December 31, 2005, Uncle Mike's quarterly membership refunds were as follows: March $54,900; June $18,715; September $8,803; and December $4,667. Memberships issued during the year were:

Month	Number	Month	Number
January	2,000	July	500
February	2,000	August	500
March	1,500	September	1,000
April	1,000	October	800
May	900	November	900
June	500	December	800

Required:

1. Prepare a schedule showing quarterly and annual membership fees earned by Uncle Mike's during 2005.
2. How would you initially classify the membership fees in Uncle Mike's financial statements?
3. How would your answer change (in Requirement 1) if Uncle Mike's could not accurately predict membership refunds?

C3 – 5

Revenue recognition—Goods shipped to distributors with right of return

GiveThree Inc., a maker of a popular series of video games for various systems, shipped several thousand units to three distributors of its games on December 20, 2005 in order to ensure that the anticipated heightened demand for its games would be met during the last two weeks of the calendar and fiscal year. The distributors were told to hold the shipments and to return any part of the shipment that they couldn't sell after the first of the new year. The company planned on booking the revenue associated with these shipments at the point of delivery to the distributors, and would make an entry debiting Sales Returns and Allowances, which is a contra-revenue account (shown as a deduction from Sales Revenue), in 2006 for any parts of the shipments that are ultimately returned.

Required:

1. Critically evaluate the accounting treatment proposed by GiveThree.
2. How should revenue related to these shipments be recognized in light of GAAP regarding revenue recognition?
3. Locate the *Wall Street Journal* article from February 14, 2002 entitled, "TakeTwo Announces SEC Investigation," and identify the primary accounting issue discussed in the article. You may be able to access through Dow Jones News Retrieval or through www.factiva.com if your library subscribes to these services.

C3 – 6

Channel stuffing

ClearOne Communications, Inc. is a provider of end-to-end video and audio conferencing services, including the manufacture and sale of video and audio conferencing products. From its inception as a manufacturer of audio and video conferencing equipment through 2001, ClearOne sold its products through a nationwide network of manufacturer's representatives. Sometime in early 2001, ClearOne made the decision to alter its business model and instead of utilizing manufacturer's representatives, ClearOne began selling its products through a nationwide network of distributors complemented by a direct sales force. Through early 2001, ClearOne experienced robust growth and increased product sales every quarter. From the selected financial data extracted from ClearOne's Form 10-Ks presented below, this growth appeared to continue through fiscal 2002. However, a complaint filed by the SEC against ClearOne alleges that things may not be as rosy as they seem.

ClearOne Communications

	Selected Financial Data Years Ended June 30		
	2002	2001	2000
Product sales	$37,215,161	$28,189,612	$22,226,504
Service sales	17,327,525	11,688,793	5,891,909
Cost of goods sold—products	15,057,167	10,633,956	8,033,867
Cost of goods sold—services	7,942,952	5,869,106	2,974,456
Operating expenses	20,809,281	14,904,460	10,568,861
Pre-tax operating income	10,733,286	8,470,883	6,541,229
Income from continuing operations	7,410,752	5,525,185	4,301,742
Net accounts receivable at June 30,	$20,316,730	$ 7,212,970	$ 4,153,677
Cost of goods sold %—products	40.5%	37.7%	36.1%

Required:

1. Retrieve the SEC's complaint against ClearOne Communications, Inc. (http://www.sec.gov/litigation/complaints/comp17934.htm). Describe management's scheme for inflating revenue.
2. The SEC alleges that by the end of fiscal 2002, ClearOne had stuffed approximately $11.5 million of inventory into the distribution channel. On the basis of this assertion, what was the approximate amount of ClearOne's alleged revenue overstatement by the end of 2002?
3. Does the financial statement data presented above support your estimate? Why or why not?

Indus International, Inc. (the "Company") develops, markets, implements and supports a proprietary line of Enterprise Asset Management ("EAM") software and service solutions for capital intensive industries (for example, the utilities and energy industry) worldwide. The following was extracted from Forms 10-Q and 10-K filed by the company for 1999.

C3 – 7

Financial reporting case: Revenue recognition— Software sales

Revenue Recognition

The Company provides its software to customers under contracts, which provide for both software license fees and system implementation services. Revenues from system implementation services, which generally are time and material-based, are recognized as direct contract costs are incurred. The revenues from software license fees have been recognized as earned revenue in accordance with AICPA Statements of Position 97-2, and 98-4 relating to software revenue recognition, when persuasive evidence of arrangement exists, delivery has occurred, the license fee is fixed and determinable, and collection is probable. Effective in the quarter ended September 30, 1997, the Company began to report applicable new license fees on standard software products not requiring substantial modification or customization as earned revenue upon shipment to customers. Previously, because substantial modification and customization of software products was expected by customers, The Indus Group, Inc. had deferred the applicable license fees initially and recognized those fees as earned over the period of modification, customization and other installation services. Maintenance and support services are subject to separate contracts for which revenue is recognized ratably over the contract period. Unbilled accounts receivable represent amounts related to revenue which has been recorded either as deferred revenue or earned revenue but which has not been billed. Generally, unbilled amounts are billed within 60 to 90 days of the sale of product or performance of services. Deferred revenue represents primarily unearned maintenance and support fees and unearned license fees, for which future performance obligations remain.

Indus International, Inc.

Condensed Consolidated Statements of Operations

($ in 000s, except per share amounts)	Three Months Ended September 30	
	1999	1998
Revenues:		
Software license fees	$ 9,935	$13,042
Service and maintenance	40,945	37,291
Total revenues	50,880	50,333
Cost of revenues	25,292	25,994
Gross profit	25,588	24,339
Operating expenses:		
Research and development	8,874	8,171
Sales and marketing	7,232	8,778
General administrative	4,930	4,379
Total operating expenses	21,036	21,328
Income from operations	4,552	3,011
Interest and other income (expense), net	1,126	(206)
Income before income taxes	5,678	2,805
Income taxes	2,158	—
Net income	$ 3,520	2,805
EPS (basic)	$ 0.11	$ 0.09
EPS (diluted)	$ 0.10	$ 0.08
Shares used in computing EPS (basic)	32,196	30,990
Shares used in computing EPS (diluted)	34,750	34,739

Required:

1. Reported third quarter income includes over $2 million in revenue from two contracts where the CEO had "side letters" written to the customers giving each a right to cancel their contracts. Should this revenue have been recognized at that time? Cite appropriate authoritative literature in support of your answer.

2. On October 28, 1999, Indus issued a press release announcing its third quarter 1999 financial results. The company reported that it had met quarterly targets with revenues of $ 50.88 million and earnings of $ 3.52 million, or 10 cents per share on a diluted basis. What would be the approximate effect on reported EPS of not including revenue from the two contracts referred to in requirement 1?

C3 – 8

Ethical issues—Earnings management

Symbol Technologies, Inc. is a leading manufacturer of bar code scanners and related information technology whose stock is traded on the New York Stock Exchange. In 2003, the SEC filed allegations that during the period 1998 to 2002, the company manipulated millions of dollars in revenue, net income, and other measures of financial performance. These manipulations were designed to meet financial projections driven by Wall Street expectations and were allegedly engineered and/or facilitated by the company's chief accounting officer (a CPA).

An example of the various ploys used by Symbol occurred in 2001 when a Symbol officer and other employees created an excessive reserve of $10 million for obsolete inventory. This $10 million cushion was a "cookie jar" reserve designed for use when the company failed to meet its quarterly forecast, and it exceeded any reasonable estimate of the company's exposure for obsolete inventory. This reserve was released into earnings in the fourth quarter of 2001. By making this and other adjustments that quarter, Symbol reported net income of $13.4 million rather than a $2.4 million loss, and hit the quarterly forecast right on the nose. The reversal of this "cookie jar" inventory reserve and the favorable impact on reported earnings were not disclosed to the public.

Required:

Identify the ethical issues involved with the "cookie jar" reserves and the economic consequences for parties affected by the chief accounting officer's actions. (*Hint:* Reference the AICPA's code of professional conduct for CPAs.)

Austins Steaks & Saloon, Inc. (Austins) operates and/or franchises restaurants. The company currently has approximately 118 franchisees operating 186 Western Sizzlin, Western Sizzlin Wood Grill, Market Street Buffet and Bakery, and Great American Steak & Buffet restaurants in 22 states.

Austins' standard franchise agreement has a 20-year term, with one ten-year renewal option. It provides for a one-time payment of an initial franchise fee and a continuing royalty fee based on gross sales. Sales reports and financial statements are regularly collected from franchisees.

Each franchisee is responsible for selecting the location for its restaurant, subject to Austins' approval (based on demographics, competition, traffic volume, etc.). Each franchised restaurant must have a designated manager and assistant manager who have completed Austins' six-week manager training program or who have been otherwise approved by the company. For the opening of a restaurant, Austins provides consultation and makes company personnel generally available to a franchisee. In addition, the company sends a team of personnel to the restaurant for up to two weeks to assist the franchisee and its managers in the opening, the initial marketing and training effort, as well as the overall operation of the restaurant.

Initial franchise fees are recognized when the company has substantially performed all material services and the restaurant has opened for business. Franchise royalties, which are based on a percentage of monthly sales, are recognized as income on the accrual basis. Costs associated with franchise operations are recognized on the accrual basis.

Assume that:

1. Austins entered into a standard franchise agreement on July 1, 2005 with Stacey Spitko to open a Market Street Buffet and Bakery in Lewisburg, PA.
2. The agreement called for an initial franchise fee of $500,000 and a 2.5% royalty. $100,000 of the fee is payable immediately; the remainder is to be paid in equal annual installments each July 1 over the life of the franchise agreement.
3. Interest of 6% on the unpaid franchise fee balance is also payable each July 1.
4. Royalty payments are to be submitted with accompanying financial statements 15 days after the end of each quarter.
5. The restaurant opened on September 30, 2005. Austins management sent a team to assist with the opening. Because Spitko felt that this assistance would be more valuable if rendered primarily after the restaurant opened, the team scheduled its arrival in Lewisburg for September 26, 2005 and was on site until October 10. Management estimated that $34,000 in costs was incurred to provide the entire package of "restaurant opening" services.
6. In keeping with the agreement, the restaurant reported the following gross sales in 2005 and 2006 and made the required payments:

| | **Quarter** | | | |
	First	**Second**	**Third**	**Fourth**
2005				$185,000
2006	$208,500	$242,000	$243,500	$271,000

Required:

1. Should Austins recognize revenue from the initial franchise fee in their quarter ending September 30, 2005? Explain.
2. For Austins, prepare summary journal entries for 2005 and 2006 necessitated by this franchise agreement.

Remember to check the book's Companion Website for additional problem and case material.

www.prenhall.com/revsine

Structure of the Balance Sheet and Statement of Cash Flows

Learning Objectives
After studying this chapter, you will understand:

1. How the various asset, liability, and stockholders' equity accounts on a typical corporate balance sheet are measured and classified.

2. How to use balance sheet information to understand key differences in the nature of firms' operations and how those operations are financed.

3. Differences in balance sheet terminology and presentation format in countries outside the United States.

4. The information provided in footnotes on significant accounting policies, subsequent events, and related party transactions.

5. How successive balance sheets and the income statement can be used to determine cash inflows and outflows for a period.

6. How information provided in the cash flow statement can be used to explain changes in noncash accounts on the balance sheet.

7. The distinction between operating, investing, and financing sources and uses of cash.

8. How changes in current asset and current liability accounts can be used to adjust accrual earnings to obtain cash flows from operations.

The **balance sheet**—sometimes called the statement of financial position—contains a summation of the assets owned by the firm, the liabilities incurred to finance these assets, and the shareholders' equity representing the amount of financing provided by owners at a specific date.

The Financial Accounting Standards Board (FASB) defines the three basic elements of the balance sheet:[1]

1. **Assets:** Probable future economic benefits obtained or controlled by an entity as a result of past transactions or events.
2. **Liabilities:** Probable future sacrifices of economic benefits arising from an entity's *present* obligations to transfer assets or provide services to other entities in the *future* as a result of *past* transactions or events.
3. **Equity:** The residual interest in the assets of an entity that remains after deducting its liabilities. For a corporate form of organization, this interest is referred to as shareholders' or stockholders' equity.

The balance sheet tells us how management has invested its money and where the money came from. It provides information for assessing rates of return, capital structure, liquidity, solvency, and financial flexibility of an enterprise.

Two **rate of return** measures for evaluating operating efficiency and profitability of an enterprise are return on assets (ROA) and return on common equity (ROCE). (The precise calculation of these two performance measures is detailed in Chapter 5.) By comparing ROA to ROCE, statement users can see whether debt financing is being used to enhance the return earned by shareholders.

The balance sheet provides critical information for understanding an entity's **capital structure**. Capital structure refers to how much of an entity's assets are financed from debt versus equity sources. An important decision in corporate finance is determining the proper mix of debt and equity financing. Management

---

[1] "Elements of Financial Statements of Business Enterprises," *Statement of Financial Accounting Concepts No. 6* (Stamford, CT: FASB, 1985), paras. 25, 35, 49.

must weigh the benefits of using debt financing (with tax-deductible interest) against the dangers of becoming over-leveraged (that is, having too much debt) and the possibility of defaulting on required interest and principal payments.

In addition to assessing the mix of debt versus equity financing, the balance sheet and related footnotes provide information for evaluating the **maturity structure** of the various obligations within the liability section. This information is critical to assessing the **liquidity** of an entity. Liquidity measures how readily assets can be converted to cash relative to how soon liabilities will have to be paid in cash. The balance sheet is the source of information for a variety of liquidity measures (detailed in Chapter 5) used by analysts and commercial lending officers to assess the credit worthiness of an entity.

> Maturity structure refers to how far into the future the obligations will come due.

In addition to the liquidity measures that focus on short-term cash inflows and cash needs, balance sheets provide information for assessing long-term **solvency**—the ability of a company to generate sufficient cash flows to maintain its productive capacity and still meet interest and principal payments on long-term debt. A company that cannot make debt payments when due is technically insolvent and may be forced to reorganize or liquidate.

Operating and financial flexibility refers to an entity's ability to adjust to unexpected downturns in the economic environment in which it operates or to take advantage of profitable investment opportunities as they arise. Balance sheets provide information for making these assessments. A firm with most of its assets invested in specialized manufacturing facilities (for example, a foundry) has limited ability to adjust to economic downturns and, thus, has limited operating flexibility. Similarly, a firm with minimal cash reserves and large amounts of high interest debt on its balance sheet will have limited ability to take advantage of profitable investment opportunities that may arise.

Now that we have outlined the information contained in balance sheets and how it is used, we next turn our attention to how various balance sheet accounts are measured and classified.

Classification Criteria and Measurement Conventions for Balance Sheet Accounts

We will use the financial statements of Motorola to illustrate the classification criteria and measurement methods used in a typical balance sheet. While many people characterize generally accepted accounting principles (GAAP) balance sheet carrying amounts as **historical costs**, what they really represent is more complicated. In fact, carrying amounts in a GAAP balance sheet are a mixture of historical costs, **current costs** (also called **fair value**), **net realizable value**, and **discounted present values**.

Exhibit 4.1 shows Motorola's balance sheet, which uses a typical U.S. disclosure format. In the "Assets" section, cash and any other assets expected to be converted into cash within the next 12 months (or within the **operating cycle**, if the operating cycle is longer than 12 months) are classified as "Current assets." Assets not expected to be converted into cash within this period are categorized separately. Within the "Current assets" category, items are disclosed in descending order of liquidity—how quickly the items will be converted into cash through the normal course of business. In the "Liabilities" section of the balance sheet, items expected to be settled from current assets within the next 12 months (or within the operating cycle, if longer) are categorized as "Current liabilities." All other liabilities appear in a separate section as noncurrent or long-term obligations. Equity claims also appear in their own separate section of the balance sheet, which is often referred to as the "Stockholders' equity" section.

> A firm's **operating cycle** is the elapsed time beginning with the initiation of production and ending with the cash collection of the receivables from the sale of the product.

EXHIBIT 4.1	Motorola Inc. and Consolidated Subsidiaries

Balance Sheet

($ in millions)	December 31 2002	December 31 2001
Assets		
Current assets		
Cash and cash equivalents	$ 6,507	$ 6,082
Short-term investments	59	80
Accounts receivable, net	4,437	4,583
Inventories	2,869	2,756
Deferred income taxes	2,358	2,633
Other current assets	904	1,015
Total current assets	17,134	17,149
Property, plant and equipment, net	6,104	8,913
Investments	2,053	2,954
Deferred income taxes	3,112	1,152
Other assets	2,749	3,230
Total assets	$31,152	$33,398
Liabilities and Stockholders' Equity		
Current liabilities		
Notes payable and current portion of long-term debt	$ 1,629	$ 870
Accounts payable	2,268	2,434
Accrued liabilities	5,913	6,394
Total current liabilities	9,810	9,698
Long-term debt	7,189	8,372
Other liabilities	2,429	1,152
Total liabilities	19,428	19,222
Company-obligated mandatorily redeemable preferred securities of subsidiary trust holding solely company-guaranteed debentures	485	485
Stockholders' equity		
Preferred stock, $100 par value issuable in series Authorized shares: 0.5 (none issued)	—	—
Common stock, $3 par value Authorized shares: 2002 and 2001, 4,200.0 Issued and outstanding: 2002, 2,315.3; 2001, 2,254.0	6,947	6,764
Additional paid-in capital	2,233	1,707
Retained earnings	2,582	5,434
Non-owner changes to equity	(523)	(214)
Total stockholders' equity	11,239	13,691
Total liabilities and stockholders' equity	$31,152	$33,398

To convey a feeling for the diversity of the measurement bases used in a typical balance sheet, we will discuss selected accounts from Motorola's 2002 comparative balance sheet (see Exhibit 4.1). Many of the measurement issues introduced in this section are explored in greater depth in subsequent chapters.

Cash The balance sheet carrying amount for cash reflects the amount of money or currency the firm has on hand or in bank accounts. If cash consists exclusively of U.S. dollar amounts, the balance sheet cash account reflects the *historical* amount of net dollar units arising from past transactions. But due to the unique liquidity of cash, this historical amount of net dollar units is identical to the current market value of the cash.

If some of the cash amounts are denominated in foreign currency units (likely for Motorola, a multinational firm), then those amounts in foreign currency units must be *translated* into U.S.

Monetary assets are fixed in dollar amounts irrespective of price changes. A $300,000 cash deposit remains fixed at $300,000 even if the general level of prices goes up and the purchasing power of that $300,000 declines. **Nonmonetary assets** like inventory and buildings are *not* fixed in dollar amounts—that is, inventory purchased for $300,000 can conceivably increase in value if prices go up. While not assured, this potential for changing value is the distinguishing characteristic of nonmonetary items—their value is *not* expressed in a fixed number of monetary units.

dollar equivalents. For **monetary assets** like cash, accounts receivable, and notes receivable, the current rate of exchange in effect at the balance sheet date is used to translate foreign currency units into dollars. As a consequence of using the current rate of exchange (rather than the historical rate of exchange that was in effect at the time of the foreign currency cash inflow), this portion of the cash account is carried at its **current market price**—*not* at its historical transaction amount. For these foreign currency deposits, current market exchange values are used irrespective of whether they are higher or lower than the historical rate. Consequently, the GAAP measurement convention for cash is, in reality, current market price rather than historical cost.

A U.S. company with 1 million pesos in the bank account of its Mexican manufacturing subsidiary would value the cash at $95,877 U.S. dollars on December 31, 2002 when the exchange rate was 10.43 pesos to the dollar. This same bank account (with 1 million pesos) would have been valued at $108,814 U.S. dollars on December 31, 2001 when the exchange rate was 9.19 pesos to the dollar.

Short-term Investments This category of assets comprises items like U.S. Treasury bills, notes, equity securities, or other financial assets that companies use to earn a return on funds not currently needed in operations. The FASB measurement rules for certain investments in debt and equity securities distinguishes between debt securities, which the reporting company intends to hold to maturity, and all other securities (both debt and equity), which an entity intends to hold only for short periods of time.[2]

The rules are:

1. Debt securities the company intends to hold to maturity are carried at amortized cost. (When debt securities are sold at a premium or discount, the premium or discount is amortized over time—hence, the term **amortized cost**.)

2. Debt and equity securities held for short-range investment purposes are carried at market value at each balance sheet date (that is, the price at which these securities can be bought and sold), irrespective of whether market is above or below cost.

When the balance sheet carrying amount of the securities investment is written up or down to current market value, the offsetting gain or loss appears on the income statement if the securities are **trading securities** where the intent is to generate profits on short-term differences in price. When less actively traded securities (termed **available-for-sale securities**) are marked-to-market, the offsetting gain or loss goes directly to stockholders' equity rather than through the income statement. (These accounting rules are discussed further in Chapter 16.)

How long the company intends to hold the debt securities determines how they are measured in the balance sheet. Some will be carried at amortized cost and others at current market prices. Equity securities held for the short-term are always measured at current market prices.

Net Accounts Receivable This account reflects credit sales that have not yet been collected. The balance sheet carrying amount for gross accounts receivable is equal to the face amount arising from past credit sales transactions. Thus, if a company sold goods with a sales price of $100,000 on November 15, 2005, the following entry would be made:

DR Accounts receivable	$100,000	
CR Sales revenue		$100,000

---

[2] "Accounting for Certain Investments in Debt and Equity Securities," *Statement of Financial Accounting Standards (SFAS) No. 115* (Norwalk, CT: FASB 1993). Under the old rules that *SFAS No. 115* replaced, short-term investments were carried at lower of cost or market.

If the receivable is still outstanding at December 31, 2005, it would be shown on the balance sheet at $100,000. However, accrual accounting requires that any future costs be matched against the revenues recognized in that period. When sales are made for credit (on account), some sales may unknowingly be made to customers who will prove incapable of making the required payment. The expense associated with these uncollectible accounts must be recognized—on an estimated basis—in the period in which the sales arise.

This compels companies to prepare an estimate of the proportion of existing accounts receivable balances that they reasonably believe will ultimately not be collected. In Motorola's case, the 2002 accounts receivable footnote disclosure shows the details behind the net Accounts receivable balance shown on its balance sheet as follows ($ in millions):

> The accounting entry to recognize estimated uncollectible accounts is:
> DR Bad debt expense $XXX
>   CR Allowance for doubtful accounts $XXX
> The debited account reduces income in the current period, while the account credited appears as a deduction from gross accounts receivable. (See again Exhibit 4.1.) Such deductions from asset accounts are called **contra-asset** accounts. (Estimating and recognizing bad debt expense is discussed in Chapter 8.)

Gross accounts receivable	$4,675
Less allowance for doubtful accounts	(238)
Net accounts receivable reported on balance sheet	$4,437

Notice that as a consequence of this "netting" of accounts, the total for net accounts receivable ($4,437 million) is carried at expected **net realizable value** as of the balance sheet date, not at original historical cost ($4,675 million).

Inventories The inventory account for a manufacturing firm like Motorola is comprised of three components: (1) raw materials; (2) work-in-process; and (3) finished goods. In the notes to its financial statements, Motorola discloses that inventories are carried at **lower of cost or market**, where cost is computed using the weighted average method (discussed in Chapter 9). Therefore, the measurement basis for inventories depends on the relationship between historical cost and current market price.

> For a wholesale or retail company, this account reflects only finished goods—that is, merchandise held for resale.

- When costs are lower than market price, the carrying amounts for inventory conform to the historical cost convention.
- When cost exceeds market, inventories on the balance sheet are carried at current market price, where that market price is the cost to replace the item (subject to special GAAP rules—see Chapter 9).

Deferred Income Taxes This asset account represents taxes paid by Motorola to the government on income that: (a) was recognized for tax purposes in the current or prior periods, but (b) will not be recognized for financial reporting purposes until some future period. Because this future expense has already been paid, it is reported as a **deferred tax asset**. In the United States, the rules used to determine income for financial reporting purposes (called **book income**) frequently do not conform to the rules used to determine income for taxation purposes (called **taxable income**). Book income also diverges from taxable income in many other industrialized countries. Income determination rules for financial reporting differ from rules for determining income for taxation purposes because of the very different objectives of the two computations. The objective in measuring book income is to reflect a firm's underlying economic success: Was the firm profitable during the period? The objective in measuring taxable income is to conform to laws designed to provide a basis for funding government operations. Since the rules that govern income determination for tax purposes result from a national political process, these rules do not necessarily measure changes in firms' underlying economic condition. Most companies maintain two sets of accounting records (or books) to facilitate both accurate financial reporting and compliance with tax laws.

The amount reported as book income is the basis for the deduction reported on the income statement for tax expense. However, the amount actually owed and paid to the government—that is, the sum of the credits to cash and to income taxes payable on the balance sheet—is determined by firms' taxable income. As a consequence, the debit to the income statement account (tax expense) and the credit to the balance sheet accounts (cash or taxes payable) **will usually be for different amounts.** To balance the entry, deferred income taxes—reflecting the difference in the *timing* of revenue and expense in computing book income versus taxable income—must be debited or credited. (The measurement and reporting rules for deferred taxes are covered in Chapter 13.)

> In 2000 Motorola also reported "Deferred income taxes" totaling $1,504 million in the liability section of its balance sheet. This amount arises because certain timing differences caused book income to be *greater* than taxable income in prior years.

In Motorola's case, the deferred income tax asset account has a debit balance of $2,358 million due to the **timing differences** that caused taxable income to exceed book income in past years.[3] Taxable income can exceed book income for at least two possible reasons:

1. Internal Revenue Service (IRS) rules do not allow Motorola to claim deductions for tax purposes until after these items are reflected as GAAP expenses on the books.
2. IRS rules require Motorola to recognize revenues on its tax return before they are recognized on its GAAP income statement.

> There are other reasons why book income may differ from taxable income—called permanent differences—but they do not give rise to deferred taxes. For example, U.S. income tax law does not tax municipal bond interest. Consequently, if a firm owns municipal bonds and receives interest on these bonds, the interest is tax free. Book income will include the interest income, but taxable income will not.

Since these timing differences are expected to reverse in subsequent years, *future* book income will exceed taxable income. Even though these reversals may be expected to take place in, say, three years in the future, GAAP reflects these amounts at their *undiscounted amount*. In other words, existing GAAP treats expected reversals in the years 2005 and 2015 identically—that is, the time-value of money is ignored.

Property, Plant and Equipment—Net This account reflects the tangible long-lived assets that Motorola uses in its operations. This item appears on the balance sheet at its net amount—historical cost minus accumulated depreciation. Motorola, like most companies, provides information about the components of this figure in the financial statement notes.

> *SFAS No. 121* (para. 7) defines *fair value* of an asset as ". . . the amount at which the asset could be bought or sold in a current transaction between willing parties, that is, other than a forced or liquidation sale."

($ in millions)	December 31 2002	December 31 2001
Land	$ 328	$ 346
Buildings	5,035	6,208
Machinery and equipment	15,069	16,254
	20,432	22,808
Less accumulated depreciation	(14,328)	(13,895)
Property, plant and equipment—net	$ 6,104	$ 8,913

When a long-lived asset becomes impaired—that is, when its carrying amount may no longer be recoverable—the fixed asset account is reduced to its lower **fair value.**[4] If available, quoted current market prices are the best measure of fair value. However, market prices for long-lived assets are not always readily available. So, fair value may need to be estimated by discounting expected future net operating cash flows. (This topic is covered in Chapter 10.)

---

[3] *Debits* to deferred income tax arise because the credit to taxes payable exceeds the debit to taxes expense. Since tax expense is based on book income and taxes payable is based on taxable income, this means that in past years book income for Motorola was less than taxable income.

[4] "Accounting for the Impairment of Long-Lived Assets and for Long-Lived Assets to Be Disposed of," *SFAS No. 121* (Norwalk, CT: FASB, 1995).

Notes Payable and Current Portion of Long-term Debt Notes payable are formal written promises to pay cash at some future date issued in connection with loans from a bank or for the purchase of goods or services. The current portion of long-term debt represents the portion of long-term borrowings that fall due within one year of the balance sheet date. Since these amounts will be paid within a relatively short period of time (within one year), they are reported at their (undiscounted) face amount—that is, the amount due at maturity.

Accounts Payable and Accrued Liabilities Accounts payable represent amounts owed to suppliers of merchandise or services purchased on open account (that is, for credit). Payment is typically due within 30 to 90 days. Accrued liabilities represent expenses that have been incurred, but not yet paid. Examples include accrued wages and accrued interest expense. These items are reflected on the balance sheet at the amount of the original liability—that is, at the amount arising at the inception of the transaction. Consequently, the numbers are shown at historical cost.

Long-term Debt This account represents obligations that fall due beyond one year from the balance sheet date. Examples include notes, bonds, lease obligations, and pension obligations. When long-term debt (typically, notes or bonds) is issued, the initial balance sheet carrying amount is determined by computing the **discounted present value** of the sum of (1) the future principal repayment *plus* (2) the periodic interest payments. The rate used for discounting these amounts is the effective yield on the notes or bonds at the date they were issued. Here, we'll simply provide a brief overview of the general measurement rules for long-term debt. More on bonds and other long-term debt instruments is presented in Chapter 11.

When bonds are sold at par, the amount received is equal to the recorded face amount of the debt. For example, if Motorola sells $100,000,000 of 15-year, 10% coupon bonds for $100,000,000, the accounting entry is:

DR Cash	$100,000,000	
CR Bonds payable		$100,000,000

The $100,000,000 carrying amount is equal to the present value of the principal *and* interest payments over the life of the bond discounted at 10%, the effective yield at the time of issue. The effective yield is 10% since the effective yield on bonds sold at par is equal to the coupon rate. (We'll show why in Chapter 11.) When bonds are sold at a premium or at a discount, the initial carrying amount is again equal to the present value of the future payments, where the discount rate is the effective yield on the bonds. In general, at balance sheet dates after the bonds' issuance date, the subsequent carrying amount of *all* bonds outstanding is equal to the present value of the future principal and interest flows discounted at the *original effective yield rate*. This carrying amount will differ from the current market price of the bonds whenever interest rates have changed subsequent to issuance. Consequently, long-term debt is also carried at historical cost, where the carrying amount is determined by calculating the discounted present value of the future principal and interest cash flows using the original effective yield on the bonds as the discount rate.

Mandatorily Redeemable Preferred Stock Motorola, like several other companies, has issued a type of preferred stock called trust preferred securities (TPS) to provide financing for their operations.[5] (We'll just provide an overview here—further details on the complicated transactions that give rise to these securities are discussed in Chapter 15.) The shares pay monthly or

[5] For a further discussion of the key features of trust preferred securities, see P. J. Frischmann, P. D. Kimmel, and T. D. Warfield, "Innovation in Preferred Stock: Current Developments and Implications for Financial Reporting," *Accounting Horizons* (September 1999), pp. 201–18.

quarterly dividends and are redeemable at Motorola's option. Because of the mandatory redemption feature and the required periodic dividend payments, these hybrid securities incorporate elements of both debt and equity. So where to classify them within the balance sheet is controversial. Notice that Motorola finessed the issue by disclosing them in a section between debt and equity—often called the "mezzanine" section. In May 2003, the FASB issued *SFAS No. 150*, which establishes standards for how an issuer classifies and measures certain financial instruments with characteristics of both liabilities and equity.[6] The Board concluded that mandatorily redeemable preferred stock should be reported in the liability section of the balance sheet unless the redemption is required to occur only upon the liquidation or termination of the reporting entity. This reporting requirement became effective after the Motorola financial statements for 2002 were issued.

Common Stock This account represents the **par value** of shares issued and outstanding. The par value is determined by the company's articles of incorporation. Par values were originally established to ensure that a corporation would maintain a minimum level of investment by shareholders to protect the interests of creditors. For example, some states preclude companies from paying dividends to shareholders that would result in a reduction of stockholders' equity below the par value of shares issued and outstanding. As a practical matter, debt covenant provisions in lending agreements of the borrower generally place restrictions on firms' distributions to shareholders that are more stringent than the statutory par-value restrictions. Therefore, the par value of shares has limited economic significance, as discussed in Chapter 15. The common stock account is carried at the historical par value of the shares.

Additional Paid-in Capital This account reflects the amounts in excess of par or stated value that were received by the corporation when the shares were originally issued. For example, if Motorola issued 100,000 shares of $3 par-value stock for $15 per share, the "Additional paid-in capital" component would be credited for

$$(\$15 - \$3) \times 100{,}000 = \$1{,}200{,}000$$

Thus, paid-in capital is also shown at historical cost (that is, the amount above par value that was paid to the firm when the shares were originally issued).

Retained Earnings This account measures the net of cumulative earnings less cumulative dividend distributions of the company since inception. Therefore, it represents the cumulative earnings that have been reinvested in the business. The "Retained earnings" account is increased (decreased) by the net income (net loss) for the period and is decreased for dividends that are declared in the period. For many firms, like Motorola, retained earnings represents the major portion of stockholders' equity. Thus, the book value of equity is largely determined by the past earnings that have been retained and reinvested in the business. As we will see in Chapters 5 and 6, book value of equity is a key element of many performance measures—like return on common equity (ROCE)—and it plays an important role in equity valuation.

Different measurement bases pervade the balance sheet. Because these items ultimately appear on the income statement, income is a mixture of historical costs, current values, and present values. This means that retained earnings is also a mixture of many different measurement bases.

---

[6] "Accounting for Certain Financial Instruments with Characteristics of both Liabilities and Equity," *Statement of Financial Accounting Standards (SFAS) No. 150* (Norwalk, CT: FASB 2003).

Non-owner Changes to Equity This account measures the cumulative unrealized gains and losses from *other comprehensive income components* recognized in current and prior years. This component of stockholders' equity is also called "Accumulated other comprehensive income." As noted in Chapter 2, the most common components of other comprehensive income are:

1. fair value adjustments made to securities classified as "available-for-sale" (see Chapter 16),
2. fair value changes on derivatives that meet certain conditions for hedge accounting (see Chapter 11),
3. foreign currency translation adjustments (see Chapter 16), and
4. unrealized losses resulting from recognition of the minimum liability provision under *SFAS No. 87* (see Chapter 14).

The non-owner changes to this equity account are credited for unrealized gains and debited for unrealized losses. All amounts are shown net of tax effects. For Motorola, this account balance increased from a $214 million debit balance at the end of 2001 to a $523 million debit balance at the end of 2002, an increase of $309 million. Motorola's consolidated statement of stockholders' equity (not shown) explains the components of this change:

($ in millions)	Unrealized Gain (Loss)	
1. Unrealized gains on available-for-sale securities	$ 245	CR
2. Foreign currency translation adjustments	94	CR
3. Minimum pension liability adjustment	(647)	DR
4. Loss on derivative instruments, net	(1)	DR
Total 2002 increase	$(309)	DR

Analytical Insights: Understanding the Nature of a Firm's Business

One tool for gaining insights into the nature of a company's operations and for analyzing its asset and financial structure is to prepare a **common-size balance sheet**. In a common-size balance sheet, each balance sheet account is expressed as a percentage of total assets or, equivalently, as a percentage of total liabilities plus shareholders' equity. Exhibit 4.2 presents common-size balance sheets for four companies operating in four distinctly different industries—E-Trade Group, an Internet company specializing in online investing services; Deere & Company, a manufacturer of agricultural and heavy construction equipment with a large finance subsidiary; Wal-Mart, a well-known discount retailer; and Potomac Electric Power Company, an electrical utility providing service to Washington, D.C., and the surrounding area. Can you match up the common-size statements with each of these companies? Think about the industry in which each firm operates and about the economic activities the firms might engage in. Then try to figure out how these activities might impact a typical balance sheet.

Note that Company C has a very large proportion of its assets in cash, marketable securities and accounts receivable with no inventory, and a relatively small amount of property, plant, and equipment (PP&E). Most of Company C's debt financing comes from short-term liabilities, as the company carries no long-term debt. Finally, note that retained earnings is negative (a deficit), indicating that the company has suffered cumulative losses since it was formed. The lack of inventory rules out Deere and Wal-Mart as the source of Company C's data since both would hold significant inventories. Also, the relatively low amount of property, plant, and equipment further rules out these two firms as well as Potomac Power since all three need significant amounts of fixed assets to conduct business. This leaves E-Trade Group as the obvious match. A corroborating piece of evidence is the deficit in retained earnings. Because of heavy start-up costs, many of the relatively young Internet companies like E-Trade have yet to turn a profit.

EXHIBIT 4.2 — Common-Sized Balance Sheet Comparison

2001 Fiscal Year

	Company A ($ in millions)	%	Company B ($ in millions)	%	Company C ($ in millions)	%	Company D ($ in millions)	%
Assets								
Current assets:								
Cash and marketable securities	$ 1,206.2	5.3	$ 2,161.0	2.6	$ 5,157.5	28.4	$ 676.7	12.8
Current receivables	12,826.9	56.6	2,000.0	2.4	10,149.7	55.8	401.2	7.6
Inventories	1,505.7	6.6	22,614.0	27.1	—	—	37.8	0.7
Other current assets	1,939.3	8.6	1,471.0	1.8	—	—	24.2	0.5
Total current assets	17,478.1	77.1	28,246.0	33.9	15,307.2	84.2	1,139.9	21.6
Noncurrent assets:								
Property, plant, and equipment, net	2,052.3	9.0	45,750.0	54.8	331.7	1.8	2,753.4	52.1
Goodwill and intangibles, net	874.0	3.9	8,595.0	10.3	684.4	3.8	—	—
Other assets, net	2,258.7	10.0	860.0	1.0	1,849.1	10.2	1,392.6	26.3
Total assets	$22,663.1	100.0%	$83,451.0	100.0%	$18,172.4	100.0%	$5,285.9	100.0%
Liabilities and Stockholders' Equity								
Current liabilities:								
Total current liabilities	$ 9,456.6	41.7	$27,282.0	32.7	$16,532.0	91.0	$965.4	18.2
Long-term liabilities:								
Total current liabilities	9,214.3	40.7	21,067.0	25.2	—	—	2,287.5	43.3
Total liabilities	18,670.9	82.4	48,349.0	57.9	16,532.0	91.0	3,252.9	61.5
Redeemable preferred stock	—	—	—	—	69.5	0.4	209.8	4.0
Stockholder's equity:								
Contributed capital and other equity items	157.4	0.7	661.0	0.8	1,818.0	10.0	849.1	16.1
Retained earnings (deficit)	3,834.8	16.9	34,441.0	41.3	(247.1)	(1.4)	974.1	18.4
Total liabilities and stockholders' equity	$22,663.1	100.0%	$83,451.0	100.0%	$18,172.4	100.0%	$5,285.9	100.0%

Both Company A and Company B have relatively high amounts of current assets, but the mix of current assets is quite different. For Company A, current receivables represent nearly 57% of total assets, while Company B has no current receivables but 27% of its assets are in inventory. Since many of Deere's agricultural and heavy construction equipment products sell for well in excess of $100,000, dealers and customers often need to finance their purchases. Deere offers this financing through John Deere Credit, its wholly-owned finance subsidiary, whose operations are included in the consolidated numbers. Thus, the large receivables balance for Company A coupled with significant amounts invested in inventories and PP&E provide strong clues that Deere is Company A.

Like most national discount retailers, Wal-Mart would be expected to have large amounts of inventory. Because most sales are for cash or paid through bank credit cards (for example, Visa or Master Card), Wal-Mart would likely have little or no current receivables on its balance sheet. Moreover, with a large number of stores either purchased or leased under capital lease arrangements, we would expect to see relatively large investments in PP&E. This profile seems to match up well with Company B's data.

This leaves Potomac Power as Company D. Note the relatively low amount of current assets and the large investment in PP&E to generate electricity. The large amount of long-term debt financing is also quite common for utilities. Regulated utilities are allowed to build a "reasonable and fair return" to stockholders into the energy rates charged customers. Therefore, they have a relatively steady and predictable earnings and cash flow stream. This allows utilities like Potomac Power to use proportionately more long-term debt to finance their operations relative to companies with more volatile earnings patterns.

The preceding exercise demonstrates how statement readers can extract useful information from common-size balance sheets to learn about the underlying economics of an industry and the nature of the firm's operations. Chapter 5 will introduce additional analytical tools for conducting in-depth analyses of companies.

International Differences in Balance Sheet Presentation

The account titles and format of balance sheets prepared in other countries can sometimes differ rather dramatically from those prepared under U.S. GAAP.[7] In contrast to the United States, where assets are presented in decreasing order of liquidity, in the United Kingdom, Germany, Netherlands, and some other European countries, fixed assets are presented first followed by the current assets displayed in increasing order of liquidity. This format is illustrated in Exhibit 4.3, which presents the 2002 balance sheet of Cadbury Schweppes PLC, a British confectionery and beverage company.

International

Note that within the fixed assets category, intangible assets are presented first followed by tangible assets (that is, property, plant, and equipment) and finally financial assets or investments. The British balance sheet format is presented in a way that emphasizes the firm's liquidity and solvency. Notice, instead of reporting a figure for total assets, Cadbury Schweppes reports a subtotal for current assets less current liabilities, which highlights their working capital or liquidity position. Also notice the presentation of a subtotal for total assets less current liabilities. This figure can readily be compared with the long-term debt obligations appearing next to assess Cadbury's solvency position.

---

[7]   In addition, the measurement bases used for various accounts can sometimes be quite different from country to country. Throughout the book, we will alert you to some of these important differences as we discuss the recognition, measurement, and disclosure rules that govern financial reporting.

| EXHIBIT 4.3 | Cadbury Schweppes PLC | | | |

Balance Sheets at 30 December 2002

	Group		Company	
(in millions of sterling pounds)	2002 £m	2001 £m	2002 £m	2001 £m
Fixed Assets				
Intangible assets and goodwill	3,919	3,721	—	—
Tangible assets	1,351	1,209	131	79
Investments in associates	308	309	9	11
Investments	237	246	5,555	4,445
	5,815	5,485	5,695	4,535
Current Assets				
Stocks	528	487	—	—
Debtors				
—Due within one year	970	908	101	152
—Due after one year	82	88	22	9
Investments	297	323	—	—
Cash at bank and in hand	175	134	—	—
	2,052	1,940	123	161
Current Liabilities				
Creditors: amounts falling due within one year				
—Borrowings	(790)	(695)	(1,764)	(1,686)
—Other	(1,795)	(1,694)	(381)	(361)
Net Current Liabilities	(533)	(449)	(2,022)	(1,886)
Total Assets less Current Liabilities	5,282	5,036	3,673	2,649
Non-Current Liabilities				
Creditors: amounts falling due after more than one year				
—Borrowings	(1,528)	(1,399)	(985)	(1,109)
—Other	(49)	(62)	—	—
Provisions for liabilities and charges	(419)	(392)	(1)	—
	(1,996)	(1,853)	(986)	(1,109)
Net Assets	3,286	3,183	2,687	1,540
Capital and Reserves				
Called up share capital	257	256	257	256
Share premium account	1,050	1,019	1,050	1,019
Revaluation reserve	59	59	1	1
Capital redemption reserve	90	90	1,249	90
Profit and loss account	1,564	1,456	130	174
Shareholders' Funds	3,020	2,880	2,687	1,540
Minority Interests				
Equity minority interests	16	28	—	—
Non-equity minority interests	250	275	—	—
	266	303	—	—
Total Capital Employed	3,286	3,183	2,687	1,540

Source: Cadbury Schweppes 2002 Annual Report and Form 20-F

The Cadbury Schweppes balance sheet also introduces some account titles unique to British accounting that can be confusing to the unwary. For example, two accounts in the current assets section that can be particularly confusing are the "Stocks" and "Debtors" accounts. In the United Kingdom, Stocks is the common term for inventory. The Debtors account is analogous to the Accounts receivable account in the United States. The Capital and Reserves section, which is analogous to the Stockholders' equity section in U.S. balance sheets, contains several account titles unique to British accounting. Exhibit 4.4 shows the accounts under U.S. GAAP that correspond to these British accounts. Two of the British equity accounts require brief elaboration since they have no U.S. counterpart:

- **Revaluation reserve:** U.K. GAAP allows companies to periodically revalue both tangible and intangible fixed assets. Any surplus arising from a revaluation is credited to a revaluation reserve in the equity section of the balance sheet.
- **Capital redemption reserve:** In the United Kingdom, when a company repurchases its own shares, these shares are cancelled. Where the repurchase is paid for from profits, an amount equivalent to the par or stated value of the shares repurchased is transferred from the Called up share capital account to a Capital redemption reserve account, which is not available for dividend distribution.

EXHIBIT 4.4	Comparison of U.K. and U.S. Account Titles
U.K. Equity Accounts	**Equivalent U.S. Accounts**
Called up share capital	Common stock—par
Share premium account	Capital in excess of par
Revaluation reserve	No equivalent in U.S. GAAP
Capital redemption reserve	No equivalent in U.S. GAAP
Profit and loss account	Retained earnings

Finally, note that Cadbury Schweppes reports two sets of numbers on its balance sheet—one for the "Group" and another for the "Company." The Group numbers reflect the financial position of Cadbury Schweppes and all of its subsidiaries. This is equivalent to the "consolidated" financial statement numbers of a parent and its subsidiaries under U.S. GAAP. The company numbers reflect the financial position of the Cadbury Schweppes holding company.

This example provides a brief glimpse of how balance sheet format and terminology used in other countries differ from those used under U.S. GAAP. Examples of differences in accounting standards across countries appear throughout the book and are discussed extensively in Chapter 18.

RECAP

The balance sheet provides a snapshot of the financial position of a company at a given point in time. It shows the various types of assets held at the balance sheet date and the claims against those assets (that is, how those assets have been financed).

Balance sheet accounts reflect a variety of measurement bases, including historical cost, current costs (also called fair value), net realizable value, and discounted present value. Therefore, users of balance sheet information must be careful to recognize the effects that these different measurement bases can have both when aggregating numbers across accounts as well as when computing ratios that are used in making inter-company comparisons.

With the tremendous growth in international business and the increased frequency of cross-border financing, it is likely that you will encounter statements prepared under non–U.S. GAAP sometime during your career. When you do, you must be aware of differences in recognition and measurement criteria, statement format, and terminology in order to properly interpret and analyze those statements.

Financial Statement Footnotes

Footnotes are an integral part of companies' financial reports. Financial statement footnotes provide a wealth of information that allows statement users to better understand and interpret the numbers presented in the body of the financial statements. In some instances, footnotes contain important information not found in the financial statements themselves. For example, the lease footnote shows a firm's future commitments under noncapitalized operating leases, which is useful in assessing a firm's future cash flow needs and creditworthiness. Throughout the remainder of the book, we will illustrate the kind of information typically found in footnotes, and we'll discuss how this information can be used to evaluate a company's future prospects and risk profile (that is, factors that affect the creditworthiness of an enterprise).

Here we briefly discuss and illustrate three important notes typically found in companies' reports:

1. summary of significant accounting policies;
2. disclosure of important subsequent events; and
3. related party transactions.

Summary of Significant Accounting Policies As you will see in later chapters, there are many areas of accounting where management is free to choose from equally acceptable alternative accounting methods. Examples include different cost flow assumptions for valuing inventory (FIFO versus LIFO), different methods for determining depreciation expense (straight-line versus accelerated), and different methods of accounting for long-term construction contracts (percentage-of-completion versus completed-contract). In order to make valid intercompany comparisons, it is important for statement users to recognize and understand the alternative accounting methods that a reporting entity has selected to account for its economic activities.

The **Summary of Significant Accounting Policies** explains the important accounting choices that the reporting entity uses to account for selected transactions and accounts.[8] Exhibit 4.5 shows excerpts from the accounting policy footnote in Motorola's 2002 annual report.

EXHIBIT 4.5	**Motorola Inc.**

Excerpts from 2002 Accounting Policies Footnote

1. **Summary of Significant Accounting Policies**

   Revenue Recognition: The Company recognizes revenue for product sales when title transfers, the risks and rewards of ownership have been transferred to the customer, the fee is fixed and determinable, and collection of the related receivable is probable which is generally at the time of shipment. Accruals are established for price protection, returns and cooperative marketing programs for distributors related to these sales. For long-term contracts, the Company uses the percentage-of-completion method to recognize revenues and costs based on the percentage of costs incurred to date compared to the total estimated contract costs. For contracts involving new unproven technologies, revenues and profits or parts thereof are deferred until technological feasibility is established, customer acceptance is obtained and other contract-specific terms have been completed. Provisions for losses are recognized during the period in which the loss first becomes apparent. Revenue for services is recognized ratably over the contract term or as services are being performed.

   Inventories: Inventories are valued at the lower of average cost (which approximates computation on a first-in, first-out basis) or market (net realizable value or replacement cost).

   Property, Plant and Equipment: Property, plant and equipment are stated at cost less accumulated depreciation. Depreciation is recorded using declining-balance and straight-line methods, based on the estimated useful lives of the assets (buildings and building equipment, 5–40 years; machinery and equipment, 2–12 years), and commences once the assets are ready for their intended use.

[8] "Disclosure of Accounting Policies," *Accounting Principles Board Opinion No. 22* (New York: AICPA, 1972).

Subsequent Events Footnote Events or transactions that have a significant effect on a company's financial position or results of operations sometimes occur subsequent to the close of a company's fiscal year-end, but before the financial statements are issued. Disclosure of these **subsequent events** is required if they are material and are likely to influence investors' appraisal of the risk and return prospects of the reporting entity.[9] Examples of such events include loss of a major customer, a business combination, issuance of debt or equity securities, or a catastrophic loss. Exhibit 4.6 illustrates a subsequent event disclosure provided by IBM Corporation in its 2002 annual report related to registration for sale of debt and equity capital and for a cash purchase of Rational Software Corporation.

EXHIBIT 4.6	IBM Corporation Footnote on Subsequent Events 2002 Annual Report

Note Y: Subsequent Events

On January 21, 2003, the company filed with the Securities and Exchange Commission a shelf registration to periodically sell up to $20 billion in debt securities, preferred and capital stock, depository shares and warrants. The company may sell securities in one or more separate offerings with the size, price and terms to be determined at the time of sale. The net proceeds from the sale of the securities will be used for general corporate purposes, which may include debt repayment, investments in or extensions of credit to its subsidiaries, redemption of any preferred stock the company may issue, or financing of possible acquisitions or business expansion. The net proceeds may be invested temporarily or applied to repay short-term debt until they are used for their stated purpose.

Consistent with the company's strategy to concentrate borrowing at the IBM level, this shelf registration eliminates the need for a shelf registration associated with its U.S. financing subsidiary, IBM Credit Corporation (ICC). The ICC shelf will be terminated shortly after the effective date of the new IBM shelf.

On February 21, 2003, the company purchased the outstanding stock of Rational Software Corp. (Rational) for approximately $2.1 billion in cash. Rational provides open, industry standard tools, best practices and services for developing business applications and building software products and systems. The Rational acquisition provides the company with the ability to offer a complete software development environment for customers. The company intends to merge Rational's business operations and employees into the IBM Software Group as a new division and brand. The results of operations of Rational will be included in the company's Consolidated Financial Statements as of February 21, 2003. The company has not completed the allocation of the purchase price related to the Rational acquisition as it is in the process of identifying and determining the fair value of all assets acquired and liabilities assumed.

Source: IBM 2002 Annual Report

Related Party Transactions A **related party transaction** occurs when a company enters into a transaction with individuals or other businesses that are in some way connected with it or its management. Examples include transactions between:

1. the reporting entity and its principal owners, management, or members of their immediate families;

> Enron's dealings with several special purpose entities set up as limited partnerships that were headed up by Andrew Fastow, Enron's chief financial officer, provide an example of this type of related party transaction.

---

[9] "Codification of Auditing Standards and Procedures," *Statement on Auditing Standards No. 1* (New York: AICPA, 1972).

2. subsidiaries of a common parent; or

3. the reporting entity and nonconsolidated affiliates in which it holds a significant ownership stake.

Because related party transactions are not entered into at arms length, these events pose greater risks. Therefore, companies are required to disclose in a footnote any related party transactions, including the nature of the relationship, a description of the transaction, and any dollar amounts involved.[10] Exhibit 4.7 illustrates a related party footnote disclosure from SAP AG, Incorporated's 2002 annual report detailing transactions that SAP AG entered into with other companies in which SAP AG board members or related family members of SAP officers hold positions of significant responsibility or significant stock ownership.

EXHIBIT 4.7	SAP AG Excerpts from 2002 Footnote on Related Party Transactions

Related Party Transactions

Certain board members of SAP AG currently hold or have held within the last year positions of significant responsibility with other entities as presented in note 35. The Company has relationships with certain of these entities in the ordinary course of business, whereby it buys and sells a wide variety of services and software at arm's length.

On May 2, 2002, SAP agreed to purchase the assets of Menahel—Management Data and Business Accounting Ltd. ("Menahel"), seated in the State of Israel, including all business intellectual property, contracts, software and related know-how and substantially all of Menahel's workforce for US $7.5 million. Menahel has been renamed to SAP Manage Ltd. Mr. Reuven Agassi, father of SAP AG Executive Board Member Shai Agassi, was the managing director as well as the indirect owner of one of Menahel's largest shareholders.

Prof. Dr. Wilhelm Haarmann is a partner in Haarmann Hemmelrath & Partner, which serves infrequently as special German tax counsel and counsels SAP AG with regard to other legal matters.

At December 31, 2002 the Company held no note receivables from any member of the Executive Board and Supervisory Board. There were no significant transactions between the Company and the major shareholders as outlined in note 23.

Source: SAP AG 2002 Annual Report

Statement of Cash Flows

The balance sheet shows a firm's investments (assets) and financial structure (liabilities and stockholders' equity) at a given *point in time*. By contrast, the **statement of cash flows** shows the user why a firm's investments and financial structure have *changed* between two balance sheet dates. The connection between successive balance sheet positions and the statement of cash flows can be demonstrated through simple manipulation of the basic accounting equation:

$$\text{Assets} = \text{Liabilities} + \text{Stockholders' equity} \qquad (4.1)$$

Partitioning the assets into cash and all other assets yields:

$$\text{Cash} + \text{Noncash assets} = \text{Liabilities} + \text{Stockholders' equity} \qquad (4.2)$$

---

[10] "Related Party Disclosures," *Statement of Financial Accounting Standards No. 57* (Stamford, CT: FASB, 1982).

Rearranging yields:

$$\text{Cash} = \text{Liabilities} - \text{Noncash assets} + \text{Stockholders' equity} \qquad (4.3)$$

From basic algebra we know that an equality like this must also hold for the algebraic sum of the changes on both sides of the equation. Representing equation (4.3) in the form of the change (Δ) in each term results in

$$\Delta\text{Cash} = \Delta\text{Liabilities} - \Delta\text{Noncash assets} + \Delta\text{Stockholders' equity} \qquad (4.4)$$

Thus, the cash flow statement—which provides an explanation of why a firm's cash position has changed between successive balance sheet dates—simultaneously explains the changes that have taken place in the firm's noncash asset, liability, and stockholders' equity accounts over the same time period.

The change in a firm's cash position between successive balance sheet dates will *not* equal the reported earnings for that period. There are three reasons for this:

1. Reported net income usually will not equal cash flow from **operating activities** because (a) noncash revenues and expenses are often recognized as part of accrual earnings, and (b) certain operating cash inflows and outflows are not recorded as revenues or expenses under accrual accounting in the same period the cash flows occur.
2. Changes in cash are also caused by nonoperating **investing activities** like the purchase or sale of fixed assets.
3. Additional changes in cash are caused by **financing activities** like the issuance of stock or bonds, the repayment of a bank loan, or dividends paid to stockholders.

Cash flows are critical to assessing a company's liquidity and creditworthiness. Firms with cash flows that are smaller than currently maturing obligations can be forced into liquidation or bankruptcy. Because cash flows and accrual earnings can differ dramatically, current reporting standards mandate that firms prepare a statement of cash flows as well as an income statement and balance sheet. The cash flow statement is designed to explain the causes for year-to-year changes in the balance of cash and cash equivalents.[11] We provide a brief introduction to the statement of cash flows here, focusing on the format of the statement and on the nature of some of the basic adjustments that are needed to convert accrual earnings to cash flow from operations. Later, after you have reviewed the accrual and cash flow effects of the transactions that affect various balance sheet and income statement accounts in the intervening chapters, you will find a more detailed explanation of the cash flow statement in Chapter 17.

> Cash equivalents include short-term, highly liquid investments that are readily convertible to cash such as demand deposits, savings accounts, certificates of deposit, money market funds, and U.S. treasury bills.

The cash flow statement summarizes the cash inflows and outflows of a company broken down into its three principal activities:

- **Operating activities:** Cash flows from operating activities result from the cash effects of transactions and events that affect operating income—both production and delivery of goods and services.
- **Investing activities:** Cash flows from investing activities include making and collecting loans; investing in and disposing of debt or equity securities of other companies; and purchasing and disposing of assets, like equipment, that are used by a company in the production of goods or services.
- **Financing activities:** Cash flows from financing activities include obtaining cash from new issues of stock or bonds, paying dividends or buying back a company's own shares (treasury stock), borrowing money, and repaying amounts borrowed.

---

[11] The format for preparing the cash flow statement is specified in "Statement of Cash Flows," *SFAS No. 95* (Stamford, CT: FASB, 1987).

Companies that are able to satisfy most of their cash needs from operating cash flows are generally considered to be in stronger financial health and better credit risks.

Exhibit 4.8 presents Wal-Mart's 2002 cash flow statement broken down into operating, investing, and financing activities. Note that operating activities generated $10.260 billion in cash flows, investing activities used $7.146 billion, and financing activities used $2.978 billion of cash, resulting in a net cash increase of $107 million after adjusting for a $29 million foreign currency exchange rate change on cash. Wal-Mart uses the so-called **indirect approach** to calculate cash flows from operations by adjusting accrual-basis earnings for differences between accrual revenues and expenses and cash inflows and outflows related to operating activities during the period. The rationale for the depreciation and amortization adjustment and why changes in various working capital accounts capture the differences between accrual earnings and operating cash flows is explained with a simplified example in the following section.

Wal-Mart's major investing cash outflow ($8.383 billion) was for purchase of property, plant, and equipment. In the financing section, the issuance of long-term debt provided $4.591 billion of cash. Major financing cash outflows were used for repayment of loans obtained through commercial paper ($1.533 billion), purchase of company stock ($1.214 billion), dividend payments ($1.249 billion), and repayment of long-term debt ($3.519 billion).

EXHIBIT 4.8	Wal-Mart Stores Inc.

Consolidated Statements of Cash Flows
($ in millions)

Fiscal years ended January 31,	2002	2001	2000
Cash flows from operating activities			
Net income	$ 6,671	$ 6,295	$ 5,377
Adjustments to reconcile net income to net cash, provided by operating activities:			
Depreciation and amortization	3,290	2,868	2,375
Cumulative effect of accounting change, net of tax	—	—	198
Increase in accounts receivable	(210)	(422)	(255)
Increase in inventories	(1,235)	(1,795)	(2,088)
Increase in accounts payable	368	2,061	1,849
Increase in accrued liabilities	1,125	11	1,015
Deferred income taxes	185	342	(138)
Other	66	244	(139)
Net cash provided by operating activities	10,260	9,604	8,194
Cash flows from investing activities			
Payments for property, plant and equipment	(8,383)	(8,042)	(6,183)
Investment in international operations (net of cash acquired, $195 million in Fiscal 2000)	—	(627)	(10,419)
Proceeds from termination of net investment hedges	1,134	—	—
Other investing activities	103	(45)	(244)
Net cash used in investing activities	(7,146)	(8,714)	(16,846)
Cash flows from financing activities			
Increase/(decrease) in commercial paper	(1,533)	(2,022)	4,316
Proceeds from issuance of long-term debt	4,591	3,778	6,000
Purchase of company stock	(1,214)	(193)	(101)
Dividends paid	(1,249)	(1,070)	(890)
Payment of long-term debt	(3,519)	(1,519)	(863)
Payment of capital lease obligations	(167)	(173)	(133)
Proceeds from issuance of company stock	—	581	—
Other financing activities	113	176	224
Net cash provided by (used in) financing activities	(2,978)	(442)	8,553
Effect of exchange rate changes on cash	(29)	(250)	76
Net increase/(decrease) in cash and cash equivalents	107	198	(23)
Cash and cash equivalents at beginning of year	2,054	1,856	1,879
Cash and cash equivalents at end of year	$ 2,161	$ 2,054	$ 1,856

Cash Flows Versus Accrual Earnings

The following example illustrates the major differences between cash flows and accrual earnings, why a cash flow statement is needed to fully understand the distinction between the two, and why certain adjustments are made to accrual earnings to obtain cash flows from operations.

HRB Advertising Company opened for business on April 1, 2005. The corporation's activities and transactions for the remainder of 2005 are summarized as follows:

1. Herb Wilson, Robin Hansen, and Barbara Reynolds each contributed $3,500 cash on April 1 for shares of the company's common stock.
2. HRB rented office space beginning April 1, and paid the full year's rental of $2,000 per month—or $24,000—in advance.
3. The company borrowed $10,000 from a bank on April 1. The principal plus accrued interest is payable January 1, 2006 with interest at the rate of 12% per year.
4. HRB purchased office equipment with a five-year life for $15,000 cash on April 1. Salvage value is zero and the equipment is being depreciated straight-line.
5. HRB sold and billed customers for $65,000 of advertising services rendered between April 1 and December 31. Of this amount, $20,000 was still uncollected by year-end.
6. By year-end, the company incurred and paid the following operating costs: (a) utilities, $650; (b) salaries, $36,250; and (c) supplies, $800.
7. The company had accrued (unpaid) expenses at year-end as follows: (a) utilities, $75; (b) salaries, $2,400; and (c) interest, $900.
8. Supplies purchased on account and unpaid at year-end amounted to $50.
9. Supplies inventory on hand at year-end amounted to $100.
10. Annual depreciation on office equipment is $15,000 ÷ 5 = $3,000. Since the equipment was acquired on April 1, the depreciation expense for 2005 is $3,000 × 9/12 = $2,250.

Herb, Robin, and Barbara were delighted to discover that the company earned a profit (before taxes) of $3,725 in 2005. However, they were shocked to learn that the company's checking account was overdrawn by $11,200 at year-end. This overdraft was particularly disconcerting since the bank loan was now due.

Is HRB Advertising Company profitable? Or is it about to go bankrupt? What are its prospects for the future? Exhibit 4.9 helps us examine these issues.

While HRB Advertising generated *positive* accrual accounting earnings of $3,725 during 2005, its operating cash flow was a *negative* $16,700. Columns (b) and (c) show the causes for the divergence between the components of accrual income (column [a]) and operating cash flows (column [d]). Because of a net infusion of cash from financing activities (column [d]), the net change in cash (a negative $11,200) was much smaller than the negative cash flow of $16,700 from operating activities.

We now discuss the rationale behind the adjustments in columns (b) and (c). We examine each adjustment in terms of how it affects "bottom-line" *accrual basis net income*—not how the adjustment affects revenues or expenses that comprise net income. Because expenses are treated as negative amounts in computing net income, an adjustment that reduces (increases) an expense is treated as a plus (negative) amount in columns (b) and (c). This way of designating positive and negative amounts will facilitate our discussion of the adjustments to accrual basis income needed to arrive at operating cash flows.

- Advertising revenues recognized under accrual accounting totaled $65,000. However, $20,000 of this remains as uncollected accounts receivable at year-end. Thus, the ending balance in the "Accounts receivable" account must be *subtracted* from the accrual-basis revenues to derive the cash received during the year for advertising services.

EXHIBIT 4.9	HRB Advertising Company

Analysis of Accrual Income versus Change in Cash for Year Ended December 31, 2005

Item	(a) Accrual Income	(b) Noncash Accruals: Revenue Earned (or Expenses Incurred)	(c) Prepayments and Supplies Buildup	(d) a + b + c Cash Received (or Paid) During 2005
Operating Activities				
Advertising revenues	$65,000	−$20,000[5]		$45,000
Salaries	−38,650	+2,400[7b]		−36,250
Rent	−18,000		−$6,000[2]	−24,000
Utilities	−725	+75[7a]		−650
Supplies	−750	+50[8]	−100[9]	−800
Interest	−900	+900[7c]		—0—
Depreciation	−2,250	+2,250[10]		—0—
Operating cash flow				−$16,700
Net income	$ 3,725			
Investing Activities				
Equipment purchase				−$15,000[4]
Financing Activities				
Stock issuance				$10,500[1]
Bank borrowing				10,000[3]
				$20,500
Change in cash				−$11,200

Note: Numbers in parentheses refer to numbered transactions on page 177.

- The salaries expense of $38,650 for the year includes the $36,250 of salaries incurred and paid in cash plus the $2,400 of salary expense accrued at year-end. Therefore, the accrued (unpaid) salaries, which is the ending balance in the "Accrued salaries payable" (liability) account, must be *added back* to total salaries expense to derive the salaries paid in cash.

- HRB recognized rent expense of $2,000 × 9 months = $18,000 in 2005. The difference between the amount paid out in cash and the amount recognized as expense under accrual accounting ($24,000 minus $18,000 or $6,000) would be the ending balance in the "Prepaid rent" (asset) account. This amount is shown as a negative adjustment (*subtraction*) in column (c), since the cash outflow for rent was greater than the amount of rent expense recognized.

- The utilities expense of $725 for the year includes the $650 of utilities paid in cash plus $75 of utilities expense accrued at year-end. The utilities expense incurred but not yet paid, which is the ending balance in the "Accrued utilities payable" (liability) account, must be *added back* to the total utilities expense to obtain the cash payments for utilities in 2005.

- Total supplies purchased during the year included $800 paid in cash and $50 purchased on account ("Accounts payable"). Of the amount purchased, $100 of supplies remains on hand in the "Supplies inventory" account at the end of the year. So, supplies expense under accrual accounting is $800 + $50 − $100 = $750. To adjust the accrual-basis expense to derive the cash outflow for supplies requires that we *add back* the ending balance in accounts payable (which was a noncash increase to the supplies expense) and *subtract* the $100 ending balance in supplies inventory (which was a noncash decrease to the supplies expense).

- Accrued interest expense for the year is $10,000 \times 12\% \times 9/12 = \$900$. Since none of this has been paid in cash, the ending balance in the "Accrued interest payable" (liability) account must be *added back* to the "Interest expense" account to obtain the cash paid out for interest in 2005.

- Depreciation is a noncash expense under accrual accounting. So, this amount, which is reflected in the increase in the "Accumulated depreciation" (contra-asset) account, must be *added back* to depreciation expense.

> Remember, for a start-up company, beginning account balances are zero.

Except for depreciation, each of the adjustments we just outlined uses the ending balance (which is also the *change* in the account balance in the first year of a company's life) of a current asset account (for example, "Accounts receivable," "Supplies inventory," or "Prepaid rent") or a current liability account (for example, "Accounts payable," "Salaries payable," "Utilities payable," or "Interest payable") to adjust accrual-basis revenues or expenses in order to derive cash flows from operations. The adjustments to accrual-basis income (revenues minus expenses) for changes in current asset and current liability accounts that represent accrued revenues, deferred (unearned) revenues, accrued expenses, or deferred (prepaid) expenses are summarized in Figure 4.1.

> Only adjustments for changes in working capital accounts are summarized in Figure 4.1. Other adjustments (such as depreciation and gains/losses on asset sales) will be discussed in Chapter 17.

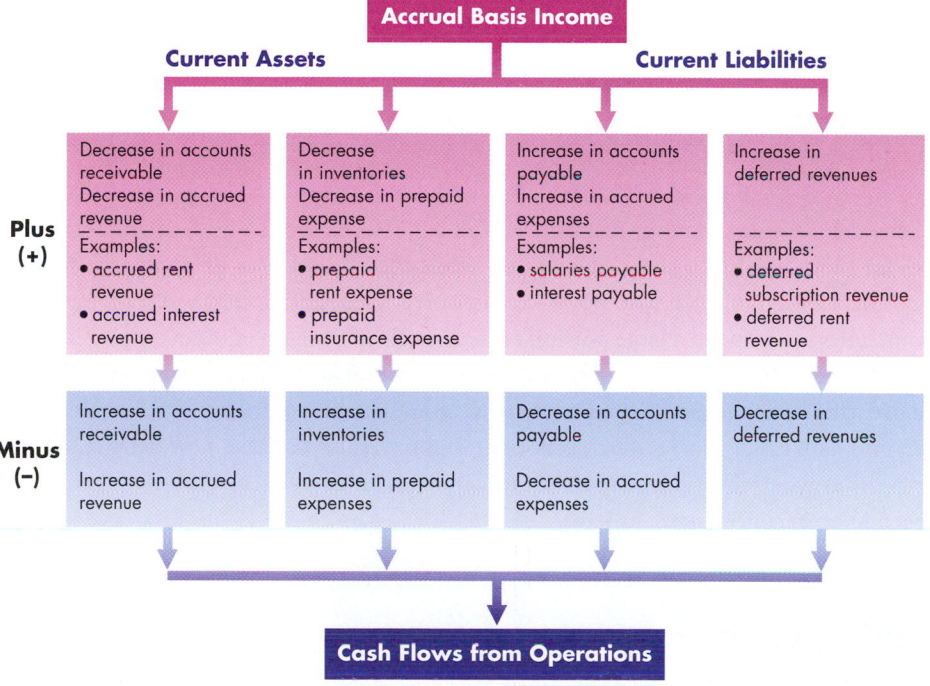

Figure 4.1

ADJUSTMENTS TO ACCRUAL EARNINGS FOR CHANGES IN WORKING CAPITAL ACCOUNTS TO OBTAIN CASH FLOWS FROM OPERATIONS

Exhibit 4.10 illustrates how the adjustments to accrual earnings due to *changes* in various current asset and liability accounts would be reflected in a GAAP statement of cash flows. The item numbers appearing next to each element in the cash flow statement correspond to the numbers in columns (b), (c), and (d) of Exhibit 4.9. The presentation format illustrated is the indirect approach (described previously), since it does not show the individual operating cash inflows and outflows *directly*. (The **direct approach**, which shows the revenues collected in cash and the expenses paid in cash, is shown in column [d] of Exhibit 4.9.) In Exhibit 4.10, net cash flows from operations is arrived at indirectly by adjusting earnings for the differences between accrual-basis revenues and expenses and cash inflows and outflows during the period.

EXHIBIT 4.10	**HRB Advertising Company**

Statement of Cash Flows for Year Ended December 31, 2005

Operating Cash Flows		
Net income		$ 3,725
Plus:		
Depreciation[10]	$ 2,250	
Increase in salaries payable[7b]	2,400	
Increase in accounts payable[8]	50	
Increase in utilities payable[7a]	75	
Increase in interest payable[7c]	900	5,675
Minus:		
Increase in receivables[5]	(20,000)	
Increase in prepaid rent[2]	(6,000)	
Increase in supplies inventory[9]	(100)	(26,100)
Cash flows from operations		($16,700)
Investing Cash Flows		
Equipment purchase[4]		($15,000)
Financing Cash Flows		
Stock issuance[1]		$10,500
Bank borrowing[3]		10,000
		$20,500
Change in cash		($11,200)

Note: Numbers in parentheses refer to numbered transactions on page 177.

The cash flow statement in Exhibit 4.10 will help Herb, Robin, and Barbara understand the causes for their overdrawn checking account. While the business was profitable from an accrual accounting standpoint, total cash flows were negative. This should not be surprising since start-up companies often spend a large portion of their available cash on equipment purchases, inventory buildup, and the production of goods and services that are frequently sold on account—and, therefore, that generate no cash immediately. Although the company is profitable, it may be forced into bankruptcy unless quick action is taken to resolve the cash flow deficit. To remain in business, the owners must infuse more equity capital, arrange for an extension of their bank loan, or speed up cash collections.

Deriving Cash Flow Information

The three owners were able to convince their banker to refinance the loan but only after they each agreed to contribute another $2,000 to the company—a total of $6,000. The loan was replaced by a three-year note, but the interest rate was increased to 13.50% to reflect the additional risk associated with the refinanced borrowing. Herb, Robin, and Barbara felt confident that with careful attention to both earnings and cash flow, they could successfully grow the business and repay the note before its maturity.

During 2006—the second year of business—revenues increased and operating cash flows were positive, but the company recorded a loss for the year. Exhibit 4.11 contains HRB Advertising's comparative balance sheets for 2005 and 2006, and Exhibit 4.12 presents the company's earnings and cash flow statements for the two years.

We can see from the balance sheet that the $10,000 bank loan was refinanced as a note ("Note payable" in Exhibit 4.11) and that additional common stock of $6,000 was issued during 2006. Also notice that the company's cash account ended the year with a positive balance of $500.

Highlights from the income statement (Exhibit 4.12[a]) include substantial growth in advertising revenues from $65,000 to $92,000, a 41.5% increase. At the same time, the company was able to speed up its collection of credit sales and reduce its "Accounts receivable" balance, as shown in Exhibit 4.11. Unfortunately, salary expense increased nearly 63%, from $38,650 to $62,875, which seems to be the major factor contributing to the company's $1,725 loss for the year. From the cash flow statement (see Exhibit 4.12[b]), we see that 2006 cash flows from operations totaled a positive $7,200 even though the business sustained a loss for the year. The company's overall cash balance increased by $11,700 during the year, with $6,000 of that amount representing cash contributed by the owners in exchange for additional common stock.

Although U.S. companies must now include a cash flow statement similar to Exhibit 4.12(b) in their annual report to shareholders, this was not always the case. Moreover, quarterly cash flow statements are not required, although some companies voluntarily make them available to shareholders. Companies that don't provide quarterly cash flow statements challenge the analyst. How can cash flow information be derived from a company's balance sheet and income statement when the cash flow statement itself is not available?

The answer is not very complicated, as we will see. Deriving information about a company's cash receipts and disbursements from balance sheet and income statement information involves little more than a careful and systematic analysis of the changes in individual balance sheet accounts and their corresponding income statement effects. From this analysis you can deduce individual cash flows and construct a summary schedule of cash receipts (inflows) and disbursements (outflows) that closely resembles the cash flow statement presented in Exhibit 4.12(b).

EXHIBIT 4.11	HRB Advertising Company

Comparative Balance Sheets December 31, 2005 and 2006

	2005	2006
Assets		
Cash	$(11,200)	$ 500
Accounts receivable	20,000	15,775
Supplies inventory	100	225
Prepaid rent	6,000	6,000
Office equipment	15,000	16,500
Less: Accumulated depreciation	(2,250)	(5,500)
Total assets	$ 27,650	$33,500
Liabilities and Equities		
Utilities payable	$ 75	$ 50
Interest payable	900	675
Accounts payable (supplies)	50	75
Salaries payable	2,400	4,200
Bank loan	10,000	—
Note payable	—	10,000
Total liabilities	$ 13,425	$15,000
Common stock	10,500	16,500
Retained earnings	3,725	2,000
Total liabilities and stockholders' equity	$ 27,650	$33,500

EXHIBIT 4.12	HRB Advertising Company

Comparative Income and Cash Flow Statements for Years Ended December 31, 2005 and 2006

	2005	2006
Panel (a)		
Income Statement		
Revenue from advertising services	$ 65,000	$ 92,000
Less:		
Salaries expense	(38,650)	(62,875)
Supplies expense	(750)	(1,200)
Rent expense	(18,000)	(24,000)
Utilities expense	(725)	(1,050)
Interest expense	(900)	(1,350)
Depreciation	(2,250)	(3,250)
Net income	$ 3,725	$ (1,725)
Panel (b)		
Cash Flow Statement		
Net income	$ 3,725	$ (1,725)
Depreciation	2,250	3,250
	5,975	1,525
Working capital adjustments:		
Accounts receivable decrease (increase)	(20,000)	4,225
Supplies inventory (increase)	(100)	(125)
Prepaid rent decrease (increase)	(6,000)	—
Utilities payable increase (decrease)	75	(25)
Accounts payable (supplies) increase	50	25
Interest payable increase (decrease)	900	(225)
Salaries payable increase	2,400	1,800
Cash flow from operations	$(16,700)	$ 7,200
Equipment purchases	$(15,000)	$ (1,500)
Cash flow from investing activities	$(15,000)	$ (1,500)
Bank loan (repayment)	$ 10,000	$(10,000)
Note payable issued	—	10,000
Common stock issued	10,500	6,000
Cash flow from financing activities	$ 20,500	$ 6,000
Change in cash balance	$(11,200)	$ 11,700

The starting point for this analysis is the cash account itself. Notice from the balance sheet (Exhibit 4.11) that the company's cash position increased by $11,700 during 2006, from the $11,200 deficit at the beginning of the year to a $500 positive balance at year-end. Consequently, we know that total cash receipts for the year must have been $11,700 greater than total cash payments. Now let's uncover some individual cash flow items.

Exhibit 4.13 illustrates the general T-account analysis that can be used to derive cash flow information from selected balance sheet accounts of HRB Advertising for 2006. From the comparative balance sheet in Exhibit 4.11, the beginning and ending balances can be obtained for each *balance sheet* account that is affected when a revenue or expense item is recorded. The accrual-basis revenue or expense that results in a debit or credit to the related balance sheet account can then be entered (see circled items in Exhibit 4.13). The cash received or cash paid, which results in an offsetting entry to each of these accounts, is the "plug" figure (in bold) that is needed to arrive at the ending balance that is given. We now illustrate this analysis for selected accounts in Exhibit 4.13.

EXHIBIT 4.13   HRB Advertising Company

Analysis of Income Statement and Balance Sheet Accounts for Year Ended December 31, 2006

INCOME STATEMENT	BALANCE SHEET

Advertising Revenues | **Accounts Receivable**

	Beginning balance $20,000
$92,000	Advertising revenues $92,000
	(accrual basis)
	Ending balance $15,775

$96,225   Collections (cash basis)

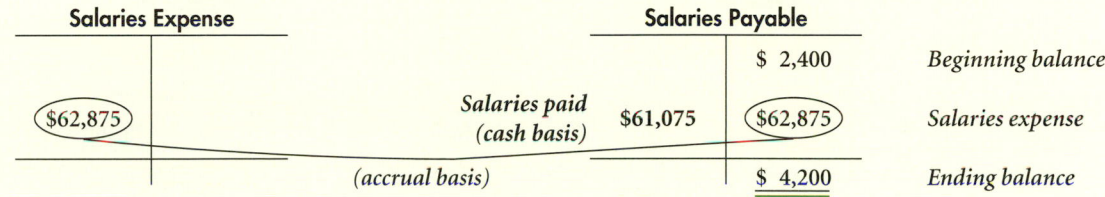

Salaries Expense | **Salaries Payable**

	$ 2,400 Beginning balance
$62,875	Salaries paid $61,075 $62,875 Salaries expense
	(cash basis) (accrual basis)
	$ 4,200 Ending balance

Rent Expense | **Prepaid Rent**

Rent expense from 1/1/06 to 3/31/06 $ 6,000

Rent expense from 4/1/06 to 12/31/06 $18,000

Total expense $24,000

Beginning balance $ 6,000	$ 6,000 Amortized from beginning balance Rent expense from 1/1/06 to 3/31/06
Rent paid in advance on 4/1/06 $24,000	$18,000 Amortized from 4/1/06 payment Rent expense from 4/1/06 to 12/31/06
(accrual basis)	
Ending balance $ 6,000	

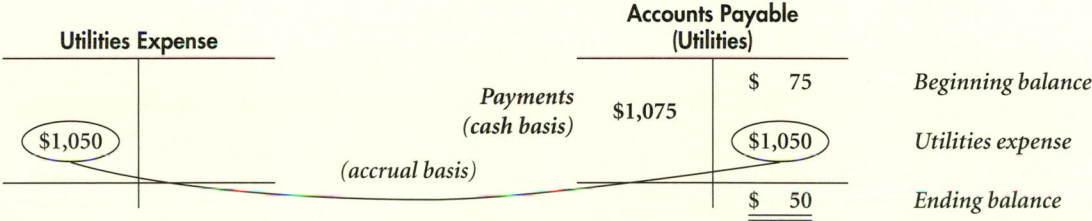

Utilities Expense | **Accounts Payable (Utilities)**

	$ 75 Beginning balance
$1,050	Payments $1,075 $1,050 Utilities expense
	(cash basis) (accrual basis)
	$ 50 Ending balance

Accounts Payable (Supplies)

Payments $1,300	$ 50 Beginning balance
(cash basis)	$1,325 Purchases on account
	$ 75 Ending balance

Supplies Expense | **Supplies Inventory**

	Beginning balance $ 100
$ 1,200	Purchases on account $1,325 $1,200 Supplies used up
	(accrual basis)
	Ending balance $ 225 (continued on next page)

EXHIBIT 4.13	HRB Advertising Company *(continued)*

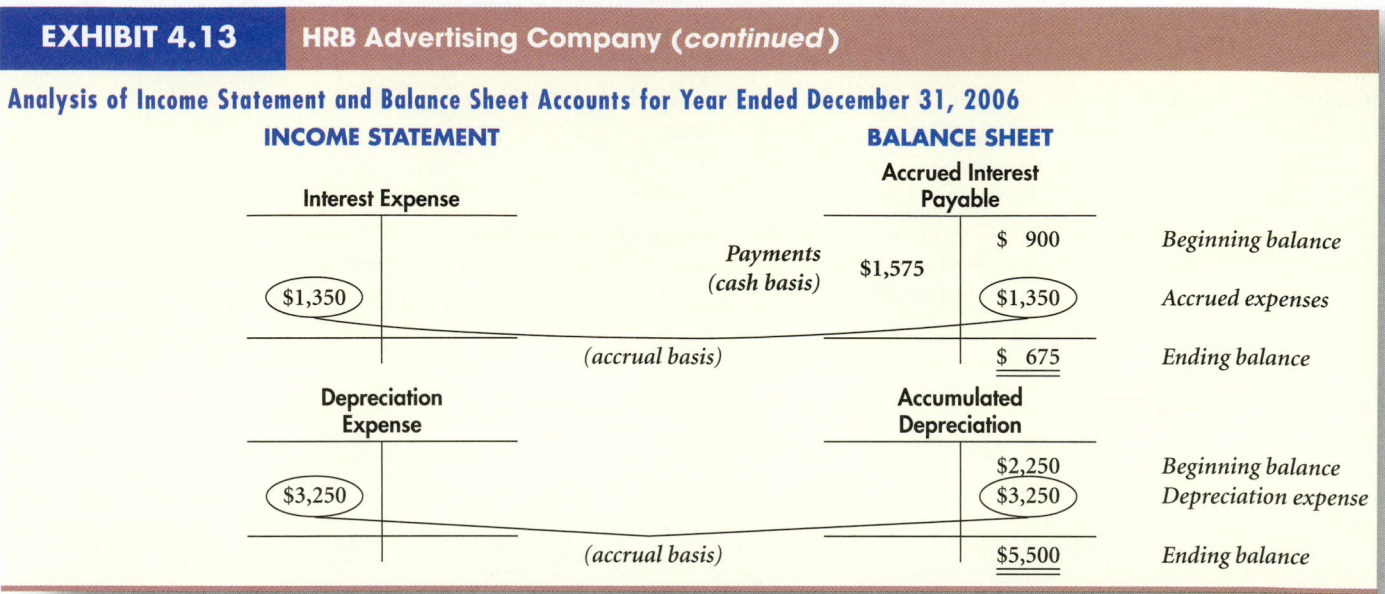

Analysis of Income Statement and Balance Sheet Accounts for Year Ended December 31, 2006

The company's only source of operating cash inflows is customer receipts, so we begin with an analysis of the "Accounts receivable" account. As shown in Exhibit 4.13, the balance in the "Accounts receivable" account declined by $4,225 during 2006, from a beginning balance of $20,000 to a year-end balance of $15,775. Since billings for advertising services performed during 2006 totaled $92,000 (that is, advertising revenues in the earnings statement of Exhibit 4.12[a]), HRB must have collected $96,225 from its customers. To see this, note that collections must have been $4,225 greater than new billings, because the "Accounts receivable" balance decreased by this amount during the year. Another way to think about this calculation is to assume that all customers pay on a timely basis. In this case, HRB would have collected $20,000 cash from customers billed in 2005 and another $76,225 from customers billed in 2006 (or $92,000 billings minus the $15,775 that was uncollected at year-end).

Salary payments represent the company's largest operating cash outflow. Exhibit 4.13 shows that salaries payable increased by $1,800 during the year, from a beginning balance of $2,400 to $4,200 at year-end. Consequently, salary payments must have been $61,075 for the year, or $1,800 less than the total salaries expense of $62,875 that shows up in the income statement in Exhibit 4.12(a).

Some cash inflows and outflows involve more than one balance sheet account. Exhibit 4.13 shows this for supplies. As shown there, "Accounts payable (supplies)" increased $25 during the year, from a beginning balance of $50 to $75 at year-end. This means that payments for supplies must have been $25 less than purchases. But, where can we find information about purchases? Certainly not from the income statement (Exhibit 4.12[a]), because it reports the cost of supplies *used* during the year regardless of when they were purchased. Since purchases increase the total supplies on hand, we turn our attention to the "Supplies inventory" account. As we see in Exhibit 4.13, supplies inventory increased by $125 during the year, from $100 at the start to $225 at year-end. Purchases must therefore have been $125 greater than the amount of supplies used during the year (that is, the supplies expense from Exhibit 4.12[a]). In other words, purchases must have totaled $1,325 (or the $1,200 supplies expense plus the $125 inventory increase), and consequently, supplier payments must have totaled $1,300 (or $1,325 purchases minus the $25 accounts payable increase).

The same kind of analysis just outlined is illustrated for the "Prepaid rent," "Accounts payable (utilities)," and "Accrued interest payable" accounts in Exhibit 4.13. The process continues until all balance sheet accounts are fully reconciled and the company's cash receipts and disbursements are identified. In addition, analysis of changes in the "Notes payable," "Common stock," and "Equipment" accounts (not shown) can identify cash inflows and outflows from financing and investing activities.

The derived cash inflows and outflows for HRB Advertising are listed in Exhibit 4.14, by major sources—operating, investing, and financing activities. This schedule explains why the company's cash balance increased by $11,700 during the year. Operating activities contributed $7,200 of cash, $1,500 was spent on new equipment, and financing activities added another $6,000. These are precisely the cash inflows and outflows listed in the company's cash flow statement in Exhibit 4.12(b).

EXHIBIT 4.14	**HRB Advertising Company**

Schedule of Cash Receipts and Disbursements for the Years Ended December 31, 2005 and 2006

	2005	2006	
Operating Activities			
Advertising services	$ 45,000	$ 96,225	from Accounts Receivable
Salaries	(36,250)	(61,075)	from Salaries Payable
Rent	(24,000)	(24,000)	from Prepaid Rent
Utilities	(650)	(1,075)	from Utilities Payable
Supplies	(800)	(1,300)	from Supplies Payable
Interest	—	(1,575)	from Interest Payable
Operating cash flow	$(16,700)	$ 7,200	
Investing Activities			
Equipment purchase	$(15,000)	$ (1,500)	from Office Equipment
Financing Activities			
Bank borrowing	$ 10,000	$(10,000)	from Notes Payable
Note issuance	—	10,000	from Notes Payable
Stock issuance	10,500	6,000	from Common Stock
	20,500	6,000	
Change in cash	$(11,200)	$ 11,700	from Cash

The analysis in Exhibit 4.14 has focused on the adjustments to accrual earnings that are required as a result of changes in various working capital (current assets minus current liabilities) accounts in order to derive operating cash flows under the indirect method. Obviously, many other adjustments are required to fully reconcile accrual earnings and cash flows from operations. These will be discussed in Chapter 17 after you have had a chance to review in some detail the accrual accounting entries related to noncurrent asset and liability accounts.

RECAP

Accrual earnings and cash flows capture different aspects of a firm's performance and often differ by a wide margin from year to year. Cash flows are critical to assessing a company's liquidity and creditworthiness. The cash flow statement provides a detailed summary of the cash inflows and outflows that are derived from a company's three primary activities—operations, investing, and financing. This section has outlined the basic techniques for deriving operating cash flows from an analysis of comparative balance sheets and income statement information. To do this, you must analyze changes in current asset and current liability accounts (as well as other noncash revenues and expenses like depreciation) that capture differences between the cash flow effects and accrual earnings effects of revenue and expense transactions.

SUMMARY

- The balance sheet and statement of cash flows are two of the primary financial statements required under GAAP.
- The balance sheet shows the assets owned by a company at a given point in time and how those assets are financed (debt versus equity). A variety of measurement bases are used to report the various asset, liability, and stockholders' equity accounts.
- When making intercompany comparisons, financial statement users must be careful to recognize how the different measurement bases affect key financial ratios and how account titles and statement formats vary across countries.
- Financial statement footnotes are an integral part of companies' financial reports and provide a wealth of information that allows statement users to better understand and interpret the numbers presented in the body of the financial statements.
- The statement of cash flows shows the change in cash for a given period, broken down into operating, investing, and financing activities.
- Successive balance sheets and the statement of cash flows articulate with one another, because changes in noncash balance sheet accounts can be used to explain changes in cash for a period.
- Analysis of changes in selected balance sheet accounts also can be used to explain why operating cash flows differ from accrual income.
- Conversely, the statement of cash flows provides information that enables users to understand changes in balance sheet accounts that have occurred over the reporting period.
- Understanding the interrelationships between successive balance sheets and the statement of cash flows, and being able to exploit these interrelationships to derive unknown account balances are important skills for analysts and lending officers.

EXERCISES

E4 – 1

Balance sheet classification

Typical balance sheet classifications appear below:

A.	Current assets	F.	Current liabilities
B.	Long-term investments and funds	G.	Long-term debt
C.	Property, plant and equipment	H.	Paid-in capital
D.	Intangible assets	I.	Retained earnings
E.	Other assets		

Required:

Use the letters above to indicate the proper classification for each of the following December 31, 2005 balance sheet items. Place brackets around the chosen letter for items that are contra-accounts.

1 _____ Accounts payable

2 _____ Accrued salaries payable

3 _____ Accumulated depreciation

4 _____ Cash

5 _____ Class B Preferred Stock

6 _____ Common Stock

7 _____ Installment note, payable in annual installments until 2009

8 _____ Investment in join venture

9 _____ Land, site of current manufacturing facility

10 _____ Leaseholds

11 _____ Long-lived assets classified as "held for sale"

12	_____	Note payable, March 25, 2006 maturity date
13	_____	Note receivable, October 12, 2007, maturity date
14	_____	Office supplies
15	_____	Prepaid rent, for 2006
16	_____	Short-term investments
17	_____	Term bonds payable, 2012 maturity date
18	_____	Trademarks
19	_____	Unearned revenue on 3-year subscriptions
20	_____	Vehicles

The following balance sheet for Northumberland Farm Machinery and Supply, Inc. was prepared by an inexperienced accountant and contains several errors.

E4 – 2

Balance sheet preparation

Northumberland Farm Machinery and Supply, Inc.

Balance Sheet December 31, 2005

Assets:

Cash	$ 15,000
Short-term investments	8,000
Inventory	175,000
Accounts receivable	70,000
Fixed assets	575,000
Trademark	5,000
Goodwill	65,000
Total assets	$913,000

Liabilities and Shareholders' Equity:

Accounts payable	$ 40,000
Wages payable	6,500
Allowance for bad debts	2,500
Mortgage payable	180,000
Bonds payable	300,000
Common stock	127,000
Retained earnings	257,000
Total liabilities and shareholders' equity	$913,000

Additional information:

1. Inventory is valued at cost (FIFO). At December 31, 2005 the inventory could have been replaced at a total cost of $165,000.
2. "Fixed assets" is comprised of land, buildings, and machinery that cost $85,000, $840,000, and $250,000, respectively. Accumulated depreciation on the buildings and machinery was $480,000 and $120,000, respectively.
3. Accounts receivable include a $5,000 note receivable from the company president due in June 2007.
4. The mortgage is payable in monthly installments. $15,000 in principal will be repaid in 2006.
5. The company's common stock has a $1 par value; 50,000 shares have been issued and are outstanding at year-end.
6. "Short-term investments" consists of shares of other companies that are appropriately valued at current market prices. These shares are appropriately classified as "available for sale" because management plans to sell them if the company needs additional operating cash in the next few months.
7. The bonds payable mature in 2010 and pay interest semiannually. The accountant forgot to record $6,000 in interest that had accrued since the last semiannual payment was made.

Required:

Prepare a classified balance sheet in proper form. Make any necessary corrections.

E4 – 3

Financial disclosures

Examples of typical disclosures that would appear in the notes accompanying financial statements are listed below.

Example		AP	Cash equivalents
1	_____		Components of inventory
2	_____		Computer software capitalization
3	_____		Depreciation methods
4	_____		Foreign currency translation
5	_____		Maturities of long-term debt issues
6	_____		Post-retirement benefits
7	_____		Restructuring and asset impairment charges
8	_____		Revenue recognition
9	_____		Schedule of other expense (income)
10	_____		Use of estimates

Required:

Indicate where the disclosure pertaining to each item would likely appear—either in the "accounting policies" note (AP) or a separate note (SN).

E4 – 4

Balance sheet classifications

A number of balance sheet accounts for Harvey's Heavy Metals, Inc. are presented below.

1. Raw materials inventory
2. Available-for-sale securities
3. 5,000 shares of XYZ common stock
4. Property taxes payable
5. Prepaid customer orders
6. Accrued salaries
7. Machinery held for sale
8. Treasury stock
9. Cash dividends payable
10. Certificates of deposit
11. Supplies
12. Accumulated depreciation
13. Franchise
14. Cash surrender value of life insurance
15. Long-term debt maturing within one year

Required:

Indicate the proper balance sheet classification for each of the accounts above. If more than one classification is potentially possible, indicate what additional information would be needed to make a determination.

E4 – 5

Classification of balance sheet accounts

Bunny's Fashions, Inc. used the following headings on the company's December 31, 2005 balance sheet.

(A) Current assets

(B) Long-term investments

(C) Property, plant and equipment

(D) Intangible assets

(E) Other assets

(F) Current liabilities

(G)   Long-term obligations

(H)   Capital stock

(I)   Additional paid-in-capital

(J)   Retained earnings

Required:

For each of the following, indicate its normal classification category. Use (NA) for items that would not appear on the face of the balance sheet, but would be discussed in the notes to the financial statements. Indicate by (NR) any items that would not be reported.

1 _____   Accounts receivable

2 _____   Accrued interest on notes payable (2006 maturity)

3 _____   Accumulated depreciation

4 _____   Bonds issued in 1976 the company plans to retire in 2006. No sinking fund exists.

5 _____   Class B common stock

6 _____   Deposits on designer fashions ordered by customers

7 _____   Depreciation methods

8 _____   Investment in affiliated company

9 _____   Maturities of long-term debt issues

10 _____   New 40-year bonds were issued on January 5, 2006

11 _____   Obsolete production machinery held for sale

12 _____   Office building owned by the company

13 _____   Preferred stock

14 _____   Premium on Class B common stock

15 _____   Prepaid insurance

16 _____   Salaries payable

17 _____   Taxes payable

18 _____   The company president announced plans to retire in 2007

19 _____   Trademarks

20 _____   Unrestricted savings account

During 2005 Kew Company, a service organization, had $200,000 in cash sales and $3,000,000 in credit sales. The accounts receivable balances were $400,000 and $485,000 at December 31, 2004 and 2005, respectively.

E4 – 6

Determining collections on account

Required:

What was Kew Company's cash receipts from sales in 2005?

The following information is available from Sand Corporation's accounting records for the year ended December 31, 2005:

E4 – 7

Determining cash from operations

Cash received from customers	$870,000
Rent received	10,000
Cash paid to suppliers and employees	510,000
Taxes paid	110,000
Cash dividends paid	30,000

Required:

Compute cash flow provided by operations for 2005.

E4 – 8

Determining cash collections on account

AICPA
ADAPTED

Fresh Company is preparing its cash budget for the month of May. The following information is available concerning its accounts receivable:

Estimated credit sales for May	$200,000
Actual credit sales for April	$150,000
Estimated collection in May for credit sales in May	20%
Estimated collection in May for credit sales in April	70%
Estimated collection in May for credit sales prior to April	$ 12,000
Estimated write-offs in May for uncollectible credit sales	$ 8,000
Estimated bad debts expense in May for credit sales in May	$ 7,000

Required:

What are the estimated cash receipts from accounts receivable collections in May?

E4 – 9

Determining ending accounts receivable

AICPA
ADAPTED

The following information is available for Alex Corporation's first year of operation:

Payment for merchandise purchases	$200,000
Ending merchandise inventory	60,000
Accounts payable (balance at end of year)	40,000
Collections from customers	170,000

All merchandise items were marked to sell at 30% above cost.

Required:

What should be the ending balance in accounts receivable, assuming all accounts are deemed collectible?

E4 – 10

Determining cash disbursements

AICPA
ADAPTED

Serven Corporation has estimated its accrual-basis revenue and expenses for June 2005 and would like your help in estimating cash disbursements. Selected data from these estimated amounts are as follows:

Sales	$700,000
Gross profit (based on sales)	30%
Increase in trade accounts receivable for the month	$ 20,000
Change in accounts payable during month	0
Increase in inventory during month	$ 10,000

Variable selling, general, and administrative expenses include a charge for uncollectible accounts of 1% of sales.

Total selling, general, and administrative expenses are $71,000 per month plus 15% of sales.

Depreciation expense of $40,000 per month is included in fixed selling, general, and administrative expense.

Required:

On the basis of the preceding data, what are the estimated cash disbursements from operations for June?

E4 – 11

Determining cash collections on account

AICPA
ADAPTED

The following information was taken from the 2005 financial statement of Planet Corporation:

Accounts receivable, January 1, 2005	$ 21,600
Accounts receivable, December 31, 2005	30,400
Sales on accounts and cash sales	438,000
Uncollectible accounts (bad debts)	1,000

No accounts receivable were written off or recovered during the year.

Required:

Determine the cash collected from customers by Planet Corporation in 2005.

Lance Corporation's statement of cash flows for the year ended September 30, 2005 was prepared using the indirect method, and it included the following items:

Net income	$60,000
Noncash adjustments	
Depreciation expense	9,000
Increase in accounts receivable	(5,000)
Decrease in inventory	40,000
Decrease in accounts payable	(12,000)
Net cash flows from operating activities	$92,000

Lance reported revenues from customers of $75,000 in its 2005 income statement.

E4 – 12

Determining cash received from customers

ADAPTED

Required:

What amount of cash did Lance receive from customers during the year ended September 30, 2005?

The following information was taken from the 2005 financial statements of Eiger Corporation, a maker of equipment for mountain and rock climbers:

Net income	$100,000
Depreciation	30,000
Increase (decrease) in	
Accounts receivable	110,000
Inventories	(50,000)
Prepaid expenses	15,000
Accounts payable	(150,000)
Salaries payable	15,000
Other current liabilities	(70,000)

E4 – 13

Determining cash from operations and reconciling with accrual net income

Required:

1. Calculate Eiger's cash flow from operating activities for 2005.
2. Explain the reasons for the difference between the firm's net income and its cash flow from operating activities in 2005.

The following information was taken from the 2005 financial statements of Zurich Corporation, a maker of fine Swiss watches:

Net income	$(200,000)
Depreciation	50,000
Increase (decrease) in	
Accounts receivable	(140,000)
Inventories	25,000
Other current assets	10,000
Accounts payable	120,000
Accrued payables	(25,000)
Interest payable	50,000

E4 – 14

Determining cash from operations and reconciling with accrual net income

Required:

1. Calculate Zurich's cash flow from operating activities for 2005.
2. Explain the reasons for the difference between the firm's net income and its cash flow from operating activities in 2005.

E4 – 15

Determining amounts shown
on statements of cash flows

The following information was taken from Abbott Laboratory's financial statements. Abbott makes a variety of healthcare products and uses the indirect method to determine cash flows from operations:

Cost of goods sold	$ 6,563,978
Acquisitions of property, plant and equipment	1,007,247
Decrease in inventories	109,087
Repayments of obligations under long-term leases	112,876
Decrease in salaries payable	534,281
Gain on sale of land	271,986
Increase in receivables	181,085
Purchases of long-term investment securities	178,727
Repayments of long-term borrowings	234,848
Increase in accrued payables	154,873
Proceeds from short-term borrowings	196,487
Decrease in accounts payable	121,741
Proceeds from sales of property, plant and equipment	23,878
Proceeds from the sale of long-term borrowings	381,848
Proceeds from sales of long-term investment securities	496,120
Decrease in other current assets	114,009
Purchases of common stock for treasury	607,598
Increase in prepaid expenses	34,875
Dividends paid	488,413
Sales	10,978,387
Depreciation and amortization	427,782
Repayments of short-term borrowings	213,833
Increase in current assets	3,978,911
Proceeds from the exercise of executive stock options	74,027

Required:

Determine which of the preceding items would appear as a separate line-item on Abbott Laboratory's statement of cash flows. In each case, indicate whether the item is related to cash flows from operations, from investing activities, or from financing activities.

PROBLEMS/DISCUSSION QUESTIONS

P4 – 1

Balance sheet preparation

Bambi's House Wares, Inc. produced the unadjusted trial balance shown below at December 31, 2005.

	Debits	Credits
Accounts payable		$ 796,050
Accounts receivable	$2,175,000	
Accrued interest payable		3,190
Accrued salaries payable		13,450
Accumulated depreciation—building		3,590,150
Accumulated depreciation—production equipment		4,750,000
Additional paid-in capital		520,000
Administrative expenses	1,377,500	
Allowance for uncollectible accounts		97,875
Available-for-sale securities (at cost, $91,000)	96,000	
Bond sinking fund	155,000	
Bonds payable (maturing 2010)		2,500,000
Buildings	9,845,000	
Cash	67,500	
Cash dividends payable		34,000
Common stock ($10 par)		4,000,000
Cost of goods sold	8,845,000	
Dividends	68,000	
Goodwill	390,000	

	Debits	Credits
Interest expense	168,750	
Inventories	1,105,625	
Investment in affiliated company	250,000	
Investment revenue		31,500
Land	417,800	
Leasehold	2,350	
Loss on discontinued operations before tax	68,500	
Notes payable (maturing 6/15/2006)		16,500
Notes payable (maturing 8/15/2009)		200,000
Production equipment	5,500,000	
Retained earnings, January 1, 2005		689,510
Sales		14,500,000
Selling expenses	1,160,000	
Trademark	8,100	
Treasury stock at cost	47,100	
Unrealized holding gain on available-for-sale securities	—	5,000
Totals	$31,747,225	$31,747,225

Required:

Prepare a balance sheet at December 31, 2005 for Bambi's House Wares, Inc. The company's tax rate is 35%.

Shawn Mikeska, Inc. prepared the following balance sheet at December 31, 2004.

P4 – 2

Preparation of a statement of cash flows and a balance sheet

Shawn Mikeska, Inc.

Balance Sheet December 31, 2004

Cash	$ 50,000
Accounts receivable	27,000
Inventory	80,000
Long-term investments	10,000
Land	32,000
Plant and equipment (net)	91,000
Total assets	$290,000
Accounts payable	$ 17,000
Taxes payable	3,000
Bonds payable	100,000
Capital stock	75,000
Retained earnings	95,000
Total liabilities and stockholders' equity	$290,000

The following occurred during 2005.

1. $25,000 in cash and a $35,000 note payable were exchanged for land valued at $60,000.
2. Bonds payable (maturing in 2009) in the amount of $20,000 were retired by paying $18,000 cash.
3. Capital stock in the amount of $50,000 was issued at par value.
4. The company sold surplus equipment for $18,000. The equipment had a book value of $14,000 at the time of the sale.
5. Net income was $31,000.
6. Cash dividends of $2,500 were paid to the stockholders.
7. 100 shares of stock (considered short-term investments) were purchased for $8,300.
8. A new building was acquired through the issuance of $50,000 in bonds.
9. $8,000 of depreciation was recorded on the plant and equipment.
10. At December 31, 2005, Cash was $87,200, Accounts receivable had a balance of $30,000, Inventory had increased to $82,000, and Accounts payable had fallen to $12,000. Long-term investments and Taxes payable were unchanged from 2004.

Required:

1. Prepare a statement of cash flows for 2005 using the indirect method.
2. Prepare the December 31, 2005 balance sheet for Shawn Mikeska, Inc.

P4 – 3

Balance sheet preparation

A December 31, 2005, post-closing trial balance for Short Erin Company appears below.

Account title	Debits	Credits
Cash	$ 61,500	
Short-term investments	47,000	
Accounts receivable	95,600	
Inventory	175,000	
Prepaid expenses	13,500	
Land	241,800	
Buildings	584,900	
Accumulated depreciation—buildings		$ 132,500
Production equipment	477,700	
Accumulated depreciation—production equipment		239,600
Patents	50,000	
Leasehold	7,000	
Accounts payable		38,400
Accrued salaries		3,400
Taxes payable		65,800
Notes payable		200,000
Installment note payable		84,200
Bonds payable		250,000
Common stock		300,000
Retained earnings		440,100
Totals	$1,754,000	$1,754,000

Additional information about Short Erin's account balances:
1. "Cash" includes $12,000 in U.S. treasury bills purchased on December 21, 2005 that mature in January 2006. The account also includes $8,500 in stock purchased just before year-end that the company plans to sell in a few days.
2. The accounts receivable balance consists of:

Trade receivables	$84,700
Allowance for doubtful trade accounts	(4,600)
Note receivable from Short Erin's president due in 2007	15,500
	$95,600

Trade receivables include $1,400 of customer accounts with credit balances.
3. "Notes payable" consists of two notes. One, in the amount of $50,000, is due on March 19, 2006. The other note matures on October 27, 2008.
4. The taxes payable account contains deferred income taxes amounting to $61,250.
5. The installment note payable bears an annual interest rate of 10%. Semiannual payments of $6,756.43 are due each June 30 and December 31 and include principal and accrued interest. These payments will reduce the installment note balance by $5,220 in 2006.
6. Of the 1,000,000 authorized shares of no par common stock, 300,000 shares are issued and outstanding.
7. The company recently announced plans to sell its operating facility in Katy, Texas, consisting of land (cost $82,000) and a building (cost $175,000; book value $110,000). Production equipment has already been removed from the Katy plant and is being used in other company facilities.

Required:

Prepare a classified balance sheet for the Short Erin Company at December 31, 2005.

P4 – 4

Preparing the income statement and statement of cash flows

Consider the following transactions pertaining to Retail Traders Company. Amounts in parentheses indicate a decrease in the account.

Explanation	Assets		=	Liabilities	+	Owners' Equity	
	Cash	Inventory		Accounts Payable		Common Stock	Retained Earnings
Beginning balance		$ 10,000		$ 5,000		$3,000	$ 2,000
Credit purchases		100,000		100,000			
Cash sales	$115,000						115,000
Cost of goods sold		(90,000)					(90,000)
Cash paid to suppliers	(85,000)			(85,000)			
Ending balance	$ 30,000	$ 20,000		$ 20,000		$3,000	$ 27,000

Required:

1. Based on this information, prepare an income statement and statement of cash flows.
2. Provide an intuitive explanation of how the adjustments made to net income in the cash flow statement converts the accrual numbers to cash flow numbers.

In reviewing the financial statements of Graceland Rock Company, you note that net income increased but cash flow from operations decreased from 2005 to 2006.

P4 – 5

Explaining the differences between cash flow from operations and accrual net income

Required:

1. Explain how net income could increase for Graceland Rock Company while cash flow from operations decreased. Your answer must include three illustrative examples.
2. Explain why cash flow from operations may be a good indicator of a firm's "quality of earnings" when analyzed in conjunction with accrual-basis earnings.

CMA
ADAPTED

Below are the common-size balance sheets from four companies: Amazon.com, an Internet book retailer; Alcoa, a major producer of aluminum products; Wendy's, a fast-food services organization; and Delta Air Lines, a major supplier of air transportation.

P4 – 6

Common-size financial statements

Required:

Based on your general business knowledge, the economic activities of these four firms, and information derived from the balance sheet analysis below, match the company with its respective balance sheet. Explain your reasoning for the choices that you make.

Common-Size Balance Sheet Comparisons

	Company A	Company B	Company C	Company D
Assets				
Current assets				
Cash and marketable securities	1.84%	6.91%	28.57%	11.19%
Current receivables	13.85	3.64	—	4.22
Inventories	9.48	—	8.93	2.14
Other current assets	2.95	5.60	3.45	1.02
Total current assets	28.12	16.15	40.95	18.57
Noncurrent assets				
Property, plant and equipment, net	53.52	69.32	12.85	73.76
Goodwill and intangibles, net	7.78	9.56	29.55	2.56
Other assets, net	10.58	4.97	16.65	5.11
Total assets	100.00%	100.00%	100.00%	100.00%
Liabilities and Stockholders' Equity				
Current liabilities				
Total current liabilities	17.60%	32.20%	29.90%	15.09%
Long-term liabilities	36.84	39.73	59.33	17.73
Total liabilities	54.44	71.93	89.23	32.82
Minority interest	8.53	—	—	—
Redeemable preferred stock	—	—	—	10.62
Stockholders' equity				
Contributed capital and other equity items	1.51	11.41	46.46	(0.18)
Retained earnings (deficit)	35.52	16.66	(35.69)	56.74
Total liabilities and stockholders' equity	100.00%	100.00%	100.00%	100.00%

P4 – 7

Common-size financial
statements

Below are the common-size balance sheets from four companies: Merck & Co., a global research-driven pharmaceutical manufacturing company; Target, a national discount retailer; Gannett, a newspaper publisher and broadcasting company; and Wisconsin Electric Power Company, a regional electric utility.

Required:

Based on your general business knowledge, the environment in which the above firms operate, and information derived from the balance sheet analysis, match the company with its respective balance sheet. Explain your reasoning for the choices that you make.

Common-Size Balance Sheet Comparisons

	Company A	Company B	Company C	Company D
Assets				
Current assets				
Cash and marketable securities	1.28%	8.99%	0.40%	0.51%
Current receivables	10.72	11.47	5.91	9.80
Inventories	22.16	7.99	3.16	1.05
Other current assets	3.66	3.15	1.61	0.58
Total current assets	37.82	31.60	11.08	11.94
Noncurrent assets				
Property, plant and equipment, net	57.74	27.15	62.75	24.69
Goodwill and intangibles, net	—	21.28	—	59.94
Other assets, net	4.44	19.97	26.17	3.43
Total assets	100.00%	100.00%	100.00%	100.00%
Liabilities and Stockholders' Equity				
Current liabilities				
Total current liabilities	34.13%	24.58%	13.41%	9.81%
Long-term liabilities	31.68	28.55	50.04	38.79
Total liabilities	65.81	53.13	63.45	48.60
Redeemable preferred stock	—	—	3.23	—
Stockholders' equity				
Contributed capital and other equity items*	4.70	(18.93)	14.37	(9.72)
Retained earnings (deficit)	29.49	65.80	18.95	61.12
Total liabilities and stockholders' equity	100.00%	100.00%	100.00%	100.00%

*Net of cost of shares repurchased for treasury.

P4 – 8

Determining cash flows from
operating and investing
activities

AICPA
ADAPTED

Karr, Inc. reported net income of $300,000 for 2005. Changes occurred in several balance sheet accounts as follows:

Equipment	$25,000 increase	Inventories	$20,000 decrease
Accumulated depreciation	40,000 increase	Accounts receivable	15,000 increase
Note payable	30,000 increase	Accounts payable	5,000 decrease

Additional Information:

- During 2005 Karr sold equipment costing $25,000, with accumulated depreciation of $12,000, for a gain of $5,000.
- In December 2005 Karr purchased equipment costing $50,000, with $20,000 cash and a 12% note payable of $30,000.
- Depreciation expense for the year was $52,000.

Required:

1. In Karr's 2005 statement of cash flows, calculate net cash provided by operating activities.
2. In Karr's 2005 statement of cash flows, calculate net cash used in investing activities.

The following data have been extracted from the financial statements of Prentiss, Inc., a calendar-year merchandising corporation:

P4 – 9

Determining operating cash flow components

ADAPTED

	December 31	
Balance sheet data	2005	2006
Trade accounts receivable—net	$ 84,000	$ 78,000
Inventory	150,000	140,000
Accounts payable—merchandise (credit)	(95,000)	(98,000)

- Total sales for 2006 were $1,200,000 and for 2005 were $1,100,000. Cash sales were 20% of total sales each year.
- Cost of goods sold was $840,000 for 2006.
- Variable general and administrative (G&A) expenses for 2006 were $120,000. These expenses have varied in proportion to sales and have been paid at the rate of 50% in the year incurred and 50% the following year. Unpaid G&A expenses are *not* included in accounts payable.
- Fixed general and administrative expenses—including $35,000 depreciation and $5,000 bad debt expense—totaled $100,000 each year. The amount of such expenses involving cash payments was paid at the rate of 80% in the year incurred and 20% the following year. In each year there was a $5,000 bad debt estimate and a $5,000 write-off. Unpaid G&A expenses are *not* included in accounts payable.

Required:

Compute the following:
1. The amount of cash collected during 2006 that resulted from total sales in 2005 and 2006.
2. The amount of cash disbursed during 2006 for purchases of merchandise.
3. The amount of cash disbursed during 2006 for variable and fixed general and administrative expenses.

The following cash flow information pertains to the 2005 operations of Matterhorn, Inc., a maker of ski equipment:

P4 – 10

Understanding the relation between the income statement, cash flow statement, and changes in balance sheet accounts

Cash collections from customers	$16,670
Cash payments to suppliers	19,428
Cash payments for various operating expenses	7,148
Cash payments for current income taxes	200
Cash provided (used) by operating activities	(10,106)

The following additional information comes from Matterhorn's 2005 income statement:

Net income	$ 609
Depreciation of equipment	2,256
Amortization of patents	399
Loss on sale of equipment	169

The following additional information comes from Matterhorn's 2004 and 2005 comparative balance sheets (decreases are in parentheses):

Change in accounts receivable	$ 3,630
Change in inventory	3,250
Change in accounts payable	(3,998)
Change in accrued operating expenses	(2,788)
Change in deferred taxes payable	127

Required:

1. Use the preceding information to derive Matterhorn's 2005 income statement.
2. Use the same information to compute Matterhorn's 2005 cash flow from operating activities under the indirect method (that is, derive cash flow from operating activities by making the necessary adjustments to net income).
3. Provide a brief explanation for the difference observed between net income and cash provided by operating activities.

P4 – 11

Understanding the relation between the income statement, cash flow statement, and changes in balance sheet accounts

The following cash flow information pertains to the 2005 operations of Divemaster, Inc., a maker of scuba diving equipment:

Cash collections from customers	$72,481
Cash payments to suppliers	51,768
Cash payments for selling and administrative expenses	9,409
Cash payments for interest	1,344
Cash payments for current income taxes	671
Cash provided by operating activities	9,289

The following additional information comes from Divemaster's 2005 income statement:

Net income	$ 1,085
Depreciation of equipment	7,380
Gain on sale of equipment	327

The following additional information comes from Divemaster's 2004 and 2005 comparative balance sheets (decreases are in parentheses):

Change in accounts receivable	$ (4,603)
Change in inventory	7,400
Change in accounts payable	3,146
Change in accrued selling and administrative expenses	772
Change in deferred taxes payable	(87)
Change in accrued interest payable	117

Required:

1. Use the preceding information to derive Divemaster's 2005 income statement.
2. Use the same information to compute Divemaster's 2005 cash flow from operating activities under the indirect method (that is, derive cash flow from operating activities by making the necessary adjustments to net income).
3. Provide a brief explanation for the difference observed between net income and cash provided by operating activities.

P4 – 12

Understanding the relation between operating cash flows and accrual earnings

The following information is taken from the operating section of the statement of cash flows (direct method) of Battery Builders, Inc.:

Collections from customers	$ 28,000
Payments to suppliers for purchases	(13,000)
Payments for operating expenses	(9,000)
Payments for current period income taxes	(4,000)
Cash provided by operating activities	2,000

The following information is obtained from the income statement of Battery Builders:

Net income	$4,000
Depreciation expense	4,000
Gain on sale of equipment	2,000
Write-off of goodwill	1,000

In addition, the following information is obtained from the comparative balance sheets of Battery Builders (+/– refers to increase/decrease):

Change in accounts receivable	$+3,000
Change in inventory	+3,000
Change in accounts payable	+2,000
Change in accrued payable (related to operating expense)	–2,000
Change in deferred income taxes payable	+1,000

Required:

1. Prepare a complete accrual-basis income statement for the current year.
2. Compute the cash flows from operations using the indirect approach (that is, start with accrual-basis net income and adjust for various items to obtain cash flows from operations).

The data listed below were taken from a recent balance sheet for American Standard Companies. The amounts indicated by question marks were intentionally omitted.

P4 – 13

Balance sheet preparation with missing elements

($ in millions)

Assets	
Current assets:	
Cash and cash equivalents	$ 96.6
Accounts receivable, less allowance	
for doubtful accounts of $38.1	881.4
Inventories	770.7
Deferred tax assets	?
Other current assets	217.0
Total current assets	2,014.4
Facilities, at cost, net of accumulated depreciation	1,430.1
Goodwill	1,012.8
Capitalized software costs, net of accumulated	
amortization of $131.7	?
Debt issuance costs, net of accumulated	
amortization of $17.4	26.5
Other assets	418.0
Total assets	?
Current liabilities:	
Loans payable to banks	36.3
Current maturities of long-term debt	4.5
Accounts payable	601.6
Accrued payrolls	281.0
Current portion of warranties	118.0
Taxes payable	?
Other accrued liabilities	525.3
Total current liabilities	1,665.6
Long-term debt	1,918.4
Other long-term liabilities:	
Post-retirement benefits	623.3
Warranty obligations	?
Deferred tax liabilities	108.9
Other	399.9
Total liabilities	4,914.0
Shareholders' equity:	
Preferred stock, 2,000,000 shares authorized, none issued	—
Common stock, $.01 par value, 200,000,000 shares	
authorized; shares issued and outstanding—72,613,736	0.7
Capital surplus	724.4
Unearned compensation	(2.3)
Treasury stock, at cost: 11.301,604 shares	(534.6)
Retained earnings	428.0
Accumulated other comprehensive income:	
Foreign currency translation effects	(309.2)
Deferred loss on hedge contracts, net of tax	(2.0)
Minimum pension liability adjustment, net of tax	(75.2)
Total shareholders' equity	?
Total liabilities and shareholders' equity	?

Required:

1. Determine the missing amounts.
2. Prepare American Standard's classified balance sheet.

P4 – 14

Microsoft (Finding missing values on a classified balance sheet and analyzing balance sheet changes)

The following information was taken from Microsoft Corporation's Year 2 balance sheet; Microsoft is one of the largest independent computer software makers in the United States.

($ in millions)	June 30, Year 2
Total current liabilities	$ 5,730
Other current assets	?
Equity investments	?
Property, plant and equipment, net	1,505
Common stock and paid-in capital	?
Other assets	260
Cash and short-term investments	13,927
Total stockholders' equity	?
Accounts payable	759
Retained earnings	7,622
Unearned revenue	?
Accrued compensation	359
Accounts receivable, net	1,460
Total assets	?
Other current liabilities	809
Preferred stock	980
Total current assets	15,889
Income taxes payable	915
Total liabilities and stockholders' equity	22,357

The following is Microsoft's Year 1 balance sheet.

Microsoft Corporation

Consolidated Balance Sheets

($ in millions)	June 30, Year 1
Assets	
Current assets	
Cash and short-term investments	$ 8,966
Accounts receivable, net	980
Other	427
Total current assets	10,373
Property, plant and equipment	1,465
Equity investments	2,346
Other assets	203
Total assets	$14,387
Liabilities and Stockholders' Equity	
Current liabilities	
Accounts payable	$ 721
Accrued compensation	336
Income taxes payable	466
Unearned revenue	1,418
Other	669
Total current liabilities	3,610
Stockholders' equity	
Convertible preferred stock: shares authorized 100; issued and outstanding 13	980
Common stock and paid-in capital: shares authorized 8,000; issued and outstanding 2,408	4,509
Retained earnings	5,288
Total stockholders' equity	10,777
Total liabilities and stockholders' equity	$14,387

Required:

1. Solve for the missing values and present Microsoft's Year 2 balance sheet in good form.
2. Microsoft has recently become a customer of your firm. In fact, their accounts receivable is one of your firm's largest current assets. The amount is so large that the chief executive officer (CEO) of

your firm is concerned because if Microsoft doesn't pay in a timely fashion your firm would experience severe cash flow problems. Use Microsoft's balance sheet to assess Microsoft's ability to make timely payment of its current liabilities.

3. Using your Year 2 balance sheet and the Year 1 balance sheet provided, compare and contrast the financial position of the firm at the end of these two years. For example, were there any major changes in Microsoft's financial position from the end of Year 1 to the end of Year 2? In what ways did the firm's financial position improve or deteriorate over this time period?

4. Assume that you are a financial analyst. Based on the financial position of Microsoft as portrayed in the Year 1 and Year 2 balance sheets, would you advise your clients to invest in the common stock of the firm? Why or why not?

5. Before advising your clients about whether or not to purchase the common stock of Microsoft, what information beyond the Year 1 and Year 2 balance sheets would you seek?

The following information was taken from one of Hewlett-Packard Company's recent balance sheets. Hewlett-Packard is a major designer and manufacturer of electronic measurement and computing equipment, including workstations, PCs, and laser printers.

P4 – 15

Finding missing values on a classified balance sheet and analyzing balance sheet accounts

www.prenhall.com/revsine

● Student Resources

☑ Template for solution

($ in millions)

Total liabilities and shareholders' equity	?
Inventories: Finished goods	$ 1,100
Other current assets	347
Employee compensation and benefits payable	837
Total current assets	6,716
Land	?
Total shareholders' equity	7,269
Long-term debt	?
Machinery and equipment	2,792
Taxes payable	381
Long-term receivables and other assets	1,912
Other long-term liabilities	210
Cash and cash equivalents	625
Total assets	11,973
Notes payable and short-term borrowings	?
Deferred revenues (current)	375
Short-term investments	495
Buildings and leasehold improvements	2,779
Total current liabilities	4,063
Inventories: Purchased parts and fabricated assemblies	1,173
Deferred taxes payable	243
Common stock and capital in excess of $1 par value	1,010
Accumulated depreciation	2,616
Other accrued liabilities	583
Retained earnings	?
Accounts and notes receivable	?
Accounts payable	686

Required:

1. Use the information in the problem to determine the missing amounts and present Hewlett-Packard's balance sheet in good form.

2. Does Hewlett-Packard obtain financing primarily from stockholders or from creditors? Explain.

3. What is Hewlett-Packard's largest current asset?

4. What is Hewlett-Packard's largest current liability?

5. Calculate the ratio of Hewlett-Packard's current assets to current liabilities and comment on Hewlett-Packard's short-term liquidity position.

6. Hewlett-Packard's balance sheet lists an item called "Other current assets." What assets might be included under this heading?

P4 – 16

Analyzing the difference between operating cash flows and accrual earnings

www

www.prenhall.com/revsine

● Student Resources

✔ Template for solution

The following are Food Tiger's 2004 and 2005 balance sheets and 2005 income statement.

Food Tiger, Inc.

Comparative Balance Sheets

	December 31	
	2005	**2004**
Assets		
Current assets		
Cash and cash equivalents	$ 6,804	$ 428
Receivables	97,106	76,961
Inventories	844,539	673,606
Prepaid expenses	9,401	16,684
Total current assets	957,850	767,679
Property, at cost	1,446,896	1,094,804
Less: Accumulated depreciation	(407,641)	(303,027)
Total assets	$1,997,105	$1,559,456
Liabilities and Shareholders' Equity		
Current liabilities		
Accounts payable—trade	$ 343,163	$ 290,064
Accrued expenses	184,017	138,921
Accrued interest payable	1,067	3,394
Income taxes payable	37,390	42,958
Total current liabilities	565,637	475,337
Long-term debt	504,913	415,561
Total liabilities	$1,070,550	$ 890,898
Shareholders' equity		
Common stock	$ 263,155	$ 162,298
Retained earnings	663,400	506,260
Total shareholders' equity	$ 926,555	$ 668,558
Total liabilities and shareholders' equity	$1,997,105	$1,559,456

Food Tiger, Inc.

Income Statement for Year Ended December 31, 2005

Net sales	$6,438,507
Cost of goods sold	(5,102,977)
Gross profit	1,335,530
Selling and administrative expenses	(855,809)
Interest expense	(34,436)
Depreciation	(104,614)
Income before income taxes	340,671
Provision for income taxes	(135,500)
Net income	$ 205,171

Additional Information:

1. The "Accounts payable, trade" account is used only for purchases of merchandise inventory.
2. The balance in the "Prepaid expenses" account represents prepaid selling and administrative expenses for the following year.
3. Except for the prepaid selling and administrative expenses noted in (2), the company records all selling and administrative expenses in the accrued expenses account prior to making payment.
4. The company records all interest expense in the "Accrued interest payable" account prior to making payment.
5. The company records all income tax expense in the "Income taxes payable" account prior to making payment.
6. Cash dividends declared and paid during 2005 were $48,031.
7. No long-term assets were disposed of in 2005.

Required:

1. Prepare an analysis of Food Tiger's 2005 operating cash flows and accrual-based net income by completing the following table. The table follows the format of Exhibit 4.9 in this chapter.
2. Prepare Food Tiger's "Statement of cash flows" for 2005. Follow the format of Exhibit 4.10 in this chapter.

Table 1 Food Tiger, Inc.

Analysis of Change in Cash versus Income for 2005

Item	(a) Accrual Income	(b) Noncash Accruals: Revenue Earned or Expenses Incurred	(c) Prepayments/ Buildups/Other Adjustments	(d) (a + b + c) Cash Received (+) or Paid (–)
Operating activities				
.				
.				
.				
Operating cash flow				
Net income				
Investing activities				
.				
.				
.				
Financing activities				
.				
.				
.				
Change in cash				

Vanguard Corporation is a distributor of food products. The corporation has approximately 1,000 stockholders; and its stock, which is traded "over-the-counter," is sold throughout 2005 at about $7 a share with little fluctuation. The corporation's balance sheet at December 31, 2004 appears below.

P4 – 17

Preparing the balance sheet and income statement

AICPA
ADAPTED

www.prenhall.com/revsine

● Student Resources

☑ Template for solution

Vanguard Corporation

Balance Sheet December 31, 2004

Assets		
Current assets		
Cash		$ 4,386,040
Accounts receivable	$3,150,000	
Less allowance for doubtful accounts	(94,500)	3,055,500
Inventories—at the lower of cost (FIFO)		
or market		2,800,000
Total current assets		10,241,540
Fixed assets—at cost	$3,300,000	
Less accumulated depreciation	(1,300,000)	2,000,000
Total assets		$12,241,540
Liabilities and Stockholders' Equity		
Current liabilities		
Notes payable due within one year		$ 1,000,000
Accounts payable and accrued liabilities		2,091,500
Federal income taxes payable		300,000
Total current liabilities		3,391,500
Notes payable due after one year		4,000,000
Stockholders' equity		
Capital stock—authorized 2,000,000 shares		
of $1 par value; issued and outstanding		
1,000,000 shares	$1,000,000	
Additional paid-in capital	1,500,000	
Retained earnings	2,350,040	
Total stockholders' equity		4,850,040
Total liabilities and stockholders' equity		$12,241,540

Information concerning the corporation and its activities during 2005 follows:

1. Sales for the year were $15,650,000. The gross profit percentage for the year was 30% of sales. Merchandise purchases and freight-in totaled $10,905,000. Depreciation and other expenses do not enter into cost of goods sold.

2. Administrative, selling, and general expenses (including provision for state taxes) other than interest, depreciation, and provision for doubtful accounts amounted to $2,403,250.

3. The December 31, 2005 accounts receivable amounted to $3,350,000, and the corporation maintains an allowance for doubtful accounts equal to 3% of the accounts receivable outstanding. During the year $50,000 of 2004 receivables were deemed uncollectible and charged off to the allowance account.

4. The rate of depreciation of fixed assets is 13% per annum, and the corporation consistently follows the policy of taking one-half year's depreciation in the year of acquisition. The depreciation expense for 2005 was $474,500.

5. The notes are payable in 20 equal quarterly installments—commencing March 31, 2005—with interest at 5% per annum also payable quarterly.

6. Accounts payable and accrued liabilities at December 31, 2005 were $2,221,000.

7. The balance of the 2005 federal income tax paid in 2005 was in exact agreement with the amount accrued on the December 31, 2004 balance sheet.

8. The 2005 estimated tax payments made in 2005 totaled $400,000. Income tax expense for 2005 on an accrual accounting basis was $530,000.

9. During the second month of each quarter of 2005, dividends of $0.10 a share were declared and paid. In addition, in July 2005 a 5% stock dividend was declared and paid.

Required:

Prepare the following statements in good form and support them by well-organized and developed computations for the year ending December 31, 2005:

a. Balance sheet

b. Income statement

P4 – 18

Snap-On-Tools Corporation (CW): Determine missing amounts on the cash flow statement

www.prenhall.com/revsine

● Student Resources

☑ Template for solution

The purpose of this case is to familiarize you with the statement of cash flows of a publicly held company. Its primary objective is to test your understanding of the relationships underlying the cash flow statement. It also serves as a natural way to expand your understanding of accounting terminology. This is an important feature because the financial statements of publicly held companies often use terms that are different from those appearing in financial accounting textbooks.

The information that follows was taken from Snap-On-Tools Corporation's Year 2 statement of cash flows. Snap-On-Tools Corporation makes and sells hand tools for mechanics, tool storage units, and related items. Most of the company's sales come from dealers who visit customer locations with their walk-in vans.

($ in thousands)	
Cash and cash equivalents at beginning of year	$ 10,930
Increase in notes payable	52,503
Decrease in deferred income taxes	6,005
Decrease in accounts payable	8,202
Net cash provided by operating activities	?
Capital expenditures	21,081
Depreciation	25,484
Acquisition of Sun Electric, net of cash acquired	110,719
Increase in receivables	5,458
Net cash used in investing activities	?
Payment of long-term debt	8,332
Increase in other noncurrent assets	3,609
Decrease in inventories	5,928
Proceeds from stock option plans	4,940
Net earnings	65,975
Increase in accruals, deposits, and other liabilities	23,330
Cash dividends paid	45,718
Increase in long-term debt	78,650
Net cash provided by (used in) financing activities	?
Effect of exchange rate changes	1,916
Increase in cash and cash equivalents	?
Disposal of property and equipment	3,379

($ in thousands)

Cash and cash equivalents at end of year	?
Amortization	3,973
Increase in prepaid expenses	4,829
Gain on sale of assets	250

Required:

Use the information provided above and on the previous page to solve for the missing values, and recast Snap-On-Tools's Year 2 statement of cash flows in proper form. (*Note:* The item "Effect of exchange rate changes" captures gains or losses that arise when a firm converts its foreign subsidiaries' financial statements from the respective currencies [for example, French francs] into U.S. dollars.) In Snap-On's case, these translations were not favorable in Year 2. While the amount of this item reflects events and transactions affecting various items in the statement of cash flows, it is not separately identified with any individual section of the statement. Rather, it is treated as an adjustment to aggregate net cash flows to arrive at the change in cash. This adjustment usually appears near the bottom of the statement of cash flows.

CASES

A major retailer recently filed the balance sheet below with the SEC.

C4 – 1

Financial disclosures

Major Retailer

Consolidated Balance Sheet for the Year Ended February 1, 2003
($ in thousands)

Assets	
Current assets	
Cash and equivalents	$3,388,514
Merchandise inventory	2,049,879
Other current assets	303,332
Total current assets	5,741,725
Property and equipment	
Leasehold improvements	2,241,831
Furniture and equipment	3,438,805
Land and buildings	942,845
Construction-in-progress	202,839
	6,826,320
Accumulated depreciation and amortization	(3,049,477)
Property and equipment, net	3,776,843
Lease rights and other assets	383,436
Total assets	$9,902,004
Liabilities and Stockholders' Equity	
Current Liabilities	
Current maturities of long-term debt	$ 499,979
Accounts payable	1,159,301
Accrued expenses and other current liabilities	1,067,294
Total current liabilities	2,726,574
Long-term liabilities	
Long-term debt	1,515,794
Senior convertible notes	1,380,000
Deferred lease credits and other liabilities	621,424
Total long-term liabilities	3,517,218
Stockholders' equity	
Common stock	48,401
Additional paid-in capital	638,306
Retained earnings	5,289,480
Accumulated other comprehensive losses	(16,766)
Deferred compensation	(13,574)
Treasury stock	(2,287,635)
Total stockholders' equity	3,658,212
Total liabilities and stockholders' equity	$9,902,004

Required:

Identify the items in the major retailer's balance sheet that probably would require additional disclosure either on the face of the financial statement or in a note. For each item you identify, specify the general contents of the required disclosure.

C4 – 2

Financial reporting research case—Subsequent events

Alpha Manufacturing, Inc. issued audited financial statements on March 10, 2006 for its year ended December 31, 2005. The following events occurred after December 31, 2005, but before the financial statements were issued.

1. Alpha Manufacturing received legal notification on January 18, 2006 that Conner Co. (one of the company's customers) had filed for bankruptcy. Alpha Manufacturing's December 31, 2005 accounts receivable balance included receivables from Conner Co. in the amount of $92,500.
2. On February 23, 2006 Alpha's board of directors voted to secure $50,000,000 in additional debt financing through an issue of 25-year debentures. Management has been working with an investment bank on this matter and plans to market the securities in the next month or two.
3. Alpha signed a contract with a major retailer on January 12, 2006 that is expected to increase sales by 20% over the next few years.
4. February 15, 2006 was not a good day for Alpha Manufacturing. On that date, a competitor introduced a new product that will render $27 million of Alpha's inventory obsolete. Alpha will also be forced to idle one of its production facilities and retool another as a result of this development.

Required:

Review *Statement on Auditing Standards No. 1* on "Subsequent Events" from your library. Determine the appropriate treatment of each of these events in Alpha Manufacturing's 2005 financial statements. Assume each of these events is considered material.

C4 – 3

Financial reporting research case—Related party matters

Golden Bear Golf, Inc., an international golf services company, was founded in 1996 when it was spun-off from Golden Bear International, Inc. (GBI). Golden Bear's initial business plan called for it to focus primarily on acquiring and operating golf centers. Paragon Construction International, Inc., a wholly owned subsidiary of Golden Bear Golf, provided golf course construction services. Paragon's financial statements were a material component of Golden Bear's consolidated financial statements. The SEC maintains that Golden Bear Golf's financial statements in 1997 and 1998 did not conform to GAAP because Paragon engaged in a scheme to artificially inflate and accelerate revenue and gross margin on its construction contracts.

Required:

1. Review *SFAS No. 57*, "Related Party Disclosures" using the FASB's Financial Accounting Research System (FARS), Pricewaterhouse Cooper's Comperio® authoritative financial reporting database or other reference sources in your local library.
2. Use Edgar (WWW.SEC.gov) to access the 1997 Form 10-K for Golden Bear Golf, Inc. Look up and read the "related party" footnote (note 13). The SEC maintains that this footnote is deficient because:

   > "Golden Bear also failed to disclose certain material terms of related party transactions it had with GBI and with GBI's owner personally. Among other things, the Company [Golden Bear Golf] failed to disclose that in October 1996, GBI guaranteed an amount owed to Paragon by the owner of a specific golf course construction project (project "A") that Paragon was building. The Company also failed to disclose that at December 31, 1997, Project A's owners defaulted on the debt, leaving a balance of $500,000 due from GBI pursuant to the guarantee. Golden Bear also failed to disclose its July 1998 forgiveness of GBI's $500,000 guarantee in connection with GBI's participation in the Company's settlement of claims relating to a separate project."[12]

3. What is the significance of this omitted disclosure?
4. Why is it important that companies disclose related party transactions?

---

[12] Securities and Exchange Commission, *Accounting and Auditing Enforcement Release No. 1676*, November 26, 2002.

A recent balance sheet for British Airways, PLC is presented below. (Footnote references—appearing on the original balance sheet—have been omitted.)

C4 – 4

International reporting case

British Airways, PLC

Balance Sheets at March 31, 2003
(£ in millions)

Fixed assets		
Intangible assets		
Goodwill	£ 99	
Landing rights	65	
	164	
Tangible assets		
Fleet	7,828	
Property	1,219	
Equipment	440	
	9,487	
Investments		
Associated undertakings	461	
Trade investments	32	
Investment in own shares	31	
	524	
	10,175	
Current assets		
Stocks	87	
Debtors	986	
Short-term loans and deposits	1,430	
Cash at bank and in hand	222	
	2,725	
Creditors: Amounts falling due within one year	(2,904)	
Net current liabilities	(179)	
Total assets less current liabilities	9,996	
Creditors: Amounts falling due after more than one year		
Borrowings and other creditors	(6,441)	
Convertible capital bonds 2005	(112)	
	(6,553)	
Provision for deferred tax	(1,062)	
Provisions for liabilities and charges	(107)	
	£ 2,274	
Capital and reserves		
Called up share capital	£ 271	
Reserves		
Share premium account	788	
Revaluation reserve	270	
Profit and loss account	729	
	1,787	
Total equity shareholders' funds	2,058	
Minority interest		
Equity minority interest	10	
Non-equity minority interest	206	
	216	
	£ 2,274	

Required:

1. Examine the British Airways balance sheet and identify at least three differences between balance sheets as presented in the United Kingdom and the United States.
2. Review British Airways' balance sheet and discuss how its format provides useful information to investors and creditors.

C4 – 5

Debbie Dress Shops, Inc.:
Determining cash flow
amounts from comparative
balance sheets and income
statement

AICPA
ADAPTED

The balance sheet and income statement for Debbie Dress Shops are presented along with some additional information about the accounts. You are to answer the questions that follow concerning cash flows for the period.

Debbie Dress Shops, Inc.

Balance Sheet

	December 31	
	2005	2004
Assets		
Current assets		
Cash	$ 300,000	$ 200,000
Accounts receivable—net	840,000	580,000
Merchandise inventory	660,000	420,000
Prepaid expenses	100,000	50,000
Total current assets	1,900,000	1,250,000
Long-term investments	80,000	—
Land, building, and fixtures	1,130,000	600,000
Less: Accumulated depreciation	(110,000)	(50,000)
	1,020,000	550,000
Total assets	$3,000,000	$1,800,000
Liabilities and Stockholders' Equity		
Current liabilities		
Accounts payable	$ 530,000	$ 440,000
Accrued expenses	140,000	130,000
Dividends payable	70,000	—
Total current liabilities	740,000	570,000
Note payable—due year 2008	500,000	—
Stockholders' Equity		
Common stock	1,200,000	900,000
Retained earnings	560,000	330,000
Total stockholders' equity	1,760,000	1,230,000
Total liabilities and stockholders' equity	$3,000,000	$1,800,000

Debbie Dress Shops, Inc.

Income Statements

	Years Ended December 31	
	2005	2004
Net credit sales	$6,400,000	$4,000,000
Cost of goods sold	5,000,000	3,200,000
Gross profit	1,400,000	800,000
Expenses (including income taxes)	1,000,000	520,000
Net income	$ 400,000	$ 280,000

1. All accounts receivable and accounts payable are related to trade merchandise. Accounts payable are recorded net and always are paid to take all the discounts allowed. The allowance for doubtful accounts at the end of 2005 was the same as at the end of 2004; no receivables were charged against the allowance during 2005.
2. The proceeds from the note payable were used to finance a new store building. Capital stock was sold to provide additional working capital.

Required:

1. Calculate cash collected during 2005 from accounts receivable.
2. Calculate cash payments during 2005 on accounts payable to suppliers.
3. Calculate cash provided from operations for 2005.
4. Calculate cash inflows during 2005 from financing activities.
5. Calculate cash outflows from investing activities during 2005.

Following is Drop Zone Corporation's balance sheet at the end of 2004 and its cash flow statement for 2005. Drop Zone manufactures equipment for sky divers.

C4 – 6

Drop Zone Corporation (CW): Understanding the relation between successive balance sheets and the cash flow statement

www.prenhall.com/revsine

● Student Resources

☑ Template for solution

STRETCH

Drop Zone Corporation

Balance Sheet December 31, 2004

Assets

Current assets

Cash	$ 7,410
Accounts receivable—net	6,270
Inventory	13,395
Prepaid assets	1,995
Total current assets	29,070
Land	27,930
Buildings and equipment	194,655
Less: Accumulated depreciation, buildings and equipment	(40,185)
Total assets	$211,470

Liabilities and Stockholders' Equity

Current liabilities

Accounts payable	$ 11,400
Accrued payables	3,135
Total current liabilities	14,535
Long-term debt	19,950

Stockholders' equity

Common stock, $10.00 par value	18,525
Paid-in capital	31,920
Retained earnings	144,780
Less: Treasury stock	(18,240)
Total liabilities and stockholders' equity	$211,470

Drop Zone Corporation

Statement of Cash Flows for Year Ended December 31, 2005

Operating Activities

Net income	$ 11,400

Plus (minus) noncash items

+Depreciation expense	5,415

Plus (minus) changes in current asset and liability accounts

+Decrease in inventory	1,425
+Decrease in prepaid assets	855
+Increase in accrued payables	1,140
−Increase in accounts receivable	(3,990)
−Decrease in accounts payable	(2,850)
Cash provided by operating activities	$ 13,395

Investing Activities

Purchase of equipment	$(39,615)
Proceeds from the sale of land	8,550
Cash used by investing activities	$(31,065)

Financing Activities

Issuance of long-term debt	$ 16,245
Issuance of common stock	12,825
Cash dividends paid	(6,270)
Purchase of treasury stock	(2,565)
Cash provided by financing activities	$ 20,235
Net cash flow	$ 2,565

Additional Information:

1. During 2005, 500 shares of common stock were sold to the public.
2. Land was sold during 2005 at an amount that equaled its original cost.

Required:

Use the preceding information to derive Drop Zone Corporation's balance sheet at the end of 2005.

C4 – 7

Long Distance Runner Corporation (CW): Understanding the relation between successive balance sheets and the cash flow statement

www.prenhall.com/revsine

● Student Resources

☑ Template for solution

Long Distance Runner Corporation manufactures footwear and clothing for runners and hikers. Its balance sheet at the end of 2005 and its cash flow statement for 2005 follow.

Long Distance Runner Corporation

Balance Sheet December 31, 2005

Assets	
Current assets	
Cash	$ 39,825
Accounts receivable—net	147,825
Inventory	27,000
Prepaid expenses	6,750
Total current assets	221,400
Land	202,500
Buildings	202,500
Equipment	40,500
Less: Accumulated depreciation, buildings and equipment	(27,000)
Patents, net	40,500
Total assets	$680,400
Liabilities and Stockholders' Equity	
Current liabilities	
Accounts payable	$ 62,100
Accrued salaries payable	20,250
Accrued interest payable	20,250
Total current liabilities	102,600
Notes payable—long term	148,500
Long-term debt	158,625
Stockholders' equity	
Common stock $1.00 par value	23,500
Paid-in capital	233,000
Retained earnings	14,175
Less: Treasury stock	—
Total liabilities and stockholders' equity	$680,400

Long Distance Runner Corporation

Statement of Cash Flows for the Year Ended December 31, 2005

Operating Activities	
Net income	$ 20,925
Plus (minus) noncash items	
+Depreciation expense	16,875
+Amortization of patent	13,500
+Loss on sale of equipment	675
	$ 51,975
Plus (minus) changes in current asset and liability accounts	
+Decrease in prepaid assets	6,750
+Increase in accrued salaries payable	13,500
−Increase in accounts receivable	(73,575)
−Increase in inventory	(6,750)
−Decrease in accounts payable	(22,275)
−Decrease in accrued interest	(10,125)
Cash used by operating activities	$ (40,500)

Investing Activities	
Purchase of land	$ (67,500)
Purchase of building	(202,500)
Proceeds from the sale of equipment	9,450
Cash used by investing activities	$(260,550)
Financing Activities	
Issuance of long-term debt	$ 158,625
Issuance of common stock	175,500
Cash dividends paid	(47,250)
Sale of treasury stock	6,750
Principal repayment on note payable	(6,750)
Cash provided by financing activities	$ 286,875
Net cash flow	$ (14,175)

Additional Information:

1. During 2005, 7,500 shares of common stock were sold to the public.
2. Equipment with an original cost of $13,500 and with accumulated depreciation of $3,375 was sold for $9,450 in 2005.

Required:

Use the preceding information to derive Long Distance Runner Corporation's balance sheet at the end of 2004 (that is, at the beginning of 2005).

COLLABORATIVE LEARNING CASE

The following information was taken from Kellogg Company's Year 2 statement of cash flows. Kellogg is the world's largest maker of ready-to-eat cereals. Its cereal products account for about 38% of the U.S. market and 52% of the non-U.S. market. Some of its more famous brand-name products include Frosted Flakes, Rice Krispies, Fruit Loops, and Apple Jacks.

C4 – 8

Kellogg Company (CW): Determine missing amounts on the cash flow statement and explain the causes for change in cash

($ in millions)	
Increase (decrease) in cash and temporary investments	$77.5
Issuance of common stock	17.7
Other noncash expenses	16.8
Decrease in accounts receivable	10.2
Additions to properties	?
Purchase of treasury stock	83.6
Depreciation	222.8
Increase in prepaid expenses	22.9
Cash and temporary investments at end of year	?
Decrease in deferred income taxes	5.4
Borrowings on notes payable	182.1
Cash used by investing activities	319.9
Issuance of long-term debt	4.3
Cash dividends	?
Property disposals	25.2
Cash provided by operations	934.4
Increase in accounts payable	42.7
Other financing activities	1.1
Reduction of long-term debt	126.0
Increase in inventories	41.4
Cash used by financing activities	?
Effect of exchange rate changes on cash	0.7
Net earnings	?
Cash and temporary investments at beginning of year	100.5
Increase in accrued liabilities	105.6
Other acquisitions	11.6
Reduction of notes payable	274.0

Required:

1. Determine the missing values and recast Kellogg's Year 2 statement of cash flows, showing in good form cash flows from operations, investing, and financing activities. (*Note:* The item "Effect of exchange rate changes on cash" captures the gains or losses that arise when a firm converts its foreign subsidiaries' financial statements from the respective currencies (for example, French francs) into U.S. dollars. In Kellogg's case, these translations were favorable in Year 2. This item should be treated as an adjustment to aggregate net cash flows to arrive at the change in cash. This adjustment usually appears near the bottom of the statement of cash flows.)

2. How did Kellogg fund its investing activities during Year 2?

3. How much cash did depreciation provide during Year 2?

4. Cash provided by operations was $934.4 million in Year 2, yet Kellogg's cash account balance only increased by $77.5 million during the year. How can this be?

www.prenhall.com/revsine

Remember to check the book's Companion Website for additional problem and case material.

CHAPTER 5

Essentials of Financial Statement Analysis

"Investors would be well advised to shut out all the yammering about earnings expectations, consensus forecasts, and whisper numbers and focus instead on the financial information reported by companies themselves."[1]

A firm's financial statements are like an optical lens. If you know how to look through them, you can more clearly see what is going on at the firm. Has profitability improved? Are customers paying their bills more promptly? How was the new manufacturing plant financed? Financial statements hold the answers to these and other questions. They can tell us how the company got to where it is today, and they can help us forecast where the company might be tomorrow.

This chapter provides an overview of three financial analysis tools—**common-size statements**, **trend statements**, and **financial ratios**. We show how each tool is used to analyze profitability and credit risk, and we explain how to interpret the results from each. But the important message in this chapter is that all financial analysis tools are built around reported accounting data, and these tools can be no better than the data from which they are constructed. ***What financial data a company chooses to report and how the data are reported affect not only the financial statements themselves but also the ratios and other numbers used to analyze those statements.***

Introducing financial analysis tools at this early point prepares you for later chapters where we describe various financial reporting alternatives and their impact on ratios, trends, and other comparisons.

Basic Approaches

Analysts use financial statements and financial data in many ways and for many different purposes. Two purposes you should know are time-series analysis and cross-sectional analysis.

Time-series analysis helps identify financial trends over time for a *single* company or business unit. The analyst might be interested in determining the rate of growth in sales for Intel Corporation, or the degree to which Intel's earnings have fluctuated historically in relation to inflation, business cycles, foreign currency exchange rates, or changes in economic growth in domestic or foreign markets.

---

[1] G. Morgenson, "Flying Blind in a Fog of Data," *New York Times* (June 18, 2000).

Learning Objectives

After studying this chapter, you will understand:

1. How competitive forces and a company's business strategy influence its profitability and the composition of its balance sheet.

2. Why analysts worry about the quality of financial statement information and how quality is determined.

3. How return on assets (ROA) can be used to analyze a company's profitability, and what insights are gained from separating ROA into its profit margin and asset turnover components.

4. How return on common equity (ROCE) can be used to assess the impact of financial leverage on a company's profitability.

5. How short-term liquidity risk differs from long-term solvency risk, and what financial ratios are helpful in assessing these two dimensions of credit risk.

6. How to interpret the results of an analysis of profitability and risk.

7. Why EBITDA (earnings before interest, taxes, depreciation, and amortization) can be a misleading indicator of profitability and cash flow.

> **Tangible net worth** is usually defined as total *tangible* assets minus total liabilities, where tangible assets exclude things like goodwill, patents, trademarks, and other *intangible* items.

Cross-sectional analysis helps identify similarities and differences *across* companies or business units at a single moment in time. The analyst might compare the 2005 profitability of one company in an industry to a competitor's profitability. A related analytic tool—**benchmark comparison**—measures a company's performance or health against some predetermined standard. For example, commercial lending agreements often require the borrowing company to maintain minimum dollar levels of working capital or tangible net worth. Once the loan has been granted, the lender—a bank or insurance company—monitors compliance by comparing the borrower's reported financial amounts and ratios to those specified in the loan agreement.

Evaluating the "Quality" of Accounting Numbers

Analysts use a mixture of time-series and cross-sectional tools when evaluating a particular company or business unit. Both can reveal meaningful details about current profitability and financial condition, and they can also reveal details about recent changes that might affect future profitability or financial condition. However, these comparisons make use of financial statement data. Hence, they are influenced by distortions of that data—if indeed the data are distorted.

Analysts use financial statement information to "get behind the numbers"—that is, to see more accurately the economic activities and condition of the company and its prospects, as depicted in Figure 5.1. However, financial statements do not always provide a complete and faithful picture of a company's activities and condition. The raw data needed for a complete and faithful picture do not always reach the financial reports because the information is filtered by generally accepted accounting principles (GAAP) and by management's accounting discretion. Both factors can distort the quality of the reported information and the analyst's view of the company.

Figure 5.1

THE FINANCIAL REPORTING FILTER AND THE ANALYST'S TASK

Let's see how the financial reporting "filter" phenomenon works with equipment leases. GAAP requires each lease to be classified as either a **capital lease** or an **operating lease**, and it requires only capital leases to be reported as balance sheet assets and liabilities. Operating leases are "off-balance sheet" items—meaning they are not included in the reported asset and liability numbers but are instead disclosed in supplemental footnotes that accompany the financial statements. (We'll see how and why this is so in Chapter 12.) So GAAP lets capital leases pass to the balance sheet, but it filters out operating leases, sending them to the statement footnotes. Analysts can—and do—use these footnotes to recast the balance sheet so that all equipment leases are treated the same way. The GAAP filter is then overcome.

Management discretion can cloud financial analysis in several ways. For example, managers who understand GAAP can use it to structure business transactions so that financial reporting goals are achieved. Do you, as a manager, want to keep equipment leases off the balance sheet? Then just make certain your company's lease contracts meet the GAAP rules for an operating lease. Doing so keeps the leases off your balance sheet and lowers reported debt.

Management discretion can also complicate the analyst's task in areas like inventory accounting, where GAAP allows managers to freely choose among several alternative reporting methods. Because each inventory method leads to a different set of reported earnings and asset numbers, financial comparisons can be affected. Here, too, the analyst can sometimes use footnote information to recast the reported financial results and thereby eliminate management discretion as an information filter.

Management also has discretion over accounting estimates and the timing of business transactions. Consider estimated "bad debt expense," management's forecast of the amount of current credit sales that will never be collected from customers. A reduction in estimated bad debt expense could mean customer credit quality has improved—that is, more credit customers are now expected to pay their bills. Or, it could mean bad debt expense was temporarily reduced to meet a quarterly earnings goal. Similar questions arise over the timing of discretionary expenditures for advertising, research and development (R&D), or information technology. Did advertising expense decline because the current ad program was a resounding success, or because management curtailed spending this quarter just to meet an earnings goal? In other words, have business fundamentals improved or is it simply "earnings management"?

> GAAP and management discretion can sometimes make the analyst's task easier by illuminating aspects of the company's activities and condition. For example, GAAP requires companies to disclose sales and operating income by business segment—information that some companies would not otherwise make available. Similarly, management sometimes goes far beyond GAAP's minimum reporting requirements by disclosing financial and nonfinancial operating details that are useful to analysts.

Conflicts of interest pose another potential threat to the quality of financial reports. Conflicts of interest arise when what is good for one party (for example, management) isn't necessarily good for another party (say, lenders or outside investors). Take the case of Adelphia Communications, a provider of cable entertainment and communication services. In March 2002, Adelphia revealed for the first time the existence of $2.6 billion in previously unreported off-balance sheet liabilities. Over the next several months, lenders and investors learned that Adelphia's top executives—including the company's founder and his family members—had deliberately shifted bank loans totalling $2.6 billion from Adelphia's books to the books of unconsolidated affiliates controlled by the family. What happened to the $2.6 billion that was originally borrowed? Family members used it to buy Adelphia stock, construct a golf course, pay off personal loans, and purchase luxury condominiums in Colorado, Mexico, and New York City—uses that were unrelated to the original business purpose of the bank loans. By June 2002, Adelphia and more than 200 of its subsidiaries and affiliates had filed bankruptcy.

> When related party transactions occur, *Statement of Financial Accounting Standards (SFAS) No. 57* requires companies to disclose the nature of the relationship, provide a description of the transactions, and report the dollar amount of the transactions and any amounts due to or from related parties. Examples of related party transactions include transactions between the company—in this case, Adelphia Communications—and (1) its subsidiaries or affiliates; (2) owners, management, and members of their families; (3) another company that is owned by management; and (4) employee benefit trusts that are under the trusteeship of management. *SFAS No. 57* requires a high level of disclosure because related party transactions cannot be presumed to have been the result of an "arm's-length" negotiation between an independent buyer and seller in a competitive marketplace. "Related Party Disclosures," *SFAS No. 57* (Stamford, CT: FASB, 1982).

Companies have an obligation to disclose business transactions that involve potential conflicts of interest. Adelphia violated FASB and SEC guidelines on **related party transactions** by concealing from lenders and investors that billions of dollars had been given to affiliates controlled by the founder's family and how the money was being spent. Adelphia violated GAAP by systematically hiding the debt on the books of the affiliates. Lenders and investors were caught unaware.

A Case in Point: Getting Behind the Numbers at Krispy Kreme

Krispy Kreme is a wholesome brand experience. Sometimes the experience comes from the simple pleasure of enjoying a Hot Original Glazed doughnut or just watching the doughnuts pass through the familiar glaze waterfall in our stores. Other times Krispy Kreme is about being part of a celebration or tradition with family and friends. We value our wholesome brand image and strive to reinforce it as we work to create more "Good Times and Warm Memories" for our customers. [Krispy Kreme Doughnuts, Inc., 2002 Annual Report]

Krispy Kreme got its start in 1937, when Vernon Rudolph bought a secret recipe for yeast-raised doughnuts from a New Orleans pastry chef, rented a building in Winston-Salem, North Carolina, and then began selling doughnuts to local grocery stores. People soon began stopping by the doughnut factory to ask if they could buy the hot doughnuts for themselves. In response, Rudolph cut a hole in the Krispy Kreme factory wall and started selling "Hot Original Glazed" doughnuts to passersby. Today, the company has more than 290 doughnut stores throughout the United States, and it makes over 7.5 million doughnuts every day.

Krispy Kreme both owns and franchises its stores. About half of the company's in-store sales occur in the morning, and half occur in the afternoon and evening. The company also delivers fresh doughnuts to supermarkets, convenience stores, and other institutions. With the purchase of Digital Java, a coffee company, in 2002, Krispy Kreme acquired considerable coffee roasting expertise and now offers a complete line of drip coffees, espresso-based coffees, and frozen drinks.

> "I say only three types of people claim they don't like Krispy Kremes: nutritionists . . . Dunkin' Donut franchisees, and compulsive liars. Fortunately for the company, that's not a large group." Andy Sewer, *Fortune* (June 23, 2003).

The U.S. doughnut industry is one that is fragmented and mature. Doughnut consumption per person in the United States remains essentially unchanged from one year to the next, although the industry has benefited from increased snack food consumption and a shift toward foods consumed away from home. Krispy Kreme competes against Dunkin' Donuts, as well as regional and local doughnut shops, and retailers of doughnuts and snacks sold through supermarkets, convenience stores, restaurants, and retail stores. Dunkin' Donuts alone has 5,500 retail stores worldwide and 3,600 in the United States. Competition within the industry centers around food quality, convenience, customer service, and value.

Krispy Kreme's management attributes the company's phenomenal sales growth—12% in fiscal 2002 for stores open 18 months or more, and 25% for its stores overall—to several key elements of the company's brand image:

- A one-of-a-kind taste based on a secret recipe and premium ingredients.
- Stores built as doughnut-making "theaters" that give customers a unique, multisensory entertainment experience.
- The "Hot Doughnuts Now" sign that, when illuminated, signals that Hot Original Glazed doughnuts are being made.

- A perception that Krispy Kreme doughnuts are an "affordable indulgence," meaning they are priced to sell to the widest market possible.
- Strong community relationships through the sponsorship of charitable events and fundraising programs for schools, clubs, and community organizations.

The company makes money in three ways. About 65% of its revenue comes from selling doughnuts through company-owned stores. Another 31% of its revenue comes from selling flour mix, doughnut-making equipment, and supplies to franchised stores. And Krispy Kreme gets another 4% of its revenue from franchise licenses and fees.

Now that you have an understanding of the business and the industry, let's take a look at the company's financial statements.

Examining Krispy Kreme's Financial Statements

Comparative income statements for Krispy Kreme Doughnuts are shown in Exhibit 5.1(a). Sales increased from $220.2 million in 1999 to $491.5 million in 2002. These figures reflect revenues from doughnuts sold through company-owned stores, royalties from doughnuts sold by franchised stores, and sales of ingredients to franchised stores. If you want to know the dollar value of all doughnuts sold at Krispy Kreme stores—company-owned and franchised—you need to locate information in the annual report about system-wide sales (usually found in a schedule of key operating results). Exhibit 5.1(a) shows that system-wide doughnut sales increased from $318.9 million in 1999 to $778.6 million in 2002.

EXHIBIT 5.1(a)	Krispy Kreme Doughnuts, Inc.			
Comparative Income Statements *($ in millions)*	**2002**	**2001**	**2000**	**1999**
Sales	$491.5	$394.4	$300.7	$220.2
Operating expenses	393.7	324.9	257.1	194.5
Gross profit	97.8	69.5	43.6	25.7
Selling, general and administrative expenses	28.9	27.6	20.1	14.9
Interest expense	1.8	0.3	0.6	1.5
Other (revenues) expenses	10.0	(2.1)	(1.6)	(0.3)
Pre-tax income	57.1	43.7	24.5	9.6
Income taxes	21.3	16.2	9.1	3.6
Minority interest	2.3	1.1	0.7	0.0
Net income	$ 33.5	$ 26.4	$ 14.7	$ 6.0
Systemwide sales	$778.6	$621.7	$448.1	$318.9

But sales growth is only part of the story at Krispy Kreme. Exhibit 5.1(a) also shows that net income increased from $6.0 million in 1999 to $33.5 million in 2002. That's a 558% increase in just four years.

A closer look at Krispy Kreme's income statements reveals that net income for 2002 would have been even larger if it weren't for a one-time special charge booked that year. Notice that "Other (revenues) expenses" increased from a *minus* (indicating net *revenue*) $2.1 million in 2001 to a *plus* (indicating net *expense*) $10.0 million in 2002. A financial statement footnote tells us why. In September 2002, the company booked a one-time, $9.1 million special charge to settle a business dispute. Based on the company's effective tax rate of 37%, this one-time charge decreased 2002 net income by $5.733 million from what it otherwise would have been. In other words, Krispy Kreme would have reported net income of $39.2 million ($33.5 + $5.7) for 2002 without the one-time charge, rather than the $33.5 million actually reported that year.

A company's **effective tax rate** is just tax expense ($21.3 million for 2002) divided by pre-tax income ($57.1 million). For Krispy Kreme, the figure works out to be 0.374 or 37% when rounded.

Common-Size and Trend Analysis Income Statements Financial analysts use *common-size* and *trend* statements of net income to help spot changes in a company's cost structure and profit performance. **Common-size income statements**, shown in Exhibit 5.1(b), recast each statement item as a percentage of sales. Common-size income statements show you how much of each sales dollar is spent on operating expenses and other business costs, and how much of each sales dollar hits the bottom line as profit. For example, Krispy Kreme's operating expenses for 2002 are shown as 80.1% of 2002 sales ($80.1\% = \$393.7$ operating expenses$_{2002} \div \$491.5$ sales$_{2002}$) instead of $393.7 million. This means that 80.1 cents of each 2002 sales dollar was spent on operating costs. That leaves only 19.9 cents of each 2002 sales dollar to cover other business costs and provide a profit for the year.

The **trend statements**, shown in Exhibit 5.1(b), also recast each statement item in percentage terms, but they do so using a base year number rather than sales. Trend statements help you spot increases (and decreases) over time in each income statement item. For instance, the trend statement of income shows Krispy Kreme's 2002 operating expenses as 202.4% of base year (1999) operating expenses ($202.4\% = \$393.7$ operating expenses$_{2002} \div \$194.5$ operating expenses$_{1999}$). This means that operating expenses in 2002 are more than twice as large as they were in 1999.

EXHIBIT 5.1(b)	Krispy Kreme Doughnuts, Inc.			

Common-Size and Trend Analysis of Income

Common-Size Statements (% of sales)	2002	2001	2000	1999
Sales	100.0	100.0	100.0	100.0
Operating expenses	80.1	82.4	85.5	88.3
Gross profit	19.9	17.6	14.5	11.7
Selling, general and administrative expenses	5.9	6.9	6.7	6.7
Interest expense	0.4	0.1	0.2	0.7
Other (revenues) expenses	2.0	(0.5)	(0.5)	(0.1)
Pre-tax income	11.6	11.1	8.1	4.4
Income taxes	4.3	4.1	3.0	1.7
Minority interest	0.5	0.3	0.2	0.0
Net income	6.8	6.7	4.9	2.7

Trend Statements (1999 = 100%)	2002	2001	2000	1999
Sales	223.2	179.1	136.6	100.0
Operating expenses	202.4	167.0	132.2	100.0
Gross profit	380.5	270.4	169.6	100.0
Selling, general and administrative expenses	194.0	185.2	134.9	100.0
Interest expense	120.0	20.0	40.0	100.0
Other (revenues) expenses	(3,333.3)	700.0	533.3	100.0
Pre-tax income	594.8	455.2	255.2	100.0
Income taxes	591.7	450.0	252.8	100.0
Minority interest	328.6	157.1	100.0	*
Net income	558.3	440.0	245.0	100.0

* Trend computed using 2000 as the base year because 1999 base year value is zero.

The common-size and trend statements of net income reveal several interesting aspects of the company's profit performance:

- From the trend statements we can see that sales in 2002 were 223.2% larger than they were in 1999, having increased steadily over the four-year period.
- From the common-size statements, we can see that operating expenses steadily declined as a percent of sales, from 88.3% in 1999 to only 80.1% in 2002. Selling, general, and administrative

expenses remained roughly constant from 1999 through 2001 as a percentage of sales, but declined to 5.9% of sales in 2002.

• The fluctuations in "Other (revenues) expenses" evident in both the common-size and trend statements are due in part to the one-time special charge recorded in 2002.

The years shown in the statements were particularly successful ones for the company and its employees. We can see from the trend statements that sales grew 223.2% over four years and that net income was up 558.3%. What factors contributed to the company's tremendous sales growth? It was a combination of increased sales at existing Krispy Kreme stores—12% in 2002 alone—plus sales from newly opened stores. Why did net income grow faster than sales? Apparently, the company benefited from operating and administrative efficiencies that resulted in lower expenses per dollar of sales. For example, operating expenses fell from 88.3 cents per dollar of sales in 1999 to only 80.1 cents in 2002 as shown on the common-size statements. This means that there was 8.2 cents more gross profit for each dollar of sales.

Common-size and trend statements can also be helpful in identifying where a company makes money. Exhibit 5.2(a) reproduces information found in Krispy Kreme's annual report footnote on its three business segments—company-owned stores that sell doughnuts to the public, franchise operations that generate license and fee income, and the manufacturing segment of the company (called "KKM&D"), which sells flour mix, doughnut-making equipment, and supplies to franchised stores. The top portion of the exhibit shows how much revenue each business segment produced each year. The bottom portion of the exhibit shows the operating income—sales minus operating expenses including selling, general, and administration costs—earned by each segment, along with corporate general and administrative expenses not allocated to the segments. For example, revenue from company-owned stores totaled $319.6 million in 2002, and operating income was $58.2 million.

EXHIBIT 5.2(a)	**Krispy Kreme Doughnuts, Inc.**		
Information about the Company's Operations by Business Segment			
($ in millions)	**2002**	**2001**	**2000**
Revenues:			
Company store operations	$319.6	$266.2	$213.7
Franchise operations	19.3	14.0	9.4
KKM&D*	152.6	114.2	77.6
Total revenues	$491.5	$394.4	$300.7
Operating income:			
Company store operations	$ 58.2	$ 42.9	$ 27.4
Franchise operations	14.3	9.0	5.7
KKM&D*	26.8	19.0	11.7
Unallocated general and administrative expenses	(39.5)	(29.0)	(21.3)
Total operating income	$ 59.8	$ 41.9	$ 23.5

*KKM&D sells flour mix, doughnut-making equipment, and supplies to franchised stores.

Exhibit 5.2(b) uses a common-size approach to isolate each segment's contribution to total company revenue and then computes an operating profit margin (that is, operating income divided by revenue) for each segment. As you can now easily see, 65% ($319.6 ÷ $491.5) of Krispy Kreme's revenue for 2002 came from company-owned stores, while only 4% came from franchise licenses and fees. But the franchise segment had a higher operating margin (74% = $14.3 ÷ $19.3) when compared to company-owned stores and KKM&D (18% each). Although the franchise segment makes a smaller contribution to overall company revenue, it makes a larger percentage contribution to overall operating income.

EXHIBIT 5.2(b)	Krispy Kreme Doughnuts, Inc.		

Revenue Contribution and Operating Margin by Business Segment

	2002	2001	2000
Revenue contribution %			
Company store operations	65	67	71
Franchise operations	4	4	3
KKM&D*	31	29	26
Operating margin %			
Company store operations	18	16	13
Franchise operations	74	64	61
KKM&D*	18	17	15

*KKM&D sells flour mix, doughnut-making equipment, and supplies to franchised stores.

Now let's see what we can learn from the balance sheet.

Common-Size and Trend Analysis Balance Sheets Exhibit 5.3(a) shows Krispy Kreme's comparative balance sheets using reported dollar amounts. The company's assets are concentrated in cash, accounts receivables, inventories (probably ingredients and supplies) as well as the

EXHIBIT 5.3(a)	Krispy Kreme Doughnuts, Inc.			

Comparative Balance Sheets

($ in millions)	2002	2001	2000	1999
Assets				
Current assets				
Cash and cash equivalents	$ 32.2	$ 21.9	$ 7.0	$ 3.2
Accounts receivable—net of allowances	46.2	38.7	24.7	20.4
Inventories	24.4	16.2	12.0	10.0
Other current assets	38.3	25.0	23.9	7.5
Total current assets	141.1	101.8	67.6	41.1
Property, plant and equipment, net	202.6	112.6	78.3	60.6
Long-term investment	11.2	16.1	20.7	1.4
Intangibles	48.7	16.6	0.0	0.0
Other assets	6.9	8.3	4.9	1.9
Total assets	$410.5	$255.4	$171.5	$105.0
Liabilities and shareholders' equity				
Current liabilities				
Current portion of long-term debt	$ 4.2	$ 4.6	$ 3.5	$ 2.4
Accounts payable	14.1	12.1	8.2	13.1
Accrued expenses	30.0	26.7	21.2	14.1
Other current liabilities	11.4	9.1	5.3	0.0
Total current liabilities	59.7	52.5	38.2	29.6
Long-term debt, less current portion	57.2	3.9	0.0	20.5
Other liabilities	15.0	8.8	6.5	7.1
Total liabilities	131.9	65.2	44.7	57.2
Minority interest	5.2	2.5	1.1	0.0
Common stock	173.2	121.1	85.1	15.5
Retained earnings	100.2	66.6	40.6	32.3
Total common shareholders' equity	273.4	187.7	125.7	47.8
Total liabilities and shareholders' equity	$410.5	$255.4	$171.5	$105.0

stores themselves (called "Property, plant and equipment"). Consumers pay cash for their dough-nuts, so Krispy Kreme's accounts receivable must represent amounts owed to the company by retail customers (like grocery and convenience stores) or franchisees. To finance its various oper-ating assets, the company has relied on a combination of vendor payables (called "Accounts payable" and "Accrued expenses"), long-term debt, and common stock along with internally gen-erated resources (represented by "Retained earnings").

Several important changes in the company's asset mix and financial structure have occurred since 1999. These changes can be easily seen from the common-size and trend statements in Exhibits 5.3(b) ("Assets") and 5.3(c) ("Liabilities and Shareholders' Equity").

EXHIBIT 5.3(b)	Krispy Kreme Doughnuts, Inc.			
Common-Size and Trend Analysis of Assets				
Common-Size Statements (% of total assets)	**2002**	**2001**	**2000**	**1999**
Assets				
Current assets				
Cash and cash equivalents	7.8	8.6	4.1	3.0
Accounts receivable—net of allowances	11.3	15.2	14.4	19.5
Inventories	5.9	6.3	7.0	9.5
Other current assets	9.3	9.8	13.9	7.1
Total current assets	34.3	39.9	39.4	39.1
Property, plant and equipment, net	49.4	44.1	45.7	57.7
Long-term investment	2.7	6.3	12.0	1.4
Intangibles	11.9	6.5	0.0	0.0
Other assets	1.7	3.2	2.9	1.8
Total assets	100.0	100.0	100.0	100.0
Trend Statements (1999 = 100%)	**2002**	**2001**	**2000**	**1999**
Assets				
Current assets				
Cash and cash equivalents	1,006.3	684.4	218.8	100.0
Accounts receivable—net of allowances	226.5	189.7	121.1	100.0
Inventories	244.0	162.0	120.0	100.0
Other current assets	510.7	333.3	318.7	100.0
Total current assets	343.3	247.7	164.5	100.0
Property, plant and equipment, net	334.3	185.8	129.2	100.0
Long-term investment	800.0	1,150.0	1,478.6	100.0
Intangibles	293.4	100.0	*	*
Other assets	363.2	436.8	257.9	100.0
Total assets	391.0	243.2	163.3	100.0

* Trend computed using a 2001 base year because the 1999 base year value is zero.

Consider the composition of Krispy Kreme's assets in 2002. The company's common-size statements in Exhibit 5.3(b) show that cash made up 7.8% of total assets that year, up from only 3.0% in 1999. Accounts receivable represented 11.3% of total 2002 assets, while inventories con-tributed another 5.9%, both down from their 1999 levels. Krispy Kreme's investment in stores and manufacturing capacity—shown under the "Property, plant and equipment" account—made up almost one-half (49.4%) of the company's total 2002 assets.

That may seem like a lot of cash ($32.2 million), and it is. But then some cash is needed to support the operations of each Krispy Kreme store because retail cus-tomers pay cash (and expect to receive change) when they buy doughnuts. A portion of the company's cash balance is also used to fund future store growth.

| EXHIBIT 5.3(c) | Krispy Kreme Doughnuts, Inc. | | | |

Common-Size and Trend Analysis of Liabilities and Shareholders' Equity

Common-Size Statements (% of total assets)	2002	2001	2000	1999
Liabilities and shareholders' equity				
Current liabilities				
Current portion of long-term debt	1.0	1.8	2.0	2.3
Accounts payable	3.4	4.7	4.8	12.5
Accrued expenses	7.3	10.5	12.4	13.4
Other current liabilities	2.8	3.6	3.1	0.0
Total current liabilities	14.5	20.6	22.3	28.2
Long-term debt, less current portion	13.9	1.5	0.0	19.5
Other liabilities	3.7	3.4	3.8	6.8
Total liabilities	32.1	25.5	26.1	54.5
Minority interest	1.3	1.0	0.6	0.0
Common stock	42.2	47.4	49.6	14.7
Retained earnings	24.4	26.1	23.7	30.8
Total common shareholders' equity	66.6	73.5	73.3	45.5
Total liabilities and shareholders' equity	100.0	100.0	100.0	100.0

Trend Statements (1999 = 100%)	2002	2001	2000	1999
Liabilities and shareholders' equity				
Current liabilities				
Current portion of long-term debt	175.0	191.7	145.8	100.0
Accounts payable	107.6	92.4	62.6	100.0
Accrued expenses	212.8	189.4	150.4	100.0
Other current liabilities	215.1	171.7	100.0	*
Total current liabilities	201.7	177.4	129.1	100.0
Long-term debt, less current portion	279.0	19.0	0.0	100.0
Other liabilities	211.3	123.9	91.5	100.0
Total liabilities	230.6	114.0	78.1	100.0
Minority interest	472.7	227.3	100.0	*
Commons stock	1,117.4	781.3	549.0	100.0
Retained earnings	310.2	206.2	125.7	100.0
Total common shareholders' equity	572.0	392.7	263.0	100.0
Total liabilities and shareholders' equity	391.0	243.2	163.3	100.0

*Trend computed using a 2000 base year because the 1999 base year value is zero.

The company had a substantial investment in "Other current assets": $38.3 million in 2002 or 9.3% of total assets. A financial statement footnote tells us that about $15.0 million of this amount represented short-term investments in money-market savings accounts and publicly traded securities. These investments could be sold off to raise cash if the company were to need money for future store growth.

Krispy Kreme's investment in intangible assets represents accounting **goodwill**—the amount in the acquisition price that represents a premium paid for the target company over and above the value of its identifiable assets. (Chapter 16 has more on goodwill.). A footnote to the annual report tells us that some of the goodwill arose when Krispy Kreme bought Digital Java. However, most of the goodwill was booked when the company bought back Krispy Kreme stores from franchisees.

What changes in the company's financial structure occurred between 1999 and 2002? Did the mix of debt and equity remain constant over the four years? And what about the proportion of short-term versus long-term borrowing? The common-size and trend statements in Exhibit 5.3(c) provide the answers. We can see the following from the common-size statements:

- Total current liabilities were 14.5%, down from 28.2% in 1999, and this reduction was concentrated in accounts payable and accrued expenses.
- Long-term debt stood at 19.5% in 1999, then declined to zero before rising back to 13.9% in 2002.
- Common stock exhibited the opposite pattern. It stood at 14.8% in 1999, and then increased to 49.6% the next year.

There are two messages from the common-size statements in Exhibit 5.3(c). First, Krispy Kreme altered its financial structure in 2000. In that year, the company issued common stock to investors and reduced its reliance on long-term bank debt and accounts payable financing. Second, Krispy Kreme issued additional long-term debt in 2002.

The trend statements in Exhibit 5.3(c) support this view of the company's changing financial structure. Total liabilities increased only 230.6% over the four-year period, a rate of increase that is smaller than the combined 391.0% increase in liabilities plus shareholders' equity. This means that Krispy Kreme reduced its reliance on debt financing. It instead relied on investors—rather than lenders—for its outside capital needs. That's why common stock increased 1,117.4% over the four-year period. In fact, the trend statements also reveal that Krispy Kreme issued a significant amount of common stock in 2002 since this statement item grew to 1,117.4% from 781.3% the previous year. ***Trend statements provide a clearer indication of a company's growth (and decline) than do common-size statements.***

Common-Size and Trend Analysis Cash Flow Statements Exhibit 5.4(a) presents comparative cash flow statements with some statement items reported as combined figures to simplify the presentation. Common-size and trends for selected cash flow items are shown in Exhibit 5.4(b). The common-size statements are constructed by dividing each cash flow item by sales for that year. For example, Krispy Kreme's operating activities generated $51.1 million cash [Exhibit 5.3(a)] in 2002, or 10.4% of $491.5 million in sales [Exhibit 5.1(a)]. In other words, cash from operations equaled 10.4 cents of each sales dollar, up from 3.9 cents in 1999 [Exhibit 5.4(b)].

EXHIBIT 5.4(a)	**Krispy Kreme Doughnuts, Inc.**			

Comparative Cash Flow Statements

($ in millions)	2002	2001	2000	1999
Net income	$33.5	$26.4	$14.7	$6.0
Adjustments	17.6	9.8	17.4	2.5
Cash from operations	51.1	36.2	32.1	8.5
Capital expenditures and acquisitions—net	(93.9)	(55.8)	(28.7)	(10.5)
Other investments	(0.7)	3.6	(38.6)	0.5
Cash used in investing activities	(94.6)	(52.2)	(67.3)	(10.0)
Cash dividends	—	—	(7.0)	(1.5)
Process from debt—net	41.4	5.0	(19.4)	1.9
Stock issuance (repurchase)	7.1	21.1	65.7	—
Other financing activities	5.3	4.8	(0.3)	—
Cash used in financing activities	53.8	30.9	39.0	0.4
Net increase (decrease) in cash	$10.3	$14.9	$ 3.8	$(1.1)

EXHIBIT 5.4(b)	Krispy Kreme Doughnuts, Inc.

Common-Size and Trend Analysis of Selected Cash Flow Items

Common-Size Statements (% of sales)	2002	2001	2000	1999
Selected Items				
Cash from operations	10.4	9.2	10.7	3.9
Capital expenditures and acquisitions—net	(19.1)	(14.1)	(9.5)	(4.8)
Other investments	(0.1)	0.9	(12.8)	0.2
Cash used in investing activities	(19.2)	(13.2)	(22.3)	(4.6)
Cash dividends	0.0	0.0	(2.3)	(0.7)
Proceeds from debt—net	8.4	1.3	(6.5)	0.9
Stock issuance (repurchase)	1.4	5.3	21.8	0.0
Other financing activities	1.1	1.2	(0.1)	0.0
Cash used in financing activities	10.9	7.8	12.9	0.2
Net increase (decrease) in cash	2.1	3.8	1.3	(0.5)

Trend Statements (1999 = 100%)	2002	2001	2000	1999
Selected Items				
Cash from operations	601.2	425.9	377.6	100.0
Capital expenditures and acquisitions—net	894.3	531.4	273.3	100.0
Other investments	(140.0)	720.0	(7,720.0)	100.0
Cash used in investing activities	946.0	522.0	673.0	100.0
Cash dividends	0.0	0.0	466.7	100.0
Proceeds from debt—net	2,178.9	263.2	(1,021.1)	100.0
Stock issuance (repurchase)	10.8	32.1	100.0	*
Other financing activities	(1,766.7)	(1,600.0)	100.0	*
Cash used in financing activities	13,450.0	7,725.0	9,750.0	100.0
Net increase (decrease) in cash	(936.4)	(1,354.5)	(345.5)	100.0

* Trend computed using a 2000 base year because the 1999 base year value is zero.

How does Krispy Kreme use these operating cash flows? Like most growing retail companies, Krispy Kreme must devote resources to expanding its store base. Therefore, a major use of its cash is capital expenditures and acquisitions. These activities consumed $93.9 million in 2002 [Exhibit 5.4(a)], or 19.1 cents per sales dollar [19.1% in Exhibit 5.4(b)]. Wait a moment! Operations generated only 10.4 cents per sales dollar but the company spent 19.1 cents on store growth and acquisitions. Where did Krispy Kreme get the other 8.7 cents (19.1 cents − 10.4 cents) it needed for growth in 2002? According to the common-size cash flow statements in Exhibit 5.4(b), the company filled its cash needs using a combination of bank borrowing (8.4 cents), stock issuance (1.4 cents), and other financing activities (1.1 cents).

The trend statements in Exhibit 5.4(b) reveal that operating cash flow grew 601.2% over four years, compared to net income growth of 558.3% [Exhibit 5.1(b)] during the same period. However, capital expenditures grew at an even faster pace of 894.3%. When operating cash flows grow more slowly than capital expenditures, companies must look to outside sources (investors and lenders) for the additional cash needed to fuel growth. And that's just what Krispy Kreme did in 2002. It borrowed money and issued some additional shares of stock. The company also curtailed its cash dividend payments in 2001.

From our analysis of Krispy Kreme and its financial statements, we can come to three conclusions:

- Informed financial statement analysis begins with knowledge of the company and its industry.
- Common-size and trend statements provide a convenient way to organize financial statement information so that major financial components and changes are easily recognized.
- Financial statements help the analyst gain a sharper understanding of the company's economic condition and its prospects for the future.

Profitability, Competition, and Business Strategy

The mechanics of running a business are not really very complicated when you get down to essentials. You have to make some stuff and sell it to somebody for more than it cost you. That's about all there is, except for a few million details.

–John L. McCaffey

Financial Ratios and Profitability Analysis

Financial ratios are another powerful tool analysts use in evaluating profit performance and assessing credit risk. Most evaluations of profit performance begin with the **return on assets (ROA)** ratio,

$$ROA = \frac{NOPAT}{Average\ assets}$$

where *NOPAT* refers to the company's **net operating profit after taxes** for a particular period (such as a year), and *average assets* is the average book value of total assets over that same time period. Before computing ROA, analysts adjust the company's reported earnings and asset figures. These adjustments fall into three broad categories:

1. Adjustments aimed at *isolating a company's sustainable operating profits* by removing nonoperating or nonrecurring items from reported income.
2. An adjustment that *eliminates after-tax interest expense* from the profit calculation so that *operating* profitability comparisons over time or across companies are not clouded by differences in financial structure.[2]

---

[2] To illustrate how financial structure can affect profitability comparisons, consider two companies that have (a) identical after-tax operating profits of $500 before interest expense is considered, and (b) the same total asset base of $5,000. One company has no interest-bearing debt, the other has $2,000 of 12% debt outstanding. Annual interest expense on this debt is $240 = $2,000 \times 0.12$, but the deductibility of interest expense for tax purposes saves the company $84 = 240×0.35 each year when the corporate income tax rate is 35%. Consequently, the company with debt would report net income of $344 or $500 - $240 \times (1 - 0.35)$. If financing costs are ignored, the all-equity company would have an ROA of 10% ($500/$5,000), while the company with debt would have an ROA of only 6.88% ($344/$5,000). The analyst might mistakenly conclude that one company's profit performance is superior to the other when, in fact, the only difference between these two companies is their choice of financing. The "adjusted" ROA for the company with debt would confirm that identical levels of *operating* profit performance had been achieved:

$$ROA = \frac{After\text{-}tax\ operating\ profits + Interest\ expense \times (1 - Tax\ rate)}{Average\ assets}$$
$$= \frac{\$344 + \$240 \times (1 - 0.35)}{\$5,000} = .10\ or\ 10\%$$

3. Adjustments for **distortions related to accounting quality concerns**, which involve potential adjustments to both income and assets for items such as nonoperating income from short-term investments or the off-balance sheet operating leases mentioned earlier.

Exhibit 5.5 summarizes the ROA calculations for Krispy Kreme using the company's earnings and balance sheet information from Exhibits 5.1(a) and 5.3(a). The adjustments made to reported earnings each year eliminate the nonrecurring business dispute charge ($9.1 million) mentioned earlier and interest ($1.8 million), on an after-tax basis. ROA for 2002 thus becomes:

EXHIBIT 5.5	Krispy Kreme Doughnuts, Inc.

Return on Assets

	2002	2001	2000	1999
Net income as reported	$ 33.5	$ 26.4	$ 14.7	$ 6.0
Nonrecurring business dispute charge	5.7	—	—	—
Interest expense (after-tax)	1.1	0.2	0.4	1.0
Net operating profit after tax (NOPAT)	$ 40.3	$ 26.6	$ 15.1	$ 7.0
Assets at year-end	$410.5	$255.4	$171.5	$105.0
Assets at beginning of year	255.4	171.5	105.0	93.3
Average assets	$333.0	$213.5	$138.3	$ 99.2
Return on assets (NOPAT/Average assets)	12.1%	12.5%	10.9%	7.1%

Note: Following common practice, the company's effective tax rate (37% in this case) is used to compute the after-tax impact of special charges and interest expense.

$$\text{ROA}_{2002} = \frac{\text{Net income} \pm \text{Charges and gains} \times (1 - \text{Tax rate}) + \text{Interest} \times (1 - \text{Tax rate})}{\text{Average assets}}$$

$$= \frac{\$33.5 + \$9.1 \times (1 - 0.37) + \$1.8 \times (1 - 0.37)}{(\$410.5 + \$255.4)/2} = .121 \text{ or } 12.1\%$$

Notice that the company's effective tax rate (37%) was used in the ROA calculation. After all adjustments, Krispy Kreme's ROA increased from 7.1% in 1999 to 12.1% in 2002. Here's why.

There are just two ways a company can increase its operating profits per asset dollar. One is to increase the profit yield on each sales dollar. The other is to expand the amount of sales generated from each asset dollar. In other words, a company that wants to **increase its rate of return on assets** can strive to do so in two different ways:

1. By increasing the operating profit margin. For instance, a large manufacturing company might use its bargaining power to negotiate favorable price reductions from raw material suppliers. Lower raw material costs would reduce operating expenses for the same level of sales, and thus yield an increase in the manufacturing company's operating profit margin.
2. By increasing the intensity of asset utilization. For instance, a restaurant that was previously open only for lunch and dinner might decide to stay open 24 hours each day. Doing so would allow the restaurant to generate more sales per dollar invested in restaurant assets, and thus yield an increase in asset utilization.

Both approaches are embedded in the ROA calculation:

$$ROA = \frac{NOPAT}{\text{Average assets}} = \left(\frac{NOPAT}{\text{Sales}}\right) \times \left(\frac{\text{Sales}}{\text{Average assets}}\right)$$

$$= \text{Operating profit margin} \times \text{Asset turnover}$$

Changes in the profit yield per sales dollar show up as changes in the *operating profit margin*, and changes in the amount of sales generated from each asset dollar are reflected as *asset turnover* changes.

Consider a company that earns $9 million of NOPAT on sales of $100 million and that has an average asset base of $50 million. The ROA for this company is:

$$ROA = \left(\frac{NOPAT}{\text{Sales}}\right) \times \left(\frac{\text{Sales}}{\text{Average assets}}\right)$$

$$= \left(\frac{\$9}{\$100}\right) \times \left(\frac{\$100}{\$50}\right) = .09 \times 2 = .18 \text{ or } 18\%$$

Now suppose that some efficiencies in inventory and accounts receivable management are achieved so that average assets can be reduced to $45 million without sacrificing sales. Assets turnover will increase to 2.22 and ROA will rise to 20%:

$$ROA = \left(\frac{NOPAT}{\text{Sales}}\right) \times \left(\frac{\text{Sales}}{\text{Average assets}}\right)$$

$$= \left(\frac{\$9}{\$100}\right) \times \left(\frac{\$100}{\$45}\right) = .09 \times 2.22 = .20 \text{ or } 20\%$$

However, there is another way to boost ROA from 18% to 20%—that is, increase the operating profit margin to 10% through aggressive expense reductions. Sales are unchanged and asset turnover stays at 2, but ROA is now:

$$ROA = \left(\frac{NOPAT}{\text{Sales}}\right) \times \left(\frac{\text{Sales}}{\text{Average assets}}\right)$$

$$= \left(\frac{\$10}{\$100}\right) \times \left(\frac{\$100}{\$50}\right) = .10 \times 2 = .20 \text{ or } 20\%$$

Exhibit 5.6 on the next page extends the ROA analysis of Krispy Kreme by presenting operating margin and asset turnover figures for each of the four years. Here we learn that the company's improved profitability stems from better operating margins because asset turnover actually declined.

Krispy Kreme's operating margin increased from 3.2% in 1999 to 8.2% in 2002. However, asset turnover fell from 2.22 to 1.48 over this same period. In other words, in 1999, Krispy Kreme generated $2.22 of sales from each asset dollar, and each sales dollar produced 3.2 cents of NOPAT, for an ROA of 7.1%. By contrast, the company generated only $1.48 of sales for each asset dollar in 2002, but each sales dollar produced 8.2 cents of NOPAT, so the ROA that year was 12.1%.

If Krispy Kreme had been able to keep its asset turnover at the 1999 level and still improve the operating margin to 8.2%, the company's ROA for 2002 would then have been 18.2%, or 8.2% times 2.22.

EXHIBIT 5.6	Krispy Kreme Doughnuts, Inc.			
ROA Decomposition				
	2002	**2001**	**2000**	**1999**
Sales	$491.5	$394.4	$300.7	$220.2
NOPAT	40.3	26.6	15.1	7.0
Average assets	333.0	213.5	138.3	99.2
Operating profit margin (NOPAT/Sales)	8.2%	6.7%	5.0%	3.2%
Asset turnover (Sales/Average assets)	1.48	1.85	2.18	2.22
ROA = Margin × Asset turnover	12.1%	12.5%	10.9%	7.1%

The explanation for Krispy Kreme's profitability improvement lies in the numbers—and in the business decisions that lurk behind the numbers. Krispy Kreme grew from 144 stores to 276 stores by the end of 2002. This expanded store base, along with increased sales from existing stores, allowed the fixed operating costs of doughnut production, distribution, and marketing to be spread over a larger number of individual stores. The result was in an improved operating profit margin. Production efficiency gains may also have played a role in the company's operating margin increase. But there is another part to the story. More stores meant more resources tied up operating cash, receivables, inventories, and facilities (property, plant, and equipment). Krispy Kreme's asset base was considerably less productive in 2002 ($1.48 of sales per dollar of assets) than it was in 1999 ($2.22 of sales per asset dollar).

Can Krispy Kreme sustain its 2002 level of profitability? It is hard to say. Increased costs of ingredients, brand erosion, and competitive price pressures may reduce the company's ROA. For example, an increase in the cost of flour and sugar could easily cause the operating margin to slip to 7.5% from its 2002 level of 8.2%. This small change when amplified by the asset turnover ratio would result in ROA declining from 12.1% to 11.1% (7.5% × 1.48). To sustain ROA at 12.1%, Krispy Kreme would then need to generate $1.61 of sales per asset dollar (12.1% ÷ 7.5%), or an additional $0.13 over its $1.48 of sales per asset dollar in 2002. However, achieving continued sales growth from existing stores is a challenge for any retail company operating in a mature industry.

Many analysts find it helpful to further decompose ROA by isolating individual factors that contribute to a company's operating profit margin and asset turnover. For example, the operating profit margin for Krispy Kreme can be expressed as:

Using the information in Krispy Kreme's 2002 income statement to illustrate the tax expense adjustment, we find that adjusted taxes would equal $25.3 instead of the reported income tax expense of $21.3 shown in the statement. The various adjustments made in arriving at NOPAT also cause the tax component of ROA to differ from the reported figure. The correct figure for *Taxes* is computed by solving:

$$NOPAT = Sales - OpEx - SG\&A - Other - Taxes$$

Substitution for NOPAT and the other statement items yields:

$$\$40.3 = \$491.5 - 393.7 - 28.9 - 3.2 - Taxes$$

meaning that *Taxes* = $25.4 that year. (Note that *Other* is other revenues and expenses after eliminating the one-time business dispute charge, plus minority interest, or 3.2 = 10.0 − 9.1 + 2.3.)

$$\text{Operating profit margin} = \frac{NOPAT}{Sales} = \frac{(Sales - OpEx - SG\&A - Other - Taxes)}{Sales}$$

$$= \left(\frac{Sales}{Sales}\right) - \left(\frac{OpEx}{Sales}\right) - \left(\frac{SG\&A}{Sales}\right) - \left(\frac{Other}{Sales}\right) - \left(\frac{Taxes}{Sales}\right)$$

$$= 100\% - \left(\frac{OpEx}{Sales}\right) - \left(\frac{SG\&A}{Sales}\right) - \left(\frac{Other}{Sales}\right) - \left(\frac{Taxes}{Sales}\right)$$

where, from Exhibit 5.1(a), OpEx is the company's operating expenses; *SG&A* is Krispy Kreme's selling, general, and administrative expense; *Other* is other expenses and revenues (including minority interest), and *Taxes* is adjusted income tax expense. These margin components (which happen to correspond to the common-size income statement items we've already described) can help the analyst identify areas where cost reductions have been achieved or where cost improvements are needed.

The asset turnover component of ROA can be decomposed as:

$$\frac{1}{\text{Asset turnover}} = \frac{\text{Average assets}}{\text{Sales}}$$

$$= \left(\frac{\text{Average current assets} + \text{Average long-term assets}}{\text{Sales}} \right)$$

$$= \left(\frac{\text{Average current assets}}{\text{Sales}} \right) + \left(\frac{\text{Average long-term assets}}{\text{Sales}} \right)$$

$$= \left(\frac{1}{\text{Current asset turnover}} \right) + \left(\frac{1}{\text{Long-term asset turnover}} \right)$$

The **current asset turnover** ratio helps the analyst spot efficiency gains from improved accounts receivable and inventory management, while the **long-term asset turnover** ratio captures information about property, plant, and equipment utilization.

ROA and Competitive Advantage

Our analysis of Krispy Kreme's profit performance has thus far revealed that the company's ROA for 2002 was 12.1%, up from 7.1% in 1999. This profitability increase was traced to a higher operating profit margin because asset utilization fell. Now we want to know how Krispy Kreme's profit performance compares with other companies in the industry.

It's easy to identify Krispy Kreme's most important direct competitors. There's Dunkin' Donuts, with over 5,000 stores worldwide, and then there's Tim Horton's, with 2,200 doughnut shops across Canada and another 160 stores in key U.S. markets. Financial data for these two competitors are difficult to obtain because Dunkin' Donuts (owned by Wendy's International) and Tim Horton's (owned by Allied Domecq PLC) do not issue their own financial statements. Instead, the financial activities of each doughnut subsidiary are combined with their respective parent companies. Analysts routinely confront this problem when trying to compare one firm with another in the same line of business. The solution is to use "similar" companies as benchmarks for the analysis even though the benchmark companies may not be direct competitors. For instance, we will use Wendy's International as our benchmark company because it's the parent company of Dunkin' Donuts. The fact that Wendy's International owns three other restaurant chains— Wendy's hamburger restaurants, Baja Fresh, and Café Express—somewhat clouds the comparison.

Exhibit 5.7 presents a decomposition of 2002 ROA for Krispy Kreme and Wendy's International. Also shown are the average ROA and component values for the industry—restaurants—to which these two companies belong. Industry data like these are available from a variety of sources, including Standard & Poor's *Industry Survey*, Robert Morris and Associates' *Annual Statement Studies*, and many online financial information services.

EXHIBIT 5.7	Krispy Kreme versus the Competition		
2002 ROA Decomposition			
	Krispy Kreme	Wendy's	Restaurant Industry
Operating profit margin (NOPAT/Sales)	8.2%	9.0%	5.3%
Asset turnover (Sales/Average assets)	1.48	1.15	1.13
Return on assets (ROA)	12.1%	10.4%	6.0%

Krispy Kreme was more profitable than Wendy's in 2002, earning an ROA of 12.1% compared to 10.4% for Wendy's. However, both companies beat the industry average ROA of 6.0%. How did Krispy Kreme achieve superior profit performance? The ROA decomposition reveals the company's NOPAT margin was 8.2 cents per sales dollar—better than the industry average margin of 5.3%, but actually slightly worse than Wendy's 9.0% margin. And the reason Krispy Kreme outperformed Wendy's? Better asset turnover. Krispy Kreme generated $1.48 in sales per asset dollar compared to only $1.15 in sales per asset dollar at Wendy's and just $1.13 for the industry.

What was the key to Krispy Kreme's success in 2002 versus the restaurant industry as a whole? The answer lies in both its profit margin and its asset turnover. Krispy Kreme outperformed the competition by earning a higher operating profit margin on each dollar of sales and by generating more sales per asset dollar.

Can Krispy Kreme maintain this level of ROA performance? The answer can be found only by identifying the company's competitive advantage—that is, the source of its superior operating profit margin and turnover rate—and by determining whether that competitive advantage is sustainable over time. There are several factors that can explain why companies operating in the same industry—and that therefore confront similar economic conditions—can earn markedly different rates of return on their assets. Some companies gain a competitive advantage over rivals by developing unique products or services (like "Hot Original Glazed" doughnuts). Others do so by providing consistent quality or exceptional customer service and convenience. Still others get ahead because of their innovative production technologies, distribution channels, or sales and marketing efforts. The sustainability of these advantages, however, varies.

Competition in an industry continually works to drive down the rate of return on assets toward the competitive floor—that is, the rate of return that would be earned in the economist's "perfectly competitive" industry.[3] Companies that consistently earn rates of return above the floor are said to have a **competitive advantage**. However, rates of return that are higher than the industry floor stimulate more competition as existing companies innovate and expand their market reach or as new companies enter the industry. These developments lead to an erosion of profitability and advantage.

To see how these forces work, consider the simplified representation of the restaurant industry comprising four firms in Figure 5.2.

Figure 5.2

ILLUSTRATION OF HOW MARGIN AND TURNOVER AFFECT RETURN ON ASSETS (ROA)

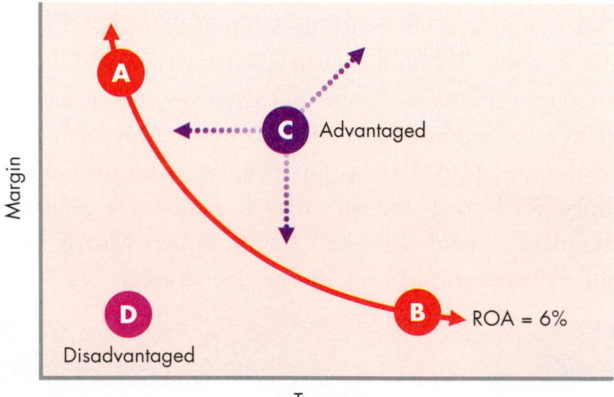

ROA = Margin × Turnover = (NOPAT/Sales) × (Sales/Assets)

---

[3] This competitive floor represents the industry-average **cost of capital** and is approximated by the yield on long-term government securities (that is, the **risk-free rate of return**), adjusted upward for the risk of business failure and capital loss in the industry.

Firm A and Firm B earn exactly the same competitive floor rate of return, which we assume to be 6%, but they do so in different ways. Firm A earns a 6% ROA by combining a high margin (say 6%) with low turnover (say 1). Firm B has a low margin (say 2%) and a high turnover (3 times). Despite their differences, both companies achieve the same level of economic success: ROA = 6% = 6% × 1 = 2% × 3.

Firm C enjoys a competitive advantage that allows it to earn a return greater than 6%; D is disadvantaged and earns a return less than 6%.

Suppose C's superior profitability stems from the widespread acceptance of its new Healthy Breakfast menu among health-conscious consumers. C's current edge is that the breakfast menu items are unique in the marketplace.

The particular competitive advantage C now enjoys may not persist. Other restaurant companies can and will develop menu items that rival the Healthy Breakfast menu in taste and nutritional benefits. As rival menu items become available, they will compete directly with Healthy Breakfast for each consumer dollar, and C's sales volume will thus decline. This will prompt a reduction in C's asset turnover, and it will shift C leftward (dotted arrow) in Figure 5.2 toward the competitive ROA of 6%. Of course, C's management is unlikely to ignore the introduction of rival breakfast items. Faced with the threatened loss of its competitive advantage, C could respond by reducing prices or by increasing advertising expenditures. Both responses could stimulate additional consumer sales and increase turnover, causing a shift back to the right. However, price reductions and increased advertising costs also lower the company's NOPAT margin, and thus they produce a downward shift (dotted arrow) toward the competitive ROA floor.

While the challenge to C is sustaining its Healthy Breakfast advantage in the face of escalating competition, D is facing different challenges. D's current level of profitability is below the industry floor of 6%. Investors and creditors will be reluctant to commit additional financial resources to D unless its profit picture improves. Why? Because D is not currently earning a rate of return large enough to compensate investors for business and financial risk. If D is unable to rectify the situation quickly, its cost of capital will increase, its profit margin will become even lower, and its long-term financial viability may be threatened. What turnaround strategies can D pursue?

According to most observers, there are only two strategies for achieving superior performance in any business. One strategy is product and service **differentiation**; the other is **low-cost leadership**.[4] A differentiation strategy focuses customer attention on "unique" product or service attributes to gain brand loyalty and attractive profit margins. The idea is quite simple: People are willing to pay premium prices for things they value and can't get elsewhere.

Differentiation can take several forms. Examples include advanced technology and performance capabilities, consistent quality, availability in multiple colors or sizes, prompt delivery, technical support services, customer financing, distribution channels, or some other factor of real or perceived importance to customers. Our hypothetical restaurant companies, for instance, are likely to focus customer attention on superior taste and nutritional benefits when introducing menu items intended to compete with Healthy Breakfast. Retailers like Bloomingdales, Neiman Marcus, and Nordstrom achieve differentiation by emphasizing customer service, merchandise quality, and a "unique" shopping experience.

A low-cost leadership strategy focuses customer attention on product pricing, often using slogans like "everyday low prices" or "the lowest price in town." The goal is to become the lowest cost producer in the marketplace so that you can underprice the competition, achieve the highest sales volumes, and still make a profit on each sale. Companies can attain a low-cost position in

---

[4] See W. K. Hall, "Survival Strategies in a Hostile Environment," *Harvard Business Review* (September–October 1980), pp. 78–85; and M. E. Porter, *Competitive Strategy* (New York: Free Press, 1980). Porter also describes a "niche" or "focused" strategy whereby companies achieve uniqueness within a narrowly defined market segment.

various ways. Examples include quantity discount purchases, a lean administrative structure, and production efficiencies from outsourcing or vigorous cost containment. Large retailing companies like Home Depot are able to negotiate steep quantity discounts with manufacturers because their size gives them more bargaining power; such discounts then allow the retailer to offer merchandise to customers at comparatively low prices.

Few companies actually pursue one strategy to the exclusion of the other. Most companies try to do both—developing customer loyalty while controlling costs. Understanding the relative emphasis a company places on differentiation versus low-cost leadership can be important for competitive analysis. *Differences in the business strategies companies adopt give rise to economic differences, which are reflected as differences in operating margins, asset utilization, and profitability.* For example, consider in Figure 5.2 the two cereal companies A and B, which earn exactly the same 6% competitive ROA. Company A achieved this profitability level through a combination of high margin (6%) and low asset turnover (1), a combination often associated with companies that adopt a differentiation strategy. Company B achieved the same ROA level through a combination of low margin (2%) and high turnover (3), a pattern consistent with low-cost leadership.

The choice confronting D's management should now be clear. There are three ways D can return to a competitive profit level: (1) improve the operating margin, (2) increase asset turnover (more sales volume or fewer assets), or (3) both. Margin improvements will shift D upward in Figure 5.2, whereas better turnover will shift it horizontally to the right. In both cases, D moves closer to the industry ROA of 6%. So, D's managers must choose one path or the other—or a combination of the two. That's all they need to do—and attend to a few million details to do it.

RECAP

Not every company in an industry earns the same rate of return on its assets. Some earn more than the industry average ROA while others earn less. Companies that fall below the industry average ROA strive to grow sales, improve operating efficiency, and better manage assets so that they can become competitive again. Those who are fortunate enough to earn more than the industry average ROA struggle to maintain their competitive advantage—through differentiation or low-cost leadership—and to stay on top. This ebb and flow of competition shows up as differences in ROA and in its profit margin and asset turnover components.

Credit Risk and Capital Structure

Credit risk refers to the risk of default by the borrower, and the resulting loss to the lender of interest payments and loan principal. Put differently, credit risk refers to the ability and willingness of a borrower (an individual or organization) to pay its debt. Ability and willingness influence the likelihood that the lender (typically a bank or insurance company) will receive promised principal and interest payments when due. In the corporate arena, two factors must be kept in mind:

- A company's *ability to repay debt* is determined by its capacity to generate cash from operations, asset sales, or external financial markets in excess of its cash needs.
- A company's *willingness to pay* depends on which of the competing cash needs management believes are most pressing at the moment. Those needs include working capital and plant capacity requirements to sustain existing operating activities, capital expenditures for new products, service development or market expansion, and shareholder dividends or debt service requirements.

Figure 5.3 summarizes these ideas.

Figure 5.3

BALANCING CASH SOURCES
AND NEEDS

There are numerous and interrelated risks that influence a company's ability to generate cash. Multinational companies, for example, must cope with possible changes in host government regulations, potential political unrest, and fluctuating currency exchange rates. Domestic companies are exposed to the kind of risk associated with political or demographic changes, recession, inflation, and interest rate fluctuations. Companies within a particular industry confront risks related to technological change, shifting competition, regulation, and availability of raw materials and labor. Management competency, litigation, and the company's strategic direction are additional sources of risk. Each of these risks ultimately affects a company's operating performance, net income, and cash flows. In fact, the statement of cash flows—which reports the net amount of cash generated or used by operating, investing, and financing activities—is an important source of information for analyzing a company's credit risk.

For instance, the comparative cash flow statements for Krispy Kreme in Exhibit 5.4(a) reveal strong, and growing, operating cash flows. However, the company's $51.1 million of operating cash flows in 2002 were not sufficient to cover its net investing needs ($94.6 million) that year. How did the company cover this $43.5 million (= $51.1 − $94.6) cash shortfall? Some of the money came from selling stock to investors ($7.1 million). But the majority of the cash needed to fund the company's continued retail expansion came from new bank loans ($41.4 million). With these new loans, the company's outstanding debt stood at only $61.4 million [$4.2 million current debt plus $57.2 million long-term debt as shown in Exhibit 5.3(a)]. Based on this cursory analysis, it appears that Krispy Kreme is a low credit risk company. Even though the company borrowed money in 2002, the total balance owed represents just a little more than one-year's worth of operating cash flow.

Although cash flow statements contain information enabling a user to assess a company's credit risk, financial ratios are also useful for this purpose. ***Credit risk analysis using financial ratios typically involves an assessment of liquidity and solvency.*** **Liquidity** refers to the company's *short-term* ability to generate cash for working capital needs and immediate debt repayment needs. **Solvency** refers to the *long-term* ability to generate cash internally or from external sources in order to satisfy plant capacity needs, fuel growth, and repay debt when due. Our discussion of financial ratios as an analytical tool for assessing credit risk is based on the distinction between concerns for short-term liquidity and for long-term solvency.

Short-Term Liquidity Short-term liquidity problems arise because operating cash inflows don't match outflows. To illustrate the mismatching problem, let's consider the *operating cycle* of a retailer like Wal-Mart. It acquires merchandise from suppliers on credit, promising to pay within 30 or 60 days. The merchandise is first shipped to Wal-Mart warehouses. Later it is sent on to Wal-Mart stores where it is displayed for purchase and promoted through in-store and regular advertising. Wal-Mart pays for some transportation, labor, and advertising costs immediately and delays payment of other costs. Eventually, Wal-Mart sells the merchandise to customers, who pay by cash or charge card; receivables (if any) are collected some time later; and the company then pays the remaining amounts owed to suppliers and others. Liquidity problems arise when cash inflows from customers lag behind the cash outflows to employees, suppliers, and others.

The operating cycle must not only generate sufficient cash to supply working capital needs, it must also provide cash to service debt as payments become due. For some companies, interest expense is their largest single cost. Such companies may discover that operating cash flows are sufficient to cover periodic interest payments but that the need to repay loan principal causes a liquidity problem. Companies that are not liquid—and are therefore not able to pay obligations as they come due—may be forced into bankruptcy.

One index of a company's short-term liquidity is its **current ratio**:

$$\text{Current ratio} = \frac{\text{Current assets}}{\text{Current liabilities}}$$

Current assets include cash and "near cash" items. For example, receivables become cash as they are collected, so they are only one step removed from cash. Inventories are converted into cash in two steps:

1. They must be sold, usually on credit.
2. The resulting receivable must later be collected.

By including receivables and inventory in current assets, the current ratio reflects existing cash as well as amounts soon to be converted to cash in the normal operating cycle.

A more short-run reflection of liquidity is the **quick ratio**:

$$\text{Quick ratio} = \frac{\text{Cash} + \text{Marketable securities} + \text{Receivables}}{\text{Current liabilities}}$$

Few businesses can instantaneously convert their inventories into cash. So, the quick ratio does not include inventory in the numerator. It therefore provides a measure of *very* immediate liquidity.

Activity ratios tell us how efficiently the company is using its assets. Activity ratios can highlight causes for operating cash flow mismatches. For example, the **accounts receivable turnover** ratio is an activity ratio that can help analysts determine whether receivables are excessive when compared to existing levels of credit sales:

$$\text{Accounts receivable turnover} = \frac{\text{Net credit sales}}{\text{Average accounts receivable}}$$

To illustrate how to interpret this ratio, suppose annual credit sales totaled $10 million and that customer accounts receivable were $2 million at the beginning of the year and $3 million at year-end. The accounts receivable turnover ratio value is then:

$$\frac{\$10}{(\$2 + \$3)/2} = 4 \text{ times per year}$$

The average annual balance of receivables ($2.5 million) represents one-fourth of yearly credit sales ($2.5/$10 = 1/4), so receivables must turn over four times per year.

The accounts receivable turnover ratio can also be used by the analyst to spot changing customer payment patterns. For example, if we divide the accounts receivable turnover ratio into 365 days, the result tells us the number of days that the average customer receivable is "on the books" before it is collected—that is:

$$\text{Days accounts receivable outstanding} = \frac{365 \text{ days}}{\text{Accounts receivable turnover}}$$

$$= \frac{365 \text{ days}}{4} = 91.25 \text{ days}$$

In our example the average accounts receivable is collected about 91 days after the credit sale occurs. This is the same as saying accounts receivable "turn over" four times per year.

Another activity ratio is the **inventory turnover ratio**, which tells us how effectively inventories are managed:

$$\text{Inventory turnover} = \frac{\text{Cost of goods sold}}{\text{Average inventory}}$$

Assume that beginning inventory was $8 million, that year-end inventory was $9 million, and that cost of goods sold was $43.35 million. Therefore inventory turnover is:

> Most companies just report a single "Sales" number that is the sum of cash plus credit sales. Using total "Sales" instead of "Credit sales" in the accounts receivable turnover calculation can sometimes produce misleading results. Companies for which cash sales comprise a large proportion of total "Sales" will have relatively low accounts receivable balances and correspondingly large receivable turnover ratios. Fortunately, cash sales are rare in a surprisingly large number of businesses today. In certain industries like discount retailing (Wal-Mart) and doughnuts (Krispy Kreme), however, cash sales are the rule rather than the exception.

$$\frac{\$43.35}{(\$8 + \$9)/2} = 5.1 \text{ times per year}$$

Take for example, the inventory turnover ratio for Amazon.com and other e-commerce companies. The business models used by e-commerce companies avoid the need to stock inventory in brick-and-mortar stores. As a result, inventory turnover ratios for e-tailers tend to be quite large. Amazon's inventory turnover ratio (14.6 in 2001) has a large numerator ($2,324 million, reflecting high sales volume) and a small denominator ($159 million, reflecting low inventory levels).

The inventory turnover ratio can also be used to determine the average **days inventory held** as follows:

$$\text{Days inventory held} = \frac{365 \text{ days}}{\text{Inventory turnover}}$$

$$= \frac{365 \text{ days}}{5.1} = 71.57 \text{ days}$$

In our example, it takes about 72 days for inventory to move from the company to its customers. In other words, average inventory is sufficient to cover almost 72 days of customer sales. This is just another way of saying that inventory turns over 5.1 times (that is, 365 days/71.57 days) each year. By contrast, Amazon's inventory is held for about 25 days (or 365 days divided by 14.6 inventory turns).

> The calculation of inventory turnover and days inventory held for a manufacturing firm is more complicated than for the merchandising firm illustrated here. That's because inventory in a manufacturing firm must pass through three stages of the operating cycle:
> 1. As *raw material*, from purchase to the start of production.
> 2. As *work-in-process*, over the length of the production cycle.
> 3. As *finished goods*, from completion of production until it is sold.
> Inventory in a merchandising firm passes only through Stage 3.
>
> To calculate how long inventory is held at each stage, analysts use the following activity ratios:
>
> Raw materials: $365 \text{ days} \times \dfrac{\text{Average raw materials inventory}}{\text{Raw materials used}}$
>
> Work-in-process: $365 \text{ days} \times \dfrac{\text{Average work-in-process inventory}}{\text{Cost of goods manufacatured}}$
>
> Finished goods: $365 \text{ days} \times \dfrac{\text{Average finished goods inventory}}{\text{Cost of goods sold}}$
>
> Cost of goods sold and the breakdown of inventory into raw materials, work-in-process, and finished goods is reported in the financial statements. Cost of goods manufactured can be calculated as "cost of goods sold" *plus* ending "finished goods inventory" *minus* beginning "finished goods inventory." However, the amount of raw materials used in production is rarely disclosed in financial statements. It may be available in the company's fact book or obtained by contacting the company's investor relations group.

The **accounts payable turnover** ratio—and its **days payable outstanding** counterpart—helps analysts understand the company's pattern of payments to suppliers:

$$\text{Accounts payable turnover} = \frac{\text{Inventory purchases}}{\text{Average accounts payable}}$$

$$\text{Days accounts payable outstanding} = \frac{365 \text{ days}}{\text{Accounts payable turnover}}$$

Suppose trade accounts payable averaged $7.3 million and inventory purchases totaled $44.350 million during the year. The accounts payable turnover ratio would then equal almost 6 (that is, it would turn over six times per year), and the days accounts payable outstanding would be about 60 days. (You should verify both calculations!) *More timely payment of accounts payable would lead to a lower average payable balance, a higher turnover ratio, and fewer days outstanding.*

> For retail companies like Amazon.com and Wal-Mart, inventory purchases equal cost of goods sold expense plus the year's inventory increase—that is, $44.350 = $43.350 + ($9 − $8) in our example.

Let's piece these activity ratios together to get a picture that will help us analyze the financial condition of our company.

- Inventory remains on hand for about 72 days.
- Inventory is sold, and another 91 days elapse before cash is collected from the customer.
- Suppliers are paid about 60 days after inventory is purchased.

Cash outflows and inflows seem dangerously mismatched. Suppliers are paid 60 days after inventory is purchased by the company, but it takes 72 days to sell the inventory and another 91 days to collect cash from customers. That's a mismatch of 103 days (72 + 91 − 60). Here's how that number was obtained: The company's **operating cycle** spans 163 days—that is how long it takes to sell inventory (72 days) and collect cash from the customers (91 days). But the company pays for inventory purchases in just 60 days, so its **cash conversion cycle** is 103 days—suppliers are paid 103 days before the company has received cash from product sales. This hypothetical company may face a short-term liquidity problem because cash outflows and inflows are mismatched by 103 days. It must rely on other cash sources—like bank loans—to sustain its operating working capital requirements over the 103-day gap.

Exhibit 5.8 reports the operating cycle and cash conversion cycle for three retailers: Amazon.com, Wal-Mart, and Nordstrom. Each company has adopted a different business model, and differences in these business models show up as differences in working capital activity ratios, operating cycles, and cash conversion cycles. Amazon.com is an e-commerce retailer that doesn't have to stock inventory on store shelves, although its distribution centers do stock inventory. Consequently, inventory levels at Amazon.com are quite low—just 25 days. Amazon's customers pay by bank credit card so Amazon gets cash (from the customer's credit card company) almost instantaneously when it makes a sale. The operating cycle at Amazon.com is 25 days but the cash conversion cycle is *minus* 49 days. That's because Amazon waits 74 days after buying inventory to pay its suppliers.

EXHIBIT 5.8	Amazon.com, Wal-Mart, and Nordstrom

Comparison of Operating and Cash Conversion Cycles

	Amazon.com	Wal-Mart	Nordstrom
Working capital activity ratios:			
1. Days inventory held	25.0	50.0	88.8
2. Days accounts receivable outstanding	0.0	3.0	46.0
3. Days accounts payable outstanding	74.0	33.9	47.1
Operating cycle (1 + 2)	25.0	53.0	134.8
Cash conversion cycle (1 + 2 − 3)	(49.0)	19.1	87.7

Wal-Mart and Nordstrom are traditional brick-and-mortar retailers that target different market segments. Wal-Mart carries a broad line of merchandise, emphasizes low prices, and most customers pay cash or use a credit card. Nordstrom is known for its fashion apparel and shoes. The company emphasizes product quality and customer service and promotes its in-store credit card. Wal-Mart has a 53-day operating cycle compared to 134.8 days at Nordstrom. It takes Nordstrom longer to sell inventory (88.8 days compared to 50 days at Wal-Mart), and longer to collect cash from customers once the sale has been made (46 days, compared to 3 days at Wal-Mart). However, Wal-Mart pays suppliers in about 34 days while Nordstom's suppliers wait over 47 days for payment. So, the difference in cash conversion cycle at the two companies—19.1 days at Wal-Mart compared to 87.7 days at Nordstrom—can be traced back to Nordstrom's emphasis on fashion apparel (slower to sell) and its in-store credit card (slower to collect cash). Both companies must carefully manage their short-term liquidity because cash outflows and inflows are mismatched.

Let's return to our analysis of Krispy Kreme Inc. Exhibit 5.9 reports data on the company's short-term liquidity ratios. Krispy Kreme's current ratio was 2.36 in 2002, up from 1.77 two years earlier. The quick ratio was 1.31, suggesting some improvement since 2000. The quick ratio means cash and receivables at Krispy Kreme were sufficient to cover 131% of the company's 2002 current liabilities. Adding inventories further improves the picture—a current ratio of 2.36 means that total current assets cover 236% of Krispy Kreme's current liabilities.

EXHIBIT 5.9	Krispy Kreme, Inc.		

Credit Risk Analysis: Short-Term Liquidity

	2002	2001	2000
Current ratio	2.36	1.94	1.77
Quick ratio	1.31	1.15	0.83
Working capital activity ratios			
1. Days inventory held	18.8	15.8	15.6
2. Days accounts receivable outstanding	31.5	29.3	27.4
3. Days accounts payable outstanding	11.9	11.3	15.0
Operating cycle (1 + 2)	50.3	45.1	43.0
Cash conversion cycle (1 + 2 − 3)	38.4	33.8	28.0

Krispy Kreme's credit customers (including franchised stores) were paying less promptly in 2002 than they did in 2000, with days receivable outstanding at 31.5 compared to 27.4 two years earlier. However, in 2002, Krispy Kreme paid its bills more promptly. Days payable outstanding fell from 15.0 in 2000 to 11.9 in 2002. Inventory turnover deteriorated slightly, and inventory levels were up from 15.6 days in 2000 to 18.8 days in 2002.

There is some misalignment of operating cash flows, since payments to suppliers occurred about 12 days after purchase; in contrast, it took 50 days (18.8 + 31.5) to generate a sale and collect cash from customers. In view of the company's overall level of positive operating cash flows, this misalignment is unlikely to cause concern.

Long-Term Solvency   Solvency refers to the ability of a company to generate a stream of cash inflows sufficient to maintain its productive capacity and still meet the interest and principal payments on its long-term debt. A company that cannot make timely payments in the amount required becomes insolvent and may be compelled to reorganize or liquidate.

Debt ratios provide information about the amount of long-term debt in a company's financial structure. The more a company relies on long-term borrowing to finance its business activities, the higher its debt ratio and the greater the long-term solvency risk. There are several variations in debt ratios. Two commonly used ratios are **long-term debt to assets** and **long-term debt to tangible assets:**

$$\text{Long-term debt to assets} = \frac{\text{Long-term debt}}{\text{Total assets}}$$

$$\text{Long-term debt to tangible assets} = \frac{\text{Long-term debt}}{\text{Total tangible assets}}$$

Suppose a company has $20 million of outstanding long-term debt and $100 million of total assets, of which $35 million are intangibles like goodwill or purchased patents, trademarks, or copyrights. The two debt ratios would be:

$$\text{Long-term debt to assets} = \frac{\$20}{\$100} = 0.200$$

$$\text{Long-term debt to tangible assets} = \frac{\$20}{\$100 - \$35} = 0.308$$

Most analysts add the "Current portion of long-term debt" to the numerator in long-term debt solvency ratios, even though this debt is classified as a current liability on the balance sheet. Some analysts go so far as to include *all* short-term interest bearing debt (like "Notes payable") in their solvency ratio calculations. Several arguments favor this approach: (1) Long-term debt that is repayable over several years will always have some portion shown as a current liability, and this current portion should not be ignored; (2) Long-term debt is shown as a current liability when loan covenants have been violated, but this does not mean that the firm's solvency risk has improved; (3) A firm with significant short-term debt but no long-term debt is not necessarily less risky than one with only long-term debt outstanding. Adding short-term debt to the ratio numerator overcomes distortions that can affect the interpretation of solvency risk.

These results tell us that only 20 cents of each asset dollar was financed using long-term debt. The remaining 80 cents came from other sources—internally generated resources, short-term borrowing, or equity capital in the form of common and preferred stock. This level of debt—only 20 cents of each asset dollar—would be surprisingly high for a discount retailer like Wal-Mart but surprisingly low for an electric utility company. Retailers use short-term debt and trade credit to finance their inventory purchases, and they usually lease (but don't own) their retail stores. Electric utilities, on the other hand, rely on long-term debt to support their sizable investment in power generating facilities and transmission lines. Electric utilities also have relatively predictable operating cash flows because energy demand is reasonably stable and competition is limited by regulators. Companies whose sales fluctuate widely due to changing economic conditions generally prefer to avoid debt, since the fixed interest charges can be difficult to meet during bad times. These cyclical companies tend to have smaller debt-to-asset ratios.

Analysts devote considerable attention to refining both the numerator and denominator of debt ratios. For example, analysts include in the numerator "hybrid" securities, or obligations that have the cash flow characteristics of regular balance-sheet debt, even though they may not be classified as such on the balance sheet. Operating leases and other off-balance sheet obligations are routinely included as debt "equivalents" in the numerator. The exclusion of intangible assets from the solvency ratio denominator is also common. This adjustment is intended to remove "soft" assets—those difficult to value reliably—from the analysis.

Comparative debt ratios for Krispy Kreme are shown in Exhibit 5.10. The company's debt-to-total-assets ratio was 0.15 in 2002, a substantial increase from the 0.02 level in 2000, and the long-term debt-to-tangible-assets ratio stood at 0.17, also up from 0.02 in 2000. The two debt ratios moved in the same direction and are consistent with a fast-growing company that, while financially sound, is relying more and more on long-term debt to finance growth in operations.

EXHIBIT 5.10	Krispy Kreme, Inc.		

Credit Risk Analysis: Long-Term Solvency

	2002	2001	2000
Long-term debt to assets ratio	0.15	0.03	0.02
Long-term debt to tangible assets ratio	0.17	0.04	0.02
Interest coverage ratio	38.28	139.67	39.17
Operating cash flow to total liabilities	0.39	0.56	0.72

Although debt ratios are useful for understanding the financial structure of a company, they provide no information about its ability to generate a stream of inflows sufficient to make principal and interest payments. One financial ratio commonly used for this purpose is the **interest coverage ratio**:

$$\text{Interest coverage} = \frac{\text{Operating income before taxes and interest}}{\text{Interest expense}}$$

This ratio indicates how many times interest expense is covered by operating profits before taxes and interest are factored in. It reflects the cushion between operating profit inflows and required interest payments. If the company must also make periodic principal payments, then the analyst could include those amounts in the calculation.

> Many analysts use an *adjusted* operating income figure that removes nonrecurring items from reported income and that corrects for accounting quality distortions.

Suppose a company has $200 million of operating income before taxes and interest, and $50 million of interest expense. The company's interest coverage ratio is:

$$\frac{\$200}{\$50} = 4$$

This shows that operating profit is four times larger than interest expense—a substantial cushion for the lender. But now suppose our company is also required to make a $100 million debt principal payment. The revised interest coverage ratio is:

$$\frac{\$200}{\$50 + \$100} = 1.33$$

When required debt payments are factored in, the lender's cushion now looks thin.

A criticism of the traditional interest coverage ratio is that it uses earnings rather than operating cash flows in the numerator. Some analysts prefer to compute a **cash flow coverage ratio** in which the numerator represents operating cash flows before interest and tax payments are factored in. When operating profits and cash flows move in tandem, both versions of the ratio will yield similar results. However, when the two measures do diverge—for example, during a period in which the company experiences rapid growth—income may be a poor substitute for cash flow. In that case the cash flow coverage ratio is preferable as a solvency measure. After all, real cash (and not just operating profits) is what the company needs to make its required interest payments.

Another useful measure of long-term solvency compares **operating cash flow** to the company's **total liabilities** (excluding deferred taxes):

$$\frac{\text{Operating cash flow}}{\text{to total liabilities}} = \frac{\text{Cash flow from continuing operations}}{\text{Average current liabilities plus long-term debt}}$$

This ratio shows the ability of a company to generate cash from operations in order to service both short-term and long-term borrowings.

Referring to Exhibit 5.10, we see an interest coverage ratio of 38.28 in 2002, almost unchanged from 39.17 two years earlier. This means that Krispy Kreme's pre-tax operating income [before interest and excluding "Other (revenues) expenses"] was about 39 times larger than interest expense, indicating that the company has ample coverage. What is striking about the interest coverage ratios in Exhibit 5.10 is the unusually high figure (139.67) shown for 2001. Two factors help explain this. First, interest expense declined in 2001 to only one-half of the amount for 2000 [Exhibit 5.1(a)]. Second, pre-tax operating income nearly doubled. As a result, Krispy Kreme's 2001 interest coverage ratio benefited from a larger income flow and a lower level of interest expense.

Krispy Kreme's operating cash flow to total liabilities ratio clearly demonstrates why the company is regarded by most analysts as financially solvent and a low credit risk. Operating cash flows in 2002 were sufficient to repay 39% of the company's total debt, meaning that Krispy Kreme could afford to repay all of its debt in about two and one-half years (100% ÷ 39% = 2.56), if it so chose. Of course the company is unlikely to do so because it needs cash—from operations and from additional borrowing—to fuel growth. That's why the company's operating cash flow to total liabilities ratio declined over three years.

Financial Ratios and Default Risk

A company is in **default** when it fails to make a required loan principal or interest payments on time. Lenders can respond to a default in one of several ways. At one end of the spectrum, lenders may simply adjust the loan payment schedule to better suit the company's anticipated operating cash flows. This response would seem appropriate when the default stems from a temporary cash flow shortfall. If the borrower's cash flow problem is more serious, lenders will modify the payment schedule while also increasing the loan interest rate and requiring loan collateral (like receivables, inventory, or equipment) as additional protection. If the borrower's cash flow problem is extreme, lenders may petition to have the borrower judged insolvent by a court. The court-appointed trustee then can either liquidate or reorganize the business—and restructure its loans—in an effort to settle all obligations in an orderly and equitable manner. Insolvency (or "bankruptcy," as it is more commonly known) thus becomes the ultimate form of default.

Credit analysis is intended to help lenders assess default risk, or the likelihood of loan default by the borrower. Financial ratios play two crucial roles in credit analysis. First, they help lenders quantify a potential borrower's default risk before a loan decision is finalized. Second, once a loan is granted, financial ratios then serve as an early warning device that alerts lenders to changes in the borrower's credit risk. But which specific financial ratios are most useful for these purposes? In other words, which particular financial ratios best predict default risk and how well do they do so?

Predicting loan default and bankruptcy is not an easy task because both events are relatively rare, especially among public companies. For example, Figure 5.4 shows the one-year default rates for 1983 to 1999 among public companies covered by Moody's Investors Services, a credit rating agency. Moody's assigns a credit rating to each of several thousand companies. For example, an "Aaa" rating represents Moody's lowest credit risk.

The power of Moody's ratings is immediately clear in the ability to group companies by low and high default rates. Companies assigned the top rating ("Aaa") by Moody's seem to never default on their loans while those assigned the bottom rating ("B3") default 12.2% of the time. In fact, the default rates associated with most of the rating categories shown in Figure 5.4 are quite small. Remember, too, that most public companies are financially sound and thus earn a relatively high credit rating; 80% of the companies covered by Moody's receive a rating of "B1" or above. This means that only a few companies fall into the high credit risk ("B3") pool, and of those, only about 12% default.

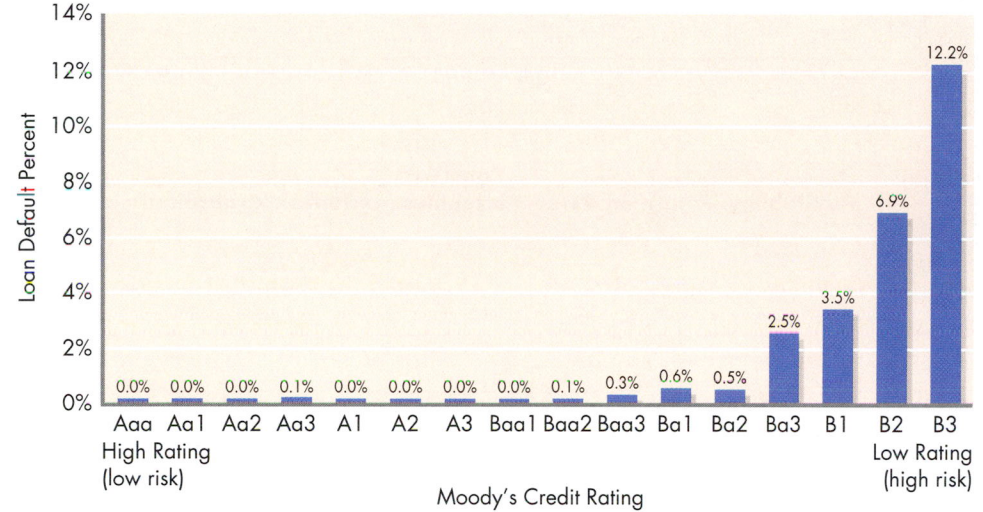

Figure 5.4

DEFAULT RATES BY MOODY'S CREDIT RATING, 1983–1999

Source: RiskCalc for Private Companies: Moody's Default Model Rating Methodology, Moody's Investors Service (May 2000).

Figure 5.5 on the next page shows default frequency graphs for four common financial ratios: return on assets (ROA), debt-to-tangible-assets, interest coverage, and the quick ratio. Notice that ROA is a profitability measure, while the other financial ratios measure solvency (debt-to-tangible-assets ratio and interest coverage ratio) or liquidity (quick ratio). Each graph was estimated using financial data from public companies in Moody's loan default database over the 1980–1999 period. To generate the ROA graph, the data were first divided into 50 groups that ranged from very low ROA to very high ROA. The companies in each group were then examined to determine whether or not a default occurred in 90 days to 5 years from the financial statement date. Default frequencies were then compiled for each group and statistically smoothed to aid interpretation. Graphs for the other three ratios were constructed in a similar manner.

The pattern of default frequencies in Figure 5.5a confirms our intuition: Default risk goes up as profitability declines. Highly *unprofitable* companies—those with the lowest ROA and shown on the far left-hand side of Figure 5.5a—have a five-year default rate of about 8% compared to only about 1.5% for the companies with the highest ROA. Notice, too, that companies in the 40th percentile have below average ROA and a 5% default rate. In other words, lower profitability means higher default risk.

Figure 5.5b tells a similar story about solvency ratios and default frequencies. Companies with low debt-to-tangible-assets (far left-hand side of the graph) and high interest coverage (far right-hand side of the graph) also have low default rates. As solvency deteriorates, because of either an increase in debt-to-tangible-assets or a decline in interest coverage decreases, default rates go up. The same holds true for liquidity and the quick ratio in Figure 5.5c. Highly liquid companies—those with the highest quick ratio and shown on the far right-hand side of Figure 5.5c—have low default rates when compared to the relatively high default rates experienced by illiquid (low quick ratio) companies.

Figure 5.5

PROBABILITY OF DEFAULT
WITHIN FIVE YEARS AMONG
PUBLIC COMPANIES: 1980
TO 1999

Source: RiskCalc for Private Companies: Moody's Default Model
Rating Methodology, Moody's
Investors Service (May 2000).

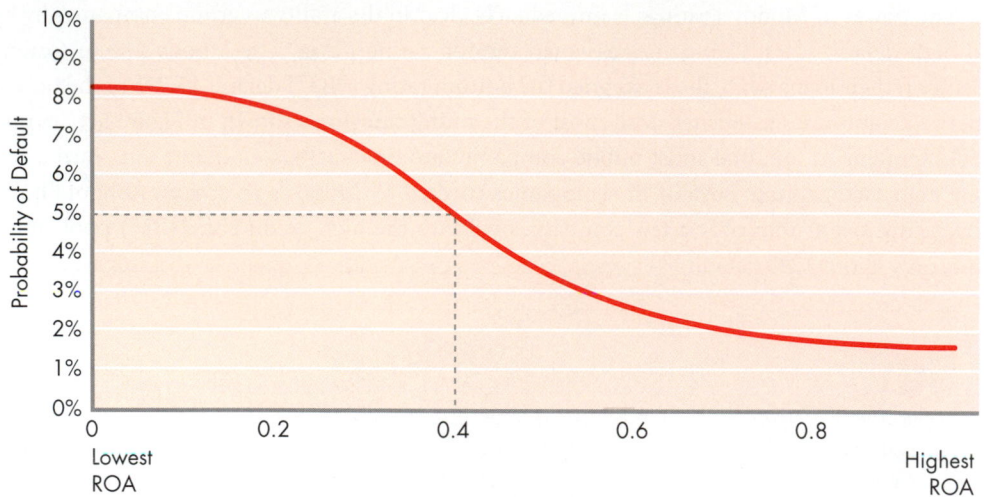

Panel (a)
Profitability: Return on Assets Percentiles (excludes extraordinary items)

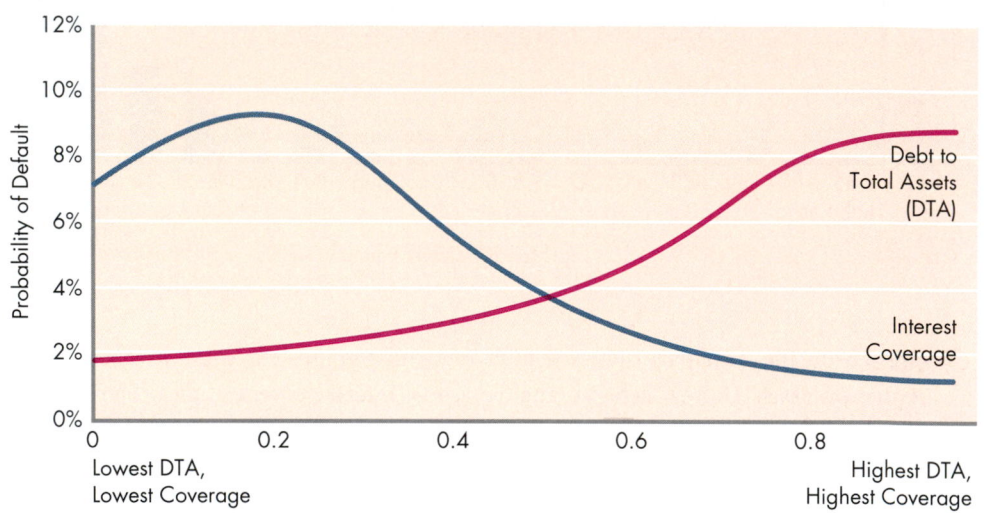

Panel (b)
Solvency: Debt-to-Tangible Assets and Interest Coverage Percentiles

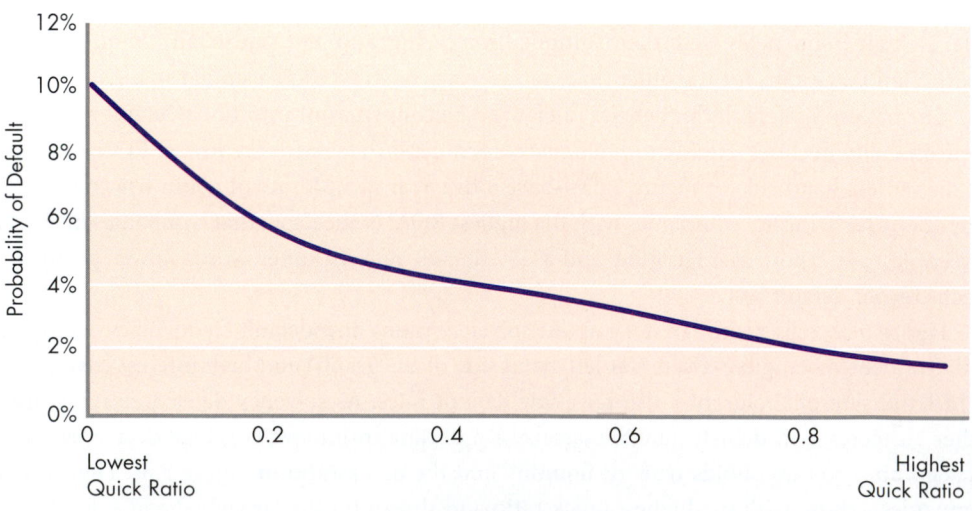

Panel (c)
Liquidity: Quick Ratio Percentiles

Now you see how financial ratios can be used to assess default risk—once you have access to default-frequency graphs like those in Figure 5.5 compiled by Moody's Investor Services. For example, if a prospective borrower falls into the very highest ROA pool in Figure 5.5a, the default risk is only about 1.5% over the next five years—a relatively safe bet for a loan. However, if the borrower's profitability suddenly declines to a below-average level (for example, to the 40th percentile), default risk increases to 5%. The ROA decline serves as an early warning signal about the increased probability of default in the future.

The appendix to this chapter describes one popular approach for combining several financial ratios into a single predictor of the ultimate default event—bankruptcy.

> **RECAP**
>
> When lenders want to know about a company's ability to pay debts on time, they assess its credit risk. A cash flow statement is often the starting point for credit risk assessment because it shows the company's operating cash flows along with its financing and investment needs. A low-credit-risk company generates operating cash flows substantially in excess of what are required to sustain its business activities. Liquidity and solvency ratios are additional tools the lender can use to assess credit risk.

Return on Equity and Financial Leverage

Profitability and credit risk both influence the return that common shareholders earn on their investment in the company. To see how, let's look at what happens when a successful company borrows money to fund its growth.

ParsTech develops and distributes home financial planning software nationwide. Assume the company has $1 million in assets and no debt—ParsTech is an "all equity" firm. Earnings in 2005 are $150,000 and the entire amount is paid to shareholders as a dividend. These events are summarized in the first row of Exhibit 5.11.

EXHIBIT 5.11	ParsTech						
Financial Leverage							
	Earnings Before Interest*	Assets	Common Shareholders' Equity	Return on Assets (ROA)	Interest Charges	Net Income Available to Common Stockholders	Return on Common Equity (ROCE)
2005	$150,000	$1 million	$1 million	15%	—	$150,000	15%
2006	300,000	2 million	1 million	15	$100,000	200,000	20
2007	450,000	3 million	1 million	15	300,000	150,000	15

*Earnings are before interest but after taxes, and they are distributed to lenders (as interest) and shareholders (as dividends) each year.

ParsTech's ROA for 2005 is 15% ($150,000 in earnings/$1 million in assets). Since the company has no debt, all the earnings belong to shareholders, so **return on common equity** (ROCE) is also 15% ($150,000 in earnings/$1 million in common equity).

Early in 2006 the company borrows $1 million to expand its manufacturing, distribution, and customer support facilities. Lenders charge only 10% interest on the loan because the company has steady cash flows and a track record of successful new product introductions.

Strong consumer demand plus expanded plant capacity produce a banner year for the company. Earnings before interest total $300,000 in 2006, and ParsTech's ROA is again 15% (shown in the second row of Exhibit 5.11). Who gets the $300,000? Lenders must receive their share—$100,000 in interest on the loan—but the rest belongs to common shareholders. Shareholders receive $200,000 and ROCE is 20%.

Why did ROCE increase while ROA was unchanged? The answer is **financial leverage**. ParsTech borrowed $1 million at 10% (or $100,000 annual interest) but earned 15% (or $150,000) on the money. After the company paid interest charges, common shareholders gained $50,000 without investing more of their own money in the company. Financial leverage benefits shareholders whenever the cost of debt (10% in our example) is less than what the company earns on the borrowed funds (15% in our example).

There's a downside here, however, because financial leverage can sometimes be costly to shareholders. For instance, suppose that ParsTech borrowed another $1 million in 2007 to further expand its facilities. But this time, lenders assign a higher credit risk to the company and charge 20% interest. Earnings before interest but after taxes are $450,000 in 2007 and ParsTech's ROA is again 15%. What is ROCE?

Now lenders receive $300,000 in interest—$100,000 for the first loan plus $200,000 for the second—leaving only $150,000 of earnings for common shareholders. ROCE in 2007 is 15% ($150,000/$1 million in common equity), down from the previous year. Stockholders are no better off now than they were two years earlier when the company was smaller and earnings were lower. What happened?

> More precisely, it's the *after-tax* cost of debt that must be less than what the company earns on borrowed funds. If the corporate income tax rate is 35%, ParsTech has an after-tax cost of debt of 6.5% $[10\% \times (1 - 0.35)]$ even though lenders are charging 10% interest. Financial leverage benefits ParsTech shareholders as long as the company earns more than 6.5% after-tax on its debt-financed investment.

The second loan cost more (20% or $200,000 in annual interest) than ParsTech was able to earn ($150,000) on the borrowed funds, and shareholders had to make up the difference. *Financial leverage is beneficial—but only when the company earns more than the incremental after-tax cost of debt.* If the cost of debt becomes too high, increased leverage can actually harm shareholders.

If you want to gauge a company's profit performance from its shareholders' viewpoint, use ROCE.

$$\text{ROCE} = \frac{\text{Net income available to common shareholders}}{\text{Average common shareholders' equity}}$$

ROCE measures a company's performance in using capital provided by common shareholders to generate earnings.[5] It explicitly considers how the company's assets are financed. Interest charged on loans and dividends on preferred stock are both subtracted in arriving at "Net income available to common shareholders." The capital provided by common shareholders during the period can be computed by averaging the aggregate par value of common stock, capital contributed in excess of par, and retained earnings (minus common treasury shares) at the beginning and end of the period. For example, using the data in Exhibit 5.1(a) and Exhibit 5.3(a), the ROCE for Krispy Kreme in 2002 is:

$$\text{ROCE} = \frac{\text{Net income} - \text{Preferred dividends}}{\text{Average common shareholders' equity}}$$

$$= \frac{\$33.5 - \$0}{(\$273.4 + \$187.7)/2} = \frac{\$33.5}{\$230.6} = 0.145 \text{ or } 14.5\%$$

Krispy Kreme's return on common equity (ROCE) was a respectable 14.5% in 2002, but less than the 16.8% the company earned in 2001. Why did the company's profitability decline? One rea-

---

[5] If the analysts' goal is to isolate *sustainable* ROCE, "Net income available to common shareholders" should be purged of nonoperating and nonrecurring items, and corrected for accounting quality distortions. These adjustments are discussed in later chapters.

son is that net income for 2002 included a $9.1 million special charge for settling a business dispute. This one-time expense distorted the company's profitability picture for 2002 when compared to ROCE in earlier years. Once this distortion is eliminated, we see that Krispy Kreme's ROCE was 17% in 2002, up from the 2001 amount. Now it's clear that the company was slightly *more* profitable in 2002 than in the previous year, not *less* profitable as the unadjusted ROCE figure suggested.

> To eliminate the distortion caused by one-time expenses (and gains), add the *after-tax* amount of the charge (but subtract the *after-tax* amount of any gain) to net income in the ROCE numerator. Assuming a 37% corporate income tax rate, the after-tax adjustment for Krispy Kreme is $5.79 million (or $9.1 million × (1 − 0.37). When this amount is added to net income, the ROCE numerator for 2002 becomes $39.29 and ROCE is then 17.0% (or $39.29 /$230.6).

Components of ROCE

We can break down ROCE into several components to aid in our interpretation, much as we did earlier with ROA. The components of ROCE are ROA, common earnings leverage, and financial leverage:

$$\text{ROCE} = \text{ROA} \times \text{Common earnings leverage} \times \text{Financial structure leverage}$$

$$= \left(\frac{\text{NOPAT}}{\text{Average assets}} \right) \times \left(\frac{\text{Net income available to common shareholders}}{\text{NOPAT}} \right)$$

$$\times \left(\frac{\text{Average assets}}{\text{Average common shareholders' equity}} \right)$$

$$= \frac{\text{Net income available to common shareholders}}{\text{Average common shareholders' equity}}$$

ROA measures the profitability of operations before considering how the company's assets are financed. The **common earnings leverage ratio** shows the proportion of NOPAT (net operating profits before interest but after taxes) that belongs to common shareholders. The **financial structure leverage ratio** measures the degree to which the company uses common shareholders' capital to finance assets.

Using the numbers from earlier exhibits, the ROCE breakdown for Krispy Kreme in 2002 (before eliminating the business dispute charge from ROCE) was:

$$\text{ROCE} = \text{ROA} \times \text{Common earnings leverage} \times \text{Financial structure leverage}$$

$$= \left(\frac{\$40.367}{(\$410.5 + \$255.4)/2} \right) \times \left(\frac{\$33.5}{\$40.367} \right) \times \left(\frac{(\$410.5 + \$255.4)/2}{(\$273.4 + \$187.7)/2} \right)$$

$$= 0.121 \times 0.830 \times 1.444$$

$$= 0.145 \text{ or } 14.5\%$$

Krispy Kreme's higher ROCE (14.5%) compared to ROA (12.1%) occurred because the company has debt in its financial structure, resulting in a moderately high financial structure leverage ratio (1.444). Interest on this debt, along with the nonrecurring charge, contributed to a moderate common earnings leverage ratio (0.830). The two factors in combination produced a return on common equity that is 1.199 (or, 0.830 x1.444) times greater than what the company earns on all assets (12.1% ROA).

To see how the components of ROCE work together, consider two companies—NoDebt and HiDebt—each with $2 million in assets. NoDebt raised all its capital from common shareholders; HiDebt borrowed $1 million at 10% interest. Both companies pay income taxes at a combined federal and state rate of 40%.

Exhibit 5.12 shows how the two companies compare in different earnings years. Let's start with a good earnings year, one in which both companies earn $240,000 before interest but after taxes. This represents an ROA of 12% for each company, and 12% is also NoDebt's ROCE. HiDebt's ROCE is 18%, since $180,000 of earnings ($240,000 − $60,000 after-tax interest) is available to common shareholders. Leverage increased the return to HiDebt's shareholders because the capital contributed by lenders earned 12% but required an after-tax interest payment of only 6%—that is, a 10% rate of interest × (1 − 40% tax rate). The extra 6% earned on each borrowed asset dollar increased the return to common shareholders.

EXHIBIT 5.12	Nodebt and Hidebt

Profitability and Financial Leverage

	Total Assets	Shareholders' Equity	Earnings Before Interest*	After-Tax Interest	Available to Common Shareholders	ROA	ROCE
Good Earnings Year							
HiDebt	$2 million	$1 million	$240,000	$60,000	$180,000	12.0%	18.0%
NoDebt	2 million	2 million	240,000	—	240,000	12.0	12.0
Neutral Earnings Year							
HiDebt	2 million	1 million	120,000	60,000	60,000	6.0	6.0
NoDebt	2 million	2 million	120,000	—	120,000	6.0	6.0
Bad Earnings Year							
HiDebt	2 million	1 million	60,000	60,000	—	3.0	0.0
NoDebt	2 million	2 million	60,000	—	60,000	3.0	3.0

*Earnings are before interest but after taxes. HiDebt has after-tax interest charges of $60,000—that is, $1 million × 10% × (1 − 40%)—each year.

But what happens when earnings are low? That situation is illustrated by the bad earnings year in Exhibit 5.12. Both companies earn $60,000 before interest but after taxes, for a 3% ROA. All of these earnings are available to NoDebt shareholders, so ROCE for that company is also 3%. At HiDebt, after-tax interest charges wipe out earnings and ROCE becomes 0% because there's nothing left for shareholders. HiDebt earns 3% on each asset dollar but must pay 6% to lenders for each dollar borrowed. In this case, leverage decreases the return to common equity and harms shareholders.

In the neutral year, leverage neither helps nor hurts shareholders. That's because the 6% return earned on each asset dollar just equals the 6% after-tax cost of borrowing. Figure 5.6 illustrates the key results from this example.

Figure 5.6

FINANCIAL LEVERAGE
AND ROCE

Financial leverage works two ways. It can make good years better by increasing the shareholders' return, but it can also make bad years worse by decreasing the shareholders' return. It all depends on whether the company earns more on each borrowed dollar than it pays out in interest.

RECAP

Financial Statement Analysis and Accounting Quality

Financial ratios, common-size statements, and trend statements are extremely powerful tools for understanding how a company got to where it is today and where the company might be tomorrow. But because these tools are built around reported accounting data, they can be no better than the data from which they are constructed. Analysts need a thorough understanding of accounting rules and a keen eye for information in the financial statement footnotes before they can use the tools to their full advantage.

The profit performance of Krispy Kreme illustrates this point. As you recall, the company's return on common equity (ROCE) appeared to have fallen from 16.8% in 2001 to just 14.5% in 2002. A careful look at the company's financial statements and footnotes uncovered the reason for this apparent decline—a one-time $9.1 million charge for settling a business dispute. Once this nonrecurring item was eliminated from the ROCE calculation, we could see that Krispy Kreme's 17% ROCE for 2002 was slightly better than it had been in the prior year.

Nonrecurring items of this sort are just the tip of the iceberg when it comes to potential accounting distortions of financial ratios, common-size percentages, and trends. Differences in accounting methods and estimates across firms or changes in those methods and estimates for a given firm can also distort financial ratio, percentage, and trend comparisons. Fail to spot a company's aggressive revenue recognition method (Chapter 3) and you may mistakenly conclude that sales at the company are growing faster than industry norms. Aggressive revenue recognition often leads to a balance sheet buildup of accounts receivable, which may further cause you to mistakenly conclude (using the quick ratio) that the company is more liquid than is actually the case. Or, fail to spot a company's off-balance-sheet leases (Chapter 12) in the financial statement footnotes, and you may mistakenly conclude (using the debt-to-equity ratio) that the company is more solvent than its competitors.

Some companies account for inventory using the first-in first-out (FIFO) method; others use last-in first-out (LIFO). These alternative methods can produce very different balance sheet and income statement figures, and, as a result, numerous financial ratios and comparisons can be affected (Chapter 9). Analysts must be alert to this possibility and know how to recognize when differences in GAAP accounting methods, rather than economic fundamentals, are affecting the analysis.

Another problem occurs because under GAAP, fixed assets are measured using historical costs (Chapter 10). Two companies with identical assets that were purchased at different times will show those assets at different amounts. The company with the older (presumably lower cost) asset would likely report a higher return on assets (ROA) as well as a higher asset turnover ratio. Here, too, the analyst must guard against accounting distortions that mask economic fundamentals.

The message here is simply that analysts must always be vigilant about the possibility that accounting distortions are present and complicate the interpretation of financial ratios, percentage relations, and trend indices. That's why each chapter of this book alerts you to potential accounting distortions, and then shows you how to eliminate those distortions so that the analysis reflects a true "apples-to-apples" comparison. Only then can you accurately assess a company's true profitability and credit risk.

Earnings, Pro Forma Earnings, or EBITDA?

It's the quarterly earnings season, that three-week period each quarter when analysts and investors nervously watch the financial wire services as companies report their results. One company whose stock you own, Millbrae Technologies, is expected to report record per share earnings of $1.50 this quarter. That's what analysts covering the company are saying. You, however, are confident that Millbrae will beat the $1.50 consensus "Wall Street" estimate. You scan your e-mail for the company's press release, and sure enough the headline reads: "Millbrae has a blockbuster quarter—earns $2.10 per share." Great news! But wait—the stock is trading down as if investors are punishing the company for reporting an earnings disappointment. What's going on?

A closer look at Millbrae's press release reveals the problem. The company's GAAP earnings for the quarter were only $1.20 per share, considerably below what analysts were expecting. No wonder the stock is trading down on the earnings disappointment. And the "$2.10 per share" the company said it earned? It turns out that the $2.10 wasn't GAAP earnings at all but instead something called "**pro forma earnings**" (earnings before certain GAAP expense items that Millbrae's management wants you to ignore).

Many companies today are highlighting a non-GAAP earnings figure in press releases, in analyst conference calls, and in quarterly and annual reports. Sometimes the earnings figure is called EBITDA—earnings before income taxes, depreciation, and amortization—sometimes it's called "adjusted earnings" and sometimes "pro forma earnings." But these distinctions are often vague, so you have to look closely to find out what's really going on. For example, here is what Amazon.com said in one of its quarterly earnings press release:

Pro forma net income (loss) excludes the following line items on the Company's statement of operations: stock-based compensation, amortization of goodwill and other intangibles, restructuring-related and other, remeasurement of 6.875% PEACS and other, equity in losses of equity-method investees (net), and cumulative effect of change in accounting principle.

Pro forma net income is provided as a complement to ["As reported"] results provided in accordance with accounting principles generally accepted in the United States (known as "GAAP"). Management uses this measure internally to evaluate the Company's performance and manage its operations.

Source: Amazon.com quarterly earnings press release, April 24, 2003.

	Three months ended March 31, 2003 (in thousands, except per share data)		Three months ended March 31, 2002 (in thousands, except per share data)	
	As reported	Pro forma	As reported	Pro forma
Net sales	$1,083,559	$1,083,559	$847,422	$847,422
Income from operations	39,225	67,460	1,774	24,658
Net income (loss)	(10,121)	40,348	(23,150)	(4,839)
Income (loss) per share	$(0.03)	$0.10	$(0.06)	$(0.01)

Amazon reported a "pro forma" profit of about $40 million or $0.10 per share for the first quarter in 2003. Of course, the profit measure Amazon highlights in its press release is one that the company itself has concocted. Pro forma profits at Amazon.com exclude a variety of costs that are routinely included in GAAP earnings. Once these costs are included, the company's quarterly pro forma profit becomes a GAAP loss of about $10 million or $0.03 per share. Was Amazon profitable that quarter? The answer depends on which profit benchmark is used—the company's own "pro forma" calculation or GAAP earnings. The more cost items Amazon excludes from its profit computation, the more "profitable" the company will appear. But appearances don't necessarily mirror reality!

Let's take a closer look at the computation and origin of these non-GAAP profit measures. Exhibit 5.13 presents a GAAP income statement for Marconi Communications, an emerging telecommunications company. Marconi has a GAAP loss of $66 million for 2005. This loss includes a charge for depreciation, amortization of intangibles, stock-based compensation, restructuring and merger costs, interest, and taxes. By selectively including or excluding these items, Marconi can highlight any of several different profit numbers. For example, Marconi adds back amortization and stock-based compensation expense along with its restructuring and merger costs to arrive at "pro forma" earnings of $99 million. The company's $175 million of EBITDA excludes interest, taxes, depreciation, and goodwill amortization. Be forewarned, however, that standard definitions for these non-GAAP profit benchmarks do not presently exist. Companies today can and do exercise considerable discretion over which cost items are included or excluded in the profit numbers they choose to highlight. Of course, the financial statements themselves must still report GAAP earnings (for example, Marconi's $66 million loss) but some firms try to overshadow these GAAP numbers with other, more creative, profit benchmarks.

> The Securities and Exchange Commission (SEC) now requires firms that highlight a non-GAAP earnings number in their press releases or other investor communications to also include a table showing how the earnings figure is calculated.

EXHIBIT 5.13 **Marconi Communications**

GAAP Earnings, "Pro forma" Earnings, and EBITDA Earnings

GAAP Earnings

($ in millions)	2005
Sales	$ 500
Cost of goods sold (excluding depreciation)	(200)
Depreciation expense	(100)
Selling, general and administrative expenses	(75)
Amortization	(100)
Stock-based compensation expense	(15)
Restructuring and merger expenses	(50)
Interest expense	(60)
Taxes	34
Net income (loss)	$ (66)

"Pro forma" earnings

Net income (loss)	$ (66)
Excluded costs:	
Amortization	100
Stock-based compensation	15
Restructuring and merger expenses	50
Pro forma earnings	$ 99

EBITDA earnings

Net income (loss)	$ (66)
Excluded costs:	
Interest expense	60
Tax expense	(34)
Depreciation expense	100
Amortization	100
EBITDA	$160

The origins of EBITDA date back to before 1980 when EBIT (earnings before interest and taxes) or *operating earnings* was often used as a key indicator of a company's ability to service its debt.[6] One important advantage of EBIT is that it "leveled the playing field" for differences in capital structure and taxation by removing interest and taxes from the profit benchmark, thus making comparisons across companies more transparent. (Recall our earlier discussion of interest coverage.) However, EBIT is not a cash flow measure—we will see why in a moment—and it may overstate or understate the degree to which operating cash is available to service debt.

EBITDA displaced EBIT in the 1980s as a financial benchmark for measuring a company's cash flow and thus its ability to service debt. EBITDA removes from the profit calculation two non-cash items—depreciation and amortization—that are major expense items for many companies

---

[6] P. Stumpp, T. Marshella, M. Rowan, R. McCreary, and M. Coppola, "Putting EBITDA in Perspective: Ten Critical Failings of EBITDA as the Principal Determinant of Cash Flow," *Global Credit Research Report*, Moody's Investors Service (June 2000).

today, especially technology and telecommunications companies. Proponents claim EBITDA really is an accurate measure of cash flow—assuming the company does not have to spend money on equipment or pay taxes and interest on debt. Critics respond that EBITDA isn't the same as cash flow. Quite simply, cash flow is what's left in the till after you account for all the cash coming in and all the cash going out during a given period. EBITDA ignores the cash required for working capital growth and for reinvestment (for example, money spent replacing worn-out equipment). EBITDA also says nothing about the quality of earnings because it takes operating revenues and expenses at face value without considering whether those revenues and expenses affect cash directly. As a result, EBITDA can easily be manipulated through aggressive accounting policies relating to revenues and expenses.

"Pro forma" earnings emerged in the late 1990s as a label for adjusted GAAP earnings where everything but the kitchen sink may be excluded from the profit figure. At firms like Amazon.com, the adjustments include the elimination of amortization, merger costs, stock-based employee pay, and losses at affiliates. Some companies also exclude interest, taxes, and depreciation to produce an "adjusted pro forma" EBITDA. These and other "pro forma" adjustments to GAAP earnings are rationalized by analysts and company managers because they involve non-cash charges, or they are nonrecurring, or because they somehow mask the company's true profitability. Skeptics argue that "pro forma" profits are nothing more than EEBS—earnings excluding bad stuff![7]

According to one recent study, investors do not focus only on the "pro forma" earnings number highlighted in company press releases. Investors instead seem to consider a richer set of information—including the GAAP items left out of "pro forma" earnings—when they price firms' shares. B. Johnson and W. Schwartz, "Are Investors Misled by 'Pro Forma' Earnings?" *Contemporary Accounting Research (forthcoming).*

Why are companies resorting to EBITDA and "pro forma" earnings instead of just highlighting their GAAP earnings performance? The answer is simple—impression management! It's a whole lot easier to transform a GAAP loss into a "profit" by changing how profits are measured rather than by changing the economics of the business itself. Just cross out a few expense items here and there, and suddenly the business looks profitable again. Sometimes the adjustments are well-intentioned attempts to describe the company's sustainable operating profits and cash flows. But not always. In either case, you will be well served to remember the following:

- There are no standard definitions for non-GAAP earnings numbers. EBITDA at one company may be labeled "pro forma" earnings at another and "adjusted" earnings at still another. Worse, a company may change its EBITDA or "pro forma" earnings definition each quarter.
- Non-GAAP earnings like EBITDA and pro forma earnings ignore some real business costs and can result in an incomplete picture of a company's profitability. For example, buildings and equipment wear out over time. GAAP accounting recognizes this economic reality as depreciation expense and requires it be included in the profit calculation. Ignoring GAAP depreciation expense understates the true costs of the business.
- EBITDA and pro forma earnings do not accurately measure firm cash flows because they ignore a company's cash requirements for working capital growth and replacement capital expenditures. They also overlook the non-cash elements of revenues and expenses (like credit sales that have not yet been collected) and can easily be manipulated using aggressive accounting policies.

RECAP   **Despite the growing acceptance of non-GAAP profit measures on Wall Street, in corporate boardrooms, and among credit analysts, informed financial statement readers must be wary and look behind the numbers to understand what's really going on in the business. For the credit analyst, the message is simple: You can't buy a cup of coffee with EBITDA or "pro forma" earnings. It takes real cash!**

[7] J. Fox, "Forget Earnings—Try Fully Diluted EEBS!" *Fortune* (May 11, 1998).

SUMMARY

Financial ratios, along with common-size and trend statements, provide analysts with powerful tools for tracking a company's performance over time, for making comparisons among different companies, and for assessing compliance with contractual benchmarks. Here are some things to remember about those tools:

- **There is no single "correct" way to compute many financial ratios.** In this chapter, we have shown you how to compute common financial ratios using the most widely accepted methods. But not every analyst calculates these ratios in the exact same way. Why? Sometimes it's a matter of personal taste or industry practice (for example, operating profit ratios for retail companies often exclude depreciation and rent). At other times, it's because the analyst is attempting to make the numbers more comparable across companies or over time.

- **Financial ratios don't provide the answers, but they can help you ask the right questions.** It's useful to know that a company's profitability or credit risk has improved (or declined), but it's even more important to know *why* the change has occurred. Has consumer demand increased or is the company stealing market share from competitors? Have operating costs been reduced, and if so, which ones? Use the financial ratios and the other tools in this chapter to guide your analysis. They can help you to ask the right questions and tell you where to look for answers.

- **Is it the economics of the business or is it the accounting?** Watch out for accounting distortions that can complicate your interpretation of financial ratios and other comparisons. Remember that the analyst's task is to "get behind the numbers"—that is, to develop a solid understanding of the company's economic activities and how industry fundamentals have shaped where the company is today and where it will be tomorrow.

APPENDIX

ALTMAN'S Z-SCORE AND THE PREDICTION OF BANKRUPTCY

The best-known bankruptcy prediction model is Altman's Z-score model—a set of five financial ratios that are combined in a precise way to estimate a company's default risk.[8] Altman faced several challenges when developing the Z-score model: which financial ratios to use; how to combine them into a composite index of bankruptcy risk; and where to draw the line between companies predicted to be financially solvent in the future and those likely to go bankrupt.

Altman first searched for individual ratios that showed promise as predictors of bankruptcy. He assembled a large sample of bankrupt and nonbankrupt firms, calculated the ratio value for each sample firm using financial statement data prior to the bankruptcy, and then compared default frequencies across the range of ratio values much as we did in Figure 5.5. If bankrupt firms tended to cluster at one extreme of the ratio (for example, at very high ratios values) while nonbankrupt firms tended to cluster at the other extreme, the ratio was retained for further consideration. Altman next used statistical techniques to further reduce the list of candidate ratios to only those that added new information to the bankruptcy risk estimate. These same techniques identified the best way to combine the surviving ratios into a composite index of bankruptcy risk.

The final Z-score model is:

$$
\begin{aligned}
\text{Z-score} \; = \; & 1.2 \times \text{Working capital/Total assets} \\
& + 1.4 \times \text{Retained earnings/Total assets} \\
& + 3.3 \times \text{EBIT/Total assets} \\
& + 0.6 \times \text{Market value of equity/Book value of debt} \\
& + 1.0 \times \text{Sales/Total assets}
\end{aligned}
$$

---

[8] E. Altman, "Financial Ratios, Discriminant Analysis and the Prediction of Corporate Bankruptcy," *Journal of Finance* (September 1968), pp. 589–609.

where EBIT is earnings before interest and taxes. Notice how the model combines information about a company's current profitability (EBIT / Total assets), long-term profitability (Retained earnings / Total assets), liquidity (Working capital / Total assets), solvency (Market value of equity / Book value of debt), and asset turnover (Sales / Total assets) into a single measure of bankruptcy risk. Notice also that the five surviving ratios are not simply added together to form the overall Z-score value. Instead, each ratio has its own unique weight in the final calculation.

Now, suppose you applied the Z-score formula to a real company and got 2.4 as your answer. As you can probably guess by looking carefully at the formula, high Z-scores are good and low Z-scores are bad. (High Z-scores arise when profitability, liquidity, solvency, and turnover are also high.) But what does a Z-score value of 2.4 mean? Is a value of 2.4 above or below the cutoff for predicted bankruptcy? Before we see how Altman answered this question, let's look at some hypothetical data so that we can better understand the problem Altman faced.

Suppose your company sells merchandise on credit and that there are only two types of credit customers: "deadbeats," who fail to pay their bills, and "prompt payers," who always pay the full amount on time. Of course, you cannot know for certain which type of customer you are dealing with until it comes time for them to pay their bills. You can, however, use historical information about your customers and their payment patterns to identify characteristics that seem to predict whether a customer will be a deadbeat or prompt payer. If your customers are companies, then financial ratios might do the trick especially if those ratios are combined according to the Z-score formula. Figure 5.7 shows the historical frequency distribution of Z-score values for our deadbeats and prompt paying customers. As you might suspect, deadbeats tend to have low Z-scores (high default risk) while prompt paying customers tend to have high Z-scores (low default risk).

Figure 5.7

FREQUENCY DISTRIBUTION
OF Z-SCORES FOR TWO TYPES
OF CREDIT CUSTOMERS

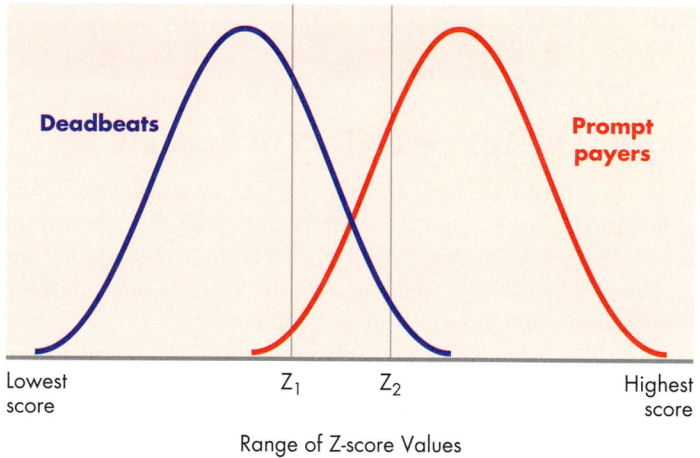

Range of Z-score Values

Now suppose you were to set the cutoff point at Z_1, meaning that customers with Z-score values below that point would be denied credit and could only buy your merchandise for cash. Almost all of your prompt paying customers would still qualify for credit at your store because the vast majority of these customers have Z-scores above Z_1. Unfortunately, so do many deadbeats. If you want to deny credit to more deadbeats, you need to set the cutoff higher. The value Z_2 shown in Figure 5.7 is one possibility. Using this cutoff, fewer deadbeats will qualify for credit, but you will also be denying credit to a larger number of prompt paying customers.

The research evidence led Altman to conclude that firms having a Z-score of greater than 2.99 (think Z_2) clearly fell into the "prompt payer" category—our label, not his—and were predicted to remain solvent. Firms having a Z-score of less than 1.81 (think Z_1), on the other hand, clearly fell into the "deadbeat" category and were predicted to go bankrupt. Firms with Z-scores that fell between these two cutoff points land in a "gray area," where classification mistakes can be large (because the two distributions overlap) and costly. Altman recommends that these firms be given additional, in-depth scrutiny using conventional financial analysis tools and information beyond just that contained in the published financial statements.

The original Z-score model was designed for publicly traded manufacturing firms. Altman has since developed models for private companies and public service-sector firms.[9] Credit rating agencies like Dun and Bradstreet have used a similar approach to develop their credit rating scores, although these agencies are often silent about the specific factors they consider and how much weight each factor is given in the composite score.

EXERCISES

E5 – 1

Inventory turnover

AICPA
ADAPTED

Motley Company's merchandise inventory and other related accounts for 2005 follow:

Sales	$3,000,000
Cost of goods sold	2,200,000
Merchandise inventory	
Beginning of year	500,000
End of year	600,000

Required:

Assuming that the merchandise-inventory buildup was relatively constant during the year, how many times did the merchandise inventory turn over during 2005?

E5 – 2

Receivable and inventory turnover

AICPA
ADAPTED

Selected data of the Islander Company follow:

	As of December 31	
Balance Sheet Data	**2005**	**2004**
Accounts receivable	$500,000	$470,000
Allowance for doubtful accounts	(25,000)	(20,000)
Net accounts receivable	$475,000	$450,000
Inventories—lower of cost or market	$600,000	$550,000

	Year Ended December 31	
Income Statement Data	**2005**	**2004**
Net credit sales	$2,500,000	$2,200,000
Net cash sales	500,000	400,000
Net sales	$3,000,000	$2,600,000
Cost of goods sold	$2,000,000	$1,800,000
Selling, general, and administrative expenses	300,000	270,000
Other	50,000	30,000
Total operating expenses	$2,350,000	$2,100,000

Required:

1. What is the accounts receivable turnover for 2005?
2. What is the inventory turnover for 2005?

E5 – 3

Inventory turnover

AICPA
ADAPTED

On January 1, 2005 River Company's beginning inventory was $400,000. During 2005 the company purchased $1,900,000 of additional inventory, and on December 31, 2005 River's ending inventory was $500,000.

Required:

What is the inventory turnover for 2005?

---

[9] See E. Altman, *Corporate Financial Distress and Bankruptcy* (New York: Wiley, 1993).

E5 – 4

Receivable turnover

AICPA
ADAPTED

Utica Company's net accounts receivable was $250,000 at December 31, 2004 and $300,000 at December 31, 2005. Net cash sales for 2005 were $100,000. The accounts receivable turnover for 2005 was 5.0, and this turnover figure was computed from net credit sales for the year.

Required:

What was Utica's total net sales for 2005?

E5 – 5

Current and quick ratios

AICPA
ADAPTED

Todd Corporation wrote off $100,000 of obsolete inventory at December 31, 2005.

Required:

What effect did this write-off have on the company's 2005 current and quick ratios?

E5 – 6

Current ratio

AICPA
ADAPTED

Gil Corporation has current assets of $90,000 and current liabilities of $180,000.

Required:

Compute the effect of each of the following transactions on Gil's current ratio:
1. Refinancing a $30,000 long-term mortgage with a short-term note.
2. Purchasing $50,000 of merchandise inventory with short-term accounts payable.
3. Paying $20,000 of short-term accounts payable.
4. Collecting $10,000 of short-term accounts receivable.

E5 – 7

Interest coverage

AICPA
ADAPTED

The following data were taken from the financial records of Glum Corporation for 2005:

Sales	$3,600,000
Bond interest expense	120,000
Income taxes	600,000
Net income	800,000

Required:

How many times was bond interest earned in 2005?

E5 – 8

Why inventory turnover increased

AICPA
ADAPTED

In a comparison of 2005 to 2004 performance, Neir Company's inventory turnover increased substantially, although sales and inventory amounts were essentially unchanged.

Required:

Which of the following statements best explains the increased inventory turnover ratio?
1. Cost of goods sold decreased.
2. Accounts receivable turnover increased.
3. Total asset turnover increased.
4. Gross profit percentage decreased.

E5 – 9

Days sales outstanding

AICPA
ADAPTED

Selected information taken from the accounting records of Vigor Company follows:

Net accounts receivable at December 31, 2004	$ 900,000
Net accounts receivable at December 31, 2005	$1,000,000
Accounts receivable turnover	5 to 1
Inventories at December 31, 2004	$1,100,000
Inventories at December 31, 2005	$1,200,000
Inventory turnover	4 to 1

Required:

1. What was Vigor's gross margin for 2005?
2. Suppose there are 360 business days in the year. What was the number of days' sales outstanding in average receivables and the number of days' sales outstanding in average inventories for 2005, respectively?

PROBLEMS/DISCUSSION QUESTIONS

The table below presents ROA calculations for three companies in the retail grocery industry using earnings (NOPAT) and balance sheet data for each company. These companies compete on price, quality of goods and service, convenience, and product mix. 7-Eleven operates convenience stores and generates approximately 25% of its revenue from gasoline sales. Publix Super Markets operates retail food supermarkets in Florida, Georgia, South Carolina, Alabama, and Tennessee. Albertson's is the second largest U.S. supermarket chain.

P5 – 1

Comparing profitability

Required:

1. Which company has shown the strongest sales growth over the past three years?
2. Which company has shown the greatest improvement in profitability over the past three years?
3. Which company was the most profitable in 2002? What was the source of that superior profitability—a profit margin advantage or better turnover?

7-Eleven Corp.

	1999	2000	2001	2002
Sales	$ 8,251,700	$ 9,178,711	$ 9,622,301	$10,109,744
Operating profit margin (NOPAT/Sales)	1.7%	1.8%	1.4%	0.9%
Asset turnover (Sales/Average assets)	3.20	3.38	3.41	3.39
ROA = Margin × Asset turnover	5.5%	6.0%	4.9%	3.1%

Publix Super Markets

	1999	2000	2001	2002
Sales	$13,068,900	$14,575,031	$15,284,229	$15,930,602
Operating profit margin (NOPAT/Sales)	3.5%	3.6%	3.5%	4.0%
Asset turnover (Sales/Average assets)	3.38	3.49	3.53	3.46
ROA = Margin × Asset turnover	11.9%	12.7%	12.3%	13.8%

Albertson's

	1999	2000	2001	2002
Sales	$37,478,000	$35,501,000	$36,605,000	$35,626,000
Operating profit margin (NOPAT/Sales)	1.6%	2.7%	2.7%	3.1%
Asset turnover (Sales/Average assets)	2.43	2.23	2.28	2.28
ROA = Margin × Asset turnover	3.9%	6.1%	6.3%	7.0%

Electronic Arts develops, markets, publishes, and distributes interactive software games. An abridged "lease commitments" footnote from the company's 2002 annual report reads:

P5 – 2

Earnings quality

> "In 2001, we renewed the lease on our headquarters facility in Redwood City, California and account for this arrangement as an operating lease. We have an option to purchase the property (land and facilities) for $145.0 million, or, at the end of the lease in 2006, to arrange for (1) an additional extension of the lease or (2) sale of the property to a third party. In December 2000, we entered into a second lease for a five-year term to expand our Redwood Shores, California headquarters facilities and develop adjacent property. We also accounted for this arrangement as an operating lease and have an option to purchase this property for $127.0 million."

Operating leases are "off-balance-sheet" obligations, meaning that GAAP does not include the debt among the liabilities shown on a company's balance sheet. Operating lease obligations are only disclosed in the financial statement footnotes. Capital leases, on the other hand, are included among balance sheet liabilities. This liability increase is offset by a corresponding increase to a balance sheet asset representing the leased property or equipment. (Chapter 12 provides the details.)

Electronic Arts

Selected financial data ($ in thousands)	2002
NOPAT	$110,374
Average assets	1,539,146
Long-term debt	0
ROA (NOPAT/Average assets)	7.17%

Required:

1. Suppose Electronic Arts had entered into a capital lease rather than an operating lease. Describe in qualitative terms how this change would alter the company's balance sheet.
2. Describe in qualitative terms what impact a capital lease would have on the company's ROA and Long-term debt to assets ratios.
3. Would the changes in these ratios, if any, be favorable from management's perspective? Why or why not?

P5 – 3

Short-term liquidity

The following table reports the operating cycle, cash conversion cycle, and current ratio for three retailers in the apparel business. The GAP built its brand name on basic, casual clothing styles (T-shirts, jeans, and khakis). Over the years the company expanded by opening Banana Republic and Old Navy stores. Spiegel is a top U.S. direct retailer, selling through its namesake catalog and its Eddie Bauer unit. The majority of J. Crew's sales come from classic-styled jeans, khakis, and other basic items sold to young professionals through catalogs, a website, and the company's retail and factory outlets.

	GAP	Spiegel	J. Crew
Working capital activity ratios:			
1. Days inventory held	73.0	108.2	93.9
2. Days accounts receivable outstanding	0.0	90.2	0.0
3. Days accounts payable outstanding	43.8	116.5	49.6
Operating cycle (1 + 2)	73.0	198.4	93.9
Cash conversion cycle (1 + 2 − 3)	29.2	81.9	44.3
Current ratio	2.11	0.74	1.32

Required:

1. Do any of these companies appear to have a short-term liquidity problem?
2. Which company has the most mismatched cash flow?
3. All three companies are in the same industry. Why is Spiegel the only one with accounts receivable?

P5 – 4

Credit risk analysis and long-term solvency

AK Steel is a fully integrated producer of steel. It operates seven manufacturing and finishing plants in Indiana, Kentucky, Ohio, and Pennsylvania. These plants produce cold-rolled and hot-rolled steel products, and specialty stainless and electrical steels that are sold to the domestic automotive, appliance, industrial machinery and equipment, and construction markets. Comparative debt ratios for AK Steel are shown in the table below.

AK Steel Holding Corporation

	1999	2000	2001	2002
Long-term debt to assets ratio	0.28	0.28	0.27	0.24
Long-term debt to tangible assets ratio	0.29	0.28	0.28	0.25
Interest coverage ratio	1.98	2.50	(0.13)	(5.44)
Cash flow coverage ratio	3.07	3.44	2.11	3.02
Operating cash flow to total liabilities	0.11	0.15	0.07	0.14

Required:

1. Does AK Steel appear to be able to easily make its interest payments? How can you tell?
2. Does AK Steel rely heavily on debt to finance asset purchases? Has the company's reliance on debt changed significantly over the past several years?
3. Does AK Steel have significant amounts of intangible assets? How can you tell?

The following table provides a breakdown of ROCE for Best Buy Co., Inc., a retailer of consumer electronics.

P5 – 5

Decomposing return on common shareholders' equity (ROCE)

Best Buy Co., Inc.

	2001	2002	2003
ROA	0.10	0.10	0.08
Common earnings leverage	0.99	0.97	0.98
Financial structure leverage	2.69	2.81	2.86
ROCE	0.27	0.27	0.22

Required:

How has Best Buy's profitability changed over the three years?

Georgia-Pacific and Weyerhaeuser are forest products companies. Georgia-Pacific manufactures and distributes building products, consumer products (Brawny, Coronet, Dixie, and Quilted Northern brand-name products), and paper and packaging. Weyerhaeuser produces wood products (lumber, plywood, oriented strand board, and engineered wood), containerboard and packaging, pulp, and papers. Weyerhaeuser also recycles paper and develops real estate. Financial statement data for these two companies follow.

P5 – 6

Interpreting accounts receivable turnover

Georgia-Pacific

($ in million)	1999	2000	2001	2002
Sales		$22,050	$25,016	$23,271
Accounts receivable	$2,158	2,705	2,352	1,777
Accounts receivable turnover		9.07	9.89	11.27

Weyerhaeuser

Sales		$14,603	$13,084	$16,771
Accounts receivable	$1,296	1,247	1,024	1,413
Accounts receivable turnover		11.48	11.52	13.76

Required:

1. Which company collects its accounts receivable more quickly?
2. Which company showed the greatest improvement in accounts receivable turnover from 2000 to 2002?
3. What factors might explain why these two companies—which appear to operate in similar markets—have different accounts receivable turnover ratios?

Danaher Corporation has two business segments. The process/environmental controls group produces monitoring, sensing, controlling, and testing products. The company's tools and components segment manufactures mechanics' hand tools, automotive specialty tools, and accessories under various brand names. Selected financial statement data and related performance indicators appear below.

P5 – 7

Analyzing inventories

Danaher Corporation

($ in thousands)	2000	2001	2002
Sales	$3,777,777	$3,782,444	$4,577,232
Cost of goods sold	2,315,731	2,338,027	2,791,175
Average inventory	392,642	434,423	446,912
Selected performance measures:			
Sales growth rate	0.18	0.00	0.21
Average inventory growth rate	0.19	0.11	0.03
Gross profit (%)	0.39	0.38	0.39
Inventory turnover ratio	5.90	5.38	6.25

Required:

How well has Danaher managed its inventories over the 2000–2002 period?

P5 – 8

Fixed asset turnover

Lennox International makes air-conditioning, heating, and fireplace systems for residential and commercial uses, as well as commercial refrigeration equipment. American Standard Companies is a leading maker of air-conditioning systems, plumbing products, and automotive braking systems. Selected financial statement data for each company appear below along with asset utilization ratios.

American Standard Companies

	2000	2001	2002
Sales	$7,598,370	$7,465,300	$7,795,400
ROA	0.09	0.08	0.09
Current assets turnover	4.22	3.96	3.99
Fixed (long-term) assets turnover	2.61	2.57	2.57
Total assets turnover	1.61	1.56	1.56

Lennox International Inc.

	2000	2001	2002
Sales	$3,242,204	$3,113,649	$3,025,767
ROA	0.05	−0.01	0.05
Current assets turnover	3.62	3.86	4.36
Fixed (long-term) assets turnover	3.33	2.79	3.14
Total assets turnover	1.73	1.62	1.83

Required:

1. Compare the asset utilization effectiveness of these two companies. Which company seems to be doing the best job? Are there any important industry trends apparent from these data?
2. Why does Lennox International have a lower ROA than does American Standard?

P5 – 9

Profitability analyses for three companies

The following table shows six profitability measures derived from the financial statements of three real companies, labeled A, B, and C in the table. (They are not listed in the table in any particular order.) The real companies are:

- Brunswick Corporation, a leader in the leisure products industry that manufactures boats and marine engines, bowling and billiards products, as well as fitness equipment.
- Consolidated Edison, an electricity and natural gas company. Its nonutility operations include energy marketing and fiber-optic telecommunications.
- Foot Locker, a shoe retailer with about 3,600 specialty stores in North America, Australia, and Europe. It also operates Champs Sports, an athletic wear retail chain, and Eastbay, a catalog retailer of athletic equipment and apparel.

	A	B	C
Operating profit margin	0.12	0.04	0.04
Asset turnover ratio	0.47	1.13	1.88
ROA	0.06	0.04	0.07
Common earnings leverage	0.68	0.79	0.90
Financial structure leverage	3.09	2.97	2.28
ROCE	0.12	0.09	0.15

Required:

Which company is which? Explain how you identified each company from the information given in the table.

Nucor Corporation produces steel and steel products at its eight mills and is a major recycler of scrap metal. The following data relate to Nucor for the years indicated.

Nucor Corporation				
($ in thousands)	1999	2000	2001	2002
Total assets	$3,729,848	$3,721,788	$3,759,348	$4,381,001
Common stockholders' equity	2,262,248	2,130,952	2,201,460	2,322,989
Sales		4,756,521	4,333,707	4,801,776
Net income		310,908	112,961	162,080
Interest expense		22,449	22,002	22,918
Income tax rate		0.37	0.37	0.296

Required:

1. Calculate Nucor's return on assets for 2000, 2001, and 2002. Decompose ROA into operating profit margin and asset turnover components.
2. Has Nucor's profitability changed over the three years? If so, how?
3. Calculate the rate of return on common stockholders' equity for 2000, 2001, and 2002. Decompose ROCE into ROA, common earnings leverage, and financial structure leverage.
4. What seem to be the reasons for the change in ROCE over the three years?

Items 1 through 6 describe what an auditor discovered about changes in a client's financial statement ratios or amounts from the prior year's figures. For each item, select the most likely explanation from the list provided. The items are independent of each other.

1. Inventory turnover increased substantially from the prior year. (Select three explanations.)
2. Accounts receivable turnover decreased substantially from the prior year. (Select three explanations.)
3. Allowance for doubtful accounts increased in dollars from the prior year, but it decreased from the prior year as a percentage of accounts receivable. (Select three explanations.)
4. Long-term debt increased from the prior year, but interest expense increased more than the percentage increase in long-term debt. (Select one explanation.)
5. Operating income increased from the prior year, although the company was less profitable than in the prior year. (Select two explanations.)
6. Gross margin percentage was unchanged from the prior year, although gross margin increased from the prior year. (Select one explanation.)

Explanations List:

a. Items shipped on consignment during the last month of the year were recorded as sales.
b. A significant number of credit memos for returned merchandise issued during the last month of the year were not recorded.
c. Year-end inventory purchases were overstated because items received in the first month of the subsequent year were incorrectly included.
d. Year-end inventory purchases were understated because items received before year-end were incorrectly excluded.
e. A larger percentage of sales occurred during the last month of the year, compared to the prior year.
f. A smaller percentage of sales occurred during the last month of the year, compared to the prior year.
g. The same percentage of sales occurred during the last month of the year, compared to the prior year.
h. Sales increased at the same percentage as cost of goods sold, compared to the prior year.
i. Sales increased at a lower percentage than cost of goods sold increased, compared to the prior year.
j. Sales increased at a higher percentage than cost of goods sold increased, compared to the prior year.
k. Interest expense decreased, compared to the prior year.
l. The effective income tax rate increased, compared to the prior year.
m. The effective income tax rate decreased, compared to the prior year.
n. Short-term borrowing was refinanced on a long-term basis at the same interest rate.
o. Short-term borrowing was refinanced on a long-term basis at lower interest rates.
p. Short-term borrowing was refinanced on a long-term basis at higher interest rates.

P5 – 12

Why financial ratios change

AICPA
ADAPTED

Daley, Inc. is consistently profitable. Daley's normal financial statement relationships are as follows:

Current ratio	3 to 1
Inventory turnover	4 times
Total debt/total assets ratio	0.5 to 1

Required:

Determine whether each transaction or event that follows increased, decreased, or had no effect on each ratio.

1. Daley declared, but did not pay, a cash dividend.
2. Customers returned invoiced goods for which they had not paid.
3. Accounts payable were paid at year-end.
4. Daley recorded both a receivable from an insurance company and a loss from fire damage to a factory building.
5. Early in the year, Daley increased the selling price of one of its products because customer demand far exceeded production capacity. The number of units sold this year was the same as last year.

P5 – 13

Working backward
to the statements

AICPA
ADAPTED

The December 31, 2005 balance sheet of Ratio, Inc. is presented next. These are the *only* accounts in Ratio's balance sheet. Amounts indicated by a question mark (?) can be calculated from the additional information given.

Assets	
Cash	$ 25,000
Accounts receivable (net)	?
Inventory	?
Property, plant, and equipment (net)	294,000
	$432,000
Liabilities and Stockholders' Equity	
Accounts payable (trade)	?
Income taxes payable (current)	25,000
Long-term debt	?
Common stock	300,000
Retained earnings	?
	$432,000

Additional Information:

Current ratio at year-end	1.5 to 1
Total liabilities divided by total stockholders' equity	0.8
Inventory turnover based on sales and ending inventory	15 times
Inventory turnover based on cost of goods sold and ending inventory	10.5 times
Gross margin for 2005	$315,000

Required:

Compute the December 31, 2005 balance for each missing item.

$$\text{Hint:} \quad \frac{\text{Gross margin}}{\text{Inventory}} = \frac{\text{Sales} - \text{CGS}}{\text{Inventory}} = \left(\frac{\text{Sales}}{\text{Inventory}}\right) - \left(\frac{\text{CGS}}{\text{Inventory}}\right)$$

P5 – 14

EBITDA and revenue
recognition

Griffin and Lasky, Inc. (G&L) supplies industrial automation equipment and machine tools to the automotive industry. G&L uses the "percentage of completion" method for recognizing revenue on its long-term contracts. Customer orders have long lead times because they involve multi-year capital investment programs. Sometimes orders are cancelled. Selected items from the company's financial statements are shown below.

($ in millions)	2003	2004	2005
Sales	$571.5	$619.5	$730.6
Accounts receivable—billed	141.6	94.5	147.9
Accounts receivable—unbilled	104.5	249.4	202.7
Total accounts receivable	246.1	343.9	350.6

($ in millions)	2003	2004	2005
Inventory	57.4	74.8	102.3
Earnings before interest and taxes (EBIT)	74.8	75.8	38.1
Depreciation and amortization	14.8	15.4	19.3
Plant write-down	–0–	–0–	30.3

Required:

1. Compute EBITDA and "adjusted EBITDA"—after excluding the plant write-down—for each year shown in the schedule.
2. Are profits at G&L keeping pace with sales?
3. Compute "days receivables outstanding"—using year-end receivables—for each year shown in the schedule.
4. Why might analysts be concerned about earnings quality at G&L?

Shown below is the comparative statements of cash flows for Toys "Я" Us for 2002, 2001, and 2000. The company reported sales (in millions) of $11,305, $11,019, and $11,332, respectively, in those years.

P5 – 15

Toys "Я" Us, Inc.: Common-size statements of cash flow

www.prenhall.com/revsine

● Student Resources

☑ Template for solution

Toys "Я" Us Inc.

Consolidated Statement of Cash Flows

($ in millions)	2002	2001	2000
Net income	$ 229	$ 67	$ 404
Adjustments:			
Depreciation and amortization	317	308	290
Deferred income taxes	99	(58)	67
Noncash operating gains and losses	(45)	56	(379)
Other gains and losses	0	0	81
Changes in operating assets and liabilities:			
Accounts receivable	8	15	(69)
Inventories	(100)	217	(486)
Accounts payable	112	(241)	(178)
Other	(46)	140	119
Cash flows from operating activities	$ 574	$ 504	$(151)
Capital expenditures	$(398)	$ (705)	$(402)
Investments	0	0	252
Cash flows from investing activities	$(398)	$ (705)	$(150)
Debt issues	$ 548	$1,214	$ 566
Stock issued	266	19	12
Debt repayments	(141)	(998)	(45)
Stock repurchased	0	(44)	(632)
Dividends	0	0	0
Other	(60)	0	97
Cash flows from financing activities	$ 613	$ 191	$ (2)
Effect of exchange rate changes	(49)	18	(6)
Change in cash	$ 740	$ 8	$(309)

Required:

1. What is the purpose of preparing common-size statements of cash flows? For example, what can a financial analyst learn about a firm by preparing a set of common-size statements of cash flows?
2. Prepare common-size statements of cash flows (expressed as a percentage of sales) for the fiscal years ending 2002, 2001, and 2000 for Toys "Я" Us.
3. Interpret your common-size statements of cash flows. For example, what interesting features of the company's operating, financing, and investing activities do they reveal?

Maytag Corporation manufactures and distributes a broad line of home appliances including gas and electric ranges, dishwashers, refrigerators, freezers, laundry equipment, and vacuum cleaning products. The home appliance segment contributes about 87% of Maytag's total sales. The company's other two segments are commercial appliances and international appliances, both of which have been scaled back over the last three years. Roughly 89% of Maytag's sales come from North American markets.

Refer to Maytag's 2002 financial statements. Consolidated sales increased 1.8% from 2000 to 2001 and 7.9% from 2001 to 2002. Earnings varied considerably over these years with net income falling from $201 million in 2000 to $48 million in 2001 and then rebounding to $188 million in 2002.

Required:

Prepare an analysis of Maytag's profitability for 2002, 2001, and 2000 following the steps outlined below. For all ratios requiring balance sheet values, use the average of beginning and ending balances. Ratios using earnings numbers should be based on net income before extraordinary items. Assume a 35% tax rate.

Step 1: Calculate average total assets, liabilities, and stockholders' equity for 2002.

	2002	2001	2000
Average total assets	?	$2,912.5	$2,653.0
Average total liabilities and minority interest	?	2,890.0	2,329.0
Average total shareholders' equity	?	22.5	224.5

Step 2: Calculate Maytag's return on assets (ROA) for each year. Use margin and turnover analysis together with common-size income statements to explain the year-to-year change in ROA.

Step 3: What is the after-tax interest rate that Maytag has been paying for its debt? Analyze the portion of average total assets that Maytag has been financing with debt over the last three years and comment on any apparent strategy.

Step 4: Calculate Maytag's return on common equity (ROCE) for each year. Has leverage benefited Maytag shareholders? How can you tell?

Maytag Corporation

Consolidated Statements of Income

($ in millions)	2002	2001	2000
Sales	$4,666	$4,324	$4,248
Cost of goods sold	3,661	3,320	3,102
Gross profit	1,005	1,004	1,146
Selling, general, and administrative expenses	578	705	678
Special items*	(67)	(21)	(67)
Operating income	360	278	401
Interest expense	62	65	64
Other expenses (income), net	2	—	4
Tax expense	101	30	115
Minority interest	4	15	16
Net income before extraordinary items and discontinued operations	191	168	202
Loss from discontinued operations	(3)	(111)	
Extraordinary Item—loss on early debt retirement	—	(5)	—
Cumulative effect of accounting change	—	(4)	—
Net income	$ 188	$ 48	$ 202

*Special items include expenses associated with plant closings and other nonrecurring charges.

Maytag Corporation

Consolidated Balance Sheets
($ in millions)

	2002	2001	2000
Cash	$ 8	$ 109	$ 27
Accounts receivable	587	619	538
Inventories	468	448	409
Other current assets	261	194	103
Current Assets	1,324	1,370	1,077
Property, plant and equipment (net)	1,066	1,036	970
Intangibles (net)	396	399	465
Other assets	318	351	157
Total assets	$3,104	$3,156	$2,669
Accounts payable	$ 364	$ 316	$ 285
Current interest-bearing debt	374	282	423
Other current liabilities	426	477	264
Current liabilities	1,164	1,075	972
Long-term debt	739	932	451
Deferred taxes	—	25	22
Minority interest	—	100	365
Other liabilities	1,159	1,001	837
Total liabilities	3,062	3,133	2,647
Common stockholders' equity	42	23	22
Total liabilities and equity	$3,104	$3,156	$2,669

Margaret O'Flaherty, a portfolio manager for MCF Investments, is considering an investment in Alpine Chemical 7% bonds, which mature in 10 years. She asks you to analyze the company to determine the riskiness of the bonds.

P5 – 17

Ratio analysis

CMA
ADAPTED

www.prenhall.com/revsine

● Student Resources

☑ Template for solution

Alpine Chemical Company Financial Statements

($ in millions)	Years Ended December 31					
	2000	2001	2002	2003	2004	2005
Assets						
Cash	$ 190	$ 55	$ –0–	$ 157	$ 249	$ –0–
Accounts receivable	1,637	2,087	1,394	2,143	3,493	3,451
	2,021	945	1,258	1,293	1,322	1,643
Inventories						
Other current assets	17	27	55	393	33	171
Current assets	3,865	3,114	2,707	3,986	5,097	5,265
Gross fixed assets	4,650	5,038	5,619	5,757	6,181	7,187
Less: Accumulated depreciation	2,177	2,543	2,841	3,138	3,465	3,893
Net fixed assets	2,473	2,495	2,778	2,619	2,716	3,294
Total assets	$6,338	$5,609	$5,485	$6,605	$7,813	$8,559
Liabilities and net worth						
Notes payable	$ 525	$ 750	$ –0–	$1,300	$1,750	$1,900
Accounts payable	673	638	681	338	743	978
Accrued liabilities	303	172	359	359	483	761
Current liabilities	1,501	1,560	1,040	1,997	2,976	3,639
Long-term debt	1,985	1,044	1,401	1,457	1,542	1,491
Deferred tax credits	352	347	363	336	345	354
Total liabilities	3,838	2,951	2,804	3,790	4,863	5,484

(*continued on next page*)

Alpine Chemical Company Financial Statements (*continued*)

($ in millions)	2000	2001	2002	2003	2004	2005
			Years Ended December 31			
Common stock	50	50	100	100	100	100
Capital surplus	100	100	–0–	–0–	–0–	–0–
Retained earnings	2,350	2,508	2,581	2,715	2,850	2,975
Net worth	2,500	2,658	2,681	2,815	2,950	3,075
Total liabilities and net worth	$6,338	$5,609	$5,485	$6,605	$7,813	$8,559

Income statement	2000	2001	2002	2003	2004	2005
Net sales	$14,100	$15,508	$13,875	$14,750	$19,133	$19,460
Cost of goods sold	10,200	11,220	9,366	10,059	13,400	13,117
Gross profit	3,900	4,288	4,509	4,691	5,733	6,343
Operating expense	2,065	2,203	2,665	2,685	3,472	3,885
Operating profit	1,835	2,085	1,844	2,006	2,261	2,458
Interest expense	275	465	275	319	376	318
Depreciation expense	475	477	479	478	495	511
Profit before tax	1,085	1,143	1,090	1,209	1,390	1,629
Income taxes	193	115	265	145	192	150
Net income	$ 892	$ 1,028	$ 825	$ 1,064	$ 1,198	$ 1,479

Required:

1. Using the data provided in the accompanying financial statement, calculate the following ratios for Alpine Chemical for 2005:

    a. EBIT/interest expense
    b. Long-term debt/total capitalization
    c. Funds from operations/total debt
    d. Operating income/sales

    Use the following conventions: EBIT is earnings before interest and taxes; total capitalization is interest-bearing long-term debt plus net worth; funds from operations means net income plus depreciation expense; and total debt includes interest-bearing short-term and long-term debt.

2. Briefly explain the significance of each ratio calculated in requirement 1 to the assessment of Alpine Chemical's creditworthiness.

3. Insert your answers to requirement 1 into Table 1 that follows. Then from Table 2, select an appropriate credit rating for Alpine Chemical.

Table 1	**Alpine Chemical Company**					
	2000	2001	2002	2003	2004	2005
EBIT/interest expense	4.95x	3.46x	4.96x	4.79x	4.70x	?
Long-term debt/total capitalization	44%	28%	34%	34%	34%	?
Funds from operations/total debt	54%	84%	93%	56%	51%	?
Operating income/sales	13%	13%	13%	14%	12%	?

Table 2	**Industry Data**					
Three-Year Medians (2003–2005) by Credit Rating Category						
	Aaa	Aa	A	Bbb	Bb	B
EBIT/interest expense	11.0	9.5	4.5	3.0	2.0	1.0
Long-term debt/total capitalization	13.0	16.5	29.5	39.0	45.5	63.5
Funds from operations/total debt	83.0	74.0	45.5	31.5	18.5	8.0
Operating income/sales	21.5	16.0	15.0	12.0	11.0	9.0

Here is a cash flow statement and partial balance sheet for Woods Company, along with supplemental information. The omitted items are numbered from (1) through (16) and can be calculated from the other information given.

Woods Company

2005 Statement of Cash Flows

Operations	
Net loss for 2005	$ (2,885)
Adjustments:	
Bond premium amortization	(500)
Deferred income taxes	(200)
Depreciation expense	3,000
Amortization of intangibles	2,000
Increase in (noncash) working capital	(700)
Total from operations	715
Proceeds from equipment sold	10,000
Proceeds from reissue of treasury stock	11,400
Par value of common stock issued to reacquire preferred stock	7,500
Purchase of land	(14,715)
Payment on long-term bond debt	(7,200)
Par value of preferred stock reacquired by issuing common stock	(7,500)
Increase in cash	$ 200

Supplemental Information—Selected 2005 Income Statement Items

Bond interest expense (net of amortization)	$ 3,500
Loss before tax adjustment	(3,900)
Less: Income tax adjustment for refund due	815
Deferred income taxes	200
Net loss after tax adjustment	$ (2,885)

Selected Ratios

	January 1, 2005*	December 31, 2005
Current ratio	?	3:1
Total stockholders' equity divided by total liabilities	4:3	?

*The above ratios were computed prior to the error correction.

Woods Company had neglected to amortize $2,000 of intangibles in 2004. The correction of this material error has been appropriately made in 2005. The book value and selling price of the equipment sold was two-thirds of the cost of the equipment.

Woods Company

Balance Sheets

	January 1, 2005*	December 31, 2005
Current assets	$22,000	$(5)
Building and equipment	92,000	(6)
Accumulated depreciation	(25,000)	(7)
Land	(1)	(8)
Intangibles and goodwill	12,000	(9)
Total assets	$ (?)	$ (?)
Current liabilities	$ (2)	(10)
Bonds payable (8%)	(3)	(11)
Bond premium	(?)	(12)
Deferred income taxes	(4)	1,700
Common stock	66,000	(13)
Paid-in capital	13,000	(14)
Preferred stock	16,000	(15)
Retained earnings (deficit)	(6,000)	(16)
Treasury stock (at cost)	(9,000)	–0–
Total liabilities and stockholders' equity	$ (?)	$ (?)

*The January 1, 2005 items are shown prior to restatement.

(*continued on next page*)

Required:

Number your answer sheet from (1) through (16). Place the correct balance for each balance sheet item next to the corresponding number on your answer sheet. Question mark (?) amounts may be needed to calculate the numbered balances. Do not restate the January 1 balance sheet for the error. Working capital was $16,500 at January 1, 2005.

P5 – 19

Financial ratios and the balance sheet

STRETCH

Required:

Use the following information along with your knowledge of financial ratios and balance sheet relationships to fill in the missing items on the balance sheet of Clapton Corporation. Round all amounts to the nearest dollar.

Additional Information:
1. Days accounts payable outstanding was 45.6 days in 2005, compared to 66.3 days in 2004.
2. The current ratio at the end of 2005 was 2.5, compared to 2.0 at the end of 2004.
3. The firm's gross profit rate was 25% in 2005 and 28% in 2004.
4. Net income for 2005 was $1,250,000, compared to $1,000,000 in 2004.
5. No common or preferred stock was issued during 2005.
6. Return on average assets was 5% for 2005, compared to 8% in 2004.
7. Cash dividends declared and paid in 2005 were $250,000; in 2004 they were $200,000.
8. Days accounts receivable outstanding was 36.5 days in 2005 and 50.5 days in 2004.
9. The long-term debt to total asset ratio at the end of 2005 was 0.40, compared to 0.30 at the end of 2004.
10. The quick ratio at the end of 2005 was 1.6875, compared to 1.5 at the end of 2004.
11. Days inventory held was 60.8 days in 2005 and 75.7 days in 2004.
12. Net sales in 2005 were $20,000,000, compared to $18,000,000 in 2004.
13. Net operating profit after taxes—but before interest—for 2005 was $1,750,000, compared to $1,400,000 in 2004.

Clapton Corporation

Consolidated Balance Sheets

	As of December 31	
	2005	**2004**
Assets		
Current assets		
Cash	$ (a)	$ 500,000
Marketable securities	3,200,000	(b)
Accounts receivable	(c)	1,800,000
Inventories	(d)	(e)
Prepaid expenses	550,000	450,000
Total current assets	10,000,000	(f)
Property, plant and equipment (net)	(g)	18,000,000
Noncurrent assets		
Long-term receivables	2,500,000	2,000,000
Investments	1,500,000	1,000,000
Other	1,000,000	(h)
Total assets	$ (i)	$ (j)
Liabilities and Stockholders' Equity		
Current liabilities		
Accounts payable	$ (k)	$ (l)
Wages and employee benefits payable	775,000	(m)
Income taxes	300,000	750,000
Advances and deposits	100,000	200,000
Other current liabilities	200,000	400,000
Total current liabilities	(n)	(o)

| | As of December 31 | |
	2005	2004
Long-term liabilities		
Long-term debt	(p)	9,000,000
Deferred income taxes	3,000,000	2,000,000
Other	(q)	500,000
Total liabilities	(r)	15,000,000
Stockholders' equity		
Preferred stock	1,000,000	(s)
Common stock	(t)	2,000,000
Paid-in capital	(u)	9,000,000
Retained earnings	(v)	(w)
Total stockholders' equity	(x)	(y)
Total liabilities and stockholders' equity	$ (z)	$ (zz)

Helpful Hints:

- Start by calculating the missing values for common and preferred stock. Then compute total assets for 2004.
- Total assets for 2005 can be found using 2004 total assets along with the additional information in items (6) and (13).
- Accounts receivable for 2005 can be found using 2004 accounts receivable along with the information in items (8) and (12).

CASES

The comparative statements of income for J.C. Penney Company, Inc. covering the years 2000–2002 are reproduced below.

C5 – 1

J.C. Penney (A) (CW): Common-size and trend income statements

www.prenhall.com/revsine

- Student Resources
  - ✔ Template for solution

Required:

1. Prepare common-size income statements for each year.
2. What do the common-size statements reveal about the company's operating results?
3. Using 2000 as the base year, prepare a trend analysis of J.C. Penney's income statement through 2002.
4. What does the trend analysis reveal about the company's operating results?
5. Which approach—common-size or trend analysis—was most revealing? Why?

J.C. Penney Company, Inc.

Consolidated Statements of Operations

($ in millions)	2002	2001	2000
Sales	$32,347	$32,004	$31,846
Costs of goods sold	22,573	22,789	23,031
Selling, general and administrative expenses	8,667	8,459	8,637
Other charges	93	46	515
Net interest expense	388	386	427
Goodwill amortization	42	121	122
Total cost and expenses	31,763	31,801	32,732
Income/(loss) from continuing operations before income taxes	584	203	(886)
Income taxes	213	89	(318)
Income/(loss) from continuing operations	$ 371	$ 114	$ (568)
Income from discontinued operations	—	—	159
Gain/(loss) on sale of discontinued operations	34	(16)	(296)
Net income (loss)	$ 405	$ 98	$(705)

This case builds on the earlier J.C. Penney (A) case (C5–1) and illustrates how common-size statements and trend analysis can be used to forecast a company's earnings. Such projections are often referred to as *pro forma* ("as if") financial statements. The following assumptions (listed in no particular order) should be used:

1. J.C. Penney's combined federal and state income tax rate was about 36% in 2002. Tax rates are expected to remain at this level.
2. Interest expense fell from 2000 to 2001 because the company retired some long-term debt. It does not intend to retire any debt (or issue new debt) during 2003.
3. Sales for the industry are expected to grow in 2003 at the average annual growth rate of the last two years.
4. No nonrecurring charges, accounting method changes, discontinued operations, or "other" charges are anticipated in 2003.
5. Because of heavy competition from discount retailers (like Wal-Mart) and full-service retail firms (like Sears), J.C. Penney will need to increase its advertising expenditures in 2003 to achieve the projected sales growth. Selling, general, and administrative expenses as a percentage of total revenue will increase by three percentage points from the 2002 level.
6. Amortization expense is expected to remain constant (unchanged) in 2003.
7. J.C. Penney expects to improve its inventory management procedures in 2003. This improvement should yield a two-percentage point increase in the 2003 gross margin when compared to 2002.

Required:

1. Prepare a projected 2003 income statement for J.C. Penney. (*Hint:* Start by forecasting sales for the year.)
2. Based on your forecast, will J.C. Penney have a better year in 2003 than it did in 2002? Why or why not?
3. How did the company do in 2003?

Iomega Corporation designs, manufactures, and markets removable data storage devices for use with personal computers and workstations. These storage devices include magnetic disk drives, tape backup drives, and ZIP removable cartridge drives.

You were recently hired by Wean Ditter, a firm providing investment advisory services to individual investors, as their head analyst for the computer industry. Next week you are scheduled to attend an analysts meeting at Iomega where the company's chief executive officer and chief financial officer will be available to field your questions.

Required:

The financial statements and related information about this company can be accessed at our website.

Prepare a list of the questions that you want answered by Iomega's chief executive officer and chief financial officer. These questions should clarify your understanding of the company's past performance, current financial condition, and future prospects.

Nike designs, develops, and markets quality footwear, apparel, athletic equipment, and accessories worldwide. The company sells its products to approximately 20,000 retail accounts in the United States and through a mix of independent distributors, licensees, and subsidiaries in approximately 110 countries around the world.

Reebok International Ltd. designs and markets sports, fitness, and "casual use" footwear and apparel. The company has four major brands: Reebok, Greg Norman, Rockport (shoes), and the Ralph Lauren Footwear Company, which manufactures footwear sold under the Ralph Lauren and Polo Shirt brands. Financial statements for Nike and Reebok appear below.

Additional Information:

1. The financial statements for both companies can be accessed at our website.
2. Reebok's cash flow from operations was $225 million in 2002, $177 million in 2001, and $184 million in 2000. Nike's cash flow from operations was $1,082 million, $657 million, and $760 million, respectively.
3. If a tax rate is needed, use a rate of 35%.

Required:

1. Using the information in the financial statements, calculate the following financial ratios for fiscal 2002 for each company. Financial ratio values for 2003 have already been computed.

	2003		2002	
	Nike	**Reebok**	**Nike**	**Reebok**
Current ratio	?	?	2.26	2.78
Quick ratio	?	?	1.30	1.84
Accounts receivable turnover	?	?	5.77	7.77
Days receivable outstanding	?	?	63.25	49.98
Inventory turnover	?	?	4.09	5.05
Days inventory held	?	?	89.14	72.27
Accounts payable turnover	?	?	12.13	13.38
Days accounts payable outstanding	?	?	30.1	27.3
Return on assets	?	?	11.2%	8.0%
Long-term debt to total assets*	?	?	17.2%	20.0%
Long-term debt to total tangible assets*	?	?	18.4%	20.8%
Interest coverage	?	?	22.4	9.05
Operating cash flow to total liabilities	?	?	41.5%	23.0%
Operating profit margin	?	?	10.8%	6.9%
Asset turnover	?	?	1.61	1.84

* Includes current portion of long-term debt, if any.

2. Use the results of the ratio analysis to identify similarities and differences in the profitability, liquidity, and long-term solvency of the two firms.
3. As a financial analyst following the two firms, what other information (beyond what's in the financial statements) would you seek to supplement the ratio analysis?

It's late Tuesday evening, and you've just received a phone call from Dennis Whiting, your boss at GE Capital. Dennis wants to know your reaction to the Argenti loan request before tomorrow's loan committee meeting. Here's what he tells you:

> We've provided seasonal loans to Argenti for the past 20 years, and they've always been a first-rate customer, but I'm troubled by several recent events. For instance, the company just reported a $141 million loss for the first quarter of 2005. This comes on top of a $237 million loss in 2004 and a $9 million loss in 2003. What's worse, Argenti changed inventory accounting methods last year, and this change reduced the 2004 loss by $22 million. I can't tell if the company's using other accounting tricks to prop up earnings, but I doubt it.
>
> I believe Argenti's problem lies in its core business—customers just aren't buying its merchandise these days. Management's aggressive price discount program in the fourth quarter of 2004 helped move inventory, but Argenti doesn't have the cost structure needed to be competitive as a discounter. Take a look at the financials I'm sending over, and let me know what you think.

Argenti Corporation operates a national chain of retail stores ("Argenti's") selling appliances and electronics, home furnishings, automotive parts, apparel, and jewelry. The company's first store opened in New York City in 1904. Today, the company owns or leases more than 900 stores located in downtown areas of larger cities and in suburban shopping malls. Customer purchases are financed in-house using ArgentiCredit cards. The company employs more than 58,000 people.

The Seasonal Credit Agreement with GE Capital—dated October 4, 2004—provides a revolving loan facility in the principal amount of $165 million. The purpose of this facility is to provide backup liquidity as Argenti reduces its inventory levels. Under the credit agreement, Argenti may select among several interest rate options, which are based on market rates. Unless GE Capital agrees, loans may be made under the seasonal credit facility only after the commitments under the company's other debt agreements are fully used.

C5 – 5

Argenti Corporation: Evaluating credit risk

www.prenhall.com/revsine

● Student Resources

☑ Template for solution

Argenti Corporation

Balance Sheets and Selected Other Data
($ in millions)

	2004	2003	2002	2001	2000
Assets					
Cash and securities	$ 35	$ 38	$ 36	$ 117	$ 92
Receivables	213	166	112	62	47
Inventories	1,545	1,770	1,625	1,242	1,038
Other current assets	13	22	6	4	312
	1,806	1,996	1,779	1,425	1,489
Property, plant and equipment—net	1,308	1,366	1,396	1,263	1,222
Investments	317	345	314	296	277
Other assets	1,448	1,177	1,048	851	445
	$4,879	$4,884	$4,537	$3,835	$3,433
Liabilities and shareholders' equity					
Notes payable	$1,028	$ 160	$ 144	$ 0	$ 0
Accounts payable	1,812	2,040	1,955	1,595	1,399
Accrued expenses	1,232	1,201	1,248	1,204	1,148
	4,072	3,401	3,347	2,799	2,547
Long-term debt	87	423	228	213	125
Other liabilities	112	185	203	216	208
Preferred stock	175	175	75	–0–	–0–
Common stock	54	46	23	19	16
Retained earnings	518	768	750	661	583
Less: Treasury stock	(139)	(114)	(89)	(73)	(46)
	$4,879	$4,884	$4,537	$3,835	$3,433
Selected earnings and cash flow data					
Sales	$6,620	$7,085	$7,029	$6,023	$5,806
Cost of goods sold	4,869	5,211	5,107	4,258	4,047
Gross margin	1,751	1,874	1,922	1,765	1,759
Net income	(237)	(9)	137	101	60
Operating cash flow	(356)	(182)	153	132	157
Dividends	9	4	24	23	19

Argenti management has asked GE Capital for a $1.5 billion refinancing package that would be used to pay off all or a substantial portion of its outstanding debt. Excerpts from the company's financial statements follow.

Management Discussion and Analysis (2004 Annual Report)

The company has obtained waivers under the Long-Term Credit Agreement and the Short-Term Credit Agreement with respect to compliance for the fiscal quarter ending March 29, 2005—with covenants requiring maintenance of minimum consolidated shareholders' equity, a minimum ratio of debt to capitalization, and minimum earnings before interest, taxes, depreciation, amortization, and rent (EBITDAR). These waivers and amendments reduce the maximum amount of debt permitted to be incurred, and the maturity of the Long-Term Agreement was changed from February 28, 2006 to August 29, 2005.

The company is currently in discussions with financing sources with a view toward both a longer term solution to its liquidity problems and obtaining refinancing for all or a substantial portion of its outstanding indebtedness, including a total of $1,008 million, which will mature on or about August 29, 2005. This would include repayment of the current bank borrowings and amounts outstanding under the Note Purchase Agreements. The company's management is highly confident that the indebtedness can be refinanced. Its largest shareholder, GE Capital, also expects the company to be able to refinance such indebtedness. However, there can be no assurance that such refinancing can be obtained or that amendments or waivers required to maintain compliance with the previous agreements can be obtained.

Footnote to Financial Statements (2004 Annual Report)

The company intends to improve its financial condition and reduce its dependence on borrowing by slowing expansion, controlling expenses, closing certain unprofitable stores and continuing to implement its inventory reduction program. Management is in the process of reevaluating the company's merchandising, marketing, store operations, and real estate strategies. The company is also considering the sale of certain operating units as a means of generating cash. Future cash is also expected to continue to be provided by ongoing operations, sale of receivables under the Accounts Receivable Purchase Agreement with GE capital, borrowings under revolving loan facilities, and vendor financing programs.

Quarterly Income

	Mar. 05	Dec. 04	Fiscal 2004 Sep. 04	Jun. 04	Mar. 04
Sales	$1,329	$2,084	$1,567	$1,534	$1,435
Cost of goods sold	997	1,525	1,096	1,210	1,038
Gross profit	$ 332	$ 559	$ 471	$ 324	$ 397
Net income	$ (141)	$ (165)	$ (35)	$ 11	$ (48)
Gross profit (% sales)	25.0%	26.8%	30.1%	21.1%	27.7%
Net income (% sales)	(10.6%)	(7.9%)	(2.2%)	0.7%	(3.3%)

Required:

1. Why did Argenti need to increase its notes payable borrowing to over $1 billion in 2004?
2. What recommendation would you make regarding the company's request for a $1.5 billion refinancing package?

Amazon.com, Inc. is the world's leading online retailer with over 17 million customer accounts in over 150 countries. The company sells books, music, DVDs, videos, toys, electronics software, video games, and home improvement products. Through its marketplace services—Amazon.com Auctions, zShops and sothebys.amazon.com—the company has created Web-based marketplaces where buyers and sellers enter into transactions involving a wide range of products. As the company states in its 1999 10-K:

> We offer our customers a superior shopping experience by providing high value through selection, convenience, ease of use, low prices, product information and an intense focus on customer service. We are a proven technology leader, having developed electronic commerce innovations such as 1-Click technology, personalized shopping services, easy-to-use search and browse features, secure payment protections, and wireless access to our stores.

The company's quarterly income statement and balance sheet appear on page 272.

C5 – 6

Amazon.com: Analysis of an Internet retailer

www.prenhall.com/revsine

● Student Resources

☑ Template for solution

Required:

1. Comment on the company's "year over year" sales growth for the March and December quarters. Why do you suppose December 1999 sales outpaced March 2000 sales?
2. Compute the gross profit margin for each quarter and comment on any trend.
3. How well has the company been managing its "Selling, general, and administrative expense"?
4. Why doesn't Amazon.com have any "Receivables" on its balance sheet?
5. Compute inventory turnover for each quarter (using the quarter-end inventory amount) and comment on any trend.
6. Analysts who cover Internet stocks use the "cash burn rate" as an index of company health. The cash burn rate (in months) is:

$$\text{Cash burn rate} = \frac{\text{Cash on hand}}{\text{Operating cash flow needs (per month)}}$$

Suppose an Internet company is generating *negative* operating cash flows of –$300 each quarter, or –$100 per month. If it has $1,000 of cash on hand, its cash burn rate is 10 months. Unless operations turn cash flow positive, the company will run out of money in 10 months. Based on Amazon's historical growth and operating cash flows, what is its cash burn rate as of March 2000?

7. Why are analysts interested in Amazon's cash burn rate?

Amazon.com, Inc.

Quarterly Income Statements
($ in millions)

	Mar. 00	Dec. 99	Sep. 99	Jun. 99	Mar. 99	Dec. 98
Sales	$ 573.9	$ 676.0	$ 355.8	$ 314.4	$ 293.6	$ 252.9
Cost of goods sold	427.6	588.2	285.3	246.8	223.6	199.5
Gross profit	146.3	87.8	70.5	67.6	70.0	53.4
Selling, general, and administrative expenses	342.2	359.5	293.9	139.5	121.6	95.4
Operating profit	(195.9)	(271.7)	(223.4)	(71.9)	(51.6)	(42.0)
Interest income (net)	27.6	18.2	21.5	28.3	16.6	8.6
Non-operating expense	(140.2)	(69.7)	4.8	(94.4)	(26.7)	(13.0)
Pre-tax income	(308.5)	(323.2)	(197.1)	(138.0)	(61.7)	(46.4)
Total income taxes	–0–	–0–	–0–	–0–	–0–	–0–
Net income	$ (308.5)	$ (323.2)	$ (197.1)	$ (138.0)	$ (61.7)	$ (46.4)
Cash flows from operations	$ (320.5)	$ 31.5	$ (75.6)	$ (29.6)	$ (17.2)	$ 38.9

Amazon.com, Inc.

Quarterly Balance Sheets
($ in millions)

	Mar. 00	Dec. 99	Sep. 99	Jun. 99	Mar. 99	Dec. 98
Cash and equivalents	$1,008.8	$ 706.3	$ 905.7	$1,144.3	$1,443.0	$ 373.4
Net receivables	–0–	–0–	–0–	–0–	–0–	–0–
Inventories	172.3	220.6	118.8	59.4	45.2	29.5
Other current assets	89.8	85.3	55.6	53.3	37.1	21.4
Total current assets	1,270.9	1,012.2	1,080.1	1,257.0	1,525.3	424.3
Net property, plant and equipment	334.4	317.6	221.2	156.3	60.6	29.8
Other assets	1,124.4	1,141.8	938.5	884.9	227.1	194.4
Total assets	$2,729.7	$2,471.6	$2,239.8	$2,298.2	$1,813.0	$ 648.5
Current portion of long-term debt	$ 16.0	$ 14.3	$ 12.8	$ 9.9	$ 7.2	$ 0.7
Accounts payable	255.8	463.0	236.7	166.0	133.0	113.4
Other current liabilities	295.4	261.6	108.2	102.0	61.4	47.6
Total current liabilities	567.2	738.9	357.7	277.9	201.6	161.7
Long-term debt	2,137.0	1,466.3	1,462.2	1,449.2	1,533.9	348.1
Common stock	3.5	3.5	3.4	1.7	1.6	0.5
Capital surplus	1,258.9	1,146.6	994.3	940.5	304.0	298.5
Retained earnings	(1,236.9)	(883.7)	(577.8)	(371.1)	(228.1)	(160.3)
Total common equity	25.5	266.4	419.9	571.1	77.5	138.7
Total liabilities and equity	$2,729.7	$2,471.6	$2,239.8	$2,298.2	$1,813.0	$ 648.5

Remember to check the book's Companion Website for additional problem and case material.

www.prenhall.com/revsine

The Role of Financial Information in Valuation, Cash Flow Analysis, and Credit Risk Assessment

Learning Objectives

After studying this chapter, you will understand:

1. The basic steps in corporate valuation.

2. What free cash flows are and how they are used to value a company.

3. How accounting earnings are used in valuation and why *current* earnings are considered more useful than *current* cash flows for assessing *future* cash flows.

4. What an earnings multiple is and what factors contribute to variation in price-earnings multiples.

5. How the permanent, transitory, and valuation-irrelevant components of earnings each affects price-earnings multiples.

6. The notion of earnings quality and what factors influence the quality of earnings.

7. The abnormal earnings approach to valuation and how it is applied in practice.

8. The notion of "earnings surprises" and how stock returns relate to "good news" and "bad news" earnings surprises.

9. The importance of cash flow analysis and credit risk assessment in lending decisions.

10. How to forecast a company's financial statements.

We introduced the key financial ratios used to assess a company's operating performance, liquidity, and solvency in the previous chapter. In this chapter we examine the role that financial accounting information plays in valuation, cash flow analysis, and credit risk assessment. Along the way, we will also build a framework for understanding what academic and professional research has to say about how useful accounting numbers are to investors and creditors.

Corporate valuation involves estimating the worth—or intrinsic value—of a company, one of its operating units, or its ownership shares. Although there are several approaches to valuation, equity investors and analysts often use **fundamental analysis** to estimate the value of a company. This valuation approach uses basic accounting measures, or "fundamentals," to assess the amount, timing, and uncertainty of a firm's *future* operating cash flows or earnings. Data from a firm's financial statements, along with industry and economy-wide data, are used to develop projections of future earnings or cash flows. These projections are then discounted at a risk-adjusted cost of capital to arrive at an initial valuation estimate. This initial estimate is further refined by adding the current value of nonoperating assets (such as a corporate art collection) and subtracting off-balance sheet obligations. This refined valuation becomes the basis for investment (buy, hold, or sell) decisions.

Cash flow assessment plays a central role in analyzing the **credit risk** of a company. Lenders and credit analysts use the firm's financial statements and other information to estimate its *future* cash flows. These cash flow projections are then compared to the firm's future debt-service requirements. Companies with projected operating cash flows that comfortably exceed required future debt principal and interest payments are deemed good credit risks. Less favorable operating cash flow prospects may suggest the firm is a high credit risk. In this case, the firm may be charged higher rates of interest, have more stringent conditions placed on its loans, or be refused credit.

Corporate Valuation

Valuing an entire company, an operating division of that company, or its ownership shares involves three basic steps:

1. **Forecasting** future amounts of some financial attribute—what we call a **value-relevant attribute**—that ultimately determine how much a company is worth. Common value-relevant attributes include:

   - Distributable or free cash flows (defined and discussed later)
   - Accounting earnings
   - Balance sheet book values

2. Determining the **risk** or **uncertainty** associated with the forecasted future amounts.
3. Determining the **discounted present value** of the expected future amounts using a discount rate that reflects the risk or uncertainty from step 2.

> Dividends are another value-relevant attribute discussed in finance texts. However, the "dividend discount" valuation approach described in finance texts is of limited practical use despite its intuitive appeal. This is because dividends represent the *distribution* of wealth. The accounting measures considered here focus on wealth *creation*, the prosperity and growth of the business.

The Discounted Free Cash Flow Approach to Equity Valuation

The **distributable—or free—cash flow valuation approach** combines the elements in these three steps to express current stock price as the discounted present value of expected future distributable cash flows. **Free cash flow**—a term popular among analysts—is sometimes defined as the company's operating cash flows (before interest) minus cash outlays for operating capacity like buildings, equipment, and furnishings. It's the amount available to finance further expansion of operating capacity, to reduce debt, to pay dividends, or to repurchase stock. This is the best way to measure free cash flows if you are interested in valuing the company as a whole without regard to its capital structure.

But what if you want to value just the company's common stock? Then you would need to refine the free cash flow measure by also subtracting cash interest payments, debt repayments, and preferred dividends. What's left is the free cash flow (denoted *CF*) that's available to common stockholders.[1] Of course, *CF* can be used to pay common dividends, buy back common stock, or expand operating capacity. The free cash flow equity valuation model can be written as:[2]

$$P_0 = \underbrace{\frac{E_0(\tilde{CF}_1)}{(1+r)^1}}_{} + \underbrace{\frac{E_0(\tilde{CF}_2)}{(1+r)^2}}_{} + \underbrace{\frac{E_0(\tilde{CF}_3)}{(1+r)^3}}_{} + \cdots \text{(continuing to infinity)} = \sum_{t=1}^{\infty} \frac{E_0(\tilde{CF}_t)}{(1+r)^t} \quad (6.1)$$

Expected free cash flow each period $\longrightarrow \infty$

Discount factor each period $\longrightarrow \infty$

---

[1] One of the earliest accounting treatments of this concept appeared in L. Revsine, *Replacement Cost Accounting* (Upper Saddle River, NJ: Prentice Hall, 1973), pp. 33–35 and 95–100.) There, free cash flow was defined as "the portion of net operating flows that can be distributed as a dividend without reducing the level of future physical operations" (p. 34).

[2] See E. F. Fama and M. H. Miller, *The Theory of Finance* (New York: Holt, Rinehart & Winston, 1972), Ch. 2; R. Brealey and S. Myers, *Principles of Corporate Finance* (New York: McGraw-Hill, 1988), Ch. 4; S. A. Ross, R. W. Westerfield, and J. F. Jaffee, *Corporate Finance* (Homewood, IL: Richard D. Irwin, 1993), Ch. 5; L. Soffer and R. Soffer, *Financial Statement Analysis: A Valuation Approach* (Upper Saddle River, NJ: Prentice Hall, 2003).

The math may look complex, but the intuition is straightforward. The free cash flow valuation model says that the price, (P_0), that the market assigns today (at time $t = 0$) to a company's stock equals the sum (Σ) of the stream of *expected future free cash flows* [the $E_0(\tilde{CF})$ terms] per share of stock *discounted back to the present* [the $(1 + r)^t$ terms].[3] Each periodic expected future free cash flow has its own unique discount factor $(1/(1 + r)^t)$, which reflects the risk (r) and timing (t) of the free cash flow. The E_0 signifies that the expected future cash flows are based on investors' *current assessment* (at time $t = 0$) of the company's future business activities.

The cash flow stream begins one period from now at $t = 1$, and it continues over an infinite horizon to $t = \infty$, but each future free cash flow is currently unknown and therefore uncertain.[4]

The discount rate (r), commonly referred to as the **equity cost of capital**, is adjusted to reflect the uncertainty or riskiness of the expected cash flow stream.[5] Streams that are more uncertain or risky will be discounted at a higher rate.

Simply put, the free cash flow valuation model in equation (6.1) says that today's market price of each common share depends on investors' current *expectations* about the future economic prospects of the firm as measured by free cash flows. These future cash flows are discounted by a factor that reflects the risk (or uncertainty) and timing of the anticipated flows.

Here's an illustration of the discounted free cash flow approach to valuation.

> Willard Brown is thinking about starting a truck rental business. He plans to buy four trucks now, and to then add a fifth truck in two years. Each truck will cost $20,000. Willard has carefully evaluated the local market for rental trucks and believes that each truck will generate $5,000 of net operating cash flows each year. At the end of five years, Willard believes he can sell the trucks for $30,000 in total. How much is the business worth?

Exhibit 6.1 shows you each step in the valuation process. First, Willard must forecast the expected future free cash flows associated with the truck rental business. These include the expected net operating cash flows of $5,000 per truck or $20,000 in the first two years (from four trucks) and then $25,000 in the final three years (when the fifth truck is added). Then there's the additional $30,000 cash flow Willard expects to receive when he sells the trucks at the end of Year 5, and the $20,000 he must spend at the end of Year 2 to buy the final truck. The expected future free cash flows range from a low of $0 in Year 2, to a high of $55,000 in Year 5.

---

[3] We denote uncertain future amounts with a tilde (˜). Thus, $E_0(\tilde{CF}_3)$ indicates the currently expected but uncertain free cash flow for period 3 in the future. By contrast, the already known past cash flow in period 0 would be shown without the tilde (that is, as CF_0).

[4] An alternative representation of the discounted cash flow valuation model presumes that the future cash flow stream continues only through some finite terminal period, T, at which point the company is liquidated and a liquidating or terminal distribution, $(\tilde{CF}_T)$ is paid to stockholders:

$$P_0 = \sum_{t=1}^{T-1} \frac{E_0(\tilde{CF}_t)}{(1+r)^t} + \frac{E_0(\tilde{CF}_T)}{(1+r)^T}$$

[5] There is no clear consensus in the finance literature on how best to estimate the cost of equity capital. However, one popular approach is to use the **capital asset pricing model** (CAPM), which expresses the equity cost of capital as the sum of the return on a riskless asset (r_f) plus an equity risk premium $[E(r_M) - r_f]$ multiplied by the company's systematic (beta) risk:

$$r_e - r_f + \beta[E(r_M) - r_f]$$

See J. Pettit, "Corporate Capital Costs: A Practitioners' Guide," *Journal of Applied Corporate Finance* (Spring 1999), pp. 115–20.

EXHIBIT 6.1	Illustration of the Discounted Free Cash Flow Approach to Valuation

Step 1: Forecast expected future free cash flows

	Year 1	Year 2	Year 3	Year 4	Year 5
Net cash flows from operations	$20,000	$20,000	$25,000	$25,000	$25,000
Cash from selling all trucks in Year 5					30,000
Capital expenditure in Year 2 for the fifth truck		(20,000)			
Future free cash flows	$20,000	$0	$25,000	$25,000	$55,000

Step 2: Determine the cash flow risk (discount rate)   10%

Step 3: Determine the discounted present value of future free cash flows

Expected future free cash flows	$20,000	$0	$25,000	$25,000	$55,000
Present value factor $1/(1 + .10)^t$	0.90909	0.82645	0.75131	0.68301	0.62092
Present value of each future free cash flow	$18,182	$0	$18,783	$17,075	$34,151

Value of business opportunity (sum of all present values)	$88,191
Value per share (1,000 shares)	$88.19

Next, Willard must assess the cash flow risk associated with the truck rental business and determine the appropriate discount rate. For now, let's just say it's 10%.

The final step involves determining the discounted present value of each future free cash flow. The discount factors shown in Exhibit 6.1 are computed as $1/(1 + .10)^t$ and thus capture information about the risk of the business opportunity (10% or .10) and about the timing of each cash flow (the exponent t). The present value of the $20,000 Year 1 free cash flow is therefore $18,182. The present value of the entire free cash flow stream (the sum of the free cash flow present values for Years 1 through 5) is $88,191. So, if there are 1,000 shares of common stock outstanding, the truck rental business is worth $88.19 per share using Willard's free cash flow forecasts.

> For example, we assumed that Willard sold all of his trucks at the end of Year 5 and ceased doing business.

To apply discounted free cash flow valuation approach as represented in equation (6.1), we would need to estimate free cash flows for each and every future period, starting one year hence and going forward forever. Obviously, this would be a daunting task. In practice some simplifying assumptions are made to facilitate the valuation process.[6]

One simplification for a mature firm with a stable cash flow pattern is to assume that the *current level* of cash flows (CF_0) will continue unchanged forever—a zero-growth perpetuity. This means the *expected* free cash flows in each future period will equal the *known* current period cash flow so that equation (6.1) becomes:

$$
\underbrace{P_0 = \frac{CF_0}{(1+r)^1} + \frac{CF_0}{(1+r)^2} + \frac{CF_0}{(1+r)^3} + \cdots}_{\text{Discount factor each year} \longrightarrow \infty} \text{(continuing to infinity)} \tag{6.2}
$$

Expected free cash flow in each year set equal to the free cash flow realized in year 0 $\longrightarrow \infty$

Discount factor each year $\longrightarrow \infty$

---

[6] These simplifying assumptions and other detailed aspects of the valuation process are described in B. Cornell, *Corporate Valuation* (Homewood, IL: R. D. Irwin, 1993); T. Copeland T. Koller, and J. Murin, *Valuation* (New York: Wiley, 2000); A. Damadoran, *Investment Valuation* (New York: Wiley, 1996); S. Penman, *Financial Statement Analysis and Security Valuation* (New York: McGraw-Hill/Irwin, 2003), and L. Soffer and R. Soffer, *Financial Statement Analysis: A Valuation Approach* (Upper Saddle River, NJ: Prentice Hall, 2003).

The present value of the same dollar cash flow over an infinite horizon—called a **constant perpetuity**—simplifies to:[7]

$$P_0 = \frac{CF_0}{r} \qquad (6.3)$$

Thus, if a company is currently generating a free cash flow of $5 per share, which is expected to continue indefinitely, and if the discount rate is 10%, the estimated share price would be $5/.10 = $50.

Goodwill Impairment and Free Cash Flow Valuation You may think that the details of free cash flow valuation are important only for stock analysts and investors. If so, you would be mistaken. Because of recent changes in U.S. financial reporting practices for goodwill, accountants and auditors must also know how to use the discounted free cash flow valuation approach.

For example, here's a footnote from the 2002 annual report of Corning, Inc., a leading manufacturer of fiber-optic cable and other equipment for the telecommunications industry.

IMPAIRMENT OF GOODWILL

SFAS No. 142, "Goodwill and Other Intangible Assets," requires management to make judgments about the fair value of its reporting unit. Corning measures fair value on the basis of **discounted expected future cash flows**. The determination of expected future cash flows involves judgment. Corning's judgment was based upon our historical experience in the telecommunications business, our current knowledge from our commercial relationships, and available external information about future trends. With this input, it is management's expectation that there will be minimal volume growth in the short term, volume growth is assumed to accelerate beginning in 2005 commensurate with overall market recovery. Terminal value of the business assumes a growth in perpetuity of 3%. These cash flows are also used to value intangible and tangible assets which determine the implied value of reporting unit goodwill . . . Corning used a discount rate of 12% in its calculation of fair value of the expected future cash flows and recorded an impairment charge of $400 million . . .

Source: Corning, Inc., 2002 Annual Report to Shareholders. Emphasis added.

---

[7] A constant perpetuity is a stream of constant cash flows without end. To see why the present value of a cash flow perpetuity

$$PV = \frac{CF}{(1+r)^1} + \frac{CF}{(1+r)^2} + \frac{CF}{(1+r)^3} + \cdots + \frac{CF}{(1+r)^\infty}$$

reduces to

$$PV = \frac{CF}{r}$$

Consider this example. Suppose the market price (that is, the present value) of an investment is $1,000 and that this investment will yield a return of 9%, or $90, forever. Because the amount of this perpetual cash flow is $PV \times r$, we can express the amount of the perpetuity as:

$$PV \times r = CF$$

Dividing both sides of the equation by r immediately yields the formula for the present value of a perpetuity:

$$PV = \frac{CF}{r}$$

In our example,

$$\$1,000 = \frac{\$90}{.09}$$

Accounting goodwill arises when one company buys another company and pays more than the fair market value of the acquired company's individual net assets. For example, suppose Corning pays $800 million for another telecommunications equipment manufacturer. If the acquired company's identifiable net assets (cash, receivables, inventories, equipment, buildings, patents, and so on *minus* debt) have a fair market value of only $50 million, then Corning must record the $750 million balance of the purchase price as goodwill.

Statement of Financial Accounting Standards (SFAS) No. 142 requires companies to "test" the impairment of this goodwill at least once a year.[8] That's what Corning's accountants and auditors did using the free cash flow valuation approach. Continuing our example, assume Corning estimated the expected future free cash flows associated with its telecommunications reporting unit (the acquired company), and discovered the unit is now worth only $400 million. Why? Because few companies today are spending money on new telecommunications equipment. This downturn in demand has lowered Corning's forecasts of the acquired company's future sales, earnings, and future free cash flows from what they were when Corning bought the unit.

If the reporting unit's fair value of identifiable net assets is still $50 million, then Corning can only show $350 million of goodwill. Corning's original goodwill ($750 million) has become impaired and must be written down by $400 million—a direct charge to net income for the year.

Corning goes on to say that the impairment charge would have been $225 million higher if the company had used a discount rate of 12.5% rather than 12% to compute the present value of the reporting unit's expected future free cash flows. On the other hand, no impairment charge would have been recorded in 2002 if an 11% discount rate had been used.

Next year, Corning's accountants and auditors will again test for goodwill impairment using the discounted free cash flow valuation approach.

> You will learn more about accounting for goodwill in Chapter 16.

> The following quote from the "Intrinsic Value" column of the *Wall Street Journal* underscores the importance of accrual earnings as an indicator of future free cash flows:
>
> "As per usual, this column values stocks by their expected future free cash flow, discounted back to the present. Earnings are a proxy—imperfect but the best we have— for free cash flow, which is the spare change that the underlying business throws off to their owners after paying for salaries, interest, capital maintenance, taxes and Danish for their chief executives, in addition to their eight-figure bonuses." [R. Lowenstein, "S&P 500: Cheap, Fair, Going, Gone. . . . ," *Wall Street Journal* (June 19, 1997)].

The Role of Earnings in Valuation

We have just described a free cash flow valuation approach linking investors' expectations about a company's future cash flow prospects to today's stock price. *But what role does earnings play in valuation?* If investors are truly interested in knowing the company's future cash flows, why would they care about current earnings? The answer hinges on the belief that *current* accrual accounting earnings are more useful than *current* cash flows in predicting *future* cash flows. The Financial Accounting Standards Board (FASB), for example, makes this assertion. It states:

> "Information about enterprise earnings and its components measured by accrual accounting generally provides a better indication of enterprise performance than information about current cash receipts and payments."[9]

The Board stresses that the primary objective of financial reporting is to provide information useful to investors and creditors in assessing the *amount*, *timing*, and *uncertainty* of future net cash flows.[10] The FASB contends that users pay attention to firms' accounting earnings because this accrual measure of periodic firm performance improves their ability to forecast companies' future cash flows.

---

[8] "Goodwill and Other Intangible Assets," *Statement of Financial Accounting Standards (SFAS) No. 142* (Norwalk, CT: FASB, 2001).

[9] "Objectives of Financial Reporting by Business Enterprises," *Statement of Financial Accounting Concepts No. 1* (Stamford, CT: FASB, 1978), para. 43.

[10] Ibid., para. 37. The term **net cash flows** refers to the difference between cash receipts (inflows) and cash payments (outflows).

The FASB's belief that *current* earnings outperform *current* cash flows in predicting *future* cash flows stems from the *forward-looking* nature of accrual accounting. To illustrate, consider this example. Under generally accepted accounting principles (GAAP), a $100,000 cash expenditure for production equipment would not be expensed in its entirety when purchased. Instead, that expenditure is charged to an asset account, and the asset is depreciated over future years as it is used to produce the products that are sold to customers. Both the depreciable life and depreciation method are chosen to reflect the *expected future benefit pattern* that arises from the use of the asset. Accrual accounting automatically incorporates this long-horizon, multiple-period view for capital expenditure transactions.

Consider another example. Under accrual accounting an up-front cash advance from a customer is recognized as income not when the cash is received but rather over a series of future periods as the advance is earned (recall the Canterbury Publishing example from Chapter 2).

Cash flows are "lumpy"—but as these examples illustrate—accrual accounting earnings measurement takes a long-horizon perspective that smooths out the "lumpiness" in year-to-year cash flows. This explains why the FASB contends that current earnings provide a much better measure of long-run expected operating performance than do current cash flows.

The FASB's contention is supported by empirical research that shows two results:

- Current earnings are a better forecast of future cash flows than are current cash flows.[11]
- Stock returns correlate better with accrual earnings than with realized operating cash flows.[12]

These results imply that investors are better able to predict a company's future free cash flows using the company's accrual earnings than by using realized cash flows.

Figure 6.1 illustrates the linkage between a company's current earnings, future free cash flows, and current stock price, as suggested by the FASB and by the empirical evidence.[13]

Figure 6.1

LINKAGE BETWEEN STOCK PRICE AND ACCRUAL EARNINGS

As Figure 6.1 shows, the analyst combines information about the company's current earnings, its business strategy, and the industry's competitive dynamics to forecast future free cash flows. ***Through the use of accruals and deferrals, accrual accounting produces an earnings number that smooths out the unevenness or "lumpiness" in year-to-year cash flows, and it provides an estimate of sustainable "annualized" long-run future free cash flows.***

The final step in this process involves using the annualized free cash flow estimate together with the risk-adjusted discount rate to arrive at an estimated value for the firm's stock.

[11] See M. Barth, C. Cram, and K. Nelson, "Accruals and the Prediction of Future Cash Flows," *The Accounting Review* (January 2001), pp. 27–58; and P. Dechow, S. P. Kothari, and R. Watts, "The Relation Between Earnings and Cash Flow," *Journal of Accounting and Economics* (May 1998), pp. 133–68. Additional evidence on the usefulness of *current earnings* in predicting *future cash flows* is provided by R. Greenberg, G. Johnson, and K. Ramesh, "Earnings Versus Cash Flow as a Predictor of Future Cash Flow," *Journal of Accounting, Auditing and Finance* (Fall 1986), pp. 266–77; and C. Finger, "The Ability of Earnings to Predict Future Earnings and Cash Flow," *Journal of Accounting Research* (Autumn 1994), pp. 210–23.

[12] P. Dechow, "Accounting Earnings and Cash Flows as Measures of Firm Performance: The Role of Accounting Accruals," *Journal of Accounting and Economics* (July 1994), pp. 3–42.

[13] For a slightly different discussion of these linkages, see W. Beaver, *Financial Reporting: An Accounting Revolution* (Upper Saddle River, NJ: Prentice Hall, 1981), Ch. 4.

To appreciate the implications of these linkages, let's revisit the simplified zero-growth perpetuity setting and our free cash flow valuation model in equation (6.2). Assuming zero growth means that one way to estimate a firm's equity value (or stock price) is to use its current period free cash flow (CF_0) as our forecast for each future period free cash flow. But according to the FASB's assertion, the current period accrual income is a better proxy for sustainable future cash flows than is the current period free cash flow. This means replacing the current period cash flow (CF_0) in equation (6.2) with the current period earnings (denoted X_0). In this case the free cash flow valuation equation simplifies to:

Free cash flow discount model from equation (6.1)

Expected future free cash flow set equal to current accrual earnings in year 0 $\longrightarrow \infty$

$$P_0 = \sum_{t=1}^{\infty} \frac{E_0(\tilde{CF}_t)}{(1+r)^t} = \frac{X_0}{(1+r)^1} + \frac{X_0}{(1+r)^2} + \frac{X_0}{(1+r)^3} + \cdots + \frac{X_0}{(1+r)^{\infty}} \tag{6.4}$$

Discount factor each year $\longrightarrow \infty$

As in equation (6.2), the right-hand side of equation (6.4) is a perpetuity with a discounted present value of X_0/r. Thus, given our simplifying assumptions, the current stock price estimate can be expressed as a capitalized rate $(1/r)$ times a perpetuity equal to current earnings:

$$P_0 = \frac{1}{r}(X_0) = \frac{X_0}{r} \tag{6.5}$$

or alternatively:

$$\frac{P_0}{X_0} = \frac{1}{r} \tag{6.6}$$

The left-hand side of equation (6.6) is the **price/earnings (P/E) ratio**—also called the **earnings multiple**—which is a measure of the relation between a firm's current earnings and its share price. Under the assumption of zero growth, the price/earnings ratio in equation (6.6) is the reciprocal of the risk-adjusted interest rate (equity cost of capital) used to discount future earnings. If the current risk-adjusted interest rate is 8%, the earnings multiple is $1/.08 = 12.5$, which is the rate at which \$1 of current earnings is capitalized into share price. If the company reports current earnings of \$5 per share and if investors believe this earnings level will persist forever as a perpetuity of \$5 per share, then the present value of the future earnings stream implies a share price of $\$5 \times 12.5 = \$62.50$.

RECAP   In theory, equity valuation involves discounting the expected value of some measure of wealth creation—like free cash flow or earnings—over an infinite horizon using a risk-adjusted discount rate (equity cost of capital). In practice, simplifying assumptions are made to facilitate the valuation process. One simplification is to assume that future periods' free cash flows will be a perpetuity equal to the current period's accrual earnings. Accrual accounting produces an earnings number that smoothes out the unevenness in the year-to-year cash flows, thereby providing a measure of firm performance that is generally a better indicator of a company's long-run sustainable free cash flows. Using this valuation approach, stock price is stated as a multiple of current period earnings, where the multiple (in the no-growth case) is the reciprocal of the firm's equity cost of capital.

Research on Earnings and Equity Valuation

Over the past 30 years, researchers have investigated the **value-relevance** of financial accounting information.[14] Many of these studies seek to further our understanding of the relation between stock prices and earnings.

To illustrate, let's consider equation (6.5). That equation says that current earnings (X_0) can "explain" current stock price (P_0) in the sense that a perpetual earnings stream of $5 per share gives rise to a $62.50 share price. It immediately follows that *differences* in current earnings across firms should help explain *differences* in stock prices across firms at a particular point in time. ***That is, if accounting earnings are viewed by investors as an important piece of information for assessing firm value, then earnings differences across firms should help explain differences in firms' stock prices.*** This is just another way of saying that earnings are value-relevant.

One way to test whether reported earnings are value-relevant is to examine the statistical association between stock prices and earnings across many firms at a given point in time. Researchers have explored this statistical association using the following simple earnings valuation equation:

$$P_i = \alpha + \beta X_i + e_i \qquad (6.7)$$

where:

- P_i is the end-of-period closing stock price for firm *i*, and X_i is the firm's reported accounting earnings per share for that same period.
- The intercept (α) and slope (β) terms in the equation represent coefficients to be estimated using standard regression analysis or similar techniques.
- e_i denotes a random error that reflects the variation in stock prices that cannot be explained by earnings.

If accounting earnings are relevant for determining stock prices, then the estimated slope coefficient β, which measures the relationship between earnings and prices, should be positive. A statistically positive β means that differences in earnings across firms explain a significant portion of the variation in share prices across firms. Moreover, if current earnings were a perfect forecast of expected future free cash flows, and if all companies had the same cost of equity capital and conformed to the zero-growth assumption, current earnings would explain 100% of the variation in share prices.

> For now, earnings per share (EPS) can be taken to mean a company's net income divided by its number of outstanding common shares. As you will discover in Chapter 15, EPS calculations are a little more complicated than this.

Figure 6.2 on the next page plots 2002 year-end stock prices (shown on the vertical axis) against annual earnings per share (EPS, shown on the horizontal axis) for 40 restaurant companies. The upward-sloping line represents the estimated price-earnings relation for the regression equation (6.7) for this group of companies at the end of 2002. The regression line has a vertical axis intercept (α) estimate of $9.54 per share and a slope (β) coefficient estimate of 8.18—that is:

---

[14] For an overview of this research, see B. Lev and J. Ohlson, "Market-Based Empirical Research in Accounting: A Review, Interpretation, and Extension," *Journal of Accounting Research* (Supplement, 1982), pp. 249–322; B. Lev, "On the Usefulness of Earnings and Earnings Research: Lessons and Directions from Two Decades of Empirical Research," *Journal of Accounting Research* (Supplement, 1989), pp., 153–92; S. Kothari, "Capital Markets Research in Accounting," *Journal of Accounting and Economics* (September 2001), pp. 105–232; and R. Holthausen and R. Watts, "The Relevance of the Value-Relevance Literature for Financial Accounting Standard Setting," *Journal of Accounting and Economics* (September 2001), pp. 3–76.

$$
P_i = \underset{\substack{\uparrow \\ \text{Stock} \\ \text{price at} \\ \$0\ \text{EPS}}}{\overset{\substack{\text{Intercept} \\ \downarrow}}{9.54}} + \underset{\substack{\uparrow \\ \text{Earnings} \\ \text{multiple}}}{\overset{\substack{\text{Slope} \\ \downarrow}}{8.18}} \times \underset{\substack{\uparrow \\ \text{EPS}}}{(\$X_i)}
$$

(6.8)

A restaurant that reported earnings per share of $X_i = \$1$ in 2002 would be predicted to have a stock price of $\$17.72 = \$9.54 + 8.18 \times \$1$. The estimated slope coefficient ($\beta = 8.18$) is positive and statistically significant, indicating that reported earnings explains some of the variation in stock prices of restaurant companies. However, the proportion of variation in share prices explained by earnings (the R^2 for the regression) is only 30.0%. Some points lie well above the average price-earnings relation in Figure 6.2, while others fall far below the regression line.[15] The next section discusses reasons why current earnings do not explain 100% of the variation in current prices and why some firms' P/E ratios are well above (or below) average.

Figure 6.2

2002 P/E RELATIONSHIP FOR 40 RESTAURANT COMPANIES

Regression Result:

$P_i = \$9.54 + 8.18X_i$

$R^2 = 30.0\%$

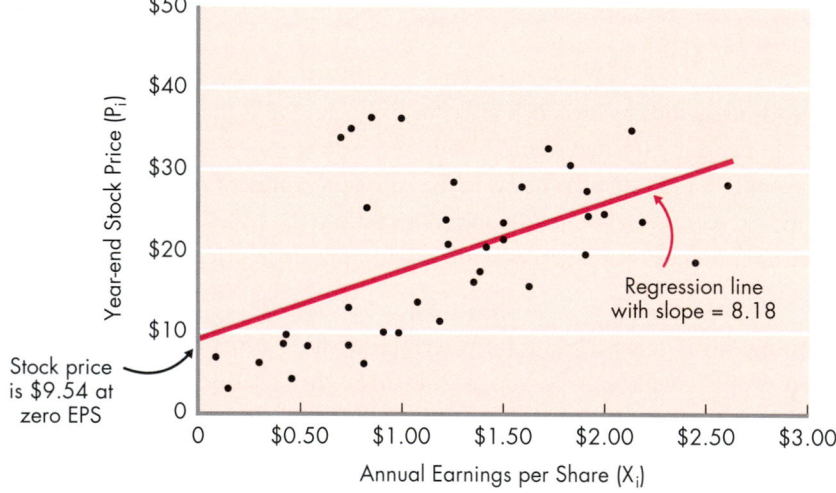

Sources of Variation in P/E Multiples

Risk Differences Two firms with the same level of current and future expected earnings can sell for different prices because of differences in the risk or uncertainty associated with those earnings. Riskier firms have a higher risk-adjusted cost of capital, which means the discount rate for capitalizing their earnings will be *higher*, resulting in *lower* share prices for those companies.

To illustrate, suppose Firm A and Firm B both report current earnings of $10 per share, and it is expected, on average, that these earnings will persist into the future forever. However, Firm A's earnings exhibit greater volatility over time—and therefore, greater risk—which results in a 15% cost of equity capital for Firm A. Firm B's earnings are more stable—that is, they represent a lower risk—so Firm B's cost of equity capital is only 10%.

---

[15] The error term (e_i) in equation (6.7) does not show up in equation (6.8). That's because equation (6.8) is the expression for the *fitted regression line*. The vertical distance between the fitted regression line and the data points for individual firms in Figure 6.2 are the e_i error terms in equation (6.7).

The estimated share price for each firm would be:

	Firm A	Firm B
	$\dfrac{\$10}{.15} = \$66.67$	$\dfrac{\$10}{.10} = \$100$

Thus, despite having equal earnings, Firm A's share price will be one-third less than Firm B's ($66.67 versus $100) because Firm A is riskier and its cost of capital (15%) is higher than Firm B's (10%).

Growth Opportunities Most firms' P/E ratios run between 10 and 30. However, it is not uncommon to find start-up companies like Brocade Communications and high-tech companies like Applied Materials trading at share prices 100 times (or more) than their current earnings per share. What explains these exceptionally high P/E ratios?

In addition to valuing earnings generated from existing assets, the market values **growth opportunities**—that is, the firm's *potential earnings* from reinvesting current earnings in new projects that will eventually earn a rate of return in excess of the cost of equity capital. The net present value of growth opportunities (NPVGO) from the reinvestment of current earnings adds a positive increment to the firm's stock price, resulting in above-average P/E multiples. For a firm with positive growth opportunities, the pricing equation (6.5) can be rewritten as:

$$P_0 = \underbrace{\frac{X_0}{r}}_{\substack{\text{Present value of earnings} \\ \text{from assets in place}}} + \underbrace{\text{NPVGO}}_{\substack{\text{Net present value of future} \\ \text{growth opportunities}}}$$

(6.9)

The first term is the current operations value of a firm that has no growth opportunities and distributes all its earnings to stockholders in the form of dividends. The second term (NPVGO) is the future growth value of a firm—the *additional* share value created if the firm retains its earnings to fund new investment projects.

To illustrate the incremental value derived from growth opportunities, suppose Firm A has 100,000 shares outstanding and can generate earnings of $1 million per year in perpetuity if it undertakes no new investment projects. Thus, its earnings per share now and in the future is $10 ($1 million divided by 100,000 shares). If Firm A's cost of equity capital is 10%, the price per share is:

> If on the one hand, investors believe the firm will put money into worthwhile projects (that is, those with a *positive* net present value), NPVGO will be positive. On the other hand, if investors believe the firm will invest in unprofitable projects (that is, those with a *negative* net present value), NPVGO will be negative.

$$P_0 = \frac{X_0}{r} = \frac{\$10}{.10} = \$100$$

Now assume that Firm A can reinvest all earnings from period 0 in a project that is expected to increase earnings in period 1 and *in every subsequent period* by $150,000, or $1.50 per share. This represents a 15% return on the reinvested earnings ($150,000/$1 million). If Firm A's cost of capital remains at 10%, the net present value of this investment project as of the start of period 1 is:

$$\underbrace{-\$1,000,000}_{\substack{\textbf{Earnings invested} \\ \textbf{at beginning of} \\ \textbf{period 1}}} \quad + \quad \underbrace{\frac{\$150,000}{.10}}_{\substack{\textbf{Present value at beginning of} \\ \textbf{period 1 of incremental return} \\ \textbf{from reinvested earnings}}} \quad = \quad \$500,000$$

Since \$500,000 is the project's net present value as of the beginning of period 1, the value of the project today (time 0) can be determined by discounting back one period:

$$\frac{\$500,000}{(1+.10)^1} = \$454,545$$

Thus, NPVGO per share is $\dfrac{\$454,545}{100,000}$ = \$4.55. The price per share of Firm A with this particular growth opportunity is:

$$P_0 = \frac{X_0}{r} + \text{NPVGO}$$

$$= \frac{\$10}{.10} + \$4.55 = \$104.55$$

Note the stock is now more valuable than it was with no-growth (\$100). That's because the firm is able to reinvest earnings in a project expected to earn a 15% rate of return (forever) when the firm's cost of capital or discount rate is only 10%. In this simplified example, the retention rate on earnings was 100%—meaning that none of the earnings were paid as dividends to shareholders. But this need not be the case for a firm to have growing earnings.

In general, the growth rate in earnings will depend on:

- the portion of earnings reinvested each period, called the **earnings retention rate**,[16] and
- the rate of return earned on new investment (r^*).

> Equation (6.7) is our simple earnings valuation equation : $P_i = \alpha + \beta X_i + e_i$ where P is stock price, X is earnings per share, α and β are regression coefficients, and e is the error term.

As long as the retention rate is positive and as long as the return earned on new investment is greater than the firm's cost of equity capital $(r^* > r)$, NPVGO will be positive and will contribute to the P/E multiple. Return on equity (ROE), one of the key accounting performance measures introduced in Chapter 5, can be used to assess whether a firm is likely to earn a return on reinvested earnings that exceeds its cost of equity capital.

Permanent, Transitory, and Valuation-Irrelevant Components of Earnings If investors view firms' current earnings levels as likely to persist in perpetuity, then the slope coefficient (β) in equation (6.7) should equal the average earnings multiple for the particular companies and time period being examined. This prediction follows directly from the equity valuation model in equation (6.5), where current earnings are translated into share price using an earnings multiple based on the risk-adjusted cost of equity capital. For example, if the average risk-

---

[16] The earnings retention rate (k) is [(earnings − dividends)/earnings]. One minus the retention rate $(1 − k)$ is the **dividend payout ratio**.

adjusted cost of capital is 8%, then β should be 1/.08 or 12.5. However, for many firms, the earnings multiple falls well below this theoretical value.[17] Why?

One explanation is that reported earnings numbers often contain three distinctly different components, each subject to a different earnings capitalization rate:[18]

1. A **permanent earnings** component (X_i^P), which is expected to persist into the future and is therefore valuation-relevant. In theory, the multiple for this component should approach $1/r$.

2. A **transitory earnings** component (X_i^T), which is valuation-relevant but is not expected to persist into the future. Since transitory earnings result from one-time events or transactions, the multiple for this component should approach 1.0.

3. A **value-irrelevant earnings** (or **noise**) component (X_i^0), which is unrelated to future free cash flows or future earnings and, therefore, is *not* pertinent to assessing current share price. Such earnings components should carry a multiple of zero.

These three earnings components correspond roughly to the three broad classifications in the multiple-step income statements as described in Chapter 2. For example:

- *Income from continuing operations* (with the possible exception of certain so-called "special" items) is generally regarded as a recurring, sustainable component of a company's profit performance, and thus it would fall into the permanent earnings category.

- *Income (loss) from discontinued operations and extraordinary gains and losses*, on the other hand, are nonrecurring. These items are more likely to be viewed as transitory components of earnings and, therefore, to be valued at a much lower multiple than those items associated with permanent earnings components.

- A *change in accounting principles*, which gives rise to a *cumulative effect adjustment* to income that has no future cash flow consequences to shareholders, may be viewed as "noise" that is valuation-irrelevant.

> Some items that comprise income from continuing operations may correctly be viewed by the investors as highly transitory and/or value-irrelevant, and would be capitalized accordingly. Analysts call these "special" items. Examples include inventory holding gains and losses embedded in First-In First-Out (FIFO) earnings and Last-In, First-Out (LIFO) liquidation profits that result when old LIFO inventory layers are sold. Later chapters discuss the value-relevance of these and other earnings and balance sheet items in considerable detail.

The idea that reported earnings may sometimes contain permanent, transitory, and value-irrelevant components suggests that X_i (total earnings) in the simple price-earnings regression model of equation (6.7) should be rewritten as the sum of permanent, transitory, and valuation-irrelevant components—that is:

$$X_i = X_i^P + X_i^T + X_i^0$$

This modification allows for a different multiple or capitalization rate for each earnings component in the valuation equation:[19]

---

[17] Notice that the slope coefficient of 9.54 for restaurants in Figure 6.2 suggests an earnings capitalization rate of 10.48% because $1/.1048 = 9.54$.

[18] For a more formal discussion of these three earnings components and their valuation implication, see R. Ramakrishnan and J. Thomas, "Valuation of Permanent, Transitory, and Price-Irrelevant Components of Reported Earnings," *Journal of Accounting, Auditing and Finance* (1998), pp. 301–36.

[19] You may wonder about the distinction between the value-irrelevant component (X_i^0) and the error term (e_i) in equation (6.10). X_i^0 is an earnings component that is not relevant to assessing share price. However, e_i represents "other information" that is *not* a component of current earnings but *is* relevant to assessing price. For example, e_i may represent news about a new scientific breakthrough or discovery the firm has just made. Such news would have a positive effect on share price, but it would not yet be reflected in current earnings.

$$
\underset{\underset{\text{of earnings}}{\uparrow}}{\overset{\overset{\text{Permanent}}{\text{component}}}{}} \quad \underset{\underset{\text{earnings}}{\uparrow}}{\overset{\overset{\text{Transitory}}{\text{component of}}}{}} \quad \underset{\underset{\text{earnings}}{\uparrow}}{\overset{\overset{\text{Value-irrelevant}}{\text{component of}}}{}}
$$

$$
P_i = \alpha + \underset{\uparrow}{\beta_P X_i^P} + \underset{\uparrow}{\beta_T X_i^T} + \underset{\uparrow}{\beta_0 X_i^0} + e_i \quad \textbf{(6.10)}
$$

Earnings multiples for permanent (β_P), transitory (β_T), and value-irrelevant (β_0) components of earnings

Equation (6.10) expresses share price as a function of the permanent, transitory, and valuation-irrelevant components of earnings. Each earnings component has a different earnings multiple—β_P, β_T, and, β_0, respectively.

In theory, permanent (sustainable) earnings should have a higher earnings multiple than transitory earnings because we expect the former to persist longer into the future—that is, β_P should be greater than β_T.[20] Likewise, the multiple for transitory earnings should exceed the multiple for value-irrelevant earnings since the latter have no bearing on future cash flows and, therefore, have no bearing on price—that is, β_0 should be 0 while β_T should be approximately 1.0. Figure 6.3 illustrates these predictions about earnings multiples for different earnings components. The slope of each line corresponds to the earnings multiple for that particular earnings component, where r equals 20%.

Figure 6.3

PRICE/EARNINGS MULTIPLES FOR PERMANENT, TRANSITORY, AND VALUE-IRRELEVANT EARNINGS COMPONENTS WITH $r = 20\%$

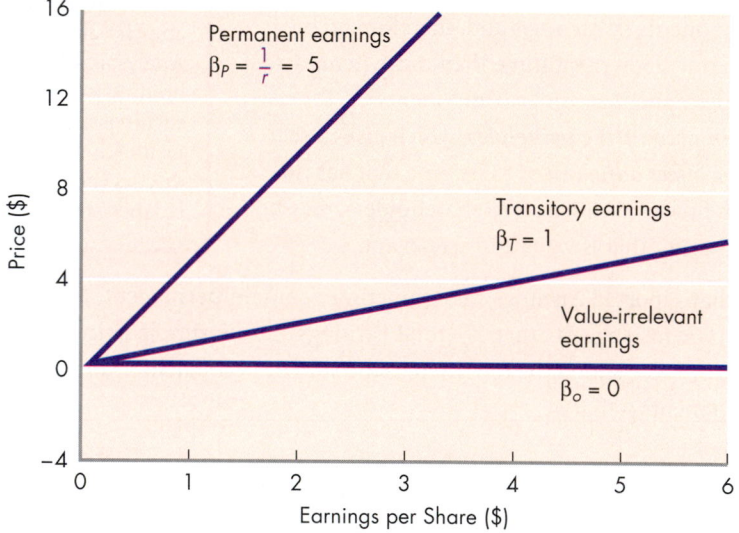

To illustrate the importance of distinguishing between permanent, transitory, and value-irrelevant earnings components, let's suppose two companies report identical bottom-line earnings of $10 per share, as in Exhibit 6.2. Does this mean they would necessarily sell for the same price? Perhaps not, as we will see.

A careful analysis of the financial statements and related footnotes of Firm A reveals that its total earnings fall into three categories: (1) 60% that is judged to be value-relevant and permanent, (2) 30% that is value-relevant but transitory, and (3) 10% that is considered value-irrelevant. Analysis of Firm B's financial report indicates its earnings composition is 50% permanent, 20% transitory, and 30% value-irrelevant. This decomposition of each firm's reported EPS is shown in Exhibit 6.2.

---

[20] Lipe presents evidence consistent with this conjecture. He finds a greater stock price reaction to earnings components that exhibit greater permanence than to those components that are more transitory in nature. See R. Lipe, "The Information Contained in the Components of Earnings," *Journal of Accounting Research* (Supplement, 1986), pp. 33–64.

EXHIBIT 6.2	Applying P/E Multiples to Earnings Components	
	Firm A	**Firm B**
EPS as reported	$10	$10
Analyst's EPS decomposition		
Permanent component	60% of $10 = $6	50% of $10 = $5
Transitory component	30% of $10 = $3	20% of $10 = $2
Value-irrelevant component	10% of $10 = $1	30% of $10 = $3
Earnings multiple applied to each earnings component at cost of capital of $r = 20\%$		
Permanent component ($\beta_P = 5 = 1/.20$)	$5 \times \$6 = 30$	$5 \times \$5 = 25$
Transitory component ($\beta_T = 1$)	$1 \times \$3 = 3$	$1 \times \$2 = 2$
Value-irrelevant component ($\beta_0 = 0$)	$0 \times \$1 = 0$	$0 \times \$3 = 0$
Implied share price	$33	$27
Implied total earnings multiple (Share price/EPS as reported)	3.3	2.7

Using a 20% cost of capital to capitalize the permanent component of earnings, we find that the valuation model in equation (6.10) implies a stock price of $33 for Firm A and $27 for Firm B. Firm A's stock price is approximately 20% greater than Firm B's price, even though both companies report the same earnings per share. In the vernacular of the analyst community, Firm A's stock sells for a higher earnings multiple because investors perceive its **earnings quality** to be superior to that of Firm B.

The Concept of Earnings Quality A *Wall Street Journal* article described earnings quality and its implications for stock prices:

> Quality of earnings measures how much the profits companies publicly report diverge from their true operating earnings. Low quality means the bottom line is padded with paper gains—such as the profit-fattening effect of inflation on a company's reported inventory values, or gains produced by "underdepreciation," when a company doesn't write off plant and equipment as fast as their real value is falling.
>
> Because a decline in quality means companies' reported earnings are weaker and less sustainable than they appear, it indicates likely trouble for future earnings—whether or not a recession arrives. If history is any guide, those lower quality earnings also will come home to roost in lower stock prices. . . .[21]

The notion of earnings quality is multifaceted, and there is no consensus on how best to measure it.[22] Basically, earnings are considered to be high quality when they are *sustainable*—for example, those that are generated from repeat customers and from high-quality products that enjoy steady consumer demand. Examples of *un*sustainable earnings items include gains or losses from debt retirement; asset write-offs from corporate restructuring and plant closings; or temporary reductions in discretionary expenditures for advertising, research and development, or employee training.

Earnings quality is also affected by the accounting methods chosen by management to describe routine, ongoing business activities (like using LIFO rather than FIFO for inventory accounting). Earnings quality is also affected by the subjectivity—it's unavoidable!—of accounting estimates (for example, the estimated allowance for future uncollectibles).

Accrual accounting treats these discretionary expenditures as expenses. One way a firm can boost earnings temporarily is by cutting back on the amount spent for these activities. However, earnings increases of this sort are not sustainable because the expenditures are critical to creating future demand for the firm's products, and to creating new products or developing competent management—all important determinants of long-run sustainable earnings.

---

[21] B. Donnelly, "Profits' 'Quality' Erodes, Making Them Less Reliable," *Wall Street Journal* (October 18, 1990).

[22] See L. Bernstein and J. Siegel, "The Concept of Earnings Quality," *Financial Analysts Journal* (July–August 1979), pp. 72–75; J. Siegel, "The 'Quality of Earnings' Concept—A Survey," *Financial Analysts Journal* (March–April 1982), pp. 60–68.

Does earnings quality matter? One study finds that when reported earnings are adjusted for quality differences—for example, subtracting (or adding back) transitory gains (or losses) or adjusting for differences in inventory methods (FIFO versus LIFO)—the "quality-adjusted" earnings numbers better explain why firms' stocks sell for different prices.[23] These results suggest that differences in earnings quality are associated with differences in the overall earnings capitalization rate (earnings multiple) that investors assign to reported earnings when determining share prices. Notice carefully that as transitory (X_i^T) or value-irrelevant (X_i^0) components become a larger part of a firm's reported earnings:

- the quality of those reported earnings is eroded,
- reported earnings become a less reliable indicator of the company's long-run sustainable cash flows, and
- hence earnings are a less reliable indicator of fundamental value.

This is illustrated in Exhibit 6.2, where we see that Firm B (with a higher proportion of transitory or value-irrelevant components of earnings) has an overall earnings multiple of 2.7 compared to 3.3 for Firm A. Suppose all the reported earnings were considered permanent. Then the stock would sell for $10/.20 = $50, and the earnings multiple would be 5. Low-quality earnings will be assigned a lower overall earnings multiple and capitalized at a lower rate.

The research to date suggests that the capital market is rather sophisticated—it does not react naively to reported earnings, but instead, it appears to distinguish among permanent, transitory, and value-irrelevant earnings components. Investors recognize differences in the quality of reported earnings numbers and take these differences into account when assessing the implications of earnings reports for share prices. From time to time throughout this book, we will come back to this idea as we discuss alternative accounting treatments, both for ongoing events and for specialized transactions, and as we review the academic and professional research literature on the valuation-relevance of alternative accounting methods and footnote disclosures.

RE CAP — **Firms' shares often sell at prices that differ from multiplying current reported earnings by the average earnings multiple for their industry. A variety of factors contribute to variation in price/earnings (P/E) multiples. These include differences in risk; in growth opportunities; and in what proportions of current earnings are considered to be permanent, transitory, and value-irrelevant. The persistence of earnings is related to earnings quality—higher quality earnings are more persistent and sustainable. Assessing earnings quality involves using information from a multiple-step income statement, a balance sheet, a cash flow statement, financial footnotes, and Management's Discussion and Analysis (MD&A) to identify components of current earnings that are likely to be sustainable in contrast to those that are transitory or price-irrelevant.**

The Abnormal Earnings Approach to Equity Valuation

In the previous section, we found that the role of accounting earnings information in equity valuation is *indirect*—earnings are only useful because they help generate forecasts of future free cash flows. These future free cash flow estimates were then discounted to arrive at an estimated value for the company and its shares. Recently, another valuation approach has emerged in practice that uses earnings and equity book value numbers themselves as *direct* inputs in the valuation

---

[23] See B. Lev and R. Thiagarajan, "Fundamental Information Analysis," *Journal of Accounting Research* (Autumn 1993), pp. 190–215. To arrive at "quality-adjusted" earnings, the researchers started with reported earnings and then eliminated revenue or expense items thought to be transitory or value-irrelevant.

process. Under many circumstances this new earnings-based approach leads to valuation esti-mates that are equivalent to the free cash flow approach. So, why is it important to learn about this new approach? Because, it helps us better understand the economic forces that influence share prices over time and across firms.

This new approach is based on the notion that the value of a company (and its share price) is driven not by the level of earnings themselves but by the level of earnings *relative to a fundamental economic benchmark*. That benchmark is the cost of capital, expressed in dollars, and it reflects the level of earnings investors demand from the company as compensation for the risks of investment. Investors willingly pay a premium only for those firms that earn more than the cost of capital—meaning firms that produce **positive abnormal earnings**. For firms whose earnings are "ordinary" or "normal"—that is, where the earnings rate is equal to the cost of capital—investors are only willing to pay an amount equal to the underlying book value of net assets. Firms that earn less than the cost of capital—that is, that produce **negative abnormal earnings**—have a share price *below* book value and thus sell at a discount. This relationship between share prices, book value, and abnormal earnings performance is expressed mathematically as:[24]

> In theory, the abnormal earnings approach and the free cash flow approach *always* produce the same valuation estimate. In practice, however, the two approaches sometimes produce different valuation estimates. When this occurs, it's because the analyst has introduced shortcuts and simplifications that produce errors in one or both valuation estimates.

$$P_0 = BV_0 + \sum_{t=1}^{\infty} \frac{E_0(\text{Abnormal earnings}_t)}{(1+r)^t} \quad (6.11)$$

where P_0 is share price at time 0, BV_0 is book value of equity at time 0, $E_0(\text{Abnormal earnings}_t)$ is expected future abnormal earnings, and $(1+r)^t$ is the discount factors for each future period.

where:

- *BV* denotes the equity book value (assets minus liabilities, or net assets) per share that shareholders have invested in the firm,
- E_0 denotes the expectation about future abnormal earnings per share formed at time 0, and
- *r* is the cost of equity capital.

The cost of equity capital, *r*, also corresponds to the risk-adjusted return stockholders *require* from their investment. So the earnings level the company must generate in period *t* to satisfy stockholders is $r \times BV_{t-1}$, or stockholders' required rate of return multiplied by the beginning of period $(t-1)$ invested capital. Any difference between actual earnings for the period (X_t) and stockholders' required dollar return on invested capital for the period $(r \times BV_{t-1})$ represents **abnormal earnings**.

[24] Several variations of the abnormal earnings valuation model have appeared in the literature. Recent examples include J. Ohlson, "Earnings, Book Values, and Dividends in Equity Valuation," *Contemporary Accounting Research* (Spring 1995), pp. 661–87; T. Copeland, T. Koller, and J. Murrin, *Valuation: Measuring and Managing the Value of Companies* (New York: Wiley, 1994); R. Lundholm and R. Sloan, *Equity Valuation and Analysis* (New York: McGraw-Hill/Irwin, 2004); B. Madden, *CFROI Valuation* (Boston, MA: Butterworth-Heinemann, 1999); S. Penman, *Financial Statement Analysis and Security Valuation* (New York: McGraw-Hill/Irwin, 2003); L. Soffer and R. Soffer, *Financial Statement Analysis: A Valuation Approach* (Upper Saddle River, NJ: Prentice Hall, 2003); and G. B. Stewart, III, *The Quest for Value* (New York: Harper Business, 1991).

$$\underset{\displaystyle\downarrow}{\overset{\text{Actual}}{\text{earnings}}} \qquad \underset{\displaystyle\downarrow}{\overset{\text{Required}}{\text{earnings}}} \tag{6.12}$$

$$\text{Abnormal earnings}_t \;=\; X_t \;-\; \overbrace{(r \times BV_{t-1})}$$

To illustrate, suppose a company's equity book value (BV) at the beginning of the year is $100 per share, and the cost of equity (r) is 15%. Stockholders therefore require earnings of at least $100 × 15% or $15 per share. If investors expect the company to report earnings equal to the benchmark earnings of $15 per share, but the company does even better and earns $20 per share—thus exceeding the benchmark—its stock price will increase to reflect its superior performance. If actual earnings are only $10—thus falling short of the benchmark expected earnings—the stock price will fall. The amount of the stock price increase (or decline) depends on the degree to which stockholders believe that abnormal earnings (earnings above *or* below the benchmark) are permanent rather than transitory.

Exhibit 6.3 shows how the abnormal earnings approach can be used to assign a value to Willard Brown's truck rental business. You remember Willard? Here's a description of the business opportunity along with some additional information pertinent to the abnormal earnings valuation approach.

Willard Brown is thinking about starting a truck rental business. If you recall, he plans to buy four trucks now, and to then add a fifth truck in two years. Each truck will cost $20,000, and he believes each will generate $5,000 of net operating cash flows every year. At the end of five years, he thinks he can sell the trucks for $30,000 in total.

Additional information:

- Willard will put $80,000 cash into the business. This amount represents his beginning equity.
- The company will pay out all excess cash as dividends each year. The cash needed to buy the last truck in Year 2 will come from operating cash flows that year. No new investment will be required.
- Net income includes truck depreciation and is estimated to be $7,830 in Years 1 and 2, and $9,780 each year in the final three years.
- The $30,000 received for the trucks at the end of five years equals their book value at that point in time. No gain or loss is to be recorded on the sale of the trucks.

If we use the abnormal earnings approach instead of the free cash flow approach to determine the value of Willard's business, how much will it be worth?

The top portion of Exhibit 6.3 describes how the book value of equity is forecasted to change over time. Equity book value is increased by net income for the year and decreased when dividends are paid to shareholders. Notice that Willard's company does not pay a dividend in Year 2. Why? Because the entire $20,000 of operating cash flows generated that year (4 trucks × $5,000 operating cash flow per truck) is needed to buy the fifth and final truck.

Step 1 of Exhibit 6.3 illustrates the computation of expected future abnormal earnings from the truck business. Each year, the beginning book value of equity is multiplied by the rate of return required by investors (10% in this example) to arrive at required or "normal" earnings. For example, the required earnings threshold in Year 1 is $8,000, or $80,000 of initial equity capital multiplied by the 10% required rate of return. The $8,000 of required earnings is then subtracted from the $7,830 of forecasted earnings for the year to arrive at expected abnormal earnings of −$170.

EXHIBIT 6.3	Illustration of the Abnormal Earnings Approach to Valuation

	Year 1	Year 2	Year 3	Year 4	Year 5
Summary earnings and equity book value					
Beginning book value of equity	$80,000	$67,830	$75,660	$60,440	$45,220
Net income for the year (NOPAT)	7,830	7,830	9,780	9,780	9,780
Dividends paid to shareholders	(20,000)	—	(25,000)	(25,000)	(25,000)
Ending book value of equity	$67,830	$75,660	$60,440	$45,220	$30,000

Step 1: Forecast expected future abnormal earnings

	Year 1	Year 2	Year 3	Year 4	Year 5
Expected future earnings (net income)	$ 7,830	$ 7,830	$ 9,780	$ 9,780	$ 9,780
Required ("normal") earnings:					
Beginning equity book value	$80,000	$67,830	$75,660	$60,440	$45,220
Investors required rate of return	10%	10%	10%	10%	10%
Required ("normal") earnings	$ 8,000	$ 6,783	$ 7,566	$ 6,044	$ 4,522
Expected future abnormal earnings	$ (170)	$ 1,047	$ 2,214	$ 3,736	$ 5,258

Step 2: Determine the present value of expected future abnormal earnings

	Year 1	Year 2	Year 3	Year 4	Year 5
Expected future abnormal earnings	$ (170)	$1,047	$2,214	$3,736	$5,258
Present value factor	0.90909	0.82645	0.75131	0.68301	0.62092
Present value of each future abnormal earnings	$ (155)	$ 865	$1,663	$2,552	$3,265

Sum of all present values	$ 8,191
Beginning equity book value	$80,000
Value of business opportunity	$88,191
Value per share	$ 88.19

Step 2 of Exhibit 6.3 then determines the present value of expected future abnormal earnings over the life of the truck rental business (5 years). The discount factors shown are the same ones used in the free cash flow approach described earlier (see Exhibit 6.1). The individual present values are then summed, and this amount ($8,191) is added to the beginning book value of equity ($80,000) to arrive at the estimated value of the truck rental business ($88,191 or $88.19 per share). This is the same value estimate we developed using the free cash flow approach!

Financial statements and related footnotes provide a wealth of information for assessing the relationships expressed by equations (6.11) and (6.12). The balance sheet provides detailed information on the book value of equity (assets minus liabilities). The income statement provides detailed information for assessing a firm's earnings. As you have seen, we can use these numbers from a firm's financial statements to determine its worth via the abnormal earnings approach.

Abnormal Earnings and ROE Return on equity (ROE) combines information about earnings and equity book value—two financial statement items essential to the abnormal earnings valuation approach. A firm's ROE can be compared to its required rate of return on equity (cost of equity capital) or to the ROEs of other companies in the industry to evaluate its prospects for generating "abnormal earnings." Companies with ROEs that consistently exceed the industry average generally will have shares that sell for a premium relative to book value (that is, a higher market-to-book ratio).

Figure 6.4 plots the relationship between the 2002 ROE (measured on the horizontal axis) and the 2002 year-end market-to-book ratio (measured on the vertical axis) for 40 restaurant companies. The upward-sloping line represents the estimated regression line of ROE versus market-to-book ratio for these companies. The regression line has an intercept estimate of 1.09 and a slope coefficient estimate of 0.09. According to the regression line, a restaurant company that earned an ROE of 20% should have a market-to-book ratio of 2.89 (or $1.09 + [0.09 \times 20]$). A market-to-book ratio of 2.89 means that the company's shares sell for a substantial premium of almost three times their equity book value.

Figure 6.4

RELATIONSHIP BETWEEN ROE PERFORMANCE AND MARKET-TO-BOOK (M/B) RATIOS FOR 40 RESTAURANT COMPANIES

Regression Result:

$M/B = 1.09 + 0.09 \text{ ROE}$
$R^2 = 18.4\%$

In making comparisons across firms, the analyst must be careful to gauge the quality and comparability of the accounting policies or methods used. For example, does the company being analyzed tend to select liberal accounting methods (those that may increase earnings and net asset values) or more conservative methods (those that may decrease earnings and net asset values). The degree of conservatism associated with a firm's accounting choices will have a direct bearing on the relationship among share price, earnings, and equity book value components of equation (6.11). To see this, let us consider a company that has a $10 share price and an $8 per share equity book value. Analysts who understand the accounting complexities described later in this book know there are two reasons why this company's stock may be valued at a $2 premium to equity book value. One reason is that shareholders believe the company will produce abnormal earnings in the future, and those future earnings are worth—according to equation (6.11)—$2 today. A second possibility, however, is that stockholders only expect the company to produce "normal" earnings in the future (that is, zero abnormal earnings), but they recognize that the company's conservative accounting methods understate equity book value by $2 per share.[25]

Much of the information needed for assessing the quality and value-relevance of a company's reported accounting numbers appears in footnotes to its financial statements. These footnotes describe accounting policies for such matters as revenue recognition (completed contract versus percentage-of-completion), depreciation (straight-line versus accelerated), and inventory valuation (LIFO versus FIFO). Later chapters will clarify the important differences in these and other accounting methods and their impact on earnings and balance sheet book values. In certain instances, we show how you can adjust reported numbers to put firms that use different methods on a more equal footing before using those numbers for valuation purposes.

---

[25] For a further discussion of these points and the implications of the abnormal earnings valuation model, see G. Feltham and J. Ohlson, "Valuation and Clean Surplus Accounting for Operating and Financial Assets," *Contemporary Accounting Research* (Spring 1995), pp. 689–731; V. Bernard, "The Feltham-Ohlson Framework: Implications for Empiricists," *Contemporary Accounting Research* (Spring 1995), pp. 733–47; Lundholm and Sloan, ibid.; Penman, ibid.; Soffer and Soffer, ibid.; and Stewart, ibid.

> **RECAP**
>
> The abnormal earnings approach to valuation says a company's future earnings are determined by (1) the resources (net assets) available to management; and (2) the rate of return or profitability earned on those net assets. If a firm can earn a return on net assets (equity book value) that *exceeds* its cost of equity capital, then it will generate positive abnormal earnings. Its stock will then sell at a premium relative to book value. However, if the firm earns a return on net assets that falls *below* its cost of equity capital, then it will generate negative abnormal earnings. Its stock will then sell at a discount relative to book value. A key feature of this valuation model is that it explicitly takes into account a cost for the capital (net assets) provided by the owners of the business. Value is added only if the earnings generated from those net assets exceed the equity cost of capital benchmark. Appendix A to this chapter illustrates how to use this valuation model for a real company.

Earnings Surprises

Both the earnings capitalization model (equation [6.4]) and the abnormal earnings model (equation [6.11]) share a common characteristic: Each requires estimates of future earnings. But estimates can (and usually do) prove to be incorrect. When this happens, an "earnings surprise" results.

If securities markets are rational and efficient in the sense that they fully and correctly impound all available information into a companys' stock price, then the price will reflect investors' *unbiased* expectations about the company's future earnings and cash flows. These expectations take into account a vast array of information available to the public, including information about the company's earnings and cash flow history, product market conditions, competitor actions, and other factors. For example, the stock prices of General Motors and Ford incorporate information about unit sales figures published weekly in the financial press, as well as expectations about changes in interest rates, because interest rates influence consumers' car-buying behavior. Stock prices move up or down as investors receive new information and then revise their expectations about the future earnings and cash flow prospects of the company. Financial reports are an important source of information that investors use to update their expectations.

> Unbiased means that, on average, the market's earnings expectations will be correct—not too high or too low.

Consider a typical General Motors' quarterly earnings announcement that is released through major financial wire services. If reported quarterly earnings correspond exactly to the earnings investors expected before the announcement, then the investors have no reason to alter their expectations about GM's future earnings or cash flows. The reported quarterly earnings simply *confirm* the market's expectations. In other words, although the earnings release may resolve market uncertainty about current earnings, it does not provide new information to investors. On the other hand, if reported quarterly earnings deviate from investors' expectations, this **earnings surprise** represents new information that investors will use to revise their expectations about the company's future earnings and cash flow prospects. Of course, this change in investor expectations will cause the company's stock price to change following the earnings announcement.

> Stock price changes can also occur because of unanticipated changes in interest (discount) rates over time.

The way stock prices change in response to new information about earnings can be expressed mathematically as follows:

$$
\underbrace{P_t - P_{t-1}}_{\substack{\text{Price change from} \\ \text{period } t-1 \text{ to } t}} = \underbrace{X_t - E_{t-1}(\tilde{X}_t)}_{\substack{\text{Current earnings} \\ \text{surprise}}} + \underbrace{\sum_{k=1}^{\infty} \frac{\Delta E_t(\tilde{X}_{t+k})}{(1+r)^k}}_{\substack{\text{Change } (\Delta) \text{ in expectations} \\ \text{about future earnings}}} \qquad (6.13)
$$

where:

- $P_t - P_{t-1}$ is the stock price change from just before to just after the earnings announcement;
- $X_t - E_{t-1}(\tilde{X}_t)$ is the earnings "surprise" or deviation of reported earnings from the market's expectation just *before* the earnings announcement; and
- $\displaystyle\sum_{k=1}^{\infty} \frac{\Delta E_t(\tilde{X}_{t+k})}{(1+r)^k}$, the summation term, represents the valuation impact of revised expectations about all future earnings.

The change in stock price from one point in time to another can also be influenced by dividends. Consequently, some versions of equation (6.13) include a dividend term so that the resulting price change (defined as $P_t + D_t - P_{t-1}$) better isolates the impact of new earnings information. A similar (but more complicated) expression for earnings announcement stock price changes can be derived from the abnormal earnings valuation equation (6.10). Until recently, however, most "earnings surprise" research has used variations of equation (6.13).

Figure 6.5 illustrates the typical behavior of stock returns—the price change divided by P_{t-1}—leading up to, and following quarterly earnings announcements for three different scenarios:

1. Reported earnings are viewed as a *"good news"* earnings surprise because they exceed market expectations.
2. Reported earnings contain *"no news"* because they correspond exactly to market expectations.
3. Reported earnings are viewed as a *"bad news"* earnings surprise because they fall below market expectations.[26]

Figure 6.5

STOCK RETURNS AND
QUARTERLY EARNINGS
"SURPRISES"

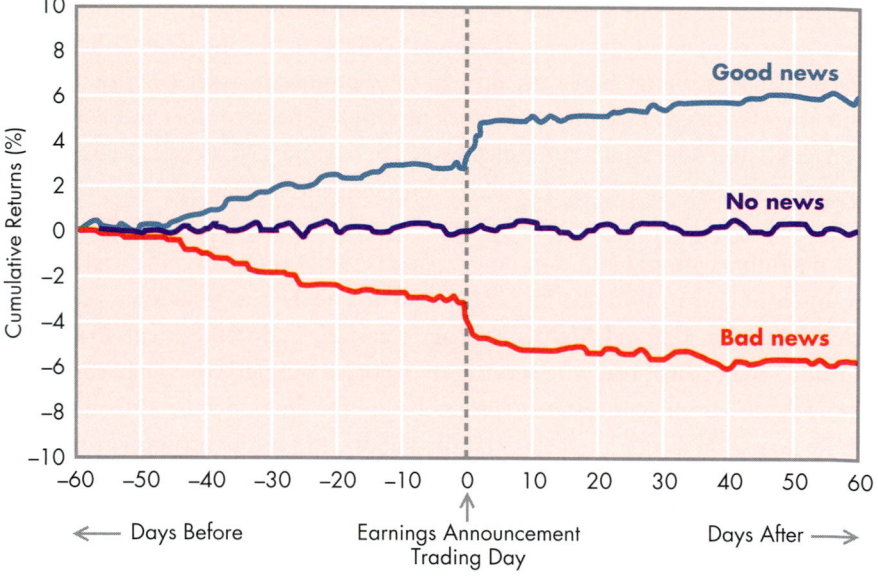

Companies that report good news earnings (a positive earnings surprise) tend to have an upward drift in stock returns before the actual earnings announcement date (day 0 in Figure 6.5), followed by another stock return increase on announcement. The stock returns of companies reporting "bad news" earnings surprises exhibit a negative drift before the announcement, followed by another decrease in stock returns at the announcement date. Modest post-announcement drifts in stock returns are also not uncommon, especially when the earnings

[26] For early research on the association between earnings surprises and stock returns, see R. Ball and P. Brown, "An Empirical Evaluation of Accounting Income Numbers," *Journal of Accounting Research* (Autumn 1968), pp. 159–78; and G. Foster, C. Olsen, and T. Shevlin, "Earnings Releases, Anomalies, and the Behavior of Security Returns," *The Accounting Review* (October 1984), pp. 574–603. Recent research is summarized in S. Kothari, "Capital Market Research in Accounting," *Journal of Accounting and Economics* (September 2001), pp. 105–232.

surprise is quite large.[27] Quarterly earnings announcements that contain "no news" lead to stock returns that hover around zero before and after announcement.

It's easy to explain why stock prices sometimes exhibit a positive or negative drift *before* the actual earnings announcement date. Take the case of General Motors. Investors learn about the company's automobile sales on a weekly basis and therefore can anticipate fairly well the actual quarterly earnings number prior to its formal announcement by GM. The fact that GM's stock price changes at the announcement date indicates that not all the information contained in the earnings release is fully anticipated by investors. Small companies—and those followed by just a few securities analysts—tend to exhibit less pre-announcement stock return drift because investors usually have very limited information about the company and its earnings prospects for the quarter. Large companies, whose performance is tracked by many analysts, are more likely to exhibit the pre-announcement stock return behavior illustrated in Figure 6.5.

RECAP

A company's stock price at any given point in time reflects investors' aggregate expectations about the company's future earnings. Information that changes investors' expectations about future earnings will cause the stock price to rise or fall depending on whether the information represents "good news" or "bad news." Research evidence demonstrates that quarterly and annual earnings announcements are important information events. Stock prices tend to increase (or decrease) when the reported earnings turn out to be greater (or less) than expected. The degree of the surprise conveyed by an earnings announcement depends on the amount of pre-earnings announcement information provided by the financial press.

Valuing a Business Opportunity (An Illustration)

Allen Ford's passion for literature motivated him to consider opening a neighborhood bookstore. Allen convinced a colleague who was an expert in market research to look at the economic viability of a general title bookstore. The results of his analysis fueled Allen's enthusiasm: The market demographics were favorable, and there was little competition. Annual sales were projected to ultimately reach $350,000.

Allen rejected the notion of opening his own independent bookstore, however, and instead focused on several franchise opportunities. By affiliating with a national or regional company, Allen would enjoy brand-name recognition, economies of scale in purchasing and advertising, and employee training and support programs. After investigating several possibilities, Allen settled on "The BookWorm," an expanding regional chain of franchised bookstores that emphasized convenience, price, selection, and neighborhood friendliness. Each store had a coffee bar surrounded by soft seating. Abundant natural light encouraged patrons to browse leisurely. The franchise had a proven record of success in similar communities, and it appealed to Allen's tastes.

Allen learned that a BookWorm store could be established for about $100,000, including the initial franchise fee of $21,000, store fixtures of $20,000 to $25,000, and an inventory cost of $55,000 to $60,000. The inventory and fixtures would be purchased from the corporate parent,

---

[27] A number of studies investigate whether post-earnings announcement drift provides opportunities to earn abnormal returns in the stock market. For a review of this literature, see V. Bernard, "Stock Price Reactions to Earnings Announcements: A Summary of Recent Anomalous Evidence and Possible Explanations," in R. Thaler (ed.), *Advances in Behavioral Finance* (New York: Russell Sage Foundation, 1992); and V. Bernard, J. Thomas, and J. Abarbanell, "How Sophisticated Is the Market in Interpreting Earnings News," *Journal of Applied Corporate Finance* (Summer 1993), pp. 54–63.

BookWorm, Inc. Corporate staff would conduct a site location study, assist in negotiating lease terms for retail space, help with store layout and renovation, train employees on operating policies and procedures, and provide all grand opening advertising and promotional materials. Once a new BookWorm franchise opened, the corporate parent received royalties (typically as a percentage of sales) determined in accordance with a 15-year renewable franchise contract.

The prospectus that Allen obtained from the parent company contained the selected financial highlights for a typical BookWorm franchise store shown in Exhibit 6.4. The notes accompanying the exhibit indicated that store fixtures are depreciated over 10 years; that the initial franchise fee is amortized over 15 years; that operating expenses include a competitive salary for a store manager; and that income taxes have been ignored because they are owner-specific, thus making them highly variable across locations.

EXHIBIT 6.4	BookWorm Franchise				

Projected Sales, Earnings, Free Cash Flows, and Owner's Investment

	Year 1	Year 2	Year 3	Year 4	Year 5
Sales	$200,000	$250,000	$300,000	$325,000	$350,000
Franchise royalty (5%)	10,000	12,500	15,000	16,250	17,500
Pre-tax earnings	(6,832)	3,600	13,750	22,000	26,000
Free cash flows*	(3,000)	5,500	15,000	16,000	24,500
Assets at year-end	100,000	100,000	100,000	100,000	100,000
Owner's investment:					
Beginning of year	100,000	100,000	100,000	100,000	100,000
+ Pre-tax earnings	(6,832)	3,600	13,750	22,000	26,000
− Distribution to owner	6,832	(3,600)	(13,750)	(22,000)	(26,000)
= End of year	$100,000	$100,000	$100,000	$100,000	$100,000

*Free cash flows are cash from operations minus required capital expenditures.

With these financial projections and his understanding of the marketplace, Allen Ford had to decide whether to invest $100,000 in a BookWorm franchise. Influencing the decision were several nonfinancial considerations, like his confidence in BookWorm's corporate staff or the proposed interior design and ambiance of the shop. However, viewed through the stark lens of economics, Allen's decision problem simplifies to the standard **net present value rule**—invest if the estimated value of the franchise (adjusted for the risk of investment) exceeds its $100,000 cost. From trade sources, Allen learned that 16% was a reasonable estimate of the cost of equity capital for franchised neighborhood bookstores. Allen used two different approaches to estimate the value of the bookstore, relying on predictions contained in the **pro forma**, or forecasted, financial statements whenever possible.

The first approach, based on expected future *free cash flows*, is summarized in Exhibit 6.5. Sales and free cash flow projections for Years 1 through 5 are taken directly from the pro forma financial statement data in Exhibit 6.4. Allen believes that sales will remain flat after Year 5 and that free cash flows will average about $24,500 per year thereafter. These assumptions produce a Year 5 **terminal value** estimate of $153,125—that is, the present value (at the end of Year 5) of the perpetual $24,500 free cash flow per year, discounted at a 16% cost of equity capital.

When the terminal value at the end of Year 5 is discounted back to the present (beginning of Year 1) and added to the sum of the present value of expected free cash flows for Year 1 through Year 5, the result is a free cash flow value estimate for the bookstore of $104,517, as shown in Exhibit 6.5. This amount is *greater* than Allen's required capital investment of $100,000—this means Allen will be earning a return in excess of 16% per year on his investment *if* he opens the bookstore and the financial projections underlying the valuation estimate prove correct.

EXHIBIT 6.5	BookWorm Franchise

Valuation of Expected Future Cash Flows

	Year 1	Year 2	Year 3	Year 4	Year 5	Beyond Year 5
(a) Financial Projections						
Sales	$200,000	$250,000	$300,000	$325,000	$350,000	$350,000
Free cash flows	$ (3,000)	$ 5,500	$ 15,000	$ 16,000	$ 24,500	$ 24,500
As a percentage of sales	−1.5%	2.2%	5.0%	4.9%	7.0%	7.0%
					Estimated terminal value = $24,500/0.16	
(b) Valuation Estimate at 16%						
Expected future cash flow	$ (3,000)	$ 5,500	$ 15,000	$ 16,000	$ 24,500	$153,125*
× Discount factor at 16%	0.86207	0.74316	0.64066	0.55229	0.47611	0.47611
= Present value of each flow	$ (2,586)	$ 4,087	$ 9,610	$ 8,837	$ 11,665	$ 72,904
(c) Estimated Value (sum of all present values above)	$104,517					

*Rounded

A second approach for estimating the value of Allen's business opportunity relies on expected future *abnormal earnings*—the amount by which operating earnings each year exceed the dollar cost of capital for the bookstore. This valuation, also based on projections contained in the pro forma financial statements, is summarized in Exhibit 6.6. In addition to flat sales and free cash flow here in Year 5, Allen is projecting flat pre-tax earnings of $25,000 for each year beyond Year 5.

EXHIBIT 6.6	BookWorm Franchise

Valuation of Expected Abnormal Earnings

	Year 1	Year 2	Year 3	Year 4	Year 5	Beyond Year 5
(a) Computation of Abnormal Earnings						
Equity book value (beginning of year)	$100,000	$100,000	$100,000	$100,000	$100,000	$100,000
× Cost of equity capital = 16%	0.16	0.16	0.16	0.16	0.16	0.16
= Normal earnings	$ 16,000	$ 16,000	$ 16,000	$ 16,000	$ 16,000	$ 16,000
Projected pre-tax earnings (loss)	$ (6,832)	$ 3,600	$ 13,750	$ 22,000	$ 26,000	$ 25,000
× Normal earnings	(16,000)	(16,000)	(16,000)	(16,000)	(16,000)	(16,000)
= Abnormal earnings (loss)	$ (22,832)	$ (12,400)	$ (2,250)	$ 6,000	$ 10,000	$ 9,000
(b) Valuation Estimate at 16%						
					Estimated terminal value = $9,000/0.16	
Expected abnormal earnings (loss)	$ (22,832)	$ (12,400)	$ (2,250)	$ 6,000	$ 10,000	$ 56,250
× Discount factor at 16%	0.86207	0.74316	0.64066	0.55229	0.47611	0.47611
= Present value of each abnormal earnings flow	$ (19,683)	$ (9,215)	$ (1,441)	$ 3,314	$ 4,761	$ 26,781
(c) Estimated Value						
Sum of all present values	$ 4,517					
Capital to start the business	100,000					
Estimated value	$104,517					

Before investing, Allen should perform a **sensitivity analysis** of the free cash flow and abnormal earnings valuation estimates. Sensitivity analysis involves constructing "best case" and "worst case" scenarios for the business that incorporate alternative assumptions about sales, costs, and competitor behavior. Each scenario produces financial forecasts that become the basis for revised free cash flow and abnormal earnings valuation estimates. In this way Allen could learn how alternative economic conditions might affect the bookstore's value and his return on investment.

Part (a) of Exhibit 6.6 describes the calculation of yearly abnormal earnings. First, the 16% "Cost of equity capital" is multiplied by the beginning book value of equity to produce a figure called **"Normal earnings"** in each year. The component "Normal earnings" is the profit level that investors (including Allen) demand from the business in order to earn their 16% per year required rate of return. Then "Normal earnings" is subtracted from "Projected pre-tax earnings" to produce an estimate of expected "Abnormal earnings" for each year.

In part (b), the Beyond Year 5 "Terminal value" estimate of $56,250 represents the present value (at the end of Year 5) of the perpetual $9,000 per year abnormal earnings flow from Year 6 to infinity, discounted at a 16% cost of equity capital. The present value (as of the beginning of Year 1) of all abnormal earnings sums to $4,517. This amount, when added to the $100,000 of capital required to start the business, yields a valuation estimate for the bookstore of $104,517. Once again, the analysis supports opening the bookstore.

Cash Flow Analysis and Credit Risk

Equity investors analyze financial statements to determine the value of a firm's shares. Creditors, on the other hand, are primarily concerned with assessing a firm's ability to meet its debt obligations through timely payment of principal and interest. Commercial banks, insurance companies, pension funds, and other lenders form opinions about a company's **credit risk** by comparing current and future debt-service requirements to estimates of the company's current and expected future cash flows.

Financing the BookWorm Franchise
After careful review, Allen Ford decided to purchase a BookWorm franchise. The evaluation process was lengthy. It included interviews with 10 current franchise owners. These interviews helped Allen gain a deeper understanding of the business and its key risks and success factors. He was able to identify several proven marketing and promotion strategies for launching the franchise. With this information and an assessment of local market conditions, Allen refined the financial projections supplied by the parent company, BookWorm, Inc., performed a valuation analysis, and concluded that the franchise was likely to earn an acceptable risk-adjusted rate of return over time. There was still one hurdle—financing a portion of the $100,000 franchise purchase price.

Allen needed a bank loan for two reasons. First, Allen's personal investment portfolio was worth only $50,000. Second, Allen's interviews with other franchise owners revealed that a $100,000 initial investment might not provide an adequate cash cushion during the first year of operation.

Allen described the business opportunity to a local banker and said his cash needs would be in the $50,000 to $100,000 range. The banker said a loan of this size would not be a problem since ample funds were currently available at attractive interest rates. Allen was asked to complete a detailed loan application, including a personal credit history and business plan, and to prepare monthly earnings and cash flow projections for the first two years of franchise operations. Filled with optimism, Allen began assembling the financial and other information required and thinking about the kind of loan he would request from the bank.

Traditional Lending Products

Commercial bank loans are a common source of cash for most companies today. These loans can be structured either as short-term or long-term, fixed or floating rate, payable on demand or with fixed maturity, and secured or unsecured.

Short-term Loans Loans with maturities of one year or less, called short-term loans, comprise more than half of all commercial bank loans. **Seasonal lines of credit** and special-purpose loans are the most common short-term borrowing. Short-term loans are used primarily to finance working capital needs when inventory or receivables increase temporarily. They may be **secured** by the inventories or receivables themselves, or they may be **unsecured**. Loan repayment usually comes from the routine conversion of these current assets into cash.

Long-term Loans Called **term lending agreements**, long-term loans have a maturity of more than one year, with maturities ranging from two to five years being the most common. The principal and interest repayment schedule, along with other conditions of the loan, are detailed in a signed contractual agreement between the borrower and the bank. Term loans are often used to finance the purchase of fixed assets, the acquisition of another company, the refinancing of existing long-term debt, or permanent working capital needs. They are frequently secured by pledging the assets acquired with the loan proceeds, although lenders rarely look to asset liquidation as the primary source of funds for loan repayment. Scheduled principal and interest payments are generally presumed to come from the borrower's future operating cash flows.

> Seasonal lines of credit are commonly used by companies with sales cycles that are also seasonal (e.g., lawn and garden equipment retailers). These loans provide the cash to support increases in current assets during the peak selling period. The borrower draws on the seasonal credit line as funds are required and later repays as seasonal sales produce net cash inflows. **Special-purpose business loans** are often used to finance, on a temporary basis, increases in current assets resulting from unusual or unexpected circumstances.

Revolving Loans Revolving loans are a variation on the seasonal credit line. They allow borrowing up to a maximum level at any time over the life (usually more than one year) of the loan commitment. Revolving loans are often used to finance cash imbalances that arise in day-to-day operations, seasonal needs, or permanent working capital needs when normal trade credit is inadequate to support a company's sales volume. Borrowers can *prepay* the revolving loan and later re-borrow those funds, but they must comply with the terms and conditions specified in the loan agreement. The interest rate on the revolving line of credit is usually the bank's prime lending rate plus an additional percentage, and the rate will usually change (or "float") as the prime rate rises or falls over the life of the credit line. In addition to interest, the borrower pays a "commitment fee" that is based on the total amount of the credit extended.

Commercial banks are not the only source of debt financing for businesses. Another source of financing is **commercial paper**—short-term notes sold directly to investors by large and financially sound companies. These notes usually mature in 270 days or less and carry a fixed interest rate. Because commercial paper is issued directly to institutional investors (like insurance companies) and is usually secured by a bank credit line, the interest rate the borrowing company pays is often significantly below the rate a bank would charge for a comparable direct loan.

> The word **bond** is commonly used to refer to all kinds of secured and unsecured debt although, strictly speaking, a bond is a secured debt. A **debenture** is an *unsecured* bond, one in which no specific pledge of property is made, although the debenture holder does have a claim on property not otherwise pledged as collateral or security. The term **note** is generally used for unsecured debt instruments issued with a maturity of 10 years or less.

Public Debt Long-term forms of public debt financing include bonds, debentures, or notes. Long-term debt securities are promises made by the issuing company to pay principal when due and to make timely interest payments on the unpaid balance. Bonds can have numerous special features. For example, **secured bonds** specify collateral that protects the bondholder if and when the borrower defaults. Other bonds contain **seniority** features that specify which bondholders will be paid first in the event of bankruptcy. Some may contain **sinking fund provisions** that require the borrowing company to make annual payments to a trustee (usually a bank), who then uses the funds to retire a portion of the debt prior to its maturity. Still others may contain **call provisions**, which allow the borrowing company to "call" (meaning repurchase) part or all of the debt at stated prices over a specific period.

Regardless of the special features attached, virtually all bonds or notes contain numerous **protective covenants** designed to protect the interests of the lender. These covenants place restrictions on the borrower's activity and are described in the **indenture**, a written agreement between the borrowing company and its lenders. The role that accounting numbers play in these debt covenants is described in Chapter 7.

Credit Analysis

To lend funds to a company, a commercial loan officer of a bank must first evaluate the prospective borrower's ability to repay the proposed loan at maturity. This evaluation typically involves financial analysis and includes the preparation of forecasted financial statements, "due diligence" (a qualitative assessment of the business, its customers and suppliers, and management's character and capability), and analysis of credit risk.

Financial analysis of a potential borrower begins with an understanding of the firm, its business, its key risks and success factors, and the competitive dynamics of the industry. Next, an evaluation of the quality of its accounting earnings and financial reporting choices is made to determine whether traditional ratios and statistics derived from the financial statements can be relied on to measure accurately the company's economic performance and financial condition. However, lenders and credit analysts will frequently adjust a company's reported financial statement numbers. For example, nonrecurring gains and losses and other transitory components of earnings are removed from the reported bottom-line earnings number to arrive at a measure of operating performance that is more representative of a firm's long-run sustainable profitability. Off-balance sheet obligations (such as operating lease commitments) are frequently added to a firm's reported debt. Finally, other adjustments are made to improve the comparability of the financial data across potential loan candidates.

The next step is evaluating the company's profit performance and balance sheet strength. Financial, operating, and leverage ratios (discussed in Chapter 5) as well as trends in revenues and expenses are examined and compared to industry averages. This phase of the analysis identifies positive and negative changes in the prospective borrower's profitability, financial health, and industry position. However, the historical performance and condition of the borrower is only a partial indication of creditworthiness. Loan approval is largely determined by the borrower's ability to repay the proposed loan from *future* operating cash flows. ***Consequently, an estimate of the company's future financial condition is indispensable to most lending decisions.*** Analysts accomplish this assessment by constructing pro forma financial statement projections (forecasts) of borrower cash flows.

> Appendix B shows how you can construct pro forma financial statement projections.

Pro forma, or "as if," financial statement projections are prepared by the credit analyst to assess the borrower's ability to generate sufficient cash flows to make interest and principal payments when due. These projections incorporate the analyst's understanding of the company's plans and business strategy, the likely responses of rival companies, and other factors that shape the prospective borrower's economic environment. The pro forma financial statements and their underlying assumptions are then tested to establish the borrower's vulnerability to changing economic circumstances. This testing involves examining plausible "worst-case" scenarios that indicate just how poorly the company can perform before it defaults. This enables the analyst to gauge the company's **financial flexibility**—that is, the degree to which the company can satisfy its cash needs during periods of fiscal stress by drawing on existing credit lines, accessing financial markets, curtailing discretionary cash expenditures, or selling assets.

A **due diligence** evaluation is like "kicking the tires" of the prospective borrower. The analyst does a due diligence evaluation by conducting plant tours, trade checks, and interviews with competitors, suppliers, customers, and employees. Comprehensive due diligence may also include asset appraisals, reviews of the company's other debt obligations, internal controls, planned capital expenditures, potential environmental liabilities, and other matters that bear on the company's future success and ability to repay debt at maturity.

The final step of credit analysis is a **comprehensive risk assessment** that involves evaluating and summarizing the various individual risks associated with the loan. Some risks will be unique to the specific borrower (for example, a pharmaceutical company may run the risk that a new drug it has developed may ultimately prove ineffective during clinical test trials); other risks will be associated with potential changes in the economy or industry, new regulations, or unanticipated events. The credit analyst evaluates the severity of each risk in terms of (1) its probability of occurrence, (2) how it could affect the borrower's ability or willingness to repay, and (3) the bank's estimated costs if the borrower defaults.

If the prospective borrower is judged to be creditworthy, the final terms and conditions of the loan are negotiated with the borrower. Obviously, a lender is compensated for *anticipated* credit risks by the interest rate it charges on the loan. The interest rate must be sufficient to cover the lender's (1) cost of borrowing funds; (2) costs of administering, monitoring, and servicing the loan; (3) normal (competitive) return on the capital needed to support the bank's lending operations; and (4) premium for exposure to default risk. Collateralized loans or loans with personal guarantees lower credit risk and enable lenders to lower the borrower's cost of debt.

> Credit evaluations performed by rating agencies such as Standard & Poor's or Moody's involve procedural steps similar to those described here for commercial bank loans. Ratings are assigned to long-term debt, medium-term notes, and commercial paper based on analysts' evaluation of (1) the likelihood of default, (2) the nature and provisions of the debt, and (3) the protection afforded debtholders in the event of bankruptcy. See *Corporate Finance Criteria* (New York: Standard & Poor's, 1994).

Interpretation of Cash Flow Components

Although a company's earnings are important, an analysis of its cash flows is central to all credit evaluations and lending decisions. This is because a company's earnings include many noncash accruals like accounts receivable. Obviously, a company cannot make interest and principal payments with its accounts receivable. Rather, the company must pay its lenders with hard, cold cash!

Consider the situation confronting your client, G. T. Wilson Company. Wilson Company has been a client of your bank for over 40 years. The company owns and operates nearly 850 retail furniture stores throughout the United States and has over 38,000 employees. Sales and earnings growth have exceeded the industry average until recently, and the company has paid dividends consistently for almost 100 years. Prior to 1997 Wilson built its reputation on sales of moderately priced upholstered furniture, case goods (wooden tables, chairs, and bookcases), and decorative accessories. The company's stores were located in large urban centers where occupancy costs were quite low. Increased competition and changing consumer tastes caused Wilson to alter its strategy beginning in 1997. One aspect of this strategic shift involved expanding the company's product line to include higher quality furniture, consumer electronics, and home entertainment systems. To complement its expanded product line, Wilson also introduced a credit card system so that customers could more easily pay for their purchases. Wilson used commercial paper, bank loans, and trade credit to finance the growth of receivables and inventories. The company's strategy also focused on closing unprofitable downtown stores; at the same time it chose to expand by opening new stores in suburban shopping centers.

Your bank has extended two loans to Wilson, a $50 million secured construction loan that matures in 2009, and a $200 million revolving credit line that is currently up for renewal. Wilson has always complied with the terms of the revolving line of credit, but the company's borrowing has been at or near the maximum amount allowed for the past two years. Exhibit 6.7 presents comparative cash flow statements for the company and Exhibit 6.8 reports selected financial statistics. What do these cash flow statements and summary statistics tell us about the company's credit risk?

EXHIBIT 6.7	G. T. Wilson Company

Comparative Statements of Cash Flow

($ in thousands)	1997	1998	1999	2000	2001	2002	2003	2004	2005
Operating:									
Net income	$ 31,600	$ 33,000	$ 38,200	$ 41,900	$ 36,400	$ 31,600	$ 34,950	$ 10,900	$(145,400)
Depreciation	7,500	8,200	8,400	9,000	9,600	10,600	12,000	13,600	14,600
Other adjustments to income	70	(850)	(1,100)	(1,600)	(2,500)	(1,800)	(1,700)	(1,350)	(17,000)
(Increase) Decrease in receivables	(57,700)	(42,000)	(40,300)	(55,500)	(12,000)	(49,900)	(60,300)	(72,200)	9,600
(Increase) in inventories	(23,300)	(9,100)	(24,900)	(13,500)	(38,400)	(38,200)	(100,850)	(51,100)	(4,350)
(Increase) Decrease in prepayments	(450)	100	(400)	(650)	(200)	(150)	(1,250)	(650)	700
Increase (Decrease) in accounts payable	17,600	3,800	22,400	2,050	13,900	6,900	(12,100)	(8,000)	42,400
Increase (Decrease) in other current liabilities	8,100	11,900	8,500	15,400	(21,900)	13,900	14,950	15,650	(1,500)
Cash flow from operations	$ (16,580)	$ 5,050	$ 10,800	$ (2,900)	$ (15,100)	$ (27,050)	$(114,300)	$ (93,150)	$(100,950)
Investing:									
Acquisition of property, plant and equipment	(15,250)	(7,800)	(10,600)	(14,400)	(16,100)	(25,900)	(26,250)	(23,150)	(15,500)
Acquisition of investments	(250)	(400)	—	—	(450)	(6,000)	(2,200)	(5,700)	(5,300)
Cash flow from investing	$ (15,500)	$ (8,200)	$ (10,600)	$ (14,400)	$ (16,550)	$ (31,900)	$ (28,450)	$ (28,850)	$ (20,800)
Financing:									
Increase (Decrease) in short-term borrowing	60,300	1,600	18,900	64,000	64,300	(8,650)	152,300	63,050	147,600
Increase (Decrease) in long-term borrowing	—	(1,500)	(1,500)	(1,650)	(1,500)	98,450	(1,600)	93,900	(4,000)
Increase (Decrease) in capital stock	2,700	4,000	850	(17,900)	(8,900)	7,400	(8,200)	1,800	850
Dividends	(14,100)	(14,400)	(17,700)	(19,700)	(20,800)	(21,100)	(21,150)	(21,100)	(4,500)
Cash flow from financing	$ 48,900	$ (10,300)	$ 550	$ 24,750	$ 33,100	$ 76,100	$ 121,350	$137,650	$ 139,950
Other	(450)	(400)	(100)	—	(400)	(1,350)	2,450	(650)	(700)
Change in cash	$ 16,370	$ (13,850)	$ 650	$ 7,450	$ 1,050	$ 15,800	$ (18,950)	$ 15,000	$ 17,500

Cash Flow From Operations A company's "cash flow from operations" is the amount of cash it is able to generate from ongoing core business activities. Generating cash from operations is essential to the long-term economic viability of the business. However, not every company can be expected to produce positive operating cash flows every year. Even financially healthy companies must sometimes spend more cash on their operating activities than they receive from customers.

EXHIBIT 6.8	G. T. Wilson Company

Selected Financial Statistics

	Years Ended January 31								
	1997	1998	1999	2000	2001	2002	2003	2004	2005
Operations:									
Sales ($ millions)	$920	$980	$1,095	$1,210	$1,250	$1,375	$1,665	$1,850	$1,762
Number of new stores (net of closures)	4	6	13	21	52	40	37	41	21
Gross profit/sales	31.8%	32.1%	32.8%	33.0%	36.5%	35.8%	35.3%	35.1%	30.1%
Selling, general, and administrative/sales	24.8%	25.1%	25.2%	25.2%	29.9%	30.7%	30.6%	30.4%	41.3%
Net income/sales	3.4%	3.4%	3.5%	3.5%	2.9%	2.3%	2.1%	0.6%	−8.3%
Dividends/net income	44.6%	43.6%	46.3%	47.0%	57.1%	66.8%	60.5%	193.6%	−3.1%
Short-term Liquidity:									
Current assets/current liabilities	3.7	3.6	3.3	3.4	3.7	4.6	4.5	5.0	6.2
Operating cash flows as a % of sales	−1.8%	0.5%	1.0%	−0.2%	−1.2%	−2.0%	−6.9%	−5.0%	−5.7%
Days receivable	91.3	95.3	104.1	115.1	126.2	131.1	130.5	140.0	142.5
Allowance for uncollectibles (%)	3.8%	4.1%	3.8%	4.0%	3.6%	3.2%	2.8%	3.0%	3.3%
Days inventory	100.9	100.2	102.7	104.3	112.8	117.1	129.6	131.2	130.5
Days payable	42.4	42.5	48.6	45.7	48.9	47.1	33.6	30.7	42.6
Long-term Solvency:									
Total debt as a % of assets	32.7%	29.3%	25.9%	30.8%	37.3%	41.8%	49.8%	56.4%	75.7%
Interest coverage	8.8	8.1	8.7	6.4	4.7	4.5	3.9	1.2	(2.4)
Short-term debt as a % of total debt	33.3%	46.5%	59.4%	70.8%	81.6%	64.0%	75.8%	70.0%	78.3%

The comparative cash flow statements in Exhibit 6.7 show that Wilson produced positive operating cash flows in 1998 and 1999. Since then, its operating cash flows have been consistently negative and declining, with the average level for the last three years approximately equal to *minus* $100 million. This sharply contrasts with the company's sales and earnings performance as shown in Exhibit 6.8. Sales have grown steadily from $920 million in 1997 to $1.85 billion in 2004, with a small decline in 2005. Net income (shown in Exhibit 6.7) increased from $31.6 million in 1997 to a peak of $41.9 million in 2000, followed by three years of relative stability where earnings averaged about $33 million each year. Net income declined in 2004 to $10.9 million, and the company reported a $145.4 million loss in 2005.

What aspects of Wilson's operations consumed cash during the company's profitable years? Exhibit 6.7 shows that the primary factors contributing to the company's negative operating cash flows were increases in accounts receivable and increases in inventories. Some growth in receivables and inventories is to be expected because of the company's decision to expand its product line and to introduce a customer credit card. However, increases in receivables or inventories can sometimes signal unfavorable business conditions. For example, the average collection period for customer accounts (days receivables in Exhibit 6.8) increased from 91.3 days in 1997 to 142.5

days in 2005. This trend could reflect expanded credit card use, more lenient credit policies toward customers, or a deterioration in customers' ability to pay. Similarly, the increase in days inventory (Exhibit 6.8) from 100.9 in 1997 to 130.5 in 2005 could be due to product-line extensions, escalating merchandise costs, or slack consumer demand. The credit analyst must evaluate each possible explanation to discover what economic forces are responsible for the company's negative operating cash flows and whether positive cash flows from operating activities are likely to be generated in the future.

> It is interesting to note that Wilson's allowance for uncollectibles actually declined in percentage terms after 2000 (Exhibit 6.8) even though the average collection period increased. So, bad debt expense accruals apparently fell.

A business like G. T. Wilson that spends more cash on its operating activities than it generates must find ways to finance the operating cash shortfall. Typically, this means using up cash reserves, borrowing additional cash, issuing additional equity, or liquidating investments like real estate and other fixed assets. None of these options can be sustained for prolonged periods of time. For example, Wilson could finance the company's continued operating cash flow deficit by selling some retail stores. Doing this might jeopardize the company's ability to generate positive operating cash flows in the future. Similarly, creditors are unlikely to keep lending to a business that continuously fails to generate an acceptable level of cash flow from its operations. In this regard, Wilson's inability to generate positive operating cash flows in recent years is troublesome.

Investing Activities   In this section of the cash flow statement, companies disclose capital expenditures, acquisitions of other firms, and investments in marketable securities. Of course, disinvestment generates cash (examples include the sale of buildings, equipment, or investment securities).

The cash flow statements of Wilson Company (Exhibit 6.7) show sustained investment in property, plant, and equipment that is consistent with the company's expansion into new stores (Exhibit 6.8). Analysts should carefully investigate the capital expenditures of the company and any fixed asset retirements during the year. Capital expenditures and asset sales should be consistent with the company's business strategy and growth opportunities. For example, consider the following scenarios.

- *Emerging companies* require substantial investments in property, plant, and equipment at a stage when operating cash flows are typically negative.
- *Established growth companies* also require substantial fixed asset investments to further expand their market presence. Operating cash flows for established growth companies can be positive or negative depending on the pace of expansion, the degree to which expansion also requires working capital investment, and the ability of the company to generate a positive operating cash flow from markets in which it is established.
- *Mature companies'* capital expenditures, on the other hand, are limited to the amount needed to sustain current levels of operation. Mature companies usually rely on internal sources (operating cash flows and fixed asset sales) to finance their capital expenditure needs.

Consequently, changes in a company's capital expenditures or fixed asset sales over time must be carefully analyzed. For example, a sharp reduction in capital expenditures for an emerging growth company may indicate that the company is suffering from a temporary cash shortage. Decreased capital expenditures may also signal a more fundamental change in management's expectations about the company's growth opportunities and its competitive environment. Similarly, an unexplained increase in fixed asset sales could mean that management needs to raise cash quickly or that it is eliminating excess production capacity. The analyst needs to evaluate each of these possibilities because they have very different implications for the company's future operating cash flows.

Financing Activities   The most significant source of external financing for most companies is debt. A large amount of research has been conducted that explores the "optimal" amount of debt financing companies should include in their capital structure. Determining this optimal debt level involves a trade-off between two competing economic forces—taxes and bankruptcy costs.[28] The

---

[28] See Ross, Westerfield, and Jaffe, op. cit., Chapter 16. These and other authors identify a third economic force that influences firms' capital structure decisions—that is, agency costs. These costs are considered in more detail in Chapter 7.

advantage of debt financing is that interest on debt is tax deductible. The disadvantage is that highly leveraged firms have a greater risk of bankruptcy. The precise point at which these two forces counterbalance one another varies from company to company and over time. One way analysts can assess the optimal level of debt is to evaluate the company's historical and estimated future ability to meet scheduled debt payments. In this regard the situation at G. T. Wilson Company would appear bleak.

The financing section of Wilson's cash flow statements (Exhibit 6.7) reveals a heavy reliance on short-term debt to finance the company's capital expenditures and operating cash flow deficits. The company issued $98.45 million of long-term debt in 2002 and $93.9 million in 2004. But the vast majority of Wilson's external financing has been in the form of short-term debt. Total debt as a percentage of assets (Exhibit 6.8) has grown from 32.7% in 1997 to 75.7% in 2005; short-term debt as a percentage of total debt has increased from 33.3% in 1997 to 78.3% in 2005, and the company's interest coverage ratio has deteriorated from 8.8 times to *minus* 2.4 times.

Wilson's cash flow needs and growing debt burden raise questions about the wisdom of its dividend policy. Recall that Wilson has paid cash dividends to shareholders for almost 100 years, and it continued to do so during 2005 when the company reported a $145.4 million loss. Cash dividend payments totaled $14.1 million in 1997, grew to $20.8 million in 2001, and then held steady at that level until falling to $4.5 million in 2005. These cash flows could instead have been used to finance the company's operating deficits and capital expenditures—or to pay down debt.

Why was management so reluctant to curtail dividends? The payment of a cash dividend is viewed as an important signal by many financial analysts and investors. Management presumably "signals" its expectations about the future through its dividend policy. A cash dividend increase is viewed as an indication that management expects future operating cash flows to be favorable—to the extent it can sustain the higher dividend. A reduction in cash dividends is interpreted as an indication that management expects future operating cash flows to decrease and remain at this decreased level. Research tends to corroborate dividend signaling. Increases and decreases in cash dividend payments are (on average) associated with subsequent earnings and operating cash flow changes in the same direction. Of course, the degree of association between dividend changes and future earnings or operating cash flow performance is less than perfect. So, financial analysts and investors must evaluate carefully the specific circumstances confronting each company.

RECOMMENDATION Wilson's use of short-term debt financing, coupled with its inability to generate positive cash flows from operations, places the company in a precarious position. Unless other external sources of financing are identified or unless operating activities start to generate positive cash flows, the company will be forced to declare bankruptcy if (and when) short-term creditors demand payment on existing loans. Wilson Company is a serious credit risk to the bank, and renewal of the $200 million revolving credit line is probably not justified. In fact, the bank may consider taking immediate steps to improve the likelihood of loan repayment and to protect its creditor position in the event of bankruptcy.

This illustration is based loosely on the financial statements of a real company, W. T. Grant for the years 1967 through 1975. At the time that it filed for bankruptcy in late 1975, Grant was the seventeenth largest retailer in the United States. The company's collapse has been traced to a failed business strategy that involved rapid store expansion, product-line extensions, and customer credit terms that contributed to delayed payment and increased customer default risk.*

*See J. Largay and C. Stickney, "Cash Flows, Ratio Analysis and the W. T. Grant Company Bankruptcy," *Financial Analysts Journal* (July–August, 1980), pp. 51–84.

RECAP

Timing differences between cash inflows and cash outflows create the need to borrow money. Cash flow analysis helps lenders identify why cash flow imbalances occur and whether the imbalance is temporary. Commercial banks, insurance companies, pension funds, and other lenders will lend the needed cash only if there is a high probability that the borrower's future cash inflows will be sufficient to repay the loan. Credit analysts rely on their understanding of the company, its business strategy and the competitive environment, and the adequacy of its past cash flows as a basis for forecasting future cash flows and assessing the company's financial flexibility under stress.

SUMMARY

In *Concepts Statement No. 1*, the FASB sets forth the primary objectives of financial reporting. One of those objectives states:

> Financial reporting should provide information to help present and potential investors and creditors and others in assessing the amounts, timing and uncertainty of prospective cash receipts from dividends or interest and the proceeds from the sale, redemption, or maturity of securities or loans. Since investors' and creditors' cash flows are related to enterprise cash flows, financial reporting should provide information to help investors, creditors, and others assess the amounts, timing, and uncertainty of prospective net cash inflows to the related enterprise.[29]

- This chapter provides a framework for understanding how financial reporting meets this important objective.
- Specifically, we show how accounting numbers are used in valuation, cash flow analysis, and credit risk assessment, and then illustrate what it means to "assess the amounts, timing, and uncertainty of prospective net cash inflows" of a business.
- A critical part of understanding the **decision-usefulness** of accounting information—a major focus of this book—is understanding *which* accounting numbers are used, *why* they are used, and *how* they are used in investment and credit decisions.
- Knowing how earnings, book values, and cash flows are used in investment and credit decisions will help you to evaluate the alternative accounting measures discussed in subsequent chapters of this book—not only those recognized in the financial statements but also those disclosed outside the financial statements in footnotes.

APPENDIX A

ABNORMAL EARNINGS VALUATION

This appendix illustrates how the abnormal earnings valuation model can be combined with security analysts' published earnings forecasts to produce an **intrinsic stock price estimate** for a company. To make this illustration real, we focus on Krispy Kreme Doughnuts, Inc. and those analysts' earnings forecasts that were available in August 2003 when the company's common stock was trading at $44.00 per share.

Share Price Valuation There are five steps to deriving a share price estimate using analysts' earnings forecasts and the abnormal earnings valuation model:

1. Obtain analysts' earnings per share (EPS) forecasts for some finite horizon, say the next five years.
2. Combine the EPS forecasts with projected dividends to forecast common equity book value over the horizon.
3. Compute yearly *abnormal* earnings by subtracting *normal* earnings (that is., beginning equity book value multiplied by the equity cost of capital) from analysts' EPS forecasts.
4. Forecast the perpetual (terminal year) *abnormal* earnings flow that will occur beyond the explicit forecast horizon.
5. Add the current book value and the present value of the two abnormal earnings components— the first five years and for years beyond the terminal period—to obtain an intrinsic value estimate of the company's share price.

Each of these steps is illustrated in the Krispy Kreme valuation in Exhibit 6.9.

---

[29] "Objectives of Financial Reporting by Business Enterprises," *Statement of Financial Accounting Concepts No. 1* (Stamford, CT: FASB, 1978), p. viii.

EXHIBIT 6.9   Krispy Kreme Doughnuts

Abnormal Earnings Valuation as of August 2003

	Actual Results		Forecasted Results					
	2001	**2002**	**2003**	**2004**	**2005**	**2006**	**2007**	**Beyond 2007**
(a) Earnings Forecasts								
Reported earnings per share[a]	$0.49	$0.70						
Last year's earnings per share			$ 0.70	$0.89	$1.16	$ 1.54	$ 2.04	
× (1 + Forecasted earnings growth)			1.2714	1.3034	1.3250	1.3250	1.3250	
= Forecasted earnings per share			$ 0.89	$1.16	$1.54	$ 2.04	$ 2.70	
(b) Equity Book Value Forecasts								
Equity book value at beginning of year	$2.32	$3.46	$ 4.87	$5.76	$6.92	$ 8.46	$10.50	
+ Earnings per share	0.49	0.70	0.89	1.16	1.54	2.04	2.70	
+ Stock issued (repurchased)	0.65	0.39	0.00	0.00	0.00	0.00	0.00	
+ Other comprehensive income per share	—	0.32	0.00	0.00	0.00	0.00	0.00	
− Dividends per share	0.00	0.00	0.00	0.00	0.00	0.00	0.00	
= Equity book value at year-end	$3.46	$4.87	$ 5.76	$6.92	$8.46	$10.50	$13.20	
ROE = EPS / Equity book value at beginning of year	21.1%	20.2%	18.3%	20.1%	22.3%	24.1%	25.7%	
(c) Abnormal Earnings								
Equity book value at beginning of year	$2.32	$3.46	$ 4.87	$5.76	$6.92	$ 8.46	$10.50	
× Equity cost of capital	11.0%	11.0%	11.0%	11.0%	11.0%	11.0%	11.0%	
= Normal earnings	$0.26	$0.38	$ 0.54	$0.63	$0.76	$ 0.93	$ 1.16	
Actual or forecasted earnings	$0.49	$0.70	$ 0.89	$1.16	$1.54	$ 2.04	$ 2.70	
− Normal earnings	0.26	0.38	0.54	0.63	0.76	0.93	1.16	
= Abnormal earnings	$0.23	$0.32	$ 0.35	$0.53	$0.78	$ 1.11	$ 1.54	
(d) Valuation								
Future abnormal earnings in forecast horizon			$ 0.35	$0.53	$0.78	$ 1.11	$ 1.54	
× Discount factor at	0.1100		0.90090	0.81162	0.73119	0.65873	0.59345	
= Abnormal earnings discounted to present			$ 0.32	$0.43	$0.57	$ 0.73	$ 0.91	
Abnormal earnings in year 2008[b]								$ 1.59
Assumed long-term growth rate								3.0%
Perpetuity factor for year 2007								12.50
Discount factor at 11%								0.59345
Present value of terminal year abnormal earnings[c]								$11.79
(e) Estimated share price								
Sum of discounted abnormal earnings over horizon			$ 2.96					
+ Present value of terminal year abnormal earnings			$11.79					
= Present value of all abnormal earnings			$14.75					
+ Current equity book value			$ 4.87					
= Estimated current share price at August, 2003			$19.62					
Actual share price at August, 2003			$44.00					

[a]Adjusted for nonrecurring gains and losses.
[b]This is forecasted abnormal earnings for 2007, multiplied by one plus the long-term growth rate: $1.54 × (1 + .03) = 1.5862, or $1.59 rounded.
[c]This is just $1.59 × 12.50 × 0.59345 = 11.794818, or $11.79 rounded.

Our forecast horizon—and the one used by analysts covering the company—is the five-year period from 2003 through 2007. There are at least three reasons why analysts focus on the short- to intermediate-term forecast horizon in valuing a company. First, competitive pressures make it difficult for the company to sustain growth in sales, profits, and cash flows in the long run. Thus, it is unrealistic to forecast that a growing company can maintain high short-term growth rates for an indefinite period. Second, long-range projections are more uncertain and, therefore, subject to greater error. Simply put, projected earnings or dividend payouts to shareholders become less and less reliable the further removed they are from the current forecast date. And third, because of the time value of money, the discounted present values of future abnormal earnings (or free cash) flows, become smaller as the forecast horizon increases. In other words, longer range forecasts often do not matter very much in terms of determining current share price. For example, the present value of a dollar received 25 years from now discounted at 15%—a very realistic estimate for the cost of equity capital—is equal to $1 \div (1 + .15)^{25} = \$0.03$.

In late August 2003 securities analysts who covered Krispy Kreme were forecasting EPS of $0.89 for 2003 and $1.16 for 2004. These same analysts were forecasting annual EPS growth of 32.5% for 2005 through 2007. Based on the company's projected EPS of $1.16 for 2004, this means that analysts were forecasting 2005 EPS of $1.54 (or 1.16×1.325). These same analysts were forecasting 2006 EPS of $2.04 (or 1.54×1.325), and so on. These EPS forecasts are presented in part (a) of Exhibit 6.9.

Next, we need to compute the book value of common equity for each year of the five-year forecast horizon. From the historical information contained in part (b) of the exhibit, we learn that Krispy Kreme has not been paying dividends for the last two years or buying back much of its common stock. We assume that no dividend distributions or additional stock repurchases will occur over the next five years. These assumptions are combined with the EPS forecasts from part (a) to produce the equity book value forecasts of $5.76 per share at the end of 2003 and $13.20 per share at the end of 2007.

The abnormal earnings calculations for each of the five years in our forecast horizon are shown in part (c) of Exhibit 6.9. Here, "normal" earnings are subtracted from the annual EPS forecasts. Normal earnings are just Krispy Kreme's common equity book value at the *beginning* of each year—as computed in part (b)—multiplied by the company's cost of equity capital, which is 11%.[30] For example, Krispy Kreme's normal earnings for 2003 would be calculated by multiplying its equity book value at the beginning of the year, which is $4.87, by the equity cost of capital, which is 0.11. The result is $0.54. These normal earnings ($.054) are then subtracted from forecasted earnings of $.089. The difference between the two, or $.035, are Krispy Kreme's abnormal earnings for 2003.

These abnormal earnings forecasts from part (c) become the basic inputs to the valuation calculation in part (d), where abnormal earnings are discounted at the company's 11% equity cost of capital. A *terminal value* calculation intended to represent the value of the company's abnormal earnings flow beyond our five-year forecast horizon is also shown in part (d). To arrive at this terminal value estimate, we assume that Krispy Kreme's abnormal earnings of $1.54 in 2007 will continue to grow by 3% each year for the foreseeable future. The present value of this growing perpetual flow at the beginning of 2008 is $19.88 (not shown in Exhibit 6.9), which is the 2007 earnings multiplied by one plus the long-term growth rate $(1 + 0.03)$, and then multiplied again by the perpetuity factor 12.50.[31] This quantity is then discounted using the present value factor for five periods discounted at 11% (0.59345), which translates the present value of abnormal earnings at the beginning of 2008 into a present value at the beginning of 2003 of $11.79. Part (e) shows that the sum of all discounted abnormal earnings flows ($14.75) plus the company's 2002 year-end equity book value ($4.87) produces an estimated share price of $19.62; this contrasts with Krispy Kreme's actual $44.00 share price in August 2003.

What does this tell us? For one thing, Krispy Kreme's $44.00 per share stock price in August 2003 was considerably higher than that implied by securities analysts' five-year EPS and dividend payout forecasts coupled with our own predictions about earnings growth beyond the forecast horizon (year 2007). In this regard, Krispy Kreme's stock may appear to be somewhat overpriced in the marketplace.

---

[30] This figure was derived from the capital asset pricing model (CAPM) using the then-current risk-free rate of 4.00% for 30-year treasury bonds, Krispy Kreme's equity beta of 1.21 as reported by *Zacks Investment Research*, and a long-term market risk premium of 6%. The CAPM formula applied to Krispy Kreme is:

$$4.00\% + (1.21 \times 6\%) = 11.26\% \text{ or about } 11\%$$

[31] This discount factor is equal to one divided by the difference between the equity cost of capital (11%) and the abnormal earnings growth rate (3%), or $1/(.11 - .03)$.

However, the market may have been anticipating abnormal earnings to increase even faster and for a longer time period than our projections would indicate. The rub, of course, is that we cannot know at the time which of the forecasts will prove correct in the future.

The abnormal earnings valuation model in Exhibit 6.9 can be used to value almost any publicly traded company. It's easy to implement because it requires just a handful of data items—earnings forecasts from analysts, a beginning book value of equity, forecasts of dividends and stock repurchases, an equity cost of capital (discount rate), and a long-term growth rate for abnormal earnings beyond the terminal year. But how well does it work?

There are several ways to answer this question. One approach compares the accuracy of stock price estimates from several different valuation models—for example, the abnormal earnings model versus the free cash flow valuation model. A recent study did just that using a sample of nearly 3,000 firm-year observations from 1989 through 1993.[32] Earnings, dividends, and cash flow forecasts were gathered from *Value Line* for each sample firm and year. These forecasts were then used as inputs to an abnormal earnings valuation model (like the one in Exhibit 6.9) and as inputs to a separate free cash flow valuation model. The two value estimates—one based on abnormal earnings and the other based on free cash flows—were then compared to actual stock prices. Which valuation model was best? Abnormal earnings value estimates were more accurate and explained more of the variation in actual stock prices than did free cash flow value estimates.

> In theory, both valuation models should produce the same stock price estimate. But in practice, the two valuation models often do not produce the same stock price estimate.

A related study asked if money can be made from the abnormal earnings valuation model in Exhibit 6.9.[33] Using a sample of nearly 18,000 firm-year observations covering 1979 to 1991, the researchers computed valuation estimates for each firm and year. These estimates were then used to construct a *value index*—it's the estimated value divided by the actual share price—for each company and year. (The value index for Krispy Kreme would be $19.62/$44.00 = 0.446.) The simulated trading strategy involved "buying" the most undervalued companies (high value index) and "selling short" the most overvalued companies (low value index). This strategy produced a three-year portfolio return of 35%, which implies investors can profit from using the abnormal earnings valuation model.

APPENDIX B

FINANCIAL STATEMENT FORECASTS

Financial statement forecasts (or projections) are essential ingredients of equity valuation and credit risk analysis. This appendix illustrates the construction of *comprehensive* financial statement forecasts.[34] Our approach has two advantages. First, it uses information about the company's complete operating, investing, and financing activities to yield a forecast of each individual financial statement item. Second, the approach ensures that the forecasted financial statements—sometimes called "pro forma" projections—are internally consistent. Nothing is overlooked, and the projected financial statements fit together as they should.

The starting point for developing comprehensive financial statement forecasts is a detailed understanding of the company, its recent financial performance, and health. (Chapter 5 shows you how!) This involves learning about the company and its industry conditions, competitors, customers, and suppliers. Armed with this knowledge, the analyst can then develop plausible predictions about future economic conditions in the industry, and about how the company and its competitors will respond to those conditions. The analyst then incorporates these predictions into the forecasted financial statements.

> Sometimes the analyst is only interested in forecasting a single financial statement item, like earnings per share (EPS). Shortcuts that circumvent the need to construct comprehensive financial statement forecasts are often used in such cases, but the resulting single item forecasts may prove highly unreliable.

[32] J. Francis, P. Olsson, and D. R. Oswald, "Comparing the Accuracy and Explainability of Dividends, Free Cash Flow, and Abnormal Earnings Equity Value Estimates," *Journal of Accounting Research* (Spring 2000), pp. 45–70.

[33] R. Frankel and C. Lee, "Accounting Valuation, Market Expectation, and Cross-Sectional Stock Returns," *Journal of Accounting and Economics* (June 1998), pp. 283–320.

[34] Techniques for constructing financial statement forecasts are described in T. Copeland, et al., op. cit.; R. Lundholm and R. Sloan, op. cit.; K. Palepu, V. Bernard, and P. Healy, *Business Analysis and Valuation* (Cincinnati, OH: South-Western Publishing, 2004); L. Soffer and R. Soffer, op. cit.; and C. Stickney and P. Brown, *Financial Statement Analysis: A Strategic Perspective* (Fort Worth, TX: Dryden Press, 1999).

There are six steps to preparing comprehensive financial statement forecasts:

1. Project sales revenue for each period in the forecast horizon (say, two years).
2. Forecast operating expenses like cost of goods sold (but not depreciation, interest, or tax expense, which are handled separately), and derive projected pre-tax operating income before depreciation and amortization. Expense margins—for example, "Cost of goods sold" expressed as a percentage of sales—are useful for this purpose.
3. Forecast the level of balance sheet operating assets and liabilities—cash, inventories, accounts receivable, accounts payable, and the like—needed to support the projected operations in steps 1 and 2. Turnover ratios (also called "utilization") ratios can help guide these projections.
4. Forecast depreciation expense and tax expense each period. These are the last items needed to construct projected income statements.
5. Forecast the company's financial structure (mix of debt and equity financing) and dividend policy each period. This information, along with an estimate of the interest rate charged on debt financing, is then used to project interest expense.
6. Derive projected cash flow statements from the forecasted income statements and balance sheets.

An Illustration of Comprehensive Financial Statement Forecasts

Veto Equipment Supply Company manufactures original equipment parts for the U.S. automobile industry. The company has been in business for over 50 years. Although sales rise and fall with the ebb and flow of consumer demand for U.S. automobiles, the company has remained profitable throughout most of its history. In 2004, Veto Equipment Supply reported sales of $25.2 million, an increase of 5% from the previous year. Net income that year was $1.056 million, an increase of 20% from 2003.

The company has a $2.5 million revolving credit loan with Commerce First Bank. At the end of 2004, Veto had only drawn $2.077 million of the available credit, but management is still concerned about the amount of money it will need to borrow over the next two years. The reason for this concern is because Veto has developed a successful new product that is expected to increase its sales significantly. However, the new product will require that Veto expand its operations. Management wants to know if Veto will need to negotiate a higher credit limit to support the planned expansion. How much more money will the company need?

Exhibit 6.10 shows the company's income statements and balance sheets for the past two years. An abbreviated statement of retained earnings is included to provide an explicit link between income statement and balance sheet amounts. Our task is to "fill in the blanks" by preparing forecasted financial statements for 2005 and 2006 using the six-step process described above. Let's get started!

Step 1:   **Project sales revenue.** Management is forecasting sales growth of 10% in 2005 and another 15% in 2006. This compares to 4% sales growth in 2003 and 5% in 2004. We will use management's sales growth estimates to compute projected sales revenue for the next two years. This means that sales in 2005 are expected to be $27.720 million (or $25.200 million × 1.10). Similarly, sales in 2006 are projected to be $31.878 million (or $27.720 × 1.15).

	Historical		Projected	
	2003	**2004**	**2005**	**2006**
Sales growth	4.0%	5.0%	10.0%	15.0%

EXHIBIT 6.10	Veto Equipment Supply Company

Historical Financial Statements

	Historical		Projected	
($ in thousands)	2003	2004	2005	2006
Income Statement				
Sales	$24,000	$25,200		
Cost of goods sold	15,760	16,380		
Research and development expense	—	—		
Selling, general, and administrative expense	5,600	5,796		
Depreciation expense	1,080	1,147		
Pre-tax operating income	1,560	1,877		
Interest expense	240	277		
Nonoperating income (loss)	—	—		
Pre-tax earnings	1,320	1,600		
Tax expense	440	544		
Net income	$ 880	$ 1,056		
Balance Sheet				
Operating cash and equivalents	$ 1,160	$ 1,134		
Accounts receivable	2,120	2,016		
Inventories	3,240	3,528		
Other current assets	—	—		
Current assets	6,520	6,678		
Property, plant and equipment (gross)	16,600	17,640		
Accumulated depreciation	(10,080)	(11,227)		
Other assets	600	756		
Total assets	$13,640	$13,847		
Current portion of long-term debt	$ 180	$ 208		
Accounts payable	2,820	2,520		
Other payables	160	252		
Current liabilities	3,160	2,980		
Long-term debt	1,800	1,869		
Other liabilities	800	504		
Shareholders' equity				
Contributed capital	5,000	5,358		
Retained earnings	2,880	3,136		
Total shareholders' equity	7,880	8,494		
Total liabilities and equity	$13,640	$13,847		
Retained Earnings				
Beginning retained earnings	$ 2,800	$ 2,880		
+ Net income	880	1,056		
− Dividends	(800)	(800)		
= Ending retained earnings	$ 2,880	$ 3,136		

Step 2: **Forecast operating expenses (except depreciation, and interest expense).** A good jumping-off point for this step in the forecasting process is to assemble information about the company's historical expense margins. These data then provide a basis for projecting future expense amounts.

Here are the historical expense margins and our projected margins.

	Historical		Projected	
	2003	**2004**	**2005**	**2006**
Expense margins				
Cost of goods sold	65.7%	65.0%	65.0%	65.0%
Research and development expense	0.0%	0.0%	0.0%	0.0%
Selling, general, and administrative expense	23.3%	23.0%	23.0%	23.0%
Nonoperating income (loss)	0.0%	0.0%	0.0%	0.0%

Notice that cost of goods sold was 65.7% of sales in 2003 but then declined to only 65.0% of sales in 2004. You can see from the table that we are projecting a continuation of this margin for the next two years. Consequently, cost of goods sold is expected to be $18.018 million in 2005, or 65.0% of the $27.720 million in projected sales for that year. The 2006 cost of goods sold forecast ($20.721 million) is constructed in a similar manner.

Research and development expenses are projected to remain at zero for the next two years, as are nonoperating items. Selling, general, and administrative expenses are projected to be 23.0% of sales. In other words, our expense forecasts presume that management will continue to operate the business over the next two years in the same manner it did in 2004.

Step 3: **Forecast the level of balance sheet operating assets and liabilities.** Here, too, information about the company's historical asset and liability utilization ratios—for example, operating cash or accounts receivable as a percent of its sales—is helpful as a starting point in this step. Here are the historical (and projected) utilization ratios for each operating asset and liability.

> To simplify the forecasting task, utilization ratios are computed using year-end balance sheet amounts.

	Historical		Projected	
	2003	**2004**	**2005**	**2006**
Operating asset and liability utilization (% of sales)				
Operating cash and equivalents/sales	4.8%	4.5%	4.5%	4.5%
Accounts receivable/sales	8.8%	8.0%	8.0%	8.0%
Inventory/sales	13.5%	14.0%	17.0%	17.0%
Other current assets/sales	0.0%	0.0%	0.0%	0.0%
Property, plant and equipment (gross)/sales	69.2%	70.0%	65.0%	70.0%
Other assets/sales	2.5%	3.0%	3.0%	3.0%
Accounts payable/sales	11.8%	10.0%	10.0%	10.0%
Other current liabilities/sales	0.7%	1.0%	1.0%	1.0%
Other liabilities/sales	3.3%	2.0%	2.0%	2.0%

Notice, for example, that accounts receivable at the end of 2003 amounted to 8.8% of sales that year. However, accounts receivable were only 8.0% of sales at the end of 2004. We are projecting that receivables will maintain their current 8.0% level over the next two years. This means that accounts receivable are forecasted to be $2.218 million at the end of 2005 (or 8.0% of the $27.720 in expected 2005 sales). A similar computation determines the forecasted balance of accounts receivable at the end of 2006.

Most of the operating assets and liabilities are forecasted to remain at their 2004 utilization ratios for the next two years. However, there are two exceptions. Inventory levels are expected to increase from 14.0% of sales in 2004 to 17.0% of sales in 2005 and 2006. At the same time, Veto's investment in gross property, plant and equipment is expected to decline from 70.0% of sales in 2004 to 65.0% of sales in 2005, and then rise back again to 70.0% in 2006.

Step 4: **Forecast depreciation expense and tax expense.** Historical and projected information about depreciation expense (as a percent of year-end cost of property, plant and equipment) and tax expense (as a percent of pre-tax earnings) is shown in the following table.

	Historical		Projected	
	2003	2004	2005	2006
Depreciation expense/PP&E cost	6.5%	6.5%	6.5%	6.5%
Tax expense/pre-tax earnings	33.3%	34.0%	34.0%	34.0%

Depreciation expense has been running at 6.5% of the company's year-end investment in property, plant and equipment. Depreciation is expected to remain at this level for the next two years. So, depreciation expense is forecasted to be $1.171 million in 2005 (or 6.5% of the $18.018 million invested in property, plant and equipment at the end of that year). This amount of depreciation expense is shown on the company's 2005 income statement, and as an increase to the "Accumulated depreciation" balance sheet account in 2005. Tax expense is projected to be 34.0% of pre-tax earnings for the next two years, a level equal to that in 2004. This means that tax expense is forecasted to be $0.634 million in 2005 (or 34% of the $1.864 million in pre-tax earnings that year including interest expense from Step 5).

Step 5: **Forecast the company's financial structure.** This forecasting step develops projections for dividends, debt, and interest expense. Here's an historical snapshot of each financial statement component and our projections for 2005 and 2006.

	Historical		Projected	
	2003	2004	2005	2006
Financial structure				
Debt/assets	14.5%	15.0%	15.0%	15.0%
Current portion of long-term debt/debt	9.1%	10.0%	10.0%	10.0%
Interest rate on beginning debt	12.1%	14.0%	14.0%	14.0%
Dividends ($ in thousands)	$800	$800	$800	$800

The debt (current portion plus long-term portion) to asset ratio at Veto Equipment Supply was 14.5% in 2003, and 9.1% of the company's debt that year was listed as a current liability on the balance sheet. The debt to asset ratio increased to 15% in 2004, and is projected to remain at that percentage level over the next two years. The current portion of long-term debt is projected to stay at 10%. This means that Veto is projected to have debt of $2.194 million in 2005 (or 15.0% of the $14.629 in forecasted total assets). Of that amount, $0.219 (or 10%) is classified as a current liability.

Interest expense as a percent of beginning debt was 12.1% in 2003 but then increased to 14.0% in 2004. We are projecting interest expense to remain at this percentage level over the next two years. So, interest expense in 2005 is projected to be $0.291 million (or 14.0% of the $2.077 million in *beginning* debt that year). Dividends have been $0.800 million each year and are expected to remain so for the next two years.

We have now completed the forecasting steps necessary to the construction of projected income statements and balance sheets for Veto Equipment Supply Company. Exhibit 6.11 contains our detailed forecasts.

The company is projected to have sales of $31.878 million in 2006, and net income of $1.365 million. However, the revolving credit line needs are expected to reach $2.823 million (or $0.282 in current debt plus another $2.541 million in long-term debt). This amount exceeds the company's existing credit limit for the Commerce First Bank loan. Let's take a look at Veto's projected cash flow statements to learn the reason for this projected increase in borrowing.

There is one financial statement item—"Contributed capital"—that we did not forecast directly. Instead, we made use of the balance sheet equation that requires total assets to equal total liabilities plus shareholders' equity. The projected contributed capital figure was set equal to an amount that ensured that the balance sheet equation held for each forecast year.

EXHIBIT 6.11	Veto Equipment Supply Company

Historical and Projected Income Statements and Balance Sheets

	Historical		Projected	
($ in thousands)	2003	2004	2005	2006
Income Statement				
Sales	$24,000	$25,200	$27,720	$31,878
Cost of goods sold	15,760	16,380	18,018	20,721
Research and development expense	—	—	—	—
Selling, general, and administrative expense	5,600	5,796	6,375	7,332
Depreciation expense	1,080	1,147	1,171	1,450
Pre-tax operating income	1,560	1,877	2,156	2,375
Interest expense	240	277	291	307
Non-operating income (loss)	—	—	—	—
Pre-tax earnings	1,320	1,600	1,865	2,068
Tax expense	440	544	634	703
Net income	$ 880	$ 1,056	$ 1,231	$ 1,365
Balance Sheet				
Operating cash and equivalents	$ 1,160	$ 1,134	$ 1,247	$ 1,435
Accounts receivable	2,120	2,016	2,218	2,550
Inventories	3,240	3,528	4,712	5,419
Other current assets	—	—	—	—
Current assets	6,520	6,678	8,177	9,404
Property, plant and equipment (gross)	16,600	17,640	18,018	22,315
Accumulated depreciation	(10,080)	(11,227)	(12,398)	(13,848)
Other assets	600	756	832	956
Total assets	$13,640	$13,847	$14,629	$18,827
Current portion of long-term debt	$ 180	$ 208	$ 219	$ 282
Accounts payable	2,820	2,520	2,772	3,188
Other payables	160	252	277	319
Current liabilities	3,160	2,980	3,268	3,789
Long-term debt	1,800	1,869	1,975	2,541
Other liabilities	800	504	554	638
Shareholders' equity:				
Contributed capital	5,000	5,358	5,265	7,727
Retained earnings	2,880	3,136	3,567	4,132
Total shareholders' equity	7,880	8,494	8,832	11,859
Total liabilities and equity	$13,640	$13,847	$14,629	$18,827
Retained Earnings				
Beginning retained earnings	$ 2,800	$ 2,880	$ 3,136	$ 3,567
+ Net income	880	1,056	1,231	1,365
– Dividends	(800)	(800)	(800)	(800)
= Ending retained earnings	$ 2,880	$ 3,136	$ 3,567	$ 4,132

Step 6: **Derive projected cash flow statements.** Projected cash flow statements can now be derived directly from the company's projected income statements and balance sheets. Exhibit 6.12 shows the historical and projected cash flows for the company.

The historical cash flow statements reveal that Veto enjoyed positive free cash flows—"Cash from operations" minus "Cash used in investing activities"—in both 2003 and 2004. The statements also indicate that the company paid dividends and increased its long-term debt in both years. From a credit risk perspective, this is not good news because it suggests that the company is borrowing money to maintain a stable dividend payout.

The projected cash flow statements indicate that Veto is facing a significant cash flow problem in 2006. Even though operating cash flows that year are projected to be $2.233 million, free cash flows that year are expected to be in a deficit position of –$2.188 million (or $2.233

EXHIBIT 6.12	Veto Equipment Supply Company

Historical and Projected Cash Flow Statements

($ in thousands)	Historical 2003	2004	Projected 2005	2006
Cash Flow Statement				
Net income	$ 880	$ 1,056	$ 1,231	$ 1,365
Non-cash expenses:				
Depreciation	1,080	1,147	1,171	1,450
Changes in non-cash working capital accounts				
Accounts receivable decrease	65	104	(202)	(332)
Inventory decrease	(158)	(288)	(1,184)	(707)
Other current asset decrease	—	—	—	—
Accounts payable increase	100	(300)	252	416
Other current liabilities increase	(20)	92	25	42
Cash from operations	$ 1,947	$ 1,811	$ 1,293	$ 2,234
Increase in property, plant and equipment	$ (985)	$(1,040)	$ (378)	$(4,297)
Increase in other assets	(67)	(156)	(76)	(124)
Cash used in investing activities	$(1,052)	$(1,196)	$ (454)	$(4,421)
Increase in long-term debt	$ 200	$ 97	$ 117	$ 629
Increase in other liabilities	(50)	(296)	50	83
Increase in contributed capital	—	358	(93)	2,463
Dividends paid	(800)	(800)	(800)	(800)
Cash from financing activities	$ (650)	$ (641)	$ (726)	$ 2,375
Net increase (decrease) in cash	$ 245	$ (26)	$ 113	$ 188

million in operating cash flows minus $4.421 million in required investment). Add the continued dividend payment of $800,000, and the cash flow deficit approaches $3 million.

According to our forecasts, Veto will make up this deficit by borrowing $0.630 million, as shown by the increase in long-term debt, and by raising another $2.463 million from stockholders, as shown by the increase in contributed capital. But, what if stockholders are unwilling to buy more shares from the company? Then management must either scale back the company's operating plans to free up more cash, or negotiate a substantially larger credit line with Commerce First Bank.

PROBLEMS/DISCUSSION QUESTIONS

P6 – 1
Quality of earning essay

1. Define the term *quality of earnings.*
2. List the techniques that management can use to improve a company's *reported* earning performance in the short run.
3. Give examples of low-quality earnings components.

P6 – 2
Discussion questions on the role of accounting numbers in valuation

1. Describe the role of accounting numbers in corporate valuation.
2. Describe the role of accounting numbers in cash flow assessment.
3. What is meant by sustainable earnings? What types of earnings are not sustainable?
4. Briefly describe what the process of valuation involves.
5. What are free cash flows? Describe the key features of the free cash flow approach to valuation.
6. Explain the difference between a company's "operating cash flow" and its "free cash flow."
7. What are abnormal earnings? Describe the key features of the abnormal earnings approach to valuation.
8. What is an earnings surprise? How does an earnings surprise impact the value of a firm's equity?

P6 – 3

Explaining differences in P/E ratios

The price/earnings (P/E) ratios in August 2003 for two groups of companies were:

Company	P/E Ratio
Group A	
Amazon.com	112
General Motors	17
Krispy Kreme Doughnuts	52
Microsoft	27
Group B	
Bob Evans Farms	13
Cheesecake Factory	31
Krispy Kreme Doughnuts	52
Wendy's International	15

Required:

1. What factors might explain the difference in the P/E ratios of the firms in Group A?
2. What factors might explain the difference in the P/E ratios of the restaurant firms in Group B?

P6 – 4

Abnormal earnings—some examples

As discussed in the chapter, abnormal earnings (AE) are:

$$AE_t = \text{Actual earnings}_t - \text{Required or "normal" earnings}_t$$

which may be expressed as

$$AE_t = \text{NOPAT}_t - (r \times BV_{t-1})$$

where NOPAT is the firm's net operating profit after taxes, r is the cost of equity capital and BV_{t-1} is the book value of equity at time $t-1$.

Required:

Solve the following problems:
1. If NOPAT is $5,000, $r = 15\%$, and BV_{t-1} is $50,000, what is AE?
2. If NOPAT is $25,000, $r = 18\%$, and BV_{t-1} is $125,000, what is AE?
3. Assume that the firm in requirement 2 can increase NOPAT to $30,000 by instituting some cost-cutting measures. What is the new AE?
4. Assume that the firm in requirement 2 can divest $25,000 of unproductive capital, with NOPAT falling by only $2,000. What is the new AE?
5. Assume that the firm in requirement 2 can add a new division at a cost of $40,000, which will increase NOPAT by $7,600 per year. Would adding the new division increase AE?
6. Assume that the firm in requirement 1 can add a new division at a cost of $25,000, which will increase NOPAT by $3,500 per year. Would adding the new division increase AE?

P6 – 5

Value creation by two companies

www.prenhall.com/revsine

● Student Resources

☑ Template for solution

As discussed in the chapter, abnormal earnings (AE) are:

$$AE_t = \text{Actual earnings}_t - \text{Required earnings}_t$$

which may be expressed as

$$AE_t = \text{NOPAT}_t - (r \times BV_{t-1})$$

where NOPAT is the firm's net operating profit after taxes, r is the cost of equity capital, and BV_{t-1} is the book value of equity at $t-1$.

Appearing next is the NOPAT, BV_{t-1} and cost of equity capital of two firms.

Company A	2001	2002	2003	2004	2005
NOPAT	$ 66,920	$ 79,632	$ 83,314	$ 89,920	$ 92,690
BV_{t-1}	$478,000	$504,000	$541,000	$562,000	$598,000
Cost of equity capital	0.152	0.167	0.159	0.172	0.166
Company B	2001	2002	2003	2004	2005
NOPAT	$192,940	$176,341	$227,700	$ 198,900	$ 282,964
BV_{t-1}	$877,000	$943,000	$989,999	$1,020,000	$1,199,000
Cost of equity capital	0.188	0.179	0.183	0.175	0.186

Required:

1. Calculate each firm's AE each year from 2001 to 2005.
2. Which firm was a better investment for its shareholders over the 2001–2005 period? Why?

A firm's P/E ratio can be written using equation (6.9) as:

P6 – 6

Determinants of P/E ratios

$$P/E = \frac{\text{Market price per share}}{\text{Earning per share}} = \frac{1}{r} + \frac{\text{Present value of growth opportunities per share}}{\text{Earning per share}}$$

where r is the cost of equity capital (discount rate).

Required:

Briefly discuss how a firm's P/E ratio is related to (a) the present value of growth opportunities, (b) risk, and (c) the firm's choice of accounting methods.

As shown in equation (6.9), the price equation for a firm with positive growth opportunities is

P6 – 7

Valuing growth opportunities

$$P_0 = \frac{X_0}{r} + \text{NPVGO}$$

where P_0 is the current stock price, X_0 is current reported earnings per share, r is the cost of equity capital, and NPVGO is the net present value of future growth opportunities. The recent values of P_0, X_0, and r for several companies are:

	P_0	X_0	r
Dell Computer	$26.74	$0.82	0.138
eBay	67.82	0.82	0.198
Ford Motor	9.30	0.99	0.114
Home Depot	24.02	1.55	0.121
Wal-Mart	50.51	1.83	0.090

Required:

1. Why does eBay have a higher cost of equity capital (r) than does Wal-Mart?
2. Compute NPVGO for each company.
3. Why is the NPVGO of eBay larger than that for Home Depot?
4. Why do Ford Motor and Wal-Mart have such different NPVGO amounts?

In each of the following situations assume a zero-growth rate for earnings and dividends (NPVGO is zero), that all earnings are paid out as dividends, and that the earnings-based valuation model in equation (6.9) is being used.

P6 – 8

Earnings-based equity valuations

1. Dennison Corporation's earnings are expected to be $7.00 per share and its stock price is $28.00. What is the required rate of return on the firm's equity?
2. Sampson Corporation's earnings are expected to be $5.00 per share and its required rate of return on equity is 22%. What is the current price of the stock?
3. Johnson Corporation's current stock price is $40.00 and its required rate of return on equity is 15%. What is the firm's expected earnings?

P6 – 9

Interpreting stock price changes

Assume that General Motors (GM) announces on September 30, 2005 that it expects its earnings per share (EPS) to be $4.50 for the year 2005. At the time of the announcement financial analysts are forecasting GM's annual EPS to be $5.00.

Required:

1. Would you expect to observe a change in GM's stock price on September 30? Explain why or why not.
2. Consider the following two scenarios:

   a. The $0.50 difference between GM's management forecast and analysts' forecast is completely attributable to a month-long labor strike at one of GM's parts plants, a strike that disrupted production at most of the firm's car manufacturing facilities.
   b. The $0.50 difference between GM's management forecast and analysts' forecast is attributable to GM's (previously undisclosed) decision to discontinue production of its line of sports utility vehicles and small trucks.

   Do you expect the magnitude of the stock price change to be greater in case (a) or case (b)? Why?

P6 – 10

Components of earnings

This chapter discusses the following three components of earnings: permanent, transitory, and valuation-irrelevant.

Required:

1. Provide a one-sentence explanation for each component.
2. Provide some examples of each component. (You might examine the income statements of two or three publicly traded companies to aid your answer.)

P6 – 11

Stock price assimilation of earnings information

Figure 6.5 in this chapter illustrates the behavior of stock returns over the period before a quarterly earnings announcement (from trading days −60 to −1); at the time of an earnings announcement (on day 0); and over the period following an earnings announcement (from trading days +1 to +60) for three groups of firms. (*Note:* A 60 trading day period is almost equal to the 90 calendar days that make up a fiscal quarter.) The three groups are "good news" firms (firms whose earnings are greater than what the market expected), "no news" firms (firms whose earnings are what the market expected), and "bad news" firms (firms whose earnings are less than what the market expected).

Required:

1. Why do the stock returns of "good news" firms drift upward before the earnings announcement date.
2. Why do the stock returns of "bad news" firms drift downward before the earnings announcement date.
3. Why don't the stock returns of "no news" firms drift upward or downward during the −60 to −1 trading day period?
4. For each group, explain the behavior of the stock returns at the time of the earnings announcement (on trading day 0).
5. While not immediately obvious from Figure 6.5, there is a tendency for the stock returns of "good news" firms to continue to drift upward after the earnings announcement, and for the stock returns of "bad news" firms to continue to drift downward after the earnings announcement. Explain why these post-announcement drifts occur.
6. Suppose a separate Figure 6.5 were produced for a sample of large publicly traded firms and for a sample of small publicly traded firms. Would you expect the two figures to look the same? Explain why or why not.

P6 – 12

Applying P/E multiples to earnings components

Consider the following information:

	ABC Corporation	XYZ Corporation
Reported EPS	$5.00	$5.00
EPS decomposition		
Permanent	75%	55%
Transitory	20%	25%
Value-irrelevant	5%	20%

Required:

1. Use a risk-adjusted cost of capital of 15% to calculate the implied share price and earnings multiples for each firm. Why are the implict share prices and earnings multiples for the two firms different?
2. Repeat requirement 1 using a risk-adjusted cost of capital of 8%.

Colonel Electric Company is one of the largest and most diversified industrial corporations in the world. From the time of its incorporation in 1892 the company has engaged in developing, manufacturing, and marketing a wide variety of products for the generation, transmission, distribution, control, and utilization of electricity.

Appearing in the accompanying table are the 2003–2005 income statements of Colonel Electric Company.

P6 – 13

Calculating sustainable earnings

www.prenhall.com/revsine

● Student Resources

☑ Template for solution

Colonel Electric Company

Comparative Income Statements for Years Ended December 31

($ in millions)	2005	2004	2003
Revenues			
Sales of goods	$54,196	$53,177	$52,767
Sales of services	11,923	10,836	8,863
Royalties and fees	1,629	753	783
Total revenues	67,748	64,766	62,413
Costs and Expenses			
Cost of goods sold	(24,594)	(24,308)	(22,775)
Cost of services sold	(8,425)	(6,785)	(6,274)
Restructuring (charges) reversals	1,000	—	(2,500)
Interest charges	(595)	(649)	(410)
Other costs and expenses	(6,274)	(5,743)	(5,211)
Litigation charges (income)	550	—	(250)
(Losses) gains on sales of investments	(75)	—	25
(Losses) gains on asset sales	25	55	(35)
Inventory write-offs	—	(18)	—
Asset impairment write-offs	—	—	(24)
Special item charges	(34)	—	(8)
Loss from labor strike	—	(20)	—
Total costs and expenses	(38,422)	(37,468)	(37,462)
Earnings from continuing operations before income taxes	29,326	27,298	24,951
Provision for income taxes (34%)	(9,971)	(9,281)	(8,483)
Earnings from continuing operations	$19,355	$18,017	$16,468
Income (loss) from discontinued operations (net of tax)	—	(250)	1,100
Gain (loss) on sale of discontinued operations (net of tax)	750	—	—
Extraordinary gain (loss) on early debt retirement (net of tax)	(50)	—	10
Cumulative gain (loss) from change in accounting methods (net of tax)	(110)	—	55
Net earnings	$19,945	$17,767	$17,633

In 2005 the company earned "Royalties and fees" revenue of $1 billion from a one-time six-month contract with the U.S. government. The company does not expect to do any further business with the U.S. government in the future.

Required:

1. Calculate Colonel Electric's sustainable earnings for each year.
2. How do Colonel Electric's sustainable earnings compare to its reported net earnings in each year?

P6 – 14

Net accruals and discretionary accruals

Companies that want to "manage" their reported earnings can do so through operating cash flows or net income accruals (the noncash revenue and expense components of GAAP earnings).

The 2004–2005 balance sheets and 2005 income statement of Runner's World follow. The company's operating cash flow for 2005 was –$38,460, a net outflow.

Runner's World, Inc.

Income Statement for the Year Ended December 31, 2005

Sales	$120,000
Cost of goods sold	(60,000)
Selling, general, and administrative expenses	(22,000)
Depreciation expense	(14,000)
Operating income	24,000
Interest expense	(6,000)
Interest income	1,000
Income before taxes	19,000
Income taxes (34%)	(6,460)
Net income	$ 12,540

Runner's World, Inc.

Balance Sheet

	December 31	
	2005	2004
Assets		
Cash	$ 100,000	$ 80,000
Accounts receivable	95,000	75,000
Inventories	120,000	90,000
Prepaid expenses	15,000	20,000
Plant, property and equipment (net)	924,000	850,000
Long-term investments	175,000	232,000
Total assets	$1,429,000	$1,347,000
Liabilities and stockholders' equity		
Liabilities		
Accounts payable	$ 220,000	$ 155,000
Accrued payables	195,000	275,000
Interest payable	22,000	10,000
Income tax payable	45,000	62,000
Long-term debt	350,000	270,000
Total liabilities	832,000	772,000
Stockholders' equity		
Common stock	175,000	145,000
Retained earnings	422,000	430,000
Total stockholders' equity	597,000	575,000
Total liabilities and stockholders' equity	$1,429,000	$1,347,000

Required:

1. Calculate the net accruals (the difference between accrual earnings and operating cash flows) recorded by Runner's World in 2005.
2. Identify the individual components of net accruals in requirement 1.
3. Which accruals identified in requirement 2 are subject to the greatest degree of management discretion?
4. Why might managers manipulate the firm's discretionary accruals?

Allison Manufacturing and BSJ Manufacturing both produce after-market accessories for sports utility vehicles. Both companies are about to launch strategic initiatives that will increase sales and net income for the foreseeable future. Allison Manufacturing has decided to launch an expensive advertising campaign that will increase sales from $20 million to $30 million a year and net income from $2 million to $2.5 million a year. BSJ Manufacturing has decided to issue an additional $10 million of common stock and then use the proceeds to buy a smaller accessories manufacturer. The acquisition is expected to increase BSJ's sales by $10 million a year and net income by $1 million. Key financial statement figures for both companies are shown below. The "Before" amounts describe each company's current operations, while the "After" amounts incorporate the expected results from the strategic initiatives.

P6 – 15

Growth, expansion, and equity valuation

	Before	After
Allison Manufacturing:		
Annual sales	$20 million	$ 30 million
Annual net income	$ 2 million	$2.5 million
Equity book value	$10 million	$ 10 million
Number of shares outstanding	100,000	100,000
BSJ Manufacturing:		
Annual sales	$20 million	$30 million
Annual net income	$ 2 million	$ 3 million
Equity book value	$10 million	$20 million
Number of shares outstanding	100,000	200,000

Both companies pay all net income out as dividends each year and have a 10% cost of equity capital. Use the abnormal earnings valuation model from equation (6.11) to answer the required questions.

Required:

1. Calculate the per share value of each company *before* they undertake their strategic initiatives assuming that their current levels of annual net income can be sustained forever.
2. Calculate the percentage growth rate in sales and net income that each company will experience as a result of its strategic initiatives. What is the return on equity (ROE) for each company before and after its strategic initiative?
3. Calculate the per share value of each company after it implements its strategic initiative assuming that the new expected level of annual net income can be sustained forever.
4. Explain why the per share value of one company increases while the per share value of the other company declines.

In October 2003, analysts were expecting sales at Krispy Kreme to be $657 million in 2003 and $819 million in 2004. Net income was expected to be $50.7 million in 2003 and $65.9 million in 2004. The company's financial statements through 2002 are described and analyzed in Chapter 5.

P6 – 16

Financial Statement Forecasts—Krispy Kreme Doughnuts

www.prenhall.com/revsine

● Student Resources

☑ Template for solution

Required:

1. Using the steps outlined in Appendix B to this chapter and the spreadsheet template available on the textbook website, prepare 2003 and 2004 forecasted financial statements (income statements, balance sheets, and cash flow statements) for Krispy Kreme. Your forecasts should incorporate the following assumptions:
   - Sales for 2003 and 2004 will equal $657 million and $819 million.
   - Nonoperating expenses and income will be zero.
   - The company's income tax rate will be 35%.
   - All other income statement items are expected to equal their 2002 levels as a percentage of sales. Depreciation expense was $12.3 million in 2002 ($10.3 in cost of goods sold and $2.0 in SG&A), and $8.0 million in 2001 ($6.0 in cost of goods sold and $2.0 in SG&A).
   - All balance sheet items except "Common stockholders' equity" are expected to equal their 2002 levels as a percentage of sales. Accumulated depreciation was $43.9 million and $50.2 million in 2001 and 2002, respectively. Combine "Long-term investments," "Intangibles," and "Other assets" into a single balance sheet item ("Other assets").
   - Debt is expected to be 15% of assets, and the current portion of long-term debt will be 10% of total debt each year. Interest expense will be 6% of debt at the beginning of each year.
   - The company will issue or buyback stock during 2003 and 2004 to meet its cash flow needs or to distribute excess cash. Dividends and "other comprehensive income" will be zero.

2. How do your net income forecasts from requirement 1 compare with those of the analysts ($50.7 million and $65.9 million)? What does this tell you about your forecasting assumptions compared to those used by the analysts?
3. Why is it important to assume the company will issue or buyback stock when constructing financial statement forecasts?
4. How do your sales, net income, accounts receiveable, total assets, and operating cash flow forecasts for 2003 and 2004 compare to the amounts actually reported by the company in those two years? What factors are likely to explain sizable differences between the actual figures and your forecasts?

P6 – 17

Abnormal earnings valuation—Dell Computer

www.prenhall.com/revsine

● Student Resources

☑ Template for solution

STRETCH

Dell Computer Corporation designs, manufactures, and markets a wide range of computer systems, including desktops, notebooks, and network servers; it also markets software, peripherals, and service and support programs. The company is the world's leading direct-computer systems company and one of the top five computer vendors in the world.

The company was founded on the principle that delivering computers custom-built to specific customer orders is the best business model for providing solutions that truly meet end-user needs. This build-to-order, flexible manufacturing process enables the company to achieve faster inventory turnover and reduced inventory levels, and it allows the company to rapidly incorporate new technologies and components into its product offerings. The company also offers a broad range of service and support programs through its own technical personnel and its direct management of specialized service suppliers. These services range from telephone support to onsite customer-dedicated systems engineers.

1. Appearing in the accompanying table are Dell's earnings per share and equity book value per share for fiscal years 2000–2002. (Dell's fiscal year ends on January 31.)
2. Dell has not been paying any dividends on its common stock. Assume that it won't in the future.
3. Dell has issued common stock and also repurchased some common stock in the open market. Assume that no stock will be issued or repurchased in the future.
4. In August 2003, financial analysts following Dell were forecasting annual earnings per share (EPS) of $1.00 in 2003, $1.21 in 2004, and an annual EPS growth rate of 15% for 2005–2007.
5. After an initial five-year horizon, assume that Dell's abnormal earnings will grow by 8% per year.
6. Dell's beta is 1.20 and the risk-free rate of return is 4%. Use this information, along with a market risk premium of 5.5% to estimate Dell's cost of equity capital. (See footnote 31 in this chapter for a description of how to calculate the equity cost of capital.)
7. Dell's actual stock price was $32.00 at the end of August 2003.

Dell Computer			
	2000	**2001**	**2002**
As reported earnings per share	$0.79	$0.46	$0.80
Equity book value beginning of year	$2.08	$2.17	$1.80
+ Earnings per share	0.79	0.46	0.80
+ Stock issued (repurchased)	(0.70)	(0.83)	(0.71)
− Dividends per share	0	0	0
= Equity book value, end of year	$2.17	$1.80	$1.89

Required:

1. Use the abnormal earnings valuation model from Appendix A of this chapter to derive an estimate of Dell's stock price as of August 2003. How does the price you derive compare to the company's actual stock price of $32.00?
2. Some analysts were forecasting the company's EPS to be $1.20 in 2003, $1.50 in 2004, and to grow at 20% each year from 2005 to 2007. Repeat requirement 1 using these analysts' forecasts in your calculation.
3. Why might Dell's actual stock price differ from the share price estimates you derived in requirements 1 and 2?

The following excerpt is from an article appearing in the *Wall Street Journal*.

The usefulness of management earnings forecasts to financial analysts and investors

LOW-BALLING: HOW SOME COMPANIES SEND STOCKS ALOFT

What makes a stock a high flyer? Consistently beating the analysts' estimates helps a lot. And many companies seem to have figured out a way to try to help ensure that happens.

Each quarter, after securities analysts estimate what the companies they follow will earn, the game begins. Chief financial officers or investor relations representatives traditionally "give guidance" to analysts, hinting whether the analysts should raise or lower their earnings projections so the analysts won't be embarrassed later.

And these days, many companies are encouraging analysts to deflate earnings projections to artificially low levels, analysts and money managers say. If the game is played right, a company's stock will rise sharply on the day it announces its earnings—and beats the analysts' too-conservative estimates.

Take U.S. Healthcare Inc. Late last year, some analysts say, executives of the health-care services company led them to figure it would post fourth-quarter earnings of about 45 cents a share. On Jan. 28, U.S. Healthcare announced a "preliminary" earnings estimate of 55 cents a share. Then, only two weeks later, U.S. Healthcare shocked Wall Street by posting a whopping 68 cents a share for the quarter. The company's stock surged 10% that day, closing at $40.625.

Several analysts think that they were misled. "U.S. Healthcare may have beat its own internal estimates, but it also wanted to guide analysts to numbers they knew they could beat," says Kenneth Abramowitz, a health-care analyst who follows the company for Sanford Bernstein and Co.

Costas Nicolaides, the company's chief financial officer, says U.S. Healthcare simply did better than it expected. "I don't guide analysts," he says. "But if someone were to come up with a ridiculous figure, I might raise my eyebrow, or my body language would be such that they'd know."

Money managers and analysts say an increasing number of companies are leading analysts to underestimate their earnings. "More companies," especially those in such growth areas as health-care and technology, "are starting to coerce us to a high degree about what our estimates should be," says Michael Stark, a research analyst with Robertson Stephens & Co. in San Francisco. "They're always low-balling."

Analysts and portfolio managers say that some companies consistently report earnings that are just a little bit better than what they lead analysts to believe. They mention T2 Medical Inc. and Cirrus Logic Inc.; both "understate by pennies," says Robert Czepial, who runs the Robertson Stephens & Co. Growth Fund. "Of course they're managing the information," he says.

A spokesman for T2 declines to comment. Cirrus's chief financial officer, Sam Srinivasan, says that "Cirrus doesn't play the game of being conservative with the numbers for the analysts."

One corporate chief financial officer, speaking on the condition of anonymity, says that analysts, not the company he works for, are to blame for the company's low-balling its projected earnings. "If the Street's looking for 10 cents and you do nine, you're a moron," he says. "If they're looking for 10 and you do 11, you're a hero."

But low-balling may not work forever. That's the conclusion that some analysts draw from the case of AST Research Inc. For more than five quarters, several analysts and money managers say, the Irvine, Calif., computer maker consistently led them to believe it would earn at least five cents a share less than the actual results.

But for this year's first quarter, analysts lifted their projections, running far ahead of the company's "guidance."

Last month, when AST announced its earnings for the quarter, its stock fell $1.875 to $28.125—even though AST's results were in line with numbers it had given analysts.

Required:

1. Briefly discuss why managers' forecasts of earnings may be useful to financial analysts and investors.
2. Why might managers steer analysts toward conservative earnings estimates by issuing earnings forecasts that they know are below the earnings they expect to report?
3. As an analyst, what action(s) would you take with firms that consistently issue conservative earnings forecasts?
4. Are there any disadvantages to firms (or their managers) issuing conservative earnings forecasts?
5. The article claims that firms can consistently "low-ball" analysts by issuing conservative earnings forecasts and then expect to see their stock prices increase when reported earnings are "higher than expected." Do you agree or disagree with this claim? Why?

P6 – 19

Restructuring charges (and reversals) and the quality of earnings

The following excerpt is from an article that appeared in the *Wall Street Journal*.

ABREAST OF THE MARKET: WRITE-OFFS MAY BECOME "WRITE-ONS"; REVERSAL OF CHARGES COULD PROVE CUSHION IN THE NEXT DOWNTURN

With the Dow Jones Industrial Average hitting another record last week, investors wonder if earnings next year can support today's stock prices. But they may be pleasantly surprised by reserves buried in some corporate balance sheets.

Companies ranging from General Motors to USAir Group took huge write-offs in the early 1990s to account for previously unrecognized liabilities, especially for retired employees' health care. Now, analysts at Goldman, Sachs & Co. say many write-offs, which wiped billions in book value from balance sheets and crushed earnings, appear overly conservative. Many companies could reduce or reverse charges in the next year or two. Such "write-ons" as Goldman calls them, could provide a cushion to profits in the next cyclical downturn, the firm says.

As a result of the write-offs, the earnings and book values investors see today are "the cleanest" in many years, writes Gabrielle Napolitano, an analyst at Goldman, in a study. And she says "many of the write-offs taken in earlier years may actually be reversed in full or in part."

Ms. Napolitano says it's difficult to forecast when and how write-ons may occur, but adds, "They could be substantial." Ms. Napolitano says she believes companies may use write-ons to smooth their earnings over the next year or two if growth in the economy and profits slows.

The problem for investors trying to predict write-ons is that the nature and size of the original write-offs were unprecedented, so it's difficult to predict how, or whether, companies will take write-ons. A reversal might show up as an unusual gain, leaving operating earnings untouched. Companies offer few details on how they might adjust write-offs. Write-off reversals or reductions would vary depending on the industry.

Goldman says conservative accounting now in place has produced the highest-quality earnings and book values in years. David Shulman, chief stock strategist at Salomon Brothers, says earlier charges "may very well have been overstated." But he's concerned that if companies bury write-ons in such things as labor costs without identifying the source of the cost reduction, investors could think earnings are stronger than conditions warrant.

Source: Republished with permission of Dow Jones & Co.; ©1996. From *Wall Street Journal* (December 30, 1996); permission conveyed through Copyright Clearance Center, Inc.

Required:

1. The *Wall Street Journal* article contains the following two statements: (a) "As a result of the write-offs, the earnings and book values investors see today are the cleanest in many years" and (b) "Conservative accounting now in place has produced the highest-quality earnings and book values in years." What is meant by these statements? Do you agree with them? Why or why not?
2. How do restructuring charges and subsequent reversals affect the quality of reported earnings?
3. Why might management tend to overestimate future restructuring costs?
4. Why might analysts be concerned about the potential for firms to make "write-ons" in future years?
5. What is the biggest difficulty that you foresee in dealing with write-ons?

CASES

C6 – 1

Illinois Tool Works (JB): Abnormal earnings valuation

www

www.prenhall.com/revsine

● Student Resources

☑ Template for solution

The abnormal earnings approach for estimating common share value is:

$$P_0 = BV_0 + \sum_{t=1}^{\infty} \frac{E_0(X_t - r \times BV_{t-1})}{(1+r)^t}$$

where P is the total value of all outstanding shares, BV is the (beginning) book value of stockholders' equity, r is the cost of equity capital, E is the expectations operator, and X is net income. In words, the model says that share value equals the book value of stockholders' equity plus the present value of future expected abnormal earnings (where abnormal earnings is net income minus the cost of equity capital multiplied by the beginning-of-period book value of stockholders' equity).

The approach is amazingly simple. Two "rubs" are that the model is silent on just how one comes up with expected net income for future years (and therefore future expected abnormal earnings) and just how many future years should be used. Owing to the way present value is calculated, abnormal earnings amounts expected for years in the distant future have a small present value and are essentially irrelevant to valuation. In addition, competitive market forces tend eventually to drive abnormal earnings to zero. Thus, it isn't important to make the forecasting horizon terribly long. Professional analysts rarely use more than 15 years, often fewer than 10.

Comparative income statements and retained earnings statements for Illinois Tool Works (ITW) for 2000–2002 are presented below.

Required:

1. Assume a 10-year forecasting horizon. Also assume that ITW's 2002 return on beginning stock-holders' equity (net income without extraordinary items divided by beginning 2002 stockholders' equity) of 9.5% is expected to persist throughout the forecasting horizon (that is, that expected net income is always equal to 0.095 multiplied by beginning-of-the-year stockholders' equity). Also assume no additional stock issuances or repurchases are made, and that dividends equal 25% of net income in each year. (This is ITW's approximate historical dividend payout ratio.) Given these assumptions, the book value of stockholders' equity at the *end* of 2003 equals book value at the *beginning* of 2003 plus (1 − .25) times 2003 net income. Finally assume that the cost of equity capital is 9%. (This is ITW's approximate cost of equity capital.) With these relatively simple assumptions, use the abnormal earnings model to estimate the total value of Illinois Tool Work's common shares as of the end of 2002. Ignore terminal values at the end of the 10-year forecast horizon in your calculations.

2. As of the end of 2002, 307 million common shares were outstanding. Convert your estimate in requirement 1 to a per share estimate. For purposes of comparison, the actual market value of ITW's common shares ranged from $56 to $64 during the first quarter of 2003.

3. Now assume that ITW will maintain a 20% return on beginning stockholders' equity over the 10-year forecast horizon. What would the company's shares then be worth?

Illinois Tool Works

Consolidated Statement of Income

($ in millions)	2002	2001	2000
Sales	$9,468	$9,293	$9,984
Cost of goods sold	5,936	5,910	6,192
Gross profit	3,532	3,383	3,792
Selling and administrative expenses	1,720	1,691	1,814
Depreciation and amortization	306	385	414
Operating profit	1,506	1,307	1,564
Interest expense	68	68	72
Nonoperating income (expense)	(4)	(7)	(13)
Special items	0	3	0
Pre-tax income	1,434	1,235	1,479
Total income taxes	502	429	521
Extraordinary items	(219)	0	0
Net income	$ 713	$ 806	$ 958

Illinois Tool Works

Consolidated Statement of Shareholders' Equity

($ in millions)	2002	2001	2000
Balance at beginning of year	$ 9,823	$9,604	$9,061
Net income (loss)	713	806	958
Stock issued (repurchased)	361	(337)	(192)
Common stock dividends	(273)	(250)	(223)
Balance at end of year	$10,624	$9,823	$9,604

Because you are president of your investment club and have a strong background in corporate financial reporting, the other club members typically rely on you to lead the discussion of the group's investment decisions. A special meeting has been called for Monday night (two days from now) to discuss the club's investment in the common stock and unsecured bonds of General Motors (GM). This previously unscheduled meeting was prompted by yesterday's announcement by GM that it had both a net loss of $651.8 million for the fourth quarter of fiscal 1992 and a net loss of $23.5 billion for the entire year (see the following *Wall Street Journal* article).

GM'S DEFICIT IN QUARTER HIT $651.8 MILLION; HUGE ONE-TIME CHARGES CAUSED THE LOSS WHILE OPERATIONS REBOUNDED DETROIT—GENERAL MOTORS CORP., WEIGHED DOWN BY HUGE ONE-TIME CHARGES, REPORTED A FOURTH-QUARTER LOSS OF $651.8 MILLION AND A WORLD RECORD-BREAKING $23.5 BILLION DEFICIT FOR THE YEAR. BUT EXCLUDING THE CHARGES, GM WAS IN THE BLACK.

Analysts called the $3.5 billion improvement in GM's annual operating performance a positive surprise, as it was accomplished despite more conservative accounting. Investors boosted the company's shares to $40.50, up $1.25, in heavy New York Stock Exchange composite trading. "It's a turnaround we can be proud of," GM's Chief Financial Officer, G. Richard Wagoner, said during a news conference. "But we've got a way to go."

Indeed, GM's unfunded pension liabilities soared to $14 billion from $8.4 billion a year earlier, representing a claim on future cash flow. And Mr. Wagoner reaffirmed GM's "aggressive but achievable target" of reversing $3.5 billion in North American Operations losses this year, even though sales aren't expected to improve strongly.

The No. 1 auto maker said it earned $273.3 million, or 10 cents a share, in the fourth quarter before two big charges and a smaller gain. That marked a rebound from a year-earlier loss of $519.8 million, or $1.09 a share, before a restructuring charge. Including charges, GM had a loss of $2.47 billion, or $4.25 a share, a year earlier. In the latest quarter, GM's net loss was $1.25 a share. Revenue rose 6.4% to $35.76 billion in the latest fourth quarter.

When GM "can earn 10 cents a share with conservative accounting, that's a major surprise," said Morgan Stanley analyst Scott Merlis. If the economy rebounds, GM "could show the same type of earnings surprises as Chrysler," he added.

More importantly, GM added $1.98 billion in cash to its coffers during the fourth quarter as cash flow from operations rebounded strongly. GM ended the year with $7.2 billion in cash, up from $3.98 billion a year earlier.

The rebound in cash flow is critical, because GM's cash outflow during the past two years had undermined its efforts to develop new products and fix its badly dented balance sheet.

For the first time, GM disclosed the magnitude of the losses that drove the auto maker's outside directors last year to oust former President Lloyd E. Reuss and then Chairman Robert C. Stempel. GM had a loss of $3.5 billion on its core North American auto business in all of 1992, on top of 1991's $6.89 billion deficit. In the fourth quarter, GM narrowed its North American loss "before interest and taxes" to $966 million from $1.27 billion a year earlier.

But the North American loss in the 1992 quarter was deepened by a one-time $333 million expense for a larger-than-expected early retirement program, and an unspecified addition to warranty-claims reserves taken as part of a broad move to make GM's accounting more conservative.

GM's overseas automotive operations earned $218.4 million in the fourth quarter, down 24% from a year earlier before a $165.1 million gain from GM's sale of its stake in South Korea's Daewoo Motor Corp. The drop reflects weakness in key European markets, and Mr. Wagoner said business will be "tougher" for GM's European operations this year.

GM's three big nonautomotive units contributed a total of $703.1 million in the latest quarter. For all of 1992, GM earned $92 million before a $22.2 billion charge to recognize liabilities for retiree medical benefits and $1.5 billion in other restructuring charges. That compares with a 1991 loss of $3.45 billion before one-time write-offs. GM's revenue for all of 1992 climbed 7.6% to $132.43 billion.

Mr. Wagoner said GM is still confident it can make good on President John F. Smith Jr.'s promise to produce break-even results in North American operations, before interest, taxes and a continuing charge for retiree medical benefits.

But he conceded that GM "has work to do" to shore up its balance sheet. The $20.8 billion charge for retiree medical benefits reduced GM's net worth to just $6.23 billion from $27.34 billion. That won't affect GM's ability to pay dividends or secure financing, Mr. Wagoner said. But it does dramatize the huge claim health care will put on GM's future cash flow, particularly as the ratio of U.S. automotive retirees to U.S. active workers rises above the current 1-to-1.

"We have at GM a very rich benefits program," Mr. Wagoner said. "We need to work with our unions" to lower medical costs that GM estimates are escalating now at about 10% annually.

That process began yesterday, as Mr. Smith met with United Auto Workers union local leaders in Detroit for an unprecedented session to discuss the state of GM's business and the impact of the retiree-benefits issue.

As for the huge unfunded pension liability, GM took steps to tighten up its pension accounting and begin contributing more to its retirement funds. "We're going to start funding more than we're expensing," a GM spokesman said. GM lowered to 10% from 11% the assumed rate of earnings on its pension assets. That move will raise the company's continuing pension expenses about $428 million a year, the spokesman said.

Although the club has investments in the common stock and bonds of 15 to 20 different companies, its investment in GM common stock and bonds represents about 15% of the total value of the club's portfolio. Several club members are concerned about GM's net losses and by other information in the earnings announcement. They wonder if it is time to sell some or all the club's GM common stock and bonds. Some of the concerns raised by club members (which are sure to come up for discussion at the meeting) include:

1. "With such a large loss, will the company still have enough cash to continue to pay dividends?"
2. "Where will the company get the cash to pay for these one-time charges?"
3. "I heard that GM could have written off the $22.2 billion charge for retiree medical benefits over 20 years rather than all in one year. Why did they write it all off in one year?"
4. "In a couple of places the article mentions 'conservative accounting.' What does that mean?"
5. "In the article, GM's chief financial officer states, 'It's a turnaround we can be proud of, . . . but we've got a way to go.' How in the world can a $23.5 billion loss for the year be a turnaround to be proud of?"
6. "Given the size of the $23.5 billion net loss for the year, I don't understand why the share price rose by $1.25 on the day of the announcement."
7. "Since its net worth (that is, assets minus liabilities or just stockholders' equity) fell from $27.34 billion to $6.23 billion for the year, isn't GM now more highly leveraged than before, and hence more risky? Won't the leverage increase mean that bond rating agencies like Moody's and Standard & Poor's will reduce GM's credit rating, thereby reducing the value of our bonds?"
8. "I'm confused by all of the 'earnings' numbers referred to in the article. Which one is the best indicator of GM's future profitability?"
9. "The article states that during 1992, GM added $3.22 billion to its cash. How can this be? They lost $23.5 billion!"
10. "The article states that the reduction in GM's net worth from $27.34 billion to $6.23 billion won't affect its ability to pay dividends or secure financing. How can this be?"

Required:

1. To focus discussion at the meeting, you decide that you should identify the key positives and negatives about GM that are contained in the *Wall Street Journal* article. What positives and negatives would you put forth for the group to consider?
2. What specific comments would you make in response to the issues raised by your fellow club members?
3. Based on your analysis of GM's earnings-related disclosures, how much (if any) of the club's GM common stock and bonds would you vote to sell?
4. If you had more time before the meeting, what other information would you gather and why?

The following excerpt is from an article that appeared in the *Wall Street Journal*.

C6 – 3

Nike (CW): Firm-specific information releases and large stock price changes

NIKE'S STOCK DROPS 13% AS FIRM SEES QUARTERLY NET FALLING SHORT OF FORECASTS

Nike Inc. warned that shifts in order patterns and other factors would drag fiscal fourth-quarter earnings below Wall Street forecasts. The news hammered the Beaverton, Ore., athletic-footwear maker's highflying shares. In New York Stock Exchange composite trading yesterday, Nike dropped $8.625, or 13%, to $55.375.

The issues crimping profits for the period ending tomorrow are relatively minor and short term, analysts said. But Wall Street and investor expectations about Nike have been high because of the company's turbocharged growth over the past several quarters. Moreover, the stock has surged in recent days on unconfirmed rumors that investor Warren Buffett has been buying Nike shares. The developments do represent the first stumble in a long time for Nike, which has had profit increases as high as 80% in recent quarters.

Nike said that it expects earnings of between 51 and 56 cents a share for the fourth quarter, including a one-time pretax charge of $18 million for the planned shutdown of a manufacturing facility. Wall Street had been expecting earnings of 69 cents a share. In the year-earlier fourth quarter, Nike earned $156.4 million, or 53 cents a share, on revenue of $1.92 billion.

Nike said several factors damped fourth-quarter profits. One was a shift in order patterns, particularly in Europe. Nike said more retailers bought more items in advance. Typically, Nike retailers buy shoes in advance, and if they sell out, make emergency "at once" orders that are delivered quickly. But Nike said retailers are making fewer "at once" orders in the current quarter. That implies that retailers' sales are lower than they expected. Some analysts said that, because of Nike's torrid growth in recent quarters, Nike retailers

(*continued*)

ordered aggressively, betting that sales would continue to surge. "Some got stuck because sales may not have gone up as rapidly as they have," said Jennifer Black Groves, an analyst with Black & Co.

Nike also said it had a "slight" increase in order cancellations in the U.S. Nike's international business has been booming, but U.S. sales still make up more than 60% of total revenue. In an analysts call, the company said it had about $30 million of canceled orders in the quarter, slightly more than it has typically had in recent quarters. Analysts said the domestic market for Nike is mature, and suggested Nike may have priced shoes at a point where competitors can cut into Nike sales. Reebok, Converse, and Adidas all have recently introduced shoes that sell in the $80 to $110 a pair range; many Nike models cost more. "They've been walking up the price ladder and they may have gone up as far as they can go," said Alice Ruth, an analyst at Montgomery Securities.

Even with pinched fourth-quarter profit, Nike said it expects a record year, with revenue and profit increasing 40% from year-earlier levels. It also said it expects revenue growth in 1998 to surpass the company's stated goal of 15%. Last fiscal year, Nike earned $553.2 million, or $3.77 a share, on sales of $6.5 billion.

Nonetheless, the fourth-quarter projection prompted many analysts to adjust their fiscal 1997 and 1998 projections. Shelly Hale Young, analyst at Hambrecht & Quist, lowered her 1997 projection to $2.68 a share from $2.83, and dropped her 1998 forecast to $3.24 from $3.40.

Source: Republished with permission of Dow Jones & Co.; ©1997. From *Wall Street Journal* (May 30, 1997); permission conveyed through Copyright Clearance Center, Inc.

Required:

1. What aspects of the *Wall Street Journal* article are likely to have caused Nike's stock price to change?
2. Assume that you are a financial analyst. Would the information in the article cause you to alter your forecast of Nike's earnings for next year (1998)? Why? Would the article alter your earnings forecasts for each of the next five years? Why?
3. Do you think that the stock prices of Nike's competitors (Reebok, Converse, L.A. Gear, and Adidas) would change on the day that Nike made the announcement? If so, how and why? If not, why not?
4. Firms often release important news after the market has closed for the day. Why might they do this? What are the costs and benefits of such a strategy?

COLLABORATIVE LEARNING CASES

C6 – 4

Microsoft Corporation (CW): Unearned revenues and earnings management

Microsoft develops, manufactures, licenses, sells, and supports a wide range of software products, including operating systems for personal computers (PCs) and servers; server applications for client/server environments; business and consumer productivity applications; software development tools; and Internet and intranet software and technologies. The company has expanded its interactive content efforts, including MSN (the Microsoft Network online service), various Internet-based services, and entertainment and information software programs. Microsoft also sells PC books and input devices, and it researches and develops advanced technologies for future software products.

The following excerpt is from an article that appeared in the *Wall Street Journal*.

MICROSOFT'S EARNINGS GROWTH SLOWED IN THE LATEST QUARTER

Microsoft Corp.'s growth juggernaut slowed in its fiscal fourth quarter, but the numbers masked a surprisingly potent performance by the software giant.

The Redmond, Wash., company's earnings barely topped Wall Street's consensus, breaking a pattern of dramatic upside surprises for the company. But the company's profit would have been considerably higher had it not salted away revenue in a special reserve account for use in future quarters. That account, dubbed "unearned revenues," continued to swell and underscore the returns Microsoft is reaping as a near-monopoly supplier of personal computer operating-software and key application programs. The account represents revenues Microsoft has collected but hadn't yet reported. It was established

because the company faces future costs to deliver up-grades and customer support for products that already have been paid for. The policy helps smooth out sharp swings in the company's quarterly results.

Microsoft reported net income of $1.06 billion, or 80 cents a share, for the quarter ended June 30, an increase of 89% from $559 million, or 43 cents a share, a year earlier. Analysts had expected per-share earnings of about 79 cents, according to First Call Corp. Quarterly revenue was $3.18 billion, up 41% from $2.26 billion a year earlier.

Source: Republished with permission of Dow Jones & Co.; ©1997. From *Wall Street Journal* (July 18, 1997); permission conveyed through Copyright Clearance Center, Inc.

Other Information:

1. Appearing in the accompanying tables are the comparative income statements for the fourth quarters of fiscal 1996 and 1997 and for the fiscal years 1996 and 1997. Also shown are comparative balance sheets for fiscal 1996 and 1997.
2. The balance in the unearned revenues account on March 31, 1997 (the end of the third fiscal quarter of 1997) was $1,285 (in millions).
3. The following description of Microsoft's unearned revenues account is taken from the company's SEC filings:

The portion of the Company's revenues that are earned later than billed is reflected in the unearned revenues account. Of the March 31, 1997 balance of $1,285 million, approximately $765 million represented the unearned portion of Windows desktop operating systems revenues and $150 million represented the unearned portion of Office 97 revenues. Unearned revenues associated with upgrade rights for Microsoft Office 97 were $190 million and the balance of unearned revenues was primarily attributable to maintenance and other subscription contracts.

Microsoft Corporation

Income Statements

($ in millions, except earnings per share)	Three Months Ended June 30		Years Ended June 30	
	1996	1997	1996	1997
Net revenues	$2,255	$3,175	$8,671	$11,358
Cost of revenues	241	242	1,188	1,085
Research and development	453	516	1,432	1,925
Sales and marketing	661	744	2,657	2,856
General and administrative	90	94	316	362
Total operating expenses	1,445	1,596	5,593	6,228
Operating income	810	1,579	3,078	5,130
Interest income	92	127	320	443
Other expenses	(42)	(80)	(19)	(259)
Income before income taxes	860	1,626	3,379	5,314
Provision for income taxes	301	569	1,184	1,860
Net income	$ 559	$1,057	$2,195	$ 3,454
Preferred stock dividends	–0–	7	–0–	15
Net income available for common shareholders	$ 559	$1,050	$2,195	$ 3,439
Earnings per share	$ 0.43	$ 0.80	$ 1.71	$ 2.63
Average shares outstanding	1,290	1,327	1,281	1,312

Balance Sheets

($ in millions)	June 30, 1996	June 30, 1997
Assets		
Current assets		
Cash and short-term investments	$ 6,940	$ 8,966
Accounts receivable	639	980
Other	260	427
Total current assets	7,839	10,373
Property, plant and equipment	1,326	1,465
Equity investments	675	2,346
Other assets	253	203
Total assets	$10,093	$14,387
Liabilities and Stockholders' Equity		
Current liabilities		
Accounts payable	$ 808	$ 721
Accrued compensation	202	336
Income taxes payable	484	466
Unearned revenues	560	1,418
Other	371	669
Total current liabilities	2,425	3,610

(*continued*)

Microsoft Corporation (*continued*)

Balance Sheets
($ in millions)

	June 30, 1996	June 30, 1997
Liabilities and Stockholders' Equity		
Minority interest	125	—
Put warrants	635	—
Stockholders' equity		
Convertible preferred stock	—	980
Common stock and paid-in capital	2,924	4,509
Retained earnings	3,984	5,288
Total stockholders' equity	6,908	10,777
Total liabilities and stockholders' equity	$10,093	$14,387

Required:

1. Calculate Microsoft's net profit margin for the fourth quarter of 1996 and 1997 and for the fiscal years 1996 and 1997. Comment on the results.
2. Calculate Microsoft's working capital and current ratio. Comment on the results.
3. Did Microsoft fall short of, meet, or exceed analysts' expectations for fourth-quarter 1997 EPS?
4. If no reductions were made from the "Unearned revenues" account during the fourth quarter of fiscal 1997, how much did Microsoft add to the account during that quarter?
5. Continuing requirement 4, how much higher or lower would Microsoft's fourth-quarter income before tax have been (on a per share basis) if this accrual adjustment had not been made?
6. Assume that Microsoft reduced its "Unearned revenues" account by $188.0 million during the first three quarters of fiscal 1997. How much did Microsoft add to the account during the fiscal year?
7. Continuing requirement 6, how much higher or lower would Microsoft's annual income before tax have been (on a per share basis) if this accrual adjustment had not been made?
8. How much income before tax (on a per share basis) does Microsoft have "stored" in the "Unearned revenues" account at the end of 1997?
9. How can the "Unearned revenues" account be used to manage EPS?
10. How can analysts monitor the extent to which the "Unearned revenues" account is being used to manage EPS?
11. Does the existence of the "Unearned revenues" account necessarily mean that Microsoft intends to manage its reported earnings? Explain.

C6 – 5

M&W Retailing (CW): Cash flow assessments and credit analysis

www.prenhall.com/revsine

● Student Resources

☑ Template for solution

Founded in 1872 and incorporated in Illinois in 1968, M&W Retailing Corporation (not its real name) is one of the nation's oldest and largest retail merchandising organizations with over $6.6 billion in annual revenues. The company operates 408 retail stores in 43 states with approximately 29 million square feet of selling space. The major product offerings by the company are: appliances and consumer electronics; furniture and home furnishings; apparel; jewelry; and automotive parts and repairs. In 1988 the company was taken private by its management in a $3.8 billion leveraged buyout.

The company has been a client of your bank for 35 years. It is early January 2005, and management has approached your bank to ask for an increase in the firm's line of credit from $1.0 to $2.0 billion.

As part of the loan application process, your bank asked M&W to provide some financial information about its operations over the last five years. Because the company's fiscal year ends on December 31, 2004, the results for 2004 are not yet available, so the company has provided information covering the 1999–2003 period. Management has provided the following information that it expects to report for the fiscal year ended December 31, 2004 ($ in millions):

Total revenues of $6,620 versus $7,085 in 2003

Net loss of ($237) versus net income of $11 in 2003

Cash flows from operating activities of −$356 versus −$182 in 2003

Cash flows from investing activities of −$148 versus −$109 in 2003

Cash flows from financing activities of $499 versus $295 in 2003

(Proceeds from the issuance of short-term debt of $588 were the primary source of the financing cash flows in 2004)

Overall a net cash flow of −$5 for 2004

The income statements and balance sheets that follow are prepared on both a trend basis and on a common-size basis. In the trend statements, 1999 serves as the base year with all subsequent years' amounts expressed as a percent of the 1999 amount. For example, in the trend income statements, sales for 1999, 2000, and 2001 are reported at $5,655,000, 102.21, and 106.14, respectively. This means sales for 2000 were 102.21% of 1999 sales, and 2001 sales were 106.14% of 1999 sales. The trend balance sheets are constructed in a similar fashion. In the common-size income statements all items are expressed as a percent of sales for that year. In the common-size balance sheets all items are expressed as a percent of total assets for that year.

Note: In responding to these questions you should provide a detailed discussion and analysis of the financial statements given in the case including appropriate trend and ratio analysis.

Required:

1. Should the increase in the firm's line of credit be granted? Why or why not?
2. What other information would you like to have before finalizing your decision?

M&W Retailing Corporation

Partial Trend Income Statement

	1999 ($ in millions)	2000 (%)	2001 (%)	2002 (%)	2003 (%)
Sales	$5,655	102.21	106.14	124.46	125.29
Cost of goods sold	(4,103)	102.53	107.90	123.86	125.74
Gross profit	1,552	101.35	101.48	126.03	124.10
Selling, general, and administrative expense	(1,243)	103.14	102.49	129.53	137.25
Operating income before depreciation	309	94.17	97.41	111.97	71.20
Depreciation	(95)	102.11	103.16	114.74	125.26
Operating profit	214	90.65	94.86	110.75	47.20
Interest expense	(75)	68.00	58.67	80.00	125.33
Nonoperating income	19	36.84	5.26	10.53	15.79
Special items	17	0.00	0.00	0.00	0.00
Pre-tax income	175	85.71	91.43	102.29	5.71
Income taxes	(40)	125.00	147.50	155.00	(2.50)
Income from continuing operations	$ 135	74.07	74.81	86.67	8.15

M&W Retailing Corporation

Partial Common-Size Income Statement

	1999	2000	2001	2002	2003
Sales	100.00%	100.00%	100.00%	100.00%	100.00%
Cost of goods sold	(72.56)	(72.79)	(73.76)	(72.21)	(72.82)
Gross profit	27.44	27.21	26.24	27.79	27.18
Selling, general, and administrative expense	(21.98)	(22.18)	(21.23)	(22.88)	(24.08)
Operating income before depreciation	5.46	5.03	5.01	4.91	3.10
Depreciation	(1.68)	(1.68)	(1.63)	(1.55)	(1.68)
Operating profit	3.78	3.35	3.38	3.36	1.42
Interest expense	(1.33)	(0.88)	(0.73)	(0.85)	(1.33)
Nonoperating income	0.34	0.12	0.02	0.03	0.04
Special items	0.30	0.00	0.00	0.00	0.00
Pre-tax income	3.09	2.59	2.67	2.54	0.13
Income taxes	(0.71)	(0.87)	(0.98)	(0.88)	0.01
Income from continuing operations	2.38%	1.72%	1.69%	1.66%	0.14%

M&W Retailing Corporation

Partial Trend Balance Sheet

	1999 ($ in millions)	2000 (%)	2001 (%)	2002 (%)	2003 (%)
Cash and equivalents	$ 623	18.94	25.04	10.75	11.24
Net receivables	73	93.15	90.41	161.64	257.53
Inventories	1,000	103.80	124.20	162.50	177.00
Accounts payable	1,227	98.61	110.68	140.10	147.03

M&W Retailing Corporation

Partial Common-Size Balance Sheet

	1999	2000	2001	2002	2003
Assets					
Cash and equivalents	16.08%	3.44%	4.07%	1.48%	1.43%
Net receivables	1.88	1.98	1.72	2.60	3.85
Inventories	25.81	30.24	32.39	35.79	36.24
Total assets	100.00%	100.00%	100.00%	100.00%	100.00%
Liabilities and Equity					
Accounts payable	31.66%	35.25%	35.41%	37.86%	36.94%
Long-term debt	13.94	5.97	7.35	6.48	9.17
Total liabilities	84.26	83.89	84.17	83.22	82.08
Total equity	15.74	16.11	15.83	16.78	17.92
Total liabilities and equity	100.00%	100.00%	100.00%	100.00%	100.00%

M&W Retailing Corporation

Annual Statement of Cash Flows

($ in millions)	1999	2000	2001	2002	2003
Operating Activities					
Income before extraordinary items	$135	$100	$101	$117	$ 11
Noncash adjustments					
Depreciation and amortization	95	97	98	109	119
Deferred taxes	(16)	32	25	29	(7)
Gain on sale of property, plant and equipment	0	0	0	0	(11)
Other	0	0	0	0	(12)
Changes in operating assets and liabilities					
Receivables	21	8	5	(40)	(70)
Inventory	(73)	(38)	(204)	(243)	(145)
Deferred taxes	(8)	(34)	(1)	5	(9)
Other assets and liabilities	70	(10)	105	179	(58)
Operating activities—net cash flow	224	155	129	156	(182)
Investing Activities					
Increase in investments	(751)	(707)	(688)	(691)	(803)
Sale of investments	729	698	669	671	775
Net change in short-term investments	55	146	(8)	16	2
Capital expenditures	(128)	(146)	(142)	(184)	(122)
Sale of property, plant and equipment	3	7	3	4	39
Acquisitions	0	0	0	(120)	0
Investing activities—other	2	2	3	0	0
Investing activities—net cash flow	(90)	0	(163)	(304)	(109)

M&W Retailing Corporation (*continued*)

Annual Statement of Cash Flows
($ in millions)

	1999	2000	2001	2002	2003
Financing Activities					
Sale of common and preferred stock	0	1	1	78	193
Purchase of common and preferred stock	(7)	(97)	(11)	(9)	(98)
Cash dividends	(13)	(19)	(23)	(24)	(4)
Long-term debt—issuance	0	0	100	168	205
Long-term debt—reduction	(137)	(403)	(18)	(275)	(17)
Current debt—changes	0	0	0	144	16
Financing activities—other	3	2	2	1	0
Financing activities—net cash flow	(154)	(516)	51	83	295
Cash and equivalents—change	$ (20)	$(361)	$ 17	$ (65)	$ 4

M&W Retailing Corporation

Selected Ratios

	1999	2000	2001	2002	2003
Liquidity and Activity					
Cash flow per share	4.98	4.31	4.46	5.10	(2.94)
Inventory turnover	4.26	4.13	3.88	3.55	3.04
Receivables turnover	67.72	81.99	89.58	76.50	46.31
Total asset turnover	1.47	1.58	1.65	1.68	1.50
Collection period (days)	5	4	4	5	8
Days to sell inventory	85	87	93	102	118
Operating cycle (days)	90	92	97	106	126
Profitability					
Pre-tax profit margin (%)	3.09	2.60	2.67	2.54	0.14
Net profit margin (%)	2.39	1.73	1.68	1.66	0.16
Return on assets (%)	3.48	2.91	2.63	2.58	0.23
Return on equity (%)	25.96	18.08	16.64	17.03	1.57
Leverage					
Interest coverage	3.33	3.94	4.64	3.98	1.11
Total debt/total assets (%)	16.13	6.41	7.87	9.98	13.29
Total assets/common equity	7.45	6.21	6.32	6.61	6.98
Long-term debt/capital	46.98	27.04	31.72	27.84	33.86
Long-term debt/common equity	103.85	37.07	46.46	42.79	64.00

Remember to check the book's Companion Website for additional problem and case material.

www.prenhall.com/revsine

C H A P T E R 7

The Role of Financial Information in Contracting

"A verbal contract isn't worth the paper it's written on."

–Sam Goldwyn, film producer

Learning Objectives

After studying this chapter, you will understand:

1. What conflicts of interest arise between managers and shareholders, lenders, or regulators.

2. How and why accounting numbers are used in debt agreements, in compensation contracts, and for regulatory purposes.

3. How managerial incentives are influenced by accounting-based contracts and regulations.

4. What role contracts and regulations play in shaping managers' accounting choices.

5. What accounting "gimmicks" are sometimes used to hide a company's true performance, and how to spot them.

Business contracts include formal written agreements, such as Allen Ford's franchise contract with BookWorm, Inc.[1] Financial accounting numbers are often used to define contract terms and to monitor compliance with those terms.

Commercial lending agreements, for example, may require the borrower to maintain an interest coverage ratio above a certain level (say, 5) for the duration of a loan. This requirement protects the lender from a deterioration of the borrower's creditworthiness. The lender then uses earnings, cash flow, and balance sheet data to monitor the borrower's compliance with the loan covenants. If the covenants are violated—for example, because the borrower's interest coverage ratio falls below 5—the lender can then act swiftly to recover the loan.

Financial data are also used in executive compensation contracts and in formal agreements with government agencies, joint-venture partners, suppliers, distributors, and customers. Figure 7.1 on the next page identifies the parties in each of these contractual relationships.

The usefulness of financial statement data for contracting purposes depends on the accounting methods used by the company and its freedom to change them. For example, an interest coverage provision is *unlikely* to protect the lender if the borrowing company can achieve the required coverage level by changing its accounting methods or through other artificial means. Contracting parties understand that financial reporting flexibility affects how contracts are written and enforced. This chapter describes these influences and addresses the following questions:

- What role do accounting numbers play in contracts?

- What incentives do accounting-based contracts create for the parties involved?

- How do these incentives help us understand why managers choose certain accounting methods and avoid others?

- How do these incentives influence when transactions are recorded?

---

[1] Chapter 6 explains why Allen Ford decided to purchase a BookWorm franchise. In this chapter, Allen must obtain a bank loan to finance the purchase.

335

Figure 7.1

SIGNIFICANT CONTRACTING
RELATIONSHIPS IN CORPORATE
ORGANIZATIONS

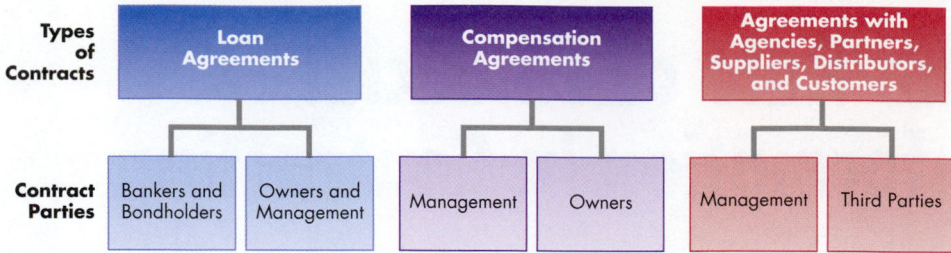

Finalizing the BookWorm Loan

Allen Ford assembled the monthly cash flow projections and other materials requested by the loan officer. This was not easy, but it produced an unintended benefit: Allen was forced again to evaluate the economic viability of the bookstore and the financial challenges ahead. His detailed financial projections revealed the need for a $75,000 loan, slightly larger than he anticipated originally. Otherwise, the prospects for the business seemed bright.

Several days after Allen completed the loan application, the bank phoned him to indicate preliminary approval of both the term loan and the revolving credit line. Allen was elated with the approval but surprised by the interest rate. It seemed higher than other local banks were charging for similar business loans. Allen and the loan officer agreed to meet to discuss the final terms and conditions of both loans. The loan officer advised Allen to consider accepting more stringent loan covenant restrictions in exchange for a lower rate of interest.

Allen was not quite sure what the loan officer had in mind, but it seemed worth exploring. Allen knew that some loan covenants were tied directly to the borrower's financial statements, and he wanted to be certain that the accounting-based covenants proposed by the bank agreed with his financial projections for the bookstore. In preparation for this negotiation, Allen decided to spend some time understanding how loan covenants work and what types of covenants are commonly used in commercial bank loans.

Conflicts of Interest in Business Relationships

Delegating decision-making authority is an essential feature of the modern corporation and most business relationships. Capital providers (stockholders and lenders) delegate authority to professional managers. In turn, managers delegate authority over aspects of a company's business affairs to others—inside and even outside the company—who have expertise or timely access to information that is critical for decision making. (Wal-Mart and Costco, for example, allow some suppliers to monitor product sales electronically at the checkout stand and to replenish shelf inventory without first seeking company approval.) But delegation of authority can cause **conflicts of interest**. Conflicts of interest arise when one party to the business relationship can take actions for his or her own benefit that harm other parties in the relationship.

Suppose that rather than operating the store himself, Allen Ford hired a bookstore manager. Would the bookstore manager always make decisions that are in Allen's (the owner's) best interest? Probably not, because some business decisions that benefit the owner may not always benefit the manager. Conversely, there will be other business decisions that directly benefit the manager at Allen's expense. Consider this example: A longtime friend of the manager arrives in town unexpectedly and suggests a leisurely lunch at the country club. The manager is tempted to agree even though it would mean closing the bookstore for several hours. Allen would prefer to keep the bookstore open because he absorbs the profit lost from closing the store and receives no benefit from the manager's luncheon reunion.

Potential conflicts of interest permeate many business relationships. Allen's franchise loans provide an illustration. The interest rate on each loan compensates the bank for credit risk and the other costs associated with providing financial capital to the BookWorm business. Once the loans are granted, however, Allen might be tempted to divert the cash toward other, more risky investment opportunities—like buying tickets in the state lottery. The chance of winning $40 million is quite remote, and if the loan proceeds are diverted, the lender's risk of nonpayment jumps.

Contract terms can be designed to eliminate or reduce conflicting incentives that arise in business relationships. Allen's loan agreements will describe the business purpose for each loan and require that the borrowed funds be used only for those purposes. By agreeing to such conditions, Allen is providing the bank with a written assurance that borrowed funds will not be diverted to other unspecified uses—such as buying lottery tickets. Business contracts specify the mutual expectations—the rights and responsibilities—of each participant in the relationship. Thus, they provide a low-cost mechanism for addressing any conflicts of interest that can occur.

Debt Covenants in Lending Agreements

Most companies have debt in the form of either commercial bank loans or bonds. In addition, managers frequently own shares of the companies they manage. Unfortunately, the interests of creditors and stockholders often diverge, particularly after the lender has handed over the cash. This divergence creates incentives for managers to take actions that transfer part of the company's value from creditors to the managers themselves as well as to other stockholders.

Here is an example that illustrates the conflicting incentives of creditors and owner-manager borrowers. Recall that Allen Ford needs about $125,000 to launch his BookWorm store. Allen plans to invest $50,000 of his own money and borrow the remaining $75,000 from the bank. Once the loan is granted, however, a natural conflict of interests arises between Allen (the borrower) and the bank (the creditor). This conflict of interests occurs because Allen—not the bank—decides just how the money will be spent.

> These conflicts of interest between creditors and owner-managers are spelled out in detail in the Appendix to this chapter.

Suppose Allen immediately pays himself a $75,000 dividend instead of using the bank's money to buy inventory and equipment for the store. After all, he is the owner-manager of the business and as such can declare a dividend at any time. A $75,000 dividend payment would increase Allen's personal wealth but surely spell disaster for the BookWorm store because the cash needed to launch the business would no longer be available. The bank would have a $75,000 loan outstanding for a business consisting of only $50,000 in cash. The dividend payment benefits Allen but harms the bank.

Creditors know that their interests will sometimes conflict with those of borrowers, and they protect themselves in several ways. One way is to charge a higher rate of interest on the loan as compensation for the risky actions that managers like Allen can take. *Another way to reduce conflicts of interest between lenders and borrowers is by writing contracts that restrict—explicitly or implicitly—the borrowers' ability to harm lenders.* For instance, the bank might require Allen to personally guarantee the business loan. A personal guarantee would require Allen to repay the bank loan from his own funds if the bookstore failed. This would certainly make paying himself a $75,000 dividend less attractive. Alternatively, the loan agreement might prohibit any dividend payments without prior approval by the bank, or it might limit dividends to some fraction (say, 50%) of net income.

Lending agreements contain restrictions called **debt covenants** that help guard against conflicts of interest between creditors and borrowers. Debt covenants benefit both creditors and borrowers. Creditors benefit because the covenants reduce default risk. Borrowers benefit because a lower default risk means a lower cost of debt. *This cost savings occurs because creditors face less default risk, and can afford to offer loans at lower rates of interest.*

Affirmative Covenants, Negative Covenants, and Default Provisions

Debt covenants are intensively negotiated. They require the borrower to maintain a certain financial status for the loan's duration, and they set minimum standards for the borrower's future conduct and performance. Covenants vary with the borrower's business characteristics, financial condition, and the length of the loan. If credit risk is high, covenants may be tied directly to detailed financial projections provided by the borrower; where credit risk is low, a few general financial benchmarks may be sufficient. In either case, covenants are designed to protect the creditor and to sound an early warning if the financial condition of the borrower deteriorates.

Affirmative covenants stipulate actions the borrower *must* take. Generally, these include:

1. Using the loan for the agreed-upon purpose
2. Financial covenants and reporting requirements
3. Compliance with laws
4. Allowing the lender to inspect business assets and business contracts
5. Maintaining business records and business properties and carrying insurance on them

For example, loan agreements place restrictions on how the money borrowed can be used, often saying that it can only be used for a specific agreed-upon purpose spelled out in the loan contract. This type of covenant can be found in a recent loan agreement involving TCBY Enterprises—"The Country's Best Yogurt":

> Borrower will use the proceeds of the term loans for the loan purposes set forth . . . in Section 1.1 of this agreement. (para. 5.5 of TCBY term loan agreement).

To keep the lender informed about the company's financial and operating performance, another covenant in TCBY's loan agreement states that the borrower (TCBY) is required to provide financial reports to the lender in a timely manner:

> [The company] will furnish . . . not later than one hundred twenty days (120) after the close of each fiscal year . . . consolidated balance sheets, income statements and statements of cash flow . . . and such other comments and financial details as are usually included in similar reports. (para. 5.1 of TCBY term loan agreement).

Financial covenants establish minimum financial tests with which a borrower must comply. These tests can specify dollar amounts (such as required minimum levels of net worth and working capital) or ratios (such as minimum debt-to-equity and interest coverage ratios). Financial covenants are intended to signal financial difficulty and to trigger intervention by the creditor—we explain how later—long before bankruptcy or liquidation become necessary. However, financial covenants often do not stipulate the accounting methods to be used when preparing the statements, except that they must comply with generally accepted accounting principles (GAAP):

> Such reports shall be prepared in accordance with GAAP and shall be audited by independent certified public accountants of recognized standing . . . and shall contain unqualified opinions . . . (para. 5.1 of TCBY term loan agreement).

The financial covenants also define the financial terms and ratios mentioned in the contract:

> Borrower will at all times maintain a ratio of Current Assets to Current Liabilities . . . that is greater than 2.0 to 1.0 . . . a Profitability Ratio greater than 1.5 to 1.0 . . . [defined as] the ratio of Net Income for the immediately preceding period of twelve calendar months to Current Maturities of Long Term Debt . . . a Fixed Charge Coverage Ratio greater than 1.0

to 1.0 . . . [defined as] the ratio of Net Income of the Borrower and Subsidiaries for the immediately preceding period of twelve calendar months plus Noncash Charges of the Borrower and Subsidiaries for the same period to Current Maturities of Long Term Debt of the Borrower and Subsidiaries plus cash dividends paid by TCBY to the shareholders of TCBY for the preceding period of twelve calendar months plus Replacement CapEx of the Borrower and Subsidiaries for the preceding twelve calendar months . . . (paras. 5.7, 5.8, and 5.9 of TCBY term loan agreement).

Notice that TCBY is required to maintain a **fixed-charge coverage** ratio greater than 1.0, measured over the most recent 12 months:

$$\text{Fixed-charge coverage} = \frac{\text{Net income} + \text{Noncash charges}}{\text{Current maturities} + \text{Dividends} + \text{Replacement CapEx}}$$

Noncash charges—like depreciation and goodwill amortization—are added back to net income because they don't reduce the cash available for debt repayment. Replacement CapEx—capital expenditures required to maintain (but not expand) the business—is viewed by TCBY's lender as a necessary cash outflow, like debt repayment.

Also notice how the fixed-charge coverage requirement indirectly limits the company's ability to pay dividends. Suppose TCBY had net income of $50, noncash charges of $35, current loan maturities of $40, and replacement capital expenditures of $30. How large a dividend could TCBY pay to shareholders? A simple calculation shows the answer to be $15.

$$\begin{aligned}\text{Fixed-charge coverage} &= \frac{\$50 + \$35}{\$40 + \text{Dividend} + \$30} = 1.0 \\[2mm] &= \frac{\$50 + \$35}{\$40 + \$15 + \$30} = 1.0\end{aligned}$$

Dividends in excess of $15 would put TCBY in violation of its fixed-charge coverage requirement.

Negative covenants tend to be more significant and even more intensively negotiated than affirmative covenants because they place direct *restrictions* on the actions borrowers can take. These restrictions prevent actions that might impair the lender's claims against the company's cash flows, earnings, and assets. Negative covenants include limits on total indebtedness, investment of funds, capital expenditures, leases, and corporate loans, as well as restrictions on the payment of cash dividends, share repurchases, mergers, asset sales, voluntary prepayment of other indebtedness, and on new business ventures. This example is from the TCBY loan agreement:

> [Borrower agrees that it will not] sell, lease, transfer, or otherwise dispose of any assets . . . except the sale of inventory in the ordinary course of business and disposition of obsolete or worn-out equipment upon the replacement thereof . . . [or to] repurchase the stock of TCBY using, directly or indirectly, the proceeds of any loan. (paras. 6.6 and 6.12 of TCBY term loan agreement).

Covenants restricting the use of funds for dividend payments, share repurchases, capital expenditures, and other business purposes are included so the creditor has greater assurance that cash will be available to make interest and principal payments when due. In limiting the borrower's ability to sell, merge, or transfer operating assets, the creditor is ensuring the survival of the borrower's repayment potential.

Restrictions on total indebtedness limit the amount of additional debt the company may incur over the term of the loan. These restrictions are stated as a dollar amount or as a ratio (examples include total debt to assets, working capital, or tangible net worth):

> [Borrower agrees that it will not take on any new loans if] the aggregate amount of all such loans, advances and extensions of credit . . . would exceed twenty-five percent (25%) of the consolidated Tangible Net Worth of the Borrower . . . (para. 6.3 of TCBY term loan agreement).

It is also common for a borrower to agree not to use any of its existing property as collateral on future loans without first obtaining consent from the current lender:

> [Borrower agrees that it will not] create, incur, assume or suffer to exist any Lien, encumbrance, or charge of any kind (including any lease required to be capitalized under GAAP) upon any of its properties and/or assets other than Permitted Liens. (para. 6.1 of TCBY term loan agreement).

An unusual feature of this **negative pledge**—a promise to not take a particular action—is that TCBY agrees to limit its property leasing activities, but it does so only for leases required to be capitalized under GAAP. The agreement does not restrict TCBY from utilizing other operating leases.

The **events of default** section of a loan agreement describes circumstances in which the creditor has the right to terminate the lending relationship. Situations leading to default include the failure to pay interest or principal when due, inaccuracy in representations, failure to abide by a covenant, failure to pay other debts when due (known as "cross default"), impairment of collateral, change in management or ownership, and bankruptcy.

Most lending agreements require the borrower to periodically provide a **Certificate of Compliance**, which affirms that the borrower's managers have reviewed the financial statements and found no violation of any covenant provision. If a covenant has been violated, the nature and status of the violation must be specified.[2] Remedies for breach of covenant restrictions include renegotiation of the debt contract terms such as an increase in the interest rate, seizure of collateral, acceleration of the maturity of the debt, or initiation of legal bankruptcy proceedings.

The common remedy creditors exercise in the event of default is renegotiation of the loan agreement. All aspects of the loan—payment schedule, interest rate, collateral, affirmative and negative covenants—may be renegotiated. In cases where the circumstances of default are considered relatively insignificant, the creditor may waive the violation or give the borrower a period of time—a "grace period"—to correct its covenant breach. In cases where the default is severe, the creditor may accelerate loan repayment (with interest) and terminate its relationship with the borrower. Although creditors rarely exercise the right to accelerate repayment, having this right substantially strengthens a lender's negotiating position with the borrower if problems arise.

> For example, TCBY would be in default on the bank loan if the company reported net income of $120 and had $100 in current maturities of long-term debt. These figures would equate to a Profitability Index (as defined in the loan agreement) of 1.2, which is less than the 1.5 required minimum.

 RECAP

> **When it comes to a company's business decisions, what's best for managers and shareholders isn't always best for creditors. Debt covenants—including those based on accounting numbers—help reduce this conflict of interest. Creditors benefit because debt covenants reduce default risk, and shareholders benefit from the lowered cost of debt financing.**

---

2   Any covenant breach that existed at the date of the most recent balance sheet and that subsequently has not been cured (that is, remedied or corrected) should be disclosed in the notes to the financial statements (Rule 4–08[c] of Securities and Exchange Commission [SEC] Regulation S-X). When covenants are violated, the related debt must be reclassified as current if it is probable that the borrower will not be able to cure the default within the next 12 months. See "Classification of Obligations that are Callable by the Creditor," *Statement of Financial Accounting Standards [SFAS] No. 78* (Stamford, CT: Financial Accounting Standards Board [FASB] 1983) and "Classification of Obligations When a Violation Is Waived by the Creditor," *Emerging Issues Task Force 86–30* (Stamford, CT: FASB, 1986).

Managers' Responses to Potential Debt Covenant Violations

Violating a covenant is costly. So managers have strong incentives to make accounting choices and/or manipulate discretionary accruals in ways that reduce the likelihood of technical default. Accounting choices include not only the selection of alternative accounting techniques (for example, LIFO versus FIFO inventory methods) but also accrual adjustments (like changing the amount of bad debt provisions), and decisions about when to initiate transactions that result in accounting gains or losses (for example, when assets are sold or the corporation is restructured). **Readers of financial statements must be able to recognize and understand these incentives and their effect on managers' accounting choices.**

> A **technical default** occurs when the borrower violates one or more loan covenants but has made all interest and principal payments. A **payment default** occurs when the borrower is unable to make the scheduled interest or principal payment.

A number of studies have examined how debt-covenant-related incentives affect managers' accounting choices. One study looked at voluntary accounting changes made by 130 companies reporting covenant violations from 1980 to 1989. The study found that net worth and working capital restrictions are the most frequently violated accounting-based covenants and that companies approaching default often make accounting changes that increase reported earnings.[3] The most common techniques used at these companies to increase earnings are changes in pension cost assumptions (discussed in Chapter 14), the liquidation of LIFO layers, and the adoption of the FIFO inventory method (discussed in Chapter 9).

Another study examined **discretionary accounting accruals**—noncash financial statement adjustments that "accrue" revenue (like debits to accounts receivable and credits to sales) or accrue expenses (such as debits to warranty expense and credits to accrued warranties payable).[4] This study, which looked at discretionary accruals by 94 companies reporting covenant violations from 1985 to 1988, found that "abnormal" accruals in the year prior to violation significantly increased reported earnings by accelerating revenue and postponing expenses. (Normal accruals were determined by examining each company's past accruals and by benchmarking against average accruals reported by other firms in the same industry that year.) Moreover, these accrual adjustments were also more likely to increase working capital in the year of the covenant violation.

These and other studies suggest that *management tends to make accounting changes and/or to manipulate discretionary accruals that increase income in order to avoid violating debt covenants.* However, earnings increases due to maneuvers to avoid covenant violations are unlikely to reflect the true economic condition of the company and, therefore, are not likely to be sustainable. Unsustainable earnings increases are unlikely to translate into permanent cash flow increases, as we discovered in Chapter 2. Consequently, these "tenuous" earnings should be interpreted with caution.

Throughout the remainder of the book, we highlight how alternative accounting methods and accrual adjustments affect earnings and key financial ratios. We'll alert you to accounting choices that can have substantial implications for debt covenants—implications you should keep in mind as you go about interpreting and using accounting numbers for making economic decisions.

---

[3] A. P. Sweeney, "Debt-Covenant Violations and Managers' Accounting Responses," *Journal of Accounting and Economics* (May 1994), pp. 281–308.

[4] M. L. DeFond and J. Jiambalvo, "Debt Covenant Violation and Manipulation of Accruals," *Journal of Accounting and Economics* (January 1994), pp. 145–76.

Management Compensation

Most modern corporations are not run by the descendants of those who founded the organization but instead are controlled by professional managers—that is, "hired hands" who may lack the passion for corporate excellence that comes with substantial share ownership. This separation of ownership and control creates potential conflicts of interest between shareholders and managers.[5]

Consider a top executive whose job requires extensive travel and who, for reasons of "comfort and convenience," prefers the corporate jet to a commercial airline. Who receives the benefits of the comfort and convenience? And who pays the cost? If the comfort and convenience that comes from using the corporate jet leads to increased managerial productivity, both parties stand to gain. Shareholders lose, however, when the benefits of comfort and convenience accrue only to the executive, and there are no productivity improvements that result from it. That's because shareholders alone bear the added cost of travel by corporate jet.

> The corporate jet example illustrates one type of conflict between owners and managers—the tendency of managers to "overconsume" corporate resources. But there are others. For example, managers who are close to retirement age may have little incentive to adopt a long-term focus by investing in R&D.

Obviously, managers have incentives to use corporate assets for their personal benefit at the expense of owners. Potential conflicts of interest can be overcome if managers are given incentives that cause them to behave like owners. One way is to give them a compensation package that links their pay to improvements in firm value.[6]

If a manager's compensation goes up as the organization's value increases, then he or she has an incentive to take actions that lead to such an increase. As a result, both the manager and the owners will benefit simultaneously.

Two ways of aligning managers' incentives with owners' interests are to link compensation to stock returns and/or financial performance measures such as accounting earnings. Both are widely used. Neither is perfect.

Consider stock returns. Managerial strategies and decisions clearly affect share prices in the long run. But in the short run, share prices could rise or fall due to factors like interest rate changes that are beyond management's control.

> Changes in interest rates affect stock prices for two reasons. To see why, consider the effect of a *decrease* in marketwide interest rates. First, notice that a decrease in marketwide interest rates will reduce the company's cost of equity capital. As you know from Chapter 6, this will increase share price. Second, as interest rates decrease, the yields on fixed-rate bond investments fall, making them less attractive to investors. Both factors contribute to an increase in the demand for stocks and to an increase in stock prices.

Similar problems cloud the linkage between compensation and financial performance measures like earnings. On the positive side, earnings are probably less susceptible to the influence of temporary and external economic forces, and unlike stock returns, accounting-based financial performance measures can be tied to a manager's specific responsibilities, such as the profitability of a single product line or geographical region. On the other hand, using accounting earnings as a measure is frequently criticized for its reliance on accruals, deferrals, allocations, and valuations that involve varying degrees of subjectivity and judgment.

A good compensation plan must overcome the incentive alignment problems we have discussed and motivate managers to act like owners.[7]

---

[5] For more information about conflicts of interest between owners and managers, see J. Boyd, R. Parrino, and G. Pritsch, "Stockholder-Manager Conflicts and Firm Value," *Financial Analysts Journal* (May/June 1998), pp. 14–30.

[6] A more complete discussion of compensation incentives and owner-manager conflicts of interest is contained in M. Jensen and W. Meckling, "Theory of the Firm: Managerial Behavior, Agency Costs and Ownership Structure," *Journal of Financial Economics* (October 1976), pp. 305–60; P. Milgrom and J. Roberts, *Economics, Organization, and Management* (Upper Saddle River, NJ: Prentice Hall, 1992); and R. Watts and J. Zimmerman, *Positive Accounting Theory* (Upper Saddle River, NJ: Prentice Hall, 1986).

[7] Certain features of executive compensation packages are also designed to reduce the combined tax liability of the company and its managers. Tax considerations undoubtedly contribute to the popularity of certain pay practices and help explain their use by some companies and not others. See C. W. Smith and R. L. Watts, "Incentive and Tax Effects of Executive Compensation Plans," in R. Ball and C. W. Smith (eds.), *The Economics of Accounting Policy Choice* (New York: McGraw-Hill, 1992).

How Executives Are Paid

Most compensation packages involve a base salary, an annual incentive, and a long-term incentive:

- **Base salary** is typically dictated by industry norms and the executive's specialized skills.
- **Annual incentives** set yearly financial performance goals that must be achieved if the executive is to earn various bonus awards. For example, a plan may stipulate that a bonus of 50% of salary is earned only if the after-tax return on assets for the company exceeds 12%. But a 100% bonus can be earned if the return on assets is 15% or more. Such plans link pay to performance; because compensation is "at risk," managers have an incentive to achieve plan goals.
- **Long-term incentives** motivate and reward executives for the company's long-term growth and prosperity (typically three to seven years). Long-term incentives are designed to counterbalance the inherently short-term orientation of other incentives.

> One of the earliest annual incentive plans was the General Motors Bonus Plan, which was adopted in 1918. According to a former CEO of the company, "the interests of the corporation and its stockholders are best served by making key employees parties in the corporation's prosperity . . . each individual should be rewarded in proportion to his [sic] contribution to the profit of his [sic] own division and of the corporation as a whole." Alfred. P. Sloan, Jr., *My Years with General Motors* (New York: Doubleday & Company, 1964), p. 407.

Figure 7.2 shows the mix of compensation for chief executive officers in 1985, 1995, and 2000 based on annual surveys of pay practices at 1,500 large U.S. companies. In 1985, base salary was 55% of the median total pay. Annual bonus payments and long-term incentive awards that year comprised 28% and 17%, respectively, of total pay. In other words, each dollar of compensation paid to CEOs in 1985 was made up of $0.55 in base salary and $0.45 in performance-related incentive pay.

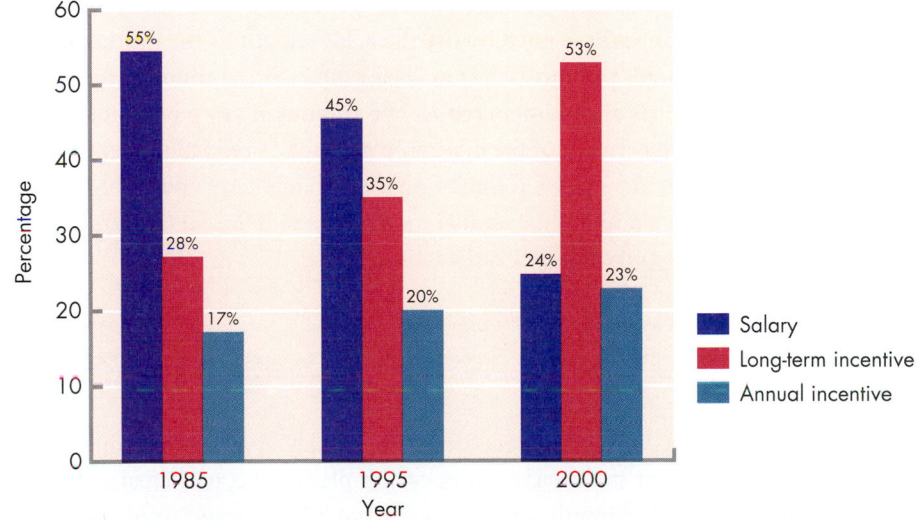

Figure 7.2

CEO COMPENSATION MIX
Annual incentive is a yearly performance-based bonus payment. Long-term incentive is a yearly award in cash, stock, or stock options for multi-year performance.

Source: The Conference Board, "Executive Annual Incentive Plans— 1996" (New York: 1997) and The Conference Board, "Top Executive Compensation in 2000," (New York: 2001).

There are several trends evident in Figure 7.2. One trend is that base salary has become a smaller component of total CEO compensation (55% in 1985 versus 24% in 2000), while long-term incentive awards have become a larger part of CEO pay (28% in 1985 versus 53% in 2000). This shift in compensation mix can be traced to the increased use of stock options in executive pay packages. Figure 7.2 also shows that $0.76 of each dollar of pay in 2000 came from annual incentives ($0.23) and long-term incentives ($0.53). This means that the amount of "at risk" pay—the combined percentage of short-term and long-term incentive compensation—is substantially greater in 2000 (76%) than it was in 1985 (45%).

Within a given organization, the proportion of pay "at risk" falls off steeply for executives on lower rungs of the corporate ladder. One compensation survey found that corporate executives in large industrial companies had 71% of their 1997 pay at risk, mid-level managers had 20%, and nonmanagerial professionals had only 8%.[8]

Annual (Short-term) Incentives   The most common financial performance measure used in these bonus plans is GAAP net income, or some variation of GAAP net income. For example, Exhibit 7.1 shows you what Computer Associates International says about its annual incentive plan.

EXHIBIT 7.1	Computer Associates International

Description of Annual Incentive Compensation Plan

Annual Incentives. [U]nder the Company's annual incentive plan ① **previously approved by the stockholders**, targeted payouts are determined at the beginning of each fiscal year based on the Company's ② achievement of (1) a minimum level of **revenue** and (2) threshold amounts of **net operating profit after taxes ("NOPAT")**, relative to the performance of the Company's peers. The NOPAT thresholds are derived from the financial forecasts of the Company that are publicly disclosed at the beginning of each fiscal year.

No payouts are made unless the minimum revenue level is achieved. If the minimum revenue level is reached, the **payout amount can range from 0% to 200%**, based on the percentage of NOPAT that is ③ achieved as compared to the threshold, as follows:

	% Target Payout
Below Threshold	0%
At Threshold	Up to 50%
Between Threshold and Target	Up to 100%
Between Target and Maximum	Up to 200%

The [Compensation] **Committee must certify the achievement of the minimum revenue level and the NOPAT thresholds** prior to each annual payout under the annual incentive plan. In addition, the ④ Committee has **discretion to reduce the amount of any payout** if it determines that, notwithstanding the achievement of the minimum amounts, a reduction is appropriate.

In fiscal 2003, the Company exceeded the minimum revenue level and the NOPAT target amounts. The ⑤ amounts paid under the annual incentive plan reflected those results, as well as **individual contributions and customer satisfaction**.

Source: Computer Associates International, 2003 Proxy Statement (emphasis added).

Notice that Computer Associates' shareholders have already approved the annual incentive plan (see ①). This means that the basic features of the plan—who participates, how performance will be measured, the maximum payout as a percent of salary, and so on—were submitted to shareholders and approved by a formal vote at an annual meeting. Most companies do not request shareholder approval of their annual incentive plans, but a growing number are doing so.

Computer Associates uses two accounting-based performance measures—revenue and net operating profit after taxes (NOPAT)—to determine managers' annual incentive pay (see ② and ③). The bonus formula has two components.

1. The company must achieve a minimum revenue goal each year before any bonus will be paid.
2. Once this revenue goal has been achieved, the amount of the bonus is determined by corporate profits (NOPAT) compared to a minimum and maximum profit threshold, and a target profit amount.

---

[8] *1998 Hay Compensation Report*, Hay Group, Inc., 1998.

Figure 7.3 illustrates how the second (or NOPAT) component of the bonus formula works. Suppose the minimum NOPAT threshold for the year is set at $10 million, the target NOPAT is $20 million, and the maximum threshold is $30 million. To complete the illustration, let's assume that the CEO's target bonus is $2 million or a 10% share of the $20 million NOPAT. One more thing: Revenue for the year is assumed to exceed the minimum requirement for bonus payments.

Figure 7.3

COMPUTER ASSOCIATES INTERNATIONAL
How the annual bonus formula works.

As Figure 7.3 shows, no bonus is paid if actual NOPAT for the year falls below the $10 million threshold. If NOPAT falls at the minimum threshold, the CEO will receive a bonus of $0.5 million (50% payout × 10% NOPAT bonus share × $10 million NOPAT). If NOPAT falls between the minimum threshold and the target, the payout rate increases from 50% up to 100%. So, if the company reports NOPAT of $20 million, the CEO earns a bonus of $2 million (100% payout × 10% NOPAT bonus share × $20 million NOPAT).

Once NOPAT exceeds the $20 million target level, the payout rate grows further from 100% up to 200%. For example, the CEO earns a bonus of $6 million when NOPAT at the company reaches $30 million ($6 million = 200% payout × 10% NOPAT bonus share × $30 million NOPAT). But there's a catch! The bonus formula puts a cap on the *maximum* amount of annual incentive pay the CEO can earn. Even though actual NOPAT may be above $30 million (the maximum threshold), the CEO's bonus will still be just $6 million that year.

At Computer Associates and most other companies today, it's the compensation committee that is responsible for implementing the executive pay plan (see ④). This committee is comprised of the company's outside (non-management) directors. It selects the performance metrics to be used and sets the annual or multi-year performance goals for each executive. (At some companies, the pay plan is then submitted to shareholders for their approval.) This avoids the conflict of interest that would naturally arise if the executives themselves were to set annual threshold and target profit levels. The committee can sometimes override the bonus formula when circumstances warrant. Computer Associates' compensation committee is allowed to reduce or eliminate the calculated award, but it may not increase the award (see ⑤). As we will see in a moment, compensation committees play an important role in reducing managers' incentives to meet the performance target using accounting "gimmickry."

> Notice how important one more profit dollar can be if it enables the company to report NOPAT of $10 million rather than $9,999,999. In our example, that one extra dollar of profit causes the CEO's bonus to jump from $0 to $500,000.

Long-term Incentives Long-term incentives comprise a large portion of total compensation for most CEOs, although many long-term plans are not tied directly to accounting numbers. Figure 7.4 shows the prevalence of long-term incentives by type.

Figure 7.4

PREVALENCE OF LONG-TERM INCENTIVES

Source: J. D. England "Executives Pay, Incentives and Performance," in D. E. Logue (ed.) *Handbook of Modern Finance* (Boston: Warren, Gorham & Lamont, 1996), p. E-93.

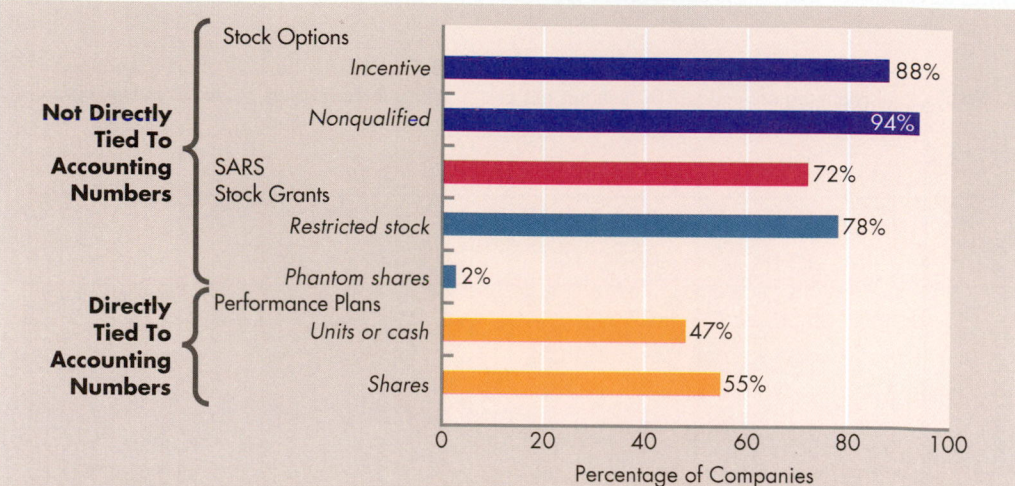

Stock options come in various forms, the choice of which is largely dependent on the tax treatment for the executive and the company. Stock options give the executive the right to buy shares at a stated (exercise) price, typically the fair market price on the grant date, for a period of years. If the stock price rises, the executive may trade in (or "exercise") each option plus pay the stated exercise price in exchange for a share of company stock. *Nonqualified stock options* require the executive to pay ordinary income tax at the exercise date on the difference between the stated exercise price and the stock's current fair market value. Under certain Internal Revenue Code provisions, *incentive stock options* may be awarded that offer capital gains tax treatment; however, the corporate tax deductability of the options is also limited by Code provisions.

Stock appreciation rights (SARs) do not require the manager to exercise the option and pay the stated exercise price in order to capture the share price gain. Instead, with SARs an executive receives an amount equal to the difference between the current stock price and the exercise price. This "appreciation" can be paid in stock, cash, or both. SARs enable companies and their executives to reduce the transaction costs associated with exercising options.

Stock grants give the executive outright ownership of company shares. With *restricted stock,* only after all restrictions lapse are the shares "earned out" and unconditionally owned by the executive. The most prevalent restriction is one of continued employment, although performance-related conditions are sometimes applied. Dividends can be paid to the executive even when the stock is restricted, and many restricted stock awards carry immediate voting rights. With *phantom* (hypothetical) *shares,* the executive "owns" the share value but not the stock itself.

Performance plans require the manager to achieve certain multiyear financial performance goals such as a three-year average return on equity above 20%. The payout could be either cash or company shares.

Stock options are the most common long-term incentive device. Because the option has value only if the market price of the underlying stock rises, the executive has an incentive to increase shareholder value as measured by stock price. So-called **incentive stock options** qualify for favorable tax treatment—that is, the executive is taxed at the capital gains rate, which is usually lower than the ordinary income tax rate. So-called **nonqualified stock options** do not have this personal tax advantage.

Stock appreciation rights (SARs) are a stock option variation developed to ease the cash flow burden faced by executives when stock options are exercised. The executive does not have to pay anything to receive the cash value of an appreciated SAR. When granted in tandem with traditional stock options, SARs can provide all of the cash needed to exercise the options, including any associated tax liability.

Restricted stock is typically an award of stock that is nontransferable or subject to forfeiture for a period of years. Restricted stock grants provide a set of "golden handcuffs" for retaining executives with desirable skills, at least during the restriction period. **Phantom stock** has all the characteristics of restricted stock, except that the executive receives the cash value of shares "earned out," not the shares themselves.

Performance plans award shares or cash units earned according to the degree of achievement of predetermined performance goals. From a financial reporting perspective, these plans are important because performance goals are often tied to financial targets like earnings-per-share growth or return-on-equity hurdles. Occasionally, the performance goals are strategic—increasing market share, reducing costs, or raising product quality. Performance goals are established at the beginning of the award period, which usually ranges from four to seven years, and may be stated in absolute terms or relative to the performance levels achieved by peer companies over the award period.

Performance unit (or cash) plans allocate to each executive a given number of "units" of fixed dollar value at the start of the award period. At the end of the award period, the executive receives cash equal to the number of units "earned out" times the fixed dollar value, with the proportion of units earned determined by the degree to which performance goals have been achieved.

Performance shares are similar to unit plans in that each executive is allocated a fixed number of common shares, with the proportion earned out again contingent upon the extent to which financial and strategic goals are met. Since performance plans comprise an important element of long-term incentive compensation, analysts and other statement readers must be aware that financial reporting choices have a potential impact on managers' long-term compensation.

> Although performance plans have been a key element of long-term incentive compensation in many companies for a number of years, passage of the Tax Reform Act of 1993 provided further impetus for pay plans linked to specific performance goals. See the discussion in Reebok's proxy statement (Exhibit 7.2).

Proxy Statements and Executive Compensation

Information about a company's executive compensation practices can be found in the annual proxy statement, a notification of the annual shareholders meeting, filed each year with the SEC. Among other disclosures, this document describes both the compensation payments and awards made to the five highest paid executives of the company and any new executive compensation plans submitted for shareholder approval. Exhibit 7.2 presents excerpts from the 1996 proxy statement of Reebok International Ltd.

EXHIBIT 7.2 — Reebok International LTD.

Notice of Annual Meeting of Shareholders
Executive Compensation

The following table sets forth the aggregate compensation paid or accrued by the Company for services rendered during the years ended December 1993, 1994 and 1995 for the Chief Executive Officer and each of the Company's four other most highly compensated executive officers. [Authors' note: Three executives are omitted for brevity.]

Name and Position	Year	Salary	Bonus	Other	Restricted Stock ($k)	Options	Other ($k)
Paul B. Fireman	1995	$1,000	none	none	none	87,300	$ 97
Chairman, President and	1994	1,000	$1,000	none	none	none	69
Chief Executive Officer	1993	1,000	650	none	none	none	231
Paul R. Duncan	1995	600	120	none	none	40,000	52
Executive Vice President	1994	583	525	none	none	none	16
	1993	500	357	none	none	25,000	77

(continued on next page)

EXHIBIT 7.2	Reebok International LTD. (*continued*)

① Certain of the Company's executive officers are required to defer twenty-five percent (25%) of their 1995 bonus award and to invest it into restricted shares of Reebok Common Stock. Fifty percent (50%) of such shares vest on each of January 1, 1997 and January 1, 1998. Any unvested portion of such shares will be forfeited if the executive officer leaves the Company prior to such vesting dates.

Approval of Executive Performance Incentive Plan

On February 15, 1996 the Compensation Committee of the Board of Directors unanimously approved, subject to approval by shareholders at the 1996 Annual Meeting, the Reebok International Ltd. Executive Performance Incentive Plan (the "Incentive Plan") which provides for the awarding of bonuses to certain executive officers or other key employees of the Company and its subsidiaries subject to attainment of certain performance criteria.

In 1993, the Internal Revenue Code was amended by adding Section 162(m) which limits to $1 million the federal income tax deduction which public corporations may claim for compensation paid to any of its top five executives except in certain limited circumstances. One such exception is for compensation based solely on the attainment of one or more performance criteria which are established by an independent compensation committee and approved by shareholders. The Incentive Plan is intended to comply with this exclusion for performance-based compensation and is being submitted to shareholders for approval in order to preserve the deductibility of compensation paid under the Incentive Plan.

The following is a brief description of certain material features of the Incentive Plan.

Term. Subject to approval by shareholders, the Incentive Plan will be effective as of January 1, 1996 and will continue until December 31, 2000 unless reapproved by the Company's shareholders or unless amended or terminated.

Participants. Participants in the Incentive Plan will be those corporate officers and other key employees of the Company and its subsidiaries who are selected annually to participate in the Plan by the Compensation Committee. It is anticipated that the participants selected by the Compensation Committee will be those officers and other key employees whose compensation may be subject to the deductibility limits of Section 162(m) of the Code and will include annually less than twenty individuals. . . .

Performance Criteria. Within 90 days after the beginning of each fiscal year of the Company, the Compensation Committee will establish for each participant an objective performance goal or goals based on one or more of the following performance criteria: net income (before or after taxes); operating income; revenue; advance orders or bookings; expenses; return on sales; gross or net margin; cash flow; earnings per share; return on assets; return on equity; total shareholder return; market share; inventory turnover; and stock price. In establishing such performance goals, the Compensation Committee may apply the performance criteria as a measure of the Company or a subsidiary, or any product category or categories. The Compensation Committee will also determine the amounts of the target awards that will be paid if the performance goal or goals are met and the method by which such amounts will be calculated. In addition, at the Committee's option, it may determine that all or any part of the award will be paid in shares of Reebok Common Stock having an equivalent value to the amount of the award, which shares will be subject to such restrictions as the Compensation Committee may determine. In any case, the maximum award that may be paid to any participant under the Incentive Plan for any year is the lesser of 300% of such participant's base salary in effect in such year or $3 million.

Determination of Award. . . . In order to reflect additional considerations relating to performance, the Compensation Committee may, in its discretion, reduce or eliminate any calculated award to be paid to a participant, but may not increase such award.

An affirmative vote of a majority of the shares present, in person or by proxy, and entitled to vote at the Annual Meeting is required to approve the Incentive Plan.

The Board of Directors unanimously recommends that shareholders vote FOR [the proposal].

Why did Reebok require its top executives to use part of their 1995 cash bonus to buy restricted shares of the company's common stock? (See ① in Exhibit 7.2.) Bonuses do not provide a very strong incentive for managers to act like owners since earnings can be "managed." Stock ownership can strengthen managers' incentives and reduce potential owner-manager conflicts of interest. The restriction on the stock—some or all of the bonus investment is lost if the executive leaves within two years—exists to make certain that the executives don't just "take the money and run." The two-year vesting provision encourages managers to worry about the company's longer-term financial success.

A second feature of Reebok's executive compensation is that both financial performance measures (such as earnings per share, cash flow, and return on assets) and nonfinancial performance measures (like bookings and market share) were used.[9] Financial metrics like last year's earnings per share tell us about the past. However, nonfinancial metrics like sales orders booked are lead indicators of future economic performance. Also, some of the financial metrics used at Reebok are accounting-based (like gross margin, operating income, and revenue) while others are market-based (like total shareholder return and stock price). The end result is a mixture of internal and external financial metrics combined with some nonfinancial metrics to produce a "balanced scorecard" for evaluating managerial performance.[10]

Incentives Tied to Accounting Numbers

Figure 7.4 showed that 47% to 55% of all companies use performance plans, which are usually tied to accounting numbers, as *long-term* compensation incentives. For *annual* bonus plans, accounting numbers become overwhelmingly important. Let's take a closer look at how these "at risk" compensation components—annual bonus plans and long-term compensation—are tied to accounting numbers.

The common performance measures used in annual and multiyear (long-term) incentive plans for senior corporate executives are shown in Figure 7.5. Most plans link incentive pay to one or more accounting-based performance measures, such as revenue, earnings per share, or return on equity. Economic value added (EVA®) is used in 12% of the plans, while operating cash flow is used in 10% of the plans.

> Economic value added or EVA® is a performance metric popularized by the consulting firm Stern Stewart & Company. In its simplest form, EVA® is just net operating profit after taxes (or NOPAT from Chapter 5) minus a charge for the financial capital lenders and investors have put into the business ($c^* \times$ Capital, where c^* is the company's weighted average cost of capital). So, a company that earns $150 of NOPAT using $1,000 of capital with a c^* of 10% will have generated $50 of EVA® ($150 - .10 \times $1,000). Stern Stewart and most other economic value practitioners advocate making a variety of adjustments to GAAP income statements and balance sheets before performing the EVA® calculation. These adjustments are intended to eliminate certain accounting "distortions," many of which we describe in later chapters of this book.

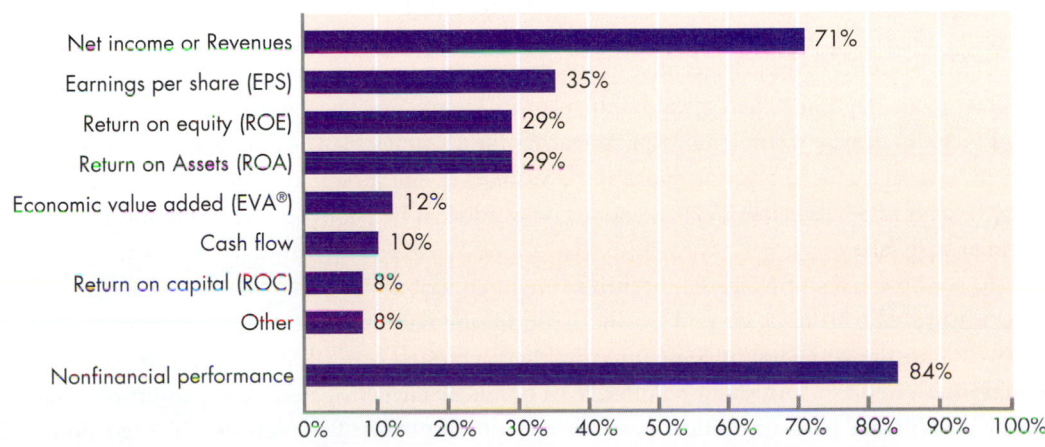

Net income or Revenues	71%
Earnings per share (EPS)	35%
Return on equity (ROE)	29%
Return on Assets (ROA)	29%
Economic value added (EVA®)	12%
Cash flow	10%
Return on capital (ROC)	8%
Other	8%
Nonfinancial performance	84%

Figure 7.5

PERFORMANCE MEASURES USED IN ANNUAL AND MULTI-YEAR CASH INCENTIVE PLANS

The individual percentages sum to more than 100% because many companies use multiple measures of performance. The results are based on a comprehensive survey of 2,700 U.S. companies.

Source: The Conference Board, "Executive Annual Incentive Plans—1996" (New York: 1997).

---

[9] To learn more about the use of nonfinancial performance measures in bonus plans, see C. D. Ittner, D. F. Larcker, and M. U. Rajan, "The Choice of Performance Measures in Annual Bonus Contracts," *The Accounting Review* (April 1997), pp. 231–55.

[10] See R. S. Kaplan and D. P. Norton, *The Balanced Scorecard* (Boston, MA: Harvard Business School Press, 1996).

In addition to accounting-based performance measures, Figure 7.5 shows that many annual and multi-year plans also use nonfinancial performance measures to determine incentive pay. These might include, for example, customer satisfaction targets, achievement of strategic goals (including merger and acquisition activities), total quality management or technology objectives, and safety or environmental goals.

This wide use of accounting-based incentives is controversial for at least four reasons:

First, earnings growth does not automatically translate into increased shareholder value. Management can "grow" earnings by expanding the size of the business through acquisitions or new investment. This strategy can produce substantial dollar increases in sales volume, operating earnings, and EPS. But these added profits don't always increase shareholder value. For shareholder value to increase, the company must earn more on new investments than its incremental cost of capital. Alas, not all acquisitions and investments clear the cost of capital "hurdle" even though they may show an accounting profit. So earnings-based incentive compensation plans can reward managers for launching new investments that increase earnings but not shareholder value. Notice that EVA® overcomes this problem by incorporating an explicit charge for the cost of capital.

Second, the accrual accounting process itself can sometimes distort traditional measures of company performance. Take return on assets (ROA), for example. Companies that show improving ROA often do so because of real profitability gains—greater revenues or lower expenses. However, some ROA improvements are due to nothing more than depreciation accounting. To see this, consider a business that generates $100 of net income each year and pays that same amount out as a dividend. The business opens on January 1, 2005 with total assets of $1,000 and no debt. Half of those assets ($500) are invested in new equipment. The annual depreciation charge for the equipment is $50. The company's ROA for 2005 is 10% ($100 of net income, divided by $1,000 of beginning assets). But next year ROA will grow to about 10.5%. And the year after that, ROA will be 11.1%. Why? Not because profits at the company have increased but instead because depreciation accounting has reduced the book value of total assets. (Inflation exacerbates this problem, as discussed in Chapter 10.)

> ROA for 2006 equals the $100 of net income, divided by net assets of $950 (after subtracting $50 of accumulated depreciation) or 10.5%. The 11.1% ROA calculation for 2007 is $100 of net income, divided by net assets of $900 (after subtracting $100 of accumulated depreciation).

As a stockholder in the company, you probably don't want to pay an ROA bonus for nothing more than depreciation accounting. It's better instead to reward management for real profitability improvement and to ignore the profit growth illusion created by depreciation accounting. That's why some companies prefer ROGI (return on gross investment, or net income divided by total *gross* assets) as a performance metric in their bonus plans.

Third, accounting-based incentive plans can encourage managers to adopt a short-term business focus. Consider the typical bonus plan in Figure 7.6. The executive receives a bonus equal to 100% of base salary if annual EPS reaches the $3.50 target. The bonus award declines to 50% of base salary for EPS performance at the $3.00 level, and it escalates to 150% for EPS at the $4.00 level. If EPS falls below $3.00, no bonus is awarded; at EPS above $4.00, the bonus remains 150% of base salary.

To see how accounting-based incentives might contribute to a short-term focus, consider an executive who believes current business conditions will only allow the company to earn $2.80 EPS for the year. Despite these unfavorable (no bonus) conditions, the executive can still achieve the $3.00 EPS minimum required for a bonus by curtailing needed expenditures—say, simply by cutting back on critical research and development. Research expenses go down, reported earnings go up, and bonuses are paid! This short-term strategy can prove costly in the long term if a competitor introduces a new product based on the technology the company had been researching. Of course, the same unsustainable short-term earnings increase can be achieved by delaying essential maintenance and repairs or by postponing other key operating expenditures.

Figure 7.6

STRUCTURE OF ANNUAL
PERFORMANCE BONUSES

Executives also have an incentive to "manage down" reported earnings when the accounting benchmark (EPS in this example) is *above* the upper bonus limit. Suppose our executive believes that current business conditions will enable the company to earn $4.20 EPS this year. Here the executive has an incentive to reduce reported earnings to $4.00, deferring the excess to the future. After all, the same bonus is awarded no matter whether EPS is at the $4.00 or $4.20 level!

How can excess earnings be deferred? It's easy! Delay some fourth-quarter customer shipments until the beginning of next year. Current year's sales decline and earnings fall without affecting this year's bonus; the delayed sales and earnings count toward next year's bonus. You don't lose anything this year, and you increase the probability of earning the bonus next year.

Fourth, executives have some discretion over the company's accounting policies, and they can use that discretion to achieve bonus goals. For example, an executive falling short of the $3.00 EPS minimum might deliberately reduce fourth-quarter inventories, report a "LIFO liquidation" gain, and boost earnings to a level above the bonus threshold. (LIFO liquidations are discussed in Chapter 9.) On the other hand, if earnings performance is so low that reaching the bonus threshold is impossible, the manager has an incentive to further reduce earnings. The objective of these deliberate earnings reductions—called "big baths"—is simple. Today's write-offs lower future expenses, thereby increasing future earnings—and future bonuses! Examples of "big bath" write-offs include higher bad debt allowances, asset impairments, and large restructuring charges. Accounting discretion also allows managers who believe earnings will exceed the $4.00 ceiling to play bonus "games"—reduce reported earnings down to the bonus maximum and defer the excess.

Research Evidence Do managers use accounting flexibility to achieve bonus goals? One study, which looked at annual bonus plans like the one in Figure 7.6, revealed two things:[11]

1. When annual earnings already exceeded the $4.00 bonus ceiling, managers used discretionary accounting options to *reduce* earnings.
2. When it was clearly evident that earnings would be below the bonus threshold ($3.00 in Figure 7.6), managers used their financial reporting flexibility to reduce earnings still further.

These reductions in earnings had no impact on that year's bonus but improved managers' chances of receiving bonuses the following year. That's because taking a larger discretionary expense this year often meant a smaller expense next year—and that helped to ensure that next year's earnings would meet or beat the bonus target.

---

[11] P. Healy, "The Effect of Bonus Schemes on Accounting Decisions," *Journal of Accounting and Economics* (April 1985), pp. 85–108. Later studies find mixed evidence on managers' use of accounting discretion around bonus thresholds. See T. Fields, T. Lys, and L. Vincent, "Empirical Research on Accounting Choice," *Journal of Accounting and Economics* (September 2001), pp. 255–308.

Another study examined motivations for a controversial, debt extinguishment transaction called **insubstance defeasances**.[12] These transactions were widely believed to generate artificial profits, and the FASB subsequently forbade them in 1996.[13] The evidence is that some firms used these transactions to "window-dress" earnings and to avoid restrictions in bond covenants. Again, the research findings show that managers sometimes use accounting flexibility to evade contract constraints in order to gain bonus benefits.

Several studies show that incoming CEOs have an incentive to decrease earnings in the year of the executive change and increase earnings in the next year.[14] Doing so presumably allows the new CEO to take credit for the company's apparent (but not necessarily real) performance improvement.

Yet another research study found evidence that R&D expenditures tend to decline during the years immediately prior to a CEO's retirement.[15] Existing GAAP requires R&D expenditures to be expensed as incurred, thereby reducing income and bonuses.[16] By reducing R&D expenditures before they retired, CEOs were able to increase their final bonus payouts.

RECAP | Compensation plans should align managers' incentives with the objectives of shareholders. Many compensation plans link incentive pay to accounting numbers. This linkage is an effective management incentive since improved financial performance generally translates into greater shareholder wealth. Unfortunately, accounting numbers can be manipulated. Consequently, compensation plans tied to financial goals sometimes backfire because of the short-term, self-interest focus of executives.

Protection Against Short-Term Focus These abuses explain why compensation plans must also be designed to include long-term incentive components (primarily stock options) that are specifically intended to mitigate the short-term focus of executives. Stock options (and stock ownership) give managers a strong incentive to avoid shortsighted business decisions and instead operate the company in ways that create shareholder value. That's why today stock and stock option portfolios, rather than cash compensation and other benefits, are the major determinants of top executives' wealth.

Some critics argue that the prevalence of stock options in executive pay packages actually contributes to—rather than moderates—managers' short-term focus. Penny differences in earnings per share matter a lot to investors—just watch what happens to a company's share price when quarterly EPS comes in one cent below analysts' expectations. And this share price decline makes executive stock options less valuable. As you will learn in later chapters, there are many ways managers can use accounting gimmicks to find a penny or two of EPS and appease investors. See K. Brown, "Tweaking Results Is Hardly a Sometime Thing," *Wall Street Journal* (February 6, 2002).

Another factor that can reduce short-term focus is the fact that incentive compensation plans are administered by a compensation committee comprised of the company's outside (nonmanagement) directors. The committee can intervene when circumstances warrant modification of the scheduled incentive award. For example, intervention might arise when a change in an accounting principle occurs since the full cumulative effect of the change on all prior years usually appears in the current year's income statement (see Chapter 2). In general, the compensation committee can adjust the

---

[12] J. R. M. Hand, P. J. Hughes, and S. E. Sefcik, "Insubstance Defeasances: Security Price Reactions and Motivations," *Journal of Accounting and Economics* (May 1990), pp. 47–89. The transaction allowed a company to account for a liability "as if extinguished" when cash or other assets were placed irrevocably in a trust that then made all remaining principal and interest payments on the debt.

[13] "Accounting for Transfers and Servicing of Financial Assets and Extinguishments of Liabilities," *SFAS No. 125* (Norwalk, CT: FASB, 1996), para. 16.

[14] J. Elliott and W. Shaw, "Write-offs as Accounting Procedures to Manage Perceptions," *Journal of Accounting Research* (Supplement 1988), pp. 91–119; J. Francis, D. Hanna, and L. Vincent, "Causes and Effects of Discretionary Accounting Write-offs," *Journal of Accounting Research* (Supplement 1996), pp. 117–34; S. Pourciau, "Earnings Management and Non-routine Executive Changes," *Journal of Accounting and Economics* (January–July 1993), pp. 317–36.

[15] P. M. Dechow and R. G. Sloan, "Executive Incentives and The Horizon Problem: An Empirical Investigation," *Journal of Accounting and Economics* (March 1991), pp. 51–89.

[16] "Accounting for Research and Development Costs," *SFAS No. 2* (Stamford, CT: FASB, 1974).

incentive award whenever it believes that current earnings have been unduly influenced by special items or other possible accounting distortions.

For example, language of the following sort is typical in many compensation agreements:

"At any time prior to the payment of performance awards, the compensation committee may adjust previously established performance targets and other terms and conditions . . . to reflect major unforeseen events such as changes in laws, regulations, or accounting practices, mergers, acquisitions, divestitures, or extraordinary, unusual, or nonrecurring items or events."[17]

Compensation committees *can* adjust incentive awards for unusual or nonrecurring items and events—but do they? One study looked at the pay practices of 376 large public companies from 1970 through 1996 and found that nonrecurring gains tend to flow through to compensation but losses do not.[18] Compensation committees apparently do shield top managers from bonus reductions when net income is decreased by nonrecurring losses. But when net income is increased by nonrecurring gains, top managers reap the benefits in the form of higher bonus awards.

Regulatory Agencies

Financial statements used by creditors and shareholders are prepared using GAAP. But banks, insurance companies, public utilities, and many others must also provide financial statements to the government agencies that regulate them. Those statements may be prepared on another basis—RAP—to satisfy specific regulatory objectives.

RAP stands for **regulatory accounting principles**, the methods and procedures that must be followed when assembling financial statements for regulatory agencies. RAP tells a company how to account for its business transactions—from when to record revenue and in what amount, to how depreciation expense must be calculated and what account title to use.

Regulators use RAP financial reports to set the prices customers are charged, as a basis for supervisory action, as a source of statistical information, and as an early warning signal for monitoring a company's financial health. To achieve these goals, regulators sometimes require the use of accounting principles that deviate from GAAP. Here's an example of a disclosure related to such a deviation:

Under regulatory accounting, the company capitalizes both interest and equity costs during periods of construction. (SBC Communications, annual report)

GAAP allows the cost of debt (called "interest") to be treated as just another construction project cost, but "equity costs" are not capitalized under GAAP (see Chapter 10). So, SBC Communications is telling annual report readers that its treatment of equity costs complies with RAP but deviates from GAAP. As a result, the company's completed construction projects—its telephone lines and related facilities—are shown at higher book values than would be the case if GAAP were used.

Why do shareholders, creditors, and other statement readers care about RAP if companies only use it when preparing financial reports for regulatory agencies? The answer is that *RAP sometimes shows up in the company's GAAP financial statements too*. Why? Because *SFAS No. 71*

[17] J. D. England, "Executive Pay, Incentives and Performance," in D. E. Logue (ed.), *Handbook of Modern Finance* (Boston: Warren, Gorham & Lamont, 1996), p. E9–18.

[18] J. J. Gaver and K. M. Gaver, "The Relation Between Nonrecurring Accounting Transactions and CEO Cash Compensation," *The Accounting Review* (April 1998), pp. 235–54.

allows rate-regulated companies like SBC Communications to account for and report assets and liabilities consistent with the way in which regulators establish rates as long as:

- the rates are designed to recover the costs of providing the regulated service, and
- the competitive environment makes it reasonable to assume that such rates can be charged and collected.[19]

So, SBC Communications not only capitalized equity costs in its financial reports to industry regulators, but also did so in its published financial statements for shareholders and creditors.

Knowing how a company accounts for its business transactions—whether it uses GAAP or RAP—is essential to gaining a clear understanding of its financial performance and condition.

There's another reason why shareholders and creditors need to understand RAP as well as GAAP. Regulated companies can suffer because financial reports affect the regulatory process—for example, a rate increase may be denied based on the reported numbers. This possibility can influence both (1) management's GAAP accounting choices and (2) when transactions are recorded.

To see how, let's take a look at banks, savings institutions, and credit unions.

> The published balance sheets of rate-regulated companies will also contain **regulatory assets and liabilities** that reflect anticipated future rate adjustments, deferred costs, and delayed obligations specific to the regulatory process.

Capital Requirements in the Banking Industry

Banks and other financial institutions are required by federal and state regulatory agencies to meet **minimum capital requirements**. The purpose of these requirements is to ensure that the bank (or institution) remains financially sound and can meet its obligations to depositors.

The test for capital adequacy is a simple one: Does the amount of investor capital (think of "adjusted" stockholders' equity) or the ratio of investor capital to gross assets—both defined by RAP—exceed the minimum level allowed by the regulator? If it does, the bank is in compliance and considered to have adequate capital. If bank capital falls below the minimum allowed, regulatory intervention can be triggered.

Suppose Hometown Bank & Trust has gross assets of $900 million and investor capital of $135 million, and suppose the bank's regulators set a 10% minimum capital ratio. Hometown is in compliance with the capital requirement because it has a capital adequacy ratio of 15%, calculated as:

$$\text{Capital adequacy ratio} = \frac{\text{Invested capital (as defined by RAP)}}{\text{Gross assets (as defined by RAP)}}$$
$$= \frac{\$135 \text{ million}}{\$900 \text{ million}} = 15\%$$

which is above the 10% minimum allowed.

Regulators have a powerful weapon to encourage compliance with minimum capital guidelines. They can impose costs on banks and financial institutions found to be in noncompliance. For example, a noncomplying bank:

- is required to submit a comprehensive plan describing how and when its capital will be increased;
- can be examined more frequently by the regulator;
- can be denied a request to merge, open new branches, or expand services; and
- can be subject to dividend payment restrictions if it has inadequate or "potentially inadequate" capital (for example., Hometown Bank & Trust might be prohibited from paying any dividends if its capital adequacy ratio falls to the minimum level allowed—10%).

Because regulators can restrict bank operations, a bank with "inadequate" capital incurs greater regulatory costs than does a bank with adequate capital.

[19] "Accounting for the Effects of Certain Types of Regulation," *SFAS No. 71* (Stamford, CT: FASB, 1982).

There are several ways bank managers can avoid the regulatory costs of failing to meet minimum capital requirements. The best approach is to operate profitably and invest wisely so that the bank remains financially sound. Another way is to choose accounting policies that increase RAP invested capital or decrease RAP gross assets so that the bank can pass its capital adequacy test. Let's examine this "artificial" approach to regulatory compliance.

The cash that banks receive from depositors is used to make loans. These loans show up as balance sheet receivables; they typically represent the bank's single largest asset. Uncollected loans are a significant cost in the banking industry. But bank managers have some discretion over the timing and amount of recorded uncollectibles. This discretion can be used to improve the bank's capital adequacy ratio. How?

> A bank's **loan loss provision** is just the estimated bad debt expense associated with its loan receivables. Loan loss provisions are expenses that reduce bank net income but (under RAP) have no impact on invested capital. **Loan charge-offs** are loans the bank no longer expects to collect. Loan charge-offs decrease bank capital but have no impact on bank net income.

It's easy: Understate the true loan loss provision and loan charge-offs for the year. This improves the bank's capital adequacy ratio, and simultaneously increases the net income figure reported to shareholders. But these improvements are just an illusion. In reality the bank expects more uncollectibles than are shown on the financial reports. Understating loan loss provisions and charge-offs may help avoid noncompliance with bank capital requirements, but this strategy hides the bank's true performance and condition from both regulators and shareholders. So evading RAP guidelines can impede accurate financial analysis.

Rate Regulation in the Electric Utilities Industry

Electric utility companies like El Paso Electric have their prices set by state and federal agencies known as public utility commissions. The rate formulas of most commissions use accounting-determined costs and asset values. A typical rate formula for an electric utility looks like this:

Allowed revenue = Operating costs + Depreciation + Taxes + (ROA × Asset base)

where ROA is the return on assets allowed by the regulator. The rate formula sets total allowed revenues equal to an amount that covers the company's operating costs (fuel, labor, and administrative expenses plus depreciation and taxes) and provides a "fair" return on the capital invested in operating assets (things like generating stations, transmission lines, fuel inventory, and so on). This "fair return" component of the rate formula is (ROA × Asset base).

Suppose Midwest Power & Light has annual operating costs, depreciation, and taxes of $300 million. Suppose also that $500 million of capital is invested in operating assets. Finally, suppose that the state public service commission sets ROA at 10%. The annual revenue allowed would be:

Allowed revenue = $300 million + (10% × $500 million)
= $300 million + $50 million = $350 million

To arrive at a rate per kilowatt-hour of electricity, the $350 million of revenue allowed is divided by the company's *estimate* of total kilowatt-hours to be sold during the year.

Industry RAP governs which items can be included in a regulated utility's operating costs and asset base—and which cannot be included. The difference is important because included items are charged to customers but disallowed items are charged to shareholders. Consider this example: Suppose Midwest Power & Light spends $10 million on customer safety advertising and $50 million on corporate "image" advertising. Customer safety advertising is an allowed operating cost, so it is included in the rate formula. Customers ultimately pay for the $10 million spent on safety advertising through higher electricity rates.

Corporate image advertising is not an allowed cost in most states, so the $50 million that Midwest Power & Light spent promoting itself cannot be passed on to customers in the form of higher electricity rates. Who pays the bill? Shareholders do, because there's $50 million less cash in the company. Regulators apparently see image advertising as unnecessary. Consequently, they do not require customers to pay for it through higher electricity rates.

The example illustrates how RAP can influence rate regulation and the revenues ultimately received by utility companies. But there's another important point to the example. Industry RAP treats customer safety advertising and corporate image advertising differently. GAAP does not—both kinds of advertising would be included in operating costs on the company's income statement. Other differences between public utility RAP and GAAP are:

- **deferring costs** that would otherwise be charged to expense by nonregulated companies—utilities can postpone expensing storm damage costs, for example, as long as it is *probable* that those specific deferred costs are subject to recovery in future revenues,
- **capitalization of equity costs** on construction projects whereas interest alone can be capitalized by nonregulated companies.

Because of *SFAS No. 71*, RAP gets included in the financial statements that utility companies prepare for shareholders and creditors.

Rate regulation also creates incentives for public utility managers to artificially increase the asset base. Suppose Midwest Power & Light signs a $700,000 one-year rental agreement for service vehicles. If the rental payment is an allowed operating cost for rate-making purposes, customers would pay $700,000 in higher electricity rates. On the other hand, if the rental could be included in the company's regulatory asset base, customers would pay $770,000, or 10% more—$700,000 for depreciation (the full cost of the one-year asset) plus another $70,000 so that shareholders receive the allowed 10% return on the $700,000 asset.

> In 2002, Duke Energy agreed to pay $25 million to its customers to settle allegations that the company had *under reported* its net income in order to avoid having to reduce its electricity rates. Profits were underreported by $123 million (pre-tax) because the company overstated RAP expenses.

Given the choice, utility company shareholders would prefer to have the rental payment treated as an asset for rate-making purposes. The company could then charge customers an extra $70,000 and use the cash to cover "disallowed" costs—like image advertising—or to pay stockholder dividends. One way to make this happen is to design the rental contract so that it qualifies for RAP treatment as an asset. (We show you how in Chapter 12.) Another approach is to lobby regulators to relax the rules governing when a rental contract qualifies for asset treatment. *Change the contract or change the accounting rules*—the result is the same. Adding more dollars to the asset base increases the allowed revenue stream for a rate-regulated company.

Taxation

All companies are "regulated" by state and federal tax agencies. When it comes to income taxes and the U.S. government, the regulators are Congress and the Internal Revenue Service (IRS). Congress writes the rules, but the IRS interprets and administers them, and it collects the income tax.

IRS regulations govern the computation of net income for tax purposes. These IRS accounting rules are just another type of RAP. Many IRS accounting rules are the same as GAAP rules. Consider this example: Revenue is generally recognized for tax and GAAP purposes at the time of sale, not later when cash is collected from customers. However, there are situations in which IRS accounting rules differ from GAAP.

> Chapter 10 explains GAAP depreciation expense and the straight-line method, while Chapter 13 sheds further light on IRS depreciation expense.

A case in point is depreciation expense. GAAP requires companies to spread the cost of assets like equipment and buildings over the entire period of intended use (or economic life). The amount charged to depreciation each year can be computed using one of several different methods. IRS rules, on the other hand, require companies to use a strict schedule called the Modified Accelerated Cost Recovery System to determine their annual depreciation tax deduction. The result is that GAAP depreciation expense will rarely (if ever) equal the IRS depreciation tax deduction, which means that taxable net income will most often differ from GAAP net income.

Sometimes the IRS requires firms to use identical tax and GAAP accounting methods. When inventory costs are rising, companies like to use LIFO for tax purposes because it lowers their taxable income. But the IRS rules on LIFO inventory accounting contain an unusual requirement—companies that elect to use LIFO for tax purposes must also use LIFO in their shareholder reports. So the tax benefits of LIFO can only be obtained when LIFO is also used in GAAP financial statements—but doing so lowers GAAP net income when prices are rising. Since the LIFO method is widely used, many corporate managers must believe that the tax benefits of LIFO outweigh its negative impact on GAAP net income.

Taxation and GAAP accounting are related in another way. Companies reporting large GAAP earnings sometimes attract the attention of politicians who threaten to impose "windfall profits" taxes. This has been true for big U.S. oil companies during periods of rapidly increasing oil prices and/or during oil "shortages" caused by governmental policies.

For example, during the 1970s the price of gasoline was controlled by the federal government in an effort to reduce consumption and to dampen the inflationary impact of escalating oil prices. In 1979 the price of gasoline at the pump was decontrolled one week before big oil companies announced record third-quarter profits that were labeled by politicians as "obscene." After the earnings announcements, a "windfall profits" tax on oil company earnings was proposed, and politicians voted to reinstate gasoline price controls. These actions occurred even though part of the reported profit increase was due to an accounting change required by the FASB; most of the rest of the increase was due to overseas operations and inventory holding gains.

Sometimes it just doesn't pay to be seen as a highly profitable company. When that's the case, managers have incentives to use accounting methods that make the company look less profitable than it really is. That way they can avoid attracting the attention of politicians and regulators who might impose a "windfall profits" tax or other cost on the company.

> LIFO means "**last-in, first-out**," and here's how it works. Suppose a start-up bicycle retailer begins the year with no inventory. Ten bicycles are purchased for $150 each during the first week of operations and another five bicycles are purchased mid-month for $180 each—same brand and model, just a higher price from the manufacturer. Eight bicycles are sold during the month, leaving seven still in inventory. Using LIFO, the retailer would calculate the cost of goods sold to be $1,350 (or five bicycles at $180 each plus three more at $150 each). Notice that this calculation presumes the *last* bicycles to come into the shop (those bought for $180 each) are the *first sold*. Notice also that with rising inventory costs, LIFO produces a larger cost of goods sold expense ($1,350 in our example) than does FIFO or "**first-in, first-out**" (eight bicycles at $150 each, or $1,200). A larger cost of goods sold expense means a lower taxable income, Chapter 9 tells you more.

RECAP

Government regulatory agencies and taxing authorities can write their own accounting rules, and many do. The result is that some financial statements for shareholders and creditors contain special regulatory items or use regulatory accounting methods that deviate from normal GAAP. Accounting-based regulations—including IRS rules—also influence the choice of GAAP accounting methods for shareholder reports and when transactions are recorded.

Analytical Insights: Identifying "Managed" Earnings

It is essential for financial statement users to identify companies that achieve incremental increases in earnings resulting from strength in business fundamentals rather than earnings management techniques or accounting 'gimmickry.'[20]

---

[20] G. Napolitano, *Earnings Management Revisited: Minimizing the Torpedoes in Financial Reports* (New York: Goldman Sachs, November 1998), p. 3.

ANALYSIS

We said in Chapter 6 that the key measure of corporate value is **permanent** ("sustainable") **earnings** from core businesses—the "above the line" income from continuing operations discussed in Chapter 2. Most analysts, investors, and lenders agree. Compared to bottom-line net income, core earnings provide a truer picture of a company's ability to generate profits from its major business activities. Core earnings are also more predictive of the company's sustainable economic performance, its long-term growth trends, and its financial viability.

But uncovering a company's core earnings and assessing its overall performance is not easy. The challenge comes from several sources. As an analyst, you must do the following:

- Wrestle with differences in accounting methods and reporting practices across companies— even in the same industry.
- Identify areas where accounting choices can hide a potential earnings surprise—or a so-called "accounting torpedo"—such as a major write-off of bad debts or intangibles.
- Assess the degree to which the firm has "managed" earnings and used accounting gimmickry.
- Adjust the reported financial statement amounts to eliminate the impact of these potential accounting "abuses."

This book is devoted to helping you meet the challenge.

The message from this chapter and from Chapter 3 is that managers sometimes have powerful incentives to "manage" the reported profitability and financial condition of their companies. These incentives are motivated by loan covenants, compensation contracts, regulatory agency oversight, tax avoidance efforts, a desire to "meet or beat" analysts' quarterly earnings forecasts, and to increase the company's stock price. Financial statement gimmicks are likely to be most prevalent when these accounting incentives are especially strong. For example, when the company is in danger of violating its debt covenants; or when a large portion of top management pay comes from bonuses tied to earnings per share or sales growth; or when management has a lengthy record of beating "the Street's" earnings forecast by a penny. What's the penalty for failing to "make" the numbers? Loan default, lost bonuses, and an abrupt stock price decline.

So now you know *when* to look for potential accounting distortions, but what exactly do you look *for* and *where* do you look? How do companies "manage" earnings? What accounting gimmicks are used?

The remaining chapters of this book explore these topics in detail. For now, we'll simply give you a "broad-brush" overview to sensitize you to the danger areas.

Look to areas where subjective judgments or estimates have a significant impact on the financial statements. For some companies, the areas to scrutinize might be revenue recognition, deferred marketing and customer acquisition costs, or reserves for bad debts and inventory obsolescence. For other companies, the critical areas may involve intangible asset valuation, asset impairment, warranty and product liability reserves, restructuring charges, or litigation and environmental contingencies. Also take a close look at areas where it is difficult to evaluate the company's accounting practices because no authoritative standards exist or because established practices are controversial. And watch out for large business transactions, especially those that are unusually complex in structure or in their financial statement effects. And take a magnifying glass to the financial statement footnotes and other financial disclosures. They should be complete and transparent— allowing you to look behind the numbers to see what's really going on in the company. If not, there may be an accounting torpedo headed in your direction.[21]

Accounting gimmicks sometimes backfire. In 1997, top officers and directors at Leslie Fay agreed to pay back $34.7 million to shareholders of the company. The payment settled shareholder lawsuits filed because of alleged accounting gimmicks used in 1991 and 1992. Among other things, the suits charged that earnings gimmicks artificially increased officers' bonuses in those years. See L. Vickery, "Leslie Fay's Ex-Financial Chief, Polishan, Is Found Guilty of Fraud," *Wall Street Journal* (July 7, 2000).

A recent professional pronouncement requires independent auditors to adopt this incentives-driven financial analytic perspective when conducting audits.

Source: "Consideration of Fraud in a Financial Statement Audit," *Statement on Auditing Standards No. 99* (New York: American Institute of Certified Public Accountants, 2002), paras. 16–17.

---

[21] Recent examples of accounting torpedoes can be found in United States General Accounting Office (GAO) report "Financial Statement Restatements: Trends, Market Impacts, Regulatory Responses, and Remaining Challenges," GAO-03-138 (October 2002). This report chronicles the accounting abuses uncovered at ENRON, Sunbeam, Xerox, and other companies.

Exhibit 7.3 contains a partial list of tell-tale signs for identifying "aggressive" accounting choices. Keep this list handy as you read the rest of the book. We have a lot more to say about the "red flags" in Exhibit 7.3 and why they are helpful. Each chapter discusses other warning signals that you may want to add to this list.

EXHIBIT 7.3	**Tell-Tale Signs of Potential Accounting Distortions**

- Unexplained changes in accounting methods like a switch from LIFO to FIFO inventory methods.
- LIFO "dipping" or excessive year-end inventory purchases for LIFO companies when prices are rising.
- Changes in estimates for asset useful life, lease residual value, and pension or post-retirement health care benefit assumptions.
- Receivables or inventory growth that outpaces sales growth.
- Bad debt reserves that are low relative to receivables, past credit losses, or peer companies.
- Sudden "off-loading" of receivables by sale or securitization.
- Unusually long depreciation lives and amortization periods.
- Increasing gap between earnings and operating cash flows.
- Increasing gap between earnings and taxable income.
- Unexplained large increases or decreases in deferred income tax balances.
- Off-balance-sheet financing arrangements including significant use of joint ventures, "take-or-pay" contracts, or operating leases.
- Unexpected write-offs of receivables and loans, inventories, buildings and equipment, or intangibles.
- Large changes in discretionary expenses such as advertising and R&D.
- Unusual business transactions that boost earnings.
- Audit qualifications or changes in the outside auditor.

Note: These (and other) accounting "red flags" are described more fully in later chapters.

SUMMARY

- Conflicts of interest among managers, shareholders, lenders, or regulators are a natural feature of business.
- Contracts and regulations help address these conflicts of interest in ways that are mutually beneficial to the parties involved.
- Accounting numbers often play an important role in contracts and regulations because they provide useful information about the company's performance and financial condition as well as about the management team's accomplishments.
- Accounting-based lending agreements, compensation contracts, and regulations shape managers' incentives—after all, that's why accounting numbers are included in contracts and regulations. They also help explain the accounting choices managers make.
- Understanding why and how managers exercise their discretion in implementing GAAP can be extremely helpful to those who are analyzing and interpreting a company's financial statements.
- And what happened to Allen Ford? The bank provided the loans Allen needed to open his first BookWorm, and the concept proved so successful he now owns three stores. Allen is currently developing a business plan for a used sports equipment store to be called Second Time Around.

APPENDIX

CONFLICTS OF INTERESTS BETWEEN CREDITORS AND OWNER-MANAGERS

The economic interests of those who borrow money and those who lend money often diverge, especially after the lender has handed over the cash. For example, retail automobile loans typically involve a direct transfer of funds from the bank to the car dealer. The borrower (you and me) never actually touches the cash. This procedural step ensures that the borrower will not divert the loan proceeds to some other purpose like gambling on the state lottery.

The inherent divergence of interests between borrowers and lenders is even more acute in the business setting. Why? One reason is that a "corporate veil" protects shareholders in the event that the company cannot pay its debts. Creditors do not have recourse to the personal financial fortunes of shareholders (or managers, for that matter) when a company defaults on its loans. Another reason is that managers, not shareholders, decide how the money is spent. This creates incentives for managers to take actions that transfer part of the company's value from creditors to the managers themselves as well as to other shareholders. *These incentives arise because business decisions affect not only the value of the firm but also the relative share of that value belonging to owners rather than to creditors.*

Loan agreements contain restrictions—called covenants—that reduce the divergence of interests between creditors (lenders) and owner-managers (borrowers). This appendix explores the types of creditor/owner conflicts that give rise to the need for covenants.

Sources of Conflict: Asset Substitution and Repayment

Two sources of conflict can arise between creditors and owners:

- **Asset substitution:** If a company borrows to engage in low-risk investment projects and the interest rate charged reflects that low risk, the value of the business to owners is increased—and the value to creditors is reduced—by substituting higher-risk projects.
- **Repayment:** If a company borrows money for a new project and the interest rate charged presumes the company's current dividend policy will be maintained, the value of the creditor's stake is reduced when the borrowed funds are used instead to pay larger dividends. At the extreme, if the company sells all its assets and pays owners a liquidating dividend, creditors are left with a worthless business.[22]

We begin by first looking at **asset substitution** and the conflicting incentives of creditors and owners. Figure 7.7 shows the probability distribution of dollar returns associated with two investment projects.[23] Each curve spans the entire range of possible dollar returns for the project, with the height of the curve at any given point indicating the probability of receiving that particular dollar return. Both investment projects have the same cost ($M), the same expected dollar return ($E), the same investment horizon (one year), and the same market risk.[24] But, as shown, the potential returns from Project 2 have greater dispersion (higher variance) than do those from Project 1. In other words, the extreme dollar returns—those at the far left and right in the figure—have a greater probability of occurrence for Project 2 than for Project 1.

> Investment outcomes cannot be known in advance with certainty. So it is convenient to represent outcome possibilities using a **probability distribution** like the one in Figure 7.7, which shows the likelihood that each investment project will yield a particular dollar outcome. For example, one project may have a 10% chance of earning $5,000 or less, a 40% chance of earning from $5,000 to $20,000, a 40% chance of earning between $20,000 and $35,000, and a 10% chance of earning more than $35,000.

---

[22] Descriptions of these—and other—creditor–stockholder conflicts of interest are contained in A. Barnea, R. Haugen, and L. Senbet, *Agency Problems and Financial Contracting* (Upper Saddle River, NJ: Prentice Hall, 1985); P. Milgrom and J. Roberts, *Economics, Organization and Management* (Upper Saddle River, NJ: Prentice Hall, 1992); C. Smith and J. Warner, "On Financial Contracting: An Analysis of Bond Covenants," *Journal of Financial Economics* (1979), pp. 117–61; and R. Watts and J. Zimmerman, *Positive Accounting Theory* (Upper Saddle River, NJ: Prentice Hall, 1986).

[23] This illustration of asset substitution is adapted from R. Watts and J. Zimmerman, ibid., p. 187.

[24] These project attributes greatly simplify the discussion. **Market risk** is the covariance of project returns with market returns in the sense commonly used when discussing capital asset pricing models. See, for example, S. A. Ross, R. W. Westerfield, and J. F. Jaffe, *Corporate Finance* (Homewood, IL: Irwin, 1993), p. 295.

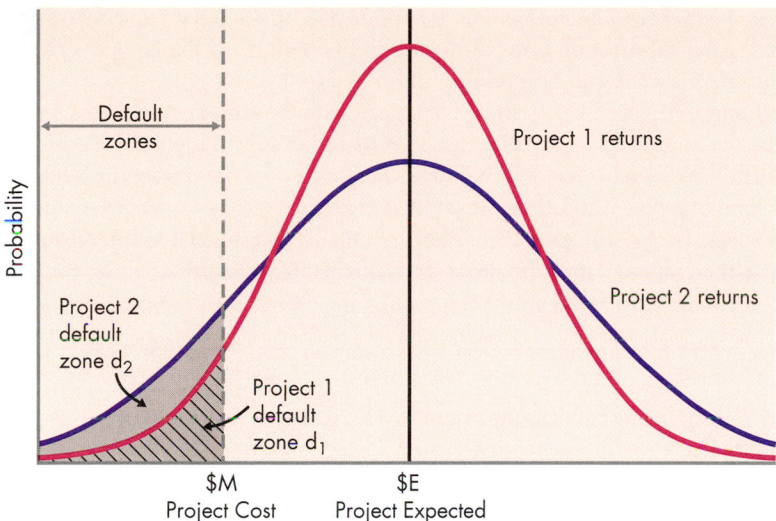

If both projects require the same dollar investment, which one would the owner-manager select? With no debt outstanding, stockholders—including the owner-manager—would be indifferent between the two projects. That's because the value of the company is the same no matter which project is chosen, since both projects have the same cost ($M), the same expected dollar return ($E), and the same market risk.

But what if the company has debt with principal and interest payments that also total $M one year from now? Would shareholders still be indifferent between the two projects? What about creditors who supplied debt financing to the company? Would they too be indifferent?

When companies have debt outstanding, the *dispersion* of dollar returns for each investment project—the likelihood of extreme outcomes—has a bearing on the **relative value** of the project to creditors and stockholders. So even though the two projects in Figure 7.7 have the same expected value ($E), one will now be worth more to some faction than the other because they don't have the same dispersion.

To see this, consider the viewpoint of creditors who expect to be paid from the dollars earned by the chosen project. Notice that the *probability* of Project 1 generating dollar returns less than the required $M loan payment is given by the crosshatched area d_1 under the Project 1 curve. We refer to this region as the "default zone" because if Project 1 produces returns to the left of $M, the company will default on part or all of its required loan payment. Since the probability of all possible dollar returns from a given project must sum to one, the probability that creditors will receive full payment is $(1 - d_1)$; this is shown by the *unshaded area* under the Project 1 curve to the right of $M.

The default zone for Project 2 is the grey area d_2 (which includes the crosshatched area d_1). The probability that creditors will receive full payment from Project 2 is $(1 - d_2)$, and because d_2 is larger than d_1, the probability of debt repayment for Project 1 is greater than the probability of debt repayment for Project 2.

Compare the default regions of the two investments. Creditors prefer Project 1 over Project 2 because Project 1 has a lower default probability than does Project 2—and thus, it has a correspondingly higher probability that creditors will be paid in full. Obviously, the value of the business to creditors will be greater if Project 1 is chosen because it has less default risk.

But what do stockholders prefer? Project 2 has a higher probability of very large dollar returns to stockholders. But, what about the project's higher risk of a large loss? Stockholders are not obligated to pay a company's debts when corporate cash flows are inadequate to cover what is owed. This limits stockholders' "downside" exposure: When project returns fall below $M, stockholders don't have to make up the shortfall so that creditors can be paid. Creditors, on the other hand, have limited "upside potential" because their **fixed claim** (the $M loan payment in our example) to corporate cash flows does not get larger when project returns exceed $M. *All other things being equal, stockholders of companies with debt financing prefer investment projects with high dispersion (like Project 2) because they receive all payoffs greater than $M while creditors absorb the loss associated with payoffs less than $M.*

If the company borrows $M for low-risk Project 1 but then invests the funds in high-risk Project 2, stockholder value is increased but creditor value falls. Substituting the high-risk Project 2 for the low-risk Project 1 leaves stockholders with more upside potential—but creditors have more "downside risk" of default. Asset substitution transfers wealth from creditors to shareholders but leaves the total value of the business unchanged. This result is illustrated in Figure 7.8(a).

The situation we've just described involved projects with the same cost, expected return, and market risk—and thus, the same total value. We've also seen that asset substitution changes how the company's total value is shared between owners and creditors—but that it does not change the value of the company.

Another kind of asset substitution—illustrated in Figure 7.8(b)—occurs when high-risk Project 2 has a lower expected value (or greater market risk) than Project 1. Here the creditors' loss is even greater because the company itself becomes less valuable. Skipping the details, we see that the end result is that borrowing for Project 1 but then putting the money into Project 2 instead makes:

- the company worth less because Project 2 has a smaller total value than Project 1 ($950 versus $1,000),
- the owners' share of the company worth more ($770 versus $750), and
- the creditors' share worth less because Project 2 has more dispersion than Project 1.

Figure 7.8

THE CONSEQUENCES OF ASSET SUBSTITUTION FOR OWNERS AND CREDITORS

(a) Investment projects with the same expected dollar returns (and market risk) but different dispersions.
(b) Investment projects with different expected dollar returns (and market risk) and different dispersions.

Stockholders are willing to substitute projects that *reduce* the total value of the company when the wealth transfer from creditors more than compensates them for the overall value loss. The company is worth less ($950 versus $1,000), but substitution results in more value for shareholders ($770 versus $750) and less for creditors ($180 versus $250).

The second source of conflict, **repayment**, involves a conflict of interest over how to use the cash generated by the company's operating activities. Managers can use the cash to:

1. Reinvest the cash back into the business
2. Repay amounts owed to lenders
3. Pay dividends to or buy back shares from stockholders

When companies are financed partially with debt, owner-managers have incentives to distribute cash to stockholders (including themselves).[25] This could be done in several ways. Management could forego investments in positive net present value projects and instead pay dividends to shareholders or repurchase outstanding shares; or management could sell existing business assets and distribute the proceeds to shareholders (again by means of dividends or share repurchases). Both actions would

---

[25] S. C. Myers, "Determinants of Corporate Borrowing," *Journal of Financial Economics* (November 1977), pp. 147–75.

leave creditors with a company of greatly reduced value—or worse—an "empty corporate shell." The value of the business to creditors is reduced because there are fewer total corporate resources available for debt repayment, making loan default more likely.

Debt Covenants

Creditors know that their interests will sometimes conflict with the interests of shareholders and owner-managers. Without protections in lending agreements, creditors will demand a higher return (interest rate) on business loans as compensation for the added risk of asset substitution and repayment. This higher interest rate is the way creditors get paid for the possibility that owner-managers will take actions that benefit shareholders but harm creditors. But this increases the cost of debt financing and shifts $M to the right in Figure 7.7—thus causing shareholder value to fall!

Another way to reduce conflicts of interest between creditors and shareholders is by writing contracts that restrict—explicitly or implicitly—the owner-manager's ability to harm creditors.[26] To do this, loan provisions are specifically designed to address asset substitution and repayment. These covenants effectively lower the default risk of creditors, and this lower risk, in turn, lowers the borrower's cost of debt financing and shifts $M loan payment to the left. *Debt covenants benefit both creditors and shareholders.* Creditors benefit because debt covenants reduce default risk, and shareholders benefit from the lowered cost of debt.

EXERCISES

Suppose you and two friends each invested $100,000 in an oil and gas partnership. The general partner—Huge Gamble, Inc.—invests no cash but makes all operating decisions for the partnership, including where and how deep to drill for oil. Drilling costs plus a management fee are charged against the $300,000 of cash you and your friends invested. If oil is found, you each get 15% of partnership net income, with the remaining 55% going to Huge Gamble. But if the wells are dry, you get nothing except any cash that remains.

E7 – 1
Conflicts of interest and agency costs

Required:
What is an agency relationship and what are agency costs? How do these concepts apply to your investment in the oil and gas partnership?

E7 – 2
Understanding debt covenants

Required:
What is a debt covenant? Why do lenders include them in loan agreements? Why do borrowers agree to include covenants in loan agreements?

E7 – 3
Affirmative and negative debt covenants

Required:
What are affirmative debt covenants? What are negative covenants? Provide two examples of each.

E7 – 4
Debt covenants and accounting methods

The debt covenants in TCBY's loan agreement do not explicitly mention the accounting methods that must be used when TCBY prepares financial statements for submission to the lender.
Required:
Why don't lenders require the use of specific accounting methods rather than letting management pick from among GAAP alternatives?

[26] See M. C. Jensen and W. H. Meckling, "Theory of the Firm: Managerial Behavior, Agency Costs, and Ownership Structure," *Journal of Financial Economics* (October 1976), pp. 305–60; or Smith and Warner, op. cit.

E7 – 5

Contracts and accounting numbers

Required:

What are the advantages of loan agreements that contain covenants tied to accounting numbers? Are there any disadvantages? Explain.

E7 – 6

Regulatory costs

Required:

What are regulatory costs and why are they important for understanding a company's financial reporting choices?

E7 – 7

Regulatory accounting principles

Some public service commissions let utilities include "Construction in progress"—construction dollars spent for projects not yet completed—in their rate-making asset bases. Other states only allow completed projects to be included.

Required:

Which approach favors shareholders? Why?

E7 – 8

TCBY's debt covenants

Which of TCBY's debt covenants address the asset substitution and repayment problems described in the appendix to this chapter?

E7 – 9

Equipment repairs and rate regulation

Illinois Power & Heat just spent $5 million repairing one of its electrical generating stations that was damaged by a tornado. The loss was uninsured. Management has asked the public service commission for approval to treat the $5 million as an asset for rate-making purposes rather than as an allowed expense.

Required:

What difference will this make to customers and shareholders?

E7 – 10

Capital adequacy

Required:

Why are banks and insurance companies required by regulators to maintain minimum levels of investor capital? What impact does this type of regulatory requirement have on the financial statements that banks and insurance companies prepare for shareholders?

E7 – 11

Incentive design

The top five executives at Marvel Manufacturing are paid annual bonuses based on predetermined earnings goals. These bonuses can be as much as 500% of salary. As a member of the company's compensation committee, you've been asked to comment on the following proposed changes to the annual bonus plan:

- Use after-tax income from continuing operations as the earnings performance measure instead of bottom-line net income.
- Set performance goals based on return on assets (ROA) rather than on earnings.
- Set performance goals—net income or ROA—based on beating the industry average rather than using an absolute performance target.

Required:

What are the advantages and disadvantages of each suggested change?

Required:

Explain the potential conflict of interest that arises when doctors own the hospitals in which they work. The following news article may help.

The executive who became the most visible symbol of profit-driven medical care stepped down yesterday as the top officer of the Columbia/HCA Healthcare Corporation amid a criminal investigation of whether the company's pursuit of profits has stretched beyond the legal limits . . . [He] will be replaced by Thomas F. Frist, Jr., a surgeon by training, who has made his career in the hospital business . . . Dr. Frist said he was ending

Columbia's practice of selling ownership stakes in its hospitals to its doctors. That has been a critical piece of the strategy that helped propel Columbia's growth but led to great legal and ethical criticism that the company was compromising the medical independence of its doctors.

Source: New York Times (July 26, 1997).

Required:

1. During the late 1990s, stock options were a substantial component of executive pay packages. How might the use of stock options contribute to accounting gimmickry and financial statement abuses?
2. GE's new "performance share" plan described below ties CEO compensation to (a) cash flow performance and (b) stock return performance over the next five years. Does the use of these performance measures—rather than net income or earnings per share—increase or reduce the likelihood of accounting gimmickry? Explain why.

SIGN OF TIMES: GE CHIEF IMMELT TO GET STOCK—NOT OPTIONS

For General Electric Co. chief Jeffrey Immelt, stock-option grants—those wealth generators of the 1990s—will be a thing of the past.

In another move to reshape its executive-compensation and corporate governance policies, General Electric said yesterday it no longer would grant its chairman and chief executive either stock options or restricted stock. Instead, it will tie the majority of his pay to a new type of stock award that requires him to meet specific performance targets.

Under the plan, which could set a precedent for other corporations, Mr. Immelt has been granted 250,000 "performance share units." These financial instruments eventually will turn into stock

shares if Mr. Immelt and the company meet two performance measures. If they miss, he will still get his base salary, currently $3 million; an undetermined bonus . . . and dividends . . . on his stock units.

Each stock unit equals one share, and under GE's current price, the value of the new grants is about $7.5 million. If Mr. Immelt meets his targets, the performance-share units would contribute a significant portion of his pay.

Half of the units will vest in five years if GE's cash flow increases at an average of at least 10% each year. The other 125,000 shares will vest at the same time if GE's shareholder return meets or outperforms the five-year cumulative total return of companies in the Standard & Poor's 500 stock index. . . .

Source: Wall Street Journal (September 18, 2003).

Required:

1. The company's bonus plan for top executives is described below. One way Krispy Kreme executives can achieve their earnings growth target is to open new stores as fast as possible. Explain why this might alarm shareholders.
2. Describe how Krispy Kreme's executive bonus plan might lead to accounting abuses at the company.

For fiscal 2003, bonuses for all executive officers were contingent upon meeting or exceeding targets for two performance measures: (1) a percentage increase in earnings per share of common stock; and (2) a percentage return on revenues as measured by dividing earnings before interest and taxes (EBIT) by total Krispy

Kreme revenues. Both targets were met or exceeded for fiscal 2003 though not to the extent they were met or exceeded in fiscal 2002 or fiscal 2001.

Source: Krispy Kreme Doughnuts, Inc. 2003 proxy.

PROBLEMS/DISCUSSION QUESTIONS

P7 – 1

Managerial incentives
and stock ownership

Required:

1. Suppose Mr. Johnson received a base salary (before personal income taxes) of $800,000 in 1993. His personal tax rate was 35% that year, and the year-end value of his Campbell stock was $1.6 million. How much of his after-tax salary for 1993 would go toward buying more stock in the company?
2. What are the advantages and disadvantages of Campbell's stock ownership plan?
3. Do you think that institutional investors like pension portfolio managers and mutual fund managers would favor or oppose Campbell's plan? Why?

CAMPBELL'S SOUP EXECUTIVES MUST OWN FIRM'S STOCK

Campbell Soup Co. said Tuesday it is introducing a stock ownership plan for its chief executive and about 70 other senior executives. Under the plan, David Johnson, president and chief executive officer, is required to hold three times his 1992 base salary of $757,500 in shares by the end of 1994. He must maintain the three times-earnings stake every year until he leaves the company. Executive or senior vice presidents are expected to buy and hold at least two times their annual base salary by 1994. Corporate vice presidents who have been with the company for three or more years will buy and hold the equivalent of one year's base salary. Senior executives will buy shares equal to at least one-half their annual salary. All corporate officers must hold at least 1,000 shares of Campbell stock by the end of this year.

Source: Reprinted with permission of Bloomberg L.P.; © 2001. *Bloomberg Business News* (May 1993). All rights reserved.

P7 – 2

Managerial incentives
and pay

Required:

1. The article below describes a shareholder proposal made by one ConAgra investor. The investor, Mr. Hudgens, has five minutes to speak on his proposal at the ConAgra shareholders' meeting. What key points do you think Mr. Hudgens will make?
2. ConAgra's vice president for human resources will also have five minutes to defend the current incentive plan and to oppose the Hudgens proposal. What arguments will the vice president make?
3. Will ConAgra's institutional investors (for example, its pension portfolio managers and mutual fund managers) favor or oppose the Hudgens plan? Why?
4. How do you think the shareholder vote turned out?

CONAGRA HOLDER IS SEEKING CHANGES IN INCENTIVE PLAN

Donald Hudgens thinks ConAgra, Inc.'s chairman and chief executive officer, Philip B. Fletcher, has it too easy. "Maybe I'm naive," says Mr. Hudgens, a retired railroad chemist. "I've never had a high-powered job." Still, he contends that ConAgra's CEO should be working harder for his millions.

As a consequence, ConAgra shareholders will vote later this month on Mr. Hudgens's proposal that the company revise a special long-term incentive plan directors approved for Mr. Fletcher last year. Under that plan, the chairman would receive 50,000 ConAgra common shares for every percentage point over 10% that the company's per-share earnings rise during the next four fiscal years.

For example, if earnings grow at a compound annual rate of 14%, as they did last year, Mr. Fletcher would get 200,000 shares of stock—that is, four percentage points times 50,000 shares. The payout would occur in July 1998. At ConAgra's current price, every 50,000 shares would be valued at $1.6 million.

"They'll do it [exceed 10%] in spite of any incentive award," Mr. Hudgens says. He has some statistical support. Prudential Securities food analyst John McMillin calculates that over the past five years ConAgra's per-share earnings have grown at a 15.4% compounded annual rate; ConAgra's longtime internal goal is for per-share earnings growth to exceed 14% a year, on average.

Thus, Mr. Hudgens wants ConAgra to compare its performance with that of other food companies, and he has drawn up a list of 13—Archer-Daniels-Midland Co., Borden, Inc., CPC International, Inc., Campbell Soup Co., General Mills, Inc., H.J. Heinz Co., Kellogg Co., PepsiCo, Inc., Philip Morris Co., Quaker Oats Co., Ralston Purina Co., Sara Lee Corp., and Tyson Foods, Inc. Moreover, per-share growth must come from continuing operations, the 54-year-old shareholder says.

"I have no problem with management making a lot of money," Mr. Hudgens says. "More power to 'em. But I want them to work their tails off for us."

Source: Republished with permission of Dow Jones & Co.; © 1994. From *Wall Street Journal* (September 6, 1994); permission conveyed through Copyright Clearance Center, Inc.

In June 1997, the Calpers pension fund announced that it wanted to strengthen the power and independence of corporate boards by urging companies to do the following:

1. Adopt a tougher definition of independent director. To count as independent, for example, a board member couldn't serve more than 10 years, hold a personal-services contract with a senior executive, or be affiliated with a nonprofit group that gets "significant contributions" from the company.
2. Appoint these independent directors to a majority of board seats. Only those directors meeting 10 strict measures of independence could serve on key board committees, such as the audit or compensation panel.
3. Pick an independent "lead" director, who would help the chairman run the board. About 36% of the biggest industrial companies had lead directors last year (1996), up from 21% in 1995, according to a survey of 1,058 directors by recruiters Korn/Ferry International in New York.
4. Publish guidelines in the annual proxy statement describing how the board handles competing time commitments when directors serve on multiple boards.
5. Decide what proportion of board members may exceed a certain age.

CALPERS TO BACK CORPORATE GOVERNANCE STANDARDS

The nation's biggest public pension fund soon will demand that the nation's biggest businesses bolster their boards' power and independence through much stronger corporate-governance practices.

Directors of the California Public Employees' Retirement System [Calpers] today are expected to endorse corporate-governance standards for the first time. The standards, which define board independence more rigidly than ever before, mark the latest burst of activism by a giant fund that played an influential role in the departure of chief executives from General Motors Corp., Eastman Kodak Co., International Business Machines Corp. and other companies.

Calpers will grade the 300 largest U.S. companies in its $113 billion stock portfolio on whether they meet its new minimum standards, dubbed "fundamental principles." Fund officials say they plan to withhold votes for the re-election of directors at concerns scoring the worst grades. Though other activist investors praised the standards, some executives said full compliance could be difficult.

. . . A majority of the 300 companies that Calpers will grade probably don't meet every fundamental principle, suggested Kayla Gillan, the fund's general counsel. But many will revamp their corporate-governance practices "simply because they don't want to get a bad grade."

. . . Some boards undoubtedly will resist Calpers's sweeping corporate-governance push. The stricter definition of director independence "doesn't make sense at all," said Terence J. Gallagher, corporate-governance vice president at Pfizer Inc. For instance, he noted, about four of Pfizer's 13 nonemployee directors have served more than a decade and they're all highly valued.

. . . The Calpers board today probably also will approve a set of tougher "ideal" principles, which Ms. Gillan said she may use to grade the 300 companies again in the future. These standards include: a) appointment of an independent director as chairman; b) board term limits; c) removal of directors who don't achieve certain performance criteria; d) limiting employees' board seats to just the chief executive officer; and e) a 10% limit on the number of directors more than 70 years old.

Source: Republished with permission of Dow Jones & Co.; © 1997. From *Wall Street Journal* (June 16, 1997); permission conveyed through Copyright Clearance Center, Inc.

Required:

1. Why do companies have boards of directors?
2. Outside board members at some companies are long-time personal friends of the CEO and own no company stock. Some serve on 10 or more boards and earn substantial fees from doing so. Company-funded retirement plans for board members are also common. How might each of these factors weaken corporate governance?
3. How will each of Calpers's proposals improve corporate governance?
4. Will these corporate governance changes help companies achieve better financial performance?
5. Will these corporate governance changes improve the credibility and transparency of corporate financial statements?

Delhaize America operates retail food supermarkets in the southeastern and mid-Atlantic regions of the United States. The Company's stores—"Food Lion," "Kash 'n' Karry," and "Save 'n' Pack"—sell a wide variety of groceries, including produce, meats, dairy products, seafood, frozen food, delicatessen and bakery foods, and nonfood items such as health and beauty care products, prescriptions, and other household and personal products.

In 1999 the company entered into a credit agreement with a group of banks. Excerpts taken from the loan agreement follow:

SECTION 6.07. FIXED CHARGES COVERAGE

At the end of each Fiscal Quarter set forth below, the ratio of (i) Consolidated EBITDAR for the period of four Fiscal Quarters then ended to (ii) Consolidated Fixed Charges for such period, shall not have been less than the ratio set forth below opposite such Fiscal Quarter:

Fiscal Quarter	Ratio
First Fiscal Quarter ended on or immediately after the Effective Date—Third Fiscal Quarter 2001	2.25:1
Fourth Fiscal Quarter 2001—Third Fiscal Quarter 2002	2.50:1
Fourth Fiscal Quarter 2002—Third Fiscal Quarter 2003	2.75:1
Fourth Fiscal Quarter 2003 and thereafter	3.00:1

SECTION 6.08. RATIO OF CONSOLIDATED ADJUSTED DEBT TO CONSOLIDATED EBITDAR

At no date will the ratio of (i) Consolidated Adjusted Debt at such date to (ii) Consolidated EBITDAR for the period of four consecutive Fiscal Quarters ended on or most recently prior to such date exceed the ratio set forth below opposite the period in which such date falls:

Period	Ratio
Effective Date—day immediately preceding last day of Fourth Fiscal Quarter 2001	4.50:1
Last day of Fourth Fiscal Quarter 2001—day immediately preceding last day of Fourth Fiscal Quarter 2002	4.00:1
Last day of Fourth Fiscal Quarter 2002—day immediately preceding last day of Fourth Fiscal Quarter 2003	3.75:1
Last day of Fourth Fiscal Quarter 2003 and thereafter	3.50:1

Source: Delhaize America loan agreement.

"EBITDAR" is Earning Before Interest, Taxes, Depreciation, Amortization, and Rent, and "Consolidated Fixed Charges" means debt payments and interest expenses plus rent payments.

Required:

1. Why does the loan agreement include rent as a "fixed charge" in the EBITDAR coverage ratio described in Section 6.07?
2. The minimum acceptable EBITDAR coverage ratio (Section 6.07) increases from 2.25 at inception of the loan to 3.00 in the fourth quarter of 2003. How does the company benefit from this requirement? How does the lender benefit?
3. The debt-to-EBITDAR ratio described in Section 6.08 serves what purpose?
4. The maximum acceptable debt-to-EBITDAR ratio (Section 6.08) decreases from 4.50 at inception of the loan to 3.50 in the fourth quarter of 2003. How does the company benefit from this requirement? How does the lender benefit?

P7 – 5

Bonus tied to EPS performance

Mr. John Brincat is the president and chief executive of Mercury Finance, an auto lender that specializes in high credit-risk customers. The company's proxy statement contains the following description of Mr. Brincat's pay package.

Mr. Brincat is eligible for an annual incentive bonus equal to 1% of Net After-tax Earnings of the Company and is eligible for an additional bonus based upon annual increases in Net After-tax Earnings per share only after earnings exceed 20% over the prior year. The additional bonus is determined as follows:

- Earnings per share increases of 0% to 19.99%, no additional bonus is paid.
- Earnings per share increases of 20% to 29.99%, additional bonus will be equal to 2.5% of the amount of increase from the prior year.

- Earnings per share increases of 30% to 39.99%, additional bonus will be equal to 3.0% of the amount of increase from the prior year.
- Earnings per share increases of 40% or more, additional bonus will be equal to 3.5% of the amount of increase from the prior year.

In addition, at the time the employment contract was entered into, Mr. Brincat was issued a stock option grant . . . of 2,500,000 shares at a price of $17.375 per share, the fair market value on the date of the grant. The options vest equally during the next five years of the contract and are exercisable in increments of 500,000 shares annually only if earnings per share each year exceeds the prior year's earnings per share by 20%. If earnings per share do not increase by 20%, Mr. Brincat forfeits that year's options and has no further right or claim to that year's options.

Source: Mercury Finance 1995 proxy.

Required:

1. Suppose Mercury Finance had $50 million of net after-tax earnings for the year. How much of a bonus would Mr. Brincat receive if the EPS increase that year was only 10%?
2. How much of a bonus would Mr. Brincat receive if the EPS increase was 30%?
3. As a shareholder, how comfortable would you be if your company's managers had contracts with these types of bonus and stock option incentives? Why?

Following your retirement as senior vice president of finance for a large company, you joined the board of Cayman Grand Cruises, Inc. You serve on the compensation committee and help set the bonuses paid to the company's top five executives. According to the annual bonus plan, each executive can earn a bonus of 1% of annual net income.

P7 – 6

Earnings quality and pay

No bonuses were paid in 2005 because the company reported a net loss of $6,588,000.

Shortly after the end of the year, the compensation committee received a letter signed by all five executives, indicating that they felt the company had performed well in 2005. The letter identified the following items from the 2005 income statement that the executives felt painted a less favorable view of their performance than was actually the case:

Proposed Adjustments to 2005 Earnings

($ in thousands)	
Restructuring and other nonrecurring charges	$63,000
Loss from discontinued operations	22,851
Extraordinary charge, early retirement of debt	6,824
Cumulative effect of required changes in accounting principles for postretirement benefits other than pensions	88,847
Cumulative effect of management-initiated changes in accounting principles for:	
Depreciation	14,180
Warehouse and catalog costs	2,110

The letter asked the compensation committee to add these items back to the reported net loss and to then recalculate the bonus awards for 2005. The fiscal year 2005 income statement follows. Assume the tax rate is 34%.

Required:

1. As a member of the compensation committee, how would you respond to each suggested adjustment? Why?
2. What 2005 net income figure do you suggest be used to determine bonuses for the year?

Cayman Grand Cruises, Inc.	
Consolidated Statement of Income	
($ in thousands)	**June 30, 2005**
Net revenues	$1,024,467
Cost of sales	535,178
Gross margin	489,289
Selling, general, and administrative	299,101
Research, development, and engineering	94,172
Gain on sale of joint venture	(33,000)
Restructuring and other nonrecurring charges	63,000
Operating income	66,016
Gain on sale of investment	40,800
Interest expense	(7,145)
Interest income	2,382
Other income (expense)—net	(2,121)
Income before income taxes	99,932
Provision for income taxes	(29,980)
Income from continuing operations	69,952
Income (loss) from discontinued operations (net of tax effect)	(22,851)
Gain on disposal of discontinued operations (net of tax effect)	38,343
Extraordinary charge, early retirement of debt (net of tax effect)	(6,824)
Income before cumulative effect of changes in accounting principles	78,620
Cumulative effect on prior years of changes in accounting principles for:	
Postretirement benefits other than pensions (net of tax effect)	(88,847)
Income taxes (net of tax effect)	19,929
Depreciation (net of tax effect)	(14,180)
Warehouse and catalog costs (net of tax effect)	(2,110)
Net income (loss)	$ (6,588)

P7 – 7

Avoiding debt covenant violations

Food Lion, Inc. operates a chain of retail supermarkets principally in the southeastern United States. The supermarket business is highly competitive, and it is characterized by low profit margins. Food Lion competes with national, regional, and local supermarket chains; discount food stores; single unit stores; convenience stores; and warehouse clubs.

Food Lion recently entered into a credit agreement with a group of banks. Excerpts taken from the loan agreement follow.

SECTION 5.19. LIMITATION ON INCURRENCE OF FUNDED DEBT

The Borrower will not create, assume or incur or in any manner be or become liable in respect of any [additional] Funded Debt . . . [unless] the ratio of Income Available for Fixed Charges for the immediately preceding four Fiscal Quarters to Pro Forma Fixed Charges for such four Fiscal Quarters shall have been at least 2.00 to 1.00.

SECTION 5.20. FIXED CHARGES COVERAGE

At the end of each Fiscal Quarter . . . the ratio of Income Available for Fixed Charges for the immediately preceding four Fiscal Quarters then ended to Consolidated Fixed Charges for the immediately preceding four Fiscal Quarters then ended, shall not be less than . . . 1.75 to 1.0.

SECTION 5.21. MINIMUM CONSOLIDATED TANGIBLE NET WORTH

Consolidated Tangible Net Worth will at no time be less than (i) $706,575,475 plus (ii) 30.0% of the cumulative Consolidated Net Income of the Borrower during any period after [the new loan agreement is signed], calculated quarterly but excluding from such calculations of Consolidated Net Income for purposes of this clause (ii), any quarter in which the Consolidated Net Income of the Borrower and its Consolidated Subsidiaries is negative.

Source: Food Lion, Inc. loan agreement.

Required:

1. In two more weeks, the company's books will be closed for the quarter and the *fixed-charges coverage* might fall below the level required by the loan agreement. How can management avoid violating this covenant?
2. The company's *tangible net worth* may also fall below the amount specified in the loan agreement. How can management avoid violating this covenant?
3. Elsewhere in the loan agreement it says that the company's *ratio of consolidated debt to total capitalization* must be no more than 0.75 to 1.0. How can management avoid violating this covenant?
4. Suppose you were one of Food Lion's bankers, and you were thinking about making changes to the loan covenants. What management activities would you most want to limit? Why?

ABC Corp. must choose between two projects, both of which require an investment of $250,000. Project A has a 0.5 probability of generating a net payoff of $250,000 and a 0.5 probability of generating a net payoff of $500,000. Project B has a 0.5 probability of generating a net payoff of $100,000 and a 0.5 probability of generating a net payoff of $650,000.

P7 – 8

Investment projects and stockholder-bondholder conflict
(Appendix)

Required:

1. What is the expected value of each project? Which project do shareholders prefer? Why?
2. ABC Corp. will issue $250,000 in bonds to finance the chosen project. The bonds will be repaid from project cash flows. Which project do bondholders prefer? Why?
3. Suppose bondholders plan to loan the company $250,000 for Project A, and they know nothing about Project B. Management knows about both projects and will invest the borrowed funds in the project that's most valuable for shareholders. What problem does Project B create for bondholders? What should bondholders do to guard against this Project B possibility before giving money to the company?

A 1999 *Wall Street Journal* article described how Microsoft records revenue from software sales.

P7 – 9

Microsoft's "unearned revenue" account

STRETCH

SOME SAVVY FANS COOL TO MICROSOFT

Some savvy investors, detecting fissures in Microsoft's armor, are pulling back from the world's most highly valued company.

The concern: the first-ever drop in an arcane but closely watched indicator of Microsoft's future results.

The balance in Microsoft's "unearned revenue" account, which declined to $4.13 billion on Sept. 30 from $4.24 billion in June, has become a lightning rod for more general concerns about the price of the company's shares. . . . Managers of several large funds . . . are shedding part of their Microsoft holdings. The immediate trigger was the first quarter-to-quarter decline in Microsoft's unearned revenue account. . . .

In the software industry, Microsoft pioneered the practice of recording a portion of the revenue from some products as "unearned," starting with the release of Windows 95. The practice is common in some other fields: Many magazine publishers, for instance, record subscription revenues only when issues are shipped.

Similarly, Microsoft now holds back a portion of revenues from Windows 98, Windows NT and Office until it "earns" the revenue by delivering interim upgrades, bug fixes and other customer support. The account also includes the value of coupons that customers receive, which entitle them to free upgrades when they buy a Microsoft product before the next version is ready.

A delay in the shipment of Office 2000 earlier this year caused the company to add $400 million to the unearned revenue account in the March quarter to cover the coupons issued to buyers of Office 97. As copies of Office 2000 were shipped, half of that amount flowed into the June quarterly results; another $150 million was transferred in the fiscal quarter ended in September.

The effect was to bolster earned revenues in those quarters and lower unearned revenues . . .   *(continued)*

FUTURE OR FALLOUT?

Microsoft's unearned revenue account consists of revenues set aside from the sales of Windows 98, Windows NT and Office to pay for future improvements. It also includes the value of coupons that entitle users to upgrade to newer versions of Microsoft software.

Source: Republished with permission of Dow Jones & Co.; © 1999. From *Wall Street Journal* (October 28, 1999); permission conveyed through Copyright Clearance Center, Inc.

($ in billions)

Required:

1. Based on the revenue recognition principles discussed in Chapter 2 and 3, explain why a company like Microsoft would set aside some software sales revenues as "unearned"?
2. How would you determine how much sales revenue to set aside each quarter? Is this number easy to calculate?
3. Suppose the "unearned revenue" account is reduced by $100 million. Where do these dollars go? (The "unearned revenue" account is reduced by a debit. What account receives the offsetting credit?)
4. Describe how contracting and regulatory incentives might influence how much revenue is set aside as "unearned." How might these incentives influence when the "unearned revenue" account is reduced and by how much?
5. Why do analysts and investors pay such close attention to changes in Microsoft's unearned revenue account?

P7 – 10

Executive pay when the CEO nears retirement

Required:

1. Why might it make sense to change a CEO's incentive pay plan as the CEO nears retirement? What conflicts of interest arise as a CEO gets close to retirement age?
2. In early 1997, Ralston Purina Company changed the way its CEO was paid. As a shareholder, what are the advantages and disadvantages of the compensation committee's new strategy for paying Mr. Stiritz?
3. Suppose you are an independent compensation consultant hired by a group of Ralston Purina shareholders. What changes would you suggest be made to the compensation committee's plan?
4. According to the committee, Mr. Stiritz's compensation was changed to "facilitate greater focus on succession planning" and to locate the right successor "so the company will do well after his retirement." In May 1997 Ralston Purina named two of its officers as co-chief executives. As a shareholder, would you be surprised by this outcome? Why or why not?

CEOS HAVE LESS SAY IN DESIGNATING SUCCESSORS

Not long ago, chief executive officers called all the shots in the crucial corporate game of "Pass the Baton."

Today, it's a whole new game. Assertive boards and influential investors are playing bigger parts in the timing of a CEO's exit and choice of successor. Their increased involvement weakens business titans' authority over abdication and can turn transfers of leadership into messy succession struggles.

Bowing to shareholder demands for tougher oversight, more boards now link a chief's pay increase or yearly performance review to succession-planning progress. Ralston Purina Co. directors gave William P. Stiritz options on 600,000 shares last fall to "facilitate

greater focus on succession planning." To make sure the 62-year-old chief executive tapped a replacement soon, Ralston froze his salary and ended certain bonuses and stock grants until he retires.

The package rewards Mr. Stiritz, ensconced in the top post since 1981, for locating the right successor "so the company will do well after his retirement," says W. H. Danforth, an outside director of the St. Louis pet-food and battery company. Late last month, Ralston finally named two officers to share the chief-executive title, but Mr. Stiritz won't relinquish it until September 30.

Source: Republished with permission of Dow Jones & Co.; © 1997. From *Wall Street Journal* (June 24, 1997); permission conveyed through Copyright Clearance Center, Inc.

Ralston Purina Company:

COMPENSATION FOR THE CHAIRMAN AND CHIEF EXECUTIVE OFFICER

The Compensation Committee recognized, as it evaluated Mr. Stiritz's overall compensation at the end of fiscal 1996, that he is likely to retire in the next few years from the position of Chief Executive Officer. Taking that into consideration, the Committee determined it to be in the best interest of the Company to change its approach to compensating Mr. Stiritz. The Committee wishes to facilitate a greater focus by Mr. Stiritz on succession planning and believes that sequential grants of long-term awards which are intended to retain key employees are not appropriate with respect to the Chief Executive Officer when there are relatively few years until retirement. To that end, the Committee decided to award Mr. Stiritz a special performance stock option grant of 600,000 shares in exchange for which it would (i) freeze Mr. Stiritz's base pay until retirement at the level it was during fiscal year 1996; (ii) exclude him from future annual stock award grants; and (iii) exclude him from any further intermediate or long-term cash bonus plans.

The purpose of the grant which, in the Committee's opinion, has an approximate value equal to the benefits described above which he will forgo, is to tie the majority of Mr. Stiritz's compensation to the Company's Common Stock price performance during the last years of his employment.

Alliant Energy just received regulatory approval for its 2005 electricity rate. The company has been authorized to charge customers $0.10 per kilowatt-hour (kwh), a rate lower than what other utilities in the state charge. Details of the rate calculation are as follows:

P7 – 11

Understanding rate regulation and accounting choices

Alliant Energy

		2005 Rate Authorization
Allowed operating costs		$ 1,120 million
Assets in service	$3,200 million	
× Allowed rate of return	8.75%	= $ 280 million
Revenue requirement		$ 1,400 million
÷ Estimated energy demand		14,000 million kwh
Rate allowed per kwh		$ 0.10

Shortly after the 2005 rate was set, the company's financial reporting staff circulated an internal memo recommending the following accounting changes:

1. Extend plant depreciation life by five years to reflect current utilization forecasts. This would add $175 million to the asset base and reduce annual depreciation (an operating cost) by $5 million.
2. Increase estimated bad debt expense from 1% to 1.5% of sales to reflect current forecasts of customer defaults. This would add $7 million to operating costs and reduce total assets by the same amount.
3. Amortize 2004 hostile takeover defense costs of $4.5 million over three years rather than take the entire expense in 2004. This would increase 2005 operating costs by $1.5 million and add $3 million to the asset base.
4. Write up fuel and materials inventories to their current replacement value. This would add $60 million to the asset base, but it would have no impact on 2005 operating costs.

Required:

1. Assess the impact of each proposed change on the company's 2005 revenue requirement and rate per kilowatt-hour, assuming that regulators will approve the accounting changes and adjust the allowed rate accordingly.
2. As a member of the state utility commission, comment on the merits of each proposed accounting change.

P7 – 12

Relative performance
and stock options

Here's how Level 3 Communication's stock option plan works. Suppose options are granted on January 1, 2000 when the company's stock is selling for $50 a share. The options cannot be exercised until January 1, 2003 and the exercise price on that date is $50 plus a factor reflecting the change in the S&P Index between the grant date and the exercise date. If the Index increases 50%, so does the exercise price (to $75). If the Index falls by 10% between the grant date and the exercise date, the exercise price also falls (to $45).

Required:

1. On January 1, 2003, the company's stock is trading at $90 a share. The S&P Index has increased 60 percent from its level at the grant date. What is the exercise price of Level 3's options? Have employees benefited from the company's stock option plan?

2. What if the January 1, 2003 stock price was only $70? Calculate the option exercise price and determine if employees have benefited from the stock option plan. How well have Level 3 stockholders done since the grant date?

3. Stock prices and the S&P Index tend to increase when Mr. Alan Greenspan, Chairman of the Federal Reserve Bank, lowers interest rates. What is the rationale for raising the exercise price when interest rates decline? What other macroeconomic risks can influence the value of employee stock options at Level 3?

4. Why hasn't the Level 3 plan been adopted by many other companies?

THE MOVING-TARGET OPTION

Nineteen ninety-eight was a good year for Harvey Golub, the chief executive of American Express. His stock options zoomed from $45 million to $60 million in value. But it was a bad year for Golub's shareholders. They underperformed the S&P 500 by 13 percentage points.

The disappointed Amex holders have a lot of company. It's common these days for executives to get rich off options even as they deliver subpar results to their investors. It's the simple arithmetic of a bull market: Options can be worth a lot of money on a stock that rises, even if it badly lags the averages. . . .

How do we stop this madness? One bold telecom executive, James Crowe, shows how. When he founded fiber-optics network Level 3 Communications three years ago, he vowed to align his interests with investors'. His option plan, which covers all employees, ties exercise prices to the S&P 500 Index. If Level 3 just keeps up with the average, the options are worthless. If it outperforms, the options are worth a decent amount to rank and file employees and big money to top managers.

Level 3 investors aren't hurting and neither is Chief Executive Crowe. Since the stock was first offered to the public just under two years ago, it has tripled in price. Crowe has a $300 million paper profit so far on his options.

Crowe thinks every company should adopt an option plan like this one. "All kinds of companies have hurt their investors, yet managements are getting enormous payoffs," he scolds.

Crowe is a lonely crusader. We don't know of a single other public company that ties option prices to the S&P.

Former Securities & Exchange Commissioner Joseph Grundfest, now a Stanford Law School professor, presented Level 3's plan at his annual directors' conference last year. Directors of companies like American International Group, Bank America, Lucent and Time Warner attended. Grundfest reports their reaction: "Many thought it was a great idea—for other companies." He adds: "A Level 3-style plan would eliminate the Lake Wobegon effect, where all CEOs are above average. Which is why it's frightening to many." . . .

Source: Reprinted by permission of *Forbes Magazine* © 2000 Forbes. From an article by T. Mack (March 20, 2000).

CASES

C7 – 1

Genesco, Inc., Worthington
Industries, Inc., and
Symantec Corporation (CW):
A tale of three dividend
constraints

Loan agreements often contain provisions that limit the borrower's ability to pay cash dividends or buy back stock to an amount called the "**inventory of payable funds**" or IPF. The IPF is increased by earnings and the proceeds from stock sales, and it is reduced by losses and cash payments to shareholders (dividends or buybacks).

Here's an example: A loan agreement signed in January 2005 says: "cash dividends and stock redemptions (buybacks) are limited to the sum of $5 million plus (i) 25% of net income after December 31, 2004 and (ii) 60% of the proceeds received from issuing common or preferred stock after February 1, 2005."

Suppose the company reports 2005 net income of $12 million and issues $10 million of stock during the year. According to the loan agreement, dividends and stock buybacks cannot exceed $14 million—the $5 million base amount plus 25% of the $12 million net income and 60% of the $10 million stock proceeds. If cash dividends of $3 million were paid out during the year and there were no stock buybacks, the IPF would total $11 million at year-end. This is the most that can be paid to shareholders without more earnings or stock sales.

Several factors in addition to earnings, stock issues, and shareholder payouts determine the level of a company's IPF. First, there's the base IPF amount described in the covenant ($5 million in our example). Next, there's the earnings cumulation date (beginning December 31, 2004) and the percentage allowed (25%). Finally, there's the stock sale cumulation date (February 1, 2005) and the percentage allowed (60%). These details are negotiated as part of the loan approval and acceptance process.

Reproduced next are dividend constraint descriptions for three companies. Genesco, Inc. manufactures and sells branded men's and women's shoes and boots, including Johnston & Murphy, Dockers, and Nautica shoes as well as Laredo, Code West, and Larry Mahan boots.

The February 1, 1993 indenture, under which the Company's $10\frac{3}{8}$% senior notes due 2003 were issued, limits the payment of dividends and redemptions of capital stock to the sum of $10 million plus (i) 50% of Consolidated Net Income (as defined) after April 30, 1993 and (ii) the aggregate Net Proceeds (as defined) received from the issuance or sale of capital stock after February 1, 1993.

At February 1, 1997, the Company was in a deficit position of $91.3 million in its ability to pay dividends. Due to the above restrictions, the Company suspended dividends ... and now has cumulative dividend arrearage in the amount of $277,494 for Series 1, $300,553 for Series 3, $253,360 for Series 4, and $146,333 for $1.50 Subordinated Cumulative Preferred Stock.

Worthington Industries, Inc. is the largest independent flat rolled steel processor in the United States with over 1,700 industrial customers.

Various debt agreements place restrictions on financial conditions and require maintenance of certain ratios. One of these restrictions limits cash dividends and certain other payments to $3,000,000 plus 75% of net earnings, as defined, subsequent to May 31, 1976. Retained earnings of $347,333,000 were unrestricted at May 31, 1996.

Symantec Corporation develops, markets, and supports a diversified line of application and system software products designed to enhance individual and workgroup productivity as well as manage networked computing environments.

On April 2, 1993, the Company issued convertible subordinated debentures totaling $25.0 million. The debentures limit the payment of cash dividends and the repurchase of capital stock to a total of $10.0 million plus 25% of cumulative net income subsequent to April 2, 1993.

The following information was taken from the Symantec Corporation's March 31, 1996 annual report to shareholders.

Symantec Corporation

Selected Financial Statement Items

($ in thousands)	1994	1995	1996
Net income (loss)	$(44,421)	$33,409	$(39,783)
Proceeds from sale of common stock	47,969	21,395	20,770
Cash dividends paid	–0–	–0–	–0–
Stock repurchases	–0–	–0–	–0–

Required:

1. Calculate Symantec's inventory of payable funds (IPF) at the end of fiscal 1996.
2. What percentage of net income (loss) is added to (subtracted from) the IPF of each company? Why does the percentage vary across companies?
3. Why do lenders treat both cash dividends and stock buybacks as a reduction to the IPF?
4. Why do lenders treat proceeds from new stock sales as an IPF increase?
5. How might Genesco's management eliminate the company's IPF deficit?
6. Why does Worthington Industries maintain such a large IPF balance?

C7 – 2

Huffy Corporation, Caesars World, and Lands' End (CW): Accounting-based incentive bonus plans

Huffy Corporation manufactures and sells recreation and leisure products through its subsidiaries— Huffy Bicycle, Huffy Sports, and True Temper Hardware. The company's profit sharing bonus plan is described in a proxy statement as follows:

Profit Sharing Bonus Plan

Bonus opportunity is extended to virtually all managerial employees of the Company, including its Executive Officers. Individual and corporate performance objectives are established at the beginning of each year. The corporate performance measure for bonus payments is based on return on average net assets ("RONA"), and for 1992 the Committee determined that the target level bonus would be achieved when RONA was 10 percent, with threshold level bonus and maximum level bonus being achieved when RONA was 8.5 percent and 14.2 percent, respectively.

The company reported 1992 net income of $4,215,000 and earnings before the cumulative effect of accounting changes of $11,843,000. An accounting change made that year explains the difference between these two numbers. In addition, the company's net assets at the end of 1991 and 1992 were $124,997,000 and $117,687,000, respectively.

Caesars World, Inc. and its subsidiaries provide domestic and international customers with a broad range of entertainment, gaming, and resort experiences at its three hotel/resort properties. The company's incentive compensation plans are described in a proxy statement as follows:

Incentive Compensation Plans

The Company has adopted Incentive Compensation Plans for fiscal 1993 with respect to certain officers of the Company. Basically, the Plans provide for incentive compensation for each officer designated to participate based on a designated percentage of corporate pre-tax income (before extraordinary and certain unusual items) in excess of 12% of shareholders' equity as of July 31, 1992 (subject to adjustment if certain stock sales or repurchases occur).

The company's financial statements show:

Caesars World

Selected Financial Statement Items

($ in thousands)	Year-End Amounts		
	1992	1993	1994
Income before taxes and extraordinary loss	$117,360	$133,976	$128,555
Extraordinary loss	6,073	–0–	–0–
Net income	66,005	83,215	78,361
Total stockholders' equity	384,648	472,890	556,867
Proceeds from stock issued	2,454	1,369	2,111
Stock repurchases	1,986	1,338	2,337

Lands' End, Inc. is a leading direct marketer of traditionally styled apparel, soft luggage, and other products offered through its regular and specialty catalogs. The company's incentive bonus plan is described in a proxy statement as follows:

Incentive Bonuses

The Plan provides participants with bonuses in the form of Company Common Stock, cash or a combination thereof in the event the Company earns pre-tax income in excess of 6% of net sales for the fiscal year of participation. The amount of each incentive bonus is a function of two factors: (i) the participant's level of eligibility ("Bonus Eligibility Amount") as determined by the Committee, and (ii) the extent to which the Company's pre-tax income exceeds 6% of net sales. Each participant's bonus will be calculated as that employee's Bonus Eligibility amount (as determined by the Committee) multiplied by the earned participation level for such year in accordance with the following table:

Pre-tax Income to Net Sales (%)	Participation Level (% of Incentive Bonus Earned)
6%	0%
7	15
8	35
9	70
10	100
11	150

The company's financial statements show:

Lands' End

Selected Financial Statement Items

($ in thousands)	1995	1994	1993	1992	1991
Net sales	$992,106	$869,975	$733,623	$683,427	$601,991
Pre-tax income	59,663	69,870	54,033	47,492	29,943

Required:

1. Why do Huffy, Caesars World, and Lands' End use bonus plans?
2. Did Huffy's managers achieve a RONA greater than 8.5% in 1992?
3. Did Caesars World's managers earn their required minimum rate of return on beginning equity in 1993? How about 1994?
4. Did executives at Lands' End meet their minimum rate of return on sales over the 1991–1995 period?
5. Why don't all companies use the same financial performance measure in their bonus plans?
6. As a member of the board's compensation committee at each company, what financial reporting decisions would you want to carefully monitor? Why?
7. Are the performance targets in these plans reasonable? What information would help you answer this question?

Sunny Day Stores operates convenience stores throughout much of the United States. The industry is highly competitive, with low profit margins. The company's competition includes national, regional, and local supermarkets; oil companies; and convenience store operators.

C7 – 3

Sunny Day Stores, Inc. (CW): Debt covenants and financial distress

A footnote to the 2005 financial statements described the company's long-term debt:

Note payable to the Prudential Insurance Company of America ("Prudential") with annual principal payments of $900,000, interest at 8.93%. Amount outstanding: $5,700,000 in 2005 and $6,600,000 in 2004.

Term note payable to First Florida Bank ("First Florida") maturing in September 2010, with quarterly principal payments of $125,000 through June 30, 2006 and $250,000 thereafter, with interest at 1% in excess of prime (5.5% at December 26, 2005). Amount outstanding: $3,563,956 in 2005 and $3,000,000 in 2004.

Revolving note payable to First Florida Bank with interest at 1% in excess of prime (5.5% at December 26, 2005). Amount outstanding: $7,400,000 in 2005 and 2004.

Certain of the Company's loan agreements pertaining to the borrowings from the Prudential Insurance Company of America ("Prudential") and First Florida Bank ("First Florida") require the Company to maintain minimum interest coverage ratio, working capital, and net worth levels, impose restrictions on additional borrowings, and prohibit the payment of dividends. Specifically, at the end of fiscal 2005 Sunny Day must have a net worth of $22,850,000, working capital (on a FIFO inventory basis) must be at least $1,300,000, and the interest coverage ratio must be at least 1.6.

The company's 2005 financial statements that follow show that Sunny Day Stores was not in compliance with these loan covenants at year end.

Sunny Day Stores, Inc.

Comparative Balance Sheets

	2005	2004		2005	2004
Cash and cash equivalents	$ 1,451,688	$ 2,971,457	Accounts payable		
Accounts receivable less			Trade	$ 9,237,416	$ 6,208,733
allowances for doubtful			Money orders	1,637,255	1,442,811
accounts of $82,000			Fuel taxes	1,106,713	635,556
and $63,000 in 2005			Accrued liabilities		
and 2004, respectively	985,987	705,923	Salaries and wages	774,519	846,131
Refundable income taxes	400,000	135,831	Self-insurance reserves	1,186,613	966,770
Inventories—FIFO basis	10,640,125	8,690,734	State and local taxes	1,136,241	569,160
Less LIFO reserve	(3,057,715)	(2,845,703)	Current portion of long-		
Total inventories	7,582,410	5,845,031	term debt	1,956,369	1,082,429
Prepaid expenses and			Total current liabilities	$17,035,126	$11,751,590
other assets	764,627	547,705			
Refundable deposits	700,000	380,522			
Total current assets	$11,884,712	$10,586,469			
Property and equipment			Deferred income taxes	400,000	1,477,323
Land	11,016,168	13,603,304	Unearned revenue	111,426	179,224
Buildings	19,673,636	19,801,221			
Fixtures and equipment	32,232,643	32,749,133	Long-term debt, less		
Leaseholds and			current portion	13,969,745	16,693,772
improvements	5,084,679	4,929,748			
	$68,007,126	$71,083,406			
Less allowances for					
depreciation and					
amortization	(31,008,778)	(28,988,173)	Stockholders' equity		
	$36,998,348	$42,095,233	Common stock	170,165	170,165
Other assets			Additional paid-in capital	5,124,245	5,124,245
Land held for sale	2,641,735		Retained earnings	15,171,001	17,735,240
Other	456,913	449,857		$20,465,411	$23,029,650
			Total liabilities and		
Total assets	$51,981,708	$53,131,559	stockholders' equity	$51,981,708	$53,131,559

Sunny Day Stores, Inc.

Statement of Cash Flows

	2005	2004	2003
Cash Flows from Operating Activities			
Net income (loss)	$(2,564,239)	$(1,042,297)	$ 613,423
Adjustments			
Depreciation and amortization	3,980,186	4,460,529	3,793,119
Deferred income taxes	(1,077,323)	(512,995)	577,235
Gain on sale of property	(532,570)	(174,657)	(100,322)
Decrease in unearned revenue	(67,798)	(83,804)	(84,235)
Changes in assets and liabilities			
(Increase) in accounts receivable	(280,064)	53,121	(358,982)
(Increase) in refundable income taxes	(264,169)	244,085	(113,675)
(Increase) in inventories	(1,737,379)	2,908,024	412,647
(Increase) in other assets	(263,981)	(141,910)	(241,347)
Increase in refundable deposits	(319,478)	(15,107)	(145,866)
Increase in accounts payable and other liabilities	4,409,596	(4,304,076)	3,807,200
Total adjustments	3,847,020	2,433,210	7,545,774
Net cash flow from operations	$ 1,282,781	$ 1,390,913	$ 8,159,197
Cash Flows from Investing Activities			
Purchase of property and equipment, net	(2,390,832)	(2,871,399)	(9,593,270)
Sale of property and equipment	1,428,051	668,656	821,641
Collections of notes and loans receivables	10,318	(103,610)	7,775
Net cash used in investing activities	$ (952,463)	$(2,306,353)	$(8,763,854)
Cash Flows from Financing Activities			
Issuance of long-term debt	82,515	2,633,454	4,528,915
Dividends	–0–	–0–	(204,198)
Payment of long-term debt	(1,932,602)	(3,108,251)	(1,588,391)
Net cash provided by financing activities	$(1,850,087)	$ (474,797)	$ 2,736,326
Net increase (Decrease) in Cash	$(1,519,769)	$(1,390,237)	$ 2,131,669

Sunny Day Stores, Inc.

Statement of Operations

	2005	2004	2003
Net revenue	$217,710,782	$202,393,136	$191,243,016
Cost and expenses			
Costs of goods sold	176,102,027	158,643,287	146,652,853
Selling, general, and administrative	44,631,749	43,687,704	41,805,330
Interest expense—net	1,551,138	1,728,650	1,658,732
Net gain from sale of property	(532,570)	(174,657)	(100,322)
	221,752,344	203,884,984	190,016,593
Income (loss) before taxes	(4,041,562)	(1,491,848)	1,226,423
Provision (benefit) for income taxes			
Current	(400,000)	63,444	50,000
Deferred	(1,077,323)	(512,995)	563,000
	(1,477,323)	(449,551)	613,000
Net income (loss)	$ (2,564,239)	$ (1,042,297)	$ 613,423
Earnings per common share	$(1.51)	$(0.61)	$0.36

Required:

It's late January 2006 and you've been hired by Prudential and First Florida to act on their behalf in negotiations with Sunny Day Stores, Inc. Both lenders want to restructure their loans to address the company's current financial problems, and the restructured loans may require covenant changes.

Prudential and First Florida seek your advice on the type and amount of collateral to be required, revised interest rates, and possible changes to the payment schedules. In addition, the lenders have asked you to suggest new minimum net worth, working capital, and interest coverage ratios for 2006 and 2007. Specifically:

1. What type and amount of collateral do you suggest be required?
2. Should a higher interest rate be charged? Why or why not?
3. What changes would you suggest be made to the payment schedule?
4. What new minimum net worth, working capital, and interest coverage limits would you suggest the lenders set?
5. Suppose the company asked permission to resume payment of its $0.12 per-share common stock dividend, which was suspended in 2004. What advice would you give Prudential and First Florida?

C7 – 4

Maxcor Manufacturing:
Compensation and earnings
quality

Margaret Magee has served both as an outside director to Maxcor Manufacturing since 1995 and as a member of the company's compensation committee since 2002. Margaret has been reviewing Maxcor's 2005 preliminary earnings statement in preparation for the February 2006 board and compensation committee meetings. She is uneasy about the company's definition and computation of "Operating profits" for 2005, particularly since management bonuses at Maxcor are based on achieving specific operating profit goals.

Maxcor Manufacturing

Consolidated Results of Operations

	Years Ended December 31	
($ in millions)	**2005**	**2004**
Sales	$98.4	$111.2
Operating costs		
Cost of goods sold	(81.5)	(92.2)
Selling, general, and administrative expenses	(12.5)	(12.9)
Operating profit	4.4	6.1
Research and development expenses (see note)	(5.7)	(2.4)
Provision for plant closings (see note)	(2.6)	–0–
Interest expense	(2.9)	(2.6)
Other income	0.7	1.2
Profit (loss) before taxes	(6.1)	2.3
Provision (credit) for income taxes	2.1	(0.8)
Profit (loss) of consolidated companies	(4.0)	1.5
Equity in profit of affiliated companies	0.2	0.3
Profit (loss)	$ (3.8)	$ 1.8

The preliminary financial statements also contained the following footnotes:

Research and Engineering Expenses. Research and engineering expenses include both "Research and development expenses" for new product development and charges originally made to "Cost of goods sold" for ongoing product improvements. The amounts (in millions) for 2005 and 2004 were:

	2005	2004
Research and development expenses	$5.7	$2.4
Cost of goods sold	2.9	6.3
Research and engineering expense	$8.6	$8.7

Plant Closing Costs. In 2005, the Company recorded provisions for plant closing and staff consolidation costs totaling $2.62 million. Included in this total are charges related to the probable closing of the Company's York, Pennsylvania facility ($1.75 million), the consolidation of the North American operations of the Building Construction Products Division ($0.63 million), and charges to reflect lower estimates of the market value of previously closed U.S. facilities ($0.24 million). These costs include the estimated costs of employee severance benefits, the estimated net losses on disposal of land, buildings, machinery and equipment, and other costs incidental to the closing and planned consolidation.

Maxcor Manufacturing is an established, privately held manufacturer that operates in two principal business segments: *Building Construction Products*, which involves the design, manufacturing, and marketing of construction and materials-handling machinery; and *Engines* for various off-highway applications. Before 2005 the company had experienced 15 years of steadily increasing sales and operating profits.

The company was founded in 1938 by Hugh Maxwell, a former Ford Motor Company engineer. Neither Mr. Maxwell nor any members of his family are currently officers of the company. Maxcor's common stock is held by the Maxwell Family Trust (35%), the Maxwell Employee Stock Ownership Plan (ESOP) Trust (50%), a venture capital firm (13%), and current management (2%). Margaret Magee also serves as an outside trustee for the Maxwell ESOP Trust.

Maxcor's senior management participates in an incentive bonus plan that was first adopted in 1996. The bonus formula for 2005 was approved by the compensation committee at its February 2004 meeting. According to the plan, each senior manager's 2005 bonus is to be determined as follows:

Bonus as Percentage of 2005 Salary	2005 Operating Profits ($ in millions)
0%	Below $4.0
100	At least $4.0
200	At least $6.0
300	At least $8.0

The compensation committee can award a lesser amount than that indicated by the plan formula if circumstances warrant such action. No bonus reductions have occurred since the plan was adopted in 1996.

Required:

Why might Ms. Magee feel uneasy about Maxcor's computation of 2005 operating profits? Should Ms. Magee approve the 100% bonus payment for 2005 as specified by the plan formula? What changes (if any) would you recommend be made to the bonus formula for next year?

Remember to check the book's Companion Website for additional problem and case material.

www.prenhall.com/revsine

Receivables

Receivables are amounts owed to a business firm by outsiders. In U.K. financial reports, receivables are called "debtors"—a term clearly connoting the legal obligation of outsiders to make payments to a firm. Most receivables arise from credit sales and are called **trade receivables** or **accounts receivable**. Receivables that result from other types of transactions and events (for example, insurance claims from casualty losses) are separately disclosed, if significant, on the balance sheet. This separate disclosure facilitates informed financial analysis.

Assessing the Net Realizable Value of Accounts Receivable

Generally accepted accounting principles (GAAP) require that accounts receivable be reflected in the balance sheet at their **net realizable value**.[1] Two things must be estimated to determine the net realizable value of receivables:

1. The amount that will not be collected because customers are unable to pay—called **uncollectibles**.
2. The amount that will not be collected because customers return the merchandise for credit or are allowed a reduction in the amount owed—called **returns** and **allowances**.

The next sections discuss financial reporting issues relating to uncollectibles, returns, and allowances.

Estimating Uncollectibles

Receivables arising from some credit sales never get collected. These losses are an unavoidable cost of doing business. Companies could adopt such stringent credit standards that "bad debt" losses would be virtually zero. But if they only sold to

---

[1] "Net realizable value" means the selling price of an item minus reasonable further costs both to make the item ready to sell and to sell it. When applied to trade receivables, net realizable value means the amount of money the business can reasonably expect to collect from its credit customers.

customers with impeccable credit records, they would forego many otherwise profitable sales opportunities.

Most companies establish credit policies by weighing the expected cost of credit sales—customer billing and collection costs plus potential bad debt losses—against the benefit of increased sales. Companies choose what they believe is a profit maximizing balance. This trade-off between increased costs and additional profits from credit sales illustrates that bad debts are often unavoidable. Consequently, the accrual accounting matching principle requires that some *estimate* of uncollectible accounts be offset against current period sales—that is, ***estimated losses from customers who are ultimately unable to pay are treated as an expense of the period in which the sale is made.*** Obviously, companies can't know at the time of sale which customers will ultimately be unable to pay. So proper matching of revenues and expenses is achieved by estimating the proportion of current period credit sales that will not be collected in the future, and then by charging this estimated amount as an expense.

Suppose Bristol Corporation estimates that, based on current industry trends and the company's experience, bad debt losses arising from first quarter 2005 sales are expected to be $30,000. The entry Bristol would make under GAAP is:

DR	Bad debt expense	$30,000	
	CR Allowance for uncollectibles		$30,000

The Allowance for uncollectibles is a contra-asset account that is subtracted from gross accounts receivable. If Bristol's gross accounts receivable and allowance for uncollectibles balances *before* recording this bad debt entry were $1,500,000 and $15,000, respectively, then after recording bad debts, its balance sheet would show:

Accounts receivable (gross)	$1,500,000	
Less: Allowance for uncollectibles	(45,000)	{ (15,000) Initial balance
Accounts receivable (net)	$1,455,000	{ (30,000) Addition

There are two alternative approaches companies can use to estimate uncollectible accounts. One multiplies a specific loss percentage by sales revenues; the other multiplies a (usually different) loss percentage by gross accounts receivable. Each approach is illustrated as follows.

1. *The sales revenue approach.* Assume that Bristol Corporation prepares quarterly financial statements and must estimate bad debt expense at the end of each quarter. Analyzing past customer payment patterns, Bristol determined that bad debt losses average about 1% of sales. If first quarter sales in 2005 total $3,000,000, then bad debt losses from those sales are expected to total $30,000. The entry previously illustrated would then be made to record the company's estimate of bad debt expenses arising from current quarter sales.

Sales Revenue Approach

Estimate the current period bad debt expense as a percentage of current period sales. For Bristol Corporation, the estimate is:

.01 × $3,000,000 Sales for the quarter = $30,000 Bad debt expense

So the entry is:

DR	Bad debt expense	$30,000	
	CR Allowance for uncollectibles		$30,000

2. *The gross accounts receivable approach.* Suppose that instead of estimating bad debts as a percentage of sales, Bristol determined that at any given time approximately 3% of gross accounts receivable eventually prove uncollectible. Gross receivables at March 31, 2005 total $1,500,000, which means that on that date the required allowance for uncollectibles is 3% of this amount, or $45,000. Because the allowance-account balance is only $15,000, $30,000 must be added to the uncollectibles account at the end of the quarter. Doing this would bring the allowance for uncollectibles balance up to $45,000.

Gross Receivables Approach

Estimate the required allowance account balance as a percentage of gross receivables, then adjust the allowance upwards or downwards to this figure. For Bristol Corporation, the required allowance account balance is:

$.03 \times \$1,500,000$ Outstanding receivables = $45,000 Allowance for uncollectibles

The allowance account currently has a $15,000 balance, so $30,000 is added:

DR Bad debt expense	$30,000	
CR Allowance for uncollectibles		$30,000

Writing Off Bad Debts When a specific account receivable is known to be definitely uncollectible, the entire account must be removed from the books. For example, if Bristol determines that a $750 receivable from Ralph Company cannot be collected, the following entry is made:

DR Allowance for uncollectibles	$750	
CR Account receivable—Ralph Company		$750

Notice that this entry has no effect on income. A specific account receivable (Ralph Company) is eliminated from the books and the allowance contra-account is reduced, *but no bad debt expense is recorded.* This is consistent with the accrual accounting philosophy of recording estimated bad debt expense when the sale was made rather than at some later date when the nonpaying customer is identified. Of course, Bristol Corporation does not know at the time of each sale which particular customers will be unable to pay. That's why the offsetting credit for bad debt expense was originally made to the contra-asset account "Allowance for uncollectibles." *Only when the seller knows which specific receivable is uncollectible can the individual account (Ralph Company) be written off.* This is what the preceding entry accomplishes.

Assessing the Adequacy of the Allowance for Uncollectibles Account Balance

No matter which method—percentage of sales or percentage of gross receivables—is used to estimate bad debts, management must periodically assess the reasonableness of the allowance for uncollectibles balance. Given existing economic conditions and customer circumstances, is the balance in the allowance-for-uncollectibles account adequate, excessive, or insufficient?

To make this judgment, management performs an **aging of accounts receivable.** As the name implies, an aging of receivables is simply a determination of how long each receivable has been on the books. Receivables that are long past due often exist because customers are experiencing financial difficulties and may ultimately be unable to pay. An aging is performed by subdividing total accounts receivable into several age categories, as shown in Exhibit 8.1.

EXHIBIT 8.1	Bristol Corporation

Allowance for Uncollectibles Based on Aging of Receivables

On December 31, 2005 Bristol Corporation's gross accounts receivable are $1,600,000, and the allowance-for-uncollectibles balance is $39,000. Bristol's normal sales terms require payment within 30 days after the sale is made and the goods are received by the buyer. Bristol determines that the receivables have the following age distribution:

	Current	31–90 days old	91–180 days old	Over 180 days old	Total
Amount	$1,450,000	$125,000	$15,000	$10,000	$1,600,000

Once the receivables have been grouped by age category, a separate estimate of uncollectibles by category is developed. Based on past experience, Bristol determines the following estimate of expected bad debt losses by category:

	Current	31–90 days old	91–180 days old	Over 180 days old
Estimated % of bad debt losses	2.5%	6%	20%	40%

The required balance in the allowance-for-uncollectibles account would then be as follows:

	Current	31–90 days old	91–180 days old	Over 180 days old	Total
Amount	$1,450,000	$125,000	$15,000	$10,000	$1,600,000
Estimated % of bad debt losses	2.5%	6%	20%	40%	
Allowance for uncollectibles	$ 36,250	$ 7,500	$ 3,000	$ 4,000	$ 50,750

Because the allowance-for-uncollectibles balance is only $39,000 on December 31, 2005, the account must be increased by $11,750. This is the difference between the $50,750 required balance (as computed) and the existing $39,000 balance. To bring the balance up to the $50,750 figure indicated by the aging, Bristol would make the following adjusting entry:

DR Bad debt expense	$11,750	
CR Allowance for uncollectibles		$11,750

Obviously, considerable judgment goes into evaluating the adequacy of the allowance-for-uncollectibles balance. Most companies make careful appraisals in this area, since audit guidelines are well developed and auditors' scrutiny is intense.

Exhibit 8.2 contains selected financial statement figures taken from the 2001 annual report of The Scotts Company, a leading manufacturer and marketer of consumer branded products for lawn and garden care.

EXHIBIT 8.2	The Scotts Company

Analysis of Uncollectible Accounts Receivable

	2001	2000
A. Reported Amounts ($ *in millions*)		
Net sales	$1,747.7	$1,709.0
Pre-tax income	28.7	116.3
Customer receivables (gross)	$ 244.7	$ 227.7
Allowance for uncollectibles	23.9	11.7
Bad debt expense	20.9	4.8
B. Analysis		
Bad debt expense as % of sales	1.2%	0.3%
Allowance as % of customer receivables	9.8%	5.1%

Source: The Scotts Company 2001 Annual Report to Shareholders.

2001 was a lackluster year for Scotts. Sales increased 2.2% (from $1,709.0 million to $1,747.7 million), but pre-tax income fell 75.3% (from $116.3 million to $28.7 million). Earnings declined because of a small decrease in gross profit and costs associated with plant closures and relocations. Despite the income decline, both the bad debt expense (as a percentage of sales) and the allowance for uncollectibles (as a percentage of gross customer receivables) increased in 2001. This suggests that Scotts was taking a more conservative view of receivable collections than it had in the past, perhaps because the customer credit quality had recently deteriorated.

ANALYSI

What impact did this conservative view have on the company's 2001 pre-tax earnings? The data in Exhibit 8.2 provide the answer.

Suppose Scotts had maintained 2001 bad debt expense at 0.3% of sales (the same rate used in 2000). Bad debt expense would then have been $5.2 million (0.3% of $1,747.7 million sales)—or $15.7 million lower. This would have meant a corresponding $15.7 million (or 54.7%) increase in pre-tax income for the year.

Now suppose Scotts had kept the allowance for uncollectibles at 5.1% of gross receivables (the rate used in 2000). In this case, the allowance account balance for 2001 would have been $12.5 million (5.1% of $244.7 million gross customer receivables)—or $11.4 million lower than what the company actually reported. Of course, this would have meant an $11.4 million reduction in bad debt expense for the year, and an $11.4 million (or 39.7%) increase in pre-tax income.

This analysis shows that the decision to be more conservative about receivable collections penalized reported earnings in what was already a down profit year.

For companies like Scotts, a modest change in the percentage rate used to estimate bad debt expense or the allowance for uncollectibles can have a big impact on reported earnings.

Determining whether the allowance for uncollectibles is adequate requires judgment. Consequently, the temptation to "manage" earnings by using bad debt accruals can be strong. As the Scotts example illustrates, not all companies succumb to this temptation. However, research evidence does show that companies tend to reduce bad debt expense (and thereby increase earnings) when earnings are otherwise low—and then to increase the expense when earnings are high.[2]

Estimating Sales Returns and Allowances

Sometimes the wrong goods are shipped to customers or the correct goods arrive damaged. In either case the customer will return the item or request a price reduction. When goods are returned or price allowances granted, the customer's account receivable must be reduced and an income statement charge made. Assume that Bristol Corporation agrees to reduce by $8,000 the price of goods that arrived damaged at Bath Company. Bristol would record this price adjustment as:

DR Sales returns and allowances		$8,000	
CR Accounts receivable—Bath Company			$8,000

[2] See M. McNichols and G. P. Wilson, "Evidence of Earnings Management From the Provision for Bad Debts," *Journal of Accounting Research* (Supplement 1988), pp. 1–31; S. Moyer, "Capital Adequacy Ratio Regulations and Accounting Choices in Commercial Banks," *Journal of Accounting and Economics* (July 1990), pp. 123–54; M. Scholes, P. Wilson, and M. Wolfson, "Tax Planning, Regulatory Capital Planning and Financial Reporting Strategy for Commercial Banks," *Review of Financial Studies* (Vol. 3, No. 4, 1990), pp. 625–50; J. Collins, D. Shackelford, and J. Wahlen, "Bank Differences in the Coordination of Regulatory Capital, Earnings, and Taxes," *Journal of Accounting Research* (Autumn 1995), pp. 263–91; A. Beatty, S. Chamberlain, and J. Magliolo, "Managing Financial Reports of Commercial Banks: The Influence of Taxes, Regulatory Capital, and Earnings," *Journal of Accounting Research* (Autumn 1995), pp. 231–61. As the titles of these studies suggest, regulatory capital requirements in commercial banks and financial services companies also influence bad debt accruals.

Bath now owes $8,000 less than the amount it was previously billed, as reflected by the reduction to Accounts receivable. The account that is debited here is an offset to sales revenues—termed a contra-revenue account. Sales revenues are not reduced directly; the contra-revenue account allows Bristol Corporation to keep a running record of the frequency and amount of returns and price reductions, since these events represent potential breakdowns in customer relations.

At the end of the reporting period, companies estimate the expected amount of future returns and allowances arising from receivables currently on the books. If the estimated number is large in relation to the accounts receivable balance or to earnings, then the adjusting entry is:

DR	Sales returns and allowances	$$$$	
CR	Allowance for sales returns and allowances		$$$$

The debit is to a contra-revenue account that reduces net sales by the estimated amount of returns and allowances. Since it is not yet known which *specific* customer accounts will require future returns and allowances, the credit entry must be made to a contra-asset account that off-sets gross accounts receivable. In practice, estimated sales returns and allowances are seldom material in relation to receivables. Consequently, no end-of-period accrual is typically made for these items.

Ordinary returns and allowances are seldom a major issue in financial reporting. On the other hand, companies occasionally adopt "aggressive" revenue recognition practices—meaning that revenue is recognized either prematurely or inappropriately. Examples include recognizing revenue on goods shipped on consignment or recognizing revenue when delivery is delayed, as discussed in Chapter 3. This revenue recognition aggressiveness generates significant returns in later periods. Aggressive revenue recognition overstates both accounts receivable and income. Consequently, analysts must understand that a sudden spurt in accounts receivable may be a danger signal, as we see next.

> Ignoring *estimated* future returns and allowances has a trivial effect on income when the amount of *actual* returns and allowances does not vary greatly from year to year.

Analytical Insight: Do Existing Receivables Represent Real Sales?

When a company's sales terms, customer creditworthiness, and accounting methods do not change from period to period, the growth rates in sales and in accounts receivable will be roughly equal. If sales grow by 10%, accounts receivable should also grow by about 10%. Statement readers who understand this will carefully monitor the relationship between sales growth and receivables growth. When receivables grow faster than sales, those statement readers will see a potential "red flag." Receivables could grow at a higher rate than sales grow for several reasons. One reason is that the disparity in growth rates might reflect something positive like a deliberate change in sales terms designed to attract new customers. Suppose that instead of requiring payment within 30 days of shipment, Hmong Company allows customers to pay in four months. Changes like this broaden the potential market for the company's products and services by allowing slightly less creditworthy customers to buy the firm's products. In this case, receivables growth will far outpace sales growth. To illustrate, consider the following example:

> Assume that before introducing more lenient credit terms, Hmong Company had annual sales of $12 million and customers, on average, paid within 30 days. Outstanding accounts receivable, therefore, represent one month's sales, or $1 million. Under the new credit program, customer receivables would represent four months' sales, or $4 million; this represents a 300% increase in receivables even if total sales remain unchanged.

Another reason for receivables growth exceeding sales growth might be due to deteriorating creditworthiness among existing customers, which could represent an emerging problem. If customers are unable to pay, receivables will not be collected when due and accounts receivable will grow at a faster rate than sales. However, this problem should be uncovered in careful audits by the company's independent auditor. Accordingly, when the cause for the unusual growth in receivables is due to an inability of customers to pay on time, GAAP financial statements would ordinarily show a large increase in estimated uncollectibles.

So growth in accounts receivables can outstrip growth in sales revenues either because firms allow customers more time to pay or because customers are unable to pay due to their own cash flow problems.

Yet another reason why receivables growth might exceed sales growth is that the firm has changed its financial reporting procedures, which determine *when* sales are recognized. To illustrate this possibility, let's consider an automobile manufacturer that builds cars and ships them to a dealer who ultimately sells them to individuals like you. Assume that the manufacturer in past years has recognized revenue from sales only when the automobile was sold to the final customer. But if the auto manufacturer in the current year suddenly decides to recognize automobile sales revenue when the cars are shipped to the dealer, ***this would represent a significant change in financial reporting principles***. To see how a financial reporting change like this would affect the relationship between receivables growth and sales growth, consider Exhibit 8.3, which presents selected financial statement data for Bausch & Lomb Inc. for the years 1990 through 1993.

> Collectibility of receivables requires forecasts of future conditions. Forecasts are often inaccurate. However, existing auditing procedures for accounts receivable are very detailed and stringent, requiring auditors to send confirmations to customers verifying the legitimacy of the recorded receivables. Aging schedules to uncover payment problems are also required. Furthermore, auditors undertake credit-checks on the company's largest customers to ascertain the probability of eventual collection. As a consequence of these procedures, while collectibility requires forecasts that could be wrong, extreme overstatement of net (collectible) receivables is rare.

EXHIBIT 8.3	**Bausch & Lomb, Inc**			
Selected Financial Statement Data, 1990–93 ($000 omitted)	**1990**	**1991**	**1992**	**1993**
Net sales	$1,368,580	$1,520,104	$1,709,086	$1,872,184
Net trade accounts receivable	$ 202,967	$ 205,262	$ 277,338	$ 384,973
Days sales outstanding*	54 days*	49 days	59 days	75 days
Receivables as a % of total assets	12.1%	11.8%	14.8%	15.3%
Year-to-year growth in				
Net sales		$151,524	$188,982	$163,098
Net trade accounts receivable		$ 2,295	$ 72,076	$107,635
Net sales		11.07%	12.43%	9.54%
Net trade accounts receivable		1.13%	35.11%	38.81%

*"Days sales outstanding" is "Net trade accounts receivables" divided by "Net sales" per day. For example, the calculation for 1990 "Days sales outstanding" is

$202,967 net trade receivables/($1,368,580 net sales/365 days) = 54 days.

Source: Bausch & Lomb Inc. Annual Reports.

Exhibit 8.3 shows that net trade accounts receivable grew dramatically in both 1992 and 1993. This growth shows up in absolute dollar amounts (an increase of $72,076 in 1992 and $107,635 in 1993) as well as in relation to total balance sheet assets (11.8% in 1991 versus 14.8% in 1992 and 15.3% in 1993). But what makes this growth seem "unusual" is the disparity in growth rates between sales and receivables. While sales grew 12.43% in 1992 and 9.54% in 1993, receivables jumped by 35.11% and 38.81% in those same years, respectively (highlighted areas in Exhibit 8.3). Clearly, something unusual was happening in both years. A partial explanation was provided one year later in the company's 1994 annual report, which stated:

In the fourth quarter of 1993, the Company adopted a business strategy to shift responsibility for the sale and distribution of a portion of the U.S. traditional contact lens business to optical distributors. A 1993 fourth quarter marketing program to implement this strategy was developed, contributing one-time net income of approximately $10 million. Subsequently, this strategy proved unsuccessful.

Prior to this change in Bausch & Lomb's business strategy, revenues and associated receivables were recognized when sales were made to retailers or ultimate consumers. In the fourth quarter of 1993, however, shipments to distributors appear to have been treated as sales. This change in revenue recognition was in keeping with the shift in sales strategy, but the worry is that if distributors are unable to sell their inventory they will return it to Bausch & Lomb for credit. This is exactly what happened, as described in the company's 1994 annual report:

> In October 1994, the Company announced it had implemented a new pricing policy for traditional contact lenses and agreed on a one-time basis to accept returns from these distributors. As a result, the Company recorded sales reserves and pricing adjustments which reduced operating earnings by approximately $20 million in the third quarter. The new pricing policy sought to enhance the Company's competitive position in a market segment where industry prices had declined since the business strategy was implemented. *The returns program allowed U.S. distributors to send back the excess portion of unsold traditional lenses and balance their overall contact lens inventories.* [Emphasis added.]

*SFAS No. 48** states that when a sales agreement contains conditions that may allow the buyer to return the product, revenue should be recognized only when:
1. the return privilege has substantially expired because of performance by the seller, or other conditions, and
2. the amount of future returns can be reasonably estimated.

But these guidelines are imprecise and abuses of the rules have occurred, as discussed in Chapter 3.

*"Revenue Recognition When Right of Return Exists" (Stamford CT: FASB, 1981).

So we see that like our hypothetical automobile manufacturer, Bausch & Lomb began recognizing revenue when output was shipped to distributors rather than waiting until units were sold to final consumers.

But the first annual report excerpt at the top of this page suggests that the changes in sales strategy and revenue recognition only began in 1993. Yet the data in Exhibit 8.3 reveal that a large disparity in sales and receivables growth rates occurred earlier. What explains this pre-1993 disparity?

A *Business Week* article published six months after Bausch & Lomb released its 1994 annual report suggests several possible explanations.[3] The article asserts that top-down pressure to achieve sales and profit goals caused Bausch & Lomb managers to loosen revenue recognition standards in the early 1990s, an assertion that was vehemently denied by top Bausch & Lomb executives. Specifically, Bausch & Lomb sales representatives allegedly "gave customers extraordinarily long payment terms, knowingly fed gray markets, and threatened to cut off distributors unless they took on huge quantities of unwanted products. Some also shipped goods before customers ordered them and booked the shipments as sales. . . . "[4] The article further contends that this type of deal making "became frantic" from the last quarter of 1992 through early 1994 and that the U.S. contact lens division "had a habit of constantly rolling over unpaid bills so that customers wouldn't return unwanted goods for credit."[5] If *Business Week*'s interpretations are correct, these practices would explain the unusual pre-1993 receivables growth.

Figure 8.1 depicts the company's days sales outstanding (DSO) for receivables by quarter for March 1989 through the end of 1995. DSO receivables is just the dollar amount of outstanding receivables divided by average daily sales. From March 1989 to March 1992, DSO receivables at Bausch & Lomb averaged about 50 days and fluctuated little from quarter to quarter. By the end of 1992, however, outstanding receivables had grown to 59 days, and by the fourth quarter of 1993 they stood at 72 days. This unusual pattern of growth in DSO receivables at Bausch & Lomb

3 M. Maremont "Blind Ambition," *Business Week* (October 23, 1995), pp. 78–92.
4 Ibid., pp. 79–80.
5 Ibid., p. 86.

undoubtedly caused some financial statement readers to become skeptical about the company's revenue recognition practices.

Figure 8.1

BAUSCH & LOMB INC.
DSO Receivables by Quarter

One last point regarding Bausch & Lomb. The *Business Week* article contends that the reported December 31, 1993 accounts receivable number of $385 million (see Exhibit 8.3) *understates* the real growth of outstanding customer credit. The understatement occurs, according to the article, because Bausch & Lomb sold some receivables to a third-party financing company for cash. Receivable sales of this sort are called **factoring**, which is discussed later in this chapter. Factored receivables are removed from the balance sheet. If the receivables had not been factored, then the accounts receivable balance would have been higher and the disparity in sales and receivables growth rates for 1992 and 1993 would have been even larger!

Scrutiny of changes in accounts receivable balances is essential. Large increases in accounts receivable relative to sales frequently represent a danger signal. The two most likely causes are (1) collection difficulties, and (2) sales contingencies or disputes that may lead to potential returns. But another possible explanation, as you just saw, is changes in revenue recognition methods.

Many revenue recognition "irregularities" can be discovered by tracking the relationship between changes in sales and changes in receivables. Another example is provided by the 1997 Sunbeam Corporation annual report.

Albert J. Dunlap joined Sunbeam Corporation as Chairman and Chief Executive Officer in July 1996. He had earned a reputation as a "turnaround" specialist because of his aggressiveness in restructuring and downsizing companies he previously ran, such as Scott Paper. By cutting costs and eliminating waste, Dunlap restored the companies to profitability. Sunbeam had mediocre performance in the years prior to Dunlap's arrival. But reported 1997 quarterly and annual financial results seemed to indicate considerable improvement.

At the start of his letter to shareholders in the 1997 annual report, Dunlap stated:

> We had an amazing year in 1997! During the past 12 months we set new records in almost every facet of the Company's operations. We experienced significant sales growth and concurrently increased margins and earnings.

The letter concluded:

> Stay tuned, the best is yet to come!

Soon after the 1997 Sunbeam annual report appeared, some analysts raised questions about the quality of the reported earnings and the economic validity of the results.[6] Sales for 1997 and 1996 and year-end receivables were:

---
[6] See Jonathan R. Laing, "Dangerous Games," *Barron's* (June 8, 1998).

($000 omitted)	1997	1996
Net sales	$1,168,182	$984,236
Gross trade accounts receivable	313,013	229,455

Sales grew by 18.69% ([$1,168,182 − $984,236] ÷ $984,236) while receivables grew by 36.42% ([$313,013 − $229,455] ÷ $229,455). The disparity in growth rates is a clue that there may be a problem. Investigation is warranted since the following notes to the 1997 annual report in Exhibit 8.4 disclose "bill and hold sales" and disposal of receivables—events that affect both sales and receivables.

EXHIBIT 8.4 **Sunbeam Corporation Footnotes**

Revenue Recognition

The Company recognizes revenues from product sales principally at the time of shipment to customers. In limited circumstances, at the customer's request the Company may sell seasonal product on a bill and hold basis provided that the goods are completed, packaged and ready for shipment, such goods are segregated and the risks of ownership and legal title have passed to the customer. *The amount of such bill and hold sales at December 29, 1997 was approximately 3% of consolidated revenues.* [Emphasis and highlighting added.]

Credit Facilities

In December 1997, the Company entered into a revolving trade accounts receivable securitization program to sell without recourse, through a wholly-owned subsidiary, certain trade accounts receivable. The maximum amount of receivables that can be sold through this program is $70 million. *At December 28, 1997, the Company had received approximately $59 million from the sale of trade accounts receivable.* [Emphasis and highlighting added.]

Source: Sunbeam Corporation 1997 Annual Report.

Let's look at **bill and hold** sales. In a bill and hold sale, the company recognizes revenue and the associated account receivable, but does not ship the product to the customer until later. One issue is whether these are real sales. The annual report note states that these bill and hold terms were at the customer's request and legal title to the inventory had passed. So it's reasonable to conclude that the sales were legitimate even though the inventory hadn't been shipped. But the other issue is whether these are really sales of 1997 or instead 1998 sales that have been pulled into 1997 by the bill and hold terms. The amount in question isn't trivial—3% of Sunbeam's 1997 sales ($1,168,182,000) is $35,045,460. This represents 19.05% of the reported $183,946,000 growth in sales between 1996 and 1997.

Furthermore, the true growth in receivables is understated by the amount of receivables sold at the end of 1997. The $59 million cash received is the book value of the receivables minus the financing charge. So $59 million roughly approximates the amount of receivables removed from the books.

Let's summarize the clues that were available to the careful analyst:

1. Receivables growth greatly exceeded sales growth.
2. Bill and hold sales raise the possibility that some of this disparity is because sales were booked too early, thus generating receivables that won't be collected quickly. Worse yet, collection may never occur if delivery of "sold" items is ultimately refused.

3. Had Sunbeam not sold approximately $59 million of receivables, the "real" growth rate of receivables would have exceeded the reported rate of 36.42%, further increasing the disparity between sales and receivables growth rates. This even larger disparity increases the likelihood that some "channel stuffing"—that is, overly aggressive revenue recognition on items "sold" to dealers—was occurring.

These, as well as other issues unrelated to receivables, prompted a reaudit of Sunbeam's financial statements from the fourth quarter of 1996 through the first quarter of 1998. The reaudit disclosed that 1997 sales were overstated by $95,092,000 and profits were $38,301,000 rather than $109,415,000, as reported.[7]

And it was careful scrutiny by informed analysts that led to inquiries which resulted in these corrections!

> Albert J. Dunlap was fired by Sunbeam's Board of Directors on June 15, 1998. He personally paid $15 million as part of a $141 million settlement of a shareholder class-action fraud lawsuit against Sunbeam. In addition, he later paid a $500,000 penalty to the SEC to settle civil allegations of accounting fraud. As part of the settlement, Mr. Dunlap agreed to a permanent ban on serving as an official of a public company. See Michael Schroeder, "Dunlap Settles Fraud Charges with the SEC," *Wall Street Journal* (September 5, 2002).

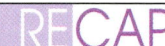

RECAP

Evaluating the net realizable value of accounts receivable requires an analysis of the adequacy of estimated uncollectibles and provisions for returns and price adjustments. When receivables growth exceeds sales growth, this could be an indication of aggressive revenue recognition policies. Statement readers who carefully examine receivables trends and levels can discern potential problems as they evolve.

Imputed Interest on Trade Notes Receivable

In certain industries the seller sometimes extends long-term credit to the buyer, who then signs a note. If the note bears an interest rate that approximates prevailing borrowing and lending rates, the accounting is straightforward. Assume that Michele Corporation manufactures and sells a machine to Texas Products Company. The cash selling price of the machine is $50,000. Michele accepts a three-year $50,000 note signed by Texas Products, with interest of 10% per annum to be paid in quarterly installments each year. Assume that 10% approximates prevailing borrowing rates for companies as creditworthy as Texas Products. Upon making the sale, Michele would record:

DR Note receivable—Texas Products Company	$50,000	
CR Sales revenues		$50,000

Interest income would accrue each quarter, and when the cash payment is received, the accrued interest receivable would be reduced. These are the entries:

DR Accrued interest receivable	$1,250	
CR Interest income		$1,250
(To accrue three months' interest = [$50,000 × .10] ÷ 4)		

DR Cash	$1,250	
CR Accrued interest receivable		$1,250
(To record receipt of the interest payment)		

A complication arises for a note that does not state an interest rate or when the stated rate is lower than prevailing rates for loans of similar risk. Suppose Monson Corporation sells equipment it manufactured to Davenport Products in exchange for a $50,000 note due in three years.

[7] See Dana Canedy, "Sunbeam Restates Results, and 'Fix' Shows Significant Warts," *New York Times* (October 21, 1998).

The note bears no explicit interest. It just says that the entire $50,000 is to be paid at the end of three years. Monson's published cash selling price for the equipment is $37,566, and the current borrowing rate for companies like Davenport is 10%.

The present value factor for a payment three years away at a 10% rate is .75132 (see Appendix 1 Table 1). Therefore, the present value of the note is $50,000 times .75132, or $37,566—which is exactly equal to the cash selling price of the equipment. Although the $50,000 note itself does not contain any mention of interest, Monson will earn a return of 10% per year for financing Davenport's long-term credit purchase. This is easily demonstrated in Exhibit 8.5.

EXHIBIT 8.5	Demonstration That Monson Earns 10% Interest for Three Years on Cash Sales Price of $37,566.00
Present value of $50,000 payment in 3 years (cash sales price)	$37,566.00
Plus: Year 1 interest: 10% × $37,566.00	3,756.60
Equals: Present value of $50,000 payment due in 2 years	41,322.60
Plus: Year 2 interest: 10% × $41,322.60	4,132.26
Equals: Present value of $50,000 payment due in 1 year	45,454.86
Plus: Year 3 interest: 10% × $45,454.86	4,545.14*
Equals: Payment by Davenport at the end of year 3	$50,000.00

*Rounded.

At the end of year 3, Monson receives a payment of $50,000, which consists of the cash sales price ($37,566) plus interest ($12,434 = $3,756.60 + $4,132.26 + $4,545.14).

Monson Corporation would record the sale to Davenport Products as:

DR Note receivable—Davenport	$37,566.00	
CR Sales revenue		$37,566.00

Over the next three years, the note receivable is increased and interest income recognized. For example, at the end of Year 1, the entry would be:[8]

DR Note receivable—Davenport	$3,756.60	
CR Interest income		$3,756.60

Notice that after Monson records interest income of $4,132.26 in Year 2 and $4,545.14 in Year 3, the carrying amount of the note receivable will be exactly $50,000, as shown in Exhibit 8.5. When Davenport makes the required payment at maturity of the note, Monson Corporation would record:

DR Cash	$50,000.00	
CR Note receivable—Davenport		$50,000.00

This process of allocating the $50,000 proceeds of the note between sales revenue and interest income is called **imputed interest**.

A complication also arises when the note receivable contains a stated interest rate *but the stated rate is lower than prevailing borrowing rates at the time of the transaction*. When this

---

[8] For simplicity, we ignore the periodic recording of interest on a monthly or quarterly basis during the year. In reality, if quarterly statements were prepared, the first year interest income of $3,756.60 would be apportioned to each quarter.

happens, interest must again be imputed. Assume that Quinones Corporation sells a machine to Linda Manufacturing in exchange for a $40,000, three-year, 2.5% note from Linda. At the time of the sale, the interest rate normally charged to companies with Linda's credit rating is 10%. Since the note's stated interest rate is far below Linda's normal borrowing rate, Quinones must determine the machine's implied sales price by computing the note's present value at the 10% rate. The computation of this implied sales price is shown in Exhibit 8.6.

EXHIBIT 8.6	Computation of Implied Sales Price in Conjunction with a Nominal Interest Bearing Note

Calculation of Present Value at 10% Effective Interest Rate

Present value of $40,000 principal repayment in three years at 10%:

$40,000	×	.75132	=	$30,052.80

Present value of three interest payments
of $1,000 (that is, $40,000 × .025), each at 10%:

Year 1:	$1,000	×	.90909	=	909.09
Year 2:	$1,000	×	.82645	=	826.45
Year 3:	$1,000	×	.75132	=	751.32
Implied sales price of machine					$32,539.66

(Note: All present value factors are from Appendix 1 Table 1, 10% column.)

This computation shows that the implied selling price of the machine is $32,539.66, because this amount equals the discounted present value of the note Quinones received in exchange for the machine. Quinones makes the following entry:

DR Note receivable—Linda Mfg.	$32,539.66	
CR Sales revenue		$32,539.66

Since payment was deferred, Quinones will earn 10% over the duration of the note on the amount of the credit sale ($32,539.66). The interest earned consists of three $1,000 payments over each of the ensuing years and another imputed interest payment of $7,460.34 ($40,000 minus the $32,539.66 implied cash selling price) at maturity. The composition of yearly interest income is shown in Exhibit 8.7, and Figure 8.2 shows the note receivable from the time of sale to maturity.

EXHIBIT 8.7	Quinones Corporation

Computation of Interest on Note Receivable

	(a) Interest Income— 10% of Column (d) Balance for Prior Year	(b) Cash Interest Received	(c) Increase in Present Value of Note (a) Minus (b)	(d) End of Year Present Value of Note
Inception	—	—	—	$32,539.66
Year 1	$ 3,253.97	$1,000.00	$2,253.97	34,793.63
Year 2	3,479.36	1,000.00	2,479.36	37,272.99
Year 3	3,727.01*	1,000.00	2,727.01	40,000.00
Total	$10,460.34			

*Rounded.

Figure 8.2

QUINONES CORPORATION
Carrying Value of Note
Receivable

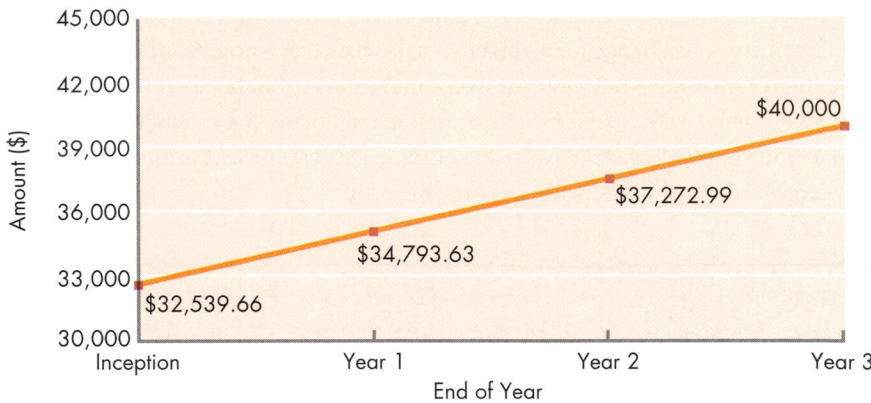

As shown in Exhibit 8.7 and Figure 8.2, the present value of the note, and thus its carrying value, increases each year (see column (d) of Exhibit 8.7). The increase in the carrying value of the note equals the difference between the annual 10% interest income earned—column (a)—and the cash received—column (b). For example, in Year 1 Quinones would record:

DR Note receivable—Linda Mfg.	$2,253.97	
DR Cash	1,000.00	
CR Interest income		$3,253.97

Similar entries would be made in Years 2 and 3 using the amounts shown in Exhibit 8.7. At the end of Year 3, the carrying amount of the note will be $40,000. When Linda pays the note on maturity, Quinones will record the payment as:

DR Cash	$40,000.00	
CR Note receivable—Linda Mfg.		$40,000.00

RECAP

For long-term credit sales transactions utilizing notes receivable:

- Sales revenue is recorded at the known cash price (Monson Corporation) or at the implied cash price (Quinones Corporation) of the item sold. The implied cash price is determined by computing the note receivable's present value using the prevailing borrowing rate (that is, the effective market rate of interest).
- Interest income is recorded each period over the note's term to maturity using the prevailing borrowing rate.

This approach achieves a clear separation between the two income sources—credit sales and interest earned. Income from the credit sale is recorded when the sale is made. Interest income from financing the customer's purchase, on the other hand, is recorded over time as it is earned. This separation of income sources makes it possible to assess the degree to which a company's overall earnings are due to profitable credit sales versus profitable customer financing—a potentially important distinction.

Accelerating Cash Collection: Sale of Receivables and Collateralized Borrowings

Companies collect cash from their credit customers according to the payment schedule called for in the note or trade receivable. Sometimes companies prefer not to wait until customer payments arrive in the normal course of business. Instead, they accelerate cash collection with the help of a bank or financing company.

There are two ways to accelerate cash collections, as depicted in Figure 8.3. One is **factoring**, where the company sells its receivables outright to the bank in exchange for cash. Customer payments flow directly to the bank in most cases. Factoring can be **without recourse** (also called **nonrecourse**), meaning that the bank cannot turn to the company for payment in the event that some customer receivables prove uncollectible. Factoring can also be **with recourse**, meaning that the company must buy back any bad receivables from the bank.

The other way to accelerate cash collection is a loan collateralized by receivables. The company gets cash from the bank and is responsible for repaying the loan.

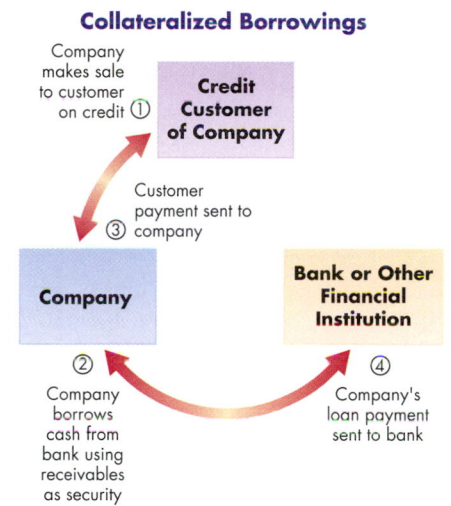

Figure 8.3

SALE OF RECEIVABLES AND COLLATERALIZED BORROWINGS

Reasons why companies might accelerate cash collections include:

1. *Competitive conditions require credit sales but the company is unwilling to bear the cost of processing and collecting receivables.* Restaurants are an example of this. Customers of upscale restaurants expect to be able to charge meals rather than pay cash. Yet, most restaurants are reluctant to incur the costs of servicing receivables. Consequently, restaurants rely on third parties like VISA, American Express, and Diners' Club, companies that, in effect, "buy" the customer receivable from the restaurant.

2. *There may be an imbalance between the credit terms of the company's suppliers and the time required to collect customer receivables.* Suppliers might extend credit on three-month terms to a company while inventory turnover plus receivables turnover total six months. To pay suppliers within the due date, cash collection must be accelerated.

3. *The company may have an immediate need for cash but be short of it.* Selling receivables to a financial institution allows the company to raise cash quickly. Using receivables as collateral for a bank loan also represents a way to obtain quick cash (and perhaps low-cost financing).

> Credit card companies "buy" the receivables at a discount—they pay the restaurant, say, 97 cents for every dollar of receivables. The three-cent "discount" is the fee charged for accelerating cash receipts.

Let's look at the accounting issues that arise when receivables are either sold or used in a collateralized borrowing.

Sale of Receivables (Factoring)

To illustrate a factoring transaction *without* recourse, suppose Hervey Corporation sells $80,000 of its customer receivables to Leslie Financing. The purchaser (Leslie Financing) is called the **factor**. Leslie charges a 5% fee (.05% × $80,000 = $4,000) for this service and pays Hervey $76,000. The entry to record the nonrecourse sale of the receivables on Hervey Corporation's books is:

DR Cash	$76,000	
DR Interest expense	4,000	
CR Accounts receivable		$80,000

Usually, the bank or financing company refuses to bear the costs of sales returns, discounts, or allowances. Consequently, a holdback to cover these items may be included in the transaction. For example, if the holdback is $3,000 and if all other facts regarding the nonrecourse sale are unchanged, the entry on Hervey's books is:

DR Cash	$73,000	
DR Interest expense	4,000	
DR Due from Leslie Financing	3,000	
CR Accounts receivable		$80,000

Any returns, discounts, or allowances reduce the amount paid to Hervey by Leslie. If these items totaled $1,800 on the sold receivables, Leslie would ultimately pay an additional $1,200 to Hervey and Hervey would make the following entry:

DR Cash	$1,200	
DR Sales returns, discounts, and allowances	1,800	
CR Due from Leslie Financing		$3,000

The $4,000 is charged to Interest expense because this amount represents the financing charge Hervey incurred to accelerate cash collection. In a sale without recourse, if some of Hervey's customers fail to pay the amount owed, Leslie Financing has no recourse against Hervey (hence the term)—and thus, Leslie bears the loss.

Next we illustrate the sale of accounts receivable *with* recourse. Again, assume Hervey Corporation sells $80,000 of trade receivables to Leslie Financing. If any of the receivables are not paid, Hervey bears the loss. Leslie's fee is reduced to 4% (.04 × $80,000 = $3,200) with a recourse transaction rather than 5% because the risk to Leslie is lower. Assume Leslie withholds $5,000 to cover possible noncollections. The entry on Hervey Corporation's books is:

DR Cash	$71,800	
DR Interest expense	3,200	
DR Due from Leslie Financing	5,000	
CR Accounts receivable		$80,000

The $5,000 holdback account "Due from Leslie Financing" represents a cushion to absorb credit losses that must ultimately be borne by Hervey in a sale with recourse.

Assume all but $3,750 of receivables are collected. Once collections are known, the financing company remits the final settlement amount. The entry on Hervey's books is:

DR Cash	$1,250	
DR Allowance for uncollectibles	3,750	
CR Due from Leslie Financing		$5,000

The $3,750 debit to Allowance for uncollectibles is appropriate if normal allowances had been accrued on the receivables that were sold. Allowance accounts are usually maintained when the sale is with recourse. If no allowance was maintained, then the debit of $3,750 would be made to an account entitled "Loss on sale of receivables" or some other similarly titled income statement loss account.

Borrowing Using Receivables as Collateral

If the transaction between Hervey Corporation and Leslie Financing had been a **collateralized loan** rather than a sale of receivables, then the accounts receivable would not be removed from Hervey's books. Instead, a liability account would be created to reflect the loan. Suppose that $80,000 of receivables were pledged as collateral for a loan; interest is 4% of $80,000. Then the entry is:

DR Cash	$76,800	
DR Prepaid interest	3,200	
CR Loan payable—Leslie Financing		$80,000

The fact that the receivables have been pledged as collateral for this loan must be disclosed in the notes to the financial statements, if material.[9] Once the loan is due, Hervey would make these entries:

[9] "Accounting for Contingencies," *Statement of Financial Accounting Standards (SFAS) No. 5* (Stamford, CT: Financial Accounting Standard Board [FASB], 1975), para. 12.

DR Loan payable—Leslie Financing	$80,000	
CR Cash		$80,000
DR Interest expense	$ 3,200	
CR Prepaid interest		$ 3,200

Notes receivable can also be assigned or sold. Accelerating cash collection on notes in this way is called **discounting**, because the financial institution advances cash to the company based on the *discounted* present value of the notes. For example, suppose Abbott Manufacturing received a $9,000 six-month, 8% per year interest-bearing note from Weaver Company, a customer. That same day, Abbott discounted the note at Second State Bank. If the bank discounts the note at 12%, Abbott would receive only $8,798.40. The cash proceeds to Abbott are computed as follows:

Face amount of the note	$9,000.00
Interest to maturity ($9,000 × .08 × 6/12)	360.00
Maturity amount of the note	9,360.00
Interest charge by bank:	
($9,360 × .12 × 6/12)	561.60
Cash proceeds	$8,798.40

Abbott would make the following entry when the note is discounted:

DR Cash	$8,798.40	
DR Interest expense	201.60	
CR Note receivable		$9,000

Accelerating cash collection generates interest expense of $201.60, the difference between the book value of the note and the cash proceeds.

At maturity, the bank will present the note to Weaver Company for payment. Notes can be discounted either with or without recourse. If discounted *with* recourse, then Second State Bank would collect $9,360 ($9,000 principal plus $360 interest) from Abbott if Weaver failed to pay the note at maturity. When notes are discounted with recourse and the note is removed from the books of the seller, a contingent liability must be disclosed in the footnotes.[10]

Ambiguities Abound: Is It a Sale or a Borrowing?

Usually, the nature of a transaction involving receivables is clear. But in some situations, it is not obvious whether the receivables have been sold or are instead being used as collateral for a loan. The ambiguity arises whenever certain obligations, duties, or rights regarding the transferred receivables are retained by the firm undertaking the transfer (which is called the **transferor**).

The FASB has provided guidelines in *SFAS No. 140* for distinguishing between sales and collateralized borrowings involving receivables.[11] The guidelines hinge on the issue of whether the transferor **surrenders control over the receivables**. If control is surrendered, then the transaction is treated as a sale, and any gain or loss is recognized in earnings. However, if the criteria for a sale

---

[10] Ibid., para. 12.
[11] "Accounting for Transfers and Servicing of Financial Assets and Extinguishments of Liabilities," *SFAS No. 140* (Norwalk, CT: FASB, 2000).

are not met because control has not been surrendered, then the transaction is accounted for as a collateralized borrowing.

> *SFAS No. 140* states that the transferor surrenders control over the receivables when *all* of the following conditions are met:
> 1. The transferred assets are beyond the reach of the transferor and its creditors.
> 2. The transferee has the right to dispose of the assets.
> 3. There is no agreement obligating the transferor to repurchase or redeem the transferred assets in the future nor can the transferor unilaterally force the holder to return the assets.
>
> (See para. 9 and para. 27–28.)

The issues addressed in *SFAS No. 140* have assumed great importance with the growth of **financial asset securitization**. *Securitization occurs when receivables (like mortgages or automobile loans) are bundled together and sold or transferred to another organization, which issues securities that are collateralized by the transferred receivables.* For example, the financing subsidiary of General Motors (General Motors Acceptance Corporation) bundles large numbers of automobile loans together. These loans are then used as collateral for interest-bearing notes that are sold to outside investors. The outside investors often earn a higher return than would otherwise be available to them since auto loans usually carry a relatively high rate of interest. By bundling large numbers of receivables, GM creates value because the risk of loss is reduced by the portfolio effect of the bundling itself.

Home mortgages, car loans, and credit card debt are just a few of the receivables that have been securitized and sold to investors. An estimated $2.5 trillion of securitized instruments were outstanding at the end of 1998.[12] As more of these transactions were undertaken, the FASB felt compelled to provide guidelines for when securitizations should be treated as sales and for when they must be treated as borrowings.

Ambiguities arise, for example, when a bank transfers a group of mortgages (which, to the bank, are receivables) to some other organization but retains the responsibility for servicing the mortgages. For example, the bank often continues to collect the mortgage payments or to handle customer inquiries, or it even promises to buy back the mortgages at some future date if certain conditions occur. How these transactions are treated has important financial reporting implications. For example:

Analysis

1. If the transaction is really a borrowing but is erroneously treated as a sale, then both assets and liabilities are understated (that is, the loan liability does not appear on the company's balance sheet and neither do the receivables that were transferred). Ratios like debt-to-equity and rate of return on assets are consequently distorted by the understatements.
2. If the transaction is really a sale, then a gain or loss on the transaction should be recognized. To erroneously treat such transactions as borrowings misrepresents the company's net assets.

A Closer Look at Securitizations

Securitizations are popular for two reasons.

- First, investors have a strong appetite for acquiring securitized assets.
- Second, firms with large amounts of receivables have powerful incentives to engage in securitizations.

It's a "win-win" situation for investors and firms; both parties benefit.

Investors benefit because they are able to obtain highly liquid financial instruments that diversify their risk. A simple example shows this. Suppose the prevailing rate of return on debt instruments with "moderate" risk is 6% per year. The 6% yield is determined by the credit standing of large corporate and government issuers of bonds and other instruments. By contrast, peo-

---

[12] Fitch IBCA, "Securitization and Its Impact on Bank Ratings," *Financial Services Special Report* (New York, March 9, 1999).

ple who take out home mortgages with banks do not have the same high credit-standing as these bond issuers. Understandably, the rates people pay on their mortgages are higher—let's say 7% per year.

Assume that a bank forms a bundled portfolio of these home mortgages and is prepared to sell them at a price that yields the investor a return of 6%. The risk associated with the individual mortgages ranges from "low" to "moderately high" *but the risk of the bundled portfolio in the aggregate is "moderate."* So the investors have a new investment option that also provides a 6% per year yield at the same "moderate" risk level but responds differently than other debt instruments to changes in interest rates and other economic events. This diversifies risk. That's attractive. Furthermore, the investors could not form a "moderate" risk, 6% return mortgage portfolio themselves since the costs of identifying potential mortgagees and doing a credit analysis are high and would lower their return below 6%. And even if they could construct their own portfolio, if investors later wanted to liquidate the investment, they'd have difficulty finding buyers for individual mortgages. So investors benefit from securitizations by gaining liquid portfolio diversification opportunities that they could not achieve on their own.

> If you don't understand this now, it's too early to panic. We'll explain why there's a gain in Chapter 11. You'll be able to follow the discussion in this section without a detailed understanding of the specifics underlying the gain.

But the bank also wins! If the bank sells the 7% mortgages at a price that yields the purchasers a return of 6%, this means that the selling price is higher than the carrying value of the mortgages on the bank's books. So the bank records a gain on the sale of the receivables. *This gain exists because the bank has created value.* As you just saw, the individual investors would never consider lending directly to, say, two or three home purchasers. (It's too risky. Who knows how many will default?) But the large portfolio is much less risky. So investors who are unable to duplicate the bank's return on their own without assuming high risks (and costs) are very willing to accept the 6% return.

Banks and other firms that engage in securitization transactions do not transact directly with the investors. The format of securitizations is somewhat convoluted, for reasons we'll soon explain. Figure 8.4 shows how a typical securitization is structured.

> It's even better for the investors! To make the securities more attractive, the bank will provide investors with a return that slightly exceeds 6%.

Figure 8.4

THE STRUCTURE OF A SECURITIZATION

Securitizations are carefully designed to enable the transferor to avoid consolidating the SPE. SPEs that meet these conditions are called **qualifying special purpose entities (QSPEs)**. To accomplish this, the SPE must meet four conditions stated in *SFAS No. 140*, para. 35:

1. *It is demonstrably distinct from the transferor.* This condition is met if the transferor cannot unilaterally dissolve the SPE and either of two other highly technical circumstances apply.
2. *Its activities are narrowly limited.* These are restricted to holding title to the transferred assets, issuing the collateralized debt securities, collecting cash flows from the transferred assets, and making interest and principal payments to holders of the debt securities.
3. *It holds only rigidly defined types of assets.* The assets must not require decision-making by the SPE.
4. *Its ability to dispose of assets is limited to narrowly defined circumstances.* This means that the SPE must be an unthinking robot that cannot exercise discretion.

Furthermore, as we go to press, the FASB has proposed further tightening the rules for what constitutes a QSPE. Among other things, these additional proposals would deny QSPE treatment when the transfer of financial assets is accompanied by guarantees to the SPE by the transferor.

Why does the FASB allow favorable off-balance sheet treatment for these contorted transactions? One reason is because they are economically beneficial. That is, the transferor creates value through the portfolio effect of bundling the assets, and the investors diversify their risk and earn slightly higher returns.

Under International Financial Reporting Standards (IFRS), SPEs must be consolidated when the enterprise that created the SPE (that is, the transferor in our example) controls the SPE. Control exists, for example, when the SPE's activities are expressly designed to satisfy the business needs of the enterprise that created it. Consequently, securitizations under IFRS do not result in "off-balance sheet" assets and liabilities since the SPE is consolidated. See "Consolidation—Special Purpose Entities," *SIC-12* (London: International Accounting Standards Board (IASB), Standing Interpretations Committee, 1998).

International

The firm doing the securitization (the transferor) forms what is called a **special purpose entity** or **SPE**. The SPE is usually a trust or corporation that is legally distinct from the transferor and is created solely for the purpose of undertaking the securitization transaction. The transferor then sells (transfers) the receivables (mortgages in our example) to the SPE (Step 1 in Figure 8.4). The SPE creates and issues debt securities (with the mortgages as collateral) that are sold to outside investors (Steps 2 and 3). The cash received from the investors by the SPE is then remitted to the transferor (Step 4). In many situations the transferor continues to service the assets (that is, handle cash collections, recordkeeping, etc.) usually for a fee that is paid by the SPE.

The cash flows from the mortgages themselves (that is, principal repayment and interest) are later used to make the periodic interest and principal repayments to the investors who bought the debt securities.

The SPE is created for two reasons. One reason is to protect the investors who bought the debt securities. Because the receivables were sold to the SPE, they are beyond the reach of the transferor and its creditors. *So even if the transferor were to declare bankruptcy, the collateral underlying the notes is safe from seizure.* The other reason for creating the SPE is because its existence allows the transferor to receive favorable financial reporting treatment for the transaction. Here's why. If there were no SPE, the transferor would issue the notes directly to investors. This would constitute a collateralized borrowing; the receivables would appear on the transferor's books and so would the notes (as a liability). But by creating the legally distinct entity, the receivables are removed from the transferor's books. Furthermore, the notes are the SPE's debt, not the transferor's. Since the SPE is not consolidated, the debt securities never appear on the transferor's balance sheet. *So both the receivables and the debt are "off balance sheet."*

To illustrate these financial statement effects of the "off-balance sheet" treatment of securitizations, consider the following example.

Doyle National Bank has the following account balances at December 31, 2005:

Assets:	
Mortgages receivable	$1,200,000
All other assets	1,800,000
Total assets	$3,000,000
Liabilities and equity:	
Liabilities	$2,700,000
Equity	300,000
Total liabilities and equity	$3,000,000
After-tax income for the year ended December 31, 2005	$ 40,000

On December 30, 2005, Doyle securitized $1,000,000 of mortgages using a QSPE it established. The cash received from the QSPE was exactly $1,000,000, so no gain or loss was recognized on the transaction. The receivables were removed from the books since this transaction conformed to the *SFAS Nos. 140* rules for securitizations.

The journal entry Doyle made to remove the receivables on December 30, 2005 was:

DR Cash $1,000,000
    CR Mortgages receivable $1,000,000

Now let's see what the financial statement effect would have been if the $1,000,000 transaction had instead been treated as a borrowing with the mortgages used as collateral. With this changed assumption, the entry *would have been*:

DR Cash $1,000,000
    CR Loan payable $1,000,000

Under this alternative scenario, the account balances at December 31, 2005 (assuming no *other* transactions) would have been:

	Amounts Under Securitization Scenario	Change in Balance If $1,000,00 Transaction Is Accounted for as a Borrowing	Amounts Under Borrowing Scenario
Assets:			
Mortgages receivable	$1,200,000	+$1,000,000	$2,200,000
All other assets	1,800,000	—	1,800,000
Total assets	$3,000,000		$4,000,000
Liabilities and equity:			
Liabilities	$2,700,000	+$1,000,000	$3,700,000
Equity	300,000	—	300,000
Total liabilities and equity	$3,000,000		$4,000,000
After tax income for the year ended December 31, 2005	$ 40,000	—	$ 40,000

The return-on-assets ratio and debt-to-equity ratio for Doyle National Bank after completing this $1,000,000 transaction are computed below as of December 31, 2005. The left column shows the ratio values that are reflected after the securitized receivables are removed from the balance sheet. The right column shows the ratio balances *that would have been reflected* if the transaction had been treated as a borrowing with the mortgages serving as collateral. (Remember, under a borrowing, the receivables remain on Doyle's books and a liability for the borrowing is recorded.)

	Ratios Under Securitization Scenario	**Ratios Under Borrowing Scenario**
Return-on-assets ratio	$\dfrac{\$40,000}{\$3,000,000} = .013$	$\dfrac{\$40,000}{\$4,000,000} = .01$
Debt-to-equity ratio	$\dfrac{\$2,700,000}{\$300,000} = 9$	$\dfrac{\$3,700,000}{\$300,000} = 12.33$

So you see that treating the transaction as a securitization (which removes the mortgage assets from the balance sheet and does not put a loan payable on the balance sheet) improves the return-on-assets ratio from 1% to 1.3%—a 30% increase. Similarly, the securitization treatment improves (reduces) the debt-to-equity ratio from 12.33 to 9—a 27% reduction.

Some Cautions for Statement Readers

Factoring, assignment, and securitization of receivables raise some issues for those who analyze financial statements. The main issue is the level of disclosure in statement footnotes when receivables have been transferred during the reporting period. When the transfer is with recourse (the "selling" company is still responsible for uncollected receivables), *SFAS No. 5* requires footnote disclosure of the contingent liability.[13] **But there is no similar unequivocal disclosure requirement when receivables are sold without recourse.** Some observers contend that receivables sold without recourse are a financing transaction that must be separately disclosed in the cash flow statement.[14] But even if this interpretation is correct, GAAP only requires that disclosures be made when they are **material**. The FASB has defined materiality as:

> A decision not to disclose certain information may be made, say, . . . because the amounts involved are too small to make a difference (they are not material). . . . The Board's present position is that no general standards of materiality can be formulated to take into account all the considerations that enter into an experienced human judgment.[15]

Materiality is defined loosely as information that, if disclosed, would change the decision-maker's conclusion. But since the guidelines are unclear, some companies might purposely not disclose sales of receivables and, if asked about the omission, declare the information "immaterial."

The Securities and Exchange Commission has issued a Staff Accounting Bulletin (SAB) on materiality to establish clearer guidelines.* (SABs inform registrants about the criteria the SEC staff will use in resolving reporting issues.) *SAB No. 99* rejects arbitrary, across-the-board percentages like 5% as the materiality threshold. Instead, through a series of examples, the SEC reaffirms that materiality is contextual. So consider a firm where the consensus analysts' quarterly EPS forecasts are $1.00 per share. The firm knows that actual earnings will fall short at 99¢ per share. If the firm evades GAAP rules to raise earnings by one cent per share, *in that specific context*, the inappropriate earnings boost is material because it is designed to change investors' perceptions of whether the firm is performing up to expectations.

*SEC Staff Accounting Bulletin: No. 99—Materiality (August 12, 1999).

Here's what this means for statement readers. Earlier in this chapter you saw that one way to assess whether reported receivables arose from legitimate sales was to compare the growth rate of sales and the growth rate of receivables. This comparison in Exhibit 8.3 for Bausch & Lomb showed that receivables growth far outstripped sales growth between 1991 and 1993. Our conclusion—based on disclosures from the 1994 Bausch & Lomb annual report—was that the leap in receivables growth arose from "forcing" inventory on distributors and treating these shipments as sales. The way to recognize these potential trouble areas is to monitor receivables growth. **But when firms sell receivables, the receivables number reported in the ending balance sheet only includes the remaining receivables and will thus understate the true growth in receivables over the period.**

This is precisely what *Business Week* says happened at Bausch & Lomb, whose "internal financial documents," they claim, show year-end 1993 receivables to be $506 million rather than the $385 million reported on the company's balance sheet (see again Exhibit 8.3). According to *Business Week*, Bausch & Lomb felt the factored receivables didn't need to be disclosed under GAAP.[16]

If the *Business Week* assertion is correct and Bausch & Lomb didn't disclose the removal of $121 million of receivables from the balance sheet (that is, $506 − $385) through factoring, assignment or securitization, then the reported 1993 receivables growth rate is understated. Specifically:

---

[13] *SFAS No. 5*, para. 12.

[14] This position is based on an interpretation of "Statement of Cash Flows," *SFAS No. 95* (Stamford, CT: FASB, 1987), para. 16.

[15] "Qualitative Characteristics of Accounting Information," *Statement of Financial Accounting Concepts No. 2* (Stamford, CT: FASB, 1980), para. 125 and 131.

[16] M. Maremont, op. cit., p. 90.

	1992	1993
Receivables growth computed in Exhibit 8.3 using Bausch & Lomb balance sheet data	$277,338	$384,973
		+38.81%
Receivables growth computed by adding $121 million to reported 1993 receivables based on the *Business Week* assertion	$277,338	$506,000
		+82.45%

So the receivables growth rate computed from the financial statements was "only" 38.81% rather than 82.45%—the figure *Business Week* claims would have resulted if Bausch & Lomb had disclosed the receivables transaction.

Irrespective of whose interpretation of disclosure requirements is correct here, the opportunity to transfer receivables provides a way for companies to disguise the *real* extent of receivables growth. Suppose a company is "aggressively" booking sales to artificially raise current earnings. To avoid discovery, the company could factor or securitize some of its "good" receivables—those that don't arise from the questionable sales—and thus understate the true disparity in the growth rates of receivables and sales. So the receivables remaining on the books are the "bad" ones and the factoring has disguised the deterioration in the *quality* of reported receivables. Consequently, statement readers must scrutinize footnotes and the financing activities section of the cash flow statement for evidence of dispositions of receivables that may be masking overly aggressive revenue recognition policies or bad receivables management.

> The Sunbeam sale of trade accounts receivable on page 392 was a securitization. Sunbeam fully disclosed the transaction. But if the securitization had not taken place, the year-to-year growth in Sunbeam's receivables would have approximated 60%, not the 36.42% reported on the comparative financial statements themselves.

The transferred receivables "disappear" from the balance sheet. Because receivables are lower, certain ratios like return on assets and receivables turnover improve when compared to previous periods. But is the ratio improvement sustainable? Should the analyst "undo" the transfer and recompute the ratios with the receivables included? At a minimum, the analyst must be aware of the extent of the disruption in the year-to-year ratio pattern and its impact on financial forecasts. Other adjustments depend on the circumstances. Also, did the transferor "cherry-pick" the best receivables in order to make the transaction attractive to the purchasers? If it did, the analyst must scrutinize the quality of the remaining receivables as well as the adequacy of the allowance for uncollectibles.

Troubled Debt Restructuring

What happens to a lender when a customer is financially unable to make the interest and principal payments required by an installment loan or other receivable? Rather than force the customer into bankruptcy, lenders frequently agree to **restructure** the loan receivable, thus allowing the customer to remain in business. The restructured loan can differ from the original loan in several ways:

- Scheduled interest and principal payments may be reduced or eliminated.
- The repayment schedule may be extended over a longer time period.
- The customer and lender can settle the loan for cash, other assets, or equity interests.

Lenders are willing to restructure a customer's loan to help the customer resolve present financial difficulties and stay in business. And lenders often receive more through restructuring than through foreclosure or bankruptcy.

To help you understand this financial instrument, we'll define each of the three words, in reverse order. **Debentures** are bonds that have no underlying collateral that could be seized if Hudson Hotels defaulted on the debt. It is an unsecured borrowing. **Subordinated** means that Hudson has other debt issues that "ranked-ahead" of this debt in the event of liquidation—that is, investors in the other debt would be paid before investors in the Convertible Subordinated Debenture. **Convertible** bonds allow the investor—at the investor's option—to convert the bond into equity shares of Hudson. A conversion price of $4.50 on December 31, 1998 means that each $1,000 bond could be converted into 222.222 shares ($1,000 ÷ $4.50 = 222.222). This is an attractive feature for bond investors because it provides a potentially valuable "up-side" option if the issuer prospers.

Consider the debt restructuring described in Exhibit 8.8. On December 31, 1999, Hudson Hotels Corporation owned and/or managed 47 hotel properties located primarily in the northeastern and southeastern United States. These investments were financed using long-term debt—a Convertible Subordinated Debenture. During 1999, the company suffered operating losses and cash flow difficulties. The Convertible Subordinated Debenture originally carried an interest rate of 7.5% per year and a maturity date of July 1, 2001. The conversion price on December 31, 1998 was $4.50 per common share. Because the Company could not make the required loan payments, the lender (a mutual fund) canceled $4.5 million of the debt in exchange for the following:

- An acceleration of the maturity date by 8 1/2 months.
- An increase in the annual interest rate from 7.5% to 18.75%.
- A decrease in the conversion price of $2.70 per share (that is, $4.50 − $1.80).

EXHIBIT 8.8	Hudson Hotels Corporation

Debt Restructuring

In July 1999, the Company replaced its outstanding $7.5 million Convertible Subordinated Debenture to Oppenheimer Convertible Securities Fund with a new Convertible Subordinated Debenture bearing the following terms: principal balance of $3.0 million; interest rate of 18.75%; maturity date of April 15, 2000; and a conversion price of $1.80 per share. As a result, the Company reported an extraordinary gain from the debt restructuring, net of expenses, of approximately $4 million or $0.64 per common share—basic.

Source: Hudson Hotels Corporation 1999 10-K Report.

Obviously, the lender would have preferred that Hudson Hotels pay the original debt principal and interest on time. Faced with the company's inability to do so, it chose to restructure the debt rather than force the company into bankruptcy. The enormous leap in the interest rate from 7.5% to 18.75% reflects the precarious financial condition of Hudson Hotels Corporation and the resulting riskiness of the restructured loan.

This example illustrates a key feature of **troubled debt restructurings** not present in ordinary debt refinancings. *SFAS No. 15* gives this definition:

> A restructuring of debt constitutes a troubled debt restructuring . . . if the creditor for economic or legal reasons related to the debtor's financial difficulties grants a **concession** to the debtor that it would not otherwise consider.[17] [Emphasis added.]

In other words, for the restructuring to be "troubled," the borrower (Hudson Hotels Corporation) must be unable to pay off the original debt and the lender (the mutual fund) must grant a concession to the borrower. What the FASB means by "concession" is quite specific: In exchange for canceling the original debt, the lender must accept *new debt or assets with an economic value less than the book value of the original debt plus any accrued interest.*

---

[17] "Accounting by Debtors and Creditors for Troubled Debt Restructurings," *SFAS No. 15* (Stamford, CT: FASB, 1977), para. 2.

Our Hudson Hotels example meets these guidelines. The company was unable to make its interest and principal payments. The lender then agreed to restructure the debt, and in so doing, it granted the company a substantial economic concession—the $4.5 million of debt cancellation.

Troubled debt restructurings can be accomplished in two different ways:

- **Settlement**, where the original loan is canceled by a transfer of cash, other assets, or equity interests (borrower's stock) to the lender.
- **Continuation with modification** of debt terms, where the original loan is canceled and a new loan agreement is signed.

Some troubled debt restructurings contain elements of both settlement and modification.

The accounting issues related to troubled debt restructuring encompass both the measurement of the new (modified) loan and a report of any gain or loss. The following examples illustrate these issues.[18]

> Assume that Harper Companies purchased $75,000 of corn milling equipment from Farmers State Cooperative on January 1, 2002. Harper paid $25,000 cash and signed a five-year 10% installment note for the remaining $50,000 of the purchase price. The note calls for annual payments of $10,000 plus interest on December 31 of each year. Harper made the first two installment payments on time but was unable to make the third annual payment on December 31, 2004. After much negotiation, Farmers State agreed to restructure the note receivable. At that time, Harper owed $30,000 in unpaid principal plus $3,000 in accrued interest. We will assume that the restructuring was agreed to on January 1, 2005 and that both companies have already recorded interest up to that date.

Settlement

Suppose Farmers State agrees to cancel the loan if Harper pays $5,000 cash and turns over the company car. The car was purchased 18 months ago for $21,000 cash, has a current fair market value of $18,000, and is carried on Harper's books at $16,000 ($21,000 original cost minus $5,000 accumulated depreciation). Notice that the combined economic value of the cash ($5,000) and automobile ($18,000) is $23,000—or $10,000 less than the $33,000 Harper owes Farmers State.

The January 1, 2005 entries made to record settlement of the troubled debt are:

Harper Companies (Borrower)

(a) To increase the net carrying amount of the automobile ($16,000) to its fair market value ($18,000):

DR Automobile	$ 2,000	
CR Gain on disposal of asset		$ 2,000

(b) To record the settlement:

DR Note payable	$30,000	
DR Interest payable	3,000	
DR Accumulated depreciation	5,000	
CR Cash		$ 5,000
CR Automobile		23,000
CR Gain on debt restructuring		10,000

[18] Troubled debt restructurings often involve complexities that are beyond the scope of our discussion here. See *SFAS No. 15*, ibid.; "Accounting by Creditors for Impairment of a Loan," *SFAS No. 114* (Norwalk, CT: FASB, 1993); and "Accounting by Creditors for Impairment of a Loan—Income Recognition and Disclosures," *SFAS No. 118* (Norwalk, CT: FASB, 1994).

Farmers State Cooperative's settlement loss would not be extraordinary but would instead be included in the computation of income from continuing operations. Because it's a lender, restructurings are a normal part of its business and are likely to recur. So these transactions meet *neither* of the two criteria for extraordinary items—unusual nature and infrequency of occurrence—discussed in Chapter 2. Harper Companies' gain would be treated as extraordinary only if it met both of these criteria for extraordinary items.

Farmers State Cooperative (Lender)

(a) To record the settlement:

DR Cash	$ 5,000	
DR Automobile	18,000	
DR Loss on receivable restructuring	10,000	
CR Note receivable		$30,000
CR Interest receivable		3,000

What do these entries accomplish? The settlement creates two earnings gains for Harper:

- a gain on asset disposal of $2,000—the difference between the car's fair market value ($18,000) and its book value ($16,000); and
- a debt restructuring gain of $10,000—the difference between the note's book value plus accrued interest ($30,000 plus $3,000) and the fair market value of assets transferred ($5,000 cash plus $18,000 automobile).

Farmers State has a debt restructuring loss for the same $10,000 figure. Both companies record all interest up to the restructuring date and then cancel the note and related interest receivable and payable.

Continuation with Modification of Debt Terms

Instead of reaching a negotiated settlement of the note receivable, Harper and Farmers State could have resolved the troubled debt by modifying the terms of the original loan. The possibilities are endless. For accounting purposes, what matters is whether the **undiscounted sum of future cash flows under the restructured note is above or below the note's carrying value (including accrued interest) at the restructuring date.**

To see this, notice that the restructured note calls for Harper to make a single payment of $39,000 on December 31, 2006—two years from the January 1, 2005 restructuring date. We need to find a discount rate that equates the present value of this $39,000 payment with the $33,000 carrying value of the note receivable. This means finding the rate r that solves the following equation:

$$\underbrace{\text{Carrying value}} = \underbrace{\text{Present value of future cash flows}}$$

$$\$33,000 = \frac{\$39,000}{(1+r)^2}$$

The value of r that satisfies this equation is .087. To verify this, go to our website—www.prenhall.com/revsine—and use the present value calculator to see that the present value factor for a single payment due in two periods at 8.7% is 0.84615, and $39,000 multiplied by this factor equals $33,000 (rounded).

Sum of restructured flows exceeds carrying value of payable Suppose Farmers State agrees to postpone all principal and interest payments on the note receivable to maturity. Harper's final (and only) payment on December 31, 2006 would total $39,000 (the $30,000 principal plus $9,000 representing three years interest at 10%). Harper and Farmers State have already recorded $3,000 in accrued interest as of January 1, 2005. So the book value of the note plus accrued interest is $33,000 at the restructuring date.

Because the sum of future cash flows on the restructured note ($39,000) is *greater* than the carrying value of the original payable ($33,000), Harper will not show a restructuring gain. Instead, Harper will compute a new (and lower) effective interest rate for the restructured note and accrue interest at that new rate until the loan is fully paid. The new effective interest rate is the rate that equates the present value of the restructured cash flows to the carrying value of the debt at the date of restructure.[19] The new effective interest rate for Harper Companies is 8.7% per year.

Farmers State will continue using the 10% interest rate on the original note.[20] To do so, it must value the restructured note payments using a 10% effective interest rate. Farmers State will then show

---

[19] *SFAS No. 15*, para. 16.
[20] *SFAS No. 114*, para. 14.

a loss for the difference between the present value of the restructured note, which is $32,232, and the carrying value of the original note ($33,000). The entries made by both companies are:

> The present value factor for a single payment due in two years at 10% is .82645. The value of the note is $39,000 × .82645, or $32,232 (rounded).

Harper Companies (Borrower)

(a) To record the modified note (when sum of restructured cash flows is greater than note carrying value):

DR Note payable	$30,000	
DR Interest payable	3,000	
CR Restructured note payable		$33,000

Farmers State Cooperative (Lender)

(a) To record the modified note (when sum of restructured cash flows is greater than note carrying value):

DR Restructured note receivable	$32,232	
DR Loss on receivable restructuring	768	
CR Note receivable		$30,000
CR Interest receivable		3,000

Both companies accrue interest beginning on the debt restructuring date (January 1, 2005) and ending on the maturity date of the restructured note (December 31, 2006). But they will *not* use the same interest rate, as you just saw. The borrower, Harper, will record annual interest at 8.7% of the note's carrying value at the beginning of each year, whereas Farmers State will use a 10% annual rate. The entries for the next two years are:

Harper Companies (Borrower)

(a) To record interest on December 31, 2005:

DR Interest expense	$2,871	
CR Restructured note payable		$2,871

($2,871 = $33,000 × .087)

(b) To record interest on December 31, 2006:

DR Interest expense	$3,121	
CR Restructured note payable		$3,121

($3,121 = [$33,000 + $2,871] × .087)

Farmers State Cooperative (Lender)

(a) To record interest on December 31, 2005:

DR Restructured note receivable	$3,223	
CR Interest income		$3,223

($3,223 = $32,232 × .10)

(b) To record interest on December 31, 2006:

DR Restructured note receivable	$3,546	
CR Interest income		$3,546

($3,546 = [$32,232 + $3,223] × .10)

Over time, Harper Companies' note payable and Farmers State Cooperative's note receivable grow to the final balance of $39,000, the required payment at maturity, as shown in Exhibit 8.9. The entry to record the payment is:

Harper Companies (Borrower)

To record payment of balance on December 31, 2006:

DR Restructured note payable	$39,000	
CR Cash		$39,000

Farmers State Cooperative (Lender)

To record receipt of balance on December 31, 2006:

DR Cash	$39,000	
CR Restructured note receivable		$39,000

EXHIBIT 8.9	Growth of Note Carrying Amount	
	Harper Companies	Farmers State Cooperative
Restructured note, initial carrying amount	$33,000	$32,232
Accrued interest expense, Harper		
2005	2,871	
2006	3,121	
Accrued interest revenue, Farmers State		
2005		3,223
2006		3,546
Note carrying amount, December 31, 2006	$39,000*	$39,000*

*Rounded.

This example illustrates a restructured loan in which the total restructured cash flows are *greater* than the carrying value of the troubled debt. Next let's examine a situation in which the sum of the future cash flows is *less* than the carrying value of the troubled debt.

Sum of restructured flows is less than carrying value of payable Suppose Farmers State waives all interest payments (that is, the $3,000 unpaid accrued interest for 2004 as well as the 2005 and 2006 interest) and defers all principal payments until December 31, 2006. The restructured cash payments (now only $30,000) are *less* than the carrying value of the original receivable ($33,000). Harper will show a gain on the debt restructuring, and the subsequent payment will be treated as a reduction of the restructured principal. No interest expense is recorded by Harper. But Farmers State follows the procedures outlined in the previous example. The restructured note is valued at $24,794 (using the 10% effective interest rate from the original note), a debt restructuring loss is recorded, and interest income is accrued to maturity. The entries made at the restructuring date are:

> The $24,794 is just the present value of $30,000 received in two years at 10%, or $24,794 = $30,000 × 0.82645.

International

> International Accounting Standards for debt restructurings from the lender's perspective are virtually identical to U.S. GAAP. (See "Financial Instruments: Recognition and Measurement," *International Accounting Standard (IAS) 39* [London, 1998], para. 113.) There are no explicit international standards governing troubled debt restructuring from the borrower's perspective.

Harper Companies (Borrower)
To record the modified note (when sum of restructured cash flows is less than note carrying value):

DR	Note payable	$30,000	
DR	Interest payable	3,000	
CR	Restructured note payable		$30,000
CR	Gain on debt restructuring		3,000

Farmers State Cooperative (Lender)
To record the modified note (when sum of restructured cash flows is less than note carrying value):

DR	Restructured note receivable	$24,794	
DR	Loss on receivable restructuring	8,206	
CR	Note receivable		$30,000
CR	Interest receivable		3,000

Harper would not record any interest over the life of the restructured note. The $30,000 cash payment on December 31, 2006 would reduce the outstanding balance of Harper's restructured note payable. Farmers State still records interest income over the life of the note. These entries would be:

Harper Companies (Borrower)

(No entries are made until the cash payment at maturity.)

DR Restructured note receivable	$30,000	
CR Cash		$30,000

Farmers State Cooperative (Lender)

(a) To record interest on December 31, 2005:

DR Restructured note receivable	$ 2,479	
CR Interest income		$ 2,479

($2,479 = $24,794 \times .10$)

(b) To record interest on December 31, 2006:

DR Restructured note receivable	$ 2,727	
CR Interest income		$ 2,727

($2,727 = [$24,794 + $2,479] \times .10$)

The note receivable balance at Farmers State has now grown to $30,000 (that is, $24,794 + $2,479 + $2,727).

(c) To record payment of receivable balance on December 31, 2006:

DR Cash	$30,000	
CR Restructured note receivable		$30,000

Evaluating Troubled Debt Restructuring Rules

The GAAP rules for troubled debt restructurings are subject to several criticisms.

First, there is an obvious (and uncomfortable) lack of symmetry in the financial reporting of the borrower and lender. Different measurement rules are used to value the borrower's restructured note payable and the lender's restructured receivable when there is continuation with modification of debt terms. Consequently, the initial book value GAAP assigns to the payable is not the same as the initial book value assigned to the receivable. This also results in a difference between the borrower's restructuring gain and the lender's restructuring loss.

Second, the GAAP restructuring gains and losses do not always correspond to real economic gains and losses for the companies involved. For one thing, GAAP often assigns the gain or loss to the wrong time period. Take the case of Farmers State Cooperative. Although the accounting loss was shown in 2005, most of the economic loss occurred earlier when Harper became unable to make the loan payments.

Third, it's possible to question GAAP's use of the original loan's effective interest rate to value the restructured receivable and the lender's restructuring loss. Turning again to Farmers State, the original 10% loan to Harper used an interest rate that reflected the borrower's credit risk at the time. Over the ensuing three years, Harper's credit risk undoubtedly increased to the point where lenders would charge a higher rate of interest (say 15%) on new loans to the company. After all, Harper failed to meet its financial obligations in 2004. A higher effective interest rate on the restructured receivable will produce a lower initial book value and a larger restructuring loss for the lender. The GAAP approach is a practical solution because it avoids the sometimes difficult task of estimating the borrower's real effective interest rate at the restructuring date. However, this approach also fails to fully reflect the economic realities of troubled debt restructurings.

Exhibit 8.10 summarizes, in general terms, the accounting illustrated in each of the Harper–Farmers State troubled debt restructurings.

RECAP

EXHIBIT 8.10	Summary of Accounting Procedures for Troubled Debt Restructurings		

		Restructured Loan Cash Flows Are:	
	Settlement Gain or Loss	Lower Than Current Carrying Value of Loan*	Higher Than Current Carrying Value of Loan*
Borrower			
New loan payable	—	Total of restructured cash flows	Current book value
Gain on debt restructuring	Ordinary#	Ordinary#	None
Gain (loss) on transfer of assets	Ordinary	—	—
Future interest expense	—	None, all payments applied to principal	Based on rate that equates current carrying value and restructured cash flows
Lender			
New loan receivable	—	Present value of new cash flows at original effective interest rate	Present value of new cash flows at original effective interest rate
Loss on debt restructuring	Ordinary	Ordinary	Ordinary
Future interest income	—	Based on original loan rate	Based on original loan rate

*Includes unpaid accrued interest.
#Unless it meets both criteria for extraordinary items.

SUMMARY

- GAAP requires that accounts receivable be shown at their net realizable value. This means gross accounts receivable must be reduced by the amount of estimated uncollectibles and returns/allowances.
- Companies use one of two methods to estimate uncollectible accounts: (1) the sales revenue approach, or (2) the gross accounts receivable approach. Under either approach, firms must periodically assess the reasonableness of the uncollectibles balance by performing an aging of accounts receivable.
- Analysts should scrutinize the allowance for uncollectibles balance over time. Increases in the allowance as a percent of accounts receivable may indicate collection problems or other customer difficulties. Decreases in the allowance percentage might be a sign of earnings management.
- Receivables growth can exceed sales growth for several reasons, including a change in customer mix or credit terms. But a disparity in the growth rate of receivables and sales could also indicate that aggressive revenue recognition practices are being used. For this reason, careful analysis of period-to-period trends is necessary to determine whether the reported receivables arise from real sales.
- In certain long-term credit sales transactions, interest must be imputed by determining the note receivable's present value. This is necessary to distinguish between income from the sale and interest income, which might be recognized in different periods.
- Firms sometimes transfer or dispose of receivables before their due date in order to accelerate cash collection.
- Sales of receivables—also called factoring—can be with or without recourse.
- Receivables are also occasionally used as collateral for a loan.
- In analyzing these receivables transactions, it is sometimes not obvious whether the transaction to accelerate cash collection represents a sale or a borrowing; however, the FASB has provided guidelines in *SFAS No. 140* for distinguishing between sales (where the transferor surrenders control over the receivables) and borrowings (where control is not surrendered).

- Receivables that are transferred get removed from the balance sheet.
- Analysts should examine receivables transfer transactions to determine whether it is a sale or a borrowing. Any divergence between the accounting treatment and the economics of the transaction misstates assets and liabilities. Furthermore, sales of receivables change ratios like receivables turnover as well as potentially masking the underlying real growth in receivables. Keep these factors in mind when using these ratios in valuations or other forecasts.
- Banks and other holders of receivables will frequently restructure the terms of the receivable when a customer is unable to make required payments.
- These troubled debt restructurings can take one of two forms: (1) settlement, or (2) continuation with modification of debt terms.
- When terms are modified, the precise accounting treatment depends on whether the sum of future cash flows under the restructured note is above or below the note's carrying value at the restructuring date.
- Remember that the interest rate used in troubled debt restructurings may not reflect the real economic loss suffered by the lender.

SELF-STUDY PROBLEM

ROOMKIN & JURIS DEPARTMENT STORES SECURITIZATION

Roomkin & Juris is a department store chain in the western United States. In September 2005 it created a legally separate trust (R & J Trust) to serve as the special purpose entity for securitizing $1,000,000 of customer receivables. Customers are charged an interest rate of 12% per year on unpaid receivable balances. The receivables were sold to the trust, which in turn issued $1,000,000 of two-year 9% per annum notes collateralized by the receivables. Interest on the notes is paid quarterly. Roomkin & Juris services the accounts and remits a portion of the cash collected to the trust. The R & J Trust uses this cash to make all required payments to the investors. Because the receivables are constantly turning over, this is what is called a **revolving securitization**. The amount of collateral must be maintained at the original amount (here $1,000,000) less any credit losses (which, we assume, are borne by the investors). Three transactions in 2005 were related to the securitization:

- *September 30:* Roomkin & Juris sells receivables with a book value of $980,000 (that is, gross receivables of $1,000,000 and an allowance for uncollectibles of $20,000) to the trust for $995,000.
- *October 1–December 29:* Roomkin & Juris collects $692,500 from customers on the receivables sold to the trust. This amount represents payment of both the principal portion of the receivables and interest.
- *December 30:* Roomkin & Juris transfers $692,500 of new receivables and cash to the trust to replenish the collateral base and to allow the trust to make required interest payments.

1. **Record the sale of the receivables on Roomkin & Juris' books.**

   The journal entry is:

DR Cash	$995,000	
DR Allowance for uncollectibles	20,000	
CR Accounts receivable		$1,000,000
CR Gain on sale of receivables		15,000

   Because the investors bear all credit losses, the allowance that relates to the sold receivables is removed from the books. The journal entry presumes that Roomkin & Juris do not charge a fee for servicing the accounts. The $15,000 gain is the value created by securitization—it's what investors are willing to pay over and above the book value of the receivables.

2. **Record Roomkin & Juris' cash collections on the sold receivables.**

   The journal entry is:

DR Cash	$692,500	
CR Due to R & J Trust		$692,500

The collateral must be maintained at $1,000,000 less any credit losses. (Remember, investors bear all credit losses in this securitization.) So Roomkin & Juris must replace the receivables principal that has been repaid by the customers, plus $22,500 cash to cover the fourth quarter 2005 interest payment on the notes ($1,000,000 × .09 × 1/4 = $22,500). This total is $692,500.

3. **Record the asset transfer to the R & J Trust.**

The journal entry is:

DR Due to R & J Trust	$692,500	
CR Accounts receivable		$670,000
CR Cash		22,500

Since some of the original accounts receivable have been collected, the collateral is now replenished by a transfer of $670,000 of *new* receivables to the R & J Trust. The $22,500 cash enables the trust to make the quarterly interest payment on the notes.

4. **What happens in September 2007 when the R & J Trust repays the principal amount of the notes?**

Over the two years, the collateral has been maintained at $1,000,000 minus any credit losses. Let's assume that the receivables collateral balance is $984,000 on September 30, 2007 when the notes are due; that is, credit losses were $16,000 ($1,000,000 − $984,000). The amount of principal repayment that the investors will receive is $984,000. Roomkin & Juris will remit that amount in cash to the R & J Trust. Since the securitization has terminated, collateral is no longer needed and the receivables are transferred back from the R & J Trust to the department store. The entry on Roomkin & Juris' books is:

DR Accounts receivable	$984,000	
CR Cash		$984,000

APPENDIX

TIME VALUE OF MONEY

Cash is an economic resource. When firms borrow cash—for example, take out a two-year bank loan—they are renting the use of that economic resource for the two-year term of that loan. The lender's charge for renting its cash to the borrower is called **interest**.

Interest is an important concept since many business transactions involve borrowing, lending, or investment. Because of interest, a dollar amount invested today grows (or accumulates) to a larger amount in the future. The amount that that dollar grows to in the future is called the **future value**. Similarly, because of interest, a dollar amount that will be received in the future—say, two years from now—is less valuable than that same dollar amount in-hand today. Calculating today's value of a future dollar amount is called **discounting**. The result of that discounting calculation is called the **present value** of that future dollar amount.

The time at which cash inflows and cash outflows take place determines the ultimate future value or the present value of those flows. Correctly valuing these flows is necessary to represent properly the value of the assets, liabilities, revenues, and expenses arising from various business transactions.

> The concepts of present value and future value are totally driven by the role of interest. These concepts are unrelated to the buying power of money—inflation or deflation—which is a distinct and separate topic that we do not discuss in this Appendix.

Future Value

Assume that Alice Han's parents give her a $1,000 check for her twenty-first birthday. Alice wants to invest the money for graduate school, which she will attend in two years. Three local banks advertise that their savings accounts pay 6% interest per year, although how that interest is computed differs among them. Bank A pays 6% **simple interest** on the cash in a depositor's savings account. Simple interest means that each year's interest is computed on the original amount invested, which is called the **principal**. So interest each year would be $1,000 × .06, or $60. At the end of two years, the account at Bank A will have a future value of $1,120, calculated as:

$$\text{Future value with simple interest} = \$1,000 + \$60 + \$60 = \$1,120$$

Bank B pays 6% **compound interest** on savings accounts. Compound interest means that interest is paid not just on the initial principal but also on the interest that has been earned each period to date. So the accumulated amount would be computed as follows:

Date	Interest Calculation	Accumulated Amount
Initial principal		$1,000.00
Year 1	$1,000 × .06 = $60.00	$1,060.00
Year 2	$1,060 × .06 = $63.60	$1,123.60

Future value with interest compounded annually = $1,123.60

Bank B has compounded the interest annually; that is, interest is computed only once a year.

Bank C pays 6% interest compounded semiannually. This means that interest is computed every six months at a rate of 3%. The accumulated amount is:

Date	Interest Calculation	Accumulated Amount
Initial principal		$1,000.00
Year 1—First 6 months	$1,000 × .03 = $30.00	$1,030.00
—Last 6 months	$1,030 × .03 = $30.90	$1,060.90
Year 2—First 6 months	$1,060.90 × .03 = $31.83	$1,092.73
—Last 6 months	$1,092.73 × .03 = $32.78	$1,125.51

Future value with interest compounded semiannually = $1,125.51

Because most business transactions use compound interest, so will our examples. The formula for computing compound interest is

$$FV = P(1 + r)^n$$

Where:

FV = future value
P = present value
r = interest rate per compounding period
n = number of compounding periods

For simplicity, let's assume that interest is compounded annually. So the compounding period is a year. Using the formula to compute the future amount of a $1,000 two-year deposit in Bank B:

$$FV = \$1,000 (1 + .06)^2$$
$$FV = \$1,123.60$$

Of course, $1,123.60 equals the same future amount computed previously by the more tedious calculation above.

Present Value

As you just saw, if interest is compounded annually at 6%, the future value of $1,000.00 after two years is $1,123.60. This means that $1,123.60 to be received two years in the future is equivalent to $1,000 today—its present value—when the interest rate is 6% per year. To be sure you understand this concept of present value, we'll look at it from another perspective.

Assume that Alice Han's parents, knowing that she wanted to enroll in graduate school in two years, gave her a choice of birthday gifts:

- $1,000 cash immediately, or
- $1,123.60 to be received in exactly two years.

Which option should Alice choose? If Alice is determined to spend the money for graduate school (that is, she doesn't need the cash immediately) and if she knows that 6% per year is the prevailing interest rate, then **she should be indifferent between the two options.** Here's why. If she chose the $1,000 today, she could put it in a savings account at Bank B at 6% per year compounded annually where it would accumulate to $1,123.60 in two years.[21] So the two alternative gift amounts are identical at 6% per year compounded annually. *Being indifferent between $1,000 today and $1,123.60 in two years means that the present value of $1,123.60 due in two years is $1,000 at a 6% interest rate compounded annually.*

By rearranging the formula for computing compound interest, we can represent this notion of present value:

$$FV = P(1 + r)^n$$

Solving this formula for P, we find the present value:

$$P = \frac{FV}{(1 + r)^n}$$

Table 1 in Appendix 1 (following Chapter 18) shows the present value factors for various compounding periods and various interest rates per period. These present value factors result from solving the present value equation for P. This table provides the factor for computing the present value of a dollar to be received n periods in the future at interest rate r. (A portion of that table is reproduced here for convenience.)

TABLE 1	Present Value of $1

(Selected Excerpts)

$$P = \frac{1}{(1 + r)^n} = (1 + r)^n$$

(n) Periods	2%	3%	4%	5%	6%	7%	8%	9%	10%	11%	12%	15%
1	0.98039	0.97087	0.96154	0.95238	0.94340	0.93458	0.92593	0.91743	0.90909	0.90090	0.89286	0.86957
2	0.96117	0.94260	0.92456	0.90703	0.89000	0.87344	0.85734	0.84168	0.82645	0.81162	0.79719	0.75614
3	0.94232	0.91514	0.88900	0.86384	0.83962	0.81630	0.79383	0.77218	0.75132	0.73119	0.71178	0.65752
4	0.92385	0.88849	0.85480	0.82270	0.79209	0.76290	0.73503	0.70843	0.68301	0.65873	0.63552	0.57175
5	0.90573	0.86261	0.82193	0.78353	0.74726	0.71299	0.68058	0.64993	0.62092	0.59345	0.56743	0.49718

[21] For simplicity, we focus on annual compounding and ignore the possibility of depositing money in Bank C.

Using Alice Han's two gift options as a concrete example, we can show you how to use Table 1. Look at the intersection of the period 2 row and the 6% column and you will see the number 0.89000 (highlighted). This number is the factor that represents the present value of a dollar to be received at the end of two years at a 6% per period **discount rate**. To verify this, notice that if 89¢ were invested at 6% compounded annually for two years, it would accumulate to:

Date	Interest Calculation	Accumulated Amount
Initial principal		$0.89
Year 1	$0.89 × 6% = 0.0534. Then, $0.89 + 0.0534	= $0.9434
Year 2	$0.9434 × 6% = 0.0566. Then, $0.9434 + 0.0566	= $1.00

> Discount rate is what the interest rate is called when computing present values.

Because 0.89000 is the present value factor for one dollar, the present value for 1,123.60 dollars (Alice's parents' second birthday choice amount) is $1,123.60 × 0.89000 = $1,000. So you see how Table 1 helps us verify that the two gift amounts have identical present values.

Careful examination of Table 1 reveals two characteristics that are general to present value computations. First, looking *down any column*, you can see that the numbers grow smaller. For example, in the 6% column, the number in the period 3 row is 0.83962, which is smaller than 0.89000—the number in the period 2 row. This illustrates that the further in the future is the dollar flow, the smaller is its present value. Second, looking to the right *across any row*, the numbers again grow smaller. For example, in the period 2 row, in the 7% column, the number 0.87344 is smaller than 0.89000—the number in the 6% column. This illustrates that the higher the discount rate is (7% versus 6%), the smaller the present value of $1 is. Why? Because the higher the discount rate is, the smaller is the amount that must be invested at *r*% to equal $1 in *n* periods. At 7% only 87.344¢ must be invested to equal $1 in two periods, whereas at 6%, 89¢ must be invested to equal $1 in two periods.

Present Value of an Ordinary Annuity

Jacquie Henderson has just won the state lottery's "One Hundred Thousand Dollar Bonanza." The winnings are paid out in four equal installments. Each $25,000 installment is mailed to the winner on the one-year anniversary of the lottery drawing beginning 365 days from now. Jacquie understands that the discounted present value of the prize is less than $100,000 and wishes to compute its exact value using a discount rate of 5%. One way she can do this is to list each of the four payments separately and use the present value factors from Table 1. Doing it this way, the computation is:

Payment Number	Payment Amount	Present Value Factor	Present Value
1	$25,000	0.95238	$23,809.50
2	25,000	0.90703	22,675.75
3	25,000	0.86384	21,596.00
4	25,000	0.82270	20,567.50
TOTAL			$88,648.75

As the computation shows, the present value of the advertised $100,000 prize is only $88,648.75. Notice that the $25,000 undiscounted dollar amount received each period is the same. When each payment in a series is the same dollar amount, the series is called an **annuity**. When each payment is made at the *end* of each period, as in our example, that payment series is called an **ordinary annuity** (also called an **annuity in arrears**).

To compute the present value of an ordinary annuity, it isn't necessary to compute the present value of each payment separately, as we just did. Instead, Table 2 of Appendix 1 following Chapter 18 provides present value factors for ordinary annuities of various lengths at selected discount rates. A portion of Table 2 is reproduced here for convenience.

TABLE 2	Present Value of an Ordinary Annuity of $1

(Selected Excerpts)

$$P_{OA} = \left(1 - \frac{1}{(1+r)^n}\right)/r$$

(n) Periods	2%	3%	4%	5%	6%	7%	8%	9%	10%	11%	12%	15%
1	0.98039	0.97087	0.96154	0.95238	0.94340	0.93458	0.92593	0.91743	0.90909	0.90090	0.89286	0.86957
2	1.94156	1.91347	1.88609	1.85941	1.83339	1.80802	1.78326	1.75911	1.73554	1.71252	1.69005	1.62571
3	2.88388	2.82861	2.77509	2.72325	2.67301	2.62432	2.57710	2.53129	2.48685	2.44371	2.40183	2.28323
4	3.80773	3.71710	3.62990	3.54595	3.46511	3.38721	3.31213	3.23972	3.16987	3.10245	3.03735	2.85498
5	4.71346	4.57971	4.45182	4.32948	4.21236	4.10020	3.99271	3.88965	3.79079	3.69590	3.60478	3.35216

Notice in Table 2 that the intersection of the period 4 row and the 5% column contains the factor 3.54595 (highlighted). This number is simply the sum of the four present value factors we just used in the lottery computation. Specifically:

Payment Number	Present Value Factor
1	0.95238
2	0.90703
3	0.86384
4	0.82270
TOTAL	3.54595

So you see that 3.54595 is the present value of an ordinary annuity of one dollar each period for four periods. To determine the present value of an ordinary annuity of 25,000 dollars each period for four periods, we multiply 3.54595 times $25,000. The product, $88,648.75, is identical to the number we just computed more tediously for the present value of Jacquie Henderson's lottery winnings.

Present Value of an Annuity Due

Let's return to the lottery example and now assume that the first lottery check is received immediately. The next three checks follow at one-year intervals, that is, at the start of each of the next three periods. When each payment is made at the *beginning* of the period, as we are now assuming in this example, that payment series is called an **annuity due** (also called an **annuity in advance**).

To determine the present value of the lottery winnings when the payout is an annuity due, we can again compute from Table 1 the present value at 5% of each of the $25,000 checks, remembering that the present value factor for the first payment received *today* is 1.0000:

> Remember: The present value of one dollar in hand today is one dollar. Hence, its present value factor is 1.0000.

Payment Number	Payment Amount	Present Value Factor	Present Value
1	$25,000	1.00000	$25,000.00
2	25,000	0.95238	23,809.50
3	25,000	0.90703	22,675.75
4	25,000	0.86384	21,596.00
TOTAL			$93,081.25

When the lottery payments are made at the start of the year rather than at the end of the year (that is, an annuity due rather than an ordinary annuity) the present value of those payments is higher— $93,081.25 versus only $88,648.75 for the ordinary annuity.

Tables for computing the present value of an annuity due are also available; see Table 3 of Appendix 1 at the back of this book. A portion of Table 3 is reproduced here for convenience.

TABLE 3	Present Value of an Annuity Due of $1

(Selected Excerpts)

$$P_{AD} = 1 + \left(1 - \frac{1}{(1+r)^{n-1}}\right)/r$$

(n) Periods	2%	3%	4%	5%	6%	7%	8%	9%	10%	11%	12%	15%
1	1.00000	1.00000	1.00000	1.00000	1.00000	1.00000	1.00000	1.00000	1.00000	1.00000	1.00000	1.00000
2	1.98039	1.97087	1.96154	1.95238	1.94340	1.93458	1.92593	1.91743	1.90909	1.90090	1.89286	1.86957
3	2.94156	2.91347	2.88609	2.85941	2.83339	2.80802	2.78326	2.75911	2.73554	2.71252	2.69005	2.62571
4	3.88388	3.82861	3.77509	3.72325	3.67301	3.62432	3.57710	3.53129	3.48685	3.44371	3.40183	3.28323
5	4.80773	4.71710	4.62990	4.54595	4.46511	4.38721	4.31213	4.23972	4.16987	4.10245	4.03735	3.85498

The highlighted present value factor at the intersection of the period 4 row and the 5% column is 3.72325. Multiplying 3.72325 times $25,000 yields $93,081.25, the answer we just computed above. And, if you have suspected that the 3.72325 factor is simply the sum of 1.00000 + 0.95238 + 0.90703 + 0.86384, your suspicion is not only correct, you are understanding annuities, discount rates, and present value.

EXERCISES

For the month of December 2005 the records of Ranger Corporation show the following information:

Cash received on accounts receivable	$35,000
Cash sales	30,000
Accounts receivable, December 1, 2005	80,000
Accounts receivable, December 31, 2005	74,000
Accounts receivable written off as uncollectible	1,000

E8 – 1

Account analysis

ADAPTED

Required:
Determine the gross sales for the month of December 2005.

At the close of its first year of operations, on December 31, 2005, the Walker Company had accounts receivable of $250,000, which were *net* of the related allowance for doubtful accounts. During 2005, the company had charges to bad debt expense of $40,000 and wrote off, as uncollectible, accounts receivable of $10,000.

E8 – 2

Account analysis

AICPA
ADAPTED

Required:
What should the company report on its balance sheet at December 31, 2005, as accounts receivable *before* the allowance for doubtful accounts?

Delta Corporation wrote off a $100 uncollectible account receivable against the $1,200 balance in its allowance account.

E8 – 3

Ratio effects of write-offs

AICPA
ADAPTED

Required:
For the following amounts or ratios, determine the relationship between the amount or ratio before the write-off (x) with the amount or ratio after the write-off (y):

Amount or Ratio	Possibilities
1. Current ratio	a. x greater than y
2. Net accounts receivable balance	b. x equals y
3. Gross accounts receivable balance	c. x less than y
	d. Cannot be determined

E8 – 4

Bad debt expense

The following information is available for the Parker Company:

Credit sales during 2005	$100,000
Allowance for doubtful accounts at December 31, 2004	1,200
Accounts receivable deemed worthless and written off during 2005	1,600

During 2005 Parker estimated that its bad debt expense should be 1% of all credit sales.

As a result of a review and aging of accounts receivable in early January 2006, it has been determined that an allowance for doubtful accounts of $1,100 is needed at December 31, 2005.

Required:

What is the total amount that Parker should record as "bad debt expense" for the year ended December 31, 2005?

E8 – 5

Amortization table

The Lake Company sold some machinery to the View Company on January 1, 2005, for which the cash selling price was $758,200. View entered into an installment sales contract with Lake at an interest rate of 10%. The contract required payments of $200,000 a year over five years, with the first payment due on December 31, 2005.

Required:

Prepare an amortization schedule that shows what portion of each $200,000 payment will be shown as interest income over the period 2005–2009.

E8 – 6

Discounted note

Weaver, Inc. received a $60,000, six-month, 12% interest-bearing note from a customer. The note was discounted the same day at Third National Bank at 15%.

Required:

Compute the amount of cash received by Weaver from the bank.

E8 – 7

Note receivable carrying amount

STRETCH

On January 1, 2005, Carpet Company loaned $100,000 to its supplier, Loom Corporation, which was evidenced by a note, payable in five years. Interest at 5% is payable annually, with the first payment due on December 31, 2005. The going rate of interest for this type of loan is 10%. The parties agreed that Carpet's inventory needs for the loan period will be met by Loom at favorable prices. Assume that the present value (at the going rate of interest) of the $100,000 note is $81,000 at January 1, 2005.

Required:

1. Show the journal entry that Carpet would make to record interest and the receipt of cash at December 31, 2005.
2. What is the nature of the account that arises as a consequence of the difference between the 5% cash interest and the effective yield of 10%?

E8 – 8

Aging analysis

On December 31, 2005, Vale Company had an unadjusted credit balance of $1,000 in its allowance for uncollectible accounts. An analysis of Vale's trade accounts receivable at that date revealed the following:

Age	Amount	Estimated Uncollectible
0–30 days	$60,000	5%
31–60 days	4,000	10
Over 60 days	2,000	70

Required:

What amount should Vale report as allowance for uncollectible accounts in its December 31, 2005 balance sheet?

The following information relates to Jay Company's accounts receivable for 2005:

Accounts receivable, 1/1/05	$ 650,000
Credit sales for 2005	2,700,000
Sales returns for 2005	75,000
Accounts written off during 2005	40,000
Collections from customers during 2005	2,150,000
Estimated future sales returns at 12/31/05	50,000
Estimated uncollectible accounts at 12/31/05	110,000

E8 – 9

Account analysis

AICPA
ADAPTED

Required:

What amount should Jay report for accounts receivable, before allowances for sales returns and uncollectible accounts, at December 31, 2005?

Mare Company's December 31, 2005 balance sheet reported the following current assets:

Cash	$ 70,000
Accounts receivable	120,000
Inventories	60,000
Total	$250,000

E8 – 10

Consignments

AICPA
ADAPTED

An analysis of the accounts disclosed that accounts receivable consisted of the following:

Trade accounts	$ 96,000
Allowance for uncollectible accounts	(2,000)
Selling price of Mare's unsold goods out on consignment, at 130% of cost, *not* included in Mare's ending inventory	26,000
Total	$120,000

Required:

What are the correct totals for cash, accounts receivable, and inventories at December 31, 2005?

Blue, Inc. sells playground equipment to schools and municipalities. Invoices are mailed at the end of each month for all goods shipped during that month; credit terms are net 30 days. Sales and accounts receivable data for 2005, 2006, and 2007 were as follows:

E8 – 11

Is it a real sale?

	Years Ending December 31		
	2005	**2006**	**2007**
Sales	$1,785,980	$1,839,559	$1,986,724
Accounts receivable at year-end	220,189	227,896	267,094

Required:

1. Calculate the growth rates in sales and receivables during 2006 and 2007.
2. Do your calculations indicate any potential problems with Interworld's receivables?
3. If so, suggest a possible explanation for your findings and indicate what action, if any, would then be needed to bring Interworld's financial statements into conformity with GAAP.

On December 31, 2005, Fenton Company sold equipment to Denver, Inc., accepting a $275,000 non-interest-bearing note receivable in full payment on December 31, 2008. Denver, Inc., normally pays 12% for its borrowed funds. The equipment is carried in Fenton's perpetual inventory records at 65% of its cash selling price.

E8 – 12

Imputed interest

Required:

1. Prepare Fenton's journal entries to record the sale on December 31, 2005.
2. Prepare Fenton's journal entry on December 31, 2006 necessitated by this transaction. (*Hint:* Prepare an amortization schedule for the loan.)
3. Show Fenton's balance sheet presentation of Denver's note at December 31, 2006.

E8 – 13

Factoring receivables

Slifer, Inc. sells $125,000 of its accounts receivable to M&T Finance with recourse. M&T charges a fee of 3% and withholds 10% of the face amount of the receivables to cover possible uncollectible accounts and sales returns.

Required:

1. Prepare the journal entry Slifer would make to record the factoring.
2. Prepare Slifer's journal entry to record any subsequent cash received from M&T if M&T collects all of the factored receivables except for two accounts: $2,500 (due to a sales return) and $2,000 (resulting from a bad debt).

E8 – 14

Troubled debt settlement

Smithfield Farms purchased a combine from John Deere for $175,000 on January 2, 2005. Smithfield paid $25,000 in cash and signed an installment note calling for five annual payments of $39,569.58 beginning on December 31, 2005. Deere based the payments on a 10% rate of interest. Smithfield made the first payment, but a failed harvest in 2006 left them unable to make the upcoming payment. Deere agreed to repossess the combine—which had a market value of $132,000—on December 31, 2006—and cancel the note. Deere accrued interest on the loan for 2006 prior to canceling the note.

Required:

Prepare the journal entry John Deere would make on December 31, 2006 to record the settlement.

E8 – 15

Troubled debt restructuring

Central Valley Construction (CVC) purchased $80,000 of sheet metal fabricating equipment from Buffalo Supply on January 1, 2005. CVC paid $15,000 cash and signed a five-year 10% note for the remaining $65,000 of the purchase price. The note specifies that payments of $13,000 plus interest be made each year on the anniversary date of the loan. CVC made the required January 1, 2006 payment, but was unable to make the second payment on January 1, 2007 because of a downturn in the construction industry. At this time CVC owed Buffalo Supply $52,000 plus $5,200 interest that had been accrued by both companies. Rather than write off the note and repossess the equipment, Buffalo Supply agreed to restructure the loan as follows: one payment of $50,000 on January 1, 2009 would satisfy the restructured note.

Required:

Prepare the entries CVC and Buffalo Supply would make on January 1, 2007 to record the restructuring.

PROBLEMS/DISCUSSION QUESTIONS

P8 – 1

Balance sheet presentation and journal entries for various receivables transactions

Aardvark, Inc. began 2005 with the following receivables related account balances:

Accounts receivable	$575,000
Allowance for uncollectibles	43,250

Aardvark's transactions during 2005 include the following:

1. On April 1, 2005, Aardvark accepted an 8%, 12-month note from Smith Bros. in settlement of a past due account of $17,775.
2. Aardvark finally ceased all efforts to collect $23,200 from various customers and wrote off their accounts.
3. Total sales for the year (80% on credit) were $1,765,000. Cash receipts from customers as reported on Aardvark's cash flow statement were $1,925,000.
4. Sales for 2005 reported above included $100,000 of merchandise Jensen, Inc. ordered from Aardvark. Unfortunately, a shipping department error resulted in items valued at $150,000 being shipped and invoiced to Jensen. Because Jensen believed that they could eventually use the unordered items, they agreed to keep them in exchange for a 10% reduction in their price to cover storage costs.
5. On February 1, 2005, Aardvark borrowed $65,000 from Sun Bank and pledged receivables in that amount as collateral for the loan. Interest of 5% was deducted from the cash proceeds. In June, Aardvark repaid the loan.
6. Aardvark estimates uncollectible accounts using the sales revenue approach. In past years, bad debt expense was estimated at 1% of gross sales revenue, but a weaker economy in 2005 leads management to increase the estimate to 1.5% of gross sales revenue.
7. On July 1, 2005, Aardvark sold equipment to Zebra Company and received a $100,000 non-interest-bearing note receivable due in three years. The equipment normally sells for $79,383. Assume the appropriate rate of interest for this transaction is 8%.

Required:

1. Prepare journal entries for each of these events. Also prepare any needed entries to accrue interest on the notes at December 31, 2005.
2. Show Aardvark's balance sheet presentation for accounts and notes receivable at December 31, 2005.

Baer Enterprises's balance sheet at October 31, 2005 (fiscal year-end) includes the following:

Accounts receivable	$379,000
Less: Allowance for uncollectible accounts	(33,000)
Accounts receivable (net)	$346,000

P8 – 2

Balance sheet presentation and journal entries for various receivables transactions

Transactions for fiscal year 2006 include the following:

1. Due to a product defect, previously sold merchandise totaling $10,500 was returned.
2. Customer accounts totaling $29,750 were written off during the year.
3. On November 1, 2005, Baer sold teleconferencing equipment and received a $75,000 non-interest-bearing note receivable due in three years. The normal cash-selling price for the equipment is $56,349. Assume the appropriate interest rate for this transaction is 10%.
4. Credit sales during the year were $395,000, while collections totaled $355,000.
5. Baer sold Hartman, Inc. $45,000 of accounts receivable without recourse. Hartman's fee for factoring receivables is 9%.
6. Utilizing the gross receivables approach, Baer determined that the 2006 fiscal year-end allowance for uncollectible accounts should be $35,000.

Required:

1. Prepare journal entries for each of these events. Also prepare the entry to accrue interest income on the note.
2. Show Baer's balance sheet presentation for accounts and notes receivable at October 31, 2006.

Avillion Corporation had a $45,000 debit balance in accounts receivable and a $3,500 credit balance in allowance for uncollectibles on December 31, 2005. The company prepared the following aging schedule to record the adjusting entry for bad debts on December 31, 2005:

P8 – 3

Allowance for uncollectibles

Age of Receivables	Amount	Expected Bad Debts
0–30 days old	$30,000	5%
31–90 days old	10,000	11
Over 90 days old	5,000	30

a. On January 1, 2006 the company was informed that one of its customers (Smith Corporation), which owed $2,000, has filed for bankruptcy and may be unable to pay the amount due.
b. On March 1, 2006 Smith Corporation's bankruptcy was finalized and the bankruptcy court notified all its creditors (including Avillion Corporation) that Smith Corporation will pay 60 cents on the dollar for the amount owed to its creditors.
c. On May 7, 2006 Avillion Corporation received a check from Smith Corporation for the amount indicated by the court.

Required:

1. Provide journal entries to record the preceding transactions in the books of Avillion Corporation. In addition, using the table format provided below, show the effects of each of the transactions on the following financial statement items. Clearly indicate the amount and the direction of the effects (use "+" for increase, "−" for decrease, and "NE" for no effect).

	Assets	Liabilities	Net Income	Cash Flow from Operations
Direction of effect				
Dollar amount of effect				

2. Assume that Avillion Corporation had instead prepared the following aging schedule on December 31, 2005:

Age of Receivables	Amount	Expected Bad Debts
0–30 days old	$30,000	3%
31–90 days old	10,000	8
Over 90 days old	5,000	22

Redo requirement (1) using the revised aging schedule.

P8 – 4

Journal entries, aging analysis and balance sheet presentation

At December 31, 2004, Oettinger Corporation, a premium kitchen cabinetmaker for the home remodeling industry, reported the following accounts receivable information on its year-end balance sheet:

Gross accounts receivable	$850,000
Less: Allowance for uncollectibles	(25,000)
Accounts receivable (net)	$825,000

During 2005, the company had credit sales of $8,200,000 of which $7,975,000 was collected. Oettinger employs the sales revenue approach to estimate bad debt expense and, continuing to use the same 1% used in previous years, made the normal adjustment at the end of 2005.

Although 2005 started off well, the industry experienced a slowdown in the last four months of the year and cash collections consequently dropped off substantially. Moreover, a major customer, who owed Oettinger $85,000, unexpectedly filed for bankruptcy and went out of business during November, at which time their account was written off. Oettinger's controller is concerned that some customers are experiencing cash flow problems and that the company's allowance for uncollectible accounts is too low. As a result, she prepared the following schedule:

% of Accounts Receivable Balance	Number of Days Past Due	Estimated % Collectible
20%	0–30	98%
40	31–60	95
35	61–90	85
3	91–120	75
2	120 or more	50

Required:

1. Determine Oettinger's accounts receivable balance at December 31, 2005. Prepare a journal entry for each of the transactions affecting the accounts receivable balance for 2005.
2. Prepare an aging analysis to compute the required balance in the allowance for uncollectible accounts at December 31, 2005.
3. Prepare any other required journal entries affecting the allowance for uncollectible accounts for the year ended December 31, 2005. (Do not duplicate any entries from part 1.)
4. Show Oettinger's balance sheet presentation of accounts receivable at December 31, 2005.

P8 – 5

Account analysis

AICPA
ADAPTED

The following information is available for the Hokum Company ($ in thousands):

	2005	2006	2007
Charge sales	$900	$1,100	$1,000
Cash sales	600	800	700
Total	$1,500	$1,900	$1,700
Accounts receivable (end of year)	$170	$230	$220
Allowance for doubtful accounts (end of year)	47	30	56
Accounts written off as uncollectible (during the year)	2	50	4

Required:

Assuming that there was *no* change in the method used for estimating doubtful accounts during 2005–2007, determine the balance in the Allowance for doubtful accounts at the beginning of 2005.

The following information pertains to the financial statements of Buffalo Supply Company, a provider of plumbing fixtures to contractors in central Pennsylvania.

P8 – 6

Account analysis

	Fiscal Years Ended October 31		
	2005	**2004**	**2003**
From Income Statements			
Revenues	$3,519,444	$3,877,135	$2,969,981
Bad debt expense	45,753	50,403	38,610
From Balance Sheets			
Gross accounts receivable	$ 345,044	$ 362,349	$ 282,855
Less: Allowance for doubtful accounts	(54,654)	(74,365)	(47,612)
Net accounts receivable	$ 290,390	$ 287,984	$ 235,243

Required:

Reconstruct all the journal entries pertaining to "Gross accounts receivable" and "Allowance for doubtful accounts" for the fiscal year ended October 31, 2005. Assume that all revenues are from credit sales. (*Hint:* Begin by doing a "T-account" analysis of both accounts, starting with the allowance account.)

On January 1, 2005 Patz Corporation reports the following information pertaining to its accounts receivable:

P8 – 7

Comprehensive receivables and allowance analysis

Accounts receivable (gross)	$20,000
Less: Allowance for uncollectibles	(2,000)
Accounts receivable (net)	$18,000

For the year ended December 31, 2005, Patz Corporation had credit sales of $100,000. Collections for the year amounted to $92,000, of which $16,000 was from 2004 sales and $76,000 was from current year's sales. Bad debts written off during the year totaled $9,000; $4,000 of this total pertained to receivables outstanding as of January 1, 2005, and $5,000 was from this year's sales. On December 31, 2005, the company prepared the following aging schedule to determine the ending balance in the Allowance for uncollectibles:

Aging Information	Book Value	Expected Bad Debts
Over 90 days old	$2,000	30%
31–90 days old	7,000	20
Current (0–30 days)	(To be computed by you)	10

Required:

1. Provide journal entries to record the preceding transactions as well as year-end Bad debt expense. Compute the ending Accounts receivable and Allowance for uncollectibles balances.
2. Show how the Accounts receivable balance you computed will be disclosed in the balance sheet as of December 31, 2005.
3. Show how much of the Bad debt expense for 2005 relates to actual and expected future write-offs from 2005 sales versus prior years' sales.

On December 31, 1995, Sea Containers Ltd., a company located in Hamilton, Bermuda, reported notes receivable of $63,930,000. This amount represents the present value of future cash flows (both principal and interest) discounted at a rate of 11.12% per annum. The schedule of collections of the receivables is provided next ($ in thousands):

P8 – 8

Interest schedule

www.prenhall.com/revsine

● Student Resources

☑ Template for solution

Year Ending December	Collections
1996	$20,724
1997	15,896
1998	11,559
1999	7,179
2000	8,559
2001	13
	$63,930

Assume that the interest due is paid along with the face value of the receivables at the end of each year.

Required:

Provide journal entries to record the interest received as well as the collection of the notes receivable.

P8 – 9

Imputed interest on a
nominal interest-bearing
note

On January 2, 2005, Healthy Farms purchased from Deerfield Ag Center a new piece of machinery that had a cash selling price of $127,255. As payment, Healthy gave Deerfield a $150,000 5-year note that provided for annual interest payments at 6%. At the time of the sale, the interest rate normally charged to farms with Healthy's credit rating is 10%.

Required:

1. Prepare Deerfield's journal entry to record the sale.
2. Prepare the journal entry to record the first interest payment received by Deerfield on December 31, 2005.
3. Determine the note receivable balance that Deerfield will report on December 31, 2006.

P8 – 10

Account analysis

The following information is adapted from the financial statements of Buck Hill Falls Company. The company provides recreational facilities, water and sewage services, and miscellaneous maintenance services to residents of Buck Hill Falls, Monroe County, Pennsylvania.

Buck Hill Falls Company			
	Fiscal Years Ended October 31		
	1996	1995	1994
From Income Statements			
Revenues	$2,175,475	$2,218,139	$2,203,529
Provision for doubtful accounts	20,585	150,631	95,241
From Balance Sheets			
Gross accounts receivable	$ 353,723	$ 325,229	$ 210,758
(−) Allowance for doubtful accounts	(100,445)	(79,860)	(35,000)
Net accounts receivable	$ 253,278	$ 245,369	$ 175,758

Note: Bad debt expense is frequently referred to as "Provision for doubtful accounts."

Required:

1. Reconstruct all the journal entries pertaining to "Gross accounts receivable" and "Allowance for doubtful accounts" (that is, "Allowance for uncollectibles") for the fiscal years ended October 31, 1995 and October 31, 1996. You may assume that all revenues are from credit sales.
2. Try to identify scenarios consistent with the allowance and write-off activity reported over the 1994–1996 period.

P8 – 11

Cash discounts and sales
returns

On February 7, 2005 Jilian Company sold 20,000 sweatshirts to customers for $130,000 using credit terms of 2/10, n/30. These credit terms mean that customers will get a cash discount of 2% of the invoice price for payments made within 10 days of the sale (this is what the 2/10 signifies). If payment is not made within 10 days, then the entire invoice price is due no later than the 30th day (this is what the n/30 signifies). On February 16, 2005 various customers made payment on one half of the total receivables (discounts are recorded in a "Cash discounts" account that is reported as a contra-revenue item on the income statement). A customer returned goods with a selling price of $5,000 on February 25, 2005. The balance due (from the remaining receivables) was paid on March 5, 2005.

Required:

1. Provide journal entries to record the preceding transactions in the books of Jilian Company; assume that Jilian records sales returns when customers actually return the goods.
2. Assume that the borrowing rate for Jilian's customers is 18%. Demonstrate that the customers not paying within 10 days would be better off borrowing the money if necessary to enable payment to be made within the discount period.

On January 1, 2005 Hillock Brewing Company sold 50,000 bottles of beer to various customers for $45,000 using credit terms of 3/10, n/30. These credit terms mean that customers will get a cash discount of 3% of invoice price for payments made within 10 days of the sale (this is what the 3/10 signifies). If payment is not made within 10 days, then the entire invoice price is due no later than the 30th day (this is what the n/30 signifies). At the time of sale, Hillock expects sales returns of 5%. On January 9, 2005 customers made payment on one half of the total receivables. They returned goods with a selling price of $2,000 on January 15, 2005. The balance due was paid on January 28, 2005.

P8 – 12

Cash discounts and sales returns

Required:

1. Provide journal entries to record the preceding transactions in the books of Hillock Company; assume that Hillock records *expected* sales returns at the time of sales.
2. Redo requirement (1) assuming that customers returned goods with a selling price of $3,000 on January 15, 2005.
3. Provide journal entries to record the preceding transactions in the books of Hillock Company; assume that Hillock records sales returns when customers *actually* return the goods.
4. Since the net sales revenue is the same under both methods—requirements (1) and (3)—what is the advantage of recording anticipated sales returns rather than waiting to record them when the customers actually return the goods?
5. Assuming that the incremental annualized borrowing rate for a customer is 18%, are customers better off paying within 10 days to get the discount or should they wait to pay until the 30th day?

Mik-Gen Corporation has a $100,000 bond sinking fund payment due in early August. In order to meet its obligation, on August 1 Mik-Gen decided to accelerate collection of accounts receivable by assigning $130,000 of specified accounts to a commercial lender as collateral for a loan. Under the agreement, Mik-Gen guarantees the accounts and will notify its customers to make their payments directly to the lender; in return, the lender will advance Mik-Gen 85% of the accounts assigned. The remaining 15% will be paid to Mik-Gen once the commercial lender has recovered its fees and related cash advances. The lender receives a fee of 5% of the total accounts assigned, which is immediately deducted from the initial cash advance. The lender also assesses a monthly finance charge of one half of 1% on any uncollected balances. Finance charges are to be deducted from the first payment due Mik-Gen after the lender has recovered its cash advances.

On August 31, Mik-Gen received a statement from the lender saying it had collected $80,000. On September 30, Mik-Gen receives a check from the lender together with a second statement saying an additional $40,000 has been collected.

P8 – 13

Collateralized borrowing

Required:

1. Prepare all necessary journal entries.
2. Show the balance sheet presentation of the assigned accounts receivable and any related liabilities at August 31.

Atherton Manufacturing Company sold $200,000 of accounts receivable to a factor. Pertinent facts about this transaction include the following:

1. The factored receivables had a corresponding $4,000 balance in the Allowance for uncollectibles.
2. The receivables were factored on a without recourse basis with notification (that is, the customers were instructed to mail their checks directly to the factor).
3. Atherton remained responsible for sales returns and a 5% holdback was retained by the factor for this purpose.
4. The factor charged 1% interest on the gross receivables factored plus a 6% factoring fee, both of which were deducted by the factor from the value of receivables.
5. The customers returned inventory with a selling price of $3,000. All remaining accounts were settled and the factor paid the balance due. Assume that Atherton records sales returns only when goods are returned (that is, it does not record an Allowance for sales returns).
6. The factor incurred actual bad debts of $7,500.

P8 – 14

Factoring receivables

Required:

Provide journal entries to record:
1. the receipt of proceeds from the factor,
2. treatment of sales returns, and
3. any other items related to the pertinent facts, including the final cash settlement from the factor.

P8 – 15

Reconstructing T-accounts

The following information is taken from the financial statements of Ramsay Health Care Inc.:

	Excerpts from Balance Sheets as of End of	
	Year 3	Year 2
Gross accounts receivable	$26,944,000	$31,651,000
Allowance for doubtful accounts	(3,925,000)	(4,955,000)
Net accounts receivable	$23,019,000	$26,696,000

	Excerpts from Income Statements for the Years Ended		
	Year 3	Year 2	Year 1
Revenue	$137,002,000	$136,354,000	$136,946,000
Provision for doubtful accounts	5,846,000	8,148,000	8,628,000
Operating income before taxes	6,900,000	(1,048,000)	9,321,000

Note: Bad debt expense is frequently referred to as "Provision for doubtful accounts."

Required:

1. Reconstruct all the journal entries relating to "Gross accounts receivable" and "Allowance for doubtful accounts" (that is, "Allowance for uncollectibles") for the year ended December 31, Year 3. You may assume that all revenues are from credit sales.
2. Assume that the company computes its bad debt expense by multiplying sales revenues by some percentage. (This is called the sales revenue approach.) Recalculate the bad debt expense (that is, "Provision for doubtful accounts") for Year 3; assume that Ramsay estimated the Year 3 bad debts at the same percentage of revenue as it did in Year 2. Based on the revised figure, show how "Gross accounts receivable" and "Allowance for doubtful accounts" would be presented as of the end of Year 3. Also calculate a revised operating income before taxes using the revised figure for bad debt expense.
3. In answering this part, assume that the company is using the gross accounts receivable approach to estimate its bad debt expense (that is, assume that "Allowance for doubtful accounts" is fixed as a percentage of gross receivables). Recalculate the bad debts expense for Year 3 *and* the ending balance in "Allowance for doubtful accounts" at the end of Year 3; assume that Ramsay estimated the expected bad debts at the same percentage of receivables as it did in Year 2. Also, calculate the revised operating income before taxes using the revised figure for bad debt expense.
4. Based on your answers to requirements (2) and (3), what inferences can be drawn about Ramsay's accounts receivables management and the adequacy of the allowance for doubtful accounts?

P8 – 16

Restructured note receivable

Fish Spotters, Inc. purchased a single-engine aircraft from National Aviation on January 1, 2005. Fish Spotters paid $55,000 cash and signed a three-year 8% note for the remaining $45,000. Terms of the note require Fish Spotters to pay accrued interest annually on December 31, with the remaining $45,000 balance due with the last interest payment on December 31, 2007. Fish Spotters made the first two interest payments but was unable to make the principal and interest payment due December 31, 2007. On January 1, 2008 National Aviation agreed to restructure the note receivable.

Required:

Provide the journal entries that National Aviation would record under each of the following independent scenarios.

1. National Aviation agrees to take the aircraft back in return for the outstanding note. Assume that the aircraft has a market value of $40,000.
2. National agrees to accept a $5,000 cash payment and a new $35,000 note receivable due in five years. The note stipulates that annual interest of $4,200 will be paid each December 31. Prepare the note receivable amortization table through December 31, 2012 and all entries through December 31, 2010.

Warren Companies purchased equipment for $72,000 from General Equipment Manufacturers on January 1, 2003. Warren Companies paid $12,000 in cash and signed a five-year, 5% installment note for the remaining $60,000 of the purchase price. The note calls for annual payments of $12,000 plus interest on December 31 of each year. Warren Companies made the first installment on time, but it was not able to make the next installment (due on December 31, 2004). On January 1, 2005 General Equipment Manufacturers agreed to restructure the note receivable.

P8 – 17

Restructured note receivable

Required:

Provide journal entries in the books of both Warren Companies and General Equipment Manufacturers for the period 2005–2007 under the following *independent* scenarios:

1. General Equipment Manufacturers accepted $20,000 in cash and old equipment fully depreciated in the books of Warren Companies (with a market value of $14,000) in exchange for the outstanding note.
2. General Equipment Manufacturers agreed to receive a total of $57,600 ($48,000 plus $9,600, representing four years interest at 5%) on December 31, 2007 in exchange for the outstanding note. (Interpolate for Warren's new effective interest rate.)
3. General Equipment decides to waive all interest and defers all principal payments until December 31, 2007.

The following footnotes are excerpted from the financial statements of three companies:

P8 – 18

Accounting for transfer of receivables

Ricoh Company Ltd., March 31, 1994

NOTE NO. 7—SHORT-TERM BORROWINGS AND TRADE NOTES RECEIVABLE DISCOUNTED WITH BANKS

The Company and certain of its domestic subsidiaries regularly discount trade notes receivable on a full recourse basis with banks. These trade notes receivable discounted are contingent liabilities. The weighted average interest rates on these trade notes receivable discounted were 4.2% and 3.2% as of March 31, 1993 and 1994, respectively.

Crown Crafts Inc., March 31, 1994

NOTE NO. 4—FINANCING ARRANGEMENTS

Factoring Agreement

The Company assigns substantially all of its trade accounts receivable to a commercial factor. Under the terms of the factoring agreement, the factor remits invoiced amounts to the Company on the approximate due dates of the factored invoices. The Company does not borrow funds from its factor or take advances against its factored receivables balances. Accounts are factored without recourse as to credit losses but with recourse as to returns, allowances, disputes and discounts. Factoring fees included in marketing and administrative expenses in the consolidated statements of earnings were: $1,501,000 (1994), $1,223,000 (1993) and $1,077,000 (1992).

Foxmeyer Corporation, March 31, 1994

NOTE C—ACCOUNTS RECEIVABLE FINANCING

On October 29, 1993, the Corporation entered into a one-year agreement to sell a percentage ownership interest in a defined pool of the Corporation's trade accounts receivable with limited recourse. Proceeds of $125.0 million from the sale were used to reduce amounts outstanding under the Corporation's revolving credit facilities. Generally, an undivided interest in new accounts receivable will be sold daily as existing accounts receivable are collected to maintain the participation interest at $125.0 million. Such accounts receivable sold are not included in the accompanying consolidated balance sheet at March 31, 1994. An allowance for doubtful accounts has been retained on the participation interest sold based on estimates of the Corporation's risk of credit loss from its obligation under the recourse provisions. The cost of the accounts receivable financing program is based on a 30-day commercial paper rate plus certain fees. The total cost of the program in 1994 was $2.2 million and was charged against "Other income" in the accompanying consolidated statements of income. Under the agreement, the Corporation also acts as agent for the purchaser by performing recordkeeping and collection functions on the participation interest sold. The agreement contains certain covenants regarding the quality of the accounts receivable portfolio, as well as other covenants which are substantially identical to those contained in the Corporation's credit facilities.

Required:

How do the three companies record the transfer of their receivables—that is, as a sale or borrowing? Is their accounting treatment consistent with the economics of the transactions? Explain.

P8 – 19

Do existing receivables represent real sales?

Moto-Lite Company is an original equipment manufacturer of high-quality aircraft engines that have traditionally been sold directly to aero clubs building their own aircraft. The engine's selling price is dependent on its size and horsepower; Moto-Lite's average gross profit per engine is 35%.

In an effort to expand its sales, Moto-Lite entered into an agreement with Macco Corporation, a British manufacturer of light aircraft, to be the sole supplier of its 80 horsepower, 2 stroke engines. Under the terms of the agreement, Moto-Lite will stock a minimum of 10 engines at Macco's production facility in order to service aircraft production requirements. Each engine has a firm selling price of $6,000. Title to the engines does not pass until the engine is used in Macco's production process.

During its quarter ending October 31, Moto-Lite shipped and billed 19 engines (DR accounts receivable, CR sales) to Macco Corporation. As of that date, Macco had used nine engines in its production process. All but three of the engines used had been paid for prior to October 31. The remaining ten engines will be used in November.

Required:

1. What type of agreement does this appear to be? Was Moto-Lite correct to record all 19 motors shipped as sales in the quarter ending October 31?
2. How should the transaction be accounted for and by how much, if at all, were Moto-Lite's sales, receivables, and gross profit overstated at October 31?

P8 – 20

Do existing receivables represent real sales?

Aurora Aluminum, a vendor to Bostian Enterprises, receives Bostian's purchase order for computer drill sheet. Bostian, a maker of electronic circuit boards, implemented a production process that is designed to take advantage of just-in-time inventory management techniques. Accordingly, their purchase order specifically states that delivery is to be made to Bostian's assembly plant at 1 P.M. on January 16, 2006 and that payment will be 30 days after delivery.

Aurora had a lull in production activity and decided to produce Bostian's order over the Christmas holidays. After producing the material on December 27, it was promptly loaded on a staged trailer, which was immediately locked and sealed. An invoice and a bill of lading were prepared. The invoice was immediately sent to Bostian on a "bill and hold" basis.

Upon receiving the invoice, Bostian contacted Aurora and was told that the material was invoiced because Aurora wanted to include the sale in its just closed calendar year-end; however, actual delivery would take place in accordance with the purchase order terms and that payment would be expected 30 days after delivery. Moreover, risk of ownership would remain with Aurora until delivery. Bostian accepted the explanation, and reminded Aurora that it could not accept the material prior to its scheduled delivery date due to space constraints.

Required:

Was Aurora correct to include the Bostian transaction as a sale and account receivable in calendar year 2005? Explain.

The following facts pertain to the year ended December 31, 2005 of Grosse Pointe Corporation, a manufacturer of power tools.

P8 – 21

Channel stuffing

1. Based on year-to-date sales through early December, management projected 2005 sales to be 5% below their forecast target for the year.
2. The 2005 sales forecast included projected sales of a new string trimmer that was introduced late in the third quarter of 2005; unfortunately for Grosse Pointe Corporation, actual customer orders for the new product through early December were disappointing.
3. Effective December 15, 2005, Grosse Pointe Corporation began providing the following incentives to boost sales of the new string trimmer: (a) normal 2/10, n/30 payment terms were extended to n/90, and (b) full right of return for 90 days was granted on all trimmers purchased during the last two weeks of December.
4. Grosse Pointe Corporation has never before been forced to offer these types of incentives and thus has no basis for estimating return rates or default rates on these sales.
5. Sales of the new trimmer for October 1 to December 15, 2005 were $1,265,000.
6. The marketing department began aggressively promoting the new trimmer by stressing the "no risk" nature of the incentives ("if you can't sell them, just return them") and generated sales for December 15 to 31, 2005 of $2,391,000. Management included all of this revenue to make the company's sales target for 2005. Grosse Pointe Corporation uses a perpetual inventory system and charged $1,650,000 to cost of goods sold when these sales were made.

Required:

1. Is Grosse Pointe Corporation correct to recognize the "incentive sales" and related accounts receivable in 2005? Explain.
2. If Grosse Pointe's auditors do not concur with management's desired accounting treatment, what correcting entries are needed?

CASES

Appearing next is information pertaining to the "Allowance for doubtful accounts" of Garrels Company. Examine this information and answer the following questions ($ in thousands).

C8 – 1

Garrels Company (CW): Comprehensive allowance analysis

| | Years Ended December 31 | | |
	2003	2002	2001
Allowance for Doubtful Accounts			
Balance, beginning of year	?	?	$1,324
Provision charged to expense	?	502	1,349
Write-offs, less recoveries	1	622	?
Balance, end of year	1,453	?	1,302

Required:

1. Solve for the unknowns in the schedule above.
2. Make all the entries related to the "Allowance for doubtful accounts" account for 2001–2003.
3. Make all entries for bad debts for 2001–2003 assuming Garrels did not accrue for estimated bad debt losses but instead recorded bad debt expense once receivables were determined to be uncollectible. (This is called the direct write-off method.)
4. Why does GAAP require the allowance method over the direct write-off method?
5. Calculate the cumulative difference in reported pre-tax income under the allowance and direct write-off methods over the 2001–2003 period.

6. Assume it is the end of 2004 and the management of Garrels Company is trying to decide on the amount of the bad debt expense for 2004. Based on an aging of accounts receivable, the accounting department feels that a provision of $400,000 is appropriate. However, the company just found out that a customer with an outstanding accounts receivable of $300,000 may have to file for bankruptcy. The decision facing Garrels Company management is whether to increase the initial provision of $400,000 by $300,000, by some lesser amount, or by nothing at all. What is your recommendation?

7. Continuing the scenario from requirement 6, now consider the following additional information. Assume that you are a member of the company's compensation committee. Assume further that the company's chief financial officer (CFO) is solely responsible for deciding the amount of bad debt expense to record, and that the CFO has a cash bonus plan that is a function of reported earnings before income taxes. Specifically, assume that the CFO receives an annual cash bonus of zero if earnings before income taxes is below $17 million and 10.0% of the amount by which earnings before income taxes exceeds $17 million and up to a maximum bonus of $1 million (that is, when net income reaches $27 million, no further bonus is earned). What adjustment to the initial $400,000 bad debt provision might the CFO make in each of the following scenarios?

   a. Earnings before income taxes (including the initial $400,000 provision for bad debts) is $11 million.
   b. Earnings before income taxes (including the initial $400,000 provision for bad debts) is $18.02 million.
   c. Earnings before income taxes (including the initial $400,000 provision for bad debts) is $38.25 million.
   d. Earnings before income taxes (including the initial $400,000 provision for bad debts) is $27.15 million.

8. What other scenarios can you identify in which managers might use the provision for bad debts to accomplish some contract-related strategy?

9. Identify other items in the financial statements (besides the bad debt provision) that managers have the ability to "manage."

C8 – 2

Great Southwest Corporation (KR): Valuing notes and recording interest

www.prenhall.com/revsine

● Student Resources

☑ Template for solution

Great Southwest Corporation, Inc. (GSC) was a real estate development company headquartered in the southwestern United States. GSC was also engaged in constructing, developing, and operating amusement parks. On January 1, 1969 GSC sold its amusement park "Six Flags over Texas," which had been carried on the books of GSC at a value of $22 million. GSC received a down payment of $2 million immediately and received a 35-year, 6.5% note for $35 million from the buyer. In addition, GSC immediately received another $3,412,500, representing prepayments of stated interest for the first three years. Beginning in 1972 payments of $2,137,500 (which include interest payment of $1,137,500 and principal payment of $1,000,000) per year were to be made for the next 35 years. Since the average book value of the note is $17.5 million (one half of $35 million), the annual stated interest payments were calculated at 6.5% of $17.5 million.

Assume that the company can justify recording the sale of the amusement park on January 1, 1969 when the contract was signed. Also, assume that all cash transactions took place on the first day of each year.

GSC recorded the following journal entries to reflect the sale:

DR Cash		$ 2,000,000	
DR Notes receivable		35,000,000	
	CR Amusement park in Dallas		$22,000,000
	CR Gain on sale		15,000,000
DR Cash		3,412,500	
	CR Unearned interest revenue		3,412,500

Required:

1. Are these journal entries consistent with GAAP? If not, explain how GSC should have recorded the sale and the receipt of initial cash payments. Show all relevant calculations.

2. Assuming that the prevailing effective interest rate for comparable transactions is 10%, redo requirement (1). In addition, provide the necessary journal entries for the first four years of the note's life (that is, 1969 to 1972) to record the interest revenue and the receipt of the periodic payments.

You have recently been hired as an equity analyst at a large mutual fund. During your first week, you receive the following memo:

Welcome to Vitality Mutual Funds. I am sure you are excited to join our firm as a financial analyst. I am currently looking at the financial statements of Spiegel, Inc., which is a multi-channel specialty company that owns Spiegel, Eddie Bauer, and Newport News. The company also owns First Consumers National Bank ("FCNB"). FCNB is a special purpose bank limited to the issuance of credit cards, primarily FCNB Preferred Charge cards for use by Spiegel, Eddie Bauer, and Newport News customers. I need your assistance in analyzing the company's accounts receivable. I did some cursory analysis and identified some very interesting trends. During 1994 and 1995, the growth in sales has outpaced the growth in receivables. In fact, during 1995, while the company's net sales grew at around 7%, its receivables decreased by more than 30%! I am quite pleased with the improvement in receivables management. In fact, the receivable collection period has dropped from around 140 days to less than 120 days. This is quite impressive given that the company relies very heavily on installment sales to generate a substantial majority of its revenue. However, I am not sure how Spiegel is accounting for the sale of receivables or how the factoring of receivables impacts my calculations. One additional thing that I can't understand is why Spiegel is showing a portion of the allowance for sales returns under accrued liabilities. I am under the impression that such allowance accounts are contra-asset accounts. What I need from you is a succinct report (with supporting analysis) addressing the issues that I have raised in this memo. To help you in your analysis, I have included below some information that I have on the company. Good luck.

Sincerely,

Maria S. Kang

Senior Analyst

Vitality Mutual Funds

The following table provides an adapted breakdown of the net receivables balance reported in comparative balance sheets:

	As of December 31		
	1995	1994	1993
Receivables generated from operations	$2,001,081	$1,683,444	$1,403,618
Receivables sold	(1,180,000)	(480,000)	(330,000)
Receivables owned	821,081	1,203,444	1,073,618
Less: Allowance for returns	(37,769)	(27,762)	(28,238)
Less: Allowance for doubtful accounts	(40,832)	(49,954)	(46,855)
Receivables—net (from balance sheet)	$ 742,480	$1,125,728	$ 998,525

During 1995, 1994, and 1993, the company transferred portions of its customer receivables to trusts, which, in turn, sold certificates representing undivided interests in the trusts to investors. These transactions are similar to the factoring of receivables, except that a group of investors, as opposed to a single factor, is investing in the receivables of Spiegel. That is, this was a securitization of the receivables. Certificates sold were $700,000 in 1995 (under two separate transactions of $350,000 each) and $150,000 and $330,000 (in 1994 and 1993, respectively). As a result of these transactions, other revenue increased by $18,637 and $10,658 in 1995 and 1994, respectively, representing the gain on the sold receivables that existed at the date of the transaction. The receivables were *sold without recourse*, and the bad debt reserve related to the net receivables sold has been reduced accordingly. Note that Spiegel is still responsible for sales returns, although the investors in the securitized receivables bear the bad debt risk. As cash is collected from the customers, Spiegel pays only the required interest portion to the investors and reinvests the remaining cash flows in new accounts receivables that are generated (that is, the investors are continually refinancing the receivables of Spiegel over the duration of the securitization agreement). The company owns the remaining undivided interest in the trusts not represented by the certificates (that is, Spiegel is retaining ownership of a portion of the securitized receivables, which is included under "Receivables Owned"). In addition, the company *will service all receivables for the trusts* (that is, Spiegel is performing the administrative aspects of collecting and distributing the cash flows from the receivables).

The company reported the following sales figures over the three-year period:

| | For the Years Ended December 31 | | |
	1995	1994	1993
Net sales	$2,886,225	$2,706,791	$2,337,235

In addition, the following table provides information on the company's allowance for doubtful accounts over the same period:

| | Allowance for Doubtful Accounts | | |
	1995	1994	1993
Beginning balance	$49,954	$46,855	$37,231
Charged to earnings	91,612	79,183	69,160
Reduction for receivables sold	(33,600)	(6,300)	(1,609)
Other	-0-	-0-	695
Accounts written off	(67,134)	(69,784)	(58,622)
Ending balance	$40,832	$49,954	$46,855

"Other" represents the beginning balance of Newport News, which was acquired in 1993.

The company's accrued liabilities at the end of 1995 include "Allowance for returns" of $31,927. This breakdown is not available for the prior two years.

The following footnote describes the company's revenue recognition policy:

Revenue Recognition

Sales made under installment accounts represent a substantial portion of net sales. The Company provides for returns at the time of sale based upon projected merchandise returns.

Required:

Provide the analysis requested by Ms. Kang including journal entries that show how Spiegel accounts for the sale of receivables.

C8 – 4

Thompson Traders (KR): Bad debt analysis

Thompson Traders started its business on January 1, 2001. The following information pertains to the company's accounts receivable during the first five years of its operations:

| | | | Bad Debts Pertaining to Sales Made During | | | | |
| | | Bad Debts | | | | | |
Year	Revenue	Written Off	2001	2002	2003	2004	2005
2001	$30,000	$ 600	$600				
2002	40,000	1,000	300	$700			
2003	60,000	1,500	-0-	500	$1,000		
2004	80,000	2,400	-0-	-0-	800	$1,600	
2005	90,000	3,000	-0-	-0-	-0-	800	$2,200

The company typically sells on credit to its customers. All sales made in a given calendar year are fully settled by the following year, by which time all uncollected receivables are written off. Since inception, Thompson has recorded bad debts expense at 2.75% of its revenue. After five years of operation, the company is now considering a reevaluation of its bad debts formula before finalizing its financial statements for the year 2005. The following are excerpts taken from a recent meeting of Thompson's managers discussing this issue:

Our experience suggests that the bad debts written off have ballooned from 2% of revenues to almost 3.5%. So, while we were being very conservative in the earlier years, currently our provisions are much below our actuals. Conservatively, I recommend a formula of 3.5% of revenues.

(Tony Barclay, Corporate Accounting)

While I agree with Tony's computations, my experience suggests that the quality of our receivables has pretty much remained the same and I don't expect them to change in the near future. Therefore, I recommend that we retain our current formula.

(Ian Spencer, Manager, Accounts Receivable)

If you believe that you have under- or over-provided for bad debts over the last four years, you have to revise the formula to reflect your past experience and current expectations. While revising the formula will lead to correct expensing in the future, you also have to adjust the allowance account for past estimation errors. More importantly, since this will be considered as a change in accounting methods, you have to restate the past financial statements.

(Brian Joshi, Outside Consultant)

Required:

You have been hired as a summer intern in the corporate controller's office to examine the bad debt accounting at Thompson. Based on the information provided, write a report to the top management providing an assessment of the company's bad debt formula and provide specific recommendations to improve its accounting, if needed. In completing the report, please address all the issues raised during the recent company meeting.

Remember to check the book's Companion Website for additional problem and case material.

www.prenhall.com/revsine

Inventories

A wholesaler or retailer buys assets like suits or shoes that are immediately saleable in their current form. Assets held for sale are called **inventories**. A typical wholesaler or retailer will have only one inventory account, called *merchandise inventory*, on its balance sheet.

A manufacturing firm making a final product like dishwashers uses inputs from many different suppliers. Consequently, manufacturers' balance sheets typically include three categories of inventory accounts:

1. **Raw materials inventory**, which consists of components like steel that will eventually be used in the completed product.
2. **Work-in-process inventory**, which contains the aggregate cost of units that have been started but not completed as of the balance sheet date. Work-in-process inventory includes the cost of the raw materials, direct labor, and overhead that has been incurred in the manufacture of the partially completed units.[1]
3. **Finished goods inventory**, which represents the total costs incorporated in completed but unsold units.

Inventories are usually a significant asset, both in absolute size and in proportion to all of a company's other assets. Furthermore, selling inventories for a price greater than their cost represents the main source of a firm's sustainable income. For these reasons, inventory accounting is exceedingly important.

An Overview of Inventory Accounting Issues

We will use an example of a retailer who sells refrigerators to illustrate the basic issues in inventory accounting. Assume the retailer started the year with a beginning inventory of one refrigerator it purchased for $300. During the year the retailer's

---

[1] Manufacturing overhead includes items such as depreciation of production equipment and buildings, power, indirect labor, and so on.

Learning Objectives

After studying this chapter, you will understand:

1. The two methods used to determine inventory quantities—the perpetual inventory system and the periodic inventory system.

2. What specific items and kinds of costs are included in inventory.

3. What absorption costing is and how it complicates financial analysis.

4. The difference between various cost flow assumptions—weighted average, FIFO, and LIFO.

5. How to use the LIFO reserve disclosure to estimate inventory holding gains and to transform LIFO firms to a FIFO basis.

6. How LIFO liquidations distort gross profit and how to adjust for these distortions to improve forecasts.

7. What research tells us about the economic incentives guiding the choice of inventory accounting methods.

8. How to eliminate realized holding gains from FIFO income.

9. How to apply the lower of cost or market method and on what assumptions the method rests.

10. How and why the dollar-value LIFO method is applied.

cost of identical refrigerators increases to $340, and the retailer purchases another refrigerator at this $340 cost. At the end of the year the retailer sells one of the refrigerators to a consumer for $500. Further assume that it is not possible to ascertain which of the two refrigerators was actually sold.

It is easy to determine the total cost of the goods that were available for sale. This total cost is determined by adding the cost of the beginning inventory and the cost of any purchases during the period—that is,

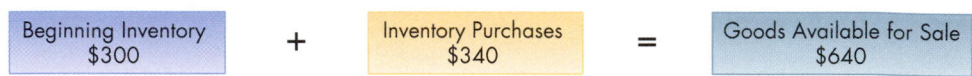

The total cost of the goods available for sale during the period was $640, a total that represents the aggregate *historical cost* of the two refrigerators.

The cost of the refrigerator that has been sold must be removed from the inventory account and charged to cost of goods sold, while the cost of the other refrigerator remains in inventory. In other words, the total cost of the goods available for sale ($640) must be allocated between ending inventory and cost of goods sold. This allocation process can be represented as follows:

The choice of the method for making this allocation between ending inventory and cost of goods sold represents the major issue in inventory accounting.

Even in this simple case, there are at least three ways the total for the goods available for sale ($640) can be allocated between ending inventory and cost of goods sold:

1. One is to assume the refrigerator that was sold should reflect the average of the cost of the two refrigerators ($640/2 = $320), which would make the allocation:

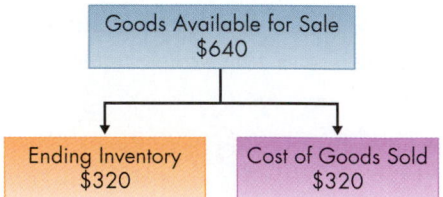

This is called the **weighted average** inventory costing method.

2. Another possibility is to assume that the refrigerator that was sold was the oldest refrigerator in stock—the $300 unit from the beginning inventory. This would mean the cost assigned to the refrigerator still on hand at the end of the year would be the $340 cost of the most recently purchased unit. Here, the allocation is:

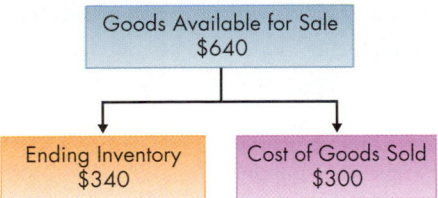

This method assumes the first unit purchased is the first unit sold. Accountants call this **first-in, first-out (FIFO).**

3. Yet another alternative is to assume the refrigerator that was sold was the most recently purchased refrigerator—the one costing $340. This would mean the cost assigned to the refrigerator still on hand at the end of the year would be the $300 cost of the oldest available unit that was in inventory at the start of the year, making the allocation:

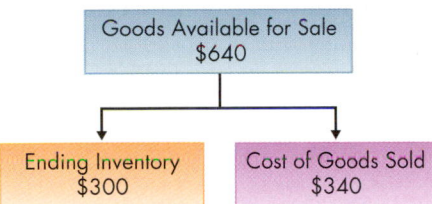

This method assumes the last unit purchased is the first unit sold. This is called **last-in, first-out (LIFO).**

Each of these cost allocations assumes a different flow of inventory costs—average cost, FIFO, or LIFO—from goods available for sale to the ending inventory account and to the cost of goods sold expense account; this is why these methods are called *cost flow assumptions*. GAAP does not require the *cost flow* assumption to correspond to the actual *physical flow* of inventory. ***If the cost of inventory never changed, all three cost flow assumptions would yield the same financial statement result.*** Also, under historical cost accounting, no matter what cost flow assumption is used, the total dollar amount allocated between cost of goods sold and ending inventory is always equal to the historical dollar cost of the goods available for sale ($640 in this case). This important point is shown in the following schedule:

> Even though the LIFO cost flow assumption is used by many firms, very few examples exist in which the real physical flow of units sold is also last-in, first-out. To see why, consider a grocery store. If the store actually sold the most recently acquired items first—a LIFO flow—the unsold items that were received earlier would soon become stale!

Cost Flow Assumption	Total Historical Cost of Goods Available for Sale	=	Amount Allocated to Ending Inventory	+	Amount Allocated to Cost of Goods Sold
Weighted average	$640	=	$320	+	$320
First-in, first-out (FIFO)	$640	=	$340	+	$300
Last-in, first-out (LIFO)	$640	=	$300	+	$340

Once an inventory cost flow assumption is selected, the cost of goods sold can be determined using the following formula:

> We don't discuss the weighted average method in the cost flow assumptions section later in the chapter because it generates numbers that are between the LIFO and FIFO approaches, and it introduces no additional issues. However, we do illustrate weighted average in more detail in the self-study problem at the end of the chapter.

Beginning Inventory	+	Inventory Purchases	=	Goods Available for Sale
Goods Available for Sale	−	Ending Inventory	=	Cost of Goods Sold

For example, assume that the FIFO cost flow assumption is selected, so ending inventory is $340. Then, cost of goods sold is calculated as:

Beginning inventory	$300
Inventory purchases	+340
Goods available for sale	640
Ending FIFO inventory	−340
Cost of goods sold	$300

This simple example should refresh your memory about basic inventory accounting points. But actual business situations are more complex and encompass issues such as:

- How should physical quantities in inventory be determined?
- What items should be included in ending inventory?
- What costs should be included in inventory purchases (and eventually in ending inventory)?
- What cost flow assumption should be used for allocating goods available for sale between cost of goods sold and ending inventory?

We discuss each of these complications next.

Determining Inventory Quantities

There are two different methods for determining inventory quantities—perpetual and periodic. A **perpetual inventory system** keeps a running (or "perpetual") record of the amount of inventory on hand. Purchases are debited to the inventory account itself, and the cost of units sold is removed from the inventory account as sales are made. Usually, these inventory records are maintained in both physical units and dollars. The physical amount of inventory on hand at any point in time should correspond to the unit balance in the inventory account.

The inventory T-account under a perpetual inventory system contains the following information at any point in time:

Inventory	
Beginning inventory (units and $s) Plus: Cost of units purchased (units and $s)	Minus: Cost of units transferred to cost of goods sold (units and $s)
Equals: Ending inventory on hand (units and $s)	

A **periodic inventory system** does not keep a running record of the amount of inventory on hand. Purchases are accumulated in a separate "inventory purchases" account and no entry is made at the time of sale to reflect cost of goods sold. The records for a periodic inventory system look like this:

Inventory		Inventory Purchases	
Beginning inventory ($s only)		Cost of units purchased ($s only)	

In a periodic inventory system, ending inventory and cost of goods must be determined by physically counting the goods on hand at the end of the period. The computation is:

To illustrate the accounting entries under each system, assume the following data:

Sales	$10,000
Beginning inventory	1,400
Inventory purchases	9,100
Ending inventory	3,500

The entries under the perpetual and periodic inventory systems are compared below.

Comparison of Entries—Perpetual Versus Periodic Inventory System

Perpetual Inventory System	Periodic Inventory System

Entry (1) To Record Purchases:

DR Inventory	$ 9,100		**DR** Inventory purchases	$ 9,100	
CR Accounts payable			**CR** Accounts payable		
(or cash)		$ 9,100	(or cash)		$ 9,100

Entry (2) To Record Sales:

DR Cash or			**DR** Cash or		
Accounts receivable	$10,000		Accounts receivable	$10,000	
CR Sales revenues		$10,000	**CR** Sales revenues		$10,000
DR Cost of goods sold	$ 7,000*		(NO ENTRY)		
CR Inventory		$ 7,000			

Entry (3) To Close the Accounts:

(NO ENTRY)		**DR** Inventory (ending)	$3,500	
		DR Cost of goods sold	7,000	
		CR Inventory (beginning)		$1,400
		CR Inventory purchases		9,100

*(Computed as Beginning inventory [$1,400] + Purchases [$9,100] – Ending inventory [$3,500] = Cost of goods sold [$7,000])

The inventory-related accounts would appear as follows under each method (entry numbers are indicated in parentheses):

PERPETUAL INVENTORY SYSTEM

Inventory					Cost of Goods Sold		
Beg. bal.	$1,400				(2)	$7,000	
(1)	9,100	(2)	$7,000				
					Sales		
End. bal.	$3,500					(2)	$10,000

PERIODIC INVENTORY SYSTEM

Inventory				Inventory Purchases			
Beg. bal.	$1,400			(1)	$9,100	(3)	$ 9,100
(3)	3,500	(3)	$1,400				
End. bal.	$3,500			End. Bal.	–0–		
Cost of Goods Sold				**Sales**			
(3)	$7,000					(2)	$10,000

Periodic inventory systems reduce recordkeeping, making these systems less costly to maintain. However, this cost advantage is achieved at the expense of far less management control over inventory. For those who use a periodic inventory system, there is no running inventory record, and quantities on hand must be determined by physical count. Furthermore, the cost of goods sold number under the periodic system is a "plug" figure—that is, the computation assumes that goods not on hand when the physical count is taken were sold. But some of the goods not on hand may have been stolen or wasted. Under the periodic system, there is no way to determine the extent of these potential losses.

A perpetual inventory system is more complicated and usually more expensive. It does not eliminate the need to take a physical inventory, since the book inventory figures must be verified for accuracy at least annually. But a perpetual system gives management greater control over inventories. For example, the running balance in inventory allows careful monitoring of stock levels. This is useful in avoiding stock-outs, particularly in manufacturing where "just-in-time" inventory purchasing is practiced. Furthermore, the comparisons that must be made between book inventories and physical count figures reveal discrepancies that may be attributable to theft, employee carelessness, or natural shrinkage.

Choosing between the two systems depends on weighing their costs and benefits. Perpetual inventory systems are typically used where:

- *a small number of inventory units, each with a high unit value, exists.* An example is vehicles at an automobile dealership.
- *continuous monitoring of inventory levels is essential.* An example is a production line where raw materials shortages would shut the operation down.

Periodic systems are used when inventory volumes are high and per-unit costs are low. However, the widespread use of computerized optical scanning equipment has led to the adoption of perpetual systems in supermarkets and other high-volume settings where such systems were previously not cost-effective. Wal-Mart and Costco were among the first companies to utilize optical scanning and perpetual inventory systems. These firms share the information captured by their electronic inventory management systems with suppliers who are authorized to automatically ship new merchandise directly to these retailers' stores when their inventory levels fall below prescribed minimum levels. This approach shortens inventory restocking cycles at Wal-Mart and Costco and reduces their need to warehouse inventories.

When the physical count reveals inventory shortages, the accounting records must be adjusted to conform to the actual amount on hand. If a shortage of $310 was indicated, the adjustment is:

DR Loss from inventory shortage $310
   (or Cost of goods sold)
   CR Inventory $310

One morning, a Costco store in Los Angeles began running a little low on size-one and size-two Huggies. Crisis loomed.

So what did Costco managers do? Nothing. They didn't have to, thanks to a special arrangement with Kimberly-Clark Corp., the company that makes the diapers.

Under this deal, responsibility for replenishing stock falls on the manufacturer, not Costco. In return, the big retailer shares detailed information about individual stores' sales. So, long before babies in Los Angeles would ever notice it, diaper dearth was averted by a Kimberly-Clark data analyst working at a computer hundreds of miles away in Neenah, Wis. . . . A Kimberly-Clark spokeswoman says the benefits of the program "more than offset" additional labor costs. Last year, Kimberly-Clark posted a 51% rise in net income to $1.67 billion on $13 billion in sales, capping three years of improving results.

For Costco, the benefits of such close cooperation with a major supplier are equally clear: Costco saves money not only on staffing in its inventory department, but also on storage.

Source: Republished with permission of Dow Jones & Co.; © 2000. From *Wall Street Journal*, "Kimberly-Clark Keeps Costco in Diapers, Absorbing Costs Itself" by E. Nelson and A. Zimmerman (September 7, 2000). Permission conveyed through Copyright Clearance Center, Inc.

Items Included in Inventory

All inventory items to which the firm has legal title should be included in the inventory account. However, in day-to-day operations, most firms do not attempt to use the passage of legal title as the criterion for including items in their inventory records, since this would be a time-consuming process. Instead, most firms record inventory only when they physically receive it.

This physical-receipt system creates no difficulties except when it comes time to prepare financial statements. At that time, the firm must determine whether all goods that were in fact legally owned have been included in the inventory account. Goods in transit are the primary concern, since legal title to such goods may transfer to the purchaser before they are physically received by the purchaser. The purchaser determines the legal status of goods in transit by examining invoices pertaining to goods received during the first few days of the next accounting period, and then uses this information to determine precisely when title passed.

Sometimes goods may be physically in the possession of a firm but not legally owned by the firm. One example is goods shipped on **consignment**. Here, the firm that holds the goods (the consignee) acts as an agent for the owner (the consignor) in selling the goods. The consignee receives a sales commission and forwards the net sales price (after deducting the commission and any selling expenses) to the consignor. Consignment goods should not be included in the inventory of the consignee; instead, they must appear as part of the inventory of the consignor, the legal owner.

> Consignment goods also raise potential revenue recognition issues for the consignor that analysts must consider. For example, manufacturers may ship products to their dealers on consignment and nevertheless try to treat such shipments as sales, thereby recognizing income prematurely. Consequently, if "sales" terms provide the "purchaser" with the right to return unsold goods or if the cash payment terms on the "sale" are unusually long, it is possible that the manufacturer has treated consignment shipments as sales, thereby overstating both sales revenues and income and understating inventory (see Chapter 3).

Costs Included in Inventory

The carrying cost of inventory should include all costs required to obtain physical possession of the merchandise and to make it saleable. This includes the purchase cost, sales taxes and transportation costs paid by the purchaser, insurance costs, and storage costs. For a manufacturing firm, inventory costs also include those production costs—such as labor and overhead—that are incurred in making a finished saleable product.[2]

In principle, inventory costs should also include the costs of the purchasing department and other general administrative costs associated with the acquisition and distribution of inventory. As a practical matter, however, such costs are extremely difficult to associate with individual purchases and would have to be allocated on some arbitrary basis. From a cost-benefit perspective, the effort that would be expended in trying to assign these indirect inventory costs to unit purchases generally exceeds the benefits. That's why inventory cost shown in the accounting records is usually limited to *direct* acquisition and processing costs that can be objectively associated with specific goods. Costs that do not meet this criterion—such as purchasing department costs—are generally treated as period costs and expensed in the period in which they arise. Furthermore, a cash purchase discount that is lost because of a late payment would be recorded as interest expense rather than as a cost of acquiring inventory.

> To illustrate, assume that on February 9, 2005 Hernandez Company purchased inventory with a list price of $1,000 subject to a 2% cash discount if the invoice was paid within ten days. Hernandez (like most companies) records the purchase at its net (after discount) cost of $980:
>
> | **DR** Inventory | $980 | |
> |---|---|---|
> | **CR** Accounts payable | | $980 |
>
> Due to an administrative oversight, the invoice is not paid until March 15, 2005. The entry Hernandez makes is:
>
> | **DR** Accounts payable | $980 | |
> |---|---|---|
> | **DR** Interest expense— | | |
> | purchase discount lost | 20 | |
> | **CR** Cash | | $1,000 |
>
> So the cost associated with the lost discount is charged to interest expense. The inventory carrying amount of these goods is $980.

---

[2] In certain cases, interest incurred during the time that inventory is being developed for sale can be capitalized, as described in Chapter 10. Examples include discrete projects such as shipbuilding or real estate development—that is, cases in which money is borrowed to finance construction over several reporting periods. See *Statement of Financial Accounting Standards (SFAS) No. 34*, "Capitalization of Interest Cost" (Stamford, CT: Financial Accounting Standards Board [FASB], October 1979).

Manufacturing Costs

The inventory costs of a manufacturer include raw material, labor, and certain overhead items. Costs of this type are called **product costs**. Product costs are assigned to inventory and treated as assets until the inventory is sold. When sold, the inventory carrying value is charged to cost of goods sold, and at that point all inventoried costs become an expense.

A manufacturer also incurs costs not considered to be closely associated with production. Examples include general administrative costs (such as the president's salary) and selling costs (say, the commissions earned by the firm's salespeople). These costs are not inventoried. Instead, they are treated as expenses of the period in which they are incurred and are called **period costs**.

The flow of product costs through the inventory accounts and, eventually, to the cost of goods sold account is illustrated in Exhibit 9.1.

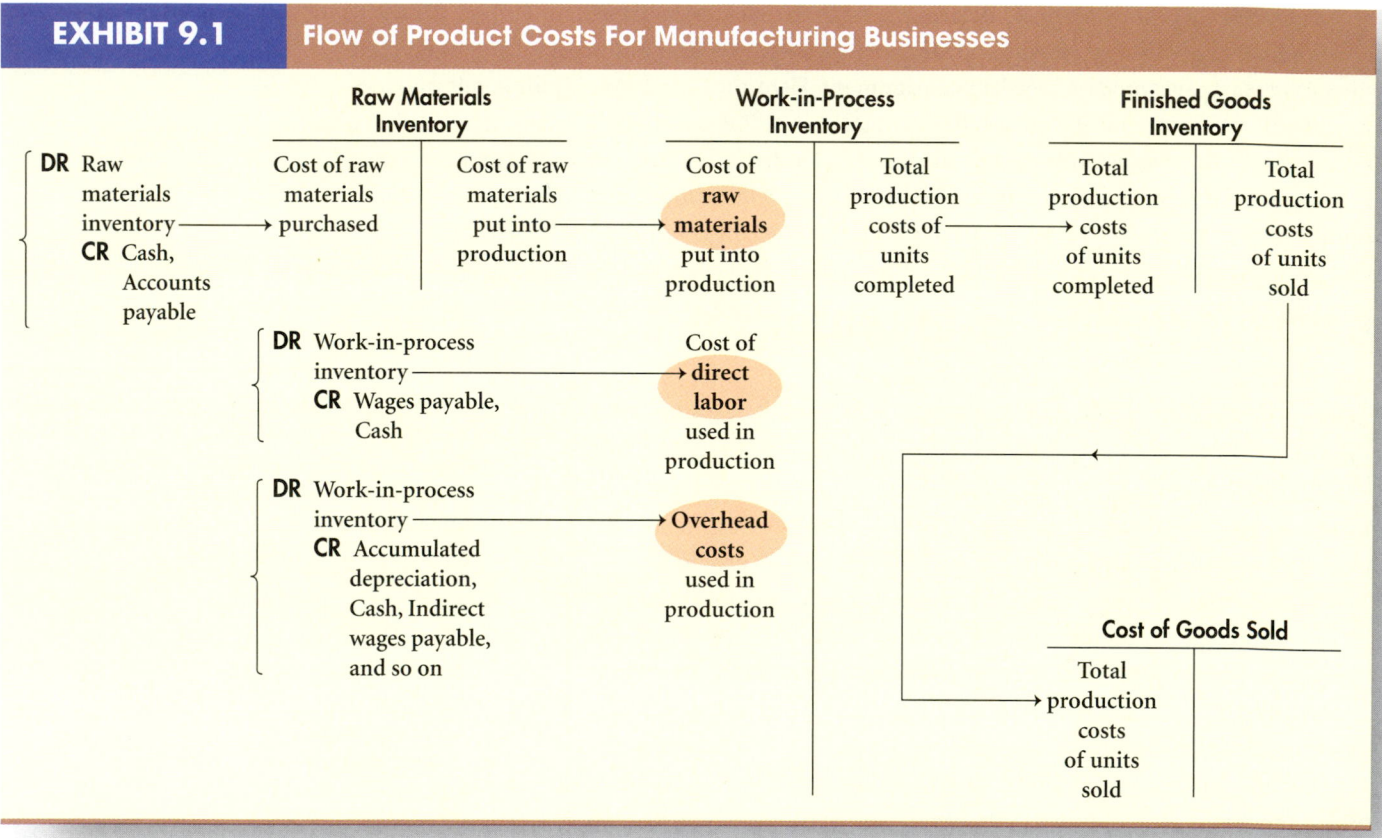

| **EXHIBIT 9.1** | **Flow of Product Costs For Manufacturing Businesses** |

Absorption Costing Versus Variable Costing

As indicated in Exhibit 9.1, manufacturing overhead costs comprise one element of product costs and are accordingly included in inventory. However, there are two views regarding the appropriate treatment of *fixed* manufacturing overhead costs. One view is called **variable costing** (or direct costing), while the other view is called **absorption costing** (or full costing).

Variable costing includes only the variable costs of production in inventory. **Variable costs** are those that change in proportion to the level of production. Examples include raw materials cost, direct labor, and certain overhead items such as electricity used in running production equipment. **Fixed costs** of production are costs that do not change as production levels change. Examples include rental of production facilities, depreciation of production equipment, and property taxes. *When variable costing is used, these fixed production overhead costs are not included as part of inventory cost.* Instead, fixed production overhead costs are treated as period costs and are expensed in the period in which they are incurred.

The logic underlying variable costing is that incurred costs are considered to be includable in inventory only if they provide future benefits to the firm. Proponents of variable costing argue that fixed production overhead costs are *not* assets since they expire in the period in which they are incurred and thus do not provide future benefit to the firm. For example, factory insurance carried in June provides no benefit after June 30; for insurance protection in July, another month's premium must be paid. But future benefits *do* derive from variable costs such as materials used in production; once materials have been purchased and used in making an inventory unit, that cost can be "stored" and will provide a future benefit when the inventory is eventually sold. These kinds of costs are considered to be includable in inventory under variable costing.

Under absorption costing, all production costs are inventoried. Fixed production overhead costs are not written off to expense as incurred. Instead they are treated as product costs and carried as assets in the appropriate inventory accounts. The rationale is that *both* variable and fixed production costs are assets since *both* are needed to produce a saleable product.

Both absorption costing and variable costing treat all selling, general, and administrative (SG&A) costs as period costs. These SG&A costs are *never* inventoried under *any* circumstances under either method. Exhibit 9.2 shows the treatment of costs by category under each inventory costing approach. The only cost category treated differently is fixed production overhead, which is highlighted in the table.

EXHIBIT 9.2	Summary of Cost Treatment by Category Under Variable and Absorption Costing	
Cost Category	**Inventoried under Variable Costing?**	**Inventoried under Absorption Costing?**
Production materials	Yes	Yes
Production labor	Yes	Yes
Variable production overhead	Yes	Yes
Fixed production overhead	No	Yes
Selling, general and administrative	No	No

The variable and absorption costing alternatives provide statement readers with potentially very different pictures of year-to-year changes in performance—that is, the trend of earnings over a series of years can differ markedly under the two approaches, as we will illustrate. These different earnings trends could influence analysts' forecasts. Analysts must understand the financial statement effects of *both* methods even though *generally accepted accounting principles do not allow variable costing to be used in external financial statements.* Accounting rules require inventory cost to include both fixed and variable production costs; therefore, *only absorption costing is permitted under GAAP.*

Unfortunately, absorption costing makes it difficult to interpret year-to-year changes in reported income. These problems arise when inventory levels change between one year and the next. This is illustrated in the example whose basic assumptions are shown in Exhibit 9.3 on page 446.

International Accounting Standards (IAS) also require the use of absorption costing. See *IAS 2* (revised 1993), "Inventories" (London: International Accounting Standards Board, 1993, para. 10.) GAAP in most non-U.S. settings also requires absorption costing. Mexican GAAP permits variable costing, but it is not widely used.

International

Valuation

| | EXHIBIT 9.3 | Absorption Versus Variable Costing Illustration |

Selling price and cost data:
Selling price = $8 per unit in both 2005 and 2006
Variable production costs = $3 per unit in both 2005 and 2006
Fixed production costs = $400,000 per year in both 2005 and 2006
Beginning inventory (FIFO basis), January 1, 2005 = 50,000 units @ $7

Production and sales volume data:	2005	2006
Units produced	100,000	125,000
Units sold	110,000	90,000
Ending inventory (in units)*	40,000	75,000

*Computations—2005: 50,000 + 100,000 − 110,000 = 40,000 units
2006: 40,000 + 125,000 − 90,000 = 75,000 units

In Exhibit 9.4, the fixed costs in inventory at January 1, 2006 totaled $160,000 (that is, 40,000 units times $4 of fixed cost per **unit**). At December 31, 2006, fixed cost included in inventory had risen to $240,000 (that is, 75,000 units times $3.20 of fixed cost per unit).

A research study found that firms in danger of producing zero earnings resort to (among other things) overproducing inventory in order to reduce cost of goods sold and thereby boost profits. So the evidence suggests that absorption costing provides opportunities for firms to manipulate profits opportunistically. See S. Roychowdhury, "Management of Earnings Through the Manipulation of Real Activities That Affect Cash Flow From Operations," unpublished paper, MIT (November 2003).

Companies rarely disclose absorption costing effects on income. But Vacu-Dry Company did in its 1996 Annual Report:

In fiscal 1995, the increase in the cost of sales percentage was predominantly due to the lower production volume as a result of the decreased sales volume and the resultant *decrease in overhead absorption.* [Emphasis added.]

Over the two years in the example, there was a constant selling price, constant variable production costs per unit and constant total fixed production costs. Units produced increased in 2006 (125,000 versus 100,000 in 2005), but units sold in 2006 dropped (90,000 versus 110,000 units in 2005).

Exhibit 9.4 shows that reported GAAP gross margin under FIFO absorption costing increases from $110,000 in 2005 to $130,000 in 2006—an 18.2% increase. Income *increases* despite the fact that variable production cost and selling price per unit were constant, fixed cost did not change in total, and unit sales decreased.

Why do we get this strange result? The answer reveals a major deficiency of absorption cost financial statements. Production increased in 2006 to 125,000 units and exceeded sales, which totaled 90,000 units. Inventory therefore increased by 35,000 units (125,000 minus 90,000) to a year-end total of 75,000 units. When inventory increases under absorption costing, as in this illustration, the amount of fixed cost assigned to inventory increases. **As inventory absorbs more fixed cost, less fixed cost gets charged to the income statement and income goes up.** Very large inventory increases produce a favorable income effect that can offset an unfavorable income effect caused, say, by a sales decrease. This is what happened in Exhibit 9.4, and it is this effect that explains the jump in 2006 income.

By contrast, variable cost income in Exhibit 9.4 falls from $150,000 in 2005 to $50,000 in 2006. Critics of absorption costing contend that in situations similar to this example, variable costing better reflects underlying economics. Nonetheless, external financial statements must conform to absorption costing, as required by GAAP.

Generalizing from this example, the mechanics of absorption costing can lead to year-to-year income changes that may delude the unwary. This can happen whenever production and sales are not in balance—that is, whenever physical inventory levels (in units) are either increasing or decreasing. When the number of units in inventory is increasing, absorption cost gross margins tend to rise. This effect may be so large that it could obscure offsetting unfavorable effects (for example, sales decreases or deteriorating efficiency) that are taking place simultaneously. When physical inventory levels are decreasing, absorption cost income tends to fall, since fixed overhead that was previously in inventory gets charged against income as part of the cost of goods sold.

EXHIBIT 9.4	Absorption Versus Variable Costing Statements: Contrasting The Outcomes

Absorption Cost Income Statements (GAAP)

	2005			2006	
Sales revenues (110,000 @ $8)		$880,000	Sales revenues (90,000 @ $8)		$720,000
Cost of goods sold:			Cost of goods sold:		
From beginning inventory			From beginning inventory		
(50,000 @ $7)	$350,000		(40,000 @ $7)	$280,000	
From 2005 production			From 2006 production		
(60,000 @ $7*)	420,000		(50,000 @ $6.20**)	310,000	
		(770,000)			(590,000)
GAAP gross margin		$110,000	GAAP gross margin		$130,000
Gross margin %		12.50%	Gross margin %		18.06%
Ending inventory: 40,000 units @ $7*			Ending inventory: 75,000 units @ $6.20**		

*This cost is determined as follows:		**This cost is determined as follows:	
Variable production		Variable production	
costs (given)	$3.00/unit	costs (given)	$3.00/unit
Fixed production		Fixed production	
costs, unitized		costs, unitized	
$400,000/100,000 =	4.00/unit	$400,000/125,000 =	3.20/unit
Total production cost		Total production cost	
for 2005	$7.00/unit	for 2006	$6.20/unit

Variable Cost Income Statements (Not GAAP)

	2005			2006	
Sales revenues (110,000 @ $8)		$880,000	Sales revenues (90,000 @ $8)		$720,000
Variable cost of goods sold:			Variable cost of goods sold:		
From beginning inventory			From beginning inventory		
(50,000 @ $3)	$150,000		(40,000 @ $3)	$120,000	
From 2005 production			From 2006 production		
(60,000 @ $3)	180,000		(50,000 @ $3)	150,000	
		(330,000)			(270,000)
Variable contribution margin		550,000	Variable contribution margin		$450,000
Less: Fixed production costs			Less: Fixed production costs		
treated as a period expense		(400,000)	treated as a period expense		(400,000)
Variable cost gross margin		$150,000	Variable cost gross margin		$ 50,000
Gross margin %		17.05%	Gross margin %		6.94%
Ending inventory: 40,000 units @ $3			Ending inventory: 75,000 units @ $3		

Here's an example of how an understanding of absorption costing can help careful analysts. In 2001 Intel Corporation's gross margin was 49.2%. According to a *New York Times* story, Intel management initially predicted that gross margins in the second quarter of 2002 would be 53%.[3] But one analyst warned his clients "that Intel's impressive margins were mostly a result of a buildup in inventory, not sales to end users, and that the margins were therefore unsustainable unless demand picked up."[4] Late in the second quarter, Intel reduced its profit margin forecast to 49% because of weak demand. "They continued to produce at high levels, which improved their gross margins, and then talked about efficiencies and productivity when it was only an inventory buildup," the analyst concluded.[5]

[3] G. Morgenson, "Far From Wall Street, Intel's Bad News Was No Surprise," *New York Times* (June 9, 2002).

[4] Ibid.

[5] Ibid.

> **RE|CAP**   To analyze comparative income statements, you must understand the mechanics of absorption costing and bear in mind that any imbalance between units produced and units sold may have a pronounced effect on reported income. Furthermore, the absorption cost income effect can obscure underlying economic changes of interest to statement readers. For example, a sudden, unexpected sales jump—clearly a good news event—may cause an inventory depletion. With GAAP absorption costing, the inventory reduction forces an additional dose of fixed overhead through the income statement, thereby masking part of the income benefit arising from the sales jump.

Cost Flow Assumptions: The Concepts

For most publicly held firms, inventory is continuously purchased in large quantities. It is difficult to determine which purchase lots correspond to the units that have been sold, especially in firms where manufacturing alters the form of the raw materials acquired. Consider an automobile manufacturer. It's not easy to know what specific steel purchase batch was used in the hood of a specific car.

But in a few industries, it is possible to identify which particular units have been sold. In retail businesses like jewelry stores and automobile dealerships, which sell a small number of high-value items, cost of goods sold can be measured by reference to the known cost of the actual units sold. This inventory accounting method is called **specific identification**. But this method suffers from a serious deficiency, since specific identification makes it relatively easy to manipulate income. Consider a large jewelry dealer with three identical watches in inventory that were acquired at three different purchase costs. Under the specific identification method, the reported profit on sale can be raised (or lowered) by simply delivering the lowest (or highest) cost watch. An inventory method allowing latitude like this is open to criticism.

Specific identification is usually not feasible for most businesses. Even when it is feasible, it has some serious drawbacks, as just illustrated. For these reasons, a **cost flow assumption** is usually required to allocate goods available for sale between ending inventory and cost of goods sold—that is,

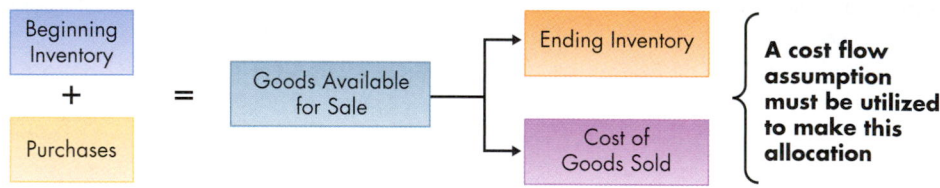

It is important to understand that GAAP does not require the cost flow assumption to conform to the actual physical flow of the goods.

<table>
<tr><td>

International Accounting Standards designate FIFO and weighted average cost as the "benchmark" treatments. LIFO is an "allowed alternative" treatment. (See *IAS 2*, paras. 21–23.)

</td></tr>
</table>

Six hundred companies were surveyed by the American Institute of Certified Public Accountants, and the inventory cost flow assumptions that they used, as shown in Exhibit 9.5, indicate two things. First, the most popular inventory costing method is FIFO, followed closely by LIFO; weighted average cost is the next most popular method. Second, the total frequencies of all methods exceed the total number of firms surveyed (600), which means most firms use a combination of inventory costing methods. For example, of the 255 firms using LIFO in 2002, only 6.7% (17 firms) exclusively used LIFO for all inventories, largely because LIFO is prohibited in most countries outside the United States. Thus, U.S.-domiciled multinational companies that use LIFO for domestic inventories would usually be required to use some other cost flow assumption for their foreign subsidiary inventories.

International

EXHIBIT 9.5	Frequency of Inventory Cost Flow Assumptions (1999–2002)			
	Number of Companies			
	2002	**2001**	**2000**	**1999**
Methods				
First-in, first-out (FIFO)	380	382	386	404
Last-in, first-out (LIFO)	255	265	283	301
Weighted average cost	165	180	180	176
Other	28	46	38	34
Use of LIFO				
All inventories	17	17	23	24
50% or more of inventories	121	130	148	159
Less than 50% of inventories	88	88	82	83
Not determinable	29	30	30	35
Companies Using LIFO	255	265	283	301

Source: Y. Iofe and M. C. Calderisi (eds.), *Accounting Trends and Techniques*, 2003. Copyright © 2003 by the American Institute of Certified Public Accountants, Inc. Reprinted with permission.

Let's revisit the refrigerator dealer to explore the underlying cost flow concepts. This simple example highlights key issues without cluttering the analysis with details that hinder comprehension. Recall the facts of the example.

> The retailer started the year with a beginning inventory of one refrigerator, which had an invoice cost of $300. During the year, the dealer-cost of identical refrigerators increased to $340. Assume that the retailer purchases another refrigerator at this $340 cost. At the end of the year, one of the two refrigerators is sold for $500.

First-In, First-Out (FIFO) Cost Flow

The first-in, first-out (FIFO) method assumes the oldest units available in inventory are the first units that are sold. This means that ending inventory on the FIFO basis will always consist of the cost of the most recently acquired units. In the refrigerator example, the computations are:

Income statement:		
Sales revenues	$500	
Cost of goods sold (FIFO)	300	(Cost of oldest unit)
Net income	$200	
Balance sheet:		
Ending inventory (FIFO)	$340	(Cost of newest unit)

FIFO cost flow for a more realistic case, one in which numerous purchases and sales are made throughout the year, is shown in Figure 9.1. The FIFO cost flow in this diagram illustrates that sales are presumed to have been made from the oldest available goods (in this case, from beginning inventory and the goods purchased in January through September) and that ending inventory consists of the most recently acquired goods (October through December).

Figure 9.1

FIFO COST FLOW

FIFO charges the oldest costs against revenues on the income statement. This characteristic is often viewed as a deficiency of the FIFO method, since the current cost of replacing the units sold is not being matched with current revenues. However, on the balance sheet, FIFO inventory represents the most recent purchases and—if inventory turnover is reasonably rapid—will usually approximate current replacement cost.

Last-In, First-Out (LIFO) Cost Flow

The last-in, first-out (LIFO) method presumes sales were made from the most recently acquired units. In the refrigerator example, the computations are:

Income statement:		
Sales revenues	$500	
Cost of goods sold (LIFO)	340	(Cost of newest unit)
Net income	$160	
Balance sheet:		
Ending inventory (LIFO)	$300	(Cost of oldest unit)

This method will seldom correspond to the actual physical flow of goods, but remember, GAAP does not require conformity between the assumed cost flow and the physical flow of units.

LIFO matches the most recently incurred costs against revenues. When purchases and sales occur continuously, the most recently incurred costs will be virtually identical to current replacement cost. So LIFO provides a good match between current costs and current revenues. But on the balance sheet, LIFO inventory consists of the oldest costs ($300 in the refrigerator example), which usually will not approximate the current replacement cost of inventory.

For firms that have used the LIFO method for many years, the LIFO inventory amount may reflect only a small fraction of what it would cost to replace this inventory at today's prices. A diagram of LIFO cost flow in Figure 9.2 shows how old **layers** can accumulate in ending inventory.

As Figure 9.2 shows, when purchases exceed sales in any year, a new LIFO layer is formed. New inventory layers are valued using the *oldest* costs incurred during that year. For example, the LIFO layer added in 2005 is comprised of the inventory purchase costs expended from January through March 2005. Since sales under LIFO are always presumed to have been made from the most recent purchases, the 2005 LIFO layer will remain on the books at the end of 2006 as long as units sold in 2006 do not exceed units purchased in 2006. As Figure 9.2 shows, not only did the 2005 LIFO layer remain, but a small additional LIFO layer was added in 2006, because unit purchases again exceeded unit sales. A firm that has been on LIFO since, say, 1954 could still be carrying a portion of its inventory at 1954 costs, a portion at 1955 costs, and so on.

Figure 9.2 LIFO COST FLOW

FIFO, LIFO, and Inventory Holding Gains

FIFO and LIFO give different financial statement results because each method treats inventory holding gains and losses in a different way. To understand the differences, we first need to understand inventory holding gains and losses.

Inventory holding gains and losses are the input cost changes that occur following the purchase of inventory. Let's go back to the refrigerator example. Assume the replacement cost of each refrigerator at the end of the year was $340. However, both FIFO and LIFO are historical cost methods, and therefore goods available for sale will reflect only the *historical cost* that was paid to acquire the two units on hand:

Beginning inventory (1 unit @ $300)	$300
Purchases (1 unit @ $340)	+ 340
Historical cost of goods available for sale	$640

Notice that historical cost accounting ignores the $40 holding gain that arose on the unit of beginning inventory as its replacement cost increased from $300 to $340. Thus, goods available for sale are shown at their historical cost of $640 rather than at their current replacement cost of $680 (that is, to replace the two units would cost $340 each).

There is an accounting method called **current cost accounting** that records holding gains on financial statements as they arise. ***Because it is a departure from historical cost, current cost accounting is not permitted in the basic financial statements.*** However, the FASB does allow voluntary supplementary disclosure of current cost data in the annual report.[6]

In a current cost (non-GAAP) accounting system, the following entry would be made at the time that inventory replacement cost increases:

DR	Inventory	$40	
	CR Unrealized holding gain		$40

---

[6] "Financial Reporting and Changing Prices," *Statement of Financial Accounting Standards No. 89* (Stamford, CT: FASB, 1986).

> The holding gain takes place as the replacement cost of the inventory increases. But since the gain has not yet been included in income, it is an **unrealized holding gain**. Once the gain gets included in income (as described in this section), it is a **realized holding gain**.

You may want to re-read Chapter 2, pp. 70–73 to review other comprehensive income.

The "Unrealized holding gain" account represents an owners' equity increase. Whether these holding gains should be treated as a component of net income or instead included in other comprehensive income is a controversial issue that we discuss in Chapter 18. In this chapter we ignore the controversy and treat holding gains as an element of other comprehensive income.

Once the holding gains entry has been made, the current cost of goods available for sale is:

Beginning inventory (1 unit @ $300)	$300
Increase in the replacement cost of beginning inventory	+40
Purchases (1 unit @ $340)	+340
Current cost of goods available for sale (2 units @ $340)	$680

When the unit is sold for $500, the partial financial statements under current cost are:

Income statement:	
Sales revenues	$500
Replacement cost of goods sold	
(1 unit @ $340)	340
Current cost operating profit	$160
Balance sheet:	
Ending inventory	$340

The current cost operating profit figure is the margin that results from matching current replacement cost against current revenues. It reflects the expected ongoing profitability of current operations at current levels of costs and selling prices.

Figure 9.3 contrasts the treatment of goods available for sale under (a) historical cost accounting and (b) current cost accounting. Notice that the total amount to be allocated between inventory and cost of goods sold is $40 higher under current costing ($680 versus $640). This difference is attributable to the holding gain that was added to goods available for sale under current costing. With current costing, the total to be allocated is carried at current cost (two units at $340 each, for a total of $680). *This means that the balance sheet inventory number and the cost of goods sold number are both shown at current cost.*

Figure 9.3

ALLOCATION OF GOODS AVAILABLE FOR SALE: HISTORICAL COSTING VERSUS CURRENT COSTING.

(a) Historical Cost of Goods Available for Sale = $640; and (b) Current Cost of Goods Available for Sale = $680.

By contrast, the historical cost figures for goods available for sale under both FIFO and LIFO ($640) are $40 less than the total current cost of the two units available ($680). This means that under either LIFO or FIFO it is impossible to simultaneously reflect both the balance sheet inventory *and* cost of goods sold at current cost: One can be shown at current cost, but the other must then be shown at historical cost. ***The primary difference between FIFO and LIFO is that each method makes a different choice regarding which element is shown at the out-of-date cost.*** FIFO shows inventory at approximately[7] current cost but is then forced to reflect cost of goods sold at historical cost. LIFO shows cost of goods sold at approximately current cost but is then forced to reflect inventory on the balance sheet at historical cost.

> Inventory quantity decreases—reductions in physical units in inventory—can produce a distortion known as a LIFO liquidation, discussed later in the chapter.

When input costs are rising, LIFO income will be lower than FIFO income as long as inventory quantities remain constant or increase. In the refrigerator example, LIFO income is $160, whereas FIFO income is $200 (see pp. 449–450). Income is *lower under LIFO because LIFO charges the new, higher cost units to cost of goods sold.*

The income number under LIFO will *usually* (but not always) closely approximate the income number under current costing:

LIFO Income		Current Cost Income	
Sales revenues	$500	Sales revenues	$500
Cost of goods sold	340	Replacement cost of goods sold	340
LIFO operating profit	$160	Current cost operating profit	$160

When purchases occur continuously, this near equivalence exists because LIFO charges the most recently acquired goods to cost of goods sold.

Now let's reexamine the FIFO income number. ***By charging the oldest costs to the income statement, FIFO automatically includes in income the holding gain on the unit that was sold.*** This result is seen by comparing the total income figures under FIFO and current costing:

FIFO Income		Current Cost Income	
Sales revenues	$500	Sales revenues	$500
Cost of goods sold	300	Replacement cost of goods sold	340
FIFO operating profit	$200	Current cost operating profit	$160

A comparison of the two income numbers shows that FIFO income is $40 higher. This $40 difference is, of course, the holding gain on the oldest refrigerator, which is the one that the FIFO assumption considers to have been sold. Another way to visualize this income difference is to decompose FIFO income into its component parts.

Components of FIFO Income	
Current cost operating profit	$160
Holding gain on unit considered sold	40
FIFO operating profit	$200

---

[7] In our example, FIFO inventory is shown at *exactly* current cost. In more complicated situations that occur in real organizations, FIFO inventory amounts will *approximate* current costs. The faster the inventory turnover (cost of goods sold divided by average inventory), the closer will be the correspondence between inventory at FIFO cost and inventory at replacement cost.

This reformulation tells us that FIFO income comprises two components:

- Current cost operating profit of $160
- A realized holding gain of $40 on the unit that was sold.

While these components are easy to extract in the refrigerator example, in actual financial statements the components of FIFO profit are not disclosed and only the total figure is reported.

Some analysts argue that by merging current cost operating profits and realized holding gains, FIFO gives misleading signals about the sustainable operating profits of the company. For example, operating profit is generally considered to be potentially sustainable if existing conditions continue. By contrast, holding gains are dependent on external price increases, which may or may not be sustainable. But FIFO gives the impression that operating profit is $200, thus suggesting that $200—not $160—is sustainable. Because the higher FIFO income number includes potentially unsustainable gains, that $40 portion of FIFO income is considered to represent low-quality earnings.[8]

But remember, LIFO is also an historical cost accounting method with its own deficiencies. There is only $640 (rather than $680) to allocate between cost of goods sold and inventory in our refrigerator example. Because LIFO allocates the most recent cost of $340 to the income statement, that leaves only $300—the old historical cost—for allocation to the balance sheet. Therefore, the LIFO balance sheet inventory number will not reflect current replacement cost. This leads to another set of issues that further cloud financial reporting. Let's examine them.

> Remember, the notion of "current cost operating profit" represents a matching against sales revenue of the then-current replacement cost of the inventory at the time of sale.

Analysis

> Technically, the SEC rule requires firms to disclose "the excess of replacement cost or current cost over stated LIFO value . . . " (see Regulation S-X, Rule 5–02). In practice, most firms do measure the LIFO reserve as the difference between the LIFO inventory carrying amount and the replacement cost of the inventory. However, some firms compute the LIFO reserve by taking the difference between inventory book value at LIFO and inventory book value at FIFO. Presumably, this is justified if inventory turnover is reasonably rapid because FIFO inventory will then approximate replacement cost. Consequently, both of these alternative computations of the LIFO reserve will usually result in similar amounts and thus comply with the SEC directive.

The LIFO Reserve Disclosure

Because LIFO inventory costs on the balance sheet frequently include old inventory layers, they are carried at amounts that are much lower than FIFO inventory amounts. This can make it very difficult to compare LIFO versus FIFO firms meaningfully. To remedy this difficulty, the Securities and Exchange Commission adopted a disclosure policy in 1974 that requires LIFO firms to disclose the dollar magnitude of the difference between LIFO and FIFO inventory costs. This disclosure is called the **LIFO reserve** and must be reported at each balance sheet date. Exhibit 9.6 illustrates a typical disclosure of this divergence between LIFO and FIFO inventory amounts for Aral Company. (This example is loosely based on the actual financial statements of a food processing firm that is no longer a free-standing entity.)

EXHIBIT 9.6	**Aral Company**	

Inventories footnote disclosure

	December 31	
	2005	2004
Raw materials	$ 792,000	$ 510,000
Work-in-process	1,808,000	1,315,000
Finished goods	4,100,000	4,425,000
Inventory at FIFO cost	6,700,000	6,250,000
Less: LIFO reserve	1,720,000	2,375,000
Inventory at LIFO cost	$4,980,000	$3,875,000

The disclosure in Exhibit 9.6 provides statement readers with an important tool. By adding the reported LIFO reserve amount at December 31, 2005 to the December 31, 2005 balance sheet LIFO

---

[8] See, for example, J. G. Siegel, "The 'Quality of Earnings' Concept—A Survey," *Financial Analysts Journal* (March–April 1982), pp. 60–68.

inventory number, one can estimate December 31, 2005 FIFO inventory. Specifically, the sum of the ending LIFO inventory ($4,980,000) and the fiscal year-end LIFO reserve ($1,720,000) totals $6,700,000. This sum represents an estimate of December 31, 2005 FIFO ending inventory of Aral Company. Notice that this result immediately follows from the definition of the LIFO reserve, which is the difference between FIFO inventory amounts and LIFO inventory amounts—that is,

$$\text{Inventory}_{\text{FIFO}} - \text{Inventory}_{\text{LIFO}} = \text{LIFO Reserve}$$
$$\$6,700,000 - \$4,980,000 = \$1,720,000$$

Therefore, rearranging the equation yields the following:

$$\text{Inventory}_{\text{FIFO}} = \text{Inventory}_{\text{LIFO}} + \text{LIFO Reserve}$$
$$\$6,700,000 = \$4,980,000 + \$1,720,000$$

Remember, this conversion to FIFO is an approximation. As long as inventory turns fairly rapidly, the approximation is close.

Thus, one can think of the FIFO inventory cost as being comprised of LIFO inventory cost plus a LIFO reserve adjustment which measures the difference between the current cost of inventory units and the historical cost of all LIFO layers. The LIFO reserve disclosure allows the analyst to convert reported LIFO inventory amounts to FIFO amounts. This adjustment can be performed for all dates for which LIFO reserve amounts are disclosed. To illustrate this point specifically, a similar adjustment using the beginning LIFO reserve disclosure in Exhibit 9.6 can also be made to estimate Aral's December 31, 2004 FIFO inventory:

$$\text{Inventory}_{\text{FIFO}} = \text{Inventory}_{\text{LIFO}} + \text{LIFO Reserve}$$
$$\$6,250,000 = \$3,875,000 + \$2,375,000$$

FIFO inventory at December 31, 2004 equals $6,250,000. This number is also, of course, the FIFO beginning inventory for January 1, 2005.

Using the LIFO reserve disclosure in this way also makes it possible for analysts to convert LIFO cost of goods sold to a FIFO basis. This is most easily understood by looking at the basic cost of goods sold formula in column (1) of Exhibit 9.7. Notice that both the beginning and ending inventory *and* the cost of goods sold amounts in column (1) are measured at LIFO. (Inventory purchases represent the actual events of the period and do not require a cost flow assumption.) Column (2) shows the addition of the respective LIFO reserves to beginning and ending LIFO inventory. As we just saw, the sum that results from this addition yields FIFO inventory amounts, which are shown in column (3). Using the basic cost of goods sold formula on the column (3) FIFO numbers plus actual purchases yields FIFO cost of goods sold. Thus, the LIFO reserve disclosures make it possible to convert LIFO cost of goods sold to a FIFO basis.

EXHIBIT 9.7	**Adjusting Cost of Goods Sold From LIFO to FIFO**	
(1)	**(2)**	**(3)**
Beginning Inventory$_{\text{LIFO}}$ Plus:	+ Beginning LIFO Reserve	= Beginning Inventory$_{\text{FIFO}}$ Plus:
Purchases Equals:		Purchases Equals:
Goods Available$_{\text{LIFO}}$ Minus:		Goods Available$_{\text{FIFO}}$ Minus:
Ending Inventory$_{\text{LIFO}}$ Equals:	+ Ending LIFO Reserve	= Ending Inventory$_{\text{FIFO}}$ Equals:
Cost of Goods Sold$_{\text{LIFO}}$	− Increase in LIFO Reserve or + Decrease in LIFO Reserve	= Costs of Goods Sold$_{\text{FIFO}}$

We apply this adjustment process to convert Aral Company's reported LIFO cost of goods sold number to a FIFO basis in Exhibit 9.8. Inventory purchases during 2005 are $22,165,000. FIFO cost of goods sold is $21,715,000. To make valid comparisons across firms that use different inventory accounting methods, you must make adjustments like those in Exhibit 9.8.

EXHIBIT 9.8	Aral Company			

Adjusting From LIFO to FIFO Cost of Goods Sold

($ in thousands)	As Reported in Financial Statements (LIFO)		LIFO Reserve		Adjusted to FIFO Basis
Beginning inventory, January 1, 2005	$ 3,875	+	$2,375	=	$ 6,250
Purchases	22,165				22,165
Goods available	26,040				28,415
Ending inventory, December 31, 2005	4,980	+	1,720	=	6,700
Cost of goods sold	$21,060	+	$ 655 decrease	=	$21,715

A shortcut procedure can be used to convert cost of goods sold from LIFO to FIFO. The shortcut focuses on the *change* in the LIFO reserve between the beginning and end of the year, as reflected in the bracketed area at the bottom of column (2) in Exhibit 9.7. (This shortcut avoids the need to successively add the respective LIFO reserve amounts to beginning and ending inventory.) Applying this shortcut adjustment to the Aral Company data given in Exhibit 9.8, we see that the change in the LIFO reserve was a *decrease* of $655,000 (that is, $2,375,000 at the start of the year versus $1,720,000 at the end of the year) and that FIFO cost of goods sold exceeds LIFO cost of goods sold by $655,000. So, when the LIFO reserve amount *decreases*, the shortcut conversion procedure is:

$$\text{Cost of goods sold}_{\text{LIFO}} \quad + \quad \text{Decrease in LIFO reserve} \quad = \quad \text{Cost of goods sold}_{\text{FIFO}}$$

When the LIFO reserve amount *increases*, the conversion is:

$$\text{Cost of goods sold}_{\text{LIFO}} \quad - \quad \text{Increase in LIFO reserve} \quad = \quad \text{Cost of goods sold}_{\text{FIFO}}$$

Aral uses LIFO for all of its inventory. But as we saw in Exhibit 9.5, most companies use a combination of inventory cost flow assumptions. This is illustrated in the following disclosure from the 2002 Winn-Dixie Stores, Inc., annual report:

Inventories are stated at the lower of cost or market. The "dollar value" last-in, first-out (LIFO) method is used to determine the cost of approximately 84% of inventories consisting primarily of merchandise in stores and distribution warehouses. Manufacturing, pharmacy and produce inventories are valued at the lower of first-in, first-out (FIFO) cost or market. . . . At June 26, 2002, inventories valued by the LIFO method would have been $215,873 higher ($220,411 higher at June 27, 2001) if they were stated at the lower of FIFO cost or market.

The LIFO-to-FIFO adjustment for a company like Winn-Dixie, which uses LIFO for only a portion of its inventory, is identical to the method used in Exhibit 9.8 for Aral Company. The beginning and ending LIFO reserves are added, respectively, to beginning and ending reported inventory amounts. It doesn't matter that LIFO was used for only 84% of the inventory. By adding the LIFO reserve to the reported inventory, *the LIFO portion is adjusted* and what results is inventory on a 100% FIFO basis.

There is no standardized GAAP format for disclosing the LIFO reserve. The format shown in 9.6 for Aral Company is often seen. Other firms disclose the LIFO reserve amount in narrative form, as Winn-Dixie did on page 456. Indeed, Winn-Dixie never used the term "LIFO reserve"; instead they revealed the reserve obliquely by stating how much higher the inventory dollar amount would have been under FIFO. Exhibit 9.9 shows yet another disclosure format from Finlay Enterprises, Inc., a jewelry retailer that uses LIFO for inventory reporting.

EXHIBIT 9.9	Illustrative LIFO Reserve Disclosure Format (Edited)

Finlay Enterprises, Inc.
NOTE 3—MERCHANDISE INVENTORIES
Merchandise inventories consisted of the following:

($ in thousands)	February 1, 2003	February 2, 2002
Jewelry goods—rings, watches and other fine jewelry (first-in, first-out ("FIFO") basis)	$275,339	$314,473
Less: Excess of FIFO cost over LIFO inventory value	11,795	9,965
LIFO Cost	$263,544	$304,508

Source: Finlay Enterprises, Inc. 2002 Annual Report.

Notice that Finlay—like Winn-Dixie—did not use the phrase "LIFO reserve" either.

A self-study problem intended to solidify your understanding of the different inventory accounting methods appears at the end of the chapter. You may wish to refer to it now.

RECAP

Under both FIFO and LIFO, the allocation of costs between ending inventory and cost of goods sold is limited to the *historical* costs incurred. As costs change, LIFO puts the "oldest" costs on the balance sheet, while FIFO runs the "oldest" costs through the income statement. The LIFO reserve disclosure permits analysts to transform LIFO financial statements to a FIFO basis, thus making comparisons between firms more meaningful when one firm is using LIFO and the other FIFO.

Inflation, LIFO Reserves, and the LIFO Effect on Income

Figure 9.4 provides descriptive statistics on the magnitude of LIFO reserves and the LIFO income effect for a broad cross-section of firms that used LIFO for all or part of their inventories from 1976 to 2001.[9] Figure 9.4(a) shows the median LIFO reserve amount stated as a percentage of stockholders' equity along with the 25th and 75th percentile values.[10] Figure 9.4(c) shows the median, 25th, and 75th percentile values of the *change* in LIFO reserve each year stated as a percentage of the absolute value of pre-tax income for that year. The change in LIFO reserve shows how much higher (or lower) the cost of goods sold is under LIFO as compared to FIFO and, hence,

[9] The 1976 to 1991 data for these graphs are adapted from R. Jennings, P. J. Simko, and R. B. Thompson, II, "Does LIFO Inventory Accounting Improve the Income Statement at the Expense of the Balance Sheet?" *Journal of Accounting Research* (Spring 1996), pp. 85–109. The data from 1992–1996 came from Standard & Poor's Research Insight,® and the 1997–2001 data came from Compustat®.

[10] The 75th percentile value is the value that is equal to or greater than the observation for 75% of the firms in the sample. Therefore, 25% of the firms will have an observed value that is *greater* than the 75th percentile.

how much lower (or higher) pre-tax LIFO income is as compared to FIFO income. Finally, Figure 9.4(b) relates the annual inflation rates (as measured by the percentage change in the Consumer Price Index) to the amounts reported in the (a) and (c) graphs over the 1976 to 2001 time period.

Figure 9.4

MAGNITUDE OF LIFO RESERVES AND LIFO EARNINGS EFFECT.

(a) Distribution of LIFO Reserve Amounts as a Percentage of Owners' Equity; (b) Percentage Change in CPI for Benchmark; and (c) LIFO Effect as Percentage of Pre-tax Income. (1976–2001).

Source: (a): R. Jennings, P. J. Simko, and R. B. Thompson, II, op. cit., 1976 to 1991; Standard & Poor's Research Insight®, 1992 to 1998; Compustat®, 1999–2001; (c) Standard and Poor's Research Insight®, 1976–1998; Compustat®, 1999–2001.

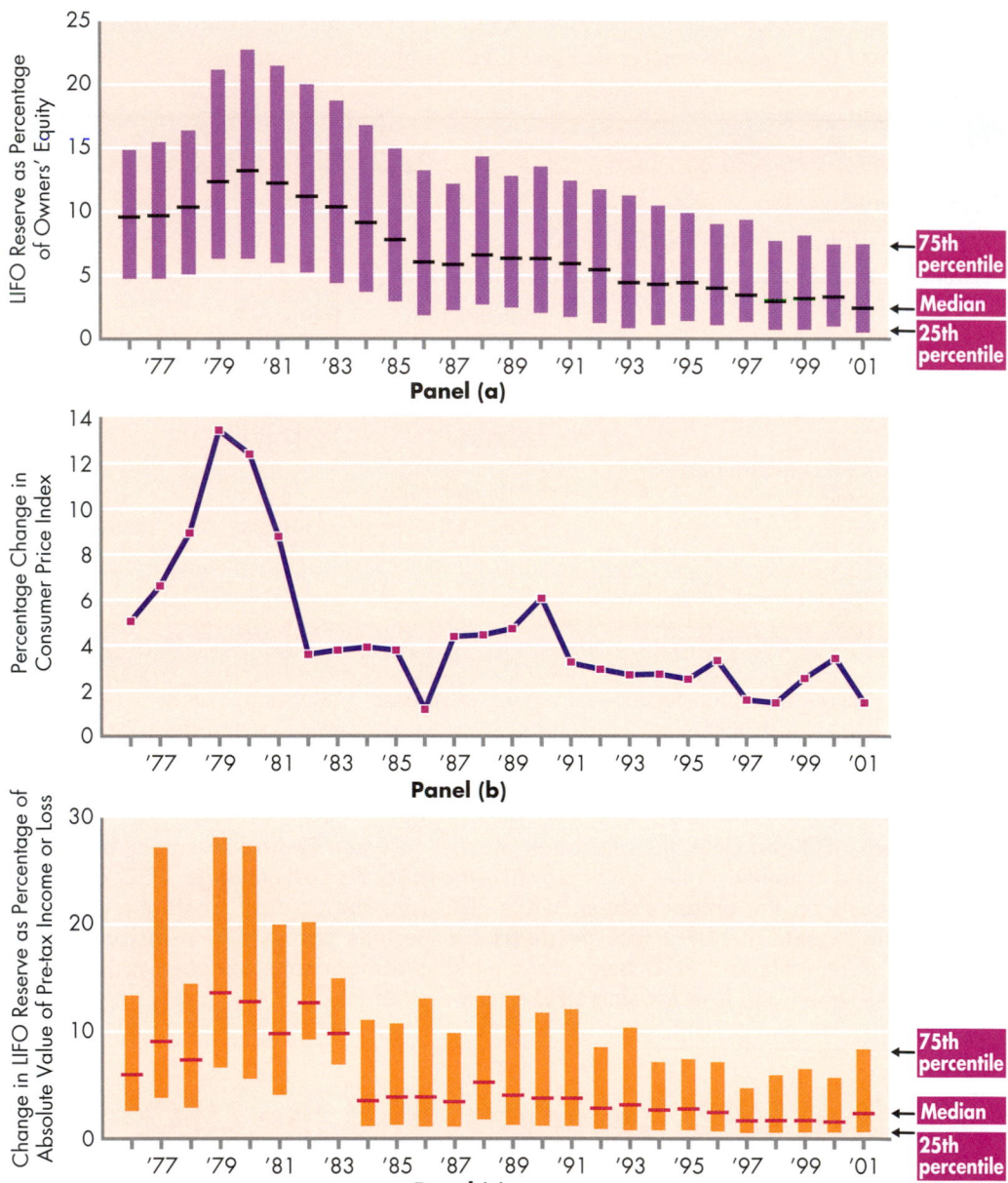

You may ask why the LIFO reserve amounts as a percentage of stockholders' equity show a general downward trend through the 1980s and early 1990s despite annual inflation rates from 4% to 6% in most years. With constant inventory levels (in units) and positive price increases from year to year, you would expect to see LIFO reserves that increase through time. The general downward trend in the LIFO reserve as a percentage of owners' equity from 1981 to 2001 can be explained by a combination of (1) the growing owners' equity through time; and (2) the increasing tendency of firms to reduce inventory *levels* throughout the 1980s and 1990s as they downsized and restructured their operations, and as they adopted just-in-time inventory management.

The median LIFO reserve in Figure 9.4(a) ranged from a high of 13.3% of stockholders' equity in 1980 to a low of 2.6% in 2001. Since stockholders' equity equals the book value of net assets (that is, assets minus liabilities), the results in Figure 9.4(a) also reveal how much *higher* the reported net assets of firms would have been had they valued their LIFO inventories under the FIFO method. Clearly, the decision to use the LIFO inventory method reduces the net asset values below what they would have reported under the FIFO inventory method.

The LIFO pre-tax income in Figure 9.4(c) was substantially *lower* than what firms would have reported under the FIFO inventory method throughout the 1976–2001 time period. The median pre-tax LIFO "earnings effect" ranged from a reduction of 13.6% in 1979 to a reduction of 1.6% in 2000. The higher LIFO reserves and larger LIFO earnings "drag" during 1976–1982 correspond to the relatively higher inflation rates in these years as compared to 1983–2001, as shown in Figure 9.4(b). This makes sense because you would expect the greatest differences between LIFO and FIFO inventory values and cost of goods sold amounts to occur during periods of significant price changes.

LIFO Liquidation

When a LIFO firm liquidates old LIFO layers, the net income number under LIFO can be seriously distorted. This is because the older (and usually lower) costs in the LIFO layers that are liquidated are "matched" against sales dollars that are stated at higher current prices. This results in an inflated or illusory profit margin. The following example illustrates the point.

> The difference between LIFO and FIFO income can still be significant for some firms even when the overall inflation rate is low. 2001 is an example. The 75th percentile value in Figure 9.4(c) for 2001 was 8.3%. This means that 25% of sample firms had a 2001 difference between LIFO income and FIFO income that exceeded 8.3% even though the rise in the consumer price index that year was only 1.55%.

The Bernazard Company had the following layers in its LIFO inventory at January 1, 2005, at which time the replacement cost of the inventory was $600 per unit.

Year LIFO Layer Added	Units	Unit Cost	Total	LIFO Reserve as of 1/1/05
2002	10	$300	$ 3,000	($600 – $300) × 10 = $ 3,000
2003	20	400	8,000	($600 – $400) × 20 = 4,000
2004	30	500	15,000	($600 – $500) × 30 = 3,000
	60		$26,000	$10,000

Bernazard sets its selling price by adding a $400 per unit markup to replacement cost at the time of sale. As of January 1, 2005, the replacement cost was $600 per unit; this cost remained constant throughout 2005. During 2005 the company purchased 45 units at a cost of $600 per unit, and it sold 80 units at a price of $1,000 per unit. Pre-tax LIFO income for 2005 is:

Sales revenues, 80 @ $1,000		$80,000
Cost of goods sold:		
2005 purchases, 45 @ $600	$27,000	
2004 purchases, 30 @ $500	15,000	
2003 purchases, 5 @ $400	2,000	
		44,000
LIFO gross margin		$36,000

Because the number of units sold (80) exceeded the number of units purchased in 2005 (45), Bernazard was forced to liquidate its entire 2004 LIFO layer (30 units) and five units from its 2003 LIFO layer. In such situations the income statement matching advantages of LIFO disappear. Indeed, a "mismatching" occurs since the reported LIFO margin per unit is $36,000 ÷ 80, or $450; this overstates the "real" current cost operating margin of $400 per unit. This $50 per unit overstatement of the margin occurs because some 2003 and 2004 purchase costs are being matched against 2005 revenues. If analysts use past margin numbers as a starting point in generating future cash flow estimates, the LIFO income number is misleading when dipping occurs. That is, the $450 *reported* LIFO unit margin overstates the current cost "*real*" margin of $400 used for pricing purposes and thus does not represent a sustainable expected future per-unit margin number. LIFO earnings that include LIFO dipping profits are considered to be lower quality earnings.[11] The illusory profit elements would generally be assigned a lower earnings multiple for valuation purposes. Research shows that security price reactions to earnings numbers that contain LIFO liquidation profits are smaller than the price reactions to earnings numbers that are devoid of these illusory profits.[12]

To understand better what happens when LIFO dipping occurs, let's examine the reported current cost operating margin for 2005:

Sales revenues (80 × $1,000)	$80,000
Replacement cost of goods sold (80 × $600)	48,000
Current cost operating margin (80 × $400)	$32,000

The 2005 LIFO income of $36,000 exceeds the 2005 current cost margin of $32,000. ***This "extra" LIFO income of $4,000 is the result of mismatching.*** In more technical terms, as LIFO layers are liquidated, some of the inventory holding gains of 2004 and 2003 that were ignored under historical cost LIFO in the years they occurred suddenly get recognized as income as the old, lower cost inventory layers are matched against current selling prices. This can be seen by examining the December 31, 2005 LIFO inventory computation:

Year LIFO Layer Added	Remaining Units	Unit Cost	Ending Inventory 12/31/05 Total	LIFO Reserve as of 12/31/05
2002	10	$300	$3,000	($600 − $300) × 10 = $3,000
2003	15	$400	6,000	($600 − $400) × 15 = 3,000
	25		$9,000	$6,000

The LIFO reserve was $10,000 at January 1, 2005 (see p. 459). Notice that the LIFO dipping has reduced the LIFO reserve to $6,000 at December 31, 2005. This $4,000 reduction in the LIFO reserve represents another way of visualizing how LIFO dipping creates a mismatching on the income statement. Previously ignored unrealized holding gains get included in income as Bernazard liquidates the old LIFO layers. The earnings "boost" of $4,000 is equal to the difference between the current cost to replace the liquidated layer of LIFO inventory (at date of sale) and the original cost of those units. This is demonstrated in Exhibit 9.10. When old LIFO layers are invaded, LIFO income jumps, but the increase is not sustainable.

EXHIBIT 9.10	Calculation of LIFO Liquidation Profits

Year Added	LIFO Layer Liquidated — Units Liquidated	Current Cost	Historical Cost	LIFO Liquidation Effect on Earnings
2004	30 ×	($600 −	$500) =	$3,000
2003	5 ×	($600 −	$400) =	1,000
Total increase in pre-tax earnings due to LIFO liquidation				$4,000

---

[11] For example, see Siegel, op. cit., pp. 60–68.

[12] T. Carroll, D. W. Collins, and W. B. Johnson, "The LIFO-FIFO Choice and the Quality of Earnings Signals" (working paper, University of Iowa, August 1997).

When the income effect of a LIFO liquidation is material, the SEC requires that the 10-K report disclose the dollar impact of LIFO dipping on income. Most companies that provide the 10-K disclosure also disclose the dollar impact of dipping in the annual report. The statement user should be alert to the fact that the earnings effect of LIFO dipping can be reported on either a *before-tax* or *after-tax* basis. Exhibit 9.11 shows this disclosure (on both a before- and after-tax basis) from Aral Company's 2005 annual report.

EXHIBIT 9.11	Aral Company

2005 Annual Report Disclosure of LIFO Dipping

During 2005, the Company liquidated certain LIFO inventories that were carried at lower costs prevailing in prior years. The effect of this liquidation was to increase earnings before income taxes by $2,600,000 ($1,690,000 increase in net earnings, or an increase of $.08 per share).

The LIFO dipping disclosure in Exhibit 9.11 indicates that 2005 earnings before income taxes were increased by $2,600,000 as a consequence of matching old LIFO layer costs against 2005 revenues. This number represents the *pre-tax* effect of LIFO liquidation, indicating that the reported LIFO gross margin in 2005 overstated sustainable earnings by $2,600,000. Equivalently, the LIFO cost of goods sold number was lower than current cost of goods sold by $2,600,000.

We are now able to explain more precisely what factors drive the LIFO–FIFO cost of goods sold (COGS) difference computed for Aral in Exhibit 9.8. As we see in that exhibit, FIFO cost of goods sold exceeds LIFO cost of goods sold by $655,000—the dollar decrease in the LIFO reserve. LIFO dipping reduces the LIFO reserve because old, lower cost LIFO layers are eliminated. But the LIFO reserve increases when input costs increase. So, to explain what causes the LIFO versus FIFO cost of goods sold difference, we need to explain what causes the change in the LIFO reserve. This is done in Exhibit 9.12.

EXHIBIT 9.12	Aral Company

Change in the LIFO Reserve

Beginning LIFO reserve, January 1, 2005	$2,375,000
Decrease in LIFO reserve due to LIFO dipping (Exhibit 9.11)	(2,600,000)
Increase in LIFO reserve due to increases in input costs during the year (Plug)	1,945,000
Ending LIFO reserve, December 31, 2005	$1,720,000

We know the beginning and ending balance of the reserve as well as the decrease caused by LIFO dipping. To reconcile to the December 31, 2005 LIFO reserve amount, the reserve had to increase by $1,945,000 (the "Plug" figure in Exhibit 9.12). This increase is attributable to rising input costs. So the $655,000 difference between the LIFO and FIFO cost of goods sold numbers can be explained as:

1. Rising input costs *increased* LIFO cost of goods sold by:	$1,945,000
2. LIFO dipping undercharged expense and thus *reduced* cost of goods sold by:	(2,600,000)
3. Result: FIFO cost of goods sold exceeds LIFO cost of goods sold by:	$ 655,000

Reconciling the LIFO reserve as in Exhibit 9.12 provides the analyst with information about the direction of input costs. When linked to other data, this cost information can be valuable. For example, if the analyst knows that input costs are rising but competition limits output price increases, the analyst can deduce that future margins will suffer.

The LIFO to FIFO adjustment is also used in trend analysis, as illustrated in Exhibit 9.13, where comparative gross profit data for Aral are shown for 2003 to 2005.

EXHIBIT 9.13	**Aral Company**		

Comparative Gross Profit Data as Reported

	Years Ended December 31		
($ in thousands)	2005	2004	2003
Net sales	$26,000	$25,000	$24,000
Cost of goods sold	21,060	21,000	20,400
Gross profit	$ 4,940	$ 4,000	$ 3,600
Gross profit as a percentage of sales	19.0%	16.0%	15.0%

The Exhibit 9.13 data show that the gross profit percentage rose slightly in 2004 and more dramatically in 2005. But we have also seen in Exhibit 9.11 that there was LIFO dipping in 2005, which increased the reported gross profit in 2005 over what it would have been without the liquidation. You might ask what the profit trend looks like after adjusting for LIFO dipping. We can extend the previous analysis to address this question, as shown in Exhibit 9.14.

EXHIBIT 9.14	**Aral Company**		

Gross Profit Data Adjusted for LIFO Dipping

	Years Ended December 31		
($ in thousands)	2005	2004	2003
Gross profit as reported	$ 4,940	$ 4,000	$ 3,600
Pre-tax effect of LIFO dipping on gross profit	2,600	—	—
Gross profit after eliminating LIFO dipping effect	$ 2,340	$ 4,000	$ 3,600
Net sales (as reported)	$26,000	$25,000	$24,000
Adjusted gross profit percentage	9.0%	16.0%	15.0%
Exhibit 9.13 gross profit percentage	19.0%	16.0%	15.0%
Difference	−10	N/A	N/A

The computations reveal that after removing the illusory income effect arising from LIFO dipping, the gross profit percentage for Aral shows a sharp decline in 2005. The adjusted gross profit percentage (highlighted in Exhibit 9.14) fell from 15.0% in 2003 to 9.0% in 2005. This deterioration is not immediately evident in the *reported* gross margin figures. Analysis of trend data provides potentially important information regarding management's performance in adapting to new market conditions. Neglecting to adjust the year-to-year data for nonsustainable factors (such as the artificial margin improvement that results from LIFO dipping) could easily lead to erroneous conclusions.

Consider one final point regarding Exhibit 9.14. Many analysts believe that the most recent margin percentage provides the least-biased estimate of the next year's margin percentage. (This belief is correct when margins follow a random-walk pattern. When they do, the best estimate of the next period's value is generated by simply extrapolating the most recently observed past value.) ***After eliminating the effects of LIFO dipping, the adjusted gross margin percentage provides a clearer picture of the underlying real sustainable gross margin in each year.*** Analysts trying to estimate Aral Company's future performance must understand that it is the 9.0% adjusted margin percentage—not the 19.0% unadjusted figure—that represents the starting point for estimating the sustainable margin in subsequent periods.

The Frequency of LIFO Liquidations

Figure 9.5 provides information regarding the frequency of LIFO liquidations from 1985 through 2001 for manufacturing and merchandising firms using LIFO. The vertical axis represents the percentage of firms that reported a LIFO liquidation in any given year. In most years, between 10% and 20% of firms using LIFO experience a LIFO liquidation; clearly, liquidations are not uncommon. Inventory costs tended to increase over this period. When LIFO dipping occurred, roughly 60% to 80% of the time the older costs that were matched against current revenues were below current replacement costs, as shown in Figure 9.6. This causes a transitory boost to earnings.

The Aral disclosure revealed both the pre-tax *and* after-tax income effect of LIFO dipping. Some companies only disclose the increase in net (after-tax) earnings. In these instances analysts can still easily convert the LIFO dipping effect to a pre-tax basis and evaluate year-to-year changes in gross margin.

Here's how. Assume that a company discloses that LIFO dipping increased its (after-tax) net income by $3,055,000. Further assume that the income tax rate is 35%. Then:

$$\text{After-tax effect} = \text{Pre-tax effect} \times (1 - \text{marginal tax rate})$$

or

$$\$3,055,000 = \text{Pre-tax effect} \times (1 - .35)$$

or

$$\frac{\$3,055,000}{.65} = \text{Pre-tax effect of } \$4,700,000$$

The $4,700,000 pre-tax impact of LIFO dipping would then be used to undertake an analysis like Exhibit 9.14.

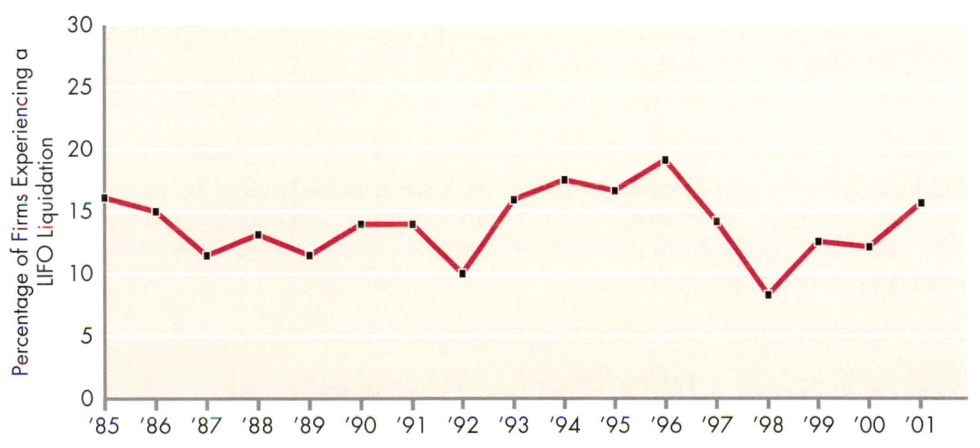

Figure 9.5

PERCENTAGE OF MANUFACTURING AND MERCHANDISING FIRMS USING LIFO AND EXPERIENCING A LIFO LIQUIDATION

Source: 1985–1993 data, *National Automated Accounting Research System (NAARS).* The NAARS service is offered jointly by Lexis-Nexis, a division of Reed Elsevier, Inc., and the American Institute of Certified Public Accountants; 1994–2001 data, 10-K Wizard® and Compustat®.

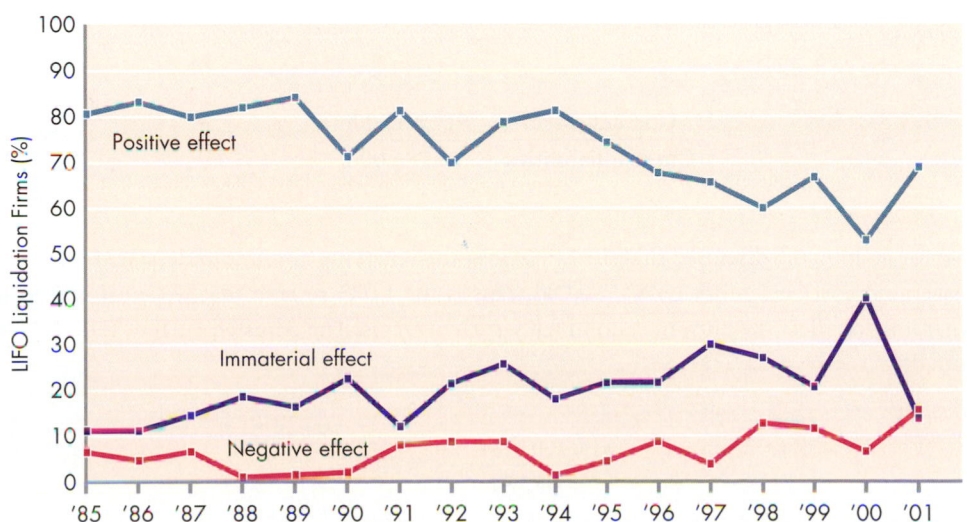

Figure 9.6

PERCENTAGE OF FIRMS WITH LIFO LIQUIDATIONS EXPERIENCING A POSITIVE, NEGATIVE, OR IMMATERIAL EFFECT ON PRE-TAX EARNINGS

Source: 1985–1993 data, *National Automated Accounting Research System (NAARS);* 1994–2001 data, 10-K Wizard®.

Figure 9.7 shows the earnings impact for those firms in the sample that reported LIFO liquidations with positive earnings effects. From 1985 to 2001, the median effect of LIFO dipping on pre-tax earnings ranged from a high of 10.4% in 1991 to a low of 2.0% in 2000. The numbers above the bars represent the 75th percentile of the distribution. So, for example, 25% of the firms with 1991 LIFO liquidations boosted pre-tax earnings by 36.8% or more. Clearly, LIFO liquidations occur frequently, and their impact on earnings is large enough to warrant close attention. To avoid being misled by transitory LIFO liquidation profits, statement users should carefully scrutinize the LIFO inventory footnote. The objective is to determine if a LIFO liquidation occurred during the period and, if so, what impact this had on reported profits for the period.

Figure 9.7

PRE-TAX EARNINGS EFFECT OF LIFO LIQUIDATIONS WITH POSITIVE EFFECTS ON EARNINGS

Source: 1985–1993 data, *National Automated Accounting Research System (NAARS)*; 1994–2001 data, 10-K Wizard®.

RECAP

LIFO liquidations occur frequently and often have a large impact on reported earnings. The earnings effect arises from a mismatching, since LIFO layers carried at "old" costs are matched against current period revenues. Reported margins are distorted and so is the income trend.

Eliminating LIFO Ratio Distortions

LIFO inventory costing can lead to ratio distortions that can be corrected easily. For example, on its December 31, 2005 balance sheet, Aral Company reported total current assets of $14,460,000 and total current liabilities of $5,784,000. Utilizing these numbers, the current ratio at December 31, 2005 is:

$$\frac{\text{Current assets}}{\text{Current liabilities}} = \frac{\$14,460,000}{\$5,784,000} = 2.5$$

However, Exhibit 9.6 disclosed that the LIFO inventory carrying amount understated FIFO (and replacement cost) inventory by $1,720,000. This is the LIFO reserve that we must add to the numerator to reflect the current ratio in truly *current* terms. The adjusted current ratio is ($000 omitted):

$$\frac{\$14,460 + \$1,720}{\$5,784} = 2.80$$

The current ratio improves after making the LIFO adjustment. Most other ratios deteriorate once the adjustments for LIFO effects are included. To illustrate the general deterioration, consider the inventory turnover ratio:

$$\frac{\text{Cost of goods sold}}{\text{Average inventory}} = \text{Inventory turnover}$$

The inventory turnover ratio is designed to reflect the physical turnover of product—that is, how long the typical unit remains in inventory. Most firms have many inventory categories. This diversity renders unit measures of inventory turnover meaningless since unit turnover is difficult to interpret in a diversified firm. That's why dollar—rather than unit—inventory measures are used to compute the turnover ratio. For Aral, using the inventory amounts from Exhibit 9.6 and cost of goods sold from Exhibit 9.8, inventory turnover for 2005 is ($000 omitted):

$$\frac{\$21,060}{(\$3,875 + \$4,980)/2} = 4.76 \text{ times per year}$$

The typical unit turns over 4.76 times per year. Another way to understand what this means is to divide 4.76 into 365, the number of days in a year. The result $365/4.76 = 76.7$ shows that the typical unit remains in inventory for 76.7 days.

The inventory turnover ratio is structured to approximate *physical* unit flow. The numerator is the cumulative dollar cost of units that have been sold; the denominator is the average cost of units on hand during the year. Under "normal" circumstances, the quotient should reflect the physical unit turnover. Unfortunately, LIFO frequently distorts the representation of physical unit flow. To see why, consider the denominator of the Aral ratio; it does *not* reflect the then-current cost of the inventory at either the beginning or end of 2005, since there was a LIFO reserve at both times—$2,375,000 and $1,720,000, respectively. For a firm using LIFO,

- the numerator of the ratio—cost of goods sold—is predominantly current period costs, here, 2005, and
- the denominator—average inventory—consists of old LIFO costs.

The quotient will not capture physical unit turnover unless an adjustment is made to the denominator. Furthermore, an adjustment to the numerator is also required here because the pre-tax impact of the LIFO dipping ($2,600,000) causes the cost of goods sold numerator to understate *current* cost of goods sold by this amount. To correctly gauge physical turnover, the analyst must *always* adjust the denominator of LIFO firms' turnover by adding the LIFO reserve amounts to beginning and ending inventory. In addition, the numerator must also be adjusted for LIFO liquidation profits whenever LIFO dipping occurs. The Aral 2005 inventory turnover ratio adjusting both the numerator and the denominator is ($000 omitted):

$$\frac{\overset{\text{(Reported cost of goods sold)}}{\$21,060} + \overset{\text{(Pre-tax effect of LIFO dipping)}}{\$2,600}}{[(\underset{\text{Beginning inventory}}{\$3,875} + \underset{\text{Beginning LIFO reserve}}{\$2,375}) + (\underset{\text{Ending inventory}}{\$4,980} + \underset{\text{Ending LIFO reserve}}{\$1,720})]/2} = 3.65$$

Dividing this LIFO adjusted turnover (3.65) into 365 days reveals that the typical unit, in fact, remains in inventory for 100 days—considerably longer than the 76.7 days suggested by the unadjusted analysis.

Tax Implications of LIFO

In the United States, the accounting principles that a firm uses in preparing its external financial statements need not be the same as the principles used in computing income taxes. The only exception to this statement occurs under LIFO. U.S. tax rules specify that if LIFO is used for tax purposes, the external financial statements must also use LIFO. This is called the **LIFO conformity rule**.

The LIFO conformity rule partially explains the widespread use of LIFO for financial reporting purposes. To gain the tax advantage of LIFO, firms must also use this method in their external financial statements.

> Footnote disclosure of the LIFO reserve, as required by GAAP, is allowed by the IRS.

LIFO's tax advantage is that it provides a lower income number than FIFO during periods of rising prices and nondecreasing inventory quantities, thus lowering the immediate tax liability. However, this effect can be reversed if LIFO layers are liquidated or if future purchase costs fall.

The dollar amount of the tax saving provided by LIFO can easily be computed by reference to the LIFO reserve number. For example, in Exhibit 9.6 we saw that Aral's LIFO reserve at December 31, 2005 was $1,720,000. This number is equal to the cumulative excess of LIFO cost of goods sold over what the cost of goods sold would have been if FIFO had been used. The $1,720,000 also represents the cumulative unrealized holding gain on the old LIFO layers. Under FIFO, the old, lower cost inventory would have been charged to cost of goods sold, thereby raising cumulative pre-tax income by this amount. Assuming an average tax rate over the past years of 40%, Aral has *postponed* approximately $688,000 in taxes (that is, $1,720,000 × 40%) since it began using LIFO.

> The marginal federal corporate tax rate immediately prior to 1986 was 46% and from 1986 to 1992 the rate was 34%. Since 1992 the rate has been 35%. With state and local taxes the overall marginal tax rates obviously would be even higher. We use a flat 40% rate to simplify the calculations.

The amount of taxes that companies can postpone by using LIFO can be substantial, as shown in Exhibit 9.15. This table lists the twelve firms with the largest LIFO reserves as of year-end 2002 together with their estimated tax savings (based on using a 40% marginal tax rate). As shown, the LIFO tax benefit ranges from $2.720 billion for Exxon Mobil Corporation to $277.6 million for Walgreen Company. The average amount of taxes postponed by these twelve firms was $647.5 million. Clearly, these companies have received a substantial cumulative cash flow benefit from using LIFO rather than FIFO.

EXHIBIT 9.15	Estimated Tax Savings for Firms with the Largest LIFO Reserves	
($ in millions)	2002 LIFO Reserve	Estimated Cumulative Tax Benefit*
Exxon Mobil Corp.	$6800	$2720.0
Caterpillar, Inc.	1977	790.8
General Motors Corp.	1807	722.8
ChevronTexaco Corp.	1578	631.2
MeadWestvaco Corp.	1130	452.0
Sunoco Inc.	962	384.8
Ford Motor Co.	957	382.8
Royal Dutch/Shell Group	955	382.0
Deere & Co.	948	379.2
Phelps Dodge Corp.	858	343.2
DaimlerChrysler AG	759	303.6
Walgreen Co.	694	277.6

*Based on an average marginal tax rate of 40%.
Source: Compustat® as data source; methodology not verified or controlled by Standard & Poor's.

Although clear cash flow benefits result from using LIFO, critics argue that LIFO may induce undesirable managerial behavior. This may happen if a firm has depleted its inventory quantities toward the end of a year. If inventories are allowed to remain at the depleted level, the tax liability could increase considerably because the liquidation of old, low-cost LIFO layers increases income. However, a manager can avoid this increase in taxes by simply purchasing a large amount of inventory at the end of the year in order to bring the inventory back up to beginning-of-year levels. Doing this to avoid tax increases may cause unwise purchasing behavior—excessive stocks may be carried, or year-end purchases may be made despite the fact that future purchase costs are expected to fall.[13]

Eliminating Realized Holding Gains for FIFO Firms

LIFO puts realized holding gains into income when old LIFO layers are eliminated. In contrast, reported income for FIFO firms *always* includes some realized holding gains during periods of rising inventory costs since FIFO charges the *oldest* inventory to cost of goods sold. Another way of saying the same thing is that FIFO cost of goods sold is understated because of the inventory holding gains that have occurred during the period. Since holding gains are potentially unsustainable, astute analysts try to remove them from reported FIFO income (or, equivalently, add them to FIFO costs of goods sold).

The size of the divergence between FIFO cost of goods sold and replacement cost of goods sold depends on two factors:

1. *The severity of input cost changes.* All other factors being equal, the greater the amount of cost change, the larger the divergence between FIFO and replacement cost of goods sold.
2. *The rapidity of physical inventory turnover.* The slower inventory turnover, the larger the divergence.

We illustrate a simple procedure to convert cost of goods sold from FIFO to replacement cost—and thereby eliminate realized holding gains from FIFO income.[14] The procedure requires an estimate of inventory cost change and assumes rapid inventory turnover. Consider the following example.

Ray Department Store experienced the following inventory transactions during 2005:

Beginning inventory (FIFO basis)	$1,000,000
Merchandise purchases	+8,000,000
Goods available for sale	9,000,000
Ending inventory (FIFO basis)	−1,100,000
Cost of goods sold (FIFO basis)	$7,900,000

Assume, on average, Ray's input costs for inventory increased by 10% during 2005. The adjustment procedure comprises three steps:

1. Determine FIFO cost of goods sold. In the example, this is $7,900,000. This amount is *not* adjusted.
2. Adjust the *beginning* inventory for one full year of specific price change. In the example, this is $1,000,000 times 10% or $100,000.
3. Determine the replacement cost of goods sold, which is the sum of the amount in step 1 ($7,900,000) and the amount in step 2 ($100,000)—that is, $8,000,000.

---

[13] Results consistent with the potential for tax-driven inventory management inefficiencies are reported in M. Frankel and R. Trezevant, "The Year-End LIFO Inventory Purchasing Decision: An Empirical Test," *The Accounting Review* (April 1994), pp. 382–398.

[14] See A. Falkenstein and R. L. Weil, "Replacement Cost Accounting: What Will Income Statements Based on the SEC Disclosures Show?—Part II," *Financial Analysts Journal* (March–April 1977), pp. 48–57. We have altered the Falkenstein and Weil procedural description slightly to simplify the exposition.

The difference between the computed replacement cost of goods sold ($8,000,000) and FIFO cost of goods sold ($7,900,000) equals the amount of realized holding gains included in the FIFO income figure ($100,000). This simple procedure gives results that accurately approximate tedious calculation approaches.

In Appendix A to this chapter, we provide an intuitive explanation for why this procedure for isolating realized holding gains for FIFO firms "works." We also discuss how analysts can use either price indices or competitors' data to estimate the rate of inventory cost change—10% in the example.)

Inventory Errors

Errors in computing inventory are rare and almost always accidental. For example, a computer programming mistake might assign the wrong costs to inventory items. But there are also occasional instances where companies deliberately (and fraudulently) misstate inventories to manipulate reported earnings. You must first understand how inventory errors affect reported results in order to understand why some managers use this misrepresentation technique.

To visualize the effect of inventory errors, let's assume that due to a miscount in the 2005 year-end physical inventory, Jones Corporation's ending inventory is *overstated* by $1 million. Further assume there are no other inventory errors. Using the cost of goods sold formula, we see that this error *understates* 2005 cost of goods sold by $1 million:

Effect of 2005 Error on:	
Beginning inventory	No error
Plus: Purchases	No error
Equals: Goods available	No error
Minus: Ending inventory	Overstated by $1 million
Equals: Cost of goods sold	Understated by $1 million

Because ending inventory is subtracted in the cost of goods sold computation, an overstatement of ending inventory leads to an understatement of cost of goods sold. By understating cost of goods sold by $1 million, pre-tax income is overstated by $1 million. Furthermore, if the error is not detected and corrected in 2005, the error will also cause 2006 pre-tax income to be misstated. The reason that the error carries over into 2006 is because the December 31, 2005 ending inventory becomes the January 1, 2006 beginning inventory. So the carryforward effect (assuming no other 2006 inventory errors) is:

Effect of 2005 Error on the 2006 COGS Computation:	
Beginning inventory	Overstated by $1 million
Plus: Purchases	No error
Equals: Goods available	Overstated by $1 million
Minus: Ending inventory	No error
Equals: Cost of goods sold	Overstated by $1 million

The overstatement of 2006 cost of goods sold (COGS) results in a $1 million understatement of 2006 pre-tax income. The carryforward effect in 2006 is equal in amount but in the opposite direction from the 2005 effect. Because the first year's income is overstated by $1 million and the second year's income is understated by the same amount, by December 31, 2006—the end of the two-year cycle—the retained earnings account (which is cumulative, of course) will be correct.

If an inventory error is discovered during the reporting year, it is corrected immediately. However, if an error is not discovered until a subsequent year (say, 2006 in our example), then the retained earnings balance as of the beginning of the discovery year (2006) is corrected. If the error has a material effect on the company's financial statements, it must be separately disclosed.

In recent years, the media have coined the phrase "accounting irregularities." Some of these irregularities simply relate to exuberant use of the flexibility within GAAP; others involve fraud. Accounting fraud is relatively rare, but it does happen. And some of the more spectacular frauds involve inventory misstatement. Leslie Fay Companies, Inc., is an example. The company manufactures women's apparel. 1992 was expected to be a difficult year for the firm because of pricing and style issues. To offset the emerging profit shortfall, quarter-end inventory was overstated. As we just saw, overstating ending inventory decreases cost of goods sold, increases income, and masks the adverse real conditions facing the company. Subsequent shareholder litigation alleged that this behavior was partly motivated by a bonus plan tied to reported profits.[15] But as our numerical example illustrates, the phony earnings boost in the overstatement year reverses in the following year. So if the economic adversity that motivated the deliberate initial inventory overstatement continues, the inventory overstatements have to continue as well.

This is exactly what happened at Comptronix Corporation, an electronics manufacturer who lost an important customer in 1989.[16] After succumbing to the temptation of overstating profits by overstating inventory, the practice could not be abandoned without causing a reversal. So the overstatement continued until late 1992.[17] The fraud was eventually discovered at both companies. Can analysts be successful detectives and uncover these situations? For outsiders, fraud is difficult to detect. But, there are sometimes clues.[18] For example, the reduction in cost of goods sold arising from inventory overstatement increases gross margins. So an unexplained increase in gross margins during troubled economic times is suspicious and warrants investigation.

> If we assume that Jones Corporation's inventory error was discovered in January 2006 and that the income tax rate is 35%, the entry to correct the error is:
>
> **DR** Retained earnings $650,000
> **DR** Income tax payable 350,000
> **CR** Inventory $1,000,000

Analysis

> Using the perpetual method defeats the purpose of LIFO. Here's why. Suppose a calendar year firm makes a sale on January 4 and uses the perpetual method; under LIFO, the units sold are presumed to come from the most recent purchase, say January 3. But if the firm instead uses the periodic method and computes cost of goods sold on December 31, those early-in-the-year January purchases will be the *oldest* purchases and less likely to be considered sold. So perpetual LIFO is seldom used.

Contracting

Analytical Insights: LIFO Dangers

LIFO makes it possible to manage earnings. To see how, consider a firm that has an executive bonus plan linked to earnings per share, as depicted in Figure 7.6 on p. 351. Assume it is December 15, 2005, the firm reports on a calendar year basis, and the managers expect EPS for 2005 to be $4.40. (Since year-end is only two weeks away, this estimate is likely to be very accurate.) As described in Chapter 7, the bonus "tops-out" at $4.00 per share. From the managers' perspective, 40¢ of expected earnings is "wasted" in the sense that it doesn't increase bonus payouts. So the executives have an incentive to "manage down" reported earnings back toward $4.00. LIFO makes this easy to do when input costs are rising. Here's why.

LIFO is applied using the periodic inventory method. Firms wait until the end of the year to compute cost of goods sold. So inventory purchased on December 31, 2005 is the "last-in" and is considered to be the "first-out" when LIFO cost of goods sold is computed. Similarly, inventory purchased on December 30 is considered to have been sold next, and so on. Since input costs are

[15] L. Vickery, "Leslie Fay's Ex-Financial Chief, Polishan, Is Found Guilty of Fraud," *Wall Street Journal* (July 7, 2000).

[16] See C. Mulford and E. Comiskey, *Financial Warnings* (New York: John Wiley & Sons, Inc., 1996), pp. 228–33.

[17] For a comprehensive discussion of the accounting issues at Comptronix, see J. L. Boockholdt, "Comptronix, Inc.: An Audit Case Involving Fraud," *Issues in Accounting Education* (February 2000), pp. 105–28.

[18] For a discussion of these clues, see Mulford and Comiskey, op. cit.

rising, if the managers buy unneeded, higher-cost inventory during the last two weeks of 2005, this will raise cost of goods sold, lower income, and drive EPS down toward $4.00. Lowering earnings in this way doesn't decrease their bonus so long as they don't let EPS fall below $4.00. But this unneeded inventory *does* increase inventory carrying costs as well as the risk of loss from obsolescence and spoilage. So managers don't suffer from the inventory buildup but shareholders do.

But the story isn't over. In 2006 the firm now has too much inventory—remember, the purchases at the end of 2005 were unneeded. So in 2006, managers reduce inventory down to proper levels—a LIFO liquidation occurs. If input costs and output prices move together (that's the norm), then 2006 selling prices are higher than those in 2005. The LIFO dipping in 2006 results in old, low-cost, early 2005 purchases being matched against higher 2006 selling prices. This artificially raises 2006 income. So it's a win-win situation for the managers! Playing this 2005 year-end LIFO game costs the managers no 2005 bonus and promises to increase 2006 income. At the end of 2005 they can't accurately forecast 2006 income. It might be below $3.00 per share, out of the bonus range. But the LIFO dipping income might be enough to raise 2006 income above $3.00 per share—back into the bonus range. The effect of the income shift from 2005 into 2006 improves the likelihood that the managers will earn a bonus in 2006.

> Remember, under LIFO, 2005 cost of goods sold assumed December purchases were sold first, then November, and so on, working backward through the year. The new LIFO inventory layers added during the last two weeks of 2005 are costed out at cost levels in effect early in 2005, say, costs incurred in January and February.

To see the full range of earnings management "dangers" using LIFO, let's go to a totally new scenario. It's November 15, 2005. Again there's a bonus plan like the one in Figure 7.6 and input costs and output prices have been rising. But here, assume that forecasted EPS is only $2.60. At this earnings level, the managers won't qualify for a bonus. But if the managers deliberately stop normal purchases for the last six weeks of the year, LIFO layers will be depleted. Again a mismatching occurs as December sales revenues are matched against pre-November 15 costs. When this is done aggressively, EPS can be driven into the bonus area above $3.00 per share. But do managers engage in this type of deliberate LIFO dipping? Unfortunately, research evidence here is sparse. However, if bonus contracts do not subtract out LIFO dipping "profits," there is an incentive to dip deliberately.

Empirical Evidence on Inventory Policy Choice

LIFO provides significant tax benefits when costs are rising. To obtain these tax benefits, Congress specified that companies must use LIFO not just for tax purposes but for financial reporting as well. Despite this constraint, only about 43% of companies in an AICPA survey use LIFO, as shown in Exhibit 9.5. Since costs have tended to rise consistently over most of the past 60 years, you can ask why the other 57% of companies do *not* use LIFO. Are they squandering available tax benefits? Why many companies do not use LIFO has intrigued accounting researchers for years. Conjectures about why some companies do not use LIFO include the following:[19]

1. The estimated tax savings from using LIFO are too small to justify the added complexity of the LIFO approach. There are two possible reasons for small tax savings:

   a. Inventory holding gains are trivial for non-LIFO firms.
   b. These non-LIFO firms have large tax loss carryforwards and are not currently paying taxes.

---

[19] See B. E. Cushing and M. J. LeClere, "Evidence on the Determinants of Inventory Accounting Policy Choice," *The Accounting Review* (April 1992), pp. 355–66.

2. Firms in cyclical industries that are subject to extreme fluctuations in physical inventory levels would find LIFO unattractive because of the high probability of LIFO liquidations and consequent adverse tax effects.

3. Inventory obsolescence poses difficult issues under LIFO; consequently, firms subject to a high rate of inventory obsolescence may be reluctant to adopt LIFO.

4. During periods of generally rising prices, LIFO leads to lower profits. Managers may be reluctant to adopt LIFO under these conditions for either one—or both—of the following reasons:

    a. They believe that lower LIFO earnings will lead to lower stock price.

    b. They believe that the lower LIFO earnings will lead to lower compensation, since management bonuses are often linked to reported earnings.

5. In a period of rising prices, LIFO causes certain ratios used in loan agreements to deteriorate—for example, the leverage ratio. Firms might be reluctant to adopt LIFO because adoption could result in loan covenant violations.

6. Smaller firms might not adopt LIFO because of the higher costs associated with maintaining the more complicated LIFO accounting records.

Research evidence is consistent with many (but not all) of these conjectures about why some firms don't use LIFO. Several studies have found that the potential inventory holding gains are much higher for LIFO firms than for non-LIFO firms.[20] Accordingly, the tax saving for LIFO adopters is much higher than the potential savings for firms not using LIFO. Furthermore, non-LIFO firms generally have significantly larger tax loss carryforwards than LIFO firms, thereby obviating the need to adopt LIFO.[21] Research evidence is also generally consistent with the fact that LIFO adopters have lower levels of inventory fluctuations[22] and lower leverage in comparison with non-LIFO adopters.[23] In the aggregate, these studies suggest rational economic explanations for the behavior of firms who do not adopt LIFO.

Another aspect of inventory accounting that has intrigued researchers is whether the stock market differentiates between LIFO earnings and FIFO earnings. In inflationary periods LIFO firms would—on average—report lower profits than FIFO firms but would have higher after-tax cash flows. From an economic perspective the LIFO firms are better off, despite the lower reported earnings. Furthermore, the quality of reported LIFO earnings is presumably higher than FIFO earnings, since LIFO earnings usually exclude inventory holding gains from net income; accordingly, LIFO earnings are presumably more sustainable than FIFO earnings during inflationary periods. Thus, the research question is whether investors differentiate between the quality of LIFO versus FIFO earnings or, instead, simply penalize LIFO firms for their lower reported earnings.

Many of the early studies of market reaction to LIFO versus FIFO examined instances in which firms switched from FIFO to LIFO as inflation accelerated. The research question frequently posed was:

> If the market simply reacts to bottom-line earnings, then stock prices of firms shifting to LIFO should, on average, fall. On the other hand, if the market considers earnings *quality,* then the relatively higher reported (and expected future) after-tax cash flows of new LIFO adopters should lead—on average—to stock price increases as the switch is announced.

---

[20] Two examples of such studies are Cushing and LeClere, ibid., and N. Dopuch and M. Pincus, "Evidence on the Choice of Inventory Accounting Methods: LIFO vs. FIFO," *Journal of Accounting Research* (Spring 1988), pp. 28–59.

[21] Cushing and LeClere, ibid., and F. W. Lindahl, "Dynamic Analysis of Inventory Accounting Choice," *Journal of Accounting Research* (Autumn 1989), pp. 201–26.

[22] Examples include Dopuch and Pincus, op. cit., and C. J. Lee and D. A. Hsieh, "Choice of Inventory Accounting Methods: Comparative Analysis of Alternative Hypotheses," *Journal of Accounting Research* (Autumn 1985), pp. 468–85.

[23] Examples include Lindahl, op. cit., and Cushing and LeClere, op. cit.

Researchers studied the stock price reaction to announcements by firms that switched to LIFO as well as to the announcements of the new LIFO earnings numbers. These studies generated conflicting results, probably because of the failure to control for other factors influencing stock price behavior during the year of the inventory switch.

A more recent study that included such controls found consistent evidence that the market perceives LIFO earnings to be of higher quality than FIFO earnings.[24] This study produced the following findings:

1. When reported earnings include highly transitory inventory holding gains (either under FIFO or when LIFO liquidation occurs), the market perceives these earnings to be of lower quality. Thus, the share price increase is small relative to when high-quality (sustainable) earnings are reported.
2. The market response to earnings news is greater after LIFO adoption. This suggests that the market believes that LIFO produces a higher quality earnings signal.
3. Across all firms, there is a higher market response to a given dollar amount of earnings-surprise under LIFO in comparison to FIFO. Again, this result is consistent with LIFO being perceived as the higher quality earnings number.

SUMMARY

This chapter helps readers understand existing GAAP inventory methods and disclosures. It can also help readers compare and analyze profitability and net asset positions across firms that use different inventory methods. Here are the important messages from this chapter.

- Absorption costing can lead to potentially misleading period-to-period income changes whenever inventories increase or decrease sharply.
- Financial reporting rules allow firms latitude in selecting a cost flow assumption for determining the cost of goods sold reported on the income statement and the inventory values reported on the balance sheet. Some firms use FIFO, some use LIFO, and some use weighted average costing; others use a combination of these methods.
- This diversity in practice can severely hinder interfirm comparisons when inventory purchase costs are changing over time, which is usually the case. Before undertaking inter-firm comparisons, numbers for the LIFO firms should be transformed to the FIFO basis.
- Reported FIFO income merges together sustainable operating profits and potentially unsustainable realized holding gains. Analysts must disentangle these elements when preparing cash flow forecasts.
- Similarly, LIFO dipping distorts reported margins because it matches "old" costs with current selling prices.
- Old, out-of-date LIFO inventory carrying amounts can distort various ratios like inventory turnover. Analysts should use the LIFO reserve to adjust inventories before computing ratio values.
- Users of financial statements must understand these differences and know how to adjust for them using various footnote disclosures. Only by doing so can valid comparisons be made across firms that utilize different inventory cost flow assumptions.

SELF-STUDY PROBLEM

MITSURU CORPORATION

Mitsuru Corporation began business operations on January 1, 2005 as a wholesaler of macadamia nuts. Its purchase and sales transactions for 2005 are listed in Exhibit 9.16. Mitsuru uses a periodic inventory system.

---

[24] Carroll, Collins, and Johnson, op. cit. Additional evidence on how the market values LIFO versus FIFO earnings can be found in Jennings, Simko, and Thompson, op. cit.

EXHIBIT 9.16	Mitsuru Corporation

Inventory Purchases and Sales

| Date | Purchases | | | Sales |
	Pounds	Dollars/Pound	Total Dollars	Pounds
January 1	1,000	$10.00	$ 10,000	
February 3	4,000	10.20	40,800	
February 9				3,600
April 1	4,000	10.30	41,200	
May 29				3,500
June 28	5,000	10.40	52,000	
July 20				4,100
September 14	5,000	10.50	52,500	
September 17				4,200
December 18	4,000	10.60	42,400	
December 22				3,600
	23,000		$238,900	19,000

1. **Compute 2005 ending inventory and cost of goods sold for Mitsuru Corporation using the weighted average cost flow assumption.**

Ending inventory totals 4,000 pounds—that is, purchases of 23,000 pounds minus sales of 19,000 pounds. The average cost per pound (rounded) is:

$$\frac{\text{Total cost of goods available for sale} \rightarrow \$238,900}{\text{Total pounds available for sale} \quad \rightarrow \quad 23,000} = \$10.39/\text{pound}$$

Ending inventory is 4,000 pounds times $10.39 or $41,560. Cost of goods sold is then determined as follows:

Total cost of goods available for sale	$238,900
Less: Ending inventory computed above	41,560
Cost of goods sold (weighted average method)	$197,340

2. **Compute 2005 ending inventory and cost of goods sold for Mitsuru Corporation using the FIFO cost flow assumption.**

Under the first-in, first-out cost flow assumption, the ending inventory consists of the 4,000 most-recently purchased pounds of macadamia nuts. This ending inventory amount consists entirely of the December 18 purchase of 4,000 pounds for $42,400. Accordingly, FIFO cost of goods sold is:

Total cost of goods available for sale	$238,900
Less: Ending FIFO inventory	42,400
FIFO cost of goods sold	$196,500

3. **Compute 2005 ending inventory and cost of goods sold for Mitsuru Corporation using the LIFO cost flow assumption.**

Under LIFO, the ending inventory is comprised of the 4,000 pounds of oldest macadamia nut purchases. This 4,000 pounds would consist of two layers:

January 1	1,000 pounds	@	$10.00	=	$10,000
February 3	3,000 pounds	@	$10.20	=	30,600
	4,000 pounds				$40,600

Then, LIFO cost of goods sold is:

Total cost of goods available for sale	$238,900
Less: Ending LIFO inventory	40,600
LIFO cost of goods sold	$198,300

4. **Assume that the December 31, 2005 macadamia nut replacement cost is $10.60 per pound. Compute Mitsuru's LIFO reserve and use the beginning and ending LIFO reserve amounts to reconcile between LIFO and FIFO cost of goods sold.**

The LIFO reserve at a given point in time is the difference between the LIFO inventory book value and its then-current replacement cost. At January 1, 2005, Mitsuru Corporation's LIFO reserve was $0 since the LIFO book value and replacement cost both equaled $10,000. At December 31, 2005, the LIFO reserve was $1,800, computed as follows:

December 31, 2005 inventory replacement cost: 4,000 pounds @ $10.60	$42,400
December 31, 2005 LIFO inventory	40,600
December 31, 2005 LIFO reserve	$ 1,800

Using the formula for converting cost of goods sold from a LIFO to FIFO basis in conjunction with the answers to parts 2 and 3 of this self-study problem yields:

$COGS_{LIFO}$	+	Beginning LIFO reserve	−	Ending LIFO reserve	=	$COGS_{FIFO}$
$198,300	+	0	−	$1,800	=	$196,500

Notice that $196,500 equals the FIFO cost of goods sold number computed in part 2.

As discussed in the text, the reconciliation procedure is an approximation. Adding the LIFO reserve to the LIFO inventory equals replacement cost. If the inventory turns quickly, then inventory replacement cost *approximates* FIFO inventory. In this self-study problem, ending FIFO inventory at $10.60 per pound exactly equals replacement cost. Hence, the adjustment is precise.

APPENDIX A

ELIMINATING REALIZED HOLDING GAINS FROM FIFO INCOME

In the chapter we show a simple way to estimate the amount of realized holding gains included in the FIFO income figure. In this appendix we provide a simple example to illustrate why this method works.

Consider a firm buying and selling inventory *in equal amounts* daily as you contemplate Figure 9.8. The *quantity* of inventory purchased during the year is the area denoted "P." Beginning inventory *quantity* is the area denoted "B," and ending inventory *quantity* is the area denoted "E." Let's assume that B equals E—that is, the firm had exactly as many units in inventory at the end of the year as it did at the start of the year. Under these conditions the *units* comprising FIFO cost of goods sold would consist of the area B + (P − E). In other words, under the FIFO cost flow assumption, cost of goods sold consists of the first—or oldest—units available, which is beginning inventory plus the earliest purchases. Under LIFO, cost of goods sold would comprise the area P—that is, the most *recently* purchased units. The difference between the units comprising the two cost of goods sold measures is the area E minus B. Expressed in units:

$$CGS_{LIFO} \quad = \quad CGS_{FIFO} \quad + \quad E - B \tag{9.1}$$

Expressed in dollars:

$$\$CGS_{LIFO} \quad = \quad \$CGS_{FIFO} \quad + \quad \$E - \$B \tag{9.2}$$

Notice that if inventory costs do not change over the year, $\$E = \$B$ and $\$CGS_{LIFO} = \$CGS_{FIFO}$. In general it's reasonable to expect inventory costs to change from the beginning to the end of the year. If we assume that inventory purchase costs changed over the year at the rate "r," then $\$E$ will not equal $\$B$, even though E units equal B units. Specifically, the dollar amount of ending inventory will equal $(1 + r)$ times the dollar amount of beginning inventory—that is,

$$\$E \quad = \quad \$B \times (1 + r) \tag{9.3}$$

Figure 9.8

FIFO TO LIFO COST
OF GOODS SOLD
APPROXIMATION
TECHNIQUE

Substituting the equation (9.3) value of $E into equation (9.2) yields:

$$\$CGS_{LIFO} = \$CGS_{FIFO} + \$B \times (1 + r) - \$B \tag{9.4}$$

or

$$\$CGS_{LIFO} = \$CGS_{FIFO} + \$B \times r \tag{9.5}$$

In this example, daily unit purchases and sales are equal. Under these conditions LIFO cost of goods sold will equal current cost of goods sold. So equation (9.5) can be rewritten:

$$\$CGS_{CC} = \$CGS_{FIFO} + \$B \times r \tag{9.6}$$

where $\$CGS_{CC}$ is current cost of goods sold. As we saw on page 453, the difference between FIFO pretax income and current cost income (or, equivalently, FIFO cost of goods sold and current cost of goods sold) is the inventory holding gain or loss. Thus, the product $\$B \times r$ provides an estimate of the inventory holding gain (or loss) that is embedded in the FIFO earnings number.[25]

Notice that equation (9.6) is equivalent to the simple holding gain estimation procedure used in the chapter. This approximation "works" as long as the total number of inventory units on hand does not fluctuate much during the year and as long as inventory purchases and sales take place frequently. If these conditions aren't met for a specific firm, the conversion from FIFO cost of goods sold to current cost of goods sold will not be accurate.

To eliminate realized holding gains from FIFO income, we must estimate "r," the percentage change in inventory purchase costs. One means for estimating this rate is to use some input cost price index, such as one of the various producer price indices (PPI) prepared by the U.S. Department of Labor, Bureau of Labor Statistics. Another approach is to select a competitor that is in the same industry as the FIFO firm being adjusted but that utilizes the LIFO inventory procedure. The rate "r" can then be estimated using the following ratio computed from the LIFO competitor's disclosures:

$$\text{Rate of inventory input cost change (“r”)} = \frac{\text{Change in LIFO reserve}}{BI_{LIFO} + \text{Beginning LIFO reserve}}$$

[25] Analysts generally perceive such inventory holding gains as low-quality earnings items because they cannot be sustained in the future unless inventory costs continue to increase; see Siegel, op. cit., situation 7, p. 68. Consistent with this view, Carroll, Collins, and Johnson, op. cit., find that the market price adjustments associated with earnings surprises of firms whose earnings contain relatively large inventory holding gains are substantially smaller than those of firms with relatively smaller FIFO inventory holding gains.

The denominator of the ratio is the initial current cost of the inventory, and the numerator is the change in current cost over the period. The quotient is an estimate of the desired rate, "*r*." However, if the competitor dipped into LIFO layers over the period, the disclosed decrease in cost of goods sold because of the dipping must be added back to the numerator. The reason is that LIFO dipping reduces the LIFO reserve. Adding back the dipping effect generates a more accurate measure of "*r*." But, if the competitor's year-to-year inventory levels changed substantially, the derived rate will differ from the true rate of inventory cost increase.

APPENDIX B

LOWER OF COST OR MARKET METHOD

This appendix covers a widely used method in inventory accounting called the lower of cost or market method.

An asset represents a cost that has been incurred to create future service potential value for a firm. If subsequent events cause the future service potential value of an asset to drop below its cost, then its carrying value must be reduced. In inventory accounting this is called the **lower of cost or market method**.

It is more complicated than its name implies, although the reasoning underlying lower of cost or market is simple. Whenever the replacement cost of inventory declines below its original cost, the presumption is that the service potential value of the inventory has been impaired and a write-down is warranted. If a unit of inventory originally cost $10 but if its replacement cost falls to $8, a decrease in carrying value of $2 would be required. *What's implied here is that inventory replacement cost and eventual selling price move together.* The decline in replacement cost is presumed to signal that the price at which the inventory can be sold—its future service potential value—has fallen. Thus, a loss has occurred that must be recognized in the accounts.

In practice the relationship between cost decreases and selling price decreases is unlikely to be perfect. For this reason the market value used in applying lower of cost or market is subject to two constraints:

1. **Ceiling.** "Market" should not exceed the inventory's **net realizable value**—that is, the estimated selling price of the inventory in the ordinary course of business less the reasonably predictable costs of completing and selling it.
2. **Floor.** "Market" should not be less than the inventory's net realizable value reduced by an allowance for an approximately normal profit margin.[26]

The ceiling constraint (that market should not exceed net realizable value) is designed to avoid overstating obsolete goods. For example, assume a motor that originally cost $80 is now obsolete and has a net realizable value of only $50. Even if its replacement cost is $65, the inventory should be valued at its net realizable value of $50. To value the motor at its replacement cost of $65 would fail to recognize the full extent of the expected loss that has occurred.

The floor constraint covers situations in which declines in input replacement cost do not move perfectly with declines in selling price. To illustrate, assume the following:

	Original Cost	Replacement Cost	Net Realizable Value	Net Realizable Value Less Normal Profit of $11
Inventory item	$60	$46	$70	$59

This scenario assumes that the normal per unit profit margin is $11. An inventory write-down to $46 would lead to an abnormally high unit profit margin of $24 (net realizable value of $70 less the $46 replacement cost) when the inventory is sold in a later period. This $24 profit exceeds the $11 normal profit margin. A write-down to $59 would still afford the company a normal profit margin; any larger write-down would result in excess profits in future periods. The floor provides a lower bound for write-downs in situations where input replacement cost and selling price do not move together.

---

[26] "Restatement and Revision of Accounting Research Bulletins," *Accounting Research Bulletin No. 43* (New York: American Institute of Accountants, 1953), Chapter 4, para. 8.

Together, these two constraints mean that "market" (the market value used in applying the lower of cost or market rule) is the *middle value* of (1) replacement cost, (2) net realizable value, and (3) net realizable value less a normal profit margin. This is depicted in Figure 9.9.

Figure 9.9

LOWER OF COST OR MARKET RULE FOR INVENTORIES

Applying the lower of cost or market rule is illustrated in Exhibit 9.17 using four scenarios. The inventory value used in each scenario is highlighted.

International Accounting Standards also incorporate a lower of cost or market rule. Market is defined as net realizable value; see *IAS 2*, paras. 25–30.

EXHIBIT 9.17	Application of Lower of Cost or Market Rule				
			Market		
Scenario	Original Cost	Replacement Cost	Net Realizable Value	Net Realizable Value Less a Normal Profit Margin	Middle of the Three Market Values	Inventory Value Used
1	$20	$23	$27	$21	$23	$20
2	20	19	24	18	19	19
3	20	19	18	12	18	18
4	20	15	25	19	19	19

Scenario 1. The inventory is valued at cost ($20). The reason is that $23 is the middle value of the three market values—$23 is between $21 and $27—and cost ($20) is lower than "market" ($23). This illustrates the straightforward "lower of cost or market" rule for inventory carrying values in historical cost accounting: Inventories are carried at original cost unless the future service potential value of the item has been impaired.

Scenario 2. The inventory is carried at replacement cost ($19). Market is defined as the middle value of the three definitions in Figure 9.9. The values are 18, 19, and 24; since 19 is between 18 and 24, it is market. Since market is less than the original cost of $20, it is presumed that a portion of the original service potential value of the inventory has been impaired. Therefore, the inventory is written down from $20 to $19.

Scenario 3. The inventory is valued at net realizable value ($18) since net realizable value is the middle "market" value (that is, 18 is between 12 and 19) and is below cost. Here we see the operation of the ceiling. This rule is intended to avoid carrying obsolete goods at a cost in excess of the net value that will be realized upon sale. If the rule were not invoked, inventory would be carried at $19 (its replacement cost), which is more than the $18 that it is expected to yield.

Scenario 4. The inventory is valued at net realizable value less a normal profit margin ($19) because this number is lower than original cost and is the middle value of the market price constraints. Scenario 4 illustrates the floor. If the rule were not invoked, inventory would be carried at $15 (its replacement cost). This would be an excessive write-down, because a $15 carrying cost would result in an above-normal margin when the goods were sold.

When a perpetual inventory system is used and inventory is written down from a cost of, say, $1,000,000 to a market value of $970,000, the entry is:

DR Loss from decline in market value of inventory	$30,000
CR Inventory	$30,000

The lower of cost or market method can be applied to:

- individual inventory items,
- classes of inventory—say, fertilizers versus weed-killers, and
- the inventory as a whole.

Companies have discretion regarding how inventories are aggregated when applying the lower of cost or market rule, as illustrated in Exhibit 9.18. Depending on whether the aggregation is by item of inventory, inventory class, or total inventory, the lower of cost or market value could be $27,000, $31,000, or $32,000.

> If a periodic inventory system is used, this entry would not be made. Instead, the ending *market* value of inventory ($970,000) would be used as ending inventory in the cost of goods sold computation. This treatment essentially "buries" the $30,000 loss as an undisclosed element of cost of goods sold.

EXHIBIT 9.18 **Aggregation Alternatives in Applying the Lower of Cost or Market Rule**

Inventory Item	Cost	Market	Lower of Cost or Market Aggregated by: Item	Class	Total
Class 1:					
Item 1	$10,000	$ 6,000	$ 6,000		
Item 2	3,000	8,000	3,000		
	$13,000	$14,000		$13,000	
Class 2:					
Item 3	20,000	18,000	18,000	18,000	
	$33,000	$32,000	$27,000	$31,000	$32,000

Income tax regulations do not permit the use of the lower of cost or market rule in conjunction with LIFO. The reason for this prohibition is that LIFO provides tax advantages when prices are rising; if LIFO firms were permitted to use lower of cost or market, then they would also gain tax advantages when prices are falling. Congress is unwilling to provide LIFO firms with tax savings that would occur regardless of the direction of input cost movements.

The Contracting Origins of the Lower of Cost or Market Method

The lower of cost or market method for inventories was widely practiced in the United States before the 1920s. Presumably, it evolved in the formative years of modern financial reporting to satisfy the information needs of what was then the most important external user group—commercial lenders. Banking in that era consisted mainly of securitized lending. Loans required collateral from the borrower, primarily in the form of inventory, accounts receivable, or fixed assets. Clearly, lenders wanted to avoid basing their decisions on overstated asset values, since overstated asset values resulted in inadequate amounts of collateral. The conservatism inherent in lower of cost or market represented a

Contracting

mechanism for protecting the then-dominant user group from unpleasant surprises—lower than expected collateral values.[27] Thus, the lower of cost or market rule evolved because of the dominant form of lending contracts in use years ago.

Evaluation of the Lower of Cost or Market Rule

Individual and institutional equity investors are now important users of financial statements. The conservative bias built into the lower of cost or market rule protects lenders but it may sometimes harm these other statement users. Suppose you own stock in a company whose inventory is written down to market. If the write-down was unwarranted (for example, because the decline in replacement cost did not portend a decline in the inventory's eventual selling price), your financial position is worsened by lower of cost or market accounting. Why? Because the share price you could get if you sold your stock may be lower than the price you could sell the shares for if the accounting were less conservative. Clearly, conservative rules designed to systematically understate asset amounts favor lenders and equity purchasers over borrowers and equity sellers. This absence of neutrality that pervades lower of cost or market has troubled numerous financial reporting experts and has led to repeated criticisms of the approach.

In addition to its bias against those seeking loans and those selling equity securities, the lower of cost or market rule has another deficiency. It assumes that input costs and output prices generally move together. Therefore, a decline in input cost triggers a loss recognition because it is presumed that the cost decrease portends a selling price decrease. But there is little empirical evidence to corroborate this assumption. It is indeed possible that input costs and selling prices will move together. But it is also possible that they may not. When input costs and selling prices do not move together, a loss may be recognized when, in fact, no loss has occurred. Consider, for example, the following illustration:

	Original Cost	Replacement Cost	Net Realizable Value	Net Realizable Value Less Normal Profit Margin
Cost relationships on January 1, 2005	$100	$100	$115	$90
Cost relationships on December 31, 2005	100	95	115	90

---

[27] Evidence about the role that lenders played in the evolution of modern financial reporting and the lower of cost or market rule is contained in a proposal from the Federal Reserve Board that was designed to standardize financial reporting (*Federal Reserve Bulletin*, April 1, 1917, p. 270):

> *Because this matter was clearly of importance to banks and bankers, and especially to the Federal Reserve Banks* which might be asked to rediscount commercial paper based on borrowers' statements, the Federal Reserve Board has taken an active interest in the consideration of the suggestions which have developed as a result of the Trade Commission's investigation, and now submits in the form of a tentative statement certain proposals in regard to suggested standard forms of statements for merchants and manufacturers. [Emphasis added]
>
> The problem naturally subdivides itself into two parts. (1) The improvement in standardization of the forms of statements; (2) the adoption of methods which will insure greater care in compiling the statements and the proper verification thereof.

The proposal (which was subsequently adopted) contained a specific reference to the importance of the lower of cost or market rule for inventories (p. 275):

> . . . The auditor should satisfy himself that inventories are stated at cost or market prices, whichever are the lower at the date of the balance sheet. No inventory must be passed which has been marked up to market prices and a profit assumed that is not and may never be realized. . . . It may be found that inventories are valued at the average prices of raw materials and supplies on hand at the end of the period. *In such cases the averages should be compared with the latest invoices in order to verify the fact that they are not in excess of the latest prices. . . .* [Emphasis added]

Strict application of the lower of cost or market rule at year-end would require a write-down of the inventory to $95 from its original cost of $100. However, the selling price of the inventory has not changed, since its net realizable value is still $115. Therefore, no loss exists but GAAP would require a $5 write-down!

In summary, the lower of cost or market rule reflects conservatism. But as financial statement users have become more diverse, the rule has been subjected to mounting criticism. First, conservatism is itself an elusive concept. While inventory write-downs may initially be conservative, the resulting higher margin in the period following the write-down provides opportunities for earnings management. Second, as the use of published financial statements has broadened over the years, conservatism strikes many observers as a violation of the neutrality posture that financial reporting rules are designed to achieve. For example, if downward changes in replacement cost are considered to be reliable evidence of a loss, logic suggests that upward changes in replacement cost should similarly be considered reliable evidence of a gain. Finally, the lower of cost or market rule relies on an implicit relationship between input costs and output prices that may not prevail. When the input/output relationship does not exist, inventory losses may be recognized even though no real loss has occurred. As a consequence of these limitations, the lower of cost or market approach constitutes GAAP, but it does not hold a secure place in accounting theory.

International

Worse yet, after a write-down, International Accounting Standards permit inventory to be *written back up* to a number not exceeding original cost if selling prices recover (see *IAS 2* [revised 1993], para. 30). So companies might conceivably recognize losses in "good" earnings years that can comfortably absorb the "hit," then write the inventory back up in "bad" earnings years (recognizing gains) to mask the real extent of earnings deterioration.

APPENDIX C

DOLLAR-VALUE LIFO

The LIFO inventory method requires data on each separate product or inventory item, and it therefore has two drawbacks. First, item-by-item inventory records are *costly* to maintain; and second, when LIFO records are kept by individual item, the likelihood of *liquidating* a LIFO layer is greatly increased.

- *Cost.* Traditional LIFO systems kept by individual item require considerable clerical work. Detailed records for each separate product or item in beginning inventory must be kept both in terms of physical units and unit cost. Similar detail must be accumulated for all purchases during the period. Finally, ending inventory must also be costed individually by item. These data requirements quickly become unwieldy for firms with numerous inventory categories.
- *Liquidation.* One of the motivations for adopting LIFO is that it tends to keep inventory holding gains out of income and thereby lowers taxes. However, when old LIFO layers are liquidated, this objective is subverted and both income and income taxes rise. The possibility of liquidating a LIFO layer is very high when item-by-item LIFO is used. Consider the case of computer stores that sell printers. As laser printers were introduced, these stores reduced their inventories of older technology dot-matrix printers. If LIFO always had to be kept on a per-item basis, this decrease in the obsolete models would cause a liquidation of old LIFO layers and negate the benefits of LIFO.

To overcome both the cost and liquidation problems associated with LIFO, a method has been developed in which LIFO cost can be estimated for broad categories of inventory from simple inventory records that are kept in terms of end-of-period costs. This method is called **dollar-value LIFO**.

Overview of Dollar-Value LIFO

Dollar-value LIFO avoids much of the detailed recordkeeping required under standard LIFO. Ending inventory is determined in terms of year-end prices, just as it is under FIFO. The ending inventory at end-of-year prices is then adjusted by a price index to estimate LIFO inventory.[28] To illustrate the procedure in simplified form, let's assume that a firm first adopts LIFO on January 1, 2005 and elects to use dollar-value LIFO. The time of initial LIFO adoption is termed the **base period**. The facts of the example are:

Beginning inventory, LIFO, at base-period (1/1/05) costs	$100,000
Ending inventory at 12/31/05 costs	$140,000
Inventory price index at base period (1/1/05)	1.00
Inventory price index at 12/31/05	1.12

Under LIFO, a new LIFO layer is added only when the unit (or physical) quantity of inventory increases. In this example we cannot compare the ending inventory dollars ($140,000) with the beginning inventory dollars ($100,000) to determine whether physical quantities increased. Why? Because the December 31 inventory is stated at end-of-year costs while the beginning inventory is stated at base-period costs.

However, we can use the inventory price index to restate ending inventory (expressed in end-of-year costs) to base-period costs by dividing $140,000 by 1.12. The result, $125,000, is the December 31, 2005 inventory expressed in base-period (January 1, 2005) costs.

Once ending inventory is restated, it is possible to determine whether the physical quantity of inventory has increased during 2005:

Ending inventory expressed in base-period costs ($140,000/1.12)	$125,000
Beginning inventory expressed in base-period costs	100,000
Inventory increase expressed in base-period costs	$ 25,000

Clearly, a new LIFO layer was added in 2005. However, the new LIFO layer must be recorded at the cost level that was in effect when the layer was added. Since the inventory increase expressed in terms of base-period costs was $25,000—and since costs went up 12% during 2005—then the new LIFO layer

---

[28] A price index is simply a ratio that compares prices during the current period with prices during some base period. Separate indices are computed for each period. If a price index for a given year is 1.12, this means that prices in that year are 12% higher than they were in the base period.

In applying dollar-value LIFO, the index used must reflect price changes for the specific inventory. General price indices are not permitted except in unusual situations. One method for computing the index is to determine the following ratio by reference to detailed purchase records:

$$\frac{\text{Cost of ending inventory at end-of-period prices}}{\text{Cost of ending inventory at base-period prices}} = \text{Index for year}$$

However, this computation can be burdensome when the inventory consists of many different types of items. In such situations an index can be computed based upon a sample of representative purchases. One such approach is:

	Ending Inventory Units (1)	Base-Period Cost Per Unit (2)	Current-Period Cost Per Unit (3)	Total Base-Period Cost (1) × (2)	End-of-Period Cost (1) × (3)
Item A	20,000	$3	$ 4	$ 60,000	$ 80,000
Item B	5,000	7	8	35,000	40,000
Item C	11,000	9	10	99,000	110,000
				$194,000	$230,000

The resulting index is:

$$\frac{\$230,000}{\$194,000} = 1.186$$

would be costed at $25,000 × 1.12, or $28,000. Therefore, the December 31, 2005 ending inventory computed under the dollar-value LIFO method would be comprised of two layers:

	Base-Period Costs	Adjustment Factor	Dollar-Value LIFO Carrying Amount
Beginning inventory (1/1/05)	$100,000	1.00	$100,000
2005 layer	25,000	1.12	28,000
Ending inventory, dollar-value LIFO			$128,000

To continue the example, let's assume that the December 31, 2006 inventory price index is 1.20 and that ending inventory at December 31, 2006 is $146,400 (expressed in year-end 2006 costs).

As before, it is necessary to determine whether a new LIFO layer was added in 2006. To do this, we must restate the December 31, 2006 inventory in terms of base-period costs and compare it to the January 1, 2006 inventory (expressed in base-period costs):

Ending inventory expressed in base-period costs ($146,400/1.20)		$122,000
Beginning inventory expressed in base-period costs:		
Base-period layer	$100,000	
2005 layer ($28,000/1.12)	25,000	
		125,000
Inventory decrease expressed in base-period costs		$ (3,000)

Expressed in base-period costs, inventory decreased in 2006. Since the cost flow is LIFO, this decrease is assumed to have come from the 2005 layer. At base-period costs, the 2005 layer would be reduced to $22,000—that is, $25,000 minus the $3,000 inventory decrease. The December 31, 2006 dollar-value LIFO inventory would again be comprised of two layers:

	Base-Period Costs	Adjustment Factor	Dollar-Value LIFO Carrying Amount
Beginning inventory	$100,000	1.00	$100,000
2005 layer	22,000	1.12	24,640
Ending inventory, dollar-value LIFO			$124,640

Finally, assume that inventory at December 31, 2007 totals $170,100 at year-end costs and that the inventory price index at that date is 1.26. In order to determine whether a new LIFO layer was added in 2007, we must restate the December 31, 2007 inventory in terms of base-period costs:

Ending inventory expressed in base-period costs: ($170,100/1.26)		$135,000
Beginning inventory expressed in base-period costs:		
Base-period layer	$100,000	
2005 layer ($24,640/1.12)	22,000	
		122,000
Inventory increase expressed in base-period costs		$ 13,000

The new 2007 LIFO layer must be added to LIFO inventory using the cost level in effect in 2007. To do this, we must multiply the inventory increase expressed in base-period costs ($13,000) by the December 31, 2007 price index, which is 1.26. Thus, the December 31, 2007 dollar-value LIFO inventory would consist of three layers:

	Base-Period Costs	Adjustment Factor	Dollar-Value LIFO Carrying Amount
Beginning inventory	$100,000	1.00	$100,000
2005 layer	22,000	1.12	24,640
2007 layer	13,000	1.26	16,380
Ending inventory, dollar-value LIFO			$141,020

The steps required to compute dollar-value LIFO are summarized as follows:

1. Ending inventory is initially computed in terms of year-end costs. This simplifies recordkeeping.
2. To determine whether a new LIFO layer had been added (or whether an existing layer has been liquidated), the ending inventory must be restated to base-period cost and compared to the beginning inventory at base-period cost. This eliminates the effect of input cost changes. After restatement, any difference between beginning and ending inventory is the inventory change expressed in base-period cost. It indicates whether inventory *quantities* have changed.
3. Any inventory change determined from step 2 must be costed as follows:

    a. New LIFO layers are valued using costs of the year in which the layer was added.
    b. Decreases in old LIFO layers are removed using costs that were in effect when the layer was originally formed.

> The procedures for costing new dollar-value LIFO layers are technically inconsistent with a strict LIFO flow assumption. For example, notice that the 2007 layer added in the example is costed at 1.26, a figure that represents 2007 *year-end* costs. Under traditional LIFO, new layers are added using beginning-of-year costs, not end-of-year costs. Since dollar-value LIFO is a computational convenience, this inconsistency in costing new layers is usually ignored in order to simplify the computations.

EXERCISES

On January 1, 2005 the merchandise inventory of Manuel Company was $300,000. During 2005 Manuel purchased $1,900,000 of merchandise and recorded sales of $2,000,000. The gross profit (gross margin) on these sales was 20%.

E9 – 1

Account analysis

AICPA
ADAPTED

Required:

What is the merchandise inventory of Manuel at December 31, 2005?

Sperry-New Holland manufactures farm machinery. During 2005, the company incurred a variety of costs, several of which appear on the following list.

E9 – 2

Product versus period costs

Nature of incurred cost

1. Comprehensive liability insurance premium on corporate headquarters
2. Depreciation on production equipment
3. Electricity consumed
4. Property and casualty insurance premiums
5. Raw materials used
6. Royalties paid to the designer of one of the company's products
7. Salaries of corporate legal counsel
8. Travel expenses for sales force
9. Wages of plant maintenance personnel
10. Wages of production workers
11. Workers compensation insurance

Required:

Classify each listed cost as a product cost, period cost, or both. For costs that are probably allocable to both classifications, suggest a reasonable allocation approach.

E9 – 3

Cost flow computations

City Stationers, Inc., had 200 calculators on hand at January 1, 2005 costing $18 each. Purchases and sales of calculators during the month of January were as follows:

Date	Purchases	Sales
January 12		150 @ $28
14	100 @ $20	
29	100 @ $22	
30		100 @ $32

City does not maintain perpetual inventory records. According to a physical count, 150 calculators were on hand at January 31, 2005.

Required:

1. What is the cost of the inventory at January 31, 2005 under the FIFO method?
2. What is the cost of the inventory at January 31, 2005 under the LIFO method?

E9 – 4

Account analysis

The following information is available for Day Company for 2005:

Cash disbursements for purchases of merchandise	$290,000
Increase in trade accounts payable	25,000
Decrease in merchandise inventory	10,000

Required:

What is the cost of goods sold for 2005?

E9 – 5

Account analysis

For the year 2005, the gross profit of Dumas Company was $96,000; the cost of goods manufactured was $340,000; the beginning inventories of goods in process and finished goods were $28,000 and $45,000, respectively; and the ending inventories of goods in process and finished goods were $38,000 and $52,000, respectively.

Required:

What is the dollar amount of Dumas Company sales for 2005?

E9 – 6

Account analysis

Hestor Company's records indicate the following information:

Merchandise inventory, January 1, 2005	$ 550,000
Purchases, January 1 through December 31, 2005	2,250,000
Sales, January 1 through December 31, 2005	3,000,000

On December 31, 2005 a physical inventory determined that ending inventory of $600,000 was in the warehouse. Hestor's gross profit on sales has remained constant at 30%. Hestor suspects some of the inventory may have been taken by some new employees.

Required:

At December 31, 2005, what is the estimated cost of missing inventory?

E9 – 7

Account analysis

On June 30, 2005 a flash-flood damaged the warehouse and factory of Padway Corporation, completely destroying the work-in-process inventory. There was no damage to either the raw materials or finished goods inventories. A physical inventory taken after the flood revealed the following valuations:

Raw materials	$ 62,000
Work-in-process	–0–
Finished goods	119,000

The inventory of January 1, 2005 consisted of the following:

Raw materials	$ 30,000
Work-in-process	100,000
Finished goods	140,000
	$270,000

A review of the books and records disclosed that the gross profit margin historically approximated 25% of sales. The sales for the first six months of 2005 were $340,000. Raw material purchases were $115,000. Direct labor costs for this period were $80,000, and manufacturing overhead has historically been applied at 50% of direct labor.

Required:

Compute the value of the work-in-process inventory lost at June 30, 2005. Show supporting computations.

The Frate Company was formed on January 1, 2005. The following information is available from Frate's inventory records for Product Ply:

	Units	Unit Cost
January 1, 2005		
(Beginning inventory)	800	$ 9.00
Purchases:		
January 5, 2005	1,500	10.00
May 25, 2005	1,200	10.50
July 16, 2005	600	11.00
November 26, 2005	900	11.50

A physical inventory on December 31, 2005 shows 1,600 units on hand.

Required:

Prepare schedules to compute the ending inventory at December 31, 2005 under each of the following inventory methods:
1. FIFO
2. LIFO
3. Weighted average

Show supporting computations in good form.

Information from Peterson Company's records for the year ended December 31, 2005 is available as follows:

Net sales	$1,400,000
Cost of goods manufactured:	
Variable	$ 630,000
Fixed	$ 315,000
Operating expenses:	
Variable	$ 98,000
Fixed	$ 140,000
Units manufactured	70,000
Units sold	60,000
Finished goods inventory, 1/1/05	None

There were no work-in-process inventories at the beginning and end of 2005.

Required:

1. What would be Peterson's finished goods inventory cost at December 31, 2005 under the variable (direct) costing method?
2. Under the absorption costing method, what would be Peterson's operating income be?

Selected information concerning the operation of Kern Company for the year ended December 31, 2005 is available as follows:

Units produced	10,000
Units sold	9,000
Direct materials used	$40,000
Direct labor incurred	$20,000
Fixed factory overhead	$25,000
Variable factory overhead	$12,000
Fixed selling and administrative expenses	$30,000
Variable selling and administrative expenses	$ 4,500
Finished goods inventory, January 1, 2005	None

There were no work-in-process inventories at the beginning and end of 2005.

Required:

1. What would be Kern's finished goods inventory cost at December 31, 2005 under the variable (direct) costing method?
2. Which costing method—absorption or variable costing—would show a higher operating income for 2005, and by what amount?

E9 – 11

Change to LIFO method

AICPA
ADAPTED

The Hastings Company began operations on January 1, 2005 and uses the FIFO method in costing its raw material inventory. Management is contemplating a change to the LIFO method in 2006 and is interested in determining what effect such a change will have on net income. Accordingly, the following information has been developed:

	2005	2006
Final inventory		
FIFO	$240,000	$270,000
LIFO	200,000	210,000
Net income		
(Computed under		
the FIFO method)	$120,000	$170,000

Required:

Based on the above information, what would 2006 net income be after the change to the LIFO method?

E9 – 12

Converting LIFO to FIFO

KW Steel Corp. uses the LIFO method of inventory valuation. Waretown Steel, KW's major competitor, instead uses the FIFO method. The following are excerpts from each company's 2005 financial statements:

($ in millions)	KW Steel Corp.		Waretown Steel	
	2005	2004	2005	2004
Total inventories	$ 797.6	$ 692.7	$ 708.2	$ 688.6
LIFO reserve	378.0	334.9		
Sales	4,284.8	4,029.7	3,584.2	3,355.8
Cost of goods sold	3,427.8	3,226.5	2,724.0	2,617.5

Required:

1. Compute each company's 2005 gross margin rate and inventory turnover using cost of goods sold as reported by each company. (Round answers to one decimal place.) For each ratio, how does KW Steel compare to Waretown Steel?
2. Restate KW's cost of goods sold and inventory balances to the FIFO basis. On the basis of KW's "adjusted" data, recompute KW's gross margin rate and inventory turnover. Explain how your earlier comparisons are altered by the revised figures.

E9 – 13

LIFO liquidation

Nathan's Grills, Inc. imports and sells premium-quality gas grills. The company had the following layers in its LIFO inventory at January 1, 2005, at which time the replacement cost of the inventory was $675 per unit.

Year LIFO Layer Added	Units	Unit Cost
2002	50	$450
2003	40	500
2004	60	600

The replacement cost of grills remained constant throughout 2005. Nathan's Grills sold 275 units during 2005. The company established the selling price of each unit by doubling its replacement cost at the time of sale.

Required:

1. Determine gross margin and the gross margin percentage for 2005 assuming Nathan's Grills purchased 280 units during the year.

2. Determine gross margin and the gross margin percentage for 2005 assuming Nathan's Grills purchased 180 units during the year.
3. Explain why the assumed number of units purchased makes a difference in your answers.

Miller's Snow Blowers, Inc. had the following layers in its LIFO inventory at January 1, 2005:

E9 – 14

Margin effects of LIFO dipping

Year LIFO Layer Added	Units	Unit Cost
2002	100	$750
2003	95	780
2004	80	800

The company sets its selling price at 180% of replacement cost at the time of the sale. Replacement cost as of January 1, 2005 was $825 per unit and remained unchanged throughout 2005. During 2005, the company purchased 475 units and sold 675 units.

Required:

Calculate the difference between Miller's Snow Blowers, Inc.'s current cost operating margin (that is, on a replacement cost basis) and the LIFO operating margin as reported by the company in 2005. What does this difference represent?

Watsontown Yacht Sales has been selling large power cruisers for 25 years. On January 1, 2005, the company had $5,950,000 in inventory (based on a FIFO valuation). While the number of yachts in Watsontown Yacht Sales' inventory remained fairly constant throughout 2005, by December 31, 2005 yacht prices were 7% higher than at the start of the year. The company reported cost of goods sold for 2005 of $23,800,000.

E9 – 15

Eliminating FIFO holding gains

Required:

Calculate the amount of realized holding gains in Watsontown Yacht Sales' income for 2005.

The following inventory valuation errors have been discovered for Knox Corporation:

E9 – 16

Inventory errors

CMA
ADAPTED

*   The 2003 year-end inventory was overstated by $23,000.
*   The 2004 year-end inventory was understated by $61,000.
*   The 2005 year-end inventory was understated by $17,000.

The reported income before taxes for Knox was:

Year	Income Before Taxes
2003	$138,000
2004	254,000
2005	168,000

Required:

Compute what income before taxes for 2003, 2004, and 2005 should have been after correcting for the errors.

Moore Corporation has two products in its ending inventory; each is accounted for at the lower of cost or market. A profit margin of 30% on selling price is considered normal for each product. Specific data with respect to each product follows:

E9 – 17

Lower of cost or market

AICPA
ADAPTED

	Product 1	Product 2
Historical cost	$17.00	$ 45.00
Replacement cost	15.00	46.00
Estimated cost to dispose	5.00	26.00
Estimated selling price	30.00	100.00

Required:

In pricing its ending inventory using the lower of cost or market rule, what unit values should Moore use for products 1 and 2, respectively?

E9 – 18

Dollar-value LIFO

ADAPTED

The Acute Company manufactures a single product. On December 31, 2002, Acute adopted the dollar-value LIFO inventory method. The inventory on that date using the dollar-value LIFO inventory method was determined to be $300,000. Inventory data for succeeding years are as follows:

Year Ended December 31	Inventory at Respective Year-End Prices	Relevant Price Index (Base Year 2002)
2003	$363,000	1.10
2004	420,000	1.20
2005	430,000	1.25

Required:

Compute the inventory amounts at December 31, 2003, 2004, and 2005, using the dollar-value LIFO inventory method for each year.

E9 – 19

Dollar-value LIFO

ADAPTED

On December 31, 2004 Fern Company adopted the dollar-value LIFO inventory method. All of Fern's inventories constitute a single pool. The inventory on December 31, 2004 using the dollar-value LIFO inventory method was $600,000. Inventory data for 2005 are as follows:

December 31, 2005 inventory at year-end prices	$780,000
Relevant price index at year-end (base year 2004)	1.20

Required:

Under the dollar-value LIFO inventory method, what would Fern's inventory be at December 31, 2005?

E9 – 20

LIFO with falling prices

JD Electronics sells sound systems and other consumer electronics through a chain of retail outlets. Joanna Danielle, president of the company, recently read that many companies were adopting the LIFO method of inventory valuation to reduce income taxes and eliminate holding gains from current period income. She wonders if switching to LIFO from the company's current periodic FIFO inventory method would be beneficial. The following data concerning a popular model of entertainment center were taken from the company's inventory records:

	Inventory Purchases		
	Units	Cost per Unit	Total
Beginning inventory	3,100	$1,875	$ 5,812,500
March 1, 2005	4,000	1,825	7,300,000
June 15, 2005	3,500	1,800	6,300,000
August 1, 2005	3,800	1,785	6,783,000
October 1, 2005	4,500	1,760	7,920,000
December 15, 2005	3,000	1,750	5,250,000
	21,900		$39,365,500

	2005 Sales		
	Units	Price per Unit	Total
First quarter	4,100	$3,400	$13,940,000
Second quarter	4,600	3,300	15,180,000
Third quarter	3,500	3,250	11,375,000
Fourth quarter	5,500	3,200	17,600,000
	17,700		$58,095,000

Required:

1. Determine cost of goods sold for the entertainment centers under (a) periodic FIFO and (b) periodic LIFO. (Ignore lower of cost or market considerations.)
2. Assume operating expenses of $15,000,000 are related to this product and that the company has a 35% income tax rate. Calculate net income under both inventory valuation methods.

3. Assume that the price trend on the entertainment centers is generally mirrored by the other items in JD Electronics' inventory. Would the company be well advised to switch to the periodic LIFO method to value its inventory?

Cost for inventory purposes should be determined by the inventory cost flow method most clearly reflecting periodic income.

E9 – 21

Inventory costing concepts

ADAPTED

Required:

1. Describe the fundamental cost flow assumptions for the average cost, FIFO, and LIFO inventory cost flow methods.
2. Discuss the reasons for using LIFO in an inflationary economy.
3. Where there is evidence that the utility of goods, in their disposal in the ordinary course of business, will be less than cost, what is the proper accounting treatment, and under what concept is that treatment justified?

PROBLEMS/DISCUSSION QUESTIONS

Keefer, Inc. began business on January 1, 2005. Information on Keefer, Inc.'s inventory purchases and sales during 2005 and 2006 are presented below:

P9 – 1

LIFO versus FIFO

	Inventory Purchases		
Date	Units	Cost per Unit	Total
January 1, 2005	85	$25	$ 2,125
March 15, 2005	100	27	2,700
May 15, 2005	90	28	2,520
August 1, 2005	100	30	3,000
September 3, 2005	125	31	3,875
December 5, 2005	50	32	1,600
Total purchases—2005	550		$15,820
February 20, 2006	150	31	4,650
March 29, 2006	100	30	3,000
July 1, 2006	100	29	2,900
August 20, 2006	100	28	2,800
November 3, 2006	80	27	2,160
Total purchases—2006	530		$15,510

	Inventory Sales		
	Units	Price per Unit	Total
March 18, 2005	65	$50	$ 3,250
August 15, 2005	200	52	10,400
October 6, 2005	175	53	9,275
Total sales—2005	440		$22,925
February 12, 2006	100	53	5,300
June 2, 2006	200	52	10,400
September 30, 2006	210	50	10,500
Total sales—2006	510		$26,200

Required:

1. Calculate ending inventory, cost of goods sold, and gross margin for 2005 and 2006 under the periodic FIFO inventory valuation method.
2. Calculate ending inventory, cost of goods sold, and gross margin for 2005 and 2006 under the periodic LIFO inventory valuation method.
3. Discuss the difference in reported results under FIFO versus LIFO for each year.

P9 – 2

Account analysis

The following information pertains to Yuji Corporation:

	January 1, 2005	December 31, 2005
Raw materials inventory	$ 34,000	$ 38,000
Work-in-process inventory	126,000	145,000
Finished goods inventory	76,000	68,000

Costs incurred during the year 2005 were as follows:

Raw material purchased	$116,000
Wages to factory workers	55,000
Salary to factory supervisors	25,000
Salary to selling and administrative staff	40,000
Depreciation on factory building and equipment	10,000
Depreciation on office building	12,000
Utilities for factory building	5,000
Utilities for office building	7,500

Required:

Sales revenue during 2005 was $300,000. The income tax rate is 40%. Compute the following:

1. Cost of raw materials used
2. Cost of goods manufactured/completed
3. Cost of goods sold
4. Gross margin
5. Net income

P9 – 3

Inventory accounting—comprehensive

www.prenhall.com/revsine

● Student Resources

☑ Template for solution

Alex Wholesalers Inc. began its business on January 1, 2005. Information on its inventory purchases and sales during 2005 are provided below:

	Inventory Purchases		
	Units	Cost per Unit	Total
January 1	10,000	$4.00	$ 40,000
March 10	8,000	4.10	32,800
April 12	12,000	4.30	51,600
September 15	7,500	4.45	33,375
November 11	6,000	4.75	28,500
December 29	6,500	5.00	32,500
Units available for sale	50,000		$218,775

	Inventory Sales		
	Units	Price per Unit	Total
March 1	7,000	$8.00	$ 56,000
September 1	20,000	8.50	170,000
December 1	11,000	9.00	99,000
Units sold	38,000		$325,000

Assume a tax rate of 40%.

Required:

1. Compute the cost of ending inventory and cost of goods sold under each of the following methods: (1) FIFO, (2) Weighted average cost, and (3) LIFO. Assume that Alex uses the periodic inventory procedure.
2. Assume that Alex uses the periodic LIFO method.

   a. Calculate the replacement cost of the ending inventory and the LIFO reserve as of the end of the year. You may assume that year-end purchase cost was still $5.00 per unit.
   b. Provide an estimate of Alex's cost of goods sold under the periodic FIFO method based only on the information that will be publicly available to the investors of Alex. Explain why your answer differs from FIFO cost of goods sold computed in requirement 1.

c. The purchasing manager of Alex was planning to acquire 10,000 units of inventory on January 5, 2006 at $5.00 per unit. The accountant for Alex suggests that the company will be better off if Alex acquires the inventory instead on December 31, 2005. What are the pros and cons of the accountant's suggestion? Wherever possible, show supporting calculations.

3. Calculate cost of goods sold assuming that Alex uses the perpetual FIFO method.

The inventory footnote to the 2005 annual report of the Ruedy Company reads in part as follows:

P9 – 4

LIFO liquidation

Because of a prolonged strike in one of our supplier's plants, inventories were unavoidably reduced during 2005. Under the LIFO system of accounting, this "eating into LIFO layers" resulted in an increase in *after-tax* net income of $36,000 over what it would have been had inventories been maintained at their physical levels that existed at the start of the year.

The price of Ruedy Company's merchandise purchases was $22 per unit for 20,000 units during 2005. Prior to 2005, inventory prices had risen steadily for many years. Ruedy Company uses the periodic inventory method. The company's inventory positions at the beginning and end of the year are summarized below. Ruedy's income tax rate is 40%.

Date	Physical Count of Inventory	LIFO Cost of Inventory
January 1, 2005	30,000 units	$?
December 31, 2005	20,000 units	$260,000

Required:

1. Was 2005 cost of goods sold higher or lower as a result of the LIFO liquidation? By how much?
2. Were 2005 income taxes higher or lower as a result of "eating into LIFO layers"? By how much?
3. What was the average cost per unit of the 10,000 units removed from the January 1, 2005 LIFO inventory?
4. What was the January 1, 2005 LIFO cost of inventory?
5. What was the reported 2005 cost of goods sold for Ruedy Company?

Courtney, Inc. began operations in 1996 as a publisher of children's books. From modest beginnings, the company grew steadily with sales reaching $52.3 million in 2005. In late 2003, management began revamping the company's production process in an effort to enhance profitability. Streamlining operations permitted the company to effectively operate with lower raw material inventory levels, so these inventories were gradually reduced during 2004 and 2005. Courtney, Inc.'s raw materials consist primarily of ink and paper, with costs of the latter rising steadily since 1996 as a result of curtailed logging operations in the United States and increased transportation costs on imported paper. The following information was excerpted from Courtney, Inc.'s 2005 annual report:

P9 – 5

LIFO liquidation and inter-year comparisons

($ in thousands)	2005	2004	2003
Net sales	$52,328	$46,931	$45,286
Cost of goods sold	34,746	31,538	31,157
Gross profit	$17,582	$15,393	$14,129

NOTE 1: INVENTORIES

During 2004 and 2005, the Company streamlined its operations, permitting the liquidation of certain LIFO inventories that were carried at costs lower than current replacement costs. These liquidations increased earnings before income taxes by $892,000 and $2,355,000 in 2004 and 2005, respectively.

Required:

1. Calculate Courtney, Inc.'s gross profit as a percentage of sales as reported for 2003 through 2005.
2. Recompute the company's gross profit percentage for 2003 through 2005 adjusting for the LIFO dipping effect.
3. Assume that Courtney, Inc.'s annual report contained a comment in the "management's discussion and analysis" section citing the company's increased gross profit as evidence that the production process changes were having the desired effect. Would such a statement be justified?

P9 – 6

Criteria for choosing a cost flow assumption

The president of Jeanette Corporation is in a dilemma regarding which inventory method (LIFO or FIFO) to use. The controller of Jeanette Corporation provides the following list of factors that should be considered before making a choice.

1. Jeanette Corporation has borrowed money during the current month and has entered into a debt contract. The covenants of this contract require Jeanette Corporation to achieve a certain amount of net income and maintain a certain amount of working capital.
2. The Board of Directors of Jeanette is contemplating a proposal to reward the top management of Jeanette Corporation with an incentive bonus that is based on accounting net income.
3. The vice president of finance suggests using the LIFO method for tax purposes and the FIFO method for financial reporting purposes. With lower taxable income, Jeanette Corporation can save on the current tax it pays, and at the same time, it can show higher income in the financial reports and "look good."
4. The controller cautions that while the LIFO method may reduce the current period tax liability, "it could hit us hard when things are not going so well." This potential problem with the LIFO method could be "avoided if we use FIFO in the first place."
5. However, the president would like to adopt the method that provides both a better application of the matching principle and a more current measure of inventory on the balance sheet.
6. The controller suggests that Jeanette should adopt the FIFO method since higher accounting income means a higher stock price.

Required:

The president of Jeanette has asked you to write a report evaluating the pros and cons of each of the issues raised above. Given her busy schedule, the president would like the report to be brief. In answering this question, assume that Jeanette Corporation expects an upward trend in inventory prices.

P9 – 7

Inventory alternatives

www.prenhall.com/revsine

● Student Resources

☑ Template for solution

Princess Retail Stores started doing business on January 1, 2005. The following data reflect its inventory purchases and sales during the year:

	Inventory Purchases		
	Units	Cost per Unit	Total
January 1	20,000	$ 7.00	$140,000
March 1	16,000	9.00	144,000
June 1	14,000	11.00	154,000
September 1	10,000	13.00	130,000
December 1	12,000	15.00	180,000
	72,000		$748,000

	Sales		
	Units	Price per Unit	Total
March 2	24,000	$14.00	$336,000
September 2	18,000	16.00	288,000
December 2	20,000	18.00	360,000
	62,000		$984,000

Required:

1. Compute gross margin and cost of ending inventory using the periodic FIFO cost flow assumption.
2. Compute gross margin and cost of ending inventory using the periodic LIFO cost flow assumption. Compute the dollar amount of the LIFO reserve. Using this additional disclosure, how might an analyst estimate the cost of goods sold of Princess under the FIFO method based only on publicly available information? Show supporting calculations.
3. Under historical cost accounting, gross margin is calculated as current output price minus historical input price. For analytical convenience, we can break the gross margin into two components:

   a. "True" operating margin = current output price – current input price, and
   b. Inventory profits = current input price – historical input price.

   Provide an estimate of the "true" operating margin for Princess Retail Stores.

4. The following are excerpts from a recent top management meeting at Princess Retail Stores. Your assignment is to clearly provide guidelines to the top management team on each of the issues raised in the meeting. Show calculations where necessary.

    a. "I am most concerned about appropriately matching revenues and expenses. I suggest that we look for an inventory accounting method that achieves this objective both during inflationary and deflationary times." (Frances Iyer, Chairman)
    b. "Frances, I think the choice is obvious. What other method can achieve better matching of revenues and expenses than the specific identification method? By choosing this method, we would send a clear signal to the stock market that we are not playing any earnings management games." (Sandra Kang, VP Investor Relations)
    c. "I would like to maximize our current profits. What inventory method might help us achieve this most important goal and why?" (Antonia Iyer, CEO)
    d. "Antonia, I know you can't stop thinking about your earnings-based bonus. My primary objective is to minimize the present value of future income tax outflows." (Juanita Kang, CFO)
    e. "I would like to have our cake and eat it too. Why don't we follow Juanita's suggestion for income tax accounting and follow Antonia's idea for external financial reporting?" (B. T. Kang, VP Operations)

Dembo, Inc., a manufacturer of office furniture, reported the following data in its 2005 annual report. Dembo uses the LIFO inventory valuation method. Interest is reported as an operating expense and is not material in amount.

P9 – 8

LIFO reserve effect on various ratios

Dembo, Inc.

Condensed Financial Statements

($ in millions)	Year Ended December 31, 2005	
Revenue	$4,800.0	
Cost of sales	2,880.0	
Operating expenses	1,056.0	
Income taxes	480.0	
Net income	$ 384.0	

($ in millions)	12/31/05	12/31/04
Current assets	$2,520.0	
Property and equipment, net	3,148.2	
Intangibles and other assets	1,001.8	
Total assets	$6,670.0	$6,130.0
Current liabilities	$1,800.0	
Long-term liabilities	2,087.2	
Stockholders' equity	2,782.8	
Total liabilities and shareholders' equity	$6,670.0	

Inventories consist of (in millions)	12/31/05	12/31/04
Finished goods	$ 389.4	$ 381.3
Work in process	215.4	215.1
Raw materials	907.2	823.6
Inventory—FIFO	1,512.0	1,420.0
Less: LIFO reserve	575.0	557.0
Inventory—LIFO	$ 937.0	$ 863.0

Required:

1. Compute Dembo's (a) current ratio, (b) return on assets, (c) debt/equity ratio, and (d) inventory turnover using the company's 2005 financial data as originally reported. Round answers to two decimal places.
2. Recompute the ratios in requirement 1 after transforming Dembo's numbers to a FIFO basis. Ignore income tax effects.
3. For each ratio computed in requirements 1 and 2, indicate which computation (LIFO-basis or FIFO-basis) best captures the underlying economics.

P9 – 9

Inventory turnover

The following is excerpted from the financial statements of Baldwin Piano and Organ Company:

Consolidated Statements of Earnings

| | Years Ended December 31 | | |
	Year 3	Year 2	Year 1
Net sales	$120,657,455	$110,076,904	$103,230,431
Cost of goods sold	89,970,702	79,637,060	74,038,724
Gross profit	$ 30,686,753	$ 30,439,844	$ 29,191,707

Inventories consist of the following:

	Year 3	Year 2
FIFO cost:		
Raw materials	$ 9,930,923	$ 9,500,765
Work in process	7,081,883	5,943,672
Finished goods	36,149,809	39,328,177
	53,162,615	54,772,614
Excess of FIFO cost over		
LIFO inventory value	(8,085,250)	(6,828,615)
	$45,077,365	$47,943,999

At December 31, Year 3, approximately 77% of the company's inventories were valued on the LIFO method.

During the past three years, certain inventories were reduced. This reduction resulted in the liquidation of LIFO inventory layers carried at the lower costs prevailing in prior years as compared with the current cost of inventories. The effect of these inventory liquidations was to increase net earnings for Year 3, Year 2, and Year 1 by approximately $694,000 ($.20 per share), $519,000 ($.15 per share), and $265,000 ($.08 per share), respectively.

Required:

1. Estimate Baldwin's cost of goods sold and the cost of goods manufactured for Year 3; assume the company had used FIFO instead of LIFO.
2. On the basis of these FIFO numbers, compute Baldwin's finished goods and work-in-process inventory turnovers (expressed in days) for Year 3. What do these turnovers tell you about Baldwin's operating cycle?

P9 – 10

Gross margins and cash flow sustainability

Parque Corporation applied to Fairview Bank early in 2005 for a $400,000 five-year loan to finance plant modernization. The company proposes that the loan be unsecured and repaid from future operating cash flows. In support of the loan application, Parque submitted an income statement for 2004. Prepared using the FIFO inventory cost flow approach, this income statement reflected annual profit that was approximately 50% of the principal amount of the loan. This was offered as evidence that the loan could easily be repaid within the five-year term.

Parque is in the business of recycling yelpin, an industrial lubricant. The company buys used yelpin from large salvage companies and, after cleaning and reconditioning it, sells it to manufacturing companies. The recycling business is very competitive and has typically generated small gross margins. The salvage companies set yelpin prices on the first day of each quarter, and Parque purchases yelpin at the established price for the entire quarter. Yelpin prices fluctuate with business conditions. Prices paid to salvage companies by Parque have risen in recent years but tend to fall during economic downturns.

Parque sells the recycled yelpin at $1 per pound above the currently prevailing price that it pays to acquire the used yelpin from salvage companies. December 31, 2003 inventory was 300,000 pounds at a cost of $7.00 per pound. Purchases and sales in 2004 were:

	Purchases	Sales
First quarter 2004	600,000 lbs. @ $7.20/lb.	700,000 lbs. @ $8.20/lb.
Second quarter 2004	700,000 lbs. @ $7.40/lb.	600,000 lbs. @ $8.40/lb.
Third quarter 2004	800,000 lbs. @ $7.80/lb.	700,000 lbs. @ $8.80/lb.
Fourth quarter 2004	600,000 lbs. @ $8.10/lb.	650,000 lbs. @ $9.10/lb.

Cash operating costs during 2004 totaled $2,800,000.

Required:

1. Compute 2004 income for Parque Corporation using the FIFO inventory flow assumption. Ignore income taxes.
2. Did Parque Corporation really earn a profit from its *operating* activities in 2004?
3. Given the circumstances described, what risks exist that could threaten ultimate repayment of the loan?

---

1. The following is an excerpt from the financial statements of Trinity Industries:

P9 – 11

Evaluating inventory cost flow changes

> Effective September 30, 1987, the Company changed its method of accounting for inventories from the LIFO method principally to the Specific Identification method, because, in the opinion of management, there is a better matching of revenues and expenses, better correlation of accounting and financial information with the method by which the Company is managed, and better presentation of inventories at values that more fairly present the inventories' cost.

Required:

Evaluate each of the justifications provided by Trinity for changing its inventory cost flow assumption.

2. During 1990, SPS Technologies changed its inventory cost flow assumption from LIFO to the average cost method. The following is an excerpt from the financial statements of SPS Technologies.

> The change to the average cost method will conform all inventories of the Company to the same method of valuation. The Company believes that the average cost method of inventory valuation provides a more meaningful presentation of the financial position of the Company since it reflects more recent costs in the balance sheet. Under the current economic environment of low inflation and an expected reduction in inventories and low production costs, the Company believes that the average cost method also results in a better matching of current costs with current revenues.

Required:

Evaluate each of the justifications provided by SPS Technologies for changing its inventory cost flow assumption.

JKW Corporation has been selling plumbing supplies since 1981. In 2000, the company adopted the LIFO method of valuing its inventory. The company has grown steadily over the years and a layer has been added to its LIFO inventory in each of the years the method has been used. The company's inventory turnover ratio has averaged 4.5 in recent years. Management attempts to maintain a stable level of inventory at each store; the growth in inventory has been due to new stores being opened each year. In 2004, the board of directors approved an incentive program that pays managers a sizeable bonus in each year that certain performance targets are met. For 2005, targeted earnings per share are $2.75. Management, in an effort to "track progress" toward meeting this target, produced the following income statement for the first nine months of 2005.

P9 – 12

Managerial opportunism

JKW Corporation

Income Statement
January 1–September 30, 2005

Sales	$13,284,000
Cost of goods sold	7,970,400
Gross margin	5,313,600
Operating expenses	2,391,120
Income before taxes	2,922,480
Income tax expense	1,022,868
Net income	$ 1,899,612
Earnings per share (1,000,000 shares outstanding)	$ 1.90

Based on past history, management expects that 30% of the company's annual sales will take place in the fourth quarter. Operating expenses and gross margin are expected to remain at 18% and 40% of sales, respectively, for the remainder of the year. The company's tax rate is 35%.

Required:

1. Assuming that management maintains a stable level of inventory, project earnings per share for 2005 based on the data provided.
2. Assume that you are JKW's independent auditor, and your analysis indicates that projected earnings per share will fall short of the bonus target. In the past, JKW's managers have used aggressive (and possibly unethical) behavior to achieve salary bonus targets. You suspect that the managers intend to deplete old LIFO layers deliberately in the fourth quarter. In order to help you detect such behavior, calculate the amount of the "LIFO dip" that would be needed in the fourth quarter to hit the EPS target in 2005.

Interfirm comparisons

Fraser Corporation uses the LIFO method of inventory valuation and is in the process of preparing its financial statements for the year 2005. The controller of Fraser Corporation provided the following income statement for the year ended December 31, 2005 to top management for review:

Sales revenue		$1,000,000
Less: Cost of goods sold		
Beginning Inventory	150,000	
Add: Purchases	650,000	
Less: Ending Inventory	(200,000)	
		(600,000)
Gross profit		400,000
Less: Selling and administrative expenses		(150,000)
Net income before taxes		250,000
Less: Income taxes		(75,000)
Net income		$ 175,000

The CEO of Fraser had mixed emotions after examining the income statement. He wanted to know how Fraser compares with its closest rival, KAS Corporation, and he instructed the controller to "compute some ratios for both companies." KAS uses the FIFO method of inventory valuation. The following are excerpts from the controller's report:

	Fraser	KAS
Gross margin rate (Gross margin/sales)	?	49%
Return on sales (Net income/sales)	?	21%
Inventory turnover (COGS/average inventory)	?	1.8

Required:

1. Complete the controller's report by computing the ratios for Fraser based on the information given in the income statement above. For each ratio, how does Fraser compare with KAS? Explain how the choice of inventory methods biases the comparisons in favor of either Fraser or KAS.
2. After reviewing the controller's report, the CEO was concerned about Fraser's performance relative to KAS on two out of the three ratios. However, the controller pointed out to the CEO that the "perceived underperformance" of Fraser is primarily driven by differences in accounting methods. In addition, the controller added that if one takes into account "our current period LIFO tax savings, Fraser has outperformed KAS." The CEO asked the controller, "Why don't you show me how an analyst might adjust our income statement to make it comparable to that of KAS?" Your task is to help the controller by preparing a pro forma income statement for Fraser, one that is comparable to that of KAS. Assume that if Fraser had used the FIFO method, the beginning and ending inventories would have been higher by $50,000 and $150,000, respectively. On the basis of the "adjusted" income statement, recompute the three ratios given in the controller's report, and explain how and why the CEO's earlier conclusions are altered by the revised figures.

The original Bacardi® rum business was founded in Cuba in 1862 by Don Facundo Bacardy Maso. The following information is excerpted from the annual report of Bacardi Corporation for the year ended December 31, Year 2. The effective tax rate of Bacardi was 17% in Year 2.

P9 – 14

LIFO and ratio effects

STRETCH

> The company follows the last-in, first-out (LIFO) method of determining inventory cost. The LIFO method is considered by management to be preferable because it more closely matches current costs with current revenues in periods of price level changes. Under this method, current costs are charged to costs of sales for the year.
>
> In Year 2, LIFO liquidation was caused primarily by a substantial reduction during the year in [the inventory of] molasses (the major raw material). This LIFO liquidation, which resulted in cost of products sold being charged with higher inventory costs from prior years, caused a decrease in Year 2 net income of approximately $1,400,000 or $0.14 per share.
>
> LIFO inventories at December 31, Year 2 and Year 1 were $51,892,000 and $53,812,000 respectively, which is approximately $700,000 and $20,800,000 less than replacement cost at those dates.
>
> In accordance with generally recognized trade practices, inventories of distilled spirits in bonded aging warehouses have been included in current assets, although the normal aging period is usually from one to three years.

[Ending] inventories consist of the following:

($ in thousands)	Year 2	Year 1
Finished goods	$ 2,684	$ 2,420
Aging rum in bond	40,285	39,921
Raw materials and supplies	8,923	11,471
	$51,892	$53,812

Cost of goods sold and net income (after tax) during Year 2 were $65,374,000 and $45,568,000, respectively.

Required:

1. Compute the cost of goods manufactured (fully aged rum) during Year 2. Without using the LIFO reserve information, compute the finished goods inventory turnover (the number of days from when inventory is completed until it is sold) and the work-in-process inventory turnover (the number of days the inventory is in the production cycle). Is the difference between the two inventory turnover ratios consistent with the nature of Bacardi's business? Explain.

2. On the basis of available information, provide an estimate of Bacardi's net income if the company had used FIFO during Year 2. By comparing the reported LIFO income with your estimate of FIFO income, what do you learn about the business conditions faced by Bacardi during Year 2?

3. Using all available information, compute a total inventory turnover measure (expressed in number of days). Does your estimate of inventory turnover capture the "true" physical turnover of Bacardi (based on what you know about the business)? Explain. If it does not capture the "true" physical turnover, provide possible reasons. Be specific.

The comparative income statements and edited inventory footnote for Oxford Industries, Inc. for 2000 follow. Located in Atlanta, Oxford designs, manufactures, markets, and sells consumer apparel products for both men and women. Its ticker symbol is OXM. Using the information provided, answer the questions at the end of this problem.

P9 – 15

LIFO inventory— comprehensive

Oxford Industries, Inc. and Subsidiaries

CONSOLIDATED STATEMENTS OF EARNINGS

($ in thousands, except per share amounts)	June 2, 2000	Years Ended May 28, 1999	May 29, 1998
Net sales	$839,533	$862,435	$774,518
Costs and expenses			
Cost of goods sold	685,841	698,170	619,690
Selling, general and administrative	112,056	116,284	111,041
Interest, net	3,827	4,713	3,421
	801,724	819,167	734,152
Earnings before income taxes	37,809	43,268	40,366
Income taxes	14,368	16,875	15,743
Net earnings	$ 23,441	$ 26,393	$ 24,623
Basic earnings per common share	$3.04	$3.15	$2.79
Diluted earnings per common share	$3.02	$3.11	$2.75

Oxford Industries, Inc. and Subsidiaries

EDITED INVENTORY FOOTNOTE*

The components of inventories are summarized as follows:

($ in thousands)	June 2, 2000	May 28, 1999
Finished goods	$ 90,961	$ 92,195
Work in process	25,903	24,579
Fabric	28,255	23,280
Trim and supplies	8,118	6,874
	$153,237	$146,928

    The excess of replacement cost over the value of inventories based upon the LIFO method was $37,154,000 at June 2, 2000, $37,367,000 at May 28, 1999, and $39,205,000 at May 29, 1998. Changes in the LIFO reserve increased earnings $0.02 per share basic in 2000, $0.13 per share basic in 1999, and decreased earnings $0.06 per share basic in 1998.

    During fiscal 2000, inventory quantities were reduced, which resulted in a liquidation of LIFO inventory layers carried at lower costs which prevailed in prior years. The effect of the liquidation was to decrease cost of goods sold by approximately $147,000 and to increase net earnings by $91,000 or $0.01 per share basic. During fiscal 1999, the effect of [the 1999] liquidation was to decrease cost of goods sold by approximately $1,174,000 and to increase net earnings by $716,000 or $0.09 per share basic. During fiscal 1998, the effect of [the 1998] liquidation was to decrease cost of goods sold by approximately $591,000 and to increase net earnings by $361,000 or $0.04 per share basic.

*The footnote was edited to include selected 1998 data. Items in the footnote *text* have no zeroes omitted. Assume that the effective tax rate is 35%.

Required:

1. Based on the available information, provide an estimate of Oxford Industries' "Earnings before income taxes" for the years 2000 and 1999 if the company had used FIFO accounting.
2. Using the available data, provide estimates of the amount of realized holding gains (inventory profits) that were included in 2000, 1999, and 1998 "Earnings before income taxes" under the LIFO method.
3. Explain why the estimated FIFO income numbers (see requirement 1) are higher or lower than those under the LIFO method. (*Hint:* To do this, prepare a reconciliation of changes in the LIFO reserve for 2000 and 1999 as illustrated on page 461 of the text.)
4. As of the end of the fiscal years 2000 and 1999, compute the total amount of income tax saved by Oxford from the time of its initial adoption of LIFO. Ignore present value effects in your calculations. For the fiscal year 2000 alone, did Oxford pay higher or lower income tax under LIFO compared to what it would have paid under FIFO? How much?

5. Compute Oxford's inventory turnover ratio (without making any adjustments) for the year 2000 under the LIFO cost flow assumption. (Express it in number of days.) Does this number provide a good estimate of the days' inventory held by Oxford Industries? If not, propose (and defend) an alternative approach to calculating the inventory turnover. Show supporting calculations.

Maple Company has used the LIFO method of inventory accounting since its inception in 1960. At December 31, 2003, the ending inventory was:

P9 – 16

LIFO reporting— comprehensive

Base layer	5,000 units @ $1.00	=	$5,000
1968 layer	2,000 units @ $1.30	=	2,600
			$7,600

The company uses the periodic inventory system in which sales are assumed to have been made from the last inventory units acquired during the year. Purchase prices for Maple Company's inventory are adjusted twice a year by its supplier—on January 1 and July 1.

Purchase and sales transactions for 2004 and 2005 were:

	Units Purchased	Units Sold
2004		
January–June	40,000 units @ $2.50	30,000 units @ $3.80
July–December	40,000 units @ $2.70	50,000 units @ $3.90
2005		
January–June	40,000 units @ $2.75	43,000 units @ $4.00
July–December	40,000 units @ $3.00	43,000 units @ $4.30

Other expenses totaled $60,000 in 2004 and $66,000 in 2005. Inventory purchase prices in effect during the last half of 2003 were $2.40 per unit.

Required:

1. Compute operating income for the Maple Company on the LIFO historical cost basis for 2004 and 2005.
2. Compute current cost income from continuing operations for the Maple Company for 2004 and 2005.
3. Determine the total increases in current cost amounts (that is, unrealized cost savings or holding gains) occurring in 2004 and 2005.
4. What portion of the reported 2004 and 2005 LIFO income consisted of realized holding gains (that is, "inventory profits")?
5. What was the dollar amount of Maple Company's LIFO reserve at December 31, 2003? Compute the increases and decreases to the LIFO reserve in 2004 and 2005. Identify the cause for each increase and decrease.
6. LIFO, a method that supposedly is designed to keep inventory profits out of income, does not accomplish this result for the Maple Company in either 2004 or 2005. Why?

Sirotka Retail Company began doing business in 2003. The following information pertains to Sirotka for the first three years of its operation:

P9 – 17

LIFO—comprehensive

		Purchases		Sales	
Year	Operating Expenses	Units	Unit Cost	Units	Unit Price
2003	$60,000	15,000	$20.00	12,000	$35.00
2004	90,000	20,000	25.00	18,000	40.00
2005	65,000	5,000	30.00	10,000	40.00

Assume the following:

- The income tax rate is 40%.
- Purchase and sale prices change only at the beginning of the year.
- Sirotka uses the LIFO cost flow assumption.
- Operating expenses are primarily selling and administrative expenses.

Required:

1. Compute cost of goods sold and the cost of ending inventory for each of the three years. (Identify the number of units and the cost per unit for each LIFO layer in the ending inventory.)
2. Prepare income statements for each of the three years.
3. Compute the LIFO reserve at the end of 2003, 2004, and 2005.
4. Compute the effect of LIFO liquidation on the net income of the company for the years 2004 and 2005.
5. Compute the inventory turnover ratio for the years 2004 and 2005. Do not make adjustments for any potential biases in LIFO accounting. Comment on the direction of the bias (that is, understated/overstated) in the inventory turnover ratio under LIFO. Is the ratio in one year more biased than in the other? Explain.
6. How best can the physical turnover of inventory (that is, "true" inventory turnover) be approximated using *all* the information available in a LIFO financial statement? Illustrate your approach by recomputing Sirotka's inventory turnover ratios for 2004 and 2005.
7. Compute the gross margin rates for the years 2004 and 2005. Explain whether the difference in the gross margin rates between 2004 and 2005 reflect the change in Sirotka's economic condition from 2004 to 2005.
8. Provide an *estimate* of the FIFO cost of goods sold for the years 2003, 2004, and 2005 using the information available in the financial statements.
9. Based on your answers to requirements 1 and 8, estimate Sirotka's tax savings for 2003, 2004, and 2005.
10. Assuming a discount rate of 10%, compute the present value as of December 31, 2002 of the tax savings over the period 2003–2005 (that is, discount the 2003 tax savings one period, and so on).

P9 – 18

Identifying FIFO holding gains

Caldwell Corporation operates an ice-cream processing plant and uses the FIFO inventory cost flow assumption. A partial income statement for the year ended December 31, 2005 appears below:

Caldwell Corporation

Statement of Income
For the Year Ended December 31, 2005

Sales revenues	$680,000,000
Cost of goods sold	360,000,000
Gross margin	320,000,000
SG&A expenses	200,000,000
Income before taxes	$120,000,000

Caldwell's physical inventory levels were virtually constant throughout 2005. The FIFO dollar amount of inventory at January 1, 2005 was $60,000,000. During 2005, the Consumer Price Index (an index of overall average purchasing power for typical urban-dwelling consumers) increased by 4%.

Caldwell Corporation's largest competitor, Cohen Confections, uses LIFO for inventory accounting. Excerpts from its December 31, 2005 inventory footnote were:

INVENTORY FOOTNOTE (COHEN CONFECTIONS):

Inventories are computed using the LIFO cost flow assumption. Comparative amounts were:

	December 31	
	2005	**2004**
Raw materials	$ 8,100,000	$ 8,000,000
Finished goods	76,000,000	80,000,000
	$84,100,000	$88,000,000

The difference between the LIFO inventory amounts and the replacement cost of the inventory at December 31, 2005 and 2004, respectively, was $18,000,000 and $12,000,000. A LIFO liquidation occurred in 2005, which increased the reported gross margin by $1,000,000.

Required:

Using the preceding information, what is the *best* estimate of the amount of realized holding gains (or inventory profits) included in Caldwell Corporation's "income before taxes"?

Ramps by Andy, Inc. manufactures skateboard ramps. The company uses independent sales representatives to market its products and pays a commission of 10% on each sale. Data regarding the five styles of ramps in the company's inventory at December 31, 2005 appear below. The normal profit margin on each item is expressed as a percentage of the item's selling price.

P9 – 19

LCM application

Inventory Item	Original Cost	Replacement Cost	Selling Price	Normal Profit Margin %
1	$125	$130	$260	35%
2	210	190	350	40
3	95	90	130	20
4	460	455	500	30
5	390	390	650	20

Required:

Determine the appropriate inventory value to use for each item in Ramps by Andy's December 31, 2005 inventory.

CASES

Barbara Trading Company has used the LIFO method of inventory accounting since its inception in 1970. At December 31, 2003 the ending inventory was:

C9 – 1

Barbara Trading Company (KR): Understanding LIFO distortions

Base layer	10,000 units @ $ 7.00	$ 70,000
1980 layer	15,000 units @ $12.00	$ 60,000
		$130,000

The company uses the periodic inventory method in which sales are assumed to have been made from the last inventory units acquired during the year (periodic LIFO). The purchase and sales prices change only once a year on January 1. Operating expenses are $600,000 per year and the income tax rate is 40%.

Year	Units Purchased	Units Sold
2004	100,000 units @ $25.00	100,000 units @ $35.00
2005	90,000 units @ $30.00	100,000 units @ $40.00

During 2005, Barbara Trading Company implemented a new inventory management program to reduce the level of inventory carried.

Required:

1. Prepare Barbara's income statements for the years 2004 and 2005.
2. The CEO of Barbara Trading Company, Ms. I. M. Greedy, examined the effect of the new inventory management program on the company's inventory turnover. After doing some quick calculations, Ms. Greedy was overjoyed. "When our competitors are turning their inventory over 12 to 15 times a year, our inventory turnover for 2005 has exceeded 30!" How did the CEO estimate the inventory turnover ratio for 2005? Based on all available information, provide an estimate of the "true" inventory turnover of Barbara Trading Company during 2005. Assume the competitors' turnovers were based on data from their financial statements. What might be the potential limitations of comparing Barbara's inventory turnover with its competitors'? Show supporting figures where necessary.
3. The CEO was also quite ecstatic about the company's overall performance during the year 2005. "I am extremely pleased with the growth in our bottom line. Although some of the growth is probably due to the increase in selling price, most of it appears to be the result of our new inventory management program." Prepare a memo to the CEO explaining the "true" reasons behind the change in net income from 2004 to 2005. Show supporting figures where necessary. Also critically evaluate the rationale provided by the CEO for the growth in earnings.

4. The CFO of Barbara Trading Company, Mr. I. M. Taxed, was rather concerned about the tax implications of reducing inventory levels. He was lamenting, "I told you all about the LIFO boomerang. We could have avoided paying a lot of taxes that resulted from our inventory liquidations had we adopted FIFO in the first place." Evaluate the CFO's analysis of the LIFO tax effects.

C9 – 2

General Electric:
Interpreting a LIFO footnote

The following inventory footnote appears in the 2002 General Electric annual report.

General Electric Company

Edited Inventory Footnote

($ in millions)	December 31 2002	December 31 2001
GE		
Raw materials and work-in-process	$4,894	$4,708
Finished goods	4,379	3,951
Unbilled shipments	372	312
	9,645	8,971
Less revaluation to LIFO	(606)	(676)
	9,039	8,295
GE Capital Services		
Finished goods	208	270
	$9,247	$8,565

LIFO revaluations decreased $70 million in 2002, compared with decreases of $169 million in 2001 and $82 million in 2000. Included in these changes were decreases of $21 million, $8 million and $6 million in 2002, 2001 and 2000, respectively, that resulted from lower LIFO inventory levels. There were net cost decreases in each of the last three years.

GE's earnings before income taxes were $18.891 billion in 2002. Assume a 35% marginal tax rate.

Required:

1. What are the total cumulative tax savings as of December 31, 2002 that GE has realized as a result of using the LIFO inventory method?
2. What would GE's pre-tax earnings have been in 2002 if it had been using FIFO?
3. What December 31, 2002 balance sheet figures would be different—and by how much—if GE had been using FIFO to account for its inventories?
4. What were the LIFO liquidation profits reported in 2002 both pre-tax and after tax?
5. Explain what factors cause the difference between the LIFO pre-tax income number and the FIFO pre-tax income number you estimated in requirement 2. (*Hint:* Reconcile the change in the LIFO reserve for 2002).

C9 – 3

Gardner Denver, Inc.:
Interpreting a LIFO footnote

The following inventory footnote is taken from Gardner Denver's 2002 annual report. You are to use this information in answering the questions that follow. Inventories are summarized as follows:

Gardner Denver, Inc.

Edited Inventory Footnote

($ in thousands)	December 31 2002	December 31 2001
Raw materials	$33,400	$33,156
Work-in-process	9,077	15,908
Finished goods	27,630	30,942
Perishable tooling and supplies	2,456	2,328
	72,563	82,334
Excess of FIFO costs over LIFO costs	(5,115)	(5,684)
Inventories net	$67,448	$76,650

During 2002, 2001 and 2000, reductions in inventory quantities (net of acquisitions) resulted in liquidations of LIFO inventory layers carried at lower costs prevailing in prior years. The effect was to increase net income in 2002, 2001 and 2000 by $268, $319 and $427, respectively.

Required:

1. By how much would net income have differed for 2002 if Gardner Denver had used FIFO to value those inventory items valued under LIFO? Assume a 35% marginal tax rate. Be sure to indicate whether FIFO income would be higher or lower than LIFO income.
2. What would the "LIFO Reserve" have been on December 31, 2002 if no LIFO liquidation had occurred in 2002?
3. What was the net difference in 2002 income taxes that Gardner Denver experienced as a result of using LIFO rather than FIFO? Assume a 35% tax rate and indicate whether FIFO or LIFO would yield the higher tax and by how much.
4. What was the approximate rate of change in input costs in 2002 for Gardner Denver's inventory?

Baines Corporation is a manufacturer of fireplace tools and accessories. The company has been prosperous since its incorporation in 1960, largely due to a small, exceptionally skilled, and highly motivated managerial staff. Baines has been able to attract and retain its excellent management team because of a very attractive managerial incentive plan. The plan allocates 23% of total pre-tax FIFO-absorption cost profits into a pool that is distributed to managers as a year-end bonus. The bonus pool is allocated to individual managers using a point system based upon each manager's performance relative to a budgeted goal.

Data relating to 2004 operations were as follows:

C9 – 4

Baines Corporation: Absorption versus variable costing

www.prenhall.com/revsine

● Student Resources

☑ Template for solution

Beginning inventory	1,500,000 units @ $2.95
Ending inventory	1,500,000 units @ $2.95
Production	4,000,000 units
Sales	4,000,000 units @ $3.50
Variable production costs	$1.45/unit
Fixed production costs	$6,000,000/year

Reported pre-tax profit for 2004 was:

Sales revenues	(4,000,000 @ $3.50)		$14,000,000
Costs of goods sold:			
Variable production costs	(4,000,000 @ $1.45)	$5,800,000	
Fixed production costs	(4,000,000 @ $1.50)	6,000,000	
			11,800,000
Operating profit			2,200,000
Interest expense			200,000
Pre-tax profit			$ 2,000,000

Early in 2005, interest rates increased and the president of Baines Corporation, Mr. Eldred, was concerned about the rising cost of financing the inventory. After a careful study of the situation, Mr. Eldred became convinced that inventory levels could be reduced considerably without adversely affecting sales or delivery performance, provided certain changes in purchasing, production, and sales procedures were adopted. Accordingly, Mr. Eldred called a meeting of the management group in February 2005 and outlined his multifaceted plan for reducing inventories.

His basic strategy met with immediate acceptance, and various additional efficiencies and other inventory management improvements were suggested by several of the participants. The meeting adjourned with each manager resolving to do all that was possible to decrease inventory levels and thereby reduce interest expenses.

As the year progressed, Mr. Eldred's proposals and the refinements suggested by the other managers were put into practice; as a result, inventory levels were significantly reduced by December 31, 2005. The managers were quite pleased with their successful implementation of the new strategy, and morale was quite high.

Basic facts concerning 2005 performance were as follows:

Beginning inventory	1,500,000 units @ $2.95
Ending inventory	700,000 units @ $3.325
Production	3,200,000 units
Sales	4,000,000 units @ $3.50
Variable production costs	$1.45/unit
Fixed production costs	$6,000,000/year
Interest expense	$100,000/year

Shortly after the final 2005 profit figures were reported early in 2006, a general management meeting was held. As he walked into the room, Mr. Eldred was somewhat surprised to see a rather sullen and dispirited group of managers confronting him. One was heard to mumble, "Well, I wonder what this year's double cross will be!"

Required:

1. What do you think caused the abrupt change in the mood of the management team at Baines Corporation? Cite figures to support your explanation.
2. How might this problem have been prevented? Cite figures to support your explanation.

COLLABORATIVE LEARNING CASE

C9 – 5

Weldotron Corporation (KR): Strategic choice of accounting methods

The following excerpts are taken from Weldotron's financial statements.

Weldotron Corporation and Subsidiaries

Condensed Consolidated Balance Sheets
February 28, 1994, and February 28, 1993

($ in thousands)	1994	1993
Assets		
Total current assets	$15,449	$16,162
Net property, plant, and equipment	3,417	3,725
Other assets	220	170
Total assets	$19,086	$20,057
Liabilities and stockholders' equity		
Total current liabilities	$ 7,144	$ 7,021
Long-term debt less current portion	1,527	1,585
Other long-term liabilities	683	637
Total liabilities	9,354	9,243
Minority interest	722	700
Stockholders' equity:		
Common stock, par value $0.05 per share; issued 2,352,720 in 1994 and 1,882,720 in 1993	118	94
Additional paid in capital	9,798	8,715
(Deficit) Retained earnings	(783)	1,428
	9,133	10,237
Less: Common stock in treasury	(123)	(123)
Total stockholders' equity	9,010	10,114
Total liabilities & stockholders' equity	$19,086	$20,057

Weldotron Corporation and Subsidiaries

Condensed Consolidated Statements of Operations
For the Years Ended February 28, 1994, February 28, 1993, and February 29, 1992

($ in thousands)	1994	1993	1992
Net sales	$30,440	$26,400	$29,061
Costs and expenses:			
Cost of sales	22,375	19,322	21,372
Selling, general, and administrative	9,258	9,471	8,902
Depreciation and amortization	558	612	678
Restructuring charges	625	–0–	–0–
	32,816	29,405	30,952
Loss from operations	(2,376)	(3,005)	(1,891)
Other income (expenses)	128	(33)	606
Income tax (benefit) provision	(59)	26	–0–
Minority interest share of (income) loss	(22)	(57)	123
Loss from continuing operations	(2,211)	(3,121)	(1,162)
Discontinued operations	–0–	–0–	(1,059)
Net loss	$ (2,211)	$ (3,121)	$ (2,221)

Excerpts from Footnotes: *($ in thousands)*

1. Summary of Significant Account Policies

   Inventories: Substantially all inventories are valued at the lower of cost, determined by the use of the first in, first out method (FIFO) or market (see Note 2).

   Income Taxes: Weldotron Corporation and its subsidiaries file a consolidated federal income tax return. Accumulated undistributed earnings of the Company's foreign subsidiary were approximately $352 at February 28, 1994. No provision has been made for U.S. income taxes on these earnings as the Company has reinvested or plans to reinvest overseas.

2. Change in Accounting Principle for Inventories

   Effective February 28, 1994, the Company changed its basis of valuing inventories from the last in, first out (LIFO) method to the first in, first out (FIFO) method.

   In previous years, the Company experienced significant operating losses and has addressed these problems by discontinuing certain products and related parts. The results of inventory reductions in previous years resulted in the liquidation of LIFO layers which resulted in a mismatching of older costs with current revenues, which defeats the primary objective of LIFO. Further reductions of inventory levels are expected from the discontinuance of products and parts as well as better manufacturing methods which will reduce production lead times. Under these circumstances, the FIFO method of inventory valuation is the preferable method due to the improved matching of revenues and expenses and the current industry practice.

   The change has been applied retroactively by restating prior years' financial statements. The effects of the reversal of the previous LIFO reserve were partially offset by the appropriate application of FIFO costing requirements. The effects of this change in the method of valuing inventory were to increase the net loss previously reported in 1993 by $128 and to decrease the net loss previously reported in 1992 by $97. The effects on 1994 were not material. The effects of this restatement were also to increase retained earnings as of March 1, 1991 by $2,356 (i.e., the retroactive effect).

7. Long Term Debt and Short Term Borrowings

   On June 25, 1991, the Company entered into a credit facility (the "Credit Facility") with Congress Financial Corporation ("Congress"), a CoreStates Company, to provide a revolving line of credit and term loan for working capital purposes not to exceed $5,000, which replaced the Company's existing credit facility. The interest rate is 3.75% over the CoreStates floating base rate, which was 6% at February 28, 1994. The Credit Facility further requires that the Company pay fees on the unused line of credit, for administration and upon early termination of the Credit Facility. On April 13, 1994, the Credit Facility was extended for one year. It expires and is due and payable on or before June 25, 1995.

The Credit Facility is collateralized by substantially all of the assets of the Company and its domestic subsidiaries. Borrowings under the Credit Facility are limited to certain percentages of eligible inventory and accounts receivable including stipulations as to the ratio of advances collateralized by receivables compared to advances collateralized by inventory.

The Credit Facility's covenants stipulate that tangible domestic net worth of greater than $8,200 and consolidated working capital greater than $9,500 be maintained. In addition, the Credit Facility restricts the payment of dividends, limits the amount of the advances to and guarantees for the Company's foreign subsidiary and limits annual capital expenditures to $500. At February 28, 1994 the Company was in compliance with the covenants of the Credit Facility.

Borrowings under the Credit Facility aggregated $3,215, including a $1,500 long-term loan at February 28, 1994. The remaining borrowing under the Credit Facility is included in current liabilities.

Tax Note:

At February 28, 1994, $8,400 of Federal tax loss carryforwards are available for regular income tax purposes.

Note 2 states that Weldotron changed its inventory method from LIFO to FIFO effective February 28, 1994. In the same note, the Company has provided justifications for the change in the inventory cost flow assumption. Note 7 discloses details of the Company's credit facility and covenants. This note states that the Company was in compliance with the covenants on February 28, 1994.

Required:

Financial reporting choices can sometimes allow companies to achieve strategic objectives and benefit shareholders. Using this perspective, evaluate the effect of Weldotron's inventory accounting change on its debt covenants, specifically on the tangible domestic net worth constraint of $8,200 and the consolidated working capital constraint of $9,500. (*Note:* In answering this question you should keep in mind that when applying the working capital constraint, lenders often ignore current liabilities related to the borrowing itself.)

www.prenhall.com/revsine

Remember to check the book's Companion Website for additional problem and case material.

10

Long-Lived Assets and Depreciation

Learning Objectives
After studying this chapter, you will understand:

1. What measurement base is used in accounting for long-lived assets and why this base is used.

2. What specific costs can be capitalized and how joint costs are allocated among assets.

3. How generally accepted accounting principles (GAAP) measurement rules complicate both trend analysis and cross-company analysis and how to avoid misinterpretations.

4. Why balance sheet carrying amounts for internally developed intangibles usually differ from their real value.

5. When long-lived asset impairment exists and how it is recorded.

6. How different depreciation methods are computed.

7. How analysts can adjust for different depreciation assumptions and improve interfirm comparisons.

8. How long-lived asset accounting and depreciation practices differ internationally.

An asset is something that generates future economic benefits and is under the exclusive control of a single entity. Assets can be tangible items like inventories and buildings or intangible items like patents and trademarks.

The previous two chapters—receivables and inventories—examined current assets. Current assets represent a large part of total assets for many companies. Recall that a current asset is expected to be converted into cash within one year or within the operating cycle, whichever is longer.

This chapter concentrates on operating assets expected to yield their economic benefits (or service potential) over a period longer than one year. Such assets are called **long-lived assets**.

Long-lived assets represent a significant percentage of total assets in industries like oil exploration and refining, automobile manufacturing, and steel. Exhibit 10.1 shows the asset portion of Sunoco, Inc.'s balance sheet in both dollar and common-sized terms at December 31, 2002. Notice that long-lived assets (properties, plants, and equipment) comprises 63.6% of total assets. Firms have latitude in how much detail they provide about separate long-lived asset components. Sunoco chose to provide a footnote breakdown of the total properties by industry segment, as shown in Exhibit 10.2. Notice that the highlighted net properties total from Exhibit 10.1 ($4,099 million) appears again in Exhibit 10.2. Statement readers can then see the breakdown of gross and net properties, plants and equipment across industry segments.

> The *operating cycle* begins with the receipt of raw materials inventory and ends when cash is received for the completed product that has been sold. If inventory turns over every 90 days and if the average receivables collection period is 50 days, then the operating cycle is 140 days (that is, 90 + 50).

Clearly, there's a high proportion of long-lived assets in some industries. However, the GAAP rules used to measure the carrying amounts of long-lived assets are frequently criticized, and we'll see why next.

EXHIBIT 10.1   Sunoco, Inc.

Partial Consolidated Statement of Financial Position
December 31, 2002

($ in millions)		Percentage
Assets:		
Cash and cash equivalents	$ 390	
Accounts and notes receivable, net	923	
Inventories	491	
Deferred income taxes	94	
Total current assets	1,898	29.5%
Investments and long-term receivables	220	3.4
Properties, plants and equipment (net)	4,099	63.6
Deferred charges and other assets	224	3.5
TOTAL	$6,441	100.0%

Source: Sunoco, Inc. 2002 Annual Report.

EXHIBIT 10.2   Sunoco, Inc.

Condensed Footnote Breakdown of Properties, Plants and Equipment
December 31, 2002

($ in millions)	Gross Investments, at Cost	Accumulated Depreciation, Depletion and Amortization	Net Investment
Refining and supply	$3,637	$2,019	$1,618
Retail marketing	1,400	639	761
Chemicals	1,072	171	901
Logistics	1,012	427	585
Coke	401	167	234
	$7,522	$3,423	$4,099

Source: Sunoco, Inc. 2002 Annual Report.

Measuring the Carrying Amount of Long-Lived Assets

There are two ways that long-lived assets could potentially be measured on balance sheets:

1. Assets could be measured at their estimated value in an **output** market. An output market refers to a market where assets are **sold**. We will call measures that use output market numbers **expected benefit approaches**.
2. Assets could be measured at their estimated cost in an **input** market. An input market refers to a market where assets are **purchased**. Measures that use input market costs will be called **economic sacrifice approaches**.

Expected benefit approaches recognize that assets are valuable because of the *future cash inflows* they are expected to generate. Consequently, these approaches measure various definitions of future cash inflows that are expected to be generated by the asset. One example of an expected benefit approach is **discounted present value**. Here, the value of an item of manufacturing equipment would be measured by estimating the discounted present value of the stream of future net operating cash inflows it's expected to generate over its operating life. Another example of an expected benefit approach is the cash inflow that the asset would bring if it were sold instead of being used in operations. Under this variant of the expected benefit approach, long-lived assets would be reported at their **net realizable value**—the amount that would be received if the asset were sold in the used asset market.

Economic sacrifice approaches to asset measurement focus on the amount of resource expenditure necessary to acquire it. One example of an economic sacrifice approach is **historical cost** (the dominant GAAP measurement method)—that is, the historical amount spent to buy the asset constitutes the *past* sacrifice incurred to bring the asset into the firm. Another example of an economic sacrifice approach involves measuring the current (or replacement) cost of the asset. Under a **replacement cost** approach, assets would be carried at their current purchase cost—the expenditure (sacrifice) needed *today* to buy the asset.

The Approach Used by GAAP

Exhibit 10.3 shows a hypothetical range of long-lived asset carrying amounts as measured under each approach—expected benefit versus economic sacrifice. Assume the fixed asset is a truck used by a freight hauler to transport heavy industrial equipment. Let's say the truck originally cost $100,000, is two years old, has a remaining useful life of eight years, is being depreciated straight-line, and is expected to have no salvage value (market value) at the end of its useful life.

EXHIBIT 10.3	**Hypothetical Long-Lived Asset Carrying Amounts**

Expected Benefit Approaches

1. Discounted present value:

    Expected net operating cash inflows = $18,000 per year (assumed) for eight remaining years, discounted at a 10% (assumed) rate

$$5.33493^* \times \$18,000 = \$96,029$$

2. Net realizable value:

    Current resale price from an over-the-road equipment listing (Purple Book) for the specific vehicle model

$$\$85,000 \text{ (Assumed)}$$

Economic Sacrifice Approaches

3. Replacement cost:

    Replacement cost of a two-year-old vehicle in equivalent condition

$$\$90,000 \text{ (Assumed)}$$

4. Historical cost less accumulated depreciation:

$$\$100,000 - \left(\frac{\$100,000}{10 \text{ years}} \times 2 \text{ years} \right) = \$80,000$$

*Discount factor for an ordinary annuity for eight years at 10%.

Contracting

GAAP uses historical cost—an economic sacrifice approach—for measuring long-lived assets in almost all circumstances. The choice of historical cost is not an accident. It results from several pragmatic aspects of the existing financial reporting environment.

As discussed in Chapter 1, financial reports play a critical role in resource allocation decisions such as equity investing and lending. Furthermore, accounting numbers are widely used in contracts such as loan agreements, incentive compensation plans, and union contracts. Because of these uses, *parties whose transactions are explicitly or implicitly tied to accounting numbers expect them to be reliable numbers.* By **reliable**, we mean the numbers must not be prone to manipulation. If the numbers were not reliable, for example, if they could be easily manipulated by one party to the contract, then cautious decision makers would be reluctant to enter into contracts using such "soft" numbers. The reason is that manipulation by one party could circumvent the contract terms.

Auditors also prefer that financial statement numbers have certain characteristics. One is that the numbers be verifiable. **Verifiability** means the numbers should arise from readily observable, corroborable facts, rather than from subjective beliefs. Verifiable numbers are important to auditors because of the many legal suits arising from audited financial statements. Auditors believe that verifiable data help provide a defense in court, reducing potential litigation losses.

As modern financial reporting evolved, reliability and verifiability were used as qualitative criteria, or guidelines, for selecting acceptable long-lived asset measurement rules. Expected benefit approaches, such as discounted present value reporting, were discarded because the resulting numbers were deemed to be neither reliable nor verifiable. That's because present value computations require inherently subjective forecasts of future net cash flows as well as an assumed discount rate. This is illustrated in Exhibit 10.3 where alternative 1—the discounted present value/expected benefit approach—requires an estimate of expected net operating cash inflows ($18,000) and a choice of discount rate (10%). Most decision makers won't tie contracts to such numbers since the other party to the contract could easily evade certain contract terms by simply altering the cash flow forecast amounts or the discount rate.

Another expected benefit approach—the net realizable value from selling the asset (alternative 2)—has also been rejected as a measurement base because of its frequent lack of verifiability. Our example in Exhibit 10.3 assumed that the long-lived asset had a readily determinable market price, as some do. However, many long-lived assets like buildings are immobile, and others are highly specialized and therefore traded in thin markets; consequently, selling prices are often not readily determinable. The current selling price for these long-lived assets would need to be estimated using past transaction prices or transactions involving similar (but not necessarily identical) assets. Numbers obtained from such procedures often fail the verifiability test.

> Depreciation is an allocation of historical cost to time periods. Except by coincidence, the net book value number at a point in time—original cost less accumulated depreciation—does not reflect the economic worth of the asset at that time.

The economic sacrifice approach that uses replacement cost, that is, the estimated current cost of *replacing* the asset (alternative 3), has also been disqualified on the basis of similar assertions that the numbers lack verifiability.

The only long-lived asset measurement method that survives the dual screens of reliability and verifiability is the economic sacrifice approach called historical cost (alternative 4). Consequently, long-lived assets are generally reflected in U.S. financial statements at the original historical cost of acquiring the asset (minus accumulated depreciation). Long-lived assets typically last for many years, and their replacement cost tends to increase. But GAAP prohibits adjustment for upward revisions in the replacement cost of the asset. However, when asset values are impaired, GAAP mandates write-downs, as you'll see later.

RECAP Since long-lived assets are predominantly carried at depreciated historical cost, statement users should not expect balance sheet numbers for such assets to necessarily approximate their real economic worth. This is a serious deficiency (with important implications for statement users) that we explore later in this chapter.

Long-Lived Asset Measurement Rules Illustrated

The initial balance sheet carrying amount of a long-lived asset is governed by two rules:

1. All costs necessary to acquire the asset and make it ready for use are included in the asset account. Costs included in the asset account are called **capitalized costs**. (Expenditures excluded from asset categories are "charged-off" to income—that is, expensed.)
2. **Joint costs** incurred in acquiring more than one asset are apportioned among the acquired assets.

Both rules are illustrated in the Canyon Corporation example that follows in Exhibit 10.4.

EXHIBIT 10.4	Canyon Corporation

Joint Cost Allocation, Fixed Asset Purchase

Canyon Corporation acquired a tract of land on June 1, 2005 by paying $6,000,000 and by assuming an existing mortgage of $1,000,000 on the land. Canyon demolished an empty structure on the property at a cost of $650,000. Bricks and other materials from the demolished building were sold for $10,000. Regrading and clearing the land cost $35,000. Canyon then began constructing a new factory on the site. Architectural fees were $800,000, and the payments to contractors for building the factory totaled $12,000,000. Canyon negotiated a bank loan to help ease the cash flow crunch during construction. Interest payments over the construction period totaled $715,000. Legal fees incurred in the transaction totaled $57,000, of which $17,000 was attributable to both examination of title covering the land purchase and legal issues linked to the assumption of the existing mortgage. The remaining $40,000 of legal fees related to contracts with the architect and the construction companies. The construction project was completed on December 31, 2005.

The amounts allocated to the land and building accounts, respectively, are:

Land

Cash payment		$ 6,000,000
Mortgage assumed		1,000,000
Demolition of existing structure	$650,000	
Less: Salvage value of material	(10,000)	
		640,000
Regrading and clearing land		35,000
Legal fees allocated		17,000
Capitalized land costs		$ 7,692,000

Building

Architectural fees	$ 800,000
Building costs	12,000,000
Interest capitalized	715,000
Legal fees allocated	40,000
Capitalized building costs	$13,555,000

Capitalized land costs include many items in addition to the $6,000,000 cash payment. For example, the cost of demolishing the existing structure (net of salvaged materials) is added to the land account, since the land had to be cleared before the new building could be erected. This illustrates initial carrying amount Rule 1—all costs necessary to prepare the asset for its intended use are capitalized—here as land costs. The legal fees illustrate Rule 2—joint costs are apportioned among assets, to both the land and building in this case.

The costs allocated to the building include the interest arising from the loan Canyon negotiated to finance construction. GAAP requires capitalizing what are called **avoidable interest** payments. *Statement of Financial Accounting Standards (SFAS) No. 34* (para. 12) defines this as interest that "could have been avoided . . . if expenditures for the assets had not been made."[1] To qualify as avoidable interest, the interest doesn't have to arise from borrowing that is directly linked to a construction loan. So long as some debt was outstanding during the construction period, a portion of the interest was avoidable and qualifies for capitalization. Here's why. Building the asset required spending cash. *If the asset had not been built, that cash could have been used to retire debt, thereby lowering interest costs.* This is why the interest is *avoidable*, and this is why the capitalized interest doesn't have to arise from a dedicated construction loan. Capitalizing interest is another application of Rule 1—interest paid to lenders during the construction period is considered to be a cost necessary to prepare the asset for its intended use.

Apportionment is also necessary when more than one asset is acquired for a lump-sum price. Assume two tracts of land are acquired for $1,000,000. For property tax purposes, the land tracts are assessed as follows:

	Assessment	Percentage
Tract 1	$240,000	40%
Tract 2	360,000	60%
Total	$600,000	100%

The $1,000,000 purchase price would be apportioned between the tracts in proportion to their assessed value— 40% to Tract 1 and 60% to Tract 2.

Interest can also be capitalized for borrowings that are outstanding when the assets are being constructed for others—that is, for inventory intended for sale or lease. To qualify for interest capitalization, the inventory being constructed must be an identifiable, discrete project (a three-year contract to construct two aircraft carriers for the navy is an example).

Avoidable interest is the product of the interest rate times cumulative weighted average expenditures. For example, assume the following timing of expenditures in Exhibit 10.4 on Canyon's construction project completed on December 31:

Date and Amount			Portion of Year		Cumulative Weighted Average Expenditures
June 1	$10,000,000	×	58.630%*	=	$5,863,000
August 22	3,555,000	×	36.203%	=	1,287,000
					$7,150,000

*June 1 through December 31 = 214 days, and 214 ÷ 365 = 58.630% of a year. The 36.203% is computed similarly.

International

International Financial Reporting Standards (IFRS) allow more latitude than FASB standards for interest capitalization. The "benchmark" (or standard) treatment is to expense all borrowing costs in the period incurred. However, the "allowed alternative treatment" permits capitalization. The guidelines for allowable capitalization are similar to those in *SFAS No. 34*; see "Borrowing Costs," *IAS 23* (revised 1993) (London: International Accounting Standards Committee [IASC] 1993, paras. 7, 13, 17).

Assuming a 10% interest rate on the outstanding debt, avoidable interest is $715,000 (10% × $7,150,000). GAAP limits the amount of interest that can be capitalized to the *lower* of (1) interest actually incurred or (2) avoidable interest. If Canyon's interest actually incurred had been $800,000, the capitalized amount would be limited to avoidable interest, $715,000. If interest actually incurred was only $600,000, then just $600,000 would be capitalized.

However, *capitalization is restricted to interest arising from actual borrowings from outsiders*. To see the financial statement effect of this restriction, let's assume that Canyon had not borrowed from a bank but had instead issued more common stock and used the proceeds to finance construction. Further assume that Canyon had absolutely no interest-bearing debt outstanding. Equity funds are not "free"—stockholders expect to earn a return, and they get angry when it doesn't materialize! Despite this, GAAP does not allow Canyon to calculate an artificial interest charge on the equity financing and capitalize this "imputed interest" as a part of the cost

---

[1] "Capitalization of Interest Cost," *Statement of Financial Accounting Standards (SFAS) No. 34* (Stamford, CT: Financial Accounting Standards Board [FASB], 1979).

of the building. *So the way the construction is financed can alter the cost capitalized under GAAP when a company initially has no outstanding debt.*

Treating equity that is issued to finance construction as "free" (when there is no interest-bearing debt outstanding) is consistent with the traditional accounting model, which ignores the cost of capital provided by owners when periodic income is computed—that is, GAAP allows no expense recognition for the cost associated with capital provided by stockholders. These funds are treated as if they are costless. In summary, the cost of equity capital is ignored under GAAP in both income determination and asset costing.

Interest capitalization can complicate the analysis of firm performance over time. Because of interest capitalization, an increase in capital expenditures can temporarily decrease the amount of interest *expense* shown on the income statement and—all other factors being equal—increase income (or partially offset an income decrease). But this change in the income pattern does not result from increased sales, lower costs, or other operating efficiencies. Consequently, the year-to-year profit change is partially unrelated to operating activities and may not be sustainable. Exhibit 10.5 shows excerpts from the 2001 financial statements of Pogo Producing Company, a New York Stock Exchange company (ticker symbol PPP) engaged in the exploration, development, and production of oil and natural gas. This exhibit illustrates how interest capitalization can alter year-to-year profit assessments.

> As discussed in Chapter 15, GAAP utilizes what is called the proprietary view of the firm. The proprietary view deems the firm and its owners to be indistinguishable. Consequently, funds contributed by owners do not come from "outsiders." *The firm can't charge itself interest on contributed ownership capital.*

EXHIBIT 10.5	**Pogo Producing Company**

Panel (a)

Effect of Capitalized Interest on Year-to-year Income Changes
Capitalized Interest

Interest costs related to financing major oil and gas projects in progress are capitalized until the projects are substantially complete and ready for their intended use if projects are evaluated as successful. The increase in capitalized interest for 2001, compared to 2000 and 1999, resulted primarily from an increase in the amount of capital expenditures subject to interest capitalization during 2001 (approximately $365,000,000), compared to 2000 (approximately $248,000,000) and 1999 (approximately $217,000,000), that was only partially offset by a decrease in the computed rate that the Company uses to apply on such capital expenditures to arrive at the total amount of capitalized interest. A substantial percentage of the Company's capitalized interest expense related to unevaluated properties acquired in the North Central acquisition and capital expenditures for the development of the Benchamas field in the Gulf of Thailand and several development projects in the Gulf of Mexico. The Company currently expects the amount of capital expenditures subject to interest capitalization to decrease during 2002 due to completion of fabrication of platforms and facilities to be installed in Thailand and in the offshore Gulf of Mexico.

Panel (b)

($ in thousands)	Years Ended December 31 2001	2000	Year-to-year Change
Income from continuing operations before taxes and cumulative effect of change in accounting principle	$149,567	$155,992	−4.1%
Minus: Capitalized interest	33,242	20,918	+58.9%
Income from continuing operations before taxes and cumulative effect of change in accounting principle and *without* interest capitalization	$116,325	$135,074	−13.9%

This adjustment is only an approximation of the effect of capitalized interest on 2001 income. It's an approximation because some portion of interest capitalized in previous years has been amortized in 2001. So the 2001 "income cushion" is smaller than $33,242,000 by the amount of this amortization. GAAP does not require disclosure of the dollar amount of prior years' capitalized interest that has been amortized in the current year.

Analysis

The financial statement footnote on capitalized interest is shown in Panel (a) of Exhibit 10.5. The highlighted portion discloses that there was a large increase in capital expenditures, which increased interest capitalization in 2001. In the highlighted portion of Panel (b) we see that capitalized interest increased from $20,918,000 in 2000 to $33,242,000 in 2001, a jump of 58.9%. Pre-tax reported income fell by 4.1% in 2001. But this income decline was cushioned by the offset of capitalized interest. That is, a portion of the interest incurred in 2001 was not expensed but was instead capitalized. Without interest capitalization, *the decline in pre-tax income would have been approximately 13.9%, not 4.1%,* as shown in Panel (b) of Exhibit 10.5. By capitalizing interest, GAAP makes year-to-year income changes a function of *both* changes in operating performance *and* changes in construction levels. This complicates the analysis of earnings sustainability.

Pogo Producing Company's capitalized interest increased because capital expenditures increased. Of course, a decrease in year-to-year capital expenditures has just the opposite effect—the dollar amount of capitalized interest falls, thereby reducing income growth. To see this, consider the following example, adapted from USX Corporation's 1999 10-K.

($ in millions)	1999	1998	Year-to-year Change
Income from continuing operations before income taxes	$1,054	$989	+ 6.6%
Minus: Capitalized interest	26	46	− 43.5%
Income from continuing operations before income taxes and *without* interest capitalization	$1,028	$943	+ 9.0%

Years Ended December 31

Notice, capitalized interest fell by $20 million, or 43.5%. With capitalization, USX income from continuing operations before income tax increased by 6.6% between 1998 and 1999. Without interest capitalization, the growth would have been 9.0%. The *decline* in capitalized interest raised net interest expense and reduced the rate of year-to-year income growth. So, again, a year-to-year change in the amount of capitalized interest (here, a *decline*) clouds year-to-year income changes.

Tax Versus Financial Reporting Incentives The way incurred costs are allocated between land and building affects the amount of income that will be reported in future periods. Land is a permanent asset so it's not depreciated. A factory building has a finite life and *is* depreciated over future years. For *financial reporting purposes,* the manner in which costs are allocated between, say, land and building, is guided by which one (land or building) generated the cost.

For *tax purposes* the incentives for allocating costs between land and building asset categories are completely different, because the objective of most firms is to minimize tax payments, not to "correctly" allocate costs. The larger the costs allocated to land for tax purposes, the *higher* the future taxable income becomes since land cannot be depreciated. Aggressive taxpayers seek to minimize the amount of joint expenditures allocated to nondepreciable assets like land. Similarly, taxpayers would prefer not to capitalize interest payments for tax purposes since the benefits of the deduction would be spread over the depreciable life of the asset rather than being deductible immediately. However, U.S. income tax rules generally parallel financial reporting rules and *require* cost allocations between land and buildings that are similar to U.S. GAAP rules. The same is true for interest capitalization—U.S. tax rules closely parallel GAAP rules and therefore require avoidable interest to be capitalized for tax purposes.

Capitalization Criteria—An Extension Businesses frequently upgrade their long-lived assets in order to increase their usefulness. For example, a trucking company might install new motors in its older vehicles. GAAP capitalizes such expenditures—that is, increases the carrying amount of a long-lived asset—when the expenditure causes any of the following conditions:

- The useful life of the asset is extended;
- The capacity of the asset is increased (that is, when there is an increase in attainable units of output);
- The efficiency of the asset is increased (that is, when fewer labor hours or raw material inputs are required);
- There is any other type of increase in the economic benefits (or future service potential value) of the asset that results as a consequence of the expenditure.

To illustrate how these capitalization criteria work, consider the example in Exhibit 10.6. In Exhibit 10.6, total expenditures that are capitalized—that is, those that are included in the carrying amount of the machine—include *all* of the highlighted costs ($88,500) associated with getting the machine ready for production use, not just the invoice cost of $80,000.

EXHIBIT 10.6	Winger Enterprises

Determination of Capitalized Costs

On January 1, 2005 Winger Enterprises purchased a machine that will be used in operations. The cash purchase price of the machine was $80,000. The freight cost to transport the machine to Winger's factory was $1,200. During the month of January 2005 Winger's employees spent considerable time calibrating the machine and making adjustments and test-runs to get it ready for use. Costs incurred in doing this were:

Allocated portion of production manager's salary for coordinating machine adjustments	$2,200
Hourly wages of production workers engaged in test-runs of the machine	3,600
Cost of raw materials that were used in test-runs (the output was not saleable)	1,500

Given these facts, the capitalized amount of the machine would be the total of all of the costs ($80,000 + $1,200 + $2,200 + $3,600 + $1,500 = $88,500).

To further illustrate the capitalization criteria, suppose that in January 2008 Winger spent an additional $8,000 on the machine. The total expenditure consisted of:

- $2,000 for ordinary repairs and maintenance, required every several years; and
- $6,000 for the installation of a new component that allowed the machine to consume less raw material and operate more efficiently.

In this example, the $2,000 would be treated as a period expense, while the $6,000 would be capitalized in 2008 and added to the carrying amount of the machine.

WorldCom, once the leading telecommunications company in the United States, is accused of deliberately misapplying the asset capitalization rules in order to boost reported pre-tax income by approximately $3.8 billion over five quarters in 2001 and 2002.[2] WorldCom's method

---

[2] See J. Sandberg, D. Solomon, and R. Blumenstein, "Inside WorldCom's Unearthing of a Vast Accounting Scandal," *Wall Street Journal* (June 27, 2002), and K. Eichenwald and S. Romero, "Inquiry Finds Effort at Delay at WorldCom," *New York Times* (July 4, 2002).

was simple. Normal operating costs of connecting to other firms' telecommunications lines—clearly period expenses—were instead capitalized. Since these items (called "line-costs") were debited to balance sheet asset accounts rather than charged to income statement expenses, income was overstated. The motive for this misrepresentation was to hide WorldCom's inherent unprofitability due to excess industry capacity. So a failure to apply the capitalization criteria correctly resulted in an enormous income misstatement as illustrated in Figure 10.1.

Figure 10.1

IMPACT OF WORLDCOM'S MISAPPLICATION OF ASSET CAPITALIZATION RULES

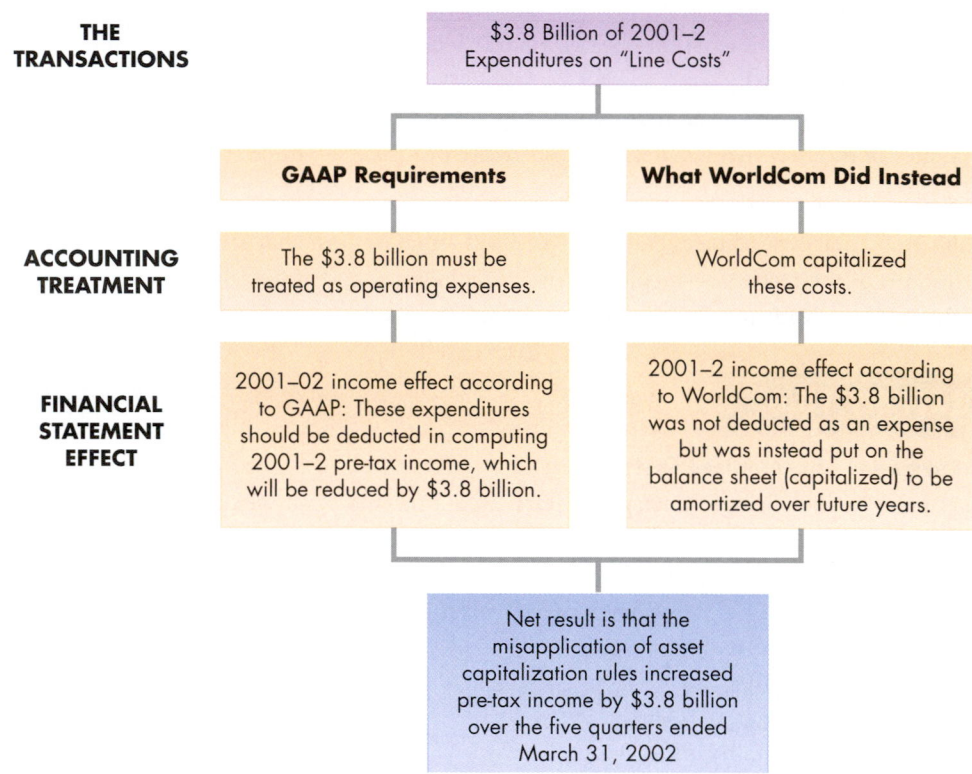

Financial Analysis and Fixed Asset Reporting

Using depreciated historical cost as the measure of fixed asset values introduces many potential pitfalls for unwary statement readers. Here's a simple example.

Chen Corporation purchases long-lived assets and begins operations on January 1, 2005. The assets cost $1,000,000, have a 10-year expected life, no salvage value, and will be depreciated using the straight-line method. Assume that net operating cash flows (that is, revenues minus variable operating expenses) for 2005 are $220,000. Chen's reported pre-tax return on beginning assets for 2005 is 12%, computed as:

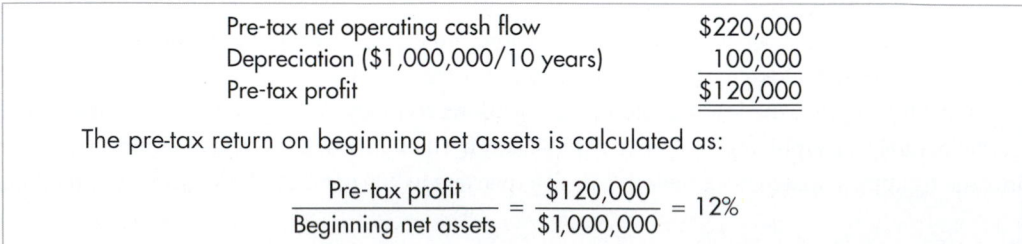

Let's assume Chen makes no additional capital expenditures over the ensuing four years. Consequently, the average age of its operating assets increases over this period. Further assume that, on average, prices in the economy are increasing at 3% per year and that Chen is able to keep pace by

increasing its net operating cash flow by 3%. Our example incorporates two features—aging assets and inflation—which complicate statement analysis. Exhibit 10.7 shows why.

EXHIBIT 10.7	Chen Corporation					
Time-Series Distortions from Aging Assets and Inflation						
	January 1, 2005	December 31, 2005	December 31, 2006	December 31, 2007	December 31, 2008	December 31, 2009
Asset net book value	$1,000,000	$900,000	$800,000	$700,000	$600,000	$500,000
Net operating cash flow (increasing by 3% per year):		$220,000	$226,600	$233,398	$240,400	$247,612
Depreciation		100,000	100,000	100,000	100,000	100,000
Pre-tax profit		$120,000	$126,600	$133,398	$140,400	$147,612
Return on beginning of year net assets*		12%	14.1%	16.7%	20.1%	24.6%
Average age of assets		1 year	2 years	3 years	4 years	5 years

*2006 calculation is $126,600 ÷ $900,000 = 14.1%. Other years' returns are computed similarly.

Notice that the return on beginning assets rises from 12% to 24.6% over the five years, highlighted in Exhibit 10.7. As we are about to explain, this increase is caused by two factors:

1. An aging asset base
2. Increasing costs and prices.

While our example is contrived, it does help us understand how historical cost reporting for fixed assets may make trend analyses misleading. Specifically, how should the increasing return be interpreted? Is Chen's year-to-year performance really improving? Is the 2009 rate of return sustainable?

"Is year-to-year performance improving?" Probably not. The upward drift in reported return on assets is caused by operating cash flows that just keep pace with inflation, while depreciation and the asset's original cost do not change under historical cost reporting. To know whether the rate of return increase is "real," we need each year's numbers expressed in terms of current year prices. That is, to determine whether the return increase from 12% to 14.1% (in 2006) represents real improvement, we would need to know the replacement cost of the assets and we would need to recompute the rate of return using replacement cost depreciation and asset value. Only then could we assess whether some portion of the year-to-year "improvement" is real—as opposed to being an artifact of the historical cost basis of accounting for fixed assets.

"Is the 2009 return sustainable?" No, it's not. If the rate of return for 2009 were recomputed on a replacement cost basis, it would be lower than 24.6%. Statement readers seldom have enough information to adjust for year-to-year distortions like those in Exhibit 10.7. However, they must understand that **when asset reinvestment is not continuous, the increasing age of the asset base in conjunction with rising prices introduces distortions** like those in Exhibit 10.7—and thus, projections must be made with caution.

Historical cost accounting for long-lived assets also creates problems for statement readers who try to make comparisons between companies like Chen Corporation and its competitors. To see why, suppose Chen's biggest competitor is Rizzo Corporation. As of January 1, 2005 Rizzo had assets with a net book value of $1,000,000. Recall that Chen also had an asset net book value of $1,000,000 on that same date. While Chen's assets were new, let's assume Rizzo's were, on average, slightly less than five years old and had a ten-year expected life. Rizzo also uses straight-line depreciation with no salvage value. Rizzo's policy is to replace 10% of its assets each year at the end of their useful lives. Further assume that the cost of replacing the assets retired each year has consistently increased by 3% annually in past years. Given these assumptions, Rizzo's asset net book value consisted of:[3]

Long-lived assets at original cost	$1,741,098
Less: Accumulated depreciation	741,098
Net asset book value	$1,000,000

Assume that Rizzo's pre-tax net operating cash flow for 2005 is $294,110 and that its pre-tax return on beginning net assets is 12%, as shown here:

Pre-tax net operating cash flow	$ 294,110
Depreciation ($1,741,098/10 years)	174,110
Pre-tax profit	$ 120,000

The pre-tax return on beginning net assets is calculated as:

$$\frac{\text{Pre-tax profit}}{\text{Beginning net assets}} = \frac{\$120,000}{(\$1,741,098 - \$741,098)} = 12\%$$

Rizzo's 2005 pre-tax return on assets is 12%, the same as Chen's. Rizzo is also able to keep pace with inflation by increasing its net operating cash flow by 3% each year. We will assume that its annual capital expenditures to replace 10% of its assets each year also continues to increase at 3%, just as in past years, and that the new assets are purchased on the last day of each year. These assumptions yield the performance data for 2005–2009 in Exhibit 10.8.

Here's what our Chen (Exhibit 10.7) versus Rizzo Corporation (Exhibit 10.8) comparison illustrates. Both firms start in identical financial reporting positions on January 1, 2005. Each has assets with a *net* book value of $1,000,000. The *only* difference is that Chen's assets are new and Rizzo's are 4.5 years old, on average. Rizzo constantly replaces a portion of its assets and maintains an average asset age of 4.5 years as highlighted in Exhibit 10.8, while the average age of Chen Corporation's assets is increasing, as highlighted in Exhibit 10.7. Rizzo's reported return on beginning assets at the end of 2009 is 12.0%; Chen's is 24.6%. Both firms experienced identical economic conditions and were able to respond identically. The only difference is that over this period Rizzo constantly maintained a long-lived asset age of 4.5 years, while the average age of Chen's assets increased from one year to five years. An analyst who is unaware of the asset age differential might erroneously conclude that Chen is more profitable than Rizzo in 2009 (a 24.6% versus a 12.0% return on assets) and that Chen's dramatic upward trend implies a rosier future. As we have just seen, such inferences are unwarranted since the difference across firms is driven by the way that historical-cost, fixed-asset accounting rules affect firms with aging assets.

[3] These numbers were determined as follows. Since Rizzo replaces 10% of its assets each year, there are ten asset layers. Furthermore, each year's layer cost 3% more than the previous layer. With these assumptions, the January 1, 2005 figures for original cost and accumulated depreciation—layer by layer—are:

Asset Purchased on Dec. 31	Cost	Accumulated Depreciation	Asset Purchased on Dec. 31	Cost	Accumulated Depreciation
1995	$151,877	$136,689	2000	$176,067	$ 70,427
1996	156,433	125,146	2001	181,349	54,405
1997	161,126	112,788	2002	186,789	37,358
1998	165,960	99,576	2003	192,393	19,239
1999	170,939	85,470	2004	198,165	—
				$1,741,098	$741,098

Average age equals 4.5 years

Source: We are grateful to Meredith Maher for formulating this example.

EXHIBIT 10.8	Rizzo Corporation

Time-Series Without Distortion from Aging Assets

	January 1, 2005	December 31, 2005	December 31, 2006	December 31, 2007	December 31, 2008	December 31, 2009
			Year Ended			
Asset net book value	$1,000,000	$1,030,000*	$1,060,900	$1,092,727	$1,125,508	$1,159,274
Capital expenditures (increasing by 3% per year)		204,110	210,233	216,540	223,036	229,727
Net operating cash flow (increasing by 3% per year):		294,110	302,933	312,021	321,382	331,023
Depreciation (see details below)		174,110	179,333	184,713	190,255	195,962
Pre-tax profit		$ 120,000	$ 123,600	$ 127,308	$ 131,127	$ 135,061
Return on beginning of year net assets		12.0%	12.0%	12.0%	12.0%	12.0%
Average age of assets		4.5 years	4.5 years	4.5 years	4.5 years	4.5 years

Depreciation details explained:	2005	2006	2007	2008	2009
1. Beginning-of-year gross original cost of assets	$1,741,098	$1,793,331	$1,847,131	$1,902,545	$1,959,621
2. Gross cost of assets retired at year-end	(151,877)	(156,433)	(161,126)	(165,960)	(170,939)
3. Capital expenditure on new assets (increases by 3%)	204,110	210,233	216,540	223,036	229,727
4. End-of-year gross original cost of assets	$1,793,331	$1,847,131	$1,902,545	$1,959,621	$2,018,409
Depreciation for year:					
Item 1 × 10%	$ 174,110	$ 179,333	$ 184,713	$ 190,255	$ 195,962

*Computed as: Beginning net book value ($1,000,000) + Capital expenditure ($204,110) − Depreciation ($174,110) = $1,030,000. All other years are computed similarly. This item is increasing by 3% per year.

Exhibit 10.7 is intended to convey the problems analysts face in doing a trend analysis for a single firm. These problems exist because of the GAAP rules used in long-lived asset financial reporting. Exhibit 10.8 extends this critique of GAAP rules by showing how firms like Rizzo Corporation whose assets are continually being replaced cannot easily be compared to firms with aging assets like Chen Corporation.

While the issues raised in Exhibits 10.7 and 10.8 are real, the problems confronting analysts in practice are not usually as extreme. To understand why, let's focus on year-to-year (time-series) analyses, like those in Exhibit 10.7. Unlike Chen, most firms replace some assets each year. Established firms with continuous capital expenditures do not experience the increasing average asset age shown in Exhibit 10.7. Instead, with regular replacement, the average age of long-lived assets remains fairly constant from year-to-year. For these firms, the year-to-year pattern of returns will not display an artificial upward drift like that of Chen Corporation. That is why we introduced an example of a firm whose average asset age remained constant, like Rizzo's. Of course, in those rare instances in which capital expenditures are "lumpy," statement readers must recognize the possibility that an aging asset base can lead to distorted returns on assets, like those of Exhibit 10.7. And, the higher is the rate of input cost and output price increases, the greater is the trend distortion.

GAAP for long-lived assets does significantly impede rate-of-return comparisons across companies in certain situations. Within the same industry, differences like those between Chen and Rizzo would be unusual, since competition often leads firms to pursue similar investment and operating strategies. Firms that don't modernize or innovate are ultimately left behind. Consequently, market forces lead to commonalities that usually make comparisons across firms *within the same industry* meaningful.

The historical cost basis used for long-lived assets does create potentially significant problems for those comparing firms in *different industries*. Operating conditions, capital expenditure policies, and the rate of input cost change can vary significantly across industries. For example, if there is little technological change in one industry, there is little incentive for firms to replace old—but still functional—assets. In stagnated industries, the average age of assets can increase, and this tendency contrasts with industries in which technological advancements have proliferated. This average age differential can lead to misleading comparisons, like those illustrated in Exhibit 10.7 (where Chen experienced an increase in asset age) as compared to Exhibit 10.8 (where Rizzo's asset age remained stable).

RECAP GAAP rules for fixed asset accounting complicate financial analysis. Statement readers need to understand what factors might cause trend and across-firm distortions and adjust for them. Often, information to make the adjustment is unavailable. In these circumstances, knowing the approximate direction of any biases may help the statement reader avoid unwarranted inferences.

Intangible Assets

Intangible assets, like patents, trademarks, and copyrights, convey future benefits to their owners. When one firm purchases an intangible asset from another—for example, a valuable trademark—few new accounting or reporting issues arise. The acquired intangible asset is recorded at the arm's-length transaction price and is amortized over its expected useful life, as described later in the chapter. (Another category of acquired intangible assets, called goodwill, arises as a consequence of certain types of corporate takeovers. This category of intangible assets is discussed in Chapter 16.)

Difficult financial reporting issues exist when the intangible asset is developed internally instead of being purchased from another company. These difficulties arise because of the accounting treatment of the expenditures that ultimately create valuable intangibles like patents or trademarks. A patent, for example, is the result of successful research and development expenditures; a valuable trademark is the result of successful advertising, a great product, clever packaging, or brand loyalty.

The recoverability of research and development expenditures is highly uncertain at the start of a project. Consequently, the FASB requires that virtually all R&D expenditures be expensed as incurred.[4] This mandated financial reporting uniformity was viewed as a practical way of dealing with the risk of nonrecoverability of R&D expenditures. Similarly, prevailing accounting principles have long required companies to treat advertising and creative product development expenditures as period costs, again because of the highly uncertain, difficult-to-predict, future benefits.

The major types of cash outflows most likely to result in intangibles-creation (R&D, advertising costs, and so forth) are immediately expensed. ***When past outflows successfully create intangible assets, these outflows have already been expensed and there are usually few remaining future outflows to capitalize!*** Consequently, the balance sheet carrying amount for intangible

---

[4] "Accounting for Research and Development Costs," *SFAS No. 2* (Stamford, CT: FASB, 1974). The only exception to immediate expensing is when the R&D expenditures will be reimbursed by some outside group.

assets is often far below the value of the property right. For example, the 1991 Annual Report of Polaroid Corporation indicates that "Patents and trademarks" are valued at $1. However, a footnote in that same annual report discloses that Polaroid was awarded a court judgment arising from a suit which alleged that Eastman Kodak Company's instant cameras and film infringed on Polaroid patents. The judgment was ultimately settled for $924.5 million. The size of the judgment and settlement indicates that the Polaroid patents were extremely valuable. Nevertheless, the real economic value of these internally developed intangible assets did not appear on Polaroid's balance sheet, since the costs incurred in developing the valuable patents were expensed as incurred. This situation is not unusual.

As software development companies proliferated in the 1980s, the FASB ultimately provided guidance in accounting for software development costs.[5] *SFAS No. 86* applies the previously described R&D rules to the particular circumstances faced by companies developing computer software products. Specifically, *prior to* establishing the **technological feasibility** of a computer software product, a company expenses *all* R&D costs incurred to develop it. After technological feasibility is established, additional costs incurred to get the product ready for general release to customers are supposed to be capitalized. Capitalization of additional costs ceases when the final product is available for sale. The costs incurred before technological feasibility is established can be considerable; because feasibility may not be assured until late in the expenditure cycle, there may be few costs left to capitalize. Accordingly, the intangible software asset may be recorded at an amount far lower than its value to the software development firm, just as in other (nonsoftware) R&D settings.

> *SFAS No. 86* states that technological feasibility has been established "when the enterprise has completed all planning, designing, coding and testing activities that are necessary to establish that the product can be produced to meet its design specifications including functions, features, and technical performance requirements" (para. 4).

The GAAP bias that leads to an understatement of internally developed intangible assets has hindered financial analysis for many years, and the problem has worsened as economic activity shifted in the 1980s from heavy manufacturing to high technology. In high-technology industries like software development and biotechnology, research has contributed to large increases in the value of intellectual property rights such as patents and trademarks. Yet accounting rules for internally developed intangibles have not kept pace.

The FASB justified expensing all R&D for three reasons:

1. The future benefits accruing from these expenditures are highly uncertain.
2. A causal relationship between current R&D and future revenue has not been demonstrated.
3. Whatever benefits may arise cannot be objectively measured.[6]

But recent research indicates that these assertions are probably incorrect. One study examined the relationship between R&D expenditures and both future earnings and share values.[7] The study found that a one-dollar increase in R&D expenditures results in a cumulative two-dollar profit increase over a seven-year period. Furthermore, a one-dollar increase in R&D expenditures leads to a five-dollar increase in the market value of a firm's shares, on average. So R&D expenditures *are* related to future benefits and logic suggests that a causal relationship exists. Another study developed statistically reliable estimates of unrecorded R&D asset costs.[8] These asset cost estimates were then used to adjust reported earnings and book values to reflect capitalization of R&D. The adjusted numbers that reflected R&D capitalization (and subsequent amortization) were strongly associated with stock prices and returns and, thus, value-relevant to investors. So investors' behavior suggests that the adjusted numbers are measuring R&D benefits. Together, the results of these two studies contradict the three reasons the FASB used to justify expensing R&D.

Valuation

---

[5] "Accounting for the Costs of Computer Software to Be Sold, Leased, or Otherwise Marketed," *SFAS No. 86* (Stamford, CT: FASB, 1985).

[6] *SFAS No. 2*, paras. 39–46.

[7] T. Sougiannis, "The Accounting Based Valuation of Corporate R&D," *The Accounting Review* (January 1994), pp. 44–68.

[8] B. Lev and T. Sougiannis, "The Capitalization, Amortization, and Value-Relevance of R&D," *Journal of Accounting and Economics* (February 1996), pp. 107–138.

Some portion (often small) of total software development costs does get capitalized once technological feasibility is established. But the proportion of total software development costs that gets capitalized is subjectively determined and varies across firms, as shown in Figure 10.2. More than 50% of the firms included in the Figure 10.2 sample capitalized between 0 to 20% of software development costs while about 5% capitalized more than 60%. So one question that arises is whether a GAAP standard that conveys such latitude also provides information that is relevant to investors. One study found that it does since the capitalization-related variables (annual amount capitalized, amount of the software asset, and annual amortization) were significantly associated with stock prices, returns, and future earnings.[9] But the next question is whether value relevance would *increase* if GAAP permitted even larger amounts of software development costs to be capitalized. Another study explored this.[10] The author found that capitalizing 100% of software development costs and amortizing them over three years produced accounting numbers that are more consistent with observed market prices than are *SFAS No. 86* partial capitalization numbers. So, ***relaxing the expense charge-off criteria improved value relevance***.

Figure 10.2

SOFTWARE CAPITALIZATION RATES

Source: Elizabeth A. Eccher, "Managerial Discretion in Financial Reporting," Working Paper, Massachusetts Institute of Technology, August 1998. Reprinted with permission.

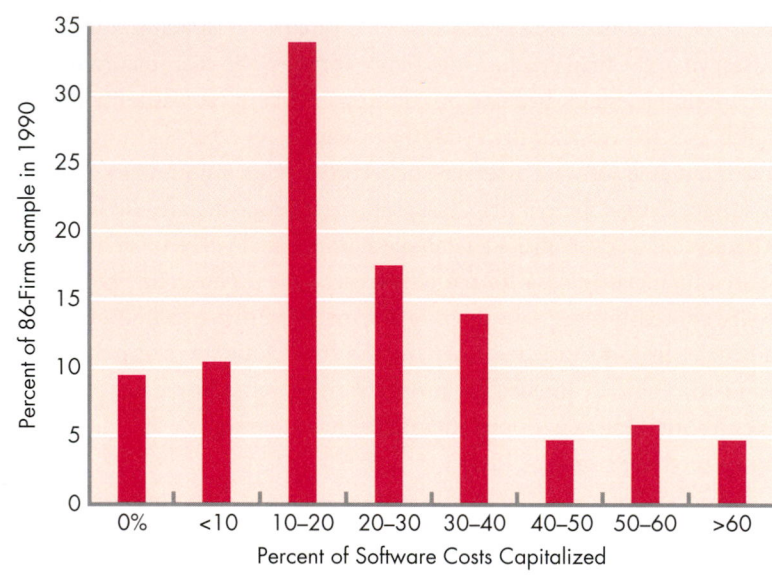

Valuation

To summarize, research findings almost uniformly indicate that existing GAAP for both R&D and software development is too conservative. The expenditures create assets that do not appear on balance sheets, and income for current as well as future years is misstated. Fortunately, analysts can adjust for these problems using required GAAP disclosures. For example, firms are required to disclose separately total expensed R&D costs.[11] Similarly, *SFAS No. 86* requires disclosure of unamortized software assets, amortization and write-downs of the assets in each period, and all costs that are expensed prior to technological feasibility.[12] ***Analysts can use these disclosures to reconstruct what asset and amortization amounts would be if GAAP allowed full capitalization.*** (Analysts can create their own estimation procedures or use the models in the articles cited in footnotes 8 and 10.) Unhappily, disclosures of marketing and advertising expenditures are too cryptic to permit a similar adjustment approach for trademarks or brands. So it's harder to undo the deficiencies of GAAP for these unrecorded intangible assets.

[9] D. Aboody and B. Lev, "The Value Relevance of Intangibles: The Case of Software Capitalization," *Journal of Accounting Research* (Supplement 1998), pp. 161–191.
[10] K. Den Adel, "The Value-Relevance of Alternative Accounting Treatments of Software Development Costs" (unpublished manuscript, Purdue University, May 2000).
[11] *SFAS No. 2*, para. 13.
[12] *SFAS No. 86*, paras. 11–12.

Intangibles and Mergers   The merger boom of the late 1990s increased the understatement of R&D assets. Here's why. When one firm acquires another and uses the **purchase method** to account for the acquisition (discussed in Chapter 16), the total purchase price must be apportioned to the individual assets acquired. The firms that were taken over often had ongoing R&D projects. Managers of the acquiring firm have strong incentives to allocate a large portion of the acquisition cost to this **purchased in-process R&D**. Why? Well, GAAP requires R&D to be written off as incurred. Allocating a large portion of the purchase price to in-process R&D provides a justification for immediately charging the *acquired* R&D to expense. Some managers of acquiring companies believe that large income statement charges arising from acquisitions are treated as transitory (or even valuation irrelevant) events by analysts. So their impact on firm valuation is presumed to be minimal. They feel that aggressively allocating much of the purchase price to in-process R&D reduces both consolidated assets and acquisition period income without reducing firm value. But the write-off will *increase* future periods' income because there are fewer dollars of asset cost to amortize later. So managers get to write off a (potentially large) portion of the acquisition price to the acquisition period income statement—presumably without penalty—and, by reducing assets, also reduce future periods' amortization expenses. From the managers' perspective, it's a win-win situation!

GAAP says that purchase price amounts assigned to in-process R&D projects that *have no alternative future use* must be charged to expense upon acquisition.[13] Purchased in-process R&D projects have alternative future use when these expenditures have achieved (or are virtually certain to achieve) a successful commercial outcome. This is an extension of the logic of *SFAS No. 2.* Accordingly, the acquiring firm must determine whether the purchased in-process R&D has "no alternative future use." If there *is* a future use, the purchased in-process R&D cannot be written off. But the criteria for ascertaining whether purchased in-process R&D has a future use are subjective and murky. So it seems likely that aggressive write-offs of purchased in-process R&D will continue.

Intangibles Accounting in the United Kingdom: Similarities and Differences

The financial reporting rules for research and development in the United Kingdom are generally similar to those in the United States. Marketing and advertising costs are treated as period costs in the United Kingdom, just as they are in the United States. As a result, U.K. balance sheet numbers for patents, trademarks, and similar intangibles are subject to the same type of understatement as those in the United States.

However, there is a difference between the application of the historical cost accounting principle in the United Kingdom and the United States. United Kingdom accounting rules allow companies to write long-lived assets up to new higher carrying values when market value exceeds cost—making adherence to the cost principle more flexible in the United Kingdom. The understatement of intangibles on U.K. firms' books prompted a few U.K. companies to abandon the historical cost treatment of trademarks (called "brands" in British English) and to write these intangible assets up to their estimated fair value. One author summarizes the U.K. treatment of brands as follows:

International

> A case can be made that the brand value should be placed on the balance sheet or at least reported to shareholders as part of a firm's financial report. In fact, several British firms have

---

[13] "Applicability of FASB Statement No. 2 to Business Combinations Accounted for by the Purchase Method," *FASB Interpretation No. 4* (Norwalk, CT: FASB, 1975). This financial reporting guidance was explicitly reiterated in *SFAS No. 141* "Business Combinations" (Norwalk, CT: FASB, 2001), para. B170.

However, the latitude for recognizing internally developed intangibles in the U.K. has recently been restricted. The U.K. standard setting group, the Accounting Standards Board, stated:

> "An internally developed intangible asset may be capitalised only if it has a readily ascertainable market value." ["Goodwill and Intangible Assets," *Financial Reporting Standard* (*FRS*) *10* (London: Accounting Standards Board, 1997), para. 14].

added brand equity to the balance sheet. For example, in 1988 Ranks Hovis McDougall decided to put a balance sheet value of $1.2 billion on its 60 brands. First, such an intangible asset can easily exceed in value that of tangible assets which are scrupulously reported and affect shareholders' valuation of firms. Second, reported brand equity can focus attention upon intangible assets and thus make it easier to justify brand building activities that are likely to pay off in the long term. Without such information, shareholders must rely upon short-term financials.

The major difficulty involves a question of whether any valuation of brand equity can be both objective and verifiable. Unless brand valuation can be defended, it will not be helpful and can result in legal liability. It is no coincidence that in England, where brand value has been placed upon the balance sheet, there is a less litigious environment.[14]

While only a few U.K. firms have actually written brands up to fair value, the fact that some have chosen to do so indicates the perceived limitations of existing accounting for intangibles.

RECAP
Balance sheet carrying amounts for internally developed intangible assets like patents or trademarks are not dependable indicators of their value to the firm. Because the assets are understated, so too is income statement amortization in later years.

A Case Study of Ambiguities in Capitalization Criteria: Oil and Gas Exploration Costs

Earlier, we described two characteristics that tend to make the book values of long-lived assets unreliable indicators of their value to the firm. First, for pragmatic reasons, historical cost is used as the primary basis for measuring long-lived assets. So past economic sacrifice—rather than current expected benefit—determines balance sheet carrying amounts. Second, the ultimate benefit from research and product development expenditures cannot be forecast at the start of a project; this uncertainty causes these items to be written off as period costs even if they eventually lead to the creation of an asset. That's why many development expenditures designed to create intangible assets never get capitalized.

Now we explain a third cause for the discrepancy between long-lived asset numbers and economic reality—***ambiguities in capitalization criteria***. Ambiguities in capitalization criteria arise in several settings, including the treatment of oil and gas exploration costs. Consider the following example.

> Calaboga Oil paid $50 million for a large oil field in Alaska. During 2005 Calaboga explored for oil throughout the field. Twenty wells were drilled at a total cost of $200 million, or $10 million per well. Nineteen of the wells proved to be unproductive dry holes, while one was found to contain a considerable amount of oil. The financial reporting question is this: What is the appropriate carrying amount of the producing well?

Over time, two different approaches to determining the cost of the producing well emerged. The two approaches differ in their treatment of the $190 million that was spent in drilling the 19 dry holes.

---

[14] D. A. Aaker, *Managing Brand Equity* (New York: Free Press, 1991), p. 28.

One alternative, called the **full-cost approach**, considers the $190 million to be a necessary cost of finding the one producing oil well. That well would be carried on the books at $250 million using the full-cost approach; this is the $50 million land purchase price plus the $200 million of total drilling costs.

Another alternative, the **successful-efforts approach**, would reflect the producing well at only $60 million. This is the sum of the $50 million land purchase price plus the $10 million cost of drilling the specific well that became a producer. The $190 million of drilling costs incurred on the unproductive wells would be written off to the 2005 income statement as a period expense.

The two approaches in this example can be summarized as follows.

Full Cost

Balance Sheet:

Petroleum production property

Land cost	$ 50,000,000
Drilling costs on dry holes	190,000,000
Drilling costs on producer	10,000,000
Capitalized Amount	$250,000,000

Income Statement:

2005 Charge	—0—

Successful Efforts

Balance Sheet:

Petroleum production property

Land cost	$ 50,000,000
Drilling costs on producer	10,000,000
Capitalized Amount	$ 60,000,000

Income Statement:

2005 Charge	$190,000,000

Because big, lump-sum expense write-offs can occur using the successful-efforts approach, year-to-year reported profits are more volatile, especially for small firms that do not have a large portfolio of drilling projects. Furthermore, small growth firms that engage in extensive exploration activities would tend to report lower near-term profits under successful efforts. To avoid this volatility and potentially lower average earnings, most smaller oil companies use the full-cost approach. Notice that under the full-cost option, unsuccessful drilling outcomes do not penalize current periods' earnings.

We focus on accounting options for oil and gas exploration because this topic contains many of the issues that typify financial reporting controversies. Specifically,

- The debate regarding the two alternative accounting treatments is endless—there is no "right" or "wrong" answer;
- The reporting options have the potential to influence managerial behavior; and
- The securities market appears to recognize that the differing managerial incentives have implications for valuing firms.

We now address these issues.

Debate Is Endless As world energy prices increased during the 1970s, public scrutiny of oil companies' profits also increased. The diversity in financial reporting within the oil industry was deemed undesirable by the U.S. Congress because it made comparisons across firms difficult and hindered effective regulation. Congress passed the Energy Policy and Conservation Act in 1975, which directed the SEC to standardize oil and gas reporting.[15] The SEC initially delegated this task to the FASB.

---

[15] Public Law 94–163, Energy Policy and Conservation Act [42 U.S. Code, Sec. 6383].

In 1977 the FASB issued *SFAS No. 19*,[16] which eliminated the choice allowed between the full-cost and successful-efforts options. *SFAS No. 19* mandated that all companies had to use successful-efforts accounting. This elicited an outcry from smaller oil companies that, remember, were predominantly using full-costing. These companies lobbied Congress by arguing that the profit volatility from successful-efforts accounting would hinder their ability to raise capital, inhibit their domestic energy exploration, and ultimately increase U.S. dependence on foreign oil, thereby negating the intent of the 1975 energy act.

These lobbying efforts were successful. The SEC was pressured to reexamine the FASB's approach. The SEC subsequently concluded that neither full-cost nor successful-efforts accounting reflected oil and gas producers' true performance. To see why, let's return to the Calaboga Oil illustration, above.

The SEC argued that if the value of the oil that had been discovered was estimated to be worth, say, $3 billion, it is pointless to debate whether this significant discovery should be reflected at $60 million or $250 million, since both totals fail to capture the economic substance. Instead, the SEC announced that statements filed with the Commission could be prepared under either full-cost or successful-efforts reporting methods. The SEC further expressed an intention to develop a new method—called **reserve recognition accounting**—which would be designed to measure the estimated worth of the discoveries. The SEC never succeeded in gaining acceptance for reserve recognition accounting, primarily because of the assumptions and forecasts it entailed.

After the SEC refused to require that *SFAS No. 19* be used in filings with the Commission, the FASB was compelled to suspend it.[17] Today, oil and gas companies continue to have the option of using either the full-cost or the successful-efforts approach. In other words, after years of endless heated debate, neither approach was considered "wrong." In addition, a footnote disclosure similar to reserve recognition accounting has been required since 1983.[18] This footnote is intended to provide approximate data regarding the estimated worth of proven oil and gas reserves.

Contracting

Reporting Options Influence Managerial Behavior The protest resulting from the FASB's attempt to eliminate full-cost accounting is revealing. The arguments raised by managers of full-cost companies were designed to evoke sentiments about U.S. energy self-sufficiency, national security, economic growth, and other emotional topics. While these issues may have been important, many observers concluded that the real reasons that firms objected to the successful-efforts accounting method were due to other factors—factors that managers were reluctant to raise openly! For example, because the successful-efforts method results in more volatile earnings numbers for small producers, managers' bonuses tied to reported earnings would be lost in certain years. Another reason (indeed, this one was raised openly by some firms) is that the lower near-term profits under the successful-efforts method could lead to violation of loan covenants tied to debt-to-equity ratios.

If one basis for the objection to *SFAS No. 19* was managers' fears of losing bonuses, then it is likely that managers would adapt their behavior if successful-efforts accounting were mandated. For example, managers of small companies might decide to forego riskier drilling projects to avoid the chance of lower successful-efforts earnings if the riskier projects failed. By limiting their drilling efforts to "surer things," the managers would increase the probability of achieving bonus targets.

[16] "Financial Accounting and Reporting by Oil and Gas Producing Companies," *SFAS No. 19* (Stamford, CT: FASB, 1977).
[17] "Suspension of Certain Accounting Requirements for Oil and Gas Producing Companies," *SFAS No. 25* (Stamford, CT: FASB, 1979).
[18] "Disclosures About Oil and Gas Producing Activities," *SFAS No. 69* (Stamford, CT: FASB, 1982).

What we have just explained underscores the issues raised in Chapters 1 and 7 regarding how reporting rules exert a potentially powerful impact on the behavior of managers. Since bonus contracts are often tied to accounting numbers like net income, managers' operating decisions can be influenced by financial reporting rules.

Securities Market Implications If securities markets are reasonably efficient, as they are believed to be, investors would be aware of the effect of these incentives on managers' behavior. Indeed, the anticipated cutback in drilling levels would be expected to lower the discounted value of affected firms' future cash flows. Why? Because the riskier drilling projects that would be eliminated would still in the aggregate have had positive expected payoffs. Following this logic, we would expect to observe an adverse price reaction for those firms whose accounting would have been altered by *SFAS No. 19*.

Several accounting researchers tested aspects of this hypothesis.[19] These studies found that as it became evident that *SFAS No. 19* would be issued, the security prices of full-cost firms fell relative to those of successful-efforts firms. This result is consistent with the market anticipating that full-cost managers will change their behavior in a way that lowers future operating cash flows. Other studies provided further evidence that the adverse share price effects for full-cost companies were related to factors like bonus payouts and bond covenant violations.[20]

RECAP

GAAP capitalization criteria for long-lived assets are sometimes ambiguous. Managers have an incentive to exploit this ambiguity in order to derive benefits for themselves and the firm in various contractual arrangements.

Asset Impairment

Here, we review guidelines for determining when and how assets that have already been capitalized should be treated once their value subsequently becomes impaired.

The notion of **asset impairment** is straightforward. A firm acquires an asset because the future benefits expected to be generated by that asset exceed its cost. Subsequently, if the asset's remaining expected future benefits fall below its net book value, that asset is considered to have become impaired.

Measuring impairment encompasses two stages. First, some threshold loss level must be established to determine *when* a write-down must be made. Second, once the threshold is triggered, the *amount* of the write-down must be determined and recorded.

> Assets are often used in combination with other assets, not just singly. When applying the impairment guidelines to groups of assets, the group should consist of the "lowest [asset] level for which identifiable cash flows are largely independent of the cash flow of other groups of assets . . ." (para. 4).

The standards for determining when assets are impaired and the guidelines for reporting impairment amounts are contained in *SFAS No. 144* and summarized in Figure 10.3.[21]

---

[19] See, for example, D. W. Collins and W. T. Dent, "The Proposed Elimination of Full Cost Accounting in the Extractive Petroleum Industry: An Empirical Assessment of the Market Consequences," *Journal of Accounting and Economics* (March 1979), pp. 3–44; and B. Lev, "The Impact of Accounting Regulation on the Stock Market: The Case of Oil and Gas Companies," *The Accounting Review* (July 1979), pp. 485–503.

[20] See, for example, D. W. Collins, M. S. Rozeff, and D. S. Dhaliwal, "The Economic Determinants of the Market Reaction to Proposed Mandatory Changes in the Oil and Gas Industry: A Cross-Sectional Analysis," *Journal of Accounting and Economics* (March 1981), pp. 37–71; T. Lys, "Mandated Accounting Changes and Debt Covenants: The Case of Oil and Gas Accounting," *Journal of Accounting and Economics* (April 1984), pp. 39–65; and D. F. Larcker and L. Revsine, "The Oil and Gas Accounting Controversy: An Analysis of Economic Consequences," *The Accounting Review* (October 1983), pp. 706–32.

[21] "Accounting for the Impairment or Disposal of Long-Lived Assets," *SFAS No. 144* (Norwalk, CT: FASB, 2001).

Figure 10.3

LONG-LIVED ASSET
IMPAIRMENT GUIDELINES

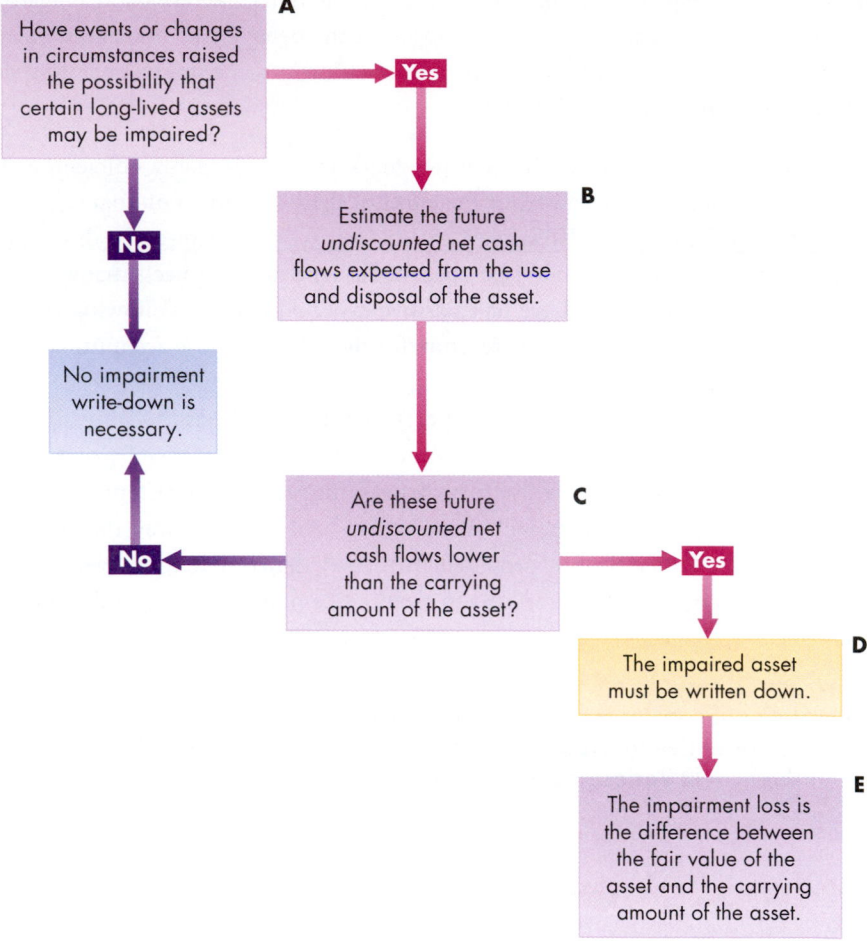

We now explain the impairment guidelines step-by-step using the lettered stages in Figure 10.3.

Stage A. *SFAS No. 144* states that an impairment review should be made whenever external events raise the possibility that an asset's carrying amount (book value) may not be recoverable. Examples of such external events include a significant decrease in the asset's market value, deterioration in the business climate, or forecasted future losses from using the asset.

Stage B. *This stage defines the threshold loss level that triggers the write-down.*

Stage C. The threshold is triggered whenever the expected future *net* cash inflow—undiscounted total future inflows minus future outflows—is *lower* than the current carrying amount of the asset.

Stage D. When an impairment loss is recognized, the long-lived asset is written down. The income statement charge is included "above the line"—that is, as a component of income from continuing operations before income taxes.

Stage E. *This stage defines the amount of the write-down that must be recognized.* The write-down loss is measured as the difference between the fair value of the asset and the current carrying amount of the asset.

The FASB defines the fair value of an asset as ". . . the amount at which that asset . . . could be bought . . . or sold . . . in a current transaction between willing parties. . . ."[22] When market prices are not available, fair value must be estimated using techniques such as discounted present values, the price of similar assets, and other information.[23]

---

[22] Ibid., para. 22.
[23] Ibid.

The following example illustrates how the impairment rules are applied.

> Solomon Corporation manufactures a variety of consumer electronics products. The growing popularity of DVD players is expected to reduce the demand for Solomon's videocassettes. The videocassettes are produced on an assembly line consisting of five special purpose assets with a carrying amount (net book value) of $2,000,000. Solomon's management believes that this change in the business climate threatens the recoverability of these assets' carrying amount; accordingly, their answer to the question in **Stage A** of Figure 10.3 is "yes." Consequently, in order to apply **Stage B**, they prepare the following estimate of future undiscounted cash flows over the expected three-year remaining life of the videocassette assembly line:
>
> | Net operating cash flows: | |
> |---|---:|
> | 2005 | $ 800,000 |
> | 2006 | 400,000 |
> | 2007 | 200,000 |
> | Expected salvage value: | 100,000 |
> | Total undiscounted cash flows | $1,500,000 |
>
> A comparison of the $2,000,000 carrying amount to the $1,500,000 undiscounted flows (**Stage C**) indicates that the asset must be written down (**Stage D**). By reference to used asset price lists, Solomon determines that the entire assembly line can be sold for $750,000. So the amount of the impairment loss (**Stage E**) is $1,250,000 (that is, $2,000,000 – $750,000).
>
> The threshold for determining whether an impairment exists (**Stage B** in Figure 10.3) is the *undiscounted* future net cash flows expected to be generated by the asset. When these undiscounted net cash flows are smaller than the asset's carrying amount, the FASB rule says the asset is impaired. By *not* discounting the future net cash flows, the threshold is higher than it would be if the flows were discounted. Obviously, the higher the threshold, the smaller is the likelihood that the impairment threshold will be triggered. So the high threshold lessens the probability of recognizing an impairment when none exists.

Impairment write-downs present managers with another set of potential earnings management opportunities. For example, in a very good earnings year, managers might be tempted to take an impairment write-down and then write the asset back up (through earnings) in some subsequent year when earnings are down. *SFAS No. 144* eliminates this opportunity for earnings management across years. The FASB prohibits firms from "restoration of a previously recognized impairment loss."[24] Once an asset is written down, it cannot later be written back up to the original higher carrying amount. But International Accounting Standards permit reversals of previously recognized impairment losses. Reversals are permitted when there has been a change in the estimates that were previously used to measure the loss.[25] The amount of the reversal increases income.[26] The IASB's greater flexibility in permitting impairment reversals represents a specific illustration of a recurring difference between IAS standards and U.S. GAAP: IAS standards typically provide more latitude than do U.S. standards. Some observers view the extra latitude favorably because it provides an opportunity for managers to convey private information about the firm's expected future performance to the investment community. Others object to the extra latitude

Contracting

International

---

[24] Ibid., para. 15.

[25] "Impairment of Assets," *IAS 36* (London: IASB, 1998).

[26] This assumes that the originally impaired asset was carried at historical cost. But as you will see later in the chapter, IAS rules allow firms to revalue assets to an amount *above* their historical cost. When the impairment reversal applies to an asset that was originally revalued and subsequently deemed to be impaired, the reversal "gain" is credited directly to owners' equity. (Ibid., para. 104.)

because it also provides managers with opportunities to manage earnings and potentially mislead analysts.

There is also research evidence regarding the timing of impairment write-offs, evidence that predates *SFAS No. 144.* This research indicates that managers used the previous absence of clear guidelines regarding the timing of impairment recognition to influence users' perceptions of how the firm was performing. One study that examined recognition of asset impairment found that these write-offs were often made during periods of sustained economic difficulty—that is, the observed behavior tended to conform to "big bath" bunching of expenses and losses.[27] But does impairment really occur only in bad times? This bunching of write-offs reinforces the need for the clear guidelines in this area that are contained in *SFAS No. 144.*

> The degree of latitude that ought to exist in financial reporting has been debated for years. It's called the **uniformity** versus **flexibility** controversy. At one extreme, some believe that all firms should report using a single (that is, uniform) approach; immediate capitalization of R&D under *SFAS No. 2* is an example of uniformity. At the opposite extreme, others believe that potentially different underlying economic circumstances justify different allowable reporting methods; LIFO versus FIFO inventory accounting illustrates flexibility. This issue is analyzed in R. A. Dye and R. E. Verrecchia, "Discretion vs. Uniformity: Choices Among GAAP," *The Accounting Review* (July 1995), pp. 389–415.

Obligations Arising from Retiring Long-Lived Assets

When an electric utility builds a nuclear plant, or an oil company constructs an offshore drilling rig, regulatory authorities require public welfare and safety expenditures at the end of the asset's life. Nuclear plants must be decontaminated and drilling rigs must be disassembled. This costs money. And by law, these expenditures must take place. *So when certain kinds of assets are built, a liability simultaneously arises.* Until recently, GAAP often ignored these required outflows at the end of an asset's life, so no liability appeared on firms' books. But this changed when the FASB issued *SFAS No. 143.* This pronouncement requires firms to record a liability when certain assets are placed into service.[28]

> Sometimes the liability arises *after* the asset is placed into service. For example, suppose a new law is passed requiring removal of gasoline storage tanks at the end of their useful lives. For firms utilizing these tanks, the liability arises when the law is passed, not when the tank was first placed into service. Also, liabilities may arise over time, as the asset is used. If a coal strip mine must be reclaimed, the liability arises proportionately as the mining occurs.

> This is the risk-free rate of interest on zero-coupon U.S. Treasury instruments plus an adjustment for the credit standing of the firm. So, if the risk-free rate is 5% and the firm's credit standing allows it to borrow at 3% over the risk-free rate, the credit adjusted risk-free rate is 8%.

Here's how the new rules work. Firms are required to estimate the expected present value of the outflows that will occur when assets are eventually retired. These outflows are discounted using what the Board terms a **credit-adjusted risk-free rate**. The discounted present value of the liability is recorded along with an increase in the carrying amount of the related long-lived asset. Consider the following example:

> The present value factor for a payment five years away at 8% is 0.68058. So rounded to the nearest thousand, the present value is $12 million × 0.68058 = $8,167,000.

> Kalai Oil Corporation constructs an oil drilling rig off the Texas coast, which is placed into service on January 1, 2005. The rig cost $300 million to build. Texas law requires that the rig be removed at the end of its estimated useful life of five years. Kalai estimates that the cost of dismantling the rig will be $12 million and its credit adjusted risk-free rate is 8%. The discounted present value of the liability is $8,167,000. Assume that Kalai has already capitalized the $300 million cost of the rig in an account called "Drilling rig."

---

[27] J. A. Elliott and W. H. Shaw, "Write-Offs as Accounting Procedures to Manage Perceptions," *Journal of Accounting Research* (Supplement 1988), pp. 91–119.

[28] "Accounting for Asset Retirement Obligations," *SFAS No.143* (Norwalk, CT: FASB, 2001).

When the asset is placed into service, Kalai records the asset retirement obligation (ARO) as:

DR	Drilling rig (asset retirement cost)	$8,167,000	
CR	ARO liability		$8,167,000

The $8,167,000 debit to the asset account is allocated to expense using some systematic method. Assuming straight-line depreciation over the expected useful life of five years, the entry is:

DR	Depreciation expense	$1,633,400	
CR	Accumulated depreciation—drilling rig		$1,633,400

The liability is initially recorded at its present value but grows over time as retirement nears. The present value of the liability will be increased by 8% per year, as the following schedule shows.

	(a) Present Value of the Liability at Start of Year	(b) Accretion Expense [8% × Column (a) Amount]	(c) Present Value of the Liability at End of Year [Column (a) + Column (b)]
2005	$ 8,167,000	$653,360	$ 8,820,360
2006	8,820,360	705,629	9,525,989
2007	9,525,989	762,079	10,288,068
2008	10,288,068	823,045	11,111,113
2009	11,111,113	888,887*	12,000,000

*Rounded.

The entry to record the increase in the liability in 2005 is:

DR	Accretion expense	$653,360	
CR	ARO liability		$653,360

"Accretion expense" is classified "above the line" in the income statement as an operating expense. It reflects the current period's growth, or *accretion*, of the liability. The FASB says that account titles other than "accretion expense" can be used so long as the nature of the expense is clearly conveyed.[29]

To complete the illustration, assume that an outside contractor dismantles the rig early in January 2010 at a cost of $11,750,000. The journal entry is:

DR	ARO liability	$12,000,000	
CR	Cash		$11,750,000
CR	Gain on settlement of ARO liability		250,000

Assets Held for Sale

Firms constantly experience changing market conditions such as the emergence of new competing products or the development of more efficient distribution systems. In responding to these innovations, firms often seek to dispose of groups of assets that are no longer suited to the new environment they face. When firms actively try to sell some of the assets they currently own, these

---

[29] Ibid., para. 14 and footnote 13.

asset groups should be classified in the balance sheet as "held for sale" if they are expected to be sold within one year.[30] When assets are held for sale, they are reported at the lower of book value or fair market value less costs to sell.[31] To illustrate, assume the following facts regarding Nebozenko Corporation's assets held for sale:

- Book value of assets (cost minus accumulated depreciation) $2,500,000
- Fair market value of assets $2,350,000
- Expected legal fees associated with sale $ 46,000

So these assets would be shown on the balance sheet at $2,304,000, that is, at fair market value minus expected legal fees ($2,350,000 − $46,000). The operating results of asset components classified as "held for sale" are reported in the discontinued operations section of the income statement in the period(s) in which they occur even if the assets have not yet been sold as of the financial statement date.[32] Once the asset group has been sold, the assets are removed from the balance sheet and the income statement disclosure policies for discontinued operations discussed in Chapter 2 are applied. That is, the firm will separately disclose "below the line" the gain or loss (net of taxes) from utilizing these assets during the period covered as well as any gain or loss on disposal of the assets themselves.

> Assets that are eligible to be separately classified must comprise "operations and cash flows that can be clearly distinguished, operationally and for financial reporting purposes, from the rest of the entity" (*SFAS No. 144*, para. 41). This is the same criterion that was used in Chapter 2 to identify elements that must be reflected in the discontinued operations section of the income statement.

Analysis

Segregating the assets held for sale on the balance sheet and separately disclosing their operating results on the income statement are designed to help analysts better understand past firm performance and assess future prospects. For example, in evaluating the efficiency of past asset utilization using the return-on-assets ratio, assets that are destined for sale should be excluded from the rate-of-return denominator and their profit or loss contribution should be excluded from the numerator. This exclusion provides a better measure of expected *future* performance based on assets expected to remain in the firm. The *SFAS No. 144* disclosure rules provide guidance on when certain assets should be segregated on the balance sheet, which alerts analysts to items that should be omitted from rate-of-return calculations. Similarly, income forecasts are enhanced insofar as the income or loss from the asset groups that have been or are about to be sold are no longer factored into the forecast.

Depreciation

Productive assets like buildings, equipment, and machinery eventually wear out. Assets like patents, which have a finite economic life, ultimately expire. Consequently, the cost of these assets must be apportioned to the periods in which they provide benefits. This is the application of the matching principle (Chapter 2) to long-lived assets. This matching process is called **depreciation**. For intangible assets, the allocation of costs to periods is referred to as **amortization**. For mineral deposits and other wasting assets, the assignment of expired costs to periods is called **depletion**. For simplicity, we will refer collectively to any of these allocations of costs to periods as the **depreciation process**.

In financial reporting, the cost to be allocated to periods through the depreciation process is the asset's original historical cost minus its expected salvage value. The objective is to spread the original cost over the period of asset use; *depreciation is not intended to track the asset's declining market value.* Realistically, the asset's end-of-period book value (its original cost minus cumulative depreciation) would approximate its market value only by sheer coincidence. We stress this *absence of correspondence* between accounting measures of depreciation and value decrement because GAAP accounting depreciation, as we have said, is a process of cost allocation, *not* asset valuation.

When applied to long-lived assets, the matching process requires the reporting entity to estimate three things:

---

[30] *SFAS No. 144*, paras. 30–33.
[31] Ibid., para. 34.
[32] Ibid., para. 43.

1. The expected useful life of the asset;
2. The depreciation pattern which will reflect the asset's declining service potential; and
3. The expected salvage value that will exist at the time the asset is retired.

Each requires estimates of future events, especially the pace of technological change and shifts in consumer tastes and preferences. Assets whose economic benefits expire evenly over time are depreciated on a straight-line basis, while those that provide more valuable services in the early years are depreciated on an accelerated basis. The following example in Exhibit 10.9 illustrates the procedures.

EXHIBIT 10.9	Depreciation Example

Facts

Cost of the asset	$10,500
Expected salvage value	$ 500
Expected useful life	5 years

Straight-line Depreciation (SL)

$$(\text{Constant rate} \times \text{Constant base}) = \frac{\text{Cost} - \text{Salvage Value}}{\text{Estimated Life}}$$

$$\left(\frac{1}{5}\right) \times (\$10{,}500 - \$500) = \$2{,}000 \text{ per year for all 5 years}$$

Double-declining Balance Depreciation (DDB)

$$(\text{Constant rate} \times \text{Changing base}) = \begin{array}{l} \text{Double the straight-line} \\ \text{rate} \times \text{Book value at beginning} \\ \text{of each period} \end{array}$$

Straight-line rate	=	20% (that is, 5 year life)
Double straight-line rate	=	20% × 2 = 40%

Year	Beginning of Year Book Value	Depreciation (40% of Beginning of Year Book Value)	End of Year Book Value
1	$10,500.00	$4,200.00	$6,300.00
2	6,300.00	2,520.00	3,780.00
3	3,780.00	1,093.33†	2,686.67
4	2,686.67	1,093.33	1,593.34
5	1,593.34	1,093.34	500.00

†Year 3: Switch to straight-line method (as explained in the text).
$3,780 − $500 = $3,280; $3,280 ÷ 3 = $1,093.33

Sum-of-the-years' Digits Depreciation (SYD)

$$\left(\begin{array}{c}\text{Changing} \\ \text{rate}\end{array} \times \begin{array}{c}\text{Constant} \\ \text{base}\end{array}\right) = \frac{\text{Years remaining in life}}{\text{Sum-of-the-years' digits*}} \times (\text{Cost} - \text{Salvage})$$

Sum-of-the-years' digits = 5 + 4 + 3 + 2 + 1 = 15

Year	Depreciable Basis ($10,500 − $500)	Applicable Fraction	Depreciation
1	$10,000	5/15	$ 3,333.33
2	10,000	4/15	2,666.67
3	10,000	3/15	2,000.00
4	10,000	2/15	1,333.33
5	10,000	1/15	666.67
Total		15/15	$10,000.00

*The formula for determining the sum-of-the-years' digits is: $n(n + 1) \div 2$ where n equals the estimated life of the asset. In our example: $5(5 + 1) \div 2 = 15$. This, of course, is the answer we get by tediously summing the years' digits—that is, $5 + 4 + 3 + 2 + 1 = 15$.

534 CHAPTER 10 Long-Lived Assets and Depreciation

The **straight-line** (SL) depreciation method simply allocates cost minus salvage value evenly over the asset's expected useful life.

The depreciation rate for the **double-declining balance** method (DDB) is double the straight-line rate (in Exhibit 10.9, 20% per year for SL, 40% per year for DDB). Applying a constant DDB depreciation percentage to a declining balance will never depreciate book value down to salvage value. To depreciate down to an asset's expected salvage value using DDB, two steps must be employed. First, in years 1 and 2, the 40% rate is applied to the book value of the assets, without subtracting the salvage value. Second, once the DDB depreciation amount falls below what it would be with straight-line depreciation, a switch to the straight-line method is made. This happens in year 3, when DDB depreciation would have been $3,780 × 40%, or $1,512, which is less than the straight-line depreciation of $2,000. Therefore, straight-line depreciation is used beginning in year 3. The SL amount of $1,093.33 is determined by taking the end of year 2 remaining DDB book value of $3,780, subtracting the salvage value of $500, and dividing the result, $3,280, by 3.

Sum-of-the-years' digits (SOYD) is another accelerated depreciation method. SOYD will depreciate an asset to precisely its salvage value, so a switch to SL is unnecessary.

Figure 10.4(a) shows the annual depreciation charges under the alternative depreciation methods; Figure 10.4(b) shows the resulting net book value at each year-end.

Figure 10.4

ALTERNATIVE DEPRECIATION METHODS

(a) Annual Depreciation Charges; and (b) Net Book Value

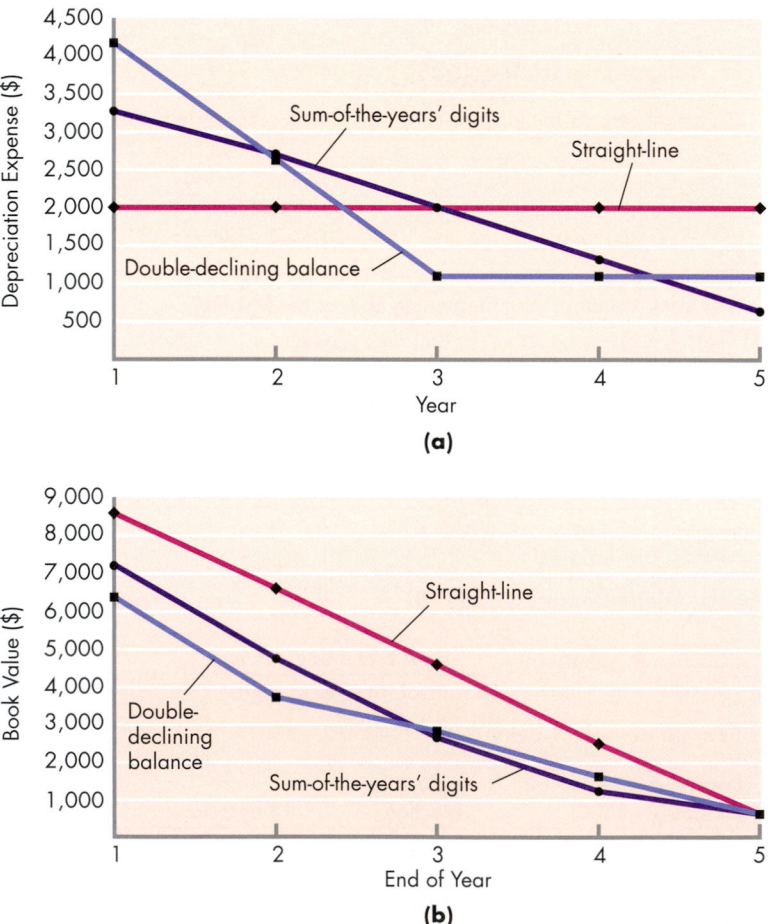

In preparing external financial reports, companies are free to select the depreciation method they believe best reflects both the pattern of an asset's use and the services it provides. Within the same industry, different companies may use different methods. Even within the same company, different types of assets may be depreciated using different methods. For example, buildings might be depreciated using the straight-line method, while trucks might be depreciated using the sum-of-the-years' digits method. Exhibit 10.10 illustrates an annual survey of book depreciation choices used by 600 companies.

EXHIBIT 10.10	Depreciation Choices			
	Number of Companies			
	2002	**2001**	**2000**	**1999**
Straight-line	579	579	576	577
Declining-balance	22	22	22	27
Sum-of-the-years' digits	5	6	7	7
Accelerated method—not specified	44	49	53	53
Units-of-production	32	32	34	31
Other	7	9	10	6

Source: Reprinted with permission from Y. Iofe and M. C. Calderisi (eds.), *Accounting Trends and Techniques*, 2003, page 422. Copyright © 2003 by the American Institute of Certified Public Accountants, Inc. The numbers for each year do not total 600 since companies use more than one depreciation method (for example, straight-line for buildings and accelerated for automobiles).

This annual AICPA survey shows that straight-line depreciation predominates for financial reporting purposes. However, accelerated depreciation is almost universally used for tax purposes. While there is some evidence that the market adjusts for differences in depreciation methods when establishing securities prices,[33] the diversity of depreciation methods across firms complicates security analysis.

Disposition of Long-Lived Assets

When individual long-lived assets are disposed of before their useful lives are completed, any difference between the net book value of the asset and the disposition proceeds is treated as a gain or loss. Assume that the asset in the Exhibit 10.9 example is being depreciated using the double-declining balance method and is sold at the end of year 2 for $5,000 when its book value is $3,780. The following entry is made:

> Firms that are not currently paying taxes because of losses or operating loss carryforwards have an incentive not to use accelerated depreciation. But even here, tax rules require certain depreciation methods. Consequently, companies are constrained in efforts to abandon accelerated tax depreciation methods when losses materialize.

DR Cash	$5,000	
DR Accumulated depreciation	6,720	
CR Long-lived asset		$10,500
CR Gain on sale of asset		1,220

Dispositions of individual assets take place frequently as firms respond to changing production and consumer-demand conditions. For this reason, gains and losses from asset sales do not satisfy the criteria for the extraordinary item treatment described in Chapter 2. Accordingly, such items are included in the income statement "above the line" as an element of pre-tax income from continuing operations.

> Gains or losses on sales of assets comprising a clearly distinguishable component of an entity, as described in the previous section "Assets Held for Sale," are shown in the discontinued operations section.

[33] W. H. Beaver and R. E. Dukes, "Interperiod Tax Allocation and δ-Depreciation Methods: Some Empirical Results," *The Accounting Review* (July 1973), pp. 549–59.

Financial Analysis and Depreciation Differences

Analysis

Most U.S. firms use straight-line depreciation for financial reporting purposes. Nevertheless, making valid comparisons across firms is often hindered by other depreciation assumptions, especially differences in useful lives. Two firms in the same industry often depreciate their otherwise similar assets over different estimated lives. When this happens, potentially significant income differences arise.

We now illustrate this problem and discuss ways to adjust depreciation to achieve greater comparability across firms. Exhibit 10.11 shows information extracted from the 2002 annual report of Wal-Mart, Inc.; Exhibit 10.12 contains similar data from the 2002 annual report of Costco Wholesale Corporation, one of Wal-Mart's competitors. Both companies depreciate all their long-lived assets using the straight-line method. However, Wal-Mart depreciates buildings and improvements over useful lives of 5 to 50 years; for Costco useful lives range from 25 to 35 years. A difference in useful life assumptions also exists for equipment and fixtures; Wal-Mart's estimated lives range from 5 to 12 years, while Costco's are from 3 to 10 years. (See highlighted sections in Exhibits 10.11 and 10.12.)

EXHIBIT 10.11	Wal-Mart Corporation

Balance Sheet Fixed Assets

	January 31	
($ in millions)	**2003**	**2002**
Property, Plant and Equipment, at Cost:		
Land	$11,228	$10,241
Building and improvements	33,750	28,527
Fixtures and equipment	15,946	14,135
Transportation equipment	1,313	1,089
	62,237	53,992
Less accumulated depreciation	13,537	11,436
Net property, plant and equipment	$48,700	$42,556
Capital Leases:		
Property under capital lease	$ 4,814	$ 4,626
Less accumulated amortization	1,610	1,432
Net property under capital leases	$ 3,204	$ 3,194

Edited Footnote on Depreciation and Amortization

Depreciation and Amortization

Depreciation and amortization for financial statement purposes are provided on the straight-line method over the estimated useful lives of the various assets. Depreciation expense, including amortization of property under capital lease, for the years 2002, 2001, and 2000 was $3.1 billion, $2.7 billion and $2.4 billion, respectively. For income tax purposes, accelerated methods are used with recognition of deferred income taxes for the resulting temporary differences. Estimated useful lives for financial statements purposes are as follows:

Building and improvements	5–50 years
Fixtures and equipment	5–12 years
Transportation equipment	2–5 years

Selected Income Statement Information

	Year Ended January 31	
($ in millions)	**2003**	**2002**
Depreciation (rounded)	$ 3,100	$ 2,700
Income before income taxes and minority interest	$12,719	$10,751

Source: Wal-Mart Corporation 2002 Annual Report

Notice that Wal-Mart rounded its depreciation expense disclosure to the nearest $100 million. As a result, all of our computations in Exhibit 10.13 and the text adjustments that follow it must unavoidably also be rounded to the nearest $100 million. This rounding reduces the precision of the resulting adjustments.

EXHIBIT 10.12   **Costco Wholesale Corporation**

Balance Sheet Fixed Assets

($ in thousands)	Sept. 1 2002	Sept. 2 2001
Property and Equipment:		
Land	$2,017,184	$1,877,158
Buildings, leaseholds and land improvements	4,367,395	3,834,714
Equipment and fixtures	1,733,979	1,529,307
Construction in progress	198,744	133,995
	8,317,302	7,375,174
Less—accumulated depreciation and amortization	(1,793,683)	(1,548,589)
Net property and equipment	$6,523,619	$5,826,585

Edited Footnote on Property and Equipment Accounting Policy

Property and equipment are stated at cost. Depreciation and amortization expenses are computed using the straight-line method for financial reporting purposes and accelerated methods for tax purposes. Buildings are depreciated over twenty-five to thirty-five years; equipment and fixtures are depreciated over three to ten years; and leasehold improvements are amortized over the initial term of the lease.

Selected Income Statement Information

	Years Ended	
($ in thousands)	Sept. 1, 2002	Sept. 2, 2001
Depreciation and amortization	$341,781	$301,297
Income before income taxes	$1,138,184	$1,003,481

Source: Costco Wholesale Corporation 2002 Annual Report

Clear differences exist but the level of disclosure is too cryptic to allow analysts to compute precise adjustments. Despite this drawback, by making reasonable assumptions, we can estimate the effect on income arising from the differences in asset lives for Wal-Mart and Costco. Let's see how.

Because both companies use straight-line depreciation, the ratio of average *gross* property, plant, and equipment divided by depreciation expense gives us a rough approximation of the estimated useful (depreciable) life of the average asset. Here's why. Straight-line depreciation expense (SL) is computed as:

$$SL = \frac{\text{Gross property, plant, and equipment (minus salvage value)}}{\text{Average useful life}} \tag{10.1}$$

Rearranging terms:

$$SL \times (\text{Average useful life}) = \text{Gross property, plant, and equipment (minus salvage value)} \tag{10.2}$$

Further rearranging yields:

$$\text{Average useful life} = \frac{\text{Gross property, plant, and equipment (minus salvage value)}}{SL} \tag{10.3}$$

The ratio in equation (10.3) is only a rough approximation for many reasons. One is that we cannot estimate the salvage values assumed by Wal-Mart and Costco. Other factors that make the computation approximate are discussed later. The computation of average useful lives using the equation (10.3) approximation is shown in Exhibit 10.13. Each company's end-of-year and start-of-year gross property are summed in Exhibit 10.13 and then divided by 2 in order to estimate its average gross property for 2002. Applying the equation (10.3) approach suggests that, *on average*, Wal-Mart is using shorter estimated lives (16.8 years) than Costco (19.0 years).[34]

EXHIBIT 10.13	Computing Approximate Average Useful Lives	
($ in millions)	**Wal-Mart**	**Costco**
Average gross property, plant and equipment* / Depreciation expense	$\dfrac{\dfrac{\$55.8 + \$48.4}{2}}{\$3.1}$	$\dfrac{\dfrac{\$6.1 + \$5.3}{2}}{\$.3}$
	$\dfrac{\$52.1}{\$3.1} = 16.8 \text{ years}$	$\dfrac{\$5.7}{\$.3} = 19.0 \text{ years}$

*Excludes land and construction in progress. For example, January 31, 2003 numbers were computed as follows using Exhibit 10.11 data for Wal-Mart (rounded to the nearest $100 million): $33.8 + $15.9 + $1.3 + $4.8 = $55.8. For Costco at September 1, 2002, the computation is: $4.4 + $1.7 = $6.1.

To improve comparisons of profitability between Wal-Mart and Costco, the analyst would like to undo these differences in depreciation lives. One way to undo these differences is to divide Wal-Mart's average gross property number by Costco's estimated depreciable life—that is,

$$\frac{\$52.1}{19.0 \text{ years}} = \$2.7$$

The quotient, $2.7 billion, is the approximate annual Wal-Mart depreciation expense number that would result from using Costco's longer estimated useful life assumption. If these rough approximations are correct, Wal-Mart's fiscal year 2002 depreciation would fall by $400 million—that is,

---

[34] To understand why the Exhibit 10.13 answer is in years (that is, 16.8 years and 19.0 years), let's express average gross property divided by depreciation expense in terms of the underlying measurement dimensions:

$\dfrac{\text{Average gross property, plant, and equipment}}{\text{Depreciation expense}}$ ← The underlying measurement dimension is $s
   ← The underlying measurement dimension is $s per year

Expressing the computation in underlying measurement dimensions, the division in Exhibit 10.13 becomes:

$$\frac{\$s}{\$s\,/\text{Year}}$$

Following algebraic rules for division by fractions, we invert the denominator and multiply it by the numerator:

$$\$s \times \frac{\text{Year}}{\$s}$$

The $s cancel and the answer is expressed dimensionally in years (for example, 16.8 years and 19.0 years).

the $3.1 billion reported in Exhibit 10.11 minus the $2.7 billion computed above—and earnings before taxes and minority interest would rise by the same amount. This represents a pre-tax earnings increase of approximately 3.1%.

This adjustment process is crude and relies on assumptions. The adjustment assumes that the useful life differences are artificial. It assumes that the salvage value proportions are roughly equivalent for both firms. It further assumes that the dollar breakdown within asset categories is similar for both Wal-Mart and Costco—that is, the computation assumes that Wal-Mart and Costco both have roughly the same proportionate dollar amount of transportation equipment, store fixtures, and so on. If these assumptions are incorrect, then the average age computation for one firm cannot legitimately be applied to the other's asset base to estimate "adjusted" depreciation. However, if these assumptions hold, the adjusted numbers should make a comparison between Wal-Mart and Costco more accurate.

> It is possible that the useful life differences reflect real economic differences rather than accounting choices. For example, Costco's gross property, plant, and equipment might be more durable and, on average, have longer useful lives. If the useful lives differences are "real," then analysts' attempts to "undo" the differences may impede, rather than improve, profit comparisons.

> Also, the two companies' fiscal years-end do not coincide. The effect of this slight deviation is probably very small.

In Chapter 13 we illustrate another adjustment approach for depreciation differences that uses data from the deferred income tax footnote.

International Perspective

The United Kingdom has financial reporting rules that are generally similar to those in the United States. Nevertheless, there are differences in long-lived asset measurement procedures between the two countries. United Kingdom companies are permitted to periodically revalue land and buildings. When this is done, the accumulated depreciation account is removed and the revalued amount becomes the new book value. The amount of the write-up is credited to an owners' equity account called **revaluation reserve**.

Assume a building that originally cost £20,000,000 and has an accumulated depreciation balance of £10,000,000 is appraised at £35,000,000 and accordingly written up, as permitted by U.K. standards. The accounting entry is:

DR Building	£15,000,000	
DR Accumulated depreciation	10,000,000	
CR Revaluation reserve		£25,000,000

The new net book value becomes £35,000,000 after this entry is made, as follows:

	Net Book Value Prior to Revaluation	Revaluation	Net Book Value After Revaluation
Building	£20,000,000	DR £15,000,000	£35,000,000
Less: Accumulated depreciation	(10,000,000)	DR £10,000,000	—
Net book value	£10,000,000		£35,000,000

The revaluation reserve account that is credited in the previous entry is an owners' equity account. Under GAAP in the United Kingdom, this amount would be disclosed as a separate line item in the owners' equity section of the balance sheet.

Depreciation in subsequent periods is based on the revaluation net book value (£35,000,000). If the building has an expected remaining useful life of 20 years at the time of the revaluation, annual depreciation on the income statement will be £1,750,000 (that is, £35,000,000 ÷ 20).

The amount in the owners' equity revaluation reserve account would be transferred year-by-year to retained earnings as the revalued asset is depreciated. For example, if we assume that the asset is not subsequently revalued over the ensuing 20 years, £1,250,000 (that is, £25,000,000 ÷ 20) would be reclassified each year. The entry is:

DR	Revaluation reserve	£1,250,000
CR	Retained earnings	£1,250,000

This reclassification entry is made in order to reduce the revaluation reserve as the asset ages. If no entry were made, there would still be a revaluation reserve amount on the books even after the asset is removed from service. The year-by-year transfer ultimately reduces the reserve to zero.

The material in this section is based on "Exchanges of Productive Assets: An Amendment of APB Opinion No. 29," *Exposure Draft* (Norwalk, CT: FASB, December, 15, 2003). The rules in this exposure draft change existing GAAP for productive asset exchanges considerably. As this book goes to press, these new rules *have not yet been formally adopted*. However, we anticipate they will be adopted, perhaps with some tweaking, in 2004. Readers are encouraged to visit the book's website, www.prenhall.com/revsine, for an update on the current status of GAAP for exchanges of productive assets.

Revaluations are not uncommon among U.K. companies. One study indicated that approximately 25% of surveyed U.K. companies revalued at least some of their long-lived assets in 1993 and 1994.[35] While revaluations are not mandatory, if a company does voluntarily revalue assets, all assets of a similar nature or function must be revalued. Furthermore, once assets are revalued, periodic reassessments are required to keep the valuations up to date.[36] However, many U.K. firms never revalue fixed assets at all. This complicates comparisons across companies in the United Kingdom since some firms' fixed assets are carried at historical costs incurred years earlier while others carry these assets at more recent revalued amounts.

A similar lack of interfirm comparability sometimes exists under International Accounting Standards (IAS) where the "benchmark treatment" is to carry property, plant and equipment at original cost less accumulated depreciation but revaluations are an "allowed alternative treatment."[37] The revaluation procedure in *IAS 16* roughly parallels the U.K. approach. *IAS 16* also requires that revaluations be updated periodically—that is, whenever the revalued carrying amount differs materially from fair value.[38]

This example illustrates that despite the general similarities among U.S., U.K., and IAS reporting rules, important differences do exist. Writing up fixed assets to reflect reappraisal increases is forbidden in the United States. Differences of this sort make financial analyses of foreign companies—even companies in "similar" reporting environments—a perilous activity.

Exchanges of Productive Assets

Occasionally firms will exchange one productive asset like inventory or equipment for another productive asset. Unless certain exceptions discussed below apply, the recorded cost of a productive asset acquired in exchange for some other productive asset is the fair value of the asset that was given-up. Any resulting gain or loss on the transaction is recognized.[39] To illustrate how the cost of a productive asset acquired in an exchange is determined, consider the following example.

Rohan Department Store exchanges a delivery truck with a fair market value of $70,000 for ten checkout scanners from Electronic Giant Warehouse, Inc. The book value of the truck is $60,000—original cost of $80,000 minus accumulated depreciation of $20,000. In addition to the truck, Rohan pays Electronic Giant $15,000.

---

[35] L. C. L. Skerratt and D. J. Tonkin (eds.), *Financial Reporting 1993–1994: A Survey of U.K. Reporting Practice* (London: The Institute of Chartered Accountants in England and Wales, 1994), p.195.

[36] "Tangible Fixed Assets," *Financial Reporting Standard (FRS) 15* (N.P.: Accounting Standards Board [ASB], 1999).

[37] "Property, Plant and Equipment," *IAS 16* (London: IASB, revised, 1998), paras. 28–29.

[38] Ibid., para. 29.

[39] "Accounting for Nonmonetary Transactions," *Accounting Principles Board (APB) Opinion No. 29* (New York: American Institute of Certified Public Accountants, 1973).

The cost of the acquired assets (scanners) is the fair value of the assets (truck and cash) that were exchanged to obtain it. So in this example, the cost of the scanners is:

Fair market value of the truck	$70,000
Cash payment	15,000
Cost of acquired assets	$85,000

> When the fair value of the asset *received* is more clearly evident than the fair value of the asset *given up*, then the fair value of the asset received is used as the new cost base. See *APB Opinion No. 29*, para. 18.

Rohan's entry is

DR Store equipment	$85,000	
DR Accumulated depreciation—		
delivery truck	20,000	
CR Delivery truck		$80,000
CR Cash		15,000
CR Gain on exchange		10,000

Notice that the "Gain on exchange" is simply the difference between the fair market value of the truck ($70,000) and its book value ($60,000).

For many years, asset exchanges occurred infrequently, so the rule we just illustrated was seldom an important part of firms' financial statements. But that all changed during the boom years of the 1990s and beyond. Asset exchanges—or swaps—proliferated. One article stated:

> When the business history of the past decade is written, perhaps nothing will sum up the outrageous financial scheming of the era as well as the frenzied swapping that marked its final years. Internet companies . . . milked revenue from complex advertising exchanges with other dot-coms in ultimately worthless deals. In Houston, equal amounts of energy were pushed back and forth between companies. . . .
>
> But the swaps rage turned out to be no bargain for investors. The bad deals contributed to an epidemic of artificially inflated revenue. In many cases, swaps slipped through legal loopholes left in place by regulators who had failed to keep pace with the ever-changing deal-making of ever-changing industries. The unraveling of those back-scratching arrangements helped usher in the market collapse and led to the realization by investors that the highest-flying industries of the boom era—telecom, energy, the Internet—were built in part on a combustible mix of wishful thinking and deceit.[40]

Here's an example of how these asset exchange rules were manipulated in order to overstate revenues and income. Telecom companies would sign agreements with other telecom companies to exchange access to each other's fiber-optic network. These deals were termed "capacity swaps"[41] and were generally structured as leases. That is, Company One would agree to lease capacity to Asia on Company Two's network for 20 years while *simultaneously* Company Two would agree to lease capacity to Europe on Company One's network for 20 years. Each company would promise to pay the other $5 million per year under the two separate leases.

Each company received cash, and the stage was therefore set for potentially recognizing revenues and income on these deals. Furthermore, Company One would structure the lease that *provided* access to its network as an operating lease while the lease in which it *obtained* access to Company Two's network was treated as a capital lease (leases are discussed in Chapter 12). What this means is that the network access Company One "sold" was treated as current period revenue

---

[40] D. K. Berman, J. Angwin, and C. Cummins, "As the Bubble Neared Its End, Bogus Swaps Padded the Books," *Wall Street Journal* (December 23, 2002).

[41] Ibid. Also see K. Brown, "Creative Accounting: How to Buff a Company," *Wall Street Journal* (February 21, 2002).

while the access it bought was capitalized and expensed over future periods. So these deals sometimes generated upfront income. Even if they didn't generate income, they did increase revenues—an important factor "since investors focused on revenue in new industries that often had little earnings to show for themselves."[42]

In order to prevent a repeat of these abuses, the FASB is formulating[43] new rules that require companies to record certain exchanges of productive assets at the existing **book value** of the relinquished asset, if any of the following conditions apply:

1. The fair value of neither the asset(s) received nor the asset(s) relinquished is determinable within reasonable limits.
2. The transaction lacks commercial substance.
3. The transaction is an exchange of inventory or property held for sale in the ordinary course of business for other inventory or property to be sold in the same line of business.

In the next section, we illustrate these three circumstances under which exchanges of productive assets must be recorded at book value.

Exchanges Recorded at Book Value

Fair Value Not Determinable To illustrate the accounting for exchanges of productive assets when the fair value of the exchanged assets cannot be determined, consider the following example.

> Denver Construction Corporation agrees to swap with Cody Company one type of crane in exchange for a slightly different model whose features are better suited for a highway bridge project it is currently engaged in. The old crane Denver is exchanging has a book value of $600,000 at the time of the transaction. Its original cost was $700,000 and accumulated depreciation is $100,000. Denver also pays Cody $40,000 to complete the transaction. It is not possible to measure the fair market value of either crane within reasonable limits.

Because neither crane's fair market value is known, the new crane is recorded at the sum of the *book value* of the old crane ($600,000) plus the cash given ($40,000). The entry is:

DR Construction crane (new)	$640,000	
DR Accumulated depreciation—		
construction crane (old)	100,000	
CR Construction crane (old)		$700,000
CR Cash		40,000

The Commercial Substance Criterion Booking exchange transactions at fair value introduces the possibility of gains (or losses) on the transaction. To preclude firms from engaging in "sham" exchanges in order to generate artificial gains, the FASB requires that the transaction must possess **commercial substance**. An exchange transaction has commercial substance when

1. The firm's future cash flows are expected to change as a result of the exchange, and
2. The amount of the cash flow change is significant relative to the fair value of the assets exchanged.[44]

If both conditions are *not* met, the transaction must be recorded using the book value of the asset(s) relinquished, using the procedure in the previous illustration. This precludes any gain recognition.

---

[42] Op. cit.
[43] "Exchanges of Productive Assets," op. cit.
[44] Ibid., para. 21.

Exchange Transaction to Facilitate Sales to Customers Sometimes firms will exchange assets with other firms—even competitors—in order to balance inventories, as in the following example.

> Lee Electronics faces a shortage of plasma television sets but has an excess of liquid crystal display sets (LCDs). It agrees to swap LCDs with a fair value of $50,000 and a book value of $40,000 in exchange for plasma sets with a fair value of $52,000 from Bonnie Enterprises.

Here, the assets being exchanged (plasma sets and LCDs) are both stocked for sale to customers. The exchange does not culminate an earning process. One asset is merely traded for another that serves a similar purpose. For this reason, Lee Electronics does not report a gain but instead records the plasma sets at $40,000—the book value of the LCDs that were relinquished in the transaction. The entry is simply:

DR Inventory—plasma sets	$40,000	
CR Inventory—LCDs		$40,000

The apparent $12,000 gain on the swap ($52,000 fair value minus $40,000 book value) will be recognized only when the plasma sets are ultimately sold to customers.

Cash Received—a Special Case Let's continue the previous example with one difference. We still assume that the fair market value of the plasma sets is $52,000 but we'll now assume that Lee Electronics also receives $5,778 from Bonnie Enterprises.

This transaction is more complicated since Lee received both cash and the plasma television sets. Indeed, cash represents 10% of the total proceeds:

> This gain is determined as follows:
>
> | | |
> |---|---|
> | Fair market value of plasma television sets | $52,000 |
> | Cash received | 5,778 |
> | Total consideration received | $57,778 |
> | Book value of LCDs relinquished | 40,000 |
> | Gain on transaction | $17,778 |

$$\frac{\text{Cash received}}{\text{Total proceeds}} = \frac{\$5,778}{\$5,778 + \$52,000} = .10$$

Because 10% of the proceeds were received in cash, 10% of the LCD assets are considered to be sold, and that portion of the earning process is complete. So 10% of the $17,778 gain on the transaction will be recognized.[45] The entry is:

DR Cash	$ 5,778	
DR Inventory—plasma sets	36,000	
CR Inventory—LCDs		$40,000
CR Recognized gain on exchange		1,778

> The carrying amount of the inventory of plasma sets is computed as follows:
>
> | | | |
> |---|---|---|
> | Fair market value of plasma sets | | $52,000 |
> | Less: Portion of gain deferred: | | |
> | Total gain | $17,778 | |
> | Gain recognized | (1,778) | |
> | Gain deferred | | (16,000) |
> | Inventory—plasma sets | | $36,000 |
>
> Notice that the $16,000 deferred gain will ultimately be recognized when the plasma sets are sold since the inventory carrying amount has been reduced by the amount of the deferred gain.

[45] *APB Opinion No. 29*, para. 22.

SUMMARY

- GAAP for long-lived assets is far from perfect. The need for reliable and verifiable numbers causes these assets to be measured in terms of the economic sacrifice incurred to obtain them—their historical cost—rather than in terms of their current expected benefit—or worth—to the firm.
- Since it is uncertain whether future benefits result from research and brand development costs, these costs are generally expensed in the period incurred. Consequently, balance sheet carrying amounts for intangible assets often differ from their real value to the firm. Analysts must scrutinize disclosures of R&D expenses to undo the overly conservative accounting.
- Managers may deliberately allocate an excessive portion of the total purchase price in a takeover to in-process R&D in order to increase post-takeover earnings.
- Changes in the amount of capitalized interest from one period to the next can distort earnings trends. A thorough understanding of how the GAAP measurement rules are applied allows statement readers to avoid pitfalls in trend analysis when investment in new assets is sporadic.
- When comparing return on assets (ROA) ratios across firms, one must remember that—all other factors being equal—there is an upward drift in reported ROA as assets age. So analysts must determine whether the average age of the long-lived assets for firms being analyzed is stable or rising. Inflation also injects an upward bias into reported ROA.
- Asset impairment write-downs depend on subjective forecasts and could be used to manage earnings, especially under IASB rules.
- An understanding of differences in depreciation choices across firms permits better inter-firm comparisons. When making inter-firm comparisons, analysts should use footnote disclosures to overcome differences in the long-lived asset useful lives chosen by each firm and where possible, in their depreciation patterns.
- International practices for long-lived assets and book depreciation charges are sometimes very different from those in the United States. Statement users who make cross-country comparisons must exercise caution.

EXERCISES

E10 – 1

Capitalized Costs

Phoenix Co. acquired a large piece of specialized machinery used in its manufacturing process. The following costs were incurred in connection with the acquisition:

Finder's fee	$ 2,000
List price	230,000
Transportation fee	4,000
Speeding ticket during transportation	65
Installation fee	2,500
Cost to repair a door damaged during installation	1,200

Required:

Which of the costs incurred by Phoenix Co. should be capitalized to the machinery account?

E10 – 2

Determining asset cost and depreciation expense

AICPA
ADAPTED

In January 2005 Action Corporation entered into a contract to acquire a new machine for its factory. The machine, which had a cash price of $150,000, was paid for as follows:

Down payment	$ 15,000
Note payable due June 1, 2005	120,000
500 Shares of Action common stock with a value of $50 per share	25,000
Total	$160,000

Prior to the machine's use, installation costs of $4,000 were incurred. The machine has an estimated useful life of 10 years and an estimated salvage value of $5,000.

Required:

What should Action record as depreciation expense for 2005 under the straight-line method?

Gonzo Co. owns a building in Georgia. The historical cost of the building is $970,000 and $440,000 of accumulated depreciation has been recorded to date. During 2005, Gonzo incurred the following expenses related to the building:

Repainted the building	$ 48,000
Major improvement to the plumbing	109,000
Replaced carpet in the plant's accounting offices	47,600
Added a 7,000 square foot lobby	234,600
Repaired a broken water main	155,800

Required:

1. Which of the costs incurred by Gonzo Co. should be capitalized to the building account?
2. What is the subsequent carrying amount of the building?

Turtle Company purchased equipment on January 2, 2005 for $50,000. The equipment had an estimated five-year service life. Turtle's policy for five-year assets is to use double-declining balance depreciation for the first two years of the asset's life and then to switch to the straight-line depreciation method.

Required:

In its December 31, 2007 balance sheet, what amount should Turtle report as accumulated depreciation for equipment?

The Apex Company purchased a tooling machine on January 3, 1995 for $30,000. The machine was being depreciated on the straight-line method over an estimated useful life of 20 years, with no salvage value.

At the beginning of 2005, when the machine had been in use for 10 years, the company paid $5,000 to overhaul the machine. As a result of this improvement, the company estimated that the remaining useful life of the machine was now 15 years.

Required:

What should be the depreciation expense recorded for this machine in 2005?

On June 18, 2005 Dell Printing Company incurred the following costs for one of its printing presses:

Purchase of collating and stapling attachment	$84,000
Installation of attachment	36,000
Replacement parts for overhaul of press	26,000
Labor and overhead in connection with overhaul	14,000

The overhaul resulted in a significant increase in production capability. Neither the attachment nor the overhaul increased the estimated useful life of the press.

Required:

What is the total amount of the preceding costs that should be capitalized?

Samson Manufacturing Company, a calendar-year company, purchased a machine for $65,000 on January 1, 2003. At the date of purchase, Samson incurred the following additional costs:

Loss on sale of old machinery	$1,000
Freight-in	500
Installation cost	2,000
Testing costs prior to regular operation	300

The estimated salvage value of the machine was $5,000, and Samson estimated the machine would have a useful life of 20 years, with depreciation being computed on the straight-line method. In January 2005 accessories costing $3,600 were added to the machine in order to reduce its operating costs. These accessories neither prolonged the machine's life nor provided any additional salvage value.

Required:

What should Samson record as depreciation expense for 2005?

E10 – 8

Deferred payment contract

On January 1, 2005 Hardy, Inc. purchased certain plant assets under a deferred payment contract. The agreement called for making annual payments of $10,000 per year for five years. The first payment is due on January 1, 2005, and the remaining payments are due on January 1 of each of the next four years. Assume an imputed interest rate of 10%.

Required:

What entry should be made to record the purchase of these plant assets on January 1, 2005?

E10 – 9

Classification of costs

On February 1, 2005 Reflection Corporation purchased a parcel of land as a factory site for $50,000. An old building on the property was demolished, and construction began on a new building, completed on November 1, 2005. Costs incurred were:

Demolition of old building	$ 4,000
Architect's fees	10,000
Legal fees for title investigation and purchase contract	2,000
Construction costs	500,000

Salvaged materials resulting from demolition were sold for $1,000.

Required:

What cost should be recorded for the land and new building, respectively?

E10 – 10

Classification of costs

On July 1, 2005 Town Company purchased for $540,000 a warehouse building and the land on which it is located. The following data were available concerning the property:

	Current Appraised Value	Seller's Original Cost
Land	$200,000	$140,000
Warehouse building	300,000	280,000
	$500,000	$420,000

Required:

At what amount should Town record the land?

E10 – 11

Capitalized interest

Clay Company started construction on a new office building on January 1, 2004, and it moved into the finished building on July 1, 2005. Of the building's $2,500,000 total cost, $2,000,000 was incurred in 2004 evenly throughout the year. Clay's incremental borrowing rate was 12% throughout 2004, and the total amount of interest incurred by Clay during 2004 was $102,000.

Required:

What amount should Clay report as capitalized interest at December 31, 2004?

E10 – 12

Capitalized interest

Cole Company began constructing a building for its own use in January 2005. During 2005 Cole incurred interest of $50,000 on specific construction debt and $20,000 on other borrowings. Interest computed on the weighted-average amount of accumulated expenditures for the building during 2005 was $40,000.

Required:

What amount of interest cost should Cole capitalize? Prepare the journal entry to record payment of the interest.

Weir Company uses straight-line depreciation for its property, plant, and equipment, which, stated at cost, consisted of the following:

E10 – 13

Account analysis

AICPA
ADAPTED

	December 31	
	2005	**2004**
Land	$ 25,000	$ 25,000
Buildings	195,000	195,000
Machinery and equipment	695,000	650,000
	915,000	870,000
Less accumulated depreciation	(400,000)	(370,000)
	$515,000	$500,000

Weir's depreciation expense for 2005 and 2004 was $55,000 and $50,000, respectively.

Required:

What amount was debited to accumulated depreciation during 2005 because of property, plant, and equipment retirements?

The following graph depicts three depreciation expense patterns over time.

E10 – 14

Depreciation expense patterns

AICPA
ADAPTED

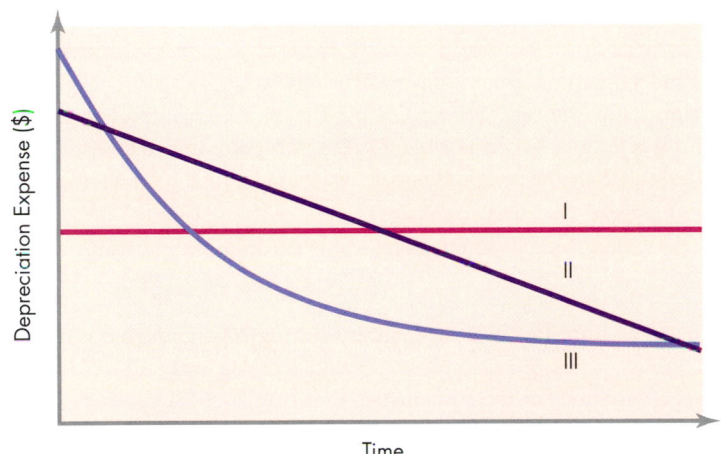

Required:

Pattern I, of course, is straight-line depreciation. Which depreciation expense pattern corresponds to the sum-of-the-years' digits method and which corresponds to the double-declining balance method? Explain why the shape of the Pattern II and Pattern III lines differs.

On January 1, 2001 Vick Company purchased a trademark for $400,000, which had an estimated useful life of 16 years. In January 2005 Vick paid $60,000 for legal fees in a successful defense of the trademark.

E10 – 15

Intangibles amortization

AICPA
ADAPTED

Required:

How much should Vick record as trademark amortization expense for 2005?

On January 2, 2002 Lava, Inc. purchased a patent for a new consumer product for $90,000. At the time of purchase, the patent was valid for 15 years; however, the patent's useful life was estimated to be only 10 years due to the competitive nature of the product. On December 31, 2005 the product was permanently withdrawn from sale under governmental order because of a potential health hazard in the product.

E10 – 16

Intangibles

AICPA
ADAPTED

Required:

What should the total charge against income be in 2005 on this patent?

E10 – 17

R&D cost treatment

AICPA
ADAPTED

During 2005 Orr Company incurred the following costs:

Research and development services performed by Key Corporation for Orr	$150,000
Design, construction, and testing of preproduction prototypes and models	200,000
Testing in search for new products or process alternatives	175,000

Required:

How much research and development expense should Orr report in 2005?

E10 – 18

R&D cost treatment

AICPA
ADAPTED

In 2005 Ball Labs incurred the following costs:

Direct costs of doing contract research and development work for the government to be reimbursed by a governmental unit	$400,000

Research and development costs not included above were:

Depreciation	$300,000
Salaries	700,000
Indirect costs appropriately allocated	200,000
Materials	180,000

Required:

What was Ball's total research and development expense in 2005?

E10 – 19

Software Development Costs

Pearl Inc. develops and markets computer software. During 2005, one of Pearl's engineers began developing a new and very innovative software product. On July 1, 2006, a team of Pearl engineers determined that the software product was technologically feasible. Pearl engineers continued to ready the software for general release and in January 2007 the first product sales were made. Total costs incurred were as follows:

2005	$3,200,000
2006	$3,600,000 (evenly throughout the year)

Required:

1. How should Pearl account for the costs incurred during 2005 and what is the rationale for your answer?
2. How should Pearl account for the costs incurred during 2006? If your answer differs from your answer in requirement 1 explain why.

E10 – 20

Depletion

AICPA
ADAPTED

In January 2005 Vorst Company purchased a mineral mine for $2,640,000, with removable ore estimated at 1,200,000 tons. After it has extracted all the ore, Vorst will be required by law to restore the land to its original condition at an estimated cost of $180,000. Vorst believes it will be able to sell the property for $300,000. During 2005 Vorst incurred $360,000 of development costs to prepare the mine for production, and it removed and sold 60,000 tons of ore.

Required:

In its 2005 income statement, what amount should Vorst report as depletion expense?

PROBLEMS/DISCUSSION QUESTIONS

P10 – 1

Depreciation expense computations

AICPA
ADAPTED

On January 2, 2004 Half, Inc. purchased a manufacturing machine for $864,000. The machine has an eight-year estimated life and a $144,000 estimated salvage value. Half expects to manufacture 1,800,000 units over the life of the machine. During 2005 Half manufactured 300,000 units.

Required:

For each item, calculate depreciation expense for 2005 (the second year of ownership) for the machine just described under the method listed:

1. Straight-line
2. Double-declining balance
3. Sum-of-the-years' digits
4. Units of production

(*Hint:* The units of production method was not discussed in the text but is easy to understand. Depreciation is based on a ratio; the ratio numerator is production during the period and the denominator is estimated total production over the life of the machine. This ratio is then multiplied by the machine's cost minus salvage value to determine depreciation expense.)

P10 – 2

Lump-sum purchases

On June 30, 2005 Macrosoft Company acquired a 10-acre tract of land. On the tract was a warehouse that Macrosoft intended to use as a distribution center. At the time of purchase, the land had an assessed tax value of $6,300,000 and the building had an assessed tax value of $11,200,000. Macrosoft paid $15,000,000 for the land and building. After the purchase the company paid $1,000,000 to have various modifications made to the building.

Required:

1. At what amount should Macrosoft record the land and building?
2. For financial reporting purposes, why might the managers of Macrosoft prefer to assign a larger portion of the $15,000,000 to the land rather than to the building?

P10 – 3

Asset cost under a deferred payment plan

Cayman Diving Inc. needs to acquire a new dive boat. The seller will accept a noninterest bearing note for $400,000 due in four years or $250,000 in cash. The company's incremental cost of borrowing is 10%.

Required:

Which option should Cayman Diving select? Would your answer change if Cayman's incremental borrowing rate was 13%? Why?

P10 – 4

Allocation of acquisition costs among asset accounts

On April 23, 2005 Starlight Department Stores Inc. acquired a 75-acre tract of land by paying $25,000,000 in cash and by issuing a six-month note payable for $5,000,000 and 1,000,000 shares of its common stock. On April 23, 2005 Starlight's common stock was selling for $80.00 a share and had a par value of $2.50. The land had two existing buildings, one that Starlight intended to renovate and use as a warehouse, and another that Starlight intended to demolish to make way for the construction of a new department store. At the time of the purchase, the assessed values for property tax purposes of the land and the building to be renovated were $105,000,000 and $20,000,000, respectively. To complete the purchase, Starlight incurred legal fees of $25,000. The cost of demolishing the unneeded building was $50,000. Starlight paid $250,000 to have the land graded so that the new store could be built. Starlight paid a total of $100,000,000 to have the new department store built and another $25,000,000 to renovate the old building. To fund the work on the renovation and the new store, Starlight obtained a loan from Gotham City Bank. Starlight made total interest payments of $10,000,000 during the period the buildings were being completed. (Assume that all of the interest payments qualify for capitalization.) Since parking would be needed for both the new department store and the warehouse, Starlight had a portion of the land covered with asphalt at a cost of $450,000. Starlight also paid $200,000 to install lighting for the parking lots and $75,000 to install decorative fencing and a parking access gate. During 2005 Starlight paid property taxes of $150,000 on the new property. All work was completed by December 31, 2005, and the new store and warehouse were placed in service on January 1, 2006.

Required:

Determine what costs should be assigned to the (1) land, (2) building, and (3) land improvements asset accounts. (*Hint:* The allocation of the original purchase price between the land and building should be made in proportion to the relative assessed values of the land and building at the time of the purchase.)

P10 – 5

Capitalize or expense various costs

Formidable Express provides overnight delivery of letters and small parcels to numerous locations throughout the United States. As part of its operations, the company maintains a sizable fleet of delivery trucks. Assume that Formidable Express made the following expenditures related to the fleet during 2005:

1. The company has the engines in its trucks serviced (that is, "tuned-up") once every two years. The cost of the servicing in 2005 was $11.0 million.

2. Due to the high mileage put on the delivery vehicles, the company normally replaces 20% of its fleet's engines every year. In 2005 the cost incurred to replace engines amounted to $7.8 million.
3. The tires on each vehicle are replaced once every three years. The cost of the new tires installed in 2005 amounted to $1.0 million.
4. In 2005 the company paid $3.5 million to have the trucks in the fleet rustproofed. Management expects that the trucks will now last an extra three years.
5. Because each truck was out of service for about a week due to the rustproofing in (4), the company estimates that it lost $12.0 million in revenue during the course of the year.

Required:

Which expenditures should Formidable capitalize and which should be expensed?

P10 – 6

Capitalize or expense various costs

Fly-by-Night is an international airline company. Its fleet includes Boeing 757s, 747s, 727s, Lockheed L-1011s, and McDonnell Douglas MD-83s, MD-80s, and DC-9s. Assume that Fly-by-Night made the following expenditures related to these aircraft in 2005:

1. New jet engines were installed on some of the MD-80s and MD-83s at a cost of $25.0 million.
2. The company paid $2.0 million to paint one-eighth of the fleet with the firm's new colors in order to create a new public image. The company intends to paint the remainder of the fleet over the next seven years.
3. Routine maintenance and repairs on various aircraft cost $8.0 million.
4. Noise abatement equipment ("hush kits") was installed on the fleet of DC-9s to meet FAA maximum allowable noise levels upon takeoff. Equipment and installation cost $7.5 million.
5. The avionics systems were replaced on the Lockheed L-1011s. This will allow the aircraft to be used four more years than originally expected.
6. The existing seats on all 747s were replaced with new, more comfortable seats at a cost of $0.5 million.
7. The jet engines on 50% of the Boeing 727s received a major overhaul at a cost of $5.0 million. As a result, the aircraft should be more fuel efficient.

Required:

1. Which of these expenditures should Fly-by-Night capitalize? Why?
2. How might Fly-by-Night use expenditures like these to manage its earnings?

P10 – 7

Determining an asset's cost

On July 23, 2005 Consolidated Parcel Service (CPS) acquired a new "de-icing" machine for use at its facility at Chicago's O'Hare airport. The machine is used to de-ice the wings of the firm's aircraft in winter months. The invoice price of the machine was $15,000,000. The seller offered CPS a 2% cash discount on the gross invoice price if CPS paid for the machine by August 1, 2005. The cost to ship the machine from the seller's warehouse was $15,000 and was paid by CPS. Insurance during transport amounted to $5,000, also paid by CPS. Many CPS employees were involved with the assembly and testing of the machine. Their wages totaled $20,000. As part of testing the machine, $35,000 worth of "de-icing" fluid was used to ensure that the machine operated properly. During testing, one of CPS's cargo planes was inadvertently damaged. The cost to repair the aircraft (not covered by insurance) amounted to $250,000. As a result of the damaged aircraft being out of service while it was being repaired, CPS lost $750,000 in revenue. Finally, because the machine was larger than the previous one, CPS had to erect a new storage facility. The cost of doing so was $75,000 for materials, $25,000 for labor, and $5,000 for salaries of the supervisory personnel who directed the construction.

Required:

Assuming that CPS paid for the machine on July 29, 2005, determine the capitalizable cost of the machine to CPS.

P10 – 8

Asset impairment

Four years ago Omega Technology Inc. acquired a machine for use in its computer chip manufacturing operations at a cost of $35,000,000. The firm expected the machine to have a seven-year useful life and a zero salvage value. The company has been using straight-line depreciation for the asset. Due to the rapid rate of technological change in the industry, at the end of Year 4, Omega estimates that the machine is capable of generating (undiscounted) future cash flows of $11,000,000. Based on the quoted market prices of similar assets, Omega estimates the machine to have a fair market value of $9,500,000.

Required:

1. What is the book value of the machine at the end of Year 4?
2. Should Omega recognize an impairment of this asset? Why or why not? If yes, what is the amount of the impairment loss that should be recognized?
3. At the end of Year 4, at what amount should the machine appear in Omega's balance sheet?

Norway Co. manufactures and sells television receivers. Due to recent innovations (plasma screens), Norway suspects that some of its equipment may be impaired. The equipment's historical cost is $4,000,000, but it has been owned, used, and depreciated for three years. When the equipment was purchased, Norway anticipated a 10-year useful life with no residual value. Norway anticipates that the equipment will generate cash sales of $1,000,000 per year for the next three years and will require operating cash expenditures of $250,000 per year during that same time period. At the end of three years the equipment will be scrapped. Similar equipment sells for $1,950,000 on the used asset market.

P10 – 9

Asset impairment test

Required:

1. What circumstances should prompt Norway Co. to perform an asset impairment test?
2. Is Norway's manufacturing equipment impaired? Why or why not?
3. Prepare any journal entry necessary based on your answer in requirement 2.
4. If two years from now there is an unexpected resurgence of demand for ordinary television receivers, will this impact any entry made in requirement 3?

In its 1995 balance sheet, IBM reported the following account:

P10 – 10

Accounting for computer software costs

($ in millions)	1995	1994
Software, less accumulated amortization (1995: $11,276; 1994: $10,793)	$2,419	$2,963

In the footnotes to its financial statements, IBM reported that it spent $2,997 on computer software-related activities. Assume that these expenditures were related to projects in which technological feasibility has been proved.

Required:

1. How is IBM required to account for computer software-related expenditures?
2. As of the end of 1995, how much has IBM spent on existing computer software-related activities in past years?
3. As of the end of 1995, how much of its computer software-related expenditures has IBM capitalized?
4. Based on the information given, estimate IBM's amortization of computer software costs in 1995.
5. Assume that IBM amortizes its capitalized software costs using the straight-line method. Estimate the average useful life of the software products developed as of the end of 1995.
6. How might firms use the accounting for computer software costs to manage their earnings?

National Sweetener Company owns the patent to the artificial sweetener known as Supersweet. Assume that National Sweetener acquired the patent on January 1, 1999 at a cost of $300 million dollars, expected the patent to have an economic useful life of 12 years, and has been amortizing the patent on a straight-line basis. Assume that at the time the patent was acquired, National Sweetener expected that the process would generate future net cash flows of $30 million the first year of its useful life and that the cash flows would grow at a rate of 10% each year over the remainder of its useful life. By the year 2011 (that is, after 12 years), National Sweetener expected that there would be several other artificial sweeteners on the market and therefore that it would sell the Supersweet patent at that time for about $60.0 million.

P10 – 11

Asset impairment

Year	Expected Future Cash Flows ($ in millions)	Year	Expected Future Cash Flows ($ in millions)
1999	$30.0	2006	$ 58.7
2000	33.0	2007	64.3
2001	36.3	2008	70.7
2002	39.9	2009	77.8
2003	43.9	2010	85.6
2004	48.3	Total	$641.6
2005	53.1		

On December 31, 2005 when the patent's book value was $160.0 million ($300.0 − $140.0), National Sweetener learned that one of its competitors had come up with a revolutionary new sweetener that could be produced much more cheaply than Supersweet. National Sweetener expects that the introduction of this product on January 1, 2006 will substantially reduce the cash flows from its Supersweet patent process.

Consider the following two independent scenarios:

> *Scenario I:* National Sweetener expects that the cash flows from Supersweet over the 2006–2010 period will be only 50% of those originally projected and that the sale of the Supersweet patent will bring only $25 million when sold. When discounted at a rate of 15% (which National Sweetener feels is appropriate), these amounts yield a present value of $129.0 million. National Sweetener estimates that the market value of the Supersweet patent on December 31, 2005 is $160.0 million.

> *Scenario II:* National Sweetener expects that the cash flows from Supersweet over the 2006–2010 period will be only 25% of those originally projected and that the sale of the Supersweet patent will bring only $25 million when sold. When discounted at a rate of 15%, these amounts yield a present value of $70.7 million. National Sweetener estimates that the market value of the Supersweet patent on December 31, 2005 is $68.0 million.

Required:

1. Should National Sweetener recognize an impairment of its Supersweet patent in Scenario I? If so, what is the amount of the loss and at what amount should the patent be reported in National Sweetener's 2005 ending balance sheet?
2. Repeat requirement 1 for the second scenario.

P10 – 12

Interest capitalization

To meet the increasing demand for its microprocessors, on January 1, 2005 Intelligent Micro Devices began construction of a new manufacturing facility. Construction costs were incurred uniformly throughout 2005 and were recorded in the firm's "Construction-in-progress" account. The average balance in the "Construction-in-progress" account during 2005 was $150,000,000.

To facilitate the construction of the facility, the firm arranged for an $80,000,000 construction loan on January 1 at a rate of 13%. The firm also issued $40,000,000 of common stock to help finance the project. Management estimates that the firm's cost of equity capital is 16%. On January 1, 2005 the firm also issued bonds in the amount of $200,000,000, carrying a weighted-average interest rate of 11.5%. Earnings before interest and taxes for 2005 is $50,000,000.

Required:

1. What is the total amount of interest incurred by the firm in 2005?
2. Assume that the firm bases the amount of capitalized interest on the average balance in the "Construction-in-progress" account. How much of the interest in requirement 1 should be capitalized?
3. How much of the amount in requirement 2 will be related to the firm's common stock issue? Why?
4. Where will the amount in requirement 2 appear in the firm's 2005 financial statements?
5. What amount of interest expense will appear in the firm's 2005 income statement?
6. Assume that the facility is completed on December 31, 2005 and that it is placed in service on January 1, 2006. How, if at all, will the amount in requirement 2 affect the future income of the firm?
7. Calculate the firm's interest coverage ratio (income before interest and taxes divided by interest expense) with and without the interest capitalization. Which coverage ratio would be more useful to a creditor in the evaluation of the firm's risk of insolvency?

Consider the following two scenarios:

> **Scenario I:** Over the 2002–2005 period, Micro Systems, Inc. spends $10,000,000 a year to develop patents on new computer hardware manufacturing technology. While some of its projects failed, the firm did develop several new patents each year during the period.

> **Scenario II:** Over the 2002–2005 period, Macro Systems, Inc., a competitor of Micro Systems, Inc., paid $10,000,000 each year to acquire patent rights from other firms. The firm assigned a five-year useful life to all of the patents.

1. Each firm had sales of $200,000,000, $242,000,000, $290,000,000, and $350,000,000, respectively, over the 2002–2005 period.
2. Each firm's operating expenses (excluding the preceding patent-related information) were $140,000,000, $170,000,000, $205,000,000, and $245,000,000, respectively, over the 2002–2005 period.
3. Assume that a 34% income tax rate applies to both firms.

Required:

1. How would the two firms account for their patent-related expenditures?
2. Calculate the net income and net income as a percent of sales (that is, profit margin) of each firm for the 2002–2005 period. Contrast the reported profitability of the two firms.
3. Assume that the firms continue to spend $10,000,000 per year in the fashion just described. How would the comparability of their income statements be affected?

P10 – 13

Accounting for internally developed patents versus purchased patents

www.prenhall.com/revsine

● Student Resources

✔ Template for solution

Assume that Major Motors Corporation, a large automobile manufacturer, reported in a recent annual report to shareholders that buildings had an original cost of $4,694,000,000.

1. Major Motors uses the straight-line depreciation method to depreciate the buildings over a useful life of 34 years.
2. Assume that the ratio of end-of-year accumulated depreciation on the buildings to their depreciable cost is 35.3%. This implies that the buildings, on average, are about 12 years old. Assume that Major Motors depreciates them to a salvage value of 5% of their original cost.
3. Assume that Major Motors' management is considering both extending the original useful lives of the buildings to 40 years from 34 years and increasing the salvage value to 10% of the buildings' original cost.
4. Assume a tax rate of 34%.

Required:

1. What is the book value of the buildings at the end of the current year (that is, before adjusting for any change in useful lives or salvage values)?
2. What would be the dollar amount and direction of the effect on Major Motors' net income if the proposed changes to the useful lives and salvage values were implemented at the start of the next fiscal year?

P10 – 14

Earnings effects of changes in useful lives and salvage values

---

The 2004 income statement and other information for Mallard Corporation, which is about to purchase a new machine at a cost of $500 and a new computer system at a cost of $300, appears next.

Sales	$1,000
Cost of goods sold	600
Gross profit	400
Operating expenses	150
Income before tax	250
Income taxes	85
Net income	$ 165

Additional Information:

- The two new assets are expected to generate a 25% annual rate of growth in the firm's sales.
- The firm will include the depreciation expense on the machine as part of cost of goods sold and the depreciation expense on the computer system as part of operating expenses.
- *Excluding* the depreciation on the new machine, the firm's cost of goods sold is expected to increase at an annual rate of 7.5%.
- *Excluding* the depreciation on the new computer system, the firm's operating expenses are expected to increase at an annual rate of 4.0%.

P10 – 15

Straight-line versus accelerated depreciation ratio effects

www.prenhall.com/revsine

● Student Resources

✔ Template for solution

- The firm's gross total assets (net of asset retirements) are expected to grow at a rate of 20% per year. Average gross total assets in 2004 were $1,000. Assume that asset retirements generate no gains or losses.
- Both the machine and the computer system have a three-year useful life and a zero salvage value.
- Assume an income tax rate of 34%.

Required:

1. Assume that the assets are purchased on January 1, 2005. Prepare pro forma income statements for 2005 through 2007. Assume the firm elects to use the straight-line depreciation method for depreciating the new assets.
2. Repeat requirement 1 assuming instead that the firm elects to use the sum-of-the-years' digits method for depreciating the new assets.
3. For both requirements 1 and 2, calculate the firm's gross profit rate (gross profit divided by sales), NOPAT margin (net operating profit after tax divided by sales), and return on assets (NOPAT divided by average total assets). How does the use of the different depreciation methods affect the behavior of the ratios over the 2005–2007 period?

P10 – 16

Asset age and intercompany comparisons

Gardenia Co. and Lantana Co. both operate in the same industry. Gardenia began its operations in 2005 with a $20 million initial investment in plant and equipment with an expected life of 10 years. Lantana's net asset base is also $20 million, but its assets are, on average, five years old with 10-year expected useful lives on January 1, 2005. Lantana replaces 10% of its assets each year at the end of the year, while Gardenia, having just entered the industry, does not have immediate plans to replace any assets.

Gardenia generates $3,000,000 per year of pre-tax net operating cash flow, while Lantana generates $5,000,000. Inflation is expected to be 2% per year and each company expects to keep pace by increasing its pre-tax net operating cash flow by 2% per year. The cost of Lantana's planned asset replacements will also increase at 2% per year. (Note: For simplicity, assume that prior to 2005, the replacement cost of Lantana's assets remained constant.)

Required:

1. Compute return on assets for Gardenia Co. for 2005 through 2009.
2. Compute return on assets for Lantana Co. for 2005 through 2009.
3. Discuss the differences between your answers to requirement 1 and requirement 2.

P10 – 17

Oil and gas accounting

On January 2, 2005, Stern Oil Company acquired the area drilling rights for 400,000 acres in Oklahoma at a cost of $30 million. During 2005 and 2006, Stern explored for oil throughout the territory by drilling 20 wells. No productive wells were discovered until December 2006 at which time two productive wells were found, both with significant oil reserves. The following costs were incurred by Stern:

	2005	2006
Exploration costs	$38,900,000	$40,400,000
Costs associated with building 2 rigs		18,000,000

Required:

1. Using the format shown on p. 525 in the text, prepare a partial income statement and a partial balance sheet for 2005 and 2006 for Stern Oil assuming the full-cost approach is used.
2. Using the format shown on p. 525 in the text, prepare a partial income statement and a partial balance sheet for 2005 and 2006 for Stern assuming the successful-efforts approach is used. (Assume that the exploration and drilling costs were the same for all wells.)
3. Contrast the financial reporting effects of the two different oil and gas accounting methods.

P10 – 18

Asset retirement obligations

Coyote Co. is building a waste landfill in the desert between Arizona and California. Coyote estimates that this landfill will be in operation for five years, will cost $250 million to build, and will generate $800 million in revenues during its useful life. Federal law requires that Coyote decommission and decontaminate the site at the end of its useful life. A team of engineers has studied the decontamination procedure and has estimated that Coyote will have to spend $15 million on the decommissioning process when the landfill is shut down five years from now. Coyote's credit-adjusted risk-free rate of interest is 10%.

Required:

1. In accordance with *SFAS No. 143*, how should Coyote Co. account for the costs associated with the decommissioning process? Prepare the journal entry required and prepare an amortization table.
2. How are the costs associated with the decommissioning process reflected on the income statement? Explain how this accounting treatment improves the matching process.

The management of Prescott Co. has committed to a plan to dispose of a group of assets associated with the manufacture of railroad cars. This group of assets qualifies as a component of an entity for financial reporting purposes. As of December 31, 2005, management has located a likely purchaser and is in negotiations to complete the sale. It's expected that the component will be sold in late 2006 for $5,900,000, and that the following costs will be incurred in conjunction with the sale:

Brokers' fees	$360,000
Legal fees	246,000
Closing costs	67,000

P10 – 19

Assets held for sale

The railroad manufacturing assets have an historical cost of $12,000,000 and accumulated depreciation, computed using the straight-line method, of $5,500,000. These assets generated a net loss during 2005 of $475,000 on sales of $1,800,000, and are expected to generate a loss of $525,000 during 2006.

During 2005, Prescott Co. had operating income, including the railroad component, of $7,400,000 and total productive assets, including the railroad component, of $94,500,000 (net of cumulative straight-line depreciation). Sales for the company as a whole for the year ended December 31, 2005 were $20,000,000.

Required:

1. Compute the carrying value at December 31, 2005 of the railroad assets held for sale. How are these assets reported on the December 31, 2005 balance sheet?
2. Prepare a partial income statement including the discontinued operations section for Prescott Co. for the year ended December 31, 2005. Ignore income taxes.
3. Ignoring income taxes, compute return on continuing operating assets and operating margin for Prescott Co. for 2005. Now, assuming that the provisions of *SFAS No. 144* did **not** apply to assets held for sale, compute ROA and operating margin for Prescott for 2005. Contrast the two sets of ratios and comment on your results.
4. How will the group of railroad assets be accounted for during 2006?

---

1. Contrast the economic sacrifice and expected benefit approaches to long-lived asset valuation.
2. GAAP requires firms to use historical cost (in most cases) to report the value of long-lived assets. As a statement reader, do you think that firms should be encouraged to voluntarily report their asset values under alternative valuation approaches? Why or why not?
3. As the manager of a publicly held company, what costs and benefits do you see associated with the voluntary disclosure of asset values using approaches other than historical cost?

P10 – 20

Approaches to long-lived asset valuation

CASES

Target Corporation is a general merchandise retailer. Its divisions include Target, an upscale discount chain; Mervyn's, a middle-market promotional department store; and upscale department stores in the Midwest (Dayton's, Hudson's, and Marshall Field's).

Wal-Mart Stores, Inc. operates retail stores in various retailing formats in all 50 states in the United States. The company's merchandising operations serve its customers primarily through the operation of three segments: the Wal-Mart stores segment includes its discount stores, Supercenters, and Neighborhood Markets in the United States; the Sam's Club segment includes the warehouse membership clubs in the United States; the international segment includes all of its operations in Argentina, Brazil, Canada, China, Japan, Germany, Korea, Mexico, Puerto Rico, and the United Kingdom.

Information taken from both firms' 2003 annual reports to shareholders follows.

C10 – 1

Target Corporation and Wal-Mart Stores: Depreciation differences and financial statement analysis

Target Corporation

Property and Equipment

($ in millions)	February 1 2003	February 2 2002
Land	$ 3,236	$ 2,833
Buildings and improvements	11,527	10,103
Fixtures and equipment	4,983	4,290
Construction in progress	1,190	1,216
Accumulated depreciation	(5,629)	(4,909)
Property and equipment—net	$15,307	$13,533

Property and equipment are recorded at cost, less accumulated depreciation. Depreciation is computed using the straight-line method over estimated useful lives. Accelerated depreciation methods are generally used for income tax purposes.

Estimated useful lives by major asset category are as follows:

Asset	Life (in Years)
Buildings and improvements	8–50
Fixtures and equipment	4–8
Computer hardware and software	4

Selected Income Statement Information

	Years Ended	
($ in millions)	February 1 2003	February 2 2002
Depreciation and amortization	$1,212	$1,079
Earnings before income taxes and extraordinary charge	2,676	2,207
Net earnings	$1,654	$1,368

Wal-Mart Corporation

Property and Equipment

($ in millions)	January 31 2003	January 31 2002
Land	$11,228	$10,241
Buildings and improvements	33,750	28,527
Fixtures and equipment	15,946	14,135
Transportation equipment	1,313	1,089
Property under capital lease	4,814	4,626
Less-accumulated depreciation and amortization:		
Property owned	(13,537)	(11,436)
Property under capital leases	(1,610)	(1,432)
Total	$51,904	$45,750

Depreciation and amortization for financial statement purposes are provided on the straight-line method over the estimated useful lives of the various assets. For income tax purposes, accelerated methods are used with recognition of deferred income taxes for the resulting temporary differences.

Estimated useful lives for financial statements purposes are as follows.

Asset	Life (in Years)
Buildings and improvements	5–50
Fixtures and equipment	5–12
Transportation equipment	2–5
Internally developed software	3

Selected Income Statement Information

($ in millions)	January 31 2003	January 31 2002
Depreciation and amortization	$ 3,432	$ 3,290
Earnings before income taxes and		
minority interests	12,719	10,751
Net income	$ 8,039	$ 6,671

Required:

Assume a 35% tax rate.

1. Estimate the average useful life of each firm's long-lived assets.
2. Calculate a revised estimate of Wal-Mart's 2003 depreciation expense using the estimated average useful life of Target's assets. Use this amount to recalculate Wal-Mart's 2003 income before taxes and net income.
3. Calculate a revised estimate of Target's 2003 depreciation expense using the estimated average useful life of Wal-Mart's assets. Use this amount to recalculate Target's 2003 income before taxes and net income.
4. Why might a financial analyst want to make the adjustments in requirements 2 and 3?
5. What factors will affect the reliability and accuracy of the adjustments performed in requirements 2 and 3?

The following information was taken from Southwest Airlines Co.'s annual report to shareholders.

C10 – 2

Southwest Airlines (CW): Financial statement effects of capitalized interest

Southwest Airlines Company

Consolidated Statement of Income

	Years Ended December 31		
($ in thousands)	1999	1998	1997
Interest expense	$ 54,145	$ 56,276	$ 63,454
Capitalized interest	(31,262)	(25,588)	(19,779)
Income before income taxes	773,611	705,112	516,956
Net income	$474,378	$433,431	$317,772

Consolidated Statement of Cash Flows

Cash payments for interest, net of			
amount capitalized	$ 26,604	$ 33,384	$ 42,372

Required:

Assume a 35% income tax rate.

1. What is the underlying rationale for the capitalization of interest?
2. Assume that none of the assets to which the 1999 capitalized interest applies have been completed and placed into service. Calculate the firm's 1999 income before income taxes, assuming that no interest had been capitalized in 1999. What is the percentage change from the reported amount?
3. Starting with net income of $474,378 as reported in 1999, assume the same facts as in requirement 2, and recalculate Southwest's *net* income.
4. Briefly discuss the impact of capitalized interest on a firm's future reported earnings.

Microsoft develops, manufactures, licenses, sells, and supports a wide range of software products, including operating systems for personal computers (PCs) and servers; server applications for client/server environments; business and consumer productivity applications; interactive media programs; and Internet platform and development tools. Microsoft also offers online services, sells PC books and input devices, and researches and develops advanced technology software products. Microsoft products are available for most PCs, including Intel microprocessor-based computers and Apple computers. Microsoft's business strategy emphasizes the development of a broad line of PC software products for business and personal use.

Income statement and balance sheet information from Microsoft's recent annual reports to shareholders follows. Assume an income tax rate of 35%.

Microsoft: Selected Financial Information					
($ in millions)	1996	1997	1998	1999	2000
Sales	$ 8,671	$11,358	$15,262	$19,747	$22,956
Net income (NOPAT)	2,195	3,454	4,490	7,785	9,421
Total assets	10,093	14,387	22,357	38,625	52,150
Total shareholders' equity	6,908	10,777	16,627	28,438	41,368
Research and development	$ 1,432	$ 1,925	$ 2,897	$ 2,970	$ 3,775

Required:

1. How does current GAAP require firms to account for their research and development expenditures?
2. Use the reported information to calculate Microsoft's NOPAT margin (net operating profit after taxes divided by sales), asset turnover (sales divided by average total assets), return on assets (NOPAT divided by average total assets), and return on shareholders' equity (NOPAT divided by average shareholders' equity) for 1998, 1999, and 2000.
3. Assume that Microsoft expects its research and development expenditures to benefit the current accounting period as well as the next two accounting periods. Briefly describe how Microsoft's 1998 income statement and balance sheet would have been different if it had capitalized rather than expensed its research and development expenditures.
4. Repeat requirement 2 after capitalizing research and development expenditures and amortizing them as described in requirement 3. As a statement reader, would you find the differences in the ratios in requirements 2 and 4 to be significant? Why?

Dallas Inc. began operations on January 1, 2005 when it purchased some long-lived assets at a cost of $120,000. The assets have a 12-year useful life and no salvage value; Dallas Inc. intends to use the straight-line depreciation method. Assume that the firm will generate net operating cash flows of $33,000 in 2005 and that its net operating cash flows will grow at an annual rate of 10%. Assume that Dallas does not intend to make any capital expenditures over the next five years.

Houston Inc. is a competitor of Dallas Inc. On January 1, 2005 the book value of Houston's assets is $120,000 (original cost of $240,000). Houston's assets, like those of Dallas Inc., have a 12-year useful life, no salvage value, and are depreciated on a straight-line basis. However, they are six years old and are halfway through their useful life of 12 years. Houston has a policy of replacing one-twelfth of its assets each year at the end of the assets' useful lives. Assume that Houston Inc. will generate net operating cash flows of $43,000 in 2005 and that the firm's net operating cash flows will grow at an annual rate of 10%. To keep pace with inflation, the management of Houston Inc. will increase the capital expenditures of the firm by 10% per year. (Note: For simplicity, assume that prior to 2005, the replacement cost of Houston's assets remained constant.)

Required:

1. Prepare a schedule of Dallas Inc.'s net book value of assets, net operating cash flow, depreciation expense, income before tax, income taxes, net income, average asset age, and return on net assets (net income divided by beginning book value of net assets) for the 2005–2009 period. Assume an income tax rate of 34%.

2. Repeat requirement 1 for Houston Inc.
3. Compare the return on net assets of the firms over the 2005–2009 period.
4. Which firm's 2009 income is more sustainable? Why?

Appearing on the following pages is information pertaining to the "Property, Plant, and Equipment" accounts of Intel Corporation. This information was taken from Intel's Year 2 10-K report. A 10-K is an annual report firms must file with the SEC within 90 days of the end of their fiscal year. (All figures are in thousands.)

C10 – 5

Intel Corporation (CW): Long-lived asset reporting

Additional Information:
All amounts under the heading "Retirements and Sales" are retirements.

Required:

1. Solve for the unknowns in Intel's "Property, Plant, and Equipment" and "Accumulated Depreciation" schedules for Year 2.
2. What was the total amount expended on the acquisition of new property, plant, and equipment in Year 2? Where would this amount appear in the financial statements?
3. What was the net gain (or net loss) reported in Year 2 on the retirement of property, plant, and equipment? Where would this amount appear in the financial statements?
4. Make all the journal entries related to the "Property, plant, and equipment" and "Accumulated Depreciation" accounts for Year 2.
5. Prepare a schedule of the depreciation expense to be taken for financial reporting purposes on the new machinery and equipment acquired in Year 2. Prepare separate schedules assuming straight-line, sum-of-the-years' digits, and double-declining balance. Assume a zero salvage value for all assets and a three-year useful life; also assume that Intel takes a full year of depreciation in the year an asset is purchased.
6. Assume that one of Intel's long-term debt contracts requires that Intel maintain a minimum interest coverage ratio of 5.0. If Intel's interest coverage ratio falls below 5.0, the lenders have the option of requiring immediate payment of their debt or renegotiating the interest rate. Assume that Intel's interest coverage ratio at the end of Year 1 was 4.9. Briefly describe how the restriction on the firm's interest coverage ratio could affect management's choice of depreciation policy for all or some of the new long-term assets acquired in Year 2.
7. What other settings can you identify in which management may be tempted to use depreciation policy strategically to influence the numbers reported in the financial statements?
8. Identify other items in the financial statements (besides depreciation expense) that management is capable of "managing." Are some easier for outside parties to observe?
9. Several years ago, the SEC decided to stop requiring firms to report the detailed information about the underlying changes in the long-term asset and accumulated depreciation accounts that appear in the following two schedules. As a financial analyst, do you approve or disapprove? Explain why.

Intel Corporation

Property, Plant and Equipment

($ in thousands)	Balance at Beginning of Year 2	Additions at Cost	Retirements and Sales	Transfers, Reclassifications and Other In (Out)	Balance at End of Year 2
Land and buildings	$ (a)	$ 24,612	$12,455	$124,001	$1,097,526
Machinery and equipment	1,764,623	596,068	(b)	30,322	2,288,200
Construction in progress	87,614	(c)	2,470	(d)	258,430

Accumulated Depreciation, Property, Plant and Equipment

($ in thousands)	Balance at Beginning of Year 2	Additions at Cost	Retirements and Sales	Transfers, Reclassifications and Other In (Out)	Balance at End of Year 2
Buildings and improvements	$226,533	$ (a)	$ 1,812	$(116)	$ 283,954
Machinery and equipment	(b)	358,903	91,044	116	1,197,479

C10 – 6

Delta Air Lines (CW):
Financial statement effects
of depreciation policy
changes

The following information is taken from Delta Air Lines Inc.'s 1995 annual report to shareholders.

DEPRECIATION AND AMORTIZATION:

Prior to April 1, 1993, the Company depreciated substantially all of its flight equipment on a straight-line basis over a 15-year period from the dates placed in service. As a result of a fleet plan review, effective April 1, 1993, the Company increased the estimated useful lives of substantially all of its flight equipment. Flight equipment that was not already fully depreciated is being depreciated on a straight-line basis over a 20-year period from the dates placed in service. The effect of this change was a $34 million decrease in depreciation expense in 1993.

Required:

Assume a 34% income tax rate.

1. Calculate the impact of the depreciation policy change on Delta's 1993 net income.
2. How will the change affect Delta's reported earnings over the next few years?
3. How might a financial analyst determine if the change made by Delta is reasonable in light of industry conditions?
4. How might firms use depreciation policy changes to manage their earnings? Is there anything to prevent rampant use of depreciation policy changes as a tool to manage reported earnings?
5. In light of the contracting issues discussed in Chapter 7, speculate as to the possible reasons Delta might have made the change in its depreciation policy.

---

www.prenhall.com/revsine

Remember to check the book's Companion Website for additional problem and case material.

Financial Instruments as Liabilities

The Financial Accounting Standards Board (FASB) says:

> Liabilities are probable future sacrifices of economic benefits arising from present obligations of a particular entity to transfer assets or to provide services to other entities in the future as a result of past transactions or events.[1]

Simply, this means a financial statement liability is

1. an existing obligation arising from past events, which calls for
2. payment of cash or provision of goods and services (say, delivery of a product for which a deposit has already been received) to some other entity at some future date.

Liabilities help businesses conduct their affairs by permitting delay—delay in payment or performance. But because "time is money," **interest** is a common feature of delayed payment liabilities. Interest is the price charged for delaying payment.

Most liabilities are **monetary liabilities** because they are payable in a fixed future amount of cash.

There are **nonmonetary liabilities** that are satisfied by the delivery of things other than cash, such as goods or services. An example of a nonmonetary liability is

---

[1] "Elements of Financial Statements," *Statement of Financial Accounting Concepts No. 6* (Stamford, CT: FASB, 1985), para. 35. In October 2000, the FASB proposed broadening this definition to include as liabilities certain obligations settled by the issuance of equity shares (see "Proposed Amendment to FASB Concepts Statement No. 6 to Revise the Definition of Liabilities," *Financial Accounting Series Exposure Draft* [Stamford, CT: FASB, 2000]).

Here's an example. Suppose a start-up Internet company, Yellowbird.com, buys $100,000 of computers from a manufacturer, say Dell Computers. Instead of paying cash, Yellowbird promises to pay Dell $100,000 worth of Yellowbird stock once the company goes public (in about six months). Yellowbird is using its stock as "currency" for the transaction because it lacks cash.

Notice that a fixed amount of value ($100,000) must be conveyed to Dell, not a fixed number of Yellowbird shares. The FASB says that this makes the relationship look more like a debtor-creditor relationship—unlike an owner, Dell cannot benefit from increases or suffer from decreases in share value—so Yellowbird should record a "liability" for the $100,000.

As this book goes to press, the FASB continues to deliberate the issue.

a product warranty. If the product fails during the warranty period, the warranty liability is satisfied by either repairing or replacing the product. The liability is paid by providing nonmonetary assets—labor and replacement parts from inventory or a new product—but not cash.

Conceptually, monetary liabilities should be shown in the financial statements at the *discounted present value* of the future cash outflows required to satisfy the obligation. This discounted present value approach allows interest to accumulate over time through accounting entries that assign interest expense—the cost of delay—to the time period(s) over which payment is delayed. In practice, this is what is done with long-term monetary liabilities.

However, **current liabilities**—obligations due within a year or within the company's operating cycle, whichever is longer—are rarely discounted. Current liabilities are rarely discounted because their short maturity makes immaterial the difference between the amount due at maturity and the present value of that maturity amount. So, current liabilities are shown at the undiscounted amount due.[2] This treatment of current liabilities departs from the conceptual "ideal" solely on pragmatic grounds—the dollar difference between maturity amount and present value amount is quite small.

Noncurrent monetary liabilities are initially recorded at their present value when incurred. There are occasional exceptions, which we will discuss in Chapter 13. But the general rule is that noncurrent monetary liabilities are first recorded at their present value.

To help you visualize how these liability valuation concepts apply in practice, look at Exhibit 11.1, which reproduces the liabilities section of Oracle Corporation's balance sheet. Oracle is one of the world's leading suppliers of software for information management.

EXHIBIT 11.1	Oracle Corporation	

Liabilities Section of Consolidated Balance Sheets

($ in millions)	2002	2001
Current liabilities:		
Current maturities of long-term debt	$ —	$ 3
Accounts payable	228	270
Income taxes payable	1,091	767
Accrued compensation and related benefits	458	735
Customer advances and unearned revenues	1,276	1,214
Value-added tax and sales tax payable	155	165
Other accrued liabilities	752	763
Total current liabilities	3,960	3,917
Long-term debt	298	301
Deferred tax liabilities	204	328
Other long-term liabilities	221	207

Listed among the company's current liabilities you will find:

- "Accounts payable" that represent amounts owed to suppliers,
- "Income taxes payable" that represent amounts owed to state and federal income tax agencies, and
- "Value added tax and sales tax payable" that represent other taxes owed to state and federal taxing authorities.

---

[2] An exception is the current portion of long-term debt.

Because these accounts are shown as current liabilities, you can be assured of two things;

1. The obligations are due within a year or within the company's operating cycle, whichever is longer—at Oracle, "current" means "due within one year."
2. These current liabilities are shown at the undiscounted amount due even though some may remain unpaid for a full year.

Oracle's current liabilities also include "Customer advances and unearned revenues," which arise when customers pay for the company's software or consulting services in advance of actual delivery. Since Oracle is obligated to provide software products or consulting services in the future—but not cash—this account is a nonmonetary liability and the amount shown represents the cash payments received from these customers.

"Accrued compensation and related benefits" represents cash owed to employees of the company, and this monetary liability is shown at the undiscounted amount due.

Oracle's long-term debt is shown in two places on the balance sheet:

- The amount due within one year is listed among current liabilities as "Current maturities of long-term debt."
- Amounts due after one year are shown separately as "Long-term debt."

> Two other noncurrent liabilities are listed on Oracle's balance sheet: "Deferred tax liabilities," which are described in Chapter 13, and "Other long-term liabilities," which arise primarily from employee pension and healthcare benefits as described in Chapter 14.

This classification helps analysts and investors spot any large debt payments that may come due next year—for Oracle, the amount of long-term debt due in 2003 (that is, next year) is zero. Long-term debt is a noncurrent monetary liability and is shown at the discounted present value of the amount due. The next section explains why.

Bonds Payable

Firms issue bonds to raise cash. A **bond** is a financial instrument that represents a formal promise to repay both the amount borrowed as well as the interest on the amount borrowed. The precise terms of the borrowing are specified in the **bond indenture agreement**—the contract between the bond's issuer (that is, the borrower) and the bond's investors (lendors). In this section we look at how companies account for this debt instrument and how to interpret debt disclosures in financial statements.

> **Debentures**, the most common type of corporate bond, are backed only by the general credit of the company. **Mortgage bonds** use real estate as collateral for repayment of the loan. **Serial bonds** require periodic payment of interest and a portion of the principal (for example, an equal amount each year to maturity). Despite these and other differences, the accounting for these debt instruments follows the general approach described here.

Characteristics of Bond Cash Flows

Bond certificates are usually issued with a **principal amount** of $1,000. The principal amount—also called the **par value**, **maturity value**, or **face value**—represents the amount that will be repaid to the investor at the maturity date specified in the indenture agreement. The bond certificate also displays the **stated interest rate**—sometimes called the **coupon** or **nominal rate**.

The annual cash interest payments on the bond are computed by multiplying the principal amount by the stated interest rate. A bond with $1,000 principal and a 9% per year stated interest rate will have annual cash interest payments of $90. Typically, the total annual cash interest is paid in installments, either quarterly or semiannually.

> Investors must be careful to read the details of a bond's interest payment terms. For example, investors who put money into a bond that pays "9% interest annually" receive a single payment of $90 (per $1,000 of face value) each year. A bond that pays "9% interest semiannually" yields two payments of $45 each year (9% ÷ 2 = 4.5% each payment period). Although the total dollar interest payment is $90 per year in both cases, the semiannual bond is slightly more valuable because investors receive half of the cash earlier each year than in the case of the annual payment bond.

While the face value is typically $1,000 per bond, the price at which it is issued can be equal to, below, or above the face value.

- When the issue price exactly equals the face value, the bond is sold at **par**.
- If the issue price is below face value, the bond is sold at a **discount**.
- If the issue price is greater than the face value, the bond is sold at a **premium**.

Market conditions dictate the relationship between what investors are willing to pay—the issue price—and the bond's face value.

Bonds Issued at Par

A bond's issue price determines its **effective yield**—or true rate of return. When the issue price of the bond equals its par value, the effective yield to investors is exactly equal to the coupon (or stated) rate. Consider this example:

> On January 1, 2005 Huff Corporation issued $1,000,000 face value of 10% per year bonds at par—that is, Huff got $1,000,000 cash from investors and promised to make interest and principal payments in the future. Since the cash interest payments on the bonds are always equal to the stated interest rate (10%) times the bond principal amount ($1,000,000), cash interest will total $100,000 per year. The bonds mature in 10 years (on December 31, 2014), and interest is paid annually on December 31 of each year.

> The accounting entry to record issuance of these bonds on Huff's books is:

DR Cash	$1,000,000	
CR Bonds payable		$1,000,000

The bond is recorded at its issue price—the $1,000,000 cash received by Huff.

When bonds are sold at par (or face value), their effective yield to the investor is exactly equal to the coupon interest rate, which is 10% in this example. To show that the effective yield equals 10% in this example, we list the cash payments and compute their present value as of the issue date—January 1, 2005—in Exhibit 11.2. The effective yield is precisely 10% because the present value of the ten annual interest payments ($614,456) plus the present value of the principal repayment ($385,544) is equal to the issue proceeds received on January 1, 2005 ($1,000,000) when discounted at a 10% rate.

EXHIBIT 11.2	Huff Corporation

Demonstration that the Yield on Bonds Issued at Par Is Equal to the Coupon Interest Rate (here 10%)

Date of Payment	Type of Payment	Amount of Payment	10% Present Value Factor	Discounted Present Value
12/31/05	Interest	$ 100,000	.90909	$ 90,909
12/31/06	Interest	100,000	.82645	82,645
12/31/07	Interest	100,000	.75131	75,131
12/31/08	Interest	100,000	.68301	68,301
12/31/09	Interest	100,000	.62092	62,092
12/31/10	Interest	100,000	.56447	56,447
12/31/11	Interest	100,000	.51316	51,316
12/31/12	Interest	100,000	.46651	46,651
12/31/13	Interest	100,000	.42410	42,410
12/31/14	Interest	100,000	.38554	38,554
Total present value of interest payments				$ 614,456
12/31/14	Principal	$1,000,000	.385544	385,544
Total issue price on January 1, 2005				$1,000,000

For bonds issued at par, the coupon interest rate on the bond is equal to the effective yield earned by bond investors. Furthermore, recording the bonds at par on the issuer's books automatically records them at their discounted present value.

In the example, the amount received for the bonds ($1,000,000) is exactly equal to the present value of the future debt-related cash outflows (interest and principal payments) discounted at the 10% effective yield on the bonds.

> The cash interest payments on the Huff bonds are an **annuity**, which means a series of payments in the same amount made at equally spaced time intervals. If the first payment is made at the start of period 1, then it's an **annuity due**. Apartment leases often have this feature—the first month's payment is due when the lease is signed. The cash interest payments on Huff's bonds are an **ordinary annuity** (in arrears) because the first payment is due at the end of period 1 (December 31, 2005).

Subsequent accounting for bonds issued at par is straightforward. Let's say Huff prepares monthly financial statements; the *monthly* journal entry to record interest expense and Huff's liability for unpaid ("accrued") interest is:

DR Interest expense	$8,333.33	
CR Accrued interest payable		$8,333.33

This (rounded) amount represents $\frac{1}{12}$ of the $100,000 annual interest. At the end of the year, the accrued (unpaid) interest would total $100,000; upon payment of the interest by Huff, the entry would be:

DR Accrued interest payable	$100,000.00	
CR Cash		$100,000.00

Bonds Issued at a Discount

Arranging for the sale of bonds can take considerable time. The terms of the indenture—the bond contract—must be drafted and printed, an investment banker must be found, and the bond certificates themselves must be engraved. Time is also consumed in waiting for the Securities Exchange Commission (SEC) to review and accept the security offering prospectus. Market interest rates may change during the time it takes to do this and before the bonds are ready to be issued.

Assume the Huff bonds are printed during late 2004 and carry a 10% coupon interest rate. The coupon rate immediately establishes the yearly cash interest payout of $100,000 (10% multiplied by the $1,000,000 face amount of the bonds).

But let's say there's a sudden increase in the anticipated rate of inflation, causing investors to demand an 11% return on the Huff bond as of the January 1, 2005 issue date. To provide the 11% return that investors now demand, the Huff bonds must be sold at a *discount* relative to face value. Here's why. The annual cash interest and maturity payments are fixed by the indenture agreement at $100,000 and $1,000,000, respectively. If investors pay the full face amount ($1,000,000) for the bonds, they will just earn a 10% return on their investment. To attract investors who expect to earn an 11% return, Huff must be willing to issue the bonds at a price that is lower than the $1,000,000 face amount. How much lower than $1,000,000 must the issue price be? It must be reduced to a level that gives prospective investors exactly the 11% return they require. *The bond's price is determined by discounting the contractual cash flows at 11%,* as shown in Exhibit 11.3. Lowering the issue price gives investors the higher return they demand.

> Bonds are seldom sold directly to investors by the issuing company. Instead, the bonds are sold through a financial intermediary—an **investment banker**. In most cases the investment banker purchases the bonds and resells them to institutional investors (for example, pension funds) at whatever price the market will bear. The investment banker's profit (or loss) is the difference between the price it pays to buy the bonds from the issuing company and the price at which it sells them to investors, plus any fees paid by the company.

EXHIBIT 11.3	Huff Corporation

Determining the Issue Price for 10% Coupon Bonds When the Market Rate Is 11%

Date of Payment	Type of Payment	Amount of Payment	11% Present Value Factor	Discounted Present Value
12/31/05	Interest	$ 100,000	.90090	$ 90,090
12/31/06	Interest	100,000	.81162	81,162
12/31/07	Interest	100,000	.73119	73,119
12/31/08	Interest	100,000	.65873	65,873
12/31/09	Interest	100,000	.59345	59,345
12/31/10	Interest	100,000	.53464	53,464
12/31/11	Interest	100,000	.48166	48,166
12/31/12	Interest	100,000	.43393	43,393
12/31/13	Interest	100,000	.39093	39,093
12/31/14	Interest	100,000	.35218	35,218
Total present value of interest payments			5.88923	$588,923
12/31/14	Principal	$1,000,000	.352185	352,185
Total issue price on January 1, 2005				**$941,108**

Equivalently

December 31	2004	2005	2006	2007	2008	2009	2010	2011	2012	2013	2014

Cash interest payments ● $100k $100k $100k $100k $100k $100k $100k $100k $100k $100k

Cash principal payment ● · · · · · · · · · $1 m

Present value of single payment at 11%: $1 million × 0.352185 = $352,185

Present value of 10-period ordinary annuity at 11%: $100 thousand × 5.88923 = $588,923

The price that yields the required 11% return, given the stipulated $100,000 annual contractual interest payments, is $941,108. Investors seeking an 11% return will not be willing to pay more than $941,108 for 10-year bonds that have a face value of $1,000,000 and a coupon interest rate of 10%. Why? Because if they pay more than $941,108, they will earn less than 11% on the bond's fixed cash flow stream. And Huff will not be willing to issue the bonds for less than $941,108 because to do so would mean paying more than 11% to investors. Thus, market forces will set the issue price at $941,108.

The accounting entry made on issuance of the 10% coupon bonds at a price that yields an 11% return to investors is:

DR Cash	$941,108	
DR Bond discount	58,892	
CR Bonds payable—par		$1,000,000

The bond discount is a **liability valuation account** that is deducted from the bonds payable account for financial reporting purposes. The net balance sheet (or carrying) value of the bonds when they are issued will be $941,108 ($1,000,000 minus $58,892)—the amount of cash Huff received. This again illustrates the basic principle that newly issued bonds are recorded at the present value of the contractual cash outflows for interest and principal repayment—where *the discount rate is the effective yield on the bonds at the issuance date* (here 11%).

When bonds are not sold at par, the calculation of annual interest expense and the accounting entry that records that expense are slightly more complicated. Consider the nature of the bond discount of $58,892. The discount amount is the difference between the cash Huff received from investors and the amount Huff promised to repay them on December 31, 2014. This $58,892 is really just additional interest—over and above the contractual cash interest of $100,000 per year—that will be *earned* over the term of the loan, but it will not be *paid* until maturity. Cumulative interest expense over the 10 years will total $1,058,892—the coupon interest of $1,000,000 paid out over the life of the bond plus the issue discount of $58,892 paid at maturity.

> **Cumulative interest expense** can also be thought of as follows: Investors will ultimately be paid total debt-related cash flows of $2,000,000 in principal plus cash interest; that is, $1,000,000 paid at maturity, and 10 annual payments of $100,000. Huff received only $941,108 when the bonds were issued. The difference ($2,000,000 minus $941,108) is $1,058,892, which must be the cumulative total interest expense over the life of the bond.

How should this "extra" interest of $58,892 be allocated across the 10 years? Generally accepted accounting principles (GAAP) recommend that the bond discount be allocated to interest expense on an **effective interest basis**. This requires the use of an amortization schedule, as shown in Exhibit 11.4. In column (a) Huff received $941,108 on January 1, 2005 in exchange for issuing the bond certificates. Bondholders require an 11% return on the amount invested. Therefore, their interest income—and Huff's interest expense—in 2005 must be 11% of $941,108 or $103,522, as shown in column (b). The difference between Huff's $103,522 interest expense and the cash interest of $100,000 is the portion of "extra" interest allocated to 2005. This "extra" interest reduces the bond discount amount. If interest is recorded annually, the entry is:

> But it's an unusual "recommendation" because GAAP allows other methods only if their results are not much different.

DR Interest expense	$103,522	
CR Accrued interest payable		$100,000
CR Bond discount		3,522

EXHIBIT 11.4 | **Huff Corporation**

Bond Discount Amortization Schedule
(amounts rounded to nearest dollar)

Year	(a) Bond Net Carrying Amount at Start of Year	(b) Interest Expense (Column a × 11%)	(c) Bond Discount Amortized (Column b − $100,000)	(d) Bond Discount Balance at End of Year	(e) Bond Net Carrying Amount at End of Year (Column a + Column c)
2005	$941,108	$ 103,522	$ 3,522	$55,370	$ 944,630
2006	944,630	103,909	3,909	51,461	948,539
2007	948,539	104,339	4,339	47,122	952,878
2008	952,878	104,817	4,817	42,305	957,695
2009	957,695	105,346	5,346	36,959	963,041
2010	963,041	105,935	5,935	31,024	968,976
2011	968,976	106,587	6,587	24,437	975,563
2012	975,563	107,312	7,312	17,125	982,875
2013	982,875	108,116	8,116	9,009	990,991
2014	990,991	109,009	9,009	—	$1,000,000.00
		$1,058,892	$58,892		

The process of "spreading" the discount on bonds to increase interest expense over the life of the bonds is called **discount amortization**. The yearly amortization amount is shown in column (c) of Exhibit 11.4. After the amortization is recorded, the year-end balance in the bond discount account—shown in column (d)—will be $55,370 (the original discount of $58,892 minus the 2005 amortization of $3,522). Notice that the smaller the balance in the bond discount account, shown in column (d), the higher the **net carrying value** of the bond liability in column (e). The balance sheet value of the bond increases as the discount is amortized.

The bond amortization schedule illustrates that annual interest expense, column (b), always equals the effective interest rate (here 11%) multiplied by the start of the year borrowing balance, column (a). The difference between the accrual accounting interest expense, column (b), and the $100,000 cash interest paid each year is the discount amortization, column (c). This effective interest amortization process is represented in Exhibit 11.5.

EXHIBIT 11.5   **Determining the Amortization Amount**

Bonds Issued at a Premium

Recording bonds that are issued at a premium is similar to the accounting for bonds issued at a discount. Assume that immediately after the Huff Corporation bonds were printed late in 2004, interest rates *fell* to 9%. If these newly issued bonds were sold at par, Huff would be paying investors 10%—the coupon interest rate as printed. But why should Huff pay 10% when investors are willing to accept 9% interest. Here's how Huff pays 9% instead of 10% despite the contractual 10% specified. Rather than selling the bonds at par, Huff will issue the bonds at a *premium*—that is, at an amount sufficiently higher than the $1,000,000 face value so that investors will get only a 9% return. The exact amount is determined, as in the previous discount example, by taking the bond-related cash flows and discounting them at the effective yield rate (here 9%), as shown in Exhibit 11.6.

The bonds would be issued for $1,064,177—the present value of the contractual principal and interest payments at a discount rate of 9%. Buying the bonds at this price will give investors a 9% effective yield.

The entry to record the bond issuance is:

DR Cash	$1,064,177	
CR Bond premium		$ 64,177
CR Bonds payable—par		1,000,000

The bond premium (like the bond discount) is also a liability valuation account; the premium balance, $64,177 in this example, is added to the bonds payable account to increase the balance sheet carrying value of the bonds. The Huff bonds will initially have a carrying value of $1,064,177. ***When bonds are sold at a premium, interest expense will always be less than the cash interest payment.*** The extra cash paid represents the amount of the premium being returned to bondholders. Exhibit 11.7 shows the amortization schedule. For example, the 2005 interest expense entry shows interest expense (from column [b]) equal to $95,776 or the $100,000 cash interest payment minus the $4,224 premium amortization (from column [c])—that is:

DR Interest expense	$95,776	
DR Bond premium	4,224	
CR Cash		$100,000

EXHIBIT 11.6	Huff Corporation

Determining the Issue Price for 10% Coupon Bonds When the Market Rate Is 9%

Date of Payment	Type of Payment	Amount of Payment	9% Present Value Factor	Discounted Present Value
12/31/05	Interest	$ 100,000	.91743	$ 91,743
12/31/06	Interest	100,000	.84168	84,168
12/31/07	Interest	100,000	.77218	77,218
12/31/08	Interest	100,000	.70843	70,843
12/31/09	Interest	100,000	.64993	64,993
12/31/10	Interest	100,000	.59627	59,627
12/31/11	Interest	100,000	.54703	54,703
12/31/12	Interest	100,000	.50187	50,187
12/31/13	Interest	100,000	.46043	46,043
12/31/14	Interest	100,000	.42241	42,241
Total present value of interest payments			6.41766	$ 641,766
12/31/14	Principal	$1,000,000	.422411	422,411
Total issue price on January 1, 2005				**$1,064,177**

Equivalently

Present value of single payment at 9%: $1 million × 0.422411 = $422,411

Present value of 10-period ordinary annuity at 9%: $100 thousand × 6.41766 = $641,766

Interest expense each year is less than the $100,000 annual cash interest payment. To see why, notice that Huff initially received more cash than it promised to pay back at the end of 10 years—that is, Huff received $1,064,177 but agreed to pay back $1,000,000. The difference—or premium—is returned to bondholders gradually over the entire period of the borrowing. For example, $4,224 of the premium is returned in 2005 (as shown in column [c]), and a different amount ($4,604) is returned in 2006.

EXHIBIT 11.7	Huff Corporation

Bond Premium Amortization Schedule
(amounts rounded to nearest dollar)

Year	(a) Bond Net Carrying Amount at Start of Year	(b) Interest Expense (Column a × 9%)	(c) Bond Premium Amortized ($100,000 − Column b)	(d) Bond Premium Balance at End of Year	(e) Bond Net Carrying Amount at End of Year (Column a − Column c)
2005	$1,064,177	$ 95,776	$ 4,224	$59,953	$1,059,953
2006	1,059,953	95,396	4,604	55,349	1,055,349
2007	1,055,349	94,981	5,019	50,330	1,050,330
2008	1,050,330	94,530	5,470	44,860	1,044,860
2009	1,044,860	94,037	5,963	38,897	1,038,897
2010	1,038,897	93,501	6,499	32,398	1,032,398
2011	1,032,398	92,916	7,084	25,314	1,025,314
2012	1,025,314	92,278	7,722	17,592	1,017,592
2013	1,017,592	91,583	8,417	9,175	1,009,175
2014	1,009,175	90,825*	9,175	—	1,000,000
		$935,823	$64,177		

*Rounded

Looking at Bonds Graphically

The bar graphs in Figure 11.1 depict the components of issue price for Huff bonds when the interest rate is 10% (from Exhibit 11.2), 11% (from Exhibit 11.3), and 9% (from Exhibit 11.6). These bar graphs illustrate that *the issue price is determined by discounting the contractual principal and interest flows at the market yield rate.*

Figure 11.1

ILLUSTRATION OF SELLING PRICES OF 10% COUPON BONDS AT DIFFERENT MARKET (EFFECTIVE) YIELDS

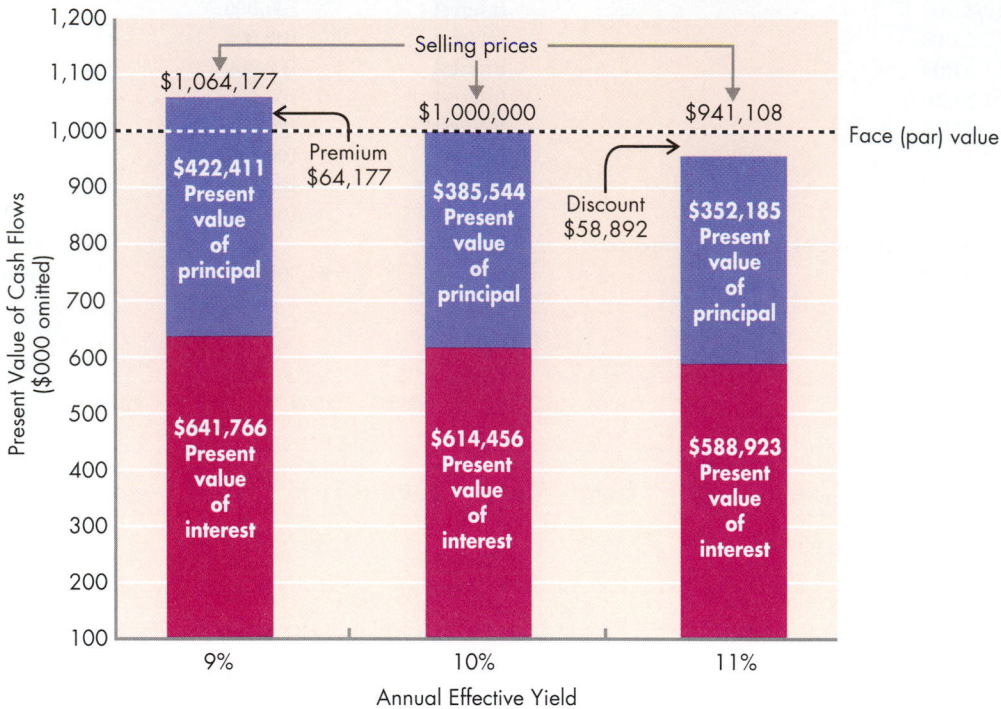

Figure 11.2 is based on the amortization schedule numbers from Exhibit 11.4, where the Huff bonds were sold at a discount because the market interest rate was 11%. Figure 11.2(a) shows the interest expense and cash interest payments for each year of the term of the bond, and the difference between the two amounts is the discount amortization. For example, $3,522, the discount amortized in 2005, is the amount from column (c) of Exhibit 11.4. The second chart (Figure 11.2(b)) shows that the net carrying value of the bonds increases as the discount is amortized each year.

Figure 11.2(a)

ILLUSTRATION OF CASH INTEREST PAYMENT AND INTEREST EXPENSE
Market yield 11%.

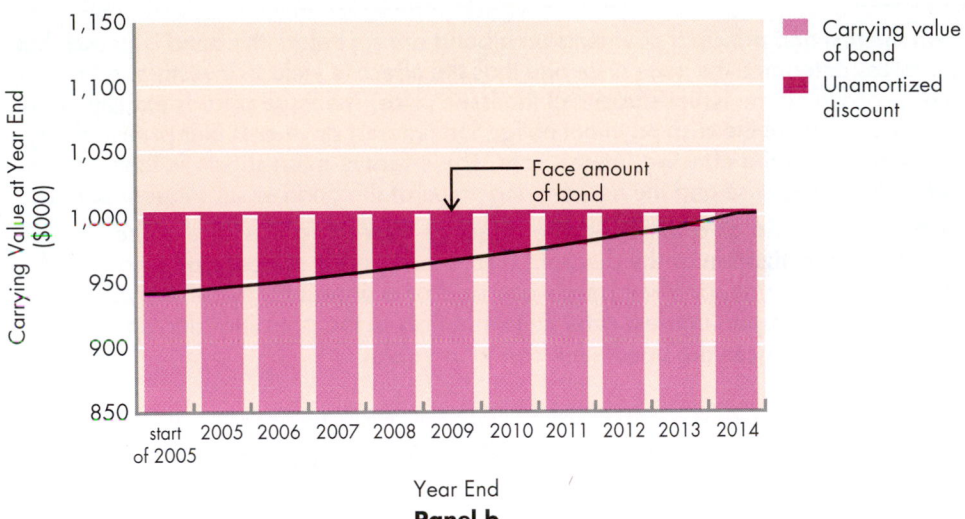

Figure 11.2(b)

ILLUSTRATION OF CARRYING
VALUE FOR 10% BONDS SOLD
AT DISCOUNT
Market yield 11%.

Figure 11.3 depicts the bond sold at a premium due to a 9% market interest rate. Figure 11.3(a) shows that interest expense each year is less than the coupon cash payment of $100,000. Figure 11.3(b) shows that the carrying value of the bond falls as the premium is amortized.

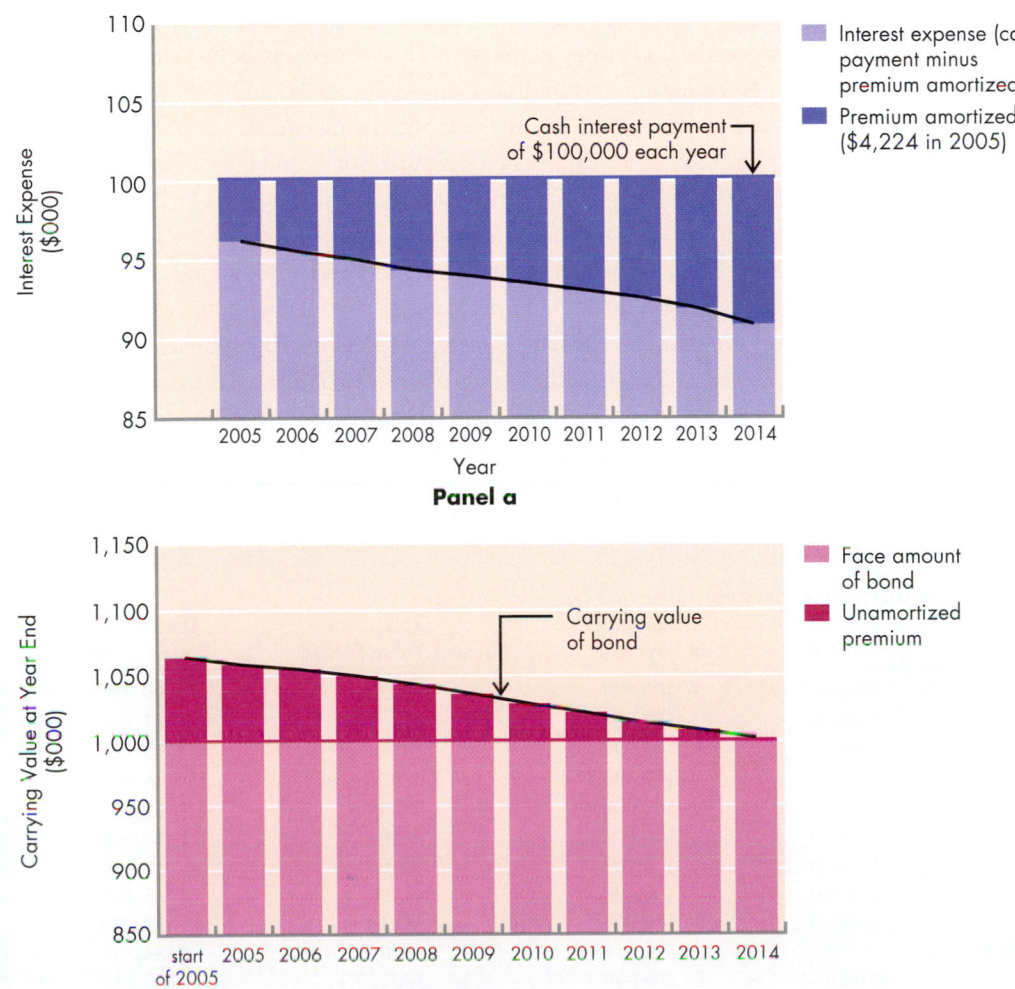

Figure 11.3

ILLUSTRATION OF (a) CASH
INTEREST PAYMENT AND
INTEREST EXPENSE, AND
(b) CARRYING VALUE FOR 10%
BONDS SOLD AT PREMIUM
Market yield 9%.

RE**CAP**

The cash interest and principal payments on a bond are set before the bond is issued, but market forces determine the issue price and thus the effective yield to investors. All bonds are first recorded on the issuer's books at the issue price. The issue price is exactly equal to the present value of the cash payment obligation (interest payments plus principal payment) discounted at the effective interest rate. The effective interest rate is then used to compute interest expense and the net carrying value of the bond in subsequent periods.

When bonds are sold at a discount, the effective interest rate is above the coupon interest rate. Amortization of the discount increases interest expense and adds to the bond's net carrying value. When bonds are sold at a premium, the effective interest rate is below the coupon interest rate. Amortization of the premium decreases interest expense and reduces the bond's net carrying value.

Book Value Versus Market Value After Issuance

Although bonds payable are shown at their market value—meaning their present value—when they are first issued, their balance sheet value will not necessarily equal their market value later. After issuance, the market value may not equal the balance sheet value because GAAP requires bonds payable to be carried on the books at **amortized historical cost**. Because market interest rates often change, that means bond prices also often change. *Thus, after issuance, the reported book value of bonds payable and their market value will likely differ.*

> Market interest rates change up or down on almost a daily basis, and thus, so do bond prices. Changes in a company's credit risk also influence bond prices. These changes are less frequent, but no less important.

To see this, let's return to the Huff Corporation example where 10% coupon bonds were issued at par on January 1, 2005. Because the bonds were issued at par, there is no discount nor premium to amortize. Hence, the book value of the bonds will always equal the principal amount of $1,000,000 each year the bonds are outstanding. Bonds payable would be shown on the balance sheet at $1,000,000 at December 31, 2005, one year after being issued.

Now it's January 1, 2006, one year after the bonds were first issued, and the market rate of interest suddenly jumps to 11%. Remember, prevailing interest rates last year "set" the price at which the bonds were originally issued. It's no different after the bonds have been issued—the market price is still set by prevailing interest rates. So the market price of Huff bonds after interest rates jump on January 1, 2006 is the remaining cash interest and principal payments discounted at the new 11% effective yield that investors now require. The market price on January 1, 2006 would be $944,630, as shown in Exhibit 11.8. However, under GAAP, the bond payable would still be shown on Huff's books at the original $1,000,000 amount. In general then, *reported book values after issuance will not necessarily equal the market value of the bonds because market interest rates fluctuate over time.*

EXHIBIT 11.8	Huff Corporation

Calculation of Bond Price After an Interest Rate Increase from 10% to 11%

Date of Payment	Type of Payment	Amount of Payment	11% Present Value Factor	Discounted Present Value
12/31/06	Interest	$ 100,000	.90090	$ 90,090
12/31/07	Interest	100,000	.81162	81,162
12/31/08	Interest	100,000	.73119	73,119
12/31/09	Interest	100,000	.65873	65,873
12/31/10	Interest	100,000	.59345	59,345
12/31/11	Interest	100,000	.53464	53,464
12/31/12	Interest	100,000	.48166	48,166
12/31/13	Interest	100,000	.43393	43,393
12/31/14	Interest	100,000	.39093	39,093
Total present value of interest payments			5.53705	$553,705
12/31/14	Principal	$1,000,000	.390925	390,925
Total market price on January 1, 2006				$944,630

Floating-Rate Debt Exhibit 11.8 illustrates that fluctuations in market interest rates change the value of financial instruments like Huff's 10% coupon bond. In our example, a one percentage point increase in the market rate of interest (from 10% to 11%) at the end of 2005 would cause the value of Huff's bond to fall by $55,370 (from $1,000,000 to $944,630). Investors who buy Huff bonds are exposed to market value losses because the coupon (stated) interest rate is fixed at 10% per year for the term of the bonds. When market interest rates increase, Huff bonds continue to pay only the fixed rate of 10% even though investors could do better elsewhere.

There are several ways investors can protect themselves from such losses; the most common is investing in **floating-rate debt**. In contrast to the Huff fixed-rate bond, floating-rate debt has a stated interest rate that fluctuates in tandem with some interest rate benchmark like the **London Interbank Offered Rate (LIBOR)**. This widely used benchmark for floating-rate debt is the base interest rate paid on deposits between European banks.

Suppose that the contractual interest rate on Huff's bonds was "LIBOR plus 4%, reset annually" and that the bonds were issued on January 1, 2005 when the LIBOR was 6%. Investors would receive a cash interest payment of $100,000 during 2005 because the contractual interest rate is 10% (LIBOR of 6% plus another 4%). If the LIBOR increased to 7% by January 1, 2006, investors would receive a cash interest payment of $110,000 (or 11%) that year because of the annual "reset" provision. The new rate equals the LIBOR of 7% plus 4% by contract. The additional $10,000 cash payment, if maintained over the life of the bond, would exactly offset in present value terms the $55,370 value decline ($1,000,000 − $944,630) we computed in Exhibit 11.8. *The market value of Huff's floating-rate debt would remain $1,000,000 and investors would be protected from losses like those associated with Huff's fixed-rate debt.*

Floating-rate debt can also benefit the issuing company. If the LIBOR falls to 5%, Huff would be able to reduce its cash interest payments to $90,000 because the contractual interest rate would be reset to 9% (LIBOR of 5% plus another 4% by contract).

Investors benefit from floating-rate debt when market interest rates increase, and issuing corporations benefit when market rates fall. Floating-rate debt allows investors and issuing companies to share in the risks and rewards of changing market interest rates. Risk sharing lowers the company's overall borrowing costs, and this translates into floating-rate debt that has a lower (expected) interest rate than would be charged on comparable fixed-rate debt.

Since virtually all floating-rate debt is issued at par, the accounting entries required are simple. Interest expense and accrued interest payable are recorded using the contractual interest rate in effect during the period. The entries made by Huff if it had issued the "LIBOR plus 4%, reset annually" bonds on January 1, 2005 are:

1/1/05:	**DR** Cash	$1,000,000	
	CR Bonds payable		$1,000,000
12/31/05:	**DR** Interest expense	$100,000	
	CR Accrued interest payable		$100,000
	2005 interest rate set at 10% (LIBOR of 6% plus 4%)		
12/31/06:	**DR** Interest expense	$110,000	
	CR Accrued interest payable		$110,000
	2006 interest rate reset to 11% (LIBOR of 7% plus 4%)		

The balance sheet would continue to show bonds payable at $1,000,000, which also equals the market value of the floating-rate debt.

> **Book value** equals **market value** on the maturity date because the principal payment is then due immediately and, consequently, is not discounted for time or risk.

Extinguishment of Debt Interest rates constantly adjust to changes in levels of economic activity and changes in expected inflation rates, among many other factors. When interest rates change, the market price of fixed-rate debt changes but in the opposite direction—as interest rates rise, the market price of debt falls; as interest rates fall, the market price of debt rises. However, as you just saw, GAAP accounting for debt is at the original transaction price using the original effective interest rate. Subsequent market price changes are not recorded on the financial statements. Because market price changes of debt are not recorded, there will be differences (nearly always) between the balance sheet value of debt and its market value. This divergence creates no accounting gain or loss for debt that is not retired before maturity—remember, book value and debt market value are always equal on the maturity date.

However, when debt is retired before maturity, book value and market value are not typically equal at the retirement date, generating an accounting gain or loss.

> When bonds are initially sold at a premium or discount, the book value is equal to the face value plus the premium or minus the discount. The premium or discount account must also be brought to zero when debt is retired. Remember that interest expense and accrued interest payable may need to be brought up to date before recording the extinguishment itself.

To see this, let's go back to Huff's $1,000,000 of 10% fixed-rate debt. On January 1, 2006, immediately after interest rates jump to 11%, Huff repurchases the 10% coupon bonds issued one year earlier. At the repurchase date, the market value of the bonds is $944,630, as you saw from Exhibit 11.8. The book value is $1,000,000. The entry to record the repurchase (ignoring possible income taxes) is:

DR Bonds payable	$1,000,000	
CR Cash		$944,630
CR Gain on debt extinguishment		55,370

The accounting gain (or loss) at retirement—more commonly called **extinguishment**—is the difference between the cash paid to extinguish the debt and the book value of the debt. Until recently, the FASB required companies to report any extinguishment gain or loss as an *extraordinary* item on the income statement.[3] But no longer. Now gains and losses from debt extinguishment are subject to the same criteria used to determine if other gains and losses qualify for extraordinary item treatment.[4]

> From Chapter 2, remember that to qualify as an extraordinary item under GAAP, the event must be both *unusual* and *infrequent*. For many firms, debt extinguishment is neither unusual nor infrequent.

One more thing! Where did Huff obtain the $944,630 cash needed to retire the old 10% fixed-rate bonds on January 1, 2006? The cash may have come from selling assets like marketable securities, from operating cash flows, or from a combination of the two. Or, Huff may have borrowed the money by issuing new nine-year 10% fixed-rate bonds with a face value of $1,000,000. Exhibit 11.8 shows that Huff would have received cash proceeds of $944,630 by issuing the new 10% bonds at a price that yields an 11% return to investors. The cash raised from selling the new bonds could then be used to retire the old 10% fixed-rate debt. The entries to record this two-step process for retiring the 10% bonds are:

DR Cash	$944,630	
CR Bonds Payable (new 10%)		$944,630

To record the issuance of nine-year 11% fixed-rate bonds with a face value of $1,000,000.

DR Bonds Payable (old 10%)	$1,000,000	
CR Cash		$944,630
CR Gain on debt extinguishment		55,370

To record the retirement of the 10% fixed-rate bonds.

---

[3] "Reporting Gains and Losses from Extinguishment of Debt," *Statement of Financial Accounting Standards (SFAS) No. 4* (Stamford, CT: FASB, 1975).

[4] "Recision of FASB Statements No. 4, 44, and 64, Amendment of FASB Statement No. 13, and Technical Corrections," *Statement of Financial Accounting Standards (SFAS) No. 145* (Norwalk, CT: FASB, 2002).

The two-step process removes a $1,000,000 liability from Huff's balance sheet but another $944,630 liability is added. Huff still reports a gain on debt retirement even though the company just replaced one debt instrument (the old 10% bonds) with a new debt instrument (the 10% bonds) of equal market value and the contractual cash flows for both bonds are the same.

> **RECAP**
>
> When interest rates change after a bond has been issued, the bond's reported book value and market value will no longer be the same. That's because GAAP requires bonds to be carried on the issuer's books at amortized historical cost using the effective yield to investors when the bonds were first issued. So when interest rates have increased and bonds are retired before maturity, market value is below book value and this generates an accounting gain. If interest rates have fallen, market value is above book value and an accounting loss results. Gains and losses from early debt retirement are sometimes treated as extraordinary items on the income statement if they qualify as such under GAAP.

Managerial Incentives and Financial Reporting for Debt

In Chapters 1 and 7 we explained that accounting numbers are widely used to enforce contracts. One example is debt covenants, which could motivate managers to manipulate accounting numbers to evade contract restrictions. Critics suggest that GAAP accounting for long-term debt makes it possible to "manage" accounting numbers to achieve this evasion.

Debt Carried at Amortized Historical Cost

Contracting

Some analysts contend that reporting debt at amortized historical cost (the $1,000,000 bond shown on Huff Corporation's books)—rather than at current market value (or $944,630 in the Huff example)—makes it easier to manipulate accounting numbers. **Debt-for-debt swaps** and **debt-for-equity swaps** illustrate the kinds of transactions that may be driven more by the financial statement effects they elicit than by any underlying economic benefits. In a debt-for-debt swap, the company offers investors the opportunity to exchange existing (old) debt for new debt issued by the company. Debt-for-equity swaps give investors the opportunity to exchange old debt for the company's common stock.

To illustrate, suppose Shifty Corporation has $1 million of outstanding 10% fixed-rate debt originally issued at par. This debt will mature in exactly one year. Since the debt was sold at par, its book value is $1 million. Assume that the current market rate for bonds of similar risk is 12%, which means Shifty's bonds have a market value of $982,146. Shifty offers bondholders the opportunity to swap their old 10% bonds for new 12% bonds that also mature in exactly one year. Just to keep things simple, let's assume bondholders are willing to swap as long as they receive 12% bonds worth $982,146, or the market value of the old 10% bonds that will be given back to the company. If the market interest rate is 12%, the new 12% bonds will be issued at par and the face value will be $982,146. This debt-for-debt swap is illustrated in Figure 11.4 on the next page.

> This $982,146 market value is computed as:
>
> Present value of $1,000,000 principal
> repayment due in one year at a 12%
> discount rate: $1,000,000 × .89286 = $892,860
>
> Present value of $100,000 interest
> payment due in one year at a 12%
> discount rate: $100,000 × .89286 = $ 89,286
>
> Market price $982,146
>
> In other words, the $982,146 market value corresponds exactly to the present value of the principal payment ($1,000,000/1.12 = $892,860 rounded) plus the present value of the final interest payment ($100,000/1.12 = $89,286 rounded), both discounted at the market rate of 12%.

Figure 11.4

SHIFTY CORPORATION
Debt-for-Debt Swap

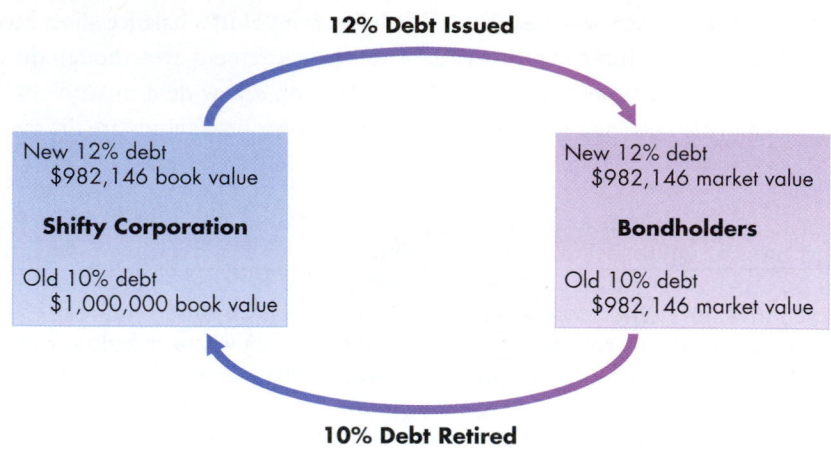

Bondholders will be presumably indifferent between the old 10% bonds and the new 12% bonds because the market values are identical. (To induce real-world bondholders to exchange the 10% bonds for 12% bonds, some "sweetener"—a slightly higher interest rate or a slightly larger face value—would have to be included.) The market values are identical precisely because the present values of the two cash flow streams are identical when discounted at the prevailing 12% market interest rate:

Old 10% Bonds at 12% Market Interest Rate	New 12% Bonds at 12% Market Interest Rate
Principal Repayment $1,000,000 × .89286 = $892,860	**Principal Repayment** $ 982,146 × .89286 = $876,919*
Interest Payment $ 100,000 × .89286 = $ 89,286 $1,100,000 $982,146	**Interest Payment** $ 117,854* × .89286 = $105,227* $1,100,000 $982,146
Interest Computation $1,000,000 × 10% = $100,000	**Interest Computation** $ 982,146 × 12% = $117,854*

Note: The present value of $1 due in one year at 12% is .89286.
*Rounded

As the computation reveals, even the *undiscounted* cash flows are identical because the principal payment plus interest payment is $1,100,000 in both cases. A debt-for-debt swap like this has no real economic benefit to Shifty (there may be income tax effects). However, if the swap was consummated, the entry on Shifty's books would be:

DR Bonds payable (old 10%)	$1,000,000	
CR Bonds payable (new 12%)		$982,146
CR Gain on debt extinguishment		17,854

Despite the absence of real economic substance, an accounting "gain" would still be reported. The gain really arose in prior periods as unanticipated inflation or other factors caused the market rate on the bonds to rise above the coupon interest rate. Because Shifty was paying interest at 10% when prevailing rates were higher, a year-by-year wealth transfer from the pockets of the original bondholders into the pockets of Shifty's shareholders was

This same financial statement result would occur if Shifty first issued the new 12% bonds for cash, and then used the cash proceeds to retire old 10% bonds. (See the Huff Corporation two-step debt retirement on page 574.) Income tax considerations and transaction costs may favor a debt-for-debt swap rather than a two-step debt extinguishment.

taking place. Historical cost accounting ignores this wealth transfer until the "artificial" swap transaction triggers recognition of the gain.

This example demonstrates the potential incentive for managerial opportunism that is introduced by historical cost accounting for debt. Critics of historical cost accounting raise the possibility that managers whose bonuses are tied to reported earnings might use swap gains to boost their firm's earnings (and thus their bonuses) in years of poor operating performance. Also, a reduction in the book value of debt (from $1,000,000 to $982,146 in our example) would improve the debt-to-equity ratio—thus providing "opportunistic" motivations for companies in danger of violating covenant restrictions tied to this ratio.

> The wealth transfer gain from bondholders to stockholders gets reflected obliquely in historical cost statements, because historical cost interest expense is lower than interest expense would be at current market rates. Accordingly, *net income is higher than it would have been at current interest rates.*

Now that you can visualize the problem, let's make the example more realistic.

To induce bondholders to swap, they must be offered some sweeteners to do so. One inducement is to offer a higher principal amount of new bonds—say, $990,000. ***This change makes the net present value of the swap negative for Shifty because it is retiring debt with a market value of $982,146 by giving bondholders something worth $990,000.*** Despite this real loss to Shifty, if the swap went through on these altered terms, Shifty would still report an accounting *gain* of $10,000—the difference between the $1 million book value of the old bonds and the $990,000 market value of the new bonds. Extinguishment gains are generally taxable, and there are fees that must be paid to investment bankers or others who orchestrate the transaction. These added costs further increase the potential disparity between the reported accounting gain and the economic effects of the swap.

On the other hand, there are sometimes real economic benefits associated with debt-for-debt exchanges. In the real world, debt-for-debt swaps are rarely designed to be a "wash" in which debt instruments with identical maturities and market values are exchanged. Typical swaps are structured to: extend debt maturity; postpone cash outflows by altering the mix of interest and principal payments; or take advantage of operating loss carryforwards (making the swap tax-free). On balance, therefore, it is entirely possible that some debt-for-debt exchanges generate real economic benefits even after factoring in transaction costs.

This is precisely what a study of debt swaps in the airline industry found. Analyzing the economic effects of swaps structured by American Airlines, Eastern Airlines, and TWA revealed economic benefits for each company in the range of $4.6 million to $5.0 million.[5] However, **the reported book gain (net of tax) for each airline was substantially higher**—for example, it was $24.65 million for Eastern, $47.1 million for TWA, and $48.4 million for American. Therefore, a large disparity exists between the reported historical cost book gains and the estimated real economic benefits. If the economic benefits of debt-for-debt exchanges are small (on average), stock prices should change little when swaps are announced. In fact, that is the case.[6]

Differences between book profits and real profits have aroused curiosity about the motives underlying another—somewhat similar—debt extinguishment transaction: debt-for-equity swaps.

The conditions for a debt-for-equity swap exist when a company has low coupon interest rate debt outstanding (say, $4\frac{1}{2}$%) and market rates are much higher (say, 12%). **The market value of that debt is much lower than its book value.** As Figure 11.5 on the next page shows, Company X retires its low coupon debt by issuing common stock of equal market value. The difference between the book value of the debt and the market value of the stock that is issued is recorded as an accounting gain. The convoluted nature of the transaction, as well as the investment banker's involvement, is required to make the gain on debt extinguishment tax free.

[5] J. R. Dietrich and J. W. Deitrick, "Bond Exchanges in the Airline Industry: Analyzing Public Disclosures," *The Accounting Review* (January 1985), pp. 109–26.

[6] See J. R. Dietrich, "Effects of Early Bond Refundings: An Empirical Investigation of Security Returns," *Journal of Accounting and Economics* (April 1984), pp. 67–96; and W. B. Johnson, "Debt Refunding and Shareholder Wealth: The Price Effects of Debt-for-Debt Exchange Offer Announcements," *The Financial Review* (February 1988), pp. 1–23.

Figure 11.5

THE SEQUENCE OF EVENTS
IN A DEBT-FOR-EQUITY SWAP

Source: From J. R. M. Hand, "Did
Firms Undertake Debt-Equity Swaps
for an Accounting Paper Profit or
True Financial Gain?" *The Accounting Review*, October 1989
(page 587–623). Reprinted
with permission.

The accounting entry on the books of Company X is:

DR	Bonds payable	$ Book value	
CR	Common stock		$ Market value
CR	Gain on debt extinguishment		$ Difference

Debt book value is greater than the market value of stock issued because the debt has a low coupon interest rate but the market interest rate is high.

Debt-for-equity swaps alter the company's capital structure and undoubtedly precipitate real economic effects. One study found that debt-for-equity swaps were associated with a 9.9% share price decline (on average) at the transaction's announcement.[7] That price decline is especially interesting since most debt-for-equity transactions result in extinguishment gains rather than losses. This prevalence of gains (and negative market reaction) raises the suspicion that earnings enhancement—rather than capital structure alteration—may be the motivation behind these transactions. Companies can use debt-for-equity swaps to smooth otherwise unexpected and transitory decreases in quarterly earnings per share or to relax otherwise binding covenant constraints.[8]

Debt-for-debt swaps, debt-for-equity swaps, and other similar transactions may serve valid economic purposes in certain instances. Nevertheless, some analysts still believe that the dominant motivation for these transactions is to increase reported income. But no matter what motivates management to swap old debt, the result is the same: an earnings boost that may not reflect economic reality but instead represents the difference between the book value and market value of the liabilities.

In response to this and other criticisms of accounting for liabilities, the FASB issued *SFAS No. 107*, which requires footnote disclosure of the market value of all financial instruments—

---

[7] See R. Masulis, "The Impact of Capital Structure Changes on Firm Value: Some Estimates," *Journal of Finance* (March 1983), pp. 107–26. Interestingly, this same study found that share prices *increase* by 14% (on average) when firms announce their willingness to retire common stock in exchange for new debt.

[8] J. R. M. Hand, "Did Firms Undertake Debt–Equity Swaps for an Accounting Paper Profit or True Financial Gain?" *The Accounting Review* (October 1989), pp. 587–623.

both financial liabilities and assets.[9] However, the FASB response is unlikely to eliminate "accounting-driven" liability transactions. Since the *SFAS No. 107* market value disclosures appear in a footnote to the financial statements, the carrying amount of liabilities on the balance sheet itself is not altered. Consequently, the swap transactions described here still generate income statement gains and favorable financial ratio effects. Managers can still use these transactions as mechanisms for altering bonus payouts, as well as for evading loan covenant restrictions or other contracting effects, whenever the contracts are tied to the financial numbers reported in the body of the statement. Only if the contract ratios and income measures are computed using the fair value footnote data would *SFAS No. 107* be effective in reducing this avenue for managerial opportunism.

RECAP

GAAP for long-term debt creates opportunities for managing reported earnings and balance sheet numbers using debt-for-debt or debt-for-equity swaps. So statement readers must be alert to the possibility that reported swap gains (and losses) are just window dressing. How can you tell? Look behind the accounting numbers and see if there are real economic benefits from the swap.

Imputed Interest on Notes Payable

Salton, Inc. designs and markets a variety of household appliances including the George Foreman Grill, the BreadMan bread machine, and Toastmaster toaster ovens. In the past, the company paid Mr. Foreman a royalty equal to 60% of the gross profit on sales of George Foreman Grills. (It's a hefty sum, but then Mr. Foreman is probably a tough negotiator.) At the beginning of 2000, the company purchased the rights to use the George Foreman name in perpetuity in exchange for shares of Salton stock valued at $23.750 million and a $113.750 million note payable in five annual installments of $22.750 million each. Mr. Foreman received a check for the first installment the same day the deal was inked. Here is how Salton recorded its purchase of the George Foreman name:

DR Intangible asset (George Foreman name)	$121.020	
CR Common stock		$ 23.750
CR Note payable		$ 97.270

To record the purchase of the rights to use the George Foreman name in perpetuity.

DR Note payable	$ 22.750	
CR Cash		$ 22.750

To record the immediate payment to Mr. Foreman of the first installment on the note.

> Imputed interest on notes receivable was discussed in Chapter 8.

And here's what Salton had to say about the transaction in its 2000 financial statements: "The effect of the acquisition of the George Foreman name related to fiscal 2000 was the elimination of royalty payments partially offset by amortization of $8.1 million and **imputed interest** of $6.3 million."

Several aspects of this accounting treatment may at first seem perplexing. For example, why did Salton record the $113.750 million note payable at a value of only $97.270 million? What is "imputed interest," how is it calculated, and when is it recorded? The answers to these questions illustrate once again that noncurrent monetary liabilities are recorded initially at their present value.

> Salton is amortizing the intangible asset over 15 years, so the $8.1 million of amortization is computed as $121.020 ÷ 15 with slight rounding.

---

[9] "Disclosures About Fair Value of Financial Instruments," *SFAS No. 107* (Norwalk, CT: FASB, 1991).

Let's start with the value assigned to the note itself, and assume that both Salton and Mr. Foreman agree that the note is worth $97.270 million at the signing date. Why isn't the note worth the full $113.750 million? Because the installment payments are spread over five years, and the extra $16.480 million is interest that Mr. Foreman will receive as compensation for delayed payment.

What is the rate of interest on the note payable? To answer that question, we need to find an interest rate that makes the value of the note ($97.270) equal to the present value of the install-ment payments. The actual calculation can be cumbersome, although a financial calculator or computer spreadsheet can make the solution easy. The following diagram illustrates how to find the imputed rate of interest on a note.

	Payment in Millions at the Beginning of the Year					
	2000	**2001**	**2002**	**2003**	**2004**	**Total payments**
	$22.750	$22.750	$22.750	$22.750	$22.750	$113.750
Present value of 2001 payment	20.968 ◄—— 0.92166					
Present value of 2001 payment	19.325 ◄—————— 0.84946					
Present value of 2001 payment	17.811 ◄———————————— 0.78291					
Present value of 2001 payment	16.416 ◄—————————————————— 0.72157 = Present					
Present value of note:	$97.270					value factor for 4 years
Imputed rate of interest:	8.50%					at 8.5%

Notice that all installment payments occur at the beginning of the year. As a result, the pre-sent value of the first $22.750 million installment payment is exactly $22.750. However, the pre-sent value of the second installment payment—which occurs at the beginning of 2001—is smaller than $22.750. How much smaller depends on the interest rate. Let's take a guess that the correct imputed interest rate is 8.50%. (In a moment we will show you why 8.50% is a reasonable "guestimate" for the imputed interest rate.) In this case, the second installment payment needs to be discounted for one year at 8.50% and the discount factor is 0.92166 (or 1/(1 + 0.085)). The present value of the 2001 payment is $20.968 million, which equals the $22.750 million cash pay-ment multiplied by the 0.92166 discount factor. A similar process is used to compute the present value for each remaining installment payment. When all five present value amounts are summed, they total $97.270 million. And that's the key step: 8.50% is the imputed rate of interest on the note precisely because it is the interest rate that makes the value of the note ($97.270) equal to the present value of the installment payments (also $97.270).

Was our 8.50% interest rate estimate just a lucky guess? Not exactly. Salton's financial state-ment indicates that interest expense on the note payable was $6.3 million in 2000. Since interest is a charge for delayed payment, and the first installment payment was made immediately, the $6.3 million in interest must represent a charge for the $74.520 million unpaid balance of the note ($74.520 = $97.270 initial note value − $22.750 first payment). We can now derive an estimate of the note's true imputed interest rate using the ratio of interest expense to the unpaid balance of the note. The result is ($6.3/$74.520) = 0.08454 or 8.45%. Why doesn't this process yield the cor-rect 8.50% imputed interest rate? Because the $6.3 million interest expense figure Salton men-tions is rounded slightly. The actual interest expense on the note that year was $6.3342 million (or $74.520 × 8.50%).

If Salton records interest expense only once a year, then the following entry is made at the end of 2000:

DR Interest Expense	$ 6.3342	
CR Note payable		$ 6.3342

To record interest expense on the unpaid balance of the Foreman note payable.

The unpaid interest is added to the note payable balance. This means that the note payable, a noncurrent monetary liability, will be shown on the 2000 year-end balance sheet at an amount ($80.8542) that corresponds to its present value (using the 8.5% imputed interest rate) as of the balance sheet date. We leave the task of verifying this fact to you.

Noncurrent monetary liabilities are initially recorded at their present value when incurred. This is true even for installment notes that make no mention of an interest rate. In such cases, an interest rate must be imputed.

Extracting Analytical Insights: Future Cash Flow Effects of Debt

Exhibit 11.9 contains excerpts from Maytag Corporation's financial statement footnote for long-term debt. This example illustrates the type of information about a company's long-term debt that is currently available in corporate annual reports.

EXHIBIT 11.9	**Maytag Corporation**

Long-term debt

Long-term debt consisted of the following:

	December 31	
($ in thousands)	2002	2001
Notes payable with interest payable semiannually:		
Due May 15, 2002 at 9.75%	$0	$125,358
Medium-term notes, maturing from 2003 to 2010 with interest payable semiannually	652,230	652,230
Public Income Notes, with interest payable quarterly:		
Due August 1, 2031 at 7.875%	250,000	250,000
Employee stock ownership plan notes payable semiannually through July 2, 2004 at 5.13%	14,120	21,180
Other	17,729	16,883
	$934,079	$1,065,651
Less current portion of long-term debt	① 195,312	133,586
	$738,767	$ 932,065

 $68.2 million of the $652.2 medium-term notes grant the holders the right to require the Company to repurchase all or any portion of these notes at 100 percent of the principal amount thereof, together with accrued interest, following the occurrence of both a change of Company control and a credit rating decline to below investment grade.

 ② Interest paid during 2002, 2001 and 2000 was $72.5 million, $70.1 million and $66.1 million, respectively. When applicable, the Company capitalizes interest incurred on funds used to construct property, plant and equipment. Interest capitalized during 2002 and 2001 was $1.1 million and $1.1 million, respectively and was not significant in 2000.

 ③ The aggregate maturities of long-term debt in each of the next five years and thereafter are as follows (in thousands): 2003—$195,312; 2004—$25,940; 2005—$3,928; 2006—$420,670; 2007—$8,000; thereafter—$280,229.

 In 2001, the Company issued $185 million in medium-term notes with a fixed interest rate of 6.875 percent due March 31, 2006; $200 million in medium-term notes with a fixed interest rate of 6.875 percent due December 1, 2006; and $250 million in Public Income Notes with a fixed interest rate of 7.875 percent due August 1, 2031. The Public Income Notes grant the Company the right to call the notes, at par, upon 30 days notice, after August 6, 2006.

Maytag provides details about interest rates and maturity dates for each major class of long-term debt. However, the company provides no information about the covenants contained in its various borrowing agreements. This nondisclosure is typical and imposes a burden on the financial analyst who must search through the lending agreements themselves to discover covenant details.

Maytag's footnote disclosure provides a wealth of information useful for determining the future cash flow implications of the company's long-term debt. For example, the table reveals current maturities (that is, the "current portion of long-term debt") of $195.312 million at the end of 2002 (see highlighted figure next to ①). This is the principal amount that Maytag must repay in 2003.

We also learn from the footnote text next to ② that Maytag paid $72.5 million in interest during 2002. This amount represents interest Maytag paid on the long-term debt shown in Exhibit 11.9 plus any short-term interest-bearing debt shown on the company's balance sheet. Dividing this cash interest payment by the average book value of outstanding long-term debt [($738.767 + $932.065)/2 = $835.416] plus average short-term debt from the balance sheet [($148.247 + $178.559)/2 = $163.403 not shown in Exhibit 11.9] suggests that the company's "cash" interest rate for 2002 was about 7.3% or [$72.5/($835.416 + $163.403)]. Using this rate as the basis for forecasting 2003 interest payments, we discover that Maytag will spend about $81.2 million (7.3% multiplied by $1,112.638 million of interest-bearing debt outstanding—comprising $934.079 million of long-term debt plus $178.559 million of short-term debt) for 2003 interest. This cash outflow is in addition to the $195.312 million of scheduled principal repayment for 2003.

Cash flow forecasts of this sort can be constructed for each year from 2003 through 2007, because Maytag, like all U.S. companies today, is required to disclose scheduled debt repayments for each of the five years after the balance sheet date. From the paragraph adjacent to ③, we can see that these repayments are particularly large in 2003 ($195.312 million) and in 2006 ($420.670 million). Analysts studying the company will want to estimate whether Maytag's operating cash flows for 2003 and 2006 will be sufficient to meet its scheduled debt interest and principal payments. Any anticipated shortfalls will necessitate asset sales or additional financing.

EXHIBIT 11.10 | **Maytag Corporation**

The fair values of long-term debt were estimated based on quoted market prices, if available, or quoted market prices of comparable instruments. . . . The carrying amounts and fair values of the Company's [long-term debt] instruments, consisted of the following:

	December 31, 2002		December 31, 2001	
	Carrying Amount	Fair Value	Carrying Amount	Fair Value
Long-term debt	$934,079	$995,804	$1,065,651	$1,085,138

In another footnote shown in Exhibit 11.10, Maytag tells us about the fair market value of its long-term debt. The fair market value of Maytag's debt is greater than its balance sheet carrying amount in both years shown. There are two reasons why this might happen.

- Maytag is a better credit risk today than it was several years ago when the debt was first issued. As a company's creditworthiness improves, the market value of its debt increases even though the book value of the debt is unchanged.
- Interest rates have fallen for reasons unrelated to the company itself (for example, lower expected inflation or a stronger economy). From our earlier discussion, you know that a decline in interest rates—whether due to company-specific factors or to macroeconomic forces—will cause the market value of fixed-rate debt to increase.

Maytag has been a financially strong company for many years. So, a falling interest rate is the most plausible explanation for why Maytag's debt has a fair market value greater than its carrying amount.

Incentives for Off-Balance Sheet Liabilities

In Chapters 1 and 7 we described modern business contracts linked to (among other things) the amount of liabilities on a company's balance sheet. Examples include loan covenants and bond indentures. These kinds of contracts usually contain terms and conditions designed to protect the lender against loss. The protection is in the form of contract terms tied to the borrower's debt-to-equity ratio, or debt-to-tangible-asset ratio, or to some other financial ratio that includes reported liabilities. Accounting-related covenants typically contain language like "the debt-to-equity ratio may not exceed 1.7 in any quarter." The intent of these covenants is to provide an early warning signal regarding deteriorating creditworthiness. In principle, the early warning allows the lender to require repayment of the loan before the borrower's condition worsens further.

Contracting

Loan contract terms of this sort create incentives for managers of borrowing companies to minimize *reported* financial statement liabilities. Reducing the total amount of reportable liabilities in the contractual ratio makes covenant violations less likely.

Consider one example of the way these incentives influence business behavior: **Unconsolidated subsidiaries** are sometimes established to finance specialized projects or **joint ventures**. Critics say these separately incorporated entities have sometimes been used to evade loan covenants linked to reported liabilities and to misrepresent the firm's total liabilities. This strategy exploits a loophole in the rules governing when subsidiaries need to be consolidated.

> As will be explained in Chapter 16, **consolidation** essentially means that the separate financial statements of the parent and subsidiary are added together line-by-line to form a single combined ("consolidated") set of financial statements. For example, the consolidated balance sheet would report as "Cash" the sum of the parent's cash plus the subsidiary's cash. Similarly, total consolidated liabilities would consist of the sum of the parent's liabilities plus those of the subsidiary. Chapter 16 provides the details and also describes the accounting rules for unconsolidated subsidiaries.

When one company owns *more* than 50% of the stock of another affiliated company, the owner (parent) is deemed to "control" the other company (subsidiary). The financial statements of subsidiaries that are under the control of a parent must be consolidated. But when one company owns 50% or *less* of another company's stock, consolidation is not required (except under special circumstances described in Chapter 16). Instead, the owner's *net investment* in the subsidiary is reported as an asset in the owner's balance sheet using what is called the **equity method** of accounting.

The equity method is described in Chapter 16. Here's an example illustrating all you need to know about it now.

Assume Blue Company and Yellow Company both use an identically manufactured input called T-spanners in their respective production processes. Manufacturing T-spanners requires a large investment in plant and equipment that must be financed by borrowing. Both Blue Company and Yellow Company wish to avoid adding further debt to their balance sheets, so they agree to form a separate jointly owned venture called Green Company.

> In real-world joint ventures, the debt is often guaranteed by the parent companies because the joint venture (for example, Green Company) is usually thinly capitalized and lenders accordingly look to the parents (Blue Company and Yellow Company) for added assurance that the loan will be repaid.

Each venture partner contributes $25 million cash to establish Green Company and receives common stock representing a 50% ownership interest in it. A bank then loans Green $300 million to purchase the plant and equipment needed to produce T-spanners. This loan is collateralized by Green's factory and guaranteed by both Blue Company and Yellow Company. Immediately after these transactions take place, the balance sheet of Green Company would appear as shown in Figure 11.6 on the next page.

Figure 11.6

JOINT VENTURE FINANCING
($ in millions)

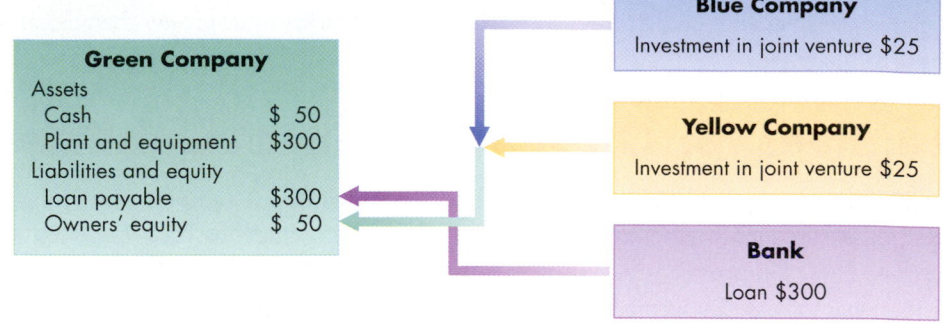

The balance sheets of Blue Company and Yellow Company would each show their $25 million investment in an asset account called "Investment in joint venture." Under the equity method, this account balance would grow if further investments were made in the joint venture or if Green earned a profit. Since Green is equally owned by Blue and Yellow, each would add 50% of Green's profit to the balance in its "Investment in joint venture" account.

The partners' balance sheets do not report any of the joint venture's $300 million bank loan! Neither Blue nor Yellow owns more than 50% of Green, so neither needs to consolidate it. Consequently, the borrowing necessary to fund the venture appears on neither partner's financial statements under the equity method. The "Investment in joint venture" account on each company's books would continue to show $25 million. Yet, both Blue and Yellow have effectively each borrowed $150 million "off-balance sheet!"

The "Investment in joint venture" account is unchanged because each partner's investment in the net assets (that is, assets minus liabilities) of the joint venture is unchanged by the borrowing. Green Company's assets increased by $300 million but so did liabilities. Consequently, Green's *net* assets remained at $50 million after the borrowing.

Prior to the issuance of "Consolidation of All Majority-Owned Subsidiaries," *SFAS No. 94* (Stamford, CT: FASB, 1987), even 100% wholly owned subsidiaries were accounted for in many cases under the equity method. This kept the subsidiaries' debt off the balance sheet in much the same manner as joint-venture debt. Here's how: In many industries, companies help customers finance the purchase of their products. One example is the automobile industry. If no financing subsidiary were formed, the cash necessary to finance the credit extended to dealers and consumers would come from bank loans or other borrowing by the parent. As a consequence, the parent's debt-to-equity ratio would be worsened. However, if a separate finance subsidiary were formed and this subsidiary borrowed the funds directly in its own name, the borrowing was effectively kept off the parent's balance sheet. The trick here was accomplished by using the equity method of accounting for subsidiaries, as will be discussed in Chapter 16. This is no longer permitted.

So-called "special purpose entities" (SPEs) represent a variation of the simple joint venture arrangement between Blue Company and Yellow Company. One common type of SPE involves assets with more or less predictable cash flows like credit card receivables. Without going into all of the details, suppose a retailer like Sears needs to borrow money and wants to do so at the best available interest rate. Instead of obtaining a traditional bank loan, Sears decides to create an SPE and then transfers a portion of its customer credit card receivables to the new entity. The SPE next obtains a low-interest loan to be repaid from the future cash flows associated with the credit card receivables, sending the money to Sears as payment for the transferred receivables. Although the transaction may seem unduly complex, the SPE structure allows Sears to isolate assets with predictable cash flows (in this case, the credit card receivables) from its other assets with less predictable cash flows. Isolating the credit card receivables in this way reduces the lender's credit risk, which in turn reduces the interest rate that Sears must pay on the loan. SPEs of this sort were often not required to be consolidated on the parent company's (that is, Sears') financial statements, so the loan was another example of "off-balance sheet" debt.

Special purpose entities became notorious following the collapse of Enron. In November 2001, Enron announced that it would restate earnings for 1997 through 2001 downward by $1.2 billion because the company and its auditors had determined that three unconsolidated SPEs should have been consolidated. As part of the restatement, Enron increased its balance sheet debt by $628 million in 2000. Over the course of the next several months, investors and creditors learned that Enron's off-balance-sheet SPEs were used to hide mounting losses and cash flow problems at the company. Several former senior officials at the company were later charged with violating the antifraud provisions of the federal securities laws.

> "Enron went too far in how it accounted for SPEs. The company was on the hook for the debt of those entities, and when the debt came due, the Enron house-of-cards came down." Randy Vitray, partner at PricewaterhouseCoopers.

The FASB has recently tightened up the rules governing the consolidation of special purpose entities, which are now called "variable interest entities" (VIEs), in an effort to avoid future Enron debacles. Chapter 16 tells you more.

RECAP

> The motivation for off-balance sheet financing transactions is strong. Managers continue to develop innovative strategies to understate reported liabilities and to ensure that certain items remain "off the balance sheet." Financial analysts and auditors must remember the motivations behind off-balance sheet financing, know how to identify peculiar and contorted borrowing arrangements, and adjust the reported financial statement numbers to better reflect economic reality.

Hedging

Businesses are exposed to **market risks** from many sources—changes in interest rates, foreign currency exchange rates, and commodity prices.[10] Suppose a bank makes numerous five-year term loans at an annual interest rate of 8%. The earnings from those loans generate the cash needed to pay interest to "money market" account depositors. The loans expose the bank to interest rate risk: If money market interest rates rise, the 8% fixed return from the loans may not be adequate to pay the new higher rates promised to depositors.

Similar risks confront manufacturers. Consider Ridge Development, a real estate development company that simultaneously constructs many single-family homes. Buyers make a down payment and agree to a fixed contract price to be paid when the home is completed. The typical home is completed in four months or less, and lumber comprises the bulk of construction costs. Since lumber prices are volatile, the developer is at risk that profits could erode (or disappear) if lumber prices were to soar during the four-month construction cycle.

> Commodities are bulk goods such as wheat, corn, lumber, jet fuel, and copper.

Or consider Southwest Airlines. It sells airline transportation services to passengers, many of whom pay a month or more in advance of the actual flight. Fuel is a major cost component in the airlines industry, and fuel prices fluctuate on almost a daily basis. Since the passenger ticket price is set prior to the flight, Southwest Airlines is at risk that escalating fuel prices may turn an otherwise profitable flight into a loss.

Managing market risk is essential to the overall business strategies of most companies today. This trend has been driven by the need to reduce cash flow volatility that arises from factors beyond management's control—the exchange rate of U.S. dollars to Japanese yen, the LIBOR interest rate (the benchmark interbank interest rate for European banks), or the price of natural gas to run a factory. In response to these and other market risks, many companies today engage in hedging—business transactions designed to insulate them from commodity price, interest rate, or exchange rate risk. **Derivative securities**, which we explain next, are often used to accomplish this insulation.

> Businesses are also exposed to **operating risks** from severe weather conditions, industrial accidents, raw material shortages, labor strikes, and so on. Insurance contracts, financial guarantees, and other business arrangements are used to hedge operating risks—but these risks do not qualify for the special hedge accounting rules described later in this section. Only certain financial risks qualify for hedge accounting.

---

[10] We gratefully acknowledge the substantial contribution of Professor Thomas Linsmeier to the material in this section.

Typical Derivative Securities and the Benefits of Hedging

Derivative securities are so named because they are securities that have no inherent value but instead represent a claim against some other asset—their value is *derived* from the value of the asset underlying that claim.[11]

A **forward contract** is one example of a derivative security. In a forward contract, two parties agree to the sale of some asset or commodity on some *future* date—called the settlement date—at a price specified today. You have been dealing with forward contracts your whole life, perhaps without knowing it. Suppose you walk into a bookstore on October 5 to buy the best-seller *Seven Unbeatable Strategies for e-Commerce*. The book is sold out, but the clerk offers to reorder it for you and call you when it arrives. The clerk says that the book should arrive in about 15 days and will cost $39.95. If you agree on October 5 to pick up and pay for the book when called, you and the clerk have agreed to a forward contract. Three elements of this contract are key: the agreed upon price ($39.95) to be paid in the future; the delivery date ("in about 15 days"); and that you will "take delivery" by paying for the book and picking it up when notified. The clerk has "sold" you a forward contract for the best-seller.

What happens if you pay for the book on October 5? Then it's a simple cash sales transaction (with a promised future delivery date)—it is not a forward contract. As long as both parties are *obligated* to perform at some future date under the agreement, it's a forward contract. Here that means the clerk is required to obtain a copy of the best-seller and deliver it to you within the specified time. And you are required to pay the agreed upon price and to take delivery when the book arrives—you have no initial investment.

Futures Contracts A variation of a forward contract takes place on financial exchanges like the New York Mercantile Exchange (COMEX) where **futures contracts** are traded daily in a market with many buyers and sellers. Futures contracts exist for commodities like corn, wheat, live hogs and cattle, cotton, copper, crude oil, lumber, and even electricity. Here is how they work.

Suppose on October 5 you "write" (meaning sell) a futures contract for 10 million pounds of February copper at 95 cents per pound—we'll show why you might want to do so in just a moment. By selling the contract, you are obligated to deliver the copper at the agreed-upon price in February. The buyer (or contract counterparty) is obliged to pay the fixed price per pound and take delivery of the copper. So far this looks like a forward contract because both parties have an obligation to perform in the future (February).

But there's more! Futures contracts do not have a predetermined settlement date—you (the seller) can choose to deliver the copper on any day during the delivery month (February). This gives sellers additional flexibility in settling the contract. When you decide to deliver the copper, you notify the COMEX clearinghouse, which then notifies an individual—let's call her Anne Smythe—who bought February copper contracts. (The clearinghouse selected Anne at random from all individuals who bought February copper contracts.) Anne is then told to be ready to accept delivery within the next several days. But what if she bought the contract as a speculative investment, has no real use for the copper, and doesn't want delivery? Futures contracts have an added advantage over forward contracts because futures are actively traded on an exchange. This means Smythe can avoid delivery by immediately selling a February copper contract for 10 million pounds, thus creating a zero net position. The first contract obligates Smythe to accept delivery of 10 million pounds of copper, but the second contract obligates her to turn over 10 million pounds to someone else. One contract cancels the other, and Smythe avoids the embarrassment of having all of that copper dumped on the floor of her garage.

How can you (the seller) avoid having to deliver the copper? From a zero net position of your own by purchasing a February copper contract from someone else—perhaps even from Anne Smythe.

---

[11] For an overview of the characteristics and uses of derivative securities, see S. A. Ross, R. W. Westerfield, and B. D. Jordan, *Fundamentals of Corporate Finance*, 2nd ed. (Homewood, IL: Irwin, 1993), Ch. 24; and C. W. Smithson, C. W. Smith, and D. S. Wilford, *Managing Financial Risk* (Homewood, IL: Irwin, 1995).

Now that you understand how futures contracts work, let's see how they can be used to hedge financial risk.

Consider the opportunities confronting Rombaurer Metals, a copper mining company. On October 1, 2005, Rombaurer has 10 million pounds of copper inventory on hand at an average cost of 65 cents per pound. The "spot" (current delivery) price for copper on October 1 is 90 cents a pound. Rombaurer could receive $9 million (10 million pounds times $0.90 per pound) by selling its entire copper inventory today. This would yield a $2.5 million gross profit ($0.90 selling price minus $0.65 average cost per pound, multiplied by 10 million pounds). However, Rombaurer has decided to hold on to its copper until February 2006 when management believes the price will return to a normal level of 95 cents a pound. The commodities market seems to agree since February copper futures are priced as though copper will sell for 95 cents in February. The decision not to sell copper in October exposes Rombaurer to **commodity price risk** from a possible future decline in copper prices.

Figure 11.7(a) illustrates the company's commodity price risk exposure. If copper prices increase to 95 cents by February as expected, Rombaurer will receive $9.5 million for its copper and earn a gross profit of $3 million ($0.95 selling price minus $0.65 average cost per pound, multiplied by 10 million pounds). That's $0.5 million more gross profit than Rombaurer would earn by selling the copper on October 1. But what if the February price of copper falls to 85 cents? The cash received from selling copper would then be only $8.5 million, and the gross profit would be only $2 million. Each 10-cent decline in the February copper price lowers the company's cash flows and expected gross profits by $1 million. At 65 cents per pound, Rombaurer just breaks even (zero gross profit) and, at any price below 65 cents, the company has a loss. These potential cash flow and gross profit declines represent the *downside risk* associated with the February price of copper.

There is *upside potential* as well. Each 10-cent increase in the February copper price will produce a $1 million increase in the company's cash flows and gross profits.

One way Rombaurer can protect itself from a decline in the price of copper is to hedge its position with futures contracts. Suppose Rombaurer sells 400 copper contracts—each contract is for 25,000 pounds—at 95 cents a pound for February delivery. The delivery month is chosen to coincide with the company's expected physical sale of the copper. The ultimate value of these contracts depends on the February price of copper as shown in Figure 11.7(b) on the next page.

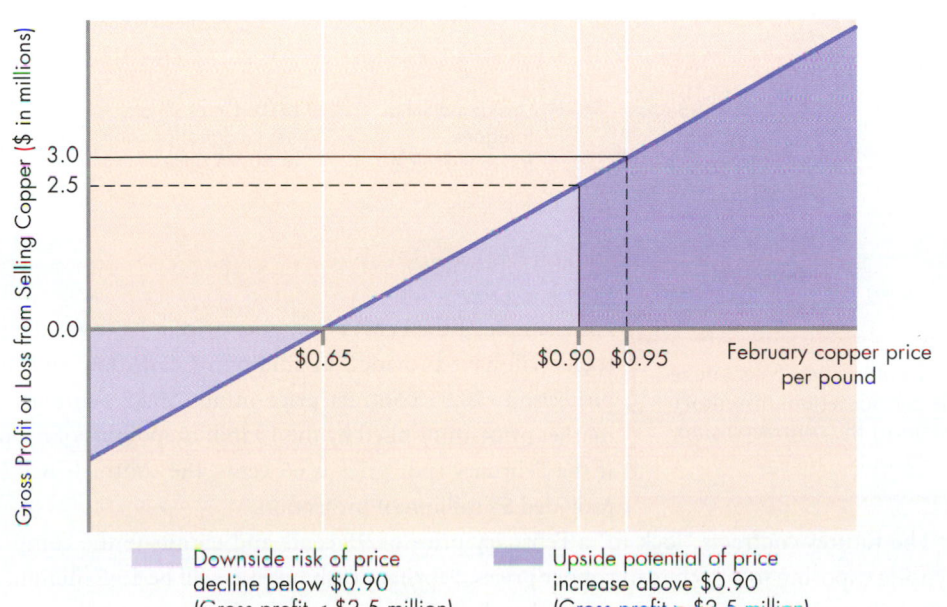

Figure 11.7 (a)

ROMBAURER METALS

Using Futures Contracts to Hedge Copper Inventory: Before the Hedge

Potential gross profit and loss from the sale of copper in February

Figure 11.7 (b)

ROMBAURER METALS
Using Futures Contracts to
Hedge Copper Inventory:
The Hedging Instrument

Potential value of forward contract
for February copper

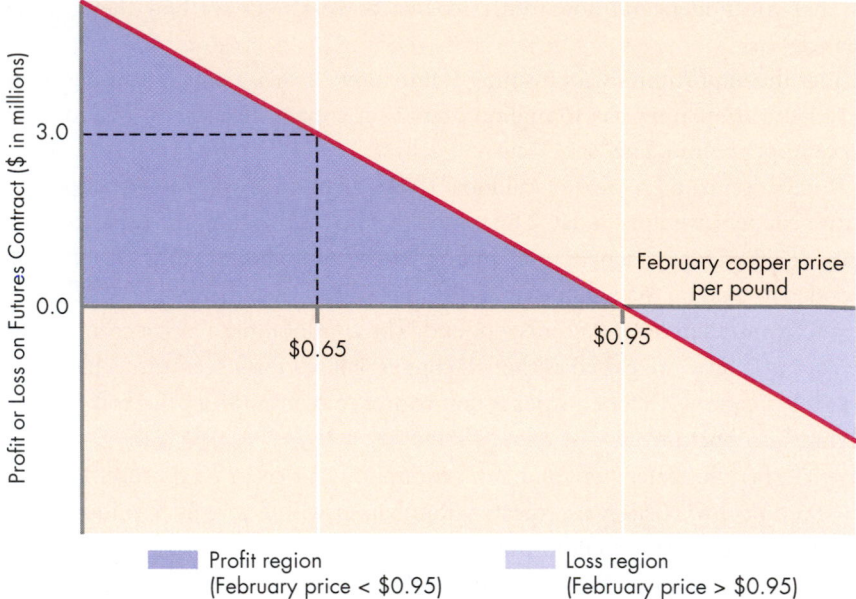

Figure 11.7 (c)

ROMBAURER METALS
Using Futures Contracts to
Hedge Copper Inventory:
After the Hedge

Gross profit from hedged position:
Combination of unhedged copper
inventory and forward contract

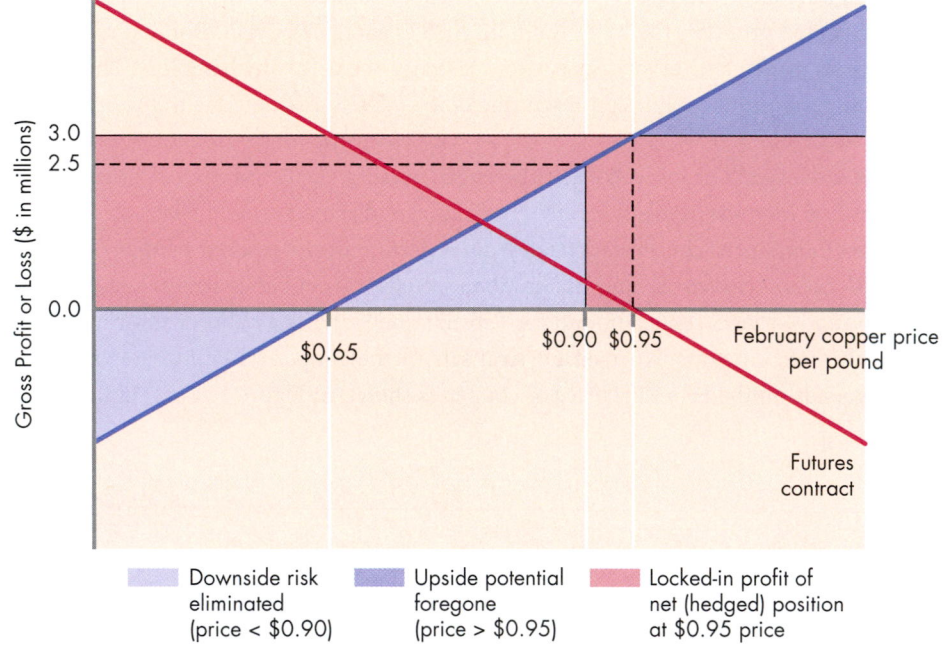

Indeed, the futures contracts provide an immediate 5 cent benefit per pound (ignoring present value considerations, inventory holding costs, and fees and commissions of the contracts) since the October 1 price of copper is only 90 cents.

For example, if the February copper price is 85 cents, the contracts will have provided $1 million of cash flow and profit protection ($0.95 contract price minus $0.85 February spot market price, multiplied by the 10 million pounds of copper). If the February spot price is 65 cents, the contracts will have provided $3 million of protection.

The futures contracts "lock in" a February price of 95 cents and eliminate the company's downside exposure to a decline in copper prices. February cash receipts will be $9.5 million, and profits will total $3.0 million, no matter what the February spot price for copper turns out to be.

Of course, there is another side to the story. By hedging its original exposure to commodity price risk with futures contracts, Rombauer has given up the cash flow and gross profit increases that could result if the February spot price is above $0.95. Figure 11.7(c) shows how the company's hedging strategy eliminates downside risk (and upside potential) and results in predictable cash flows and gross profits.

Swap Contract Another common derivative security is a **swap contract**. These contracts are a popular way to hedge interest rate or foreign currency exchange rate risk. Let's say Kistler Manufacturing has issued $100 million of long-term 8% fixed-rate debt and wants to protect itself against a *decline* in market interest rates. There are several ways the company could reduce its exposure. We already discussed one earlier in this chapter, using a debt-for-debt exchange offer to replace the fixed-rate debt with a floating-rate loan. A second—and perhaps less costly—way that Kistler Manufacturing can reduce its interest rate risk exposure is to create *synthetic* floating-rate debt using an interest rate swap.

> One reason protection might be needed is that Kistler's operating cash flows are positively correlated with interest rates. In this case a decline in market rates would be accompanied by a decrease in operating cash flows, and the company may lack the cash flow needed to meet its payment obligations under the 8% fixed-rate loan.

This form of hedging is accomplished with a "swap dealer." Swap dealers are typically banks who locate another company—called a "counterparty"—who is willing to make fixed-rate interest *payments* in exchange for floating-rate interest *receipts*. (Recall that Kistler wants to make floating-rate interest payments.) The swap transaction in Figure 11.8 includes Kistler with fixed-rate debt outstanding, the swap dealer, and the counterparty company with outstanding floating-rate debt where interest payments are linked to the one-year U.S. Treasury bill rate. This is exactly the kind of interest payment Kistler seeks.

> What's in it for the counterparty? By replacing floating-rate interest payments with synthetic fixed-rate payments, the counterparty has reduced its exposure to cash flow volatility from interest rate changes.

Kistler and the counterparty agree to swap interest payments on $100 million of debt for the next three years, with settlement every year. At the settlement date the counterparty gives Kistler the fixed-rate payment of $8 million, which is then passed on to Kistler's lender. At the same time Kistler gives the counterparty cash equal to the floating-rate payment (say $7 million based on a Treasury rate of 7%), and this too is passed on to the floating-rate lender. In reality only the $1 million difference in interest payments would be exchanged between the two parties to the swap.

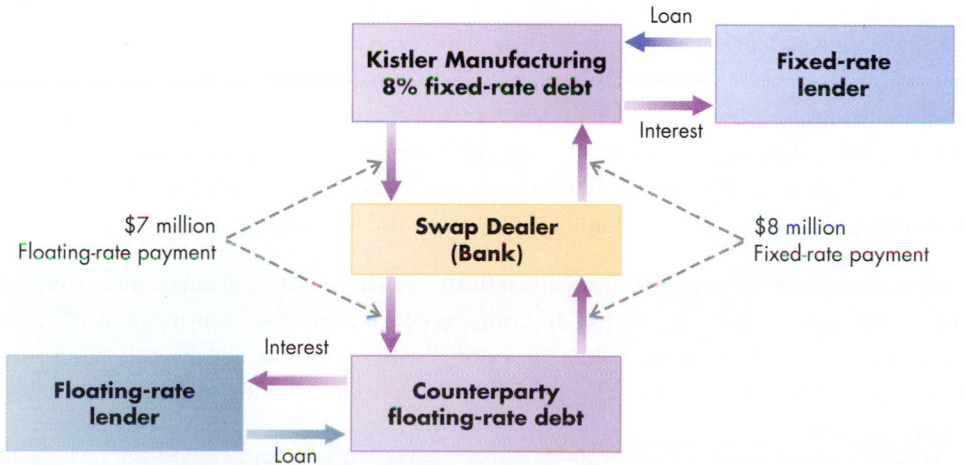

Figure 11.8

KISTLER MANUFACTURING

An Interest Rate Swap that Creates Synthetic Floating-Rate Debt

The swap transforms Kistler's fixed-rate debt into floating rate, because the money Kistler receives from the counterparty offsets the fixed payment Kistler is obligated to make to the lender. Figure 11.9 on the next page shows how the swap transaction eliminates Kistler's downside exposure to interest rate risk. If the Treasury rate falls to 7%, Kistler will receive a net cash inflow of $1 million from the swap counterparty. This net cash inflow is Kistler's $8 million fixed-rate payment minus the counterparty's $7 million floating-rate payment. Kistler then pays its lender $8 million as required, with $1 million of the payment coming from the swap counterparty. Kistler's out-of-pocket interest cost is just $7 million, the amount it would have been required to pay if it had issued floating-rate debt in the first place.[12]

Figure 11.9

KISTLER MANUFACTURING
Using a Swap to Hedge Interest Rate Risk

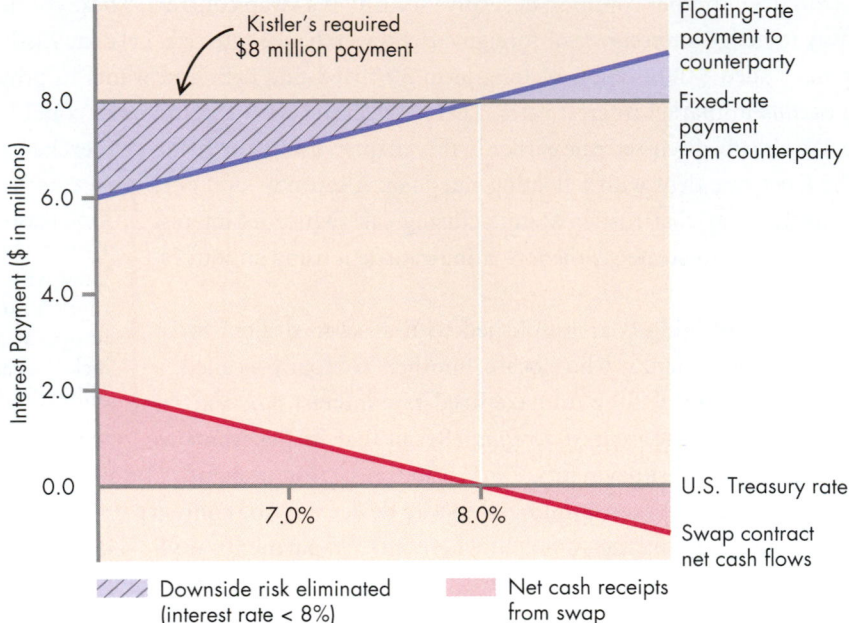

Kistler ends up with floating-rate debt that it could perhaps not otherwise obtain at attractive rates. The counterparty ends up with fixed interest payments, and the bank gets a fee for arranging the swap transaction. Everybody wins—as long as all parties fulfill their payment obligations.

A foreign exchange (currency) swap has the same structural features as those outlined in Exhibits 11.8 and 11.9 except that the loans are denominated in different currencies. Suppose St. Jean Inc. manufactures products in France but sells exclusively in the United States. The company borrows francs to finance construction of a manufacturing plant in France, and it wants to hedge its foreign exchange exposure on the loan. The company's exposure arises because its operating cash flows are in U.S. dollars but its loan payments are in francs. With the aid of a swap dealer, the company can identify a counterparty willing to exchange franc-denominated payments for dollar-denominated payments. The pattern of swapped cash flows would be identical to the flows depicted in Figure 11.8. St. Jean ends up with *synthetic* U.S. dollar-denominated debt and eliminates its exposure to fluctuations in the franc-dollar exchange rate.

Options Contract Futures and swaps are derivatives that require each party to the contract to complete the agreed-upon transaction. But other types of derivative securities exist. One is an option contract, which gives the holder an "option"—the right but not the obligation—to do something. To illustrate how options work, let's revisit our homebuilder discussed at the beginning of this section.

Suppose it is now January and Ridge Development needs 10 million board feet of lumber on hand in three months (April) to construct homes that the company has already sold to residential

---

[12] An **interest rate "collar"** may be part of the swap agreement as well—for example, the two parties could agree that the swap remains in force as long as the Treasury rate is less than 8.5% and greater than 6%.

homebuyers. Lumber currently sells for $250 per 1,000 board feet, so Ridge would have to purchase $2.5 million of lumber at the current (January) price to meet its April construction commitment. But Ridge has no place to store the lumber and lumber prices are expected to increase over the next few months. How can the company eliminate its commodity price risk from its *anticipated* lumber purchase three months from now?

One approach is to buy a futures contract for April lumber. Ridge can "lock in" the profit margin on unbuilt homes it has sold by agreeing to pay a set price now (in January) for lumber delivered in April. But if lumber prices fall over the next three months, the builder—now locked into higher lumber prices by the futures contract—would forego the increased profits from lower lumber prices.

> Some option contracts give the holder the right to *buy* a specific underlying asset at a specified price during a specified time. These are referred to as **call options**. Other option contracts give the holder the option to *sell* an asset at a specified price during a specified time period. These are called **put options**.

By using options instead of futures, the builder can protect against lumber cost increases without sacrificing potential gains if lumber prices decline. This can be done by purchasing a call option on lumber—an option to buy lumber at a specified price over the option period. The call option protects the builder against lumber cost increases. But because it is an option, Ridge is not obligated to exercise the option should lumber prices fall. Options enable Ridge to hedge unfavorable price movements and still participate in the upside possibility of increased profit margins if lumber prices fall. Figure 11.10 shows how.

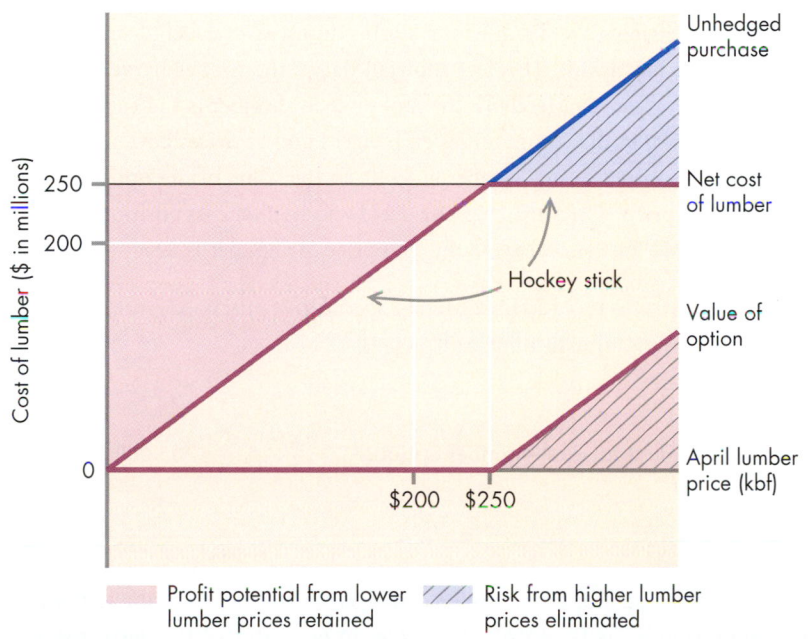

Figure 11.10

RIDGE DEVELOPMENT COMPANY
Using an Option to Hedge Commodity Price Risk

Without hedging its anticipated lumber purchase, Ridge is exposed to commodity price risk if lumber prices rise above the current $250 level over the next three months. To eliminate this exposure, Ridge buys a call option for 10 million board feet of April lumber at $250 per 1,000 board feet. If the April price of lumber is more than $250 per 1,000 board feet, Ridge will exercise the option and pay just the $250 contract price. But if the April price is, say, $200, Ridge will let the option expire and instead buy lumber in the open market—saving $500,000 in lumber costs ($50 per 1,000 board feet). The net result of the option hedge is a "hockey stick" shape (see Figure 11.10)—the *downside risk* of a lumber price increase is eliminated but the *upside potential* of a lumber price decrease is retained.

When options are used in this way, they do not necessarily "lock in" a specified profit margin or price. Instead, they provide a hedge that resembles insurance. Options allow companies to hedge against downside risk—value losses—while retaining the opportunity to benefit from favorable price movements. Insurance does the same thing. It provides protection against losses.

Financial Reporting for Derivative Securities

Before we turn our attention to hedge accounting, let's consider first how GAAP treats stand-alone derivative securities in the absence of a hedging transaction. Here's a quick synopsis:

- All derivatives must be carried on the balance sheet at fair value—no exceptions. Fair value is the market price of the derivative at the balance sheet date.
- Generally, changes in the fair value of derivatives must be recognized in income when they occur. The only exception is for derivatives that qualify as hedges (explained below) according to GAAP.

Here's an example that illustrates the basic accounting treatment for derivatives that do not qualify for special "hedge accounting" rules:

> On March 1, 2005 Heitz Metals buys call options (that is, options to purchase) for 10 million board feet of June lumber. Each call option gives Heitz the opportunity to purchase 1,000 board feet of lumber, so the firm bought a total of 10,000 option contracts (10 million board feet divided by 1,000 per contract). Heitz has no use for the lumber nor is the company hedging a financial risk. ***Instead, Heitz is just speculating that lumber prices will increase during the next several months.*** The settlement price is $240 per 1,000 board feet, the current spot price is $240, and Heitz pays $5,000 for the contracts.
>
> Over the next 30 days, a series of winter storms dump several feet of snow in the mountains of the Pacific Northwest. This late snowfall delays the timber-harvesting season and creates a lumber shortage. By March 31, the spot price for lumber is $245 and June contracts are trading for $7,500 at the commodities exchange. Lumber prices have increased to $245 but Heitz owns an option to buy lumber at $240, so the value of the option has increased along with lumber prices. On April 15, Heitz decides to liquidate its position. The June lumber contracts are sold for $12,000 when the spot price for lumber is $252.

The accounting entry to record Heitz Metals' *speculative* purchase—remember, Heitz has no real use for the lumber—of June lumber contracts is:

DR	Marketable securities—lumber options	$5,000	
CR	Cash		$5,000

The derivative securities (call options) are recorded as an asset at fair value—the purchase price paid. At the end of March, Heitz records the *change* in fair value of the derivative for the month ($7,500 fair value at the start of March − $5,000 fair value at the end of March, or $2,500):

The unrealized gain (or loss) would be included in "Income from continuing operations" on the Heitz income statement.				
	DR	Market adjustment—lumber options	$2,500	
	CR	Unrealized holding gain on lumber options (to income)		$2,500

The "Market adjustment" of $2,500 is added to the $5,000 balance in "Marketable securities." The contracts are now carried on the balance sheet at $7,500—which is their fair market value as of the end of March—and a $2,500 unrealized gain has been recorded in income for March. (If the options had declined in value, an unrealized holding loss would have been recorded along with a downward adjustment in the carrying value of the options.) Heitz then liquidates the options contracts on April 15:

DR Cash	$12,000	
CR Marketable securities—lumber options		$5,000
CR Market adjustment—lumber options		2,500
CR Realized holding gain on lumber options		
(to income)		4,500

These accounting entries are used for all types of derivatives—forwards, futures, swaps, and options—unless the special "hedge accounting" rules described next apply. Three key points about derivatives and their GAAP accounting rules should be remembered:

1. Derivative contracts represent balance sheet assets and liabilities.
2. The carrying value of the derivative is adjusted to fair value at each balance sheet date.
3. The amount of the adjustment—the change in fair value—flows to the income statement as a holding gain (or loss).

As a result of these GAAP rules, speculative investments in derivative contracts can increase the volatility of reported earnings. But the earnings volatility that results from this accounting treatment perfectly reflects the derivative's inherent economic risk.

Hedge Accounting

When a company successfully hedges its exposure to market risk, any economic loss on the hedged item (for example, copper inventory) will be offset by an economic gain on the derivative securities (for example, copper futures contracts). *To accurately reflect the underlying economics of the hedge, the company should match the loss on the hedged item with the derivative's offsetting gain in the income statement of the same period.* This matching is what the GAAP rules governing hedge accounting try to accomplish.[13] The special hedge accounting rules eliminate or reduce the earnings volatility that would otherwise result from reporting the change in the derivative's fair value in income.

> The matching process works like this. If an economic gain (or loss) on the *hedged item* flows to accounting income in the current period, so does the offsetting loss (or gain) on the derivative. But if the hedged item's economic gain (or loss) flows to accounting income some time later, then income statement recognition of the derivative's offsetting loss (or gain) is also postponed to that later period.

The type of special hedge accounting to be applied varies depending on the nature of the exposure that is being hedged. In some cases, changes in the fair value of the derivative are reported in income as they occur, but the earnings impact is then offset by a corresponding charge (or credit) from adjusting the carrying value of the asset or liability being hedged. In other cases, earnings volatility is avoided by recording changes in the fair value of the derivative directly in "Other comprehensive income."

When can hedge accounting be used? The answer depends on four considerations:

- Hedged item
- Hedging instrument
- Risk being hedged
- Effectiveness of hedge

> You may want to review Chapter 2 for a discussion of **other comprehensive income** and the income statement.

Stringent GAAP criteria must be met to qualify for hedge accounting. To fulfill the criteria, management must do three things: designate the derivative security as a hedging instrument; describe the hedging strategy; and document its effectiveness in eliminating a specific market risk for a specific hedged item. The details are voluminous and complex, so we cannot possibly cover all the bases here. What we can do is provide an overview of the most common hedging situations and how hedge accounting works. The basics are outlined in Figure 11.11 on the next page.

---

[13] "Accounting for Derivative Instruments and Hedging Activities," *SFAS No. 133* (Norwalk, CT: FASB, 1998); "Accounting for Certain Derivative Instruments and Certain Hedging Activities," *SFAS No. 138* (Norwalk, CT: FASB, 2000). These statements are summarized and interpreted in the 540-page implementation guide *Accounting for Derivative Instruments and Hedging Activities* (Norwalk, CT: FASB, 2000).

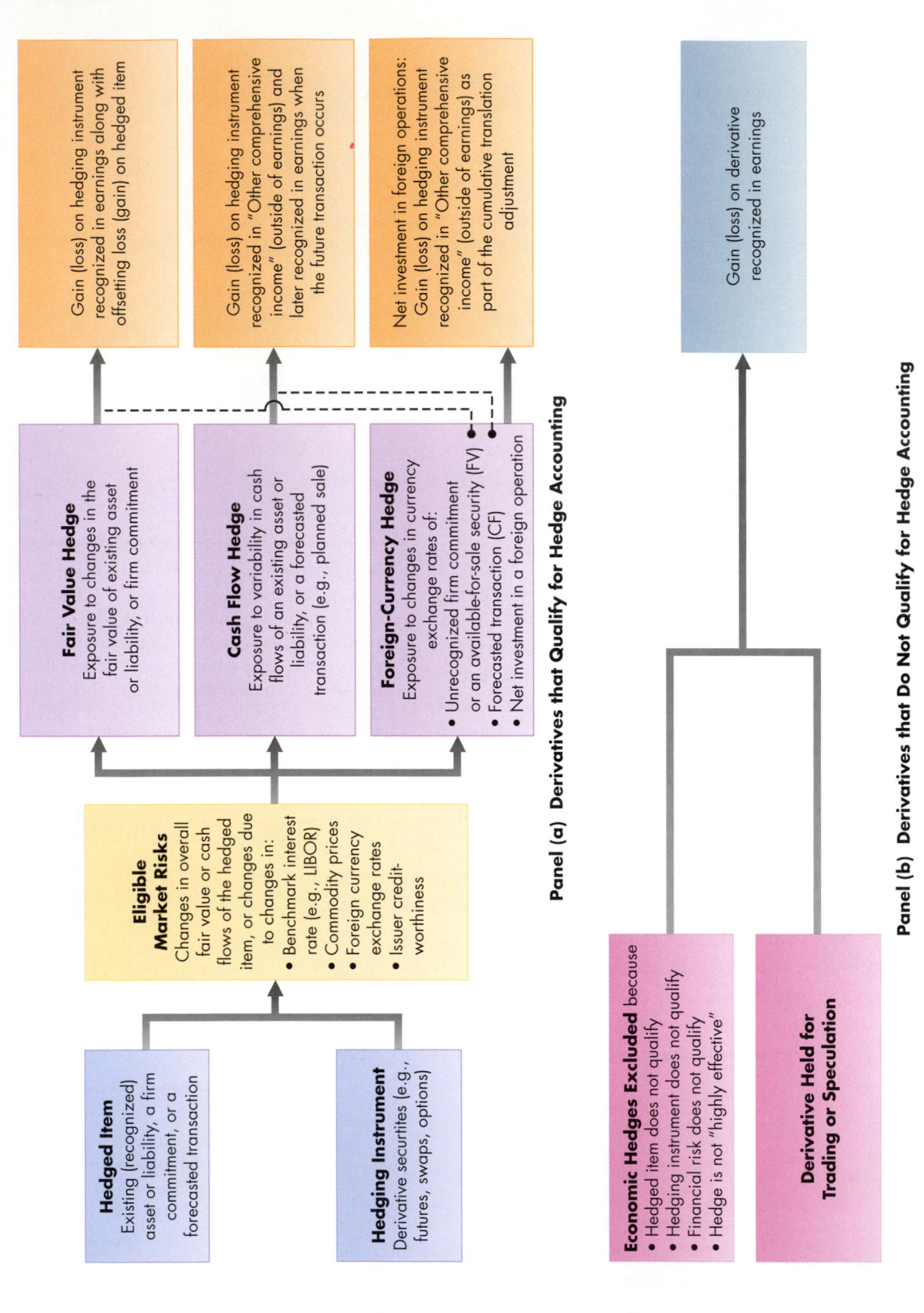

Hedged Item
Existing (recognized) asset or liability, a firm commitment, or a forecasted transaction

Hedging Instrument
Derivative securities (e.g., futures, swaps, options)

Eligible Market Risks
Changes in overall fair value or cash flows of the hedged item, or changes due to changes in:
• Benchmark interest rate (e.g., LIBOR)
• Commodity prices
• Foreign currency exchange rates
• Issuer credit-worthiness

Fair Value Hedge
Exposure to changes in the fair value of existing asset or liability, or firm commitment

Cash Flow Hedge
Exposure to variability in cash flows of an existing asset or liability, or a forecasted transaction (e.g., planned sale)

Foreign-Currency Hedge
Exposure to changes in currency exchange rates of:
• Unrecognized firm commitment or an available-for-sale security (FV)
• Forecasted transaction (CF)
• Net investment in a foreign operation

Gain (loss) on hedging instrument recognized in earnings along with offsetting loss (gain) on hedged item

Gain (loss) on hedging instrument recognized in "Other comprehensive income" (outside of earnings) and later recognized in earnings when the future transaction occurs

Net investment in foreign operations: Gain (loss) on hedging instrument recognized in "Other comprehensive income" (outside of earnings) as part of the cumulative translation adjustment

Panel (a) Derivatives that Qualify for Hedge Accounting

Economic Hedges Excluded because
• Hedged item does not qualify
• Hedging instrument does not qualify
• Financial risk does not qualify
• Hedge is not "highly effective"

Derivative Held for Trading or Speculation

Gain (loss) on derivative recognized in earnings

Panel (b) Derivatives that Do Not Qualify for Hedge Accounting

Figure 11.11

FINANCIAL REPORTING FOR DERIVATIVE SECURITIES

The **hedged item** can be either (1) an existing asset or liability on the company's books, (2) a firm commitment, or (3) an anticipated (forecasted) future transaction. Inventories of commodities like copper and lumber, receivables and loans, and debt obligations are examples of *existing assets and liabilities* that qualify as hedged items. If Hess Company agrees in June to buy network storage equipment from another company at a specific price with delivery in the future (say, August), that's a *firm commitment*. If, on the other hand, Hess just knows in June that it must buy the equipment by August but no purchase agreement has been signed, then it's a *anticipated transaction.*

The **hedging instrument** is commonly a derivative security, although not all derivatives meet the strict GAAP rules and some qualifying hedges (for example, the call provision of a callable bond) do not involve derivatives as the term is commonly used. Qualifying hedging instruments include options to purchase or sell an exchange-traded security, futures and forward contracts, and interest rate and currency swaps. *Insurance contracts, options to purchase real estate, traditional equity and debt securities, and financial guarantee contracts do not qualify as hedging instruments.*

The **risk being hedged** must meet certain GAAP criteria. The eligible market risks are limited to: risks arising from overall changes in the fair value or cash flow of the hedged item; or risks from changes in benchmark interest rates (for example, LIBOR), commodity prices (for example, copper), foreign-currency exchange rates (for example, Japanese yen to U.S. dollar), and the creditworthiness of the party (a company, institution, or government agency) that issued a financial security. Other sorts of financial and operating risks (for example, risks from weather conditions, industrial accidents, or labor strikes) do not qualify for hedge accounting. (We will discuss the effectiveness of the hedge later.)

> Derivatives that fail to meet the GAAP rules for hedge accounting—because either the hedged item, the derivative itself, or the hedged risk doesn't qualify—are treated as though they were speculative investments.

GAAP groups the risks being hedged into three categories:

1. **A fair value hedge** is a hedge of the exposure to changes in the *fair market value* of an *existing* asset or liability, or a *firm commitment.* Common examples of a fair value hedge include:

   - an interest rate swap that synthetically converts fixed-rate debt into floating rate debt (interest-rate risk exposure of an existing liability), or
   - a gold futures contract that "unlocks" a gold mining company's agreement to sell refined gold to a jewelry manufacturer next year at a fixed price (commodity price risk exposure of a firm commitment).

2. **A cash flow hedge** is a hedge of the exposure to changes in *cash flows* of an *existing* asset or liability, or an *anticipated transaction.* Common examples of a cash flow hedge include:

   - an interest rate swap that synthetically converts floating-rate debt into fixed-rate debt (interest-rate risk exposure of an existing liability), or
   - a lumber futures contract that "locks in" the price a building contractor will pay in two months for lumber (commodity price risk exposure for an anticipated transaction).

3. **A foreign currency exposure hedge** is a hedge of the exposure to changes in currency exchange rates of an existing asset or liability, a firm commitment, a forecasted transaction, or a multinational company's net investment in a foreign operation. Here GAAP applies the fair value and cash flow hedge accounting rules to foreign currency exchange exposure. The unique element of this exposure is a net investment in foreign operations. In Chapter 16 we describe the accounting and reporting issues unique to foreign subsidiaries.

> How can an interest rate swap qualify as both a fair value hedge and a cash flow hedge? The answer lies in understanding how interest rate changes affect the market values and cash flows of debt obligations. For fixed-rate debt, interest rate changes produce market value changes in the opposite direction but debt cash flows are "fixed" (meaning unchanged). So, an interest rate swap that converts fixed-rate debt into floating-rate debt eliminates fluctuations in market values and thus becomes a fair value hedge. For floating-rate debt, interest rate changes produce changes in debt cash flows—if rates increase the borrower must pay additional interest—but debt market value is unaffected. So, an interest rate swap that converts floating-rate debt into fixed-rate debt eliminates fluctuations in cash flows and thus becomes a cash flow hedge.

Figure 11.11 describes the accounting procedures for (a) derivatives that qualify for hedge accounting, and (b) derivatives that do not qualify for hedge accounting. GAAP requires all derivative securities—whether held for trading and speculation or as financial hedges—to be **marked-to-market**, meaning that they are carried at fair value on the balance sheet as assets or liabilities. The offsetting debit or credit that results from marked-to-market accounting then flows either to current income (for fair value hedges, certain foreign currency hedges, and derivatives that do not qualify for hedge accounting) or to "Other comprehensive income" (for cash flow hedges and most other foreign currency hedges).

Fair Value Hedge Accounting

Hedge accounting makes it possible for companies engaged in financial risk management to recognize the gain (or loss) on the hedged item in the same period as the offsetting loss (or gain) on the derivative security. To see how this is done, let's return to Rombaurer Metals and its copper inventory hedge:

On October 1, 2005 Rombaurer has 10 million pounds of copper inventory on hand at an average cost of $0.65 a pound. The spot price for copper is $0.90 a pound. Instead of selling copper now, Rombaurer decides to hold on to the inventory until February 2006 when management believes the price will return to a normal level of $0.95 a pound. To hedge its position, Rombaurer sells futures contracts for 10 million pounds at $0.95 for February delivery. The margin deposit on the contracts is $280,000—the amount the commodities broker requires as a good-faith cash deposit on the contracts. The market's spot and futures prices over the next several months are:

	COMEX Copper Prices	
	Spot Price	February 2002 Futures Price
October 1, 2005	$0.90	$0.95
December 31, 2005	0.85	0.91
February 26, 2006	0.94	0.94

Rombaurer has successfully hedged its exposure to commodity price risk—and the fair value of its existing copper inventory—by selling the futures contracts. Then, Rombaurer designates the futures contracts (the hedging instrument) as a **fair value hedge** of its exposure to market price fluctuations (the hedged risk) for existing copper inventory (the hedged item). As long as the futures contracts pass the GAAP test for hedge effectiveness—and they do, as you will see later—Rombaurer can use the special **fair value hedge accounting** rules. Here are the accounting entries.

On October 1, 2005 Rombaurer records the initial margin deposit on its fair value hedge:

| **DR** Amount due from broker (a receivable) | $280,000 | |
| **CR** Cash | | $280,000 |

No entry is made that day for the futures contracts themselves because they have zero value at inception—the February contract price ($0.95) equals the current $0.95 market price of February copper.

The spot price and the February futures price of copper both decline over the next several months. Rombaurer makes two journal entries at year-end, December 31. The first entry records the fair value increase for the hedging instrument:

| **DR** Amount due from broker | $400,000 | |
| **CR** Gain on hedge activity (to income) | | $400,000 |

The futures contracts are worth $400,000 on December 31, 2005. This amount is the difference between the copper price guaranteed by the contracts ($0.95) and the current futures price of February copper ($0.91), multiplied by the 10 million pounds of copper being hedged. Copper prices have fallen, but the hedge has provided $400,000 of commodity price protection. Notice too that the broker receivable now has a balance of $680,000 representing the initial margin deposit ($280,000) *plus* the fair value of the futures contracts ($400,000).

The second year-end entry adjusts the carrying value of the hedged item—copper inventory— for the change in fair value ($0.91 minus $0.95, a $0.04 loss, multiplied by 10 million pounds):

DR Loss on hedge activity (to income)	$400,000	
CR Copper inventory		$400,000

The carrying value of the copper inventory is now $6.1 million, that's the inventory's $6.5 million historical cost *minus* the $400,000 decline in the February fair value since October 1, 2005. (Note that GAAP measures this fair value decline using the October 1 $0.95 *futures* contract price as the benchmark. The October 1 *spot* price of $0.90 does not enter into the GAAP calculation of the fair value decline.)

In the first December 31 entry, the derivative is marked-to-market and a gain on the hedging instrument is recorded to income. But the gain from the futures contracts is fully offset by Rombaurer's loss on copper inventory in the second entry. (In practice, only one "Gain or loss on hedge activity" account is used to record the gain and the loss.) These offsetting gains and losses eliminate earnings volatility.

On February 26, 2006 Rombaurer sells the copper on the spot market for $0.94 a pound and cancels the futures contracts. Rombaurer makes three journal entries at this time.

The first entry records the fair value change for the hedging instrument ($0.91 minus $0.94, a $0.03 loss, multiplied by 10 million pounds), the cash returned from the broker, and eliminates the broker receivable:

DR Cash	$380,000	
DR Loss on hedge activity (to income)	300,000	
CR Amount due from broker		$680,000

February copper prices have increased $0.03 a pound since December and the futures contracts are now worth only $100,000 ($0.95 minus $0.94, multiplied by 10 million pounds), so Rombaurer records a loss of $300,000. This $300,000 loss is fair value change in the futures contracts since December 31. Rombaurer also receives $380,000 from the broker. This amount is the sum of the returned margin deposit ($280,000) and the settlement value of the contracts ($100,000).

The second entry adjusts the carrying value of the hedged copper inventory for the fair value change ($0.94 minus $0.91, multiplied by 10 million pounds):

DR Copper inventory	$300,000	
CR Gain on hedge activity (to income)		$300,000

In this case, the loss from the futures contracts (the first entry) is offset by a gain on copper inventory (the second entry).

The third and final entry records the credit sale of copper inventory at the spot market price:

DR Accounts receivable	$9,400,000	
DR Cost of goods sold	6,400,000	
CR Sales revenue		$9,400,000
CR Copper inventory		6,400,000

The $6.4 million adjusted carrying value ($0.64 per pound) is determined as:

10/5/05	cost at $0.65 per pound	$6.5 million
12/31/05	adjustment for $0.04 decline	(.4) million
2/26/06	adjustment for $0.03 increase	.3 million
2/26/06	adjusted carrying value	$6.4 million

Rombaurer's gross profit from selling copper is $3 million (the $9.4 million selling price minus the $6.4 million adjusted carrying value of the inventory sold). This is exactly the gross profit Rombaurer would have reported if the inventory—originally carried on the books at $6.5 million—had been sold at the anticipated February price of $0.95 a pound, or $9.5 million. By selling futures contracts, Rombaurer "locked in" the February price of $0.95 a pound and eliminated its exposure to commodity price risk.

That's the economics behind Rombaurer's hedging activities and that's what the accounting statements report.

What if Rombaurer did not (or could not) use hedge accounting rules for the copper futures contracts. In that case, GAAP still requires the derivative security to be marked-to-market. So Rombaurer would record a $400,000 gain on December 31, 2005 followed by a $300,000 loss on February 26, 2006—the change in fair value of the futures contracts. But GAAP would not allow an offsetting loss (on December 31, 2005) or gain (on February 26, 2006) to be recorded on the copper inventory itself. Instead, the inventory would continue to be carried at its historical cost of $6,500,000 until sold. The net result is increased earnings volatility: Net income for 2005 would include a $400,000 gain, while net income for 2006 would include a $300,000 loss and a $100,000 gross margin reduction due to the higher carrying value of inventory ($0.65 per pound original cost rather than $0.64 per pound adjusted carrying value).

Cash Flow Hedge Accounting

Exhibit 11.11 illustrates the accounting for a **cash flow hedge**. Chalk Hill Inc. issues a $10 million three-year floating-rate note with interest equal to the LIBOR rate, reset annually. To hedge its exposure to cash flow variability from changes in the LIBOR, Chalk Hill enters into an interest-rate swap with a bank. The bank agrees to make the required floating-rate interest payments and Chalk Hill agrees to pay the bank 7.5% fixed-rate interest annually for the entire three years. The interest-rate swap allows Chalk Hill to "lock in" the 7.5% fixed-rate cash payment for interest even though the actual interest rate charged on the note will rise or fall with changes in the LIBOR rate.

EXHIBIT 11.11	**Chalk Hill's Cash Flow Hedge**

Using an Interest-Rate Swap to Hedge Variable-Rate Debt

On January 1, 2005 Chalk Hill borrows $10 million signing a three-year note with interest equal to the LIBOR (currently at 7.5%), reset annually on December 31. To hedge its exposure to the variability in cash flows associated with the floating-rate note, Chalk Hill enters into a three-year interest-rate swap with Beringer Bank. Under the swap contract, Chalk Hill pays interest to the bank at the fixed rate of 7.5% and receives interest payments from the bank at a variable rate equal to the LIBOR, based on a notional amount of $10 million. Both the note and swap require that payments be made or received annually on December 31 of each year.

Chalk Hill designates the swap (hedging instrument) as a *cash flow hedge* of its exposure to variability in the cash flows of the floating-rate note (hedged item), with the specific risk being changes in cash flows due to changes in the LIBOR rate. This hedge is fully effective because the key terms of the note and swap are identical. The LIBOR rates, cash payments made and received, and the fair value of the swap contract (based on dealer quotes) are:

		Gross Cash Flow			Swap Fair Value
	LIBOR Rate	To Beringer Bank	From Beringer Bank	Net Cash Flow	Asset (Liability) from Dealer Quotes
January 1, 2005	7.50%	$750,000	$750,000	—	—
December 31, 2005	8.50	750,000	850,000	$100,000	$323,000
December 31, 2006	7.00	750,000	700,000	(50,000)	(55,000)

Swap contracts are not traded in an organized exchange (like the New York Mercantile Exchange where copper futures contracts are traded), so contract fair values can be difficult to determine. Chalk Hill's fair value estimates ("quotes") are from knowledgeable "dealers" (usually investment bankers) who are actively involved in structuring swap transactions.*

*To learn more about how practitioners value swaps and other derivatives, see C. W. Smithson, C. W. Smith, and D. S. Wilford, *Managing Financial Risk* (New York: Irwin, 1995).

EXHIBIT 11.11   Chalk Hill's Cash Flow Hedge (*continued*)

Chalk Hill makes the following entries over the life of the swap contract and note:

January 1, 2005:

DR Cash	$10,000,000	
CR Note payable		$10,000,000

(To record the initial borrowing by the company. There is no entry for the swap contract because it has no initial value—the "pay" and "receive" rates for both parties are the same, 7.5% times $10 million.)

December 31, 2005:

DR Interest expense	$750,000	
CR Interest payable		$750,000

(To accrue annual interest at a variable rate of 7.5%—the LIBOR rate on January 1, 2005.)

DR Interest payable	$750,000	
CR Cash		$750,000

(To record the annual interest payment on the note. There is no entry for the swap settlement this year because the "pay" and "receive" amounts are the same, $750,000.)

DR Swap contract	$323,000	
CR Other comprehensive income		$323,000

(To record the change in fair value of the swap based on dealer quotes.)

December 31, 2006:

DR Interest expense	$850,000	
CR Interest payable		$850,000

(To accrue annual interest at a variable rate of 8.5%—the LIBOR rate on December 31, 2005.)

DR Interest payable	$850,000	
CR Cash		$850,000

(To record the annual interest payment on the note.)

DR Cash	$100,000	
CR Interest expense		$100,000

(To record the swap settlement net receipt from Beringer Bank.)

DR Other comprehensive income	$378,000	
CR Swap contract		$378,000

(To record the change in fair value of the swap based on dealer quotes. The swap contract account now has a $55,000 credit balance.)

December 31, 2007:

DR Interest expense	$700,000	
CR Interest payable		$700,000

(To accrue annual interest at a variable rate of 7.0%—the LIBOR rate on December 31, 2006.)

DR Interest payable	$700,000	
CR Cash		$700,000

(To record the annual interest payment on the note.)

DR Interest expense	$50,000	
CR Cash		$50,000

(To record the swap settlement net payment to Beringer Bank.)

DR Swap contract	$55,000	
CR Other comprehensive income		$55,000

(To record the change in fair value of the swap. The swap agreement has now been concluded, and the contract has no further value to either party.)

DR Note payable	$10,000,000	
CR Cash		$10,000,000

(To record payment of the note principal.)

As you work through the journal entries in Exhibit 11.11, notice that the hedging instrument (swap contract) shows up as a balance sheet asset or liability. (If the account has a debit balance, it's an asset; if the balance is a credit, it's a liability.) The carrying value of the swap is its fair value at each balance sheet date. This means that changes in the swap's fair value are recorded when they occur—**but they do not flow directly to the income statement**. Instead, gains and losses on the swap contract flow to "Other comprehensive income" and shareholders' equity, as shown in Figure 11.11. What's the reason for this accounting treatment? Changes in the LIBOR rate do not affect the underlying economic value of the floating-rate note—as interest rates on a floating-rate liability change, the market price of the liability remains constant. So, we are unable to offset fair value changes in the hedging instrument with changes in the fair value of the hedged item. The only way earnings volatility can be avoided is to keep swap gains and losses off the income statement by allowing them to flow to "Other comprehensive income."

There is one more feature of the Chalk Hill example you need to observe. Interest expense is $750,000 each year, or the 7.5% fixed-rate of interest multiplied by the $10 million note principal amount. This may at first seem surprising because Chalk Hill makes a floating-rate interest payment each year, and the amount paid varies from $700,000 to $850,000 over the three years. But the interest-rate swap insulates Chalk Hill from this cash flow volatility. For example, in 2006 Chalk Hill pays $850,000 in interest on the note but receives $100,000 from the swap counterparty. Chalk Hill's net cash payment for interest that year is $750,000, which is also the amount of interest expense reported.

> Problem 11.9 looks at the accounting for Chalk Hill's swap when it does not qualify for hedge accounting.

Hedge Accounting for a Forecasted Transaction

Now let's see how hedge accounting works for a **forecasted transaction**. In this example, Vintage Construction uses lumber options contracts as a *cash flow* hedge for its projected lumber needs during the year:

> Vintage Construction Corporation builds residential homes in the far northern United States from April through November. No homes are built on speculation. Building begins only after a firm contract is signed. Construction on average takes four months. Since contract prices with home purchasers are fixed at the inception of the sale, Vintage is vulnerable to lumber price increases. To protect its margins during the 2005 construction season, Vintage buys 20 lumber futures contracts on April 1, 2005. The expiration dates on these contracts are staggered over the April through November season to approximate the monthly level of construction activity.
>
> Lumber prices rise during the 2005 construction season. Because of these unanticipated higher costs, gross profits from home construction are reduced by $600,000. However, Vintage realized a gain of $580,000 on the futures contracts due to the lumber price increase. How was this gain reflected on the company's financial statements?

> Because Vintage doesn't yet own the lumber, the futures contracts cannot qualify as a fair value hedge of an existing asset.

Vintage designates the lumber contracts as a *cash flow hedge* of forecasted lumber purchases, with commodity price volatility being the source of market risk. At inception, the futures contracts are recorded as an asset at the purchase price. At each monthly balance sheet date, the contracts are marked-to-market with the change in fair value flowing to "Other comprehensive income" and then shareholders' equity. As homes are completed each month, Vintage records the revenues and expenses from the construction business. At the same time, the cumulative gain and loss on the lumber contracts for completed homes is transferred out of "Other comprehensive income" to the income statement.

This accounting treatment offsets changes in the gross profit from construction due to lumber price fluctuations (the hedged item) with realized gains and losses from lumber futures contracts (the hedging instrument). Earnings volatility is avoided by allowing the futures contracts gains and losses to initially flow to shareholders' equity. These gains and losses eventually flow to earnings, but only when the forecasted transaction is completed and affects earnings. For Vintage Construction, that means when the homes are finished and sold—not earlier when lumber is purchased.

Because all of the options contracts were realized in 2005, the $580,000 gain would be included in income and would largely offset the $600,000 gross margin reduction that is reflected in income that same period. This income statement result corresponds to the almost perfect hedging strategy followed by Vintage Construction. A "perfect" hedge would have exactly offset the $600,000 margin shortfall.

Hedge Effectiveness

Few hedges are perfect. When they are not—as here—notice that reported income corresponds to the underlying economics. That is, while Vintage insulated itself from most of the lumber price increase, it did experience a $20,000 earnings reduction. This is precisely the reported income statement effect (that is, a $580,000 gain on the options and a $600,000 gross margin reduction).

Hedge effectiveness—the derivative's ability to generate offsetting changes in the fair value or cash flows of the hedged item—is a key qualifying criterion for hedge accounting. If critical terms of the hedging instrument and hedged item are the same, changes in the fair value or cash flow of the derivative (for example, a $1 gain) will completely offset changes in the fair value or cash flow of the hedged item (a $1 loss). In this case, the hedge will be "fully effective." Except for Vintage Construction, all of our examples have involved fully effective hedges.

> For interest-rate swaps like the one described in Exhibit 11.11, the critical terms include the notional (that is, principal) amount, contract term and loan maturity date, "pay" and "receive" rates on the benchmark interest rate, and the interest rate reset dates.

But what if the hedge is not fully effective? Does that disqualify the derivative from special hedge accounting rules? Not necessarily, because GAAP only requires the hedge to be "highly effective"—as defined by GAAP—in offsetting changes in those fair values or cash flows that are due to the hedged risk. This requirement must be met both at the inception of the hedge and on an ongoing basis. *SFAS No. 133* provides general guidelines but does not say exactly how effectiveness should be determined.

How effective is "highly effective"? The hedging instrument should offset somewhere between 80% and 125% of the hedged item's fair value or cash flow changes attributable to the hedged risk. For Vintage Construction, this means that the company must purchase enough staggered lumber futures contracts to hedge at least 80% of its exposure to lumber price fluctuations. Purchase less than this amount and the futures contracts are an "ineffective" hedge according to GAAP. On the other hand, if Vintage buys too many contracts, the hedge is also considered ineffective. That's because the futures contracts are excessive and more like a speculative investment than a true hedge of underlying market risk.

> *SFAS No. 133* and *No. 138* do not provide a bright line that defines "highly effective" so interpretation of this phrase will often be a matter of professional judgment. The range of 80% to 125% is becoming an accepted threshold for high effectiveness, but it has not been sanctioned by the FASB. There's one more feature of hedge effectiveness you should know about. Vintage Construction can instead purchase 10 lumber futures contracts and still have a "highly effective" hedge if (1) Vintage designates the contracts as a "partial hedge" of its risk exposure (for example, 50% of its lumber purchases), and (2) the contracts are "highly effective" in hedging that partial exposure.

The GAAP distinction between *highly effective* and *ineffective* hedges determines when gains and losses on the hedging instrument flow to current income. A highly effective hedge qualifies for special hedge accounting treatment; an ineffective hedge does not. Even if the highly effective test is met, some ineffectiveness may occur. And when it does, the ineffective portion of the hedge must flow directly to income. So, if Vintage Construction buys futures contracts that hedge just 50% of its full exposure, all of the gains and losses from this *ineffective* hedge flow directly to current income. That's because the contracts are ineffective and do not qualify for hedge accounting. And if the company buys futures contracts to hedge 110% of its exposure, the gains and losses on the *ineffective* portion of the hedge (the portion over 100% coverage) also flow directly to current income. Gains and losses on the remaining effective portion (equal to 100% coverage) of the hedge flow to other comprehensive income since

In a letter to the FASB, Al Wargo of Eastman Chemical said that hedge accounting could cause his company's quarterly earnings per share (EPS) to fluctuate by roughly 100% in either direction—from a $0.12 loss to a $2.24 profit based on Eastman's $1.12 EPS for the second quarter of 2000. The only way Eastman can eliminate this EPS volatility is to change how it hedges financial risk. But this means replacing a sound economic hedging transaction with a less effective hedge. EPS would then be less volatile but the company may be more exposed to financial risks. See P. A. McKay and J. Niedzielski, "New Accounting Standard Gets Mixed Reviews," *Wall Street Journal* (October 23, 2000).

the contracts qualify as a "highly effective" hedge and hedge accounting rules apply.

Critics of hedge accounting claim that additional income statement and balance sheet volatility is created when the gains and losses on the hedging instrument exceed the losses and gains on the hedged item. *This added volatility may force managers to choose between achieving sound economic results—meaning hedges that effectively address real financial risks—or minimizing accounting volatility using risk management approaches that are less efficient or simply not prudent.*

RECAP

Derivatives, when used properly, allow companies to stabilize their operating cash flows by eliminating specific sources of volatility such as fluctuations in interest rates, exchange rates, and commodity prices. The GAAP rules for derivatives are detailed and complex, but the essential points are simple. Derivative contracts represent balance sheet assets and liabilities that must be marked-to-market at each balance sheet date. The resulting mark-to-market adjustment—the change in fair value—then flows either to current earnings (for fair value hedges, certain foreign currency hedges, and derivatives held for trading and speculation) or to "Other comprehensive income" (for cash flow hedges and most other foreign currency hedges). Other aspects of hedge accounting then match gains (or losses) on the derivative with offsetting losses (or gains) on the hedged item. This allows the financial statements to reflect accurately the underlying economics of the hedge.

Contingent Liabilities

Contingent liabilities differ in one important way from the liabilities described elsewhere in this chapter—contingent liabilities are shrouded in uncertainty as to whether or not an obligation really exists. And the uncertainty will only be resolved at some future date when an event does or does not occur. For example, suppose that Whiffle Toy is being sued for $10 million in alleged damages related to its Whamo lawn dart game. If the court rules against Whiffle, an obligation exists because the company will then owe plaintiffs the $10 million in damages. But, if the court rules for Whiffle, no obligation exists. Loss contingencies of this sort arise from factors like litigation, industrial accidents, debt guarantees, and product warranties. For financial reporting purposes, two questions about contingent liabilities must be resolved: (1) When do loss contingencies need to be measured and recognized in the financial statements? (2) Under what circumstances do these contingencies need to be disclosed in footnotes, even when no liability is recorded on the balance sheet itself?

Measuring and Recognizing Loss Contingencies

The rules for measuring and recognizing loss contingencies in the financial statements are virtually identical to the rules governing revenue recognition. *SFAS No. 5* states that a loss contingency shall be accrued by a charge to income if *both* of the following conditions exist:

1. It is *probable* that an asset has been impaired or a liability has been incurred at the date of the financial statements.
2. The amount of loss can be *reasonably estimated.*[14]

---

[14] "Accounting for Contingencies," *SFAS No. 5* (Stamford, CT: FASB, 1975), para. 8.

The FASB established a range representing the likelihood of losses occurring, which is depicted in Figure 11.12, where "probable" indicates the highest likelihood. Notice that the two loss contingency recognition conditions correspond to the two income recognition conditions—"critical event" and "measurability"—discussed in Chapter 2. Specifically, the critical event for loss recognition is that it is probable that a loss has or will occur; similarly, the measurability criterion corresponds closely to how well the loss can be estimated. In this sense, the criteria that trigger income and loss recognition are roughly parallel.

Figure 11.12

SFAS NO. 5 LOSS PROBABILITY CONTINUUM

For certain categories of events, applying the loss contingency rules has become routine. One example of a routine loss contingency is the expense for **estimated uncollectible receivables** described in Chapter 8. Uncollectibles are a normal cost of business when companies sell goods or services on credit, but the amount of the uncollectible loss is unknown at the time of sale. Since some loss is probable, and since the amount can be estimated, an expense (estimated loss) is recorded in the same period that the sale occurs.

In other situations the issue of whether to recognize a loss contingency is highly subjective and complicated by the fact that recognizing and disclosing the loss could itself cause further harm. Consider a company that is being sued for actions that allegedly harmed others.

> Wren Corporation manufactures a wide range of chemical food additives sold to numerous food processors throughout the country. Due to a serious production error, a highly toxic batch of a flavor enhancer was produced by Wren and sold in October 2001. Thousands of consumers were made seriously ill; some died. A class-action law-suit seeking $10 billion in damages has been filed.

The fictitious Wren scenario illustrates a setting in which a straightforward application of the *SFAS No. 5* loss contingency rules could prove harmful to the company. Let's say Wren's management was indeed negligent and expects to negotiate an out-of-court settlement that is approximately $2 billion. If Wren accrued a charge for this expected payout, its negotiating position could be seriously weakened by a disclosure to the plaintiffs that it is prepared to pay at least $2 billion. Because the plaintiffs might be willing to settle for less than $2 billion, candid disclosure of the minimum estimated loss by Wren could raise the ultimate loss payout. Companies like Wren have strong incentives to either:

1. accrue a loss that is significantly *smaller* than the real estimated loss, or
2. disclose that while a loss may have occurred, its amount is not yet measurable.

Consequently, the *SFAS No. 5* rules for loss contingencies arising from litigation are difficult to enforce. ***Statement readers must be aware of the potential understatement of litigation losses and liabilities.***

Loss Contingency Disclosures

When a loss contingency is accrued, companies also usually disclose other information regarding the loss separately in footnotes to the financial statements. *SFAS No. 5* requires this disclosure when a failure to provide additional supplemental data could lead to misleading inferences.

Here's an example of an accrued loss contingency disclosure:

> In the normal course of business, . . . the company is party to a number of proceedings before federal and state regulatory agencies relating to environmental matters. . . . The company's policy is to accrue environmental investigatory and remediation costs for identified sites when it is probable that a liability has been incurred and the amount of loss can be reasonably estimated. . . . As of December 29, 2001, the company had reserves of $14.6 million, primarily for remediation activities associated with company-owned properties as well as for Superfund sites. (*Source:* Stanley Inc., 2001 annual report.)

Stanley has recorded a $14.6 million loss contingency for environmental clean-up at some of the company's current and former manufacturing sites. And, there is a corresponding $14.6 million contingent liability shown on the company's balance sheet. Stanley also explains why it has already accrued the loss: The company believes that it is probable that an obligation to clean up these sites exists, and the amounts involved can be reasonably estimated. Under these circumstances, *SFAS No. 5* requires that a contingent loss and corresponding liability be recorded.

Loss contingency disclosures are also sometimes made even when no loss has been recognized in the income statement itself. For example, if the loss probability is only "reasonably possible" or "remote" (refer to Figure 11.12), then no loss accrual needs to be made in the financial statements. ***Nevertheless, footnote disclosure of loss contingencies is necessary when the loss is both reasonably possible and can be estimated.*** Furthermore, even contingencies arising from remote possibilities must be disclosed in certain circumstances, such as when one company guarantees another company's debt—that is, it agrees to repay a loan if the borrower cannot.

Here's an example of a loss contingency disclosure when no loss has been recognized on the income statement. As you will notice, current and former shareholders are suing Mattel, Inc. for reasons described in the financial statement footnote.

> Following Mattel's announcement in October 1999 of the expected results of its Learning Company division for the third quarter of 1999, several of Mattel's stockholders filed purported class action complaints naming Mattel and certain of its present and former officers and directors as defendants. The complaints generally allege, among other things, that the defendants made false or misleading statements, in the joint proxy statement for the merger of Mattel and Learning Company and elsewhere, that artificially inflated the price of Mattel's common stock. . . . Mattel believes that the actions are without merit and intends to defend them vigorously. (*Source:* Mattel Inc., 2001 annual report.)

Mattel does not specifically mention a dollar amount for its contingent obligation (perhaps because it cannot be reasonably estimated), nor does the company reveal its internal assessment of the probability that the court will uphold the shareholders' claims. But the language used by Mattel—"actions are without merit" and "defend them vigorously"—suggests that management believes the court will decide the matter in favor of Mattel. Accordingly, Mattel has not yet accrued a contingent loss for the ongoing litigation.

Gain Contingencies

When they are recorded, the gain flows to income and there is a corresponding receivable shown on the balance sheet.

While the defendant in a lawsuit (for example, Mattel Corporation) faces a contingent loss, the other side—the plaintiff—has a contingent gain reflecting the possibility that the court will decide that monetary damages must be paid to the plaintiff. As you now know, loss contingencies are accrued when the event confirming the obligation is probable and the amount can be reasonably estimated. **Gain contingencies**, on the other hand, are not recorded until the event actually occurs and the obligation is confirmed. This differing treatment of loss contingencies and gain contingencies illustrates **accounting conservatism**—the notion that it's desirable to anticipate losses, but recognizing gains should wait until their confirmation and realization.

SUMMARY

- An astounding variety of financial instruments, derivatives, and nontraditional financing arrangements are now used to fund corporate activities and to manage risk. Statement readers face a daunting task when trying to grasp the economic implications of some financial innovations.
- Off-balance sheet obligations and loss contingencies are difficult to evaluate because the information needed for that evaluation is often not disclosed.
- Derivatives—whether used for hedging or speculation—pose special problems because of both their complexity and the involved details of hedge accounting.
- For many companies, the most important long-term obligation is still traditional debt financing. GAAP in this area is quite clear. Noncurrent monetary liabilities are initially recorded at the discounted present value of the contractual cash flows—that is, the issue price. The effective interest method is then used to compute interest expense and net carrying value in each period. Interest rate changes occurring after the debt has been issued are ignored.
- GAAP accounting for long-term debt makes it possible to "manage" reported income statement and balance sheet numbers when debt is retired before maturity. The opportunity to "manage" those numbers comes from the difference between debt book value and market value when interest rates have changed.
- The incentives for "managing" income statement and balance sheet numbers may be related to debt covenants, compensation, regulation, or just the desire to paint a favorable picture of the company's performance and health.
- Extinguishment gains and losses from early debt retirement and swaps require careful scrutiny. Statement readers need to know whether real economic benefits for the company and its shareholders are produced—or if the gains or losses are just window dressing.

SELF-STUDY PROBLEM

MALLARD CORPORATION

Mallard Corporation constructs and operates private waterfowl hunting facilities throughout the western United States. On July 1, 2005 the company issued $5 million of par value 10-year bonds to finance construction of a guest lodge at its newest site in Klamath, Oregon. The bonds pay interest semiannually (on December 31 and June 30) at an annual rate of 8% and are callable by Mallard at 102% of par value. The bonds were issued at a price that yields 10% annually to maturity.

1. **Compute the issue price of the bonds.**

   The bond cash flows include a semiannual interest payment of $200,000 (or $5 million at 4%) plus the principal payment of $5 million at maturity. With an effective (market) interest rate of 5% for each six-month interval, the present value factors are:

   $$\textbf{20-period ordinary annuity at 5\%} = 12.46221$$
   $$\textbf{20-period single payment} = .37689$$

   Multiplying each factor by the corresponding cash flow gives the issue price as:

   $$
   \begin{aligned}
   \$\ 200,000 \times 12.46221 &= \$2,492,442 \\
   + \$5,000,000 \times \quad .37689 &= \underline{1,884,450} \\
   &\quad\ \ \$4,376,892
   \end{aligned}
   $$

   The bonds were thus issued at a discount of $623,108 (or $5,000,000 − $4,376,892).

2. **Compute the amount of interest expense on the bonds for 2005. Mallard Corporation uses the effective interest method for amortizing bond discounts and premiums.**

   Because the bonds were issued on July 1, 2005, only six months of interest needs to be recorded for the year. Interest expense is computed at the effective interest rate of 5%. This rate is multiplied by the amount borrowed (beginning book value) to get interest expense:

   $$\$4,376,892 \times 5\% = \$218,845 \textbf{ (rounded)}$$

Computed interest expense is more than the required $200,000 cash payment. The $18,845 difference represents amortization of the bond discount—that is, an increase to the book value of the bond. The year-end financial statements of Mallard Corporation would show the bond at $4,395,737 ($4,376,892 + $18,845).

3. **Mallard uses the indirect method of computing cash flows from operations on its cash flow statement. Indicate how much will be added to (or subtracted from) the 2005 accrual basis net income figure that is related to the bonds to obtain cash flows from operations.**

The accrual income figure contains interest expense of $218,845, but the cash interest payment is only $200,000. The additional interest expense of $18,845 does not represent an operating cash outflow for the year, and so it is added back to net income to arrive at cash flows from operations. Notice that this amount equals the discount amortization for the year.

4. **Assume that the market yield on the bonds had fallen to 9% by July 1, 2007 and that Mallard decided to retire the debt on that date either by purchasing the bonds on the open market or by exercising its 102% call option. Which method of debt retirement is the least expensive for Mallard?**

Under the terms of the call option, Mallard can retire the debt by paying bond holders 102% of par value or:

$$\$5,000,000 \times 1.02 = \$5,100,000$$

However, the current market value of the bonds at an annual yield of 9% is:

$$\$200,000 \times 11.23402 = \$2,246,804$$
$$+ \$5,000,000 \times \quad .49447 = \underline{2,472,350}$$
$$\underline{4,719,154}$$

The open-market purchase is the least expensive way for Mallard to retire its debt. (Notice that the present value factors used to compute the current market price are based on a 4.5% semiannual yield and 16 six-month periods to July 1, 2015.)

5. **Produce the journal entry that Mallard Corporation would record on July 1, 2007 when it retired the bonds through an open market purchase.**

Assume that all interest expense and cash interest payments have been recorded. Then the book value of the bonds on July 1, 2007 is $4,458,115, as shown in the amortization table.

	Period (Six-month Interval)	Liability at Start of Period	Effective Interest: 5% per Period	Coupon Rate: 4% of Par	Increase in Recorded Book Value	Liability at End of Period
7/1/05	0					$4,376,892
1/1/06	1	$4,376,892	$218,845	$200,000	$18,845	4,395,737
7/1/06	2	4,395,737	219,787	200,000	19,787	4,415,524
1/1/07	3	4,415,523	220,776	200,000	20,776	4,436,300
7/1/07	4	4,436,300	221,815	200,000	21,815	4,458,115

Based on our previous calculation, we find that Mallard would pay $4,719,154 to retire the bonds on that date, so the entry is:

DR	Bonds payable	$5,000,000	
DR	Loss on debt retirement	261,039	
	CR Discount on bonds		$ 541,885
	CR Cash		4,719,154

where $541,885 represents the remaining (unamortized) balance of the original issue discount ($5,000,000 face value minus $4,458,115 book value).

SELF-STUDY PROBLEM

SNAP-ON INC.

Exhibit 11.12 is taken from the 2002 Shareholder Report of Snap-On Inc., a manufacturer and marketer of high-quality professional automotive and industrial tools. The exhibit typifies the required disclosures for long-term debt, although Snap-On also devotes a portion of this footnote to a discussion of its short-term debt. The various categories of debt are identified and key characteristics of major debt instruments—such as covenants tied to financial statement ratios—are described. An enumeration of scheduled principal repayments over the ensuing five years is also provided. The intent of the disclosure is to provide data on future cash outflows and credit risk; these data help analysts and others generate cash flow forecasts.

EXHIBIT 11.12	Snap-On Inc.

2002 Short-term and Long-term Debt Footnote

Notes payable and long-term debt at the end of 2002 totaled $360.7 million, down $113.9 million from the $474.6 million reported at year-end 2001. Notes payable to banks under bank lines of credit totaled $22.3 million and $26.5 million at the end of 2002 and 2001. At the end of 2002, Snap-On had commercial paper outstanding denominated in U.S. dollars of $25.0 million and Japanese yen of $7.9 million compared to commercial paper outstanding denominated in U.S. dollars of $135.0 million and Japanese yen of $7.2 million at year-end 2001. Snap-On classified its outstanding commercial paper as long-term debt at year-end 2001 as it was Snap-On's intent, and it had the ability (supported by its long-term revolving credit facilities), to refinance this debt on a long-term basis. Snap-On's increased cash provided by operating activities in 2002 was used primarily to reduce commercial paper borrowings. The company currently anticipates that it will continue to have positive cash flow and debt reduction for the foreseeable future and, as a result, commercial paper borrowings at December 28, 2002, of $32.9 million are included in "Notes payable and current maturities of long-term debt" on the accompanying Consolidated Balance Sheets.

At December 28, 2002, Snap-On had $408 million of multi-currency revolving credit facilities that also serve to back its commercial paper programs, including a $200 million, 364-day revolving credit facility with a one-year term-out option that terminates on August 8, 2003. The term-out option allows Snap-On to elect to borrow under the credit facility for an additional year after the termination date. In addition, Snap-On has a five-year, $208 million revolving credit facility that terminates on August 20, 2005. At the end of 2002 and 2001, Snap-On was in compliance with all covenants of the revolving credit facilities and there were no borrowings under either revolving credit commitment. The most restrictive financial covenant requires that Snap-On maintain a total debt to total capital (defined as total debt plus shareholders' equity) ratio that does not exceed 60%. Snap-On's total debt to total capital ratio, computed as defined by the financial covenant, was 30.3% at December 28, 2002, and 38.0% at December 29, 2001. At December 28, 2002, Snap-On also had an unused committed $20 million bank line of credit that expires on August 1, 2003. At December 28, 2002, Snap-On had approximately $395 million of unused available debt capacity under the terms of its revolving credit facilities and committed bank line of credit.

Average commercial paper and bank notes outstanding were $189.6 million in 2002 and $389.2 million in 2001. The weighted-average interest rate on these instruments was 1.7% in 2002 and 4.3% in 2001. As of December 28, 2002, and December 29, 2001, commercial paper and bank notes outstanding had a weighted-average interest rate of 1.3% and 2.1%.

In August 2001, Snap-On issued $200 million of unsecured notes pursuant to a $300 million shelf registration statement filed with the Securities and Exchange Commission in 1994. In October 1995, Snap-On issued $100 million of unsecured notes to the public under this shelf registration. The August 2001 notes require semiannual interest payments at the rate of 6.25% and mature in their entirety on August 15, 2011. The October 1995 notes require semiannual interest payments at a rate of 6.625% and mature in their entirety on October 1, 2005. The proceeds from these issuances were used to repay a portion of Snap-On's outstanding commercial paper and for working capital and general corporate purposes.

Snap-On's long-term debt at year-end 2002 and 2001 consisted of the following:

(Amounts in millions)	2002	2001
Senior unsecured indebtedness	$300.0	$300.0
Borrowings under commercial paper programs	—	142.2
Other long-term debt	5.5	5.9
	305.5	448.1
Current maturities	(1.2)	(2.6)
Total long-term debt	$304.3	$445.5

The annual maturities of Snap-On's long-term debt due in the next five years are $1.2 million in 2003, $.5 million in 2004, and $100.2 million in 2005, with no maturities of long-term debt in 2006 and 2007.

1. **The first paragraph of the footnote indicates that "notes payable and long-term debt" totaled $360.7 million at the end of 2002. What are the individual components that make up this total amount?**

   The company's short-term and long-term debt at year-end 2002 consists of notes payable to banks ($22.3 million), commercial paper denominated in U.S. dollars ($25.0 million), commercial paper denominated in Japanese yen ($7.9 million), senior unsecured indebtedness ($300 million), and "other" long-term debt ($5.5 million). Add these amounts together and they total $360.7 million, an amount that includes $1.2 million in current maturities of long-term debt.

2. **Why did the company classify its commercial paper as long-term debt in 2001 but as short-term debt in 2002?**

   As 2001 ended, Snap-On was planning to replace the commercial paper loans with long-term debt in early 2002. So the company included commercial paper along with its other long-term debt to alert analysts and investors about the planned refinancing. Apparently, management changed its mind in 2002 and decided not to refinance the debt. Accordingly, the company's commercial paper is now shown as a short-term obligation.

> Commercial paper refers to short-term debt obligations with maturities ranging from 2 days to 270 days issued by banks, corporations (for example, Snap-On), and other borrowers to investors with temporarily idle cash.

3. **The third paragraph of the footnote discloses the "average" commercial paper and bank notes outstanding for 2002, along with the weighted-average interest rate on those instruments. Why might this information be of use to an analyst?**

   The average outstanding balance of these short-term obligations ($189.6 million) for 2002 is substantially above the year-end amount outstanding ($55.2 million as described in the answer to question 1). Snap-On apparently has seasonal borrowing needs, in which case the average outstanding balance is a better indicator of the company's true debt during the year. Since the weighted-average interest rate on commercial paper was 1.7% in 2002, the interest expense for these short-term obligations must have been about $3.2 million (or $189.6 average outstanding balance multiplied by the 1.7% weighted-average interest rate).

4. **How much cash did the company receive in 2001 when it issued the $200 million of "Senior unsecured debt"?**

   The footnote describes two occasions when Snap-On issued senior unsecured debt: $200 million issued in 2001 and another $100 million issued in 1995. The amounts described in the footnote represent the face value of the debt. But the footnote table reveals that the book value of the debt is also $300 million. Apparently, Snap-On issued the debt at face value and thus received $200 million of cash in 2001 (and $100 million in 1995).

5. **How much interest expense did the company record on the senior unsecured debt in 2002?**

   The 1995 senior unsecured debt has an interest rate of 6.625% and the entire $100 million principal amount was outstanding for 2002. So, Snap-On recorded interest expense in the amount of $6.625 million ($100 million multiplied by the 6.625% interest rate) for the 1995 debt. The same line of reasoning indicates that Snap-On recorded interest expense of $12.500 million ($200 million multiplied by the 6.25% interest rate) for the 2001 debt. Total interest expense for these two long-term obligations in 2002 would thus be $19.125 million.

6. **Does the company face any near-term cash flow problems as a consequence of its current borrowings?**

   The final paragraph of the footnote describes the company's scheduled debt payments for the next five years. Here we see that Snap-On is required to make a $100.2 million payment in 2005, so this could be a critical cash flow year.

7. **Is Snap-On close to violating any debt covenants?**

   Apparently not. The second paragraph of the footnote indicates the company was "in compliance" with all covenants of its revolving credit facilities. In fact, the most restrictive covenant requires Snap-On to maintain a total debt to capital ratio that does not exceed 60%. But the company seems to have considerable slack in this covenant because its actual total-debt-to-capital ratio is only 30.3%. There is no mention of covenants for the company's other debt instruments—and there surely are some—but they may be less restrictive than are those of its revolving credit line.

Akers Company sold bonds on July 1, 2005, with a face value of $100,000. These bonds are due in 10 years. The stated annual interest rate is 6% per year, payable semiannually on June 30 and December 31. These bonds were sold to yield 8%.

E11–1

Finding the issue price

Required:

How much did these bonds sell for on July 1, 2005?

www.prenhall.com/revsine

● Student Resources

☑ Template for solution

By July 1, 2006 the market yield on the Akers Company bonds described in E11–1 had risen to 10%.

E11–2

Market price following a change in interest rates

Required:

What was the market price of the bonds on July 1, 2006?

www.prenhall.com/revsine

● Student Resources

☑ Template for solution

On January 1, 2005, when the market interest rate was 14%, Luba Corporation issued bonds in the face amount of $500,000, with interest at 12% payable semiannually. The bonds mature on December 31, 2014.

E11–3

Finding the discount at issuance

Required:

Calculate the bond discount at issuance. How much of the discount should be amortized by the effective interest method on July 1, 2005?

On January 2, 2005 West Company issued 9% bonds in the amount of $500,000, which mature on December 31, 2014. The bonds were issued for $469,500 to yield 10%. Interest is payable annually on December 31. West uses the effective interest method of amortizing bond discounts.

E11–4

Balance sheet value of a bond

Required:

In its June 30, 2005 balance sheet, what net amount should West report as bonds payable?

On February 1, 2002 Davis Corporation issued 12%, $1,000,000 par, 10-year bonds for $1,117,000. Davis reacquired all of these bonds at 102% of par, plus accrued interest, on May 1, 2005 and retired them. The unamortized bond premium on that date was $78,000.

E11–5

Gain or loss at early retirement

Required:

Before income taxes, what was Davis's gain or loss on the bond retirement?

E11 – 6

Amortizing a premium

Webb Company has outstanding a 7% annual, 10-year, $100,000 face-value bond that was issued by the company several years ago. The bond was originally sold to yield 6% annual interest. Webb uses the effective interest rate method to amortize the bond premium. On June 30, 2005 the carrying amount of the outstanding bond was $105,000.

Required:

What amount of unamortized premium on the bond should Webb report in its June 30, 2006 balance sheet?

E11 – 7

Loss contingencies

Brower Corporation owns a manufacturing plant in the country of Oust. On December 31, 2005 the plant had a book value of $5,000,000 and an estimated fair market value of $8,000,000. The government of Oust has clearly indicated that it will expropriate the plant during the coming year and will reimburse Brower for only 40% of the plant's estimated fair market value.

Required:

What journal entry should Brower make on December 31, 2005 to record the intended expropriation?

E11 – 8

Bonds sold at par

On January 1, 2005 Buckingham Corporation issued $10 million of 8% coupon bonds. The bonds pay interest semiannually on June 30 and December 31, and they mature in 10 years. They were issued to yield a market interest rate of 8%.

Required:

Compute the issue price of the bonds on January 1, 2005. Why is there no discount or premium to record?

E11 – 9

Debt-for-equity swap

www.prenhall.com/revsine

● Student Resources

☑ Template for solution

On January 1, 2005 Tusk Corporation issued $100 million of 10% coupon bonds at par value. Interest is paid semiannually on June 30 and December 31 of each year. The bonds mature in 10 years. On January 1, 2008 the market yield on Tusk bonds is 14%.

Required:

1. What is the market value of the bonds on January 1, 2008?
2. Suppose Tusk retired the bonds on January 1, 2008 by exchanging common stock of equal value with bondholders. What journal entry would Tusk record to retire the bonds?

E11 – 10

Imputed interest

Greg Miller wants to buy a new automobile. The dealer has the exact car Greg wants, and has given Greg two payment options: (1) pay the full cash price of $19,326 today, or (2) pay only $2,000 down today and then make four more annual payments of $5,000 each beginning one year from today. Greg doesn't have the cash needed to pay the full price of the car, but he does have enough for the down payment. He can also obtain an automobile loan from his bank at 5% interest per year.

Required:

1. Verify that the imputed interest rate on the dealer's loan is 6%. That is, show that the present value of Greg's payments equals $19,326 (rounded to the nearest dollar) when discounted at 6%.
2. Which payment option should Greg accept?

E11 – 11

Zero coupon bonds

www.prenhall.com/revsine

● Student Resources

☑ Template for solution

Zero coupon bonds pay no interest—the only cash investors receive is the lump-sum principal payment at maturity. On January 1, 2005 The Ledge Inc. issued $250 million of zero coupon bonds at a market yield rate of 12%. The bonds mature in 20 years.

Required:

1. What was the January 1, 2005 issue price of these zero coupon bonds?
2. How much interest expense will The Ledge record on the bonds in 2005?

On January 1, 2005 3Way Energy issued $200 million of 15-year floating-rate debentures at par value. The debentures pay interest on June 30 and December 31 of each year. The floating interest rate is set equal to "LIBOR plus 6%" on January 1 of each year. The LIBOR was 6% when the bonds were issued and 8% on January 1, 2006.

E11 – 12

Floating-rate debt

Required:

1. How much cash interest did 3Way Energy pay on the debentures in 2005? How much will it pay in 2006?
2. How much interest expense did the company record on the debentures in 2005? How much will it record in 2006?

On January 1, 2004 Roland Inc. issued $125 million of 8% coupon bonds at par. The bonds pay interest semiannually on June 30 and December 31 of each year, and they mature in 15 years. On December 31, 2005 (one day before the next interest payment is made), the bonds are trading at a market yield of 12% plus accrued interest.

E11 – 13

Incentives for early debt retirement

www.prenhall.com/revsine

● Student Resources

☑ Template for solution

Required:

1. Suppose Roland Inc. repurchased the entire $125 million bonds for cash at the market price on December 31, 2005. Using a 40% corporate tax rate, how much of a gain or loss would the company record on this transaction?
2. Why might the company want to retire the debt early?

Wood Company and Willie Inc. form a joint venture—Woodly Partners—to manufacture and distribute agricultural pesticides. Wood and Willie each contribute $20 million cash and receive 50% of Woodly's common stock. Woodly then borrows $200 million from a consortium of banks and uses the money to build its manufacturing and distribution facilities. The loan is made on December 31, 2005 and is fully guaranteed by both Wood and Willie.

E11 – 14

Off-balance sheet debt

Required:

How much of the $200 million debt shows up on the December 31, 2005 balance sheet of Wood Company? Why?

McClelland Corporation agreed to purchase some landscaping equipment from Agri-Products for a cash price of $500,000. Before accepting delivery of the equipment, McClelland learned that the same equipment could be purchased from another dealer for $460,000. To avoid losing the sale, Agri-Products has offered McClelland a "no interest" payment plan—McClelland would pay $100,000 at delivery, $200,000 one year later, and the final $200,000 in two years.

E11 – 15

Non-interest-bearing loan

Required:

1. McClelland would usually pay annual interest of 9% on a loan of this type. What is the present value of the Agri-Products loan at the delivery date?
2. What journal entry would McClelland make if it accepts the deal and buys from Agri-Products?
3. What should McClelland do?

Required:

1. Which of the following qualifies as a hedged item?
   a. A company's work-in-process inventory of unfinished washers, dryers, and refrigerators.
   b. Credit card receivables at Sears, Roebuck and Company.
   c. Bushels of corn owned by the Farmers' Cooperative.
   d. Salaries payable to employees of Ford Motor Company.
   e. A three-year note issued by General Motors and payable in U.S. dollars.
   f. A three-year note issued by DaimlerChrysler and payable in Euros.

E11 – 16

Understanding GAAP hedges

2. Which of the following qualifies as a hedging instrument?

   a. An electricity futures contract purchased by Alliant Energy, an electrical power company.
   b. A crop insurance contract purchased by Farmers' Cooperative that pays the co-op for crop losses from drought or flood.
   c. An option to buy shares of common stock in Ford Motor Company.
   d. An option to sell shares of common stock in General Motors.
   e. A four-year lease for office space in downtown Toronto.

3. Which of the following qualifies as an eligible risk for hedge accounting?

   a. Alliant Energy's risk that summer demand for electricity may exceed the company's power generating capacity.
   b. Ford Motor Company's risk that not enough steel will be available in six months when the company must purchase steel to produce a new sports utility vehicle.
   c. The risk to American Express that its members won't pay their credit card bills.
   d. The risk to Farmers' Cooperative that corn mold will destroy its inventory of corn held in silos for sale next year.
   e. The possibility of changes in the exchange rate of U.S. dollars for Mexican pesos for Coca Cola Company, which has a major foreign investment in Mexico.

PROBLEMS/DISCUSSION QUESTIONS

P11 – 1

Bonds issued at a discount

www.prenhall.com/revsine

● Student Resources

☑ Template for solution

On July 1, 2005 McVay Corporation issued $15 million of 10-year bonds with a coupon interest rate of 8%. The bonds pay interest semiannually on June 30 and December 31 of each year. The market rate of interest on July 1, 2005 for bonds of this type was 10%. McVay closes its books on December 31.

Required:

1. At what price were the bonds issued?
2. Using the effective interest method, prepare an amortization schedule showing interest expense, discount or premium amortization, and bond carrying value for each of the first four semiannual interest payment periods.
3. Prepare journal entries to record the first four semiannual interest payments.
4. How should the bonds be shown on McVay's December 31, 2005 balance sheet, and on its December 31, 2006 balance sheet?

P11 – 2

Bonds issued at a premium

www.prenhall.com/revsine

● Student Resources

☑ Template for solution

On January 1, 2005 Fleetwood Inc. issued bonds with a face amount of $25 million and a coupon interest rate of 8%. The bonds mature in 10 years and pay interest semiannually on June 30 and December 31 of each year. The market rate of interest on January 1, 2005 for bonds of this type was 6%. Fleetwood closes its books on December 31.

Required:

1. At what price were the bonds issued?
2. Using the effective interest method, prepare an amortization schedule showing interest expense, amortization, and bond carrying value for each of the first four semiannual interest payment periods.
3. Prepare journal entries to record the first four semiannual interest payments.
4. How would the bonds be shown on Fleetwood's December 31, 2005 balance sheet, and on its December 31, 2006 balance sheet?

P11 – 3

Installment note and imputed interest

On January 1, 2005 Newell Manufacturing purchased a new drill press. The drill press had a cash purchase price of $6,340 but Newell decided instead to pay on an installment basis. The installment contract calls for four annual payments of $2,000 each beginning in one year. Newell was not required to make an initial downpayment for the drill press.

Required:

1. Verify that the imputed interest rate on the installment loan is 10%. That is, show that the present value of the payments Newell must make is $6,340 (rounded to the nearest dollar) when discounted at a 10% rate of interest.
2. What journal entry would Newell Manufacturing make on January 1, 2005 to record the drill press purchase?
3. How much interest expense would Newell record in 2005 for the installment loan? What would the loan balance be on January 1, 2006 after Newell made the first loan payment?
4. How much interest expense would Newell record in 2006 for the installment loan? What would the loan balance be on December 31, 2006—one day before Newell makes the second loan payment?

Cory Company needs to raise about $500,000 to finance the expansion of its office building. Three alternative loan arrangements are being considered:

- *Alternative A:* Issue a $500,000, 20-year bond with an interest rate of 10%.
- *Alternative B:* Issue a $700,000, 20-year bond with an interest rate of 6%.
- *Alternative C:* Issue a $400,000, 20-year bond with an interest rate of 12%.

Each bond pays interest annually. The market interest rate for bonds of this risk and duration is 9%, and the company needs to raise the money on January 1, 2005.

P11 – 4

Understanding the numbers

www.prenhall.com/revsine

● Student Resources

☑ Template for solution

Required:

1. What is the issue price of each bond?
2. How much cash would the company have to pay out in 2005 for each bond?
3. For each alternative, how much interest expense would be recorded in 2006 and in 2011?
4. For each alternative, how much interest expense would Cory Company record over the entire 20-year life of the loan?
5. For each alternative, how much cash would Cory Company pay to bondholders over the entire 20-year life of the loan?
6. If Cory Company's marginal tax rate is 40%, which alternative do you recommend? Why?

On July 1, 2005 Stan Getz, Inc. bought call option contracts for 500 shares of Selmer Manufacturing common stock. The contracts cost $200, expire on September 15th, and have an exercise price of $40 per share. The market price of Selmer's stock that day was also $40 a share. On July 31, 2005 Selmer shares were trading at $38 a share and the fair value of the option contracts was $125—that is, Getz could buy the identical $40 strike price contracts on July 31 for $125. On August 31, 2005 the market price of Selmer stock was $44 a share and the fair value of the options contracts was $2,075.

P11 – 5

Call options as investments

Required:

1. Prepare the journal entry to record Getz's purchase of call option contracts on July 1, 2005.
2. Prepare the journal entry to record the change in fair value of the option contracts on July 31, 2005.
3. Prepare the journal entry to record the change in fair value of the option contracts on August 31, 2005.
4. Why are the option contracts worth so much more on August 31 ($2,075) than they were worth on July 31 ($125)?
5. What entry would Getz make to record exercising the options on September 15, 2005 when Selmer's shares were trading at $46?
6. Suppose instead that Getz allowed the option contracts to expire on September 15, 2005 without exercising them. What entry would Getz then make?

On March 1, 2005 Kenton Company bought put option contracts for 500 shares of Rugolo Manufacturing common stock. The contracts cost $300, expire on May 15th, and have an exercise price of $50 per share. The market price of Rugolo's stock that day was also $50 a share. On March 31, 2005 Rugolo shares were trading at $52 a share and the fair value of the option contracts was $200—that is, Kenton could buy the identical $50 strike price contracts on March 31 for $200. On April 30, 2005 the market price of Rugolo stock was $46 a share and the fair value of the options contracts was $2,100.

P11 – 6

Put options as investments

Required:

1. Prepare the journal entry to record Kenton's purchase of put option contracts on March 1, 2005.
2. Prepare the journal entry to record the change in fair value of the option contracts on March 31, 2005.
3. Prepare the journal entry to record the change in fair value of the option contracts on April 30, 2005.
4. Why are the option contracts worth so much more on April 30 ($2,100) than they were worth on March 31 ($200)?
5. What entry would Kenton make to record exercising the options on May 15, 2005 when Rugolo's shares were trading at $42?
6. Suppose instead that Kenton allowed the option contracts to expire on May 15, 2005 without exercising them. What entry would Kenton then make?

P11 – 7

Early debt retirement

www.prenhall.com/revsine

● Student Resources

☑ Template for solution

On January 1, 2005 Tango-In-The-Night, Inc. issued $75 million of bonds with a coupon interest rate of 9%. The bonds mature in 10 years and pay interest semiannually on June 30 and December 31 of each year. The market rate of interest on January 1, 2005 for bonds of this type was 11%. The company closes its books on December 31.

Required:

1. At what price were the bonds issued?
2. What is the book value of the bonds on January 1, 2007?
3. On January 1, 2007 the market interest rate for bonds of this type is 10%. What is the market value of the bonds on this date?
4. Suppose the bonds were repurchased for cash on January 1, 2007 at the market price. If you ignore taxes, what journal entry would the company make to record the debt retirement?

P11 – 8

Partial debt retirement

www.prenhall.com/revsine

● Student Resources

☑ Template for solution

On July 1, 2006 Mirage Company issued $250 million of bonds with a coupon interest rate of 8.5%. The bonds mature in 10 years and pay interest semiannually on June 30 and December 31 of each year. The market rate of interest on July 1, 2006 for bonds of this risk class was 7%. Mirage closes its books on December 31.

Required:

1. At what price were the bonds issued?
2. Using the effective interest method, prepare an amortization schedule showing interest expense, amortization, and bond carrying value for each of the first four semiannual payment periods.
3. Prepare journal entries to record the first four semiannual interest payments and related interest accruals.
4. On July 1, 2008 the market interest rate for bonds of this risk class is 8.0%. What is the market value of the bonds on this date?
5. Suppose 50% of the bonds were repurchased for cash on July 1, 2008 at the market price. If you ignore taxes, what journal entry would the company make to record this partial retirement?

P11 – 9

Chalk Hill: Interest-rate swap as a speculative investment

Exhibit 11.11 describes Chalk Hill's use of an interest-rate swap to hedge its cash flow exposure to interest rate risk from variable rate debt. The journal entries shown in the exhibit illustrate how special "hedge accounting" rules apply to the swap. Suppose instead that the swap *did not qualify* for special hedge accounting—but that all other aspects of the transaction remain as described in the exhibit. Prepare the journal entries needed to account for the variable-rate debt and swap transaction for January 1, 2005 through December 31, 2007.

P11 – 10

Hedging fuel costs

AIRLINES SHOW DISPARITY IN HEDGING FOR FUEL COSTS

Jet fuel, now more than twice as expensive as a year ago, is emerging as a major factor in the survival and bankruptcy for airlines as several carriers, including some of the weakest, find themselves with few protective price hedges in place.

Airlines typically hedge by locking in fuel at prearranged prices or buying securities that rise in value when oil climbs. Yet the industry finds itself with wide disparity in hedging, with some airlines fully hedged at low prices, and others completely exposed to huge price increases.

UAL Corp.'s United Airlines, operating under bankruptcy-court protection, has no hedges in place this year. That will likely cost the nation's second-largest airline more than $100 million in added fuel costs during the current quarter alone. . . .

By contrast, Southwest Airlines, the only profitable major carrier, hedged 100% of its jet-fuel needs for the current quarter at prices that are the equivalent of $23 a barrel for crude oil, compared with recent crude-oil prices hovering around $35 a barrel. . . . Continental Airlines has 95% of its fuel for the quarter hedged . . . and AMR Corp.'s American Airlines has 40% hedged. . . .

United says bankruptcy hurt it in the hedging game. The carrier had some hedges in place at the time of its bankruptcy filing in December, but the filing put the airline in default of those hedges so they had to be liquidated. . . .

Good credit, on the other hand, helps Southwest because many hedges revolve around futures contracts, and those on the other side of the contract may be gambling on the credit of the airlines. "If you're not a good credit then you may not be able to find a counterparty who's willing to enter into a hedging contract with you," Southwest's chief financial officer, Gary Kelly, says. . . .

Hedging can be a tricky business, and costly to an airline if fuel buyers guess wrong. There is no futures market for jet fuel, but airlines can buy contracts that lock in set prices of crude and heating oil, whose price moves most closely in line with that of jet fuel.

Source: Wall Street Journal (March 10, 2003).

Required:

1. Why do most airlines hedge at least a portion of their jet-fuel costs? What risk are the airlines trying to reduce?
2. Suppose the futures contracts used by Southwest Airlines to hedge jet-fuel costs satisfy all of the GAAP requirements for special hedge accounting. What type of hedge accounting (fair value or cash flow) would apply to these contracts? Why?
3. Can the futures contracts used by American Airlines to hedge jet-fuel costs satisfy the GAAP requirements for special hedge accounting? Why or why not?

Information taken from a Sears, Roebuck and Company annual report is shown below.

Sears: Reading the financials

Required:

1. How much interest expense did the company record during Year 2 on the 7% debentures? How much of the original issue discount was amortized during Year 2?
2. How much interest expense did the company record during Year 2 on the zero coupon bonds?
3. Suppose that interest payments on the participating mortgages are made on December 31 of each year. What journal entry did the company make in Year 2 to recognize interest expense on this debt?
4. How much cash interest did the company pay out during Year 2 on the 7% debentures and the zero coupon bonds?

	December 31	
Long-Term Debt (*$ in millions*)	Year 2	Year 1
7% Debentures, $300 million face value, due Year 11, effective rate $14.6%	$ 188.6	$ 182.7
Zero coupon bonds, $500 million face value, due Year 8, effective rate 12.0%	267.9	239.2
Participating mortgages, $850 million face value, due Year 5, effective rate 8.7%, collateralized by Sears Tower and related properties	834.5	833.9
Various other long-term debt	12,444.2	16,329.2
Total long-term debt	$13,735.2	$17,585.0

P11 – 12

Reading the financials

Information taken from the Mead Corporation annual report is shown below.

Required:

1. How much interest expense did the company record during 1999 on the $8\frac{1}{8}\%$ debentures? How much of the original issue discount was amortized during 1999?
2. How much interest expense did the company record during 1999 on the 6.60% notes? How much of the original issue discount was amortized during 1999?
3. What is the "weighted-average" effective interest rate on long-term debt at December 31, 1999?
4. If Mead calls the $8\frac{1}{8}\%$ debentures at the beginning of 2003, how much cash will the company pay to debt holders?
5. If debt holders "put" the 6.84% debentures back to the company, how much cash will Mead pay out?

Long-Term Debt December 31 ($ in millions)	1999	1998
Capital lease obligations	$ 287.4	$ 288.3
Variable-rate Industrial Development Revenue Bonds, due from 2001 through 2023, average effective rate 3.2%	165.4	165.4
$8\frac{1}{8}\%$ debentures, face amount of $150.0, due 2023 (effective rate 8.4%)	148.0	147.9
$7\frac{1}{8}\%$ debentures, face amount of $150.0, due 2025 (effective rate 7.4%)	147.3	147.2
7.35% debentures, face amount of $150.0, due 2017 (effective rate 7.4%)	148.6	148.5
6.84% debentures, face amount of $150.0, due 2037 (effective rate 7.0%)	148.4	148.2
7.55% debentures, face amount of $150.0, due 2047 (effective rate 7.7%)	143.7	143.6
6.60% notes, face amount of $100.0, due 2002 (effective rate 6.9%)	99.3	99.0
Medium-term notes, 7.3% to 9.8%, face amount of $78.5, due from 2000 through 2020 (effective rate 10.0%)	76.8	75.9
Other	3.9	11.3
	1,368.8	1,375.3
Less current portion	35.1	7.9
	$1,333.7	$1,367.4

The $8\frac{1}{8}\%$ and $7\frac{1}{8}\%$ debentures are callable by the company at approximately 103% beginning in 2003. The 6.84% debentures can be put to the company at par value in 2007. Maturities of long-term debt for the next five years are $35.1 million in 2000, $12.6 million in 2001, $135.3 million in 2002, $.7 million in 2003, and $6.7 million in 2004.

P11 – 13

Hedging

The following excerpts were taken from a recent annual report of Quaker Oats Company:

FOREIGN CURRENCY SWAPS

[Several years ago] the Company swapped $15.0 million of long-term debt for 27.9 million in deutsche mark (DM) denominated long-term debt, effectively hedging part of the German net investment. . . . Due to the sale of the European pet food business last year, the net investment in Germany was reduced to the point where the DM swap was no longer effective as a net investment hedge, requiring any subsequent revaluation adjustments to be charged or credited to the consolidated income statement. To offset this charge or credit, the Company entered into a foreign exchange forward contract and the net effect on the consolidated income statements . . . was not material. . . .

COMMODITY OPTIONS AND FUTURES

The Company uses commodity options and futures contracts to reduce its exposure to commodity price changes. The Company regularly hedges purchases of oats, corn, corn sweetener, wheat, coffee beans, and orange juice concentrate. Of the $2.81 billion in cost of goods sold, approximately $275 million to $325 million is in commodities that may be hedged. The Company's strategy is typically to hedge certain production requirements for various periods up to 12 months. As of December 31, . . . approximately 32% . . . of hedgeable production requirements for the next 12 months were hedged. . . .

INTEREST RATE HEDGES

The Company actively monitors its interest rate exposure. Last year the Company entered into interest rate swap agreements with a notional value of $150.0 million. The swap agreements were used to hedge fixed interest rate risk related to anticipated issuance of long-term debt. The swap agreements were subsequently terminated at a cost of $11.9 million as long-term debt was issued. Included in the consolidated balance sheets as of December 31, [this year and last year] were $8.9 million and $10.8 million, respectively, of prepaid interest expense as settlement of all the interest rate swap agreements. . . . [Two years ago] the Company entered into interest rate cap agreements with a notional value of $600.0 million to hedge floating interest rate risk. . . .

Required:

1. What did Quaker accomplish by swapping $15.0 million of its long-term debt for 27.9 million in deutsche mark (DM) denominated long-term debt?
2. Why was the DM swap "no longer effective" after Quaker sold its European pet food business?
3. What is a foreign exchange forward contract, and how can it be used to hedge a company's foreign currency exposure?
4. What are commodity options and futures contracts, and how do they reduce Quaker's exposure to commodity price changes?
5. What is an interest-rate swap, and how can it reduce a company's exposure to interest-rate risk?
6. What is an interest-rate cap, and how is it used to reduce a company's exposure to interest-rate changes?

On January 1, 2005 Merrill Corporation issued $2 million of par value 10-year bonds. The bonds pay interest semiannually on January 1 and July 1 at an annual rate of 10% and are callable at 102% of par. The bonds were issued to yield 8% annually.

P11 – 14

Callable bonds

www.prenhall.com/revsine

● Student Resources
☑ Template for solution

Required:

1. Compute the issue price of the bonds.
2. Compute the amount of interest expense on the bonds for 2005, assuming the effective interest method is used.
3. Merrill uses the *indirect method* of computing cash flows from operations on its cash flow statement (see Chapter 4). How much will be added to or subtracted from reported net income in 2005 for these bonds to obtain cash flows from operations?
4. On January 1, 2006 the market yield on the bonds increased to 9%, and Merrill decided to retire the debt early. Indicate how much Merrill would save by exercising the call option rather than by purchasing the debt in the open market.
5. What entry would Merrill make on January 1, 2006 to record the bond retirement, assuming it exercises the call option?

Clovis Company recently issued $500,000 (face value) bonds to finance a new construction project. The company's chief accountant prepared the following bond amortization schedule:

P11 – 15

Working backward from an amortization table

Date	Interest Expense	Semiannual Payment	Premium Amortization	Net Liability
7/1/05				$540,554
12/31/05	$21,622	$25,000	$(3,378)	537,176
6/30/06	21,487	25,000	(3,513)	533,663
12/31/06	21,347	25,000	(3,653)	530,010
6/30/07	21,200	25,000	(3,800)	526,210
12/31/07	21,048	25,000	(3,952)	522,258
6/30/08	20,890	25,000	(4,110)	518,148
12/31/08	20,726	25,000	(4,274)	513,874
6/30/09	20,555	25,000	(4,445)	509,429
12/31/09	20,377	25,000	(4,623)	504,806
6/30/10	20,194	25,000	(4,806)	500,000

Required:

1. Compute the discount or premium on the sale of the bonds, the semiannual coupon interest rate, and the semiannual effective interest rate.
2. The company's vice president of finance wants any discount (or premium) at issuance of the bonds to be recorded immediately as a loss (or gain) at the issue date. Do you agree with this approach? Why or why not?
3. On December 31, 2007 the net carrying value of the bonds is $522,258. In present value terms, what does this amount represent?
4. Suppose market interest rates were 6% semiannually on January 1, 2008, or 12.36% annually. (This 12.36% annual rate of interest is equal to the 6% semiannual rate, compounded: 0.1236 = [1.06 × 1.06] − 1.) What is the market price of the bond on that date? Is the company better off or worse off because of the interest-rate change? Explain.

How notes affect cash flows

On January 1, 2005 Prism Corporation issued $5 million of two-year, 10% per year notes. The market interest rate at issuance was 14%. Interest is payable semiannually on June 30 and December 31 of each year.

Required:

1. How much cash did the company receive by issuing the notes?
2. Prepare an amortization schedule showing interest expense, semiannual cash payments, amortization, and carrying value of the notes at each payment date to maturity.
3. Prepare journal entries to record issuance of notes; accrual and payment of interest on December 31, 2005; and payment of face value on maturity.
4. Describe how each of the following affects the company's cash flow statement: issuance of notes; payment of interest on December 31, 2005; and payment of face value on maturity.
5. Suppose the annual market interest rate falls to 10% on December 31, 2005. What is the market price of the notes on that date? Is the company better off or worse off because of the change in interest rates? Explain.

Serial bonds

On January 1, 2005 MyKoo Corporation issued $1 million in five-year, 5% serial bonds to be repaid in the amount of $200,000 on January 1 of 2006, 2007, 2008, 2009, and 2010. Interest on the unpaid balance of the bonds is due at the end of each year. The bonds were sold to yield 6%.

Required:

1. Prepare a schedule showing the computation of the total amount received from the issuance of the serial bonds.
2. Prepare a schedule of amortization of the bond discount through 2010 using the effective interest-rate method.

Discount and premium amortization

The following information appeared in the 1999 annual report of Rumours, Inc.:

LONG-TERM DEBT

$10 million 10% coupon bonds issued on January 1, 1996 and due on December 31, 2000. The prevailing market interest rate on January 1, 1996 was 12%, and the bonds pay interest on June 30 and December 31 of each year.

$10 million 10% coupon bonds issued January 1, 1997 and due on December 31, 2001. The prevailing market interest rate on January 1, 1997 was 8%, and the bonds pay interest on June 30 and December 31 of each year.

Required:

1. The carrying value of each bond is shown in the following (incomplete) table. Calculate the missing values.

	Carrying Value	
	December 31, 1998	December 31, 1999
10% bonds due in 2000	$9,653,550	?
10% bonds due in 2001	?	$10,362,950

2. How much interest expense did Rumours record in 1999 on the bond due in 2000?
3. How much interest expense did Rumours record in 1999 on the bond due in 2001?

The following information appeared in the annual reports of Apparel America, Borden, Inc., and Exxon Corporation.

P11 – 19

Loss contingencies

APPAREL AMERICA, INC.

In December 1994 the Company entered into an agreement to pay $460,000 to a former executive in settlement of certain litigation. According to the terms of the agreement, an initial payment of $150,000 was made in December 1994, with the balance payable in five semiannual installments of $50,000 commencing June 30, 1995 and a final payment of $60,000 on December 31, 1997. The settlement has been discounted at an annual effective interest rate of 9% to reflect its present value at July 31, 1996. [Excerpt from the company's 1996 annual report.]

BORDEN, INC.

The Company and Combined Companies, like others in similar businesses, is subject to extensive Federal, state and local environmental laws and regulations. Although Company and Combined Companies environmental policies and practices are designed to ensure compliance with these laws and regulations, future developments and increasingly stringent regulation could require the Company and Combined Companies to make additional unforeseen environmental expenditures.

Accruals for environmental matters are recorded when it is probable that a liability has been incurred and the amount of the liability can be reasonably estimated. Environmental accruals are routinely reviewed on an interim basis as events and developments warrant and are subjected to a comprehensive review annually during the fiscal fourth quarter. The Company and the Combined Companies have each accrued approximately $26 million (including those costs related to legal proceedings) at December 31, 2000 and 1999, for probable environmental remediation and restoration liabilities. This is management's best estimate of these liabilities. Based on currently available information and analysis, the Company believes that it is reasonably possible that costs associated with such liabilities may exceed current reserves by amounts that may prove insignificant, or by amounts, in the aggregate, of up to approximately $16 million. [Excerpt from the company's 2000 annual report.]

EXXON CORPORATION

A number of lawsuits, including class actions, have been brought in various courts against Exxon Corporation and certain of its subsidiaries relating to the release of crude oil from the tanker Exxon Valdez in 1989. Most of these lawsuits seek unspecified compensatory and punitive damages; several lawsuits seek damages in varying specified amounts. Certain of the lawsuits seek injunctive relief. The claims of many individuals have been dismissed or settled. Most of the remaining actions are scheduled for trial in federal court commencing May 2, 1994. Other actions will likely be tried in state court later in 1994. The cost to the corporation from these lawsuits is not possible to predict; however, it is believed that the final outcome will not have a materially adverse effect upon the corporation's operations or financial condition. [Excerpt from the company's 1993 annual report.]

Required:

1. What is a loss contingency, and why is it disclosed in financial statements? Which of the preceding examples represents a loss contingency?
2. What was the December 1994 present value of Apparel America's settlement with its former executive? What is the July 31, 1996 present value, and where is it shown in the financial statements?

3. Borden has a $26 million liability on its 2000 balance sheet for "probable environmental remediation and restoration." But the company says actual remediation and restoration costs could be up to $16 million more than this amount. Why doesn't Borden's balance sheet liability include the additional $16 million?

4. Why doesn't Exxon report a dollar amount for its litigation case like the one reported by Apparel America?

5. Does the lack of a specific dollar amount in Exxon's case mean that stock analysts will just ignore the litigation when valuing the company? Why or why not?

6. In a subsequent annual report, Exxon (now ExxonMobile) had more to say about the Exxon Valdez incident.

> [O]n September 24, 1996, the United States District Court for the District of Alaska entered a judgment in the amount of $5.058 billion. The District Court awarded approximately $19.6 million in compensatory damages to fisher plaintiffs, $38 million in prejudgment interest on the compensatory damages, and $5 billion in punitive damages. . . . The District Court stayed execution on the judgment pending appeal. . . . ExxonMobile appealed the judgment. On November 7, 2001, the United States Court of Appeals for the Ninth Circuit vacated the punitive damage award as being excessive under the Constitution and remanded the case to the District Court for it to determine the amount of the punitive damage award. . . . On December 6, 2002, the District Court reduced the punitive damages from $5 billion to $4 billion. . . . [Excerpt from the company's 2002 annual report.]

Based on the information provided, when did Exxon first report a balance sheet liability for the Exxon Valdez litigation? What was the amount of that liability?

P11 – 20

Floating-rate debt

On January 1, 2005 Nicks Corporation issued $250 million of floating-rate debt. The debt carries a contractual interest rate of "LIBOR plus 5.5%" and this rate is reset annually on January 1 of each year. The LIBOR rates on January 1, 2005, January 1, 2006, and January 1, 2007 were 6.5%, 7.0%, and 5.5%, respectively.

Required:

1. Prepare a journal entry to record the issuance of the bonds on January 1, 2005 at par. What was the effective (or market) interest rate when the bonds were issued?

2. Prepare a journal entry to record interest expense for 2005, 2006, and 2007. Assume that interest is paid annually on December 31.

3. What is the market value of the debt at December 31, 2007 assuming there has been no change in the credit risk of Nicks Corporation.

P11 – 21

Unconditional purchase obligations

The following information appeared in the 2002 annual report of Lyondell Petrochemical Company, a manufacturer of petrochemicals and refined petroleum products such as gasoline, heating oil, jet fuel, aromatics, and lubricants:

> The Company is party to various unconditional purchase obligation contracts as a purchaser for products and services, principally for steam and power. At December 31, 2002, future minimum payments under these contracts with noncancelable contract terms in excess of one year and fixed minimum payments were as follows ($ in millions):
>
> | | |
> |---|---:|
> | 2003 | $ 164 |
> | 2004 | 168 |
> | 2005 | 169 |
> | 2006 | 157 |
> | 2007 | 151 |
> | Thereafter | 1,749 |
> | **Total minimum payments** | **$2,558** |

Required:

1. Suppose the company was obligated to purchase $349.8 million per year in 2008 and each of the next four years for a total of $1,749. If Lyondell's normal rate of interest for a 10-year loan is 8%, what is the present value of the company's purchase commitments?

2. The company's 2002 balance sheet shows long-term debt of $3,926 million and shareholders' equity of $1,179 million. The unconditional purchase obligation is not shown on the balance sheet. What impact would including the present value of unconditional purchase obligations as part of long-term debt have on the company's 2002 ratio of long-term debt to shareholders' equity?

3. Why are unconditional purchase obligations an "off-balance sheet" liability? Why might some companies prefer to keep the purchase commitment off the balance sheet?

On January 1, 1995 Chain Corporation issued $5 million of 7% coupon bonds at par. The bonds mature in 20 years and pay interest semiannually on June 30 and December 31 of each year. On December 31, 2005 the market interest rate for bonds of similar risk was 14%, and the market value of Chain Corporation bonds (after the December 31 interest payment) was $3,146,052.

Although the company's books are not yet closed for the year, a preliminary estimate shows net income to be $500,000. This amount is substantially below the $3 million management had expected the company to earn. The company has long-term debt totaling $7.5 million (including the $5 million bond issue) and shareholders' equity of $12.5 million (including the $500,000 of estimated net income). This means the company's long-term debt-to-equity ratio is 60%.

Unfortunately, a covenant in one of the company's loan agreements requires a long-term debt-to-equity ratio of 55% or less. Violating this covenant gives lenders the right to demand immediate repayment of the loan principal. Worse yet, a "cross default" provision in the $5 million bond makes it immediately due and payable if the company violates any of its lending agreements.

Since the company does not have the cash needed to repurchase the bonds, management is considering a debt-for-debt exchange in which the outstanding 7% bonds would be replaced by new 14% bonds with a face amount of $3.2 million. The interest rate on the new bonds is equal to the market interest rate.

P11 – 22

Debt-for-debt swaps

Required:

1. Prepare a journal entry to record the swap on December 31, 2005. (Any gain or loss to the company would be taxed at 35%, and the tax should be included in your entry.)
2. What would the company's debt-to-equity ratio be after the swap?
3. What impact would the transaction have on net income for the year?
4. How else could management have avoided violation of the loan covenant?

The following information was taken from the financial statements of ALZA Corporation.

P11 – 23

Zero coupon bonds

NOTE 6: BORROWINGS

On July 28, 2000, ALZA completed a private offering of the 3% Zero Coupon Convertible Subordinated Debentures which were issued at a price of $551.26 per $1,000 principal amount at maturity. At December 29, 2002, the outstanding 3% Debentures had a total principal amount at maturity of $1.0 billion with a yield to maturity of 3% per annum, computed on a semiannual bond equivalent basis. . . . At December 29, 2002 the fair value based on quoted market value of the 3% Debentures was $813 million. . . .

Required:

1. ALZA issued zero coupon debentures with a total maturity value of $1.0 billion at a price of $551.26 per $1,000 principal amount at maturity. How much cash did the company receive when it issued these debentures?
2. The debentures mature in twenty years from the date of issuance, but no interest payments are made until maturity. Show that the issue price of $551.26 gives investors a yield to maturity of 3%.
3. Suppose the debentures were issued on January 1, 2000 instead of July 28, 2000. Reproduce the journal entries ALZA would record in 2000 for the debentures. For each *cash entry*, indicate whether the cash increase or decrease represents an operating, investing, or financing activity.
4. Explain why the debentures have a market value of $813 million at the end of 2002, almost $300 million more than the 2000 issue price.

P11 – 24

Comprehensive problem on bond premium

www.prenhall.com/revsine

● Student Resources

✔ Template for solution

On July 1, 2005 LekTech Corporation issued $20 million of 12%, 20-year bonds. Interest on the bonds is paid semiannually on December 31 and June 30 of each year, and the bonds were issued at a market interest rate of 8%.

Required:

1. Compute the issue price of the bonds on July 1, 2005.
2. Prepare an amortization schedule that shows interest expense, premium or discount amortization, bond carrying value, and cash interest payment for each interest payment period through December 31, 2010.
3. Prepare the journal entries to record all interest expense and all cash interest payments for 2006.
4. A new employee in the accounting group at LekTech has asked you to explain why interest expense on the bond changes each year. Write a two-paragraph memo that helps the employee understand interest recognition for this bond.
5. LekTech used the proceeds of the bond to construct a new manufacturing facility near Waterloo, Iowa. The company will make taillight lenses for tractors manufactured by Deere & Company at its Waterloo plant. In fact, Deere has signed a letter guaranteeing payment of the LekTech bonds. How is the guarantee shown in Deere's financial statements?
6. On January 1, 2011 the company exercised a call provision in the debenture agreement and redeemed 40% of the bonds at 105% of par. What journal entry did the company make to record this partial redemption?
7. The market yield for the bonds on January 1, 2011 was 10%. How much less did the company pay to retire bonds using the call provision than it would have paid using an open market purchase?

P11 – 25

Hedging a purchase commitment (TL)

Silverado Inc. buys titanium from a supplier who requires a six-month firm commitment on all purchases. On January 1, 2005 Silverado signs a contract with the supplier to purchase 10,000 pounds of titanium at the current forward rate of $310 per pound with settlement on June 30, 2005. However, Silverado wants to actually pay the June 30 market price for titanium. To achieve this goal, the company enters into a forward contract to sell 10,000 pounds of titanium at the current forward price of $310 per unit. The firm commitment contract and the forward contract both have zero value at inception. Titanium spot prices and the contract fair values are:

	Spot Price	Forward Price (June 30)	Contract Fair Value	
			Forward	Firm Commitment
January 1, 2005	$300	$310	0	0
March 31, 2005	292	297	$128,079	($128,079)
June 30, 2005	285	n.a.	250,000	(250,000)

Required:

1. Why did Silverado hedge its firm commitment with the supplier? After the fact, was it a good idea to do so?
2. What journal entries are made when the two contracts are signed on January 1, 2005?
3. Silverado designates the forward contract as a fair value hedge of its future titanium purchase. What journal entries are made on March 31, 2005?
4. What journal entries are made on June 30, 2005 when the contracts are settled and Silverado pays for the titanium?

P11 – 26

Hedging a planned sale (TL)

Newton Grains plans to sell 100,000 bushels of corn from its current inventory in March 2006. The company paid $1 million for the corn during the fall 2005 harvest season. On October 1, 2005 Newton writes a forward contract to sell 100,000 bushels of corn on March 15, 2006 for $1,100,000. The forward contract has zero value at inception. On December 31, 2005 the March forward price for corn is $1,050,000 and the forward contract has a fair value of $95,000. On March 15, 2006 Newton sells the corn for $1,075,000 and settles the forward contract (now valued at $25,000).

Required:

1. Why did Newton hedge its planned sale of corn? Was it a good idea to do so?
2. Newton designates the forward contract as a cash flow hedge of its exposure to corn price fluctuations. What journal entries are made when the forward contract is signed on October 1, 2005?
3. What journal entries are made on December 31, 2005?
4. What journal entries are made on March 15, 2006 when the forward contract is settled and Newton sells the corn?
5. How would your original journal entries change if the forward contract covered only 50,000 bushels of corn? (Contract fair values would then have been $47,500 on December 31, 2005 and $12,500 on March 15, 2006.)

Basie Business Forms borrowed $5 million on July 1, 2005 from First Kansas City Bank. The loan required annual interest payments at the LIBOR rate, reset annually each June 30. The loan principal is due in five years. The LIBOR rate for the first year is 6.0%.

Basie decided to swap its variable-interest payments for fixed-interest payments of 6.0%. Basie will pay 6.0% interest to the swap counterparty—Quincy Bank & Trust—and receive LIBOR payments based on a $5 million notional amount for the entire five-year term of the original loan. The swap has no value at its inception on July 1, 2005.

Basie designates the swap as a hedge of its cash flow exposure to interest rate risk on its variable-rate debt. The hedge is fully effective because the key terms of the loan and swap are identical. The variable rate was reset to 6.25% on June 30, 2006 and to 5.75% on June 30, 2007. Basie uses a June 30 fiscal year-end and records interest expense annually.

P11 – 27

Interest-rate swap as a cash flow hedge

Required:

1. How much is the net cash settlement that Basie will pay to (or receive from) Quincy Bank & Trust on July 1, 2006? On July 1, 2007?
2. How much cash will Basie pay to First Kansas City Bank on July 1, 2006? On July 1, 2007?
3. On June 30, 2006 the swap had a fair value of $40,000 based on dealer quotes. Prepare journal entries to record Basie's cash interest payments and receipts, and interest expense for the year ended June 30, 2006.
4. On June 30, 2007 the swap had a fair value of ($28,000), a negative amount. Prepare journal entries to record Basie's cash interest payments and receipts, and interest expense for the year ended June 30, 2007.

On January 1, 2005 Four Brothers Manufacturing borrowed $10 million from Guiffrie Bank by signing a three-year 8.0% fixed-rate note. The note calls for interest to be paid annually on December 31. The company then entered into an interest-rate swap agreement with Herman Bank. The agreement is that Four Brothers will receive from Herman a fixed-rate interest payment of 8.0% based on a $10 million notional amount each December 31 for three years. Four Brothers will pay Herman a variable LIBOR rate reset every December 31. The LIBOR rate for the first year is 8.0%.

Four Brothers designates the swap as a hedge of its fair value exposure to interest-rate risk on its fixed-rate note. The hedge is fully effective because the key terms of the note and swap are identical. The variable rate was reset to 8.25% on December 31, 2005 and to 7.75% on December 31, 2006. Four Brothers uses a December 31 year-end and records interest expense annually.

P11 – 28

Interest-rate swap as a fair value hedge

Required:

1. How much is the net cash settlement that Four Brothers will pay to (or receive from) Herman Bank on December 31, 2005? On December 31, 2006?
2. How much cash will Four Brothers pay to Guiffrie Bank December 31, 2005? On December 31, 2006?
3. On December 31, 2005 the swap had a fair value of ($45,000), a negative amount, and the fair value of the $10 million note was $9,955,000. Prepare journal entries to record Four Brothers' cash interest payments and receipts, and interest expense for the year ended December 31, 2005.
4. On December 31, 2006 the swap had a fair value of $23,000, and the fair value of the $10 million note was $10,023,000. Prepare journal entries to record Four Brothers' cash interest payments and receipts, and interest expense for the year ended December 31, 2006.

P11 – 29

Hedge effectiveness

Recall the Rombaurer Metals example described in the chapter: On October 5, 2005 Rombaurer has 10 million pounds of copper inventory on hand at an average cost of $0.65 a pound. The spot price for copper is $0.90 a pound. Instead of selling copper now, Rombaurer decides to hold on to the inventory until February 2006 when management believes the price will return to a normal level of $0.95 a pound. To hedge its position, Rombaurer sells futures contracts at $0.95 for February delivery. Spot and futures prices over the next several months are as follows:

	COMEX Copper Prices	
	Spot Price	February 2006 Futures Price
October 5, 2005	$0.90	$0.95
December 31, 2005	0.85	0.91
February 26, 2006	0.94	0.94

On February 26, 2006 Rombaurer sells its copper on the spot market for $0.94 a pound and cancels the futures contracts.

The chapter described how "hedge accounting" rules are used when Rombaurer hedges its entire 10 million pounds of copper inventory.

Required:

1. Suppose Rombaurer sells futures contracts for only 5 million pounds of copper. (Management had decided that it is prudent to only hedge half of the company's economic exposure.) The margin requirement on these contracts is $140,000. Because the futures contracts are now "ineffective" in hedging the company's entire fair value exposure to copper price fluctuations, Rombaurer cannot use "hedge accounting." Prepare all journal entries needed to account for the futures contracts and sale of copper from October 5, 2005 through February 26, 2006.

2. Now assume that Rombaurer designates these futures contracts as a "fully effective" hedge of its risk exposure for 5 million pounds of copper inventory. (The remaining 5 million pounds of inventory is not being hedged.) Rombaurer can now use "hedge accounting" for the futures contracts. Prepare all journal entries needed to account for the futures contracts and sale of copper from October 5, 2005 through February 26, 2006.

3. What impact does changing the definition of the hedged item (10 million pounds of copper inventory versus 5 million pounds) have on the company's financial statements for 2005 and 2006?

CASES

C11 – 1

Risk management

The following information was taken from the 2000 annual report of H.J. Heinz Company:

INTEREST RATE SWAP AGREEMENTS

The company may utilize interest rate swap agreements to lower funding costs or to alter interest rate exposure. Amounts paid or received on interest rate swap agreements are deferred and recognized as adjustments to interest expense. Gains and losses realized upon the settlement of such contracts are deferred and amortized to interest expense over the remaining term of the debt instrument or are recognized immediately if the underlying instrument is settled.

FOREIGN CURRENCY CONTRACTS

The company enters into forward, purchased option and swap contracts to hedge transactions denominated in foreign currencies in order to reduce the currency risk associated with fluctuating exchange rates. Such contracts are used primarily to hedge certain intercompany cash flows, purchases and sales of certain raw materials and finished goods and for payments arising from certain foreign currency denominated obligations. Realized and unrealized gains and losses from instruments qualifying as hedges are deferred as part of the cost basis of the underlying transaction.

Realized and unrealized gains and losses from foreign currency contracts used as economic hedges but not qualifying for hedge accounting are recognized currently in miscellaneous income and expense.

COMMODITY CONTRACTS

In connection with purchasing certain commodities for future manufacturing requirements, the company enters into commodities futures and option contracts, as deemed appropriate, to reduce the effect of price fluctuations. Such contracts are accounted for as hedges, with gains and losses recognized as part of cost of products sold, and generally have a term of less than one year.

Required:

1. How does an interest-rate swap reduce market risk?
2. Suppose Heinz only has fixed-rate debt. Is the company's interest-rate swap a cash flow hedge or a fair value hedge? Explain.
3. Why are gains and losses on settlement of the interest-rate swaps recognized immediately when the underlying instrument is settled?
4. How does a foreign currency forward contract reduce market risk from the sale of finished goods?
5. Why are some foreign currency hedge gains and losses "deferred" while others are "recognized currently" in income?
6. Explain the advantage of an option over a futures contract for reducing the market risk of a future commodity purchase.
7. Is the company's commodities futures contract a cash flow hedge or a fair value hedge? Explain.

Tuesday Morning Corporation operates a chain of discount retail stores. The company purchases close-out merchandise at prices generally ranging from 10% to 50% of the normal wholesale price and sells the merchandise at prices that are 50% to 80% lower than retail prices generally charged by department and specialty stores.

Appearing next is information taken from a recent Tuesday Morning annual report.

 C11 – 2

Tuesday Morning Corporation (CW): Interpreting long-term debt disclosures

Note 5: Mortgages on Property, Plant, and Equipment

($ in thousands)	Year 2	Year 1
Industrial development bond, payable in quarterly installments of $108 plus interest at 91.656% of prime (not to exceed 15%), maturing March 31, Year 6;	$1,401	$1,834
Payable to bank, payable in quarterly installments of $104 plus interest at LIBOR plus 2.50%, maturing September 30, Year 5, with remaining principal due at that time;	4,504	4,920
Payable to bank, payable in quarterly installments of $112 plus interest at LIBOR plus 2.50% through October 15, Year 2, with the remaining principal and interest due April 30, Year 3;	1,794	2,243

In connection with these mortgages, the Company is required to maintain minimum net worth and comply with other financial covenants, including a restriction limiting loans to officers to less than $2,000,000. At December 31, Year 2 the Company is in compliance with these covenants.

The $1,794,000 note payable to bank due on April 30, Year 3 is classified as a current liability at December 31, Year 2. The aggregate maturities of mortgages are as follows ($ in thousands):

Year	Amount
Year 3	$2,747
Year 4	849
Year 5	4,003
Year 6	100

Consolidated Balance Sheet
($ in thousands)

	Year 2	Year 1
Current liabilities:		
Current installments on mortgages	$ 2,747	$ 1,402
Current installments on capital lease obligation	607	–0–
Accounts payable	12,916	15,859
Accrued sales tax	1,574	1,760
Other accrued expenses	1,945	3,118
Deferred income taxes	303	146
Due to officer	–0–	599
Income taxes payable	988	–0–
Total current liabilities	$21,080	$22,884

Consolidated Statement of Cash Flows
($ in thousands)

	Year 2	Year 1
Cash flows from financing activities:		
Net increase (decrease) in notes payable	–0–	$(3,500)
Principal payments on mortgages	$(1,298)	(1,194)
Principal payments under capital lease obligation	(214)	–0–
Proceeds from common stock offering	–0–	–0–
Proceeds from exercise of common stock options	255	145
Repurchase of common stock	–0–	(3,383)
Net cash provided by (used in) financing activities	$(1,257)	$(7,932)

Required:

1. What was the *current portion* of Tuesday Morning's mortgage payable at the end of Year 1?
2. How much did Tuesday Morning pay in cash to reduce its mortgage payable during Year 2?
3. Explain the difference between your answer to requirement 1 and your answer to requirement 2.
4. What are the components of the current portion of the mortgage payable as of the end of Year 2?
5. Assume the next quarterly installment on the industrial development bond is due on March 31, Year 3. Prepare a journal entry to record the installment payment and any interest. Assume the effective interest rate for the bond is 14% per year.
6. The company has a mortgage note payable for $1,794,000 that comes due on April 30, Year 3. Suppose that this note is paid by the signing of a new 14% note for the amount due. Prepare the April 30, Year 3 journal entry to record this refinancing of the old note.
7. Instead of refinancing the note, suppose the company pays the principal along with any remaining interest on April 30, Year 3. Prepare a journal entry to record this cash payment.

C11 – 3

Delhaize American, Inc. (CW): Fair value disclosure of long-term debt

Delhaize American, Inc. operates retail supermarkets in the Southeastern and Mid-Atlantic regions of the United States. The company offers nationally and regionally advertised brand-name merchandise as well as products manufactured and packaged for the company under the private label of "Food Lion" and "Kash n' Karry."

The following information appeared as a footnote to the company's 1999 annual report:

6. Long-Term Debt
Long-term debt consists of the following:

($ in thousands)	1999	1998
Medium-term notes, due from 2000 to 2006		
Interest ranges from 8.40% to 8.73%	$123,300	$150,300
Debt securities, 7.55%, due 2007	150,000	150,000
Debt securities, 8.05%, due 2027	150,000	150,000
Mortgage payables due from 2000 through 2011		
Interest ranges from 7.50% to 9.30%	5,148	19,029
Other	1,316	2,952
	429,764	472,281
Less current portion	2,834	42,518
	$426,930	$429,763

At January 1, 2000, $10.7 million (net book value) in property was pledged as collateral for mortgage payables. At January 1, 2000 and January 2, 1999, the Company estimated that the fair value of its long-term debt was approximately $413.6 million and $522.0 million, respectively. The fair value of the Company's long-term debt is estimated based on the current rates offered to the Company for debt with the same remaining maturities.

Required:

1. How much would Delhaize American have to pay to retire all of its long-term debt at the end of 1999 by purchasing the debt in the market?
2. Prepare a journal entry to record the open market purchase and retirement of the company's long-term debt at the end of 1999.
3. How would the gain or loss on retirement be shown on the company's 1999 income statement? What impact would the retirement have on net income for 2000?
4. Suppose that, at the end of 1996, the company had $495 million of long-term debt outstanding. The fair market value of the debt was $536 million. Prepare a journal entry to record the open market purchase and retirement of the company's long-term debt at the end of 1996.
5. Suppose the company could instead retire all of its 1996 long-term debt at 103% of par using a call provision. How would this approach affect the company's 1996 income statement?
6. Some of the company's debt is collateralized by property, plant, and equipment (PP&E). What does this mean? Why might bondholders prefer such an arrangement? Why might management agree? In what industries are you likely to see "collateralized" loans?

ShopKo Stores Inc. is a leading regional discount store chain. ShopKo stores carry a wide selection of branded and private label nondurable "hardline" goods—housewares, music/videos, health and beauty aids, toys, and sporting goods—and "softline" goods such as home textiles, men's, women's, and children's apparel, shoes, jewelry, cosmetics, and accessories. In addition, many of the company's stores include pharmacy departments and optical departments.

C11 – 4

ShopKo Stores Inc. (CW): Comprehensive case on long-term debt

Appearing next is information taken from ShopKo's annual report for the year ended February 2, 2002.

E. Long-term obligations and leases

($ in thousands)	February 2, 2002	February 3, 2001
Senior unsecured notes, 9.0% due November 15, 2004 less unamortized discount of $12 and $49, respectively	$ 72,698	$ 72,661
Senior unsecured notes, 8.5% due March 15, 2002 less unamortized discount of $0 and $18, respectively	70,207	70,189
Senior unsecured notes, 9.25% due March 15, 2002 less unamortized discount of $386 and $405, respectively	99,614	99,595
Senior unsecured notes, 6.5% due August 15, 2003 less unamortized discount of $42 and $70, respectively	99,958	99,930
Senior Credit Facility—term loan, 5.3% at February 2, 2002	100,000	—
Mortgage and other obligations	15,637	19,919
Revolving credit facility	—	170,000
Capital lease obligations	127,295	132,897
	585,409	665,191
Less current portion	79,942	6,910
Long-term obligations	$505,467	$658,281

I. Fair values of financial instruments

The carrying amounts and fair values of the Company's long-term obligations (excluding capital leases) at February 2, 2002 and February 3, 2001 are as follows:

($ in thousands)	February 2, 2002	February 3, 2001
Carrying amount	$458,114	$532,294
Fair value	$399,652	$426,727

Required:

1. How much long-term debt was issued during the year ended February 2, 2002?
2. Does the newly issued debt carry a fixed rate of interest or a floating interest rate?
3. Prepare a journal entry to record the long-term debt issued during that year.
4. How much of the discount or premium (state which) on long-term debt was amortized during that year?
5. What did the company do with the cash it received from the long-term debt it issued during the year ended February 2, 2002?
6. Which (if any) of the company's obligations are classified as a current liability?
7. How much would ShopKo have to pay to retire all of its outstanding debt (excluding capital leases) as of February 2, 2002 by purchasing the debt in the open market? Prepare a journal entry to record the purchase and retirement of the company's debt on that date.

C11 – 5

Coca-Cola Company (CW): Using long-term debt footnotes

The following information is from Coca-Cola Company's 2001 annual report:

6. Long-term Debt

($ in millions)	2001	2000
6⅝% U.S. dollar notes due 2002	150	150
6% U.S. dollar notes due 2003	150	150
5¾% U.S. dollar notes due 2009	399	399
5¾% U.S. dollar notes due 2011	498	—
7⅜% U.S. dollar notes due 2013	116	116
Other, due 2002 to 2013	62	41
	1,375	856
Less current portion	156	21
	$1,219	$835

After giving effect to interest rate management instruments, the principal amount of our long-term debt that had fixed and variable interest rates, respectively, was $1,262 million and $113 million on December 31, 2001, and $706 million and $150 million on December 31, 2000. The weighted-average interest rate on our Company's long-term debt was 5.8 percent and 5.9 percent for the years ended December 31, 2001 and 2000, respectively. Total interest paid was approximately $304 million, $458 million, and $314 million in 2001, 2000, and 1999, respectively. Maturities of long-term debt for the five years succeeding December 31, 2001, are as follows (in millions): 2002—$156; 2003—$155; 2004—$2; 2005—$1; and 2006—$1.

Required:

1. How much of Coca-Cola's long-term debt is due in 2002?
2. How much of Coca-Cola's long-term debt is due in each of the next five years (2002–2006)?
3. Why might financial analysts be interested in these scheduled debt payments? What options does the company have with regard to making its payments?
4. Compute the company's effective interest rate for 2001 using the reported cash interest payments and the average amount of debt outstanding during the year. In addition to long-term debt shown above, the company had $3,717 million in average short-term debt outstanding.
5. What will the company's interest expense be for 2002?
6. Why might the effective interest rate calculation described in requirement 4 misstate a company's true interest cost when debt is issued at a premium or discount?
7. What does the phrase "interest rate management instruments" refer to, and why is the company using those instruments?
8. Approximately $156 million of long-term debt is due in 2002. Describe how the company might obtain the cash needed to make this payment.

The following article raises questions about Cardinal Health's accounting for an expected legal settlement. Management responded to the accusations by sending a letter to all shareholders and to analysts who covered the firm.

C11 – 6

Cardinal Health: Contingent receivables

CARDINAL HEALTH'S ACCOUNTING RAISES SOME QUESTIONS

It's a cardinal rule of accounting: Don't count your chickens before they hatch. Yet new disclosures in Cardinal Health Inc.'s latest annual report suggest that is what the drug wholesaler has done not just once, but twice, independent accounting specialists say.

As the disclosures show, Cardinal recorded $22 million of an expected legal settlement with certain vitamin manufacturers that it had accused of overcharging for products—in advance of an actual settlement. Specifically, Cardinal recorded a $10 million pre-tax gain, as well as a corresponding receivable on its balance sheet, during its December 2000 quarter. It recorded a further $12 million gain during the quarter ended Sept. 30, 2001, after concluding that its minimum future recovery would be that much bigger.

Cardinal, which says it has done nothing improper, did reach a $35.3 million settlement in the vitamin antitrust litigation last spring. The company recorded the remaining $13.3 million during the final quarter of its past fiscal year, ended June 30.

To those unfamiliar with accounting rules, the posting of the two initial sums might not raise obvious questions. Yet even first-year accounting students are taught this: Under generally accepted accounting principles, companies aren't supposed to record expected gains as current income until they are certain the gains will be realized. When it comes to litigation settlements, that means waiting until an actual settlement agreement has been reached with a party that is able to pay, independent accounting specialists say.

Now consider this twist: Had Cardinal not recorded the two initial gains when it did, it would have fallen short of Wall Street analysts' earnings targets by two cents a share for both the December 2000 and September 2001 quarters; Cardinal's earnings met analysts' targets for each of the quarters. Cardinal didn't disclose the size of the gains until September 2002, when it filed its latest annual report.

"That's abracadabra accounting," says Walter Schuetze, a former chief accountant for the Securities and Exchange Commission. "Cardinal should not have recognized a receivable and a gain until June 2002." Before then, "it was all a matter of speculation," he says, adding, "Cardinal's actions explain what is meant by the term earnings management. This is diddling the numbers." . . .

"Cardinal Health is absolutely confident in our accounting and report practices and our adherence to high ethical standards," Mr. Miller [Cardinal's chief financial officer] says. "With regard to GAAP and SEC regulations, we are in full compliance in all material respects." . . .

Source: Wall Street Journal (April 2, 2003).

CARDINAL HEALTH

A Note from Steve Fischbach, VP Investor Relations

I wanted to make sure all of our investors and analysts received some information that responds to today's *Wall Street Journal* Heard on the Street article titled "Cardinal Health's Accounting Raises a Number of Questions." . . .

Here are the facts:

As we have explained to the reporter, this item was not a recording of a contingent gain under *SFAS 5*. The recoveries that Cardinal Health recorded related to vendor overcharges in our vitamin business were based on the virtual certainty of the recovery as supported by numerous external factors.

The reporter questioned the timing of two items recorded by the company ($10 million in the second quarter of fiscal year 2001 and $12 million in the first quarter of fiscal year 2002) related to the vitamin overcharge situation. This event was the recognition of an asset related to recoveries for vendor overcharges, based on the following five factors:

1. Vendors had admitted overcharging and plead guilty in a criminal proceeding. In prior periods Cardinal Health was in fact overcharged by those vendors and those charges were reflected in prior periods as higher cost of sales.
2. Vendors had settled with a number of plaintiffs, based on their admission of guilt.
3. Vendors were all major pharmaceutical companies with a clear ability to pay.
4. Issue was not "if" we would recover, but "how much."
5. Quantification of the amount of recovery that was virtually certain was supported by written legal opinions from independent outside legal counsel that served as substantial audit evidence.

As it turned out, Cardinal Health received over $120 million from the defendants in the case which exceeded what was actually recorded by over $100 million. That is a very important point because it demonstrates the conservatism with which Cardinal Health dealt with the issue. . . .

Source: Cardinal Health Letter to Shareholders (April 2, 2003).

Required:

1. Consult *SFAS No. 5* "Accounting for Contingencies." Are the GAAP rules for recognizing contingent gains (and a corresponding receivable) the same or different from those for recognizing contingent losses (and a corresponding liability)?
2. In view of the details outlined in Cardinal Health's letter to analysts and investors, do you believe the company fully complied with *SFAS No. 5* as it pertains to recognizing contingent gains? Why or why not?
3. If asked, how might management respond to questions about the timing of the gain recognition in 2001 and 2002?
4. Suppose management was intent on informing analysts and investors about an expected litigation settlement amount. How might this be done in situations where *SFAS No. 5* precluded recognizing the gain on the financial statements?

Remember to check the book's Companion Website for additional problem and case material.

www.prenhall.com/revsine

Financial Reporting for Leases

Humans have three basic needs: food, shelter, and . . . keeping debt off the balance sheet.

–Author unknown

A lease is a contract in which the owner of an asset—the **lessor**—conveys to another party—the **lessee**—the right to use that asset. This right is granted in exchange for a fee—the **lease payment**—that is usually paid in installments. Legal title to the asset is typically retained by the lessor. The duration of a lease may be short, such as a one-week car rental agreement, or long, such as a 20-year lease for retail space in a shopping center.

At its inception, a lease is what is called a **mutually unperformed contract**. This means neither party to the lease arrangement has yet performed all of the duties called for in the contract. For example, the lessor has an obligation to provide the lessee with the right to use the asset for the entire duration of the lease; in exchange, the lessee has an obligation to pay the stipulated periodic fee to the lessor during the lease term. When the lease contract is first signed, the right to use the asset has not been provided nor have the required periodic contract payments been made. As you will see, the accounting for these unperformed contracts is controversial.

Evolution of Lease Accounting

Statement of Financial Accounting Standards (SFAS) No. 13 spells out the current generally accepted accounting principles (GAAP) for leases.[1] Before it was issued in 1976, virtually all leases were accounted for using the **operating lease approach**.

The following example illustrates the operating lease approach.

> Crest Company owns a building with a book value of $200,000. This building is leased to Iris Company under a five-year lease for a monthly rental of $2,000, which is to be paid at the end of each month.

---

[1] "Accounting for Leases," *SFAS No. 13* (Stamford, CT: Financial Accounting Standards Board [FASB], 1976).

Learning Objectives

After studying this chapter, you will understand:

1. The difference between capital leases and operating leases.

2. Lessees' incentives to keep leases off the balance sheet.

3. The criteria used to classify leases on the lessee's books.

4. The treatment of executory costs, residual values, and other aspects of lease contracts.

5. The effects of capital lease versus operating lease treatment on lessees' financial statements.

6. How analysts can adjust for ratio distortions from off-balance sheet leases when comparing firms.

7. That lessors also classify leases either as capital leases or as operating leases but that their reporting incentives are very different from those of lessees.

8. The difference among sales-type, direct financing, and operating lease treatment by lessors and the criteria for choosing the accounting treatment.

9. How the different lessor accounting treatments can affect income and net asset balances.

10. Sale/leaseback arrangements and other special leasing situations.

11. How to use footnote disclosures to estimate the increase in assets and liabilities that would ensue if operating leases had been capitalized instead.

Upon signing the lease, Iris Company, the lessee, makes no entry on its books. Here, the accounting conforms to the legal structure of lease arrangements. Since lease contracts typically do not convey title, the asset remains on the books of the lessor and no asset is reflected on the lessee's books. Further, under the operating lease approach, the lessee does not immediately record as a liability the stream of future payments specified in the contract. No liability is recorded because the lessee is not legally obligated to make the payments until the lessor performs the duties specified in the contract. Because these are mutually unperformed contracts— sometimes called **executory** contracts—accounting entries are made over time in piecemeal fashion only as partial performance under the contract takes place. *As each party performs its respective duties, that portion of the contract that has been performed is no longer considered executory and is accordingly recognized in the financial records.*

Each month, as Crest performs its part of the agreement by making the premises available to Iris Company, Iris accrues a liability for that portion of the contract that has been performed:

DR	Rent expense	$2,000	
	CR Lease liability		$2,000

Upon payment of the stipulated rental fee at the end of the month, Iris makes the following entry:

DR	Lease liability	$2,000	
	CR Cash		$2,000

In practice, the accrual for the lease liability is seldom made. Instead, only one entry is made at the time of cash payment:

DR	Rent expense	$2,000	
	CR Cash		$2,000

Iris does not record any liability on its books for *future* rental payments— neither at the time of signing the lease nor afterward. The reason is that these future rental payments are contingent upon future performance by Crest, the lessor. The stipulated payments do not become a liability to Iris under the operating lease approach until time passes and performance takes place. As each party to the mutually unperformed contract performs its duties specified in the contract, the "performed" portion is no longer considered executory. So, as you just saw, the stipulated rental for the month over which performance took place is recorded as an expense and accrued as a liability; the liability is reduced when payment is made.

Similarly, no entry would be made on the books of Crest, the lessor, at the time this operating lease was signed. However, as piecemeal performance takes place month-by-month and payment is received, the following entry is made on Crest's books:

DR	Cash	$2,000	
	CR Rental revenue		$2,000

Because the building remains an asset on the books of Crest Company, periodic depreciation is also recorded:

DR	Depreciation expense—leased building	$XXX	
	CR Accumulated depreciation—leased building		$XXX

RECAP The operating lease approach conforms to the legal structure of lease arrangements. Journal entries are made piecemeal over time as partial performance takes place.

Why Lessees Like the Operating Lease Method

Lessees like the operating lease method for lease accounting. One obvious reason is that the operating lease method doesn't reflect the cumulative liability for all future lease payments on the balance sheet of the lessee. Instead, only a portion of the obligation gets accrued piecemeal as partial performance takes place under the lease. The phrase **off-balance sheet financing** is used to reflect the fact that the lessee has financed the acquisition of asset services without recognizing a liability on the financial statement.

As we will show you, GAAP requires *footnote* disclosure of the lessee's future cash outflows arising from operating leases. And because reasonably informed financial decision makers do read statement footnotes, the liability isn't really "hidden." Nevertheless, it is easy to envision circumstances in which lessees will be made better off by using the operating lease method. To see how they are made better off, recall that many contracts are linked to financial statement numbers. One example is bank lending agreements that contain **covenants**—safety measures to protect banks against financial deterioration of the borrower. Since most covenants are based on financial statement numbers—not on footnote numbers—keeping liabilities off the balance sheet may convey benefits to borrowers even if the liabilities aren't hidden in a real sense. For example, the numerator of the lessee's debt-to-equity ratio is unaffected at the inception of an operating lease, since no liability is recorded on signing. Keeping the liability off the balance sheet strengthens the debt-to-equity ratio. The off-balance sheet liability reduces the likelihood that the lessee-borrower will violate a debt-to-equity loan covenant.

Furthermore, some lessees believe that omitting the lease liability improves their ability to obtain *future* credit. Here's why. Lenders use leverage ratios as a rule of thumb in assessing borrowing capacity—that means the amount that can safely be borrowed. Keeping the lease liability off the books lowers reported leverage. Supposedly, the lower the firm's reported leverage, the greater is that firm's perceived borrowing capacity.

Lessees also like the operating lease accounting method because it keeps the leased *asset* off the balance sheet. Certain long-term leases give lessees the *exclusive* right to use assets for most of their economic life. Nevertheless, despite the "ownership-like" property rights conveyed to the lessee, no balance sheet asset is recorded with operating leases.

Keeping leased assets off the books produces a favorable impact on lessee's financial statements that is just as substantial as the benefit that arises from omitting lease liabilities. Consider an airline that leases a portion of its aircraft fleet and accounts for the leases using the operating lease method. The leased aircraft generate gross revenues and net profits just as the owned aircraft do. However, not reporting the leased aircraft as assets under the operating lease approach raises the return-on-assets (ROA) ratio:

> Operating leases for office or retail store space often have noncancellable terms like 12 or 15 years. But if the lessee experiences a decrease in demand during the noncancellable lease term, the leased facility may become unneeded. Periodic lease payments continue without any corresponding economic benefits to the lessee. Once the leased item becomes superfluous, the lessee should recognize a liability at its fair value as well as an offsetting debit to expense. The fair value of the liability is the discounted present value of the remaining lease rentals. As time passes, the liability is increased (and an expense is recognized) using accretion procedures like those described for asset retirement obligations in Chapter 10, pp. 530–531. See "Accounting for Costs Associated with Exit or Disposal Activities," *SFAS No. 146* (Norwalk, CT: FASB, 2002), paras. 14–16.

Contracting

> On the other hand, off-balance sheet liabilities are disclosed in the lease footnote; if lenders read these footnotes, then off-balance sheet items aren't really "hidden." So this perception by lessees may be incorrect.

Analysis

$$ROA = \frac{NOPAT}{\text{Average assets}}$$

Income generated by the leased assets will appear in the numerator, net operating profit after taxes (NOPAT); however, the leased assets will not appear in the denominator. The net effect increases the return on *reported* average assets.

Investors and others use ratios like return on assets to evaluate a firm's performance. The operating lease method makes the ROA for companies that lease a significant portion of their assets *appear* to be higher than the corresponding return for companies that own their assets outright. (See the example illustrated in the Appendix to this chapter.)

The Securities and Exchange Commission's Initiative

Throughout the 1960s and early 1970s, leasing became an important financing vehicle for two reasons. First, leasing provided firms the opportunity to use assets without expending the entire cash purchase price. Second, if the leased asset became technologically obsolete, the lessee could simply lease a newer model. But the virtually exclusive use of the operating lease approach was criticized, especially by the Securities and Exchange Commission (SEC), since it felt that this accounting approach did not portray the economics of many leasing transactions.

The SEC issued *Accounting Series Release (ASR) No. 147* in 1973 to improve financial reporting for leases.[2] The SEC took what is called a **property rights** approach to lease accounting. Under this approach, leases are viewed as conveying property rights in the asset to the lessee, and the payment stream represents the lessee's liability. Following this accounting method, the lessee would record both an asset and a liability on its books equal to the present value of future lease payments when a lease is signed:

> **DR** Leased asset (to reflect the property right the lessee now has in the asset) $XXX
> **CR** Lease obligation (to reflect the liability arising from the future lease
>   payments) $XXX

This is called the **capital lease** approach since the lease is capitalized (put on the books) by the lessee.[3] The FASB soon extended and embellished the SEC property rights approach, as we discuss next.

Figure 12.1 provides an overview of the two different lease accounting approaches.

Lessee Accounting

Under *SFAS No. 13*, leases meeting certain specified criteria *must* be treated as capital leases. So a lease asset and lease liability appear on the lessee's balance sheet. Leases not meeting the *SFAS No. 13* criteria *cannot* be capitalized. Noncapitalized leases are called **operating leases** and are accounted for using the procedures we just described.

SFAS No. 13 Criteria for Capital Lease Treatment

If, at its inception, a lease satisfies *any one or more* of the following criteria, it must be treated as a capital lease on the books of the lessee:

1. The lease transfers ownership of the asset to the lessee by the end of the lease term.
2. The lease contains a bargain purchase option.
3. The noncancelable lease term is 75% or more of the estimated economic life of the leased asset.
4. The present value of the minimum lease payments equals or exceeds 90% of the current fair market value of the leased asset.

---

[2] "Notice of Adoption of Amendments to Regulations S-X Requiring Improved Disclosure of Leases," *ASR No. 14* (Washington, DC: SEC, 1973).

[3] However, *ASR No. 147* emphasized footnote *disclosure* and thus stopped short of requiring balance sheet *recognition* of leases that conveyed property rights.

Figure 12.1

DIFFERENCES BETWEEN OPERATING AND CAPITAL LEASES

Operating Leases

		Capital Leases
Used when property rights in the asset have *not* been transferred to the lessee (for example, a "short-term" rental).	**WHEN IS THIS METHOD USED?**	Used when property rights in the asset *have* been transferred to the lessee (for example, the lease spans most of the asset's life).
The leased asset remains on the lessor's books. No asset or liability appears on the lessee's books since the lease is considered to be an unperformed contract.	**WHOSE BOOKS IS THE LEASED ASSET ON?**	The leased asset is treated as being sold and is removed from the lessor's books. (Details described later in the chapter.) Lessee puts both the leased asset and the liability for future payments on its books.

As time passes—and as partial performance takes place—the lessee makes the following entry:
DR Rent (or lease) expense xx
  CR Cash   xx
(To reflect the portion of the contract that has now been performed.)
 	
At the same time, the lessor makes the following entries:
DR Cash   xx
  CR Rental revenue   xx
(To reflect revenue on the performed portion of the contract.)
 	
DR Depreciation expense   xx
  CR Accumulated
      Depreciation   xx
(To depreciate the leased asset which is on the lessor's books.)
	WHAT ENTRIES ARE MADE?	The accounting for both the leased asset and the lease liability are described in detail later in the chapter.

Each criterion represents a situation under which property rights in the leased asset have been transferred to the lessee. The transfer of property rights is easily seen in criterion (1). If a lease transfers ownership, title to the asset will eventually pass to the lessee, and the FASB requires that the accounting method conform to the substance of the transaction—an installment purchase—rather than to its form—a long-term rental agreement. Similarly, in lease arrangements where a **bargain purchase option** exists—criterion (2)—there is a strong probability the lessee will exercise the option and obtain ownership. These two criteria represent instances in which ownership will likely transfer, thus conveying significant property rights in the leased asset. This is the reason *SFAS No. 13* requires that such leases be treated as capital leases.

The philosophy underlying the third criterion—economic life—is different since legal ownership of the asset does not pass to the lessee. Nevertheless, *SFAS No. 13* indicates that criterion (3) also conveys significant property rights. The

International

International Accounting Standards (IAS) also differentiate between operating leases and capital leases. (The latter are called "finance leases.") Classification is based on which party has the risks and rewards of ownership. Criteria that are similar to (but less precise than) the four *SFAS No. 13* criteria are cited as examples of situations where a lease should be classified as a finance lease. In addition, IAS identifies other potential capitalization criteria. For example, if the leased asset is so specialized that only the lessee can use it, or if the lessee must compensate the lessor for losses from canceling the lease, capital lease treatment may be needed. See "Accounting for Leases," *IAS 17* (London: International Accounting Standards Board [IASB], 1997), paras. 8–9.

reason is that the *right to use* a leased asset for 75% or more of its expected economic life is *itself* an asset—a valuable property right representing an exclusive claim to the asset's services for the preponderance of its benefit period.

Criterion (4), sometimes called the **recovery of investment criterion**, is the most technically complicated but easy to understand in principle. A good indication that the lessor is recovering virtually all of the investment in the asset occurs when the present value of the minimum lease payments is equal to or greater than 90% of the fair market value of the asset itself. The relative magnitude of the payment schedule and the willingness of the lessee to engage in the transaction are both considered evidence that substantial property rights have been transferred to the lessee.

> For example, criterion (4) is triggered, if a lessee leases an asset with a fair market value of $100,000 and agrees to a payment stream whose present value is $93,000, since $93,000 is more than 90% of $100,000.

These four criteria for capital leases suggest the FASB has moved part of the way toward the property rights approach. But it's not a "pure" property rights approach, since these criteria do not consider *all* leases to convey property rights. Only leases that satisfy certain arbitrary conditions (for example, the 75% rule or the 90% rule) qualify. *So SFAS No. 13 is a compromise between the operating lease approach, where no leases appear on the lessee's balance sheet, and a strict property rights approach, where all leases would be shown as assets and liabilities.*

To summarize, leases that satisfy at least one of the four criteria are treated as capital leases, and the following entry is made on the books of the lessee at the inception of the lease:

DR Leased asset—capital lease	$XXX
CR Obligation under capital lease	$XXX

Leases that do not satisfy *any* of the previously discussed criteria must be accounted for as operating leases.

Capital Lease Treatment Illustrated

To illustrate the accounting for leases that qualify as capital leases, consider the following example.

> Lessee Company signs a five-year noncancelable lease with Lessor Company on January 1, 2005 when the lease begins. Several other facts pertain to the lease:
>
> 1. The lease calls for five payments of $79,139.18 to be made at the end of each year.
> 2. The leased asset has a fair market value of $315,000 on January 1, 2005.
> 3. The lease has no renewal option and possession of the asset reverts to the lessor on January 1, 2010.
> 4. Lessee Company regularly uses the straight-line method to depreciate assets of this type that it owns.
> 5. The leased asset has an expected economic life of six years.

> Minimum lease payments are defined as the noncontingent, fixed payments specified in the lease agreement. For example, if the payment schedule called for a fixed fee of $79,139.18 per year plus an additional fee of five cents per unit for each unit manufactured using the leased asset, only the $79,139.18 would be included in the computation of minimum lease payments. The five cents per unit for each unit manufactured is *a contingency that is ignored in the calculation*. In more complicated leases, the minimum lease payments also include:
> 1. the amount of any **residual value guarantee** by the lessee (as discussed later),
> 2. any penalties that must be paid if the lessee chooses not to renew the lease, and
> 3. the amount of any bargain purchase option payment, if the lease contains a bargain purchase option.

Since the five-year lease term covers more than 75% of the asset's six-year expected economic life (5/6 = 83.3%), this lease must be treated as a capital lease, following criterion (3). That means Lessee Company must recognize both an asset and a liability on its books.

But what is the asset and liability dollar amount that should be recorded? *SFAS No. 13* requires that the dollar amount be equal to the discounted present value of the **minimum lease payments** specified in the lease. Contingent payments are ignored. The discount rate that is used to determine the present value is the *lower* of the lessee's incremental borrowing rate[4] or the lessor's rate of return implicit in the lease.[5] But if the lessee can't determine the lessor's rate of return, the lessee uses the incremental borrowing rate.

Assume Lessee Company's incremental borrowing rate is 10% and the lessee can't determine the lessor's implicit rate of return on the lease. The discount rate is accordingly 10%, and the present value of the minimum lease payments in our example is:

> International standards differ here. The interest rate implicit to the lease should be used, if known; if not, the incremental borrowing rate is used. See *IAS 17*, para. 12.

International

Present value of minimum lease payments		Minimum lease payment	×	Present value factor for an ordinary annuity for five years at 10%
$300,000	=	$79,139.18	×	3.79079 (from Appendix I, Table 2)

Lessee Company makes the following entry on January 1, 2005 at the inception of the lease:

DR Leased asset—capital lease $300,000
    CR Obligation under capital lease $300,000

It is important to understand that the amount shown for the asset and the amount shown for the related liability ($300,000) are equal only at the inception of the lease. Thereafter, as the term of the lease progresses, the amount in the asset account will equal the amount in the liability account only by sheer coincidence. The reason that the two amounts will differ subsequently is that the asset account is reduced in accordance with Lessee Company's depreciation schedule for assets of this type, whereas the liability account is reduced in accordance with the payment schedule contained in the lease. The asset account and liability account are reduced at independent—and usually different—rates over the life of the lease. (The effect of these different reduction rates on the carrying value of the lease asset and liability is illustrated in the Appendix to this chapter.)

> The lease also meets criterion (4) since 90% of the $315,000 fair market value of the asset equals $283,500 and the present value of the minimum lease payments ($300,000) is greater than $283,500.

Each lease payment of $79,139.18 is composed of two elements. One represents interest on the present value of the obligation that was outstanding during the year. The other represents a repayment of a portion of the principal amount of the obligation. *SFAS No. 13* requires that the interest and principal repayment portions of each $79,139.18 outflow be measured using the **effective interest method**. The amortization schedule in Exhibit 12.1 shows this breakdown in column (b), Interest Expense, and column (c), Principal Payment. For example, the $79,139.18 payment made on 12/31/05 consists of an interest component of $30,000 and a principal payment component of $49,139.18.

---

[4] The FASB defines the **lessee's incremental borrowing rate** as the rate that the lessee "would have incurred to borrow the funds necessary to buy the leased asset on a secured loan with repayment terms similar to the payment schedule called for in the lease" (*SFAS No. 13*, para. 5 [1]).

[5] The **lessor's rate of return** is the pre-tax internal yield on the lease contract (that is, the rate that equates the fair value of the asset and the present value of the payments accruing to the lessor). Ibid., para. 5(k).

EXHIBIT 12.1	Lessee Company

Amortization Schedule—Effective Interest Method

Date	(a) Total Payment	(b) Interest Expense[1]	(c) Principal Payment[2]	(d) Lease Obligation Balance	(e) Amortization of Asset	(f) Total Annual Capital Lease Expense [Col. (b) + Col. (e)]
1/1/05				$300,000.00		
12/31/05	$ 79,139.18	$30,000.00	$ 49,139.18	250,860.82	$ 60,000.00	$ 90,000.00
12/31/06	79,139.18	25,086.08	54,053.10	196,807.72	60,000.00	85,086.08
12/31/07	79,139.18	19,680.77	59,458.41	137,349.31	60,000.00	79,680.77
12/31/08	79,139.18	13,734.93	65,404.25	71,945.06	60,000.00	73,734.93
12/31/09	79,139.18	7,194.12[3]	71,945.06	—	60,000.00	67,194.12
	$395,695.90	$95,695.90	$300,000.00	$ −0−	$300,000.00	$395,695.90

[1]Column (d) for preceding year times 10%.
[2]Column (a) minus column (b).
[3]Rounded.

On December 31, 2005 Lessee Company records both the cash payment of $79,139.18 (column [a], Total Payment), and the amortization of the capitalized leased asset (column [e], Amortization of Asset). Based upon the figures in Exhibit 12.1, the entries are:

DR Obligation under capital lease	$49,139.18	
DR Interest expense	30,000.00	
CR Cash		$79,139.18

DR Depreciation expense—capital lease	$60,000.00	
CR Accumulated depreciation—capital lease		$60,000.00

If a lease meets either the first or second capital lease criterion on p. 634, the leased asset is depreciated over the life of the *asset* since legal title to the asset ultimately passes to the lessee. If the lease is a capital lease because it meets either the third or fourth criterion, it is depreciated over the life of the *lease* since the asset reverts to the lessor at lease-end. In Exhibit 12.1, the asset is depreciated over five years since it qualified under the third criterion.

The amount of interest expense recognized each year is equal to 10% (the discount rate) times the present value of the obligation outstanding at the start of the year. Since the present value of the lease obligation at the start of the lease on January 1, 2005 was $300,000 (column [d], Lease Obligation Balance), the interest expense for 2005 is $300,000 times 10%, or $30,000. The difference between the cash payment of $79,139.18 and the interest expense of $30,000 represents repayment of principal. This 2005 difference—$49,139.18 (column [c])—reduces the remaining principal balance of the lease at December 31, 2005 to $250,860.82 ($300,000—$49,139.18) as shown in column [d]. Interest expense for 2006 would then be $250,860.82 times 10%, or $25,086.08. The 2006 journal entry for the cash payment is:

DR Obligation under capital lease	$54,053.10	
DR Interest expense	25,086.08	
CR Cash		$79,139.18

Notice that the entry to record depreciation expense would be the same in all years of the lease since Lessee Company uses the straight-line depreciation method.

Figure 12.2 summarizes lessees' accounting for capital leases.

Figure 12.2

LESSEES' ACCOUNTING
FOR CAPITAL LEASES

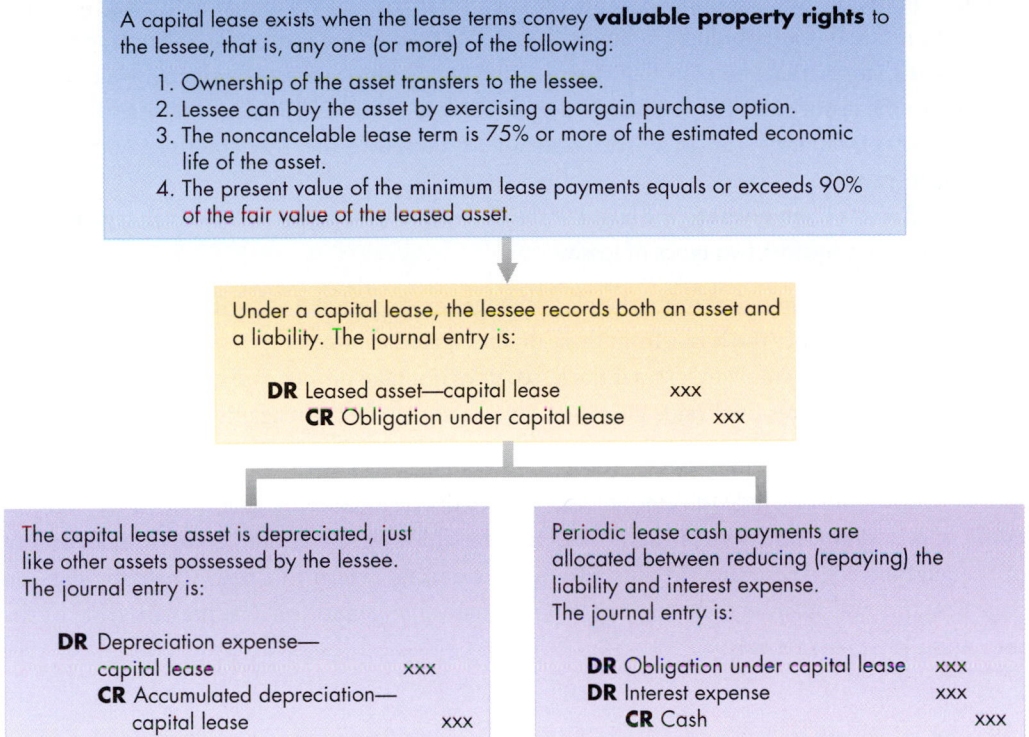

Executory Costs

Executory costs represent costs of *using* assets, such as maintenance, taxes, and insurance. Often, these costs are paid directly by the lessee. Sometimes they are paid by the lessor and passed along to the lessee as an additional lease payment. For example, if executory costs paid by Lessor Company total $2,000 per year, Lessor would include an added yearly charge of $2,000 in the lease, in addition to the basic $79,139.18 rental fee.

Since executory costs represent a cost of using assets—rather than a cost of the assets themselves—these costs are omitted when determining minimum lease payments, and thus they are not a component of the capitalized amount shown in the "Leased asset—capital leases" account. Consider this extension of the previous example. If Lessee Company's annual rental fee totals $81,139.18, which includes a $2,000 per year maintenance contract with the lessor, the minimum lease payments to be capitalized would be $79,139.18 (that is, $81,139.18 − $2,000). Under this assumption, the capitalized amount would still total $300,000 and the amortization schedule would be identical to Exhibit 12.1. The $2,000 of executory costs from the maintenance contract would be treated as a period cost by Lessee Company and charged to expense when paid. For example, the payment of $81,139.18 on December 31, 2005 would trigger this entry:

Residual Value Guarantees

Lease contracts sometimes contain a provision under which the lessee guarantees that the leased asset will have a certain value at the end of the lease. If the actual market value of the asset is less than this **residual value guarantee**, the lessee must pay the difference to the lessor.

Continuing the previous example, assume the lease required Lessee Company to guarantee that the asset's residual value would be no lower than $20,000 when the lease ends on January 1, 2010. If the asset's fair market value on that date is $20,000 or higher, Lessee Company would simply return it to the lessor since the residual value guarantee is satisfied. But if the fair market value is only $15,000 on January 1, 2010, Lessee Company would return the asset and pay $5,000 cash to Lessor Company.

Leased assets often revert to the lessor at the end of the lease term. Residual value guarantees protect the lessor against two types of losses:

- Unforeseen technological or marketplace changes erode residual value; the residual value guarantee insulates the lessor from these unanticipated changes.
- The lessor is vulnerable to losses if the lessee does not take proper care of the asset over the lease period; the residual value guarantee gives lessors protection against lessees who abuse leased assets.

The lessee must include the amount specified as the residual value guarantee in the computation of minimum lease payments. The reason is that the lessee potentially owes the full amount of the guarantee to the lessor. To illustrate the accounting, return to Lessee Company data on page 636 and now assume there is a $20,000 residual value guarantee. The present value of the minimum lease payments is:

Present value of minimum lease payments		Minimum lease payment	×	Present value factor at 10%
$300,000.00	=	$79,139.18	×	3.79079 (Present value factor for five-year ordinary annuity)
12,418.40	=	$20,000.00	×	.62092 (Present value factor for $1 due in five years, from Appendix I, Table 1)
$312,418.40				

With the residual value guarantee, Lessee Company makes the following entry on January 1, 2005 at the inception of the lease:

DR Leased asset—capital lease	$312,418.40	
CR Obligation under capital lease		$312,418.40

Exhibit 12.2 shows the amortization schedule that Lessee Company uses when this residual value guarantee is included in the lease. After making the December 31, 2009 cash payment of $79,139.18, the lease obligation balance (column [d]) and the lease asset balance (column [f]) both are $20,000 (see highlighted numbers). We're assuming that the asset's value at the end of the lease on January 1, 2010 equals or exceeds $20,000—the amount of the residual value guarantee. When Lessee Company returns the asset on that date, its obligation to Lessor Company is satisfied and the following entry results:

DR Obligation under capital lease	$20,000.00	
CR Leased asset—capital lease		$20,000.00

EXHIBIT 12.2	Lessee Company

Amortization Schedule—Effective Interest Method
With Guaranteed Residual Value

Date	(a) Total Cash Payment	(b) Interest Expense[1]	(c) Principal Payment[2]	(d) Lease Obligation Balance	(e) Amortization of Asset; Residual Value Return	(f) Lease Asset Balance	(g) Total Annual Capital Lease Expense (b) + (e)
1/1/05	—	—	—	$312,418.40	—	$312,418.40	—
12/31/05	$ 79,139.18	$ 31,241.84	$ 47,897.34	264,521.06	$ 58,483.68[3]	253,934.72	$ 89,725.52
12/31/06	79,139.18	26,452.11	52,687.07	211,833.99	58,483.68	195,451.04	84,935.79
12/31/07	79,139.18	21,183.40	57,955.78	153,878.21	58,483.68	136,967.36	79,667.08
12/31/08	79,139.18	15,387.82	63,751.36	90,126.85	58,483.68	78,483.68	73,871.50
12/31/09	79,139.18	9,012.33[4]	70,126.85	20,000.00	58,483.68	20,000.00	67,496.01
1/1/10[5]	—	—	20,000.00	—	20,000.00	—	—
	$395,695.90	$103,277.50	$312,418.40	$ -0-	$312,418.40	$ -0-	$395,695.90

[1]Column (d) for preceding year times 10%.
[2]Column (a) minus column (b).
[3]($312,418.40 − $20,000) ÷ 5
[4]Rounded.
[5]Asset returned.

Now let's alter the example and assume that the asset has a fair market value of only $15,000 at December 31, 2009. Lessee Company would have to pay $5,000 in addition to relinquishing the asset. The entry is:

DR Obligation under capital lease	$20,000.00	
DR Loss on residual value guarantee	5,000.00	
CR Leased asset—capital lease		$20,000.00
CR Cash		5,000.00

In summary, minimum lease payments include the present value of any *guaranteed* residual value. If no residual value guarantee exists in the lease contract, the minimum lease payments will contain no residual value adjustment.

Payments in Advance

When lease payments are due at the *start* of each lease period, the journal entries and amortization tables differ slightly. We'll use the original Lessee Company example on page 636 to illustrate this. Assume that the annual payment is due at the start of each year and, because the payments are received earlier, the lessor lowers the required annual payment to $71,945. Under these slightly altered conditions, the present value of the minimum lease payments is:

Present value of minimum lease payments	=	Minimum lease payment	×	Present value factor for an annuity in advance for five years at 10%
$300,000	=	$71,945	×	4.16987 (from Appendix I, Table 3)

Exhibit 12.3 shows the amortization schedule for this lease with up-front payments. Lessee Company records the following two entries on January 1, 2005 upon signing the lease and making the required lease payment:

DR Leased asset—capital lease	$300,000	
CR Obligation under capital lease		$300,000
DR Obligation under capital lease	$ 71,945	
CR Cash		$ 71,945

Notice from both the second journal entry and from Exhibit 12.3 that no portion of the January 1, 2005 payment represents interest expense; instead, all of the $71,945 payment reduces the principal balance. The reason is that interest expense ensues only as time passes, not at the inception of the lease.

EXHIBIT 12.3   **Lessee Company**

Amortization Schedule—Effective Interest Method With Payments at the Start of Each Period

Date	(a) Total Payment	(b) Interest Expense[1]	(c) Principal Payment[2]	(d) Lease Obligation Balance	(e) Amortization of Asset	(f) Total Annual Capital Lease Expense (b) + (e)
1/1/05				$300,000.00		
1/1/05	$ 71,945.00	—	$ 71,945.00	228,055.00	$ 60,000.00	$ 60,000.00
1/1/06	71,945.00	$22,805.50	49,139.50	178,915.50	60,000.00	82,805.50
1/1/07	71,945.00	17,891.55	54,053.45	124,862.05	60,000.00	77,891.55
1/1/08	71,945.00	12,486.21	59,458.79	65,403.26	60,000.00	72,486.21
1/1/09	71,945.00	6,541.74[3]	65,403.26	—	60,000.00	66,541.74
	$359,725.00	$59,725.00	$300,000.00	$ –0–	$300,000.00	$359,725.00

[1]Column (d) for preceding year times 10%.
[2]Column (a) minus column (b).
[3]Rounded.

Financial Statement Effects of Treating a Lease as a Capital Lease Versus Treating It as an Operating Lease

> Assuming zero executory costs is equivalent to assuming that the executory costs are paid directly by the lessee and are not included in the payments due to the lessor.

In order to understand the financial statement effects of lease capitalization, we need to compare the numbers that result from the capital lease approach with the numbers that would have resulted had the operating lease method been used instead.

To make that comparison, return to the beginning of Lessee Company example (p. 636) where we assumed that lease payments were due at the end of the year, executory costs were zero, and there was no residual value guarantee. If that lease had been accounted for as an operating lease, the following journal entry would have been made in each of the five years of the lease:

DR Lease expense	$79,139.18	
CR Cash		$79,139.18

Under the operating lease method, the total lease expense over the life of the lease is equal to the total cash outflow. This total expense number under the operating lease method is $395,695.90 and is shown at the bottom of column (a) of Exhibit 12.1.

Under the capital lease method, the total lease expense over the life of the lease comprises both (1) the interest payments, and (2) the amortization of the capitalized asset amount. The sum of these two elements is shown at the bottom of column (f) of the amortization schedule in Exhibit 12.1. This total is also $395,695.90.

A comparison of the Exhibit 12.1 column (a) total (lifetime expense under the operating lease method) and the column (f) total (lifetime expense under the capital lease method) demonstrates that **the two methods give rise to identical cumulative total lifetime charges to expense.** Over the life of a lease, total expense is unaffected by the choice of lease accounting method. However, a comparison of the year-by-year numbers in columns (a) and (f) demonstrates that the *timing* of the expense charge differs between the two methods. The capital lease approach leads to higher expense in the earlier years of the lease and lower lease expense in the later years, as shown in Figure 12.3. From the graphical representation you can see that in the early lease years expenses under the capital lease approach exceed lease expenses that would be recognized under the operating lease approach. Ultimately, capital lease expense drops below operating lease expense.

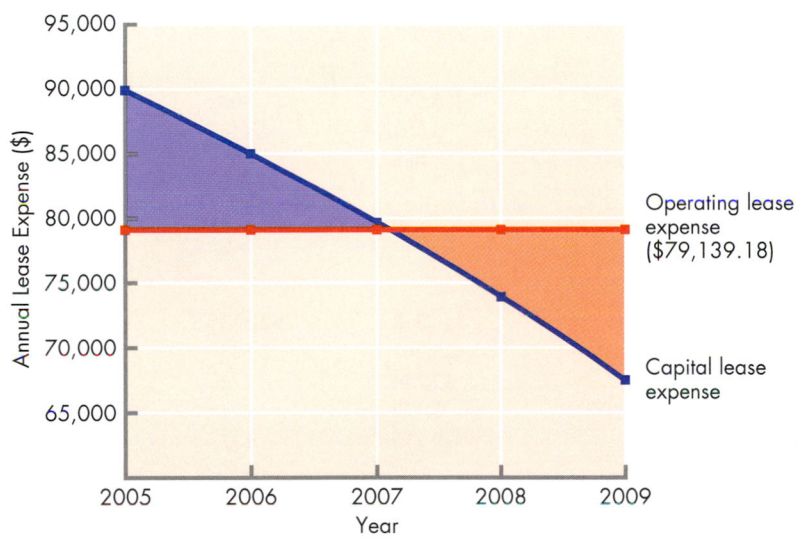

Figure 12.3

LESSEE COMPANY PATTERN OF EXPENSE RECOGNITION: CAPITAL VERSUS OPERATING LEASE METHOD

This accelerated recognition of lease expenses under the capital lease approach provides yet another reason why many lessees prefer the operating lease method. Consider the incentives of a manager whose performance evaluations and bonuses are tied to financial numbers. Since the capital lease accounting method loads the lease expenses at the front-end of the lease term, it lowers income during that front-end period and thus also reduces the discounted present value of expected bonuses. Worse yet, if managers' accomplishments are evaluated "strictly by the numbers," the higher expenses and lower profitability may jeopardize their continuing employment and advancement. So managers have a strong incentive to structure lease contracts in ways that circumvent the capitalization rules.

Exhibit 12.4 shows the total amount of scheduled capital lease payments versus operating lease payments for the five largest firms in each of five industries that use leases extensively. Notice that the dollar amount of the minimum lease payments arising from operating leases is, on average, almost 28 times larger than the capital lease payments for supermarket companies and almost 26 times larger for airlines. This demonstrates that capital leases arise infrequently even in industries that utilize leasing heavily.

Contracting

EXHIBIT 12.4	Comparison of Undiscounted Dollar Magnitudes of Capital and Operating Lease Payments		

(2002 Fiscal Year)

($ in millions)	Total Scheduled Minimum Lease Payments		Ratio of Operating to Capital Lease Payments
	Operating Leases	Capital Leases	
Department/Variety Stores			
Wal-Mart	$ 7,988	$5,225	1.53
Sears, Roebuck and Company	2,293	992	2.31
Target	1,528	244	6.26
Kmart Corp.	5,643	1,633	3.46
Costco Wholesale	1,096	14	78.29
Average			18.37
Supermarkets			
Kroger	$ 8,067	$ 814	9.91
Albertson's Inc.	3,618	745	4.86
Safeway	4,113	1,134	3.63
Publix Supermarkets	3,382	—	*
Winn-Dixie	4,213	46	91.59
Average			27.50
Railroads			
Burlington Northern Santa Fe	$ 5,537	$ 803	6.90
Union Pacific	3,301	2,446	1.35
Norfolk Southern Corporation	880	352	2.50
Florida East Coast Industries, Inc.	132	—	*
RailAmerica Inc.	98	2	49.00
Average			14.94
Airlines			
AMR	$16,318	$2,313	7.05
UAL	23,262	2,865	8.12
Delta Airlines	12,744	172	74.09
Northwest Airlines	9,122	921	9.90
Continental Airlines	19,115	637	30.01
Average			25.83
Communications			
Verizon Communications, Inc.	$ 4,305	$ 331	13.01
AT&T Corporation	2,124	153	13.88
MCI WorldCom	8,653	1,577	5.49
Sprint Corporation	2,899	339	8.55
Qwest Communications	1,272	241	5.28
Average			9.24

*Ratio cannot be calculated due to lack of capitalized leases.
Source: Company SEC filings and annual reports.

One possible explanation for the preponderance of operating leases in Exhibit 12.4 is that the criteria for capitalizing lease commitments in *SFAS No. 13* can be readily circumvented. For example, a lessee can simply refuse to sign a lease contract that transfers legal title or contains a bargain purchase option. This avoids triggering the first and second capitalization criteria. Criterion (3)— the 75% rule—can also be circumvented by bargaining with the lessor to shorten the lease term until it is less than 75% of the expected economic life of the asset. However, criterion (4)—the 90% rule (or recovery of investment criterion)—is the most difficult to circumvent and undoubtedly accounts for many of the capital leases that ultimately appear on financial statements. ─────────────

We can only infer why companies in these five industries that extensively use leases have so few capital leases. A reasonable conjecture is that they have chosen to keep these leases "off the balance sheet" to improve ratios like debt-to-equity and return-on-assets.

> Because the first three criteria are easy to evade and because the fourth is not, U.K. accounting standards for leases—which were heavily influenced by the U.S. experience with *SFAS No. 13*—use only the fourth criterion for differentiating between operating and capital leases. (See "Accounting For Leases and Hire Purchase Contracts," *Statement of Standard Accounting Practice (SSAP) No. 21*, Institute of Chartered Accountants in England and Wales, 1984, para. 15.)

International

RECAP

> Lessees have incentives to keep leases off the balance sheet. Criteria exist for identifying capital leases. However, the terms of a lease can easily be designed to evade these criteria. So operating leases far outnumber capital leases for most firms.

Lessees' Footnote Disclosures

The ratio of operating lease payments to capital lease payments in Exhibit 12.4 is typical of other industries as well. Operating leases predominate by a wide margin. However, capital leases *do* exist, and their frequency does differ across companies, even within the same industry. For this reason, analysts try to adjust financial statements to include the effects of off-balance sheet operating leases in order to enhance comparisons between firms in an industry. The footnote disclosures required by *SFAS No. 13* make these adjustments possible. Exhibit 12.5 shows portions of the leases footnote from Albertson's, Inc.'s 2002 annual report.

Analysis

EXHIBIT 12.5	Albertson's, Inc.

Edited Excerpts from Leases Footnote
January 30, 2003

Future minimum lease payments for noncancelable operating leases . . . and capital leases at January 30, 2003, are as follows:

($ in millions)	Operating Leases*	Capital Leases
2003	$ 303	$ 47
2004	303	46
2005	285	42
2006	263	40
2007	247	39
After 2007	2,217	531
Total minimum lease payments	$3,618	745
Interest		(424)
Present value of net minimum obligations		321
Current portion		(14)
Long-term obligations at January 30, 2003		$307

* Net of sublease inflows

Exhibit 12.5 contains the disclosures required of all lessees. Notice that a schedule of future minimum lease payments must be reported both for capital leases and for operating leases. (We used these schedules to develop the data in Exhibit 12.4.) Payments for each of the ensuing five years must be separately disclosed, as Albertson's has done for 2003 through 2007. Minimum lease payments for all later years may be aggregated (for example, $531 million for capital leases and $2,217 million for operating leases). These scheduled payments on operating leases make it possible for analysts to estimate the discounted present value of the off-balance sheet leases. In the Appendix to this chapter, we use the Albertson's disclosures to illustrate this computation step-by-step. Once the present value of the off-balance sheet leases is determined, the computed dollar amount can be added to both the asset account (Leased asset—capital lease) and the liability account (Obligation under capital lease). This adjustment allows analysts to compensate for distortions that can arise from off-balance sheet leases when making interfirm comparisons.

Adjusting Income

If one company has structured its lease contracts to keep these commitments off the balance sheet while a competitor has not, how do analysts make the two companies' income numbers comparable? It is not difficult to make such adjustments for companies whose average lease is approximately 50% expired. Figure 12.1 shows that halfway through the life of the lease (December 31, 2007), Lessee Company's lease expense under the operating lease approach will be very close to the lease expense under the capital lease approach. Exhibit 12.1 indicates that operating lease expense in 2007 is $79,139.18 while capital lease expense is $79,680.77—virtually the same.

The intuition behind the intersecting operating lease and capital lease curves in Figure 12.1 can be extended to financial analysis by reference to Exhibit 12.6. This is an excerpt from Kmart's 1995 annual report lease footnote. In it, Kmart voluntarily disclosed the difference between its *reported* capital lease expense and the lease expense that *would have been reported* if those capital leases had, instead, been treated as operating leases.[6] These expense differences for 1992 through 1994 (highlighted in Exhibit 12.6) are $4 million in 1992 and $3 million in 1993 and 1994. What is important to see is that the $3 million expense difference is less than 1% of 1994 capital lease expense of $315 million. This small difference reflects the fact that Kmart was a mature company with a stable portfolio of leases that were, on average, close to the midpoint of their contractual life. So the income statement lease expense charge would be virtually the same under either the capital lease approach or operating lease approach.

EXHIBIT 12.6	Kmart Corporation

Excerpts from Leases Footnote
January 25, 1995

Reconciliation of capital lease information: The impact of recording amortization and interest expense versus rent expense on capital leases follows:

($ in millions)	1994	1993	1992
Amortization of capital lease property	$119	$117	$113
Interest expense related to obligations under capital leases	196	192	185
Amounts charged to earnings	315	309	298
Related minimum lease payments net of executory costs	(312)	(306)	(294)
Excess of amounts charged over related minimum lease payments	$ 3	$ 3	$ 4

Related minimum lease payments above exclude executory costs for 1994, 1993, and 1992 in the amounts of $97, $91, and $96, respectively.

---

[6] Kmart abandoned this disclosure in its 1996 annual report. This information was useful and explains why we continue to use the 1995 report even though more recent reports are now available.

We can extend this intuition to comparisons between companies. Assume that two competitors in the same industry have capitalized different percentages of their leases and that both companies have a stable portfolio of leases. Then, generalizing from the Kmart illustration, despite these different capitalization policies, the two firms will, nevertheless, have comparable lease expense numbers. *For mature firms, the income statement effects of capital lease versus operating lease treatment will often not be significantly different.*

We will show in the next subsection that this is not true for balance sheet effects. On the contrary, capital lease versus operating lease treatment can significantly alter balance sheet numbers and resulting ratios.

Balance Sheet and Ratio Effects: Capital Lease Versus Operating Lease Approach

Accounting for leases using the capital lease approach invariably worsens certain key ratios on the lessee's balance sheet—thus providing yet another explanation for lessees' resistance to lease capitalization.[7]

One ratio that deteriorates under capital lease accounting is the current ratio. Using numbers in the Lessee Company example from Exhibit 12.1, *we will demonstrate that the current ratio over the term of the lease will be lower under the capital lease approach than it would be under the operating lease approach*. To see this, assume Lessee Company is preparing a balance sheet on January 1, 2005 immediately after signing the lease. Under the operating lease approach, the first cash payment of $79,139.18 due on December 31, 2005 is not considered to be a liability; it will accrue as a liability only as time passes and as the lessor performs its duties under the lease. Since no part of the year-end 2005 payment of $79,139.18 is recognized as a liability at January 1, 2005 under the operating lease approach, the current ratio would be unaffected on signing if Lessee Company were somehow able to avoid capitalization and were allowed to treat this as an operating lease.

By contrast, at the inception of the lease, the capital lease approach *does* recognize a liability—called "Obligation under capital lease." As shown in Exhibit 12.1, the balance in this liability account at January 1, 2005 is $300,000.00. Furthermore, *SFAS No. 13* requires that a portion of this $300,000.00 balance be classified as a current liability. The current portion of the "Obligation under capital lease" is the reduction in the principal balance that will take place over the ensuing 12 months of 2005. Exhibit 12.1 shows the current portion to be $49,139.18, since this is the expected 2005 reduction in the principal balance. Thus, treating the lease as a capital lease rather than as an operating lease will increase Lessee Company's current liabilities by $49,139.18 and thereby lower its January 1, 2005 current ratio. Exhibit 12.1 illustrates that this negative effect on the current ratio *increases* as the lease grows older, since the portion of each $79,139.18 cash outflow that represents principal repayment grows over time.

To protect the lender, many loan agreements require borrowers to maintain a certain prespecified current ratio level. It is not surprising, therefore, that lessees resist lease capitalization. As the preceding discussion illustrates, treating a lease as a capital lease lowers the current ratio; therefore, capitalization could push financially struggling lessees into

You may wonder why the current portion at January 1, 2005 is only $49,139.18 and not the entire $79,139.18 cash payment due on December 31, 2005. The difference between the two numbers is 2005 interest expense of $30,000. Interest is an expense that *accrues* as time passes. Since we are computing the current ratio at January 1, 2005, none of this 2005 interest expense nor the associated liability has yet accrued. So the current portion is limited to $49,139.18. If we were to recompute the current ratio one month later on February 1, 2005, the current liability would then be the sum of $49,139.18 plus the dollar interest that accrued during January, 2005.

When lease payments must be paid in *advance*, there is also a current ratio *numerator* effect under the capital lease approach. The advance payment reduces cash as well as the liability account "Obligation under capital lease," as shown in the journal entry on page 642. The net effect is to lower the numerator of the current ratio. By contrast, if the same lease were treated as an operating lease, when cash is credited the offsetting debit is to "Prepaid expense"—a current asset account. Accordingly, the current ratio numerator is unchanged.

[7] See E. A. Imhoff, Jr., R. C. Lipe, and D. W. Wright, "Operating Leases: Impact of Constructive Capitalization," *Accounting Horizons* (March 1991), pp. 51–63.

technical violation of their existing loan agreements by lowering their current ratio below the prespecified limit.

Contracting

Two far more obvious cases of ratio deterioration under capital lease accounting relate to the leverage ratio and the return-on-assets ratio. These effects were discussed at the start of the chapter and will not be repeated here.

In the recent past, several telecom firms artificially increased reported revenues by simultaneously leasing line capacity *to* a competitor (thereby generating revenue) while at the same time leasing an equivalent amount of capacity *from* that same competitor. The cash inflows from one lease were exactly equal to the cash outflows on the other. These transactions were designed to overstate not just revenues but *operating* cash flows too. Here's how it worked. The lease of line capacity *to* the competitor was treated as an operating lease. So these cash inflows were classified as operating cash inflows on the cash flow statement. But the lease of line capacity *from* the competitor was treated as a capital lease. As you just saw, the principal payment component of the cash outflow is a *financing* flow on the cash flow statement. So from a cash flow statement perspective, this "round-trip" pair of leases with equal cash inflows and outflows nevertheless increased reported operating cash inflows. (See K. Brown, "Creative Accounting: How to Buff a Company," *Wall Street Journal*, February 21, 2002.)

There are also cash flow statement implications arising from lease treatment. To see this, refer back to Exhibit 12.1, which shows the amortization schedule for a capital lease. On the cash flow statement, the interest expense component—column (b)—of each yearly payment would be classified as an *operating* cash flow while the principal payment component—column (c)—would be classified as a *financing* cash flow. In contrast, if the lease had been treated as an operating lease, the entire annual payment of $79,139.18 would be classified as an operating cash flow. So when lessees successfully keep leases off the balance sheet, reported cash flow from operations is lower than it would be under the capital lease approach. This is the only adverse financial statement effect lessees experience under the operating lease approach.

RECAP We have shown that lease capitalization affects balance sheet ratios and that the *SFAS No. 13* capitalization criteria can be circumvented. Since different firms can conceivably treat virtually identical leases dissimilarly, financial statements may not be immediately comparable across firms. To make comparisons, statement users need to adjust for these differences. The Appendix to this chapter outlines procedures for capitalizing off-balance sheet (operating leases) and thereby increasing interfirm statement comparability.

Lessor Accounting

In addition to outlining rules for lessees, *SFAS No. 13* specifies the treatment of leases on the books of lessors. While lessees have been reluctant to treat leases as capital leases, lessors have not. When a lease is treated as a capital lease on the books of the lessor, the timing of the recognition of leasing income is accelerated—thus creating favorable financial statement effects for the lessor, as we'll show in the following sections.

Sales-type and Direct Financing Leases

From the perspective of the lessor, if a lease arrangement:

1. transfers property rights in the leased asset to the lessee, *and*
2. allows reasonably accurate estimates regarding the amount and collectibility of the eventual net cash flows to the lessor,

then the lease is treated as a capital lease by the lessor. In a lessor's capital lease, the leased asset is considered to be "sold" and is removed from the lessor's books. For lessors, there are two types of capital leases:

1. A **sales-type lease**, which exists when the lessor is a manufacturer or dealer.
2. A **direct financing lease**, which exists when the lessor is a financial institution (for example, an insurance firm, bank, or financing company).

When both conditions—the transfer of property rights *and* reasonably accurate estimates of net cash flows—are *not simultaneously* met, the lease must be treated as an operating lease.

Figure 12.4 diagrams the various possibilities for lessor accounting, which we are about to explain in detail.

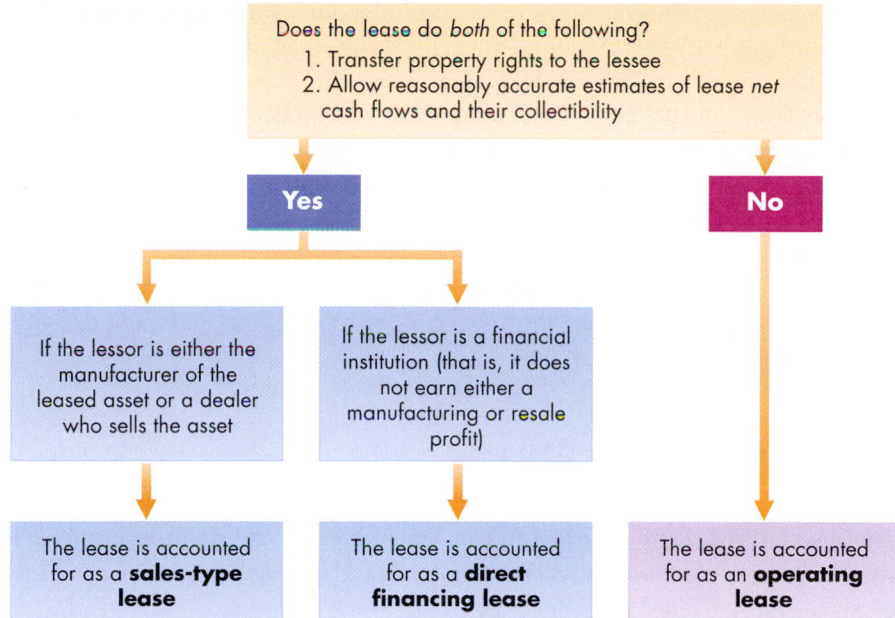

Figure 12.4

DECISION TREE FOR LESSOR'S TREATMENT OF LEASES

Sales-type Leases For manufacturers or dealers, leases can serve as a marketing vehicle since leasing arrangements generate "sales" from potential customers who are unwilling or unable to buy the assets outright for cash. For example, Deere & Company manufactures farm equipment for sale and also leases farm equipment through its wholly owned subsidiary, John Deere Credit. A lessor who uses leasing as a means for marketing products earns a profit from two sources:

1. One component of the total return on the lease is called the **manufacturer's or dealer's profit**—the difference between the fair market value (*cash* sales price) of the asset and its cost to the manufacturer or dealer.
2. Another component of the lessor's return is called **financing profit**—the difference between the total (undiscounted) minimum lease payments plus unguaranteed residual value and the fair market value of the leased asset.

The following sales-type lease example illustrates these components.

ABC Company manufactures tractors. Each tractor has a total production cost of $36,000 and a cash sales price of $50,000. ABC Company "sells" some of these tractors under five-year sales-type leases, which call for annual lease payments of $15,000. At the end of the fifth year, legal ownership of the tractor transfers to the lessee.

ABC Company's total profit over the five years of the lease is $39,000—that is, the lessee's payments of $75,000 ($15,000 per year times five years) minus the production cost of $36,000. This total profit is comprised of two components:

Manufacturer's profit: Cash sales price of $50,000 minus production cost of $36,000	$14,000
Financing profit: The difference between the cash sales price of the tractor ($50,000) and the gross inflows from the lessee ($15,000 × 5 years = $75,000)	25,000
Total profit	$39,000

Direct Financing Leases Some lessors are not manufacturers or dealers; instead, they are organizations like banks, insurance firms, or financing companies that provide lessees with a means for financing asset acquisitions. These banks and other organizations acquire assets from manufacturers by paying the fair market value and then leasing the asset to lessees. Lessors who are neither manufacturers nor dealers earn their profit from a single source—the finance fee that they charge the lessee for financing the asset acquisition. A direct financing lease example follows to illustrate lessor profit arising solely from financing the transaction.

> The Pleasant City National Bank leases tractors to local farmers. Tractors are purchased from ABC Company, the manufacturer, at their fair market value of $50,000. The tractors are then leased under five-year direct financing leases, which call for annual lease payments of $15,000. At the end of the fifth year, legal ownership of the tractor transfers to the lessee.
>
> The Bank's total profit (finance fee) on this lease is $25,000, which represents the difference between the cost of the tractor to the bank ($50,000) and the gross inflows from the lessee ($75,000).

Lessors' Operating Leases

Some lease arrangements do not transfer property rights in the asset to the lessee; or if they do transfer property rights, there may be great uncertainty about the ultimate profit or its collectibility. In either case, the leased asset is not considered to be "sold" and *remains on the books of the lessor*. Such leases are called operating leases.

Distinguishing Between Capital and Operating Leases

SFAS No. 13 identifies two types of characteristics that must be met for a lease to be treated as a capital lease—either a sales-type lease or a direct financing lease—on the books of the lessor. For ease of reference, these will be called Type I and Type II characteristics. A lease meeting *at least one* of the Type I characteristics and *both* of the Type II characteristics is a capital lease. The Type I characteristics are identical to the lessee's criteria for capital lease treatment.

Type I Characteristics
1. The lease transfers ownership of the asset to the lessee by the end of the lease term.
2. The lease contains a bargain purchase option.
3. The noncancelable lease term is 75% or more of the estimated economic life of the leased asset.
4. The present value of the minimum lease payments equals or exceeds 90% of the fair market value of the leased asset.

Type II Characteristics
1. The collectibility of the minimum lease payments is reasonably predictable.
2. There are no important uncertainties surrounding the amount of unreimbursable costs yet to be incurred by the lessor under the lease.

The purpose of these Type I and Type II characteristics is to establish the appropriate time for recognizing revenue and income on the lessor's books. We already know from Chapter 2 that revenue should be recognized when both of the following conditions exist:

1. The "critical event" in the process of earning the revenue has taken place.
2. The amount of the revenue that has been earned is measurable with a reasonable degree of assurance.

Accounting rules for the lessor in *SFAS No. 13* are directly linked to these two revenue recognition criteria. The Type I characteristics dealing with transfer of property rights identify the critical event in determining whether a lease is in substance a "sale of assets." That is, if any one of the four

Type I characteristics are met, valuable property rights have been transferred to the lessee. This transfer of property rights constitutes the "critical event." The Type II characteristics in *SFAS No. 13* relate to the predictability and riskiness of cash flows and thus to the measurability of revenue.

When at least one of the Type I characteristics and both of the Type II characteristics are satisfied by a lease, then the criteria for revenue recognition are met. This means that manufacturers or dealers can immediately recognize the sale, match costs, and reflect manufacturer's or dealer's profit. (By contrast, under the operating lease treatment, this profit recognition occurs over the life of the lease as each party performs its duties.) Furthermore, lessors can begin to recognize financing profit using an effective interest approach when the Type I and Type II characteristics exist in a lease.

When a lease does not meet *any* of the Type I characteristics, or when it meets at least one of the Type I characteristics but not *both* of the Type II characteristics, then that lease must be accounted for as an operating lease on the lessor's books. Under the operating lease approach, the lessor's recognition of income takes place piecemeal as contractual performance progresses, as we illustrate later.

Figure 12.5 summarizes the rules for how to classify and record leases on the books of the lessor. This figure is a more detailed expansion of Figure 12.4.

> Under the operating lease treatment, the recognition of financing profit is related to performance (that is, passage of time). As we will see, the recognition of financing profit is accelerated when it is recognized using an effective interest approach rather than as a function of performance.

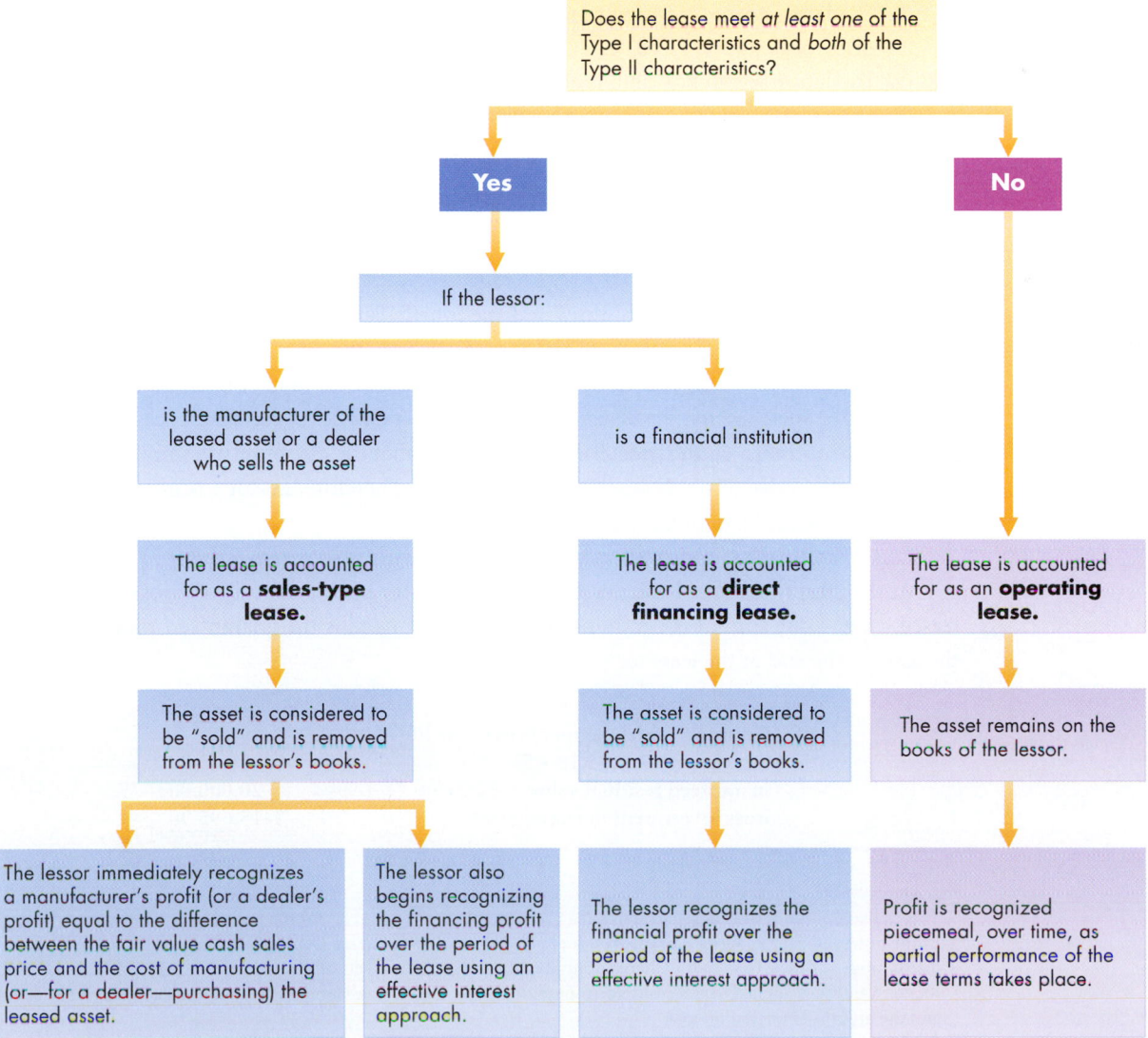

Figure 12.5 DETAILED EXPANSION OF FIGURE 12.4—DECISION TREE FOR LESSOR'S TREATMENT OF LEASES

SFAS No. 13 tries to establish symmetry in the accounting for leases by lessors and lessees. If a lease qualifies as a "sale" from the perspective of the lessor, then the property rights inherent in the lease require asset recognition by the lessee. Of course, this symmetry is not perfect, since a particular lease may meet at least one of the Type I characteristics but not both of the Type II characteristics. In such cases, the asset would appear on *both* the lessor's and the lessee's books. Another factor that inhibits symmetry is that the discount rate used by the lessor and the lessee may differ. ***The lessor is required to use the rate of return that is implicit to the lease.*** If this rate is *higher* than the lessee's incremental borrowing rate, then the lessor and the lessee will use different discount rates when accounting for the lease.

Direct-Financing Lease Treatment Illustrated

To illustrate the accounting for leases that qualify as direct financing leases, we will use a variation of our earlier lease example.

> Assume that Lessee Company signs a noncancelable five-year lease on January 1, 2005 with Lessor Company. The lease begins on January 1, 2005 and has the following terms:
>
> 1. The lease calls for five payments of $79,139.18 to be made at the end of each year.
> 2. The leased asset has a fair market value of $304,359.49 on January 1, 2005.[8]
> 3. The lease has no renewal option and possession of the asset reverts to Lessor Company on January 1, 2010.
> 4. The leased asset has an expected economic life of six years.
> 5. The collectibility of the lease payments is reasonably predictable.
> 6. There are no important uncertainties regarding unreimbursable costs yet to be incurred by Lessor Company.
> 7. The lease contract requires the lessee to guarantee a residual value of $20,000 at the end of the fifth year of the lease.

These lease terms satisfy both the third and the fourth Type I characteristics. We'll assume the lease also satisfies both Type II characteristics. Therefore, this is a capital lease. Assume Lessor Company is not a manufacturer or dealer, so this lease is a direct financing capital lease. *SFAS No. 13* (para. 17b) specifies that the discount rate that the lessor uses to record the lease is the lessor's implicit rate of return on the lease. Exhibit 12.7 shows that the rate of return implicit to this lease from the perspective of the Lessor Company is 11%.[9] Therefore, Lessor Company must use an 11% interest factor in accounting for this lease.

Lessor Company's amortization schedule for this lease is shown in Exhibit 12.8.

At the inception of the lease, Lessor Company creates an account called "Gross investment in leased asset"—the sum of the minimum rental payments plus the guaranteed residual value of the asset at the end of the lease term.

Minimum rental payments over the life of the lease ($79,139.18 × 5)	$395,695.90
Guaranteed residual value at 12/31/09	20,000.00
Gross investment in leased asset	$415,695.90

---

[8] This unusual amount was chosen to arrive at a round number (exactly 11%) for the rate of return implicit to the lease. In the previous residual value guarantee example on pages 639–641, Lessee Company capitalized $312,418.40 using a discount rate of 10%. Here in this altered example, we see that the market value of the asset is only $304,359.49. If this market value also applied to the example on pages 639–641, then Lessee Company would only capitalize $304,359.49 and use an 11% amortization rate.

[9] Exhibit 12.7 merely "proves" that the internal rate of return on this lease is 11%. When the rate is unknown and must be determined, standard procedures for computing the internal rate of return on an investment project must be used. For a step-by-step review of this computation, see R. A. Brealey and S. C. Myers, *Principles of Corporate Finance*, 7th ed. (Burr Ridge, IL: 2003), McGraw-Hill/Irwin, pp. 96–105.

EXHIBIT 12.7	**Lessor Company**

Computation of Implicit Rate of Return on Lease

Rate of return implicit to the lease is the rate that equates the present value of lease inflows and outflows.
Present value of outflows at 1/1/05
  Fair market value of the leased asset $304,359.49

Present value of inflows at 1/1/05
  Five annual payments times 11% ordinary
    annuity factor:
          $79,139.18 × 3.69590* = $292,490.49
  Guaranteed residual value times 11% five-year
    single payment factor:
          $20,000.00 × .59345† =   11,869.00
                                                    $304,359.49

Present value of inflows exactly equals present value of outflows at a discount rate of 11%. Hence,
Lessor Company's rate of return is 11%.

---

*Present value factor for a five-year ordinary annuity at 11%.
†Present value factor for $1 due in five years at 11%.

EXHIBIT 12.8	**Lessor Company**

Amortization Schedule—Effective Interest Method

Date	(a) Total Receipts	(b) Interest (Financing) Income[1]	(c) Principal Reduction[2]	(d) Remaining Principal Amount
1/1/05				$304,359.49
12/31/05	$ 79,139.18	$ 33,479.54	$ 45,659.64	258,699.85
12/31/06	79,139.18	28,456.98	50,682.20	208,017.65
12/31/07	79,139.18	22,881.94	56,257.24	151,760.41
12/31/08	79,139.18	16,693.65	62,445.53	89,314.88
12/31/09	79,139.18	9,824.30[3]	69,314.88	20,000.00
	$395,695.90	$111,336.41	$284,359.49	

---

[1]Column (d) for preceding year times 11%.
[2]Column (a) minus column (b).
[3]Rounded.

The journal entry on January 1, 2005 is:

DR	Gross investment in leased asset	$415,695.90	
	CR Equipment		$304,359.49
	CR Unearned financing income—leases		111,336.41

The credit to unearned financing income is the difference between the gross investment in leased asset and the $304,359.49 Lessor paid to purchase the asset. "Unearned financing income," a contra-account to "Gross investment in leased asset," is used to arrive at "Net investment in leased asset." Only the "Net investment in leased asset" would appear on the balance sheet but the lessor's footnote disclosure for leases would show:

Gross investment in leased asset	$415,695.90
Less: Unearned financing income–leases	(111,336.41)
Net investment in leased asset	$304,359.49

The effect of this entry is to remove the asset account representing the equipment being leased and to replace it with two accounts that together reflect the net investment in the lease. The dollar amount for the equipment removed ($304,359.49) is equal to the dollar amount for the net investment in leased asset ($415,695.90 − $111,336.41).

At December 31, 2005, when the first cash payment is received from the lessee, Lessor Company makes the following journal entries:

DR Cash	$79,139.18	
CR Gross investment in leased asset		$79,139.18

DR Unearned financing income—leases	$33,479.54	
CR Financing income—leases		$33,479.54

The amount of financing income recognized in each year is equal to the amounts shown in column (b) of Exhibit 12.8, Lessor Company's amortization schedule. For example, the $33,479.54 is the product of the January 1, 2005 net investment in leased asset ($304,359.49 from column [d]) multiplied by 11%, Lessor Company's rate of return on the lease. Lessor Company records no depreciation since the equipment itself was removed from its books (see the January 1, 2005 journal entry above).

After the last payment is received at the end of the lease term on December 31, 2009, the balance in the "Gross investment in leased asset" account will be $20,000.00, shown in column (d) of the amortization schedule. This amount represents the guaranteed residual value of the asset on the date that possession of the asset reverts to Lessor Company. Assume that the fair market value of the asset equals or exceeds $20,000; then the following entry would be made on December 31, 2009 to reflect the end of the lease and physical repossession of the asset.

DR Equipment—residual value	$20,000.00	
CR Gross investment in leased asset		$20,000.00

If the residual value of the equipment is less than $20,000, the lessee must remit the deficiency in cash when the asset is returned to Lessor Company. So if the residual value of the asset is only $15,000 on December 31, 2009, the entry is:

DR Cash	$ 5,000	
DR Equipment—residual value	15,000	
CR Gross investment in leased asset		$20,000

Guaranteed Versus Unguaranteed Residual Values

Lease contracts do not always require the lessee to guarantee that the residual value will exceed a certain dollar amount. When there is no such contract clause, then the residual value is **unguaranteed**.

If the asset reverts to the lessor at the end of the lease term, the initial entry to record the lease is identical irrespective of whether the residual value is guaranteed or unguaranteed. To see why, return to Exhibit 12.7. The example in Exhibit 12.7 assumed that the residual value would be $20,000 and that the lessee would make up any deficiency if the December 31, 2009 value were less than $20,000. So the discounted present value at 11% of the $20,000 residual value ($11,869) belongs to the lessor and is added to the present value of inflows. Now if we alter the example and assume that the expected asset residual value of $20,000 is *un*guaranteed, the asset still reverts to the lessor at December 31, 2009 and the expected (but now unguaranteed) net present value of the residual value ($11,869) still belongs to the lessor. So the $11,869 is still added to the present value of inflows just as it would be if it were guaranteed.

> Of course, with an unguaranteed residual value, the lessor bears higher risk. If the December 31, 2009 residual value is less than $20,000, the lessor loses since the lessee does not make up the difference. So the actually achieved rate of return to the lessor will be less than the Exhibit 12.7 expected return of 11%.

From the lessee's perspective, the initial entry to record the lease *is* different if the residual value is unguaranteed. Only *guaranteed* residual values are an obligation to the lessee and thereby included in the computation of minimum lease payments, as discussed on page 640.

Financial Statement Effects of Direct Financing Versus Operating Leases

Comparing the financial statement effects of direct financing versus operating lease treatment allows a more complete understanding of lessor accounting.

Had the previous lease been accounted for by Lessor Company as an operating lease, the following journal entry would have been made each year:

DR Cash	$79,139.18	
CR Rental revenue		$79,139.18

Since the leased asset remains on the lessor's books under the operating method, annual depreciation must be recognized. Assume the asset is depreciated down to a $20,000 residual value on a straight-line basis; then the annual depreciation expense is $56,871.90 ([$304,359.49 − $20,000.00] ÷ 5), and the entry each year would be:

DR Depreciation expense	$56,871.90	
CR Accumulated depreciation		$56,871.90

Exhibit 12.9 shows operating method amounts in columns (a), (b), (c) and (f) and contrasts these numbers with direct financing amounts in columns (d) and (g). Income for the operating method totals $111,336.41 over the life of the lease, as shown in column (c) of Exhibit 12.9. This total is identical to the income recognized under the direct financing method, as the total in column (d) reflects. *So income over the life of the lease is unaffected by which accounting method—the operating lease method or the direct financing method—is used. However, the timing of income does differ between the two methods*, as indicated in the highlighted column (e) of Exhibit 12.9. The direct financing method recognizes income sooner. Notice that the income timing difference would widen if an accelerated depreciation method were used in conjunction with the operating method, as opposed to the straight-line method employed in the example.

EXHIBIT 12.9	Lessor Company

Operating Method Versus Direct Financing Method
Income and Asset Balance Comparison

	Operating Method					Net Asset Balance at End of Year		
Year	(a) Lease Payment Received	(b) Depreciation	(c) Operating Method Income[1]	(d) Direct Financing Method Income[2]	(e) Income Difference Between Methods	(f) Operating Method[3]	(g) Direct Financing Method[4]	(h) Asset Balance Difference Between Methods
2005	$ 79,139.18	$ 56,871.90	$ 22,267.28	$ 33,479.54	+$11,212.26	$247,487.59	$258,699.85	+$11,212.26
2006	79,139.18	56,871.90	22,267.28	28,456.98	+ 6,189.70	190,615.69	208,017.65	+ 17,401.96
2007	79,139.18	56,871.90	22,267.28	22,881.94	+ 614.66	133,743.79	151,760.41	+ 18,016.62
2008	79,139.18	56,871.90	22,267.28	16,693.65	− 5,573.63	76,871.89	89,314.88	+ 12,442.99
2009	79,139.18	56,871.89	22,267.29	9,824.30	− 12,442.99	20,000.00	20,000.00	$ −0−
	$395,695.90	$284,359.49	$111,336.41	$111,336.41	$ −0−			

[1]Column (a) minus column (b).
[2]From column (b) of Exhibit 12.8.
[3]$304,359.49 minus the period-to-date cumulative depreciation amount from column (b).
[4]From column (d) of Exhibit 12.8.

The "front-ending" of income under the direct financing method may explain why lessors—unlike lessees—have never seriously opposed the capital lease approach to lease accounting. Furthermore, the direct financing method results in other favorable financial statement effects. For example, the lessor's rate of return on assets ratio is usually improved under the direct financing method in the early years of a lease. Highlighted columns (e) and (h) in Exhibit 12.9 illustrate this effect. Income and the end-of-year asset balance are both $11,212.26 higher under the direct financing method in 2005. An equal dollar increase in the numerator and denominator of a ratio will increase the ratio value as long as the initial value of the ratio is under 100%. Since reported rates of return on assets are almost always far less than 100%, the adoption of the direct financing method will almost always increase the lessor's reported rate of return in the early years of the lease.

Of course, Exhibit 12.9 also illustrates that this effect reverses as the lease grows older. In 2009, for example, income is $12,442.99 lower under the direct financing method while the end-of-year asset value is equal to what it would have been under the operating lease treatment. This would make the 2009 return on the direct financing method lower than the return that would have been reported on the operating lease approach.[10]

The current ratio of a lessor that uses the direct financing method will also be improved. Consider the current ratio at December 31, 2005. Under the operating lease method, the December 31, 2006 expected lease cash receipt of $79,139.18 would not be shown as an asset

Contracting
Analysis

---

[10] The ratio effect described here holds for each lease in isolation. However, most lessors have many leases of various ages outstanding. In these situations, the number of leases outstanding over time determines the effect on the return ratio. Assume Lessor Company's total number of leases is constant over time. Initially, when Lessor Company uses the direct financing method for new leases, its reported rate of return will increase. However, with a constant volume of leases, the average age of the leases accounted for on the direct financing method will eventually stabilize. When this happens, the return-on-assets ratio under the direct financing method will essentially be equal to what it would have been under the operating approach. If Lessor Company's leasing business is expanding over time, then there will be a constant infusion of new leases, and the average age of the leases in place will be falling. When this situation exists, the rate of return on assets will be higher under the direct financing method.

on Lessor Company's books on December 31, 2005, since performance under the lease contract has not yet taken place and will not take place until 2006. Under the direct financing method, however, the 2006 lease payment would be included as a component of the "Net investment in leased assets" account. Returning to Exhibit 12.8, look at the December 31, 2005 balance in this account (column [d]), which is $258,699.85; of this amount, $50,682.20 (the principal reduction in the next 12 months) is classified as a current asset. This amount is shown in column (c) of Exhibit 12.8 and represents the difference between the gross December 31, 2006 cash receipt of $79,139.18 from the lessee and the interest income of $28,456.98 that will be recognized in 2006. Thus, current assets on the direct financing basis would be higher than they would have been under the operating lease approach—and the current ratio is accordingly improved.

Sales-type Lease Treatment Illustrated

Accounting for sales-type leases is a simple extension of the direct financing method. A sales-type lease includes a manufacturer's or dealer's profit *in addition to* financing profit; a direct financing lease has only the financing profit component.

To illustrate the accounting for sales-type leases, we'll now assume Lessor Company is the *manufacturer* of the leased equipment. Prior to the start of the lease on January 1, 2005, the equipment was carried on Lessor Company's books at its manufactured cost of $240,000. All other facts in the original example (page 652) remain unchanged.

Lessor Company records the transaction on January 1, 2005 as:

DR Gross investment in leased asset	$415,695.90	
DR Cost of goods sold	$240,000.00	
CR Sales revenue		$304,359.49
CR Unearned financing income—leases		111,336.41
CR Inventory		240,000.00

The net effect of these entries is to recognize $64,359.49 of manufacturing profit ($304,359.49 − $240,000.00) immediately. The $111,336.41 of financing profit will be recognized over the life of the lease, as shown in column (b) of the amortization schedule in Exhibit 12.8. The entries for recording this financing profit are absolutely identical to the entries for the direct financing method on page 654.

Let's extend the example by assuming that Lessor Company also promises to provide maintenance services on the leased asset for an additional annual fee of $2,000. So the annual payments by Lessee Company now total $81,139.18—that is, the $79,139.18 basic fee plus the $2,000 executory maintenance costs. But the amount recorded by the lessor as "Gross investment in leased asset" is still $415,695.90; that is:

This entry assumes that the residual value is guaranteed. If it is not, then the discounted present value of the residual value—which at 11% is 0.59345 × $20,000 = $11,869—is deducted from both sales revenue and cost of goods sold. The reason $11,869 is deducted is that if the residual value is unguaranteed, the "critical event" in recognizing revenue on the residual value has not yet taken place. There is no assurance that the residual value will ultimately be realized. Only a portion of the asset has been "sold." So both "Sales revenue" and "Cost of goods sold" are reduced by $11,869. The entries with an unguaranteed residual value are:

DR Gross investment in leased asset	$415,695.90	
DR Cost of goods sold	228,131.00[a]	
CR Sales revenue		$292,490.49[b]
CR Unearned financing income—leases		111,336.41
CR Inventory		240,000.00

[a]$240,000 − $11,869 = $228,131.00
[b]$304,359.49 − $11,869 = $292,490.49

Notice that the amount of "Gross investment in leased asset" is $415,695.90 irrespective of whether the residual value is unguaranteed or guaranteed. Similarly, the amount of manufacturing profit is $64,359.49 (that is, $292,490.49 − $228,131.00), the same net amount as when the residual value is guaranteed (that is, $304,359.49 − $240,000.00 = $64,359.49).

Annual total payments	$ 81,139.18
Less: Executory cost	(2,000.00)
Payments net of executory cost	79,139.18
Number of years	× 5
	$395,695.90
Plus: Residual value	20,000.00
Gross investment in leased assets	$415,695.90

Notice that the executory costs are subtracted in computing the capitalized amount.

At December 31, 2005, when the first cash payment is received from Lessee Company, Lessor Company makes the following journal entries:

DR Cash	$81,139.18	
CR Gross investment in leased asset		$79,139.18
CR Maintenance revenue		2,000.00
DR Unearned financing income—leases	$33,479.54	
CR Financing income—leases		$33,479.54

The costs incurred over the year in fulfilling the maintenance contract (not shown) will be expensed and offset against the "Maintenance revenue" of $2,000.

RECAP   The capital lease versus operating lease dichotomy also exists for lessors. The criteria for classifying these leases include the same four criteria that apply to lessees plus two additional criteria. Lessors' incentives regarding how to classify leases are very different from lessees' incentives since capital lease treatment accelerates the timing of income recognition for lessors. In addition, capital lease treatment improves many ratios for lessors in comparison to the level of these ratios under the operating lease approach.

Additional Leasing Aspects

Sale and Leaseback

A sale and leaseback occurs when one company sells an asset to another company and immediately leases it back. This is done as a way to finance asset acquisition and/or for tax reasons. For example:

> First Company sells a manufacturing plant (excluding land) with a book value of $800,000 to Second Company for $1,000,000. First Company immediately leases the plant from Second Company for 20 years at an annual rental of $120,000.

First Company (the seller-lessee) can treat the entire annual rental of $120,000 as a deductible expense for tax purposes; if it had continued to own the asset, it could deduct depreciation only for the building itself but not for the land on which the building is located. Thus, total tax deductions may be higher under sale and leaseback arrangements. Also, the cash infusion of $1,000,000 may help meet cash flow needs.

No new *lease* accounting issues arise in sale and leaseback transactions. If the lease satisfies any of the four lessees' criteria on page 634, First Company must account for the lease as a capital lease; if none of the criteria are met, it must be treated as an operating lease. If the lease satisfies at least one of the lessor's Type I characteristics and both of the Type II characteristics (page 650), Second Company (the buyer-lessor) treats the lease as a direct financing lease; otherwise, it is an operating lease on Second Company's books.

The only complication in sale and leaseback arrangements is the treatment of the difference between the sale price of $1,000,000 and the $800,000 carrying value of the manufacturing plant on First Company's books. Typically, when assets are sold, this $200,000 would be recognized immediately on First Company's books as a gain on sale.

But this is not the way gains are treated in sale and leaseback transactions. Instead, First Company must record the $200,000 as a balance sheet credit, called a **deferred gain**. If the lease is a capital lease to First Company, this gain is then amortized into income using the same rate and life used to amortize the asset itself. If the lease is an operating lease to First Company, the gain is amortized in proportion to the rental payments.

Assume that the lease qualifies as a capital lease; then First Company's entries would initially be:

DR Cash (or receivable)	$1,000,000	
CR Property		$ 800,000
CR Deferred gain		200,000
DR Leased asset—capital lease	$1,000,000	
CR Obligation under capital lease		$1,000,000

(This assumes that the discounted present value of the minimum lease payments is equal to $1,000,000.)

The rationale for deferring the gain is simple. Notice that at the time of "sale," the sales price of $1,000,000 and the annual lease payment schedule of $120,000 are simultaneously set, and the transaction will continue for 20 years. It may be that the property is only "worth" $800,000 and that Second Company is effectively loaning $200,000 to First Company, which will be recovered over time through the $120,000 annual payments on the lease. Recognizing a gain in such circumstances would allow First Company to initially overstate its income by $200,000; this would be offset in later years by overstating its expenses by an identical amount. Thus, the U.S. GAAP requirement of deferring the gain protects against income manipulation possibilities such as creating artificial "gains on sale" by overstating the asset's "sale" price. However, the conservatism inherent to GAAP requires that losses in sale and leaseback transactions be recognized immediately on the seller's books.

> International standards do allow the seller-lessee to recognize the gain if (1) the leaseback is an operating lease *and* (2) the sale price clearly is at the asset's fair value. See *IAS 17*, para. 52.

Notice that if the sale and leaseback terms do not trigger any of the four lessees' criteria (p. 634), the transaction is an operating lease to First Company (the lessee). So carefully structured transactions allow firms to:

1. remove *existing* assets from their books using sale and leaseback accounting, and
2. keep the asset and associated liability from reappearing by treating the lease as an operating lease.

> In the past, the continuing involvement rule was sometimes circumvented through the use of a special purpose entity (SPE) that technically received the residual value. But the FASB has recently tried to close such loopholes by requiring that these SPEs (now also called **variable interest entities—VIEs**) be consolidated in many circumstances. If the VIE is consolidated, the "off-balance sheet" treatment of the sale and leaseback is reversed. See "Consolidation of Variable Interest Entities: An Interpretation of ARB No. 51," *FASB Interpretation No. 46* (Stamford, CT: FASB, 2003).

Sales and leaseback accounting cannot be used when the seller-lessee (First Company in our example) retains some of the risks and rewards of ownership, such as the right to participate in any future appreciation in the value of the leased property. Such **continuing involvement** with ownership-like characteristics is inconsistent with a "sale." That's why the existence of any such features disqualifies a transaction from sale and leaseback treatment.[11]

---

[11] "Accounting for Leases," *SFAS No. 98* (Norwalk, CT: FASB, 1988), paras. 7–13.

Other Special Lease Accounting Rules

SFAS No. 13 also covers a number of highly specialized leasing situations and outlines in detail the rules for handling these situations. Real estate leases are an example of situations requiring specialized rules in *SFAS No. 13*.[12] Leveraged leases represent another example. In a **leveraged lease**, the lessor obtains nonrecourse financing for the leased asset from a third party, such as a bank. The lease is "leveraged" because the lessor borrows to finance the transaction. A leveraged lease does not affect the lessee's accounting. For these leases, lessees use the standard lease classification procedures outlined earlier. However, the lessor must account for leveraged leases using the direct financing approach, and there are special details—outlined at length in *SFAS No. 13*—which apply.

Financial Reporting Versus Tax Accounting for Leases

The U.S. income tax rules also distinguish between operating leases and capital leases. However, the tax criteria for differentiating between them are not the same as the *SFAS No. 13* criteria. Further, the lessor's and the lessee's incentives are reversed for tax purposes. *Lessees* prefer the capital lease approach because it accelerates recognition of expenses and thereby lowers the discounted present value of their tax liability. *Lessors* prefer the operating lease approach on the tax return because it delays recognition of revenue and lowers the present value of the tax liability. So book-versus-tax differences are frequent for both lessors and lessees.

The divergence between book accounting and tax accounting for lessees widened in recent years with the invention of **synthetic leases**. Synthetic leases result from complicated arrangements that include a lender, outside investors, a special purpose entity (SPE), and the lessee. We'll skip the gory details of the legal arrangement and give you the punchline. A synthetic lease was structured to achieve the best of both worlds from the lessee's perspective: operating lease treatment on the books and capital lease treatment on the tax return. The lease contract carefully avoided triggering any of the four *SFAS No. 13* criteria, so it was an operating lease for financial reporting purposes. But for tax purposes, the lessee is considered the owner of the asset because the contractual arrangement gives the lessee the proceeds of any appreciation in the asset value at the end of the lease term.

> We encountered special purpose entities in Chapter 8, pages 401–403, when examining securitization transactions.

The special purpose entity played a crucial role in keeping the asset and liability off the lessee's books. However, after the Enron scandal, the FASB tightened the rules for consolidating SPEs, now also called variable interest entities (VIEs).[13] Under these new rules, when the lessee is the potential beneficiary of the appreciation rights, the SPE must be consolidated. This effectively puts the lease asset and liability on the lessee's books thereby negating the off-balance sheet treatment of synthetic leases. But it is too soon to know whether these FASB rules will successfully halt the off-balance sheet treatment of synthetic leases or whether loopholes will be invented to circumvent these rules.

Lessors' Disclosures

Exhibit 12.10 is taken from the notes to the December 31, 2002 financial statements of Boeing Corporation, the aircraft manufacturer. The exhibit illustrates *SFAS No. 13* disclosure requirements for lessors. Capital and operating leases must be disclosed separately, and lessors must provide a minimum lease payment schedule—just as lessees must do. Furthermore, the components of the net investment in capital leases (minimum lease payments, estimated residual values, etc.) are delineated, as are the cost and accumulated depreciation of assets under operating leases. The proportion of capital leases to operating leases for lessors is frequently greater than one—a stark

---

[12] Op. cit., para. 24–27.
[13] See *FASB Interpretation No. 46*, cited above.

contrast with lessees. Lessors like capital lease treatment since it accelerates income recognition and improves certain financial statement ratios in comparison to the operating lease approach. Exhibit 12.10 illustrates a typical footnote disclosure for a lessor.

EXHIBIT 12.10	**Boeing Corporation**

Illustration of Lessor's Financial Statement Note Disclosures
December 31, 2002

Note 10. **Customer and Commercial Financing**

Customer and commercial financing at December 31 consisted of the following:

	2002	2001
Investment in Sales-type/Financing Leases		
Aircraft financing	$3,529	$2,796
Commercial equipment financing	880	776
Total	$4,409	$3,572
Operating Leases		
Operating lease equipment cost:		
Aircraft financing	$4,906	$4,180
Commercial equipment financing	936	801
Cost	$5,842	$4,981
Less: Accumulated depreciation:		
Aircraft financing	(553)	(337)
Commercial equipment financing	(99)	(85)
	(652)	(422)
Net investment	$5,190	$4,559

Customer and commercial financing assets that are leased by the Company under capital leases and have been subleased to others totaled $533 and $437 as of December 31, 2002 and 2001. Commercial equipment consists of executive aircraft, machine tools and production equipment, containers and marine equipment, chemical, oil and gas equipment and other equipment, which the Company believes has adequate collateral value.

Scheduled payments on customer and commercial financing are as follows:

Year	Sales-type/ Financing Lease Payments Receivable	Operating Lease Payments Receivable
2003	$ 561	$ 497
2004	539	413
2005	513	380
2006	485	341
2007	452	257
Beyond 2007	3,633	1,038
Total	$6,183	$2,926

The components of investment in sales-type/financing leases at December 31 were as follows:

	2002	2001
Minimum lease payments receivable	$6,183	$5,221
Estimated residual value of leased assets	1,302	970
Unearned income	(3,098)	(2,640)
Definitive initial direct costs	22	21
Total	$4,409	$3,572

Authors' note: This financial statement note has been edited and a portion of the disclosure format has been modified slightly. The unedited footnote also includes notes receivable from customers. There is a December 31, 2002 (2001) valuation allowance of $342 ($142) deducted from the investment in leases and notes receivable combined.

SUMMARY

- The treatment of leases in *SFAS No. 13* represents a compromise between the unperformed-contracts and property-rights approaches.
- *SFAS No. 13* adopted a middle-of-the-road position that neither capitalized all leases nor prohibited capitalization.
- The FASB developed criteria for determining the precise intermediate circumstances under which leases would be capitalized.
- Several of the lease capitalization criteria that the FASB decided on are arbitrary; examples are the 75% economic life rule and the 90% recovery of investment rule. Since lease capitalization adversely affects lessees' financial statements, many lessees have tried to circumvent the *SFAS No. 13* rules and thus avoid lease capitalization. Unfortunately, some of these arbitrary rules are easy to circumvent in a way that cannot be prevented. For example, a lessee who wants to avoid lease capitalization could simply negotiate lease terms that span only 74% of the estimated economic life of the property rather than 75%. As a result, the number of leases capitalized on lessees' books pursuant to *SFAS No. 13* has been small.
- But the proportion of operating lease payments to capital lease payments can vary greatly even between firms in the same industry. This complicates financial analysis because keeping leases off the balance sheet improves various ratios like return on assets, debt-to-equity, and the current ratio. Consequently, analysts must constructively capitalize operating leases to make valid comparisons between firms with different proportions of capitalized leases.
- The FASB has been compelled to issue 10 statements on leases subsequent to *SFAS No. 13* and numerous interpretations of the original statement in an effort to close loopholes for keeping leases off the balance sheet as soon as those loopholes are perceived. But this process demonstrates the inherent weakness of a compromise approach that must rely on essentially arbitrary criteria for implementation.
- The ingenuity of lessees who wish to keep leases off the balance sheet suggests that new loopholes will continue to be invented and that new rules designed to plug these loopholes will be forthcoming.
- When lessors use the capital lease approach, income recognition is accelerated, in contrast to the timing of income recognition under the operating lease approach. Lessors' financial statement ratios are also improved. It is perhaps not surprising, therefore, that capital leases appear frequently on lessors' financial statements.

APPENDIX

MAKING BALANCE SHEET DATA COMPARABLE BY ADJUSTING FOR OFF-BALANCE SHEET LEASES

To make their debt burden appear lower, some lessees carefully design their lease contracts to evade capital lease criteria, thereby keeping most of their leases off the balance sheet. Other companies structure their leases and apply the lease accounting rules less aggressively and have a larger proportion of capital leases. This complicates comparisons between companies since each may have similar lease contract terms but very dissimilar lease balance sheet numbers. But comparisons can still be made, despite this complication.

The most straightforward method for making lessees' balance sheet data comparable is to treat *all* leases as if they were capital leases. That is, analysts should use the disclosed minimum *operating* lease payment schedule as a basis for approximating what the balance sheet numbers would have been had those operating leases been treated instead as capital leases. This is called **constructive capitalization**. We use the Albertson's, Inc. fiscal year 2002 data from Exhibit 12.5 to illustrate how this is done. For convenience, these numbers for Albertson's are reproduced in the following exhibit.

The liability that would appear on the balance sheet if these operating leases were instead treated as capital leases is the *discounted present value* of the stream of minimum operating lease payments. This payment stream (undiscounted) totals $3,618 million. Two items must be estimated to compute this present value. First, an appropriate discount rate must be determined. Second, each year's payments beyond 2007 must be estimated, since lease payments for all years after 2007 are aggregated.

Albertson's, Inc.

Operating Lease Payments from Lease Footnote
January 31, 2003 Annual Report
($ in millions)

Fiscal Year	Minimum Operating Lease Payments
2003	$ 303
2004	303
2005	285
2006	263
2007	247
After 2007	2,217
Total minimum lease payments	$3,618

Determining the Discount Rate: Two alternatives exist for determining the discount rate for computing the present value of operating lease payments:

- The weighted average discount rate implicit in capital leases.
- The weighted average discount rate on long-term debt (including capital lease commitments).

In some cases, a company will disclose the weighted average discount rate used for capital leases in its lease footnote. If this rate is not disclosed, it can be estimated provided the current portion of capital leases (that is, that portion that represents a current liability) is disclosed. This information is often provided either on the balance sheet or in the lease footnote.

Here's how the calculation is made. Recall from the earlier discussion in the chapter that each periodic lease payment is comprised of two elements: (1) interest based on the present value of the lease obligation at the beginning of the period; and (2) the principal payment on the unpaid lease obligation. The current portion of the capital lease obligation represents the second component—that is, the amount of next year's lease payment that reduces the principal balance of the lease obligation. Therefore, subtracting this principal reduction amount from the total scheduled lease payment for the coming year leaves the interest expense component. Dividing the interest expense component by the present value of the capital lease obligation shown in the footnote on the current balance sheet date (which is also the present value of the lease obligation at the beginning of the next fiscal year) yields the average implicit interest rate for capital leases. To summarize:

> For example, Target Corporation disclosed in its fiscal year 2001 lease footnote that the present value of minimum lease payments was "calculated using the interest rate at inception for each lease (the weighted average interest rate was 8.7 percent)."
>
> *Source:* Target Corporation February 1, 2003 annual report.

> This number is always provided in the schedule of lease payments found in the lease footnote.

$$\text{Interest expense on capital leases} = \text{Implicit interest rate in capital lease contracts} \times \text{Present value of lease obligation at beginning of year}$$

Rearranging we get:

$$\frac{\text{Interest expense on capital leases}}{\text{Present value of lease obligation at beginning of year}} = \text{Implicit interest rate in capital lease contracts}$$

Albertson's lease footnote shown in Exhibit 12.5 reveals that the current portion of capital leases is $14 million. Subtracting this from the $47 million scheduled capital lease payment in 2003 leaves $33 million as the interest expense component of the 2003 lease payment. Dividing this number by the $321 million present value of total capital lease commitments as of January 30, 2003 yields an average implicit interest rate of 10.28%. This rate can then be used to compute the present value of the scheduled operating lease payments (shown on page 663).

A second estimate of the discount rate can be derived from the lessee's financial statement footnote for long-term debt. The interest rate on each debt issue is disclosed in this footnote. The weighted average rate on long-term debt provides an alternative rate for discounting the operating lease payments. Another, and somewhat easier, way to approximate the weighted average interest rate on long-term debt is to compute the ratio of total interest expense (often shown on the income statement or in statement footnotes) by the average of beginning and end-of-year long-term debt outstanding (including the long-term portion of capital leases). Doing this using data from Albertson's January 30, 2003 debt footnote yields an estimated rate of 7.3%.

> Albertson's discloses interest expense in its fiscal year 2002 annual report of $.386 billion. Long-term debt (including capitalized lease obligations) at the beginning of 2002 was $5.336 billion and at the end of 2002 was $5.257 billion. So a simple estimate of average debt outstanding is $5.297 billion. The estimate of the long-term debt rate is:
>
> $$\frac{\$.386 \text{ billion}}{\$5.297 \text{ billion}} \cong 7.3\%$$

Because the first discount estimation approach is more accurate, we will round the 10.28% figure to 10% and use this rate for capitalizing the operating leases of Albertson's shown below.

Estimating Payments Beyond Five Years Procedures for estimating annual operating lease payments for periods after 2007 can also be developed. One approach is as follows. Notice from page 663 that the annual *decline* in minimum operating lease payments between 2005 and 2006 is $22 million (that is, $285 − $263); between 2006 and 2007 the decline is $16 million (that is, $263 − $247). So the average annual decline over the three-year period is $19 million (that is, [$22 + $16] ÷ 2). This suggests that the undisclosed minimum operating lease payment for 2008 is probably in the vicinity of $228 million—the $247 million 2007 payment minus approximately $19 million of estimated yearly decline. The simplest approach for estimating a schedule of annual payments for 2008 and beyond is to assume that all subsequent payments are also somewhere near $228 million per year. Dividing the total later years' minimum operating lease payments ($2,217 million, the highlighted figure) by $228 million yields an *initial* estimate of how many years beyond 2007 the existing operating leases run. The computation is:

> Because the payments after 2007 are assumed to be spread evenly over a 10-year period, we adjust our estimated yearly lease payment to be $2,217 ÷ 10 years ≅ $222 million per year.

$$\frac{\text{Minimum operating lease payments for years after 2007}}{\begin{array}{c}\text{Estimated yearly lease payment} \\ \text{(assumed to be the same for all years)}\end{array}} = \frac{\$2{,}217 \text{ million}}{\$228 \text{ million per year}} = 9.72 \text{ years}$$

The initial estimate is 9.72 years, which we round to 10 years. Based on this estimate, the net minimum lease payments will be discounted over a 15-year period—that is, 2003 through 2007 (5 years) plus the estimated 10 years we just computed.

> The current liability of $111 million is determined as follows. Interest expense in fiscal year 2003 on these capitalized operating leases would be $1,920.0 × 10%, or approximately $192 million. The 2003 minimum operating lease payment is $303 million in Exhibit 12.11. Since interest is a liability that accrues over time, only the difference between the total 2003 payment of $303 million and the as-yet unaccrued interest of $192 million (that is, $111 million) is a current liability as of January 30, 2003.

Our estimate of the amount of additional liability that would appear on Albertson's balance sheet at January 30, 2003 if all operating leases were capitalized is the highlighted amount of $1,920.0 million shown in Exhibit 12.11. A small portion ($111 million) would be a current liability and $1,920.0 million − $111 million, or $1,809.0 million, would be a long-term liability.

EXHIBIT 12.11	Albertson's Inc.

Estimate of Capitalized Operating Lease Liability as of January 30, 2003

($ in millions) Fiscal Year	Minimum Operating Lease Payment	Present Value Factor* at 10%	Discounted Present Value
2003	$303	.90909	$ 275.5
2004	303	.82645	250.4
2005	285	.75132	214.1
2006	263	.68301	179.6
2007	247	.62092	153.4
2008 } 2017 }	222	3.81529[1]	847.0
Total			$1,920.0

[1]Present value of an ordinary annuity for 15 years at 10% minus present value of an ordinary annuity for 5 years at 10%, or 7.60608 minus 3.79079.
*Present value factors for interest rates not included in Appendix I can be found at the text website: www.prenhall.com/revsine.

Once the capitalized operating lease liability has been estimated, the next task is to estimate the capitalized operating lease *asset* amount. One approach is to assume that the amount of the asset equals the amount of the computed operating lease liability. Since the asset and liability amounts are equal at the inception of a capital lease, this approach assumes that this initial equality is maintained over the entire life of the lease. But a more precise estimate can easily be made, as shown in Figure 12.6.

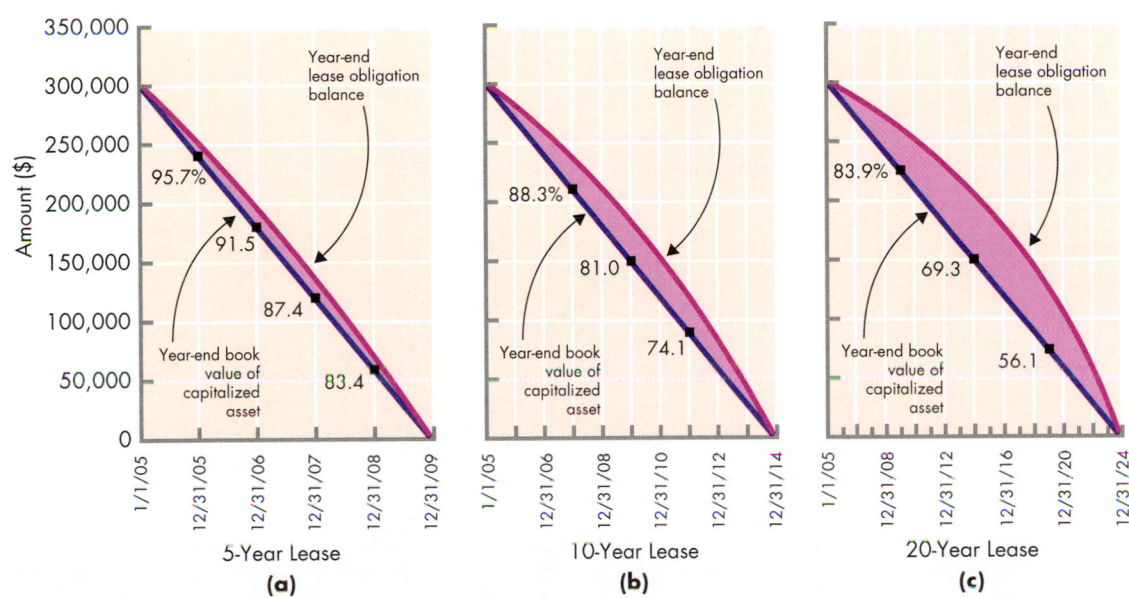

Figure 12.6 LESSEE COMPANY

General Relationship Between Capital Lease Asset and Liability When Payments Are at *End* of Period
(a) 5-Year Lease; (b) 10-Year Lease; (c) 20-Year Lease

Figure 12.6(a) graphically represents data from the Lessee Company illustration from Exhibit 12.1 where lease payments are due at the end of each period. The year-end book value of the capitalized asset (the purple line in the graph) starts at $300,000 and declines yearly by $60,000—the straight-line amortization amount from column (e) in Exhibit 12.1—until it reaches zero at the end of 2009. The magenta line depicts the year-end lease obligation balance from column (d) in Exhibit 12.1. While the two balances are obviously equal at the beginning and end of the lease, for all intermediate periods, the asset amount is lower than the liability. This relationship holds in general, since early-year payments do not reduce the liability by as much as later-year payments do (compare columns [c] and [e] of Exhibit 12.1). Notice that Figure 12.6(a) includes the percentage relationship between the capitalized asset and liability balances for all intermediate lease years. For example, at December 31, 2005, the asset balance is 95.7% of the obligation balance for the five-year lease.

Parts (b) and (c) in the figure show the relationship between the lease asset and lease liability balances for the same basic facts as in (a), but here the lease period is for 10 years and 20 years, respectively. The *difference* between the asset and liability balances *increases* the longer the life of the lease. The reason is that the lease liability balance decreases at a lower rate when lease payments are spread over longer periods—that is, a greater portion of each early lease payment is for interest and a correspondingly smaller portion goes toward reducing the lease obligation the longer the term of the lease.

Lease Payments in Advance Leases frequently require the lessee to make an up-front payment when the lease is signed. Advance payments in a capital lease mean that at the inception of the lease the amount of the recorded asset will exceed the liability. Using the Exhibit 12.3 example (p. 642), we assume a 10% discount rate and that Lessee Company makes its five annual payments in advance. Each payment is $71,945. The journal entry on January 1, 2005 is:

> Lessee Company's interest expense for 2006 would be 10% times $228,055 or $22,805.50.

DR Capital lease asset	$300,000	
CR Cash		$ 71,945
CR Obligation under capital lease		228,055

Figure 12.7 depicts the general relationship between the lease asset and lease liability for a five-, ten- and twenty-year lease at a 10% discount rate where the contract calls for payments at the beginning of each lease period.

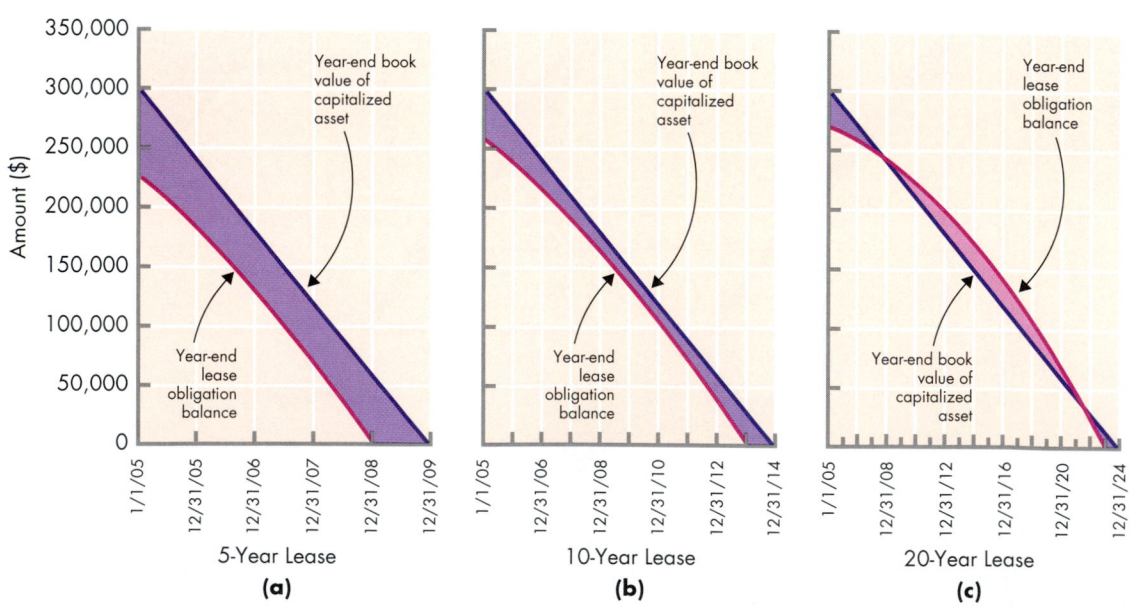

Figure 12.7 LESSEE COMPANY

General Relationship Between Capital Lease Asset and Liability When *Up-Front* Payments Are Made for a (a) 5-Year Lease; (b) 10-Year Lease; (c) 20-Year Lease.

With a $300,000 present value at 10%, the annual payments for a 5-year, 10-year, and 20-year lease are $71,945.00, $44,385.11, and $32,034.44, respectively. The vertical distance between the lease asset and obligation lines on 1/1/05 represent these initial payments.

In contrast to the situation depicted in Figure 12.6 where payments are at the end of each lease period, the up-front payment means that the asset carrying amount initially *exceeds* the liability amount, as shown in both the journal entry and in Figure 12.7. With payments in advance, in periods subsequent to the lease signing, the relationship between the leased asset and liability carrying amounts depends on the length of the lease term. With five- and ten-year leases and a 10% discount rate, the carrying value of the lease liability is always less than the asset book value throughout the lease term. However, as shown for a 20-year lease, the liability amount quickly exceeds the asset amount, and this relationship is maintained until the last two years of the lease. This excess is the magenta shaded area in Figure 12.7(c). The liability quickly "overtakes" the asset because early year payments on an amortization schedule do not reduce the liability by as much as later year payments do. For a given lease length, the higher the interest rate, the quicker the liability exceeds the asset.

> The relationship also will depend on the discount rate. With higher discount rates, the lease liability balance will decrease at a slower rate. Accordingly, the curvature of the lease liability book value line depicted in Figure 12.7 will be more pronounced.

Most companies have a portfolio of operating leases with different ages, interest rates, and payment timing. Therefore, on average across the entire portfolio, many companies' asset-to-liability ratio will be somewhere in the magenta shaded area of Figure 12.7(c). **The capital lease liability will often exceed the asset as illustrated in both Figure 12.6 and 12.7(c).** However, there are exceptions. When most of a firm's leases have up-front payments, the interest rate is low, and/or the life of the average lease is relatively short, then the asset amount *can* exceed the liability amount.

> *SFAS No. 13* (para. 16) requires that lessees disclose the net capital lease asset and liability.

The percentage relationship between the asset and the liability is a function of payment timing, the interest rate, and the length of the lease.[14] Furthermore, the precise relationship *at any specific date* depends upon the average age of existing leases. Rather than attempting to estimate the percentage relationship between the asset and liability for capitalized operating leases, we can use the disclosure the company makes for capital leases. For example, at January 30, 2003 Albertson's disclosed that its net capital lease assets totaled $257 million and its net capital lease obligations were $321 million. This results in an asset-to-liability ratio for capital leases of 80%. It may be reasonable to use this same percentage to estimate the operating lease asset to be capitalized. Our estimate of the balance sheet asset that would arise from capitalized operating leases is therefore the computed liability from Exhibit 12.11—$1,920.0 million—times 80%, or $1,536 million.

Exhibit 12.12 illustrates the estimated ratio effects for fiscal year 2002 that result from capitalizing operating leases for Albertson's. Exhibit 12.12(a) column (1) shows financial statement numbers as reported in Albertson's fiscal year 2002 statements. Column (2) shows the adjustments for operating lease capitalization. Notice, in addition to the capital lease asset and liability adjustments, there is a "net debit to balance" of $384 million— simply the difference between the $1,536 million estimated asset amount minus the $1,920 million liability amount. The debit of $384 comprises two items: (1) a debit to a deferred tax asset and (2) a debit to owners' equity.

> Of course, this is only a rough approximation. The higher the proportion of leases with up-front payments, the shorter the lease life, and/or the lower the interest rate, the higher the asset-to-liability ratio. So, if operating leases differ along these dimensions from capital leases, using the disclosed capital leases asset-to-liability ratio will tend to misstate the asset carrying value after capitalizing operating leases.

A deferred tax asset arises because capitalization accelerates expense recognition. Accordingly, capitalizing these leases means that expenses are recognized earlier on the books than on the tax return and a deferred tax asset consequently results. The amount of the deferred tax asset is determined by the cumulative capital versus operating lease expense difference. Unfortunately, this cumulative difference cannot be estimated easily or accurately. As a result we cannot subdivide the $384 between the deferred tax asset and the owners' equity debit.

As discussed in the chapter, the income statement effects of capital lease treatment versus operating lease treatment often will not be significantly different for mature firms. Consequently, we do not adjust income in Exhibit 12.12(a).

> This paragraph assumes you are comfortable with deferred tax concepts. If you are not, you can safely skip this paragraph and return to Exhibit 12.12 after reading Chapter 13.

The adjusted ratios after capitalization are shown in Exhibit 12.12(b). Notice that the adjustments from capitalizing operating leases alter Albertson's ratios. Return on assets (ROA) is lowered from 7.22% to 6.56%, a decrease of approximately 9.1% and the total

---

[14] See Imhoff, Lipe, and Wright, op. cit., pp. 51–63. A table in this article computes the asset-to-liability ratio for leases of various duration and interest rates. The table presumes that lease payments are made at the *end* of each period.

EXHIBIT 12.12	Albertson's, Inc.

Effect on Selected Ratios of Capitalizing Operating Leases
January 30, 2003

Panel (a)
FINANCIAL STATEMENT DATA

($ in millions) Statement Item	(1) January 30, 2003 Financial Statements	(2) Adjustments for Capitalization		(3) Total, After Capitalization
Total assets	$15,211	Capital lease asset	+$1,536	$16,747
Current portion lease obligation	14	Current portion lease obligation	+ 111	125
Total long-term obligations	6,566	Long-term lease obligation	+ 1,809	8,375
Owners' equity	5,197	Net debit to balance	− 384	4,813
NOPAT[1]	1,098		0	$ 1,098

[1]NOPAT refers to the company's net operating profit after taxes. To compute NOPAT, you should: 1. eliminate nonoperating or nonrecurring items from reported income; 2. add back after-tax interest expense. (See below)

Panel (b)
ADJUSTED RATIOS AFTER CAPITALIZATION

Ratio	As Reported in 1/30/03 Financial Statements	Ratio After Capitalization
Total long-term obligations to equity ratio	1.26	1.74*
ROA	7.22%	6.56%[‡]

*Computed by adding $1,809 to column (1) obligations and subtracting $384 from column (1) equity. This ignores the unknown deferred tax effect and distorts the adjusted ratio slightly.

[‡]Computed by adding $1,536 to column (1) total assets. This ignores the unknown deferred tax effect and distorts the adjusted ratio slightly. The ending balance of adjusted total assets was used to compute ROA as shown below. The tax rate was assumed to be 35%.

$$ \text{ROA} = \frac{\text{NOPAT}}{\text{Total assets}} = \frac{\text{Net income} + \text{Charges and gains} \times (1 - \text{Tax rate}) + \text{Interest} \times (1 - \text{Tax rate})}{\text{Total assets}} $$

long-term obligations to equity ratio is increased from 1.26 to 1.74, an increase of approximately 38%. It is important to make adjustments like these if you're making financial comparisons *across* firms. While the effect on Albertson's is not trivial, some of Albertson's competitors may be even more aggressive in keeping leases off the balance sheet. So interfirm comparisons may be misleading unless adjustments are also made to the competitors' statements. The underlying real economic differences are revealed only when the adjusted statements for all firms are compared. The easiest way to overcome these capitalization differences between firms is to treat all leases that convey significant property rights as though they were capital leases.

A movement to do this in the financial statements themselves is emerging internationally. The FASB published a special report formulated by a working group comprising standard-setters from Australia, Canada, the International Accounting Standards Board (IASB), New Zealand, the United Kingdom, and the United States in 1996. This report proposed that many leases that are now treated as operating leases should be treated as capital leases.[15]

> Exhibit 12.4 shows that three of the other firms in the "Supermarkets" industry have a higher ratio of operating to capital lease payments than Albertson's. This difference underscores the importance of making adjustments to Albertson's competitors before undertaking financial comparisons.

[15] See W. McGregor (Principal Author), *Accounting for Leases: A New Approach*, Financial Accounting Series, Special Report No. 163–A (Norwalk, CT: FASB, 1996).

Fox Company, a dealer in machinery and equipment, leased equipment to Tiger, Inc. on July 1, 2005. The lease is appropriately accounted for as a sale by Fox and as a purchase by Tiger. The lease is for a 10-year period (the useful life of the asset), expiring June 30, 2015. The first of 10 equal payments of $500,000 was made on July 1, 2005. Fox had purchased the equipment for $2,675,000 on January 1, 2005 and established a list selling price of $3,375,000 on the equipment. Assume that the present value at July 1, 2005 of the rent payments over the lease term discounted at 12% (the appropriate interest rate) was $3,165,000.

E12 – 1

Lessee and lessor accounting

AICPA
ADAPTED

Required:

1. What is the amount of profit on the sale and the amount of interest income that Fox should record for the year ended December 31, 2005? How much interest income should Fox record in 2006?
2. Assume that Tiger uses straight-line depreciation and a 12% discount rate. What is the amount of depreciation and interest expense that Tiger should record for the year ended December 31, 2005 and for the year ended December 31, 2006?

On January 2, 2005 Lafayette Machine Shops, Inc. signed a 10-year noncancelable lease for a heavy-duty drill press, stipulating annual payments of $15,000 starting at the end of the first year, with title passing to Lafayette at the expiration of the lease. Lafayette treated this transaction as a capital lease. The drill press has an estimated useful life of 15 years, with no salvage value. Lafayette uses straight-line depreciation for all its fixed assets. Aggregate lease payments were determined to have a present value of $92,170, based on implicit interest of 10%.

E12 – 2

Lessee accounting

AICPA
ADAPTED

Required:

What amount should Lafayette record for interest expense and depreciation expense for 2005?

East Company leased a new machine from North Company on May 1, 2005 under a lease with the following information:

E12 – 3

Lessee accounting: Purchase option

AICPA
ADAPTED

Lease term	10 years
Annual rental payable at beginning of each lease year	$40,000
Useful life of machine	12 years
Implicit interest rate	14%
Present value of an annuity of $1 paid at the beginning of each of 10 periods at 14%	5.95
Present value of $1 due at the end of 10 periods at 14%	0.27

East has the option to purchase the machine on May 1, 2015 by paying $50,000, which approximates the expected fair market value of the machine on the option exercise date.

Required:

What is the amount of the capitalized leased asset on May 1, 2005?

On December 31, 2005 Ball Company leased a machine from Cook for a 10-year period, expiring December 30, 2015. Annual payments of $100,000 are due on December 31. The first payment was made on December 31, 2005, and the second payment was made on December 31, 2006. The present value at the inception of the lease for the 10 lease payments discounted at 10% was $676,000. The lease is appropriately accounted for as a capital lease by Ball.

E12 – 4

Lessee accounting and classification

AICPA
ADAPTED

Required:

1. Compute the December 31, 2006 amount that Ball should report as lease liability.
2. What portion of this total liability should be classified as a current liability?

E12 – 5

Lessor accounting

AICPA
ADAPTED

Grady Company purchased a machine on January 1, 2005 for $720,000. The machine is expected to have a ten-year life, no residual value, and will be depreciated by the straight-line method. On January 1, 2005 the machine was leased to Lesch Company for a three-year period at an annual rental of $125,000. Grady could have sold the machine for $860,000 instead of leasing it. Grady incurred maintenance and other executory costs of $15,000 in 2005 under the terms of the lease.

Required:

What amount should Grady report as operating profit on this leased asset for the year ended December 31, 2005?

E12 – 6

Lessor accounting:
Sales-type lease

AICPA
ADAPTED

Benedict Company leased equipment to Mark Inc. on January 1, 2005. The lease is for an eight-year period, expiring December 31, 2012. The first of eight equal annual payments of $600,000 was made on January 1, 2005. Benedict had purchased the equipment on December 29, 2004 for $3,200,000. The lease is appropriately accounted for as a sales-type lease by Benedict. Assume that the present value at January 1, 2005 of all rental payments over the lease term discounted at a 10% interest rate was $3,520,000.

Required:

What amount of interest income should Benedict record in 2006 (the second year of the lease period) as a result of the lease?

E12 – 7

Lessor accounting:
Direct financing leases

AICPA
ADAPTED

Glade Company leases computer equipment to customers under direct financing leases. The equipment has no residual value at the end of the lease term, and the leases do not contain bargain purchase options. Glade wishes to earn 8% interest on a five-year lease of equipment with a fair value of $323,400. The present value of an annuity of $1 paid at the start of each period for five years at 8% is 4.312.

Required:

Compute the total amount of interest revenue that Glade will earn over the life of the lease.

E12 – 8

Lessor accounting:
Sales-type lease

AICPA
ADAPTED

Peg Company leased equipment from Howe Corporation on July 1, 2005 for an eight-year period, expiring June 30, 2013. Equal payments under the lease are $600,000 and are due on July 1 of each year. The first payment was made on July 1, 2005. The rate of interest contemplated by Peg and Howe is 10%. The cash selling price of the equipment is $3,520,000, and the cost of the equipment on Howe's accounting records is $2,800,000. The lease is appropriately recorded as a sales-type lease.

Required:

Determine the amount of profit on the sale and interest revenue that Howe should record for the year ended December 31, 2005.

E12 – 9

Lessee accounting:
Discount rate

AICPA
ADAPTED

On December 31, 2005 Day Company leased a new machine from Parr with the following pertinent information:

Lease term	6 years
Annual rental payable at beginning of each year	$50,000
Useful life of machine	8 years
Day's incremental borrowing rate	15%
Implicit interest rate in lease (this rate was known by Day)	12%
Present value of annuity of $1 paid at the start of each of six periods at	
12%	4.61
15%	4.35

The lease is not renewable, and the machine reverts to Parr at the termination of the lease. The cost of the machine on Parr's accounting records is $375,500.

Required:

Compute the amount of Day's lease liability at the beginning of the lease term.

Robbins, Inc. leased a machine from Ready Leasing Company. The lease qualifies as a capital lease and requires 10 annual payments of $10,000, beginning immediately. The lease specifies an interest rate of 12% (the lessor's return) and a purchase option of $10,000 at the end of the tenth year even though the machine's estimated value on that date is $20,000. Robbins' incremental borrowing rate is 14%.

The present value of an annuity paid at the start of each period at:

12% for 10 years is 6.328

14% for 10 years is 5.946

The present value of $1 at:

12% for 10 years is 0.322

14% for 10 years is 0.270

E12 – 10

Lessee accounting:
Purchase option

AICPA
ADAPTED

Required:

Compute the amount that Robbins should record as the lease liability at the beginning of the lease term.

On January 1, 2005 Babson, Inc. leased two automobiles for executive use. The lease requires Babson to make five annual payments of $13,000, beginning January 1, 2005. At the end of the lease term, on December 31, 2009, Babson guarantees the residual value of the automobiles will total $10,000. The lease qualifies as a capital lease. The interest rate implicit in the lease is 9%. Present value factors for the 9% rate implicit in the lease are as follows:

E12 – 11

Lessee accounting

AICPA
ADAPTED

For a five-period annuity paid at the start of each period	4.240
For a five-period annuity paid at the end of each period	3.890
Present value of $1 due in five periods	0.650

Required:

Compute Babson's recorded capital lease liability immediately after the first required payment.

On December 31, 2005 Roe Company leased a machine from Colt for a five-year period. Equal annual payments under the lease are $105,000 (including $5,000 annual executory costs) and are due on December 31 of each year. The first payment was made on December 31, 2005, and the second payment was made on December 31, 2006. The five lease payments are discounted at 10% over the lease term. The present value of minimum lease payments at the inception of the lease and before the first annual payment was $417,000. The lease is appropriately accounted for as a capital lease by Roe.

E12 – 12

Lessee reporting:
Executory costs

AICPA
ADAPTED

Required:

What is the lease liability that Roe should report in its December 31, 2006 balance sheet?

On December 31, 2005 Lane, Inc. sold equipment to Noll and simultaneously leased it back for 12 years. Pertinent information at this date is as follows:

E12 – 13

Sale and leaseback

AICPA
ADAPTED

Sales price	$480,000
Carrying amount	$360,000
Estimated remaining economic life	15 years

Required:

1. At December 31, 2005 should Lane report a gain from the sale of the equipment?
2. If not, how should the sale and leaseback be accounted for?

Coates Corporation is planning to enter into a three-year lease with annual payments of $30,000 due at the beginning of each year. If the lease qualified as a capital lease, the breakdown of the payments would be as follows:

E12 – 14

Cash flow statement effects of capital versus operating leases

Present value of an annuity due factor for 3 years at 8%	2.78326
Annual lease payment	× $30,000
DPV of lease payments	$83,498

Amortization Table

Date	Total Payment	Interest Expense	Principal Payment	Lease Obligation Balance
Inception				$83,498
Year 1	$30,000	$ 0	$30,000	53,498
Year 2	30,000	4,280	25,720	27,778
Year 3	30,000	2,222	27,778	0

Required:

1. If the lease were an operating lease, what would be the year-by-year effects on operating and financing cash flows?
2. If the lease were a capital lease, what would be the year-by-year effects on operating and financing cash flows?

E12 – 15

Ratio effects of capital versus operating leases

Sandra Company and Nova Inc. each signed lease agreements on January 1, 2005. Nova's lease qualified for capital lease treatment, while Sandra's lease did not. All other information for both companies is identical. Payments on each lease were due at the end of each year. The following information is from each company's December 31, 2004 financial statements:

	Sandra	Nova
Current assets	$2,000	$2,000
Total assets	5,000	5,000
Current liabilities	2,000	2,000
Total liabilities	2,500	2,500
Net income	500	500

Required:

1. Based on this information, what will be the impact of the lease transaction on Nova's current ratio, and debt-to-equity ratio on January 1, 2005 immediately after signing the lease?
2. What will be the impact on the return on assets ratio for 2005?
3. How would Sandra's ratio effects differ from Nova's? (*Hint:* Compute Nova's ratios before and after the capital lease transaction and assume the lease liability and asset were recorded at $1,000.)

PROBLEMS/DISCUSSION QUESTIONS

P12 – 1

Lessee accounting: Computations and journal entries

Bunker Company negotiated a lease with Gilbreth Company which begins on January 1, 2005. The lease term is three years, and the economic life of the asset is four years. The annual lease payments are $7,500, payable at the end of the year. The cost and fair market value of the asset are $21,000. The asset will have no residual value at the end of the lease term. The lessee's cost of borrowing is 9%.

Required:

1. Determine whether this lease must be treated as an operating lease or a capital lease by Bunker Company.
2. Prepare an amortization table for the lease.
3. Prepare Bunker Company's journal entries for the life of the lease.
4. Assume all facts remain the same except that the useful life of the asset is six years. Is this an operating lease or a capital lease? Prepare journal entries for the life of the lease.
5. Compare the financial statement effects of the lease treatment you selected in requirement 3 with the financial statement effects of the treatment you selected in requirement 4. Specifically, compare the effects on assets, liabilities, and equity under the two alternative sets of assumptions as of December 31, 2005 immediately *after* the first lease payment is made.

Lessor Company has a machine with a cost and fair market value of $100,000 that it leases for a 10-year period to Lessee Company. The machine has a 12-year expected economic life. Payments are received at the beginning of each year. The machine is expected to have a $10,000 residual value at the end of the lease term. (The residual value is not guaranteed by the Lessee.)

P12 – 2

Lease accounting overview: Lessors and lessees

Required:

1. What would the lease payments be if Lessor Company wants to earn a 10% return on its net investment?
2. What would be the lease obligation reported by Lessee Company when the lease is signed?
3. What would be the interest revenue reported by Lessor Company and the interest expense reported by Lessee Company in the first year, assuming they both use the 10% discount rate?
4. How would the answers to requirements 2 and 3 change for Lessee Company if the residual value is guaranteed by Lessee Company?

On January 1, 2005 Seven Wonders Inc. signed a five-year noncancelable lease with Moss Company. The lease calls for five payments of $277,409.44 to be made at the end of each year. The leased asset has a fair market value of $1,200,000 on January 1, 2005. Seven Wonders cannot renew the lease, there is no bargain purchase option, and ownership of the leased asset reverts to Moss at the end of the lease. The leased asset has an expected useful life of six years, and Seven Wonders uses straight-line depreciation for financial reporting purposes. Seven Wonders' incremental borrowing rate is 12%. Moss' implicit rate of return on the lease is unknown. Seven Wonders uses a calendar year for financial reporting purposes.

P12 – 3

Lessees' accounting for capital leases

www.prenhall.com/revsine

● Student Resources

☑ Template for solution

Required:

1. Why must Seven Wonders account for the lease as a capital lease?
2. Prepare a schedule for the amortization of the lease liability. Round the amount of the initial lease liability at January 1, 2005 to the nearest dollar. Round all amounts in the amortization table to the nearest cent.
3. Make the journal entry to record: (a) the lease as a capital lease on January 1, 2005; (b) the lease payments on December 31, 2005 and 2006; and (c) the depreciation of the leased asset in 2005 and 2006.
4. What is the total amount of expense reported on Seven Wonders' 2005 income statement from the lease? Is this amount the same as, more than, or less than the amount that would have been reported if the lease had been classified as an operating lease? Why?

Required:

1. Repeat requirement 2 of P12–3. Assume that the lease payments are due at the beginning of the year rather than at the end of the year. In this case the first payment of $277,409.44 would be made on January 1, 2005. Round the amount of the initial lease liability at January 1, 2005 to the nearest dollar. Round all amounts in the amortization table to the nearest cent.
2. Make the journal entry to record the lease as a capital lease on January 1, 2005. In addition, prepare the lessee's adjusting entries for December 31, 2005 and 2006 as well as the entries to record the lease payments on January 1, 2006 and 2007, and the depreciation of the leased asset in 2005 and 2006.

P12 – 4

Lessees' accounting for capital leases

www.prenhall.com/revsine

● Student Resources

☑ Template for solution

On January 1, 2005 Bare Trees Company signed a three-year noncancelable lease with Dreams Inc. The lease calls for three payments of $62,258.09 to be made at the end of each year. The lease payments include $3,000 of executory costs. The lease is nonrenewable, and there is no bargain purchase option. Ownership of the leased asset reverts to Dreams at the end of the lease period, at which time Bare Trees has guaranteed that the leased asset will be worth at least $15,000. The leased asset has an expected useful life of four years, and Bare Trees uses straight-line depreciation for financial reporting purposes. Bare Trees' incremental borrowing rate is 9%, which is less than Dreams' implicit rate of return on the lease.

P12 – 5

Lessees' accounting for capital leases including executory costs and residual value guarantee

Required:

1. Prepare a schedule for the amortization of the lease liability. Round the amount of the initial lease liability at January 1, 2005 to the nearest dollar. Round all amounts in the amortization table to the nearest cent.
2. Make the journal entry to record: (a) the lease on January 1, 2005; (b) the lease payments on December 31, 2005 and 2006; and (c) the depreciation of the leased asset in 2005 and 2006.
3. Assume that at the end of the lease term the leased asset is worth $16,000. Make the journal entry to account for the residual value guarantee.
4. Repeat requirement 3, but assume that the leased asset is worth only $12,000 at the end of the lease term.

P12 – 6

Guaranteed versus
unguaranteed residual
value: Lessee's perspective

On January 1, 2005, Task Co. signs an agreement to lease office equipment from Coleman, Inc. for three years, with payments of $193,357 beginning December 31, 2005. The fair value of the equipment is $500,000 with an expected useful life of four years. At the end of three years, the equipment is expected to have a $50,000 residual value, which is not guaranteed by Task. Both Task and Coleman use a 12% rate of return in evaluating this transaction. Task uses straight-line depreciation.

Required:

1. What type of a lease is this for Task and why?
2. Prepare a schedule to amortize the lease liability. Round the amount of the initial lease liability to the nearest dollar, and all amounts in the schedule to the nearest cent.
3. Prepare the journal entries required on Task's books for 2005 and 2007.
4. Assume now that Task guarantees the residual value. Prepare an amortization table and the journal entries necessary on Task's books for 2005 and 2007. Further assume that the residual value of the equipment on December 31, 2007 is $40,000.

P12 – 7

Guaranteed versus
unguaranteed residual
value: Lessor's perspective

Using the data in P12–6 above, prepare the journal entries required by Coleman, Inc. on January 1, 2005 assuming (a) the residual value is not guaranteed by Task, and (b) the residual value is guaranteed by Task. Coleman paid $500,000 to acquire the office equipment several weeks prior to the leasing transaction.

P12 – 8

Capital lease effects on
ratios and income

On December 31, 2005 Thomas Henley, financial vice president of Kingston Corporation, signed a noncancelable three-year lease for an item of manufacturing equipment. The lease called for annual payments of $41,635 per year due at the *end* of each of the next three years. The expected economic life of the leased equipment was four years. No cash changed hands since the first payment wasn't due until December 31, 2006.

Mr. Henley was talking with his auditor that afternoon and was surprised to learn that the lease qualified as a capital lease and would have to be put on the balance sheet. Although his intuition told him that capitalization adversely affected certain ratios, the size of these adverse effects was unclear to him. Because similar leases on other equipment were up for renewal in 2006, he wanted a precise measure of the ratio deterioration. "If these effects are excessive," he said, "I'll try to get similar leases on the other machinery to qualify as operating leases when they come up for renewal next year."

Assume that the appropriate rate for discounting the minimum lease payments is 12%. (The present value of an ordinary annuity of $1 per period for three periods at 12% is 2.40183.) Also assume that the asset "Leased equipment under capital leases" will be depreciated on a straight-line basis.

Required:

1. Prepare an amortization schedule for the lease.
2. The effect of lease capitalization on the current ratio worried Mr. Henley. *Before factoring in the capital lease signed on December 31, 2005,* Kingston Corporation's current ratio at December 31, 2005 was:

$$\frac{\text{Current assets } \$500,000}{\text{Current liabilities } \$294,118} = 1.7$$

Once this lease is capitalized on December 31, 2005, what is the adjusted December 31, 2005 current ratio?

3. Mr. Henley was also concerned about the effect that lease capitalization would have on net income. He estimated that if the lease previously described were treated as an *operating* lease, 2006 pre-tax income would be $225,000. Determine the 2006 pre-tax income on a capital lease basis if this lease were treated as a capital lease and if the leased equipment were depreciated on a straight-line basis over the life of the lease.

Rankin Corporation, a lessor of office machines, purchased a new machine for $725,000 on December 31, 2005, which was delivered the same day (by prior arrangement) to Liska Company, the lessee. The following information relating to the lease transaction is available:

- The leased asset has an estimated useful life of five years, which coincides with the lease term.
- At the end of the lease term, the machine will revert to Rankin, at which time it is expected to have a salvage value of $60,000 (which is not guaranteed by Liska).
- Rankin's implicit rate of return on its net lease investment is 8%, which is known by Liska.
- Liska's incremental borrowing rate is 12% at December 31, 2005.
- Lease rentals consist of five equal annual payments, the first of which was paid on December 31, 2005.
- The lease is appropriately accounted for as a direct financing lease by Rankin and as a capital lease by Liska. Both lessor and lessee are calendar-year corporations and depreciate all fixed assets on the straight-line basis.

P12-9

Lessors' direct financing lease

AICPA
ADAPTED

Required:

Round all amounts to the nearest dollar.
1. Compute the annual rental under the lease.
2. Compute the amounts of the "Gross rentals receivable" and the "Unearned interest revenue" that Rankin should disclose at the inception of the lease on December 31, 2005.
3. What expense should Liska record for the year ended December 31, 2006?

On January 1, 2005 Railcar Leasing Inc. (the lessor) purchased 10 used boxcars from Railroad Equipment Consolidators at a price of $8,345,640. Railcar Leasing Inc. immediately leased the boxcars to the Reading Railroad Company (the lessee) on the same date. The lease calls for eight annual payments of $1,500,000 to be made at the beginning of each year (that is, the first payment is due at the inception of the lease on January 1, 2005). The boxcars have a remaining useful life of eight years, the lease contains no renewal or bargain purchase option, and possession of the boxcars reverts to the lessor at the end of the lease. The lease does not require the lessee to guarantee any residual value for the boxcars. The collectibility of the payments is reasonably certain, and there are no important uncertainties regarding unreimbursable costs to be incurred by the lessor. The lessor has structured the lease to earn a rate of return of 12.0%.

P12-10

Lessors' direct financing lease

www.prenhall.com/revsine

● Student Resources

☑ Template for solution

Required:

1. What method must Railcar Leasing Inc. use to account for the lease?
2. Prepare an amortization schedule for the lease for Railcar Leasing Inc. (Round all amounts to the nearest cent.)
3. Make all journal entries for Railcar Leasing Inc. for 2005 and 2006. Assume that the company reports on a calendar-year basis.

Refer to the information contained in P12–10. Assume that collectibility of the payments is *not* reasonably certain and that the lessor uses the straight-line depreciation method.

P12-11

Lessor accounting

Required:

1. Make the necessary journal entries for Railcar Leasing Inc. for 2005 and 2006 under the lease.
2. How much income before tax does the firm expect to recognize in total over the life of the lease in these altered circumstances?
3. Is the amount in requirement 2 the same as, more than, or less than the total amount of income before tax that is recognized in P12–10?

P12 – 12

Lessor accounting
for sales-type leases

www.prenhall.com/revsine

● Student Resources

☑ Template for solution

On January 1, 2005 ABC Builders Inc. (the lessor) entered into a lease with Winged Foot Company (the lessee) for an asset that ABC Builders had manufactured at a cost of $15,000,000. The fair market value of the asset on January 1, 2005 is $19,354,730. The lease calls for six annual payments of $5,000,000 to be made at the end of each year. The asset has a useful life of six years. The lease contains no renewal or bargain purchase option, and possession of the asset reverts to ABC Builders at the end of the lease. The lease requires that Winged Foot Company guarantee that the residual value of the asset will be at least $1,000,000 at the end of the lease. The collectibility of the payments is reasonably certain, and there are no important uncertainties regarding unreimbursable costs to be incurred by the lessor. ABC Builders has structured the lease so as to earn a rate of return of 15.0%.

Required:

1. Why must ABC Builders account for the lease as a sales-type lease?
2. Prepare an amortization schedule for the lease for ABC Builders. (Round all amounts to the nearest cent.)
3. Make the journal entries for ABC Builders at the inception of the lease and for the payments received in 2005 and 2006.
4. Make the journal entry for ABC Builders at the expiration of the lease. Assume the leased asset's residual value is $0.

P12 – 13

Financial statement effects
for lessees: Capital versus
operating leases

www.prenhall.com/revsine

● Student Resources

☑ Template for solution

Assume that on January 1, 2005 Trans Global Airlines leases two used Boeing 727s from Aircraft Lessors Inc. The eight-year lease calls for payments of $10,000,000 at the end of each year. On January 1, 2005 the Boeing 727s have a total fair market value of $55,000,000 and a remaining useful life of 10 years. Assume that Trans Global's incremental borrowing rate is 12% and that it uses straight-line depreciation for financial reporting purposes. The lease is noncancelable, and it cannot be renewed by Trans Global. In addition, there is no bargain purchase option, and ownership of the leased asset reverts to Aircraft Lessors at the end of the lease. Aircraft Lessors' implicit rate of return on the lease is unknown.

Required:

1. Should Trans Global account for the lease as a capital or an operating lease? Why?
2. Based on your answer to requirement 1, make all the journal entries that Trans Global would make related to the lease for 2005, 2006, 2007, and 2012. Round all amounts to the nearest cent.
3. Assume that Trans Global accounts for the lease using whichever method (capital or operating) that you did not select in requirement 1. Make all journal entries related to the lease for 2005, 2006, 2007, and 2012.
4. Prepare a schedule of the year-to-year and total (before-tax) income differences that would result from accounting for the lease as a capital lease versus an operating lease. Round all amounts to the nearest cent.
5. Why might Trans Global's managers prefer the lease to be accounted for as an operating lease rather than as a capital lease?

P12 – 14

Direct financing versus
operating leases: Lessors'
income statement and
balance sheet effects

www.prenhall.com/revsine

● Student Resources

☑ Template for solution

On January 1, 2005 Overseas Leasing Inc. (the lessor) purchased five used oil tankers from Seven Seas Shipping Company at a price of $99,817,750. Overseas Leasing immediately leased the oil tankers to Pacific Ocean Oil Company (the lessee) on the same date. The lease calls for five annual payments of $25,000,000 to be made at the end of each year. The tankers have a remaining useful life of five years with no salvage value, and the lease does not require the lessee to guarantee any residual value for the tankers. The lessor has structured the lease to earn a rate of return of 8.0%.

Required:

Prepare a schedule like the one appearing in Exhibit 12.9 of the text. This schedule should contain the year-to-year income statement and balance sheet differences that would arise depending on whether this lease is accounted for as a direct financing lease or as an operating lease.

On January 1, 2005 Corporal Motors Corporation needs to acquire a vehicle painting machine. The company is considering three alternative methods for acquiring the machine.

P12 – 15

Asset acquisition: Cash purchase versus lease versus note payable

> *Option 1:* Issue a $125,000 noninterest-bearing note to the seller on January 1, 2005 (due date: December 31, 2009).
>
> *Option 2:* Lease the machine from the seller. The lease would require five equal annual payments of $22,000 to be made on December 31 each year from 2005 to 2009.
>
> *Option 3:* Purchase the machine outright by paying $90,000 in cash on January 1, 2005.

Other Information:

- Corporal Motors uses straight-line depreciation for financial reporting purposes.
- The machine has a five-year useful life with no salvage value.
- Round all amounts to the nearest whole dollar.
- Corporal Motors incremental borrowing rate is 8% (compounded annually).
- Corporal Motors reports on a calendar-year basis.

Required:

1. Which of the three alternatives should be selected and why?
2. What will be the total expense (and components making up the total expense) for the first year if Option 1 is adopted?
3. What will be the total expense (and components making up the total expense) for all five years together if Option 1 is adopted?
4. What will be the total expense (and components making up the total expense) for the first year if Option 2 is adopted and if the lease is accounted for as an operating lease?
5. What will be the total expense (and components making up the total expense) for all five years together if Option 2 is adopted and if the lease is accounted for as an operating lease?
6. What will be the total expense (and components making up the total expense) for the first year if Option 2 is adopted and if the lease is accounted for as a capital lease?
7. What will be the total expense (and components making up the total expense) for all five years together if Option 2 is adopted and if the lease is accounted for as a capital lease?
8. What will be the total expense (and components making up the total expense) for the first year if Option 3 is adopted?
9. What will be the total expense (and components making up the total expense) for all five years together if Option 3 is adopted?

As a loan officer for First Bank, you're evaluating the financial statements of Newton Co. Your evaluation reveals that Newton has no capital leases recorded on its financial statements while most other companies in its industry do have such leases. In order to effectively evaluate Newton's financial position and compare it to industry standards, you've decided to constructively capitalize Newton's operating leases. The following information is available from Newton's financial statements for the year ended December 31, 2005:

P12 – 16

Constructive capitalization of operating leases

Operating Lease Payments	
Year	**Minimum operating lease payments**
2006	$ 500
2007	450
2008	410
2009	380
2010	350
After 2010	2,880
Total	$4,970

Required:

1. Assuming that Newton's long-term debt rate is 10%, estimate Newton's constructively capitalized operating lease liability.
2. How might you estimate the capitalized operating lease asset amount?

P12 – 17

Constructive capitalization of operating leases

The following lease footnote disclosure is provided by Penguin Corporation:

Lease Commitments

The Company leases certain of its facilities and equipment under various operating and capital leases. The lease agreements frequently include renewal and purchase provisions and require the Company to pay taxes, insurance, and maintenance costs.

Total rental expense under operating leases was $11,243,000, $9,985,000, and $8,853,000 in 2004, 2003, and 2002, respectively.

The following is a schedule of future minimum lease payments under capital leases and rental payments required under long-term operating leases at the end of the 2004 fiscal year:

Fiscal Years	Operating Leases	Capital Leases
2005	$ 8,494	$77
2006	6,835	–0–
2007	4,952	–0–
2008	4,740	–0–
2009	4,023	–0–
Later years	12,979	–0–
Total	$42,023	$77
Less: Amount representing interest		(7)
Present value of minimum lease payments		$70

Assume that all lease payments are made at the end of the year.

Required:

1. Estimate the interest rate implicit in the firm's capital lease obligation.
2. Based on the rate in requirement 1, make the journal entry to record the 2005 capital lease payment.
3. Use the interest rate in requirement 1 to estimate the present value of the operating leases as of the end of the 2004 fiscal year. When doing so, assume that the payments due after 2009 are equal and will be made over a four-year period.
4. Prepare a 2004 end-of-year journal entry that would capitalize (that is, convert from operating to capital) the present value of Penguin's 2004 end-of-year operating leases computed in requirement 3.
5. Make the journal entry for the 2005 operating lease payment. Assume that the operating leases are being accounted for as capital leases.
6. Describe the impact on the firm's interest coverage ratio in the 2005 fiscal year if the operating leases were instead accounted for as capital leases at the end of 2004.
7. Describe the impact on the firm's leverage ratios (for example, total debt to stockholders' equity and long-term debt to stockholders' equity) at the end of 2004 if the operating leases were instead being accounted for as capital leases.
8. If the operating leases were instead being accounted for as capital leases, how would the 2005 payment affect the firm's 2005 statement of cash flows?
9. Is the answer to requirement 8 the same as or different from what the effect on the statement of cash flows would be if the leases were to be accounted for as operating leases?
10. Describe the rationale for treating some leases as capital leases and others as operating leases.

On January 1, 2005, Merchant Co. sold a tractor to Swanson, Inc. and simultaneously leased it back for five years. The tractor's fair market value is $250,000, but its carrying value on Merchant's books prior to the transaction was $200,000. The tractor has a remaining estimated useful life of six years and Merchant and Swanson both used 8% interest in evaluating the transaction. Merchant has agreed to make five payments of $57,976 beginning January 1, 2005.

P12 – 18

Sale and leaseback

Required:

1. What type of a lease is this for Merchant and why?
2. Compute the amount of Merchant's gain on the transaction. Explain how Merchant will account for this gain.
3. Prepare the January 1, 2005 entries on Merchant's books to account for the sale and leaseback.
4. Assume the tractor's carrying value on Merchant's books was $260,000. Explain how Merchant would account for the loss.

This problem is designed to allow you to see how different lease durations and interest rates affect the relationship between the capitalized lease asset and lease liability. Of course, these same asset–liability relationships apply if one wishes to constructively capitalize a lease that the lessee has treated as an operating lease.

Assume that Cambria Corporation signs a noncancelable lease that obliges it to make annual payments of $10,000. This amount excludes all executory costs, and there is no residual value guarantee included in the lease terms. The lease will be treated as a capital lease and Cambria uses straight-line depreciation for the leased asset.

P12 – 19

Capital leases: Visualizing the asset-liability relationship over time

www.prenhall.com/revsine

● Student Resources

☑ Template for solution

Required:

1. Assume that the lease payments are made at the *beginning* of each period.

   a. If the discount rate is 8% and the lease runs for 20 years, approximately when—if at all—does the capitalized lease liability first exceed the depreciated net carrying value of the leased asset?
   b. Repeat this calculation using a 12% discount rate for 20 years.
   c. Repeat this calculation using a 12% discount rate for 12 years.

2. Assume that the lease payments are made at the *end* of each period.

   a. If the discount rate is 8% and the lease runs for 20 years, does the depreciated carrying value of the leased asset ever exceed the capitalized lease liability?
   b. Will this result change if you raise the interest rate and/or shorten the duration of the lease?

CASES

May Department Stores operates department stores in 37 states and the District of Columbia. The company's department stores operate under the following names: Lord & Taylor, Filene's, Kauffmann's, Robinsons-May, Meier & Frank, Hecht's, Strawbridges, Foley's, Famous Barr, L.S. Ayres, The Jones Store, David's Bridal, After Hours, and Priscilla of Boston.

The following information is taken from a recent annual report of the company:

C12 – 1

May Department Stores (CW): Constructive capitalization of operating leases

Lease Obligations

The company leases approximately 26% of its gross retail square footage. Rental expense for the company's operating leases consisted of:

($ in millions)	2002	2001	2000
Minimum rentals	$ 97	$80	$63
Contingent rentals based on sales	13	15	18
Real property rentals	110	95	81
Equipment rentals	3	4	4
Total	$113	$99	$85

Future minimum lease payments at February 1, 2003, were:

($ in millions)	Capital Leases	Operating Leases	Total
2003	$ 7	96	103
2004	7	90	97
2005	7	83	90
2006	7	76	83
2007	7	69	76
After 2007	63	375	438
Minimum lease payments	98	$789	$887
Less imputed interest component	49		
Present value of net minimum lease payments, of which $2 million is included in current liabilities.	$49		

The present value of operating leases was $534 million at February 1, 2003.

Other Information /Assumptions:

- Assume that the amount of May's operating lease payments due each year after 2007 are equal and that these leases all terminate in the year 2013.
- Excerpted balance sheet data

	February 1, 2003	February 2, 2002
Long-term debt	$4,035	$4,403
Total shareowners' equity	4,035	3,841

- Assume that all operating lease payments are made at the end of May Department Store's fiscal year.

Required:

1. Make the journal entry to record May's operating leases as if they were being treated as capital leases as of February 1, 2003. Assume that the asset amount is set equal to the lease obligation.
2. Calculate May's ratio of long-term debt to stockholders' equity as of February 1, 2003 using the information reported in the balance sheet. Ignore income tax effects.
3. Repeat requirement 2 after capitalizing the firm's operating leases as in requirement 1. Comment on the difference between the two ratio results.
4. Demonstrate that the rate of return implicit in the present value of May's operating leases at February 1, 2003 is closer to 8% than to 7%.
5. Assume that the interest rate implicit in the present value of May's operating leases is 8%. Make the journal entry for the operating lease payment of $96 million in fiscal year 2003 assuming that the leases had been treated as capital leases rather than as operating leases. Further assume that the leased assets have an 11-year useful life, zero salvage value, and straight-line depreciation is used.

C12 – 2

Wal-Mart: Comprehensive lessee reporting—Capital versus operating treatment

Wal-Mart Stores, Inc. operates retail stores in various retailing formats in all 50 states in the United States. The Company's mass merchandising operations serve its customers primarily through the operation of three segments. The Wal-Mart Stores segment includes its discount stores, Supercenters and Neighborhood Markets in the United States. The SAM's Clubs segment includes the warehouse membership clubs in the United States. The International segment includes all of its operations in Argentina, Brazil, Canada, China, Japan, Germany, Korea, Mexico, Puerto Rico, and the United Kingdom. The Company's subsidiary, McLane Company, Inc. provides products and distribution services to retail industry and institutional foodservice customers.

Appearing next is information taken from Wal-Mart's fiscal year 2003 annual report.

Note 9: Commitments

The Company and certain of its subsidiaries have long-term leases for stores and equipment. Rentals (including, for certain leases, amounts applicable to taxes, insurance, maintenance, other operating expenses and contingent rentals) under all operating leases were $1,091 million, $1,043 million, and $893 million in 2003, 2002, and 2001, respectively. Aggregate minimum annual rentals at January 31, 2003, under noncancelable leases are as follows (in millions):

Fiscal Year	Operating Leases	Capital Leases
2004	$ 589	$ 440
2005	576	431
2006	560	428
2007	546	419
2008	515	412
Thereafter	5,202	3,152
Total minimum rentals	$7,988	A
Less estimated executory costs		$ 57
Net minimum lease payments		B
Less imputed interest at rates ranging from 6.1% to 14.0%		C
Present value of minimum lease payments		D

Excerpts from Wal-Mart's 2003 Consolidated Balance Sheets:

($ in millions)	1/31/2003
Liabilities and Shareholders Equity:	
Current Liabilities	
Commercial paper	$ 1,079
Accounts payable	17,140
Accrued liabilities	8,945
Accrued income taxes	739
Long-term debt due within one year	4,538
Obligations under capital leases due within one year	176
Total Current Liabilities	$32,617
Long-term debt	$16,607
Long-term obligations under capital leases	3,001
Deferred income taxes and other	1,761
Total Long-term Liabilities	$21,369

Required:

1. Solve for the unknowns (A, B, C, and D) in Note 9.
2. Make the journal entry to account for Wal-Mart's fiscal year 2004 capital lease payment. (Ignore allocating the executory cost portion since there is insufficient information to do so.)
3. Assume that the amount of Wal-Mart's operating lease payment due each year after 2008 is equal and is paid at the end of each fiscal year. Assume that these leases all terminate at the end of 2019. Using an interest rate of 8%, calculate the present value of the operating lease payments at January 31, 2003.
4. Make the journal entry that would be necessary at January 31, 2003 to account for the operating leases as if they were being treated as capital leases. (Ignore income taxes and assume that the amount of the capitalized asset equals the capitalized liability.)
5. Based on your answer to requirement 3, make the necessary journal entries for the fiscal year ended January 31, 2004 assuming operating leases are being accounted for as capital leases. Assume a 16-year useful life, zero salvage value, and straight-line depreciation for all capitalized leased assets.
6. Wal-Mart's total shareholders' equity listed on its January 31, 2003 Consolidated Balance Sheet was $39,337 million. This gives a long-term debt-to-shareholders' equity ratio of 54.3%. Calculate Wal-Mart's total long-term debt-to-shareholders' equity ratio after treating its operating leases as if they were capital leases. (Ignore tax effects.)
7. Comment on the differences between the unadjusted and adjusted ratios.

In a recent lending agreement (dated March 3, 1997), Nationsbank of Texas, N.A., included the following definitions for terms used in its loan covenants with a borrower:

"Fixed Charges" means the sum of, for Borrower and its Subsidiaries, determined in accordance with GAAP on a consolidated basis, (a) interest expense (including interest expense pursuant to Capital Leases), plus (b) lease expense payable for Operating Leases, determined for the four fiscal quarters preceding the date of calculation.

"Net Earnings Available for Fixed Charges" means, for Borrower and its Subsidiaries, determined in accordance with GAAP on a consolidated basis, (a) Net Income before Taxes, plus (b) extraordinary noncash charges, plus (c) interest expense (including interest expense pursuant to Capital Leases), plus (d) lease expense pursuant to Operating Leases, determined for the fiscal quarter preceding the date of calculation.

"Fixed Charges Coverage Ratio" means the ratio of Net Earnings Available for Fixed Charges to Fixed Charges.

Borrower shall not permit the Fixed Charges Coverage Ratio to be less than the following ratios for the fiscal quarters ending as follows:

December 31, 1996	0.70 to 1.00
March 31, 1997	1.00 to 1.00
June 30, 1997	1.20 to 1.00
September 30, 1997	1.50 to 1.00
December 31, 1997	1.75 to 1.00

Notice that the definitions of "Fixed charges" and "Net earnings available for fixed charges" *both* add back lease expenses under operating leases. The objective of this case is to allow you to see why astute lenders carefully design covenants to protect themselves against borrowers who might use the latitude in GAAP lease accounting rules to circumvent covenant restrictions.

Assume the following initial conditions for the borrower on June 30, 1997:

Income before interest and taxes	$120,000
Interest on capital lease	$ 60,000
Interest on other borrowings	40,000
Fixed charges	$100,000
Fixed charges coverage ratio	1.20

Notice that the fixed charges coverage ratio equals the covenant constraint at June 30, 1997; even minor adversity might cause a covenant violation in the next quarter. In addition, the borrower is required to increase the ratio to 1.50 by September 30, 1997.

Required:

1. Assume that the borrower "somehow" restructures the existing lease to have it qualify as an operating lease. What effect will this change in lease classification have on the times interest earned ratio as typically defined? (See Chapter 5.) What effect will this change have on the fixed charges coverage ratio as defined in the lending agreement? What does your answer to this part tell you about the vigilance that credit analysts must exert in designing and monitoring financial contractual restrictions?

2. Now assume that the initial times interest earned ratio was less than 1.00 to 1.00. Would changing the capital lease to an operating lease benefit the borrower's compliance with lending covenants?

Note: In answering both parts, make assumptions when sufficient information is not available.

The following information is drawn from recent annual reports of three firms in the retail industry: JC Penney Company, Inc., Dillard Department Stores, Inc., and Federated Department Stores, Inc.

A. JC Penney is a major retailer, operating 1,049 department stores in 49 states, Puerto Rico, and Mexico. In addition, it operates 54 Renner department stores in Brazil. A major portion of JC Penney Company's business consists of providing merchandise and services to consumers through department stores, catalog departments, and the Internet. Selected financial information follows:

($ in millions)	January 25, 2003	January 26, 2002
Long-term debt	$ 4,940	$ 5,179
Total shareholders' equity	6,370	6,129
Total liabilities and shareholders' equity	17,867	18,048

An excerpt from its leases footnote follows:

The company conducts the major parts of its operations from leased premises that include retail stores, catalog fulfillment centers, warehouses, offices, and other facilities. Future minimum lease obligations as of January 25, 2003, were:

($ in millions)	Operating Leases	Capital Leases
2003	$ 671	$17
2004	611	16
2005	544	12
2006	494	4
2007	455	2
Thereafter	4,128	–
Minimum payments	$6,903	$51
Present value of minimum payments		$43

B. Dillard Department Stores, Inc. is a company that operates retail department stores located primarily in the Southwest, Southeast, and Midwest. Selected financial information follows:

($ in thousands)	February 1, 2003	February 2, 2002
Long-term debt	$2,193,006	$2,124,577
Total shareholders' equity	2,264,196	2,668,397
Total liabilities and shareholders' equity	6,675,932	7,074,559

An excerpt from its leases footnote follows:

Future minimum payments under capital leases and the future minimum rental commitments for all noncancelable operating leases as of February 1, 2003 are as follows ($ in thousands):

Fiscal Year	Capital Leases Amount	Operating Leases Amount
2003	$ 3,806	$ 59,299
2004	3,622	50,479
2005	3,339	41,797
2006	3,232	38,588
2007	2,578	29,482
After 2007	21,595	105,323
Total minimum lease payments	38,172	
Less amount representing interest	(17,716)	
Present value of net minimum payments	$20,456	

C. Federated Department Stores Inc. is one of the leading operators of full-line department stores in the United States, with more than 450 department stores in 34 states. The company's department stores are located at urban or suburban sites, principally in densely populated areas across the United States. Selected financial information follows:

($ in millions)	February 1, 2003	February 2, 2002
Long-term debt	$ 3,408	$ 3,859
Total shareholders' equity	5,762	5,564
Total liabilities and shareholders' equity	14,441	16,112

An excerpt from its leases footnote follows:

Minimum rental commitments as of February 1, 2003 for noncancelable leases are:

($ in millions)	Operating Leases	Capital Leases
2003	$ 162	$ 11
2004	159	11
2005	149	9
2006	151	8
2007	145	8
Thereafter	1,943	69
Minimum payments	$2,709	116
Less amount representing interest		56
Present value of minimum payments		$ 60

Additional Information:

1. For JC Penney, assume that the operating lease payments due after 2007 are equal and will be made over a ten-year period.
2. For Dillard's, assume that the operating lease payments due after 2007 are equal and will be made over a five-year period.
3. For Federated, assume that the operating lease payments due after 2007 are equal and will be made over a 14-year period.

Required:

1. Show that the interest rate implicit in the capital lease obligations of JC Penney is closer to 8.5% than to 10%.
2. Using the 8.5% rate from requirement 1, calculate the present value of the operating lease obligations of JC Penney.
3. Using the approach followed in requirement 1, we can determine that the interest rate implicit in the capital lease obligations of Dillard's is close to 10%. Use this rate to calculate the present value of the firm's operating lease payments.
4. The approach in requirement 1 allows us to determine that the interest rate implicit in the capital lease obligations of Federated is close to 11.5%. Use this rate to calculate the present value of the firm's operating lease payments.
5. Using the balance sheet information reported earlier, calculate the long-term debt-to-shareholders'-equity ratio and the long-term debt-to-total-assets ratio of the three firms for the most recent fiscal year.
6. Repeat requirement 5 after treating the operating leases as if they are being accounted for as capital leases. How do the results compare with those in requirement 5? (Ignore taxes and assume that the capitalized asset equals the capitalized liability.)

COLLABORATIVE LEARNING CASE

C12-5

Xerox Corporation: Lessors' revenue allocations in bundled lease arrangements

Xerox Corporation, one of the world's largest manufacturers of office equipment and copiers, engages in numerous leasing transactions with customers. Many of these are sales-type leases. Its accounting for these transactions was challenged by the SEC, as excerpts from the following news account relate:

Xerox Corp. said the Securities and Exchange Commission's main accounting unit disagrees with the way the office-equipment company accounts for certain lease transactions. The news, which came in a Xerox regulatory filing, is another blow to the credibility of Xerox's accounting practices, which have been under investigation by the SEC since mid-2000. . . .

In the filing, Xerox said it had been advised by the SEC's Office of the Chief Accountant that it believed Xerox's method for booking certain office-equipment leases "does not follow the methodology" required under accounting rules.

Leasing accounts for a substantial portion of Xerox's revenues, because many customers prefer to pay for costly office equipment in increments over time instead of buying it all at once.

...

The disagreement referred to in yesterday's filing centers on changes Xerox had made to the way it allocates the various components of equipment leases.

When Xerox leases a copier to a customer, it typically bundles into a single monthly fee a payment for equipment, financing, service and supplies. By shifting its assumptions about the value assigned to these lease components, Xerox was able to book more income upfront instead of over time. . . . [16]

Assume that Northbrook Corporation signs a four-year noncancelable lease with Xerox to lease a copier. The monthly fee of $700 covers the equipment, financing, as well as executory costs like maintenance service, and all copier supplies. Further assume that the lease will be treated as a sales-type lease by Xerox Corporation, which makes the following entry to book the transaction:

DR Gross investment in leased asset	A	
CR Sales revenue		B
CR Unearned financing income–leases		C
DR Cost of goods sold	D	
CR Inventory		D

Required:

1. Explain how the dollar amounts associated with each of the letters in the journal entries are computed in accordance with *SFAS No. 13*. Be specific regarding what economic information about the copier is needed in order to book the transaction.

2. The article states that "by shifting its assumptions about the value assigned to these lease components, Xerox was able to book more income upfront instead of over time." Using the entry as a template, explain how a company could pull income forward under sales-type lease accounting. Be specific about how different assumptions regarding equipment value, rates of return, and executory costs affect the timing of revenue and income.

Remember to check the book's Companion Website for additional problem and case material.

www.prenhall.com/revsine

---

[16] M. Maremont, "Xerox Says SEC Unit Disagrees With Way It Accounts for Certain Lease Transactions," *Wall Street Journal*, (January 8, 2002).

Income Tax Reporting

In the United States and many other industrialized countries, the rules for computing income for financial reporting purposes—known as **book income**—do not correspond to the rules for computing income for taxation purposes—referred to as **taxable income**. This divergence is allowable and makes sense because of the different objectives underlying book income versus taxable income.[1] Book income is intended to reflect increases in a firm's "well-offness"; it includes all increases in net assets that meet the GAAP criteria for revenue recognition (critical event and measurable) and for costs that have expired according to the expense matching principle outlined in Chapter 2. ***Book income includes all earned inflows of net assets, even inflows not immediately convertible into cash; and it reflects expenses as they accrue, not just when they are paid.***

Determining income for tax purposes does not always focus on changes in well-offness. Instead, taxable income is governed by the "constructive receipt/ability to pay" doctrine. This means the timing of taxation usually (but not always) follows the inflow of cash or cash equivalents. That is, when liquid assets enter the firm, they are frequently taxed, since it is easiest to collect money at that time. For example, rent received in advance is taxed when received even though it is not yet earned from an accounting standpoint. Similarly, tax deductions generally are allowed only when expenditures are made or when a loss occurs. ***Because of different underlying objectives, the rules for determining book income (according to GAAP) diverge from the rules for determining taxable income (according to the Internal Revenue Service or IRS). This divergence complicates the way that income taxes are reflected in financial reports.***

This chapter describes the major differences between U.S. book income and taxable income and how these differences complicate the reporting of tax expense and tax obligations. First, we outline the major categories of differences between book income and taxable income, and we illustrate the distortions that would result on GAAP income statements if tax expense were to be set equal to taxes owed the IRS. Next, we explain and illustrate the GAAP solution for avoiding these distortions—

Learning Objectives

After studying this chapter, you will understand:

1. The different objectives underlying income determination for financial reporting (book) purposes versus tax purposes.

2. The distinction between temporary (timing) and permanent differences and the items that cause each of these differences, and how each affects book income versus taxable income.

3. The distortions created when the deferred tax effects of temporary differences are ignored.

4. How tax expense is determined with interperiod tax allocation.

5. How changes in tax rates are measured and recorded.

6. The reporting rules for net operating loss carrybacks and carryforwards.

7. How to read and interpret tax footnote disclosures and how these footnotes can be used to enhance interfirm comparability.

8. How tax footnotes can be used to evaluate the degree of conservatism in firms' book (GAAP) accounting choices.

---

[1] Countries where the rules for determining accounting (book) income and taxable income for parent companies are essentially the same include, for example, Germany, Japan, and Switzerland.

referred to as **deferred income tax accounting** or **interperiod tax allocation**. We also explore what happens from an accounting standpoint when income tax rates are changed by Congress, and we discuss how the accounting works for special U.S. tax laws that apply to unprofitable firms.

The second part of the chapter guides you through an analysis of typical income tax footnote disclosures. Our purpose is to explain the wealth of information that can be extracted from these disclosures. We demonstrate how analysts can use tax footnotes to glean information not provided elsewhere in the financial statements to better understand a firm's performance and future prospects.

> Interperiod tax allocation refers to the allocation of income tax expense *across periods* when book and tax income differ. **Intraperiod tax allocation**, introduced in Chapter 2, refers to the allocation of the tax cost (benefit) across various components of book income *within a given period*. For example, the current tax provision (expense) is related to (pre-tax) income from continuing operations, while extraordinary items and cumulative effects of accounting changes are reported *net of tax* on the income statement.

Understanding Income Tax Reporting

Temporary and Permanent Differences Between Book Income and Taxable Income

The differences that result from determining income reported in external financial statements on the one hand and determining taxable income for tax purposes on the other fall into two broad categories:

1. **Temporary** or **timing differences**
2. **Permanent differences**

> In this chapter we use the terms "temporary" and "timing" differences interchangeably. They mean the same thing. *Accounting Principles Board (APB) Opinion No. 11*, "Accounting for Income Taxes," used the term "timing difference," while *Statement of Financial Accounting Standards (SFAS) No. 109*, "Accounting for Income Taxes," which superseded *APB Opinion No. 11*, uses the term "temporary differences." The same term should have been used in both standards but, unfortunately, it wasn't.

A timing difference results when a revenue (gain) or expense (loss) enters into the determination of book income in one period but affects taxable income in a different (earlier or later) period. A brief summary of common temporary differences is provided in Exhibit 13.1. Timing differences are considered "temporary" because they eventually reverse. That is, a revenue (or expense) item that causes book income to be greater than (less than) taxable income when it is initially recorded—called an **originating** **timing difference**—will eventually reverse. These reversals cause book income to be less than (greater than) taxable income in future periods and are called *reversing* **timing differences**.

Temporary differences that will cause taxable income to be *higher* than book income in future periods give rise to a **deferred tax liability**. Conversely, temporary differences that will cause taxable income to be *lower* than book income in future periods when those differences reverse give rise to a **deferred tax asset**. Deferred tax liabilities and assets are explained in the following sections.

A **permanent difference** between taxable income and book income is caused by income items that:

> This special treatment of dividend income was put into the tax code largely to avoid double taxation of corporate profits. For ownership interests of less than 20%, U.S. corporations are permitted to deduct 70% of dividends received from other U.S. companies. For ownership interests between 20% and 80%, the deduction is 80%; and for interests of 80% or greater, corporations are allowed to deduct 100% of the dividends received from their U.S. subsidiaries.

1. Enter into the determination of accounting income but *never* affect taxable income. For example, interest income received on municipal bonds is included in accounting income but is not included in taxable income under current tax rules.
2. Enter into the determination of taxable income but *never* affect accounting income. For example, the **dividends-received deduction** in the U.S. tax laws allows one U.S. corporation to deduct from taxable income a portion of the dividends received from another U.S. corporation.

Because permanent differences between book income and taxable income do not reverse and are not offset by corresponding differences in subsequent periods, they do *not* give rise to deferred tax assets or liabilities. Exhibit 13.2 provides examples of permanent differences.

EXHIBIT 13.1	Examples of Temporary (Timing) Differences Between Book Income and Taxable Income

Depreciation Expense

Accelerated depreciation is used for taxable income; straight-line is used for book income. Modified Accelerated Cost Recovery System (MACRS) useful lives are used for taxable income and useful economic lives are used for book income. Both of these items result in larger depreciation deductions for tax purposes than for book purposes in the early years of an asset's life, and the opposite effect occurs in later years.

Bad Debts Expense

Bad debts are accrued and recognized under the allowance method for book purposes, but tax rules follow the direct write-off method, allowing a deduction only when a particular account is deemed to be uncollectible and written off.

Warranty Expense

Warranty expenses are accrued and recorded in the year the product is sold for book purposes, but for tax purposes the deduction is allowed when the actual warranty expenditures are made to correct the defect.

Prepaid Expenses

Some business expenses, like insurance premiums and rent, are paid in advance. For book purposes these expenditures are initially recorded as assets—"prepaid insurance," or "prepaid rent"—but later they are expensed over the periods when the benefits are received. Tax rules allow the deduction in the period the payment is made.

Pension and Other Post-Retirement Benefits (OPEB) Expenses

For book purposes, the deduction is based on the amount of pension or OPEB expense accrued. For pensions, a tax deduction is allowed for the amounts funded (that is, contributed to the pension fund) each period, and for OPEB costs, a deduction is allowed for amounts actually paid during the period.

Purchased Goodwill

The Revenue Reconciliation Act of 1993 allows firms a deduction for goodwill amortization on a 15-year straight-line basis under certain special conditions. But in most situations goodwill is *not* deductible. For book purposes, purchased goodwill is subject to periodic impairment tests (see Chapter 16). If impaired, goodwill is written down to fair value with an offsetting charge to earnings.

Installment Sales

Sales are generally recognized for book purposes when the goods are delivered to the customer regardless of when collections are made. If collections are made over an extended period, tax rules record the sales revenue as payments are received.

(*continued on next page*)

". . . A great deal of confusion surrounds the tax deductibility of goodwill. The financial press and even financial analysts often assume that goodwill that is recorded on a firm's financial statements is deductible for tax purposes, but in most cases, it is not. Tax-deductible goodwill arises only in acquisitions in which the *tax basis* of the target's (firm being acquired) assets are stepped-up (recorded at fair value). . . . It is rare for the target's assets to be stepped-up for *tax purposes* in acquisitions of freestanding C corporations (that is, conventional corporate entities that are taxed at the entity level): in other words, tax-deductible goodwill is rare. In contrast, with the purchase method of accounting large amounts of financial accounting goodwill typically arise. This accounting goodwill does not necessarily appear on the *tax-basis* balance sheets; that is, it is not tax-deductible goodwill.

When then is goodwill tax deductible? Goodwill is tax deductible when the *tax basis* of the acquired firm's assets are stepped-up. A step-up in the acquired firm's assets occurs frequently in acquisitions of conduits, such as S corporations (that is, corporations that elect to be taxed as partnerships) or partnerships, and in subsidiary sales, but not in acquisitions of freestanding C corporations."* (Italics and parenthetical remarks added by authors of this textbook for clarification.)

Whether goodwill is deductible for tax purposes hinges on whether the acquiring entity is buying the assets of another entity directly (for example, ABC Company buys a division of XYZ Company) or whether the acquiring entity gains control over the assets of another entity by buying the voting stock of that entity (for example, ABC Company acquires 80% of the common stock of XYZ Company). Goodwill that arises from the former type of transaction is deductible for tax purposes, while it is not deductible for the latter type of transaction. The reason that it is rare for the target's assets to be stepped-up for tax purposes (and, therefore, goodwill becomes deductible for tax purposes) in acquisitions of freestanding C corporations is because in these transactions the acquiring firm is typically buying the outstanding voting stock of the target firm, not specific assets of that entity. Since most goodwill on consolidated balance sheets arises from stock transactions rather than outright asset purchases, it is not deductible for tax purposes.

*M. Scholes, M. Wolfson, M. Erickson, E. Maydew, and T. Shevlin, *Taxes and Business Strategy: A Planning Approach* (Upper Saddle River, NJ: Prentice Hall, 2002).

EXHIBIT 13.1	Examples of Temporary (Timing) Differences Between Book Income and Taxable Income *(continued)*

Long-Term Construction Contracts

For long-term construction contracts (Chapter 3), firms may elect to use either the percentage-of-completion or the completed-contract method of revenue recognition for book purposes. In general, taxpayers may only use the percentage-of-completion method to account for long-term contracts entered into after July 11, 1989.

Revenues Received in Advance

Revenues received in advance (for example, rent revenue or subscription revenue) are initially recorded as a liability for book purposes and are transferred to income as those revenues are "earned." For tax purposes, these amounts are taxed when received.

Equity in Undistributed Earnings of Investees

If a company (Investor) owns 20% or more of the outstanding voting stock of another corporation (Investee), the equity method of accounting is used for book purposes (Chapter 16). Under the equity method, the Investor records as income its share of Investee profits for the period. For tax purposes, income is recognized when Investee dividends are received, but this recognition is subject to special dividends-received deduction rules discussed below under permanent differences.

EXHIBIT 13.2	Examples of Permanent Differences Between Book Income and Taxable Income

Items Recognized for Book Purposes but *Not* for Tax Purposes

- Interest received on state and municipal bonds is not subject to federal or state tax but is included in book income.
- If a company pays fines or expenses resulting from violations of the law (for example, environmental damages), these payments are not deductible for tax purposes but would be deducted from book income.
- Goodwill write-offs generally are not deductible for tax purposes unless they meet certain special conditions.* Goodwill writedown as a result of impairment is subtracted in determining book income (see Chapter 16).
- Premiums for life insurance on executives paid for by a company that is the designated beneficiary on these policies are not deductible for tax purposes. Similarly, any benefits collected are not taxed. For book purposes, both the premiums paid and proceeds received on such policies are used in determining income.

> Unless otherwise specified, you should assume for purposes of working problems in this chapter that goodwill write-off is treated as a permanent difference item—that is, it is *not* deductible for tax purposes.

- Compensation expense associated with certain employee stock options is not deductible for tax purposes but is deductible in determining book income.

Items Recognized for Tax Purposes but *Not* for Book Purposes

- Tax laws allow a statutory depletion deduction on certain natural resources that may be in excess of the cost-based depletion recorded for book purposes. This excess statutory depletion is a permanent difference between book and taxable income.
- U.S. corporations that own stock in other U.S. companies are allowed to deduct a portion of the dividends received from these Investees from taxable income according to the following schedule:

Ownership	Deductible Portion of Dividends
Less than 20%	70%
Equal to or greater than 20%, but less than 80%	80%
Equal to or greater than 80%	100%

*See P. McConnell, "Goodwill: The Facts," *Accounting Issues* (New York: Bear, Stearns & Co., August 26, 1994); and sections 1060 and 338 of the Internal Revenue Code.

Temporary differences occur when a revenue (gain) or expense (loss) enters into the determination of book (GAAP) income and taxable income in different periods. Temporary differences that cause taxable income to be higher (lower) than book income in future periods give rise to a deferred tax liability (asset). Permanent differences are revenue or expense items that are recognized as part of book income but are *never* recognized as part of taxable income, or vice versa. Permanent differences do *not* give rise to deferred tax assets or liabilities.

Problems Caused by Temporary Differences

To illustrate the issues related to interperiod tax allocation, consider the most prevalent temporary book/tax timing difference: depreciation expense. For tax purposes, profit-maximizing firms try to *minimize* the discounted present value of their future tax payments. Each dollar of tax deduction today is more valuable than a dollar of tax deduction in the future. This time-value-of-money principle is why most firms use accelerated depreciation for tax purposes. But many of these same firms use straight-line depreciation for financial reporting purposes. This creates a temporary difference between book income and taxable income.

Consider this illustration. Assume Mitchell Corporation buys new equipment for $10,000 on January 1, 2005. The asset has a five-year life and no salvage value. It will be depreciated using the straight-line method for book purposes, but for tax purposes the sum-of-the-years'-digits (SOYD) method will be used. Exhibit 13.3 and Figure 13.1(a) show the two depreciation schedules.

> Technically, firms are required to use Modified Accelerated Cost Recovery System depreciation schedules for tax purposes, and these differ by type of asset and useful life. We use SOYD here to simplify the illustration of depreciation temporary differences.

EXHIBIT 13.3	Mitchell Corporation

Book-Versus-Tax Depreciation

Year	(a) Book Depreciation	(b) Tax Return Depreciation	(c) Excess of Tax Over Book Depreciation	
2005	$ 2,000	$ 3,333	$1,333	Originating timing
2006	2,000	2,667	667	differences
2007	2,000	2,000	—	
2008	2,000	1,333	(667)	Reversing timing
2009	2,000	667	(1,333)	differences
	$10,000	$10,000	–0–	

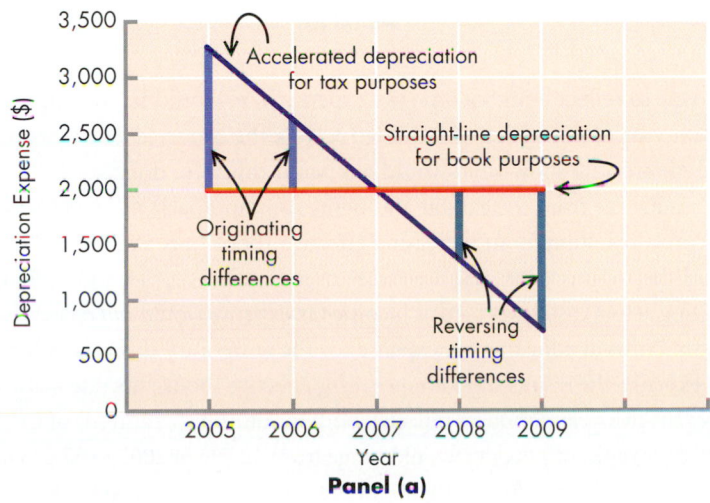

Figure 13.1(a)

MITCHELL CORPORATION
Comparison of Book-Versus-Tax Depreciation Expense

Panel (a)

Let's assume for Mitchell Corporation that depreciation constitutes the only book versus tax difference; income before depreciation is expected to be $22,000 each year over the next five years; and the statutory tax rate is 35%. Pre-tax book income, taxable income per Mitchell's tax return, and taxes payable are reflected in Exhibit 13.4. Figure 13.1(b) displays graphically the relation between taxable income and pre-tax book income over the five-year period.

> The **statutory tax rate** for corporations is the rate set by law—in this case, 35%.

EXHIBIT 13.4	Mitchell Corporation		
Income and Income Tax Payable			
Year	**(a)** **Pre-Tax** **Book Income** **($22,000 – Book Depreciation)**	**(b)** **Taxable Income** **per Tax Return** **($22,000 – Tax Depreciation)**	**(c)** **Income** **Tax Payable** **(35% of Col. [b])**
2005	$ 20,000	$ 18,667*	$ 6,533
2006	20,000	19,333	6,767
2007	20,000	20,000	7,000
2008	20,000	20,667	7,233
2009	20,000	21,333	7,467
Total	$100,000	$100,000	$35,000

*For example, in 2005, $22,000 – $3,333 (Exhibit 13.3, column [b]) = $18,667.

Figure 13.1(b)

MITCHELL CORPORATION

Pre-tax Book Income and Taxable Income

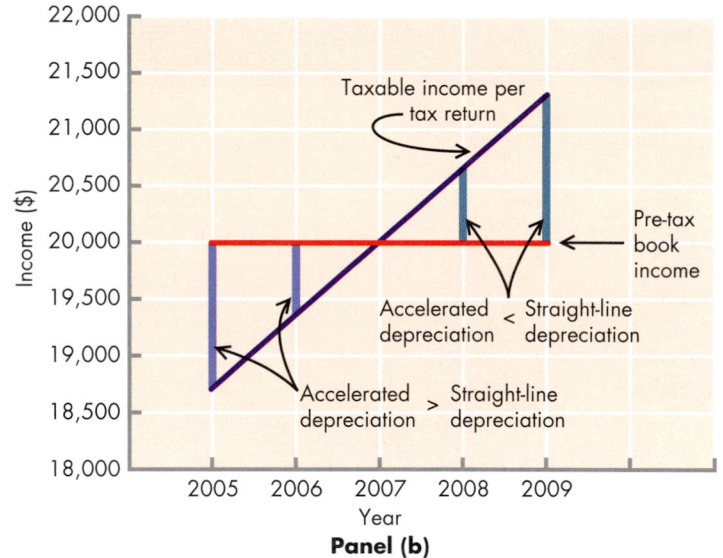

Panel (b)

The easiest way to reflect book income tax expense here would be to simply treat the actual taxes payable each year (column [c] of Exhibit 13.4) as the reported *book* income tax expense. Exhibit 13.5 and Figure 13.2 show what would happen if this were done.

As you can readily see from the exhibit and figure, this approach *mismatches* tax expense with pre-tax book income, resulting in an increasing effective (book) tax rate even though the pre-tax book income and the statutory tax rate are stable over the five-year period at $20,000 and 35%, respectively. Treating actual cash taxes paid as income tax expense would *not* reflect the true economics of the situation. Without adjusting tax expense for the temporary differences between book and tax depreciation expense, the results show an *increasing* effective (book) tax rate—and *declining* after-tax income—over the five-year period, as reflected both in columns (c) and (d) of Exhibit 13.5 and in Figure 13.2. The effective (book) tax rate would range from 32.7% in 2005 to 37.3% in 2009, and the after-tax earnings would decline from $13,467 in 2005 to $12,533 in 2009. Clearly, this approach leads to an inappropriate matching between pre-tax book income and income tax expense.

> The **effective (book) tax rate** is the tax expense divided by pre-tax income that is reported on the GAAP income statement.

EXHIBIT 13.5	Mitchell Corporation

Result from Treating Actual Taxes Paid as Income Tax Expense

Year	(a) Pre-Tax Book Income	(b) Tax Expense = Income Tax Payable	(c) Reported Tax Rate (b ÷ a)	(d) After-Tax Book Income
2005	$20,000	$6,533	32.7%	$13,467
2006	20,000	6,767	33.8	13,233
2007	20,000	7,000	35.0	13,000
2008	20,000	7,233	36.2	12,767
2009	20,000	7,467	37.3	12,533

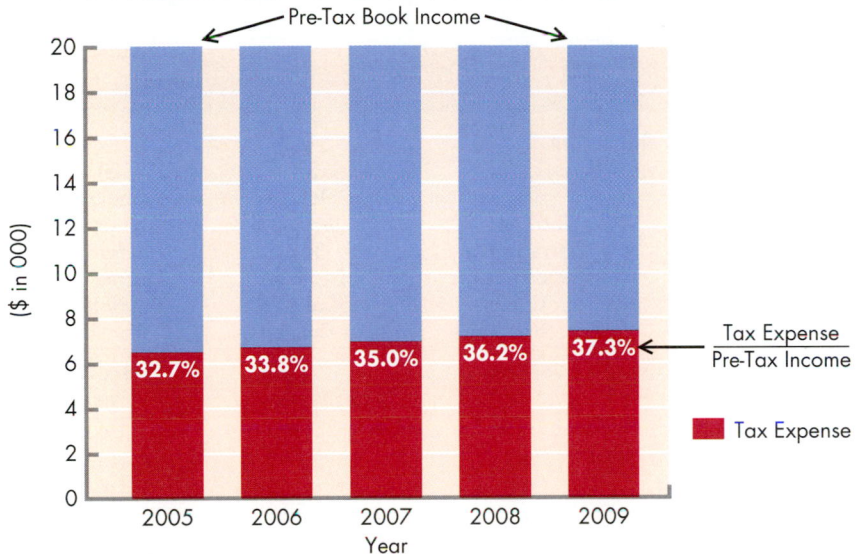

Figure 13.2

MITCHELL CORPORATION

Tax Expense *Without* Interperiod Tax Allocation

Besides leading to a mismatch on the income statement, treating actual cash taxes paid as income tax expense introduces a reporting distortion on the balance sheet. This distortion occurs because total tax depreciation deductions on an asset cannot exceed the asset's cost minus its salvage value. Accordingly, "extra" tax depreciation in early years will be offset by lower allowable tax depreciation in later years. As shown in column (c) of Exhibit 13.3, during 2005 tax depreciation ($3,333) exceeds book depreciation ($2,000). The "extra" tax depreciation of $1,333 means that future years' *tax* depreciation must be $1,333 lower than future years' *book* depreciation. Thus, the extra tax depreciation taken in 2005 generates a liability for future taxes of $1,333 times 35%, or $467.

There is another way to visualize how the extra tax depreciation creates a liability for future taxes. The Financial Accounting Standards Board (FASB) states that GAAP assumes "... the reported amounts of assets ... will be recovered. ... Based on that assumption, a difference between the tax basis of an asset ... and its reported amount ... will result in taxable ... amounts ... when the reported amounts ... are recovered. ..."[2] In our example, at the end of 2005, the reported (book) amount of the asset is $8,000 (that is, $10,000 minus book depreciation of $2,000), while the tax basis is $6,667 (that is, $10,000 minus tax depreciation of $3,333). Notice that if the asset was sold for its net book value of $8,000, a taxable gain of $1,333 would ensue, measured as the difference between the $8,000 cash received and the asset's $6,667 *tax* basis. Thus, given the GAAP assumption that reported amounts of assets will be recovered, the extra depreciation in 2005 would generate a liability for future taxes of $1,333 times 35%, or $467.

---

[2] "Accounting for Income Taxes," *Statement of Financial Accounting Standards (SFAS) No. 109* (Norwalk, CT: FASB, 1992), para. 11.

Setting tax expense equal to current taxes payable (as in column [b] of Exhibit 13.5) ignores the future tax liability that results from temporary (timing) differences between book and taxable income, and it results in a mismatching of tax expense with the related revenue and expense items reported on the GAAP income statement.

Deferred Income Tax Accounting: Interperiod Tax Allocation

To avoid the drawbacks just illustrated, income tax accounting does not simply equate tax expense with current taxes paid (or payable). Instead, the journal entry for income taxes reflects both taxes currently due as well as any liability for future taxes arising from current period book-versus-tax temporary differences that will reverse in later periods. The GAAP rules are specified in *SFAS No. 109*.[3] To illustrate them we continue the Mitchell Corporation example in Exhibit 13.6.

EXHIBIT 13.6	Mitchell Corporation

Computation of Income Tax Expense With Interperiod Tax Allocation

Year	(a) Current Income Tax Payable (Exhibit 13.4, Col. [c])	(b) Excess (Deficiency) of Tax Depreciation Relative to Book Depreciation (Exhibit 13.3, Col. [c])	(c) Increase (Decrease) in Deferred Income Tax Liability (Col. [b] × 35%)	(d) Total Income Tax Expense (Col. [a] + Col. [c])	(e) Cumulative Balance in Deferred Income Tax Payable at Year-End
2005	$ 6,533	$1,333	$467	$ 7,000	$467
2006	6,767	667	233	7,000	700
2007	7,000	–0–	–0–	7,000	700
2008	7,233	(667)	(233)	7,000	467
2009	7,467	(1,333)	(467)	7,000	–0–
	$35,000	–0–	–0–	$35,000	

Column (c) shows that for 2005 the *change* in the liability for future taxes is an increase of $467 (35% tax rate × $1,333 depreciation timing difference). Income tax currently payable is 35% of tax return income of $18,667, or $6,533. Under *SFAS No. 109*, income tax expense equals the total of the current taxes owed and the *change* in the deferred tax liability. The computation is:

Computation of Income Tax Expense for 2005	
1. Current income tax payable (35% × $18,667)	$6,533
plus	
2. *Increase* in liability for future taxes arising during the year ($1,333 × 35%)	467
Total income tax expense for 2005 = sum of steps (1) and (2)	**$7,000**

The accounting entry for 2005 income taxes is:

DR	Income tax expense	$7,000	
CR	Income tax payable		$6,533
CR	Deferred income taxes payable		467

---

[3] Ibid.

When tax rates do not change from year to year, this entry simultaneously overcomes both of the drawbacks that would exist if we simply measured tax expense as cash taxes paid—the liability for future taxes is explicitly recognized, and the reported tax expense is exactly 35% of pre-tax book income of $20,000 (that is, $7,000/$20,000 equals 35%). Thus, tax expense is also "matched" with book income. (This is true provided there are no permanent book/tax differences. When there are permanent differences between book and taxable income, then tax expense will *not* equal the tax rate times the pre-tax book income—a point demonstrated later in the chapter.)

You can readily see what this entry simultaneously accomplishes by carefully analyzing how each of the debits and credits of the entry are computed:

> In any year Congress changes U.S. tax rates, this matching disappears under *SFAS No. 109.* The reason is that *SFAS No. 109* focuses on the liability for future taxes, which changes as tax rates change.

DR Income tax expense	$7,000	
(Equal to the sum of taxes payable and the increase in deferred taxes payable. However, when tax rates are constant and there are no permanent book/tax differences, this debit will equal the tax rate [35%] times pre-tax book income [$20,000])		
CR Income tax payable		$6,533
(35% times taxable income per tax return of $18,667)		
CR Deferred income taxes payable		467
(35% times the depreciation temporary difference of $1,333 in 2005—Exhibit 13.6 column [b] "excess" depreciation)		

As illustrated here, the debit to income tax expense is a "plug" number that represents the combination of current taxes payable and any *change* in the deferred tax balance (in this case, a deferred tax liability) that arises from timing differences during the year. When the deferred income tax liability increases, the increase is *added* to current income tax payable to arrive at income tax expense. When the deferred income tax liability decreases, the decrease is *subtracted* from current income tax payable in order to determine income tax expense. This relation is summarized in Figure 13.3.

> Sometimes the originating timing differences generate deferred income tax *assets* because taxable income will be lower than book income in future periods when those differences reverse. In that circumstance the debit to income tax expense represents the sum of current taxes payable plus the decrease (minus the increase) in the deferred tax *asset* account for the period. This is discussed more fully on pages 697–699.

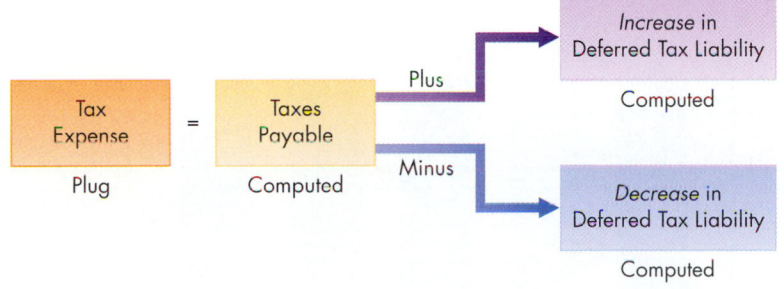

Figure 13.3

RELATION BETWEEN TAX EXPENSE, TAXES PAYABLE, AND CHANGES IN DEFERRED TAX LIABILITIES

In any year that the tax rate remains constant (say, at 35%) and there are no permanent book/tax differences, the debit to tax expense will automatically equal pre-tax book income times the 35% tax rate.

Column (b) of Exhibit 13.6 shows that the *original* book-versus-tax depreciation differences—called *originating timing differences*, and shown as the bars shaded blue in Figure 13.1(a)—increase the liability for future taxes (the deferred tax liability) in 2005 and 2006 (column [c] of Exhibit 13.6).

But all originating differences ultimately reverse. This occurs in the Mitchell Corporation illustration when tax depreciation drops below book depreciation in 2008 and 2009. The reversals of originating differences are called *reversing timing differences* and are shown as the bars that fall below the red line in Figure 13.1(a).

To show what happens when book-versus-tax temporary differences reverse, let's consider the income tax entry in 2008. From Figure 13.3, the formula for computing income tax expense is as shown below.

> 1. Current income tax payable
>   **minus**
> 2. *Decrease* in liability for future taxes arising during the year
>   = Income tax expense

Since book depreciation exceeds tax depreciation in 2008 by $667, the liability for future taxes *decreases* by $667 times 35%, or $233. Therefore, tax expense for 2008 is:

Computation of Income Tax Expense for 2008	
1. Current income tax payable:	
$20,667 × 35%	$7,233
minus	
2. *Decrease* in liability for future taxes:	
$667 × 35%	(233)
Total income tax expense for 2008	**$7,000**

The journal entry for 2008 taxes is:

DR	Income tax expense	$7,000	
DR	Deferred income taxes payable	233	
CR	Income tax payable		$7,233

Column (d) of Exhibit 13.6 as well as Figure 13.4 show the computation of income tax expense for Mitchell Corporation for the entire five-year period (2005–2009) using interperiod tax allocation. Notice that in 2005 and 2006 the deferred tax liability *increases* and these

Figure 13.4

MITCHELL CORPORATION
Tax Expense *With* Interperiod
Tax Allocation

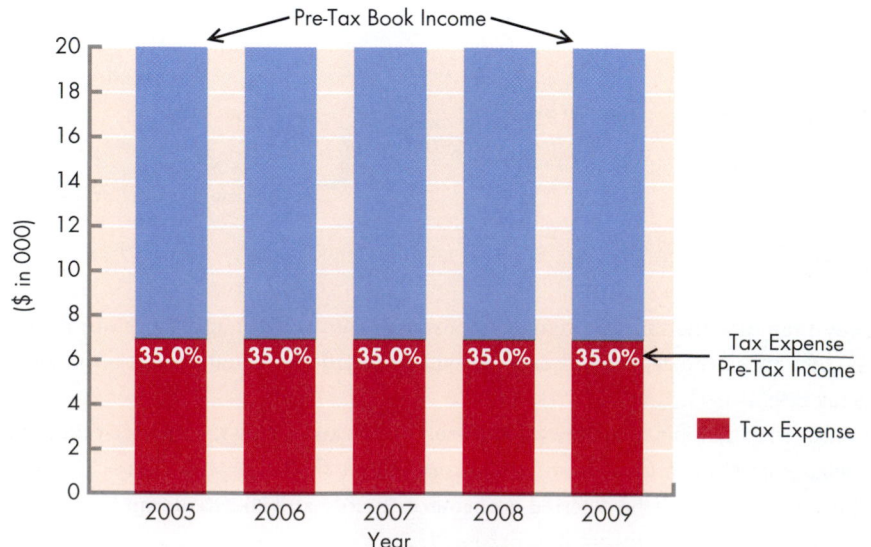

increases are *added* to taxes payable to arrive at the tax expense reported on the income statement for those years. In 2008 and 2009 the depreciation timing differences reverse, resulting in *decreases* in the deferred tax liability (since the additional taxes are now being paid), and these decreases are *subtracted* from taxes payable to arrive at tax expense for those years. By the end of 2009 the depreciation book-versus-tax timing differences have totally reversed, and the balance in deferred income tax payable is zero. With constant tax rates of 35% over the entire period, income tax expense (column [d] in Exhibit 13.6) is always 35% times pre-tax book income of $20,000, and the pattern of tax expense matches the pattern of pre-tax book income.

RECAP

With interperiod tax allocation, tax expense equals current taxes payable to the IRS plus (minus) the increase (decrease) in deferred tax liabilities. This results in a tax expense number that is matched with the revenue and expense amounts that are recognized for book purposes.

Deferred Income Tax Assets

The Mitchell Corporation example illustrated a situation in which pre-tax book income initially exceeded taxable income, creating a deferred income tax liability. Because this temporary difference later reverses, the liability ultimately is eliminated. But temporary differences can go in the opposite direction as well. In certain circumstances taxable income can initially exceed pre-tax book income, thereby giving rise to deferred income tax assets.

To illustrate how a deferred income tax asset comes about, let's assume that in December 2005 Paul Corporation owns an office building that it leases to another company for $100,000. The lease covers all of 2006 and specifies that the tenant pays the $100,000 to Paul Corporation immediately on signing the lease in 2005. On an accrual basis, rental income will be earned only in 2006. Accordingly, Paul Corporation makes the following entry on receiving the cash:

> *SFAS No. 109* calls temporary differences that result in deferred tax liabilities **future taxable amounts**, since future tax return income will be higher than future book income; temporary differences that result in deferred tax assets are called **future deductible amounts**, since future tax return income—all other factors being equal—will be lower than future book income.

DR Cash	$100,000	
CR Rent received in advance		$100,000

The account "Rent received in advance" is a liability account that will be reduced monthly by $8,333 (with an offsetting credit to the "Earned lease revenue" account) in 2006 as Paul provides the tenant with the use of the facility and earns the lease revenue. For tax purposes, the entire $100,000 rent prepayment by the tenant is included in Paul Corporation's taxable income in 2005 when it is received. Assume that the lease receipt represents the only book/tax temporary difference for Paul and that 2005 pre-tax book income totals $1,500,000. Taxable income in the tax return will accordingly total $1,600,000 in 2005—$1,500,000 plus the immediately taxable advance rental payment of $100,000. In 2006, the $100,000 lease payment received in 2005 will be "earned" for book purposes and will be included in book income. However, since this amount was already included in taxable income in 2005, it will *not* be included in Paul's 2006 taxable income. Thus, the temporary difference that originated in 2005 reverses in 2006. If book income is once again $1,500,000 in 2006, then book income will exceed taxable income by $100,000 due to the reversal of this temporary difference. Taxable income will therefore be $1,400,000 in 2006. These relationships are summarized in Exhibit 13.7.

EXHIBIT 13.7 | **Paul Corporation**

Book Versus Tax Timing Differences That Give Rise to a Deferred Tax Asset

	Book Income	2001 Lease Receipt of $100,000 Included in Book Income?	Included in Tax Return Income?	Tax Return Income
2005	$1,500,000	No	Yes	$1,600,000
2006	1,500,000	Yes	No	1,400,000

Exhibit 13.8 shows that when the rent is earned in 2006 for book purposes, accounting income will exceed taxable income by $100,000—but no tax will be due on this difference because the tax has already been paid in 2005. Thus, the temporary difference that originates in 2005 because of book/tax differences in lease revenue represents a deferred income tax asset at the end of 2005. If we assume the income tax rate is 35%, then the computation of 2005 tax expense is composed of the current taxes payable *minus* the increase in the deferred tax asset account computed as follows:

Computation of Income Tax Expense for 2005

1. Current income tax payable
   (Taxable income × 35% = $1,600,000 × 35%) $560,000
                          minus
2. *Increase* in deferred tax asset ($100,000 × 35%)   (35,000)
   Total income tax expense for 2005 $525,000

Paul Corporation makes the following 2005 entry for income taxes:

DR Income tax expense	$525,000	
DR Deferred income tax asset	35,000	
CR Income tax payable		$560,000

EXHIBIT 13.8 | **Paul Corporation**

Computation of Tax Expense *With* Interperiod Tax Allocation

Year	(a) Taxable Income per Tax Return	(b) Book Income	(c) Excess (Deficiency) of Tax Lease Revenue over Book Lease Revenue	(d) Taxes Payable (35% of Col. [a])	(e) Increase (Decrease) in Deferred Tax Asset (Col. [c] × 35%)	(f) Total Income Tax Expense (Col. [d] – Col. [e])
2005	$1,600,000	$1,500,000	$100,000	$560,000	$35,000	$525,000
2006	1,400,000	1,500,000	(100,000)	490,000	(35,000)	525,000

In column (b) of Exhibit 13.8, book income is $1,500,000 in 2006 after the $100,000 of rent revenue *earned* during the year is included. If we assume that there are no other book/tax temporary differences, then taxable income in the tax return will be $1,400,000, since the $100,000 advance rental receipt was included in taxable income in 2005—the previous year—when the rent revenue was *collected*. The $100,000 temporary difference in lease revenue that originated in 2005 reverses in 2006. The related deferred tax asset of $35,000 that was created in 2005 (column [e]) is decreased and eliminated in 2006. As shown in column (f), the decrease in the deferred tax asset of $35,000 is added to the taxes payable for that year to arrive at the tax expense number of $525,000. Paul will record the following income tax expense entry in 2006 when the timing difference reverses:

Notice that income tax expense in both 2005 and 2006 is 35% of each year's book income (that is, $525,000 ÷ $1,500,000). Thus, income tax expense is properly matched with pre-tax income.

DR	Income tax expense	$525,000	
CR	Deferred income tax asset		$ 35,000
CR	Income tax payable		490,000

Figure 13.5 depicts the relationships for computing *SFAS No. 109* income tax expense by adjusting taxes payable for changes in deferred income tax assets and liabilities.

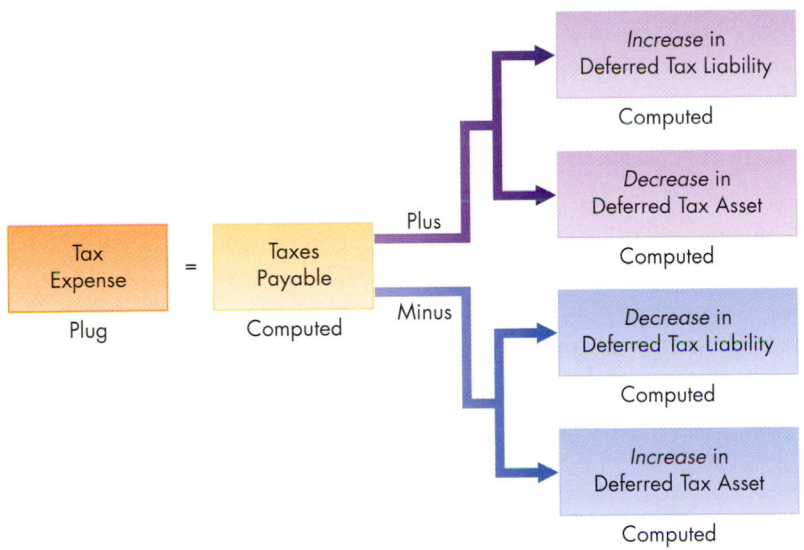

Figure 13.5

RELATION BETWEEN TAX EXPENSE, TAXES PAYABLE, AND CHANGES IN DEFERRED TAX ASSETS AND LIABILITIES

Deferred Income Tax Asset Valuation Allowances

If Paul Corporation experienced adversity in 2006 and had no taxable income in that year, the $35,000 deferred income tax asset would generate no benefit—that is, if 2006 taxes were zero, the "benefits" arising from the $35,000 tax payment on the 2005 advance rental receipt would be lost. Thus, it is always possible that a firm that has recognized deferred income tax assets may not receive tax payment reductions in future years. For this reason the FASB requires firms with deferred income tax assets to assess the likelihood that these assets may not be fully realized in future periods.

The realization of tax benefits from existing deferred income tax assets depends on whether or not the firm has future taxable income. If management believes that the probability of future taxable income is greater than 50%, deferred income tax assets can be recognized (without adjustment) in their entirety. However, if management's assessment indicates that *it is more likely than not* that some portion of the benefit will not be realized in its entirety, a **deferred tax asset valuation allowance** is required. The FASB stated that this valuation allowance *"should be sufficient to reduce the deferred tax asset to the amount that is more likely than not to be realized."*[4]

Later in this chapter, we'll see that the U.S. Income Tax Code allows unprofitable companies to recapture previously paid taxes. We temporarily ignore this provision in the tax code in order to sharpen your understanding of the possibility that deferred income tax assets may not generate future benefits.

---

[4] Ibid., para. 17. Operationally, "more likely than not" means greater than a 50% probability of happening.

To illustrate the procedure for establishing a valuation allowance for deferred tax assets, let's assume (1) that for book purposes Norman Corporation accrued $900,000 of estimated warranty expenses associated with product sales in 2005, and (2) that the actual warranty parts and services from these sales are provided in 2006 and beyond. Since the U.S. Income Tax Code only allows companies to deduct warranty expense when the warranty services are provided, this timing difference gives rise to a deferred tax asset of $315,000 (35% tax rate × $900,000 timing difference) that would be recorded in 2005. If we assume Norman's pre-tax book income is $600,000, taxable income is $1,500,000 and the 2005 entry for tax expense is:

DR Income tax expense ($600,000 × .35)	$210,000	
DR Deferred income tax asset ($900,000 × .35)	315,000	
CR Income tax payable ($1,500,000 × .35)		$525,000

Now assume that early in 2006 Norman Corporation determines that it is unlikely to earn enough taxable income in future years to realize more than $200,000 of the deferred tax asset. The entry made in 2006 is:

DR Income tax expense ($315,000 – $200,000)	$115,000	
CR Allowance to reduce deferred tax asset to expected realizable value		$115,000

The credit to the allowance account reduces the net carrying amount of the deferred tax asset from $315,000 to $200,000—its estimated realizable value. This occurs because the allowance account is shown on the balance sheet as a contra-account to the deferred tax asset. Notice that income tax expense is increased in the year during which it is determined that a portion of the income tax asset is unlikely to be recovered. Accordingly, income tax expense will exceed pre-tax book income multiplied by the tax rate in years when allowance accounts are established or increased. If Norman Corporation's future prospects improve and if in 2007 it is determined that an allowance account is no longer needed, the allowance account is reduced to zero and a *credit* to income tax expense is made.

Illustration of Footnote Disclosure for Valuation Allowances

Exhibit 13.9 contains an excerpt from eBay Inc.'s 2002 tax footnote. As noted, eBay had federal and state operating loss carryforwards resulting primarily from the exercise of employee stock options that raised questions about the recoverability of the deferred tax asset of $245.4 million recorded on the company's December 31, 2002 balance sheet. In this excerpt, eBay discusses the need for its valuation allowance of $145.2 million and the reasons why this adjustment was deemed necessary. Notice that this disclosure provides information about the company's expected future taxable income and uncertainties about its future stock price performance. Consequently, it can be used by analysts to refine estimates of eBay's future profitability and market performance.

The determination of whether a valuation allowance is necessary requires subjective assessments. Similarly, the amount of the allowance is also not based on readily observable criteria. When a valuation allowance is established, the offsetting debit is to income tax expense, which reduces income; similarly, when a previously existing allowance is lowered, the offsetting credit to income tax expense increases income. Because of the subjective judgments used when determining the need for (and the amount of) valuation allowances, the possibility of income manipulation exists. Specifically, valuation allowances could be used to smooth year-to-year earnings fluctuations. For example, in a "good" earnings year management might decide to establish an allowance account, assuming the offsetting charge to earnings is relatively small.

EXHIBIT 13.9 eBay Inc.

Excerpt from 2002 Annual Report
Income Tax Footnote

Significant deferred tax assets and liabilities consist of the following:

	December 31	
($ in thousands)	2001	2002
Deferred tax assets:		
Net operating loss and credits	$129,211	$207,276
Accruals and allowances	21,405	40,941
Depreciation and amortization	11,381	(5,708)
Net unrealized losses	2,372	2,921
Net deferred tax assets	164,369	245,430
Valuation allowance	(129,212)	(145,182)
	35,157	100,248
Deferred tax liabilities:		
Acquisition-related intangibles	(3,629)	(111,843)
	$ 31,528	$ (11,595)

As of December 31, 2002, our federal and state net operating loss carryforwards for income tax purposes were approximately $559.4 million and $133.1 million, respectively. If not utilized, the federal net operating loss carryforwards will begin to expire in 2019, and the state net operating loss carryforwards will begin to expire in 2006. The Company's federal and state research tax credit carryforwards for income tax purposes are approximately $2.1 million and $2.3 million, respectively. If not utilized, the federal tax credit carryforwards will begin to expire in 2021. Deferred tax assets of approximately $202.9 million at December 31, 2002 pertain primarily to certain net operating loss carryforwards resulting from the exercise of employee stock options of $145.2 million and the remainder relates to losses at certain subsidiaries. We have a full valuation allowance against the amounts relating to the exercise of employee stock options due to the impact that uncertainties associated with our future stock price and timing of employee stock option exercises have on the likelihood that we will realize future benefits from these amounts. To the extent that we generate taxable income in future years, we will have the ability, subject to carryforward limitations, to benefit from these amounts. When recognized, the tax benefit related to stock options will be accounted for as a credit to additional paid-in-capital rather than a reduction of the income tax provision.

Once the allowance is established, it can be diminished or even eliminated in subsequent "bad" earnings years. Notice that the credit arising from the allowance reversal increases income, thereby partially offsetting the bad earnings. The result is that income fluctuations are smoothed across years. Two recent studies investigate whether managers use the valuation allowance on deferred tax assets to manage earnings. One study finds that bank managers appear to use the valuation allowance to manage earnings toward consensus analysts' forecasts and toward average historical earnings.[5] Another study using a broader sample of manufacturing firms finds that managers use the valuation allowance to manage earnings up (down) when analysts' earnings forecasts are above (below) the premanaged earnings number.[6] Taken together, these two studies

[5] C. Schrand and F. Wong, "Earnings management using the Valuation Allowance for Deferred Tax Assets under *SFAS No. 109*," *Contemporary Accounting Research* (Fall 2003), pp. 579–611.
[6] S. Rego and M. Frank, "Do Managers Use the Valuation Allowance Account to Manage Earnings Around Certain Earnings Targets?" (working paper, University of Iowa, July 2003).

provide compelling evidence that mangers take advantage of the discretion associated with setting the valuation allowance on deferred tax assets to manage earnings in both a positive and negative direction.

RECAP

When circumstances indicate that it is "more likely than not" that some portion of the future tax benefit from a deferred tax asset will not be realized, then a deferred tax asset valuation allowance must be established to reduce the deferred tax asset book value to the amount expected to be realized.

Deferred Income Tax Accounting When Tax Rates Change

Tax rates periodically get changed by Congress. When this happens, the tax effects of the reversals change as well. To measure deferred income taxes, *SFAS No. 109* adopts the so-called **"liability approach"**—*in any year current or future tax rates are changed, the income tax expense number absorbs the full effect of the change, and the relationship between that year's tax expense and book income is destroyed.*

Returning to the Mitchell Corporation example in Exhibit 13.6, let's assume that on December 31, 2007, a new income tax law raises the income tax rate from 35% to 38% beginning January 1, 2008. Reference to column (e) of Exhibit 13.6 shows that just prior to the tax law change on December 31, 2007 the amount of deferred income tax payable for Mitchell was $700. That number represents the cumulative excess of tax over book depreciation in 2005 and 2006 (the dollar amount of temporary depreciation differences = $1,333 + $667, or $2000) times the initial tax rate of 35%. But because future tax rates have been increased, the liability for future taxes is actually larger than the $700 amount currently reported. At the new, higher income tax rate that will be in effect in 2008 and 2009, the liability for future taxes becomes $760, not $700. This future liability represents the cumulative excess of tax over book depreciation ($2,000) multiplied by the new 38% tax rate that will be in effect beginning January 1, 2008.

Under the liability approach of SFAS No. 109, the full change in the amount of future liability for income taxes (in this case, $60) is recognized as an increase or decrease in income tax expense in the year that the tax rate change becomes known. Accordingly, income tax expense for 2007 is computed as:

1. Current 2007 income tax payable (35% × $20,000 [see Exhibit 13.4])	$7,000
plus	
2. *Increase* in the liability for future taxes arising during 2007	
($1,333 + $667) × (.38 − .35)	60
Total income tax expense for 2007	**$7,060**

The accounting entry for 2007 income taxes is:

DR Income tax expense	$7,060	
CR Income tax payable		$7,000
CR Deferred income taxes payable		60

After this entry is made, the balance in deferred income taxes payable will total $760, which is the liability for future taxes at the new 38% rate. Also, because tax rates for future years were changed in 2007, the debit to income tax expense does not equal the $20,000 pre-tax book income times the 2007 tax rate of 35%.

Exhibit 13.10 shows the revised computation of income tax expense and deferred taxes payable for Mitchell Corporation for 2007 through 2009 after reflecting the income tax rate increase. The journal entry for income taxes in 2008 is:

DR Income tax expense	$7,600	
DR Deferred income tax payable	253	
CR Income tax payable		$7,853

EXHIBIT 13.10   Mitchell Corporation

Revised Computation of Income Tax Expense

Year	(a) Taxable Income (Exhibit 13.4, Col. [b])	(b) Current Income Tax Payable = 38% of Col. (a)	(c) Difference Between Tax and Book Depreciation (Exhibit 13.3, Col. [c])	(d) Increase (Decrease) in Liability for Future Taxes = Col. (c) × 38%	(e) Total Income Tax Expense = Col. (b) + Col. (d)	(f) Cumulative Balance in Deferred Income Tax Payable at Year-End
2007	$20,000	$7,000[a]	—	$ 60[b]	$7,060	$760
2008	20,667	7,853	(667)	(253)	7,600	507
2009	21,333	8,107	(1,333)	(507)	7,600	–0–

[a]Tax rate is still 35% in 2007 so this is $20,000 × 35%.
[b]This is the increase that arose in 2007 when the rate went from 35% to 38% (that is, 3% × $2,000 cumulative depreciation differences in column [b] of Exhibit 13.6).

Similarly, the 2009 entry is:

DR Income tax expense	$7,600	
DR Deferred income tax payable	507	
CR Income tax payable		$8,107

As shown in column (f) of Exhibit 13.10, the balance in the deferred income tax payable account will be zero after the year 2009 entry is made.

Because of the oblique way accounting rules recognize the effects of tax rate changes—through an adjustment to the tax expense number—analysts must be alert to recognize how these tax changes can inject one-shot (transitory) adjustments to earnings in the year Congress passes the new tax rates. Moreover, it is important to recognize that the effect of a tax rate change on bottom-line earnings can vary considerably across companies depending on three factors:

> A change in tax rates of this magnitude is not that uncommon. For example, the 1986 Tax Reform Act lowered the marginal corporate tax rate for large firms from 46% to 34%.

1. Whether the tax rates are increased or decreased.
2. Whether the firm has net deferred tax assets or net deferred tax liabilities.
3. The magnitude of the deferred tax balance.

Consider how differently a tax rate change can affect firms' bottom-line earnings: Suppose Congress passes a new tax law in 2006, one that raises the marginal statutory corporate tax rate from 35% to 45% effective in 2008. Further assume that Companies A, B, and C have the following net deferred tax asset (liability) balances on their books when the new tax law is passed:

($ in millions)	Company A	Company B	Company C
Net deferred tax asset (liability) balance in year 2006	$100	$0	($100)

Exhibit 13.11 shows how the change in tax rate will affect the after-tax earnings of these three companies in 2006—the year the new tax rate is passed. We first divide the net deferred tax asset (liability) balance by the old marginal tax rate to get the dollar magnitude of the timing differences that gave rise to the balances in these accounts. (Recall that the balances in the deferred tax asset [liability] accounts equal the cumulative dollar amount of the timing differences giving rise to future deductible [taxable] amounts times the marginal corporate tax rate when those timing differences originated. Therefore, to derive the dollar amount of the timing differences, we simply divide the deferred tax asset or liability balance by the relevant tax rate.)

EXHIBIT 13.11	Computation of How Change in Tax Rate Affects Earnings in Year That Rate Change Is Passed		
($ in millions)	Company A	Company B	Company C
Net deferred tax asset (liability) balance in 2006	$ 100	$0	$ (100)
Divide by old marginal tax rate	÷ 35%	÷ 35%	÷ 35%
Dollar amount of timing difference	$285.71 ← Future Deductible Amount	$0	$(285.71) ← Future Taxable Amount
Multiply by difference between old and new tax rates (45% − 35%)	× 10%	× 10%	× 10%
Increase (decrease) to after-tax earnings in year of rate change	$28.571	$0	$(28.571)

Company A has $285.71 ($100/.35) million of future *deductible* amounts, Company C has $285.71 of future *taxable* amounts, and Company B has neither future deductible nor taxable amounts. These timing differences are then multiplied by the *difference* between the new tax rate and the old tax rate (that is, 10%) to obtain the increase in the deferred tax asset (liability) balance and the corresponding increase (decrease) in reported after-tax earnings.

Analysis

As shown, Company A's 2006 earnings will *increase* by $28.571 million. This is because each dollar of future deductible amounts will yield an additional $0.10 in tax savings under the newly enacted tax rates (that is, when these timing differences reverse). Company C, on the other hand, will report a $28.571 million *decrease* to its after-tax earnings number, since each dollar of future taxable amounts will generate $0.10 of additional taxes as these timing differences reverse in future years (when the tax rates will be higher). Company B's 2006 after-tax earnings are unaffected by the tax rate change because there are no temporary differences.

If the tax rates had been reduced from 35% to 25%, the earnings impacts reported above for Companies A and C would be reversed. As this example demonstrates, tax rate changes can have very different effects on firms' reported earnings depending on their deferred tax status and the direction of the tax rate change.

RECAP Under *SFAS No. 109*, when tax rates change, the additional tax benefits or costs are recognized as an adjustment to tax expense in the year that the tax rate changes are *passed*, not when they *become effective*. These one-shot earnings effects are often difficult to detect, since they are reported as part of the tax expense line on the income statement. However, a careful reading of the tax footnote that reconciles the book-effective tax rate with the marginal statutory tax rate (described in greater detail later in this chapter) can reveal the magnitude of earnings increases or decreases due to tax rate changes.

Net Operating Losses: Carrybacks and Carryforwards

Since firms pay taxes during profitable years, it would be inequitable to deny them some form of tax relief in unprofitable years. Therefore, the U.S. Income Tax Code provides an opportunity for firms reporting operating losses to offset those losses against either past or future tax payments—that is, when an operating loss occurs (for example, when deductible expenses exceed taxable revenues), firms can elect one of two options described in the following sections:

1. *Both* carryback and carryforward incurred losses.
2. *Only* carryforward incurred losses.

> Prior to 1998, the loss carryback period was three years and the carryforward period was 15 years.

Carryback and Carryforward Assume that Unfortunato Corporation experienced a $1,000,000 pre-tax operating loss in 2006. Under the U.S. Income Tax Code, Unfortunato can elect to carry back the operating loss and offset it against taxable income in the previous two years—2004 and 2005. The loss must be offset against the earliest year first—in this case, 2004. If the loss exceeds the total taxable income for the 2004–2005 period, then the remaining portion of the loss can be carried forward and offset against *future* taxable income in the ensuing 20 years—2007 through 2026—as shown in Figure 13.6.

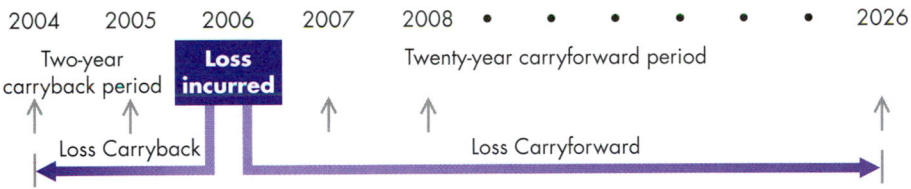

Figure 13.6

UNFORTUNATO CORPORATION
Illustration of Tax Loss Carryback/ Carryforward Provision

Carryforward Only Another alternative is available to Unfortunato Corporation. Rather than first carrying the loss back and then carrying forward any unused amounts, Unfortunato could elect *only* to carry the loss forward against taxable profits in the next 20 years, as shown in Figure 13.7.

> Why would firms elect the carryforward-only option, thereby foregoing an immediate income tax refund? Most companies *do* elect to carryback first, since this strategy usually maximizes the discounted present value of the benefit. In unusual situations—for example, where a firm expects to be profitable in the future and expects future tax rates to be much higher than past rates—the carryforward-only option may be preferred.

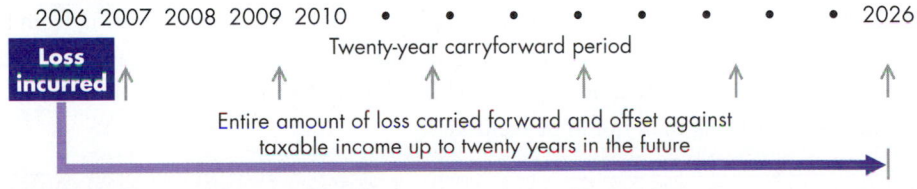

Figure 13.7

UNFORTUNATO CORPORATION
Illustration of Tax Loss Carryforward

To illustrate how the two options work, let's assume that the tax rate in effect from 2003 through 2006 was 35% and that Unfortunato had the following operating profits in those years:

Year	Taxable Profit (Loss)	Tax (at 35%)
2003	$ 300,000	$105,000
2004	400,000	140,000
2005	350,000	122,500
2006	(1,000,000)	—

If Unfortunato Corporation elects to use the combined carryback/carryforward option, losses must first be offset against 2004 income ($400,000), the earliest year in the two-year carryback time frame, and then against 2005 income ($350,000). This offsets $750,000 of the 2006 loss and generates a tax refund of $262,500 ($750,000 × 35%). Unfortunato makes the following entry in 2006 to reflect the refund due:

DR Income tax refund receivable	$262,500	
CR Income tax expense (*carryback* benefit)		$262,500

The loss in excess of the combined prior two-years' profits ($1,000,000 – $400,000 – $350,000 = $250,000) will result in future tax benefits—if Unfortunato becomes profitable again before 2026. If we assume that future tax rates remained at 35%, these potential future benefits would total $87,500 ($250,000 × 35%). If Unfortunato expects that pre-tax income in the ensuing 20 years will exceed $250,000, then an additional entry would be made in 2006:

DR Deferred income tax asset	$87,500	
CR Income tax expense (*carryforward* benefit)		$87,500

The "Income tax refund receivable" asset account would be shown among current assets on the balance sheet, and the deferred tax asset would be apportioned between current and noncurrent categories in accordance with the expected timing of the future income. If we assume the pre-tax book loss equaled the taxable loss, then the credits would be reflected on the accompanying income statement for 2006 as:

Pre-tax operating loss	$(1,000,000)
Income tax benefit due to	
operating loss *carryback*	262,500
Income tax benefit due to	
operating loss *carryforward*	87,500
After-tax operating loss	$ (650,000)

Deferred income tax assets that result from operating loss carryforwards will generate future benefits only if the firm earns profits in the ensuing 20 years. Because future profits are never assured, the probability of realizing deferred income tax assets arising from operating loss carryforwards must be carefully evaluated. The criterion here for deciding whether a valuation allowance is needed is identical to the criterion applied to deferred tax assets arising from book-versus-tax timing differences—if *it is more likely than not* that the benefit will not be realized in its entirety, a valuation allowance is required. This allowance should reduce the asset to a net amount that is more likely than not to be realized.

 RECAP U.S. tax rules allow firms to offset operating losses against taxable income. Firms can elect to carry back losses up to two years, with any unused loss carried forward up to 20 years; or they can elect to only carry forward the loss up to 20 years. The tax benefit associated with the loss carryback or carryforward is recorded as an adjustment to tax expense in the year of the loss.

Using Footnote Disclosures to Improve Financial Analysis

Understanding Footnote Disclosures

Typical income tax footnote disclosures provide financial statement users with a wealth of data. If you understand these disclosures, you'll be able to extract useful insights about a firm's performance and prospects. To illustrate, let's look at the income tax footnote from the 2002 annual report of Merck & Co., Inc., shown in Exhibit 13.12 below and on page 708. To make things easy to refer to, we have subdivided the footnote into panels (a) through (d) and numbered key lines or sections in these schedules.

Exhibit 13.12(a) shows the components of Merck's tax expense provision for the years 2000 through 2002. Notice how Merck differentiates between the portion of tax expense that is currently payable (denoted Item ①) and the portion that is deferred taxes (Item ②). Within each category, separate amounts for U.S. federal, foreign, and state taxes are disclosed. In the aggregate, the 2002 entry for taxes ($ in millions) was:

DR Income tax expense (Item ③)	$3,064.1	
CR Deferred tax liability or asset (Item ②)		$444.8
CR Income tax currently payable (Item ①)		2,619.3

The $444.8 million credit to deferred taxes arises because of temporary differences in revenue and expense items reported on Merck's GAAP income statement versus what was reported on its tax return in 2002. In aggregate, these temporary differences caused book income to be larger than taxable income in 2002. The result was either an increase in deferred tax liabilities or a decrease in deferred tax assets (both credits).

EXHIBIT 13.12	**Merck & Co., Inc.**

2002 Annual Report Footnote on Income Taxes

Panel (a)

Taxes on income consist of:

	Years Ended December 31		
($ in millions)	**2002**	**2001**	**2000**
Current Provision:			
Federal	$1,691.6	$1,692.4	$2,239.0
Foreign ①	609.3	635.7	591.0
State	318.4	326.8	266.7
	2,619.3	2,654.9	3,096.7
Deferred Provision:			
Federal	409.8	332.3	(64.4)
Foreign ②	(8.0)	57.9	(34.9)
State	43.0	75.7	5.0
	444.8	465.9	(94.3)
[Current period tax provision*] ◄ ③ ➤	$3,064.1	$3,120.8	$3,002.4

Panel (b)

A reconciliation between the Company's effective tax rate and the U.S. statutory rate is as follows:

	2002		Tax Rate	
($ in millions)	**Amount**	**2002**	**2001**	**2000**
U.S. statutory rate applied				
to pretax income	$3,574.7	35.0%	35.0%	35.0%
Differential arising from				
Foreign earnings	(602.3)	(5.9)	(5.1)	(4.7)
Tax exemption for				
Puerto Rico operations ④	(86.8)	(0.9) ⑤	(0.9)	(1.1)
State taxes	220.8	2.2	2.2	1.7
Other	(42.3)	(0.4)	(1.2)	(0.3)
[Reported tax expense*]	$3,064.1	30.0% **	30.0%	30.6%

*Description added by authors for clarity.
**Reported pre-tax income of Merck was $ 10,213.6 million, so $3,064.6 / $10,213.6 = 30.0%   (*continued on next page*)

EXHIBIT 13.12 Merck & Co., Inc. (*continued*)

Panel (c)

Deferred income taxes at December 31 consisted of:

		2002		2001	
($ in millions)		Assets	Liabilities	Assets	Liabilities
Other intangibles		$ 108.7	$1,189.0	$ 133.0	$1,263.2
Inventory related		700.5	354.1	594.1	300.9
Accelerated depreciation		—	1,459.3	—	1,230.8
Advanced payment		338.6	—	338.6	—
Equity investment	⑥	57.8	443.2	57.8	408.0
Pensions and OPEB		109.5	291.6	165.0	240.4
Accrued rebates		187.7	—	199.2	—
Compensation related		131.2	—	138.1	—
Environmental related		74.6	—	85.3	—
Other		1,299.9	441.5	1,256.0	382.8
Subtotal		3,008.5	4,178.7	2,967.1	3,826.1
Valuation allowance ← ⑧ →		2.4	—	2.1	—
Total deferred taxes		$3,006.1	$4,178.7	$2,965.0	$3,826.1
Net deferred tax liabilities ← ⑨ →			1,172.6		$ 861.1

Item ⑦ applies to the 2002 Liabilities and 2001 Liabilities columns.

Panel (d)

Recognized as:

		2002	2001
Prepaid expenses and taxes		$(764.1)	$(613.7)
Other assets		(33.3)	(65.2)
Income taxes payable	⑩	98.7	12.9
Deferred income taxes and non-current liabilities		1,871.3	1,527.1
		1,172.6	861.1

Exhibit 13.12(b) explains why the debit to tax expense in the 2000–2002 period was less than the U.S. statutory corporate tax rate of 35% times pre-tax book income. For example, the $3,064.1 million debit to tax expense in the previous entry is 30.0% of $10,213.6 million, Merck's reported pre-tax income in 2002. The reconciliation in this portion of Exhibit 13.12(b) (Item ④) explains what caused the divergence between Merck's effective tax rate of 30.0% and the 35% statutory rate (Item ⑤).

The reconciliation in Exhibit 13.12(b) is required under *SFAS 109*.[7] It is potentially useful to analysts because it provides information about the firm's tax policy. Specifically, the divergence between the **statutory tax rate** (the tax rate set forth in federal tax laws) and **effective tax rate** (measured by book tax expense divided by book pre-tax income) arises from two types of tax policy decisions:

1. The tax jurisdictions in which the firm chooses to operate.
2. Special characteristics of the income tax law.

One frequent cause for differences between effective and statutory rates is that tax rates differ across countries. For example, certain countries levy extremely low (or no) taxes on income earned within their boundaries to attract investment. And other countries' tax rates may exceed U.S. rates. Furthermore, many U.S. states impose income taxes on income earned within the state, which causes a firm's effective tax rate to exceed the 35% federal statutory rate. One important

---

[7] *SFAS 109*, para. 47.

element of a firm's tax planning strategy is choosing to operate subsidiaries within lower marginal tax rate jurisdictions. This lowers the firm's overall tax burden, thereby increasing after-tax returns to shareholders.[8] Merck apparently did this in 2002.

Another reason for differences between effective and statutory rates is due to special tax law characteristics that treat certain GAAP revenue items as nontaxable and certain GAAP expenses as nondeductible for tax purposes. Remember, book-versus-tax differences that never reverse are referred to as *permanent differences*. Permanent difference items that cause book income to be *higher* but are not taxed (such as, interest on municipal bonds) will cause the effective tax rate per books to be *lower* than the statutory tax rate. Conversely, permanent differences that cause book income to be *lower* but that are not deductible for tax purposes will cause the effective tax rate per books to be *higher* than the statutory rate (examples include fines levied for law violations and most types of goodwill amortization).

> Exhibit 13.12(b) reveals that Merck saved $86.8 million in taxes for 2002 because it had earnings from Puerto Rico operations that were tax exempt. We can determine the dollar amount of these tax-exempt earnings by dividing the tax savings by the U.S. statutory tax rate ($86.8 ÷ .35 = $248.0 million).

The reconciliation between effective and statutory tax rates, like that shown in Exhibit 13.12 (b) (Item ④), can reflect important elements of a firm's tax policy decisions. Effective tax rates that are far lower than statutory tax rates might indicate aggressive tax postures. This could benefit shareholders. But aggressive tax positions might also generate future tax audits and additional tax assessments.[9]

Items ⑥ and ⑦ of Exhibit 13.12(c) show year-end balances in deferred tax asset and deferred tax liability accounts and the source of those amounts. After deducting the valuation allowance of $2.4 million on deferred tax assets (Item ⑧), Merck had a *net* deferred tax liability balance at December 31, 2002 of $1,172.6 million (Item ⑨), or $4,178.7 million of deferred tax liabilities minus $3,006.1 million of deferred tax assets. One year earlier, Merck had a *net* deferred tax liability balance (after allowance) of $861.1 million ($3,826.1 million liability minus $2,965.0 million asset). Thus, the year-to-year change in *net* deferred tax liabilities was $1,172.6 − $861.1 = $311.5 million increase.

Notice the $311.5 million increase in Merck's net deferred tax liability on its balance sheet in Exhibit 13.12(c) does *not* equal the $444.8 million journal entry credit to deferred taxes shown earlier. The $133.3 million difference is partially explained by reference to **intraperiod income tax allocation,** discussed briefly in Chapter 2. Recall that all income statement items shown below income from continuing operations and direct charges or credits to stockholders' equity *are shown net of any related income tax effects*. Accordingly, tax effects (including deferred tax effects) that arose from discontinued operations, extraordinary items, cumulative effects of accounting changes, or direct charges or credits to stockholders' equity for prior period adjustments or other comprehensive income items are not included in Merck's tax journal entry on page 707. This journal entry is limited to income tax effects that relate to income from continuing operations.

Merck has no discontinued operations, no extraordinary items, and no accounting changes reported in its 2002 income statement. However, scrutiny of Merck's Statement of Comprehensive Income (not shown) reveals three "Other comprehensive income" items—market value adjustments on derivatives and available for sale securities and pension liability adjustments—that decreased stockholders' equity by $109.4 million net of tax effects. The net deferred tax asset associated with these three items would be approximately $58.9 million.

> This amount is determined in two steps. First, we divide the after-tax amount of $109.4 million by one minus the statutory tax rate [$109.4 ÷ (1 − .35) = $168.3 million]. This gives the before-tax amount of other comprehensive income components. Next, taking the difference between the before-tax amount of $168.3 million and the after-tax amount of $109.4 million gives the *increase* in deferred tax assets ($58.9 million) related to these other comprehensive income components.

---

[8] For an expanded discussion of this point, see M. Scholes, M. Wolfson, M. Erickson, E. Maydew, and T. Shevlin, *Tax and Corporate Financial Strategy: A Global Planning Approach* (Upper Saddle River, NJ: Prentice Hall, 2002).

[9] For an analysis of tax footnote disclosures from the perspective of tax aggressiveness and future tax audit risk, see R. Weber and J. Wheeler, "Using Income Tax Disclosures to Explore Significant Economic Transactions," *Accounting Horizons* (September 1992), pp. 14–29.

This $58.9 million is included in deferred tax assets on the balance sheet, but is not included in the 2002 journal entry for taxes. Thus, it provides a partial explanation for why the $444.8 credit to deferred taxes in Merck's 2002 tax expense entry (see p. 707) exceeds the increase in net deferred tax liabilities of $311.5 million reflected on its balance sheet ($1,172.6 − $861.1) in Exhibit 13.12(c). But this still leaves an unexplained difference of $74.4 million—that is, the original difference of $133.3 million minus the $58.9 million. The most likely source of this remaining difference is various acquisitions and divestitures made during the year, which are discussed elsewhere in Merck's 2002 annual report. When the acquired or divested subsidiary holds assets having a tax basis that differs from their financial accounting basis, changes occur in deferred tax accounts on the consolidated balance sheet. These deferred tax changes are not reflected in the deferred portion of the current period's tax provision. Unfortunately, Merck's disclosures do not allow us to determine this amount directly. The lesson here is that certain events, like acquisitions or divestitures of subsidiaries, can complicate full reconciliation of the deferred tax accounts.

Exhibit 13.12(c) also shows the specific items that collectively comprise the deferred tax asset (Item ⑥) and deferred tax liability (Item ⑦) balances at December 31, 2002. The major items giving rise to deferred tax assets are inventory and advance payments, while the major items giving rise to deferred tax liabilities are other intangibles and depreciation differences. Finally, Exhibit 13.12(d) shows in which specific accounts the net deferred tax asset and liability amounts of $1,172.6 million are reported on Merck's December 31, 2002 balance sheet (Item ⑩).

Extracting Analytical Insights from Footnote Disclosures

Analysis

As we saw in Exhibit 13.12(c) for Merck, companies are required to disclose details about individual temporary differences that give rise to the deferred tax asset and deferred tax liability balances on the balance sheet. Scrutiny of the details comprising deferred taxes can reveal important analytical insights about the actions management has taken to boost short-term earnings. To illustrate, refer to Exhibit 13.13, which contains excerpts from the 2000 income tax footnote for ChipPAC Company, one of the world's largest independent providers of semiconductor packaging, testing, and distribution services. This excerpt identifies major elements of the deferred tax asset and liability balances. Notice that the deferred income taxes attributable to book-versus-tax depreciation differences (highlighted area) went from a $92 thousand *debit* balance (asset) in 1999 to $10.870 million *credit* balance (liability) in 2000, an increase of $10.962 million. Some portion of this increase is likely due to acquisitions of new property, plant, and equipment during the year that were depreciated at a faster rate for tax purposes than for book purposes (ChipPAC's cash flow statement reveals that $93.174 million was spent in 2000 for acquisition of property and equipment). However, fixed asset growth explains only a small part of the increase in this segment of deferred tax liabilities. What else might explain the rather large increase in this component of deferred tax liabilities? In another note in its 2000 annual report, ChipPAC states:

Effective January 1, 2000, the Company re-evaluated the estimated useful lives of equipment. Based on an independent appraisal to evaluate the useful lives of such equipment and the Company's internal assessment, the Company changed the estimated useful lives of assembly and test product equipment and furniture and fixtures from five to eight years. Previously, such equipment was depreciated on a straight-line basis over an estimated useful life of five years.

The net book values of assembly and test product equipment and furniture and fixtures, as of January 1, 2000, are now being depreciated over the remaining useful life, based on eight years from the date such assets were originally placed into service. This change resulted in a decrease in depreciation expense for the year ended December 31, 2000 being $29.0 million lower than would have been recorded using five years.

By extending the useful lives of fixed assets, ChipPAC lowered book depreciation and widened the excess of 2000 book income over tax return income. This increased the deferred tax liability related to depreciation timing differences by $.35 \times \$29$ million = $10.15 million, or 92.6% of the $10.962 million increase from the prior year. Interestingly, ChipPAC reported a pre-tax *profit* of $18 million in 2000. Therefore, without the $29 million boost to earnings that resulted from lengthening the useful lives, ChipPAC would have reported an $11 million ($18 − $29) pre-tax *loss*.

EXHIBIT 13.13	ChipPAC Inc.

Excerpt from 2000 Annual Report
Income Tax Footnote

The tax effects of temporary differences that give rise to significant portions of the deferred tax assets and deferred liabilities at December 31, 2000 and December 31, 1999 are presented below:

($ in thousands)	2000	1999
Deferred tax assets:		
Income recognized for tax but not for books	$ 7,598	$ —
Tax credits	2,663	—
NOL carryforward	3,490	—
Other	3,381	6,270
Total gross deferred assets	17,132	6,270
Less: Valuation allowance	(6,122)	
Net deferred tax assets	11,010	6,270
Deferred tax liabilities:		
Depreciation	(10,870)	92
Reserves deducted for tax and not for books	(570)	(621)
Total deferred tax liabilities	(11,440)	(529)
Net deferred tax liabilities	$ (430)	$5,741

A financial statement reader can glean important information from changes in deferred tax balances, as demonstrated in Exhibit 13.13. It was possible to infer that depreciable lives were extended because of the relatively large increase in deferred taxes arising from book-versus-tax depreciation differences. As we saw, ChipPAC clearly disclosed this change in estimated useful lives. *APB Opinion No. 20* requires disclosure of a change in an accounting estimate only if the impact of the change is material.[10]

Regrettably, widely accepted guidelines for assessing materiality do not exist. Consequently, firms that are not as candid as ChipPAC could conceivably decide to extend asset lives and not disclose the change. Their motive could be to manipulate or smooth income, and they would justify nondisclosure by contending that the impact of the change is immaterial. Since materiality guidelines are subjective, careful scrutiny of the income tax footnote provides analysts with a way of detecting subtle changes in accounting estimates that affect bottom-line earnings but are not separately disclosed. This avenue is especially useful to auditors. A detailed examination of deferred income tax balances provides auditors with evidence for evaluating management's candor.[11]

---

[10] "Accounting Changes," *APB Opinion No. 20* (New York: American Institute of CPAs [AICPA], 1971), para. 38.

[11] For readers who are neither auditors nor studying to be auditors, some elaboration is necessary. At the start of an audit, the auditor discusses significant issues with the client's managers in order to identify potential problem areas. When managers do not voluntarily disclose things like income-increasing changes in accounting estimates, auditors consider this to be a potential danger signal that warrants an expansion in the scope of the audit. Scrutiny of the tax footnote provides auditors with another tool for identifying problem areas.

Increases in deferred income tax liability balances result from a widening excess of book income over taxable income. These increases represent a potential danger signal that should be investigated, because an increase in a deferred tax liability might be an indication of deteriorating earnings quality. One way to uncover such subtle deterioration in earnings quality is to investigate all large, sudden changes in deferred tax balances. The analyst should try to understand *why* the deferred tax liability balance increased.

Using Deferred Tax Footnotes to Assess Earnings Quality

To illustrate how deferred tax footnotes can be used to assess earnings quality, consider the relatively large increase in the deferred tax liability related to depreciation—$10.962 million—that was highlighted in Exhibit 13.13. We know that if a company lengthens the estimated useful lives of its fixed assets, book depreciation will be lowered and the excess of book income over taxable income will be widened, causing an increase in deferred tax liabilities. Other depreciation-related explanations for the increase in the deferred tax liability include growth in capital expenditures and tax law changes that permit more accelerated depreciation. If investigation reveals that the deferral increased without either a corresponding increase in capital expenditures or a change in tax depreciation schedules, then the analyst should try to determine whether an undisclosed change in useful lives has been made to raise income. Similar investigations should be undertaken for any sudden increase in other types of deferred income tax liabilities.

Sudden decreases in deferred income tax assets are also a potential sign of deteriorating earnings quality. Using warranty expense as an example, we will explain why a sudden decrease in a deferred tax asset may be a danger signal.

Analysis

We saw earlier that accruals for product warranties generate deferred tax assets. The reason is that GAAP requires warranty expenses to be matched against the revenues of the products to which the warranty applies. But income tax rules do not allow deductions for warranty expenses until the costs of providing the warranty services are actually incurred. This is often later than the period in which the revenues have been recognized. Accordingly, for growing companies, GAAP warranty expenses exceed tax return warranty expenses, giving rise to a deferred tax asset.

Assume that on January 1, 2005 Carson Company begins offering a one-year warranty on all sales. Its 2005 sales were $20,000,000, and Carson estimates that warranty expenses will be 1% of sales; therefore, $200,000 of warranty expense is deducted on Carson's books in 2005.

Assume that tax deductions for warranties in 2005 were zero. If tax rates in 2005 are 35%, Carson will have a deferred tax asset of $70,000 for warranties at December 31, 2005—the $200,000 book-versus-tax warranty difference times 35%. If the *actual* warranty costs incurred in 2006 that are associated with 2005 sales were precisely $200,000, this would indicate that Carson's warranty estimate was accurate and should be maintained in 2006.

Exhibit 13.14(a) shows what will happen if Carson Company uses the same warranty expense estimate of 1% of sales in 2006. Here it is assumed that sales in 2006 are again $20,000,000 and that actual warranty costs on 2006 sales are not incurred until 2007. Using these assumptions, notice that Carson's December 31, 2006 deferred tax asset balance will still be $70,000. That is, the 2005 book-versus-tax timing difference reversed in 2006 (see arrow in Exhibit 13.14[a]), but a new $200,000 timing difference on warranties associated with 2006 sales originated. *The example in Exhibit 13.14(a) is designed to demonstrate that the deferred income tax asset balance will remain stable if the warranty estimate is accurate and if sales volume is unchanged.*

EXHIBIT 13.14	Carson Company

Illustration of Decline in Deferred Tax Assets

Panel (a)

Warranty Percentage Unchanged

	2006	2005
Sales revenues	$20,000,000	$20,000,000
Estimated warranty cost percentage	.01	.01
Warranty expense per books	200,000	200,000
Warranty expense per tax return		
Attributable to 2005 sales	200,000	—
Attributable to 2006 sales	—	—
Excess of book over tax expense		
Arising from 2005 sales	—	200,000
Arising from 2006 sales	200,000	—
Tax rate	.35	.35
December 31 deferred tax asset balance	$ 70,000	$ 70,000

2006 Reversal

Panel (b)

Warranty Percentage Lowered in 2006

	2006	2005
Sales revenues	$20,000,000	$20,000,000
Estimated warranty cost percentage	.005	.01
Warranty expense per books	100,000	200,000
Warranty expense per tax return		
Attributable to 2005 sales	200,000	—
Attributable to 2006 sales	—	—
Excess of book over tax expense		
Arising from 2005 sales	—	200,000
Arising from 2006 sales	100,000	—
Tax rate	.35	.35
December 31 deferred tax asset balance	$ 35,000	$ 70,000

2006 Reversal

To illustrate why it is also important to scrutinize deferred tax asset balances, let us now assume that instead of maintaining the warranty expense estimate at 1% of sales, Carson lowers the estimate to 0.5% of sales in 2006. Carson does this because its managers wish to increase 2006 income despite the fact that the 1% number reflects actual warranty experience. Notice that since the 1% estimate accurately reflects estimated warranty costs in 2005, this change of an accounting estimate in 2006 represents a deterioration in earnings quality.

Exhibit 13.14(b) shows that the deferred tax asset balance will decrease from $70,000 to $35,000 under these circumstances. The reason for the decrease in the deferred income tax asset balance is that the book-versus-tax difference narrowed from $200,000 in 2005 to $100,000 in 2006 as a consequence of the reduction in estimated warranty expense from 1% to 0.5% of sales.

RECAP

This example demonstrates why shrinkage in a deferred tax asset balance should be investigated. Year-to-year changes in warranty expense estimates are just like other changes in accounting estimates in that they need to be disclosed only if they are material. Since materiality guidelines are subjective, companies can conceivably use undisclosed estimate changes as a way to artificially increase earnings. Decreases in deferred tax asset balances can provide clues of such possibilities to statement readers.[12]

---

[12] Changes in deferred balances can also provide evidence regarding aggressive tax behavior that could result in subsequent additional assessments; see Weber and Wheeler, op. cit.

Using Tax Footnotes to Improve Interfirm Comparability

The deferred tax portion of the income tax footnote can be used to undo differences in financial reporting choices across firms and thus to improve interfirm comparisons.

Here's a specific illustration. Lubrizol and Cambrex are both classified in the same Standard Industrial Classification (SIC) code and compete in many product categories. But each uses different depreciation methods. A recent Lubrizol 10-K states the following:

> Accelerated depreciation methods are used in computing depreciation on certain machinery and equipment, which comprise approximately 21% of the depreciable assets. The remaining assets are depreciated using the straight-line method. The estimated useful lives are 10 to 40 years for buildings and land improvements and range from 3 to 20 years for machinery and equipment.

So Lubrizol is using accelerated depreciation for some of its assets. By contrast, Cambrex's 10-K report for the same year says:

> Property, plant and equipment is stated at cost, net of accumulated depreciation. Plant and equipment are depreciated on a straight-line basis over the estimated useful lives for each applicable asset group as follows:

Buildings and improvements	15 to 20 years
Machinery and equipment	5 to 10 years
Furniture and fixtures	3 to 5 years

> SIC is a system maintained by the Office of Federal Statistical Policy and Standards in the Department of Commerce to classify firms by the nature of their operations. Lubrizol and Cambrex are both in SIC Code 2860—Industrial Organic Chemicals.

Exhibit 13.15 gives several key financial statement figures for each company from their respective 10-Ks and excerpts from their income tax footnotes. It's possible that the different depreciation choices of each firm conform perfectly to differences in the service-potential of each firm's assets. But what if they don't? How can an analyst adjust the numbers to improve interfirm comparisons?

Let's begin by looking at Exhibit 13.15(a), which shows the balances in the subcomponents of the deferred tax liability account for Lubrizol. The highlighted depreciation item reflects the $99.9 million cumulative deferred tax liability arising from book-versus-tax depreciation expense at year-end.

Companies like Lubrizol have an incentive to use the most accelerated depreciation method that the tax law allows and to depreciate the assets over the shortest allowable tax life. This minimizes the discounted present value of their tax liability by accelerating deductions to the fullest legal extent. These *tax* depreciation rate and useful life deductions exceed the *book* accelerated method and useful lives chosen by Lubrizol, so a deferred liability results. The liability declined by $1.7 million going from $101.6 million in the previous year (which we have labeled Year 1) to $99.9 million in the current year (labeled Year 2).

> A reduction in the deferred tax liability related to depreciation timing differences probably arises because either: (1) accelerated methods used for books gives higher depreciation than allowed for tax purposes, or (2) assets for which Lubrizol uses straight-line depreciation for books have reached a point in their useful lives where the straight-line depreciation exceeds the accelerated depreciation per tax return (see again Figure 13.1).

The change in the deferred income tax liability arising from depreciation is:

$$\text{Change} = (\text{Tax depreciation} - \text{Book depreciation}) \times \text{Statutory tax rate}$$

Lubrizol's statutory tax rate is 35%, and the depreciation deferred tax *change* was −$1.7 million (a decrease), as shown in Exhibit 13.15(a). Substituting these values into the preceding equation, we get:

$$-\$1.7 \text{ million} = (\text{Tax depreciation} - \text{Book depreciation}) \times .35$$

Dividing both sides by .35 yields:

$$-\$4.9 \text{ million} = (\text{Tax depreciation} - \text{Book depreciation})$$

EXHIBIT 13.15	Selected Financial Statement Disclosures from Recent 10-K Reports of Lubrizol and Cambrex

Panel (a)

	December 31	
Lubrizol: ($ in thousands)	Year 2	Year 1
Book depreciation	$ 88,300	$ 79,700
Income before income taxes	195,350	118,814
Property, plant and equipment, net of accumulated depreciation (at year-end)	670,512	718,850
Significant deferred tax liabilities	**Year 2**	**Year 1**
Depreciation and other basis differences	$ 99,938	$101,658
Undistributed foreign equity income	5,566	3,894
Inventory basis difference	1,497	3,706
Other	3,977	2,986

Panel (b)

	December 31	
Cambrex: ($ in thousands)	Year 2	Year 1
Book depreciation	$ 33,118	$ 30,547
Income before income taxes	58,901	61,695
Property, plant and equipment, net of accumulated depreciation (at year-end)	280,163	255,016
Significant deferred tax liabilities	**Year 2**	**Year 1**
Depreciation	$ 30,967	$ 29,591
Environmental reserves	796	—
Intangibles	14,963	14,839
Italian intangibles	4,581	6,086
Other benefits	2,143	—
Other	1,722	1,667

Since Exhibit 13.15(a) shows that Lubrizol's book depreciation was $88.3 million, tax depreciation must have been $88.3 million − $4.9 million = $83.4 million, which was 5.5% lower.

We can now perform the same analysis on Cambrex and determine what its tax depreciation was in Year 2. The highlighted portion of Exhibit 13.15(b) shows that Cambrex's depreciation-related deferred income tax liability was slightly less than $31.0 million in Year 2—an increase of $1.4 million over the previous year. Repeating the analytical approach we used for Lubrizol yields:

$$\text{Change} = (\text{Tax depreciation} - \text{Book depreciation}) \times \text{Statutory tax rate}$$

or:

$$\$1.4 \text{ million} = (\text{Tax depreciation} - \text{Book depreciation}) \times .35$$

or:

$$\$4 \text{ million} = (\text{Tax depreciation} - \text{Book depreciation})$$

Cambrex's book depreciation was $33.1 million (Exhibit 13.15[b]), so tax depreciation must have been $33.1 million + $4 million = $37.1 million, an increase of 12.1%.

We have now approximated the tax return depreciation taken by each firm and established a "common denominator" for interfirm analysis. While we do not have enough information to put Cambrex on Lubrizol's book depreciation basis, we do have enough information to put each firm on an identical tax depreciation basis, thereby facilitating comparisons.

Adjusting each firm's financial reporting to the same rate as well as the useful lives used for tax purposes increases Lubrizol's pre-tax income by 2.5% ($4.9 million ÷ $195.4 million). Cambrex's pre-tax income is lowered by 6.8% ($4 million ÷ $58.9 million). In any setting, the difference may—or may not—be significant. But making interfirm comparisons using comparable data is better than basing the analysis on diverse financial reporting choices.

It is important to note that the preceding analysis works only in those situations where firms have not had major asset disposals during the year. When depreciable assets are sold, the deferred tax amounts for these assets are eliminated from the deferred tax liability account. Moreover, the amount eliminated due to asset sales is rarely disclosed. So the year-to-year change in the deferred tax liability balance for depreciation no longer reflects only current period book-versus-tax depreciation differences. We can determine if the firm sold assets during the period by looking in the "Investing activity" section of the cash flow statement to see if cash was generated from asset sales. In this illustration, neither Lubrizol nor Cambrex reported major asset sales in their 1999 cash flow statement.

Using Income Tax Footnotes to Assess the Degree of Conservatism in Firms' Accounting Choices

Determining the degree of conservatism in a firm's set of accounting choices is an important part of assessing the earnings quality for that company. Conservative choices, like accelerated depreciation, decrease earnings and asset values relative to more liberal techniques, like straight-line depreciation. Ceteris paribus, the more conservative the set of accounting choices, the higher the quality of earnings.

Useful information for assessing the degree of conservatism in a firm's portfolio of accounting choices can be extracted from the income tax footnote by comparing the ratio of pre-tax book income to taxable income. While this is admittedly a relatively coarse way of assessing accounting conservatism, it can be useful in selected settings. The ratio is computed as

$$EC = \frac{\text{Pre-tax book income (adjusted for permanent differences)}}{\text{Taxable income per tax return}}$$

where EC is the current period's **earnings conservatism** ratio.

Consider the denominator, "Taxable income per tax return." In most instances firms seek to minimize tax return income. Because of this income minimization incentive, the denominator represents a very conservative income benchmark. Usually, it is the lowest permissible—meaning "legal"—taxable income number for the period.

The numerator—pre-tax GAAP income—incorporates the latitude available to firms in selecting accounting method choices, accounting estimates for things like bad debts expense and asset useful lives, and discretionary expenses such as advertising and research and development (R&D) that we have outlined elsewhere in the book. Consequently, the numerator can range from a highly aggressive (income increasing) number to a highly conservative (income decreasing) number.

To illustrate how this ratio is used, we will compute the EC ratio for Merck & Co. for 2002 (EC_{02}). Exhibit 13.12(b) on page 707 indicates that 2002 income before income taxes was $10,213.6 million. *This number needs adjustment for net permanent difference items that do not enter into the computation of taxable income and, therefore, would distort the comparison between book and taxable income made below.* From Exhibit 13.12(b), Merck reported the tax

The only exceptions will arise where firms either (1) have unused operating loss carryforwards that are about to expire, or (2) expect future tax rates to rise sharply.

Analysis

effects of net permanent difference items to be $510.6 million ($3,574.7 − $3,064.1). We divide this amount by the 35% statutory tax rate to get the before-tax amount of permanent differences ($510.6 ÷ 0.35 = $1,458.9). Since Merck's effective tax rate of 30.0% is lower than the statutory rate, this $1,458.9 million of permanent differences represents income reported on Merck's books that will never be taxed. For comparability, we need to subtract this amount from Merck's reported pre-tax book income of $10,213.6 million. This yields $8,754.7 million as the company's adjusted pre-tax book income. This is the numerator of EC_{02}.

Since most companies do not disclose details of their income tax returns, we need to estimate the denominator, "Taxable income per tax return." We do this by "grossing up" the current portion of tax expense ($2,619.3 million) shown in Exhibit 13.12(a) for Merck. That is, we approximate taxable income per tax return by dividing the current portion of the current period's tax provision by the statutory marginal federal tax rate. We saw in Exhibit 13.12(a) that income taxes currently payable in 2002 totaled $2,619.3 million. Taxable income can then be estimated as:

> A recent study points out three reasons why this simple procedure for estimating taxable income may not fully capture the taxes paid in that period by the reporting entity.*
> - Certain items may cause the current portion of tax expense to over- or understate the actual tax liabilities of the firm. For example, items like profits or losses from discontinued operations or extraordinary gains or losses, which are reported below net income from continuing operations, are shown net of tax. While these items affect the entity's taxable income (and thus, taxes paid) in the current period, they are not reported as part of pre-tax income per books under intraperiod tax allocation.
> - The current portion of tax expense is reported after tax credits like research and development credits and foreign tax credits. In the presence of credits, the estimate of taxable income from grossing-up the current tax expense will be measured with error.
> - Differing consolidation rules for book and tax purposes can cause the financial statements to include a different group of related corporations than the tax return includes.
>
> *M. Hanlon, "What Can We Infer About a Firm's Taxable Income from its Financial Statements?" (working paper, University of Michigan, 2003).

2002 Income taxes currently payable		2002 Taxable income per tax return		2002 Statutory tax rate
	=		×	

Substituting the two pieces of data from Merck's tax footnote, we get:

2002 Income taxes currently payable		2002 Taxable income per tax return		2002 Statutory tax rate
	=		×	
$2,619.3 million	=	?	×	.35

Rearranging, in order to isolate the unknown taxable income per tax return on the left side, we get:

2002 Taxable income = $2,619.3 million ÷ .35 = $7,483.7 million

Thus, EC_{02} for Merck is ($ in millions):

$$EC_{02} = \frac{2002 \text{ Pre-tax book income (adjusted)}}{2002 \text{ Taxable income}}$$

$$EC_{02} = \frac{\$8,754.7}{\$7,483.7}$$

$$EC_{02} = 1.17$$

In general, an EC ratio close to 1.0 indicates relatively conservative financial reporting choices. (Remember, companies have an incentive to minimize the denominator, "Taxable income per tax return.") When the EC ratio is greater than 1.0, this suggests that earnings conservatism per books is relatively low. In Merck's case, book income is estimated to be roughly 17% higher than taxable income in 2002.

Analysts can also compare EC ratios for a single company over time to monitor overall earnings conservatism. For example, using Exhibit 13.12, we can compute Merck's 2001 taxable income—the denominator of its EC_{01} ratio as follows:

$$
\begin{array}{ccccc}
\text{2001} & & \text{2001 Income} & & \text{2001} \\
\text{Taxable} & = & \text{taxes currently} & \div & \text{Statutory} \\
\text{income} & & \text{payable} & & \text{tax rate}
\end{array}
$$

$$
\begin{array}{ccccc}
\text{2001} & & & & \\
\text{Taxable} & = & \$2{,}654.9 \text{ million} & \div & .35 \\
\text{income} & & & &
\end{array}
$$

$$
\begin{array}{ccc}
\text{2001} & & \\
\text{Taxable} & = & \$7{,}585.4 \text{ million} \\
\text{income} & &
\end{array}
$$

Merck's 2001 pre-tax book income was $10,402.6 million. After adjusting Merck's pre-tax book income for $520.1 million of permanent difference items, Merck's EC_{01} is computed as follows:

$$ EC_{01} = \frac{\text{2001 Pre-tax book income (adjusted)}}{\text{2001 Taxable income}} $$

$$ EC_{01} = \frac{\$9{,}882.50}{\$7{,}585.4} $$

$$ EC_{01} = 1.30 $$

The decrease from EC_{01} (1.30) to EC_{02} (1.17) suggests that Merck may have been somewhat less aggressive in its financial reporting choices for 2002 relative to 2001. However, year-to-year changes in EC ratios must be interpreted with caution when dramatic changes in economic conditions or the tax law occur.

The earnings conservatism ratio can also be used to compare reporting choices across companies. For example, Merck's EC_{02} might be compared with the EC_{02} ratio of a competitor, like Pfizer, to assess whether each has similar earnings conservatism.

Having introduced the EC ratio, we now need to emphasize its three primary limitations.

1. EC ratio comparisons for a single company over time (for example, EC_{02} versus EC_{01}) can be misleading if the tax law has changed over the period of comparison. For example, if the U.S. Congress allows more accelerated tax depreciation schedules, this will cause the EC ratio to rise (that is, showing *lower* earnings conservatism) even though the firm's real earnings conservatism has remained constant.
2. Comparisons across companies in different industries should be made cautiously. Specifically, tax burdens can vary because of differences in capital intensity or specific tax rules (like the oil depletion allowance), which affect only certain industries.
3. One category of deterioration in earnings conservatism is not captured by the EC ratio. Whenever companies dip into old LIFO layers, the impact of the earnings increase affects both the numerator and the denominator of the ratio because of the LIFO conformity rule discussed in Chapter 9. That's why earnings conservatism deterioration arising from LIFO dipping is not reliably captured in EC.

Tax footnotes provide information that allows the analyst to estimate firms' taxable income. By comparing pre-tax accounting income with the estimate of taxable income, analysts can develop a rough index (subject to the limitations noted above) of the overall degree of conservatism in a firm's set of GAAP accounting choices. The degree of conservatism in a firm's set of accounting choices is an important part of assessing the earnings quality of that company.

SUMMARY

- The rules for computing income for financial reporting purposes—book income—differ from the rules for computing income for tax purposes.
- The differences between book income and taxable income are caused by both permanent and temporary (timing) differences in the revenue and expense items reported on a company's books versus its tax return.
- Temporary differences give rise to both deferred tax assets and deferred tax liabilities.
- Deferred tax accounting generally allows firms to report tax costs or benefits on the income statement in the period in which the related revenue and expense items are recognized for book purposes irrespective of when these amounts are recorded on the tax return.
- The income tax footnote provides useful information for understanding how much of the current period's tax provision (expense) is actually payable to the federal and state governments, and how much is deferred. Tax footnotes also allow users to understand why firms' effective tax rates may differ from the statutory rate.
- Finally, tax footnotes provide a wealth of information that can be exploited to improve interfirm comparability and evaluate firms' earnings quality.

APPENDIX

A COMPREHENSIVE INTERPERIOD TAX ALLOCATION PROBLEM

The following example for Hawkeye Corporation combines the various aspects of accounting for income taxes discussed in this chapter to demonstrate the interrelation between pre-tax accounting income, taxable income, taxes payable, deferred taxes, and tax expense. Working through this example will demonstrate the following points:

1. How to convert a pre-tax accounting income number to a taxable income number.
2. How taxes payable are determined.
3. How the change in deferred tax assets and deferred tax liabilities are determined.
4. How tax expense is determined.
5. How to reconcile the total tax costs (benefits) reported in the income statement with the total taxes payable according to the tax return for the period.

Before working through the Hawkeye Corporation example, look at Figure 13.8, which provides a road map for understanding how the various book and taxable income numbers and tax amounts relate to one another.

Computation of Taxable Income and Taxes Payable

Reading from left to right across the top of Figure 13.8, we see three categories of items that cause differences between pre-tax book income and taxable income on the tax return:

1. Permanent differences,
2. Operating loss carryforwards and,
3. Temporary differences.

Taxable income is determined by making adjustments to the reported pre-tax book income numbers for each of these items.

Technically, operating loss carryforwards are treated as a temporary difference under *SFAS No. 109*. Although a deferred tax asset will be reported on the company's books, the operating losses themselves are not carried over from previous periods and, thus, are not included as part of the current period's book income computation. Therefore, to reconcile pre-tax book income to taxable income requires an adjustment for the dollar amount of the loss carryforward. We have chosen to discuss the loss carryforward separately from the other temporary differences, which are discussed later.

Figure 13.8

OVERVIEW OF INTERPERIOD
TAX ALLOCATION

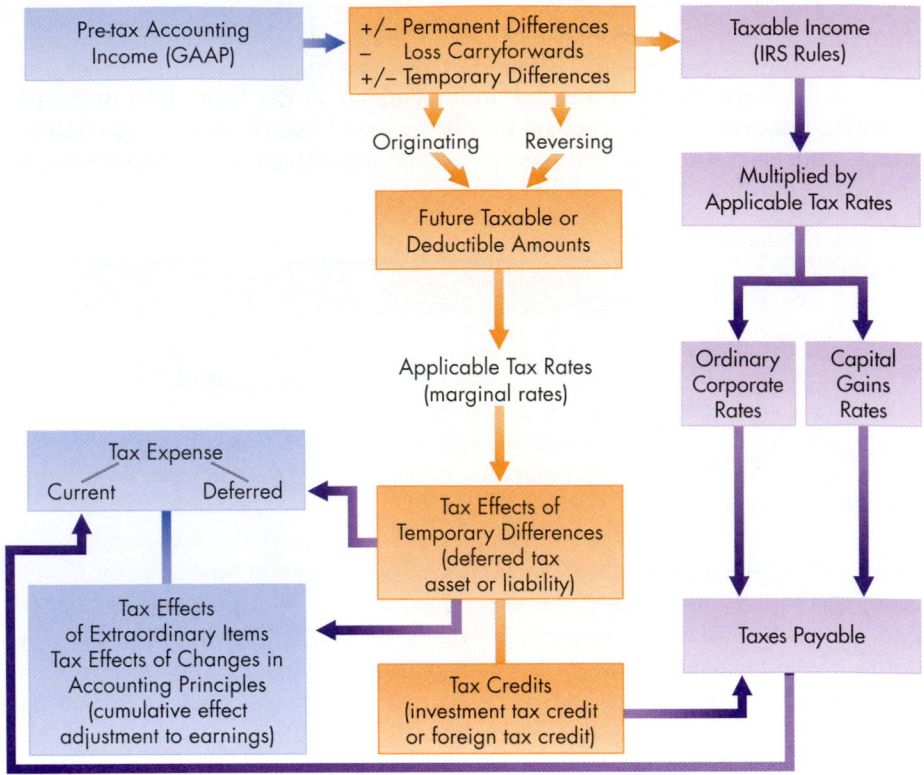

The first category of reconciling items is permanent differences. We know these are revenue or expense items that the tax rules treat differently—on a permanent basis—than the GAAP (book) rules treat them for income determination purposes. As shown below, Hawkeye Corporation has two permanent difference items—Item ①, "Interest earned on municipal bonds"; and Item ⑥, "Executive life insurance premiums paid by the company."

To arrive at taxable income, the municipal bond interest must be *subtracted* from the reported pre-tax book income number, since it is not taxable but has been included in book income. In addition, the executive life insurance premiums that were subtracted in arriving at pre-tax book income must be *added back* since they are not deductible for tax purposes when the company is the named beneficiary.

Example: Interperiod Tax Allocation

Hawkeye Corporation starts the current year, 2005, with a deferred tax asset balance of $20,000 and a deferred tax liability balance of $30,000. The current tax rate is 40% and is projected to be in effect when all temporary differences reverse. The reported pre-tax accounting income is $500,000. Analyze the following items to determine taxable income, the *change* in deferred taxes payable (future taxable and deductible amounts), and the tax expense to be reported on the income statement for 2005. Assume that there is no need for a valuation allowance provision for deferred tax assets.

Item Description

① Book income includes $12,000 of interest revenue from municipal bonds.

② Straight-line depreciation for book purposes is $100,000 in the current year, and $140,000 is deductible for tax purposes under the Modified Accelerated Cost Recovery System (MACRS).

③ Hawkeye collected $60,000 of rent for a warehouse it leases to a local manufacturer. Of this amount, $40,000 is deferred for accounting purposes and will be recognized in 2006 when it is earned.

④ Hawkeye accrued $50,000 for estimated future warranty costs in 2005 and paid $35,000 in warranty expenses in the current period.

⑤ Bad debts written off in the current period totaled $20,000, and the provision for bad debts under the allowance method amounted to $15,000. Hawkeye uses the direct write-off method for tax purposes and the allowance method for book purposes.

⑥ Book income includes an $18,000 deduction for premiums paid on executive life insurance in which the company is the named beneficiary.

⑦ In 2005 Hawkeye collected $15,000 on an installment land sale made several years earlier. The profit on the sale, all of which was recorded at the time of sale for book purposes, amounted to 30% of the selling price. The installment method of recognizing profit is being used for tax purposes. Ignore any imputed interest on the deferred payments.

⑧ Hawkeye has $35,000 of operating loss carryforward at the beginning of 2005.

The second general category of reconciling items is operating loss carryforwards. As shown in Item ⑧, Hawkeye has a $35,000 operating loss carryforward. This represents losses reported on previous years' tax returns (that is, tax deductible expenses and losses exceeded taxable income and gains) that can be offset against the 2005 taxable income. Thus, this amount is subtracted from pre-tax book income to arrive at taxable income in 2005.

The last category of reconciling items is temporary differences. These are revenue and expense items that enter into the determination of book income in one period and taxable income in a different period. There are several temporary differences for Hawkeye:

- Item ②: *Depreciation expense.* Hawkeye's pre-tax book income includes a deduction for $100,000 of straight-line depreciation expense. But for tax purposes, Hawkeye is using an accelerated depreciation method, which produces a deduction of $140,000 in the current period. To arrive at taxable income, this $40,000 dollar originating timing difference must be subtracted from pre-tax book income because it represents an additional amount that is deductible on the 2005 tax return that was not deducted in arriving at pre-tax book income.

- Item ③: *Rent collections.* In 2005, Hawkeye collected $60,000 of lease rent, and all of this amount is taxable when received. However, for book purposes, $40,000 of this amount is deferred and will be recognized in future periods when it is earned. This leaves $20,000 that was included in the $500,000 of pre-tax book income. Therefore, this $40,000 originating timing difference must be added to the pre-tax income number to arrive at 2005 taxable income.

- Item ④: *Warranty expenses.* Hawkeye accrued $50,000 for estimated warranty costs that were subtracted in arriving at the pre-tax book income number. For tax purposes, Hawkeye is allowed to deduct only the $35,000 of warranty costs that were actually paid. The $15,000 difference represents an originating timing difference that must be added back to the pre-tax book income number to yield taxable income.

- Item ⑤: *Bad debt provisions.* For book income purposes, Hawkeye uses the allowance method (described in Chapter 8) to determine the $15,000 bad debts deduction in 2005. For tax purposes, Hawkeye is allowed to take a deduction only when accounts are actually written off; this is the direct write-off method. As shown, Hawkeye wrote off $20,000 of accounts receivable in 2005. Note that all or a portion of the accounts written off in 2005 would have been deducted as an expense to arrive at GAAP/book income in prior accounting periods. Accordingly, the additional $5,000 that is deductible for tax purposes, an amount that represents a reversing timing difference, must be subtracted from pre-tax book income to arrive at taxable income for 2005.

- Item ⑦: *Profit on installment sale.* Hawkeye is using the installment method for tax purposes (Chapter 3) to record profit on a land sale made in a previous period. All of this profit was recorded in a previous period's book income number. Thus, the gross profit on the amounts collected in 2005 (30% × $15,000 collected = $4,500) represents a reversing timing difference that must be added to the pre-tax book income number to arrive at taxable income.

After adjustments for the operating loss carryforward and the temporary difference items, Hawkeye's taxable income for 2005 is determined to be $485,500, as shown in Schedule 13.1 below. To arrive at taxes payable, the taxable income number must be multiplied by the applicable tax rates, as illustrated in the right-hand column of Figure 13.8. If some of the components of taxable income are subject to special tax rates (for example, capital gains rates), then these amounts would need to be isolated and multiplied by the appropriate special rates. For simplicity, we have assumed that a flat tax rate of 40% applies to all components of taxable income, yielding taxes payable to the IRS in 2005 of $194,200 (as shown in Schedule 13.1).

SCHEDULE 13.1	Hawkeye Corporation

Calculation of Taxable Income and Taxes Payable

Computation of taxable income

Pre-tax accounting income (given)	$500,000
Adjustments for permanent differences	
−Interest on municipal bonds (Item ①)	(12,000)
+Premium on executive life insurance (Item ⑥)	18,000
Income before adjustment for temporary differences	$506,000
Adjustment for operating loss carryforward (Item ⑧)	(35,000)
Adjustments for temporary differences	
−Excess of accelerated over straight-line depreciation (Item ②)	
($140,000 − $100,000)	(40,000)
+Rent received in excess of rent earned (Item ③)	
($60,000 − $20,000)	40,000
+Excess of accrued warranty costs over actual costs incurred on warranties (Item ④)	
($50,000 − $35,000)	15,000
−Excess of accounts written off over current provision for bad debts (Item ⑤)	
($20,000 − $15,000)	(5,000)
+Installment profit recognized for tax purposes in 2005 but recognized in earlier periods for book purposes (Item ⑦)	
(30% × $15,000)	4,500
Taxable income	$485,500
Tax rate	× 40%
Taxes payable for 2005	$194,200

Calculation of Change in Deferred Tax Asset and Liability Accounts

The next step in determining the tax provision (expense) that will be reported on Hawkeye's GAAP (book) income statement for 2005 is to determine the *change* in the deferred tax asset and deferred tax liability accounts. These calculations are represented in the center column of Figure 13.8 and the details are provided in Schedule 13.2. For each temporary difference (including operating loss carryforwards), we must determine three things:

1. Whether an item is an originating or reversing temporary difference.
2. Whether it affects a deferred tax asset or a deferred tax liability balance.
3. What the applicable tax rate is for determining the tax effect of the temporary difference.

Originating temporary differences are "new" differences between book and taxable income that cause *increases* in either the deferred tax asset or the deferred tax liability balance. Reversing temporary differences are realizations or reversals of "old" temporary differences that gave rise to deferred tax assets or liabilities in previous accounting periods. Because they represent reversals of previously recorded temporary differences, reversing temporary differences are recorded as *decreases* in either the deferred tax asset or the deferred tax liability accounts.

SCHEDULE 13.2 **Hawkeye Corporation**

Calculation of Changes in Deferred Tax Accounts

	Deferred Tax Asset	Deferred Tax Liability
Operating loss carryforward (Item ⑧)		
Realization of Future Deductible Amount		
40% × $35,000	$(14,000) **CR**	
Depreciation (Item ②)		
Future Taxable Amount		
($140,000 − $100,000 = $40,000) × 40%		$(16,000) **CR**
Rent received in advance of rent earned (Item ③)		
Future Deductible Amount		
($60,000 − $20,000 = $40,000) × 40%	16,000 **DR**	
Excess of accrued warranty costs over cash warranty expenses (Item ④)		
Future Deductible Amount		
($50,000 − $35,000 = $15,000) × 40%	6,000 **DR**	
Bad debts written off (Item ⑤)		
Realization of Future Deductible Amount		
$20,000 × 40%	(8,000) **CR**	
New bad debt provisions in 2005 (Item ⑤)		
Future Deductible Amount		
$15,000 × 40%	6,000 **DR**	
Installment profit recognized for tax (Item ⑦)		
Realization of Future Taxable Amount		
(30% × $15,000 = $4,500) × 40%		1,800 **DR**
← Gross profit rate ← Tax rate		
Change in Deferred Tax Asset/Liability	6,000 **DR**	(14,200) **CR**
Beginning balance	20,000 **DR**	(30,000) **CR**
Ending balance	$ 26,000 **DR**	$(44,200) **CR**

Determining whether a particular temporary difference affects a deferred tax asset or liability balance hinges on whether the item causes taxable income to be higher or lower than book income in the current period and whether it is an originating or reversing temporary difference.

Hawkeye has one originating temporary difference that causes taxable income to be *lower* than book income in the *current* period:

• Item ②. Accelerated depreciation expense deductions for tax purposes ($140,000) exceed the straight-line depreciation deductions for book purposes ($100,000). This temporary difference gives rise to a future taxable amount—that is, taxable income will be *higher* than book income in future periods when this temporary difference reverses. Therefore, this temporary difference causes an increase (credit) to deferred tax liabilities of $16,000, as shown in Schedule 13.2.

Hawkeye has two reversing temporary differences that cause taxable income to be *lower* than book income in the *current* period:

• Item ⑧. The operating loss carryforward is $35,000.
• Item ⑤. The bad debts write-off is $20,000.

Both of these items represent realizations of future deductible amounts and result in a decrease (credit) to the deferred tax asset account, as we see in Schedule 13.2.

Hawkeye has three originating temporary differences that cause taxable income to be *higher* than book income in the *current* period:

• Item ③. Rent received ($60,000) is in excess of rent earned for book purposes ($20,000).
• Item ④. Accrued warranty expenses for book purposes ($50,000) is in excess of warranty expenditures for tax purposes ($35,000).

- Item ⑤. Bad debts expense of $15,000 that is accrued under the allowance method for book purposes will not be deductible for tax purposes until specific accounts are written off in future periods.

Each of these items gives rise to a future deductible amount and accordingly causes increases (debits) to the deferred tax asset account, as shown in Schedule 13.2.

The one remaining temporary difference for Hawkeye is the profit on the land sale that is recognized under the installment method for tax purposes.

- Item ⑦. This $4,500 amount represents a reversing temporary difference that causes taxable income to be higher than book income in 2005. Since a deferred tax liability would have been set up in a previous period (when the land was sold and the entire profit was recognized for book purposes), the deferred tax liability account is being reduced (debited) now because the tax will be paid in the current period.

The assumed marginal corporate tax rate of 40% is applied to all temporary differences to determine the dollar amount of the change in the deferred tax asset or liability accounts. This is appropriate when there are no enacted changes in the tax rates scheduled to go into effect in future periods. Using the 40% rate, the net effect of the temporary differences for Hawkeye is to increase deferred tax assets by $6,000 and increase deferred tax liabilities by $14,200, as shown in Schedule 13.2.

Calculation of Tax Expense

The calculation of tax expense that Hawkeye will report on its 2005 GAAP income statement (assuming a 40% tax rate for all periods) follows the formulas presented in Figure 13.5 and is reproduced below in Figure 13.9. The numbers appearing below the appropriate boxes are taken from Schedules 13.1 and 13.2.

Figure 13.9

CALCULATION OF TAX
EXPENSE: INDIRECT
APPROACH

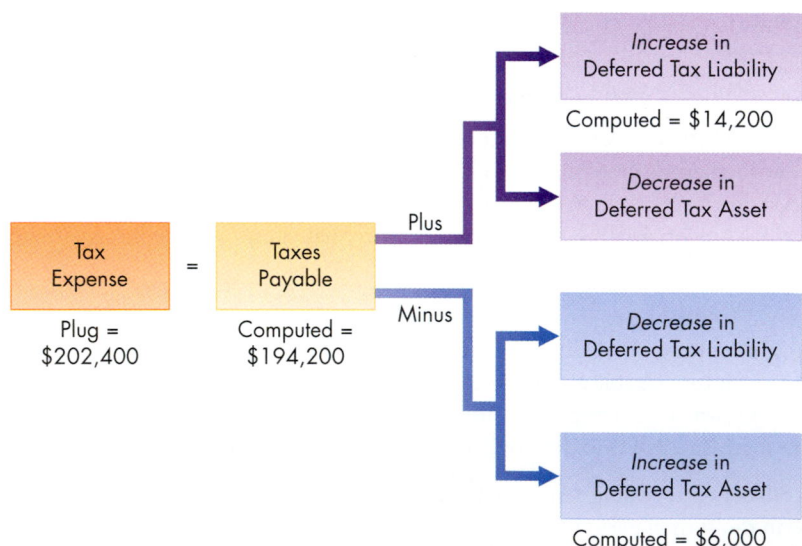

When tax rates are *not* scheduled to change in the future, the tax expense reported for book purposes can be computed directly by multiplying the pre-tax book income number that is adjusted for permanent difference items by the current tax rate. The pre-tax book income number of Hawkeye adjusted for permanent differences is $506,000 (Schedule 13.1); and the current tax rate is 40%, thus yielding a tax expense of $202,400, which is the same number arrived at under the indirect approach shown in Figure 13.9. When tax rates are scheduled to change, then tax expense must be determined using the indirect approach, which adjusts taxes payable for changes in the deferred tax asset and liability accounts, as shown in Figure 13.9.

On January 2, 2004 Allen Company purchased a machine for $70,000. This machine has a five-year useful life, a residual value of $10,000, and it is depreciated using the straight-line method for financial statement purposes. For tax purposes, depreciation expense was $25,000 for 2004 and $20,000 for 2005. Allen's 2005 book income, before income taxes and depreciation expense, was $100,000, and its tax rate was 30%.

E13 – 1

Determining current taxes payable

Required:

If Allen had made *no* estimated tax payments during 2005, what amount of current income tax liability would Allen report in its December 31, 2005 balance sheet?

Huff Corporation began operations on January 1, 2005. Huff recognizes revenues from all sales under the accrual method for financial reporting purposes and appropriately uses the installment method for income tax purposes. Huff's gross margin on installment sales under each method was as follows:

E13 – 2

Determining deferred tax liability

Year	Accrual Method	Installment Method
2005	$ 800,000	$300,000
2006	1,300,000	700,000

Enacted income tax rates are 30% for 2005 and 2006 and 25% thereafter. There are no other temporary differences.

Required:

In Huff's December 31, 2006 balance sheet, the deferred income tax liability should be how much?

In its 2005 income statement, Tow, Inc. reported proceeds from an officer's life insurance policy of $90,000 and depreciation of $250,000. Tow was the owner and beneficiary of the life insurance on its officer. Tow deducted depreciation of $370,000 in its 2005 income tax return when the tax rate was 30%. Data related to the reversal of the excess tax deduction for depreciation follow:

E13 – 3

Determining deferred tax liability

Year	Reversal of Excess Tax Deduction for Depreciation	Enacted Tax Rates
2006	$50,000	35%
2007	40,000	35
2008	20,000	25
2009	10,000	25

There are no other temporary differences.

Required:

In its December 31, 2005 balance sheet, what amount should Tow report as a deferred income tax liability?

As a result of differences between depreciation for financial reporting purposes and tax purposes, the financial reporting basis of Noor Company's sole depreciable asset, acquired in 2005, exceeded its tax basis by $250,000 at December 31, 2005. This difference will reverse in future years. The enacted tax rate is 30% for 2005, and 40% for future years. Noor has no other temporary differences.

E13 – 4

Deferred tax effects on balance sheet

Required:

In its December 31, 2005, balance sheet, how much should Noor report as the deferred tax effect of this difference? Indicate the amount and whether it is an asset or a liability.

E13 – 5

Deferred tax effects on long-term contracts

AICPA
ADAPTED

Mill Company began operations on January 1, 2005 and recognized income from construction-type contracts under the percentage-of-completion method for tax purposes and the completed-contract method for financial reporting purposes. Information concerning income recognition under each method is as follows:

Year	Percentage-of-Completion (Tax Purposes)	Completed Contract (Book Purposes)
2005	$400,000	$ 0
2006	625,000	375,000
2007	750,000	850,000

Required:

For all years, assume that the income tax rate is 40% and that there are no other timing differences. In its December 31, 2007 balance sheet, Mill should report deferred income taxes of how much? Indicate whether the amount is an asset or a liability.

E13 – 6

Determining current portion of tax expense

AICPA
ADAPTED

For the year ended December 31, 2005 Tyre Company reported pre-tax financial statement income of $750,000. Its taxable income was $650,000. The difference is due to accelerated depreciation for income tax purposes. Tyre's income tax rate is 30%, and Tyre made estimated tax payments during 2005 of $90,000.

Required:

1. What amount should Tyre report as the current portion of income tax expense for 2005?
2. What amount should Tyre report as the deferred portion of income tax expense for 2005?
3. Give the journal entry Tyre would make to record 2005 taxes.

E13 – 7

Determining current taxes payable

AICPA
ADAPTED

Dunn Company's 2005 income statement reported $90,000 income before provision for income taxes. To aid in the computation of the provision for federal income taxes, the following 2005 data are provided:

Rent received in advance	$16,000
Income from exempt municipal bonds	20,000
Depreciation deducted for income tax purposes in excess of depreciation reported for financial statement purposes	10,000
Enacted corporate income tax rate	35%

Required:

What amount of current federal income tax liability should be reported in Dunn's December 31, 2005 balance sheet?

E13 – 8

Determining deferred tax liability and current portion of tax expense

AICPA
ADAPTED

Kent, Inc.'s reconciliation between financial statement and taxable income for 2005 follows:

Pre-tax financial income	$150,000
Permanent difference	(12,000)
	138,000
Temporary difference—depreciation	(9,000)
Taxable income	$129,000

Additional information:

	At December 31	
	2004	2005
Cumulative temporary difference (future taxable amounts)	$11,000	$20,000

The enacted tax rate was 35% for 2004 and 40% for 2005 and years thereafter.

Required:

1. In its December 31, 2005 balance sheet, what amount should Kent report as its deferred income tax liability?
2. In its 2005 income statement, what amount should Kent report as the current portion of income tax expense?

West Corporation leased a building and received the $36,000 annual rental payment on June 15, 2005. The beginning of the lease was July 1, 2005. Rental income is taxable when received. West's tax rates are 30% for 2005 and 40% thereafter. West had no other permanent or temporary differences. West determined that no valuation allowance was needed.

E13 – 9

Determining deferred tax asset amounts

Required:

What amount of deferred tax asset should West report in its December 31, 2005 balance sheet?

Black Company, organized on January 2, 2005, had pre-tax accounting income of $500,000 and taxable income of $800,000 for the year ended December 31, 2005. The only temporary difference is accrued product warranty costs, which are expected to be paid as follows:

2006	$100,000
2007	50,000
2008	50,000
2009	100,000

E13 – 10

Determining deferred tax asset amounts

Circumstances indicate that it is highly likely that Black will have taxable income in the future. There were no temporary differences in prior years. The enacted income tax rates are 35% for 2005, 30% for 2006 through 2008, and 25% for 2009.

Required:

In Black's December 31, 2005 balance sheet, the deferred income tax asset should be how much?

Quinn Company reported a net deferred tax asset of $9,000 in its December 31, 2005 balance sheet. For 2006 Quinn reported pre-tax financial statement income of $300,000. Temporary differences of $100,000 resulted in taxable income of $200,000 for 2006. At December 31, 2006 Quinn had cumulative taxable differences of $70,000. The income tax rate is 30%.

E13 – 11

Deferred portion of tax expense

Required:

In its December 31, 2006 income statement, what should Quinn report as the deferred portion of income tax expense?

Note: Students may want to review the material on the equity method of accounting in Chapter 16 before beginning work on this exercise. Tara Corporation uses the equity method of accounting for its 40% investment in Flax's common stock. During 2005 Flax reported earnings of $750,000 and paid dividends of $250,000. Assume that:

E13 – 12

Temporary and permanent differences

- All the undistributed earnings of Flax will be distributed as dividends in future periods.
- The dividends received from Flax are eligible for the 80% dividends received deduction.
- There are no other temporary differences.
- Tara's 2005 income tax rate is 30%.
- Enacted income tax rates after 2005 are 25%.

Required:

In Tara's December 31, 2005 balance sheet, the increase in the deferred income tax liability from the preceding transactions would be how much?

Town, a calendar-year corporation that was incorporated in January 2004, experienced a $600,000 net operating loss (NOL) in 2006. For the years 2004 and 2005, Town reported taxable income in each year and a total of $450,000 for the two years combined. Assume that (1) there are no differences between pre-tax book income and taxable income for all years; (2) the income tax rate is 40% for all years; (3) the NOL will be carried back to the profit years (2004–2005) to the extent of $450,000, and $150,000 will be carried forward to future periods; and (4) Town expects to report taxable income for the foreseeable future.

E13 – 13

Loss carrybacks and carryforwards

Required:

1. What amounts should Town report as "Tax benefit due to NOL carryback and carryforward" in its 2006 income statement?
2. How much will Town report as a deferred tax asset on its December 31, 2006 balance sheet?

E13 – 14

Tax effects of loss carryback and carryforward

AICPA
ADAPTED

Dix Company reported operating income/loss before income tax in its first three years of operations as follows:

2004	$100,000
2005	(200,000)
2006	400,000

There are no permanent or temporary differences between book income and taxable income in these years. Dix elected to use the loss carryback in 2005 and to apply unused losses against future taxable income. Assume a 40% tax rate for all years.

Required:

1. What amount should Dix report as a tax benefit on its 2005 income statement?
2. What amount of deferred tax asset should Dix report on its December 31, 2005 balance sheet?
3. What amount should Dix report as current taxes payable on December 31, 2006 (the year after the loss)?

E13 – 15

Accounting for loss carryforwards

AICPA
ADAPTED

For the year ended December 31, 2005 Colt Corporation had a loss carryforward of $180,000 available to offset future taxable income. At December 31, 2005 the company believes that realization of the tax benefit related to the loss carryforward is probable. The tax rate is 30%.

Required:

1. What amount of the tax benefit should be reported in Colt's 2005 income statement?
2. What additional account(s) would be affected when the loss carryforward is recognized?

E13 – 16

Accounting for loss carrybacks and carryforwards

AICPA
ADAPTED

Operating income in Mobe's first three years of operations were as follows:

2004	$ 300,000
2005	(700,000)
2006	1,200,000

There were no other deferred income taxes in any year, and Mobe's income tax rate is 30%. In 2005 Mobe elected to carry back the maximum amount of loss possible and expected to have sufficient taxable income in future years to take full advantage of the loss carryforward tax benefits.

Required:

1. What would be the amount of tax benefit reported in Mobe's 2005 income statement? Give the entry to record this tax benefit.
2. In 2006 what amount should Mobe report as its current income tax liability after taking into account the loss carryforward?

E13 – 17

Deferred tax asset and valuation allowance

AICPA
ADAPTED

In Figland Company's first year of operations (2005), the company had pre-tax book income of $500,000 and taxable income of $800,000 at the December year-end. Figland expected to maintain this level of taxable income in future years. Figland's only temporary difference is for accrued product warranty costs, which are expected to be paid as follows:

2006	$100,000
2007	$200,000

The enacted income tax rate for these years is 30%. Figland believes there is a high likelihood that one third of the tax benefit associated with this future deductible amount will not be realized.

Required:

Compute the amount of deferred tax asset and related valuation allowance that would be reported in Figland's 2005 tax footnote.

E13 – 18

Deferred tax asset and valuation allowance

AICPA
ADAPTED

Note: Students may want to review the material on the equity method of accounting in Chapter 16 before beginning work on this exercise. Taft Corporation uses the equity method to account for its 25% investment in Flame, Inc. During 2005 Taft received dividends of $30,000 from Flame and recorded $180,000 as its equity in the earnings of Flame. Additional information follows:

- All the undistributed earnings of Flame will be distributed as dividends in future periods.
- The dividends received from Flame are eligible for the 80% dividends received deduction.
- There are no other temporary differences.
- Enacted income tax rates are 30% for 2005 and thereafter.

Required:

In its December 31, 2005 balance sheet, what amount should Taft report for deferred income tax liability?

The following information is provided for Lally Corporation for 2005 and 2006:

	2005	2006
Book income before income taxes	$4,000,000	$5,000,000
Interest income included above that was not subject to income taxes	100,000	100,000

E13 – 19

Determining tax expense, taxes payable, and deferred taxes

CMA
ADAPTED

- Income before income taxes in 2005 included accrued rent revenue of $80,000 that was not subject to income taxes until its receipt in 2006.
- Lally was subject to an income tax rate of 40% in 2005 and 2006.

Required:

1. What was Lally's taxable income for 2005?
2. Lally Corporation's taxes payable for 2005 was how much?
3. What was the change in Lally's deferred tax asset (liability) balance for 2005?
4. What amount of income tax expense would Lally report on its 2005 income statement?
5. Repeat requirements 1 through 4 for 2006.

Millie Co. has just completed its first year of operations on December 31, 2005 with pre-tax financial income of $400,000. Millie accrued a contingent liability of $900,000 for financial reporting purposes; however, the $900,000 will be paid and therefore deductible for tax purposes in 2006. There is also gross profit from installment sales of $800,000 that is recognized currently for financial reporting purposes, but will be taxable in 2006 and 2007 when the cash is received ($400,000 each year). Millie Co.'s pre-tax financial income includes $38,000 interest earned on its holdings of the bonds of the State of Montana. The tax rate is 30% for all years.

E13 – 20

Computing tax payable, deferred taxes, and tax expense

Required:

1. Determine Millie Co.'s taxable income and taxes payable for 2005.
2. Determine the changes in Millie Co.'s deferred tax amounts for 2005.
3. Calculate tax expense for Millie Co. for 2005.

PROBLEMS/DISCUSSION QUESTIONS

Moss, Inc. uses the accrual method of accounting for financial reporting purposes and appropriately uses the installment method of accounting for income tax purposes. Installment income of $250,000 will be collected in the following years when the enacted tax rates are as indicated.

P13 – 1

Deferred tax amounts with different tax rates

AICPA
ADAPTED

	Collection of Income	Enacted Tax Rates
2004	$ 25,000	35%
2005	50,000	30
2006	75,000	30
2007	100,000	25

The installment income is Moss's only temporary difference.

Required:

What amount should be included as the deferred income tax liability in Moss's December 31, 2004 balance sheet?

The following information pertains to Ramesh Company for the current year:

Book income before income taxes	$106,000
Income tax expense	52,000
Income taxes payable for this year	32,000
Statutory income tax rate	40%

P13 – 2

Temporary and permanent differences and tax entry

The company has both a permanent and a temporary difference between book and taxable income. The permanent difference relates to goodwill (that is, assume that amortization of goodwill is not allowed as an expense for tax purposes) and the temporary difference relates to depreciation expense.

Required:

1. Calculate the amount of temporary difference for the year and indicate whether it causes the book income to be larger or smaller than the taxable income.
2. Calculate the amount of permanent difference for the year and indicate whether it causes the book income to be larger or smaller than the taxable income.
3. Provide the journal entry to record the income tax expense for the year.
4. Compute the effective tax rate (that is, income tax expense divided by book income before taxes). Explain why this rate is different from the statutory tax rate of 40%.

P13 – 3

Deferred tax amount on income statement

For financial statement reporting, the Lexington Corporation recognizes royalty income in the period earned. For income tax reporting, royalties are taxed when collected. At December 31, 2004 unearned royalties of $400,000 were included in Lexington's balance sheet. All these royalties had been collected in 2004. During 2005 royalties of $600,000 were collected. Unearned royalties in Lexington's December 31, 2005 balance sheet amounted to $350,000. Assume that the income tax rate was 50%.

Required:

What amount should be reported as the provision for deferred income taxes in Lexington's income statement for the year ended December 31, 2005?

P13 – 4

Current and deferred portion of tax expense

Joy Corporation prepared the following reconciliation of income per books with income per tax return for the year ended December 31, 2005:

Book income before income taxes	$750,000
Add temporary difference:	
Construction contract revenue that will reverse in 2006	100,000
Deduct temporary difference:	
Depreciation expense that will reverse	
in equal amounts in each of the next four years	(400,000)
Taxable income	$450,000

Joy's income tax rate is 35% for 2005.

Required:

1. What amount should Joy report in its 2005 income statement as the current provision for income taxes?
2. How much should Joy report as deferred income taxes on the income statement in 2005?

P13 – 5

Tax expense and deferred tax calculations

Nelson Inc. purchased machinery at the beginning of 2005 for $90,000. Management used the straight-line method to depreciate the cost for financial reporting purposes and the sum-of-the-years'-digits method to depreciate the cost for tax purposes. The life of the machinery was estimated to be two years, and the salvage value was estimated at zero. Revenues less expenses other than depreciation expense and amortization of goodwill equaled $500,000 for 2005 and 2006. Nelson pays income tax at the rate of 20% of taxable income. The amortization of goodwill equaled $50,000 for 2005 and 2006.

Required:

1. Compute the taxable income and the financial reporting income (before tax) for the years 2005 and 2006.
2. What are the permanent and timing differences? Give an example of each for Nelson Inc.
3. Complete the following table on your answer to requirement 1.

Year	Ending Balance in Tax Liability	Tax Expense	Ending Balance in Deferred Income Taxes
2005			
2006			

[**Note:** Be sure to identify whether it is a debit or credit balance for deferred income taxes.]

4. Assume that the tax rate was changed by the federal government to 30% at the beginning of 2006. Compute the following:

    Increase/decrease in deferred income taxes

    Income tax liability for 2006

    Income tax expense for 2006

Metge Corporation's worksheet for calculating taxable income for 2005 is as follows:

($ in thousands)	2005
Pre-tax income	$1,000
Permanent differences	
Goodwill amortization	400
Interest on municipal bonds	(200)
Temporary differences	
Depreciation	(800)
Warranty costs	400
Rent received in advance	600
Taxable income	$1,400

P13 – 6

Determining current and deferred portion of tax expense and reconciling statutory and effective tax rates

The enacted tax rate for 2005 is 35%, but it is scheduled to increase to 40% in 2006 and subsequent years. All temporary differences are originating differences.

Required:

1. Determine Metge's 2005 taxes payable.
2. What is the change in deferred tax assets (liabilities) for 2005?
3. Determine tax expense for 2005.
4. Provide a schedule that reconciles Metge's statutory and effective tax rates (both in percentages and dollar amounts).

Smith Corporation started doing business in 2004. The following table summarizes the taxable income (loss) of the company over the 2004- 2016 period, along with the statutory tax rate effective in each of the years:

P13 – 7

Entries for loss carrybacks and carryforwards

Year	Taxable Income (Loss)	Enacted Tax Rate
2004	$100,000	40%
2005	200,000	40
2006	250,000	35
2007	400,000	32
2008	(350,000)	30
2009	(275,000)	30
2010	125,000	30
2011	175,000	30
2012	275,000	30
2013	300,000	35
2014	(800,000)	35
2015	(250,000)	35
2016	150,000	35

Since the company had no permanent or timing differences during this period, its pre-tax financial reporting income was identical to its taxable income in each of these years. During the 2013–2016 period, the company expected the current and future tax rates to be 35%. Whenever possible, the company took advantage of the loss carryback provision of the tax law. When recording the tax benefits of the loss carryforward provision, the company felt it was more likely than not that the tax benefits will be fully realized.

Required:

1. Provide journal entries to record income tax expense for the years 2008, 2009, 2014, 2015, and 2016.
2. In answering this requirement, make the following assumptions. During 2014 and 2015, Smith Corporation felt it was more likely than not that only 40% of the tax benefits will be realized

through a loss carryforward. However, during 2016 the company revised its expectation and felt that it was more likely than not that 100% of the tax benefits will be fully realized through a loss carryforward. Provide journal entries to record income tax expense for the years 2014, 2015, and 2016. Also show how the deferred tax asset will be reported as of the end of 2014, 2015, and 2016.

P13 – 8

Entries for loss carrybacks and carryforwards

Barron Corporation started doing business in 2004. The following table summarizes the taxable income (loss) of the company over the period 2004–2012:

Year	Taxable Income (Loss)
2004	$200,000
2005	150,000
2006	125,000
2007	90,000
2008	200,000
2009	(150,000)
2010	(180,000)
2011	125,000
2012	(120,000)

Since the company had no permanent or timing differences during this period, its pre-tax financial reporting income was identical to its taxable income in each of the preceding years. During the entire period, the company's current as well as its expected future tax rate was 40%. Whenever possible, the company took advantage of the loss carryback provision of the tax law. When recording the tax benefits of the loss carryforward provision, the company felt it was more likely than not that the tax benefits will be fully realized.

Required:

Provide journal entries to record income tax expense for the years 2009 through 2012.

P13 – 9

Reconciling statutory and effective tax rates

The following information pertains to Enis Corporation for the year ended December 31, 2005. The company reported a loss before taxes of $1,500,000 in its GAAP income statement, which included the effects of the following items:

*   On January 1, 2005 Enis Corporation acquired Hansen Technology Group for $5,000,000 in cash. The breakdown for the acquisition cost is:

Marketable securities	$1,800,000
Other current assets	200,000
Value of in-process technology	2,000,000
Goodwill	1,000,000
	$5,000,000

    Under GAAP, if a portion of the acquisition price can be allocated to the value of "in-process technology" (that is, technology under development), that portion should be expensed as a part of the R&D expense of the acquiring company (that is, Enis Corporation) in the year of the acquisition. However, the value of the in-process technology is not considered as an expense for tax purposes.

    In its 2005 GAAP income statement, Enis Corporation wrote off $50,000 of the goodwill acquired in the Hansen Technology acquisition because it was determined to be impaired. However, none of the goodwill write-off qualifies for a deduction in the tax statement of Enis Corporation.

*   The bad debts written off during the year was $75,000 more than the provision for uncollectibles (or bad debt expense) recorded during the year.
*   Enis Corporation earned $80,000 during 2005 from income on municipal bonds. The company has hired an investment management company to manage its portfolio of municipal bonds. Enis Corporation paid a $10,000 fee to the management company during 2005. This fee is nondeductible for tax purposes, since the income is nontaxable.
*   Enis Corporation recorded a straight-line depreciation expense of $140,000 in its GAAP income statement. The corresponding accelerated tax depreciation was $210,000.
*   Enis Corporation incurred an insurance expense of $15,000 during 2005; this expense was the premium on the life insurance policies of its senior executives. Enis Corporation is the beneficiary on these policies. During 2005 one of the senior executives passed away and Enis Corporation received $250,000 from the insurance company as death benefits.

Required:

1. Determine the taxable income and taxes payable for Enis in 2005. Assume a 35% statutory tax rate.
2. Determine the change in deferred tax assets (liabilities) for 2005.
3. Calculate the income tax expense of Enis Corporation for the year 2005.
4. Determine the effective book tax rate for Enis in 2005, and prepare a schedule to explain why the effective tax rate is different from the statutory tax rate.
5. Provide the journal entry to record the income tax expense, taxes payable, and deferred taxes for the year 2005.

Weber Manufacturing Company started doing business on January 1, 2005. The company's current business plan predicts significant growth in sales over the next several years. To respond to this predicted growth, Weber is planning to buy annually new factory equipment at a cost of $60,000 during the first six years of its operations (2005 through 2010). The first piece of equipment was purchased on January 1, 2005. The company plans to use the straight-line method to depreciate the equipment cost for financial reporting purposes and the sum-of-the-years'-digits method for tax purposes. The useful life of the factory equipment was estimated to be three years, with no salvage value for both tax and financial reporting purposes. Weber expects to pay taxes at the rate of 35% of its taxable income. Apart from the depreciation expense, Weber expects no other temporary or timing differences.

P13 – 10

Analytical insights from deferred tax account

www.prenhall.com/revsine

● Student Resources

☑ Template for solution

Required:

1. Calculate the balance in the deferred income tax liability account as of the end of years 2005 through 2010.
2. In answering this part, assume that Weber purchased the factory equipment at the beginning of each year (starting from 2005) for six years. However, the equipment costs $60,000 in 2005, which is expected to increase by $6,000 each year over the following five years ($66,000 in 2006, $72,000 in 2007, and so on). Calculate the balance in the deferred income tax liability as of the end of 2005 through 2010.
3. Consider the facts given in requirement 2. Due to expected changes in business technology, the company expects the demand for its current products to start falling in 2011. Consequently, it plans to cut down substantially its production after 2011. In fact, Weber expects to purchase no more machinery after 2010. With this new information, compute the balance in the deferred income tax liability account for 2011 and 2012.
4. Based both on your answers to requirements 1 through 3, and on changes in its deferred tax liability account, what conclusions might you draw about the financial condition of Weber?

[**Note:** Students may want to review the material on accounting for trading securities in Chapter 16 before beginning work on this problem.]

Over the past two years, Madison Corporation has accumulated operating loss carryforwards of $66,000. This year, 2005, Madison's pre-tax book income is $101,500. Madison is subject to a 40% corporate tax rate. The following items are relevant to Madison's deferred tax computations for 2005:

a. Equipment purchased in 2002 is depreciated on a straight-line basis for financial reporting purposes and using an accelerated method for tax purposes as follows:

P13 – 11

Converting book income to taxable income and computation of taxes payable

	Book	Tax
2002	$100,000	$200,000
2003	100,000	150,000
2004	100,000	100,000
2005	100,000	50,000
2006	100,000	–0–

b. Madison's trading securities portfolio generated a $13,000 unrealized gain. This gain is not recognized for tax purposes until the security is sold.

c. Madison has not yet paid its rent for November and December of 2005, a total of $25,000. The expense was accrued for book purposes and is included in pre-tax book income.

d. During 2005, Madison paid a fine of $6,500 to its state corporation commission for alleged violations of state security laws. Madison neither denied nor admitted guilt related to the charges. The expense is not deductible for tax purposes, but has been included in the computation of pre-tax book income.

Required:

1. Determine Madison Corporation's taxable income for 2005.
2. Calculate the amount of tax payable for Madison Corporation for 2005.

P13 – 12

Calculating taxes payable, deferred taxes and tax expense

[**Note:** Students may want to review the material on accounting for trading securities in Chapter 16 before beginning work on this problem.]

At the end of its third year of operations, December 31, 2005, Delilah Corp. is reporting pre-tax book income of $223,000. The following items are relevant to Delilah's deferred tax computations:

a. A $55,000 unrealized holding gain on its trading securities. This gain is not recognized for tax purposes until the securities are sold.
b. Bad debt expense of $24,000 was recorded on its accounts receivable, although during 2005 no actual write-offs took place.
c. During 2005, Delilah received $19,000 cash from one of its customers. The payment received relates to a product that will be completed and delivered to the customer in late January 2006.

Delilah is subject to a 40% corporate tax rate.

Required:

1. Determine Delilah Corp.'s taxable income and taxes payable for 2005.
2. Determine the changes in Delilah Corp.'s deferred tax amounts for 2005.
3. Calculate tax expense for Delilah Corp. for 2005.

P13 – 13

Converting from taxable income to book income

Mozart Inc.'s taxable income for 2005 of $98,000 will be taxed at the 40% corporate tax rate. For tax purposes, its depreciation expense exceeded the depreciation used for financial reporting purposes by $27,000. Mozart has $45,000 of purchased goodwill on its books; during 2005 Mozart determined that the goodwill had suffered a $3,000 impairment of value for financial reporting purposes. None of the goodwill impairment is deductible for tax purposes. Mozart purchased a 3-year corporate liability insurance policy on July 1, 2005 for $36,000 cash. The entire premium was deducted for tax purposes in 2005.

Required:

1. Determine Mozart Inc.'s pre-tax book income for 2005.
2. Determine the changes in Mozart Inc.'s deferred tax amounts for 2005.
3. Calculate tax expense for Mozart Inc. for 2005.

P13 – 14

Comprehensive tax allocation problem

Bush Inc. started its retail business on January 1, 2005. The following information is extracted from the financial reporting income statement of the company for the years 2005 and 2006:

Bush Incorporated

**Income Statements
for the Years Ended December 31**

	2005	2006
Sales revenue	$1,000,000	$1,200,000
Income from municipal bonds	60,000	75,000
Cost of goods sold	(400,000)	(504,000)
Depreciation expense	?	?
Warranty expense	(100,000)	(110,000)
Provision for uncollectibles	?	?
Life insurance premium for senior executives	(30,000)	(30,000)
Other operating expenses	(300,000)	(350,000)
Income before income taxes	?	?
Income tax expense	?	?
Net income	?	?

Required:

1. Using the following additional information, complete the income statements for 2005 and 2006:

   a. The company purchased a piece of computer equipment on January 1, 2005 for $330,000. The equipment has a useful life of five years and an estimated salvage value of $30,000. The company uses the straight-line method of depreciation for financial reporting purposes.

   b. The company estimates bad debt expense (or provision for uncollectibles) at 8% of sales revenue.

   c. Bush Inc. is the beneficiary on the life insurance policies of its senior executives.

   d. The income tax rate is 35%.

2. Using the following additional information, calculate taxable income and the income tax liability for the years 2005 and 2006:

   a. The company uses the sum-of-the-years'-digits method of depreciation for tax.

   b. The warranty liability account had balances of $15,000 and $25,000 at the end of 2005 and 2006, respectively.

   c. The allowance for uncollectibles had balances of $50,000 and $21,000 at the end of 2005 and 2006, respectively.

3. Provide a schedule showing why the effective tax rates for the company during 2005 and 2006 are different from the statutory tax rate of 35%.
4. Calculate the balances in the deferred tax accounts at the end of 2005 and 2006.
5. Provide a schedule reconciling the income tax expense with the income tax liability for both 2005 and 2006.
6. Provide journal entries to record income tax expense for 2005 and 2006.

P13 – 15

Comprehensive tax allocation problem

Flower Company started doing business on January 1, 2004. For the year ended December 31, 2005, Flower reported pre-tax book income of $450,000 on its income statement and is subject to a corporate tax rate of 40% for this year and the foreseeable future. Additionally, Flower has the following issues that impact its tax situation:

a. During 2005, Flower acquired $600,000 of specialized productive machinery that it depreciates using the straight-line method over five years with no salvage value for accounting purposes. For tax purposes, this specialized equipment is being depreciated $200,000 per year for the first three years of its productive life.

b. During 2005, Flower was fined $100,000 by the federal government for violations of environmental laws. The amount was paid on November 15, 2005 and was deducted in determining this year's book income.

c. Flower received $40,000 of interest revenue as a result of its investment in the bonds issued by the State of Arizona.

d. On January 2, 2005, Flower leased warehouse space for $2,000 per month for a three-year period. On January 2, 2005, as a condition of the lease, Flower paid $30,000 to the building's lessor to cover the first 15 months of rent. Since Flower leased space in excess of its needs, it immediately (January 2, 2005) subleased out part of the warehouse to a small, local company. The sublease was also for a period of three years and required the tenant to make $800 monthly rent payments to Flower. During 2005, Flower received $8,800 in monthly rental payments from the sublessee. Pre-tax book income includes an accrual for rent revenue earned but not yet received in cash.

e. During the year, the CEO of Flower was killed in an automobile accident. The company had a $200,000 life insurance policy on the CEO, and collected the proceeds of the policy during October 2005.

f. During 2005, Flower sold a parcel of land held for speculative purposes. The historical cost of the land was $320,000 and it was sold for $680,000. The cash will be collected from the purchaser in ten monthly installments of $68,000 each. During 2005, Flower collected five of these $68,000 payments and the remaining payments are assumed to be fully collectible during 2006.

g. During 2004, Flower accumulated an operating loss carryforward of $22,000 that can be used to offset 2005 taxable income.

h. The beginning balance in the deferred tax asset account is $8,800 and there was no beginning balance in the deferred tax liability account.

Required:

1. Beginning with pre-tax accounting income, compute taxable income and taxes payable for 2005. Clearly label all amounts used in arriving at taxable income.

2. Using the following schedule, compute the change in the deferred tax asset and deferred tax liability accounts for 2005. The depreciation temporary difference has been completed as an example.

Temporary Difference	Deferred Tax Asset	Deferred Tax Liability
Depreciation ($200,000 − $120,000) × 40%		$32,000 **CR**

3. Determine tax expense for 2005.

Comprehensive tax allocation problem

Jarvis Co. reported $90,000 pre-tax earnings on its income statement for the year ended December 31, 2005. The company has a $500,000 net operating loss carryforward from last year that may be used to offset taxable income for the next 20 years. The corporate tax rate applicable to Jarvis Co. for 2005 and all foreseeable years is 40%.

Additionally Jarvis has the following issues relevant to its 2005 tax situation:

a. Jarvis acquired equipment during 2004 for $1,000,000 that is being depreciated for books and taxes as follows:

	Books	Taxes
2004	$200,000	$550,000
2005	200,000	150,000
2006	200,000	150,000
2007	200,000	150,000
2008	200,000	−0−

b. The company carries a life insurance policy on Kevin Jarvis, president and CEO. For 2005, premiums were $42,000.

c. During 2005, Jarvis Co. earned $100,000 interest on tax-exempt municipal bonds.

d. Jarvis Co. builds luxury ocean liners and recognizes revenue using the completed contract method in computing its pre-tax GAAP earnings. For tax purposes Jarvis uses the percentage-of-completion method. Currently Jarvis has only one project that has a contract price of $2,000,000, will cost $1,640,000 to construct, and is 50% complete. Work began in early January 2005 and will be complete in late 2006.

e. Jarvis estimates that it is more likely than not that 25% of any deferred tax asset at the end of 2005 will not be realized.

f. The beginning balance in the deferred tax asset was $200,000 and the beginning balance in the deferred tax liability was $140,000.

Required:

1. Beginning with pre-tax accounting income, compute taxable income and taxes payable for 2005. Clearly label all amounts used in arriving at taxable income.

2. Using the following schedule, compute the change in the deferred tax asset and deferred tax liability accounts for 2005. The depreciation temporary difference has been completed as an example.

Temporary Difference	Deferred Tax Asset	Deferred Tax Liability
Depreciation ($200,000 − $150,000) × 40%		$20,000 **DR**

3. Determine tax expense for 2005.

[**Note:** Students may want to review the material on the equity method of accounting in Chapter 16 before beginning work on this problem.]

In the current year, 2005, Reality Corporation reported $200,000 of pre-tax earnings on its income statement. The corporate tax rate is 40% in the current year and next year, and it is scheduled to remain at this level for the foreseeable future. Additional information relevant to figuring taxes is as follows:

a. Reality acquired $500,000 of machinery in 2004. The machinery is being depreciated on a straight-line basis over five years (zero salvage) for accounting purposes and on a modified accelerated cost recovery system (MACRS) for tax purposes. A comparison of depreciation charges under these two methods is as follows:

	2004	2005	2006	2007	2008
Straight-line	$100,000	$100,000	$100,000	$100,000	$100,000
MACRS	165,000	225,000	75,000	35,000	–0–

b. Investment income from a 30% ownership of an investee company carried under the equity method is shown on the income statement as $80,000. The investee paid dividends to Reality in the amount of $30,000 in the current year. The remaining undistributed earnings for 2005 are expected to be received in equal amounts over the next two years in the form of dividends. All dividends are subject to the 80% dividend exclusion rule.

c. During the year, Reality recognized $4,000 of rental income that had been collected and taxed in 2004. In addition, $10,000 of rent revenue was received in advance in the current year. This amount was deferred for accounting purposes and will be recognized as income in 2006.

d. Reality received $5,000 of interest on State of North Carolina bonds in the current year, which is included in pre-tax income.

e. Reality sold land in the current year for $50,000 that had a $20,000 book value and tax basis. The entire gain (*not* considered extraordinary) was recognized for accounting purposes in 2005. However, since collections are to be received in three equal installments, Reality elected to use the installment sales method for tax purposes and picked up one-third of the gain on its tax return in 2005. The remaining amount of the gain will be recognized equally in 2006 and 2007.

f. Reality provided for future product warranty costs in the amount of $50,000 in the current year for book purposes. For tax purposes, such costs are deductible when paid. Actual warranty costs paid in 2005 were $15,000. It is expected that the remainder of the accrued warranty costs will be paid in 2006.

g. Included in pre-tax accounting income is a deduction for $3,000 for insurance premiums paid on Mr. Reality's life.

h. Reality made charges to bad debts expense in the current year of $15,000. The beginning balance in the "Allowance for bad debts" account was $12,000, and $6,000 of accounts was written off in the current year. It is expected that the 2005 year-end balance in the allowance account will be written off in 2006.

i. Reality has a $10,000 operating loss carryforward that can be used to offset the current period's taxable income.

j. The balance in the deferred tax asset (liability) account was $40,000 ($50,000) at the beginning of 2005.

k. Assume that it is estimated that it is more likely than not that 20% of the deferred tax asset at the end of 2005 will not be realized.

Required:

1. Starting with pre-tax accounting income, compute taxable income and taxes payable for 2005. Clearly label all amounts used in arriving at taxable income.

2. Using the following schedule, compute the change in the deferred tax asset (liability) account for 2005. The depreciation temporary difference has been completed as an example.

Temporary Difference Item	Deferred Tax Asset	Deferred Tax Liability
Depreciation ($225,000 − $100,000) × 40%		$50,000 **CR**

3. Determine the tax expense for 2005.

P13 – 18

Leasing and deferred taxes

The following information pertains to Crum International Corporation.

The company entered into the following lease agreement with Capital Leases, Inc. as of January 1, 2005. In accordance with the agreement, Crum leased a piece of computer equipment with a fair market value of $24,869 for its entire useful life of three years. In return, Crum promised to pay $10,000 per year *payable at the end of each year*, with the first payment to be made on December 31, 2005. At the end of the lease agreement, the estimated salvage value of the asset is zero.

For both tax and financial reporting purposes, Crum has *annual* income of $100,000 before taxes and before recording any expense on this lease transaction during each of the years 2005, 2006, and 2007. The tax rate is 40%.

Required:

1. Assuming that Crum treats the lease transaction as an *operating lease for tax purposes*, compute the taxable income for 2005 through 2007. Also calculate the amount of tax liability in each of the three years.
2. Assume Crum treats the lease transaction as a *capital lease for financial reporting purposes*. (The implicit interest rate in the lease contract is 10%.) Prepare a lease amortization schedule allocating the annual payments between interest expense and repayment of lease obligation. Clearly indicate the outstanding lease liability at the end of each period. Assuming further that Crum uses the straight-line method of depreciation for financial reporting purposes, prepare *income statements for financial reporting purposes*, clearly indicating the amount of tax expense for each of the three years.
3. Using all the assumptions up to this point, prepare journal entries to record the tax expense for each of the three years.

CASES

C13 – 1

Mandalay Resort Group and Subsidiaries: Analysis of tax footnote

The following is adapted from the 2003 financial statements of the Mandalay Resort Group, one of the largest hotel/casino operators in the United States. The components of the provision for income taxes in fiscal years ended January 31, 2003, 2002, and 2001 were as follows:

($ in thousands)	Years Ended January 31		
	2003	2002	2001
Current income tax expense (benefit):			
Federal	$46,446	$39,147	$53,716
State	1,504	1,438	1,417
Current income tax expense	47,950	40,585	55,133
Deferred income tax expense (benefit):			
Federal	29,919	(623)	19,559
Income tax expense	$77,869	$39,962	$74,692

The income tax effects of temporary differences between financial and income tax reporting that gave rise to deferred income tax assets and liabilities at January 31, 2003 and 2002 were as follows:

($ in thousands)	January 31	
	2003	2002
Deferred tax liabilities		
Property and equipment	$221,662	$205,434
Investments in unconsolidated affiliates	14,205	10,671
Other	12,982	1,061
Gross deferred tax liabilities	248,849	217,166
Deferred tax assets		
Accrued vacation benefits	8,137	9,232
Bad debt reserve	9,159	3,510
Preopening expenses	4,875	9,762
Pension plan	8,122	5,176
Other	7,427	7,784
Gross deferred tax assets	37,720	35,464
Net Deferred tax liabilities	$211,129	$181,702
Comprehensive Income		

Other comprehensive income for the Company includes adjustments for minimum pension liability and adjustments to interest rate swaps, net of tax. The accumulated other comprehensive loss reflected on the balance sheet consisted of the following:

($ in thousands)	January 31, 2003	January 31, 2002
Minimum pension liability adjustment	$11,370	$ 5,799
Adjustment to interest rate swaps	5,550	16,103
Accumulated other comprehensive loss	$16,920	$21,902

Note: Mandalay reports its swap-related assets and liabilities on a net basis in "Other long-term liabilities."

Required:

1. Provide journal entries to record the income tax expense for fiscal years 2001 through 2003. You may indicate the sum of the changes in the various deferred tax assets/liabilities by a single debit or credit to the "Net deferred tax asset/liability" account.

2. Refer to the deferred income tax asset and liability items reported by Mandalay at December 31, 2003 and 2002. For each item (except "Other"), determine whether the balance changed because of a net originating or net reversing timing difference. Provide a likely explanation for each of the timing differences and clearly discuss whether it is indicative of a higher or lower financial reporting revenue or expense relative to the amount reported on the fiscal 2003 tax return.

3. Mandalay's reported deferred tax expense in 2003 ($29,919) does not equal the reported increase in net deferred tax liability ($211,129 − $181,702 = $29,427) over the course of fiscal 2003. Is this difference explained by Mandalay's comprehensive income disclosure? Provide calculations in support of your answer.

Edited excerpts from Sara Lee Corporation's 2002 tax footnote follow:

C13 – 2

Sara Lee Corporation: Analysis of tax footnotes

Sara Lee Corporation

Excerpts from Tax Footnote

($ in millions)	2002	2001
Effective Income Tax Rates		
Tax expense at U.S. statutory rate*	$415	$648
State taxes, net of federal benefit	5	9
Difference between U.S. and foreign rates	(144)	(169)
Gain on disposal of Coach business		(338)
Exit activities and business dispositions	(10)	140
Nondeductible amortization		50
Benefit of foreign tax credits	(69)	(38)
Other, net	(22)	(54)
Taxes at effective worldwide tax rates	$175	$248

Current and deferred tax provisions (benefits) were:

	2002 Current	2002 Deferred	2001 Current	2001 Deferred
United States	$ 27	$(95)	$(12)	$29
Foreign	105	130	169	48
State	22	(14)	3	11
	$154	$ 21	$160	$88

The following are components of the deferred tax (benefit) provisions occurring as a result of transactions being reported in different years for financial and tax reporting:

($ in millions)	2002	2001
Depreciation	$(27)	$ 11
Inventory valuation methods	7	22
Nondeductible reserves	7	31
Other, net	34	24
Net deferred tax provision	$ 21	$ 88
Cash payments for income taxes	$266	$259

*Assume a statutory rate of 35%.

Required:

1. Prepare the book journal entry for income tax expense for 2002 (combine U.S., foreign, and state income taxes). Clearly indicate both the account title and whether the account is being debited or credited.
2. Using information given in the segment "Effective Income Tax Rates" regarding the statutory marginal tax rate for 2002, estimate Sara Lee Corporation's pre-tax book income for 2002. Show your work.
3. What was the 2002 effective overall tax rate for Sara Lee Corporation after taking into account differences arising from state and foreign income taxes, nondeductible amortization, etc? Show your work.
4. Estimate Sara Lee Corporation's taxable income. (**Note:** You do not have enough information to do this by category; therefore, combine U.S., foreign, and state taxes.) Show and clearly label all work.
5. Using information found in the tax footnote, determine whether depreciation expense was higher for book or tax purposes in 2002 and by how much.
6. Using information found in the tax footnote, determine whether expenses related to "Nondeductible reserves" were higher for book or tax purposes in 2002 and by how much.

C13 – 3

Motorola vs. Intel: Adjusting for depreciation differences

Motorola and Intel are both in the semiconductor industry and compete in many of the same product sectors. But each uses different depreciation methods. Motorola's Year 2 10-K states the following:

> Depreciation is recorded principally using the declining-balance method based on the estimated useful lives of the assets (buildings and building equipment, 5–50 years; machinery and equipment, 2–12 years).

So Motorola is using accelerated depreciation for most of its assets. By contrast, Intel's Year 2 report says:

> Depreciation is computed for financial reporting purposes principally by use of the straight-line method over the following estimated useful lives: machinery and equipment, 2 to 4 years; land and buildings, 4 to 45 years.

The table below gives several key financial statement figures for each company from their respective Year 2 10-Ks and excerpts from their income tax footnote:

From the Year 2 10-Ks of Motorola and Intel

Selected, Edited Financial Statement Disclosures

Motorola

($ in millions)	Year 2	Year 1
Book depreciation	$2,308	$1,919
Income before income taxes	1,775	3,225
Property, plant and equipment, net of accumulated depreciation (at year-end)	9,768	9,356

	December 31	
Significant deferred tax assets (liabilities)	Year 2	Year 1
Inventory reserves	$440	$345
Contract accounting methods	231	157
Employee benefits	291	286
Capitalized items	138	89
Tax basis differences on investments	(199)	(176)
Depreciation	(213)	(197)
Deferred taxes on non-U.S. earnings	(545)	(382)
Other deferred income taxes	329	132
Net deferred tax asset	$472	$254

From the Year 2 10-Ks of Motorola and Intel

Selected, Edited Financial Statement Disclosures

Intel

($ in millions)	Year 2	Year 1
Book depreciation	$1,888	$1,371
Income before income taxes	7,934	5,638
Property, plant and equipment, less accumulated depreciation (at year-end)	8,487	7,471

	December 31	
Significant deferred tax assets (liabilities)	Year 2	Year 1
Deferred tax assets:		
Accrued compensation and benefits	$ 71	$ 61
Deferred income	147	127
Inventory valuation and related reserves	187	104
Interest and taxes	54	61
Other, net	111	55
	$ 570	$ 408
Deferred tax liabilities:		
Depreciation	(573)	(475)
Unremitted earnings of certain subsidiaries	(359)	(116)
Other, net	(65)	(29)
	$(997)	$(620)

Assume a statutory tax rate of 35% for all years.

Required:

1. Using the information provided and the analytical techniques illustrated in the chapter, determine the tax depreciation for Motorola and Intel for Year 2.
2. Adjust each firm's pre-tax income to reflect the same depreciation method and useful lives used for tax purposes.
3. Explain why the adjusted numbers provide a better basis for comparing the operating performance of the two companies.

The following information is from the annual reports of Circuit City Stores, Inc. The components of the provision for income taxes (that is, income tax expense) are as follows:

C13 – 4

Circuit City Stores, Inc.: Analysis of tax footnotes

Tax Footnote:

	Years Ended February 28		
($ in thousands)	2003	2002	2001
Current:			
Federal	$17,220	$38,854	$52,846
State	2,538	11,588	7,993
	19,758	50,442	60,839
Deferred:			
Federal	5,546	27,164	9,505
State	171	840	293
	5,717	28,004	9,798
Provision for income taxes	$25,475	$78,446	$70,637

The components of deferred income taxes are as follows:

($ in thousands)	February 28 2003	February 28 2002
Deferred tax assets:		
Accrued expenses	$75,551	$61,299
Other	14,774	8,639
Total gross deferred tax assets	90,325	69,938

($ in thousands)	February 28 2003	February 28 2002
Deferred tax liabilities:		
Deferred revenue	$ 79,719	$ 75,079
Depreciation and amortization	36,168	36,123
Securitized receivables	53,718	36,749
Merchandise inventory	14,173	22,338
Prepaid expenses	23,361	10,197
Other	2,553	3,102
Total gross deferred tax liabilities	209,692	183,588
Net deferred tax liability	$119,367	$113,650

The following excerpt is from the financial statements of the company:

SUMMARY OF SIGNIFICANT ACCOUNTING POLICIES: REVENUE RECOGNITION.

The company also sells gift cards and records related deferred revenue at the time of sale. For gift cards with an unredeemed balance after 24 months, a monthly service fee is assessed. The liability associated with the sale of gift cards was $46.0 million at February 28, 2003, and $32.4 million at February 28, 2002, and is included in accounts payable on the consolidated balance sheets. Service fee revenue totaled $2.3 million in fiscal 2003, $1.3 million in fiscal 2002 and $0.7 million in fiscal 2001.

When necessary, assume a statutory tax rate of 35%.

Required:

1. Provide journal entries to record the income tax expense for 2001 through 2003. You may indicate the sum of the changes in the various deferred tax assets/liabilities by a single debit or credit to the "Net deferred tax asset/liability" account.
2. Note that the deferred portion of the tax provision in 2003 ($5,717) equals the change in the deferred tax liability from 2002 to 2003 on Circuit City's balance sheet ($119,367 − $113,650). Will this always be the case? If not, provide possible explanations for why the deferred portion of the tax provision in 2003 might not equal the change in the net deferred liability.
3. Is there a deferred tax asset associated with sales of Circuit City's gift cards? If so, where is this asset reported?
4. Estimate and comment on Circuit City's earnings conservatism ratio for 2001 to 2003.

C13 – 5

ABC Inc. (KR): Interpreting tax footnotes and reconciling statutory and effective rates

The following information is adapted from the 2005 financial statements of ABC Inc.:

ABC Inc. is in the business of airframe maintenance, modification and retrofit services, avionics and aircraft interior installations, the overhaul and repair of aircraft engines, and other related services.

The following are excerpted from its income statement for the year ended December 31, 2005.

($ in thousands)	2005
Earnings (loss) before income taxes	$10,891
Income tax benefit (provision)	(3,267)
Net earnings (loss)	$ 7,624

The details for the income tax expense or provision are provided next.

Income Tax Expense	2005
Current	$1,756
Deferred	1,511
Income tax expense	$3,267

Due to the nondeductibility of amortization of goodwill, the company's tax expense was higher by $1,076 than would be expected based on the statutory tax rate of 35%. State taxes further added another $927 to the tax expense. However, the reduction in the valuation allowance decreased the accounting income tax expense. In addition, several other items caused the tax expense to deviate from the tax liability. Since these items by themselves are immaterial, no separate breakdowns are available.

The following breakdowns are available for the balance sheet values of deferred tax assets and liabilities:

($ in thousands)	December 31 2005	December 31 2004
Deferred Tax Assets		
Accounts receivable	$ 977	$ 1,070
Inventories, principally due to additional costs inventoried for tax purposes and financial statement allowances	3,523	1,679
Employee benefits, principally due to accrual for financial reporting purposes	9,814	13,510
Accrual for costs of restructuring	5,392	8,750
Accrual for disposal of discontinued operations	4,312	5,020
Others	23,634	19,257
Gross deferred tax assets	$47,652	$49,286
Less: Valuation allowance	(13,588)	(15,710)
Total deferred tax asset	$34,064	$33,576
Deferred Tax Liability		
Plant and equipment	$ (7,770)	$ (8,993)
Others	(5,187)	(1,964)
Total deferred tax liability	(12,957)	(10,957)
Net deferred tax asset	$21,107	$22,619

The book value of the company's inventories increased from $91,130 at the end of 2004 to $127,777 at the end of 2005.

Required:

1. Prepare a schedule reconciling the statutory and effective tax rates of ABC Inc. for the year ended 2005.
2. Provide the journal entry to record the income tax expense for 2005, showing separately the effects on deferred tax asset, valuation allowance, and deferred tax liability.
3. For each component of deferred tax asset/liability, provide possible reasons for the change in its values from 2004 to 2005.

Excerpts from Wrigley Company's 2002 tax footnote follow.

C13 – 6

Understanding footnote disclosures

Wrigley Company

2002 Annual Report Footnote on Income Taxes

($ in thousands)	Years Ended December 31 2002	2001	2000
Current Provision			
Federal	$ 21,401	$ 30,142	$ 30,704
Foreign	135,901	121,137	109,184
State	6,786	6,770	7,954
	164,088	158,049	147,842
Deferred Provision			
Federal	16,113	2,384	961
Foreign	908	2,704	2,170
State	787	1,243	(603)
	17,808	6,331	2,528
Total	$181,896	$164,380	$150,370

Reconciliation of the provision for income taxes computed at the U.S. federal statutory rate of 35% for 2002, 2001, and 2000 to the reported provision for income taxes is as follows:

($ in thousands)	2002	2001	2000
Provision at U.S. Federal Statutory Rate	$204,197	$184,578	$167,759
State Taxes—Net	4,922	4,401	5,351
Foreign Tax Rates	(27,045)	(23,832)	(19,546)
Tax Credits (principally foreign)	(2,438)	(1,400)	(1,675)
Other—Net	2,260	633	(1,519)
Reported Tax Expense	$181,896	$164,380	$150,370

Components of net deferred tax balances are as follows:

($ in thousands)	2002	2001
Accrued Compensation, Pension and Post-retirement Benefits	$ 15,493	$ 26,419
Depreciation	(28,888)	(21,898)
Unrealized Holding Gains	(5,488)	(7,638)
All Other—Net	(2,361)	(317)
Net Deferred Tax Liability	$(21,244)	$ (3,434)

Balance sheet classifications of deferred taxes are as follows:

($ in thousands)	2002	2001
Deferred Tax Asset		
Current	$ 19,560	$ 14,846
Noncurrent	33,000	29,605
Deferred Tax Liability		
Current	(3,215)	(1,455)
Noncurrent	(70,589)	(46,430)
Net Deferred Tax Liability	$(21,244)	$ (3,434)

Required:

1. Provide a journal entry to record the aggregate income tax expense for 2002.
2. What amount of Wrigley's 2002 tax expense was deferred? Did this deferral result in an increase in deferred tax liabilities or a decrease in deferred tax assets?
3. Determine Wrigley's effective tax rate for 2002.
4. What tax policy or operating decision accounts for the majority of the divergence between Wrigley's statutory tax rate and effective tax rate?
5. Did Wrigley report any deferred tax assets in 2002? If so, what temporary differences between the carrying amounts of assets and liabilities for financial reporting purposes and the amounts used for income tax purposes gave rise to these assets?
6. Did Wrigley have any significant changes in its net deferred tax liability during 2002 related to nonoperating items? Explain.

COLLABORATIVE LEARNING CASE

C13 – 7

Waste Management: Analysis of tax footnotes

Waste Management is one of the largest trash haulers in the United States. In the late 1980s, the firm was widely viewed as a growth company. In an article about the company written 10 years later, *Fortune* stated that Waste Management "used improper, overly aggressive accounting tactics in an effort to boost sagging earnings . . . to retain its status as a Wall Street highflier. . . ."[13] In early 1998, the firm announced they would take a $3.54 billion pre-tax charge to correct these "accounting irregularities." The two largest charge-offs resulted from aggressive extensions of the expected depreciable lives of trucks and dumpsters and understated reserves for federal environmental liabilities. One magazine article reported that the earnings "hit" taken by Waste Management "stunned the investment community." Reproduced below are selected excerpts from Waste Management's financial statements over the period 1993–1996. Using your understanding of financial reporting and your ability to make inferences from these pre-1998 disclosures, should knowledgeable investors have been "stunned" by the early 1998 write-off? More explicit questions to guide your analysis follow the statement excerpts.

[13] Peter Elkind, "Garbage In; Garbage Out," *Fortune* (May 25, 1998).

Waste Management

Consolidated Condensed Income Statement Data (Before Correction)

($ in thousands)	Years Ended December 31			
	1993	1994	1995	1996
Revenue	$ 7,827,280	$ 8,482,718	$ 9,053,018	$ 9,186,970
Costs and expenses	6,361,233	6,824,806	7,225,747	7,352,037
Special charges	550,000	—	335,193	471,635
Gains from stock transactions of subsidiaries And exchange of exchangeable LYONs	(15,109)	—	—	—
Other expense	193,272	363,000	390,165	320,460
Income from continuing operations before income taxes	737,884	1,294,912	1,101,913	1,042,838
Provision for income taxes	319,798	552,606	483,670	565,047
Income from continuing operations	418,086	742,306	618,243	477,791
Income (loss) from discontinued operations	34,690	42,075	(14,344)	(285,706)
Net income	$ 452,776	$ 784,381	$ 603,899	$ 192,085

Condensed Balance Sheet

	1993	1994	1995	1996
Total Current Assets	$ 2,777,520	$ 3,088,844	$ 2,608,085	$ 3,093,224
Property and equipment, at cost				
Land, primarily disposal sites	3,625,412	4,162,418	4,553,717	5,019,065
Buildings	1,223,139	1,372,782	1,532,305	1,495,252
Vehicles and equipment	6,856,044	7,162,217	7,164,767	7,520,902
Leasehold improvements	100,262	91,554	84,587	85,998
	11,804,857	12,788,971	13,335,376	14,121,217
Less—Accumulated depreciation and amortization	(3,035,398)	(3,503,219)	(3,829,658)	(4,399,508)
Total property and equipment, net	8,769,459	9,285,752	9,505,718	9,721,709
Total other assets	4,717,497	5,164,318	6,250,471	5,551,659
Total Assets	$16,264,476	$17,538,914	$18,364,274	$18,366,592
Total current liabilities	$ 2,677,562	$ 3,179,731	$ 3,192,484	$ 3,038,708
Total deferred items	1,933,319	1,985,298	2,192,150	2,197,234
Long-term debt, less portion payable within one year	6,145,584	6,044,411	6,390,041	6,971,607
Minority interest in subsidiaries	1,348,559	1,536,165	1,385,301	1,186,955
Put options	—	252,328	261,959	95,789
Total stockholders' equity	4,159,452	4,540,981	4,942,339	4,876,299
Total Liabilities and Stockholders' Equity	$16,264,476	$17,538,914	$18,364,274	$18,366,592

Additional Financial Disclosures (Before Correction)

($ in thousands)	1993	1994	1995	1996
From the Consolidated Statement of Cash Flows:				
Depreciation and amortization	$796,691	$880,466	$885,384	$920,685

From Management's Discussion and Analysis:[14] (Before Correction)

Acquisitions and Capital Expenditures Capital expenditures, including [$443.5 million,] $56.8 million, $154.1 million, and $91.8 million for property and equipment of purchased businesses in [1993,] 1994, 1995, and 1996, respectively, are shown in the following table:

($ in millions)	1993	1994	1995	1996
Land (primarily disposal sites)	$ 660.2	$ 582.3	$ 517.2	$ 467.7
Buildings and leasehold improvements	195.5	141.2	148.8	109.3
Vehicles	373.0	226.0	345.8	204.9
Containers	231.6	167.9	181.2	115.8
Other equipment	702.4	395.0	348.1	319.2
Total	$2,162.7	$1,512.4	$1,541.1	$1,216.9

[14] The text is from the 1996 Annual Report and is edited to include 1993 data.

From the summary of Accounting Policies Footnote: (Before Correction)

Property and Equipment Property and equipment (including major repairs and improvements) are capitalized and stated at cost. Items of an ordinary maintenance or repair nature are charged directly to operations. Disposal sites are carried at cost and to the extent this exceeds end use realizable value, such excess is amortized over the estimated life of the disposal site. Disposal site improvement costs are capitalized and charged to operations over the shorter of the estimated usable life of the site or the improvement.

Depreciation and Amortization The cost, less estimated salvage value, of property and equipment is depreciated over the estimated useful lives on the straight-line method as follows: buildings—10 to 40 years; vehicles and equipment—3 to 20 years; leasehold improvements—over the life of the applicable lease.

Annual Report Condensed Note on Income Taxes (Before Correction)*

($ in thousands)	1993	1994	1995	1996
Deferred tax assets				
Reserves not deductible until paid	$ (538,062)	$ (494,549)	$ (503,074)	$ (495,940)
Deferred revenue	(27,714)	(25,708)	(37,284)	(16,158)
Net operating losses and tax credit carryforwards	(43,028)	(110,073)	(266,916)	(233,008)
Other	(104,059)	(70,281)	(78,474)	(73,229)
Subtotal	$ (712,863)	$ (700,611)	$ (885,748)	$ (818,335)
Deferred tax liabilities				
Depreciation and amortization	$ 948,024	$1,106,155	$1,335,559	$1,384,164
Other	183,655	233,178	374,084	359,035
Subtotal	1,131,679	1,339,333	1,709,643	1,743,199
Valuation allowance	29,890	26,955	98,605	86,729
Net deferred tax liabilities	$ 448,706	$ 665,677	$ 922,500	$1,011,593

**Note:* In the notes accompanying its pre-correction 1996 Annual Report, the Company says: "Certain amounts in previously issued financial statements have been restated to conform to 1996 classifications." Similar statements were made in the 1994 and 1995 annual reports relating to those reporting years. Since only two years of comparative data were given in each report, the 1994 data are not strictly classified in conformity with the 1996 classifications. The differences from year to year appear to be minor. However, the reader should be aware that adjacent years' data are not always perfectly comparable.

Annual Report Note on Environmental Costs and Liabilities (text from 1996 Annual Report, Before Correction)

The continuing business in which the Company is engaged is intrinsically connected with the protection of the environment. As such, a significant portion of the Company's operating costs and capital expenditures could be characterized as costs of environmental protection. . . .

Estimates of the extent of the Company's degree of responsibility for remediation of a particular site and the method and ultimate cost of remediation require a number of assumptions and are inherently difficult, and the ultimate outcome may differ from current estimates. However, the Company believes that its extensive experience in the environmental services business, as well as its involvement with a large number of sites, provides a reasonable basis for estimating its aggregate liability. As additional information becomes available, estimates are adjusted as necessary. While the Company does not anticipate that any such adjustment would be material to its financial statements, it is reasonably possible that technological, regulatory, or enforcement developments, the results of environmental studies, or other factors could necessitate the recording of additional liabilities, which could be material.

Where the Company believes that both the amount of a particular environmental liability and the timing of the payments are reliably determinable, the cost in current dollars is inflated at 3% until expected time of payment and then discounted to present value at 7%. Had the Company not discounted any portion of its liability, the amount recorded would have been increased by approximately $160 million at December 31, 1996.

The Company's active landfill sites have estimated remaining lives ranging from 1 to over 100 years based upon current site plans and annual volumes of waste. During this remaining site life, the Company will provide for an additional $1.03 billion of closure and post-closure costs, including accretion for the discount recognized to date.

As of December 31, the Company's liabilities for closure, post-closure monitoring and environmental remediation costs were as follows:

($ in thousands)	1993	1994	1995	1996
Current portion, included in accrued expenses	$ 130,863	$ 108,750	$ 138,533	$122,209
Non-current portion	745,637	704,015	621,186	543,723
Total recorded	876,500	812,765	759,719	665,932
Amount to be provided over remaining life of active sites,				
including discount of $154 million in 1993 and $169 million in 1994	987,000	1,149,617		
including discount of $171 million in 1995 and $160 million in 1996			1,118,739	1,028,437
Expected aggregate undiscounted environmental liabilities	$1,863,500	$1,962,382	$1,878,458	$1,694,369

Anticipated payments of environmental liabilities at December 31, 1996, are as follows:

($ in thousands)	
1997	$ 122,209
1998	56,000
1999	47,450
2000	33,571
2001	38,429
Thereafter	1,396,710
	$1,694,369

Required:

What elements in the Waste Management financial data and footnote excerpts included in the case might have given analysts an inkling of the excessive depreciable lives estimates and understated environmental reserves? (*Hints:* (1) Explain why the deferred tax liability for depreciation and amortization is increasing. Is this increasing CR balance consistent with year-to-year capital expenditure patterns? (2) Carefully compare recorded environmental liabilities with asset amounts.)

Remember to check the book's Companion Website for additional problem and case material.

www.prenhall.com/revsine

CHAPTER 14

Pensions and Postretirement Benefits

A **pension plan** is an agreement by an organization to provide a series of payments—called a **pension**—to employees when they retire. In most instances these company pension payments supplement payments from government-sponsored pension plans—such as Social Security in the United States. A pension plan represents a valuable benefit to employees. Employers create these plans as a way of attracting a qualified workforce. Firms derive benefits from pension plans, since they help them retain a more capable workforce with higher morale. The benefit is realized by the firm in the form of higher productivity from employees. For this reason, the cost of a worker's pension plan is treated as an expense over that worker's period of employment.

Pension plans can be divided into two categories—**defined contribution** plans and **defined benefit** plans—based on the nature of the promise embedded in the plan.

Defined contribution plans specify the amount of cash that the employer puts *into* the plan for the benefit of the employee. In a defined contribution plan, no explicit promise is made about the size of the periodic payments the employee will receive on retirement. The amount that will ultimately be paid out to the employee is determined by the accumulated value at retirement of the amounts contributed to the plan over the period of employment. In defined contribution plans, the *employee* bears the risk that the ultimate pension payments will be large enough to sustain a comfortable retirement income. Accounting for defined contribution plans is straightforward, as shown in the following example.

DEFINED CONTRIBUTION PLAN

XYZ Company sponsors a defined contribution pension plan under which it makes an annual contribution equal to 10% of employees' salaries into a fund **whose accumulated proceeds will be paid to the employees at retirement**. Employees' salaries in 2005 total $10 million. Accordingly, XYZ records pension expense equal to the amount of cash contributed to the plan ($10,000,000 × 10%) as follows:

DR Pension expense	$1,000,000	
CR Cash		$1,000,000

The $1,000,000 is transferred to a **plan trustee**—a legal entity that invests and holds the assets for the benefit of the employees. Upon retirement, individual employees receive their share of the accumulated balance from the investments.

So a defined contribution plan specifies the initial level of pay-*in* to the plan. A defined benefit plan is quite different. These agreements specify the formula for determining the amount that will be paid *out* to the employee after retirement rather than the amount that will be put into the plan. To illustrate:

DEFINED BENEFIT PLAN

ABC Company sponsors a pension plan in which employees qualify for a pension equal to **3% of their salary at retirement for each year of service**. An employee with 25 years of service and with an annual salary at retirement of $60,000 would receive an annual pension benefit of $45,000 (25 years of service times 3% for each year—75%—multiplied by the ending salary of $60,000).

Determining how much should be charged to pension expense each year and how much cash must be contributed to the fund in order to provide the annual pension benefit of $45,000 is complex. These amounts must be computed using assumptions and procedures described below.

A defined benefit plan specifies the formula for determining pension pay*outs*. Because the pension payout formula is specified in advance in a defined benefit plan, typically, the employee bears less risk regarding the adequacy of pension payments. Instead, the biggest risk in these plans is borne by the employer who must accurately estimate the amount that must be contributed to fund the plan.

Exhibit 14.1 shows the total dollar amount of assets in each of the two types of pension plans over the years from 1985 to 2002. The proportion of assets in defined benefit plans as a percent of total pension assets has declined over this period. Nevertheless, 45.9% of all pension plan assets were still in defined benefit plans at the end of 2002.

In defined contribution pension plans, employees are sometimes also required to contribute to the plan. For example, a plan might specify that the employer is to contribute 10% of the employee's salary to the plan and that the employee is to contribute 5%, for a total of 15%. The employees' 5% contributions are typically deducted from their paychecks and directly transferred to the plan trustee.

EXHIBIT 14.1	Assets by Type of Pension Plan			

($ in billions) End of Year	Defined Benefit	Defined Contribution	Defined Benefit	Defined Contribution
1985	$ 814	$ 417	66.1%	33.9%
1986	885	478	64.9	35.1
1987	883	523	62.8	37.2
1988	883	549	61.7	38.3
1989	942	672	58.4	41.6
1990	896	676	57.0	43.0
1991	1,048	829	55.8	44.2
1992	1,043	892	53.9	46.1
1993	1,170	1,014	53.6	46.4
1994	1,193	1,076	52.6	47.4
1995	1,444	1,312	52.4	47.6
1996	1,542	1,520	50.4	49.6
1997	1,783	1,853	49.0	51.0
1998	1,945	2,105	48.0	52.0
1999	2,085	2,272	47.9	52.1
2000	2,014	2,272	47.0	53.0
2001	1,820	2,141	45.9	54.1
2002	1,612	1,902	45.9	54.1

Source: Employee Benefit Research Institute, Washington, D.C.

A defined benefit pension plan raises many financial reporting complications. The main one is how much should be charged to pension expense in each year while covered employees are working.

Financial reporting for defined benefit plans is further complicated because only the benefit *formula* is specified, not the benefit *amount*. In the ABC Company example, at the time the plan was adopted it was known that retiring employees with 25 years of service would receive a pension equal to 75% of their annual salary at the time of retirement. However, to determine what the periodic pension expense should be over the span of the employees' working careers, the following factors must be estimated:

1. What proportion of the workforce will remain with the company long enough to qualify for benefits under the plan? Qualifying for benefits is called **vesting**. A forecast of the length of employee service requires actuarial assumptions regarding personnel turnover, mortality rates, and disability.
2. At what rate will salaries rise over the period until eventual retirement?
3. What is the anticipated life span of covered employees after retirement—that is, over what length of time will the pension benefits be paid?
4. What rate of return will be earned on the investments made with the cash contributed by the employer to fund the plan?
5. What is the appropriate discount rate that should be used to reflect the present value of the future benefits earned by employees in the current period?

Statement of Financial Accounting Standards (SFAS) No. 87, which was issued in December 1985, specifies measurement and disclosure requirements for defined benefit pension plans.[1] The disclosure aspects of *SFAS No. 87* were amended by *SFAS No. 132* in 1998 and amended again in 2003; the latest amended version is *SFAS No. 132* (revised 2003).[2] *SFAS No. 87* was designed to avoid volatility in pension expense since companies' financial managers abhor bottom-line volatility. This volatility-avoidance objective was achieved by using numerous smoothing devices and deferrals in computing pension expense. The result is arguably the most technically complicated financial reporting pronouncement ever issued. Consequently, analysts and other external users have experienced considerable difficulty in comprehending the concepts underlying the reported numbers. We try to clarify the topic by providing a less technical, more intuitive overview of the financial reporting rules for defined benefit pension plans.[3]

Financial Reporting for Defined Benefit Pension Plans

Under current GAAP, pension expense is comprised of six separate components. These components are (+ indicates increase in expense and − indicates decrease in expense):[4]

1. Service cost (+)
2. Interest cost (+)

---

[1] Entitled "Employers' Accounting for Pensions," *SFAS No. 87* replaced both *Accounting Principles Board (APB) Opinion No. 8* ("Accounting for the Cost of Pension Plans," 1966) and *SFAS No. 36* ("Disclosure of Pension Information," 1980), which previously governed pension accounting and disclosure.

[2] "Employers' Disclosures About Pensions and Other Postretirement Benefits," *SFAS No. 132* (Norwalk, CT: Financial Accounting Standards Board [FASB], 1998), and *SFAS No. 132* (revised 2003). The revised version of *SFAS No. 132* has the same title as the 1998 version and was issued in December 2003. For simplicity, citations throughout the chapter will simply reference *SFAS No. 132*. Where warranted, we will reference significant new disclosures mandated in the December 2003 revision of *SFAS No. 132*.

[3] The material on pp. 751–765, 773–775, and 779–780 is adapted from L. Revsine, "Understanding Financial Accounting Standard 87," *Financial Analysts Journal* (January–February 1989), pp. 61–8, and is presented here with permission from the publisher.

[4] If a company either (1) curtails a plan, or (2) settles a plan's liabilities by purchasing an annuity contract and generates a gain or loss from either event, that gain or loss would also be included in pension expense as a seventh element. Measuring the gain or loss on plan settlements or curtailments is outlined in "Employers' Accounting for Settlements and Curtailments of Defined Benefit Pension Plans and for Termination Benefits," *SFAS No. 88* (Stamford, CT: FASB, 1985).

3. Expected return on pension plan assets (−)
4. Recognized gains or losses (− or +)
5. Amortization of unrecognized transition asset or obligation (− or +)
6. Recognized prior service cost (− or +).

First, we use a simple example to illustrate how pension expense components 1 through 3 are computed and disclosed under the *SFAS Nos. 87* and *132* rules. The example assumes an environment characterized by *complete certainty*. This assumption simplifies the setting and clarifies the relationship between the various pension expense components. The complete certainty assumption makes it easy to see that there would be no need for components 4 through 6 in an environment with no surprises. Second, we show how components 4 through 6 come into play in a world of *uncertainty*, one where expectations are often not realized and where changes in assumptions occur frequently.

A Simple Example in a World of Complete Certainty

Consider the following example:[5]

> On January 1, 2005, Wildcat Corporation decides to provide a lump-sum pension payment equal to $10,000 for each year of service to its sole employee, Ed Cate. No previous pension plan existed. Wildcat expects Cate to retire on December 31, 2006 and desires to pay him the pension in one lump sum on December 31, 2007.
>
> Further assume that Wildcat operates in an environment of complete certainty where the interest rate and the rate of return on investments are both equal and known. Furthermore, Cate's life expectancy and the duration of his employment service are also known in advance. Wildcat's discount rate is 7%, and the pension trust will also earn exactly 7% on all contributions to the pension fund, which are funded fully as soon as Cate qualifies for benefits.

We'll now show how to compute components 1 through 3 for this simple example.

Component 1—Service Cost In a typical defined benefit pension plan, the pension payout increases for each additional year of service. This increase in the expected payout results in an increase in the discounted present value of the liability. This increase is **service cost**. Stated more rigorously, *service cost is the increase in the discounted present value of the pension benefits ultimately payable that is attributable to an additional year's employment*.

Most pension plans create a trust—a legal entity that takes custody of assets contributed by the employer and manages them for the benefit of the employees. Contributing assets to the plan is termed **funding**. When the employer funds the plan, these assets are transferred to the trustee.

In the simplified example, Cate worked throughout 2005 and according to the terms of the pension benefit formula became eligible for a $10,000 pension payable on December 31, 2007. The discounted present value of this obligation on December 31, 2005 (at a 7% annual discount rate) is $8,734. Because no obligation existed at the start of the year, the *increase* in the discounted present value of the obligation during the year is $8,734—this is the service cost element of pension expense on Wildcat's books for 2005 and the pension obligation at the end of the year. Because Wildcat fully funds the pension expense, the economic status of the pension plan at December 31, 2005 is:

---

[5] This example is adapted from a pre-*SFAS No. 87* illustration that was prepared by Professor Norman Bartczak of Columbia University.

Wildcat Corporation

Pension expense = Pension obligation = $\dfrac{\$10,000}{(1.07)^2}$ = $8,734 = Service cost

┌─── Pension funding $8,734 = Cash transferred to trust

│ **Wildcat Employees' Pension Trust**

└─→ Pension fund assets and obligation $8,734 = Cash received from
                                                        Wildcat Corporation

Wildcat makes the following journal entry on December 31, 2005:

DR Pension expense	$8,734	
CR Cash		$8,734

Ed Cate's continued employment throughout 2006 qualifies him for a $20,000 pension payable on December 31, 2007. The service cost element of pension expense for the year 2006 is the increase in the present value of the amount ultimately payable that is attributable to an additional year's employment. Exhibit 14.2 shows the computation.

EXHIBIT 14.2	Wildcat Corporation

Computation of Service Cost for 2006

Pension payout to Cate with two years of service (2005 and 2006)		$20,000
Less: Pension payout to Cate with one year of service (2005)	−	10,000
Undiscounted increase attributable to 2006 service	=	10,000
Discount factor at 7% for one year (this increase is discounted since the additional payout is one year away)	×	.9346
Service cost for 2006	=	$ 9,346

The ultimate pension payout has grown by $10,000, since Cate earned additional benefits by working in 2006. As shown in Exhibit 14.2, the discounted present value of this increase is $10,000 × .9346—or $9,346. By definition, this is service cost.

In addition to service cost, the 2006 *total* pension expense for Wildcat Corporation includes two other items—interest cost and return on plan assets.

Component 2—Interest Cost Service cost for 2005 was initially recorded at $8,734, the discounted present value of the pension payment due on December 31, 2007. Because the payment of this liability drew one year closer by the end of 2006, its present value has increased by $611 ($8,734 × 0.07). Therefore, in addition to service cost, there is interest cost in 2006. The **interest cost** component of pension expense (and the increase in the liability) arises from the passage of time. *Interest cost is computed by taking the pension liability at the beginning of the period ($8,734) and multiplying it by the annual interest rate factor (here, 7%).*

Component 3—Expected Return on Plan Assets At December 31, 2005 the pension fund assets (held by the trustee) also had a balance of $8,734. During 2006 these assets earned a return of $611 ($8,734 × 0.07). (Because our example is set in a world of complete certainty, the expected return and the actual return on plan assets are equal.) The **expected return on plan assets** reduces pension expense. As a consequence of all of these events, total pension expense for 2006 is $9,346 ($9,346 + $611 − $611). Exhibit 14.3 on page 754 gives the 2006 pension expense components and pension fund asset balance at December 31, 2006.

> By contrast, the service cost element arises because the pension liability grows as workers accumulate additional years of service.

The journal entry for 2006 pension expense is:

DR	Pension expense	$9,346	
	CR Cash		$9,346

If Cate retires at the end of 2006, there will be no service cost component of pension expense in 2007 since Cate didn't work during 2007. There will be interest cost of $1,308 because the present value of the amount owed at the pension payout date increases as time passes. There will also be a return on plan assets in 2007. *Exhibit 14.4 shows that the $1,308 interest cost and the $1,308 return on plan assets offset each other, so 2007 pension expense is zero.* Notice that the December 31, 2007 accumulated asset balance of $20,000 is exactly equal to the required pension payment.

In this example perfect certainty meant:

1. The exact **date of retirement was known** at the time the plan was initiated. In technical terms, the precise service life of employees was known with certainty.

2. The ultimate **amount of the pension was also known in advance.** No unexpected salary increases raised the amount of the final payment, nor were there unforeseen actuarial events such as turnover or death.

3. **Discount rates and earnings rates were equal and could be perfectly forecast over the entire period.**

With these simple (but unrealistic) circumstances, pension expense is equal to service cost in every period over which the pension plan is in effect, as shown next:

Year	Service Cost	Total Pension Expense
2005	$8,734	$8,734
2006	9,346	9,346
2007	–0–	–0–

EXHIBIT 14.4   Wildcat Pension Plan

Pension Expense and Assets for 2007

Wildcat Corporation
Pension Expense

Interest cost (that is, present value of pension obligation at 12/31/06 × discount rate: $18,692 × 7%)	=	$ 1,308
Expected return on plan assets ($18,692 × 7%)	=	(1,308)
2007 pension expense	=	–0–

Pension Funding	=	–0–

Wildcat Employees' Pension Trust
Pension Fund Assets and Obligations

Accumulated balance of 12/31/06 pension assets as of 12/31/07: ($18,692 × 1.07)	=	$20,000
Less: 12/31/07 payment to Cate	=	(20,000)
Balance of pension assets at 12/31/07	=	–0–
Present value of pension obligation as of 12/31/07	=	$20,000
Less: 12/31/07 payment to Cate	=	(20,000)
Balance of pension obligation at 12/31/07	=	–0–

Pension expense equals service cost when there is complete certainty because interest cost is exactly offset by the return on plan assets. When cash funding equals service cost, this also means that the accumulated amount of pension assets is exactly sufficient to pay the liability. *But relaxing these certainty assumptions complicates pension financial reporting considerably.*

We use perfect certainty in this example to help you see the relationship between the components comprising pension expense. There is no perfect certainty in the real pension world. On the contrary, unforeseen pension events arise continuously. Examples include the following:

1. Higher or lower than anticipated employee turnover.
2. Unusually high or low preretirement mortality.
3. The return earned on pension plan assets could differ significantly from expectations.
4. Changes in social and economic conditions may prompt companies to retroactively alter the level of benefits promised upon retirement or to alter the discount rate assumptions.

All these factors explain why, in the real world, there is no simple equality between pension plan assets and pension plan liabilities and why pension expense does not equal service cost. Depending on the age distribution of the workforce and the amount of retroactive plan alterations, interest cost—not service cost—could be the dominant part of pension expense.

Our example does capture one real-world characteristic of pension plans. Wildcat Corporation (the plan sponsor) recognized on its books only the pension expense and the cash payout when funding the pension. For example, Wildcat made the following type of entry to record pension expense and funding in 2005 and 2006:

> The reason that pension expense does not equal service cost when unexpected events occur is that past funding (which was based on the original actuarial and earnings assumptions) generates returns that are larger or smaller than interest cost (which is based on the revised actuarial assumptions).

DR Pension expense	$X,XXX	
CR Cash		$X,XXX

The assets and liabilities of the pension plan are not included in Wildcat's financial statements—a real-world characteristic. Instead, the assets and liabilities are reflected on the statements of the **plan trustee**. The plan trustee receives the payments and disburses pension benefits. The relationship between the firm that establishes the pension plan (the plan sponsor), the plan trustee, and the plan beneficiaries (the eventual retirees) is shown in Figure 14.1.

Figure 14.1

PENSION PLAN ENTITIES
AND RELATIONSHIPS

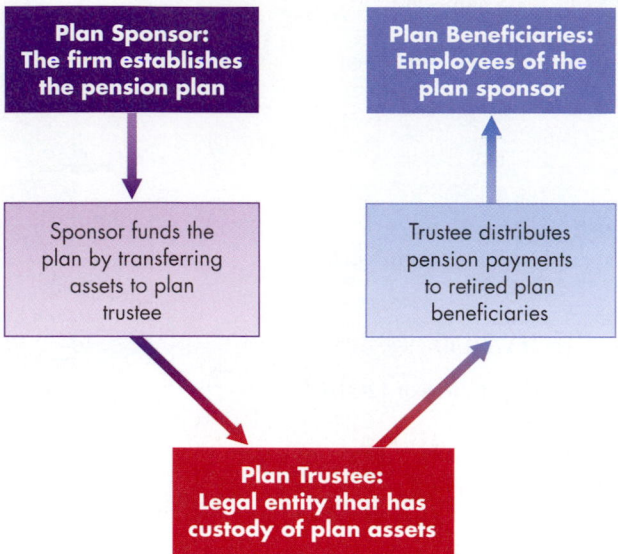

> RE CAP If the future were known with certainty, pension expense would always equal service cost and pension plan assets would always equal pension plan liabilities. Starting with this simple setting will help you understand the complications that uncertainty introduces.

Uncertainty Introduces Deferrals and Amortizations

Uncertainty requires estimates of future discount rates, expected return on plan assets, and numerous other future events like employee turnover and longevity beyond retirement. *SFAS No. 87* requires that the same interest rate be used for computing both the service cost *and* the interest cost components of pension expense. However, companies are free to choose some other interest rate for computing the *expected* rate of return on pension plan assets and many do.

The simplified complete certainty example shows that the higher the interest rate initially chosen for computing service cost, the lower the reported service cost component of pension expense, as you can see from Exhibit 14.5. This reduction in service cost is offset by an increase in the interest cost component of pension expense, which is due to the higher interest rate. In our Wildcat Corporation example, if the same higher rate is *also* used for computing the expected return on plan assets, then pension expense is reduced. Exhibit 14.5 illustrates the decrease in pension expense that results from using an 8% rate rather than 7% in the Wildcat Corporation example.

If the assumed 8% interest rate is not actually *earned* on plan assets, the accumulated pension fund assets will be too small to fund Cate's pension. But generalizing from Exhibit 14.5, you see that companies can temporarily alter pension expense (either up or down) by choosing a higher or lower discount rate, as well as by choosing a higher or lower expected rate of return on plan assets.

EXHIBIT 14.5	Wildcat Corporation			

Pension Expense at Two Different Interest Rates

			Interest Rate	
2005 Pension Expense			**8%**	**7%**
2005 Service cost	$10,000/(1.08)^2$	=	$8,573	
	$10,000/(1.07)^2$	=		$8,734
2006 Pension Expense				
2006 Service cost	($20,000 − $10,000)/1.08	=	$9,259	
	($20,000 − $10,000)/1.07	=		$9,346
Interest cost	$8,573 × 8%	=	686	
	$8,734 × 7%	=		611
Return on plan assets	$8,573 × 8%	=	(686)	
	$8,734 × 7%	=		(611)
			$9,259	$9,346

SFAS No. 87 provides explicit criteria for estimating discount rates. Paragraph 44 of the Standard states, "assumed discount rates shall reflect the rates at which the pension benefits could effectively be settled." This discount rate is referred to as the **settlement rate**. This guideline reduces managers' ability to manipulate pension expense; unfortunately it does not eliminate it.

Figure 14.2 graphically compares settlement rates (used to discount pension obligations and also used to compute pension service cost and interest cost) and the expected long-term rate of return on plan assets used by a sample of Compustat® firms from 1997 to 2002.[6] The top and bottom of each bar represent the high and low rates used by firms in that year; the line crossing each bar represents the median rate. As you can see, there is considerable variation in both the settlement rate and the expected long-term rate of return across firms within a given year. For example, the settlement rates in 1999 range from 3.5% to 8.5%, with a median of 7.5%; the expected long-term rate of return on plan assets in 1999 ranges from 4.0% to 11%, with a median of 9%. Throughout most of this six-year period the median expected rate of return on plan assets remained at 9%, dropping to 8.5% in 2002; the median settlement rate varied from 6.8% in 1998 and 2002 to 7.5% in 1999 and 2000. Since interest costs can comprise a large portion of total pension charges (see Figure 14.5 on p. 766), even small changes in the discount rate can have a material impact on pension expense. Changes in interest rate assumptions can have an even more dramatic effect on the estimated present value of pension obligations (see Exhibit 14.9 on p. 778).[7]

> The FASB provides the following guidance for estimating the settlement rate: "It is appropriate in estimating those rates to look to available information about rates implicit in current prices of annuity contracts that could be used to effect settlement of the obligation. . . . [E]mployers may also look to rates of return on high-quality fixed-income investments currently available and expected to be available during the period to maturity of the pension benefits" (para. 44). In other words, the settlement rate is the currently prevailing rate of return on high-quality bonds.

Components 4 through 6 — Smoothing Devices Uncertainty not only complicates the measurement of service cost and interest cost, it also means actual outcomes will likely differ from expectations. For example, the actual return on pension plan assets will differ from the expected return, and actual turnover and pay increases will differ from actuarial assumptions.

---

[6] Compustat® is a computerized financial database for over 7,000 firms listed on the New York Stock Exchange (NYSE), American Stock Exchange (AMEX), and National Association of Securities Dealers Automated Quotations (NASDAQ) exchanges, which is developed and distributed by Standard & Poor's Corporation. The sample excludes American Depositary Receipts (ADRs), which are non-U.S. common stock listings on these exchanges.

[7] An article in *Forbes* estimates that a 1% decrease in the discount rate can boost the estimated pension liability by as much as 10% to 15% for the typical firm. See "The Surplus Vanishes," *Forbes* (November 17, 1986), p. 94. The reason for this large multiplier effect is discussed more fully later in the chapter.

Figure 14.2

PENSION SETTLEMENT RATE
AND EXPECTED LONG-RUN
RATE OF RETURN ON PLAN
ASSETS 1997–2002

Sample consists of all AMEX
and NYSE firms with defined
benefit plans.

Source: Standard & Poor's Research
Insight^(SM) as data source; methodology not verified or controlled by
Standard & Poor's.

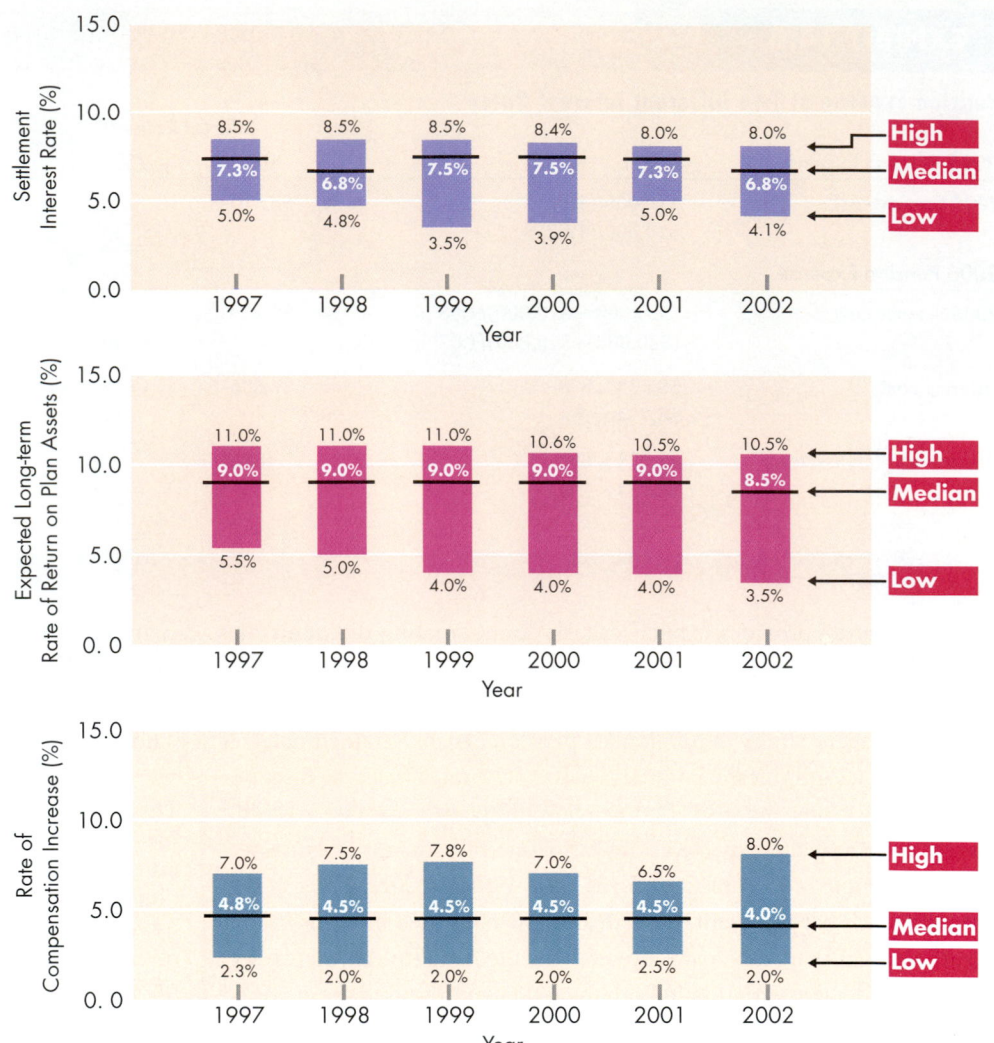

These deviations between expected and actual events—if recognized immediately—would inject volatility into the periodic measure of pension expense, as we are about to show you. Managers abhor earnings volatility, and, not surprisingly, strong sentiments for reducing this volatility emerged early in the exposure draft stage of *SFAS No. 87.* Components 4 through 6 of the annual pension expense calculation are designed to smooth this volatility.

Our discussion now turns to each of these smoothing components of pension expense.

COMPONENT 4—RECOGNIZED GAINS OR LOSSES In a real-world environment that contains uncertainty, the actual return on pension plan assets can differ considerably from the expected return in any year. Volatility in asset returns—without some smoothing mechanism—would translate directly into net income volatility since the return on plan assets reduces pension expense.

To illustrate this volatility, let's assume Anna Corporation's service cost and interest cost components of pension expense in 2006 and 2007 were:

	2006	2007
Service cost	$1,000	$1,050
Interest cost	1,000	1,050

In addition, assume that the *actual* return on plan assets in 2006 was $1,500 but was only $100 in 2007 because of adverse market conditions. If no smoothing were permitted, Anna's pension expense in the two years would be:

	2006	2007
Service cost	$1,000	$1,050
Interest cost	1,000	1,050
Less: Actual return on plan assets	(1,500)	(100)
Pension expense	$ 500	$2,000

The extreme change in year-to-year pension expense ($500 versus $2,000) would cause year-to-year volatility in the firm's earnings.

SFAS No. 87 makes it possible to avert this volatility by allowing firms to reduce pension expense by the *expected* return on plan assets rather than by the actual return. This result is accomplished in two steps:

- First, firms select a target return that they *expect* to earn on plan assets in the long run.
- Second, any difference between this expected return and the actual return that is earned in a given year is kept track of "off the balance sheet."

The cumulative balance of these unrecognized gains (losses) is monitored periodically for possible inclusion in pension expense at a later time.

To show how the smoothing mechanism works, assume that Anna's pension plan assets were $10,000 and $11,500 at the start of 2006 and 2007, respectively. Further assume that given the riskiness of the investment strategy selected, Anna expects to earn a return of 9% on average each year. Under the *SFAS No. 87* smoothing approach, Anna's pension expense would be reduced by the *expected* return in each year—$900 in 2006 ($10,000 × 9%) and $1,035 in 2007 ($11,500 × 9%). This expected return is pension expense component 3, discussed earlier. The difference between the expected and actual return in each year is deferred using an off-balance sheet smoothing device called the **unrecognized gain or loss**. Specifically:

		2006		2007
Service cost		$1,000		$1,050
Interest cost		1,000		1,050
Less:				
Actual return on plan assets (see above)	($1,500)		($100)	
Unrecognized gain (loss)	600		(935)	
Expected return on plan assets (component 3)		(900)		(1,035)
Pension expense		$1,100		$1,065

In years like 2006 when the actual return ($1,500) exceeds the expected return ($900), there is an unrecognized gain of $600 (see highlight). In years like 2007, there is an unrecognized loss of $935 since the actual return ($100) is less than the expected return ($1,035). By using the *expected* return to compute pension expense and deferring the unrecognized gain or loss, the year-to-year change in Anna Corporation's pension expense was only $35 ($1,100 – $1,065). This is much smaller than the $1,500 year-to-year change in pension expense if *actual* return on plan assets had been subtracted ($2,000 – $500, as you saw above).

Figure 14.3 graphically shows how large the differences between the actual return and expected return on pension plan assets can be. The data in Figure 14.3 come from the pension footnotes for General Electric Company (GE) for the years 1993 through 2001, excerpts of which follow the figure in Exhibit 14.6. While GE's long-term expected rate of return on plan assets was

9.5% per year over the entire period, the actual rate of return ranged from a high of 20.8% in 1995 to a low of −5.8% in 2001. Figure 14.3 depicts the actual dollar return and expected dollar return on plan assets by year. The actual return displays considerable variability from year to year; the expected dollar return gradually increases, reflecting a stable expected return rate (9.5% per year) times an increasing pension asset base. For the 1999–2001 period, the actual dollar return on GE's plan assets goes from $8.472 billion in 1999 to $1.287 billion in 2000 to negative $2.876 billion in 2001. GE's earnings before taxes and accounting changes for the 1999–2001 period were ($ in billions) $15.577, $18.446, and $19.701, respectively. Clearly, without some mechanism to smooth out the big swings in the yearly actual returns on pension assets, considerable volatility would be introduced into GE's bottom line.

Figure 14.3

GENERAL ELECTRIC COMPANY
COMPARISON OF ACTUAL
AND EXPECTED RETURN ON
PENSION PLAN ASSETS
(1993–2001)

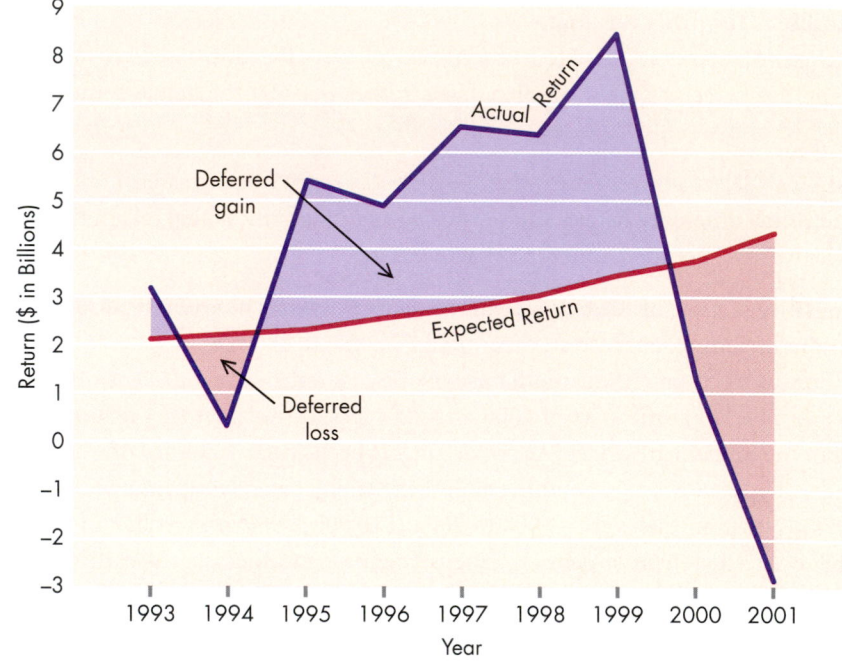

EXHIBIT 14.6	Excerpts from General Electric Company Footnotes Underlying Figure 14.3 Data								
($ in billions)	1993	1994	1995	1996	1997	1998	1999	2000	2001
Actual dollar return on pension plan assets	$3.221	$0.316	$5.439	$4.916	$6.587	$6.363	$8.472	$1.287	$(2.876)
Market value of plan assets[1]	$26.466	$27.193	$26.166	$30.200	$33.686	$38.742	$43.447	$50.243	$49.757
Actual return on plan assets	12.2%	1.2%	20.8%	16.3%	19.6%	16.4%	19.5%	2.6%	(5.8%)
Long-term expected return	9.5%	9.5%	9.5%	9.5%	9.5%	9.5%	9.5%	9.5%	9.5%
Expected dollar return on plan assets[2]	$2.155	$2.267	$2.352	$2.587	$2.721	$3.024	$3.407	$3.754	$4.327
Unrecognized gains or losses (actual minus expected return)	$1.066	$(1.951)	$3.087	$2.329	$3.866	$3.339	$5.065	$(2.467)	$(7.203)

[1]This is the value of the plan assets at the *start* of each year.
[2]You may notice that the expected dollar return for any year is not equal to the beginning market value of plan assets times the expected return rate. To illustrate using 1999, we get:

Market value of plan assets ($43.447) × expected return (.095) = $4.127 Expected dollar return

This amount differs from the $3.407 reported by GE. Why? The reason is that firms are allowed to compute the expected return on a moving-average of the market value of plan assets over a period not exceeding the preceding five years. GE apparently did this, so the 9.5% expected return was applied to some measure of late 1990s average plan assets. We do not have enough information to compute the $3.407 directly.

Source: General Electric Company Annual Reports, 1993–2001.

The data highlighted in the bottom row of Exhibit 14.6 on page 760 is the deferred portion of each year's actual return. This is the unrecognized gain or loss, and it is represented by the vertical distance between the actual return line and expected return line in Figure 14.3. Note that in six of the years (1993, 1995, 1996, 1997, 1998, and 1999), this deferral increases pension expense since it *reduces* the pension expense return deduction *down* to the expected return. In 1994, 2000, and 2001, the deferral adjustments reduce pension expense since these amounts *increase* the return that is deducted in computing pension expense.

The smoothing effect that results from the deferral component of the current period's actual return on plan assets is illustrated in Exhibit 14.7 (the data there are taken from GE's 1999 and 2000 pension footnotes). We first compute pension expense without deferring the unexpected return, then we calculate pension expense with adjustment for the deferral.

EXHIBIT 14.7	**General Electric Company**

Smoothing Effect of Deferring Unexpected Gains or Losses

($ in millions)		1999		2000
Without Deferral				
Component 1: Service cost		$ 693		$ 780
Component 2: Interest cost		1,804		1,966
Actual return on plan assets		(8,472)		(1,287)
Pension expense (income) *without deferral*				
of unexpected gain or loss		$(5,975) **CR**		$1,459 **DR**

Year-to-year "swing" of $7,434

With Deferral				
Component 1: Service cost		$ 693		$ 780
Component 2: Interest cost		1,804		1,966
Actual return on plan assets	(8,472)		(1,287)	
Deferral of unexpected gain (or loss)	5,065		(2,467)	
Component 3: Expected return on plan assets		(3,407)		(3,754)
Pension expense (income) *with deferral*				
of unexpected return		$(910) **CR**		$(1,008) **CR**

Year-to-year "swing" of $98

Looking at the data in Exhibit 14.6 on the opposite page, in 2000 the actual return on plan assets was $1.287 million, which was $2.467 billion *below* the expected return of $3.754 billion. In 1999 the actual return was $8.472 billion, which was $5.065 billion *higher* than the expected return of $3.407 billion. As these two years illustrate, the deferred portion of the current period's return can either increase or decrease pension expense. Without deferral, GE's pension expense would have gone from a $5.975 billion *credit* in 1999 to a $1.459 billion *debit* in 2000, a swing of $7.434 billion.[8] By deferring the unexpected gain or loss, the year-to-year change is reduced to only $98 million, as shown in Exhibit 14.7.

Companies are free to use a rate for computing the *expected* return on plan assets that differs from the discount rate used for service and interest cost. That makes it possible to lower pension expense in the short-run by using an expected asset return rate that is higher than the discount rate. Large disparities between the two rates affect the pension expense calculation and should be

ANALYSIS

---

[8] These numbers ignore any additional amortization due to components 4, 5, or 6. GE's earnings before taxes and accounting changes were $15.577 billion and $18.446 billion in 1999 and 2000, respectively. So reducing the pension expense "swing" by $7.336 billion (that is, $7.434 billion versus $98 million) is significant in relation to pre-tax earnings.

carefully monitored by analysts since these disparities represent a possible earnings management vehicle.

The December 2003 revision of *SFAS No. 132* has made it easier for statement readers to evaluate the reasonableness of the assumptions firms use in selecting the expected return on plan assets. Firms must now provide a table showing the percentage composition of the fair value of plan assets broken down by categories—equity securities, debt securities, real estate and all other assets—at each balance sheet date. In addition, *SFAS No. 132* now requires a narrative description of both:

1. the assumptions used to determine the expected long-term rate of return on assets, and
2. the investment policies and strategies used for plan assets including target allocation percentages for major categories of plan assets.

This information should allow analysts to assess the correspondence between the expected return rate used and the composition of the pension plan's assets and investment strategy.

HOW COMPONENT 4 IS MEASURED The cumulative amount of the deferred gains and losses are recorded off the books and monitored. If gains and losses do not offset one another over time, the cumulative off-balance sheet deferred amounts will grow excessively large. When this happens, some adjustment is needed to correct for the past smoothing. This is the role of component 4—recognized gains or losses.

Cumulative off-balance sheet net gains or losses can arise from three causes:

1. Cumulative differences between actual and expected returns on pension plan assets—as illustrated previously
2. Cumulative differences between actuarial assumptions and actual experience—for example, employee turnover, pay increases, and longevity beyond retirement
3. Changes in assumptions—for example, a change in the discount rate used for computing service cost and interest cost.

Because pension accounting requires numerous estimates of future events, differences between forecasted amounts and subsequent occurrences should be expected. These differences mean that *past* measures of pension expense were misstated:

- Cumulative asset return differences mean that the difference between actual return on plan assets and expected return on plan assets did not offset one another over time.
- Cumulative actuarial assumption differences mean that service cost (component 1) was either over- or understated.
- Changes in the assumed discount rate mean both service cost (component 1) and interest cost (component 2) were misstated in some previous years.

Rather than requiring the total correction be made at one time, the FASB again opted for a smoothing approach and allowed the correction for cumulative *past* errors to be spread over a series of *future* years. This is illustrated in the computation of the amounts of components 4 through 6, which follows.

These misstatements of *past* pension expense exist because the FASB acceded to corporate managers' dislike for income volatility and opted to smooth period-to-period fluctuations. *SFAS No. 87* does not require each year's results to reflect actual returns on plan assets or observed actuarial outcomes. *However, if the smoothing adjustments do not offset one another over time, the periodic differences will ultimately accumulate and exceed some threshold level. The FASB believes these past errors must be corrected once this threshold is exceeded.*

Here's how the component 4 adjustment mechanism threshold works. First, at the *start* of each reporting year, the cumulative unrecognized off-balance sheet gain (or loss) is computed.

Second, a materiality threshold called the **corridor** is created. This threshold is defined as 10% of the *larger* of the following two numbers:

1. The present value of pension obligations based on assumed future compensation levels—called the **projected benefit obligation (PBO)**, or
2. The **market-related value (MRV)** of pension plan assets.

> In *SFAS No. 87*, "market-related value" of pension plan assets is a technical term. It can be either (1) the fair market value of the assets, or (2) some moving-average type smoothed value that recognizes changes in value more slowly (over not more than five years).

Third, a portion of this cumulative gain or loss will be amortized over current and future years if it exceeds the 10% threshold. That is, a portion of the excess cumulative gain or loss above the 10% corridor is amortized straight-line over the estimated **average remaining service period** of active employees. We'll now illustrate the operation of this threshold corridor step-by-step:

> The average remaining service period is an actuarial computation—it's an estimate of the average number of years over which existing employees are expected to continue on the job.

On January 1, 2005 Dore Corporation had a cumulative unrecognized gain of $1,600,000 arising from (1) differences between actual and expected returns on plan assets, (2) differences between actuarial assumptions and actual experience, and (3) changes in interest rate assumptions. The market-related value (MRV) of pension plan assets on that date was $10,000,000, and the projected benefit obligation (PBO) was $8,500,000. The estimated average remaining service period of active employees is 15 years.

Figure 14.4 shows the steps in computing component 4—recognized gains or losses.

Figure 14.4

COMPUTING COMPONENT 4—RECOGNIZED GAINS OR LOSSES

Step 1. Compute the 10% threshold.
  a. Compare beginning of year amounts of market-related asset value (MRAV) of pension plan assets and projected benefit obligation (PBO).

MRAV $10,000,000	⟷	PBO $8,500,000

  b. Select the larger one, that is, MRAV of $10,000,000.
  c. Multiply the larger one by 10%; so $10,000,000 x 10% = $1,000,000. *This is the 10% threshold.*

Step 2. Determine whether the threshold is triggered.
  a. Compare beginning of year cumulative unrecognized gain or loss (CUGOL) to the threshold computed in Step 1.c.

CUGOL $1,600,000	⟷	Threshold $1,000,000

  b. The threshold is triggered because CUGOL—a cumulative gain in this example—exceeds the threshold by $600,000.
  c. So component 4—recognized gains or losses—will appear in pension expense for the current year.

Step 3. Compute the current year component 4 amortization.
  a. Obtain the average remaining service period (ARSP) figure from the actuary. Here, ARSP equals 15 years.
  b. Divide the amount by which CUGOL exceeds the threshold (Step 2.b) by ARSP.

  c. The quotient from Step 3.b, $40,000 (that is $600,000 ÷ 15), is the component 4 amount for the current year. Pension expense will be reduced by $40,000 in the current year.

The 10% threshold is computed by first comparing the size of the MRV ($10,000,000) with the PBO ($8,500,000) and choosing the larger—the $10,000,000 MRV in this instance. This $10,000,000 is then multiplied by 10% to arrive at the threshold of $1,000,000 (see step 1 in Figure 14.4). Because the cumulative unrecognized gain of $1,600,000 is larger than the $1,000,000 threshold, the threshold is triggered (see step 2). This means that component 4—recognized gains or losses—will be included in computing pension expense for the year. The $600,000 amount in excess of the threshold will be amortized over 15 years. This amortization means that pension expense component 4 will be *credited* for $40,000 of the unrecognized gain ($600,000 ÷ 15) thereby *reducing* pension expense (see step 3).

If there were no future misestimates, the $560,000 unamortized excess—$600,000 minus the $40,000 of 2005 amortization—would be totally taken into income over the ensuing 14 years. Realistically, pension accounting requires many estimates of uncertain future events. Uncertainty means that further misestimates are likely. Consequently, *SFAS No. 87* requires that the computation illustrated in the example be redone at the start of each subsequent year to determine that year's pension expense component 4. So, just because component 4 was triggered in 2005 doesn't necessarily mean it will be triggered again in 2006.

We hope that this example will help you understand why the FASB chose the projected benefit obligation and the market-related value of pension plan assets as the two benchmarks that potentially trigger the component 4 amortization. Measures of projected benefit obligations and plan assets constitute the "critical 10% corridor" because the factors giving rise to the cumulative gain or loss represent misestimates of the "real" pension plan obligations and assets.

In other words, **cumulative asset gains or losses** occur because the annual interest rate chosen for the expected return on plan assets in the computation of pension expense either understated or overstated the actual increase in pension assets. Similarly, **cumulative obligation gains or losses** occur because the amount of service cost and/or interest cost included in pension expense either understated or overstated the actual increase in pension obligations. Thus, obligations and assets constitute the appropriate benchmarks for assessing when the cumulative error is "excessive." The 10% threshold is simply an arbitrary measure of this "excessiveness."

COMPONENT 5—AMORTIZATION OF UNRECOGNIZED TRANSITION ASSET OR OBLIGATION

Before *SFAS No. 87* was issued, there was usually a disparity between the value of pension plan assets and the present value of the pension obligation. Some plans were overfunded (that is, assets exceeded obligations), while others were underfunded (obligations exceeded assets). The FASB sought to reduce future periods' pension expense charges for overfunded plans and to increase future pension expense for underfunded plans.

The following example illustrates the FASB's approach:

Rett Corporation adopted *SFAS No. 87* on January 1, 1987. On that date the fair value of the pension plan assets was $238,000,000, and the projected benefit obligation was $202,000,000. The actuarial estimate of the average remaining service period of employees who are expected to receive benefits under the plan was 18 years.

The FASB required that the amount of overfunding or underfunding be computed at the time *SFAS No. 87* was first adopted. To determine the funding status, a firm must compare the amount of the pension liability and the pension plan assets. The difference—the **transition asset or transition liability**—is amortized over the average remaining service period of employees who are expected to receive benefits under the plan. Rett's $202,000,000 projected benefit obligation (PBO) is the discounted present value of the expected pension payments, which takes into account expected pay raises over future years. This PBO is then compared to the fair value of plan assets—here $238,000,000. The funded status of the plan at adoption was an *overfunding* of $36,000,000. This transition asset amount will be amortized as component 5 over 18 years on a straight-line basis. Therefore, component 5 for Rett Corporation will be a $2,000,000 *credit* (reduction) to pension expense for each of the years 1987 through 2004. (Amortization of a transition liability results in a debit—addition—to pension expense.)

> However, if the average remaining service period is less than 15 years, the firm may still elect to use a 15-year amortization period.

Components 5 and 4 both represent a smoothing approach for correcting *past* errors in the computation of pension expense. In the case of component 5, the pension expense errors arose prior to the adoption of *SFAS No. 87*—that is, a plan that was overfunded at transition presumably used asset earnings rate assumptions that were too low, or service cost estimates that were too high, or both. In the case of component 4, similar errors arose *after* the adoption of *SFAS No. 87*. In either case the effect is the same: Past errors in computing pension expense are corrected in a smoothed fashion over current and *future* years.

> Since *SFAS No. 87* was issued in 1987, the transition asset or liability is now fully amortized for many firms. Consequently, component 5 appears infrequently today.

COMPONENT 6—RECOGNIZED PRIOR SERVICE COST Pension plans are frequently amended to provide increased benefits to employees. A firm may do this because increases in retirees' living costs warrant an increase in pension benefits. When a firm retroactively enhances the benefits provided by its pension plan, it means past pension expense and pension funding—which were both based on the "old" pension plan terms—were too low. This also means that when a firm enhances its pension plan, it immediately increases its projected benefit obligation under the plan. The dollar amount of the increase in the projected benefit obligation due to plan enhancements is called **prior service cost**.

> Pension plan amendments sometimes reduce benefits—for instance, when unions "give back" previously obtained benefits to help the firm avoid bankruptcy and preserve jobs.

Here's an example that illustrates how prior service cost arises:

> Schiller Corporation's pension plan granted employees a pension of 2% of ending salary at retirement for each year of service to a maximum of 30 years. Therefore, an employee with 30 years of service at Schiller could retire with a pension equal to 60% of his or her salary at retirement.
>
> Management at Schiller Corporation now believes that the 60% pension maximum is inadequate given existing general economic conditions. The pension plan is retroactively changed on January 1, 2005. Under the revised plan, employees qualify for a pension of 2.25% of ending salary at retirement for each year of service, again to a maximum of 30 years. Under the revised plan, the maximum pension is 67.5% of the employee's salary at retirement (2.25% × 30 years).
>
> Schiller's plan enhancement increased the projected benefit obligation by $14,000,000. The average remaining service period of employees expected to receive benefits under the plan is 10 years.

Firms retroactively enhance—or "sweeten"—pension plans for various reasons. One is to generate employee goodwill and loyalty to the organization, thereby retaining a quality workforce. Another reason for retroactive pension enhancement is a result of union demands in labor negotiations.

Even though these sweeteners are computed on the basis of services rendered in prior periods, the benefits to the firm will be realized in future periods. The benefits of retroactive plan enhancements are realized by the firm in future periods because of decreased employee turnover or better labor relations. Accordingly, *SFAS No. 87* allows these $14,000,000 of prior service costs to be amortized into pension expense on a straight-line basis over the expected remaining 10-year service lives of employees who are expected to receive benefits under the plan. So $1,400,000 would be added to pension expense over each of the next 10 years (that is, $14,000,000 ÷ 10). This is the role of component 6.

Relative Magnitude of Pension Expense Components

Figure 14.5 shows the relative magnitude of the various components of pension expense for a sample of firms over the 1987–1990 period.[9] The bars above the zero line represent debits that *increased* pension expense; the bars below the line depict credits that *decreased* pension expense. The bar at the end of each year's data (PENX) represents that portion of the total charges to pension expense that remain after offsetting the credit items against the debit items (the **net pension expense** reported on the income statement).

Figure 14.5

PENSION EXPENSE
COMPONENTS (1987–1990)

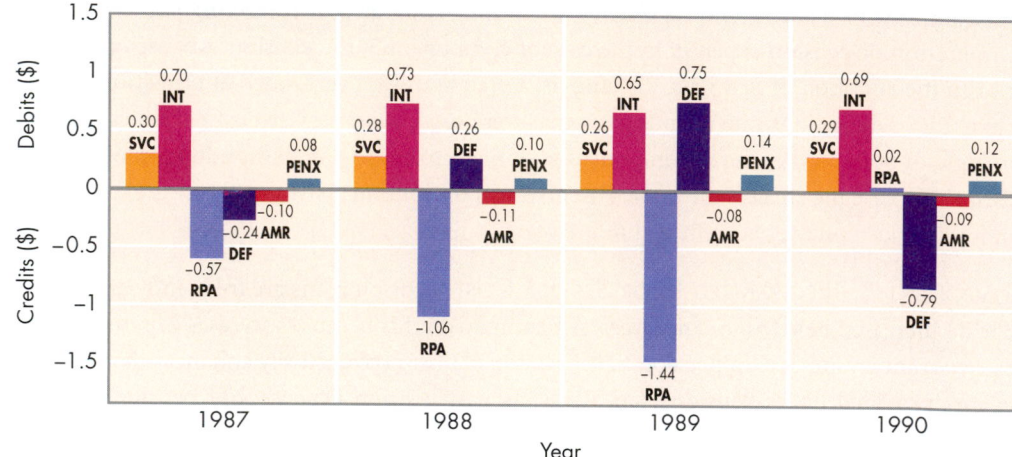

SVC = Service cost
INT = Interest cost
RPA = Actual return on plan assets
DEF = Deferred portion of current period return (actual – expected)
AMR = Net amortization of cumulative unrecognized gains (losses)
        and net transition assets (liability)
PENX = Net pension expense

All amounts are shown in dollars per share.

Be sure you observe three items in Figure 14.5. First, for the average firm, the service cost (SVC) and interest cost (INT) components are fairly stable through time. The interest component is more than twice as large as the service cost component (an average of $0.69 per share versus $0.28 per share, respectively, over the four years), which means the cumulative pension obligation from past years of service far exceeds the obligation that arises from the current period employee service. One potential explanation for this is the prevalence of retroactive plan enhancements; another is an aging workforce.

Second, in contrast to the stable service and interest cost components, the actual return on plan assets (RPA) varies considerably over this four-year period, ranging from a high of $1.44 per share in 1989 to a low of −$0.02 per share in 1990. This variability reflects the general fortunes of stocks during this period, which comprise a major portion of many pension fund portfolios. Without the smoothing effects that result from deferring the unexpected return on plan assets (as *SFAS No. 87* allows), pension expense would have been quite volatile over this period. With the deferral (DEF) of unrecognized gains or losses (note that in some years this increases pension expense while in other years it decreases pension expense), the volatility in actual return is offset, leaving a relatively stable credit adjustment to pension expense for the *expected* return on plan assets.

Third, the net amortization of components 4 through 6 (AMR) is a credit to pension expense of roughly $0.09 per share. This suggests that the average firm's pension plan was overfunded at

---

[9] The average values for the 1987–1990 period are based on a sample of 300 firms representing a broad cross section of industries. See M. E. Barth, W. H. Beaver, and W. R. Landsman, "A Structural Analysis of Pension Disclosures Under *SFAS 87* and Their Relation to Share Prices," *Financial Analysts Journal* (January–February, 1993), pp. 18–26.

transition and/or that there are cumulative unrecognized gains being amortized as a reduction to pension expense.

The net effect of the various smoothing procedures allowed under *SFAS No. 87* is apparent in the pattern of *net* pension expense amounts—the PENX bar—in Figure 14.5. Although individual components of pension expense are relatively large and actual return on plan assets is quite volatile, the net pension expense amount is relatively stable, averaging about $0.11 per share over the period.

RECAP

Estimates pervade pension accounting. When these estimates need to be adjusted, the adjustment could conceivably be recorded all at once. Doing this would make pension expense volatile from year to year. The FASB chose a different approach for adjusting pension estimates and plan changes. Components 4 through 6 are designed to be smoothing devices. When an adjustment is made, its effect is initially deferred and brought into pension expense slowly over a series of future years.

The Journal Entry to Record Pension Expense and Funding

To illustrate the journal entry for pension expense, let's assume that Adess Corporation disclosed the following components in its pension footnote at December 31, 2005:

Service cost	$23,000
Interest cost	42,500
Expected return on plan assets	(38,250)
Components 4–6	22,750
2005 Pension expense	$50,000

In years in which the entire amount of pension expense—$50,000 in this example—is funded by payments to the plan trustee, the entry is straightforward:

DR Pension expense	$50,000	
CR Cash		$50,000

However, a firm is not required to fund the full amount of the pension expense provision each period. (Factors that affect firms' funding policies are discussed in the next section.) When the amount of funding differs from the recognized expense, an additional balancing debit or credit must be established. If Adess Corporation chose to fund $53,000 in 2005, the entry would be:

DR Pension expense	$50,000	
DR Prepaid pension cost	3,000	
CR Cash		$53,000

The "Prepaid pension cost" account would be shown as an *asset* on the December 31, 2005 balance sheet.

If Adess had chosen to make a funding payment of only $44,000 in 2005, the entry would be:

DR Pension expense	$50,000	
CR Cash		$44,000
CR Unfunded accrued pension cost		6,000

The "Unfunded accrued pension cost" account in this entry would appear on the balance sheet as a *liability*.

If the funding ratio falls below an average of 90% for three consecutive plan years, or 80% in any one year, additional funding requirements may apply. In addition, when pension plans have been retroactively "sweetened," the prior service costs generated by the sweetening must be funded over 30 to 40 years. Furthermore, shortfalls arising from changes in assumptions and actuarial gains and losses must be funded over periods ranging from 5 to 30 years. The rules are very complex, so for details, see H. E. Winklevoss, *Pension Mathematics With Numerical Illustrations*, 2nd ed. (Philadelphia: University of Pennsylvania Press, 1993). Also see C. Bryan-Low, "Gloom Lifting for Pension Plans," *Wall Street Journal* (August 15, 2003).

ERISA has its own guidelines for determining whether a plan is over-funded or underfunded. These guidelines differ from those in *SFAS No. 87* because ERISA allows plan sponsors to use a broader range of actuarial and other assumptions.

The Pension Funding Decision

Legislation and income tax rules have a strong impact on pension plan funding. We first explain why. Then we outline the factors that firms with defined benefit pension plans use to determine the amount of annual pension funding.

The U.S. Congress enacted legislation to regulate private U.S. pension plans in 1974. The Employees Retirement Income Security Act (ERISA) was designed to protect workers covered by company- or industry-sponsored pension plans. This legislation was deemed necessary because some companies with largely unfunded pension plans went out of business. When Studebaker Corporation—once a major automobile manufacturer—experienced severe economic hardship and declared bankruptcy in 1964, its pension liabilities greatly exceeded its plan assets. The Studebaker retirees were unprotected and consequently lost most of their promised pension. Such hardships ultimately motivated legislation designed to prevent recurrences. ERISA established minimum funding guidelines. A pension plan sponsor is obliged to fund at least the annual service cost computed under the plan. The requirement to fund service cost is suspended if the plan is *over*funded at the start of the plan year.

The U.S. income tax law also influences pension plan funding. Because plan contributions are tax deductible—subject to a constraint discussed later—and plan earnings are nontaxable to the plan sponsor, there is a tax incentive to overfund pension plans. Because of this incentive, the tax law places limits on the deductibility of contributions to already overfunded pension plans. Consequently, firms with overfunded plans limit subsequent funding to an amount that is deductible for tax purposes.

Finally, firms with pension plans have a wide range of other uses for cash flows generated by operating activities. Examples include plant expansion, corporate acquisitions, debt retirement, and dividend increases. So firms sometimes reduce or even forego funding of the current period's pension expense—provided minimum ERISA funding guidelines are satisfied—to meet competing investment or financing cash needs.

The longer term pension funding strategy that a firm chooses to follow is determined not only by its internal cash flow needs but also by many complex economic forces. Two studies seek to explain firms' funding strategies by examining the relationship between **funding ratios**—plan assets divided by accrued pension obligations—and a variety of variables that represent the economic incentives (and costs) associated with pension funding.[10] These economic incentives can be broadly classified as (1) tax incentives, (2) finance incentives, (3) labor incentives, and (4) contracting/political cost incentives.[11]

The findings were:

- Firms with high marginal tax rates tend to have higher funding ratios—higher marginal tax rates provide an incentive to overfund.
- Firms with less stringent capital constraints and larger union membership tend to have higher funding ratios.
- Firms with more "precarious" debt/equity ratios (that is, firms close to violating debt covenant restrictions) tend to fund a lower proportion of their pension obligations.

In general, variables designed to measure political costs were not found to be significant determinants of pension funding ratios.

---

[10] See J. R. Francis and S. A. Reiter, "Determinants of Corporate Pension Funding Strategy," *Journal of Accounting and Economics* (April 1987), pp. 35–60; and J. K. Thomas, "Corporate Taxes and Defined Benefit Pension Plans," *Journal of Accounting and Economics* (July 1988), pp. 199–238.

[11] The reader is referred to the articles cited in footnote 10 for a more complete discussion of each of these incentives and their hypothesized effect on firms' pension funding strategy.

While economic incentives appear to influence long-run corporate pension funding strategies, our understanding of this multidimensional decision is far from complete.

RECAP

The Pension Footnote

Exhibit 14.8 on this and the following page reproduces the pension footnote from the 2001 Annual Report of General Electric Company. We will use this disclosure to discuss several elements of pension reporting.

EXHIBIT 14.8	General Electric Company

Edited, Condensed 2001 Annual Report Pension Benefits Footnote

Principal pension plans are the GE Pension Plan and the GE Supplementary Pension Plan.

The GE Pension Plan provides benefits to certain U.S. employees based on the greater of a formula recognizing career earnings or a formula recognizing length of service and final average earnings. Benefit provisions are subject to collective bargaining. The GE Pension Plan covers approximately 503,000 participants. . . .

The GE Supplementary Pension Plan is a pay-as-you-go plan providing supplementary retirement benefits primarily to higher-level, longer-service U.S. employees.

Details of the effect on operations of principal pension plans . . . follow:

Effect on Operations

($ in millions)	2001	2000
Service cost for benefits earned[a]	$ 884	$ 780
Interest cost on benefit obligation	2,065	1,966
Expected return on plan assets	(4,327)	(3,754)
Net actuarial gain recognized	(961)	(819)
SFAS No. 87 transition gain	—	(154)
Prior service cost	244	237
Income from pensions	$(2,095)	$(1,744)

[a]Net of participant contributions.

Funding policy for the GE Pension Plan is to contribute amounts sufficient to meet minimum funding requirements as set forth in employee benefit and tax laws plus such additional amounts as GE may determine to be appropriate. GE has not made contributions to the GE Pension Plan since 1987 because the fully funded status of the Plan precludes a current tax deduction and because any GE contribution would require payment of excise taxes.

Changes in the projected benefit obligation for principal pension plans follow.

Projected Benefit Obligation

($ in millions)	2001	2000
Balance at January 1	$28,535	$25,522
Service cost for benefits earned[a]	884	780
Interest cost on benefit obligation	2,065	1,966
Plan amendments	—	1,155
Participant contributions	141	140
Actuarial loss[b]	889	970
Benefits paid	(2,091)	(1,998)
Balance at December 31	$30,423	$28,535

[a]Net of participant contributions.
[b]Principally associated with discount rate changes.

(*continued on next page*)

EXHIBIT 14.8	General Electric Company *(continued)*

Changes in the fair value of assets for principal pension plans follow.

Fair Value of Assets

($ in millions)	2001	2000
Balance at January 1	$49,757	$50,243
Actual return on plan assets	(2,876)	1,287
Employer contributions	75	85
Participant contributions	141	140
Benefits paid	(2,091)	(1,998)
Balance at December 31	$45,006	$49,757

Plan assets are held in trust and consist mainly of common stock and fixed-income investments. GE common stock represented 8.6% and 9.2% of trust assets at year-end 2001 and 2000, respectively.

GE recorded assets and liabilities for principal pension plans as follows:

Prepaid Pension Asset/Liability

December 31 ($ in millions)	2001	2000
Funded status[a]	$14,583	$21,222
Unrecognized prior service cost	1,373	1,617
Unrecognized net actuarial gain	(3,541)	(12,594)
Net asset recognized	$12,415	$10,245
Amounts recorded in the Statement of Financial Position:		
→ Prepaid pension asset	$13,740	$11,377
→ Accrued pension liability	(1,325)	(1,132)
Net asset recognized	$12,415	$10,245

[a]Fair value of assets less PBO, as shown in the preceding tables.

Actuarial assumptions used to determine costs and benefit obligations for principal pension plans follow.

Actuarial Assumptions

December 31	2001	2000
Discount rate	7.25%	7.5%
Compensation increases	5.0	5.0
Return on assets for the year	9.5	9.5

Experience gains and losses, as well as the effects of changes in actuarial assumptions and plan provisions, are amortized over the average future service period of employees.

The actuarial assumptions portion of G.E.'s footnote in Exhibit 14.8 on this page provides information about the discount rate (7.25% in 2001 and 7.5% in 2000) used in measuring components 1 and 2 of pension expense, the assumed rate of increase in salary levels built into the projected benefit obligation computation (5%), and the expected return on plan assets (9.5%).

In the next section, we discuss other information contained in Exhibit 14.8 and explain how we can determine the funded status of the pension plans.

Funded Status Disclosure

We explained earlier that neither pension plan assets nor liabilities appear on the balance sheet of the plan sponsor but are instead shown on the separate statements of the plan trustee. The Wildcat Corporation example (Exhibits 14.2 through 14.4) showed that when the future was known with certainty the (off-balance sheet) pension assets are exactly equal to the (off-balance sheet) pension liability. In the more complex real world, where future events are uncertain and changes in pension assumptions occur, ***the off-balance sheet pension assets and liabilities will usually differ.*** When pension assets exceed liabilities, a plan is **overfunded**. If pension liabilities exceed plan assets, a plan is **underfunded**. Since both the pension plan assets and liabilities are off the plan sponsor's balance sheet, the **funded status** of the plan can only be determined from footnote disclosures. This funded status disclosure is important to statement readers, since the plan sponsor— the reporting entity—is ultimately responsible for underfunded pension plans. Moreover, sometimes the reporting entity can reclaim a portion of the excess in overfunded plans. So, information about the funded status helps analysts assess the financial condition of the sponsor. In this section we illustrate and interpret the funded status footnote disclosure.

To understand the funded status of a plan, we must first understand what factors cause the pension plan assets and liabilities to change over time. Figure 14.6 displays the causes for increases and decreases in plan assets. *SFAS No. 132* requires that plan sponsors disclose these increases and decreases in the pension footnote.[12] Using G.E.'s fair value of assets disclosures on page 770 in Exhibit 14.8 as a concrete example, we discuss the separate elements of Figure 14.6:

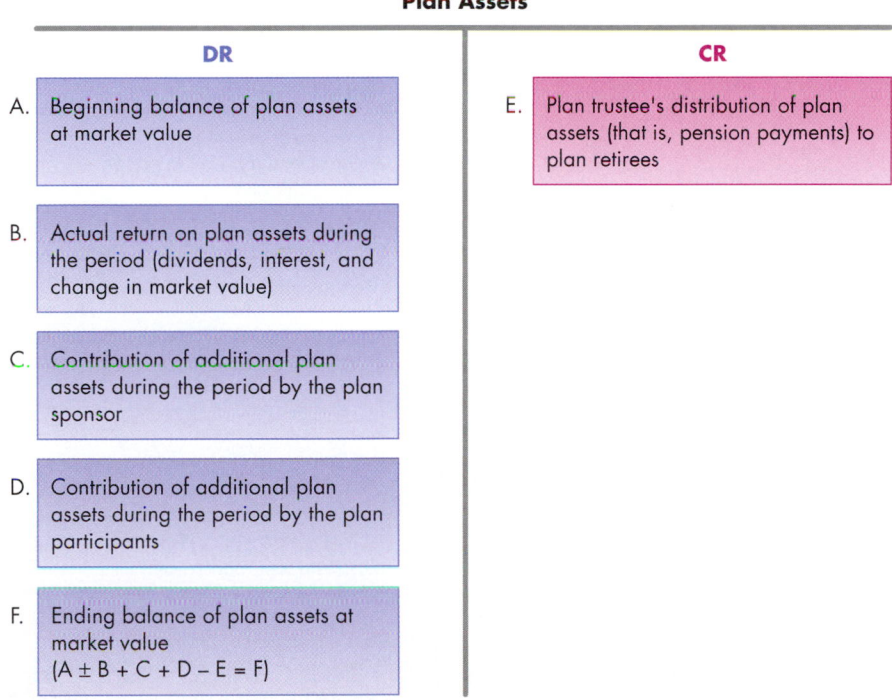

Plan Assets

DR	CR
A. Beginning balance of plan assets at market value	E. Plan trustee's distribution of plan assets (that is, pension payments) to plan retirees
B. Actual return on plan assets during the period (dividends, interest, and change in market value)	
C. Contribution of additional plan assets during the period by the plan sponsor	
D. Contribution of additional plan assets during the period by the plan participants	
F. Ending balance of plan assets at market value ($A \pm B + C + D - E = F$)	

Figure 14.6

CAUSES OF INCREASES AND DECREASES IN PLAN ASSETS

- Item A represents the beginning-of-period market value of the pension plan assets. For G.E., the January 1, 2001 amount totaled $49,757 million.
- The dollar value of plan assets is increased by Item B, the actual return on plan assets. In very bad investment years, Item B can be negative, thereby reducing plan assets. G.E.'s 2001 actual return on plan assets was a negative $2,876 million.
- Plan assets are further increased by Item C, the amount that the plan sponsor funds during the period. G.E.'s 2001 contributions were $75 million.[13]

---

[12] In addition to the items shown in Figure 14.6, *SFAS No. 132* (para. 5) requires—if applicable—disclosure of (1) changes in plan assets arising from exchange rate changes for pension plans of certain foreign subsidiaries, and (2) changes in plan assets arising from business combinations, divestitures, and plan settlements.

[13] The contributions were made to the GE Supplementary Pension Plan, which is a pay-as-you-go plan. The other plan— the GE Pension Plan—is fully funded. We are told in Exhibit 14.8 that G.E. has not contributed to this plan since 1987 because doing so yields no tax deduction and triggers payment of excise taxes.

Another measure of the pension liability is called the **accumulated benefit obligation**, or **ABO**. The ABO differs from the PBO because the ABO does not include projected salary increases between the statement date and the expected retirement date of employees. The PBO does.

- Plan assets are also increased by Item D, contributions by plan participants. During 2001, contributions by G.E. plan participants totaled $141 million.
- Retirees receive benefits during the period; these benefits are disbursed by the plan trustee and reduce plan assets, as indicated by Item E. Benefits paid to participants by the plan trustee in 2001 were $2,091 million.
- The end-of-period market value of plan assets is Item F. This amount totaled $45,006 million for the G.E. plans.

Figure 14.7 shows changes in the pension plan liability—the PBO. *SFAS No. 132* also requires that plan sponsors disclose these increases and decreases in the pension footnote.[14] We use G.E.'s projected benefit obligation disclosures in Exhibit 14.8 on page 769 to explain the elements in Figure 14.7:

Figure 14.7

CAUSES OF INCREASES AND DECREASES IN PROJECTED BENEFIT OBLIGATION (PBO)

Projected Benefit Obligation

DR	CR
M. Plan trustee's distribution of plan assets (that is, pension payments) to plan retirees	G. Beginning balance. Start-of-period discounted present value of expected pension benefits that will ultimately be paid
	H. Service cost during the period
	I. Interest cost during the period
	J. Change in promised benefits arising from plan amendments or curtailments during the period
	K. Contribution of additional plan assets during the period by plan participants
	L. Actuarial gains or losses during the period from changes in assumptions (that is, mortality and turnover rates, interest rates, and so on.)
	N. Ending balance. End-of-period discounted present value of expected pension benefits $(G + H + I \pm J + K \pm L - M = N)$

- Item G is the start-of-period present value of expected future benefits that will ultimately be paid both to currently active and already retired employees. The 2001 G.E. beginning amount is $28,535 million.
- Item H represents the increase in benefits that active employees continue to earn from additional years of work. This increase in the projected benefit obligation is service cost. G.E.'s service cost in 2001 was $884 million.

---

[14] In addition to the items shown in Figure 14.7, *SFAS No. 132* (para. 5) requires—if applicable—disclosure of (1) changes in the PBO arising from exchange rate changes for pension plans of certain foreign subsidiaries, and (2) changes in the PBO arising from business combinations, divestitures, curtailments, plan settlements, and special termination benefits.

- As time passes, the present value of future pension benefit payouts becomes larger because the number of discount periods is getting smaller as employees approach retirement. This increase in the discounted present value of the liability represents interest cost, which increases the PBO (as shown in Item I). G.E.'s 2001 interest cost was $2,065 million.
- Changes in economic and other social conditions cause firms to adjust promised benefits, as indicated by Item J. These prior service cost adjustments either raise the PBO (when the plan is sweetened) or reduce the PBO (when benefits are curtailed). G.E. did not alter promised benefits in 2001. Consequently, this amount is zero.
- The projected benefit obligation is also increased by Item K, contributions by plan participants. During 2001, such contributions totaled $141 million.
- The assumptions used in estimating the pension liability lead to gains or losses due to changing medical, lifestyle, and economic conditions. Denoted by Item L, these increases (or decreases) in the PBO can also arise from revised interest rate assumptions. Because of discount rate decreases, this loss totaled $889 million in 2001.
- Item M represents the payout of retirement benefits to participants. This is the offsetting debit to the Item E credit in Figure 14.6. The 2001 amount for G.E. was $2,091 million.
- Finally, the ending PBO balance (Item N) is the net result of each of the preceding items. This amount totaled $30,423 million for the G.E. plans.

Because the pension assets and pension liabilities do not appear on the sponsor's balance sheet and because the plan can be either over- or underfunded, disclosure of the funded status of the plan is required under GAAP. Next, we examine this disclosure.

Reconciling Funded Status to Balance Sheet Amounts

The smoothing objective that pervades *SFAS No. 87* keeps numerous gains and losses that have already occurred off the balance sheet and income statement. These deferred gains and losses are brought into income slowly over current and future years via components 4 through 6:

- Recognized gains or losses
- Amortization of unrecognized transition asset or obligation
- Recognized prior service cost

Until these past gains and losses are totally amortized, the balance sheet will not reflect the current *funded status* of the pension plan. *The current funded status of a pension plan at a given date is the difference between the fair value of the plan assets at that date and the discounted present value of the expected liability.* This liability is computed using projected future compensation levels—this is the projected benefit obligation (PBO) previously discussed in conjunction with component 4. Exhibit 14.8 shows the current economic status of General Electric Company's pension plan at December 31, 2001. Plan assets totaled $45,006 million (highlighted on p. 770) while the projected benefit obligation was only $30,423 million (highlighted on p. 769). Therefore, the G.E. plan was overfunded by the excess of plan assets over plan liabilities—$14,583 million. *This $14,583 million represents the current funded status of the pension plan at December 31, 2001.*

Because of the recognition delays that pervade *SFAS No. 87*, this $14,583 million does not correspond to the pension amounts shown on the December 31, 2001 balance sheet. The FASB believes the current funded status of the pension plan at the balance sheet date constitutes the benchmark against which companies' balance sheet pension accounts ought to be compared. For this reason, the FASB requires a footnote disclosure that reconciles—explains the difference between—the *current* funded status of the pension plan and the *recorded* balance sheet amounts. The table labeled "Prepaid pension asset/liability" in Exhibit 14.8 (p. 770) is designed to provide this reconciliation.[15] Scrutiny of this table confirms that the plan is overfunded by $14,583 million (see highlight), that is, assets of $45,006 million minus PBO of $30,423 million. Despite this overfunding, there is an accrued pension *liability* of $1,325 million on the balance sheet as well as a prepaid pension asset (see arrows in Exhibit 14.8, p. 770). The purpose of this G.E. footnote section is to provide a reconciliation between the $14,583 million current overfunded status of the plan and the $12,415 million net pension asset shown on the balance sheet (that is, the net of the two arrows: $13,740 − $1,325 = $12,415).

G.E.'s Exhibit 14.8 "Prepaid pension asset/liability" disclosure closely mirrors the *SFAS No. 132* format for this reconciliation. Unfortunately, the FASB's "preferred" format is not intuitively easy to understand. So we have rearranged the G.E. "Prepaid pension asset/liability" disclosure section of Exhibit 14.8 into a somewhat easier-to-understand format shown in Figure 14.8 for December 31, 2001.

Figure 14.8

GENERAL ELECTRIC COMPANY

Understanding the Funded Status Disclosure

Funded Status of Plans			Recognized / Unrecognized Amounts		
Plan assets at fair value	$45,006	DR	**Recognized amounts**		
Projected benefit obligation	(30,423)	CR	1. Prepaid pension asset included in consolidated balance sheet	$13,740	DR
			2. Accrued pension liability included in consolidated balance sheet	(1,325)	CR
			Unrecognized amounts		
			3. Unrecognized prior service cost	(1,373)	CR
			4. Unrecognized actuarial gain	3,541	DR
Plan assets in excess of projected benefit obligation	$14,583	DR	Plan assets in excess of projected benefit obligation	$14,583	DR

This account is also called "unfunded accrued pension cost" and was illustrated in the journal entry on page 767. G.E. has both a prepaid pension asset and an accrued pension liability because cumulative funding exceeded cumulative pension expense on some plans and expense exceeded funding on the G.E. Supplementary Pension Plan, which the footnote indicates is a pay-as-you-go plan. *SFAS No. 132* (para. 6) requires separate disclosure of both the prepaid pension asset and the accrued pension liability.

The left side of the Figure 14.8 "T" account shows the funded status of G.E's pension plans at December 31, 2001. This $14,583 total represents the "real" economic position of the plan. But this $14,583 number differs from the net pension asset ($13,740 − $1,325 = $12,415) shown on the balance sheet (see "arrowed" items in Exhibit 14.8). The right side of the "T" account explains the items that cause this difference. Simply stated, the difference exists because only some of the items ("Recognized amounts") appear on the balance sheet. Other items ("Unrecognized amounts") are "off-balance sheet." These items explain the difference between the $14,583 real economic position of the plan and the $12,415 net amount that appears on the balance sheet.

We now discuss each of the numbered items on the right side of the reconciliation in Figure 14.8:

1. *Prepaid pension asset included in consolidated balance sheet.* This is the debit that is made to balance the journal entry when pension expense is less than pension funding. (See second entry on p. 767.) The cumulative amount of this excess of funding over expense in past years is $13,740 million at December 31, 2001.
2. *Accrued pension liability included in consolidated balance sheet.* This item represents the credit that arises when pension *expense* exceeds the amount of pension *funding*. (See third entry on p. 767.) The cumulative amount of this excess of expense over funding that occurred in past years totals $1,325 million at December 31, 2001.

---

[15] Typically, the terminology "funded status" is used by companies to identify this reconciliation in the footnote. G.E. is in the minority in not using this terminology.

3. *Unrecognized prior service cost.* General Electric enhanced the benefits provided to employees subsequent to adopting *SFAS No. 87*. This item is being amortized into pension expense over time in component 6—recognized prior service cost. Consequently, the as-yet unrecognized portion ($1,373 million) at December 31, 2001 is an off-balance sheet liability.

> The unrecognized *SFAS 87* transition asset was totally amortized by the end of 2000 (see Exhibit 14.8 p. 769). Consequently, this is no longer an off-balance sheet item and does not appear on the reconciliation.

4. *Unrecognized actuarial gain.* This $3,541 million number represents the cumulative amount of three elements: (1) the difference between the expected return on plan assets and the actual return; (2) the difference between actuarial assumptions and actual experience regarding mortality, turnover, etc.; and (3) the effects of changes in discount rate and other assumptions. Since the total is within the 10% corridor on December 31, 2001, none of this item will be amortized into income during 2002. Because the cumulative amount is an unrecognized gain, it represents an off-balance sheet asset.

By focusing on the funded status of the plan, the funded status portion of the pension footnote overcomes some of the confusing smoothing-driven complexities that pervade pension accounting. For example, General Electric's December 31, 2001 balance sheet reflects a net pension asset of $12,415 million (that is, a prepaid pension asset of $13,740 million minus an accrued pension liability of $1,325 million)

> At December 31, 2001, the fair value of plan assets is larger than the PBO. The corridor is therefore $4,500.6 million—that is, 10% of the assets of $45,006 million. The unrecognized actuarial gain of $3,541 million is smaller than this, so no portion of the gain will be amortized in 2002. Notice that the 10% corridor threshold was exceeded at the start of 2001 so amortization took place in 2001.

although the pension plan was overfunded by a larger amount—$14,583 million—on that date. The net on-balance sheet pension asset of $12,415 million exists because cash funding in certain past years was greater than the amount of those years' pension expense by $12,415 million. The reconciliation directs attention to the more important *current* funded status of the plan rather than to *past* funding decisions.

A thorough understanding of pension reporting rules and disclosures enables analysts to reconstruct the pension journal entry that General Electric made in 2001. The entry ($ in millions) was:

DR	Prepaid pension asset	$2,363	
CR	Income from pensions		$2,095
CR	Accrued pension liability		193
CR	Cash		75

The amount of the debit to the "Prepaid pension asset" account ($2,363 million) is the change in this account balance between the beginning and end of 2001—that is, $13,740 million minus $11,377 million (see the orange arrow in Exhibit 14.8). Similarly, the credit to "Accrued pension liability" is the 2001 change in that account, $1,325 million minus $1,132 million (see the red arrow in Exhibit 14.8).[16] The $2,095 credit to "Income from pensions" is the total shown in the "Effect on operations" portion of the footnote on p. 769 while the $75 credit to "Cash" is the amount of employer contributions reported in the "Fair value of assets" section on p. 770.[17]

---

[16] There is a separate debit to a prepaid asset account and credit to an accrued liability account because General Electric maintains several pension plans. For some plan(s), the amount of the plan pension expense apparently exceeded the amount of G.E.'s funding.

[17] Sometimes the journal entry for a particular firm won't balance using this change in statement amounts approach. The two most frequent explanations for the failure to balance are (1) foreign currency exchange rate changes and (2) acquisitions accounted for using the purchase method (discussed in Chapter 16).

Extracting Analytic Insights From the Footnote Disclosures

The funded status reconciliation in Exhibit 14.8 and Figure 14.8 provides insights regarding expected *future* pension-related cash flows. Firms with greatly overfunded pension plans have been tempting takeover targets in the past.[18] After such takeovers, acquirers could terminate the overfunded plan, set up a new plan whose funding just equaled the liability, and use the excess funds from the terminated plan to help finance the takeover. To prevent this from happening, many potential takeover targets with overfunded pension plans voluntarily terminated the over-funded plans themselves and redeployed the excess cash proceeds. Some used the cash proceeds to pay dividends to shareholders; others increased capital expenditures, or otherwise spent the funds. After doing this, they were no longer a tempting target. The Tax Reform Act of 1986 increased the tax on the gains from plan termination; consequently, terminations of overfunded plans are somewhat less attractive to both acquirers and targets, but they still constitute a potential source of cash.[19]

By scrutinizing the causes for increases and decreases in plan assets in the pension foot-note (see Figure 14.6), analysts can often make more refined estimates of future cash flows. For example, let's assume the plan assets disclosure shows that a firm did not contribute additional funding during the reporting period. Further assume that the funded status rec-onciliation shows that the market value of plan assets barely exceeds the PBO at the end of the year. Because the plan was overfunded, the firm could *temporarily* suspend funding. But can it continue to not fund? Depending upon the extent of the overfunding and future asset returns, the answer may be "no." If its funded status were to change in future periods, the firm would be compelled to fund the plan in future years, **thereby decreasing future net operating cash flows**. Lenders and others who forecast future cash flows to estimate "safety cushions" must consider these factors when preparing their forecasts. Merely extrapolating the most recent net operating cash flow into future years would overlook the possibly unsus-tainable "boost" provided by the absence of current pension funding. But companies with greatly overfunded plans can suspend funding for long periods and use the cash for other operating purposes. On the other hand, underfunded plans may reflect past and continuing cash flow difficulties. A new disclosure in *SFAS No. 132* (revised 2003) requires firms to pro-vide their best estimate of the amount of funding expected to be paid into the plan in the ensuing year (see para. 5g). This disclosure will help analysts forecast firms' future funding requirements.

Because the enhanced disclosures in *SFAS No. 132* (revised 2003) were issued as this book was going to press, readers are encouraged to check our website— www.prenhall.com/revsine—for actual illustrations of the new company disclosures.

Another 2003 revision to *SFAS No. 132* is intended to help analysts determine whether fund assets are large enough to satisfy cur-rently anticipated pension benefit payouts. To accomplish this, firms are now required to provide a table that lists the dollar benefits expected to be paid in each of the ensuing five years and in the aggregate for the five years thereafter.

---

[18] L. Asinof, "Excess Pension Assets Lure Corporate Raiders," *Wall Street Journal* (September 11, 1985).

[19] Empirical studies investigate what factors underlie firms' decisions to remove excess pension assets from overfunded pension plans. See J. K. Thomas, "Why Do Firms Terminate Their Overfunded Pension Plans?" *Journal of Accounting and Economics* (November 1989), pp. 361–98; and H. F. Mittelstaedt, "An Empirical Analysis of the Factors Underlying the Decision to Remove Excess Assets from Overfunded Pension Plans," *Journal of Accounting and Economics* (November 1989), pp. 399–418.

If a plan is seriously underfunded and if there are insufficient funds to pay retirees, the Pension Benefit Guarantee Corporation (PBGC)—an agency set up under ERISA—pays the promised benefits. But the PBGC tries to recover the pension payments from the pension plan sponsor. The PBGC claim ranks on an equal footing alongside those of unsecured creditors; accordingly, the funded status reconciliation could serve as an early warning device for signaling other cash demands on the firm.

> In 1977 International Harvester Company (now Navistar International Corporation) sold its Wisconsin Steel division to a subsidiary of Envirodyne Industries. At the time of the sale, Wisconsin Steel's pension plans were underfunded. The Envirodyne subsidiary declared bankruptcy in 1980, and the PBGC terminated and assumed responsibility for the Wisconsin Steel pension plans. The PBGC subsequently sued Navistar, contending that the sale of Wisconsin Steel was motivated by a desire to evade its responsibility for the pension plans. Navistar was found to be liable and agreed to a $65 million settlement to be paid to the PBGC. See "Navistar Will Pay $65 Million to Settle Pension Fund Claims," *Wall Street Journal* (August 21, 1992).

Because pension funding status is important for assessing current and future cash flows of a firm, we need to stress how sensitive the asset and liability measures are to changes in interest rates. A 1% decrease in the discount rate will typically boost the estimated pension obligation by 10% to 15%.[20] For firms with a young workforce where the pension commitments will be paid 20 to 30 years in the future, small changes in interest (settlement) rate assumptions can cause large increases in the present value of these estimated obligations. Why is there this relatively large multiplier effect from small changes in interest rates? This effect is due to the impact of duration—the further into the future the cash flows are to be paid out, the greater the impact of a change in interest rates on the present value of those cash flows.

> For example, Saks, Incorporated disclosed that a 0.25% decrease in its discount rate would increase its accumulated benefit obligation at November 1, 2001 by $7.5 million. This translates into an increase in the ABO of 9.76% as the discount rate decreases by 1%.

The effect of a 1% change in interest rates on the asset side is typically much smaller since fixed income investments generally represent only a fraction of the pension asset portfolio and the maturity of those investments is typically much shorter. *Therefore, even modest declines in interest rates can easily shift the funded status of pension plans from year-to-year.*

Exhibit 14.9 provides data on the proportion of firms with defined benefit pension plans falling into either of two funded status categories for the 1997–2002 period:[21]

1. *Overfunded plans:* The fair value of plan assets (FVPA) exceeds the projected benefit obligation (PBO) (that is, FVPA > PBO).
2. *Underfunded plans:* PBO > FVPA.

> Deere & Company maintains several separate pension plans for various groups of employees. To illustrate how dramatically interest rate and asset return changes can affect funded status, consider the following. At October 31, 2001 Deere reported that only .005 percent of its pension plans (measured by plan assets) were severely underfunded (that is, ABO > FVPA); just one year later .965 percent were severely underfunded. (Review definition of ABO on p. 772.)
>
> *Source:* Deere & Company 10-K dated October 31, 2002.

Over the six-year period, an average of 42.6% of the firms were in a net overfunded position. Note that the proportion of overfunded plans rose from 47.8% in 1997 to 68.1% in 1999 and dropped steeply to 9.2% in 2002. The increase in the proportion of overfunded firms from 1997 through 1999 was primarily driven by the return performance of pension assets during this bull market period. The plunge in the proportion of firms with overfunded plans from 55.1% in 2000 to 9.2% in 2002 resulted from two factors: (1) the sharp drop in equity market prices, and (2) the decline in settlement rates (the median settlement rate declined from 7.5% in 2000 to 6.8% in 2002, as noted in Figure 14.2). As the data show, the return performance of pension assets from year to year and changes in settlement rates can quickly—and materially—alter funded status.

---

[20] See the articles by L. Jeresky, "Tapping the Golden Pool," *Forbes* (April 21, 1986), pp. 35–36; and "The Surplus Vanishes," *Forbes* (November 17, 1986), p. 94.

[21] These summary statistics are based on all AMEX/NYSE firms on Standard & Poor's Compustat® PC Plus with funded status data required under *SFAS No. 87*.

EXHIBIT 14.9	Funded Status of Pension Plans (1997–2002)	
	Proportion Overfunded (FVPA > PBO)	**Proportion Underfunded (PBO > FVPA)**
1997	47.8%	52.2%
1998	47.9	52.1
1999	68.1	31.9
2000	55.1	44.9
2001	27.3	72.7
2002	9.2	90.8
Average	42.6	57.4

Source: Standard & Poor's Research Insight[SM] as data source; methodology not verified or controlled by Standard & Poor's.

> This assumes that the discount rate (settlement rate) is higher than the assumed rate of compensation increase, which is the typical relationship.

Changes in various pension rate assumptions also affect pension expense. An increase in the discount rate lowers service cost and raises interest cost. Whether pension expense goes up or down depends upon the number of years to retirement (that is, average age of the workforce) and other factors. If the assumed rate of compensation increase used in determining the PBO is lowered, then service cost is reduced too. Also, an increase (decrease) in the *spread* between the discount rate and the assumed rate of compensation increase will lower (raise) service cost. Finally, an increase (decrease) in the expected return on plan assets will decrease (increase) pension expense.

RECAP

The pension footnote provides information about the current economic status of the pension plan. This allows insight regarding expected future pension-related cash flows.

Cash-Balance Plans

Toward the end of the 1990s, more than 400 U.S. companies with defined benefit pension plans modified their existing plan and adopted a new method for determining the rate at which pension benefits accumulate. These modified plans are called **cash-balance plans**. Here, employers contribute a fixed amount per year (say, 5% of annual pay) to the account of individual employees. Interest is earned at approximately the rate on long-term U.S. Treasury bonds. Cash-balance plans are defined benefit plans "because the employer [still ultimately] bears the investment risks and rewards and the mortality risk if the employee elects to receive benefits in the form of an annuity."[22] However, should employees leave the firm prior to retirement, the accumulated vested balance belongs to them and can be rolled-over into another pension plan.

Cash-balance pension plans are attractive to firms because, after switching, service cost usually decreases for firms with older employees. Here's why. In traditional defined benefit pension plans, the largest benefits accrue in the later years of employment. But when older workers are switched to a cash-balance plan, they usually receive the same benefit accumulation percent as do younger workers.

While popular with firms, these plans have been challenged as discriminating against older employees. Bills have been introduced in Congress to require firms to give older affected employees a choice between the pre-existing plan and the new cash-balance plan. Proposed new regula-

---

[22] A. T. Arcady and F. Mellors, "Cash Balance Conversions," *Journal of Accountancy* (February 2000), pp. 22–28.

tions for cash-balance pension plans have been issued by the Department of the Treasury.[23] These proposals state that cash-balance conversions are not inherently age discriminatory provided certain guidelines are met. A public hearing on the proposal took place in April, 2003. Critics argue that the Treasury proposals contain too much latitude to protect affected employees fully.[24] Furthermore, a federal court recently ruled that one company's cash-balance plan was age discriminatory.[25] Until the issues are resolved, the move to cash-balance plans will assuredly slow.

Minimum Balance Sheet Liability

While the funded status footnote explains the difference between balance sheet disclosures and the funded status of the plan, it does not introduce any amounts into the balance sheet itself. The FASB believed that footnote disclosure alone was inadequate for *severely* underfunded plans. The FASB defined a severely underfunded plan as one in which the liability *without* considering future pay raises—the previously defined ABO—exceeds the fair value of plan assets (FVPA). The Board mandated that a **minimum balance sheet liability** equal to the difference between the ABO and the FVPA appear on the balance sheet for firms with severely underfunded plans.

To illustrate the computation of the minimum liability provision, assume that at December 31, 2005 Nguyen Corporation's defined benefit pension plan had the following component values:

Fair value of plan assets (FVPA)	$10,000,000
Accumulated benefit obligation (ABO)	12,000,000
Projected benefit obligation (PBO)	17,000,000
Unrecognized prior service cost	3,000,000

Further assume that in all prior years the amount of pension plan funding was equal to the amount of recorded pension plan expense. Therefore, there was no prepaid pension asset or accrued pension liability on Nguyen's books at December 31, 2005.

The minimum balance sheet liability provision would be triggered here. *SFAS No. 87* requires that a liability of at least $2,000,000 (the difference between the ABO and the FVPA) appear on Nguyen's books to "flag" the serious underfunding. Because there is currently no liability on the books, an entry must be made to put one there. The accounting entry would be:

DR	Intangible asset	$2,000,000	
	CR Minimum pension liability		$2,000,000

You may ask why the offset to the "Minimum pension liability" is to an "Intangible asset" account. An asset is debited because it is presumed that the serious underfunding exists because Nguyen retroactively "sweetened" benefits (thereby increasing both the ABO and PBO) to maintain employee morale. The intangible asset account represents the future benefits that will presumably be conveyed to the firm by the happy employees whose pension plan was sweetened.

Once recorded, neither the minimum liability nor the offsetting asset are amortized over future years. Instead, the entry for each year is reversed after the financial statements are prepared

---

[23] Department of the Treasury, Internal Revenue Service, 26 CFR Part 1 (Reg-209500-86), December 10, 2002.

[24] M. W. Walsh, "It May Be Time to Plumb Your Pension's Depths," *New York Times* (December 15, 2002).

[25] M. W. Walsh, "Judge Says I.B.M. Pension Illegally Harmed Older Workers," *New York Times* (August 1, 2003).

and *the computation is redone at the end of the ensuing year.* Plans with continuing, serious under-funding problems would therefore again display intangible asset and minimum liability amounts based on the ensuing year's computations at December 31, 2006.

The rationale for not carrying the intangible asset forward for amortization relates to why seriously underfunded plans exist. The two primary reasons are (1) cumulative unrecorded losses in past years and (2) unrecognized prior service cost. Cumulative unrecorded losses are already being amortized under component 4—recognized gains or losses—while unrecognized prior service cost is being amortized under either component 5—amortization of unrecognized transition asset or obligation—or component 6—recognized prior service cost (depending on when the sweetener was adopted). Thus, to amortize the asset that arises as an offset to the minimum balance sheet liability would result in double counting.

Additional Computational Considerations There are two other factors that also affect how an additional minimum pension liability is recorded: (1) the amount of pension asset or liability already recorded on the balance sheet, and (2) the amount of prior service cost that is off the balance sheet. We'll now discuss these sequentially.

First, when firms whose ABO exceeds FVPA also have an "Accrued pension liability" or a "Prepaid pension asset" on their balance sheet, the additional minimum pension liability computation is altered. To illustrate, if Nguyen had an "Accrued pension liability" of, say, $400,000 on its books at December 31, 2005, the entry would be different than shown earlier since *SFAS No. 87* requires a *total* pension liability of $2,000,000—and $400,000 is already on the books. So an additional liability of only $1,600,000 (that is, $2,000,000 − $400,000) would need to be recorded. The entry is:

DR Intangible asset	$1,600,000	
CR Minimum pension liability		$1,600,000

On the other hand, if Nguyen had a "Prepaid pension asset" of $400,000 on its books at December 31, 2005, the entry to get to a total *net* liability of $2,000,000 is:

DR Intangible asset	$2,400,000	
CR Minimum pension liability		$2,400,000

The credit of $2,400,000, when offset against the "Prepaid pension asset" of $400,000, yields the required $2,000,000 minimum liability balance.

Second, let's examine how prior service cost affects the minimum pension liability journal entry. The dollar amount of the debit to the intangible asset account cannot exceed the dollar amount of the unrecognized prior service cost (UPSC) at the balance sheet date. The debit to the intangible asset is limited to UPSC because only this portion of the underfunding can be the result of plan "sweeteners" that generated employee goodwill (that is, the intangible asset); the rest of the underfunding must be attributable to cumulative unrecorded past losses. To see how this limitation works, let's assume Nguyen's unrecognized prior service cost is $1,500,000 rather than $3,000,000. So now the minimum liability of $2,000,000 exceeds prior service costs by $500,000. In these altered circumstances, the entry to recognize the minimum liability would be:

> More precisely, the debit to the intangible asset account cannot exceed the sum of UPSC *plus* any unrecognized transition liability arising from the initial adoption of *SFAS No. 87*. (See para. 37.) For many firms, any transition liability has by now been totally amortized through component 5.

DR Intangible asset	$1,500,000	
DR Accumulated comprehensive loss	500,000	
CR Minimum pension liability		$2,000,000

The intangible asset is limited to the amount of prior service cost ($1,500,000) and the $500,000 excess would be shown as an element of comprehensive income, as discussed in Chapter 2.

Contracting

The AMR Corporation (parent of American Airlines) 2002 Annual Report illustrates the minimum liability computation when both of these special circumstances exist. The report discloses that the ABO is $7.344 billion and the fair value of plan assets is $5.323 billion. So the minimum liability at December 31, 2002 is $2.021 billion (that is, $7.344 billion – $5.323 billion).

The decline in both equity prices and interest rates over the 2001–2002 period reduced the funded status of virtually all defined benefit pension plans. Many become severely underfunded, and firm sponsors were consequently required to record a minimum pension liability and absorb a charge to comprehensive income. Since financial convenants are sensitive to levels of debt and equity, the required recognition of a minimum pension liability put some firms in jeopardy of covenant violations. See C. Bryan-Low, "Pension Liability Raises a Flag Among Bankers," *Wall Street Journal* (November 26, 2002).

AMR discloses the following additional information as of December 31, 2002 in the pension footnote (in millions):

Prepaid pension asset	$ 54	**DR**	On balance sheet
Accrued pension liability	453	**CR**	On balance sheet
Additional minimum liability	1,623	**CR**	On balance sheet
Intangible asset	330	**DR**	On balance sheet
Accumulated comprehensive loss	1,293	**DR**	On balance sheet (in owners' equity)

This disclosure allows us to understand how the additional minimum liability ($1,623) and intangible asset ($330) amounts were determined. First, AMR already has a *net* pension liability of $399 on the balance sheet (that is, an accrued liability of $453 minus a prepaid asset of $54). So the additional liability that must be recorded is computed as follows:

Disclosed total minimum liability	$2.021 billion
Net pension liability already recorded	.399 billion
Additional liability to be recorded	$1,623 billion*

*Rounded by $1 million to conform to reported amount

Using the data in AMR's footnote disclosure above, the journal entry to record the additional minimum liability for December 31, 2002 was:

DR	Intangible asset	$ 330	
DR	Accumulated comprehensive loss	1,293	
	CR Additional minimum liability		$1,623

International

The "Intangible asset" was debited for only $330 because AMR also disclosed that its unrecognized prior service cost is $330—remember, the intangible asset cannot exceed the prior service cost amount. The difference between the "Additional minimum liability" of $1,623 and the "Intangible asset" of $330 must be debited to "Accumulated comprehensive loss," as discussed in the context of the Nguyen Corporation example, and charged to retained earnings.

International financial reporting rules for pensions are specified by "Employee Benefits," *IAS 19* (London, U.K.: International Accounting Standards Committee, 1998). These rules roughly parallel those of *SFAS No. 87*. The primary differences are that *IAS 19* contains fewer smoothing provisions than *SFAS No. 87* and does not require recognition of a minimum liability. Required financial statement disclosures are also similar.

Funded Status and Operating Cash Flows

The funded status of a pension plan appears to be an indicator of potential cash flow problems. Figure 14.9 provides evidence that firms with underfunded plans are not only experiencing lower *current* cash flows but are also likely to experience lower *future* cash flows than firms with overfunded plans. To demonstrate this, we form two portfolios based on firms' funded status at the end of 1998: (1) firms in an overfunded position (FVPA > PBO) and (2) firms in an underfunded position (PBO > FVPA).[26] The bar graph in Figure 14.9 displays the median cash flow from operations (on a per share basis) for the year of the portfolio formation (1998) and for the subsequent four years.

Figure 14.9

OPERATING CASH FLOWS
BY FUNDED STATUS GROUP
1998–2002

Source: Standard & Poor's Research Insight[(SM)] as data source; methodology not verified or controlled by Standard & Poor's.

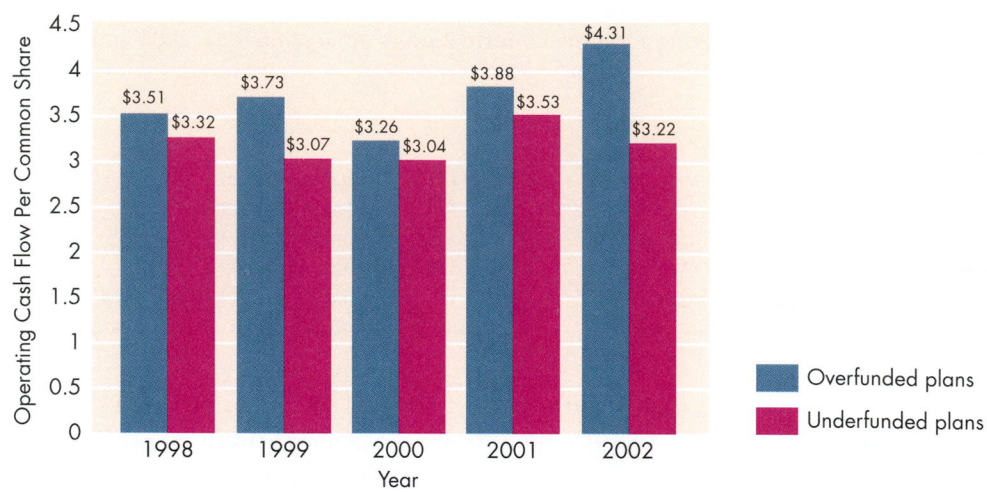

Firms whose pension plans were underfunded in 1998 experienced lower operating cash flows in that year ($3.32 per share) in comparison to firms with overfunded plans ($3.51 per share). Moreover, the operating cash flows of the underfunded firms continued to lag behind those of the overfunded firms in the subsequent four years. This suggests that pension funded status is a potentially useful indicator of the level of future cash flows.[27]

Postretirement Benefits Other Than Pensions

Many companies promise to provide healthcare and life insurance to employees and their spouses during retirement. The intent of these benefits is to attract and retain a highly qualified workforce, just like pensions are intended to do. Under the matching principle of accrual accounting, an expense should be recognized over the period of employment as employees qualify for these **other postretirement benefits (OPEB)**. Historically, however, few companies with postretirement benefit plans made expense accruals. Instead, "pay-as-you-go" accounting was employed—that is, as cash payments were made to provide the healthcare benefit coverage to retired employees, the amount of

---

[26] All firms listed on either the AMEX or NYSE with valid data for computing pension funded status in 1998 are included.

[27] Prior to the issuance of *SFAS No. 132* in 1998, it was possible to form three portfolios: (1) firms in an overfunded position, (2) firms in a moderately underfunded position (PBO > FVPA > ABO), and (3) firms in a severely underfunded position (ABO > FVPA). But *SFAS No. 132* reduced the ABO disclosure so it was no longer possible to identify firms that were severely underfunded in the aggregate. Consequently, the accuracy of cash flow forecasting using pension funded status declined. See M. Cipriano, D. W. Collins, and L. Revsine, "*SFAS No. 132* and Disclosure Effectiveness: An Examination" (unpublished manuscript, February 2000) for a detailed analysis of the deterioration in the accuracy of operating cash flow forecasts as a result of the disclosure cutbacks in the 1998 version of *SFAS No. 132*. Fortunately, the 2003 revision of *SFAS No. 132* restored the ABO disclosure, so the potential for more accurate cash flow forecasts using pension funding status is improved.

the cash outflow was charged to expense. No liability appeared on the books. Worse yet, few companies funded these OPEB plans as benefits were earned. There are two reasons for this lack of funding:

- First, in contrast to pension plans, there is no ERISA requirement that says these benefits have to be funded.
- Second, even if firms did consider voluntarily funding their plans, these payments would not be deductible for U.S. income tax purposes, thus creating a disincentive to fund.

As a result of both of these circumstances, by the mid-1980s enormous unrecorded (off-balance sheet) liabilities for postretirement benefits existed, but no periodic debits to expense nor credits to a liability account were made to reflect the continued growth of these obligations. To give some idea of the size of these previously unrecorded postretirement benefit liabilities, when General Motors adopted *SFAS No. 106* in 1992, the liability totaled $33.116 billion and the after-tax charge to the income statement was $20.838 billion. (GM's pre-tax loss *before* the cumulative effect of the change in accounting principle was $3.333 billion in 1992.)

To correct situations like this, the FASB issued *SFAS No. 106* in December 1990.[28] This standard became effective in 1993, although earlier application was permitted. Exhibit 14.10 contains excerpts from the postretirement benefit plans footnote in the 2001 annual report of General Electric Company.

EXHIBIT 14.10	General Electric Company

Edited, Condensed 2001 Annual Report Health and Life Benefits Footnote

Principal retiree benefit plans generally provide health and life insurance benefits to employees who retire under the GE Pension Plan . . . with 10 or more years of service. Retirees share in the cost of health care benefits. Benefit provisions are subject to collective bargaining. These plans cover approximately 250,000 retirees and dependents.

The effect on operations of principal retiree benefit plans is shown in the following table.

Effect on operations

($ in millions)	2001	2000
Service cost for benefits earned	$191	$165
Interest cost on benefit obligation	459	402
Expected return on plan assets	(185)	(178)
Prior service cost	90	49
Net actuarial loss recognized	60	40
Total cost	$615	$478

Funding policy for retiree health benefits is generally to pay covered expenses as they are incurred. GE funds retiree life insurance benefits at its discretion.

Changes in the accumulated postretirement benefit obligation for retiree benefit plans follow.

Accumulated postretirement benefit obligation (APBO)

($ in millions)	2001	2000
Balance at January 1	$6,422	$4,926
Service cost for benefits earned	191	165
Interest cost on benefit obligation	459	402
Participant contributions	30	25
Actuarial loss	287	534
Benefits paid	(593)	(578)
Plan amendments	—	948
Balance at December 31	$6,796	$6,422

(*continued on next page*)

---

[28] "Employers' Accounting for Postretirement Benefits Other Than Pensions," *SFAS No. 106* (Norwalk, CT: FASB, 1990).

EXHIBIT 14.10	General Electric Company (*continued*)

Changes in the fair value of assets for retiree benefit plans follow.

Fair value of assets

($ in millions)	2001	2000
Balance at January 1	$2,031	$2,369
Actual return on plan assets	(163)	(85)
Employer contributions	466	300
Participant contributions	30	25
Benefits paid	(593)	(578)
Balance at December 31	$1,771	$2,031

Plan assets are held in trust and consist mainly of common stock and fixed-income investments. GE common stock represented 6.4% and 6.9% of trust assets at year-end 2001 and 2000, respectively.

GE recorded assets and liabilities for retiree benefit plans are as follows:

Retiree benefit asset/(liability)

December 31 ($ in millions)	2001	2000
Funded status[a]	$(5,025)	$(4,391)
Unrecognized prior service cost	909	999
Unrecognized net actuarial loss	1,393	818
Net liability recognized	$(2,723)	$(2,574)
Amounts recorded in the Statement of Financial Position:		
Prepaid retiree life plans asset	$ 66	$ 8
Retiree health plans liability	(2,789)	(2,582)
Net liability recognized	$(2,723)	$(2,574)

[a]Fair value of assets less APBO, as shown in the preceding tables.

Actuarial assumptions used to determine costs and benefit obligations for principal retiree benefit plans follow.

Actuarial assumptions

December 31	2001	2000
Discount rate	7.25%	7.5%
Compensation increases	5.0	5.0
Healthcare cost trend[a]	11.6	10.0
Return on assets for the year[b]	9.5	9.5

[a]For 2001, gradually declining to 5.0% after 2009.
[b]For 2002, the return on assets actuarial assumption will be 8.5%.

Increasing or decreasing the healthcare cost trend rates by one percentage point would have had an insignificant effect on the December 31, 2001, accumulated postretirement benefit obligation and the annual cost of retiree health plans.

Experience gains and losses, as well as the effects of changes in actuarial assumptions and plan provisions, are amortized over the average future service period of employees.

The computations for postretirement benefits expense and measures of the liability generally parallel the format for pension expense and liability. Notice in Exhibit 14.10 that G.E. maintains both retiree health and life insurance benefit plans. The net postretirement benefit cost of $615 million for 2001 (as shown in the "Effect on operations" section of Exhibit 14.10 on p. 783) includes service cost plus interest cost components and expected return on plan assets.

Further scrutiny of this section shows that *SFAS No. 106* also incorporates smoothing devices that are virtually identical to components 4 through 6 in pension accounting. Specifically, when OPEB plans have been funded and thus have plan assets, postretirement benefit expense is reduced by the *expected* return on plan assets; to accomplish this smoothing, asset gains or losses are deferred off-balance sheet. Similarly, these gains and losses are accumulated and amortized as component 4 if they exceed a 10% corridor, just as they are in pension accounting. Pension component 5—amortization of transition liability—also exists in postretirement benefits accounting if the firm adopting *SFAS No. 106* chose to recognize the liability over a period of future years rather than all at once, as you will see next. Finally, a counterpart to pension component 6—amortization of prior service costs—exists as well in instances in which firms enhance or reduce the level of postretirement benefits subsequent to adopting *SFAS No. 106*.

One difference between accounting for pensions and accounting for other postretirement benefits (OPEB) is that OPEB benefits are rarely tied to salary at retirement. Consequently, *SFAS No. 106* contains no projected benefit obligation calculation. The typical postretirement benefit plan promises employees full coverage (for example, comprehensive postretirement health insurance) after a certain period

> The actuarial and other assumptions required encompass factors such as (1) what proportion of employees will work for at least 10 years and thereby qualify for benefits, (2) how long after retirement will the employee live to receive benefits, and (3) what will be the annual cost of providing the benefit over the retirement years.

of employment—say, 10 years. In such circumstances, the actuarially determined service cost of the plan will also be accrued over the first 10 years of the employee's service. The liability attributed to service to date is called the **accumulated postretirement benefit obligation (APBO)**.

The FASB permitted companies to adopt the provisions of *SFAS No. 106* in one of two ways:

1. Recognize the transition obligation or transition asset (the difference between the accumulated postretirement benefit obligation and the fair value of plan assets) immediately in net income of the period in which *SFAS No. 106* is adopted (immediate recognition).
2. Amortize the transition obligation or transition asset as a component of OPEB expense on a straight-line basis over the *longer* of (a) the average remaining service period of active plan participants, or (b) 20 years (deferred recognition).

These alternative approaches for initially adopting *SFAS No. 106* are shown in Figure 14.10.

Immediate Recognition

(Most firms used this method)

Recognize the full APBO (and any assets) immediately upon adoption.

Account for the OPEB plans using procedures that are virtually identical to those for pension accounting. (But there is no component 5—amortization of transition liability—when the immediate recognition option is used.)

Deferred Recognition Over Future Years

Amortize the transition obligation (or, rarely, the asset) on a straight-line basis, over the *longer* of (1) average remaining service period of active plan participants, or (2) 20 years.

Account for the OPEB plans using procedures that are virtually identical to those for pension accounting.

Component 5—amortization of transition liability—will typically comprise a large portion of annual OPEB expense for firms that chose deferred recognition.

Figure 14.10

THE TWO PERMITTED *SFAS NO. 106* ALTERNATIVE ADOPTION METHODS

Like most U.S. firms, G.E. chose to recognize the *SFAS No. 106* transition obligation immediately. Why did most firms choose to take the earnings "hit" all at once, rather than amortizing it over a period of future years?[29] The best explanation is that firms wanted to avoid the "drag" on future earnings that would result from amortizing the usually very large unrecorded liability over, say, the ensuing 15 years. One reason for taking the "hit" all at once is that future years' bonuses tied to earnings would be reduced by the "drag." Another is that firms may have feared that investors would soon forget the source of the earnings "drag" and bid share prices lower. Those few firms that chose not to recognize the liability all at once now have an expense charge that is a counterpart to pension component 5, as shown in Figure 14.10. Exhibit 14.11 contains a 1991 footnote excerpt that describes how G.E. recognized the full *SFAS No. 106* liability immediately. It made the following entry retroactive to the start of 1991:

Contracting

> Case C14–4 covers G.E.'s initial adoption of *SFAS No. 106*.

DR Cumulative effect of a change in accounting principle	$1,799,000,000	
DR Deferred income tax asset	911,000,000	
CR Accumulated postretirement benefit obligation		$2,710,000,000

EXHIBIT 14.11   **General Electric Company**

Excerpt from 1991 Annual Report

1991 Accounting Change. Statement of Financial Accounting Standards *(SFAS) No. 106*—"Employers' Accounting for Postretirement Benefits Other Than Pensions"—was implemented using the immediate recognition transition option, effective as of January 1, 1991.

    SFAS No. 106 requires recognition during employees' service with the Company, of the cost of their retiree health and life insurance benefits. At January 1, 1991, the accumulated postretirement benefit obligation was $4,287 million; however, $1,577 million of this obligation had been provided through the fair market value of related trust assets ($1,037 million) and recorded liabilities ($540 million), thus resulting in a pre-tax adjustment (i.e., transition obligation) of $2,710 million. The effect on net earnings and share owners' equity was $1,799 million ($2.07 per share) after [a] deferred tax benefit of $911 million. Aside from the one-time effect of the adjustment, adoption of *SFAS No. 106* was not material to 1991 financial results.

The cumulative effect of this accounting change ($1,799 million) was shown as a charge on the 1991 income statement. Deferred taxes are debited because the U.S. income tax law does not permit a tax deduction for postretirement benefits until the benefit premiums are paid. Consequently, a timing difference exists because book income for 1991 is lower than taxable income as a consequence of this item.

    Exhibit 14.10 in the section "Retiree benefit asset/(liability)" on p. 784 also shows General Electric's disclosure of the plans' status at the end of 2001. Reformulating the reconciliation using the approach we used for pensions in Figure 14.8 shows:

---

[29] For example, see E. Amir and J. Livnat, "Adoption Choices of *SFAS No. 106*: Implications for Financial Analysis," *The Journal of Financial Statement Analysis* (Winter, 1997) pp. 51–60; and K. Ramesh and L. Revsine, "The Effects of Regulatory and Contracting Costs on Banks' Choice of Accounting Method for Other Postretirement Employee Benefits," *Journal of Accounting and Economics* (October, 2000) pp. 159–86.

Funded Status of Plans		Recognized and Unrecognized Amounts	
Accumulated postretirement		**Recognized amounts**	
benefit obligation	$(6,796) **CR**	Prepaid retiree life plans asset	$66 **DR**
		Retiree health plans liability	(2,789) **CR**
Fair value of plan assets	1,771 **DR**	**Unrecognized amounts**	
		Prior service cost	(909) **CR**
		Unrecognized net actuarial loss	(1,393) **CR**
Excess of accumulated		Excess of accumulated	
postretirement benefit		postretirement benefit	
obligation over plan assets	$(5,025) **CR**	obligation over plan assets	$(5,025) **CR**

RECAP

The financial reporting and disclosures for postretirement benefit plans are similar to pension reporting and disclosures. However, most postretirement benefit plans are unfunded. Consequently, statement readers must be mindful of future cash outflows that these unfunded plans might precipitate.

Are Pension and Other Postretirement Benefits (OPEB) Disclosures Useful? The Research Evidence

Pension and other postretirement benefits (OPEB) disclosures and measurement rules are not simple. Detailed breakdowns of expense components abound (service cost, interest cost, etc.). But, are the detailed components of pension and postretirement benefits expense, as well as footnote disclosures of asset and liability amounts, useful to statement readers in equity valuation? This section describes research evidence regarding the value relevance of the rules in *SFAS No. 87*, *No. 106*, and *No. 132*.

Do the Components of Net Periodic Pension Cost Have Different Equity Pricing Implications?

The decision of the FASB to require separate disclosure of the various components of net periodic pension expense, as detailed earlier in this chapter, raises an interesting question: Is the distinction between these pension expense components important to investors and other statement users? In valuing a company's stock, does the market assign different multiples to the various components of net periodic pension cost? For example, does a dollar of service cost have the same impact on share price as a dollar of amortization of unrecognized transition asset or obligation? If not, why not?

These questions were addressed in a study that used the simple earnings capitalization equity valuation model presented in Chapter 6—that is, equation (6.7), which expresses the market value of equity as the capitalized value of a firm's "permanent" or sustainable earnings.[30] The study conjectures that the various components of net periodic pension expense (service cost, interest cost, expected return on plan assets, and so on) convey different information regarding the firm's permanent earnings potential, and, therefore, each will have a different multiple applied to it. Specifically, service cost, interest cost, and *expected* return on plan assets

Valuation

[30] M. E. Barth, W. H. Beaver, and W. R. Landsman, "The Market Valuation Implication of Net Periodic Pension Cost Components," *Journal of Accounting and Economics* (March 1992), pp. 27–62.

are relatively permanent components of earnings that are likely to persist into the future. Consequently, these components are expected to have multiples approximating $1/r$, where r is the firm's cost of equity capital. Thus, if r is 8%, the multiple applied to these earnings components would be $1/.08$, or 12.5—that is, each dollar of these expenses would lower permanent earnings and thus lower market value by $12.50, while each dollar of expected return would raise market value by $12.50.

Other components of pension expense are viewed as more transitory, and, therefore, they are expected to have a lower multiple. This lower multiple reflects the presumably less sustainable nature of these other components. For example, a lower multiple would be expected for the deferred portion of the current period's actual return on plan assets. The deferred portion reflects the difference between the actual and expected return in the current period (the unexpected return), **which is expected to net to zero in the long run**. Because the unexpected gain or loss in a given year is *not* expected to recur in the future, the multiple for this component of pension expense is expected to be approximately 1. A multiple of 1—which is far below 12.5—would reflect the one-time transitory effect of this item on the market value of equity.

The researchers hypothesize that components 4, 5, and 6 provide no incremental information about future permanent earnings that is not already reflected in other pension expense components. For example, the recognition of total net deferrals of gains and losses from previous periods (component 4) and the amortization of the net transition asset or liability (component 5) are viewed as "stale" numbers, since they derive from past gains and losses. Accordingly, these components of pension expense are viewed as irrelevant to the pricing of a firm's stock, so the multiple applied to these amounts is expected to be zero.

To see whether different multiples are applied to different components of pension cost in the determination of security prices, the researchers express market value of equity as a function of various nonpension and pension-related components of net income, as depicted in Figure 14.11. Overall, the variables depicted in the figure (including the nonpension variables) explain roughly 55% to 65% of the variation in year-end share prices across firms in the sample. The study found that the multiples applied to the pension variables in Figure 14.11 are **significantly different from one another**.[31] This difference in multiples implies that the various components of pension expense affect share price differently. In particular, the multiple on the amortization of the transition amount (component 5) is essentially zero, thus suggesting that this item is viewed by the market as a low-quality component of earnings that is price-irrelevant. This finding is noteworthy because many of the firms that adopted *SFAS No. 87* early (in 1986) were in large overfunded positions—the fair market value of plan assets exceeded the projected benefit obligation. This overfunding resulted in a large and significant reduction in reported pension expense in the adoption year and in subsequent periods (as this

Figure 14.11

RESEARCH DESIGN
ON THE RELATIONSHIP
BETWEEN STOCK PRICES
AND COMPONENTS
OF PENSION EXPENSE

[31] Ibid.

transition asset was amortized).[32] Research findings suggest that the market views this earnings boost to be largely transitory and not a significant determinant of equity prices. Further evidence shows that the multiple applied to the interest cost and return on plan assets components of pension expense generally has the predicted sign and magnitude but the service cost multiple does not.[33]

> Research results suggest that the breakdown of the components of pension expense—as called for under *SFAS No. 87* and *SFAS No. 132*—is useful to investors, since these components appear to have different share price implications.

RECAP

Equity Pricing Implications of Pension Cost: An Alternative View

The research just described tells us how the stock market appears to use pension disclosures in valuing firms. More recent articles have argued for a different approach.[34]

During the "bull market" of the late 1990s, "pension expense" gradually became "pension income" for some firms with greatly overfunded pension plans. This happened because rising equity values raised the base on which the expected return on plan assets is computed.[35] Consequently, the expected return—*which lowers pension expense*—ultimately exceeded charges to pension expense like service cost and interest cost. For example, in Exhibit 14.8 (p. 769) you can see that G.E. had pension *income* of $2,095 million in 2001. Pension income grew so large that, for many firms, it had a discernible positive effect on operating income. Exhibit 14.12 shows pension income as a percentage of pre-tax operating income in 1998 for several firms with a very high ratio of pension income to operating income.

Valuation

EXHIBIT 14.12	Ratio of 1998 Pension Income to 1998 Pre-tax Operating Income for Selected Firms
Firm	**Ratio**
Boeing Company	8%
Crown Cork & Seal Company	12
Eaton Corporation	10
General Electric Company	7
GTE Corporation	8
International Business Machines Corporation	6
International Paper Company	8
Lucent Technologies Incorporated	15
Nicor Incorporated	10
PG&E Corporation	11
Tenneco Incorporated	10
Unocal Corporation	38

Source: Bear Stearns *Accounting Issues*, September 17, 1999.

---

[32] One study reports that 92% of 192 firms that adopted *SFAS No. 87* in 1986 sponsored at least one overfunded pension plan. For this set of firms, the fair value of plan assets exceeded the projected benefit obligation at transition by an average of $165.6 million. This transition asset typically is amortized over 15 years, thus resulting in an average reduction of pension expense of slightly over $11 million. See M. Stone and R. W. Ingram, "The Effect of *Statement No. 87* on the Financial Reports of Early Adopters," *Accounting Horizons* (September 1988), pp. 48–61.

[33] Barth, et al., op. cit.

[34] For example, see R. McGough and E. E. Schultz, "How Pension Surpluses Lift Profits," *Wall Street Journal* (September 20, 1999); and G. Morgenson, "What's Hiding in Big Blue's Small Print," *New York Times* (June 4, 2000).

[35] Recall, this pension plan asset base is termed the market-related asset value. Firms can compute this in either of two ways. One is to use the fair market value (FMV) of the plan assets at the start of the reporting period. The other is to use some sort of moving average (not to exceed five years), which smooths out the year-to-year volatility inherent in a point estimate like FMV on a specific date.

These proponents further contend that OPEB items—other than service cost—also should not be included in operating income. Since OPEB obligations are seldom funded, return on assets is not a significant issue here; only interest cost is. Consequently, critics contend that the OPEB effect in isolation tends to *understate* operating income.

Some analysts and financial writers have argued that deducting pension expense or adding pension income in the operating section of the income statement misstates *operating* income. They maintain that only service cost is a true current period *operating* item since service cost represents the present value of the increased pension payout arising from current services. Interest cost (component 2 of pension expense) is thought to be a financing cost and not an element of operating income. Similarly, these critics feel that the expected return on plan assets (component 3) should be shown in other income, just like the return on investment securities firms may hold.[36] Consistent with the research result in the previous section, amortization components 4 through 6 are considered valuation irrelevant. In these critics' view, only service cost is related to core operations and, accordingly, should receive a different valuation multiple than interest cost and return on plan assets.

Exhibit 14.13 shows how the adjustments just described for pensions and OPEB would alter the year-to-year percentage increase in General Electric's 2001 and 2000 operating income. Rather than a 6.8% increase in continuing, core operating income, the adjusted increase is 5.6%.

EXHIBIT 14.13	General Electric's Growth Rate Comparison		
($ in millions)	2001	2000	Year-Over-Year Growth Rate
Reported operating income	$19,701	$18,446	+6.8%
Add back:			
Net postretirement benefit cost	615	478	
Deduct:			
Net income from pensions	(2,095)	(1,744)	
Service cost—pensions	(884)	(780)	
Service cost—postretirement benefits	(191)	(165)	
Adjusted operating income	$17,146	$16,235	+5.6%

Source: General Electric Company 2001 Annual Report.

This view of pension/OPEB expense (income) as being comprised of several nonoperating elements is controversial. Here's why. At the start of this chapter we showed that in a world of certainty the return on plan assets would exactly offset interest cost. Pension expense would consist exclusively of service cost. In the real world, this offset won't be precise. Sometimes the actual return on plan assets will be lower than the expected return. If this shortfall persists for extended periods, pension expense will grow. This growing charge to pension expense means the firm will have to make up the shortfall by expending cash in later periods to adequately fund pension payouts. In this scenario, it seems that the entirety of pension expense (that is, service cost, interest cost, and the reduction for return on plan assets) should be included as an expense in determining operating income. A growing year-to-year charge to pension expense means that events of the current and recent past periods point to the need for increased *future* pension funding to deliver the promised benefits.

At the other extreme, sometimes the actual return on plan assets will greatly exceed expected returns. When this persists, pension expense may reverse and become pension income and even grow over time, as happened in the late 1990s for some firms. This growing excess means that the firm's need to use additional resources in the future to fund benefits currently earned is shrinking. In this

[36] See Bear Stearns, "Retirement Benefits Impact Operating Income," *Accounting Issues* (Bear, Stearns & Co. Inc.: September 17, 1999) for a thorough exposition of this position.

scenario of rising returns, it also seems appropriate to treat the entirety of pension income as an increase in operating income since future pension funding requirements are diminished.

How to treat interest cost and return on pension plan assets in equity valuations is an unsettled issue. We expect continuing debate among financial observers.

Reliability and the Valuation Relevance of Alternative Pension Asset and Liability Measures

Among the several alternative pension asset and liability measures we have discussed, some are reported on the balance sheet while others appear in the pension footnote. For example, the cumulative difference between asset funding and the amounts charged to pension expense each year is included directly on the balance sheet. If cumulative past pension expense exceeds cumulative past funding, an accrued pension liability is shown on the balance sheet. Alternatively, if cumulative past pension funding exceeds cumulative past expense, the balance sheet will reflect a prepaid pension asset.

Footnote disclosures under *SFAS No. 87* and *SFAS No. 132* (revised 2003) include the accumulated benefit obligation and the projected benefit obligation as measures of pension obligations, and they also include the fair value of plan assets as the relevant measure of plan assets.

From an accounting measurement perspective, an important question is this: Which of these alternative liability and asset measures best captures the true pension obligations and resources of the firm and which are measured with the greatest reliability? From a user perspective, do the net pension amounts reported in the balance sheet or the amounts reported in the footnotes more closely reflect the asset and liability measures that investors implicitly use when they value the firm? Both sets of questions are addressed in a research study.[37]

Overall, the results of the study suggest that the pension asset and liability measures in the pension *footnotes* are more closely associated with security prices than are the measures recognized in the balance sheet. These results underscore the fact that footnotes to the financial statements often contain useful information for investors' valuation decisions—and, therefore, they should be carefully scrutinized.

Reliability and Valuation Relevance of Postretirement Benefit Obligations

Accumulated postretirement benefit obligations (APBOs) represent significant off-balance sheet obligations for many firms. Several questions can be raised about estimated APBO amounts, both from an accounting measurement perspective and from a user perspective:

- Are APBO amounts sufficiently reliable to be useful in assessing share prices?
- Are APBO amounts less reliable than pension ABO amounts?
- Do APBO amounts provide incremental information over and above ABO amounts when assessing share prices?

> These studies were done before the FASB reduced pension ABO disclosures in *SFAS No. 132*.

These questions are addressed in several studies.[38] Before summarizing the results of these studies, we briefly consider objections that were raised about reporting postretirement benefit obligations.

---

[37] M. E. Barth, "Relative Measurement Errors Among Alternative Pension Asset and Liability Measures," *The Accounting Review* (July 1991), pp. 443–63. Another measure tested in the study—the vested benefit obligation—is no longer reported under *SFAS No. 132*.

[38] H. F. Mittelstaedt and M. J. Warshawsky, "The Impact of Liabilities for Retiree Health Benefits on Share Prices," *Journal of Risk and Insurance* 60, no. 1 (1993), pp. 13–35; E. Amir, "The Market Valuation of Accounting Information: The Case of Postretirement Benefits Other Than Pensions," *The Accounting Review* (October 1993), pp. 703–24; and B. Choi, D. W. Collins, and W. B. Johnson, "Valuation Implications of Reliability Differences: The Case of Non-pension Postretirement Obligations," *The Accounting Review* (July 1997), pp. 351–83.

While there is general agreement that postretirement obligations are an economic liability of a firm promising them, questions have been raised about the reliability of the accounting estimates of this liability. This concern about reliability of APBO estimates arises from difficulties encountered in measuring future healthcare benefits granted to employees. Unlike employee pension obligations, which are contractually defined in terms of dollar payments (for example, 60% of salary at retirement), employee healthcare benefits are typically defined in terms of future services to be provided in kind. While both ABO and APBO estimates require numerous actuarial assumptions, there are more uncertainties associated with measuring the costs of future healthcare benefits. The three most important factors contributing to uncertainty in estimating APBO amounts are the following:

- Per-capita claims cost by age
- Future healthcare cost trend rates
- Future medicare reimbursement rates[39]

Escalating healthcare costs and the new *SFAS No. 106* reporting requirements have caused some firms to alter or terminate their contractual obligations under existing postretirement healthcare benefit plans. One compensation consulting firm estimated that as many as 80% of the employers surveyed were likely to reduce or terminate healthcare benefits in the future.[40] These contemplated changes in benefits contribute another source of uncertainty about reported APBO amounts. Corporate decisions to reduce or terminate healthcare benefits are reflected in accounting estimates of APBO only after the cutback occurs, but the possibility of such actions makes the original APBO figures reported by firms less reliable as a measure of their expected ultimate liability for healthcare benefits.

In summary, opponents of *SFAS No. 106* argue that the additional assumptions required to estimate future healthcare benefits and the possibility that these benefits will be curtailed in the future lower the precision of the resulting APBO estimates. Thus, concern is raised about the reliability of APBO amounts both in absolute terms and in comparison to the reliability of employee pension obligations. Clearly, by issuing *SFAS No. 106*, the FASB felt that including estimates of employee postretirement benefit obligations in the financial statements would be useful and informative. Which of these opposing positions is most consistent with empirical evidence is the subject of the studies to which we now turn our attention.

Empirical Evidence Two studies use a variant of the earnings and book value valuation model equation (6.11) introduced in Chapter 6 to determine whether investors were adjusting share prices for estimates of APBO amounts even before firms began disclosing their own estimates of APBO amounts under *SFAS No. 106*.[41] The results of both studies suggest that estimated APBO amounts are valuation relevant and were apparently being impounded into share prices prior to the *SFAS No. 106* disclosures. However, these studies find that a dollar of the estimated OPEB obligation reduces the market value of equity by only $0.40 to $0.60. One explanation for why these reductions are smaller than the theoretical (expected) reduction of one dollar is that these estimated obligations contain substantial measurement error and, therefore, lack the necessary reliability to affect share values dollar for dollar.

---

[39] *SFAS No. 106*, para. 30, op. cit.

[40] UNYSIS announced it would curtail all payments of retiree benefits within three years, thereby reducing the APBO obligation it would have otherwise reported by approximately $700 million. See "UNYSIS Corp. Says It Will Stop Paying Retiree Medical Benefits in Three Years," *Wall Street Journal* (November 4, 1992).

[41] H. F. Mittelstaedt and M. J. Warshawsky, op. cit.; and E. Amir, op. cit. The researcher-derived estimates of APBO amounts used in these studies were based on firm-specific annual pay-as-you-go costs and other publicly available information about discount rates, healthcare cost trend rates, and employee age profiles.

Another study used actual APBO amounts that were computed by firms themselves to investigate whether these obligations contain greater measurement error (less reliability) than pension ABO amounts and whether these OPEB obligations are helpful in explaining share prices.

The study finds that postretirement APBO amounts are negatively and significantly correlated with equity market values.[42] However, the multiple applied to these OPEB obligations appears to be roughly half as large as the multiple associated with the pension ABO amounts. The study concludes that *SFAS No. 106* APBO amounts are significantly less reliable than are pension ABO measures and are less reliable for firms with relatively few retirees. This is consistent with the conjecture that it is more difficult to reliably estimate healthcare benefits that are to be provided farther into the future. Thus, the results of this study suggest that the APBO measures reported under *SFAS No. 106* do not have the same reliability that *SFAS No. 87* pension disclosures have in valuing equity securities.

SUMMARY

- Under *SFAS Nos. 87* and *132*, pension expense consists of service cost, interest cost, expected return on plan assets, and three other components.
- The three other components are smoothing mechanisms that avoid year-to-year volatility in pension expense but make pension accounting exceedingly complex, since many pension-related items are "off-balance sheet."
- Because some pension items are "off-balance sheet," the FASB requires firms to disclose the funded status of the plan—the difference between the market value of plan assets and the projected benefit obligation—and to reconcile funded status to reported balance sheet amounts.
- An understanding of the funded status disclosure provides readers with an improved basis for assessing future operating cash flow.
- The reporting rules for postretirement benefit plans (OPEB) closely parallel the pension accounting rules.
- Prior to the issuance of *SFAS No. 106*, only a few companies funded postretirement benefits other than pensions. Consequently, significant amounts of off-balance sheet liabilities exist for many firms. Careful scrutiny of the *SFAS No. 106* footnote disclosures provides analysts with an improved basis for assessing the future cash outflows that are associated with existing promises to provide postretirement benefits.
- Research evidence suggests that the equity valuation impact of these estimated OPEB obligations is less than dollar-for-dollar due to the considerable uncertainty and measurement error associated with these estimates.
- Statement readers should view the following circumstances as potential warning signals or indicators of earnings management:
  1. A significant divergence between any of the various pension and OPEB rates selected by a firm (that is, the discount rate, the expected rate of return on plan assets, or the rate of increase in future compensation levels or healthcare costs) and the rates chosen by other firms in its industry.
  2. A very large difference between the chosen expected rate of return on plan assets and the discount rate used.
  3. An increase in the year-to-year expected rate of return on plan assets that seems unrelated to changes in market conditions.
  4. A decrease in the assumed rate of increase in future compensation levels (or—for OPEB—future health cost trends) that cannot be explained by changing industry or labor market conditions.

Each of these items can change reported income. Furthermore, they also affect the reported PBO or APBO.

---

[42] Choi, et al., op. cit.

SELF-STUDY PROBLEM

ILLUSTRATION OF PENSION COMPUTATIONS

The pension benefit formula of Hayes Corporation provides a pension benefit of $400 per year for each year of service to the company plus 40% of the employee's salary at the time of retirement, which is age 68. Payments begin one year after retirement and are paid annually thereafter. The actuarially determined life expectancy of employees is 78 years.

Hayes Corporation adopts the pension plan on January 1, 2005. One of Hayes Corporation's employees, Scott Schaefer, is granted credit for 10 years of prior service. He is exactly 48 years old on the date the plan is adopted. His salary on January 1, 2005 is $75,000; his salary at retirement in 20 years is expected to be $130,000.

Hayes uses a 7% interest rate for both the discounting ("settlement rate") and earnings rate on plan assets.

1. **Compute the projected benefit obligation (PBO) related to Mr. Schaefer's benefits as of January 1, 2025.**

   Mr. Schaefer will retire on his 68th birthday, which is January 1, 2025. The first pension benefit will be paid one year later and additional benefits are expected to continue to January 1, 2035 for a total of ten payments.

   To compute the PBO, first determine the undiscounted annual expected pension benefits as of January 1, 2025, the retirement date:

Years of service credit as of 1/1/05:		
10 years × $400 per year	= $	4,000
Benefits tied to expected salary at retirement:		
0.40 × $130,000	=	52,000
Total annual pension benefit based on service		
credit as of 1/1/05	= $	56,000

   This $56,000 annual pension benefit will be paid for 10 years beginning on January 1, 2026. The present value of an ordinary annuity of $56,000 per period for 10 periods at 7% (Appendix I, Table 2) is:

$56,000 × 7.02358	=	$393,320.48

   So $393,320.48 is the present value of the annuity at the retirement date, January 1, 2025. To determine the PBO, we must compute the present value of this annuity as of January 1, 2005—that is, discount the still distant annuity back to the present. To do this we take the present value factor for a payment to be received in 20 periods at 7%, which Appendix I, Table 1 indicates is 0.25842:

$393,320.48 × 0.25842	=	$101,641.87

   The PBO related to Mr. Schaefer's benefits as of January 1, 2005 is $101,641.87.

2. **Compute the accumulated benefit obligation (ABO) related to Mr. Schaefer's benefits as of January 1, 2005.**

   This computation is similar to the PBO computation *except* the annual pension benefit is based on Mr. Schaefer's current salary of $75,000, not on his expected salary at retirement. The computation is:

Years of service credit as of 1/1/05:		
10 years × $400 per year	= $	4,000
Benefits tied to current salary:		
0.40 × $75,000	=	30,000
Total annual pension benefit based on service		
credit as of 1/1/05	= $	34,000

   This is the annual pension benefit that Mr. Schaefer would receive if his salary at retirement equals his current salary. The present value at 7% as of January 1, 2025 of a 10-year annuity of $34,000 per year with the first payment on January 1, 2026 is:

$34,000 × 7.02358	=	$238,801.72

Since $238,801.72 is the present value 20 years in the future, we must now determine the present value at January 1, 2005. To do this, we multiply $238,801.72 by the 7% present value factor for a flow 20 years distant:

$$\$238,801.72 \times 0.25842 \qquad = \qquad \$61,711.14$$

So the ABO related to Mr. Schaefer's benefits as of January 1, 2005 is $61,711.14.

3. **Compute the projected benefit obligation (PBO) related to Mr. Schaefer's benefits as of January 1, 2006.**

The January 1, 2006 PBO will exceed the January 1, 2005 figure because: (a) Schaefer's additional year of service adds $400 to his annual pension benefit, and (b) the present value of the pension stream has increased because one year has elapsed.

a. Increase in annual pension benefit:

Years of service credit as of 1/1/06:		
11 years × $400 per year	=	$ 4,400
Benefits tied to expected salary at retirement:		
0.40 × $130,000	=	52,000
Total annual pension benefit based on service credit as of 1/1/06		$ 56,400

b. Increase in present value:
The present value of the 10-year annuity at January 1, 2025 is simply:

$$\$56,400 \times 7.02358 \qquad = \qquad \$396,129.91$$

But this annuity is now only 19 years away, not 20. So its present value at January 1, 2006 is:

$$\$396,129.91 \times 0.27651 \qquad = \qquad \$109,533.88$$

Note that the present value factor is from the 19 period row of the 7% column from Appendix I, Table 1. Over 2005, the PBO has grown to $109,533.88.

4. **Compute pension expense for 2005 attributable to Mr. Schaefer's employment. Show the components of pension expense.**

a. Service cost:
On page 752, service cost is defined as the increase in the discounted present value of the pension benefit ultimately payable (PBO) that is attributable to an additional year's employment.

In our example, Mr. Schaefer's annual pension benefit increased by $400 (that is, $56,400 − $56,000) by virtue of his having accrued an additional year of service credit in 2005. The present value of this increase in the ten expected pension benefit payments as of January 1, 2025 is:

$$\$400 \times 7.02358 \qquad = \qquad \$ 2,809.43$$

This $2,809.43 is the increase in the present value as measured 19 periods in the future—that is, at January 1, 2025. The increase in the present value during 2005 measured as of January 1, 2006 is:

$$\$2,809.43 \times 0.27651 \qquad = \qquad \$ 776.84$$

So service cost for 2005 is $776.84.

b. Interest cost:
This is determined by multiplying the start of the period PBO by the settlement rate. The PBO at January 1, 2005 was $101,641.87. So interest cost for 2005 is:[43]

$$\$101,641.87 \times .07 \qquad = \qquad \$ 7,114.93$$

[43] Notice that the change in the PBO during 2005 was $109,533.88 minus $101,641.87 or $7,892.01. Since there were no changes in actuarial assumptions, plan benefits, or discount rates, the PBO change is totally attributable to 2005 service cost plus interest cost. As computed above, service cost plus interest cost totals $7,891.77, which differs from $7,892.01 only because of rounding error.

c. Recognized prior service cost:

Because the plan was adopted on January 1, 2005 and because Mr. Schaefer was given credit for prior service, the entirety of the PBO at January 1, 2005 is composed of *un*recognized prior service cost. Since Schaefer's expected remaining service period is 20 years (January 1, 2005 through January 1, 2025), the *recognized* prior service cost in 2005 is:

$$\$101,641.87 \div 20 \text{ years} \qquad = \qquad \$\ 5,082.09$$

d. Other pension expense elements for 2005:

Since there were no plan assets at the start of 2005 and since there were no actuarial gains or losses or transitional amounts, there are no other pension expense elements for 2005. **So total pension expense for 2005 attributable to Mr. Schaefer's employment is:**

$$\$776.84 + \$7,114.93 + \$5,082.09 \qquad = \qquad \$\ 12,973.86$$

EXERCISES

E14 – 1
Determining projected benefit obligation

The following information pertains to Seda Company's pension plan:

Actuarial estimate of projected benefit obligation at 1/1/05	$72,000
Assumed discount rate	10%
Service cost for 2005	18,000
Pension benefits paid during 2005	15,000

Required:

If no change in actuarial estimates occurred during 2005, how much would Seda's projected benefit obligation be at December 31, 2005?

E14 – 2
Pension liability on balance sheet

At December 31, 2005 the following information was provided by Kerr Corporation's pension plan administrator:

Fair value of plan assets	$3,450,000
Accumulated benefit obligation	4,300,000
Projected benefit obligation	5,700,000

Required:

What is the amount of the pension liability that should be shown on Kerr's December 31, 2005 balance sheet?

E14 – 3
Determining prepaid pension cost

On January 2, 2005 Loch Company established a noncontributory defined benefit plan covering all employees, and it contributed $1,000,000 to the plan. At December 31, 2005 Loch determined that the 2005 service and interest costs on the plan were $620,000. The expected and the actual rate of return on plan assets for 2005 was 10%. There are no other components of Loch's pension expense.

Required:

What amount should Loch report in its December 31, 2005 balance sheet as prepaid pension cost?

E14 – 4
Determining employer's pension contribution

Webb Company implemented a defined benefit pension plan for its employees on January 1, 2002. During 2002 and 2003, Webb's contributions fully funded the plan. The following data are provided for 2004 and 2005:

	2005 Estimated	2004 Actual
Projected benefit obligation, December 31	$750,000	$700,000
Plan assets at fair value, December 31	675,000	600,000
Projected benefit obligation in excess of plan assets	75,000	100,000
Pension expense	90,000	75,000
Employer's contribution	?	50,000

Required:

What amount should Webb contribute in order to report an accrued pension liability of $15,000 in its December 31, 2005 balance sheet?

Nome Company sponsors a defined benefit plan covering all employees. Benefits are based on years of service and compensation levels at the time of retirement. Nome determined that as of September 30, 2005 its accumulated benefit obligation was $380,000 and its plan assets had a $290,000 fair value. Nome's September 30, 2005 trial balance showed a prepaid pension cost of $20,000.

E14 – 5

Required additional pension liability

Required:

In its September 30, 2005 balance sheet, what amount should Nome report as *additional* pension liability?

The following information pertains to Gali Company's defined benefit pension plan for 2005:

Fair value of plan assets, beginning of year	$350,000
Fair value of plan assets, end of year	525,000
Employer contributions	110,000
Benefits paid	85,000

E14 – 6

Determining actual return on plan assets

Required:

What was the dollar amount of actual return on plan assets for Gali Company in 2005?

The following information pertains to Kane Company's defined benefit pension plan:

Prepaid pension cost, 1/1/05	$ 2,000
Service cost	19,000
Interest cost	38,000
Expected return on plan assets	22,000
Amortization of unrecognized prior service cost	52,000
Employer contributions	40,000

The fair value of plan assets exceeds the accumulated benefit obligation.

E14 – 7

Determining accrued pension liability on balance sheet

Required:

In its December 31, 2005 balance sheet, what amount should Kane report as unfunded accrued pension cost?

Dell Company adopted a defined benefit pension plan on January 1, 2005. Dell amortizes the prior service cost over 16 years and funds prior service cost by making equal payments to the fund trustee at the end of each of the first 10 years. The service cost is fully funded at the end of each year. The following data are available for 2005:

Service cost for 2005	$220,000	
Prior service cost		
Amortized		83,400
Funded		114,400

E14 – 8

Prepaid pension cost on balance sheet

Required:

How much is Dell's prepaid pension cost at December 31, 2005?

On January 1, 2005 East Corporation adopted a defined benefit pension plan. The plan's service cost of $150,000 was fully funded at the end of 2005. Prior service cost was funded by a contribution of $60,000 in 2005. Amortization of prior service cost was $24,000 for 2005.

E14 – 9

Prepaid pension cost on balance sheet

Required:

At December 31, 2005 what amount should East report as prepaid pension cost?

E14 – 10

Minimum pension liability

AICPA
ADAPTED

Payne, Inc. implemented a defined benefit pension plan for its employees on January 1, 2005. The following data are provided for 2005, as of December 31, 2005:

Accumulated benefit obligation	$103,000
Plan assets at fair value	78,000
Net periodic pension cost	90,000
Employer's contribution	70,000

Required:

What amount should Payne record as additional minimum pension liability at December 31, 2005?

E14 – 11

Determining postretirement expense

AICPA
ADAPTED

Hukle Company has provided the following information pertaining to its postretirement plan for 2005:

Service cost	$240,000
Benefit payment	110,000
Interest on accumulated postretirement benefit obligation	40,000
Unrecognized transition obligation (being amortized over 20 years)	200,000

Required:

Calculate Hukle Company's 2005 net periodic postretirement benefit cost.

E14 – 12

Determining pension expense

AICPA
ADAPTED

The following information pertains to Lee Corporation's defined benefit pension plan for 2005:

Service cost	$160,000
Actual and expected return on plan assets	35,000
Unexpected loss on plan assets due to 2005 disposal of a subsidiary	40,000
Amortization of unrecognized prior service costs	5,000
Annual interest on pension obligation	50,000

Required:

Determine Lee Corporation's pension expense that would be reported on its 2005 income statement.

E14 – 13

Determining pension expense, actual and deferred return on plan assets

Bostonian Company provided the following information related to its defined benefit pension plan for 2005:

Projected benefit obligation (PBO) on 1/1/05	$2,500,000
Fair value of plan assets on 1/1/05	2,000,000
Interest rate for discounting pension obligations	10%
Service cost	120,000
Fair value of plan assets on 12/31/05	2,300,000
Payments made to retirees during the year	100,000
Amortization of transition asset	40,000
Recognized actuarial losses	50,000
Expected return on plan assets	12%
Contributions made to plan during 2005	80,000

Required:

1. What amount of pension expense should Bostonian report for 2005?
2. What is the actual dollar return on plan assets for 2005?
3. What was the dollar amount of return on plan assets that was deferred in 2005?

On December 31, 2005 Nelson Corporation reported the following balances related to its defined benefit pension plan:

E14 – 14

Funded status reconciliation

Accumulated benefit obligation	$825,000
Projected benefit obligation	900,000
Accrued pension cost	112,500
Plan assets (fair value)	307,500
Market-related asset value	301,250
Unrecognized prior service cost	190,000
Unamortized transition obligation	160,000
Unrecognized net (gain) loss	?

Required:

Prepare a funded status reconciliation and determine the missing amount for the "Unrecognized net (gain) loss."

Jones Company has a postretirement benefit (healthcare) plan for its employees. On January 1, 2005 the balance in the "Accumulated postretirement benefit obligation" account was $300 million. The assumed discount rate—for purposes of determining postretirement obligations and expenses—is 8%. Jones does not prefund postretirement benefits, so there are no plan assets. The unrecognized transition obligation that existed on January 1, 2003 (when *SFAS No. 106*, "Employer's Accounting for Postretirement Benefits Other than Pensions," was adopted by Jones) was $240 million; this amount is being amortized over 20 years. A prior service cost *credit* of $45 million was created in 2004 when Jones modified the healthcare plan to reduce the maximum benefits paid to each employee. This amount is being amortized over 15 years. The service cost component of postretirement benefits for 2005 is $35 million.

E14 – 15

Determining postretirement (healthcare) benefits expense and obligation

Required:

1. Determine the amount of postretirement benefits cost for 2005.
2. If benefits paid out to retirees totaled $64 million in 2005, determine the balance in the "Accumulated postretirement benefit obligation" account on December 31, 2005.

Zeff Manufacturing provides the following information about its postretirement healthcare plan for 2005:

E14 – 16

Postretirement healthcare expenses and liability balance

Accumulated benefit obligation on 1/1/05	$300,000
Fair value of plan assets on 1/1/05	30,000
Fair value of plan assets on 12/31/05	40,000
Service cost for 2005	20,000
Discount rate	8%
Expected long-run rate of return on plan assets	10%
Recognized prior service cost *credit*	5,000
Recognized loss	7,000
Amortization of transition net liability (loss)	15,000
Actual return on plan assets	4,500
Contributions to the plan	12,000

Required:

1. Determine the postretirement healthcare expense for Zeff in 2005.
2. Determine the amount of benefits paid out to employees in 2005.
3. Determine the amount of accumulated benefit obligation at December 31, 2005.

Bonny Corp. has a defined benefit pension plan for its employees who have an average remaining service life of 10 years. The following information is available for 2005 and 2006 related to the pension plan:

E14 – 17

Components of unrecognized net gain or loss

	2006	2005
Projected benefit obligation, 1/1	$829,400	$750,000
Service cost	70,000	60,000
Actual return on plan assets	66,400	72,000
Bonny Corp. contributions for year ended 12/31	74,000	68,000
Benefits paid during year	67,000	60,000
Fair value of plan assets, 1/1	680,000	600,000
Expected return on plan assets	10%	10%
Settlement rate	10%	10%
Actuarial loss during year	(13,000)	(4,400)

Bonny Corp. had no beginning balance in its unrecognized gains and losses account on January 1, 2005. The actuarial losses arose due to changes in assumptions made by the actuaries regarding both salary increases (2005) and mortality estimates (2006).

Required:

1. Compute the year-end balance in unrecognized net gain or loss for Bonny Corp. for 2005 and 2006.
2. Compute the projected benefit obligation for Bonny Corp. at December 31, 2006.
3. Compute the fair value of plan assets at December 31, 2006.

E14 – 18

Determining amount of recognized net gain or loss using the corridor approach

At January 1, 2005, Milo Co.'s projected benefit obligation is $300,000 and the fair market value of its pension plan assets is $340,000. The average remaining service period of Milo Co.'s employees is 10 years. The following additional information is available related to Milo's unrecognized gains and losses:

	2005	2006	2007
Unrecognized gain (loss) at 1/1	$ 40,000	$ 28,000	$ 53,000
PBO at 12/31	341,000	402,000	416,000
Fair value of plan assets at 12/31	323,000	419,000	438,000

Required:

For each year, 2005 through 2007, compute the amount of recognized gain or loss to be included in pension expense. Indicate whether the amount recognized would increase or decrease pension expense.

E14 – 19

Funded status reconciliation

On December 31, 2005, Johnson Corporation reported the following information related to its defined benefit pension plan:

Projected benefit obligation	$(540,000)
Fair value of plan assets	?
Prepaid pension cost	22,000
Accumulated benefit obligation	(270,000)
Unrecognized prior service cost	(120,000)
Unamortized transition obligation	(88,000)
Unrecognized net gain	116,000

Required:

Prepare a funded status reconciliation using the format in Figure 14.8 on p. 774 and determine the amount of the missing value, "Fair value of plan assets."

E14 – 20

Determining pension elements

George Corporation has a defined benefit pension plan for its employees. The following information is available for 2005:

Projected benefit obligation at 1/1	$ 930,000
Payments made to retirees during 2005	204,000
Service cost	196,000
Discount rate	10%
Expected return on plan assets	6%
Actual return on plan assets	30,000
Plan contributions during 2005	130,000
Fair value of plan assets at 12/31/05	880,000
Amortization of prior service cost	36,000
Amortization of transition obligation	40,000

Required:

1. What was the January 1, 2005 fair value of the plan assets?
2. What is the expected dollar return on plan assets for 2005?
3. What amount of pension expense should George Corporation report for the year ended December 31, 2005? Prepare the journal entry to record pension expense.
4. What was the dollar amount of return (loss) on plan assets that was deferred during 2005?

Ray Inc. has a defined benefit pension plan for its 300 employees. These employees have an average remaining service life of 20 years. At January 1, 2005 Ray Inc. has a projected benefit obligation of $700,000 and unrecognized prior service cost of $200,000. At January 1, 2006, Ray's balance sheet shows a $50,000 prepaid pension cost asset as a result of the company's funding an amount in excess of pension expense over the past several years. Additional information follows:

E14 – 21

Determining pension elements

	December 31	
	2006	**2005**
Accumulated benefit obligation	$545,000	$530,000
Projected benefit obligation	?	?
Benefits paid during the year	82,000	75,000
Fair value of plan assets	380,000	?
Contributions	106,000	99,000
Unrecognized prior service cost	?	190,000
Service cost	97,000	95,000
Actual return on plan assets	18,000	60,000
Expected rate of return on plan assets	10%	10%
Discount rate	10%	10%

Required:

1. Compute the amount of unrecognized prior service cost to be included as a component of pension expense for 2005 and 2006.
2. Compute the fair value of the plan assets at December 31, 2005.
3. Compute the amount of return on plan assets to be included as a component of pension expense for 2006.
4. Compute the balance in the projected benefit obligation at December 31, 2005 and 2006.
5. Compute the amount of unrecognized prior service cost at December 31, 2006.
6. Compute pension expense for 2006.
7. Prepare the company's required pension journal entry for 2006.
8. Compute the amount of prepaid pension cost or accrued pension cost (whichever applies) at December 31, 2006.

On January 1, 2005, Cello Co. established a defined benefit pension plan for its employees. At January 1, 2005, Cello estimates that the service cost for 2005 is $45,000, and at January 1, 2006 it estimates 2006 service cost to be $49,000. On the plan inception date, prior service credit was granted to employees for five years, the period of time between the formation of the company and the plan inception date. The prior service cost was estimated as $650,000 at January 1, 2005. Cello uses a 10% discount rate and assumes a return on plan assets of 9%. The average remaining service life of employees is 20 years and the company will fund an amount equal to service cost plus interest cost for 2005 and 2006.

E14 – 22

Determining pension elements and reconciliation schedule

	December 31	
	2006	**2005**
Projected benefit obligation	?	?
Benefits paid during the year	2,000	–0–
Fair value of plan assets	?	–0–
Contributions	?	?
Actual return on plan assets	3,200	–0–

Required:

1. Compute the amount of unrecognized prior service cost to be included as a component of pension expense for 2005.
2. Compute pension expense for 2005.

3. Prepare the company's required pension journal entry for 2005.
4. Compute the fair value of the plan assets at December 31, 2005.
5. Compute the balance of the projected benefit obligation at December 31, 2005.
6. Repeat requirements 2 through 5 for 2006.
7. Compute the amount of prepaid pension cost or accrued pension cost (whichever applies) at December 31, 2006.
8. Reconcile the funded status of the plan with the pension amounts reported in the financial statements as of December 31, 2006.

PROBLEMS/DISCUSSION QUESTIONS

P14 – 1

Determining components of pension expense

The following information pertains to Sparta Company's defined benefit pension plan:

Discount rate	8%
Expected rate of return on plan assets	10%
Average service life	12 years

At 1/1/05

Projected benefit obligation	$600,000
Fair value of pension plan assets	720,000
Unrecognized prior service cost	240,000
Unrecognized prior pension gain	96,000

At 12/31/05

Projected benefit obligation	910,000
Fair value of pension plan assets	825,000

Service cost for 2005 was $90,000. There were no contributions made or benefits paid during the year. Sparta's unfunded accrued pension liability was $8,000 at January 1, 2005. Sparta uses the straight-line method of amortization over the maximum period permitted.

Required:

Determine the amount for each of the following items:
1. Interest cost
2. Expected dollar return on plan assets
3. Actual return on plan assets
4. Balance in "Unrecognized prior pension gain" account on December 31, 2005
5. Recognized prior service costs
6. Recognized pension gain (minimum amortization)

P14 – 2

Comprehensive pension reporting computations

Turner Inc. provides a defined benefit pension plan to its employees. The company has 150 employees. The average remaining service life of employees is 10 years. Prior to 2005, the net pension expense recognized has always equaled the company's contributions to the plan. However, in 2005 the company changed its funding policy to make at least the minimum annual contribution required by applicable regulations. The cumulative unrecognized net gain or loss was zero at December 31, 2004. Additional information follows:

	December 31	
Description	2005	2004
Projected benefit obligation	$1,450,000	$1,377,000
Accumulated benefit obligation	1,425,000	1,350,000
Fair value of plan assets	1,395,000	1,085,000
Moving average (smoothed) value of plan assets	1,180,000	1,085,000
Unrecognized prior service cost	?	292,000
Service cost	117,400	
Contribution	169,000	
Settlement rate	10%	10%
Expected rate of return	10%	10%
Benefit payments made	None	None

Required:

Round all amounts to nearest dollar:

1. Compute unrecognized prior service cost that would be amortized as a component of pension expense for 2005 and 2006.
2. Compute the actual return on plan assets for 2005.
3. Compute the unexpected net gain or loss for 2005.
4. Compute pension expense for 2005.
5. Prepare the company's required pension journal entries for 2005.
6. Compute the 2005 increase/decrease in unrecognized net gains or losses and the amount to be amortized in 2005 and 2006. (Assume Turner uses the moving average value of plan assets in computing the 10% corridor.)
7. Reconcile the funded status of the plan with the pension amounts reported in the financial statements as of December 31, 2005.

Puhlman Inc. provides a defined benefit pension plan to its employees. Prior to 2005, the net pension expense recognized has always equaled the company's contributions to the plan. However, in 2005 the company changed its funding policy to make at least the minimum annual contribution required by applicable regulations. Additional information follows:

P14 – 3

Comprehensive pension reporting computations

	December 31	
Description	**2005**	**2004**
Projected benefit obligation	$2,700,000	$2,500,000
Accumulated benefit obligation	2,335,000	2,150,000
Fair value of plan assets	?	2,100,000
Moving average (smoothed) value of plan assets	2,140,000	2,100,000
Benefit payments made	?	231,000
Unrecognized net loss	114,000	–0–
Unrecognized prior service cost	?	400,000
Average remaining service life of employees	15 years	15 years
Service cost	214,000	
Contribution	321,000	
Settlement rate	9%	10%
Expected rate of return	10%	10%

During 2005 the PBO increased by $33,000 due to a decrease in the settlement rate from the previous year. Assume for 2006 that the expected rate of return remains at 10% and the expected return is $227,800.

Required:

Round all amounts to nearest dollar:

1. Compute the fair value of plan assets at December 31, 2005.
2. Compute unrecognized prior service cost that would be amortized as a component of pension expense for 2005 and 2006.
3. Compute the actual return on plan assets for 2005.
4. Compute the benefit payments made in 2005.
5. Compute pension expense for 2005.
6. Prepare the company's required pension journal entries for 2005.
7. Compute the 2005 increase/decrease in unrecognized net gains or losses and the amount to be amortized in 2005 and 2006. (Assume Puhlman uses the moving average value of plan assets in computing the 10% corridor.)
8. Reconcile the funded status of the plan with the pension amounts reported in the financial statements as of December 31, 2005.

Mary Abbott is a long-time employee of Love Enterprises, a manufacturer and distributor of farm implements. Mary plans to retire on her sixty-fifth birthday (January 1, 2010) five years from today. Mary's current salary is $48,000 per year and her projected salary for her last year of employment is $60,000.

P14 – 4

Determining PBO and ABO

Love Enterprises sponsors a defined benefit pension plan. The plan provides for an annual pension benefit equal to 60% of the employee's annual salary immediately prior to retirement. Payments commence on the employee's sixty-sixth birthday or one year after the anniversary date of their retirement. The discount ("settlement") and earnings rate on plan assets is 8%. The average life expectancy for female employees is 80 and for males is 76.

Required:

1. Compute the projected benefit obligation related to Ms. Abbott's pension benefits as of January 1, 2005.
2. Compute the accumulated benefit obligation related to Ms. Abbott's pension benefits as of January 1, 2005.
3. Repeat requirement 1, assuming the discount and earnings rate are 11%.

P14 – 5

PBO, ABO, and pension expense

Assume the pension benefit formula of ABC Corporation calls for paying a pension benefit of $250/year for each year of service with the company plus 50% of the projected last year's salary just prior to retirement. Payments begin one year after the employee attains the age of 65 and are paid annually thereafter. The average life expectancy of employees is 76.

The pension plan is adopted on January 1, 2005. One of the company's employees, Ima Workaholic, is granted credit for 10 years of prior service. He is 50 years old at the date the plan is adopted. His current annual salary is $20,000, but his salary level when he retires in 15 years is expected to be $30,000.

Assume a 10% rate of interest for both the discounting ("settlement rate") and earnings rate on plan assets.

Required:

1. Determine the projected benefit obligation and accumulated benefit obligation related to Mr. Workaholic's pension benefits as of January 1, 2005.
2. What would the projected benefit obligation be on January 1, 2006?
3. How much pension expense should ABC Corporation recognize in 2005 for Workaholic? Show the components of pension expense.

P14 – 6

PBO, ABO, and pension expense

Assume the same facts for ABC Corporation that were cited in P14-5, with the following exceptions:

- Assume both that ABC Corporation fully funds the estimated PBO on January 1, 2005 and that invested funds earn an actual return of 12% in 2005.
- Suppose that in addition to funding the estimated PBO on January 1, 2005, ABC Corporation follows a policy of contributing to the pension fund (at the end of each year) an amount equal to the estimated pension expense less the prior service cost component, which was prefunded. On January 1, 2006 the settlement rate drops from 10% to 9%, while the expected return on plan assets remains at 10% for 2006.

Required:

1. How much pension expense should ABC Corporation recognize in 2005? Show the components of pension expense. Explain how this differs from your answer in requirement 3 of P14-5.
2. Compute the pension expense and amount funded in 2006. (Assume the actual return on plan assets was 10% in 2002.) Compare the funded status of the plans at the end of 2006 and 2005. Explain the change.

P14 – 7

Effect of funding and discount rate assumption on pension expense

On January 1, 2005 Magee Corporation started doing business by hiring R. Walker as an employee at an annual salary of $50,000, with an annual salary increment of $10,000. Based on his current age and the company's retirement program, Mr. Walker is required to retire at the end of the year in 2008. However, at his option, Mr. Walker could retire any time after completing one full year of service. Regardless of when he retires, the company will pay a lump-sum pension at the end of the year in 2009. The lump-sum payment is calculated to be 25% of the cumulative lifetime salary earned by Mr. Walker. Magee's annual discount rate is 10%. Assume that Mr. Walker retires at the end of the year in 2008.

Required:

1. Assuming that Magee Corporation does not fund its pension expense, calculate the pension expense for the years 2005 through 2008. Clearly identify the service and interest cost components. Based on your calculations, provide journal entries both to record the pension expense during the 2005–2009 period as well as to record the lump-sum payment of Mr. Walker's pension at the end of the year in 2009.
2. Assume that Magee Corporation fully funds its pension cost as soon as it vests and that the contributions to the pension fund earn exactly a 10% rate of return annually. Based on these revised assumptions, redo requirement 1.
3. Explain why the total pension expense in requirement 1 is different from that in requirement 2.
4. Assume that Magee Corporation does not fund its pension expense. Discuss how different assumptions regarding the discount rate affect the pension expense. Compare the pension expense with discount rates of 5%, 10%, and 15%.

Use the same set of facts as in P14-7. In addition, assume that based on ERISA rules, Magee Corporation must contribute the following amounts to the pension fund:

	2005	2006	2007	2008
Contributions	$8,475	$11,000	$15,000	$18,000

Magee Corporation intends to fund the pension plan only to the extent required by the ERISA rules. Assume that the contributions to the pension fund earn exactly a 10% rate of return annually.

P14 – 8

Determining effect of discount rate assumption on pension expense and PBO

www.prenhall.com/revsine

● Student Resources

☑ Template for solution

Required:

1. The CEO of the company, Mr. R. Magee, is considering three possible discount rates (8%, 10%, and 12%) for calculating the annual pension expense. Provide schedules showing how much pension expense will be reported under each of the three scenarios during the 2005–2009 period.
2. Provide schedules showing the funded status of the pension plan during the 2005–2008 period.
3. Mr. Magee is wondering which of the three discount rate assumptions would be considered the most and least conservative for the purposes of determining net income. Prepare a schedule that shows how total pension expense compares across the three discount rate assumptions. Explain your results.

The following is the funded status of the pension plan of Saddington, Inc. as of December 31, 2005:

	End of Year 2005
Projected benefit obligation	$(1,000,000)
Fair value of plan assets	1,000,000
Fair value in excess of PBO	–0–
Unrecognized gain	–0–
Accrued pension liability	–0–

P14 – 9

Components of pension liability and pension expense

www.prenhall.com/revsine

● Student Resources

☑ Template for solution

The following information is provided for the years 2006 through 2009:

	2006	2007	2008	2009
Actual rate of return on plan assets	22%	20%	12%	10%
Contribution to pension fund	$220,000	$260,000	$300,000	$340,000
Pension payments	200,000	260,000	320,000	380,000
Service cost	300,000	350,000	400,000	450,000
Average remaining service period of active employees (in years)	10	10	10	10

The "Contribution to pension fund" component represents the cash flows from the company to the pension fund. The "Pension payments" component represents the payments made by the pension fund to the retired employees. The income earned by the pension fund in a given year is found by multiplying the fair value of the plan assets at the beginning of the year by the actual rate of return on plan assets for that year. The discount rate is 10% and the expected rate of return is 12% during each year from 2006 to 2009. Assume that the pension fund is not considered to be severely underfunded in any of the years over the 2006–2009 period.

Required:

1. Prepare schedules showing the changes in the following pension components over the 2006–2009 period:

   a. Projected benefit obligation
   b. Fair value of plan assets
   c. Unrecognized gain

2. Based on your answer to requirement 1, show the funded status of the plan at the end of years 2006 through 2009.
3. Calculate pension expense for the years 2006 through 2009 and provide breakdowns for service cost, interest cost, actual return on plan assets, unrecognized portion of return, and recognized gain or loss amounts.
4. Prepare all necessary journal entries pertaining to the accrued pension liability for the years 2006 through 2009. On the basis of the journal entries, construct the T-account for accrued pension liability over the same period.

P14 – 10

Effect of actual versus expected return on pension funded status and pension expense

On December 31, 2005 Muller Corporation eliminated its employee pension plan. The company has currently funded its pension plan for $100,000 (which is the value of the pension plan assets and PBO as of December 31, 2005). The expected return on plan assets and the settlement rate are both 10%. As part of the agreement with the current employees, the company expects to pay a lump sum of $133,100 on January 1, 2009 for pension obligations existing under the canceled pension plan. While the annual expected rate of return is 10%, the realized rates of return on pension assets depend on the state of the U.S. economy over the next three years. Assume that depending on whether the economy is stable, growing, or declining, the pension assets earn the following rates of return over the next three years:

| | Actual Rates of Return for | | |
State of the Economy	2006	2007	2008
Scenario 1: Stable economy	10.00%	10.00%	10.00%
Scenario 2: Growth	5.00%	10.00%	15.24%
Scenario 3: Decline	15.00%	10.00%	5.22%

Required:

1. Show for each state of the economy over the next three years that the pension plan will have sufficient funds to meet the pension obligation at the end of the year 2008. Indicate the value of the pension plan assets at the end of the years 2006 through 2008. Over the three-year period, what is the difference between the actual and expected annual rates of return under each state of the economy?
2. Ignoring the deferral of unexpected gains or losses, calculate the pension expense of Muller Corporation over the next three years under each of the three states of the economy.
3. Recalculate the pension expense of Muller Corporation over the next three years under each of the three states of the economy after incorporating the deferral of unexpected gains or losses. Also show the funded status of the pension plan at the end of 2006, 2007, and 2008.
4. Based on your answers so far, discuss the potential benefit of deferring unexpected gains or losses in the calculation of pension expense.

P14 – 11

Components of OPEB and journal entries

Excerpts from Unicom Corporation's footnotes for the year ended December 31, 1999 follow:

ComEd and certain of Unicom's subsidiaries provide certain postretirement medical, dental and vision care, and life insurance for retirees and their dependents and for the surviving dependents of eligible employees and retirees. Generally, the employees become eligible for postretirement benefits if they retire no earlier than age 55 with ten years of service. The liability for postretirement benefits is funded through trust funds based upon actuarially determined contributions that take into account the amount deductible for income tax purposes. The health care plans are contributory, funded jointly by the companies and the participating retirees. The December 31, 1999 and 1998 postretirement benefit liabilities and related data were determined using the January 1, 1999 actuarial valuations.

Reconciliation of the beginning and ending balances of the accumulated postretirement benefit obligation, and the funded status of the plan for the years 1999 and 1998 follows:

($ in thousands)	Years Ended December 31	
	1999	1998
Change in benefit obligation		
Benefit obligation at beginning of period	$1,236,000	$1,139,000
Service cost	41,000	38,000
Interest cost	82,000	78,000
Plan participants' contributions	4,000	3,000
Actuarial loss (gain)	(188,000)	25,000
Benefits paid	(51,000)	(47,000)
Special termination benefits	27,000	—
Benefit obligation at end of period	1,151,000	1,236,000
Change in plan assets		
Fair value of plan assets at beginning of period	865,000	767,000
Actual return on plan assets	105,000	122,000
Employer contributions	24,000	20,000
Plan participants' contributions	4,000	3,000
Benefits paid	(51,000)	(47,000)
Fair value of plan assets at end of period	947,000	865,000
Plan assets less than benefit obligations	(204,000)	(371,000)
Unrecognized net actuarial gain	(555,000)	(371,000)
Unrecognized prior service cost	41,000	48,000
Unrecognized transition obligation	276,000	323,000
Accrued liability for benefits	$ (442,000)	$ (371,000)

The assumed discount rate used to determine the benefit obligation as of December 31, 1999 and 1998 was 7.75% and 6.75%, respectively. The fair value of plan assets excludes $9 million and $7 million held in a grantor trust as of December 31, 1999 and 1998, respectively, for the payment of postretirement medical benefits.

The components of other postretirement benefit costs, portions of which were recorded as components of construction costs for the years 1999, 1998, and 1997 were as follows:

($ in thousands)	1999	1998	1997
Service cost	$?	$?	$34,000
Interest cost on accumulated benefit obligation	?	?	76,000
Expected return on plan assets	?	?	(61,000)
Amortization of transition obligation	22,000	22,000	22,000
Amortization of prior service costs	4,000	4,000	4,000
Recognized gain	(14,000)	(14,000)	(13,000)
Severance plan costs	1,000	6,000	8,000
Curtailment loss	35,000	–0–	–0–
Net periodic benefit cost	$?	$?	$70,000

The other postretirement benefit curtailment losses in December 1999 represent the recognition of prior service costs and transition obligations, and an increase in the benefit obligations resulting from special termination benefits, related to the reduction in the number of employees due to ComEd's sale of the fossil stations.

The healthcare cost trend rates used to measure the expected cost of the postretirement medical benefits are assumed to be 8.0% for pre-Medicare recipients and 6.0% for Medicare recipients for 1999. Those rates are assumed to decrease in 0.5% annual increments to 5% for the years 2005 and 2001, respectively, and to remain level thereafter. The healthcare cost trend rates, used to measure the expected cost of postretirement dental and vision benefits, are a level 3.5% and 2.0% per year, respectively. Assumed healthcare cost trend rates have a significant effect on the amounts reported for the healthcare plans. A one-percentage point change in the assumed healthcare cost trend rates would have the following effects:

($ in thousands)	1 Percentage Point	
	Increase	Decrease
Effect on total 1999 service and interest cost components	$ 26,000	$(20,000)
Effect on postretirement benefit obligation as of 12/31/1999	190,000	151,000

Required:

1. Assuming an expected rate of return on plan assets for 1999 and 1998 of 8.8% and 9%, compute the missing amounts in the preceding table and determine the "Net periodic benefit cost" for years 1999 and 1998. (Round amounts to nearest million.)
2. Assuming that the $4,000,000 of participant contributions were submitted directly to the trustee by the employees, show the journal entry that Unicom would make to record the 1999 company (employer) contribution and its related "Net periodic benefit cost."
3. What amount (if any) would appear on Unicom's 1999 balance sheet relating to its OPEB plans and how would it be classified?

P14 – 12

Amortization of actuarial gains (losses) and minimum pension liability

www.prenhall.com/revsine

● Student Resources

☑ Template for solution

The following information pertains to the pension plan of Beatty Business Group:

| | Beginning of the Year | | |
Year (1)	Projected Benefit Obligation (2)	Fair Value of Pension Plan Assets (3)	Gain (Loss) for the Year (4)
2006	$ 400,000	$ 390,000	
2007	450,000	410,000	$ (60,000)
2008	570,000	500,000	(120,000)
2009	840,000	800,000	120,000
2010	1,000,000	1,100,000	175,000
2011	1,200,000	1,280,000	250,000
2012	1,450,000	1,310,000	80,000

Note that the information in columns (2) and (3) are as of the beginning of the year, whereas the information in column (4) is measured *over* the year.

The cumulative unrecognized *loss* at the end of 2006 was $70,000. The "Gain (loss) for the year" represents the excess of the realized return on pension plan assets over the expected return for the specific year. When a gain (loss) was reported, then the realized return was higher (lower) than the expected return during that year. The estimated remaining service period of active employees is five years for each of the calendar years.

Required:

1. Provide a schedule showing how the gain (or loss) is amortized over the 2007–2012 period. Clearly indicate whether the amortization increases or decreases the pension expense in each year.
2. Based on available information, prepare a schedule showing the funded status of the plan at the end of the years 2006 through 2011.
3. In answering this requirement, assume that the *accumulated* benefit obligation is 95% of the *projected* benefit obligation in each year. Using this additional information, prepare a schedule showing the funded status of the plan at the end of the years 2006 through 2011. (*Note:* You may have to calculate the minimum pension liability.) Also provide journal entries to reflect the minimum pension liability over the 2006–2011 period.

P14 – 13

Pension expense and funded status

The following is the funded status of the pension plan of McKeown Consulting Company at December 31, 2005:

	2005
Projected benefit obligation	$ (900,000)
Fair value of plan assets	1,000,000
Fair value in excess of PBO	100,000
Unrecognized prior service cost	–0–
Unrecognized (gain) loss	–0–
Accrued pension asset (liability)	$ 100,000

The following information is available for the years 2006 and 2007:

	Years Ended December 31	
	2006	2007
Discount rate	10%	10%
Expected rate of return on plan assets	9%	11%

The service cost for 2006 and 2007 are $125,000 and $145,000, respectively. The interest cost for a given year is estimated by multiplying the PBO at the beginning of the year by the discount rate for the year. Similarly, the expected return on plan assets is computed by multiplying the fair value of plan assets at the beginning of the year by the assumed expected rate of return for the year. During the years 2006 and 2007 the pension fund's actual earnings are $100,000 and $64,740, respectively.

At the end of 2006, McKeown Consulting Company retroactively enhanced the benefits provided under its pension plan, and this increased the projected benefit obligation by $110,000. The average remaining service period of employees expected to receive these retroactive benefits under the plan was 10 years.

During 2006 and 2007 the company made contributions of $99,000 and $123,000, respectively, to the pension fund. In turn, the pension fund made payments of $120,000 and $85,000 to the retired employees during the same periods.

Required:

1. Compute pension expense for the years 2006 and 2007. Show the funded status of the pension plan and the funded status reconciliation as of the end of each of these years. (*Hint:* You will need to calculate the ending balances for PBO, fair value of plan assets, unrecognized prior service costs, and the unrecognized gain or loss at the end of the year.)
2. Provide necessary journal entries in the books of McKeown Consulting Company for the years 2006 and 2007 to record all transactions relating to its pension plan. Also, explain the changes in the accrued pension asset (liability) over the same period.
3. Explain the cause(s) for the difference between the funded status of the pension plan and the reported balance sheet status as of the end of the years 2005 through 2007.

The following information pertains to Kothari Manufacturing Company:

P14 – 14

Solving for pension cost and funded status components

	As of December 31		
	2005	**2006**	**2007**
Projected benefit obligation	$(550,000)	$(684,000)	$(768,720)
Less: Fair value of plan assets	550,000	595,000	686,400
PBO in excess of fair value	–0–	(89,000)	(82,320)
Unrecognized prior service cost	–0–	80,000	64,000
Unrecognized gain	–0–	–0–	(11,900)
Accrued pension asset (liability)	–0–	$ (9,000)	$ (30,220)

www.prenhall.com/revsine

● Student Resources

☑ Template for solution

	Years Ended December 31	
	2006	**2007**
Discount rate	8%	8%
Expected rate of return on plan assets	10%	10%
Actual rate of return on plan assets	10%	12%

The following additional information is available on the annual pension cost:

	Years Ended December 31	
	2006	**2007**
Service cost	$110,000	$130,000
Interest cost	?	?
– Actual return on plan assets	?	?
+/– Deferral of unrecognized gain/loss	?	?
+ Recognized prior service cost	–0–	16,000
Annual pension cost	?	?

Breakdown of the annual pension cost	**2006**	**2007**
Manufacturing employees	$63,000	$85,000
Administrative employees	?	?
Annual pension cost	?	?

At the end of 2006 Kothari Manufacturing Company retroactively enhanced the benefits provided under its pension plan. The average remaining service period of employees expected to receive these retroactive benefits under the plan was five years.

Required:

1. Calculate the missing information required to solve for the annual pension cost for the years 2006 and 2007. Based on this information, complete the breakdown of the annual pension cost between manufacturing and administrative employees.
2. Provide schedules reconciling the changes in the components of the funded status of the pension plan over the years 2006 and 2007 (PBO, fair value of plan assets, unrecognized prior service cost, and unrecognized gain). (*Hint:* You need to prepare the schedule to reconcile beginning and ending PBO before preparing the schedule for the fair value of plan assets.)
3. Provide necessary journal entries in the books of Kothari Manufacturing Company for the years 2006 and 2007 to record all transactions relating to its pension plan. (*Hint:* The annual pension cost for the manufacturing employees is a product cost.)

P14 – 15

OPEB expense
and journal entries

On January 1, 2005 Eccher Retail Stores adopted the provisions of *SFAS No. 106*, "Employers' Accounting for Postretirement Benefits Other Than Pensions." At that time, the company estimated its accumulated benefit obligation for postretirement medical expenses to be $2,000,000. The company elected to amortize this transition obligation over a 20-year period. The service and interest costs during 2005 were $210,000 and $175,000, respectively. The company made cash payments of $245,000 to retired employees for medical expenses.

Required:

1. Calculate the OPEB expense for the year 2005. Provide appropriate disclosures for the components of accrued OPEB liability as of the end of 2005.
2. Provide journal entries to record transactions pertaining to postretirement benefits during the year 2005.
3. Repeat requirements 1 and 2, but assume that the company had elected to immediately recognize the entire transition obligation as of January 1, 2005. Assume a tax rate of 35%.

P14 – 16

Reconciling accumulated
postretirement benefit
obligations and preparing
journal entries

The following information on postretirement benefit obligations is excerpted from Ordonez Corporation's Form 10-K for the fiscal year ending June 30, 2005. (This is a real company whose name has been disguised.)

	As of June 30	
	2005	**2004**
Accumulated benefit obligation (APBO)	$(21,743,000)	$(20,494,000)
Unrecognized transition obligation	12,577,000	13,475,000
Unrecognized net gain	(699,000)	(1,192,000)
Accrued cost (OPEB liability)	$ (9,865,000)	$ (8,211,000)

Assumptions	**2005**	**2004**
Discount rate used to determine APBO	7.00%	7.25%

	Year Ended June 30, 2005
Service cost	$ 467,000
Interest cost	1,444,000
Amortization of transition obligation	898,000
Amortization of unrecognized net gain	0
Net periodic benefit (OPEB) cost	$2,809,000

Benefit payments in 2005 totaled $1,155,000.

Required:

1. Using the format in the chapter on page 787, reconcile the funded status of the plan with the amounts that are recognized/unrecognized on the balance sheet.
2. Assume that only administrative employees are eligible for postretirement benefits. Provide the journal entry to record all transactions pertaining to the OPEB liability during fiscal 2005.
3. Prepare a schedule showing the changes in the accumulated postretirement benefit obligation from 2004 to 2005.
4. What would have been the OPEB expense had the company used the cash basis approach?
5. Prepare a schedule showing the changes in the accrued OPEB liability from 2004 to 2005.

The following is based on information obtained from the 2002–2005 annual reports of the E. L. Baer Company. (These numbers have been modified but are based on the activities of a real company whose name has been disguised.)

C14 – 1

OPEB reconciliation of funded status and expense components

		Years Ended December 31		
($ in thousands)	**2005**	**2004**	**2003**	**2002**
Accumulated postretirement benefit obligation	$15,894	$16,675	$17,815	$15,502
Unrecognized net gain	5,082	3,477	2,789	3,913
Prior service cost (plan curtailments)	2,314	3,070	3,826	4,582
Accrued OPEB liability	$23,290	$23,222	$24,430	$23,997

Other information	Years Ended December 31		
($ in thousands)	**2005**	**2004**	**2003**
Net periodic OPEB cost	$ 883	$ 791	$1,308
Service cost	681	642	998
Interest cost	1,140	1,113	1,199

At the end of years 2002 through 2005, the company had made the following assumptions in measuring the accumulated benefit obligation:

	Years Ended December 31			
Assumptions	**2005**	**2004**	**2003**	**2002**
Discount rate	7.50%	7.25%	7.25%	7.50%
Healthcare cost trend rate (near-term)	6.5–7.0%	7.0–8.5%	8.0–9.5%	8.5–10%

The discount rate is used to find the present value of the expected future payments to employees under the company's OPEB Plan. The healthcare cost trend rate is used to forecast the expected growth in the future medical payments due to inflation in medical costs. Assume there have been no amendments to the plan after 2001 and that the plan is totally unfunded.

Required:

1. Prepare a schedule like the one on page 787, which reconciles the funded status of the OPEB plans with the recognized and unrecognized amounts at December 31, 2005.
2. Complete the following schedule to determine net periodic OPEB cost for 2003, 2004, and 2005.

Net periodic OPEB cost	2005	2004	2003
Service cost	$	$	$
Interest cost			
Amortization of prior service cost			
Recognized net actuarial (gain) loss			
Net periodic OPEB cost	$	$	$

3. Complete the following schedule to explain changes in the accumulated benefit obligation over the period 2003 through 2005.

Accumulated postretirement benefit obligation	2005	2004	2003
APBO at beginning of year	$	$	$
Service cost			
Interest cost			
Actuarial losses (gains)			
Benefits paid			
APBO at end of year	$	$	$

4. Prepare journal entries to record transactions pertaining to the accrued OPEB liability for the period 2003 through 2005. Based on the journal entries, prepare a schedule that shows the changes in the accrued OPEB liability from the beginning to the end of the year for 2003 through 2005.
5. In each of the years 2003 through 2005, the company experienced some unrecognized gain (or loss) from changes in assumptions. Explain the year-to-year changes in unrecognized gain (or loss) by relating them to specific changes in the assumptions made by the company.

C14 – 2

Interpreting pension footnote disclosures

Selected pension information extracted from the retirement benefits footnote that appeared in Aeromed's 2005 annual report follows.

All employees of Aeromed and employees of certain other subsidiaries are eligible to participate in the company's pension plans. The defined benefit plans provide benefits for participating employees based on years of service and average compensation for a specified period of time before retirement.

The following table provides a reconciliation of the changes in the plans' benefit obligations and fair value of assets for the years ended December 31, 2005 and 2004:

Reconciliation of projected benefit obligation ($ in millions)	2005	2004
Obligation at January 1	$6,117	$5,666
Service cost	236	213
Interest cost	433	418
Actuarial loss (gain)	?	300
Plan amendments	?	–0–
Benefit payments	?	(480)
Obligation at December 31	$5,624	$6,117

Reconciliation of fair value of plan assets ($ in millions)	2005	2004
Fair value of plan assets at January 1	$5,564	$5,127
Actual return on plan assets	7	847
Employer contributions	?	70
Benefit payments	?	(480)
Fair value of plan assets at December 31	?	$5,564

The following table provides a statement of funded status of the plans as of December 31, 2005 and 2004:

Funded status ($ in millions)	2005	2004
Projected benefit obligation	$(5,624)	$(6,117)
Fair value of assets	?	5,564
Funded status at December 31:	(341)	(553)
Unrecognized loss	288	651
Unrecognized prior service costs	138	68
Unrecognized transition asset	(7)	(11)
Prepaid pension cost	$ 78	$ 155

The following table provides the components of net periodic pension cost for the years ended December 31, 2005, 2004, and 2003:

Components of net periodic pension cost ($ in millions)	2005	2004	2003
Defined benefit plans:			
Service cost	$ 236	$ 213	$ 179
Interest cost	433	418	393
Expected return on assets	(514)	(472)	(421)
Amortization of:			
Transition asset	(4)	(11)	(12)
Prior service cost	5	4	4
Unrecognized loss	21	22	26
Net periodic benefit cost	$ 177	$ 174	$ 169

The following assumptions were used by the Company in the measurement of the benefit obligation as of December 31:

Weighted-average assumptions	2005	2004
Discount rate	8.25%	7.00%
Salary growth rate	4.26%	4.26%
Expected return on plan assets	9.50%	9.50%

Required:

Show supporting computations with clear labels for all calculations.
1. What is the journal entry to record the amount of cash contributed to the pension plan in 2005?
2. What was the amount of benefit payments distributed to retirees in 2005?
3. Determine the amount of increase (decrease) in the projected benefit obligation (PBO) as a result of amendments to the plan during 2005 and reconcile it with unrecognized prior service costs.
4. Determine the effect of the actuarial loss (gain) on the PBO in 2005. Reconcile the unrecognized loss at December 31, 2004 to the balance at December 31, 2005.
5. What was the effect of increasing the discount rate from 7.00% in 2004 to 8.25% in 2005?
6. Reconcile the funded status of the plan as of December 31, 2005 with the amounts that are recognized/unrecognized on the balance sheet, using the format illustrated on page 774 of the chapter.

The retirement benefit footnote that appeared in Shileny & Cribbs' 2005 annual report follows. The firm is primarily engaged in the exploration, production, and sale of crude oil and natural gas.

All employees of Shileny & Cribbs are eligible to participate in the company's pension plan. The defined benefit plan provides benefits for participating employees based on years of service and average compensation for a specified period of time before retirement.

The following tables provide information about the pension plan:

C14 – 3

Interpreting pension footnote disclosures

Projected benefit obligation ($ in thousands)	Years Ended September 30	
	2005	2004
PBO at beginning of year	$36,954	$33,913
Service cost	3,700	2,836
Interest cost	2,468	2,430
Actuarial (gain) loss	(4,468)	231
Benefit paid	?	(2,456)
PBO at end of year	?	$36,954

Fair value of plan assets and funded status ($ in thousands)	Years Ended September 30	
	2005	2004
Fair value of plan assets at beginning of year	$51,572	$53,834
Actual return on plan assets	?	194
Benefits paid	?	(2,456)
Fair value of plan assets at end of year	$58,517	$51,572
Funded status of the plan (FVPA > PBO)	21,522	14,618
Unrecognized net actuarial gain	(10,127)	(1,647)
Unrecognized prior service cost	1,025	1,263
Unrecognized net transition asset	(1,619)	(2,159)
Prepaid pension cost	$10,801	$12,075

Pension plan assumptions	Years Ended September 30		
	2005	2004	2003
Discount rate	7.50%	6.75%	7.25%
Expected return on plan assets	9.00%	8.50%	9.00%
Rate of compensation increase	5.00%	5.00%	5.50%

Components of net pension expense	Years Ended September 30		
($ in thousands)	**2005**	**2004**	**2003**
Service cost	$3,700	$2,836	$2,114
Interest cost	2,468	2,430	1,797
Expected return on assets	(4,606)	(4,542)	(3,592)
Amortization of prior service cost	238	238	239
Amortization of transition asset	(540)	(540)	(540)
Recognized net actuarial loss (gain)	14	(65)	(66)
Net pension expense (income)	$1,274	$ 357	$ (48)

Required:

Show supporting computations with clear labels for all calculations.

1. What is the required journal entry to record the 2005 net pension expense? What is the primary reason for the $917,000 increase from 2004?
2. You determined the 2005 cash funding of the plan in answering requirement 1. Explain why the company chose to contribute this amount.
3. Compute the PBO at September 30, 2005.
4. Prepare a schedule like the one on page 774 which reconciles the funded status of the pension plan with the recognized and unrecognized amounts at September 30, 2005.
5. Assuming the firm had an unexpected gain of $3,998,000, what was 2005's actual return on plan assets in both dollars and as a percentage?
6. What was the amount of benefit payments distributed to retirees in 2005?
7. Prepare a schedule that reconciles the beginning and ending balances of the unrecognized net actuarial gain number between 2004 and 2005.

C14 – 4

General Electric—
Interpreting OPEB footnote
disclosures

Excerpts from General Electric's 1991 Annual Report footnote for retiree insurance benefits follow:

GE and its affiliates sponsor a number of . . . retiree health and life insurance plans. Principal plans are discussed below; other plans are not significant individually or in the aggregate.

1991 Accounting Change. Statement of Financial Accounting Standards (*SFAS*) *No. 106*—"Employers' Accounting for Postretirement Benefits Other Than Pensions"—was implemented using the immediate recognition transition option, effective as of January 1, 1991.

    SFAS No. 106 requires recognition during employees' service with the Company, of the cost of their retiree health and life insurance benefits. At January 1, 1991, the accumulated postretirement benefit obligation was $4,287 million; however, $1,577 million of this obligation had been provided through the fair market value of related trust assets ($1,037 million) and recorded liabilities ($540 million), thus resulting in a pre-tax adjustment (i.e., transition obligation) of $2,710 million. The effect on net earnings and share owners' equity was $1,799 million ($2.07 per share) after [a] deferred tax benefit of $911 million. Aside from the one-time effect of the adjustment, adoption of *SFAS No. 106* was not material to 1991 financial results.

    Prior to 1991, GE health benefits for eligible retirees under age 65 and eligible dependents were generally included in costs as covered expenses were actually incurred. For eligible retirees and spouses over age 65, the present value of future health benefits was included in costs in the year the retiree became eligible for benefits. The present value of future life insurance benefits for each eligible retiree was included in costs in the year of retirement.

Principal retiree insurance plans generally provide health and life insurance benefits to employees who retire under the GE Pension Plan with 10 or more years of service. Benefit provisions are subject to collective bargaining. At the end of 1991, the plans covered approximately 237,000 retirees and dependents.

Employer costs for principal retiree insurance plans follow.

Cost (income) for retiree insurance plans ($ in millions)	For the year 1991		
	Total	Health	Life
Benefit cost for service during the year—net of retiree contributions	$ 88	$ 65	$ 23
Interest cost on benefit obligations	318	214	104
Actual return on plan assets	(138)	(9)	(129)
Unrecognized portion of return	44	5	39
Amortization	(33)	(33)	–0–
Retiree insurance cost	$279[1]	$242	$ 37

[1]Retiree insurance cost was $249 million in 1990 and $283 million in 1989.

Actuarial assumptions used to determine 1991 costs and benefit obligations for principal plans include a discount rate of 9.0% (8.5% in 1990 and 1989). . . . Recognized return on plan assets for 1991 was determined by applying the expected long-term rate of return of 9.5% (8.5% in 1990 and 1989) to the market-related value of assets. The assumed rate of future increases in per capita cost of healthcare benefits (the healthcare cost trend rate) was 13.0% for 1991, decreasing gradually to 6.6% by the year 2050. These trend rates reflect GE's prior experience and management's expectation that future rates will decline. Increasing the healthcare cost trend rates by one percentage point would increase the accumulated postretirement benefit obligation by $50 million and would increase annual aggregate service and interest costs by $5 million. In connection with its 1992 annual funding review, GE may revise certain actuarial assumptions effective January 1, 1992; however, it is anticipated that any such revision would increase benefit obligations by no more than 5%.

Pension gains and losses that occur because actual experience differs from that assumed are amortized over the average future service period of employees. Amounts allocable to prior service for amendments to . . . retiree insurance plans are amortized in a similar manner.

Funding policy . . . The present value of future life insurance benefits for each eligible retiree is funded in the year of retirement. In general, retiree health benefits are paid as covered expenses are incurred.

The following table compares the market-related value of assets with the value of benefit obligations, recognizing the effects of future . . . service. The market-related value of assets is based on cost plus recognition of market appreciation and depreciation in the portfolio over five years, a method that reduces the impact of short-term market fluctuations.

Funded status for principal plans ($ in millions)	December 31	
	1991	1990
Retiree insurance plans		
Market-related value of assets	$1,124	$1,037
Accumulated postretirement benefit obligation	3,675	4,110

Schedules reconciling the benefit obligations for principal plans with GE's recorded liabilities in the Statement of Financial Position follow.

Reconciliation of benefit obligation with recorded liability ($ in millions)	Retiree Insurance Plans December 31	
	1991	1990[1]
Benefit obligation	$3,675	$4,110
Fair value of trust assets	(1,171)	(1,037)
Unamortized balances		
Experience gains (losses)	(351)	–0–
Plan amendments	829	–0–
Recorded liability	$2,982	$3,073

[1]1990 amounts include the pro forma effects of adopting *SFAS No. 106* as of January 1, 1991.

Unamortized balances for amendments include the effects of changes in retiree insurance plan provisions during 1991.

Required:

1. Explain the nature of the "plan amendments" element in the funded status portion of General Electric's footnote disclosure.
2. Discuss some possible explanations for why a company would initiate changes in plan benefits immediately *after* adopting *SFAS No. 106.*

C14 – 5

Groupe Schneider (KR): Effect of postretirement benefits on company valuation

The following information is excerpted from the footnotes to the 1990 financial statements of Square D:

> **Note P: Post-Retirement Benefits** (*$ in 000*)
>
> The company provides health-plan coverage and life insurance benefits for retired employees of substantially all of its domestic operations. Substantially all of the company's employees may become eligible for these benefits when they retire from active employment with the company. The cost of retiree health coverage is recognized as an expense when claims are paid. The cost of life insurance benefits is recognized as an expense as premiums are paid. These costs totaled $6,165 in 1990, $5,075 in 1989, and $3,982 in 1988.
>
> The Financial Accounting Standards Board has issued *Statement of Financial Accounting Standards No. 106,* "Employers' Accounting for Postretirement Benefits Other Than Pensions." This Statement will require accrual of postretirement benefits during the years an employee provides services. While the impact of this new standard has not been fully determined, the change will result in significantly greater expense being recognized for these benefits. The company plans to adopt this Statement in 1993.

The company had also provided similar footnote disclosures during the previous three years. An article related to Groupe Schneider's investment in Square D appears below.

Required:

What does the article consider as one main reason for the fall in the stock price of Groupe Schneider? What might have been the economic impact if the accounting standard for postretirement benefits (*SFAS No. 106*) were in place when Groupe Schneider acquired Square D Company?

SQUARE D OWNER'S STOCK FALLS BY JACQUES NEHER

The stock of Groupe Schneider, which acquired Palatine-based Square D Co. last summer, dropped sharply last week on the Paris stock exchange. Market sources said that, among other things, Schneider failed to assess correctly the impact of retiree health-benefit liabilities facing Square D.

Under new rules adopted by the Financial Accounting Standards Board, U.S. companies are required by 1993 to record their liability for retiree health benefits on their balance sheets, either as a one-time charge to earnings or spread out over 20 years.

Although it is based in France, Schneider will have to follow U.S. accounting rules, at least for its operations here, if it plans to borrow money or otherwise raise capital in the United States, accounting sources said.

Groupe Schneider, a giant French electrical-equipment and construction firm, acquired Square D this summer for $1.3 billion. At one point last week Schneider stock was off 10 percent in Paris, about twice the decline of the overall market.

The stock closed Monday in Paris at 639.5 French francs, up 2.5 francs from Friday but off from a recent high of 703 earlier this month.

Ian Furnivall, an analyst with UBS/Phillips & Drew in Paris, recently wrote a negative report on the company, saying that Schneider was going to have to increase its so-called goodwill write-offs (reflecting the premium over market value that Schneider paid for Square D) "principally [because of] an unforeseen exceptional charge for staff postretirement health benefits."

The report came about the same time Schneider's finance director, Alain Bommelaer, was replaced.

Jean de Courcel, who took the post of finance director, downplayed the market reports and said the accounting rule change was known to the company when it bought Square D. A Schneider spokesman added that replacing Bommelaer, who is still with the company awaiting a new assignment, had nothing to do with a miscalculation of the Square D purchase price.

Another Schneider financial source, who asked not to be named, described the effect of the accounting change as "a big problem. We've been considering it for three months, like other French companies with operations in the United States, and we still haven't decided what to do."

A spokesman for Square D in Palatine confirmed that the treatment of the accounting rule remains under consideration. One question, he said, is whether to account for the charge on the books of the French company or of Schneider North America, the U.S. subsidiary that includes Square D.

But the Square D spokesman said, "I would not tie [Schneider] stock being down to retiree health benefits." He said a more likely problem is the economic slump in France and the United States. On the other hand, he acknowledged that France's system of socialized health care creates a gulf between company operations in that country and in the United States. "They're not used to doing what we do," he said.

"The acquisition of Square D strategically is a good move, but unfortunately it's going to cost Schneider a lot of money," said Andrew Haskins, an analyst with James Capel, a London brokerage firm. "We predict a very significant dilution of earnings this year and next and maybe even in 1993."

Source: Chicago Tribune (November 26, 1991).

Selected information from Houston Marine Corporation's 2005 postretirement benefits footnote
follows.

Other postretirement benefits, including certain healthcare and life insurance benefits, are provided to retired employees. The amount of healthcare benefits is limited to lifetime maximums as
outlined in the plan. Substantially all employees of Houston Marine may become eligible for these
benefits if they satisfy eligibility requirements during their working lives.

The following table provides a reconciliation of the changes in the plan's benefit obligations
and fair value of assets for the years ended December 31, 2005 and 2004:

Accumulated postretirement benefit obligation ($ in millions)	2005	2004
APBO at beginning of year	$1,523	$1,353
Service cost	?	52
Interest cost	?	99
Actuarial loss (gain)	?	84
Benefit payments	?	(65)
APBO at end of year	$?	$1,523

Fair value of plan assets ($ in millions)	2005	2004
Fair value of plan assets at beginning of year	$62	$49
Actual return on plan assets	1	4
Employer contributions	?	74
Benefit payments	?	(65)
Fair value of plan assets at end of year	$72	$62

The following table provides a statement of funded status of the plan as of December 31, 2005
and 2004:

Funded status ($ in millions)	2005	2004
Accumulated postretirement benefit obligation	$?	$(1,523)
Fair value of assets	72	62
Funded status at December 31	?	(1,461)
Unrecognized gain	(395)	(89)
Unrecognized prior service cost	?	(45)
Accrued OPEB liability	$(1,669)	$(1,595)

The following table provides the components of net periodic OPEB cost for the years ended
December 31, 2005, 2004, and 2003:

Net periodic OPEB cost ($ in millions)	2005	2004	2003
Service cost	$?	$ 52	$ 44
Interest cost	?	99	92
Expected return on assets	?	(5)	(4)
Amortization of prior service cost	(5)	(5)	(5)
Amortization of unrecognized net gain	?	(2)	(9)
Net periodic OPEB cost	$153	$139	$118

The following assumptions were used by the Company in the measurement of the benefit obligation as of December 31:

OPEB plan assumptions	2005
Discount rate	7.10%
Expected return on plan assets	9.50%

Required:

Round all calculations to nearest million.

1. Compute 2005 interest cost.
2. Compute 2005 expected return on assets.
3. What was the employer contribution for 2005?
4. Determine 2005 benefit payments.
5. Assuming there were no plan amendments, compute the unrecognized prior service cost at December 31, 2005.
6. Determine the accumulated postretirement benefit obligation at December 31, 2005.
7. Compute 2005 actuarial gain or loss.
8. Assuming an average remaining service life of ten years, determine the 2005 amortization of unrecognized gain.
9. What was the service cost for 2005?
10. Prepare a schedule like the one on page 787, which reconciles the funded status of the postretirement benefit plan with the recognized and unrecognized amounts at December 31, 2005.
11. Redo Houston Marine's postretirement benefits footnote (in good form), filling in all missing 2005 components.

COLLABORATIVE LEARNING CASE

C14 – 7

Chrysler Corporation (KR): OPEB expense and management incentive compensation

The following text is excerpted from the 1993 proxy statement of Chrysler Corporation. A proxy is a document prepared by management to obtain authorization from shareholders to act on their behalf. In the following passage, the management of Chrysler Corporation is requesting its shareholders' permission to modify the method of computing the incentive compensation awarded to its officers and executives.

Under a resolution adopted by the stockholders in 1929, and since amended from time to time, it has been a continuing practice of the Corporation to provide incentive compensation awards to officers and executives of the Corporation and its subsidiaries whenever permitted by the formula in the stockholders' resolution as then in effect. The authority to award incentive compensation under the stockholders' resolution as last amended extended through the fiscal year ended December 31, 1992. Stockholder action is required at this time to permit the Corporation to continue its practice with respect to awards of incentive compensation for fiscal years commencing on and after January 1, 1993, subject to certain modifications in the resolution which would eliminate the effect of a mandated change in accounting for certain postretirement benefits. . . .

The formula in the resolution as most recently amended on June 7, 1984 (the "Stockholders' Resolution") provides that awards may be made only for those years in which the consolidated net earnings of the Corporation and consolidated subsidiaries (as reported in the annual report to the stockholders) plus the provision for incentive compensation exceed earnings of $0.4444 per share (adjusted from $1.00 per share for two three-for-two stock splits since 1984) on the average number of shares of Common Stock outstanding during the year. The total provision for any year is limited to 8% of such excess. The Board may set aside such total provision or any lesser amount for incentive compensation. Any part of the amount set aside for any year that is not awarded for that year, as well as any amount awarded that is subsequently forfeited, may be carried forward to and awarded in a subsequent year.

AMENDMENT FOR NEW ACCOUNTING STANDARD

The ability of the Corporation to award incentive compensation has been a significant factor in attracting, retaining, and motivating competent and experienced executive personnel; and in competing for their services with the Corporation's larger competitors and other companies that are able to offer comparable total compensation, including bonuses and other incentive based compensation.

As stated above, under the Stockholders' Resolution, incentive compensation may be awarded only out of consolidated net earnings of the Corporation and its consolidated subsidiaries (as reported in the annual report to the stockholders). However, the Financial Accounting Standards Board has issued a new accounting standard (*SFAS No. 106*), "Employers' Accounting for Postretirement Benefits Other Than Pensions" ("OPEB"), that will significantly reduce or eliminate the Corporation's ability to award incentive compensation unless its effect is excluded by an amendment to the Stockholders' Resolution.

The Corporation provides health and life insurance benefits to its eligible employees and retirees. The costs of these benefits are currently accounted for as expenses in the Corporation's financial statements in the periods in which they are paid, except that the cost of life insurance provided to retirees after age 65 is accrued. The new OPEB accounting standard will instead require accrual of retiree benefits for both U.S. and Canadian employees during the years the employees provide services. *SFAS No. 106* is effective for fiscal years beginning after December 15, 1992.

Implementation of the new standard will result in the Corporation's recognition of a transition obligation that can either be taken as a one-time charge in determining net income for the period in which the new standard is adopted or be recognized as an expense on a straight-line basis over a 20-year period. The transition obligation is the aggregate amount that would have been accrued in the years prior to adoption of *SFAS No. 106* had the OPEB standard been in effect for those years. The Corporation will adopt the new standard in both the United States and Canada effective in the first quarter of 1993.

The Corporation estimates that the transition obligation was approximately $7.5 billion at January 1, 1993. If, when the OPEB standard is adopted effective in the first quarter of 1993, the transition obligation is recognized as a one-time charge, the Corporation estimates that there would be a $4.7 billion reduction (after applicable income taxes) in the Corporation's net earnings and shareholders' equity.

The Corporation estimates that its annual expense for postretirement health and life insurance benefits after adoption of the OPEB standard will increase by $380 million per year on a pre-tax basis, or by $240 million per year on an after-tax basis, assuming that the entire transition obligation is recognized as a one-time charge in 1993. If the transition obligation is accrued over a 20-year period, the Corporation's annual expense is estimated to increase by $750 million per year on a pre-tax basis, or by $470 million per year on an after-tax basis.

The Corporation has announced that it intends to recognize the transition obligation as a one-time charge that will result in an approximately $4.7 billion (after applicable income taxes) reduction in its shareholders' equity and in its 1993 first quarter and annual net results. Although implementation of the new standard will result in Chrysler reporting a net loss in the first quarter and for [all of] 1993 after the effects of this accounting adjustment, it will have no cash impact and Chrysler does not anticipate that it will adversely affect Chrysler's payment of dividends or compliance with its debt covenants.

The Board of Directors deems it essential to be able to award incentive compensation in the future on the basis of consolidated net earnings (losses) adjusted to exclude the effect of *SFAS No. 106*, in order to avoid a significant reduction or elimination of funds available for incentive compensation as a result of this mandated new accounting standard. Accordingly, the Board of Directors recommends that the stockholders adopt a resolution . . . to continue the authority to award incentive compensation on the same basis (except as further provided below) as in the recent past, by adjusting consolidated net earnings (losses) to exclude any amounts accrued to recognize postretirement benefit obligations, other than pensions, prior to the period in which such benefits are paid by the Corporation and its subsidiaries. The adjustment to exclude the OPEB accrual will be made in 1993 and each year thereafter to the extent that the amount accrued is different than the amount paid. The incentive compensation formula would continue to limit the incentive compensation fund for any year to 8% of the sum of (1) consolidated net earnings (losses) of the Corporation and consolidated subsidiaries (provided that such net earnings [losses] would be adjusted as described above), and (2) the provision for incentive compensation, after deducting from such sum an amount equal to $0.4444 per share times the average number of shares of Common Stock outstanding during the year.

Required:

If you were a stockholder of Chrysler Corporation, would you have agreed to the management's proposal? What factor(s) did you consider in making your decision?

Remember to check the book's Companion Website for additional problem and case material.

Financial Reporting for Owners' Equity

Statement readers must understand the accounting procedures and reporting conventions for owners' equity for these reasons:

1. *Appropriate income measurement.* Differentiating between owners' equity changes that increase income or decrease income and changes that don't increase or decrease income will help answer: "Why are bond interest payments an expense that reduces income, while dividend payments on common and preferred stock are not an expense that reduces income?" "Why do certain financing transactions—like early debt retirements—generate accounting gains and losses, while others—like stock repurchases—do not generate accounting gains and losses?"

2. *Compliance with contract terms and restrictions.* Many "exotic" securities having characteristics of both debt and equity have been developed over the years by investment bankers. How should these hybrid securities be classified for monitoring compliance with contractual restrictions such as, maximum allowable debt-to-equity ratios?

3. *Legality of corporate distributions to owners.* Owners' equity is generally regarded as a financial "cushion" protecting corporate creditors. Cash distributions to shareholders—dividends and stock repurchases—reduce this cushion. How much of this cushion can legally be distributed as dividends? When a company liquidates, in what order of priority can cash payouts be made to its various claimants?

4. *Linkage to equity valuation.* Analyzing the true worth of equity shares requires an understanding of the amount of earnings that accrue to each share. Equity valuation thus depends on how a company's options, warrants, and convertible instruments affect its earnings per share.

After discussing each of these issues, we will look at existing GAAP for employee stock options, the controversy surrounding current reporting practice, and how that practice may soon change.

Appropriate Income Measurement

Some increases (decreases) in owners' equity are considered to be income (loss), while other increases (decreases) are not income (loss). To see why, you must understand the modern GAAP definition of the "firm."

What Constitutes the "Firm"? Entity View versus Proprietary View

Recall the basic accounting equation—it depicts the resources available to management as the sum total of all assets in the firm:

Entity view of the firm:

$$\underbrace{\text{Assets}}_{\text{Capital Deployed}} = \underbrace{\text{Liabilities} + \text{Owners' Equity}}_{\text{Capital Sources}}$$

This **entity view** of the firm focuses on the firm's *assets*. Capital sources (debt and shareholder financing) are lumped together. The firm's assets are considered to drive economic performance, so the *firm* is considered to be the capital deployed—the assets themselves. Who provided those assets (whether creditors or shareholders) is of secondary importance.

Prevailing GAAP is based on a different perspective—called the **proprietary view** of the firm—where the basic accounting equation is transformed to focus on the net resources (assets *minus* liabilities) available to management and the capital provided by owners of the firm. The proprietary view sharply differentiates between capital provided by owners and capital provided by creditors.

Proprietary view of the firm:

$$\underbrace{\text{Assets} - \text{Liabilities}}_{\text{Net Capital Deployed}} = \underbrace{\text{Owners' Equity}}_{\text{Owners' Capital}}$$

The proprietary view isolates the capital provided by owners. In this perspective, the firm and its owners are inseparable—the *firm* is considered to be the owner's equity investment or net assets.

The prevalence of the proprietary view in GAAP greatly influences income measurement. To see why and how it influences the way income is measured, consider the basic accounting principle that income can be earned (or expenses incurred) *only* through transactions between the firm and "outsiders." But who is "inside" the firm and who are the outsiders? *Under the proprietary view, the firm and its owners are one and the same.* The firm is the net capital deployed (net assets) and owners are the "insiders" who provided that net capital. Consequently, no income or loss can arise from transactions between the firm and its owners, because owners are *not* outsiders. This perspective explains why interest payments to banks or bondholders are expenses that reduce income, while dividend payments to common and preferred shareholders are *not* expenses that reduce income.

- Banks and bondholders are outsiders—hence, interest costs are expenses.
- Shareholders are not outsiders—thus, dividends are a *distribution of earnings* to owners and not an expense of the company.

The proprietary view helps us understand why certain financing transactions generate income or losses, while other transactions do not.

Financing Transactions   One way corporations raise capital is by selling equity shares to investors. Called **common stock**, equity shares provide the opportunity for purchasers to participate in the company's future profitability. In addition to conveying ownership rights, common stock has **limited liability**. As long as each share is initially sold for more than the per-share dollar amount—called **par value**—printed on each share, the shareholder's potential loss is limited to the original purchase price of the common share. Limited liability makes investing in common stock attractive because although potential gains from ownership are unlimited, the risk of loss is limited to the share purchase price.

> Investors who buy **preferred stock** (discussed later in the chapter) also participate in the company's future profitability. However, investors who buy debt instruments do not participate in the company's future profitability. Instead, debtholders gain only a specified fixed (or variable) rate of return—for example, "7% interest per annum," or in the case of variable rate debt, "prime plus ½%."

To see how the accounting for common stock works, assume that at its creation Nahigian Corporation issues (meaning "sells to investors") 5,000 shares of common stock at $50 per share and that the shares have a par value of $1 each. Nahigian records the stock issuance as:

> The term *par value* refers to the **nominal** value or **face value** of a security—a dollar amount printed on the face of each stock certificate. With common stock, par value is set by the company issuing the stock. At one time, par value represented the original investment in cash, goods, or services behind each share of stock. Today, par value is an assigned amount (such as $1 per share) used to compute the dollar accounting value of the common shares on the company's balance sheet. *Par value has no relation to market value.*

DR Cash	$250,000	
CR Common stock—$1 par value		$ 5,000
CR Paid-in capital in excess of par		245,000

The $1 par value per share bears no necessary relationship to the *market value* of the shares. (Remember, par value is just the dollar amount printed on each stock certificate.) The difference between the issue price of $50 and the par value of $1 is credited to a separate owners' equity account called "Paid-in capital in excess of par"—sometimes called "Additional paid-in capital."

Suppose that several years later, Nahigian Corporation reacquires 200 of these shares at a cost of $48 each. When a corporation buys back its own shares, the repurchased shares are called **treasury stock** because the shares are held in the corporate treasury for later use. The accounting entry is:

> What if rather than held in treasury for later use, the repurchased shares are to be permanently retired by Nahigian? When shares are retired, the "Common stock" account is reduced for the par value of shares retired ($200 in our example) and the "Paid-in capital" account is reduced for the "excess" purchase price ($9,600 − $200 = $9,400). The share certificates are then cancelled, thus reducing the total number of shares issued.

DR Treasury stock	$9,600	
CR Cash		$9,600

Notice that no gain or loss is recorded for the difference between the $50 per-share price at which the shares were first issued and the $48 repurchase price. *The reason stock repurchases do not involve accounting gains and losses is that they are transactions between the company and its owners.*

When treasury stock is acquired, it is not considered a corporate asset. Instead, treasury stock is treated as a reduction in owners' equity. Treasury stock is debited, as shown earlier, and it then appears on the balance sheet as a **contra-equity** account. Here's how the owners' equity section of Nahigian's balance sheet looks after the company repurchased 200 shares of common stock for $9,600:

Nahigian Corporation	
Owners' Equity	
Common stock, $1 par value, 5,000 shares issued	$ 5,000
Paid-in capital in excess of par	245,000
Retained earnings (assumed for illustration)	700,000
Total paid-in capital and retained earnings	$950,000
Less: Treasury stock (at cost)	(9,600)
Total owners' equity	$940,400

Now let's say Nahigian decides to raise more equity capital by reselling all 200 treasury shares several months later at $53 per share. The entry would be:

DR Cash	$10,600	
CR Treasury stock		$9,600
CR Paid-in capital in excess of par		1,000

This entry eliminates the contra-equity account called "Treasury stock." The per-share selling price of $53 is $5 per share higher than the $48 paid to reacquire the shares. Despite this "excess," *no income is recognized on the transaction*. No income is recognized because GAAP adopts the proprietary view of the firm, and thus no income or loss can arise from transactions between the firm and its owners. Instead, the difference of $1,000 (or 200 shares × [$53 − 48]) is added to the "Paid-in capital in excess of par" account.

But if Nahigian had reacquired outstanding *debt* at a price lower than its book value, then a gain *would* be recorded, as described in Chapter 11. Debt repurchases generate gains (and losses) while stock repurchases do not, because debtholders are outsiders under the GAAP proprietary view while shareholders are insiders.

RE**CAP**   No income (or loss) arises from treasury stock transactions—not in the proprietary view, which equates the firm with its owners. Because treasury stock transactions are between the company and its shareholders (owners) and not outsiders, no income is recognized—not even when the successive stock transactions are favorable, like those in the Nahigian Corporation illustration.

Suppose Raider Company intends to acquire Target Company for $150 million in cash. Raider already has $30 million cash set aside for the takeover, and has lined up another $100 million bank loan. But that still leaves Raider $20 million short. Where can Raider find the money it needs to complete the takeover? One possibility is to tap into the Target's surplus cash. In other words, the more surplus cash that Target has, the easier it becomes for Raider to use the money to help pay for the takeover.

Why Companies Repurchase Their Stock

Firms reacquire their own common stock for many reasons. Sometimes a company needs shares for employee stock options. Sometimes a company's management may conclude that the company's shares are undervalued at the prevailing market price and that the best use of corporate funds is to invest in those shares by buying some of them back from stockholders. Other times, perhaps management just wants to distribute surplus cash to shareholders rather than to keep it inside the company.

A company's *surplus* cash—the amount over and above the cash needed for day-to-day operating activities—can be a problem for management and for shareholders. Management worries that another company or investor group might launch a hostile takeover of the business, using the company's own cash surplus to partially finance the takeover. If a hostile takeover is successful, some managers will inevitably lose their jobs. Shareholders, on the other hand, worry that management might spend the company's surplus cash on unprofitable—negative net present value—projects and on lavish "perks" such as corporate speedboats or race cars. So, it is better to give the money to shareholders—after all, it is their money.

Stock repurchases have one other advantage: Shareholders who take the cash are taxed at capital gain rates. If the cash is paid out as dividends, shareholders would be taxed at ordinary income rates, which are usually higher than capital gain tax rates.

The popularity of stock repurchases has varied over time as a result of changes in the economic climate, stock market price levels, and the availability of surplus corporate cash. Only 87 U.S. companies announced stock buyback plans in 1980, with the dollar value totaling $1.4 billion. In 1998, stock repurchases were announced by 1,570 U.S. companies and totaled $222.0 billion.[1] Figure 15.1 shows (a) the number of stock repurchase announcements each year, and (b) the total dollar value of the buybacks, for 1980 through 1999.

Panel (a)

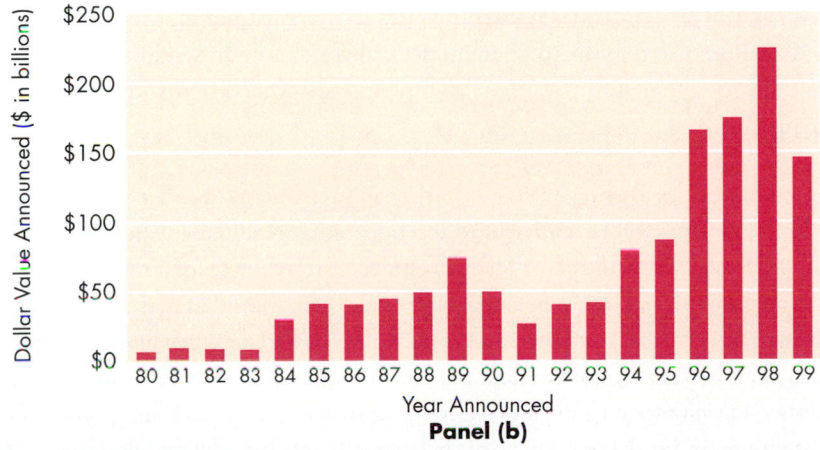

Panel (b)

Figure 15.1

THE NUMBER AND DOLLAR VALUE OF STOCK REPURCHASES ANNOUNCED BY U.S. COMPANIES FROM 1980 THROUGH 1999

The charts do not include stock repurchases announced in the last quarter of 1987 because so many U.S. companies announced repurchases that quarter as a response to the October 1987 stock market crash.

Source: From G. Grullon and D. Ikenberry, "What Do We Know About Stock Repurchases?" *Journal of Applied Corporate Finance* (Spring 2000). Reprinted with permission.

There are a number of ways a company can repurchase its shares. The most common is an **open market repurchase**—the company buys back its stock a little at a time over a period, sometimes two to three years. Open market repurchase programs are approved by company boards and disclosed to the public. However, companies do not disclose each and every stock repurchase transaction so it is difficult for analysts and investors to track completion of the buyback.

---

[1] G. Grullon and D. Ikenberry, "What Do We Know About Stock Repurchases?" *Journal of Applied Corporate Finance* (Spring 2000), pp. 31–51.

Another common way a company repurchases its own stock is the **fixed-price tender offer**—the company announces both the number of shares it wants to repurchase and the price it will pay for those shares. The offer is typically valid for a limited time and may be withdrawn if not enough shares are tendered. If the offer is oversubscribed—meaning too many shares are tendered—management has the option to increase the number of shares comprising the repurchase.

In the 1980s the **Dutch auction** became a popular way for firms to repurchase their own stock. In a Dutch auction, the company announces the total number of shares it will repurchase and sets a range of prices within which it is willing to buy back its stock. Shareholders responding to the offer must specify how many shares they are willing to sell and at what price within the range. The company then determines the lowest offered price that allows it to repurchase the number of shares it seeks. All the shares are purchased at this single price.[2]

The Dutch auction looks like the most satisfactory way to treat shareholders fairly. If a shareholder names too high a price, that shareholder may have no shares accepted. Naming too low a price simply increases the likelihood that the price paid will be low. Consequently, the Dutch auction approach encourages shareholders to be truthful and to name a price that reflects their personal valuation of the stock.

The typical share repurchase is at a price about 23% greater than the stock's market value just before the repurchase offer is announced.[3] Those shareholders who sell their stock back to the company capture this price premium. But what about the shareholders who don't sell? According to perhaps the best-known study on the subject, the stock of the average corporation that repurchases its shares outperforms the rest of the market by 12% over the four years following the announcement of the repurchase program. Even better, high book-to-market price stocks that are repurchased beat the market by 45% over the next four years.[4] So, it would seem that everybody wins when shares are repurchased. Those who sell shares back to the company capture a price premium for doing so, and those who don't sell but instead continue to own the shares capture an above-market return on their investment over the next four years.

But not all buybacks are created equal. While share repurchases as a whole help to boost investor returns, not all companies use repurchases to demonstrate that their stock is undervalued or to distribute excess cash to shareholders, skeptics say. Instead, share repurchases are sometimes used for other purposes. For example, here's what Microsoft said about its stock repurchase program:

Analysis

Management believes existing cash and short-term investments together with funds generated from operations will be sufficient to meet operating requirements for the next twelve months. Microsoft's cash and short-term investments are available for strategic investments, mergers and acquisitions, other potential large-scale cash needs that may arise, and to fund an increased stock buyback program over historical levels to reduce the dilutive impact of the Company's employee stock option and purchase programs. *Despite recent increases in stock repurchases, the buyback program has not kept pace with employee stock option grants or exercises.* Beginning in fiscal 1990, Microsoft has repurchased 134 million common shares for $4.2 billion while 336 million shares were issued under the Company's employee stock option and purchase plans. (Microsoft Corporation, Quarterly Report to Shareholders [10-Q filing], March 31, 1997. Emphasis added.)

---

[2] See D. B. Hausch, D. E. Logue, and J. K. Seward, "Dutch Auction Share Repurchases: Theory and Evidence," *Journal of Applied Corporate Finance* (Spring 1992), pp. 44–49.

[3] D. Ikenberry, J. Lakonishok, and T. Vermaelen, "Market Underreaction to Open Market Share Repurchases," *Journal of Financial Economics* (October 1995), pp. 181–208.

[4] Ibid.

Microsoft's buyback program partially offsets **share dilution**[5] caused by the company's stock option and repurchase plans. But what does a company gain from buying back its shares with one hand while issuing shares through options with the other hand? Some analysts answer: not much. While an employee usually buys shares for less than the market price under option programs, the company pays the market price to buy them back. In dollar terms, the number of shares outstanding may seem to be shrinking, because the company has spent more to buy back shares than employees have spent to acquire them. But in fact, the number of shares could remain unchanged or even grow.

> Intel's experience highlights the issue. Every year since 1992 this semiconductor manufacturer has bought back stock. But in 1999, for example, while it issued only $543 million of stock and bought back a whopping $4.6 billion of stock under its share repurchase plan, its common shares outstanding actually grew to 3,334 million from 3,315 million. What is the reason for this growth in shares? The company paid $64.95 a share for the stock it repurchased—but it received only $9.70 for each share issued through options. (Intel also issued some shares in connection with an acquisition.)

Another concern for analysts is that many companies are now borrowing to finance their stock repurchase programs. While such moves might have tax or other advantages, these companies simply replace equity with debt, so shareholders get the buyback's benefits only at the expense of owning a more leveraged company—one with more debt and less equity than before the repurchase. Also, these companies face the risk that an economic downturn could make it harder to service debt.

Even more worrisome is that *some stock buybacks are motivated solely by a desire to boost earnings per share (EPS).* Consider Rocket Software. The company just completed a successful third quarter with earnings of $220,000 and EPS of $1.00. This is the ninth consecutive quarter that Rocket Software's EPS has grown by 10% or more. But it looks like this string of EPS increases is about to be broken—fourth quarter earnings are projected to be only $220,000, unchanged from the third quarter.

> Microsoft terminated its stock buyback program in January 2000. Before doing so, the company sold "put" warrants for 157 million shares. The warrants—an off-balance-sheet liability—entitle the holders to sell shares of Microsoft back to the company at a price of about $74 per share. If Microsoft shares are trading at $54 when the warrants are exercised, and the average purchase price is $74, the company will have to come up with $20 a share—or $3.14 billion—to settle the warrants. That's a lot of cash!

How can the company keep its EPS record intact? Management could increase earnings (as well as EPS) by finding ways to grow sales revenues or reduce expenses. Or, Rocket Software could buy back some of its common stock:

	Without Buyback	With Buyback
Projected fourth quarter earnings	$220,000	$220,000
÷ Common shares outstanding	220,000	200,000
Projected EPS	$ 1.00	$ 1.10

If the buyback reduces total shares outstanding from 220,000 to 200,000, fourth quarter EPS will be $1.10 and the company can claim another quarter of 10% EPS growth.

Sounds simple? It's not! There is a hidden assumption. Stock buybacks consume cash. Where did Rocket Software get the cash needed for its buyback? Suppose the company had to borrow the cash. Then the (after-tax) interest expense on the loan—let's say it's $5,500—would reduce projected fourth quarter earnings to $214,500. The company would then have to buy

---

[5] Share dilution is akin to taking an apple pie that is already cut into six large pieces, and then slicing each piece in half again so that the pie ends up divided into twelve much smaller pieces. Here is a simplified example of share dilution. Suppose a company is worth $60 million, and there are 6 million shares of stock in the hands of investors. Each share is then worth $10. Next, suppose management gives stock options for 6 million shares to employees, who then exercise their options and receive the new shares. If the value of the company is unchanged, each outstanding share is now worth only $5 because the same $60 million pie (that is, the company) is now divided into twice as many slices (the 12 million shares outstanding). That's share dilution in a nutshell.

back 25,000 shares—or 5,000 more than originally anticipated—to reach its $1.10 EPS goal ($1.10 EPS = $214,500/195,000 shares outstanding after the expanded buyback). Instead of borrowing the cash, Rocket Software could sell some of its marketable securities, investments, or other productive assets. But asset sales may also have a dampening effect on future earnings.

As long as earnings fall by less (in percentage terms) than the buyback percentage reduction in shares outstanding, EPS will indeed go up! But this EPS increase may actually mask deteriorating business fundamentals. When it comes to stock buybacks and EPS growth, it pays to look behind the numbers.[6] That is why it has become increasingly important for prudent investors and analysts to sort through the individual share repurchase plans and to determine the reasons behind each buyback. Only then can investors and analysts figure out whether a repurchase plan is a sign to buy—or not to buy—the stock.

RECAP **Stock repurchases don't produce accounting gains or losses, but they can produce above-market returns for investors. Still, it's important to look behind the numbers and determine why and how a company is buying back its stock.**

Compliance with Contract Terms

Owners' equity is one of the accounting numbers used in many contracts with lenders, suppliers, and others (Chapter 7). For example, lending agreements usually include covenants that restrict maximum allowable debt-to-equity levels, where equity refers to the book value amount disclosed on the company's balance sheet. Firms have incentives to use their financial reporting latitude to circumvent these contractual restrictions. Consequently, financial statement analysts must understand how owners' equity is reported to determine whether a company they are evaluating is in compliance with its contract terms.

For example, the annual report of Sears Roebuck and Company contained the following statement:

Contracting

> The Illinois Insurance Holding Company Systems Act permits Allstate Insurance Company to pay, without regulatory approval, dividends to Sears Roebuck and Co. during any 12-month period in an amount up to the greater of 10% of surplus (as regards policyholders) or its net income (as defined) as of the preceding Dec. 31. Approximately $477 million of Allstate's **retained income** at Dec. 31, 1992 had no restriction relating to distribution during 1993 which would require prior approval. As of Dec. 31, 1992, subsidiary companies could remit to Sears Roebuck and Co. in the form of dividends approximately $5.6 billion, after payment of all related taxes, without prior approval of regulatory bodies or violation of contractual restrictions.
>
> *Source:* Sears Roebuck and Company, 1992 Annual Report. Allstate was a wholly owned subsidiary of Sears in 1992 but was sold by the company in 1995.

In this case, insurance regulators are using policyholder surplus (as defined by state insurance regulators), net income, and an owners' equity item—retained earnings—to restrict Allstate's ability to distribute cash to stockholders (in this case, the only stockholder is Sears Roebuck and Company). This restriction was intended to ensure that Allstate maintains a cash cushion for payment of insurance claims. Monitoring compliance with the form and substance of this regulation requires an understanding of accounting for owners' equity.

---

[6] In July 2003, AutoNation reported record second quarter EPS of $0.37, an increase of 16% from its quarterly EPS one year earlier. But the company's second quarter net income was up only a paltry 2.4% from the year ago figure. How did AutoNation achieve the added jump in EPS? The company had repurchased 47.8 million of its shares over the year—shrinking its outstanding shares by nearly 14% and thus boosting its earnings per share.

Some financial experts suggest that certain equity instruments, like **preferred stock**, are popular because they can be used to avoid various contractual restrictions. Preferred stock gets its name because relative to common stock, it confers on investors certain *preferences* to dividend payments and the distribution of corporate assets. Preferred shareholders must be paid their dividends in full before *any* cash distribution can be made to common shareholders; and if the company is liquidated, preferred stockholders must receive cash or other assets at least equal to the **stated (par) value** of their shares before any assets are distributed to common shareholders.

> Preferred stock does not ordinarily carry voting rights. *Participating* preferred stock entitles its holders to share in profits above the declared dividend, along with common shareholders. Most preferred stock is *nonparticipating*, meaning that holders are entitled to receive only the stipulated dividends.

The stated value of preferred stock is typically $100 per share. The dividend is often expressed as a percentage of the stated value. A typical 8% preferred issue would promise a dividend of $8 per share ($100 stated value × 8%). Unlike bond interest expense, however, preferred stock dividends are not contractual obligations that, if unpaid, could precipitate steps toward bankruptcy. Instead, preferred dividends are declared quarterly by the company's board of directors and can be omitted even in profitable years. Bank loans do not provide the flexibility to omit payments when cash flows are tight.

> An alternative to the 8% fixed-rate preferred stock is an **adjustable-rate preferred**, which pays a dividend that is adjusted, usually quarterly, based on changes in the Treasury bill rate or other money market rates.

However, preferred shares are usually *cumulative*. This means that if for any reason a particular quarter's preferred dividend is not paid, then no dividends on common shares can be paid until all unpaid past and current preferred dividends are paid. This feature protects purchasers of preferred shares from excessive cash distributions to common stockholders. Also because it's okay to occasionally "skip" a preferred dividend, preferred shares are less risky to issuing corporations than is debt.

Figure 15.2 shows the dollar value of preferred stock issued by U.S. companies each year from 1980 through 1997. Sixty-nine companies issued $3.1 billion of preferred stock in 1980, compared to $55.4 billion issued by 386 companies in 1997.

Figure 15.2

THE DOLLAR VALUE OF PREFERRED STOCK ISSUED BY U.S. COMPANIES FROM 1980 THROUGH 1997

Source: From K. A. Carow, G. R. Erwin, and J. J. McConnell, "A Survey of U.S. Corporate Financing Innovations: 1970–1997," *Journal of Applied Corporate Finance* (Spring 1999). Reprinted with permission.

The widespread use of preferred stock by companies is a curious phenomenon. Preferred dividends—unlike bond interest expense—are not a deductible corporate expense for tax purposes. Why do companies choose to raise capital through preferred stock rather than through debt where tax deductible interest payments reduce financing costs relative to preferred stock?

One reason preferred stock is attractive to *corporate investors* is because 70% to 80% of the dividends that corporations receive from their stock investments can be tax free (Chapter 13), whereas the interest income corporations receive from debt investments is fully taxable. But what about the companies that issue preferred stock?

Corporations that *issue* preferred stock do so because:

1. Preferred stock is less risky than debt because missing a preferred dividend payment, unlike missing an interest payment, will not trigger bankruptcy. This feature of preferred stock appeals to financially weak companies.
2. Companies with a history of operating losses usually don't pay income taxes because of their operating loss carryforwards. For these companies, debt no longer has a tax advantage, and thus preferred stock becomes more attractive as a source of new money.
3. Preferred stock is treated as equity rather than debt on financial statements. Companies precluded from issuing more debt because of covenant restrictions can sometimes issue preferred stock instead and side-step these restrictions.

The distinction between preferred stock and debt can be murky because: preferred stock (like debt) usually does not grant its holders voting rights, and preferred shareholders have no direct control over the affairs of the company.

The distinction between debt and preferred stock has been further blurred recently as companies began issuing **mandatorily redeemable preferred stock**. Although called preferred *stock*, manditorily redeemable preferred stock *requires* the issuing company to retire it (just like debt) at some future date—usually in five or ten years. This kind of preferred stock represents what many consider to be debt "disguised" as equity.

Exhibit 15.1 shows excerpts from Sealed Air's footnote disclosure for mandatorily redeemable preferred stock. Notice that the preferred shares: (a) are convertible into common stock, (b) carry voting rights as if they had already been converted, and (c) have a mandatory redemption price of $50 per share.

EXHIBIT 15.1 **Sealed Air Corporation**

Footnote Disclosure of Mandatorily Redeemable Preferred Stock

The Company's Series A preferred stock is listed on the New York Stock Exchange and is convertible at any time into approximately 0.885 of a share of common stock for each share of preferred stock. These shares vote with the common stock on an as-converted basis and are entitled to receive cumulative cash dividends, when and as declared by the Board of Directors, at an annual rate of $2.00 per share, payable quarterly in arrears on the first business day of the succeeding calendar quarter. The Series A preferred stock ranks senior to the Company's common stock and junior to the Company's indebtedness. On and after March 31, 2003, the Series A preferred stock is redeemable at the option of the Company at a price of $51.00 per share declining ratably on each March 31 thereafter to $50.00 per share on and after March 31, 2008, plus any accrued and unpaid dividends. The Series A preferred stock is subject to **mandatory redemption** on March 31, 2018 at $50.00 per share, plus any accrued and unpaid dividends, to the extent these shares remain outstanding.

Because it is subject to mandatory redemption, the Series A convertible preferred stock is classified outside of the shareholders' equity section of the consolidated balance sheets. At its date of issuance, the fair value of the Series A preferred stock exceeded its mandatory redemption amount primarily due to the common stock conversion feature. Accordingly, the book value of the Series A preferred stock is reflected in the consolidated balance sheets at its mandatory redemption value.

Source: Sealed Air Corporation 2002 Annual Report. Emphasis added.

The Securities and Exchange Commission (SEC) does not consider mandatorily redeemable preferred stock to be equity. So it prohibits firms issuing such securities from including them under the caption "Owners' equity" on the balance sheet.[7] This prohibition means that amounts for redeemable preferred stock cannot be combined with true owners' equity items like nonredeemable preferred stock and common stock in financial statements that are filed with the SEC. Exhibit 15.2 illustrates the required SEC treatment in Sealed Air's condensed balance sheet. Notice that the $1.327 billion of mandatorily redeemable preferred stock is shown on a separate line *between* liabilities and shareholders' equity. The company's preferred shares are more than half as large as its total liabilities.

EXHIBIT 15.2	Sealed Air Corporation	
Balance Sheet Excerpts ($ in thousands)	**2002**	**2001**
Current liabilities:		
Short-term borrowings	$ 53,355	$ 135,548
Current portion of long-term debt	2,049	1,943
Accounts payable	167,039	135,533
Deferred income taxes	4,239	5,097
Asbestos settlement liability	512,500	—
Other current liabilities	413,572	348,859
Total current liabilities	1,152,754	626,980
Long-term debt, less current portion	868,030	788,111
Deferred income taxes	31,037	210,830
Other liabilities	68,980	65,682
Total Liabilities	2,120,801	1,691,603
Series A convertible preferred stock mandatory redemption in 2018	1,327,005	1,366,154
Shareholders' equity:		
Common stock, $.10 par value per share	8,476	8,449
Treasury common stock at cost	(31,139)	(31,133)
Common stock reserved for issuance related to asbestos settlement	900	—
Additional paid-in capital	1,037,150	699,088
Retained earnings	31,885	394,799
Deferred compensation	(9,853)	(10,973)
	1,037,419	1,060,230
Accumulated other comprehensive loss	(224,459)	(210,078)
Total Shareholders' Equity	812,960	850,152
Total Liabilities, Preferred Stock and Shareholders' Equity	$4,260,766	$3,907,909

In May 2003, the Financial Accounting Standards Board (FASB) went one step further by requiring "liability" treatment for most mandatorily redeemable preferred stock.[8] The FASB concluded that, even though the securities are called "preferred stock," they meet the definition of a balance sheet liability and should be classified as such. In other words, if it looks like a duck and quacks like a duck, it must indeed be a duck!

What does this mean for Sealed Air and its $1.327 billion of mandatorily redeemable preferred stock? The answer is quite simple. Beginning in 2003, these securities can no longer be shown on the balance sheet in the "mezzanine" between liabilities and owners' equity (as illustrated in Exhibit 15.2).

---

[7] *Accounting Series Release No. 268* (Washington, DC: Securities and Exchange Commission [SEC], 1979).
[8] "Accounting for Certain Financial Instruments with Characteristics of Both Liabilities and Equity," *Statement of Financial Accounting Standards (SFAS) No. 150* (Stamford, CT: Financial Accounting Standards Board [FASB], 2003).

Instead, mandatorily redeemable preferred stock must now be shown as a balance sheet liability and included along side long-term debt. Had this been the case in 2002, Sealed Air would have reported total liabilities of $3.448 billion ($1.327 billion plus $2.121 billion) rather than the $2.121 billion shown in Exhibit 15.2. The FASB's "liability" treatment for mandatorily redeemable preferred stock also requires Sealed Air and other companies to record as interest expense any dividends on the preferred stock.[9]

SEC rules require companies to differentiate clearly between common stock and any type of preferred stock, whether redeemable or not. That means preferred stock must always be shown separately from common stock on the balance sheet. Finally, *Statement of Financial Accounting Standards (SFAS) No. 47* requires companies to disclose the dollar amount of preferred stock redemption requirements for each of the five years following the balance sheet date.[10] Accordingly, future cash flow commitments for redeemable preferred stock are clearly highlighted for statement users.

Here's what Samsonite Corporation said about its preferred stock redemption schedule:

> The Company is required to redeem all of the Senior Redeemable preferred Stock outstanding on June 15, 2010, at a redemption price equal to 100% of the liquidation preference thereof, plus, without duplication, all accumulated and unpaid dividends to the redemption date. The Senior Redeemable Preferred Stock is redeemable at the option of the Company in whole or in part, at any time and from time to time on or after June 15, 2001, at redemption prices ranging from 110% of the liquidation preference to 100% of the liquidation preference depending on the redemption date.

Samsonite has about $286 million of mandatorily redeemable preferred stock outstanding. The redemption provision requires Samsonite to redeem all of the outstanding shares on June 15, 2010 at 100% of the liquidation preference ($286 million). Samsonite has the option of redeeming shares as early as 2001, but it must pay a higher price for the shares (up to 110%).

The SEC and the FASB exclude mandatorily redeemable preferred stock from the owners' equity section of the balance sheet. However, this classification exclusion may not capture the real economic characteristics of these securities because many companies—including Sealed Air—have issued mandatorily redeemable preferred shares that are convertible into common stock. It's possible that preferred shares with this convertibility feature may never be redeemed for cash by the company. If instead, the preferred shares are retired by converting them into common shares, then they truly represent equity not debt—and thus their SEC and FASB status as nonequity may be arguable.[11]

Investors seem to be aware of the possibility that some redeemable preferred shares are a lot like debt while other redeemable preferred shares are a lot like equity. One study confirmed that the stock price behavior of companies whose redeemable preferred shares had clear debt-like characteristics was different from the behavior of companies whose shares had equity-like characteristics.[12] Investors apparently use disclosures about redeemable preferred shares to assess whether a particular issue should be regarded as debt or equity for valuation purposes.

---

[9] Buried in the details of *SFAS No. 150* is an exception to the required liability treatment, and the exception applies to Sealed Air. Recall that the preferred shares can be converted into common stock. The conversion option makes the preferred stock **conditionally** (not mandatorily) redeemable in the eyes of the FASB—the stock must be redeemed only if stockholders do not exercise their option to convert the preferred into common shares. Because the company's ultimate obligation to redeem the preferred shares is uncertain, *SFAS No. 150* does not require immediate "liability" treatment for conditionally redeemable preferred stock. This means that Sealed Air can continue to classify its redeemable preferred stock in the balance sheet mezzanine between liabilities and owners' equity, and that preferred dividends need not be reflected as interest expense. "Liability" treatment is required, however, once the conversion privilege expires and the preferred stock becomes mandatorily redeemable.

[10] "Disclosure of Long-Term Obligations," *SFAS No. 47* (Stamford, CT: FASB, 1981).

[11] See P. Kimmel and T. D. Warfield, "Variation in Attributes of Redeemable Preferred Stock: Implications for Accounting Standards," *Accounting Horizons* (June 1993), pp. 30–40. These authors report that almost 69% of the mandatorily redeemable preferred stock issued in 1989 and included in their sample was convertible into common stock.

[12] P. Kimmel and T. D. Warfield, "The Usefulness of Hybrid Security Classifications: Evidence from Redeemable Preferred Stock," *The Accounting Review* (January 1995), pp. 151–67.

A new form of mandatorily redeemable preferred stock has become popular in recent years, and it's called a **trust preferred security**. The company first creates a special purpose entity—the trust—which then sells redeemable preferred stock to outside investors. The company then borrows money from the trust, with repayment terms identical to those of the preferred stock issued by the trust. Outside investors own "trust preferred" stock, but the company itself has issued debt—not preferred stock—and thus gains the tax advantages associated with debt.

Here's what Motorola said about its newly issued trust preferred securities:

> In February 1999, Motorola Capital Trust I, a . . . wholly-owned subsidiary of Motorola, sold 20 million Trust Originated Preferred Securities ("TOPrS") to the public at an aggregate offering price of $500 million. The Trust used the proceeds from this sale . . . to buy . . . Subordinated Debentures from Motorola with the same payment terms as the TOPrS. Motorola, in turn, used the $484 million of net proceeds from the sale of the Subordinated Debentures to reduce short-term indebtedness.

Motorola formed a wholly owned subsidiary—Motorola Capital Trust—which sold $500 million of trust preferred stock to the public. Motorola then borrowed $484 million of cash (the $500 million proceeds minus $16 million in investment banking fees and other transaction costs) from the Trust in exchange for Motorola's subordinated debentures. Motorola has the cash and debt, its wholly owned subsidiary has the debentures receivable, and outside investors have trust preferred stock. Sounds complicated, but it's really simple. And here's the final piece of the puzzle—the interest and principal payments on the loan are matched to the dividend and mandatory redemption payments on the preferred stock. So, when Motorola makes an interest (or principal) payment to the trust, the trust then makes a dividend (or redemption) payment to outside investors.[13]

> Motorola's debt held by the wholly owned trust is eliminated when the company prepares its consolidated financial statements (Chapter 16 tells you why this occurs when the trust—a subsidiary—is wholly owned by Motorola—the parent company). That leaves only the redeemable preferred stock sold to outside investors on the consolidated balance sheet.

The benefit to Motorola should now be clear—interest expense is tax deductible but preferred dividends are not. By issuing trust preferred securities instead of traditional preferred stock, Motorola has transformed what would otherwise be a nondeductible preferred dividend payment into an interest expense tax deduction.

How are trust preferred securities shown on the balance sheet? Despite having the characteristics of debt—a required payment each period (called a "dividend" instead of "interest") and a final payment at the end (called a "mandatory redemption payment" instead of a "principal payment")—these hybrid securities have *not* always been classified as debt on the balance sheet. Instead, they have often been listed in the "mezzanine" section of the balance sheet between debt and equity along with all other mandatorily redeemable preferred stock. Beginning in 2003, however, most trust preferred securities—as well as most mandatorily redeemable preferred stock—must be shown as balance sheet liabilities.[14]

RECAP

Equity or debt? When it comes to mandatorily redeemable preferred stock, the answer isn't obvious. That's why preferred stock with a mandatory redemption feature was shown on a separate balance sheet line between liabilities and owners' equity. The FASB now requires redeemable preferred stock to be classified as a balance sheet liability as long as the obligation to redeem is unconditional. When redemption is conditional—say, because the preferred can be converted into common shares—liability treatment is not required.

---

[13] The key features of trust preferred securities are described in P. J. Frischmann, P. D. Kimmel, and T. D. Warfield, "Innovation in Preferred Stock: Current Developments and Implications for Financial Reporting," *Accounting Horizons* (September 1999), pp. 201–18.

[14] *SFAS No. 150*, op cit.

Legality of Corporate Dividend Distributions

State laws govern corporate dividend distributions to shareholders and these laws vary from state to state. The intent of these laws is to prohibit companies from distributing "excessive" assets to owners and thereby making themselves insolvent—that is, incapable of paying creditor claims. In some states, dividend distributions to owners are limited to the amount of retained earnings; in other states, the limit is retained earnings plus paid-in capital in excess of par. These laws protect creditors by ensuring that only solvent companies distribute cash to owners. (Stock repurchases, another way companies can distribute cash to owners, are not subject to these dividend distribution limitations.)

Assume Delores Corporation's balance sheet owners' equity section appears on December 31, 2005 as:

> Remember the repayment problem described in Chapter 7? Managers have incentives to borrow money and then pay all the cash out to shareholders, leaving the company insolvent and the bank with a loan receivable that will never be repaid!

Common stock, $1 par value	$20,000,000
Paid-in capital in excess of par	35,000,000
Retained earnings	43,000,000
Owners' equity	$98,000,000

In some states, Delores Corporation could only distribute up to $43,000,000 of assets—the retained earnings amount—as dividends to owners. The dividend distribution could be in the form of cash dividends or other assets such as inventory, equipment, or even land. In other states the maximum might be $78,000,000—retained earnings ($35,000,000) plus paid-in capital ($43,000,000). Many states would require corporations to give public notice if their dividends were "paid" from paid-in capital.

> If the distribution involves inventory, equipment, or land, it's called a **property dividend**.

Existing GAAP disclosures focus on the *source* of owners' equity—*contributed* capital (par plus capital in excess of par) versus *earned* capital (retained earnings, from which GAAP deducts dividends)—under the often erroneous presumption that this distinction informs analysts about legally permitted asset distributions. But many states have now adopted the **1984 Revised Model Business Corporation Act** as a guide to the legality of dividend distributions. This act redefined solvency. Under this act, as long as the *fair value of assets* exceeds the *fair value of liabilities* after the distribution, the company is considered to be solvent. In extreme cases, this means that an asset distribution would be legal even if the *book value* of net assets is *negative* after the distribution. If Delores Corporation's fair value of assets minus fair value of liabilities totaled $200 million, then $200 million (rather than $43 million or $78 million) would be the maximum legal asset distribution. Notice that a $200 million distribution would result in negative owners' equity of $102 million. ***The point is that the book value of owners' equity may not give an accurate picture of potentially legal distributions in states that have adopted the 1984 Act.***

The potential irrelevance of traditional equity disclosures is forcefully made in an article by Michael Roberts, William Samson, and Michael Dugan.

> As an example of the inadequacies of existing accounting disclosures, consider the 1987 and 1988 stockholders' equity balance sheet sections of Holiday Corporation, the parent corporation of Holiday Inns of America [see Exhibit 15.3]. The January 2, 1987 stockholders' equity section reports the traditional segregation of stockholders' equity items: par value of common stock, additional paid-in capital, and retained earnings, less treasury stock at cost, and foreign currency adjustments. Total stockholders' equity is $639 million. However, the January 1, 1988 stockholders' equity section reveals a $770 million deficit in Holiday's total stockholders' equity. How did this deficit occur? The explanation lies in the $65 per share dividend that Holiday distributed in 1987 to prevent a hostile takeover. This aggregate $1.55 billion dividend, financed with borrowed funds, not only exceeded the corporation's retained earnings but total stockholders' equity as well by more than three quarters of a billion dollars.

EXHIBIT 15.3	Holiday Corporation and Consolidated Subsidiaries		

Balance Sheet Excerpts
($ in thousands, except share amounts)

	January 1, 1988	January 2, 1987
Stockholders' equity		
Preferred stock, $100.00 par value, authorized—150,000 shares, none issued		
Special stock, authorized—5,000,000 shares	—	—
Series A—$1.125 par value, redeemable at $105.00, convertible into		
1.5 shares of common stock, outstanding—none and 170,171 shares		
(excluding none and 98,072 shares held in treasury)	—	$ 191
Series B—$1.25 par value, none issued	—	—
Common stock, $1.50 par value, authorized—120,000,000 shares,		
outstanding—26,225,980 and 23,592,569 shares (excluding 14,613,417		
and 17,246,828 shares held in treasury)	$ 39,339	35,389
Capital surplus	12,625	205,717
Retained earnings (deficit)	(791,021)	404,655
Cumulative foreign currency translation adjustment	7,972	(63)
Restricted stock	(38,861)	(7,156)
Total stockholders' equity	$(769,946)	$638,733

Holiday was able to borrow a large portion of the amount required for the dividend by using the fair value (that is, appraised value) of its real estate assets as collateral. Holiday was able to distribute the dividend (legally, according to Delaware law) because the fair value of its assets exceeded its liabilities after the distribution, and therefore it has positive equity on a fair value basis. ***However, the traditional accounting disclosures of par value, additional paid-in capital, and retained earnings do not contain any information (either before or after the dividend distribution) enabling financial statement users to assess the corporation's capacity for making such distributions.*** While stockholders and other interested parties may have had notice of Holiday's intent to leverage its assets to make the massive dividend, only Holiday's management had information about the fair values of the assets involved.

The point of the Holiday example is that state laws governing a corporation's ability to make distributions to stockholders have continued to evolve from the time when minimum legal capital was considered to be equivalent to the par value of the corporation's stock. Thus, the traditional stockholders' equity presentation of par value, additional paid-in capital, and retained earnings is obsolete because it implies that some amount, represented by a portion of stockholders' equity, exists to protect creditors.[15]

As the Holiday Corporation example illustrates, existing disclosure rules for owners' equity "*. . . focus attention on the source of capital, but ignore the capacity of the corporation for making distributions to stockholders.*"[16] To ascertain the amount of potential distributions,

Holiday Corporation paid a cash dividend to owners, but what happens when companies distribute stock instead of cash? Under current U.S. GAAP, stock *dividends* reduce retained earnings but stock *splits* may not. Small stock distributions (less than 25% of shares outstanding) are required to be recorded as stock dividends: The market value of the distributed shares is transferred from retained earnings to the par value and paid-in capital account. Distributions that equal or exceed 25% of shares outstanding—commonly called stock splits—can be treated in either of two ways: (1) like a true split, which reduces the per-share par value and increases the number of shares proportionately; or (2) like a stock dividend. Consequently, stock dividends—and stock splits recorded as stock dividends—reduce the company's future cash dividend paying ability in states where cash dividends are limited by retained earnings. Peterson, Millar, and Rimbey (1996) report that 83% of the 285 "stock split" companies in their study actually accounted for the distribution as stock dividends.* They also found that the stock market does indeed recognize that retained earnings reductions may restrict future dividends in some states but *not* in others.

The United States is the only country that records stock dividends at market value. All other countries record the "dividend"—a distribution in name only—at a nominal amount, either par value or book value.

*C. A. Peterson, J. A. Millar, and J. N. Rimbey, "The Economic Consequences of Accounting for Stock Splits and Large Stock Dividends," *The Accounting Review* (April 1996), pp. 241–53.

---

[15] M. L. Roberts, W. D. Samson, and M. T. Dugan, "The Stockholders' Equity Section: Form Without Substance?" *Accounting Horizons* (December 1990), pp. 36–37. Emphasis added.

[16] Ibid., p. 35. According to Standard and Poor's Compustat database, fourteen publicly traded U.S. companies—including Campbell Soup Company and United Airlines Inc.—paid cash dividends in 2002 despite having negative stockholders' equity.

statement analysts would need to know two things: (1) The distribution law in the state where the firm is incorporated, and (2) Fair value information if state law permits distributions based on the excess fair value of net assets. Unfortunately, this fair value information may be difficult to obtain because GAAP does not require that information to be disclosured except for marketable securities and certain investments (Chapter 16) and limited other items.

Certain limited disclosures regarding potential distributions are required by GAAP. When mandatorily redeemable preferred stock has been issued, the dollar amount of the redemption requirement for each of the ensuing five years after the balance sheet date must be disclosed. Similarly, preferred stock dividend and liquidation preferences must be disclosed, along with significant differences between the liquidation amount and the par or stated value of the underlying shares.[17] Nevertheless, these disclosures still do not allow interested readers to compute the *total* potential distribution to owners.

RE**CAP** **GAAP reporting rules usually may not be sufficient to allow analysts to ascertain the maximum legal dividend distribution available to common stockholders. Analysts must be aware that other data may have to be gathered to ascertain the dollar amount that can be distributed.**

Earnings Per Share

The amount of future income and cash flow that a company is expected to generate is a major determinant of the value of that company (Chapter 6). Valuing the firm *as a whole* is crucial during merger negotiations, corporate takeovers, and buyouts—relatively rare events in the ongoing life of a firm. For day-to-day valuations, many analysts prefer to focus on the value of *individual* common shares. For this purpose it is helpful to know how much of the company's total earnings accrue to each share. This is why **earnings per share** (**EPS**) is computed.

Computing EPS is straightforward when the company has a simple capital structure. We'll first describe the procedures for computing EPS for a simple capital structure, and then we will extend those procedures to situations involving more complicated capital structures.

Simple Capital Structure

A simple capital structure exists when a company has no convertible securities (neither convertible debt nor convertible preferred stock) and no stock options nor warrants outstanding. In these circumstances, a straightforward formula is used to compute **basic earnings per common share**:[18]

Basic earnings per common share:

$$\text{EPS} = \frac{\text{Net income} - \text{Preferred dividends}}{\text{Weighted average number of common shares outstanding}}$$

---

[17] "Disclosure of Information about Capital Structure," *SFAS No. 129* (Norwalk, CT: FASB, 1997).
[18] The guidelines for computing EPS are contained in "Earnings per Share," *SFAS No. 128* (Norwalk, CT: FASB, 1997).

To illustrate, assume Solomon Corporation had the following capital structure in 2005:

	January 1	December 31
Preferred stock, $100 par value, 7%, 10,000 shares issued and outstanding	$ 1,000,000	$ 1,000,000
Common stock, $1 par value		
160,000 shares issued and outstanding	160,000	
200,000 shares issued and outstanding		200,000
Paid-in capital in excess of par	12,000,000	16,000,000
Retained earnings	1,100,000	1,800,000
Total stockholders' equity	$14,260,000	$19,000,000

The 40,000 additional common shares were issued on September 1 and thus were outstanding for the last third of the year. The change in retained earnings during 2005 is:

Retained earnings, January 1	$1,100,000
Net income for the year	1,257,331
Preferred stock dividends	(70,000)
Common stock dividends	(487,331)
Retained earnings, December 31	$1,800,000

The denominator of the basic EPS formula uses the **weighted average** number of common shares outstanding. Since additional shares were issued in September, this weighted average number of outstanding shares is computed as:

Time Span	(a) Shares Outstanding	(b) Portion of Year	(c) Weighted Shares (Col. a × Col. b)
January 1–August 31	160,000	$\frac{2}{3}$	106,667
September 1–December 31	200,000	$\frac{1}{3}$	66,667
			173,334

Solomon Corporation's basic EPS for the year 2005 is:

$$\text{Basic EPS} = \frac{\text{Net income} - \text{Preferred dividends}}{\text{Weighted average number of common shares outstanding}}$$

$$= \frac{\$1,257,331 - \$70,000}{173,334 \text{ shares}} = \$6.85 \text{ per share}$$

There's a new wrinkle in the computation of basic EPS that you should know about. As we saw in the previous section, sometimes companies issue securities—most commonly it's preferred stock—that *must* be converted into common shares. The FASB and the International Accounting Standards Board (IASB) have recently agreed that these **mandatorily convertible securities** should also be included in the computation of basic EPS as soon as conversion becomes mandatory.[19] The rationale for doing so is that mandatorily convertible securities will eventually be included in the basic EPS computation anyway once they are converted into common stock. But why wait until the conversion actually occurs since conversion is mandatory and

[19] As this book goes to press, this change to the computation of basic EPS has yet to be formally ratified by the FASB and IASB but it is expected to become effective in 2005. As you are about to discover, convertible securities have always been considered in the computation of diluted EPS.

thus inevitable? It makes more sense to include them in the weighted average common shares outstanding from their date of issuance as if they had already been converted.

To see how mandatorily convertible securities alter the computation of basic EPS, suppose that Solomon Corporation's 10,000 shares of preferred stock mandatorily convert into 20,000 shares of common stock on January 1, 2010. (Notice that preferred stockholders have no say in the matter—the preferred shares will automatically convert into common stock in 2010.) Two adjustments to our basic EPS computation are required to accommodate the mandatorily convertible preferred:

1. Increase the weighted average common shares outstanding by 20,000 shares to reflect the "as if" conversion of preferred into common as of the first day of the reporting period (here, January 1, 2005) because the preferred shares were outstanding for the entire period.
2. Eliminate the preferred dividend adjustment to net income because preferred stockholders are now viewed as though they are common stockholders.

Solomon Corporation's basic EPS for the year 2005 now becomes:

$$\text{Basic EPS} = \frac{\text{Net income}}{\text{Weighted average number of common shares outstanding}}$$

$$= \frac{\$1,257,331}{173,334 \text{ shares} + 20,000 \text{ converted shares}} = \$6.50 \text{ per share}$$

Complex Capital Structure

A firm has a **complex capital structure** when its financing includes either securities that are convertible into common stock, or options and warrants that entitle holders to obtain common stock under specified conditions. These financial instruments increase the likelihood that additional common shares will be issued in the future. This possible increase in the number of shares is called potential **dilution** because, once the additional common shares are issued, current shareholders—those who did not receive any of the new shares—will then own a smaller slice of the company.

Convertibles are corporate securities—usually preferred shares or bonds—that are exchangeable for a set number of other securities—usually common shares—at a prestated price and at the option of the security holder. From the issuer's standpoint the convertible feature "sweetens" the marketability of the bond or preferred stock. A **call option** gives the holder the right to buy shares (typically 100) of the underlying stock at a fixed price before a specified date in the future—usually three, six, or nine months. **Employee stock options** are often of three to five years in duration. If the stock option is not exercised, the right to buy common shares expires. A **subscription warrant** is a security usually issued together with a bond or preferred stock that entitles the holder to buy a proportionate amount of common stock at a specified price—usually higher than market price at the time of issuance—for a period of years or in perpetuity.

To illustrate the EPS calculation for a complex capital structure, suppose Jackson Products has 20,000 shares of common stock outstanding along with $100,000 of convertible debentures—that is, bonds that can be converted into common stock at a specified price (say, $5.00 per share of common stock) at anytime at the option of the bondholder. According to the terms of the debenture agreement, each $1,000 face value bond can be exchanged for 200 shares of common stock (200 shares = $1,000 bond / $5.00 per share conversion price). If all debentures were exchanged, bondholders would receive 20,000 new shares of common stock. The effect on current common shareholders would be to *dilute* their claim to earnings from 100% (when they own all of the common shares outstanding) to 50% (when they own only half of the common shares outstanding).

Remember Microsoft's stock repurchase program cited earlier? Between 1990 and 1996 the company bought back 134 million shares of common stock for $4.2 billion, while 336 million shares were issued under the company's employee stock option and purchases plan. But there's more! At the end of 1996 Microsoft employees owned stock options worth $21.8 billion, so the potential future dilution was even greater.

Computed basic EPS overlooks this potential dilution of current shareholders' ownership interest in the company. To recognize the increase in outstanding shares that would ensue from conversion or options exercise, *SFAS No. 128* requires companies with complex capital structures to compute another measure, called **diluted EPS**.

The diluted EPS figure is a conservative measure of the earnings flow to each share of stock. It's conservative because the diluted EPS measure presumes the *maximum* possible new share creation—and thus the *minimum* earnings flow to each share. The computation of diluted EPS also requires that certain reasonable assumptions be made. For example, consider the potential conversion of convertible debentures into common shares. Once the bonds are converted to common stock, the company no longer needs to make further debt principal and interest payments. Consequently, the diluted EPS computation recognizes the following:

1. New shares are issued upon conversion (a denominator effect).
2. An increase in after-tax net income results when the debt interest payments are eliminated after conversion (a numerator effect).

Assumptions must also be made for employee stock options or warrants when computing diluted EPS. When holders of options or warrants exercise them, they receive common shares; but at the same time, the company receives cash in an amount representing the exercise price of the options or warrants. In the computation of diluted EPS, this cash is assumed to be used to acquire already outstanding common shares in the market. Because of adjustments for assumptions like these, the diluted EPS formula is slightly more complicated, as shown next:

$$\text{Diluted EPS} = \frac{\text{Net income} - \text{Preferred dividends} + \begin{array}{c}\text{Income adjustments due to}\\\text{dilutive financial instruments}\end{array}}{\begin{array}{c}\text{Weighted average number of}\\\text{common shares outstanding}\end{array} + \begin{array}{c}\text{Newly issuable shares due to}\\\text{dilutive financial instruments}\end{array}}$$

To illustrate how the diluted EPS computation works, we will extend the Solomon Corporation example. Assume that as of January 1, 2005 Solomon also had the following financial instruments outstanding:

- $1,000,000 of 5% convertible debenture bonds due in 15 years, which were sold at par ($1,000 per bond). Each $1,000 bond pays interest of $50 per year and is convertible into 10 shares of common stock.
- Options to buy 20,000 shares of common stock at $100 per share. These options were issued on February 9, 2003 and expire on February 9, 2006.

Assume the tax rate is 35% and Solomon stock sold for an average market price of $114 during 2005. Each of these two financial instruments is potentially dilutive and must be incorporated into the diluted EPS computation as shown below. (To keep things simple, assume also that Solomon's preferred stock does not have a mandatory conversion feature so basic EPS is still $6.85.)

The convertible debentures are included in diluted EPS by assuming conversion on the first day of the reporting period (here, January 1, 2005). The after-tax effect of interest payments on the debt is *added back* in the EPS numerator, and the additional shares that would be issued on conversion are added to the denominator. *SFAS No. 128* calls this the **"if-converted" method**. We now illustrate the computation of diluted EPS in the presence of convertible debt.

> There are 1,000 bond certificates outstanding ($1,000,000 ÷ $1,000 par value = 1,000 certificates), each convertible into 10 shares of common stock. Conversion of all bond certificates results in 10,000 new shares (or 1,000 certificates × 10 shares per certificate).

The convertible debentures are presumed to have been converted into 10,000 additional shares of stock at the beginning of the year (January 1, 2005). Accordingly, 10,000 new common shares are added to the diluted EPS denominator. Under the if-converted method, no interest would have been paid on the debentures this year because all bonds are assumed to be converted as of January 1. This means that interest of $50,000 would not have been paid on the presumptively converted bonds. With a 35% tax rate, net income would increase by $32,500 ($50,000 × [1 − 0.35]), and this amount is added to the diluted EPS numerator.

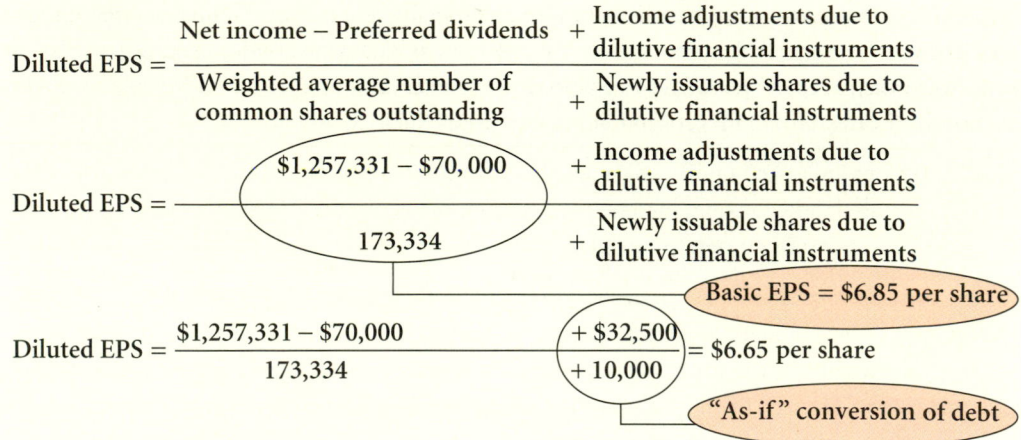

This is not always the case. If the options are issued as employee compensation, then the after-tax portion already charged to expense during the period (described later in this chapter) must be reversed in the EPS numerator.

The outstanding stock options in our example will affect only the denominator of the diluted EPS computation. This adjustment reflects the difference between the option **exercise price** ($100 per common share) and the **average market price** ($114 per common share) during the period. *SFAS No. 128* assumes that any proceeds received on exercise of the options ($100 per share) are used to buy back already outstanding common shares at the average market price for the period. This is called the **treasury stock method**.

We next illustrate the adjustment to compute diluted EPS under the treasury stock method.

Stock options are dilutive when they are "in the money"—that is, when the average market price (here, $114) exceeds the option exercise price ($100). Using the treasury stock method, we assume that the $2,000,000 proceeds to the company from presumptive exercise of the options (that is, 20,000 shares at $100 per share) are used to repurchase previously issued common shares at the $114 average market price. The cash from the options is sufficient to acquire 17,544 shares (that is, $2,000,000 ÷ $114 per share = 17,544 shares). Since 20,000 shares are presumed issued and 17,544 are presumed acquired, the difference (2,456 net new common shares) is added to the diluted EPS denominator:

In-the-money options are dilutive because the number of shares that can be repurchased with the proceeds from the options is smaller than the number of new shares issued on exercise of the options. To see this dilution, suppose that employees exercise options for 1,000 shares of common stock at an exercise price of $10 per share when the stock is trading at $20 per share. The company will receive proceeds of $10,000 cash from employees ($10 per share exercise price × 1,000 options) and issue 1,000 new shares of stock. The company can then use the cash proceeds to buy back at most 500 shares ($10,000 / $20 market price per share) from other investors. The net result is dilution because 500 additional shares of common stock are now outstanding.

$$\text{Diluted EPS} = \frac{\$1,257,331 - \$70,000 + \$32,500}{173,334 + 10,000 + 2,456} = \$6.57 \text{ per share}$$

Treasury stock conversion of options

Notice that diluted EPS equals $6.57, which is lower than the basic EPS number $6.85. It is this potential decrease in the computed earnings flow to each common share that motivates the diluted EPS computation. Diluted EPS allows current stockholders to see how small their slice of earnings will be when the potential dilution from convertible securities, options, and warrants is considered.[20]

[20] One study suggests *SFAS No. 128* systematically underestimates the economic dilution from stock options. See J. Core, W. Guay and S.P. Kothari, "The Economic Dilution of Employee Stock Options: Diluted EPS for Valuation and Financial Reporting," *The Accounting Review* (July 2002), pp. 627–652.

Analytical Insights

Now that you understand the guidelines in *SFAS No. 128* for computing diluted EPS, let's revisit our earlier claim that the diluted EPS figure is a conservative measure of the potential dilution from convertible securities. To see why this is so, consider how the "if-converted" method is applied in computing diluted EPS for Solomon Corporation. Recall that the company's convertible bonds were issued with a conversion price of $100 per share of common stock, meaning that each $1,000 bond certificate can be exchanged for 10 shares of common stock at any time by the bondholder. Remember too that the "if-converted" method assumes that all of the bonds are exchanged for common shares at the beginning of the reporting period (January 1, 2005).

But what if Jackson Product's common stock is worth only $75 per share on January 1, 2005? Are bondholders willing to exchange their certificates for common shares under these conditions?

Probably not. If bondholders surrender their certificates, they will receive 10 shares of stock for each certificate. Each share of stock is worth only $75, so the total value of shares received is just $750 per certificate. That's what bondholders get when they elect to convert a certificate into common shares, but what do they give up? By surrendering the certificate, bondholders forego the right to collect $1,000 in cash later when the bonds mature. Unless the risk of nonpayment is extremely high, bondholders will hold on to their certificates rather than exchange them for common shares.

The message here is that conversion—and thus EPS dilution—is unlikely when a company's stock price ($75 in our example) is substantially below the conversion price ($100). Conversion becomes much more attractive to bondholders once the underlying stock price rises above the conversion price. For example, if Jackson Product's common stock was trading at $150 per share, bondholders would then receive $1,500 worth of stock for each $1,000 bond certificate surrendered.

The "if-converted" method for computing EPS dilution ignores the fact that bondholders are unwilling to convert their debt certificates into shares of common stock when the share price is below the conversion price. Instead, the "if-converted" method presumes that all convertible debt certificates are exchanged for common shares at the beginning of the reporting period regardless of the prevailing share price. This approach yields a diluted EPS figure that is conservative because it reflects the maximum potential new common shares from conversion. The resulting EPS figure overstates earnings dilution—and understates diluted earnings per share—when a company's share price is substantially below the conversion price of the debt.

The treasury stock method suffers from the opposite problem. The treasury stock method tends to understate potential earnings dilution—and overstate diluted EPS—from employee stock options in some situations. To see why, recall from the Solomon Corporation example that the treasury stock method for computing diluted EPS involves a numerator adjustment that reflects the difference between the option exercise price ($100 per common share) and the average market price ($114 per common share) during the period. *SFAS No. 128* assumes that any proceeds received on exercise of the options ($100 per share) are used to buy back already outstanding common shares at the average market price for the period.

But what if the average market price of Solomon shares is slightly *below* the exercise price, say $99.95 per share? According to the treasury stock method, employee stock options are no longer dilutive when the average share price during the period falls below the exercise price. So, no adjustment at all is made to the numerator in computing diluted EPS. This approach ignores the possibility that Solomon's share price may rise above the exercise price ($100) sometime in the near future. As a result, the treasury stock method understates potential earnings dilution—and overstates diluted EPS—from employee stock options when the average share price for the period is slightly below the exercise price.

Is Earnings Per Share a Meaningful Number?

EPS data are reported in the financial news and are prominent in corporate financial reports even though EPS can be a misleading financial performance measure.

EPS ignores the amount of *capital* required to generate the reported earnings. This is easy to show. Consider the 2005 financial performance of two companies:

	Company A	Company B
Net income available to common shareholders	$ 1,000,000	$ 1,000,000
Weighted average common shares outstanding	100,000	100,000
Basic earnings per share	$ 10	$ 10
Gross assets	$20,000,000	$30,000,000
Liabilities	10,000,000	10,000,000
Equity capital (assets – liabilities)	10,000,000	20,000,000
Return on equity	10%	5%

Company A and Company B report identical basic EPS of $10. But Company B needed twice as much equity capital and 50% more gross assets to attain the $1,000,000 net income. Even though both A and B report the same *level* of net income and EPS, B has a return on equity of only 5%, while A's figure is 10%. Company A generates more earnings from existing resources—that is, from its equity capital.

Because EPS ignores capital commitments, problems can arise when trying to interpret EPS. The narrow focus of the EPS ratio clouds comparisons between companies as well as year-to-year EPS changes for a single company. For example, even if year-to-year earnings' levels are the same, a company can "improve" its reported EPS by simply repurchasing some previously outstanding common shares.

RECAP   Earnings per share (EPS) is a popular and useful summary measure of a company's profit performance. It tells you how much profit (or loss) each share of common stock has earned after adjustments for potential dilution from employee stock options, warrants, and convertible securities are factored in to the calculation. But EPS has its limitations.

Accounting for Stock-Based Compensation

Many U.S. companies compensate managers and other salaried employees with a combination of cash and stock options—that is, options to purchase equity shares in the company. A typical employee stock option gives the employee the right to purchase a specified number of common shares at a specified price within some specified time period. The specified price—called the **exercise price**—is usually equal to or higher than the market price of the company's shares at the time the options are issued. An option to buy 100 shares at $50 per share at any time within the next five years might be issued when the shares themselves are selling for $30. When the exercise price exceeds the current share price, the stock option is "out of the money." Nevertheless, an option to purchase common shares at $50 is valuable even though the shares are currently selling for only $30 because there's a chance the stock price will climb above $50 sometime during the ensuing five years.

The number of U.S. employees holding stock options has risen dramatically in the past decade, as shown in Figure 15.3. Back in 1992, only about 1 million employees held stock options. Ten years later, stock options were an important part of the com-

In 2002, Microsoft gave its employees stock options that can be converted into 41 million shares of the company's common stock at $62.50 per share. Employees have until 2012 to decide if they will exercise the options. Microsoft scrapped its employee stock option program in 2003 in favor of direct stock grants.

pensation paid to roughly 10 million employees. According to one estimate, companies in the Standard & Poor's 500 stock index awarded $126 billion in employee stock options in 2002 alone, more than the 2002 gross domestic product of Ireland.[21] Senior executives in these companies are not the only ones who receive part of their pay in the form of stock options. Almost all of Amazon.com's 7,700 full- and part-time employees receive options and at Microsoft, a "very large percentage" of the company's 50,500 employees have been granted stock options. In most companies, however, only between 10% and 20% of options go to nonmanagement employees.

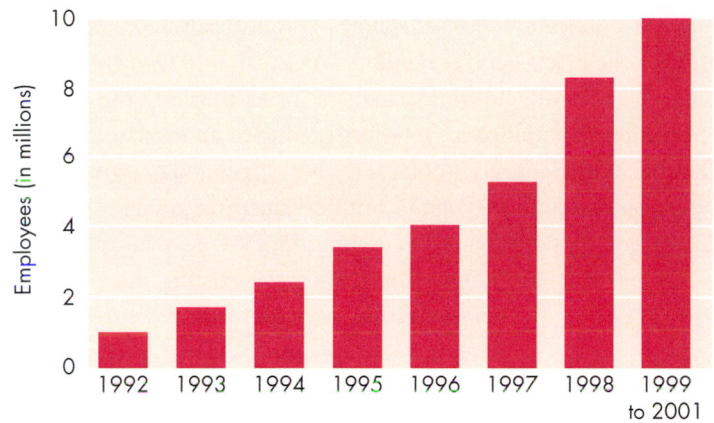

Figure 15.3

THE NUMBER OF U.S. EMPLOYEES HOLDING STOCK OPTIONS

Source: National Center for Employee Ownership.

Companies use stock options to augment cash compensation for several reasons:

- Options help align employees' interests with the interests of owners (stockholders). Employees with stock options have an incentive to make decisions that ultimately cause the share price to exceed the option exercise price.
- Many "start-up" high-growth companies are "cash starved" and cannot afford to pay competitive cash salaries. Stock options provide a way for them to attract talented employees while conserving cash.
- As long as the exercise price is equal to or greater than the market price of the underlying stock when the option is issued, this compensation is not taxable to the employee until the option is exercised. This is an attractive feature, because it allows employees to accumulate wealth while postponing taxes.

> Granting employee stock options with an exercise price *below* the current market price of the firm's common stock—for instance, an exercise price of $10 per share when the grant date market price is $15 per share—imposes a tax cost on employees. This is because the excess of market price over exercise price ($5 in our example) must be included in employees' taxable income when the options are granted.

As this book goes to press, financial reporting for employee stock options granted as compensation is still governed by *SFAS No. 123*.[22] The controversy over stock options reporting that raged during the evolution of this FASB rule was unprecedented in the history of U.S. accounting standard setting. Companies that issued employee stock options, their auditors, the SEC, and ultimately, the U.S. Senate lobbied the FASB to influence the final reporting rules. The intense debate over stock options presents an opportunity to discuss financial reporting incentives (Chapters 1 and 7) in a concrete setting and to illustrate how politics often enters the standard-setting process.

---

[21] L. Lavelle, A. Borrus, R. D. Hof, and J. Weber, "Options Grow Onerous," *BusinessWeek* (December 1, 2003).

[22] "Accounting for Stock-Based Compensation," *SFAS No. 123* (Norwalk, CT: FASB, 1995). In October 2003, the FASB proposed ending by 2005 the favorable accounting treatment employee stock options receive under *SFAS No. 123*. Barring Congressional intervention, U.S. companies may soon be forced to account for options as an expense.

Historical Perspective

Suppose an employee agrees to work this year in exchange for a small current salary and the promise of additional cash compensation to be paid five years later. No one disputes the notion that the employee's salary should be recorded on the company's books as an expense of the current year. But what about promised compensation? Should it be recorded as a current year expense, or should the expense be postponed five years until the employee actually receives the cash? This question is at the heart of the employee stock options debate.

Before *SFAS No. 123* was adopted in 1995, accounting for stock-based compensation was governed by *Accounting Principles Board (APB) Opinion No. 25*.[23] The Opinion was issued in 1972, one year prior to publication of what is now the universally accepted approach for valuing traded stock options—the Black–Scholes method.[24] Because *APB Opinion No. 25* preceded modern option pricing theory, it offered no mechanism for establishing the value of stock options granted as compensation to employees. Options issued with an exercise price equal to or above the market price of the underlying common shares *were assumed to have no value* for compensation expense purposes because they could not be valued reasonably objectively. Under *APB Opinion No. 25*, if Ramos Corporation issued on June 28, 1972 10-year options to employees that entitled each to buy 100 shares at $10 per share when the existing share price was also $10, *no compensation expense would be recognized because the value of these options could not be established reliably*.

Obviously, options with terms like those in the Ramos Corporation example are valuable; the price of the company's common stock could easily rise above the $10 exercise price sometime during the 10-year life of the option. Over the 1970s and early 1980s, option pricing *theory* evolved into option pricing *practice* using the Black–Scholes model as the standard for valuing traded options. Despite this post-*APB Opinion No. 25* breakthrough, options issued as compensation were generally treated as being valueless at the grant date for accounting purposes. Compensation expense *was* recognized in rare instances.

> An expense would be recorded under *APB Opinion No. 25* if the option exercise price was *below* the market price of the shares at the grant date. For example, Ramos would record $200 of compensation expense (and a corresponding increase to owners' equity) if the option exercise price was $8 per share and the grant-date market price was $10 per share. This pattern of exercise price and market price rarely occurs, so most companies do not record an expense under *APB Opinion No. 25*. This feature of *APB Opinion No. 25* was retained in *SFAS No. 123*.

During the 1980s U.S. companies increasingly adopted employee compensation packages designed to link employee pay to company performance. Stock option plans proliferated as an element of employee compensation. Many auditors and other financial experts considered the *APB Opinion No. 25* presumption that options were valueless to be simply incorrect. Because these beliefs were widespread, the FASB began reconsidering the accounting for stock options in 1984.

Strong and widespread opposition to the FASB's stock options initiative surfaced quickly as it became clear to the business community that the new proposal would result in expenses being recognized on the income statement when stock options were granted. Those opposed to the FASB's proposal raised arguments against expense recognition that roughly parallel the four themes of this chapter:

1. Appropriate income measurement
2. Compliance with contract terms and restrictions
3. Legality of corporate distributions to owners
4. Linkage to equity valuation

---

[23] "Accounting for Stock Issued to Employees," *APB Opinion No. 25* (New York: American Institute of Certified Public Accountants [AICPA], 1972).

[24] F. Black and M. Scholes, "The Pricing of Options and Corporate Liabilities," *Journal of Political Economy* (May–June, 1973), pp. 637–54. Corporate finance books explore the derivation of the Black–Scholes method and other option valuation techniques in detail; for example, see R. A. Brealey and S. C. Meyers, *Principles of Corporate Finance*, 5th ed. (New York: McGraw-Hill, 1996), pp. 577–599.

Objections to the FASB's stock option approach reflected each of these themes. Next, we survey those objections.

Opposition to the FASB

Some opponents of the FASB's proposal questioned whether providing stock options to employees constituted an accounting expense. These opponents said that treating stock options as an expense would violate **appropriate income measurement** because stock options do not involve a cash outflow. On the contrary, they argued, when—and if—the options were eventually exercised, cash would flow *into* the company, not *out*.[25] Supporters of the FASB counterargued that cash was not the issue. Expenses often arise independently of cash outflows. One prominent advocate of this position was Warren Buffett, Chairman of Berkshire Hathaway, Inc., who said:

> [Some contend] that options should not be viewed as a cost because they "aren't dollars out of a company's coffers." I see this line of reasoning as offering exciting possibilities to American corporations for instantly improving their reported profits. For example, they could eliminate the cost of insurance by paying for it with options. So if you're a CEO and subscribe to this "no cash–no cost" theory of accounting, I'll make you an offer you can't refuse: Give us a call at Berkshire and we will happily sell you insurance in exchange for a bundle of long-term options on your company's stock.
>
> Shareholders should understand that companies incur costs when they deliver something of value to another party and not just when cash changes hands. (Warren Buffett, Letter to Shareholders, Berkshire Hathaway, Inc., 1992 Annual Report.)

Buffett's position that expenses arise when stock options are issued is consistent with how we account for issued stock. When stock is issued, shareholders give up something of value—a portion of their ownership interest—in exchange for something else of value—usually cash from new investors. The value given up and the value received both get recorded. Buffett argues that the same accounting rules should apply for employee stock options. Shareholders are giving up a portion of their ownership interest by having the company issue additional stock—or options for stock—to employees. In exchange, shareholders receive valuable services from the employees—services that are paid for in stock options rather than in cash. From this perspective, issuing stock options to employees represents an expense to the company.

Another argument raised by opponents to the FASB's proposal was that treating employee stock options as an expense could jeopardize **compliance with contract terms and conditions**. Companies with large employee stock option awards might, under the FASB's proposal, violate loan covenants tied to reported earnings. For example, the "times-interest-earned" ratio would deteriorate if option grants were expensed because the recorded expense would reduce the earnings number used in this ratio.

Impartial observers who understand contracting incentives can see why companies with significant employee options would raise this objection. Their interests would be harmed by the FASB proposal, and economic intuition tells us that companies would resist such initiatives. But you can appreciate the FASB's mission to "do the right thing"—to draft rules that closely mirror underlying economic circumstances. If a particular accounting approach correctly captures these economic effects, it presumably should be used even though some companies may be harmed. Furthermore, many of the FASB's most vocal opponents were companies whose

Contracting

---

[25] To illustrate the point, there is no cash outflow or inflow to the company when Ramos Corporation first grants 100 options with a $10 exercise price to an employee. But there may be a cash inflow to Ramos at some later date, if (and when) the employee exercises the options. At the exercise date, Ramos will receive $1,000 cash ($10 per option × 100 options) from the employee if all of the options are exercised.

employee stock options—if expensed—would have decreased earnings by a trivial amount. Since the potential impact of the FASB proposal on these firms' covenants was insignificant, what was really motivating their opposition? Perhaps the answer lies in how (and how much) corporate executives are paid.

The compensation paid to top corporate executives was under intense scrutiny in the early 1990s. Corporate restructurings and layoffs were widespread, a recession was in progress, and many companies demonstrated lackluster financial performance. In this climate some critics questioned whether top corporate executives should continue to enjoy increasingly large salaries and bonuses while their employees were experiencing financial hardship. The issue quickly became political.

In 1993 the U.S. Congress limited the tax deductibility of executive compensation to $1,000,000 per employee—any excess over that amount could not be claimed as a deduction on the corporate tax return except when compensation was tied to the achievement of explicit and preset performance goals. (See Reebok International's discussion of the tax limitation on executive pay in Exhibit 7.2.) The passage of this law clearly illustrates public sentiment on this issue. Corporate leaders, sensitive to the growing scrutiny of executive compensation levels, may have felt that the FASB's plan to expense stock options would draw unwanted attention to executive pay.

The *legality of corporate distributions to owners* was never at issue regarding executive compensation. Political considerations aside, companies are free under the law to pay corporate executives whatever amounts are deemed appropriate by their board of directors. However, an issue did arise—whether large executive salaries were *proper*. Some companies were perceived to oppose the FASB's stock options expense proposal because it would add the value of options to cash compensation and thus make it easier for critics of "excessive" pay to spotlight certain companies and executives.

Opponents to the FASB's proposal also invoked an argument based on *equity valuation*. They believed that a simple "price–earnings multiple" relationship exists between reported earnings and common stock values. Under the FASB's plan, they argued, employee stock option grants would increase compensation expense and lower earnings—and thus lower stock price. (Our discussion of equity valuation in Chapter 6 suggests that the relationship between earnings and share price is more complicated than this.) Opponents of the FASB's plan argued that as stock prices fell, small companies who were heavy users of stock options would have difficulty raising new equity capital. This position was voiced by Senator Dianne Feinstein (Democrat, California) when she introduced legislation designed to block the FASB. She said:

> [The Bill] will also require the Financial Accounting Standards Board (FASB) to reexamine [its] recent decision to impose huge new accounting charges on the use of employee stock options. I am seriously concerned that if FASB's rule is adopted, tens of thousands of desperately needed jobs in California and the Nation will never be created. (Congressional Record—Senate, June 29, 1993, S8252.)

Senator Feinstein believed that the FASB's proposed stock options expense rule would make it more difficult for high-technology companies to raise new equity capital, thereby inhibiting expansion and job creation.

Despite growing business opposition, the FASB persisted and continued to move toward expense treatment of stock-based compensation. In response to intense business lobbying, Congress later initiated legislation which would have eliminated the FASB's independence by requiring the SEC to approve all new FASB standards.[26] Faced with this threat, the FASB was compelled to abandon its proposal and implement a compromise treatment.

---

[26] Called the Accounting Standards Reform Act of 1994, this bill was introduced by Senator Joe Lieberman (Democrat, Connecticut). Congressional Record—Senate, October 6, 1994, S14510.

The Compromise—*SFAS No. 123*

The widespread, powerful opposition to recognizing stock-based compensation as an expense caused the FASB to allow a choice of accounting methods:

1. Companies could choose to continue using the *APB Opinion No. 25* approach, under which compensation expense was rarely recognized.
2. Alternatively, companies could measure the **fair value** of the stock option at the grant date, and charge this amount to expense.[27]

The fair value of a stock option is measured using standard option-pricing models, with adjustments for factors unique to employee stock options. The FASB encouraged companies to adopt the fair value approach rather than to continue using *APB Opinion No. 25*, since it considered the fair value approach to be preferable.[28] Companies that chose to continue using *APB Opinion No. 25* accounting were also required to disclose in a footnote what net income would have been if compensation expense had been recognized under the fair value approach. The stock option reporting alternatives are represented graphically in Figure 15.4.

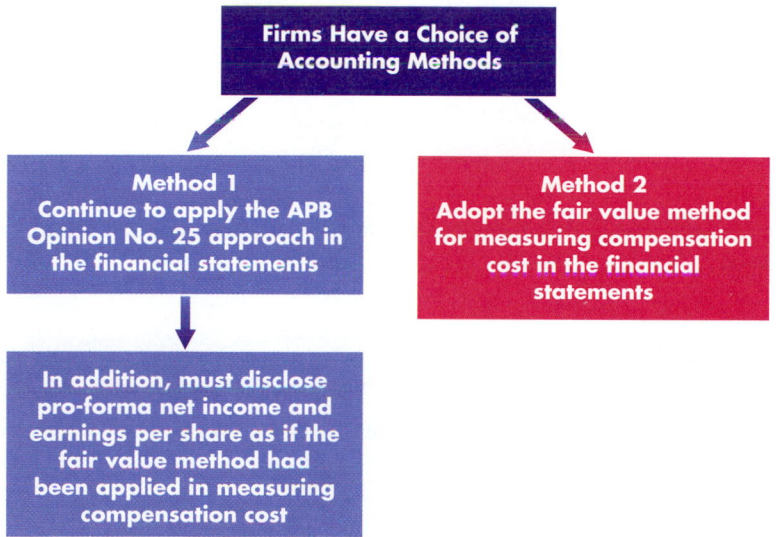

Figure 15.4

EMPLOYEE STOCK OPTION REPORTING ALTERNATIVES UNDER *SFAS NO. 123*

Implementing the fair value approach of *SFAS No. 123* is not difficult. However, the standard contains many detailed guidelines for measuring compensation expense. We describe these procedures tersely using a "big-picture" approach—that's all you need to grasp the overall impact of the fair value approach on financial numbers.

Assume that Guyton Corporation grants 100 common stock options to each of its top 300 managers on January 1, 2005. At that date, both the exercise price of the options and the market price of Guyton's stock is $30. To provide managers with an incentive to remain at Guyton, the options cannot be exercised before January 1, 2008. This time span between the grant date and the first available exercise date is called the **vesting period**. Guyton's options do not expire until January 1, 2015, giving the options a ten-year legal life. But *SFAS No. 123* requires that we

> For most companies today, the expected life of employee stock options is somewhere between three and ten years.

---

[27] *SFAS No. 123*, para. 11.

[28] Suppose Ramos Corporation used the fair value approach for its employee stock options. Recall that Ramos granted 100 options with a $10 exercise price to an employee. Let's assume that these options vest immediately—meaning they can be exercised by the employee at any time after the grant date—and have a fair value of $1.50 each (or $150 in total), as determined by an appropriate options-pricing model. Under the fair value approach, Ramos would record $150 of compensation expense on the date the options were granted.

estimate the **expected life of the options**—meaning we must forecast when the options are likely to be exercised by employees. Factors to consider in estimating the expected life include the average length of time similar grants have remained outstanding in the past and the expected volatility of the company's common stock price. Let's assume Guyton's options have an expected life of five years.

SFAS No. 123 specifies that the fair value of stock options is to be measured at the **grant date**—the date when both the terms of the grant are set and the stock options are awarded to individual employees. Here's how the fair value of a stock option should be determined:

> The fair value of a stock option . . . shall be estimated using an option-pricing model (for example, the Black–Scholes or a binomial model) that takes into account as of the grant date the exercise price and expected life of the option, the current price of the underlying stock and its expected volatility, expected dividends on the stock . . . and the risk-free interest rate for the expected term of the option. (*SFAS No. 123*, para. 19.)

Volatility in option pricing models is measured using a benchmark of one standard deviation of a stock's return over a specified time period. Assume Guyton stock has experienced a return of 10%. Since one standard deviation is roughly 66% of a normal distribution, the 20% expected volatility means there is a 66% probability that the return on Guyton's stock will be 10% ± 20% in any one year—that is, there is a two-thirds chance that the return in any one year will range between a low of −10% to a high of +30%.

It is not necessary to understand the theory behind option pricing models to understand the financial reporting for employee stock options. As the preceding excerpt indicates, the measurement of fair value requires estimates of several other variables that we have not yet specified in the Guyton example. We will assume: the risk-free interest rate is 6.75%, no dividends are forecasted for the company's common stock, and the expected volatility of Guyton's common stock is 20%. These facts are summarized in Exhibit 15.4.

EXHIBIT 15.4	Guyton Corporation

Variables Used to Estimate the Value of Employee Stock Options

Options granted (100 shares × 300 employees)	30,000
Exercise price	$30
Stock price at grant date	$30
Expected life of options	5 years
Risk-free interest rate	6.75%
Expected volatility of common stock	20%
Expected dividends on common stock	–0–

Using the Black–Scholes Option Valuation formula, the fair market value of each Guyton option is estimated to be $10.05 at the grant date.

Looking at Exhibit 15.4, inserting the numbers from the top into the Black–Scholes option pricing model indicates that each option has a fair value of $10.05 at the grant date.[29] The total

---

[29] Designed for valuing options traded in open stock exchanges, the standard Black–Scholes formula doesn't take into consideration the added restrictions of employee options, such as vesting and lack of transferability. Those limits make employee options worth much less than exchange-traded options. So, companies that use the standard Black–Scholes formula to expense options would take a much bigger charge to earnings than is necessary. Another way to calculate option expense is called the binomial model. This uses a different mathematical formula and requires more assumptions—including assumptions that explicitly address vesting and other features unique to employee stock options. A key advantage of the binomial model is that it takes into account the possibility that changes in the stock price may influence the timing of when employees exercise options.

compensation cost of all employee stock option awards is $301,500 ($10.05 × 30,000 options). Let's assume that all 300 managers will meet the vesting requirements and ultimately exercise all 30,000 options.

Stock-based compensation is intended to increase the employees' stake in the firm, creating an incentive for employees to work in the best interests of all the owners. The vesting requirements provide an extra incentive to stay with the company long enough to benefit from the anticipated value of the options. For these reasons *SFAS No. 123* charges total compensation cost of $301,500 to expense on a ***straight-line basis over the vesting period***. Guyton Corporation would recognize $100,500 ($301,500 ÷ 3 years) as compensation expense in each of the years 2005 through 2007:

> *SFAS No. 123* (para. 28) requires firms to estimate what proportion of the options originally granted will never vest due to employee turnover. Compensation expense includes only those options that are not forfeited. For example, if Guyton Corporation estimated that only 29,000 options would ultimately vest, total compensation cost would be $291,450 (that is, $10.05 × 29,000) rather than $301,500.

> We ignore deferred income tax considerations (discussed in Chapter 13) for simplicity. Deferred taxes arise because compensation expense is recognized in the financial statements and for income tax purposes at different amounts and in different periods. For income tax purposes, employers can deduct the *tax cost of* options—calculated as the difference between the exercise price and the stock price on the day the options are exercised by the employee—from taxable income. This means that companies using the *APB Opinion No. 25* intrinsic value approach for employee stock options almost never recognize any compensation expense for financial report purposes but they do recognize a tax benefit when the options are exercised.

DR Compensation expense	$100,500	
CR Paid-in capital—stock options		$100,500

This same entry is made each year even though the market value of the company's stock—and therefore the fair value of outstanding employee stock options—will undoubtedly change over time. ***SFAS No. 123 specifies that compensation cost—option fair value—is measured only once, at the grant date.***

Let's say Guyton's share price rises above the $30 exercise price after the vesting period and all 30,000 options are exercised by managers on the same day. The entry to record the exercise of employee stock options is (assuming $20 par value stock):

DR Cash (30,000 × $30)	$900,000	
DR Paid-in capital—stock options ($100,500 × 3 years)	301,500	
CR Common stock—par ($20 × 30,000)		$600,000
CR Paid-in capital in excess of par		601,500

Notice that: (1) compensation expense is recognized in the same amount each year over the vesting period; and (2) if the options are exercised, the total amount added to the common stock and capital in excess of par is $1,201,500—the sum of the cash received when the options are exercised plus the calculated fair value of the options at the grant date.

If we assume that Guyton's share price never rises above the exercise price, then the options will never be exercised. No cash will flow in. The offset to cumulative three-year compensation expense ($301,500) will remain in the "Paid-in capital—stock options" account. This dollar figure represents the estimated value of employee productivity (measured at the option grant date) that in effect was "donated" to the company without any corresponding ownership claim being given up to Guyton's employees.

The Stock Options Debate Rekindled

"It's going to happen, and quite appropriately so."

–Alan Greenspan, referring to the growing momentum for
counting stock options as an expense, in testimony before
the Senate Banking Committee on July 16, 2002.

In April 2003, the FASB reached a tentative decision to require all companies to expense the fair value of employee stock options at the grant date. This decision eliminates further use of the "intrinsic value" approach first introduced in *APB Opinion No. 25* and then later incorporated as a compromise in *SFAS No. 123*. For most U.S. companies, the FASB's decision means that they must abandon the intrinsic value method and begin using the fair value method. The dollar impact of this required accounting change would be substantial for many U.S. companies. For example, the composite 2001 earnings per share of firms in the Standard & Poors' 500 Index would have been reduced by 24.5% if the fair value of options granted that year was expensed.

Congress reacted swiftly to forestall the FASB's move. Representatives David Dreier (Republican, California) and Anna Eshoo (Democrat, California) introduced legislation entitled the "Broad-Based Stock Option Plan Transparency Act of 2003" (H.R. 1372). If enacted, the bill would direct the SEC to require enhanced reporting disclosures for employee stock options. It would also prevent the SEC from recognizing any new stock option accounting standard until the SEC submitted a report to Congress on the effectiveness of the new disclosures *following a three year period of study.*

The International Accounting Standards Board (IASB) opposed the bill and expressed concern about the impact it could have on accounting standards in general: "If the U.S. Congress or political authorities in other countries seek to override the decisions of the competent professional standard setters . . . accounting standards will inevitably lose consistency, coherence, and credibility."[30] In testimony before a house committee, FASB chairman Robert Herz warned in June 2003 that the bill to delay new rules on stock options would set a "dangerous precedent" of congressional interference in accounting standard setting.[31]

What sparked renewed debate over stock option accounting? Two factors seem to have brought the issue back into the political and regulatory arena:

1. The explosive growth in stock option grants during the late 1990s
2. Public outrage over the accounting abuses uncovered subsequently at many companies

Stock option "overload" was widely regarded as one factor—perhaps the most important factor—contributing to the accounting fiascoes at companies like Enron and WorldCom. The prevailing view was that managers who were eager to cash in their options resorted to questionable accounting practices designed to inflate earnings and revenues, and boost share prices. Rather than align the interests of shareholders and managers, options were thought to have done the opposite: transferring vast amounts of wealth to executives even as outside shareholders suffered. These concerns spawned a reform movement aimed at curbing the use of options by forcing companies to count them as an expense.

---

[30] Paul A. Volcker, former Federal Reserve Board chairman and current chairman of the foundation that oversees the IASB, in written testimony to Congress, as quoted in C. Schneider, "Who Rules Accounting," *CFO Magazine* (August 2003).

[31] A companion bill was introduced in the Senate in May 2003. A third bill, introduced in November 2003 by Senator Michael Enzi (Republican, Wyoming) would limit expensing to options granted to a company's five highest paid executives.

But not everyone agreed! The battle between those who favored and those who opposed stock options expensing involved familiar arguments:

Why Critics Say Options Should be Expensed	Why Options Expensing Defenders Disagree
• Some 75% to 80% of executive pay now comes in the form of options. Since all other forms of compensation must be deducted from earnings, options should be treated the same.	• Unlike salaries or other perks, granting options requires no cash outlay from companies. Since there is no real (cash) cost to the company to deduct, doing so will unjustly penalize earnings.
• Deducting the cost of options will yield more accurate earnings numbers, which should help restore investor confidence.	• There are no universal standards for expensing options; all valuation methods require big assumptions and estimates. So expensing them will reduce the accuracy of income statements and leave them open to manipulation.
• Since options are now all but free to companies, excessive grants to top execs have been encouraged. But options do have costs: They dilute shareholders' stakes and deprive companies of the funds they would otherwise get by selling those shares in the open market. Such costs should be reflected in earnings.	• Deducting the cost of options will reduce earnings, which is likely to drive down share prices.
• Bringing more discipline to options grants will also reduce the incentives top execs now have to pump their stocks through short-term earnings maneuvers in hopes of cashing in big option gains.	• Rather than take the hit to earnings, companies can issue far fewer options. That would hurt morale, limit a key tool used to lure talent, and inhibit companies from aligning employee and shareholder interests.
	• Tech firms argue that generous option grants have spurred the risk-taking and entrepreneurship so crucial to innovation. Expensing options risks damaging that benefit.

Source: A. Borrus, P. Dwyer, D. Foust, and L. Lavelle, "To Expense or Not to Expense," *Business Week* (July 29, 2002).

As the options reform movement gained steam in 2003, nearly 500 U.S. companies—including Amazon.com, Bank One, Coca-Cola, Computer Associates, and Procter & Gamble—said that they would soon begin expensing stock options voluntarily using the fair value method in *SFAS No. 123*. (Boeing and Winn Dixie had been doing so already for several years.) Other companies like General Electric and Microsoft curtailed their employee stock options programs in favor of outright stock grants.[32] Still others, most notably Intel and Sun Microsystems, remained steadfast in their opposition to counting stock options as an expense.

Many observers believe that stock option expensing will become a reality for U.S. companies in 2005. As this book goes to press, the FASB is formulating methods and guidelines for transitioning to stock option expensing. Policy deliberations at the IASB also favor expensing stock options, and European companies are likely to do so beginning in 2005.

As television news anchors say, "Stay tuned for more late-breaking developments!"

> "It's an accounting issue that shouldn't be resolved by our yelling, that shouldn't be political, that shouldn't be settled in op-ed columns—it should [be] settled by [the] FASB going away on a deserted island and thinking about it. A lot of emotion has blocked this rational accounting issue. A lot of what people are pissed about is executive compensation. The distinction between executive compensation and option expensing kind of gets lost." Andy Grove, CEO of Intel Corporation, as quoted in *Fortune* (September 16, 2002).

RECAP

SFAS No. 123 is a political compromise. The FASB was unanimous in its belief that expenses are incurred when companies grant stock options to employees as a part of a compensation package. Nevertheless, companies are not required to record this expense in the financial statements (although a growing number of companies do so voluntarily). Instead, the compromise requires firms to disclose the fair value amount of stock-based compensation in a footnote to the statements. But this may soon change!

---

[32] Under a stock grant program, employees receive shares of common stock as part of their compensation packages. The employer (say, Microsoft) must record as compensation expense the fair value of the shares granted.

Stock Option Disclosures

Most companies are still accounting for employee stock options as they have in the past. This means that no compensation expense is recorded unless the option exercise price is *below* the stock price on the grant date.

SFAS No. 123 requires companies to provide *pro forma*—"as if"—disclosures of net income and EPS that are calculated with a charge to compensation expense for options granted. Exhibit 15.5 shows the impact on 2002 EPS for a representative sample of companies. Citrix Systems, for example, would have reported a $0.35 per share loss that year instead of a $0.53 profit.

EXHIBIT 15.5	Earnings Per Share (EPS) Impact of Expensing the Value of Employee Stock Option Grants for Selected Companies in 2002			
	EPS as Reported	EPS Adjusted for Compensation Expense	EPS Decrease in $	Percent Decrease
Adaptec	$(1.92)	$(2.68)	$0.76	40%
AOL Time Warner	(22.15)	(22.39)	0.24	1
Autodesk	0.28	0.13	0.15	54
Biogen	1.33	1.00	0.33	25
Bristol Myers	1.07	0.94	0.13	12
Cisco Systems	0.26	0.05	0.21	81
Citrix Systems	0.53	(0.35)	0.88	166
First Data	1.63	1.49	0.14	9
Fluor	2.06	1.99	0.07	3
Hewlett Packard	(0.37)	(0.68)	0.31	84
Intel	0.47	0.29	0.18	38
Kroger	1.65	1.49	0.16	10
Lucent Technologies	(3.49)	(4.22)	0.73	21
Microsoft	1.81	1.57	0.24	13
Pepsico	1.89	1.68	0.21	11
Schering Plough	1.35	1.29	0.06	4
Texas Instruments	(0.20)	(0.43)	0.23	115
United Technologies	4.67	4.42	0.25	5
Verizon Communications	1.49	1.32	0.17	11

Source: Company annual reports.

The dollar impact of stock compensation expense for some companies can be staggering.
Here's what Cisco Systems says about its employee stock options:

The Company is required under Statement of Financial Accounting Standards No. 123, "Accounting for Stock Based Compensations" ("SFAS 123"), to disclose pro forma information regarding option grants made to its employees based on specified valuation techniques that produce estimated compensation charges.

Year Ended	July 27, 2002	July 28, 2001	July 29, 2000
Net income (loss)—as reported	$1,893	($1,014)	$2,668
Net income (loss)—pro forma	373	(2,705)	1,549
Basic net income (loss) per common share—as reported	$0.26	($0.14)	$0.39
Diluted net income (loss) per common share—as reported	0.25	(0.14)	0.36
Basic net income (loss) per common share—pro forma	0.05	(0.38)	0.22
Diluted net income (loss) per common share—pro forma	0.05	(0.38)	0.21

The fair value of stock option grants is estimated on the date of grant using the Black–Scholes option pricing model with the following weighted average assumptions:

	Employee Stock Option Plan			Employee Stock Purchase Plan		
	July 27, 2002	July 28, 2001	July 29, 2000	July 27, 2002	July 28, 2001	July 29, 2000
Expected dividend yield	0.0%	0.0%	0.0%	0.0%	0.0%	0.0%
Risk-free interest rate	4.7%	5.4%	6.4%	3.1%	5.3%	5.3%
Expected volatility	47.5%	34.8%	33.9%	58.1%	35.0%	43.3%
Expected life (in years)	5.5	3.6	3.1	0.5	0.5	0.5

The Black–Scholes options pricing model was developed for use in estimating the fair value of traded options that have no vesting restrictions and are fully transferable. In addition, options pricing models require the input of highly subjective assumptions including the expected stock price volatility. The Company uses projected volatility rates which are based upon historical volatility rates and other economic data trended into future years. Because the Company's employee stock options have characteristics significantly different from those of traded options, and because changes in the subjective input assumptions can materially affect the estimate, in management's opinion, the existing models do not necessarily provide a reliable single measure of the fair value of the Company's options. Under the Black–Scholes option pricing model, the weighted average estimated values of employee stock options granted during fiscal 2002, 2001 and 2000 were $8.60, $13.31, and $19.44, respectively. (Cisco Systems, Inc., 2002 Annual Report.)

Cisco Systems' net income for 2002 was $1,893 million. But, this figure does not include compensation expense for employee stock options. If compensation expense was included, Cisco Systems' 2002 net income would have been only $393 million (the *pro forma* amount shown in the annual report note). Cisco Systems' 2002 basic EPS would have been reduced from $0.26 to $0.05, a decrease of $0.21 per share. This 81% decline represents $1,520 million of Cisco's 2002 earnings. Of course, for many companies the dollar impact is much smaller.

Most companies are like Cisco Systems. They use the Black–Scholes options pricing model to estimate the cost (fair value) of employee stock options when constructing the pro forma net income and EPS figures required by *SFAS No. 123*. To use the Black–Scholes model, assumptions about expected dividend yield, risk-free interest rate, expected stock price volatility, and expected option life are required. (Cisco Systems follows the *SFAS No. 123* disclosure guidelines and reports its assumptions in the financial statement footnote.) Assumptions about future stock price volatility and expected option life are highly subjective. Some companies use assumptions that make the estimated cost of employee stock options look quite low. Others are more conservative and estimate a high cost. These differences can make comparisons difficult across companies.

Exhibit 15.6 on the next page illustrates how dramatically the EPS figure for a company can change when stock price volatility and option life assumptions of another company in the industry are used to recalculate stock option expense. For example, JDS Uniphase reported a $6.50 per share loss in 2002 using the *APB Opinion No. 25* "intrinsic value" approach where no stock option expense is recorded. The company's *SFAS No. 123*

> Although Cisco Systems does not record an expense for stock option compensation, the company does receive a tax break when employees exercise options. Cisco's cash flow statement reveals a stock options tax benefit of $61 million in 2002, compared to $1,397 million and $2,495 million in 2001 and 2000, respectively. Why was the tax savings so small in 2002? The company's stock price had fallen precipitously and many employees found that their options were "under water"—meaning that the exercise price was above the prevailing market price for Cisco shares. Fewer options were being exercised that year, and the company's tax benefit was correspondingly reduced.

> Recall that stock price volatility measures the degree to which the company's stock price changes over time. Expected option life refers to the speed with which employees will exercise their options in the future.

footnote indicates that JDS Uniphase would have reported a $6.92 pro forma loss per share under the "fair value" approach—the difference being the (net-of-tax) stock option expense of $0.42 per share estimated using the company's own Black–Scholes assumptions. However, if JDS Uniphase had instead used the stock price volatility and option life assumptions of its competitor (Lucent Technologies) to compute the options expense, the 2002 pro forma loss would have narrowed to only $6.72 per share.

EXHIBIT 15.6	Earnings Per Share Impact of Replacing One Company's Stock Option Assumptions With Those of a Competitor			
	Earnings (loss) per Share for 2002			
	As Reported	SFAS No. 123 Pro forma	Using Competitor's Assumptions	Change Using Competitor's Assumptions
JDS Uniphase	$(6.50)	$(6.92)	$(6.72)	$ 0.20
Lucent Technologies	$(3.49)	$(4.22)	$(4.70)	$(0.48)
Ford Motor	$(0.55)	$(0.65)	$(0.61)	$ 0.04
General Motors	$ 3.37	$ 3.01	$ 2.83	$(0.18)
SBC Communications	$ 1.70	$ 1.70	$ 1.67	$(0.03)
Verizon Communications	$ 1.49	$ 1.32	$ 1.38	$ 0.06

Note: SBC Communications used the intrinsic value method and expensed stock option costs in 2002.
Source: D. Leonhardt, "Stock Options Calculus: Who Is Getting It Right?" *New York Times* (March 30, 2003).

The option pricing assumptions made by JDS Uniphase produce a higher—more conservative—stock option expense estimate than do those of Lucent Technologies. The difference adds $0.20 per share to the pro forma earnings of JDS Uniphase and subtracts $0.48 per share from Lucent's pro forma earnings. Ford Motor and Verizon Communications seem to use conservative assumptions. Of course, there are sound reasons why the more liberal assumptions at Lucent, General Motors, and SBC Communications produce a smaller expense estimate—these companies may simply have less volatile stock prices and shorter option lives. As an analyst, the question to ask is whether or not there are real economic forces that contribute to differences in option pricing assumptions for similar firms.

RECAP

Stock options are an important part of employee pay at many companies today—and for good reason. They save cash, they motivate employees, and companies are not currently required to record compensation expense for employee stock options except in a footnote to the financial statements.

Convertible Debt

In late 1999 VerticalNet offered investors the opportunity to purchase up to $100 million of convertible bonds. These bonds paid a stated interest rate of 5.25% annually, matured in 5 years, and could be exchanged at any time for VerticalNet stock at a conversion price of $20 per common share. Because the bonds were issued in units of $1,000 face value, the conversion price meant investors could exchange each bond for 50 shares of stock ($1,000 face value ÷ $20 per share conversion price = 50 shares). Investors snapped up the entire $100 million of VerticalNet convertible bonds.

What price do you suppose VerticalNet received for each $1,000 face value bond?

To put this question in context, the average yield to maturity—that's the effective interest rate—on newly issued high-grade industrial debt in late 1999 was about 8% per year. Given the economic climate of the time, it may surprise you to learn that VerticalNet was able to sell its 5.25% bonds at par, receiving $1,000 in cash for each $1,000 face value issued. By contrast, the promised cash flows associated with each bond—$52.50 each year plus another $1,000 at maturity in the year 2004—have a discounted present value at 8% of only $890.20. ***Investors were willing to pay $109.80 more than the present value of each VerticalNet bond because of the conversion feature attached to the debt.***

We now explain the financial reporting for convertible debt and its implications for those who use financial statements.

Background

Convertible bonds give investors the opportunity—but not the obligation—to exchange a company's debt for common stock in accordance with terms in the bond indenture. The **conversion price**—the dollar value at which the debt can be converted into common stock—is typically above the prevailing market price of the company's common shares at the time the debt is issued. The option to convert is solely at the discretion of the investor, and it will only be exercised when and if the investor finds the exchange desirable. Shares of VerticalNet were trading around $16 in September 1999—or about $4 below the conversion price. Investors had little incentive to exchange their bonds for stock immediately. The real value of the conversion feature to investors was the possibility that the stock price might climb above $20 sometime over the next 5 years.

Figure 15.5 reports the dollar value of new convertible debt issues in the United States between 1980 and 1997. Industrial corporations have been the primary issuers of convertible debt.

Figure 15.5

THE DOLLAR VALUE OF CONVERTIBLE DEBT ISSUED BY U.S. COMPANIES FROM 1980 THROUGH 1997

Source: K. A. Carow, G. R. Erwin, and J. J. McConnell, "A Survey of U.S. Corporate Financing Innovations: 1970–1997," *Journal of Applied Corporate Finance* (Spring 1999). Reprinted with permission.

Convertible debt offerings increase during periods of rising stock prices, which explains much of the year-to-year variation in Figure 15.5. The opportunity to share in future stock price increases is more attractive during a period of bullish market expectations for common stocks. This sentiment is what makes it possible for companies to issue convertibles on favorable terms.

Convertible bonds are also usually **callable**, or redeemable, by the issuer at a specified price before maturity. When convertible bonds are called, investors must either convert or have the debt redeemed for a cash price that is generally less than the value of the common stock into which the debt can be converted. Call provisions protect the company against extreme price increases by forcing investor action. Otherwise, investors would simply continue holding the debt in anticipation of further share price increases.

To illustrate, suppose that VerticalNet's stock price reached $25 per share in 2000. Each $1,000 par value convertible bond would then represent a claim to $1,250 in common stock (50 shares × $25 per share). Suppose that VerticalNet's bonds were callable at a redemption price of $1,027.50 each. VerticalNet could force conversion by "calling" the debt— investors would then take the more valuable common stock ($1,250) rather than the less valuable redemption cash payment ($1,027.50).

Financial Reporting Issues

Convertible debt poses this financial reporting dilemma: Should a value be assigned to the debt's conversion feature? Clearly, conversion features are valuable to both the issuing company and investors. The conversion option enabled VerticalNet to borrow $100 million at 5.25% annual interest when other more established companies were paying 8% annual interest. Moreover, the availability of Black–Scholes and other option pricing models means that we now have well-established methods for assigning values to option features—like the VerticalNet conversion privilege. However, GAAP for convertible debt is outlined in *APB Opinion No. 14*, which predates the development of modern option pricing theory.[33]

APB Opinion No. 14 specifies that convertible bonds must be recorded as *debt only*, with no value assigned to the conversion privilege. Two reasons for not assigning a value to the conversion privilege are cited:

1. The inseparability of the conversion feature from the debt component of the convertible security
2. The practical problems of determining separate values for the debt and the conversion option in the absence of separability

On the absence of separability, the APB concluded:

In the absence of separate transferability, values are not established in the marketplace, and accordingly, the value assigned to each feature is necessarily subjective. A determination of the value of the conversion feature poses problems because of the uncertain duration of the right to obtain the stock and the uncertainty as to the future value of the stock obtainable upon conversion. Furthermore, issuers often claim that a subjective valuation of a debt security without the conversion option but with identical other terms . . . is difficult because such a security could not be sold at a price which the issuer would regard as producing an acceptable cost of financing. (*APB Opinion No. 14*, para. 8.)

Given modern option pricing methods, it is unlikely that accounting standard setters would reach the same conclusion today. Nevertheless, APB Opinion No. 14 *continues to be GAAP for convertible debt.*

Here's how VerticalNet records the issuance of all $100 million of its convertible subordinated debentures at par value:

DR Cash	$100,000,000	
CR Convertible subordinated debentures		$100,000,000

---

[33] "Accounting for Convertible Debt and Debt Issued with Stock Purchase Warrants," *APB Opinion No. 14* (New York: AICPA, 1969).

This entry assigns the entire $100 million to the convertible debt liability. One year later, Vertical-Net records interest expense of $5,250,000 (or .0525 × $100 million) and the cash interest payment, which also occurs that day:

DR	Interest expense	$5,250,000	
CR	Cash		$5,250,000

(This entry ignores the real-world complication that arises when companies accrue interest throughout the year.)

Thus far, the accounting for convertible debt parallels the accounting for the straight-debt securities described in Chapter 11. VerticalNet will continue to record interest expense at the rate of 5.25% annually until the debt is retired or converted. Let's move several years forward to see what happens at conversion.

Suppose that some (but not all) investors have now chosen to exercise their conversion privilege by exchanging $50 million of the debentures. Furthermore, the company's stock has a current market value of $30 per share, which is above the $20 conversion price. This means that investors will surrender bonds with a face value (and book value) of $50 million in exchange for common stock with a market value of $75 million. *APB Opinion No. 14* permits companies to record debt conversion in either of two ways:

> At the stated conversion price, investors will receive 2,500,000 common shares for their $50 million of debentures ($50 million divided by $20 price per share). Since each share has a market value of $30, investors receive stock worth $75 million.

1. The **book value method** records the newly issued stock at the book value of debt retired.

DR	Convertible subordinated debentures	$50,000,000	
CR	Common stock ($1 par)		$ 2,500,000
CR	Paid-in capital in excess of par		47,500,000

2. The **market value method** records the newly issued shares at their current market value. Any difference between that $30 market value and the $20 conversion price is recognized as a loss (or gain) on conversion.

DR	Convertible subordinated debentures	$50,000,000	
DR	Loss on debt conversion	25,000,000	
CR	Common stock ($1 par)		$ 2,500,000
CR	Paid-in capital in excess of par		72,500,000

The conversion loss is not classified as an extraordinary item because it is neither *unusual in nature* nor *infrequent in occurrence*.[34] Of course, VerticalNet would continue to record interest expense on the remaining $50 million of outstanding convertible debentures.

Under the book value approach, no accounting gain or loss is recognized at retirement because the debt book value is just transferred to the common stock accounts. Under the market value approach, however, common stock is credited at full market value *as if* the shares issued were sold for cash on the conversion date. It is easy to see why the book value method is more popular. Almost all debt conversions occur when the company's stock price is above the conversion price, and this situation triggers recognition of an accounting loss under the market value method. Managers can avoid recording this loss by instead selecting the book value approach.

---

[34] From Chapter 2, remember that to qualify as an extraordinary item under GAAP, the event must be both unusual *and* infrequent.

Analytical Insights

Analysis

There are two messages in this discussion of convertible debt for financial statement readers.

One message: ***Estimating the future cash flow implications of convertible debt is difficult.*** It's difficult because it is necessary to consider both the scheduled interest and principal payments for the debt, as well as the likelihood of conversion prior to maturity. Option pricing methods can be used to evaluate the probability of conversion over long time intervals. For near-term projections, however, a simple comparison of the conversion price with the current market price of common stock can prove informative—that is, if the exercise price is above the current share price and the options are close to expiration, it is unlikely they will be exercised. The bond indenture agreement should also be examined for call provision details.

The other message: ***Recorded interest expense may seriously understate the true cost of debt financing for companies that issue convertible bonds or notes.*** Few people would argue that VerticalNet is more creditworthy than the U.S. government. Yet the company borrowed money at 5.25% annually when investors were charging the federal government 5.9% annual interest for loans of similar duration. By ignoring the value of conversion features, current GAAP understates interest expense.

The recent appearance of "zero-coupon, zero-yield"[35] convertible debt issued by U.S. companies has only served to underscore the inherent deficiencies of *APB Opinion No. 14* when it comes to interest expense. To see why, consider this example. In April 2003, Yahoo Inc. sold $750 million of "zero-coupon" convertible notes and received proceeds equal to their $750 million face value of the notes. The notes mature in 2008 and can be converted into shares of Yahoo common stock at the option of the note holder.

Recall from Chapter 11, that "zero-coupon" notes do not require the borrower (in this case, it's Yahoo) to make periodic interest payments over the life of the loan. And, because the notes were issued at par—meaning Yahoo received cash equal to the $750 million face value—there is no discount to amortize over the life of the loan. No periodic coupon interest and no discount amortization mean no interest expense under *APB Opinion No. 14*. In short, Yahoo will not recognize any interest expense on the loan even though the notes may never be converted into shares of common stock.

The lesson for corporate managers is clear: Current GAAP allows you to avoid interest expense as long as you issue zero-coupon convertible debt and structure the conversion features so that the debt sells for par (face) value. The lesson for analysts is equally clear: Interest expense computed under *APB Opinion No. 14* can seriously understate a company's true cost of debt.

U.S. GAAP for convertible debt securities may soon change. In October 2000, the FASB proposed that a convertible debt instrument should be separated into both its debt and equity components.[36] In Yahoo's case, for example, this would mean assigning a portion of the $750 million proceeds to debt (say, $600 million for the "zero-coupon" loan) and the remainder to equity ($150 million for the conversion option) based on the relative fair value of each component. The separated debt would then be classified as a liability, and the conversion option (or "warrant") would be classified as equity. Under the FASB's proposal, Yahoo would record periodic interest expense on the discounted "zero-coupon" loan even though no cash interest payment is required.[37] This approach overcomes the deficiencies of *APB Opinion No. 14*.

---

[35] Because the debt pays no interest ("zero coupon") and is issued at no discount ("zero yield"), it's known as "no-no" debt.

[36] "Accounting for Financial Instruments with Characteristics of Liabilities, Equity or Both," *Exposure Draft* (Stamford, CT: FASB 2000).

[37] The periodic interest expense that Yahoo would record is the discount amortization amount computed using the effective interest method described in Chapter 11.

One of the reasons the FASB proposed separating convertible debt into its debt and equity components was to bring U.S. GAAP into line with International Financial Reporting Standards. Those standards have required the separation of convertible securities into debt and equity components since 1996.[38] Canadian GAAP also requires a similar treatment. As this book goes to press, the FASB is expected to issue a revised proposal in early 2004 and a final statement later that year.

RECAP

Convertible debt gives investors the upside potential of common stock and the safety net of debt. That's why the interest rate on convertible debt is so low—the option value of the conversion feature compensates for the lower interest paid to investors. Because GAAP ignores the conversion option, interest expense may be understated and cash flow forecasting may be impeded.

SUMMARY

- Many aspects of financial reporting for owners' equity transactions are built on technical rules and procedures that have evolved over time.
- Other aspects of owners' equity accounting have not changed despite changing economic and legal environments.
- Still other aspects of owners' equity accounting involve complicated pronouncements that reflect political compromises.
- Financial statement readers must recognize these influences and avoid unwarranted inferences based on the reported figures.
- Stock buybacks don't produce accounting gains and losses, but they can be used to artificially inflate a company's reported earnings per share (EPS).
- Preferred stock that has a mandatory redemption feature looks a lot like debt, so GAAP now requires it to be classified as debt in most cases.
- Some companies can pay dividends in excess of their retained earnings balance, but their ability to do so depends on state law.
- Earnings-per-share (EPS) numbers are adjusted for potential dilution from stock options, warrants, and convertible securities.
- GAAP doesn't yet require companies to record compensation expense when stock options are given to employees (but this could soon change) and GAAP ignores the option value in convertible debt.
- GAAP can understate interest expense when companies issue convertible debt, but new GAAP rules may soon correct this problem.
- While some rules for owners' equity accounting may seem arbitrary—and therefore insignificant—these financial statement items have a profound impact on lending agreements, regulation, and the cost of equity capital.

APPENDIX

EMPLOYEE STOCK OWNERSHIP PLANS

An **employee stock ownership plan (ESOP)** is an employee pension plan that invests primarily in the common stock of the employer company. To establish an ESOP, the company first sets up a trust to hold the ESOP assets and makes contributions of up to 25% of payroll for employees in the plan. Stock contributed to (or purchased by) the trust is allocated to the accounts of employees who have met certain eligibility requirements—like having worked at the company for at least three years. ESOPs are

---

[38] "Financial Instruments: Disclosure and Presentation," *International Accounting Standard No. 32* (London: International Accounting Standards Committee, 1996). International Accounting Standards are now known as International Financial Reporting Standards, and the International Accounting Standards Committee (IASC) is now the International Accounting Standards Board (IASB).

subject to vesting like other pensions. Plan enrollees are not taxed on the income earned by the plan, nor on contributions to the plan, nor on other amounts added to their accounts, until the time of distribution. So ESOPs enable employees to gain a tax-free ownership stake in their company. Figure 15.6 illustrates the relationships among the ESOP, employer company, employees, and external funding sources like banks.

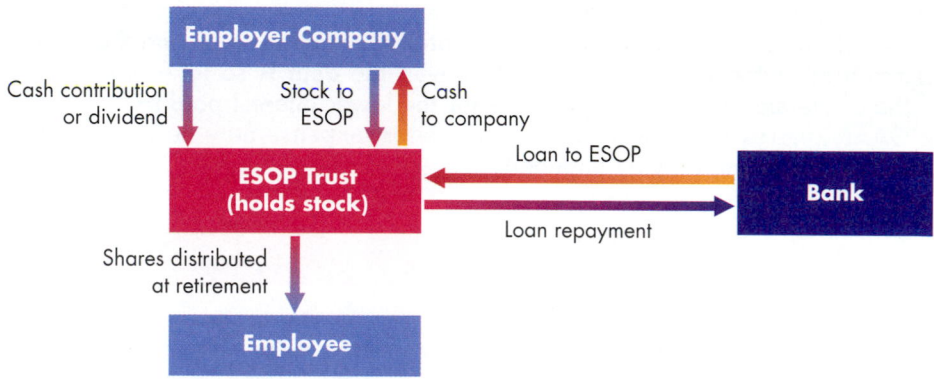

Figure 15.6 RELATIONSHIP BETWEEN THE ESOP, EMPLOYER COMPANY, EMPLOYEES, AND EXTERNAL FUNDING SOURCES

Cash contributions and dividends paid by employer company to trust are deductible for income tax purposes, within certain limits. Hence the sponsoring company can lower the cost of debt financing when compared to direct borrowing by the company.

ESOPs are attractive to employer companies for three reasons:

1. ESOPs have considerable tax advantages.
2. ESOPs can provide a source of low-cost debt financing for firms.
3. ESOPs have been used to finance management buyouts and as part of a takeover defense.

> Company payments into the ESOP trust are tax deductible within certain limits. The employer company can contribute its own stock to the ESOP and take a tax deduction for the fair value of the stock contributed. In addition, as the company makes payments to the trust to repay principal and interest on trust borrowing, *both* payments are tax deductible. Similarly, dividend payments on shares held by the trust are also tax deductible—to the extent that the trust uses the dividend payments to repay the loan. The money borrowed by the ESOP trust goes to the company as payment for the shares issued to the trust.

In a **leveraged ESOP**, the trust borrows money from a bank or other financial institution to purchase shares of stock of the employer company. As an example, suppose Buchner Manufacturing sets up an ESOP trust that then obtains a $20 million bank loan to purchase shares of Buchner stock. Next, the trust hands the cash over to Buchner in exchange for the stock. Buchner then makes annual or quarterly tax-deductible cash contributions to the trust, and the trust uses those contributions to make the interest and principal payments on the bank loan. In other words, loan proceeds flow directly to the company as ESOP shares are purchased, and loan repayment occurs over time with the ESOP shares serving as collateral for the loan. Employee ownership of the shares accrues according to the rate at which the loan principal is repaid.

Apart from their tax advantages, ESOPs have been used to take companies private, to acquire divested subsidiaries or divisions, to provide takeover defenses, and to save failed companies. ESOPs were widely used as takeover defenses because ESOP shares are relatively impervious to buyout by a hostile acquirer. Thus, a corporate raider who wants to accumulate a controlling interest in Buchner Manufacturing—for example, by owning 51% of the company's common stock—will find it hard to do so when Buchner's ESOP trust already owns 60% of the company's shares. The raider's only hope is to convince the ESOP to sell its shares—an unlikely event because the decision to sell shares rests with the ESOP trustees including typically one or more of the company's (in our example, that's Buchner Manufacturing) top executives.

The financial statement implications of ESOPs are described in Exhibit 15.7, which reprints the footnote from Maytag Company's 2002 annual report.

EXHIBIT 15.7 — Maytag Company

Footnote Disclosure for Employee Stock Ownership Plan (ESOP)

The Company established an Employee Stock Option Plan (ESOP), and a related trust issued debt and used the proceeds to acquire shares of the Company's stock for future allocation to ESOP participants. ESOP participants generally consist of all U.S. employees except certain groups covered by a collective bargaining agreement. The Company guarantees the ESOP debt and reflects it in the Consolidated Balance Sheets as Long-term debt with a related amount shown in the Shareowners' equity section as part of Employee stock plans. Dividends earned on the allocated and unallocated ESOP shares are used to service the debt. The Company is obligated to make annual contributions to the ESOP trust to the extent the dividends earned on the shares are less than the debt service requirements. As the debt is repaid, shares are released and allocated to plan participants based on the ratio of the current year debt service payment to the total debt service payments over the life of the loan. If the shares released are less than the shares earned by the employees, the Company contributes additional shares to the ESOP trust to meet the shortfall. All shares held by the ESOP trust are considered outstanding for earnings per share computations and dividends earned on the shares are recorded as a reduction of retained earnings.

The ESOP shares held in trust consisted of the following:

	December 31	
	2002	2001
Original shares held in trust:		
Released and allocated	2,469,377	2,366,589
Unreleased shares (fair value; 2002—$11,051,331; 2001—$15,221,891)	387,766	490,554
	2,857,143	2,857,143
Additional shares contributed and allocated	1,172,471	895,144
Shares withdrawn	(1,085,719)	(861,564)
Total shares held in trust	2,943,895	2,890,723

The components of the total contribution to the ESOP trust consisted of the following:

	Years Ended December 31		
($ in thousands)	2002	2001	2000
Debt service requirement	$ 3,983	$ 8,238	$8,600
Dividends earned on ESOP shares	(1,014)	(2,042)	(2,086)
Cash contribution to ESOP trust	2,969	6,196	6,514
Fair market value of additional shares contributed	8,194	4,257	3,133
Total contribution to ESOP trust	$11,163	$10,453	$9,647

The components of expense recognized by the Company for the ESOP contribution consisted of the following:

	Years Ended December 31		
($ in thousands)	2002	2001	2000
Contribution classified as interest expense	$ 453	$ 1,178	$1,540
Contribution classified as compensation expense	10,710	9,275	8,107
Total expense for the ESOP contribution	$11,163	$10,453	$9,647

Source: Maytag Company 2002 annual report.

The top portion of Maytag's footnote describes: the company's ESOP; who participates in the plan; and the flow of cash and Maytag shares between the company and the ESOP trust. The middle panel of the footnote tracks the year-to-year change in Maytag shares held by the trust. Here you learn that the trust held roughly 2.9 million shares of Maytag common stock—with a fair market value of more than $11 million—at the end of 2002, and that the company contributed nearly 1.2 million shares to the trust that year. The final two panels of the footnote provide information about ESOP-related cash flow and expense components. Maytag made a $2.969 million cash contribution to the trust in 2002 as well as an $8.194 million stock contribution, for a total contribution of $11.163 million. Maytag also recorded a corresponding $11.163 million ESOP expense, comprised of $0.453 million classified as interest expense and the remaining $10.710 million classified as compensation expense.

In addition to this footnote, Maytag Company's 2002 balance sheet included $14.1 million of ESOP debt as part of long-term liabilities and a corresponding $14.1 million owners' equity *reduction* labeled "Employee stock plans."

The following example illustrates how these two balance sheet items—ESOP debt as part of long-term liabilities and the owners' equity reduction from employee stock plans—arise, and it also illustrates how employers account for ESOPs.[39]

Assume Chittendon Manufacturing established an ESOP for hourly employees on January 1, 2005. The following transactions summarize the activities of the ESOP over its first year:

1. On January 1 the ESOP borrowed $20 million from a large regional bank, signing a ten-year installment note with annual interest payments equal to 9% of the outstanding balance. The note is guaranteed by the company.
2. That same day, the ESOP purchased 400,000 unissued shares of $10 par common stock from Chittendon Manufacturing at the current market price of $50 per share. These shares of stock are collateral for the bank loan.
3. During 2005 Chittendon Manufacturing declared and paid common dividends of $3 per share. The company also contributed $2.6 million in cash to the ESOP.
4. At the end of 2005 the ESOP "released and allocated" 40,000 shares to employees of the company.

> These shares actually remain in the ESOP trust until distributed to employees at retirement or when they leave the company.

Keep in mind that the following accounting entries are made on the books of Chittendon Manufacturing—they are not the accounting entries made by the ESOP trust itself.

The first two transactions are recorded by Chittendon as:

1. **DR** Employee stock plan	$20,000,000	
CR ESOP note payable		$20,000,000
2. **DR** Cash	$20,000,000	
CR Common stock—$10 par		$ 4,000,000
CR Paid-in capital in excess of par		16,000,000

Entry 1 records the ESOP borrowing. The debit is to a balance sheet contra-equity account called "Employee stock plan" (the same account title used by Maytag). It tracks the cost ($50 per share multiplied by 400,000 common shares) of unreleased ESOP shares, as you will see. Entry 2 records the sale of 400,000 shares of common stock to the ESOP. Chittendon declared and paid cash dividends of $3 per share during the year.

Entry 3 that follows reflects this transfer of $1.2 million ($3 per share multiplied by 400,000 ESOP shares) to the ESOP trust. However, the trust is required to make a $2.0 million principal payment on the note ($20 million ÷ 10 years) and to pay $1.8 million in interest ($20 million outstanding multiplied by 9%) at year-end. Consequently, the company must contribute $2.6 million in cash to the ESOP in addition to the $1.2 million in cash already in the trust. Entry 4 records this $2,600,000 contribution by the company to the ESOP.

---

[39] The accounting standards for ESOPs are described in "Accounting Practices for Certain Employee Stock Ownership Plans," *Statement of Position No. 76–3* (New York: AICPA, 1976).

3. **DR** Dividends		$1,200,000	
CR Cash (to ESOP trust)			$1,200,000
4. **DR** Interest expense		$1,800,000	
DR Compensation expense		800,000	
CR Cash (to ESOP trust)			$2,600,000

When the trust makes the $3.8 million payment to the bank and allocates shares to employees, Chittendon reduces the carrying value of the ESOP debt and the contra-equity account by the amount of the loan *principal* payment and shares allocated:

DR ESOP Note payable	$2,000,000	
CR Employee stock plan		$2,000,000

At this point the balance sheet of Chittendon Manufacturing shows an $18 million liability for the unpaid ESOP note and a corresponding $18 million contra-equity item labeled "Employee stock plan." The income statement shows $800,000 of compensation expense and $1.8 million of interest expense, but the other $1.2 million paid out by Chittendon is shown as a dividend distribution.

There are three points financial statement readers must keep in mind when examining ESOPs.

1. ***ESOP debt is not hidden in financial statement footnotes as an off-balance sheet item.*** Instead, the debt is carried on the books of the employer like any other long-term liability. Consequently, the future cash flow implications of ESOP debt are no more difficult to assess than for other long-term debt obligations of the company.
2. ***ESOP accounting produces an unusual balance sheet item, called "Employee stock plan" in our example.*** This account tracks the cost of ESOP shares not yet allocated to employees but still held by the trust. All common shares purchased by the ESOP—whether allocated to employees or not—are included in the "Common stock par" and "Paid-in capital in excess of par" accounts as outstanding stock.
3. ***Some analysts argue that ESOP accounting understates the company's true cost of employee compensation.*** To see why they argue there is understatement, notice that Chittendon employees "earned"—that is, they were allocated—40,000 ESOP shares during 2001 for a total cost of $2 million at $50 per share. This $2 million equals the ESOP debt principal repayment made during the year. Since the only source of ESOP cash is the employer company, Chittendon effectively made the $2 million debt payment using $1.2 million of cash labeled "dividends" and another $800,000 labeled "compensation expense." Chittendon's total cash outlay for stock-based compensation was $2 million—excluding ESOP debt interest—even though only $800,000 is recorded as an expense. This treatment *understates* employee compensation expense by $1.2 million, and so it also *overstates* the company's gross margin and net income for the year. Analysts must be aware of this possibility when evaluating companies that have large ESOPs.

EXERCISES

Spridget Company has 1,000,000 shares of common stock authorized with a par value of $3 per share, of which 600,000 shares are outstanding. The company received $7 per share when it issued shares to the public.

E15 – 1

Issuing common stock

Required:

What is the book value of the common stock par account and the additional paid-in capital account?

E15 – 2

Stockholders' equity

AICPA
ADAPTED

The stockholders' equity section of Peter Corporation's balance sheet at December 31, 2005 was as follows:

Common stock ($10 par value); authorized 1,000,000 shares, issued and outstanding 900,000 shares	$ 9,000,000
Additional paid-in capital	2,700,000
Retained earnings	1,300,000
Total stockholders' equity	$14,000,000

On January 2, 2006 Peter purchased and retired 100,000 shares of its stock for $1,800,000.

Required:

What was the balance in additional paid-in capital *and* in retained earnings immediately after retirement of the shares?

E15 – 3

Debt and redeemable preferred stock

ForeEver Yours, Inc., a manufacturer of wedding rings, issued two financial instruments at the beginning of 2005: a $10 million, forty-year bond that pays interest at the rate of 11% annually, and 10,000 shares of $100 preferred stock that pays a dividend of 7.5% annually. The preferred stock has a mandatory redemption feature that requires the company to repurchase all outstanding shares at par ($100 per share) in 40 years.

Required:

Describe how each financial instrument will affect the company's balance sheet and income statement in 2005.

E15 – 4

Various stock transactions

AICPA
ADAPTED

Warren Corporation was organized on January 1, 2005 with an authorization of 500,000 shares of common stock ($5 par value per share). During 2005 the company had the following capital transactions:

January 5	Issued 100,000 shares at $5 per share
April 6	Issued 50,000 shares at $7 per share
June 8	Issued 15,000 shares at $10 per share
July 28	Purchased 25,000 shares at $4 per share
December 31	Sold 25,000 shares held in treasury at $8 per share

Required:

What should be the balance in the additional paid-in capital account at December 31, 2005?

E15 – 5

Return on common equity

AICPA
ADAPTED

Selected information for Irvington Company is as follows:

	December 31	
	2004	2005
Preferred stock, 8%, par $100	$125,000	$125,000
Common stock	300,000	400,000
Retained earnings	75,000	185,000
Dividends paid on preferred stock	10,000	10,000
Net income	60,000	120,000

Required:

What is Irvington's return on common stockholders' equity for 2005, rounded to the nearest percentage point?

E15 – 6

How many shares?

AICPA
ADAPTED

Munn Corporation's records included the following stockholders' equity accounts:

Preferred stock, par value $15, authorized 20,000 shares	$255,000
Additional paid-in capital—preferred stock	15,000
Common stock, no par, $5 stated value, 100,000 shares authorized	300,000

Required:

How many shares of preferred stock and how many shares of common stock have been issued?

Newton Corporation was organized on January 1, 2005. On that date, it issued 200,000 shares of its $10 par-value common stock at $15 per share (400,000 shares were authorized). During the period from January 1, 2005 through December 31, 2007, Newton reported net income of $750,000 and paid cash dividends of $380,000. On January 5, 2007 Newton purchased 12,000 shares of its common stock at $12 per share. On December 31, 2007 the company sold 8,000 treasury shares at $8 per share.

E15 – 7

Stockholders' equity after a stock repurchase

AICPA
ADAPTED

Required:

What is the book value of total shareholders' equity as of December 31, 2007?

On December 31, 2005 the stockholders' equity section of Mercedes Corporation was as follows:

Common stock, par value $5; authorized 30,000 shares;	
issued and outstanding, 9,000 shares	$ 45,000
Additional paid-in capital	58,000
Retained earnings	73,000
Total stockholders' equity	$176,000

E15 – 8

Stock dividends and retained earnings

AICPA
ADAPTED

On March 1, 2006 the board of directors declared a 10% stock dividend and accordingly, 900 additional shares were issued. The fair value of the stock at that time was $8 per share. For the three months ended March 31, 2006 Mercedes sustained a net loss of $16,000.

Required:

What amount should the company report as retained earnings on its quarterly financial statement dated March 31, 2006?

On June 30, 2005 the stockholders' equity section of Comet Corporation's balance sheet was as follows:

Common stock, par value $25; authorized 500,000 shares;	
issued and outstanding 300,000 shares	$7,500,000
Additional paid-in capital	1,400,000
Retained earnings	1,890,000

E15 – 9

Stock dividends and market prices

AICPA
ADAPTED

On July 1, 2005 the board of directors of Comet declared a 5% stock dividend on common stock, to be distributed on August 10, 2005 to shareholders of record on July 31, 2005. The market price of Comet's common stock on each of these dates was as follows:

July 1	$30 per share
July 31	$31 per share
August 10	$32 per share

Required:

Prepare the general journal entry to record the stock dividend on Comet's books.

Effective April 27, 2005 the stockholders of Dorr Corporation approved a two-for-one split of the company's common stock and an increase in authorized common shares from 100,000 shares (par value of $20 per share) to 200,000 shares (par value of $10 per share). The stock split shares were issued on June 30, 2005. Dorr's stockholders' equity accounts immediately before issuance of the stock split shares were:

Common stock, par value $20; 100,000 shares authorized;	
50,000 shares outstanding	$1,000,000
Additional paid-in capital	150,000
Retained earnings	1,350,000

E15 – 10

Stockholders' equity after a stock split

AICPA
ADAPTED

Required:

After issuing the stock split shares, what are the balances of additional paid-in capital and retained earnings in Dorr's June 30, 2005 statement of stockholders' equity?

E15 – 11

Employee stock options

On July 1, 2005 Austin Company granted Harry Ross, an employee, an option to buy 500 shares of Austin common stock at $30 per share. The option was exercisable for five years from the date of the grant. Ross exercised his option on October 1, 2005 and sold his shares on December 2, 2005. The quoted market prices for Austin common stock during the year were:

July 1	$30 per share
October 1	$35 per share
December 2	$37 per share

Required:

How much compensation expense should Austin recognize in 2005 as a result of the option granted to Ross? (*Note*: Austin has elected to follow *APB Opinion No. 25*.)

E15 – 12

Computing basic EPS

The Tam Company's net income for the year ending December 31, 2005 was $10,000. During the year, Tam declared and paid $1,000 cash dividends on preferred stock and $1,750 cash dividends on common stock. At December 31, 2005 the company had 12,000 shares of common stock issued and outstanding—10,000 had been issued and outstanding throughout the year and 2,000 were issued on July 1, 2005. There were no other common stock transactions during the year, and the 5,000 shares of preferred stock are not convertible into common shares.

Required:

What should be the 2005 earnings per common share of Tam Company, rounded to the nearest penny?

E15 – 13

Finding the number of shares for EPS

Fountain Inc. has 5,000,000 shares of common stock outstanding on January 1, 2005. An additional 1,000,000 shares of common stock were issued on April 1, 2005, and 500,000 more were issued on July 1, 2005. On October 1, 2005 Fountain issued 10,000 convertible bonds; each one had a face value of $1,000 and paid 7% interest. Each bond is convertible into 40 shares of common stock. No bonds were converted into common stock during 2005.

Required:

What is the number of shares that is to be used in computing basic EPS and diluted EPS, respectively?

E15 – 14

Earnings per share

Information concerning the capital structure of the Petrock Corporation is as follows:

	December 31	
	2004	**2005**
Common stock	90,000 shares	90,000 shares
Convertible preferred stock	10,000 shares	10,000 shares
8% convertible bonds	$1,000,000	$1,000,000

During 2005 Petrock paid dividends of $1 per share on its common stock and $2.40 per share on its preferred stock. The preferred stock is convertible into 20,000 shares of common stock. The 8% convertible bonds are convertible into 30,000 shares of common stock. The net income for the year ending December 31, 2005 was $285,000, and the company's income tax rate was 40%.

Required:

1. What was basic EPS for 2005, rounded to the nearest penny?
2. What was diluted EPS for 2005, rounded to the nearest penny?

E15 – 15

Employee stock options

On July 18, 2005 the Amos Corporation granted nontransferable options to certain key employees as additional compensation. The options permitted the purchase of 20,000 shares of Amos's common stock at a price of $30 per share. On the grant date, the market value of the stock was $42 per share. The options are exercisable beginning January 1, 2006 and expire on December 31, 2014. On February 3, 2006 when the stock was selling for $45 per share, all the options were exercised.

Required:

How much compensation expense should Amos record from the issuance of these options in 2005 and in 2006? (*Note*: Amos has chosen to follow *APB Opinion No. 25*.)

Keystone Enterprises just announced record 2005 EPS of $5.00, up $0.25 from last year. This makes the tenth consecutive year the company has increased its EPS, an enviable record to be sure. Unfortunately, it looks to management like this string of EPS increases is about to be broken. Keystone is forecasting net income for 2006 and 2007 at $10 million each year, the same level earned in 2005. The company has 2,000,000 shares of common stock outstanding, no preferred stock, and no convertible debt.

E15 – 16

Incentives for stock repurchases

Required:

1. How many common shares does Keystone need to buy back at the beginning of 2006 *and* 2007 to maintain EPS growth of $0.25 per share each year? (*Note:* Keystone will use excess cash from operations to pay for the stock.)
2. Explain why your answer to requirement 1 would change if the buybacks were to occur in the middle of each year.
3. Why do you think Keystone's management would be concerned about maintaining the company's record of EPS growth?

The 2002 annual report of Procter & Gamble Company contained the following information:

E15 – 17

ESOPs

> The ESOP borrowed $1,000 in 1989, which has been guaranteed by the Company. The proceeds were used to purchase Series A ESOP Convertible Class A Preferred Stock. . . . Principal and interest requirements are $117 per year, paid by the trust from dividends on the preferred shares and from cash contributions by the Company. . . . In 1991 the ESOP borrowed an additional $1,000, also guaranteed by the Company. The proceeds were used to purchase Series B ESOP Convertible Class A Preferred Stock. . . . Debt service requirements are $94 per year, funded by preferred stock dividends and cash contributions from the Company.

Required:

1. What journal entry is made on the books of Procter & Gamble when its ESOP trust borrows money?
2. How will the ESOP affect Procter & Gamble's cash flows?
3. How will the ESOP affect Procter & Gamble's income statement?

PROBLEMS/DISCUSSION QUESTIONS

The stockholders' equity section of Warm Ways Inc.'s balance sheet at January 1, 2005 shows:

P15 – 1

Cash and stock dividends

Preferred stock, $100 par value, 10% dividend, 50,000 shares issued and outstanding	$ 5,000,000
Common stock, $6 par value, 1 million shares issued and outstanding	6,000,000
Paid-in capital in excess of par	119,000,000
Retained earnings	50,000,000
Total stockholders' equity	$180,000,000

Warm Ways reported net income of $9,250,000 for 2005, declared and paid the preferred stock cash dividend, and declared and paid a $0.25 per-share cash dividend on 1 million shares of common stock. The company also declared and paid a 10% stock dividend on its common shares. There were 1 million common shares outstanding when the stock dividend was declared, and the market price of common stock at that time was $135 per share.

Required:

1. Prepare journal entries to record the three dividend "events" that took place during 2005.
2. If the company's common stock was valued at $135 per share when the stock dividend was declared, what would the stock price be just after the dividend shares were distributed?

P15 – 2

Splits, dividends, and
retained earnings

It's July 1, 2006, and the market price of Warm Ways' common stock is $175 per share. There are 1.1 million common shares outstanding, and the retained earnings account shows a balance of $45,000,000. Management wants to declare and pay a 20% common stock dividend, but this would mean halting the company's cash dividend payments. That's because a 20% stock dividend would cause retained earnings to fall by $38,500,000 (that is, 20% × 1.1 million shares × $175 per share). This would leave a balance of only $6,500,000, far below the $25,000,000 minimum required for cash dividends as specified in the company's loan agreement. It would take several years to build up retained earnings to the point where Warm Ways could again pay cash dividends.

The company's chief financial officer (CFO) has proposed two ways the company could distribute common shares and still manage to pay cash dividends:

- Option A: Split the stock 12 for 10.
- Option B: Increase the size of the stock dividend from 20% to 30%, and record the share distribution as a stock split.

Required:

1. How will these two approaches affect the company's retained earnings?
2. As a common stockholder, would you prefer a 20% stock dividend, a 12-for-10 stock split, or a 30% stock dividend? Why?

P15 – 3

Convertible debt

On January 1, 2003 when its $30 par-value common stock was selling for $80 per share, Hershey Corporation issued $10 million of 4% convertible debentures that were due in 10 years. The conversion option allowed the holder of each $1,000 bond to convert the bond into five shares of the company's $30 par-value common stock. The debentures were issued for $10 million. Without the conversion feature, the bonds would have been issued for $8.5 million.

On January 1, 2005 the company's $30 par-value common stock was split three for one. On January 1, 2006 when the company's $10 par-value common stock was selling for $90 per share, holders of 40% of the convertible debentures exercised their conversion options.

Required:

1. Prepare a journal entry to record the original issuance of the convertible debentures.
2. How much interest expense would the company recognize on the convertible debentures in 2003?
3. Prepare a journal entry to record the exercise of the conversion option.
4. Why do many companies use the book value method to record debt conversions?

P15 – 4

EPS computations

The shareholders' equity section of the balance sheet for Holiday Roads Company shows:

	December 31 2004	December 31 2005
Preferred stock, $200 par value, 5% dividend, 20,000 shares issued and outstanding	$ 4,000,000	$ 4,000,000
Common stock, $2 par value	400,000	520,000
Paid-in capital in excess of par	19,600,000	26,800,000
Retained earnings	3,000,000	4,000,000
Total stockholders' equity	$27,000,000	$35,320,000

Net income for 2005 was $1,700,000, preferred stock dividends were $200,000, and common stock dividends were $500,000. The company issued 60,000 shares of common stock on July 1, 2005.

Required:

1. What is the company's basic EPS for 2005?
2. Suppose Holiday Roads also had $500,000 of 10% convertible subordinated debentures outstanding at the beginning and end of 2005. Each $1,000 bond is convertible into 100 shares of common stock, and the company's income tax rate is 34%. What is the company's diluted EPS for 2005?
3. What other types of securities—in addition to convertible debt—can affect the calculation of diluted EPS?

P15 – 5

Limits on dividends

Tredegar Industries Inc. makes plastic films and molded plastic products, produces soft alloy aluminum extrusions, distributes business applications software, and provides proprietary chemistry services. A footnote to the company's 1996 annual report stated:

While certain of the Company's subsidiaries' debt facilities are outstanding, the Company's subsidiaries must meet specific financial tests on an ongoing basis, which are customary for these types of facilities. Except as provided by applicable corporate law, there are no restrictions on the Company's ability to pay dividends from retained earnings. However, the payment of cash dividends by the Company's subsidiaries to the Company are subject to certain restrictions under the terms of various agreements covering the Company's subsidiaries' long-term debt. Toledo, PDI, and Balcrank [three of Tredegar's subsidiaries] are not permitted under each subsidiary's respective debt agreements to pay cash dividends. Assuming certain financial covenants are met, General Chemical [another subsidiary] is permitted to pay cash dividends of up to 50 percent of the net income (subject to certain adjustments) of General Chemical for the applicable period. Consequently, the Company's ability to pay cash dividends on Common Stock may effectively be limited by such agreements. At December 31, 1996 approximately $51,000 was available for dividend payments in accordance with these covenants.

The company's 1996 financial statements showed net income of $45,035, dividends of $3,176, and year-end retained earnings of $99,027. (All dollar amounts here and in the footnote are in thousands.)

Required:

1. Explain why and how lenders restrict a subsidiary's ability to pay dividends to the parent corporation.
2. What was Tredegar Industries' dividend payout ratio for 1996?
3. What is the maximum amount of dividends the company could have paid to common stockholders that year without violating the terms of its lending agreements?
4. Suppose Tredegar Industries' loan agreements contained no restrictions on dividend payments by subsidiaries or the parent company. What is the maximum legal amount of dividends the company could have paid to common stockholders in 1996?
5. Do contractual or legal restrictions on dividend payments seem to be influencing the company's dividend policy?

Schlumberger Ltd. provides exploration and production services to the petroleum industry. The following footnote appeared in the company's 2002 annual report:

P15 – 6

Stock options

As of December 31, 2002, the Company has two types of stock-based compensation plans. . . . Schlumberger applies APB Opinion 25 and related Interpretations in accounting for its plans. Accordingly, no compensation cost has been recognized for its stock option plans and its stock purchase plan. Had compensation cost for Schlumberger's stock-based plans been determined based on the fair value at the grant dates for awards under those plans, consistent with the method of FASB Statement 123, Schlumberger's net income and earnings per share would have been the pro forma amounts indicated below:

($ in millions except per share amounts)	2002	2001
Net income (loss)		
As reported	$(2,320)	$522
Pro forma	$(2,476)	$386
Basic earnings (loss) per share		
As reported	$ (4.01)	$0.91
Pro forma	$ (4.28)	$0.67

STOCK OPTION PLANS

During 2002, 2001, and in prior years, officers and key employees were granted stock options under Schlumberger stock option plans. For all of the stock options granted, the exercise price of each option equals the market price of the Schlumberger stock on the date of grant, an option's maximum life is ten years, and options generally vest in 20% increments over five years. . . . As required by FASB Statement 123, the fair value of each grant is estimated on the date of grant using the multiple option Black–Scholes option-pricing model. A [abbreviated] summary of the status of the Schlumberger stock option plans [follows]:

	Number of Shares	Weighted-Average Exercise Price
Outstanding 12/31/2001	32,836,340	$55.80
Granted	7,314,617	55.14
Exercised	(2,296,593)	30.02
Forfeited	(984,680)	66.69
Outstanding 12/31/2002	36,869,684	$57.03

Elsewhere in the footnote, the company says that options for 21,142,473 shares were exercisable at year-end, and that the weighted-average fair value of options granted during the year was $20.22.

Required:

1. Why doesn't Schlumberger Ltd. grant stock options with a shorter term (say, three years) and vesting period (say, one year)?
2. How much compensation expense would the company have recorded in 2002 under *APB No. 25* if the stock options granted that year had an exercise price $2 below the market price at the grant date?
3. What costs would Schlumberger employees have incurred if stock options granted in 2002 had an exercise price $2 below the market price at the grant date?
4. What journal entry would the company have made to record compensation expense for options granted in 2002 if it had used the fair value method of *FASB No. 123*?
5. Based on the footnote information, why were some options exercised in 2002 while others were forfeited?

P15 – 7

Equity management

Abbott Stores must raise $100 million on January 1, 2006 to finance its expansion into the lucrative Boston metropolitan market. The money will be used to finance construction of five retail stores and a distribution center. The stores are expected to open later this year. Three alternatives for raising the money are being considered:

1. Issue $100 million of 8% nonconvertible debt due in 20 years.
2. Issue $100 million of 6% nonconvertible preferred stock (100,000 shares).
3. Issue $100 million of common stock (1 million shares).

The company's internal forecasts indicate the following 2006 year-end amounts (before the impact of the $100 million of new financing is considered):

($ in millions)	
Total debt	$425
Total shareholders' equity	250
Net income for the year	10

Abbott has no preferred stock outstanding. There are 10 million shares of common stock outstanding, and EPS has been declining for the past several years. Earnings in 2005 were $1 per share, down from $1.10 the year before, and management wants to avoid another decline this year. One of the company's existing loan agreements requires its debt-to-equity ratio to be less than two. Abbott pays taxes at a 40% rate.

Required:

1. Assess the impact of each financing alternative on 2006 EPS and the year-end debt-to-equity ratio.
2. Which financing alternative would you recommend?

P15 – 8

Stock repurchases and EPS

Central Sprinkler Corporation manufactures and sells automatic fire sprinkler heads and valves, and it distributes components for automatic sprinkler systems. The company's 2005 financial statements show:

	Years Ended October 31			
($ in thousands except per share amounts)	2002	2003	2004	2005
Earnings available to common	$2,376	$4,018	$8,458	$3,763
Average common shares outstanding	4,752	5,023	3,383	3,330
Earnings per share (EPS)	$ 0.50	$ 0.80	$ 2.50	$ 1.13

In late December 2003 Central Sprinkler bought back 1,237,000 shares of common stock for $11,750,000.

Required:

1. What would EPS have been in 2004 and 2005 had the company not repurchased its common shares? (Assume the stock buyback occurred on December 31, 2003, and notice the company has an October 31 fiscal year-end.)
2. Compare the company's profit performance in 2005 to earlier years, and comment on this comparison.
3. The stock buyback isn't the only reason average common shares declined from 2003 to 2004. What else do you think might have contributed to this decline in average common shares?

General Electric (GE) Company has two major parts: an industrial conglomerate and a financial-services conglomerate. In the past decade, GE's EPS have risen almost every year. How does GE do it? One reason is the real growth in earnings of its business units. But another way is what the *Wall Street Journal* calls "earnings management, the orchestrated timing of gains and losses to smooth out bumps." Shown next is information taken from the company's annual reports to shareholders.

P15–9

Earnings management

www.prenhall.com/revsine

● Student Resources

☑ Template for solution

($ in millions except per share amounts)	1999	1998	1997	1996	1995	1994	1993
Earnings available for common shares	$10,717	$9,296	$8,203	$7,280	$6,573	$5,905	$4,424
Restructuring charges	(265)	–0–	(2,322)	–0–	–0–	(1,189)	(1,101)
Special gains	653	–0–	1,538	–0–	–0–	–0–	1,430
Average common shares outstanding	9,834	9,807	9,824	9,922	10,102	10,252	10,240
Earnings per share	$ 1.07	$ 0.93	$ 0.82	$ 0.72	$ 0.64	$ 0.57	$ 0.42
($ in millions except per share amounts)	1992	1991	1990	1989	1988	1987	1986
Earnings available for common shares	$ 4,305	$4,435	$4,303	$3,939	$3,386	$2,119	$2,492
Restructuring charges	–0–	–0–	–0–	–0–	–0–	(1,027)	(311)
Special gains	–0–	–0–	–0–	–0–	–0–	850	50
Average common shares outstanding	10,282	10,426	10,659	10,833	10,797	10,953	10,905
Earnings per share	$ 0.41	$ 0.42	$ 0.40	$ 0.36	$ 0.31	$ 0.19	$ 0.22

Restructuring charges include such items as the costs of employee severance packages and plant closings, as well as losses sustained on shuttered business units like Kidder Peabody, GE's discontinued securities broker–dealer. Special gains include profits from the sale of business units, properties, or investments. Restructuring charges and special gains are both included in earnings available for common shares.

Required:

1. Suppose GE had not recorded any of the special gains shown in the table. What would its EPS have been each year?
2. Suppose GE had not recorded any of the restructuring charges shown in the table. What would its EPS have been each year?
3. How do the EPS amounts from requirements 1 and 2 compare to the company's reported EPS amounts? Why might an analyst conclude that GE has engaged in earnings management?
4. Companies can smooth their reported EPS in several ways. One approach is to orchestrate the timing of gains and losses. What other ways can EPS be managed?
5. What was GE's EPS for 2000? Were restructuring charges or special gains reported that year? What impact (if any) did they have on the pattern of EPS increases?

Hershey Foods Corporation manufactures and sells consumer food products including chocolate bars, chocolate drink mixes, refrigerated puddings, beverages, pasta, cough drops, and jelly beans. In August 1995 the company repurchased 9,049,773 shares of common stock from a single stockholder—Milton Hershey School Trust—for $500 million. This stock buyback, plus other repurchases that year, reduced shareholders' equity by 25%.

Excerpts from Hershey Foods' 1995 annual report follow:

P15–10

Stock buyback incentives

As of December 31, 1995, the Corporation had 530,000,000 authorized shares of capital stock. Of this total, 450,000,000 shares were designated as Common Stock, 75,000,000 shares as Class B Common Stock (Class B Stock), and 5,000,000 shares as Preferred Stock, each class having a par value of one dollar per share. As of December 31, 1995, a combined total of 89,975,436 shares of both classes of common stock had been issued, of which 77,265,883 shares were outstanding. No shares of the Preferred Stock were issued or outstanding during the three-year period ended December 31, 1995.

Holders of the Common Stock and the Class B Stock generally vote together without regard to class on matters submitted to stockholders, including the election of directors, with the Common Stock having one vote per share and the Class B stock having ten votes per share. However, the Common Stock, voting separately as a class, is entitled to elect one-sixth of the Board of Directors. With respect to dividend rights, the Common Stock is entitled to cash dividends 10% higher than those declared and paid on the Class B Stock . . . Class B Stock can be converted into Common Stock on a share-for-share basis at any time.

Hershey Trust Company, as Trustee for the benefit of Milton Hershey School . . . and as direct owner of investment shares . . . was entitled to cast approximately 76% of the total votes of both classes of the Corporation's common stock [as of December 31, 1995]. The Milton Hershey School Trust must approve the issuance of shares of Common Stock or any other action which would result in the Milton Hershey School Trust not continuing to have voting control of the Corporation.

In August 1995, the Corporation purchased an additional 9,049,773 shares of its Common Stock to be held as Treasury Stock from the Milton Hershey School Trust for $500.0 million. In connection with the share repurchase program begun in 1993, a total of 2,000,000 shares were also acquired from the Milton Hershey School Trust in 1993 for approximately $103.1 million.

	Years Ended December 31	
($ in thousands)	1995	1994
Cash flows from operating activities	$494,929	$337,306
Common stock book value	$137,707	139,802
Treasury stock book value	$685,076	158,711
Common shares outstanding	74,733.9	74,679.4
Class B shares outstanding	15,241.4	15,242.9
	89,975.3	89,922.3
Treasury shares held	12,709.5	3,187.1

Required:

1. Why has Hershey Food Corporation issued two classes of common stock? Both types of common stock have a $1 par value. Do they have the same market price?
2. On the basis of the 1995 year-end balance sheet amounts, compute the average price per share that Hershey Food received for its common and Class B shares.
3. Compute the average price Hershey Food paid for treasury stock held at the end of 1994. How does this price compare to the average price paid for treasury shares held at the end of 1995?
4. What was the per-share price Hershey Food paid for the shares it bought back from Milton Hershey School Trust in 1995 and in 1993?
5. Why did the company buy back its shares? What are some other reasons companies repurchase their common stock?
6. As a credit analyst, how would you react to the company's announcement of its 1995 stock buyback?

P15 – 11

Preferred stock and credit analysis

AT&T Wireless Services is one of the largest wireless communication—think "cell phones"—service providers in the United States.

Information taken from the company's 2002 annual report to shareholders follows:

	December 31	
($ in millions)	2002	2001
Long-term debt	$ 6,705	$ 2,547
Preferred stock	7,644	3,000
Common stockholders' equity	19,281	21,887
Total stockholders' equity	$26,925	$24,887
Net income before interest and taxes	$ 972	$ 771
Interest expense	$ 386	$ 85
Long-term debt/total equity	0.25	0.10
Times interest earned	2.52	9.07

The company's preferred stock pays dividends at the rate of 8% annually.

Required:

1. Suppose the increase in the preferred stock account was due to the issuance of new preferred shares at par on January 1, 2002. What journal entry would the company make on that date to record the new preferred stock?
2. What journal entry would the company make to record preferred dividends for 2002 and for 2001?
3. Suppose AT&T Wireless had issued 8% debt (at par) rather than *any* preferred stock. What general journal entry would the company make to record interest on the debt for 2002 and for 2001?
4. Compute the company's long-term debt-to-total-equity ratio and its interest coverage ratio for 2002 and 2001 *as if* AT&T Wireless had issued 8% debt rather than preferred stock.
5. Lenders generally do not restrict a company's ability to raise more equity capital. That's because the dollars raised from selling stock provide a cash cushion that protects the lender's debt claim. Under what conditions might lenders want to limit a company's ability to issue preferred stock?
6. How would the preferred stock be shown on the company's balance sheet if the shares contained a mandatory redemption feature?

Kadri Corporation reported basic EPS of $3.00 and diluted EPS of $2.40 for 2005. The company's EPS calculations are shown next:

P15 – 12

Comprehensive EPS calculations

	EPS Calculation for 2005	
	Numerator	**Denominator**
Net income	$3,500,000	
Less dividend on 10% convertible preferred stock	(500,000)	
Weighted-average common shares outstanding		1,000,000
Basic EPS = $3.00	$3,000,000	1,000,000
Stock option dilution	—	33,334
Series A convertible debt dilution	240,000	250,000
Series B convertible debt dilution	300,000	200,000
10% Convertible preferred stock dilution	500,000	200,000
Diluted EPS = $2.40	$4,040,000	1,683,334

The convertible preferred stock was issued at the beginning of 2005. The Series A and Series B convertible debt was issued at par in late 2004. No stock options were granted or exercised in 2005.

Required:

1. The convertible preferred stock has a $100 par value per share. How many preferred shares were issued, and what is the common stock conversion rate for each preferred share?
2. The Series B convertible debt pays interest at 10% annually, and Kadri's marginal income tax rate for 2005 was 40%. How much Series B debt was outstanding, and what is the common stock conversion rate for each $1,000 face Series B bond?
3. What is the interest rate and common stock conversion rate for the $5 million par of Series A debt?
4. There were 50,000 shares under option during the year, and the average exercise price was $20 per share. What was the average market price of the company's common stock during 2005?
5. Explain why Series A debt carries a lower interest rate than Series B debt even though both were issued at par on the same day in 2004.

Trask Corporation, a public company whose shares are traded in the over-the-counter market, had the following stockholders' equity account balances at December 31, 2004:

P15 – 13

Stockholders' equity

ADAPTED

Common stock	$ 7,875,000
Additional paid-in capital	15,750,000
Retained earnings	16,445,000
Treasury common stock	750,000

Transactions during 2005 and other information relating to the stockholders' equity accounts were as follows:

- As of January 1, 2005 Trask had 4,000,000 authorized shares of $5 par-value common stock; 1,575,000 shares were issued, of which 75,000 were held in treasury.
- On January 21, 2005 Trask issued 50,000 shares of $100 par value, 6% cumulative preferred stock at par in exchange for all of Rover Company's assets and liabilities. On that date the net carrying

amount of Rover Company's assets and liabilities equaled their fair values. On January 22, 2005 Rover distributed the Trask shares to its stockholders in a complete liquidation and dissolution of Rover. Trask had 150,000 authorized shares of preferred stock.

- On February 17, 2005 Trask formally retired 25,000 of 75,000 treasury common stock shares. The shares were originally issued at $15 per share and had been acquired on September 25, 2004 for $10 per share.

- Trask owned 15,000 shares of Harbor, Inc. common stock, which was purchased in 2004 for $600,000. The shares of Harbor stock were trading securities. On March 5, 2005 Trask declared a property dividend of one share of Harbor common stock for every 100 shares of Trask common stock that were held by a stockholder of record on April 16, 2005. The market price of Harbor stock on March 5, 2005 was $60 per share. The property dividend was distributed on April 29, 2005.

- On January 2, 2003 Trask granted stock options to employees to purchase 200,000 shares of the company's common stock at $12 per share, which was also the market price on that date. The options are exercisable within a three-year period, beginning January 2, 2005. On June 1, 2005 employees exercised 150,000 options when the market value of the stock was $25 per share. Trask issued new shares to settle the transaction.

- On October 27, 2005 Trask declared a two-for-one stock split on its common stock and reduced the per-share par value accordingly. Trask stockholders of record on August 2, 2005 received one additional share of Trask common stock for each share of Trask common stock held. The laws of Trask's state of incorporation protect treasury stock from dilution.

- On December 12, 2005 Trask declared the yearly cash dividend on preferred stock, payable on January 11, 2006 to stockholders of record on December 31, 2005.

- On January 16, 2006 before the accounting records were closed for 2005, Trask became aware of the fact that depreciation expense was understated by $350,000 for the year ended December 31, 2004. The after-tax effect on 2004 net income was $245,000. The appropriate correcting entry was recorded on the same day.

Net income for 2005 was $2,400,000.

Required:

1. Prepare Trask's statement of retained earnings for the year ended December 31, 2005.
2. Prepare the stockholders' equity section of Trask's balance sheet at December 31, 2005.
3. Compute the book value per share of common stock at December 31, 2005.

P15 – 14

Stockholders' equity

Nike Inc. is one of the largest sellers of athletic footwear and athletic apparel in the world. The company sells its products—athletic footwear, apparel, equipment, and accessories—to retail accounts in the United States and through a mix of independent distributors, licenses, and subsidiaries in numerous countries throughout the world.

Appearing next is information taken from Nike's annual report for the year ended May 31, 2002.

NOTE 7: REDEEMABLE PREFERRED STOCK

NIAC is the sole owner of the Company's authorized Redeemable Preferred Stock, $1 par value, which is redeemable at the option of NIAC or the Company at par value aggregating $0.3 million.

NOTE 8: COMMON STOCK

The authorized number of shares of Class A Common Stock, no par value, and Class B Common Stock, no par value, are 110 million and 350 million, respectively. Each share of Class A Common Stock is convertible into one share of Class B Common Stock. Voting rights of Class B Common Stock are limited in certain circumstances with respect to the election of directors.

FROM THE BALANCE SHEET:

Class A Convertible Common Stock—98.1 and 99.1 million shares outstanding at May 31, 2002 and 2001, respectively. Class B Common Stock—168.0 and 169.5 million shares outstanding at May 31, 2002 and 2001, respectively.

FROM THE STATEMENT OF CASH FLOW

($ in millions)	Years Ended May 31		
	2002	**2001**	**2000**
Cash provided by operations:			
Net earnings	$ 663.3	$ 589.7	$ 579.1
Adjustments	417.2	66.8	120.5
Net cash provided by operating activities	$1,080.5	$ 656.5	$ 699.6
Cash provided (used) by investing activities:	$ (302.8)	$(342.3)	$(440.0)
Cash used by financing activities:			
Proceeds from long-term debt issuance	$ 329.9	$ 0.0	$ 505.1
Reductions in long-term debt	(511.8)	(119.2)	(1.7)
Proceeds from exercise of stock options	59.5	56.0	23.9
Repurchase of stock	(226.9)	(157.0)	(646.3)
Dividends—common and preferred	(128.9)	(129.7)	(133.1)
Net cash provided (used) by financing activities	$ (478.2)	$(349.9)	$(252.1)

Required: Part A

1. How many shares of redeemable preferred stock were outstanding on May 31, 2002? What is the par value of each share of preferred stock?
2. Suppose Nike sold 10,000 shares of preferred stock for $25 per share on June 1, 2002. Prepare the journal entry to record this sale of preferred stock.
3. Assume the preferred stock described in [2] pays a $0.10 per share annual dividend, on May 15 of each year. Prepare the journal entry to record the dividend payment on May 15, 2002.
4. How many shares of common stock were outstanding on May 31, 2002?
5. Explain why the number of shares outstanding might be different from the number of shares authorized or the number issued.
6. Why do some companies issue two classes of common stock?
7. Did Nike issue any common stock in the year ended May 31, 2002? Why?

Required: Part B

Ignore your answers to all of Part A, and instead assume the following hypothetical situation:

- Nike had 14,750,000 shares outstanding at the end of May 2002. On this date the balance in (a) the common stock account was $147,500; (b) the additional-paid-in capital account was $2,282,000; and (c) the retained earnings account was $226,069,000.
- All cash dividends are paid in the year they are declared. Cash dividends in millions were $14.080, $240.830, and $0 in 2005, 2004, and 2003, respectively.
- Net income in millions was $50.059, $49.589, and $45.080 for 2005, 2004, and 2003, respectively.
- During the year ended May 31, 2004, the company issued 17,250,000 common shares to the public as a stock dividend.

Determine the balances of common stock, additional paid-in capital, and retained earnings accounts for the years ended May 31, 2003, 2004, and 2005.

CASES

Amazon.com, Inc. is the world's leading online retailer with over 17 million customer accounts in over 150 countries. The company sells books, music, DVDs, videos, toys, electronics, software, video games, and home improvement products. Amazon.com also offers several e-commerce auction sites. The following footnote appeared in the company's 1999 annual report:

C15–1

Amazon.com: Stock options at a dot.com

The Company follows the intrinsic value method in accounting for its stock options. Had compensation cost been recognized based on the fair value at the date of grant for options granted in 1999, 1998 and 1997, the pro forma amounts of the Company's net loss and net loss per share for the years ended December 31, 1999, 1998 and 1997 would have been as follows:

($ in thousands, except per share data)	For the Years Ended December 31		
	1999	**1998**	**1997**
Net loss—as reported	$ (719,968)	$(124,546)	$(31,020)
Net loss—pro forma	(1,031,925)	(194,269)	(35,983)
Basic and diluted loss per share—as reported	$ (2.20)	$ (0.84)	$ (0.24)
Basic and diluted loss per share—pro forma	(3.16)	(1.31)	(0.28)

The fair value for each option granted was estimated at the date of grant using a Black–Scholes option pricing model, assuming no expected dividends and the following weighted average assumptions:

	For the Years Ended December 31		
	1999	**1998**	**1997**
Average risk-free interest rates	5.5%	4.7%	6.3%
Average expected life (in years)	3.5%	3.0%	3.0%
Volatility	84.9%	81.6%	50.0%

The weighted average fair value of options granted during 1999, 1998 and 1997 was $43.36, $19.07 and $2.07, respectively, for options granted with exercise prices at the current fair value of the underlying stock. During 1998 and 1997, some options were granted with exercise prices that were below the current fair value of the underlying stock. The weighted average fair value of options granted with exercise prices below the current fair value of the underlying stock during 1998 and 1997 was $4.61 and $0.55, respectively. Compensation expense that is recognized in providing pro forma disclosures might not be representative of the effects on pro forma earnings for future years because *SFAS No. 123* does not apply to stock option grants made prior to 1995.

Required:

1. The average exercise price for employee stock options granted in 1999 was $63.60. Suppose that Amazon.com's stock now trades at only $30 per share. Are the options worthless?
2. Some companies "reprice" their stock options when the exercise price gets too high. As a shareholder, do you favor repricing the Amazon.com options so that the exercise price is $30? Why or why not?
3. Why do you think Amazon.com uses the "intrinsic value" (*APB Opinion No. 25*) method of accounting for employee stock options rather than the fair value method allowed in *SFAS No. 123*?

C15 – 2

A study in political processes—Financial reporting for executive stock options

In March 1984 dissatisfaction with the accounting treatment of incentive stock option plans prompted the FASB to place reexamination of this topic on its agenda. As discussed earlier in this chapter, GAAP at that time was based on *APB Opinion No. 25*, which ignored the inherent value of "out of the money" options. After being placed on the agenda in 1984, no new FASB Statement or Exposure Draft emerged. The adverse publicity surrounding allegedly excessive executive compensation prompted the U.S. Senate Subcommittee on Oversight of Government Management (chaired by Senator Carl Levin, Democrat, Michigan) to hold hearings on stock compensation plans in January 1992. The vice chairman of the FASB, James J. Leisenring, testified at that hearing. In the FASB's written submission that was prepared for the hearing, the slow progress that the FASB was making in addressing accounting for stock options was explained as follows:

Existing models are designed for tradeable, usually short-term, options. Employee stock options are nontransferable, usually long-term, and generally are subject to other conditions like continued employment of the holder. The existing models, therefore, may not be directly applicable to employee stock options.

The problems of applying existing pricing models are especially acute in nonpublic companies, since their stock is not publicly traded. Nonpublic companies, in particular emerging growth companies and "start-up" companies, frequently use stock options to attract skilled employees.

The issues proved to be complex and highly controversial. Still, each time the issue was raised, board members voted unanimously that employee stock options result in compensation expense that should be recognized in the employer corporation's financial statements. Deciding just how and when to measure the compensation expense—the measurement method and measurement date—always has been the hard part.

Perhaps because of these hearings, the FASB accelerated its consideration of new rules for accounting for employee stock options. Opposition to the FASB's renewed initiative quickly emerged. Since all FASB meetings are open to the public, it is easy for interested parties to follow (and to try to later influence) the board's deliberations. With this in mind, those opposed to expense recognition for options argued that since no cash is expended when options are issued, no expense exists. Taking a contrary view in his 1992 letter to shareholders of Berkshire Hathaway, Inc., CEO Warren Buffett argued that options *are* an expense even though no cash is paid to employees:

[Some contend] that options should not be viewed as a cost because they "aren't dollars out of a company's coffers." I see this line of reasoning as offering exciting possibilities to American corporations for instantly improving their reported profits. For example, they could eliminate the cost of insurance by paying for it with options. So if you're a CEO and subscribe to this "no cash–no cost" theory of accounting, I'll make you an offer you can't refuse: Give us a call at Berkshire and we will happily sell you insurance in exchange for a bundle of long-term options on your company's stock.

Shareholders should understand that companies incur costs when they deliver something of value to another party and not just when cash changes hands.

Source: Berkshire Hathaway 1992 Annual Report.

While the FASB concurred with the view expressed by Mr. Buffett, progress continued to be slow on the employee stock option project. Because of the political visibility of the "excess" executive compensation issue, the SEC on October 15, 1992 issued rules for disclosure of option grants in the proxy mailed to shareholders. These SEC rules do *not* affect reported income; instead, companies are required to disclose the potential realizable value of the options at two assumed rates of stock price appreciation—that is, at 5% and 10%. However, the SEC also provided an alternative disclosure avenue. Rather than computing potential value at the 5% and 10% appreciation rates, companies could alternatively disclose the estimated value of the options at the grant date using some options pricing model such as Black–Scholes.

The SEC rules represent what is termed a "disclosure" approach. Under a disclosure approach, the financial statements themselves are unaffected. Only footnotes and supplemental schedules include the required data. By contrast, once the FASB resumed work on the options project, its approach concentrated on "measurement"—that is, the development of numbers that would appear in the financial statements and result in a charge to earnings for compensation expense. To this end, in early 1992 the FASB began exploring the range of estimates that would arise from attempting to measure the value inherent in various option scenarios. To gather such information, the FASB asked five compensation consulting firms to provide option value estimates for *artificial* scenarios it had developed. Then the FASB used the dispersion of these estimates to assess whether a measurement-based approach was feasible. As the FASB deliberated and publicized this continuing effort to change the accounting for stock options, influential sectors of the business community expressed strong opposition to expense recognition.

The Business Community's Response

In an article that appeared in August 1992, the *New York Times* reported that consulting firms that participated in the FASB valuation scenarios in March 1992 experienced subtle negative feedback from their clients. It said,

"The Business Roundtable let a number of consultants know in no uncertain terms that they would not view this as responsive to clients' needs, which is a buzzword," said Michael J. Halloran, the head of the Wyatt Company's executive compensation practice, referring to the help consultants have given to reporters or regulators. . . . Compensation consultants say Arthur Andersen, the accounting and consulting firm, was the target of some of the most pointed letters, perhaps because the valuations it had supplied to the accounting standards board in March came in on the high side.

Some of the letter writers reportedly went so far as to threaten to drop Andersen as their auditor unless the firm cooperated more on the options issue, the consultants said.

Source: Republished with permission of The New York Times Co.; ©1992. From A. L. Cowan, "Executives Are Fuming Over Data on Their Pay," *New York Times* (August 25, 1992); permission conveyed through Copyright Clearance Center, Inc.

Once the SEC proxy disclosure rules were issued in October 1992, the Business Roundtable endorsed the SEC's disclosure approach. Disclosure was viewed as preferable to the FASB's measurement initiative, which would cause an expense to appear in the income statement. The Business Roundtable sent a memo to its members and other interested parties on January 18, 1993 regarding strategies for complying with the SEC disclosure rules. The opening sentence of this document set the tone. It said:

In light of the efforts by FASB to require that companies value stock options as a basis for a charge to earnings for options granted, it is important that proxy statements be structured to reinforce the fact that the present value of an option at the time of grant is not accurately determinable and that future options [sic] values are not predictable.

Source: Business Roundtable memorandum, January 18, 1993.

The Roundtable memo outlined a strategy for conveying the message that the FASB's approach was flawed. It juxtaposed the 5% and 10% stock price appreciation rates approach proposed by the SEC with the alternative point-estimate valuation model approach favored by the FASB, and then stated:

Even though this valuation model may produce a smaller reportable dollar amount, we urge caution in adopting this approach. [Emphasis in original.]

The Roundtable memo communicates a preference for supplemental disclosures over income statement compensation expense deductions. Members are urged to avoid point estimates of option value—*even if lower than the 5% and 10% range estimates*—as part of a long-run strategy to forestall the FASB initiative. The Roundtable memo further contends:

To use the Black–Scholes model could place the company in the position of predicting a future stock price that would almost certainly be wrong and potentially misleading to investors.

Weeks later, the American Compensation Association (ACA) circulated a copy of the Business Roundtable memo to its members along with a cover memo that supported the Roundtable position. The ACA memo cautioned firms:

Clearly, the more companies that "endorse" the notion of a definitive stock option value [that is, "measurement approach"] that can be calculated at grant, the easier it will be for [the] FASB to conclude that such a value is appropriate for accounting purposes.

Source: American Compensation Association memorandum, January 29, 1993.

These efforts by the Roundtable and ACA appear to have been persuasive. As reported in the *New York Times* on March 26, 1993, Sibson & Company found that 56% of large clients, which it surveyed, intended to use the higher range-based numbers urged by the Roundtable and ACA. The *New York Times* article further said:

At least five large companies also borrow heavily from the Roundtable's playbook in their willingness to use their proxy statements to hammer home the Roundtable's contention that options are almost impossible to value accurately: Ameritech, B.F. Goodrich, Pfizer, PPG, and Anheuser-Busch.

All five proxy statements dutifully recite verbatim the Roundtable's assertion that no known model values options "with reasonable accuracy." They also remind shareholders that the options may be duds if their stocks fail to appreciate, and they include tables that claim to show how trivial the options are compared with how much shareholders stand to gain from a [5% and 10%] rise in their stock price.

Source: Republished with permission from The New York Times Co.; ©1993. From "Methods in Stock Options Madness," *New York Times* (March 26, 1993); permission conveyed through Copyright Clearance Center, Inc.

Taking an opposite position to the Roundtable, Buffett also commented on the accuracy of options valuation in his 1992 letter to shareholders:

Moreover, it is both silly and cynical to say that an important item of cost should not be recognized simply because it can't be quantified with pinpoint precision. Right now, accounting abounds with imprecision. After all, no manager or auditor knows how long a 747 is going to last, which means he also does not know what the yearly depreciation charge for the plane should be. No one knows with any certainty what a bank's annual loan loss charge ought to be. And the estimates of losses that property-casualty companies make are notoriously inaccurate.

Does this mean that these important items of cost should be ignored simply because they can't be quantified with absolute accuracy? Of course not. Rather, these costs should be estimated by honest and experienced people and then recorded. When you get right down to it, what other item of major but hard-to-precisely-calculate cost—other, that is, than stock options—does the accounting profession say should be ignored in the calculation of earnings?

Source: Berkshire Hathaway 1992 Annual Report.

The FASB also received two letters on the employee stock options issue dated February 17, 1993. One was from a group of preparers and users of financial statements. Signatories included, among others, the Council of Institutional Investors, General Mills, General Electric, B.F. Goodrich, the United Shareholders Association, and the National Association of Corporate Directors. The letter included a six-page listing of recommended disclosure requirements for traditional fixed stock options. In the letter, the group wrote:

Our proposal calls for complete, clear, and accurate disclosure of information that investors of all types need to protect and evaluate their investments. *This disclosure is in lieu of, not in addition to, any new charge to earnings for stock options.* [Emphasis added.]

The second letter was signed by all of the Big Six public accounting firms. This letter endorsed the views expressed by the group of preparers and users in its February 17 letter and urged the FASB to "leave the current accounting standards in place."

Even the U.S. Congress joined the fray. In the first six months of 1993, three resolutions and bills were introduced regarding the accounting for stock options. One bill, S.259, which was sponsored by Senator Carl Levin (Democrat, Michigan), required that stock options be treated as compensation expense in financial reports filed with the SEC. Senator Levin was a long-time opponent of the failure to recognize the value of options as an expense; he called this "stealth compensation." However, his was a clear minority sentiment.

Two proposals against expense treatment were introduced. One of these, H.C.R 98, which was sponsored by Congresswoman Anna Eshoo (Democrat, California), was designed to send a message to the FASB regarding the opposition of Congress to its stock option accounting initiative. The other legislation opposing expense treatment, S.1175, was cosponsored by Senators Lieberman (Democrat, Connecticut), Mack (Republican, Florida), Feinstein (Democrat, California), and Boxer (Democrat, California). In introducing the bill, Senator Lieberman said:

> . . . estimating the value of an option to purchase stock in the future requires predicting the company's future earnings, cash flow, market share, capital spending, as well as future Government policy. A high degree of subjectivity is simply unavoidable. Yet the FASB proposes to force such guesses about the future onto the company's income statement as a reduction of its hard-won earnings.
>
> *Source:* Congressional Record—Senate, June 29, 1993, S8250.

Notwithstanding H.C.R 98 and S.259, on June 30, 1993, the FASB issued an exposure draft entitled "Accounting for Stock-Based Compensation," which proposed that the estimated value of stock options issued to employees be recognized as an expense in the income statement.

The FASB scheduled a public hearing on the Exposure Draft in San Jose, California, in the heart of Silicon Valley, home of many high-tech, start-up firms that use stock options as an important part of total employee compensation. These firms organized a rally—which included a high school marching band—to coincide with the hearings in order to show opposition to the FASB proposal. Numerous employees were given time off and encouraged to attend the rally.

Despite this widespread, persistent opposition, the FASB pressed ahead with the stock option project. Opponents then "raised the stakes" considerably. First, a sense of the Senate resolution was introduced and passed by a vote of 88 to 9 (with 3 not voting). Sixteen senators—ten Democrats and six Republicans—cosponsored the legislation, which was orchestrated by Senator Joe Lieberman of Connecticut. In speaking in favor of the resolution, he stated:

> . . . accurately estimating the present value of an employee stock option at the date on which it is granted is, as I have said, simply not possible. The option is granted on a given day. It is only later that it is determined by market forces whether the option is worth anything and what it is worth. How can we possibly have a system which values that option on the day on which it is granted before there is any clear understanding of its value?
>
> *Source:* Congressional Record—Senate, May 3, 1994, S5033.

Another proponent, Senator Dianne Feinstein (Democrat, California) contended:

> I am concerned that if FASB's rule is adopted, tens of thousands of desperately needed jobs in California and the Nation will never, in fact, be created.
>
> *Source:* Congressional Record—Senate, May 3, 1994, S5036.

Despite the passage of the resolution, the FASB continued to move toward issuing a final statement that would require stock options to be recognized as an expense. To prevent this, Senator Lieberman introduced another bill on October 6, 1994, called the Accounting Standards Reform Act of 1994. This bill would require that any new FASB standard "shall become effective only following an affirmative vote of a majority of a quorum of the members of the [Securities and Exchange] Commission." If enacted, this bill would have effectively destroyed private-sector accounting standard-setting. The FASB understood that if it persisted, this legislation would likely be enacted. Consequently, in December 1994 the FASB said it was relenting to pursue a footnote disclosure approach despite the fact that

> . . . [t]he Board remains convinced that employee options have value and are compensation.
>
> *Source: Status Report No. 259* (Norwalk, CT: FASB, 1994), p. 1.

In October 1995 *SFAS No. 123*, a disclosure approach described earlier in this chapter, was issued.

Required:

1. Analyze the reaction of business executives and their membership associations to the FASB initiative regarding accounting for executive stock options. What factors motivated the strong opposition? Were the methods used surprising?
2. What motivations appear to underlie the position of the Big Six accounting firms and sponsors of the various bills introduced in the U.S. Congress?
3. In *Statement of Financial Accounting Concepts No. 2* ("Qualitative Characteristics of Accounting Information"), **representational faithfulness** is identified as an important element in financial reporting. The FASB defined representational faithfulness as "correspondence or agreement between a measure or description and the phenomenon it purports to represent." Evaluate the various parties' adherence to this objective in the context of the debate over accounting for stock options.
4. What are the current FASB and IASB standards for stock option compensation expense?

C15 – 3

RN Nabisco Group: Dividends and agency costs

Several years ago, RJR Nabisco Holdings Corporation (Holdings) offered for sale 93 million shares of its subsidiary RN-Nabisco Group. According to the prospectus, the estimated initial public offering price for RN-Nabisco common stock would be in the range of $17 to $19 per share. Holdings hoped to raise about $1.7 billion from the stock offering and to use the proceeds to reduce its debt burden. But investors weren't buying—at least not at the prospectus price—and Holdings scuttled the stock offer twenty-three days after it was first announced.

At the time the Nabisco Group was one of the world's leading packaged foods businesses, with sales of over $6.7 billion. The Group's Nabisco Biscuit Division was the largest cookie and cracker manufacturer and marketer in the United States, with eight of the nine top selling brands.

Holdings was comprised of the Nabisco Group and the Reynolds Group, which included the R.J. Reynolds Tobacco Company, the second largest manufacturer of cigarettes. The Reynolds Group's net sales as a percentage of Holdings' total consolidated net sales were 57%. Holdings was formed in 1989 when its predecessor company—RJR Nabisco, Inc. (RJRN)—was taken private in a leveraged buyout transaction. Holdings was taken public again in 1991 with the buyout group retaining 49% of Holdings' stock.

The plan at the time was to split off Nabisco Group from Reynolds Group and thereby improve the company's share price. Holdings had seen its stock price fall 36% that year for two reasons: R.J. Reynolds' earnings had been hurt by a brutal cigarette price war that began in early April, and investors had become increasingly concerned about the uncertainty over tobacco liability.

The Proposal: The Nabisco Stock offered to the public would initially represent 25% of the equity of the Nabisco Group. The Reynolds Group would retain the balance of the equity of Nabisco. Each outstanding share of common stock of Holdings would be redesignated into a common share of Reynolds Stock, which was intended to reflect separately the performance of the Reynolds Group as well as the retained interest of the Reynolds Group in the Nabisco Group.

The offering prospectus described the company's dividend policy as:

> The Board of Directors of Holdings currently intends to pay regular quarterly dividends on the Nabisco Stock in an aggregate annual amount equal to approximately 45% of the prior year's earnings of Holdings attributable to the outstanding Nabisco Stock. Consistent with this policy, Holdings currently intends to pay in the fourth quarter of 1993 an initial regular quarterly dividend of $0.13 per share of Nabisco Stock. While the Board of Directors does not currently intend to change such initial quarterly dividend rate or dividend policy, it reserves the right to do so at any time and from time to time. Under the Certificate of Incorporation and Delaware law, the Board of Directors is not required to pay dividends in accordance with such policy.
>
> Dividends on the Nabisco Stock are limited by the Certificate of Incorporation and will be payable when, as and if declared by the Board of Directors out of the lessor of (i) the Available Nabisco Dividend Amount and (ii) funds of Holdings legally available therefor. Payment of dividends on the Nabisco Stock is also subject to the prior payment of dividends on the outstanding shares of Preferred Stock of Holdings (and any new class or series of capital stock of Holdings with similar preferential dividend provisions) and to restrictions contained in the Credit Agreements and certain other debt instruments of RJRN. . . . The "Available Nabisco Dividend Amount" is similar to that amount that would be legally available for the payment of dividends on Nabisco

Stock under Delaware law if the Nabisco Group were a separate company, and will be increased or decreased as appropriate by, among other things, Holdings Earnings Attributable to the Nabisco Group. "Holdings Earnings Attributable to the Nabisco Group," for any period, means the net income or loss of the Nabisco Group during such period determined in accordance with generally accepted accounting principles (including income and expenses of Holdings allocated to the Nabisco Group on a substantially consistent basis). . . .

Holdings has never paid any cash dividends on shares of Common Stock. . . . The Board of Directors currently intends to pay future quarterly "pass-through" dividends on the Reynolds Stock with respect to the Reynolds Group's Retained Interest in the Nabisco Group. Holdings currently intends to pay in the fourth quarter of 1993 an initial quarterly pass-through dividend of approximately $0.03 per share of Reynolds Stock. . . . Subject to [certain limitations], the Board of Directors would be able, in its sole discretion, to declare and pay dividends exclusively on the Nabisco Stock or exclusively on the Reynolds Stock, or on both, in equal or unequal amounts, notwithstanding the respective amount of funds available for dividends on each series, the amount of prior dividends declared on each series or any other factor.

Required:

As a potential investor in Nabisco Group stock, what agency problems do you face that are not present when you buy common stock in most other companies?

COLLABORATIVE LEARNING CASE

C15 – 4

Is it equity or debt?

[A] Aon Corporation's Mezzanine Preferred Stock

In its 2002 annual report to shareholders, Aon Corporation described its mandatorily redeemable preferred stock as follows:

In January 1997, Aon created Aon Capital A, a wholly-owned statutory business trust, for the purpose of issuing mandatorily redeemable preferred capital securities (Capital Securities). The sole asset of Aon Capital A is $726 million aggregate principal amount of Aon's 8.205% Junior Subordinated Deferrable Interest Debentures due January 1, 2027.

Aon Capital A issued $800 million of 8.205% Capital Securities in January 1997. The Capital Securities are subject to mandatory redemption on January 1, 2027 or are redeemable in whole, but not in part, at the option of Aon upon the occurrence of certain events. . . . During 2002, approximately $98 million of the Capital Securities were repurchased on the open market for $87 million, excluding accrued interest. . . .

Source: Aon Corporation 2002 Annual Report.

Aon's 2002 balance sheet showed the following amounts:

Liabilities and Stockholders' Equity ($ millions)	2002	2001
Insurance premiums payable	$9,904	$8,233
Insurance policy liabilities	5,310	4,990
General liabilities		
General expenses	2,012	1,770
Short-term borrowings	117	257
Notes payable	1,671	1,694
Other liabilities	1,673	1,071
Total Liabilities	20,687	18,015
Redeemable Preferred Stock	50	50
Mandatorily Redeemable Preferred Capital Securities	702	800
Total Common Stockholders' Equity	3,895	3,465

Required:

1. Aon's Capital Securities are a form of preferred stock. Assume that the securities were issued by Aon Capital A (the trustee) on January 1, 1997 for $800 million cash, the same day that Aon Corporation issued $800 million of its junior debentures to the trust. Describe the cash flows associated with these two transactions—that is, explain who received cash and who gave up cash in each case.

2. One year later (on December 31, 1997), Aon Corporation must pay 8.205% interest to debt holders and Aon Capital A must pay an 8.205% dividend to preferred stockholders. Describe the cash flows associated with each of these payments—that is, explain who received cash, who gave up cash, and how much cash was exchanged.

3. For financial reporting purposes, how will Aon Corporation show its cash interest payment on December 31, 1997?

4. Why did Aon Corporation create Aon Capital A?

5. Why does Aon Corporation's 2002 balance sheet show the capital securities in the "mezzanine" section between total liabilities and stockholders' equity?

6. Aon Corporation is an insurance company, so most of its liabilities relate to insurance policy premiums and policy liabilities. The company's debt includes "Short-term borrowings" and "Notes payable." Compute Aon's debt-to-equity ratio for 2002 assuming that the Capital Securities are treated as part of equity. Repeat the calculation, this time assuming the Capital Securities are part of debt. Which debt-to-equity ratio provides the most accurate measure of the company's true debt and equity position? Why?

[B] Cephalon Inc.'s Zero-Coupon, Zero Yield-to-Maturity Convertible Notes

In June 2003, Cephalon Inc. issued $750 million of zero-coupon convertible notes. Because the notes were issued at par, meaning Cephalon received $750 million cash for the notes, they have a zero yield-to-maturity. Here is what Cephalon said about the notes:

> On June 11, 2003, we issued and sold in a private placement $750.0 million of Zero Coupon Convertible Subordinated Notes (the "Notes"). The interest rate on the Notes is zero and the Notes will not accrete interest . . . The Notes are subordinate to our existing and future senior indebtedness. The Notes were issued in two tranches and have the following salient terms:
>
> - $375.0 million of Zero Coupon Convertible Subordinated Notes due June 15, 2023 . . . are convertible prior to maturity, subject to certain conditions described below, into shares of our common stock at a conversion price of $59.50 per share (a conversion rate of approximately 16.8067 shares per $1,000 principal amount of notes) . . .
> - $375.0 million of Zero Coupon Convertible Subordinated Notes due June 15, 2023 . . . are convertible prior to maturity, subject to certain conditions described below, into shares of our common stock at a conversion price of $56.50 per share (a conversion rate of approximately 17.6691 shares per $1,000 principal amount of notes) . . .
>
> The Notes also contain a restricted convertibility feature that does not affect the conversion price of the notes but, instead, places restrictions on a holder's ability to convert their notes into shares of our common stock ("conversion shares"). A holder may convert the notes if one or more of the following conditions is satisfied:
>
> - if, on the trading day prior to the date of surrender, the closing sale price of our common stock is more than 120% of the applicable conversion price per share (the "conversion price premium");
> - if we have called the notes for redemption;
> - if the average trading prices of the notes for a specified period is less than 100% of the average of the conversion values of the notes during that period . . . ;
> - if we make certain significant distributions to our holders of common stock or we enter into specified corporate transactions.
>
> Because of the inclusion of the restricted convertibility feature of the Notes, our diluted income per common share calculation does not give effect to the dilution from the conversion of the Notes until our share price exceeds the 20% conversion price premium or one of the other conditions above is satisfied.
>
> *Source:* 10-Q filing for Cephalon Inc., June 2003.

Required:

1. What accounting entry did Cephalon make to record the proceeds received from issuing the Notes on June 11, 2003? Over the next year, what other accounting entries (if any) related to these Notes did the company make?

2. The Notes mature in 2023, approximately 20 years from the date they were issued. At a 6% rate of annual interest, the present value of $1,000 to be received 20 years from today is only $311.805. [You might want to verify this conclusion.] Suppose Cephalon's true cost of borrowing money is 6% per year. How much did Note holders pay for Cephalon debt and how much did they pay for the option to convert the Notes into shares of common stock?

3. Suppose Cephalon separated the Notes into debt and equity components, and then recorded each component separately. What accounting entry would the company make to record the proceeds received from issuing the Notes on June 11, 2003? Over the next year, what other accounting entries (if any) related to these Notes would the company make?

4. Describe the financial reporting advantages to Cephalon of issuing zero-coupon, zero yield-to-maturity Notes rather than a more traditional debt instrument. Why aren't the Notes included in the company's computation of diluted earnings per share?

5. If Cephalon were to issue those same Notes today, would it still be able to use the accounting entries outlined in your answer to requirement 1?

Intercorporate Equity Investments

Learning Objectives

After studying this chapter, you will understand:

1. How a company benefits from owning another company's common stock.

2. How an investor's ownership share is used to determine the accounting treatment of equity investments and why.

3. How the accounting for short-term speculative investments differs from the accounting for long-term investments.

4. The equity method and when to use it.

5. What consolidated financial statements are, and how they are compiled.

6. What goodwill is, and when it is shown on the financial statements.

7. How business acquisitions and mergers are recorded and why the recording method matters to statement readers.

8. How foreign subsidiaries are treated when financial statements in U.S. dollars are prepared.

One company will buy equity shares in another company to earn an investment return or to improve its competitive position. When a company buys equity shares for investment purposes, its return comes from share price increases and dividends. But when a company buys shares to improve its competitive position, its return comes from increased operating profits and growth. A company that owns shares in another company that is a supplier or customer gains influence over that company as well as access to new markets or greater production capacity.

Under existing GAAP, the method of accounting for intercorporate investments depends on the size of the ownership share of the investor corporation. Does the investor own 10% or 40% of the other company? As we will see, the ownership proportion is used to infer the purpose of the investment.

We first discuss minority ownership, cases in which the corporate investor owns less than 50% of the voting shares of another company. Then we analyze majority (more than 50%) ownership, and we look at the special reporting problems created by subsidiaries in foreign countries. Figure 16.1 depicts the financial reporting methods that are used under different percentage ownership conditions.

Minority Ownership

Share ownership usually entitles the shareholder (the corporate investor) to vote at the company's shareholder meetings. Shareholders vote to elect company directors and to approve or reject proposals put forth by management or by shareholders. Management will ask shareholders to approve the company's outside auditor, proposed mergers and buyouts, compensation plan changes, and corporate charter amendments. Shareholder proposals often address environmental, social, and political issues such as prohibiting the company from doing business in unfavored countries.

Figure 16.1 FINANCIAL REPORTING ALTERNATIVES FOR INTERCORPORATE EQUITY INVESTMENTS

A "one share, one vote" rule governs shareholder voting procedures in most companies. This means that each shareholder's influence over the company is proportional to the shares (votes) owned. A majority shareholder—one who owns more than 50% of the votes—can often dictate the company's business strategy and its major operating, investment, and financing decisions. A minority investor—one who owns less than 50% of the votes—has less influence over the company but still may be able to elect a corporate director or gain the ear of management.

For financial reporting purposes, minority investments fall into one of two categories: **minority passive** investments—those in which the shareholder has no ability to influence the acquired company; or **minority active** investments—those in which the ownership percentage is large enough for the acquiring shareholder to influence the decisions of the acquired company. Consider these examples: Owning a single share of stock is a minority passive investment, but owning 49.9% of the company's voting shares is a minority active investment. Deciding where to draw the line between passive and active minority investments can be difficult, as we shall see.

> Each share of **common stock** usually entitles the owner to one vote, while those who own **preferred stock** usually have no voting rights. There are exceptions. Some companies issue dual-class common stock (often denoted Common A and Common B), in which one class has voting rights and the other does not. In addition, some companies do issue voting preferred stock.

Minority Passive Investments: Mark-to-Market Accounting

When one company owns a small proportion of the voting shares of another company, it's safe to presume the investment was made for speculation—that is, the investor hopes to earn a return from dividends and share price increases. We may presume this because owning a small proportion of a public company does not convey the power to elect directors or influence the company's operating policies. What the investor company hopes is to earn a return on cash not currently needed in its own business. Existing GAAP presumes that ownership of less than 20% of another company's voting shares constitutes a passive investment because owning less than 20% of a company seldom provides the investor with an opportunity to significantly influence its activities. As Figure 16.1 shows, minority passive investments are classified on the investor's books in one of two ways, depending upon the expected duration of the investment.[1]

Equity securities designated by the investor as intended to be held for a short time are classified as **trading securities**. Trading securities are typically purchased to generate profits on short-term differences in price and they are generally actively managed in order to achieve trading gains.[2] All trading securities are shown on the balance sheet as current assets. Equity investments of less than 20% that are not trading securities are called **available-for-sale securities**. These securities are usually shown as noncurrent on the balance sheet. Both trading securities and available-for-sale securities are reported at fair value—current market price—not at historical cost on the balance sheet. The process of adjusting the carrying value of these securities to their market values is called **mark-to-market**.

Trading Securities Market price increases of trading securities are debited to a **market adjustment account** that is *added* to the trading securities asset account (reported at original cost). Market price decreases are credited to the same market adjustment account and *deducted* from the trading securities asset account. The offsetting credit for market price increases is made to the unrealized gain on trading securities account on the income statement; market price decreases are offset as a debit to the unrealized loss on trading securities account. Here's an example of securities that were purchased by Principal Financial Corporation for **short-term speculation**:

Purchases and Sales of Trading Securities by Principal Financial Corporation

Security	Date Acquired	Acquisition Cost	Market Value December 31			
			2005	2006	2007	2008
A Company common	1/1/05	$10,000	$11,000	$13,000	$ 14,000	$12,000
B Company preferred	1/1/05	20,000	18,000	17,000	18,000	*
C Company common	7/1/06	30,000	—	26,000	33,000	34,000
D Company options	7/1/06	40,000	—	41,000	37,000	30,000
			$29,000	$97,000	$102,000	$76,000

*B Company preferred stock was sold on January 1, 2008 for $18,500.

Let's first consider the entry to record the purchase of Company A common shares and Company B preferred shares on January 1, 2005:

DR	Trading securities—A Company common	$10,000	
DR	Trading securities—B Company preferred	20,000	
	CR Cash		$30,000

Dividends on these securities are recorded as income when declared—if dividends of $1,000 were declared by Company A on December 15, 2005, the entry would be:

DR	Dividends receivable	$1,000	
	CR Dividend income		$1,000

---

[1] The reporting rules for minority passive investments are contained in "The Equity Method of Accounting for Investments in Common Stock," *Accounting Principles Board (APB) Opinion No. 18* (New York: APB, 1971); and "Accounting for Certain Investments in Debt and Equity Securities," *Statement of Financial Accounting Standards (SFAS) No. 115* (Norwalk, CT: Financial Accounting Standards Board [FASB], 1993).

[2] *SFAS No. 115*, para. 12. Bond investments made to generate short-run trading gains are also classified as trading securities, and they are accounted for in a manner identical to equity securities in the trading portfolio.

When Principal Financial receives the cash dividend in January 2006, cash for $1,000 will be debited and the dividends receivable account will be credited for $1,000.

The 2005 year-end mark-to-market adjustment entry requires two steps:

Step 1:   The total market value of all trading securities is compared to the total cost of the securities. Any difference becomes the **target balance** for the market adjustment account.

Step 2:   The market adjustment account must be increased (or decreased) to equal its target balance, and then an unrealized gain (or loss) for the same amount must be recorded.

The 2005 year-end adjustment by Principal Financial would be:

	Step 1 Trading Securities Portfolio			Step 2 Market Adjustment Account
Total market value	$29,000	($1,000)	Target balance (CR)	
– Total cost	(30,000)	– 0	Current balance	
= Difference	($1,000)	($1,000)	Adjustment needed (CR)	

DR Unrealized holding loss on trading securities
      (income statement) $1,000
   CR Market adjustment—trading securities $1,000

Once this entry is recorded, the balance sheet section for trading securities appears as:

Trading securities (at cost)	$30,000
Less: Market adjustment—trading securities	(1,000)
Trading securities at market	$29,000

Now let's look at the entry to record the purchase of Company C common shares and Company D stock options on July 1, 2006:

DR Trading securities—Company C common stock $30,000
DR Trading securities—Company D stock options   40,000
   CR Cash $70,000

Following the two-step process, Principal Financial's 2006 year-end mark-to-market adjustment is:

	Step 1 Trading Securities Portfolio			Step 2 Market Adjustment Account
Total market value	$ 97,000	($3,000)	Target balance (CR)	
– Total cost	(100,000)	– (1,000)	Current balance (CR)	
= Difference	($ 3,000)	($2,000)	Adjustment needed (CR)	

DR Unrealized holding loss on trading securities
      (income statement) $2,000
   CR Market adjustment—trading securities $2,000

This entry highlights why it is necessary to use the two-step procedure. Comparing the portfolio market value to the *cost* of the underlying shares at each valuation date (as shown in Step 1), rather than comparing the total portfolio market value at two successive dates, corrects for changes in the number of shares at successive valuation dates.

The mark-to-market adjustment for 2007 is:

Step 1 Trading Securities Portfolio			Step 2 Market Adjustment Account
Total market value	$102,000	$2,000	Target balance (DR)
– Total cost	(100,000)	– (3,000)	Current balance (CR)
= Difference	$ 2,000	$5,000	Adjustment needed (DR)

DR Market adjustment—trading securities $5,000
  CR Unrealized holding gain on trading securities—
    (income statement) $5,000

When trading securities are sold, the *realized* gain or loss is recorded. The amount of the realized gain or loss is the sale price of the securities *minus* the most recent mark-to-market price. The original cost of the securities sold and the related portion of the market adjustment account are removed from the accounts. This is illustrated for the sale of Company B preferred stock on January 1, 2008 as follows:

> Using the most recent mark-to-market price in computing the realized gain or loss avoids double counting any unrealized gain or loss recorded in previous periods' income statements.

Computation of Realized Gain or Loss

Sale price of Company B preferred stock	$18,500
Mark-to-market value at 12/31/07 balance sheet date	(18,000)
Realized gain	$ 500

Entry to Record the Sale of Company B Common Stock

DR Cash	$18,500	
DR Market adjustment—trading securities	2,000[1]	
CR Realized gain on sale of trading securities		$ 500
CR Trading securities—Company B preferred		20,000

[1] $20,000 cost – $18,000 market value at 12/31/07 = $2,000.

After this entry is recorded, the balances in the "Trading securities" account and the "Market adjustment" account are:

Trading securities account at cost ($100,000 – $20,000)	$80,000
Market adjustment account ($2,000 **DR** balance	
on 12/31/ 07 + $2,000 **DR** from sale)	4,000
Trading securities at market	$84,000

The mark-to-market adjustment entry at the end of 2008 compares the target balance for the market adjustment account to the balance that will appear in this account after the sale of the Company B preferred stock, as in the following computation:

Step 1 Trading Securities Portfolio			Step 2 Market Adjustment Account
Total market value	$ 76,000	($4,000)	Target balance (CR)
– Total cost	(80,000)	– 4,000	Current balance (DR)
= Difference	($ 4,000)	($8,000)	Adjustment needed (CR)

DR Unrealized holding loss on trading securities
  (income statement) $8,000
  CR Market adjustment—trading securities $8,000

After this entry is recorded, the trading securities section of Principal Financial's balance sheet on December 31, 2008 would show:

Trading securities (at cost)	$80,000
Less: Market adjustment—trading securities	(4,000)
Trading securities (at market)	$76,000

Available-for-Sale Securities Now assume Principal Financial bought the equity securities described earlier because of their perceived **longer-term investment potential**—not for short-term speculation purposes. In this case the securities would be classified as "available for sale" and shown (usually) as noncurrent investments on the balance sheet. The entries to record the purchase, dividend, and mark-to-market adjustment for available-for-sale securities are very similar to the entries for trading securities.

The only significant difference between treating investment securities as "available for sale" rather than "trading" is that the *mark-to-market adjustment is not included in income. Instead, the upward or downward adjustment to reflect fair value for available-for-sale securities is a direct (net of tax) credit or debit to a special owners' equity account.* These unrealized gains or losses on available-for-sale securities are one of the "Other comprehensive income" components described in Chapter 2.

Returning to our example, we find that the 2005 year-end downward market adjustment for Principal Financial's available-for-sale portfolio is:

DR Unrealized change in value of available-for-sale		
securities (owners' equity)	$650	
DR Deferred income taxes (assumed 35% tax rate × $1,000)	350	
CR Market adjustment—available-for-sale securities		$1,000

As before, a credit balance in the "Market adjustment" account is treated as a contra-asset so that the net book value of the available-for-sale portfolio on the December 31, 2005 balance sheet is $29,000 ($30,000 cost minus the $1,000 market adjustment).

If market prices rise as they did in 2007, the upward adjustment at December 31, 2007 would be:

DR Market adjustment—available-for-sale securities	$5,000	
CR Unrealized change in value of available-for-sale		
securities (owners' equity)		$3,250
CR Deferred income taxes (assumed 35% tax rate × $5,000)		1,750

The FASB excluded unrealized gains and losses on available-for-sale securities from earnings because the securities are not held for active trading. Running the debit or credit directly into owners' equity—rather than through income—alleviates the potential for earnings volatility unrelated to eventual investment performance. When available-for-sale securities are later sold, then the cumulative unrealized gain or loss is realized and gets included in income.

RE CAP   Trading securities and available-for-sale securities—the two types of minority passive investments—are carried at fair value on the balance sheet. The unrealized holding gain or loss on trading securities is run through income in the period of the security price change. Unrealized gains and losses on available-for-sale securities do not affect income in the period of the price change; instead these gains and losses go directly to a special owners' equity account and are reported as a component of other comprehensive income.

Minority Active Investments: Equity Method

When the ownership percentage equals or exceeds 20%, GAAP presumes two elements:

1. A significant ownership position like 20% implies that the investor has the capability to exert influence over the company. This influence could encompass operating decisions, such as which research and development projects should be undertaken, and financing decisions, such as dividend payouts.

2. A substantial ownership percentage also implies a continuing relationship between the two companies, since investments of this magnitude are usually entered into in order to achieve some long-run strategic objective.

> The 20% threshold is only a guideline. It is possible that ownership of less than 20% would, under certain circumstances, allow the investor to influence the company's activities. This could happen when share ownership is widely distributed across a large number of individual investors. An investor who owns, say, 18% of a widely held company could still influence management's decisions. Accordingly, judgment must be used to categorize minority investments between passive and active in certain situations.

Both elements are present in GM's ownership stake in Fuji Heavy Industries (hereafter Fuji).

Once the ownership percentage becomes large enough for investor influence, the simple accounting system introduced for passive investments is no longer suitable. To see why, recall that the entry made on a minority passive investor's books when dividends are declared is:

DR	Dividends receivable	$1,000	
CR	Dividend income		$1,000

When the investor can influence the company's dividend policy, the minority passive accounting treatment would allow the investor to augment its own reported income. Suppose GM wants to increase its reported earnings during the period. It owns enough Fuji stock to influence the company's dividend policy, and it uses that influence to raise Fuji's dividend. This higher dividend would immediately run through GM's income statement.

To preclude this avenue for income distortion, minority active investments are accounted for through the **equity method**, as shown earlier in Figure 16.1. Under the equity method, GM records its initial investment in Fuji at cost. Subsequently, however, the investment account is increased for the pro rata share of Fuji's income, and there is a corresponding credit to the investment income account—or, in the case of a loss, GM's investment account decreases and there's a corresponding debit to the investment loss account.

Since GM's earnings are increased for its share of Fuji's earnings each period, it would be inappropriate to record dividend distributions received from Fuji as income too. This would "double-count" Fuji's earnings on GM's books. Under the equity method, dividends from Fuji are recorded as an increase (debit) to cash—or dividends receivable—and a decrease (credit) to the investment account. ***Thus, the investment account is increased for GM's share of Fuji's earnings and decreased when those earnings are received in the form of dividends.***

The following example illustrates the entries under the equity method:

> On January 1, 2005 Willis Company purchases 30% of the outstanding common shares of Planet Burbank, Inc. for $9,000,000. The book value and market value of Planet Burbank's net assets (assets minus liabilities) is $30,000,000. During 2005 Planet Burbank earns a net profit of $10,000,000, and the company declares a dividend of $500,000 on December 31, 2005. Using the equity method, the entries made by Willis are:

January 1, 2005

DR	Investment in Planet Burbank	$9,000,000	
CR	Cash		$9,000,000

December 31, 2005

DR	Investment in Planet Burbank	$3,000,000	
CR	Income from affiliate		$3,000,000

(To recognize 30% of Planet Burbank's total reported income of $10,000,000)

December 31, 2005

DR	Dividend receivable from affiliate	$150,000	
CR	Investment in Planet Burbank		$150,000

(To reduce the investment account for dividends declared—30% of $500,000)

The example shows how the equity method reduces possibilities for income distortion. Willis Company's income statement is affected only by its pro rata share of Planet Burbank's income. ***The dividend declaration—and subsequent payment—by Planet Burbank has no effect on Willis' income.*** Thus, while Willis could conceivably use the influence arising from its 30% ownership share to increase Planet Burbank's dividend declaration, doing so would leave its income unchanged ***when the equity method is used.*** Under the equity method, the carrying amount in the investment account at any point in time is comprised of the following items:

Initial investment amount	$ 9,000,000
Plus: Willis' cumulative pro rata share of Planet Burbank's income	3,000,000
Minus: Willis' cumulative pro rata share of dividends declared by Planet Burbank	(150,000)
Investment account carrying amount	$11,850,000

> This is the *rationale* for not reporting fair values under the equity method. Whether, in fact, statement readers are uninterested in the fair value of minority active investments is an empirical issue for which limited evidence is available.

In contrast to balance sheet amounts for minority passive investments, the carrying amount under equity method accounting is *not* marked-to-market. Why? A substantial ownership percentage—equal to or greater than 20%—signals an intended continuing relationship between investor and investee. Since ownership of this magnitude implies some long-term strategic intent, sale of the investment is not imminent, and fair value is presumably less important to statement readers.

When Cost and Book Value Differ In contrast to our Planet Burbank example, investors rarely buy shares at a price exactly equal to the book value of those shares, and when the investor's cost differs from book value, a new issue surfaces.

To illustrate, let's return to the Willis Company purchase of Planet Burbank stock. Here book value is $30,000,000, but let's say Willis paid $24,000,000 for its 30% stake. Why would Willis pay $24,000,000 when the book value of the shares purchased is only $9,000,000 (30% of $30,000,000)? Why would an informed buyer pay $15,000,000 more than book value?

There are two reasons. First, Planet Burbank's books are prepared using GAAP, which reflects balance sheet items at historical cost rather than at current value. As shown in Exhibit 16.1(a), the fair market value of Planet Burbank's *net* assets is $70,000,000, or $40,000,000 above the $30,000,000 book value (see the highlighted area). Sellers of Planet Burbank stock presumably know that the company's *net* assets are worth $70,000,000 rather than the lower $30,000,000 book value. On the basis of this knowledge, the asking price for the shares acquired by Willis Company will be higher than book value. But how much higher?

Willis decided to pay $24,000,000, or $15,000,000 more than book value. Exhibit 16.1(b) shows that $12,000,000 of the $15,000,000 excess of cost over book value is explained by the difference between fair value and book value of inventories and fixed assets (see highlighted area). This still leaves $3,000,000 of the disparity unexplained. The remaining difference brings us to the second reason why an informed buyer would knowingly pay a premium to acquire influence over another company.

EXHIBIT 16.1	Willis Company

Panel (a)

Investment with Goodwill

On January 1, 2005 Willis Company purchases 30% of the outstanding shares of common stock of Planet Burbank for $24,000,000. The book value and fair value of Planet Burbank's net assets on this date are as follows:

($ in millions)	Book Value	Fair Value	Difference	Investor's Share (30%)
Cash and receivables	$10	$10	$ 0	$ 0
Inventories (FIFO cost flow)	15	25	10	3
Depreciable assets (net of depreciation)*	25	55	30	9
Total assets	50	90	40	12
Minus liabilities	(20)	(20)	0	0
Net assets	$30	$70	$40	$12

*Average remaining useful life of 10 years.

During 2005 Planet Burbank reported net profit of $10,000,000, and the company declared a dividend of $500,000 on December 31, 2005.

Panel (b)

Analysis of Willis' investment cost over book value	($ in millions)
Cost of 30% investment	$24
30% of Planet Burbank's net asset book value (30% × $30)	(9)
Excess of cost over book value of Willis' shares	$15
Amount of excess attributable to	
Inventories—30% × ($25 − $15)	$ 3
Depreciable assets—30% × ($55 − $25)	9
Remainder attributable to implicit goodwill (plug figure)	3
	$15

This second potential explanation relates to **goodwill**. Goodwill exists because thriving, successful companies are frequently worth more than the sum of their individual net assets. Planet Burbank has developed a reputation for product quality, prompt service, and fair treatment of both employees and customers. Consequently, employees like to work for the company, and customers actively seek out its products. The result is that Planet Burbank is exceptionally profitable—it earns a very large return on its investment base. The capitalized value of this earning potential is what gives rise to the remaining $3,000,000 difference. This "extraordinary" earnings potential is called goodwill.

A summary of the factors comprising the $24,000,000 purchase price for 30% of Planet Burbank is as follows ($ in millions):

Recorded historical book value of the company's net assets ($50 − $20) × 30%	$ 9
Difference between fair value and cost of net assets ($40 × 30%)	12
Amount attributable to goodwill (plug figure)	3
Purchase price	$24

When the cost of the shares exceeds the underlying book value at the acquisition date, as it does in this case, the investor is required to amortize any excess that is attributable to (1) inventory, and (2) depreciable assets.[3] Amortization is recorded as a reduction (debit) to investment income and a reduction (credit) to the investment account. The rationale for amortizing the excess of the investor's cost over book value is based on the matching principle. Since Willis is picking up its share of Planet Burbank's reported earnings each period as investment income, it follows that Willis should write off any amount paid in excess of Planet Burbank's book value as a cost of gaining access to those earnings.

Using the equity method, the entries based on the preceding set of facts are:

January 1, 2005: Initial investment in Planet Burbank

DR Investment in Planet Burbank	$24,000,000	
CR Cash		$24,000,000

December 31, 2005: Investor's share of earnings

DR Investment in Planet Burbank	$3,000,000	
CR Income from affiliate		$3,000,000

(To recognize 30% of Planet Burbank's total reported income of $10,000,000)

December 31, 2005: Investor's share of dividends declared

DR Dividend receivable from Planet Burbank	$1,200,000	
CR Investment in Planet Burbank		$1,200,000

(To reduce the investment account for dividend declared—30% of $4,000,000)

December 31, 2005: Amortization of excess cost over book value attributable to inventory and depreciable assets

DR Income from affiliate	$3,900,000	
CR Investment in Planet Burbank		$3,900,000

Amortization is computed as:	Amount	Amortization
Attributed to inventory (all sold during the year)	$3,000,000	$3,000,000
Attributed to depreciable assets (over 10 years)	9,000,000	900,000
		$3,900,000

[3] Under *SFAS No. 142*, any excess attributable to implicit goodwill is not amortized, nor is it subject to an annual impairment test. For further details see paras. 40 and 59, "Goodwill and Other Intangible Assets," *SFAS No. 142* (Norwalk, CT: FASB, 2001).

The excess investment cost over book value attributable to inventory is assigned to inventory items on hand on January 1, 2005, when Willis purchased Planet Burbank's stock. This inventory is presumed to have been sold during 2005 under the FIFO cost flow assumption (see Chapter 9). The amount attributed to depreciable assets is amortized over the average remaining 10-year life of those assets. The amount attributed to goodwill is no longer amortized under *SFAS No. 142.*

The December 31, 2005 balance in the investment in Planet Burbank's account is $21,900,000 ($24,000,000 + $3,000,000 − $1,200,000 − $3,900,000).

RECAP

Under existing financial reporting practice, the general guidelines for intercorporate investments with less than majority ownership are:

1. **Less than 20% ownership requires the use of either the trading securities method or the available-for-sale method. Both methods use mark-to-market accounting.**

2. **Ownership between 20% and 50% requires use of the equity method—not the mark-to-market approach.**

3. **Under the equity method, the excess cost of purchased shares over their book value is amortized as a charge to income and a reduction to the investment account.**

Majority Ownership

Following current GAAP, when a **parent** company owns more than 50% of the voting shares of another company (**subsidiary**), the subsidiary is controlled by the parent. Under these circumstances the financial statements of the subsidiary are combined—line by line—with those of the parent using a process called **consolidation**.

Currently, consolidated statements are required only when the parent company owns *more than 50% of* the outstanding voting stock of the subsidiary. If exactly 50% of the voting shares are owned, the equity method is used and no line-by-line consolidation is necessary. In February 1999, the FASB issued an *Exposure Draft* that called for changing the existing definition of control.[4] **Control** was defined as the "ability of one entity to direct the policies and management that guide the ongoing activities of another entity." The *Exposure Draft* presumes that control exists if any of the following conditions are met:[5]

> When two companies form a **joint venture** and each company owns exactly 50% of the joint-venture entity, neither "parent" consolidates the joint venture. Chapter 11 described how this allows the joint-venture entity to incur debt—usually guaranteed by the "parents"—*but the debt does not appear on either parent's balance sheet* because consolidation is not required. Intercorporate investment reporting rules can be skillfully used to create "off-balance sheet" assets and liabilities that impedes accurate financial analysis.

- An entity has a majority voting interest in the election of a corporation's board of directors or the right to appoint a majority of the board.
- An entity has a large minority voting interest (that is, more than 50% of the votes typically cast in electing directors) and no other significant voting interest exists.
- An entity owns convertible securities, which, if exercised, would give it the right to obtain a majority in board elections or the right to appoint a majority of the board.

> Control of a newly acquired subsidiary is considered temporary if at the date of acquisition the parent (1) has committed to a plan to relinquish control of the subsidiary, or (2) is obligated to do so and it is likely that the loss of control will occur within one year.

This proposed new broader definition of control means companies owning less than 50% of the voting stock of another corporation will sometimes be required to consolidate that entity. However, consolidation is not required if the parent's control is "temporary." As we go to press, this proposal is still being deliberated.

---

[4] "Consolidated Financial Statements: Purpose and Policy," *FASB Exposure Draft, Revised* (Norwalk, CT: FASB, February 23, 1999).
[5] Ibid., para. 18.

When control exists (more than 50% ownership under current rules), the parent and subsidiary are really one in an economic sense. **Consolidated financial statements** are designed to cut across artificial corporate boundaries to portray the economic activities of the parent and subsidiary as if it were one entity. Let's see how this happens using a simple example. On December 31, 2004 the balance sheet of Alphonse Corporation looks as follows:

Assets

Current assets	$ 5,000,000
Fixed assets minus accumulated depreciation	20,000,000
Total assets	$25,000,000

Liabilities and equity

Current liabilities	$ 1,000,000
Common stock ($1 par)	24,000,000
Total liabilities and equity	$25,000,000

On January 1, 2005 Alphonse issues 8,000,000 additional shares of its stock to new outside investors for $10,000,000 cash. Immediately after the stock issue, the balance sheet of Alphonse Corporation is:

Assets

Current assets	$15,000,000
Fixed assets minus accumulated depreciation	20,000,000
Total assets	$35,000,000

Liabilities and equity

Current liabilities	$ 1,000,000
Common stock ($1 par)	32,000,000
Capital in excess of par	2,000,000
Total liabilities and equity	$35,000,000

Alphonse immediately uses the cash to buy all of the outstanding shares of Gaston Corporation for $10,000,000. Since Alphonse has used its cash to make an investment, after buying Gaston's shares Alphonse's current assets will be $10,000,000 lower than before and an investment account of $10,000,000 will exist. Alphonse's balance sheet after the stock purchase, as well as Gaston's, are shown in Exhibit 16.2.

EXHIBIT 16.2	**Alphonse and Gaston**

Preparation of Consolidated Balance Sheet
(Purchase Method — 100% acquisition)

| | After the Acquisition | | Adjustments and Eliminations | | Consolidated |
	Alphonse	Gaston	Dr.	Cr.	Balance Sheet
Assets					
Current assets	$ 5,000,000	$2,000,000			$ 7,000,000
Fixed assets, net	20,000,000	6,500,000	$ 1,500,000 (B)		28,000,000
Investment in Gaston	10,000,000	—		$ 1,500,000 (B)	—
				8,000,000 (A)	
				500,000 (C)	
Goodwill			500,000 (C)		500,000
	$35,000,000	$8,500,000			$35,500,000
Liabilities and Equity					
Current Liabilities	$ 1,000,000	$ 500,000			$ 1,500,000
Common Stock	32,000,000	8,000,000	8,000,000 (A)		32,000,000
Capital in excess of par	2,000,000	—			2,000,000
	$35,000,000	$8,500,000	$10,000,000	$10,000,000	$35,500,000

The steps that follow describe the procedures for preparing the consolidated balance sheet for Alphonse and Gaston in Exhibit 16.2. The individual balance sheets of the two companies are *not* simply added together; doing that would result in double-counting, as we'll see.

Adjustments to the Consolidated Balance Sheet

Step 1: **Analysis of the "Investment in Gaston" Account** Alphonse paid $10,000,000 for Gaston, a company whose *net* assets total only $8,000,000 (assets of $8,500,000 minus $500,000 of liabilities). Why did Alphonse pay more than $8,000,000? There are two reasons why an informed buyer would pay more than book value: (1) the fair market value of Gaston's individual assets is greater than their combined book value (we assume this excess is $1,500,000 here and is attributable to the fixed assets); and (2) goodwill, which is the remaining $500,000.

The factors comprising the $10,000,000 purchase price for Gaston are:

Recorded book value of Gaston's *net* assets	$ 8,000,000
Unrecorded difference between fair value and book value of Gaston's fixed assets ($8,000,000 – $6,500,000)	1,500,000
Unrecorded value of Gaston's goodwill	500,000
Purchase price	$10,000,000

This purchase price breakdown explains why we do not add the two balance sheets together to get the consolidated balance sheet. Adding the two balance sheets together would double-count the $8,000,000 book value of Gaston's net assets. To see why, notice that the full purchase price of $10,000,000 is already on Alphonse's balance sheet (under "Investment in Gaston" in Exhibit 16.2); but as we have just seen, $8,000,000 of this purchase price represents the book value of Gaston's net assets. Since this $8,000,000 already appears on Gaston's balance sheet (assets of $8,500,000 minus $500,000 of liabilities), simply adding the two balance sheets together would double-count the $8,000,000. To avoid doing this, we have to remove $8,000,000 from Alphonse's "Investment in Gaston" account, leaving a balance of $2,000,000. Notice that this is done in Exhibit 16.2 in the "Adjustments and Eliminations" column (next to notation "A").

Step 2: **Elimination of the "Investment in Gaston" Account** The remaining balance in the "Investment in Gaston" account represents the amount of the purchase price that is *not* reflected in Gaston's balance sheet book values. As shown in the purchase price breakdown, this $2,000,000 remaining balance represents unrecorded fixed asset appreciation of $1,500,000 and goodwill of $500,000. These amounts must stay on the consolidated balance sheet, since Alphonse paid for them. However, they must be assigned to the items they actually represent: (1) an increase to fixed assets, and (2) the acquisition of goodwill. This is done in Exhibit 16.2 in the "Adjustments and Eliminations" column (next to the notations "B" and "C"). After these adjustments are made, notice that the "Investment in Gaston" account has been eliminated and thus does not appear in the consolidated column of Exhibit 16.2. Also, consolidated fixed assets have been increased by $1,500,000, and goodwill of $500,000 is separately reported.

Step 3: **Analysis of the Common Stock Account** To consolidate both balance sheets, we need to eliminate one more element of potential double-counting. Consider the $32,000,000 common stock account on the books of Alphonse. Since Alphonse owns Gaston, Alphonse's common stock account shows the ownership of *both* companies.

Now consider the $8,000,000 balance in the common stock account of Gaston. These shares represent ownership of Gaston. **If the two common stock accounts were simply added together, ownership of Gaston would be counted twice**—once as a part of the $32,000,000 on Alphonse's books and once again in the $8,000,000 on Gaston's books.

To avoid this double-counting, the equity of Gaston is eliminated when the consolidated balance sheet is prepared. This is done opposite notation "A" in the "Adjustments and Eliminations" column in Exhibit 16.2. After this is done, consolidated owners' equity is comprised only of Alphonse's common stock, since this alone represents ownership of the entire consolidated entity.

The adjustment process described here can also be expressed in journal entry form. For example, the entry to avoid double-counting both the book value of Gaston's net assets and its owners' equity (Adjustment notation "A" in Exhibit 16.2) is:

> **DR** Common stock $8,000,000
>   **CR** Investment in Gaston $8,000,000
> (To avoid double-counting Gaston's net assets and its owners' equity
> [Adjustment notation "A"].)

Similarly, reclassification of the remaining $2,000,000 in the "Investment in Gaston" account can also be expressed in journal entry form:

> **DR** Fixed assets $1,500,000
> **DR** Goodwill   500,000
>   **CR** Investment in Gaston $2,000,000
> (To eliminate the remaining investment account balance [Adjustment
> notations "B" and "C"].)

The acquisition of Gaston by Alphonse was accomplished using cash. The accounting for cash buyouts using the procedures outlined here is called **purchase accounting**.

Other Consolidation Adjustments—Intercompany Transactions

Suppose that several months prior to the Gaston acquisition, Alphonse had borrowed $300,000 from Gaston; this borrowing had not been repaid at the time of the acquisition on January 1, 2005. Under these circumstances, another adjustment is needed to consolidate the financial statements. *This adjustment is necessary because Alphonse and Gaston are now part of the same economic unit.* The *Alphonse loan receivable* on Gaston's books and the *Gaston loan payable* on Alphonse's books are not owed to outsiders. To include the intercompany receivable and payable in the consolidated balance sheet would overstate assets and overstate liabilities, each by $300,000. That's why the following adjustment is made in preparing the consolidated statements:

> **DR** Loan payable—Gaston (on Alphonse's books) $300,000
>   **CR** Loan receivable—Alphonse (on Gaston's books) $300,000
> (To eliminate the intercompany loan from Gaston to Alphonse.)

Another frequently encountered consolidation adjustment arises when Gaston and Alphonse make sales to one another. Suppose Alphonse sold goods to Gaston on March 15, 2005 after the January 1, 2005 acquisition, and then Gaston resold all these goods to outside customers. The facts are as follows:

Intercompany Sale

	Alphonse's Sale to Gaston	Gaston's Resale to "Outsiders"	Total
Selling price	$25,000	$34,000	$59,000
Cost of goods sold	20,000	25,000	45,000
Profit	$ 5,000	$ 9,000	$14,000

If Alphonse's and Gaston's income statements were merely added together to form the consolidated income statement, double-counting would result. This happens because neither Alphonse's $25,000 sale to Gaston nor the $25,000 of cost of goods sold on Gaston's income statement represents a transaction with outsiders. This means that the intercompany sales transaction must be eliminated in preparing the consolidated income statement, as follows:

Elimination of $25,000 Intercompany Sale

| | Income Statement Totals | | Sale | |
	Alphonse	Gaston	Elimination	Consolidated
Sales	$250,000,000	$150,000,000	$(25,000)	$399,975,000
Cost of goods sold	(200,000,000)	(109,000,000)	25,000	(308,975,000)
Gross margin	$ 50,000,000	$ 41,000,000	—	$ 91,000,000

After this elimination, all that remains of the intercompany sale and Gaston's subsequent resale of the goods to outsiders is the following:

	Alphonse's Sale to Gaston	Gaston's Resale to "Outsiders"	Sale Elimination	Net
Selling price	$25,000	$34,000	$(25,000)	$34,000
Cost of goods sold	(20,000)	(25,000)	25,000	(20,000)
Profit	$ 5,000	$ 9,000	—	$14,000

Notice that the consolidated income statement now only reflects revenues realized from outsiders ($34,000) and costs paid to outsiders ($20,000). The double-counting of the intercompany sales and cost of goods sold has been eliminated.

Minority Interest—When a Parent Company Owns Less than 100% Interest in a Subsidiary

The previous example illustrates the consolidation entries for the case where Alphonse acquired a 100% interest in Gaston's outstanding common shares. But what happens if Alphonse owns less than 100% of Gaston's shares? If Alphonse's ownership exceeds 50%, it must still consolidate, but now there are other shareholders called "non-controlling" or "minority" shareholders to consider. The claim that these shareholders have in the subsidiary's net assets and income is referred to as **minority interest**. Because the *total* assets, liabilities, and income of Gaston are included in the consolidated statements, the minority shareholders' interest in these amounts must also be reported in the consolidated statements. The portion of Gaston's earnings assigned to minority shareholders is normally deducted from the total combined earnings of Alphonse and Gaston to arrive at consolidated net income. Likewise, the minority shareholders' claim in the net assets of Gaston is subtracted from the total combined net assets of Alphonse and Gaston to arrive at consolidated shareholders' equity. This minority interest claim on the consolidated net assets is either shown between the liabilities and stockholders' equity section or in the stockholders' equity section on the consolidated balance sheet.

As we go to press, the FASB has proposed a number of changes in purchase accounting for business combinations. Among the proposals are: (1) a change in the way a company records the net assets when the acquisition is less than 100%; and (2) a change in the balance sheet and income statement display of "minority interests." Specifically the FASB's proposal calls for the assets and liabilities of the acquired entity to be recorded at their full (100%) fair values on the acquisition date as compared to current GAAP, which allows a blend of fair value for the portion of the net assets acquired by the parent and book values for the portion attributable to the minority interest. Under the proposal, all (100%) of the goodwill of the acquired entity would be recognized on the consolidated balance sheet as opposed to just the acquirer's share as under current GAAP. This will result in higher consolidated assets and will lower financial ratios like return on assets and asset turnover. On the income statement, consolidated net income will be broken into two pieces: (1) income attributable to minority interest; and (2) income attributable to controlling equity. Under the proposed new accounting rules, minority interest in the net assets of the consolidated subsidiaries would be presented separately within the equity section of the consolidated balance sheet in contrast to the current classification of minority interest as a quasi-liability between liabilities and stockholders' equity. (FASB Board Meeting dated August 12, 2003.)

The following example illustrates how minority interests are computed and reported on the consolidated income statement and balance sheet. Referring back to the data underlying Exhibit 16.2 on page 896, assume that after selling 8,000,000 additional shares of its own stock on January 1, 2005 for $10,000,000, Alphonse immediately uses the $10,000,000 to acquire 80% of Gaston's outstanding shares whose book value of net assets totals $8,000,000 ($8,500,000 of assets minus $500,000 of liabilities). The difference between the amount paid by Alphonse ($10,000,000) and its equity in the book value of Gaston's net assets (80% × $8,000,000 = $6,400,000) is $3,600,000, which is attributable to two factors determined as follows: (1) the excess of the fair market value over book value of Gaston's depreciable fixed assets, which we assume to be $3,000,000 × 80% = $2,400,000; and (2) goodwill, which we assume to be $1,500,000 × 80% = $1,200,000. Immediately after this acquisition, the worksheet to prepare the consolidated balance sheet of Alphonse and its 80%-owned subsidiary, Gaston, is shown in Exhibit 16.3.

EXHIBIT 16.3	Alphonse and Gaston

Preparation of Consolidated Balance Sheet
(Purchase Method—80% acquisition)

	After the Acquisition		Eliminations		Consolidated
	Alphonse	Gaston	Dr.	Cr.	Balance Sheet
Assets					
Current assets	$ 5,000,000	$2,000,000			$ 7,000,000
Fixed assets, net	20,000,000	6,500,000	$ 2,400,000 (B)		28,900,000
Investment in Gaston	10,000,000	—		$ 2,400,000 (B)	—
				6,400,000 (A)	
				1,200,000 (C)	
Goodwill			1,200,000 (C)		1,200,000
	$35,000,000	$8,500,000			$37,100,000
Liabilities					
Current Liabilities	$ 1,000,000	$500,000			$1,500,000
Minority Interest in Gaston				1,600,000 (A)	1,600,000
Equity					
Common Stock	32,000,000	8,000,000	8,000,000 (A)		32,000,000
Capital in excess of par	2,000,000	—			2,000,000
	$35,000,000	$8,500,000	$11,600,000	$11,600,000	$37,100,000

The two adjustment and elimination entries reflected in the consolidated worksheet in Exhibit 16.3 are reproduced below in journal entry form along with brief explanations:

Adjustments and Eliminations entry (A):

DR Common stock	$8,000,000	
CR Investment in Gaston		$6,400,000
CR Minority Interest in Gaston*		1,600,000

(To eliminate 100% of Gaston's stockholders' equity against Alphonse's proportionate [80%] investment in the net assets of Gaston and to set up the 20% minority interest in Gaston shown on the consolidated balance sheet.)

*20% minority interest × $8,000,000 book value of Gaston's net assets

Adjustments and Eliminations entries (B) and (C):

DR Fixed assets	$2,400,000	
DR Goodwill	1,200,000	
CR Investment in Gaston		$3,600,000

(To allocate the excess [$3,600,000] of the price paid for Gaston's shares [$10,000,000] over Alphonse's proportionate interest in the book value of Gaston's net assets [80% × $8,000,000 = $6,400,000] and to revalue Fixed assets and set up Goodwill on the consolidated balance sheet.)

For example, the *book value* of Alphonse's proportionate interest in the net assets of Gaston was $6,400,000. Entry (B) increases this carrying amount by $2,400,000—Alphonse's proportionate share of the difference between the fair value and book value of Gaston's fixed assets (80% × $3,000,000). So 80% of the fixed assets are written up to $8,900,000. But 20% of the fixed assets are not written up and remain at their book value at time of acquisition as recorded on Gaston's books.

Under the purchase method of accounting, when a parent company acquires *all* of a subsidiary's common stock and pays more than book value for the subsidiary's net assets, the excess is allocated in the consolidated worksheet so that *all* of the subsidiary's assets and liabilities are reflected at their fair values on the consolidated balance sheet (see Exhibit 16.2, adjusting entries B and C). If, however, the parent acquires less than 100% of the subsidiary's stock and pays more than the book value for its *proportionate interest* in the subsidiary's net assets, the assets and liabilities of the subsidiary are shown on the consolidated balance sheet at their book values (on the subsidiary's books) plus the parent's proportionate share of the difference between the fair values and book values (see Exhibit 16.3). Thus, the assets and liabilities of the subsidiary are not valued at their full fair values on the consolidated balance sheet when minority interests are present. In essence, the net assets of the subsidiary are valued at the parent's proportional interest in the fair values, plus the minority interest proportion of the book value of the subsidiary's net assets at the acquisition date.

RECAP

Consolidated financial statements portray the parent company and its majority-owned subsidiaries as a single economic unit. But the individual balance sheets (and income statements) of each subsidiary and the parent are not simply added together. Instead, consolidated adjustments are made to avoid double-counting internal business transactions as well as various balance sheet items. When the parent company acquires less than 100% interest in a subsidiary, a minority interest in the subsidiary's net assets and income is created. Because the consolidated statements include the total assets, liabilities and income of the subsidiary, the minority shareholders' interest in these amounts must be recorded in the consolidated statements.

Accounting for Goodwill in Purchase Transactions

As illustrated in the previous examples, purchase accounting typically results in goodwill being recognized on the consolidated financial statements. Prior to 2002, goodwill acquired in a purchase transaction was amortized (charged to income) over a period not exceeding 40 years.[6] *SFAS No. 142*, "Goodwill and Other Intangible Assets," which became effective on January 1, 2002, dramatically changed the accounting for purchased goodwill. *SFAS No. 142* no longer permits amortization of goodwill for purchase transactions.[7] Instead, goodwill must be tested for impairment at least annually or when there is reason to suspect that its value has diminished. Goodwill is then expensed only when it is deemed to be impaired. In order to implement the new impairment test, firms are required to first allocate goodwill arising from an acquisition to one or more reporting units (firm segments) at the acquisition date. Once allocated, the two-step impairment test outlined in Figure 16.2 is applied at the reporting unit level.

Examples of circumstances that would trigger impairment testing include:
- A significant adverse change in legal factors or in the business climate,
- An adverse action or assessment by a regulator,
- Unanticipated competition,
- A loss of key personnel,
- A likelihood that a reporting unit or a significant portion of a reporting unit will be sold or disposed of,
- A significant asset group is being tested for recoverability under *SFAS No. 121*, and
- Recognition of a goodwill impairment loss in the financial statements of a subsidiary that is a component of a reporting unit.

---

[6] "Intangible Assets," *APB Opinion No. 17*, para. 9 (New York: Accounting Principles Board [APB], 1970).

[7] "Goodwill and Other Intangible Assets," *Statement of Financial Accounting Standards No. 142*, para. 18 (Norwalk, CT: FASB, 2001).

Figure 16.2

SFAS NO. 142 GOODWILL IMPAIRMENT TEST

Source: SFAS No. 142, Goodwill and Other Intangible Assets, op. cit.

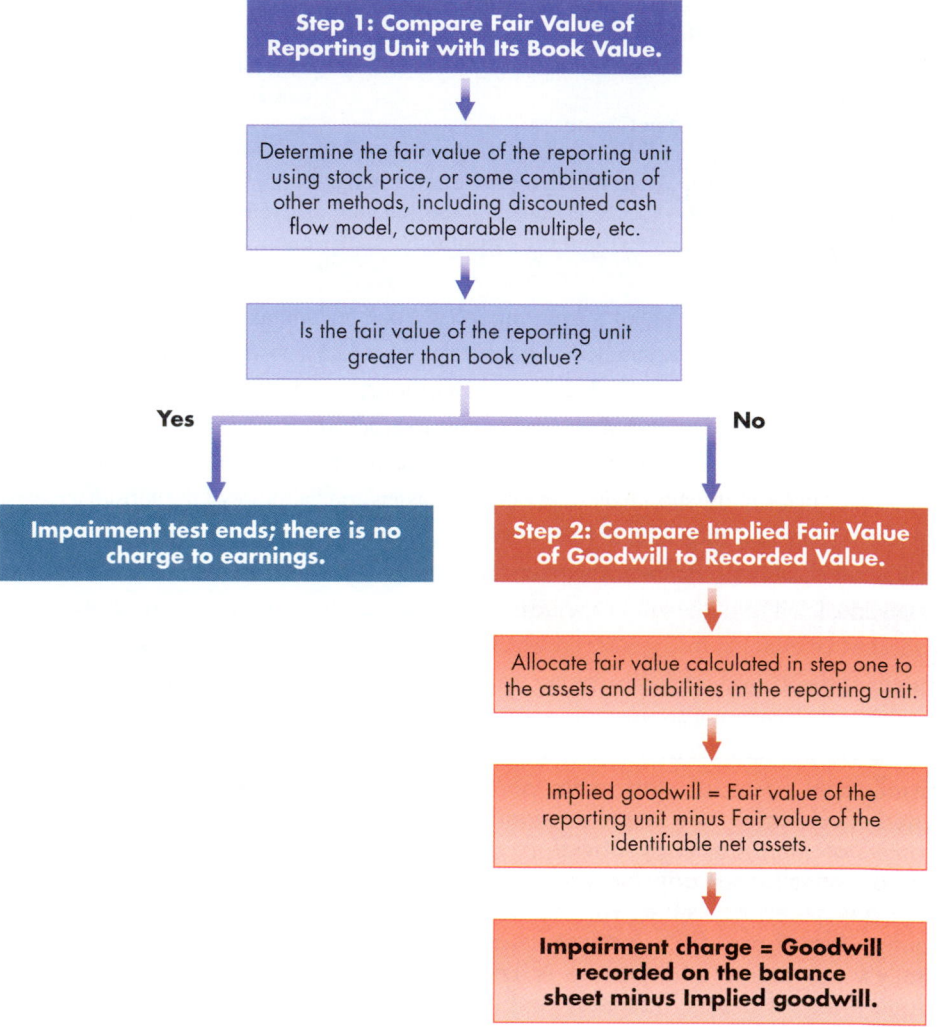

The first step is used to determine if goodwill has been impaired, and the second step establishes the amount of the impairment charge. In the first step, goodwill is considered impaired if the book value of the reporting unit's net assets (including allocated goodwill) exceed their fair value. To determine the amount of the impairment charge, the recorded goodwill for each reporting unit is compared to its implied fair value. The implied fair value of goodwill—called **implied goodwill**—is the difference between the fair value of the reporting unit as a whole (established in step 1) minus the fair value of the identifiable tangible and intangible assets (exclusive of goodwill) assigned to that reporting unit. The impairment charge is the difference between the goodwill recorded on the balance sheet and the implied goodwill. The following numerical example illustrates how goodwill impairment would be determined under *SFAS No. 142*:

Fair value of a reporting unit "refers to the amount at which the unit could be bought or sold in a current transaction between willing parties" [*SFAS No. 142*, para. 23]. If the reporting unit is publicly traded, then the stock price would provide the best evidence of fair value. If stock prices are not available, fair values are to be determined using one or more other methods including discounted cash flow analysis or a multiple of earnings or some other performance measure such as revenues or EBITDA.

Assume that Aggressive Company acquires all of the outstanding voting stock of Slow Growth Company early in 2005 for $100 million. On that date, the identifiable tangible and intangible net assets of Slow Growth had a fair value of $80 million resulting in recorded goodwill of $20 million. Aggressive assigned $15 million of the goodwill to reporting unit A and $5 million to reporting unit B. On December 31, 2005, Aggressive performs an impairment test and determines the following:

($ in millions)	Unit A	Unit B
(a) Fair value of reporting unit (including goodwill)	$60	$45
(b) Book value of reporting unit	75	35
(c) Is goodwill impaired?	Yes	No
(d) Sum of fair values of identifiable net assets of unit A, exclusive of goodwill	50	—
(e) Implied fair value of goodwill (a)–(d)	10	—
(f) Book value of goodwill	15	—
(g) Impairment charge (f)–(e)	$ 5	—

The *SFAS No. 142* rules for determining goodwill impairment coupled with the rather dramatic downturn in the stock market in 2002 resulted in a significant number of firms reporting goodwill impairments totaling hundreds of billions of dollars in their 2002 annual reports. Exhibit 16.4 reports some of the larger goodwill impairment charges taken by firms during this period.

EXHIBIT 16.4	**List of Ten Largest Goodwill Impairment Write-offs in Fiscal Year 2002**	
Company Name	**For Year End**	**Amount of Goodwill Impairment** ($ amounts in millions)
AOL Time Warner Inc.	12/31/2002	$98,920
Clear Channel Communications Inc.	12/31/2002	16,800
Tyco International Ltd.	9/30/2002	7,626
Du Pont El de Nemours & Co.	12/31/2002	2,944
Solectron Corp.	8/30/2002	2,500
Boeing Co.	12/31/2002	1,827
SBC Communications Inc.	12/31/2002	1,820
AT&T Wireless Services Inc.	12/31/2002	1,495
Viacom Inc.	12/31/2002	1,481
BellSouth Corp.	12/31/2002	1,285

Source: Bear Stearns

The following excerpt taken from a special equity research report prepared by Bear Stearns, a leading international investment banking and brokerage firm, discusses the possible valuation implications of such write-downs:

"The facts and circumstances surrounding each goodwill impairment charge will need to be evaluated for their investment significance. The new FASB rule will require information about goodwill to be provided at the segment level, increasing the likelihood that the market will be cognizant of potential changes in fundamentals diminishing the value of goodwill. If the market is aware of this deterioration from other information, the impairment charge is unlikely to affect the company's stock price. However, if there is an impairment in a reporting unit that previously had been thought to have good fundamentals, it will be news to the market and could have a negative impact on stock price."[8]

---

[8] "Goodbye, Goodwill," *Equity Research Special Report* (New York: Bear Stearns & Company, Inc., 2001).

Under *SFAS No. 142*, periodic amortization of goodwill is no longer allowed. Instead, goodwill is subject to an impairment test at least annually. As a result, goodwill impairment charges are likely to occur more frequently under *SFAS No. 142* reporting rules than was the case in the past. Statement users will need to carefully assess whether the charge is a sign of a bad acquisition, a miscalculation of the value of the target (that is, the acquirer overpaid), or due to an unexpected deterioration in the fundamentals of the business acquired.

Purchase Method versus Pooling-of-Interests Method

The examples illustrated to this point in the chapter show how business combinations are accounted for under the **purchase method** of accounting. The central idea underlying purchase accounting is that there is a change in ownership when one entity (parent) acquires all, or substantially all, of the ownership interests and net assets of another company (subsidiary). Like any other purchase of an asset—such as inventory or machinery—the parent records the investment in the common stock of the subsidiary at the fair market value of the consideration given. As shown in the consolidation worksheets in Exhibits 16.2 and 16.3, if the purchase price exceeds the book value of the net assets acquired, this excess is allocated to the identifiable assets and liabilities of the acquired entity: That's the role of the adjustment and elimination entries. What results is that the identifiable net assets of the acquired entity are revalued to their fair market values at the date of acquisition.[9] Any remaining excess is allocated to goodwill.[10] Post-consolidation earnings will often be lower than the combined earnings of the pre-consolidated entities under the purchase method of accounting for two reasons:

> A write-up of the acquired company's assets is called a "step up in basis" of those assets.

1. Various assets of the acquired company (for example, inventory and depreciable assets) are frequently written up on the date of acquisition from their carrying value to their market value—so subsequent cost of goods sold and depreciation is higher, and

2. Goodwill may subsequently become impaired and need to be written off.

Prior to the issuance of *SFAS No. 141* in June 2001, GAAP allowed a second method of accounting for business combinations, called the **pooling-of-interests method**. This method was allowed when the acquisition was achieved through an exchange of shares and certain other stringent criteria were met. The basic idea underlying pooling accounting is that the ownership interests of the two combining firms are united, and both sets of stockholders therefore share jointly in the rewards and risks of ownership of the new combined entity. Since no new assets are invested, nor do owners in the pre-combination entities withdraw assets or give up their ownership rights, *there is no transfer or sale of ownership. Consequently, there are no grounds for establishing a new basis of accounting for the net assets of the consolidated entity.* This means that the book values of the net assets of the combining entities are carried forward on the consolidated entity's books and no goodwill is recorded. Because there is no increase in the basis of the combined entity's net assets and no goodwill to be written off, the post-consolidated earnings of the consolidated entity would be higher than they would otherwise be under the purchase method.

> For instance, the combining entities could not dispose of significant operations shortly before or after the combination, and there could be no additional issuances, exchanges, or retirements of securities in contemplation of effecting the combination. Additional criteria that needed to be satisfied in order to use the pooling-of-interests method of accounting are set forth in paras. 46–48 of *APB Opinion No. 16*, "Business Combinations" (New York: Accounting Principles Board [APB], 1970).

---

9 If the acquisition is less than 100%, thus creating a minority interest in the consolidated net assets, then the revaluation of the net assets of the subsidiary reflects only the parent's percentage interest in the fair values of the subsidiary's net assets. The minority interest portion of the subsidiary's net assets is recorded at their book values at date of acquisition, as illustrated in Exhibit 16.3 on page 900.

10 This goodwill is subject to an annual impairment test and, if met, results in a charge to consolidated earnings. See "Goodwill and Other Intangible Assets," *Statement of Financial Accounting Standards No. 142* (Norwalk, CT: FASB, 2001).

Even though the pooling-of-interests method is no longer allowed, we discuss and illustrate its application in the Appendix to this chapter because a significant number of combinations (particularly the larger mergers) were accounted for as poolings prior to the issuance of *SFAS No. 141*. Since the effects of this treatment will be found in financial statements for years to come, it is important for you to understand the impact of this method and how it complicates comparisons with consolidated statements accounted for under the purchase method.

Analysis

RECAP

Under the purchase method of accounting, there is a change in ownership when the parent acquires all, or substantially all, of the ownership interests and net assets of the subsidiary. The investment in the common stock of the subsidiary is recorded at the fair value of the consideration given. Through the adjustment and elimination entries on the consolidated worksheet, the excess of the purchase price over the book value of the subsidiary's net assets is allocated to the identifiable assets and liabilities of the subsidiary. This results in the identifiable net assets of the subsidiary being recorded at their fair values at date of acquisition on the consolidated balance sheet. Under the pooling-of-interest method of accounting (which is no longer allowed pursuant to *SFAS No. 141*) equity interests are exchanged and the shareholders of the two previously separate companies become shareholders of the combined entity. No buyout occurs and, therefore, no new accounting basis—no asset write-up to fair value—is recognized in the consolidated statements. Instead, the book values of the previously separate companies are carried forward on the consolidated financial statements.

Purchase Accounting Complicates Financial Analysis

The disclosure rules for business combinations accounted for as purchases complicate financial analysis. Trend analysis becomes difficult. Why? Because under U.S. GAAP, comparative financial statements are not retroactively adjusted to include data for the acquired company for periods prior to the acquisition. To illustrate, Exhibit 16.5(a) presents comparative income statements from the 2001 annual report of Schlumberger Limited, a global technology services company incorporated in the Netherlands Antilles. In April 2001, Schlumberger acquired a 100% interest in Sema PLC, an information technology services company headquartered in London, in an acquisition accounted for as a purchase. Accordingly, Schlumberger's *2001* consolidated income statement numbers include the revenues and expenses of Sema PLC from the acquisition date (April 1) through December 31, 2001, Schlumberger's fiscal year-end. However, under the rules for purchase accounting,[11] the *2000* numbers presented in Schlumberger's 2001 comparative income statement do not include any of Sema's results for that fiscal year. But Sema's *full-year* revenues and expenses are included in Schlumberger's *2002* consolidated income statement numbers. *Thus, the income statements over the three years are noncomparable—Schlumberger's 2002 statements include Sema's results for twelve months, 2001 statements reflect Sema's performance for nine months, and 2000 statements exclude Sema's results entirely!*

To aid inter-period comparisons, existing disclosure rules require a **pro forma** (meaning *as if*) footnote that gives information for key income statement items as if the acquisition had taken place on the first day of the *previous* fiscal year, in this case January 1, 2000. Therefore, these pro forma footnote numbers for Schlumberger reflect full-year results for Sema both in 2001 and 2000. Notice, however, that these pro forma data do *not* encompass all income statement items and do not include periods prior to 2000. Consequently, even with the footnote disclosure, it is usually not possible for analysts to make comparisons of *complete* income statements adjusted for the acquisition. This is a serious deficiency that destroys the comparability of the time-series

---

[11] *APB Opinion 16*, op. cit.

financial statement data used by lenders and other financial analysts. Indeed, if the acquired company is large in relation to the size of the acquirer, the consolidated financial statements seriously distort trends and other comparative data.

EXHIBIT 16.5	Schlumberger, Ltd. and Subsidiaries

Disclosures Subsequent to a Business Combination: Purchase Accounting

Panel (a)

Consolidated Statement of Earnings

	Fiscal Years Ended December 31,	
($ in thousands)	2001	2000
Revenue		
Operating	$13,745,806	$ 9,611,462
Interest and other income	242,258	423,255
	13,988,064	10,034,717
Expenses		
Cost of goods sold and services	10,641,768	7,514,621
Research and engineering	704,336	540,698
Marketing	447,265	316,816
General	683,613	425,820
Interest	384,896	276,081
	12,861,878	9,074,036
Income from continuing operations before taxes and minority interest	1,126,186	960,681
Taxes on income	575,424	228,248
Income from continuing operations before minority interest	550,762	732,433
Minority interest	(28,545)	2,163
Income from continuing operations	522,217	734,596
Discontinued operations, net of tax	—	—
Net Income	$ 522,217	$ 734,596

Panel (b)

Excerpts from Annual Report Footnote:

On February 12, 2001, Schlumberger announced that it had reached an agreement with the board of directors of Sema PLC on the terms of a recommended offer for the entire issued and to be issued share capital of Sema PLC.

On April 6, 2001, the offer for the shares of Sema PLC was declared unconditional in all respects. The aggregate consideration for the acquisition of 100% of the issued Sema shares was $5.15 billion (including expenses of the transaction) which was financed from existing cash resources and borrowings under a $3 billion credit facility.

On October 3, 2001, wholly owned subsidiaries of Schlumberger issued $1.9 billion European bonds (Euro 1.4 billion and (pound) 425 million). The average rate of these bonds is 5.9% with maturity from 2008 through 2032. The proceeds from the issues were used to repay short-term bank loans originally taken out by those subsidiaries to finance the acquisition of Sema PLC.

For financial reporting purposes, Schlumberger included the results of operations of Sema in its consolidated accounts commencing April 1, 2001. If Sema had been included in the consolidated financial statements of Schlumberger from January 1, consolidated revenue for the twelve months ended December 31, 2001 would have increased by $538 million to $14.3 billion and consolidated net income would have decreased by approximately $140 million, to $382 million, related primarily to increased interest expense, amortization of intangibles and lower interest income. On a pro forma basis, Schlumberger 2000 operating revenue and net income would have been $12 billion and $300 million, respectively.

To illustrate the problem of trying to perform time-series comparisons for a business combination accounted for as a purchase, we concentrate on the operating revenue disclosures in Exhibit 16.5(a). The three-year operating revenue data from Schlumberger's consolidated statement of income, along with a computation of year-to-year growth in this measure is:

($ in thousands)	2002	2001	2000
Operating revenue as reported in consolidated financial statements	$13,473,662	$13,745,806	$9,611,462
Rate of growth in operating revenue compared to prior year	−2.0%	43.0%	14.5%*

*Based on 1999 operating revenue of $8,394,947.

The computed growth rates in operating revenues for 2002 and 2001 are misleading because the basic operating revenue data—and all other items in the income statement—are noncomparable. Again, the reason is that Schlumberger's 2002 data include Sema's results for the full year, the 2001 figures incorporate Sema's results for nine months, while the 2000 data exclude it altogether. To perform a valid comparison of operating revenue growth, the 2001 and 2000 numbers must be restated "as if" the combination had occurred at the beginning of each of these two fiscal years. These pro forma numbers are reported in Exhibit 16.5(b) and are reproduced below:

	2002	2001	2000
Operating revenue from consolidated statements	$13,473,662	—	—
Operating revenue from pro forma disclosure	—	$14,283,805	$12,000,000
Rate of growth in operating revenue compared to prior year	−5.7%	19.0%	*

*Cannot be calculated because 1999 pro forma data are not required to be reported.

The actual rate of operating revenue growth for 2001 and 2002 was 19.0% and −5.7%, respectively—assuming the combination occurred at the beginning of 2000. This is much lower than the rate computed from the operating revenue numbers actually reported in the financial statements—43.0% and −2.0%. Also notice from Exhibit 16.5(b) how the sparseness of pro forma disclosures makes it possible to compare only one other income statement line item besides operating revenue: bottom-line net income. The only way to overcome this problem is to gather past financial statement data for Sema and consolidate its past results with those of Schlumberger (using appropriate assumptions about intercompany sales and loans, of course). It's easy to obtain these data when the acquired company is publicly held. However, if the acquired company is not publicly held, these data may be difficult or even impossible to obtain.

For business combinations accounted for as a pooling-of-interests (allowed until July 1, 2002), this comparability problem did not occur. That's because under pooling all past financial statement data were retroactively consolidated to include both parties to the combination. Keep in mind, however, that while the pooling-of-interests approach overcomes some income statement comparability problems, the reported financial data using this approach are still fraught with the deficiencies that we describe in the Appendix to this chapter.

RECAP Trend analysis under purchase accounting becomes difficult because U.S. GAAP comparative financial statements are not retroactively adjusted to include data for the acquired company for periods prior to the acquisition. In the year of the acquisition, the consolidated income statement includes the parent company results for the full year and the results of the subsidiary from the time the acquisition took place to the end of the year (that is, for a fraction of a year the subsidiary was owned by the parent). In the year following acquisition, the consolidated income statement includes the full year results for both the parent and the subsidiary. In the year prior to the acquisition, the income statement includes the results of the parent company only and does not include any of the results of the subsidiary. This can lead to distortions in year-to-year growth rates in revenues and profits that statement users need to be aware of. Supplemental disclosures allow analysts to make adjustments to the reported numbers to make more valid comparisons, but only for selected statement items.

Consolidation of Variable Interest Entities

The collapse of Enron in 2001 created a demand for increased disclosure and transparency about companies' interests in *special purpose entities (SPE)* or *variable interest entities (VIE)*. A VIE is a corporation, partnership, trust, or any other legal structure used for business purposes that either (a) does not have equity investors with voting rights, or (b) has equity investors that do not provide sufficient financial resources for the entity to support its activities. VIEs are typically formed to engage in what is called structured financing arrangements, which offer an opportunity for a company to borrow money based on the value of a specific project or asset rather than on its own credit rating. Major uses of VIEs include synthetic leasing (see Chapter 12), securitizing loans and mortgages (see Chapter 8), selling receivables (see Chapter 8), or setting up **take-or-pay contracts** or **throughput arrangements**.

The accounting for VIEs is difficult because the rules are complex and cover a variety of transactions. Therefore, we do not go into details here. *The critical issue is determining when VIEs have to be consolidated into the financial statements of the sponsoring entity.* FASB Interpretation No. 46 requires a company to consolidate a VIE if that company is subject to a majority of the risk of loss from the VIE's activities, is entitled to receive a majority of the entity's residual returns, or both.[12] Generally, a third party has to maintain at least a 10% equity interest in the market value of the VIE's assets in order for the sponsoring entity to *avoid* consolidation. A company that consolidates a VIE is called the *primary beneficiary* of that entity.

Enron, with the help of its chief financial officer, Andrew Fastow, set up a number of limited partnerships through which it engaged in billions of dollars of complex transactions to hedge fluctuating values in some of Enron's broadband telecommunications and other technology investments. Under existing reporting rules at the time, Enron was able to avoid consolidation of these SPEs, thereby keeping hundreds of millions of dollars of debt and losses off of their financial statements.

For example, a company building a factory can borrow money based on the worth of the factory or on expectations of its future revenue.

Source: www.computerworld.com.

A take-or-pay contract is: "An agreement between a purchaser and a seller that provides for the purchaser to pay specified amounts periodically in return for products or services. The purchaser must make specified minimum payments even if it does not take delivery of the contracted products or services."*

For example, two companies may form an SPE with a nominal investment to build an oil refinery that will be used by both companies. The SPE borrows money to build the refinery with the note being guaranteed by one or both companies. Both companies agree to make minimum payments to the SPE each quarter in exchange for a specified number of barrels of refined oil on which they may or may not take delivery.

A throughput agreement is: "An agreement between a shipper (processor) and the owner of a transportation facility (such as an oil or natural gas pipeline or a ship) or a manufacturing facility that provides for the shipper (processor) to pay specified amounts periodically in return for the transportation (processing) of the product. The shipper (processor) is obligated to provide specified minimum quantities to be transported (processed) in each period and is required to make cash payments even if it does not provide the contracted quantities."**

*"Disclosure of Long-Term Obligations," *SFAS No. 47*, para. 23 (c) (Stamford, CT: FASB, 1981).
**Ibid., para. 23 (d).

---

[12] "Consolidation of Variable Interest Entities: An interpretation of ARB No. 51," *FASB Interpretation No. 46* (revised December 2003) (Norwalk, CT: FASB, December, 2003).

The FASB believes that requiring the primary beneficiary of the assets, liabilities, and operating results of VIEs to consolidate them will provide financial statement users with more complete information about the resources, obligations, risks, and opportunities facing the firm. As this book goes to press, the first disclosures under this new standard are just beginning to be provided. Time will tell whether the disclosures will provide the benefits hoped for by the FASB.

Accounting for Foreign Subsidiaries

All majority-owned subsidiaries—foreign and domestic—must be consolidated using the methods we've just described. Regrettably, there's an additional complication when consolidating foreign subsidiaries—that is, the financial records of the subsidiary will be expressed in foreign currency units. The subsidiary's numbers must first be *transformed* into the parent's currency units—into dollars, if it has a U.S. parent—before the consolidation process begins.

The transformation under U.S. GAAP (*SFAS No. 52*) specifies one of two procedures, depending on the operating characteristics of the foreign subsidiary:[13]

1. Foreign subsidiaries that are mere extensions of the parent with no self-sufficiency are **remeasured** using the **temporal method**. For example, in the case of a European sales subsidiary of a U.S. seed company, the subsidiary sells seed produced by the U.S. parent to European farmers and sends the sale proceeds back to the United States. In other words, the revenue the subsidiary collects is remitted to the parent company.

2. Foreign subsidiaries that are essentially freestanding units with self-contained foreign operations are **translated** using the **current rate method**. For example, in the case of a European manufacturing and sales subsidiary of a U.S. computer company, the subsidiary buys parts in Europe, assembles the final product, and sells it to European businesses, retaining the cash proceeds for growth and expansion locally.

The procedure selected to transform subsidiary statements expressed in foreign currency units into the parent's currency units is called the **functional currency choice**. What guides this choice is subtle;[14] foreign subsidiaries whose operations are not self-sufficient are considered to be engaging in a continuing series of **foreign currency transactions**. The consolidation process accordingly treats the financial results of these subsidiaries in the same way foreign currency transactions are treated. To illustrate, we must digress briefly to explain the accounting for foreign currency transactions.

Foreign Currency Transactions

Foreign currency transactions are simply business transactions denominated in units of a foreign currency. Examples include a U.S. company taking out a bank loan denominated in Norwegian kroner or purchasing inventory on credit for a price expressed in Dutch guilder. The accounting for foreign currency transactions depends on the type of asset acquired or liability incurred. Let's consider a foreign currency transaction that involves the acquisition of a **monetary asset**—that is, an asset like cash or accounts receivable whose value is derived from the number of monetary units into which it is convertible.

---

[13] "Foreign Currency Translation," *SFAS No. 52* (Stamford, CT: FASB, 1981). Although our discussion centers on *consolidation* of a foreign subsidiary, the rules described here must also be used in conjunction with the *equity method* when the parent owns between 20% and 50% of a foreign company.

[14] See L. Revsine, "The Rationale Underlying the Functional Currency Choice," *The Accounting Review* (July 1984), pp. 504–14.

Assume that on January 1, 2005 Yankee Corporation (a U.S. company) sells 100 units of its product to a U.K. customer. The selling price is £10 per unit, or £1,000 total. Payment is due on April 1, 2005. On January 1, 2005 let's say that one British pound is worth $2 U.S., and that the per-unit cost of production incurred by Yankee is $8.00. Given this information, we would record the foreign currency transaction on Yankee's books in this way:

DR Accounts receivable	$2,000	
CR Sales revenue		$2,000
(To record the receivable of £1,000 at its 1/1/05 U.S. dollar equivalent of $2,000.)		
DR Cost of goods sold	$800	
CR Inventory		$800
(100 units @ $8.00)		

The receivable is denominated in pounds—which is what makes this a foreign currency transaction. Since Yankee keeps its books in dollars, the receivable must be reexpressed in home-currency units when preparing financial statements. This is done using the exchange rate in effect at the transaction date—£1 = $2 U.S. It is important to understand that while the receivable is initially reflected on the books at $2,000, in reality what's owed by the customer is £1,000.

By the end of the quarter, the pound has fallen relative to the dollar, so that on March 31, 2005 the exchange rate is £1 = $1.80 U.S. This means that at current exchange rates the receivable is worth only $1,800, and so Yankee would book the following entry when preparing its quarterly statements:

DR Foreign currency transaction loss	$200	
CR Accounts receivable		$200
(To reflect the £1,000 receivable at its end-of-quarter dollar equivalent of $1,800.)		

Yankee has a loss because it was owed pounds but the pound has fallen in value. This loss is reflected in the income statement of the period in which the loss occurs. Monetary assets (like accounts receivable) that arise from foreign currency transactions are shown in the financial statements at their dollar equivalent using **the exchange rate in effect at the financial statement date**. Monetary liabilities (like accounts or bonds payable) are similarly translated using the exchange rate in effect at the statement date. The statement date exchange rate is referred to as the **current rate**.

Suppose the exchange rate on April 1, 2005, when the receivable is paid, is still £1 = $1.80 U.S. The customer remits £1,000, which Yankee then converts into dollars. The entry on Yankee's books is:

> Most liabilities are monetary since they are expressed in units of currency (for example, a Japanese yen account payable of ¥9,000,000) and will be settled using foreign currency monetary assets. However, there are a few liabilities that are settled by using *nonmonetary* assets; this small class of liabilities is considered to be nonmonetary. Examples include estimated product warranty liabilities and customer deposits for products to be produced and delivered in future periods.

DR Cash	$1,800	
CR Accounts receivable		$1,800
(To remove the receivable from the books. The initial $2,000 minus the 3/31/05 write-down of $200 equals the carrying amount of $1,800.)		

We next illustrate the accounting for a foreign currency transaction that involves a nonmonetary asset. Nonmonetary assets are items like inventory, equipment, land, buildings, and trucks whose value is determined by supply and demand.

Suppose Yankee—because of its growing volume of sales to U.K. customers—decides to purchase a warehouse in London to store inventory awaiting shipment to customers. A building is purchased on June 30, 2005 for £300,000; on that date the exchange rate is £1 = $1.75 U.S. The building is recorded on Yankee's books at the U.S. dollar equivalent of the foreign currency transaction price at the purchase date:

DR Warehouse building $525,000

    CR Cash $525,000

(To record the acquisition of the London warehouse at the U.S. dollar equivalent of the foreign currency transaction price: £300,000 × 1.75 = $525,000.)

The subsequent accounting for nonmonetary assets acquired in a foreign currency transaction is identical to the accounting for nonmonetary assets acquired in the domestic currency. Specifically, the historical cost of the fixed asset in dollars is used as the measurement basis in subsequent financial statements throughout the asset's life. Even if the value of the pound falls to £1 = $1.60 U.S. by year-end 2005, the London warehouse would still be shown on Yankee's books at $525,000—that is, at its acquisition cost in dollars (minus depreciation, of course). Thus, to reflect the gross carrying amount of nonmonetary assets acquired in a foreign currency transaction, Yankee would use the exchange rate in effect at the time of the transaction. This rate is called the **historical exchange rate.**

RECAP

The accounting for assets and liabilities arising from foreign currency transactions depends on the nature of the item—that is,

1. **Foreign currency monetary assets and liabilities are remeasured using the current rate of exchange in effect at the balance sheet date.**
2. **Foreign currency nonmonetary assets (and liabilities) are remeasured using the historical rate of exchange that was in effect at the time the item was acquired or incurred.**

Accounting for Non-Freestanding Foreign Subsidiaries

Now that we've outlined the accounting for foreign currency transactions, we can return to our main theme—that is, accounting for foreign subsidiaries. When we introduced this topic, we said the method used to transform the foreign currency accounts of foreign subsidiaries depends on the nature of the subsidiary. Subsidiaries that are not freestanding—that is, subsidiaries whose operations are simply an extension of the parent—are remeasured using the temporal method. We now explain why.

To see what it means when we say a foreign subsidiary is not freestanding, let us consider a U.S. company, Doodle Corporation, with a U.K. subsidiary called Dandy Ltd. The role of Dandy is to serve as the U.K. marketing arm of Doodle. Doodle manufactures a product in the United States using U.S. sourced materials and labor. Some of the production is shipped from the United States to the United Kingdom where it is sold to U.K. customers at a price denominated in pounds sterling. The distribution of the product and collection of the receivables are coordinated by two U.K. employees of Dandy Ltd. Upon collection of the receivables, the pounds are remitted to the United States. This cycle is repeated as the pounds are converted into dollars, the dollars are used in the United States to manufacture more inventory, and some portion of the inventory is again shipped to the United Kingdom for sale to customers there. Dandy's only U.K. assets are (1) a small amount of cash to pay expenses, (2) inventory from Doodle that has not yet been shipped to customers, and (3) a building that serves as both a warehouse and an office for the two employees.

The situation described here is a classic illustration of a foreign subsidiary that is merely an extension of the parent. Dandy Ltd. is a marketing arm of Doodle rather than a viable, freestanding company. It is a conduit for administering foreign sales, and it has no independent life of its own.

Under *SFAS No. 52*, subsidiaries like Dandy Ltd. are treated as if they were created for the sole purpose of facilitating foreign currency transactions. Because such subsidiaries are a conduit for foreign transactions, upon consolidation they are treated as if the parent company had engaged in the foreign transactions directly. That is, **the numbers included when consolidating a non-freestanding subsidiary are identical to the numbers that would have been included had the subsidiary not existed and instead the parent had engaged in the foreign currency transactions directly.**

To achieve this effect in the financial statements, the temporal method is used to translate the subsidiary's foreign currency statements into dollars.[15] The exchange rates for translating various accounts under the temporal method are shown in Exhibit 16.6.

EXHIBIT 16.6	Translation Exchange Rates Under the Temporal Method

Account Category	Rate Used
Balance Sheet	
Monetary assets and liabilities	Current rate
Nonmonetary assets and liabilities	Historical rate
Income Statement	
All revenue and expense accounts except those listed below	Rate at time of transaction
Cost of goods sold and depreciation	Historical rate

To illustrate the temporal method, consider the following transactions for Dandy Ltd. during 2005:

1. On January 1, 2005 it received inventory costing $800 from Doodle when £1 = $2 U.S, and sold these goods on credit for £1,000.
2. The pound falls to £1 = $1.80 U.S. on March 31, 2001. Receivables of £1,000 were collected on April 1, 2005, when £1 = $1.80 U.S.
3. The company purchased a building in London for £300,000 on June 30, 2005 when £1 = $1.75 U.S.

These transactions are identical to the foreign currency transactions entered into by Yankee Corporation earlier in this section. In Exhibit 16.7 we show the result of using the temporal method to translate Dandy Ltd.'s statements. The results under GAAP for Yankee's foreign currency transactions is displayed in the shaded column for comparison.

Comparing the Dandy statement numbers with those of Yankee in Exhibit 16.7 demonstrates the point of the example. Using the temporal method results in Dandy statements being denominated in dollar figures that are equal to those of Yankee. This is no coincidence. **Both Dandy and Yankee are considered to have engaged in identical foreign currency transactions, so the two sets of results should be equal.** Notice how the translation rules under the temporal method help achieve this result.

---

[15] *SFAS No. 52* uses the term **remeasure** when describing the conversion from foreign currency units to home currency units under the temporal method. For simplicity, we ignore this nuance and refer to the process as translation.

EXHIBIT 16.7	Comparison of Temporal Method Results with Accounting for Foreign Currency Transactions

| | Temporal Method Translation | | | Foreign Currency Transactions |
	Dandy Ltd. in £s	Exchange Rate	Dandy Ltd in $s	Yankee Corporation
Income Statement				
Sales	£ 1,000	1£ = $2	$ 2,000	$ 2,000
Cost of sales	400	1£ = $2	800	800
Gross margin	£ 600		$ 1,200	$ 1,200
Loss on receivables*	—		200	200
Gross income	£ 600		$ 1,000	$ 1,000
Selected Balance Sheet Accounts				
At 3/31/05				
Account receivable	£ 1,000	1£ = $1.80	$ 1,800	$ 1,800
At 4/1/05				
Cash	£ 1,000	1£ = $1.80	$ 1,800	$ 1,800
At 6/30/05				
Building	£300,000	1£ = $1.75	$525,000	$525,000

*Computed as:

Monetary asset on acquisition,	£1,000 when 1£ = $2.00 =	$2,000
Monetary asset at March 31, 2005	£1,000 when 1£ = $1.80 =	1,800
Loss on receivables		$ 200

Accounting for Self-Contained Foreign Subsidiaries

When the majority-owned foreign subsidiary and its parent operate independently, the translation of the subsidiary's financial statements into dollars uses the current rate method. To understand why, let us consider a self-contained subsidiary whose operations do not rely extensively on the parent.

A U.S. food company has a Swiss subsidiary that was formed by a capital infusion from the U.S. parent. Once the equity cushion was in place, the remainder of the Swiss subsidiary's long-term capital was raised using Swiss franc borrowing. The subsidiary engages in no transactions with the parent. Operations are entirely contained in Switzerland, where the company hires employees, buys inventory, manufactures its product line, and sells to Swiss and other European customers. Operating profits are plowed back into the Swiss operation to expand into new product lines and to increase production capacity. While the parent may periodically receive dividends from the subsidiary, its investment will remain until the subsidiary is either sold or liquidated.

For self-contained foreign subsidiaries, the effect of changes in exchange rates on future dollar cash flows is uncertain. Consider a rise in the Swiss franc. One possible effect of the rise is that it will make the subsidiary's products more expensive to foreign purchasers and could adversely affect profits. But, the rise in the Swiss franc also means that input purchases in other currencies are cheaper, so a favorable profit effect could ensue. The possibilities are many and depend on the individual characteristics of the subsidiary and on the characteristics of the markets in which it operates. These include:

1. Does the subsidiary price its product sales in countries outside Switzerland in Swiss francs or in units of the foreign currencies?
2. Does the subsidiary adjust its Swiss franc selling price when the value of the franc rises or falls?
3. What proportion of the product input is purchased locally in Switzerland in francs?
4. Does the Swiss franc borrowing have a floating rate of interest that would be sensitive to exchange rate changes?

> This is another example of an element of **comprehensive income**, discussed in Chapter 2.

These are only a few of the many possibilities that could influence the magnitude and direction of the effect of the exchange rate change on ultimate dollar cash flows from the subsidiary. *Because the ultimate exchange rate effects on U.S. dollar cash flows are uncertain, the FASB decided that such subsidiaries should be translated using the current rate method and that any debit or credit arising from translation "gains" or "losses" should be put directly into an owners' equity account and not run through the income statement.* Under the current rate method, *all* balance sheet accounts are translated at the current exchange rate in effect at the balance sheet date and *all* income statement accounts are translated at the weighted average rate of exchange that was in effect over the period covered by the statement.

> Ratio proportionality between foreign currency and translated dollar numbers is maintained *precisely* for any ratio for which the numerator and denominator are confined to a single statement. Examples include the current ratio—both balance sheet accounts—and gross margin ratio—both income statement accounts. This is true because the current rate method translates all accounts within a single statement at the same rate—weighted average rate for income statement items and end-of-year rate for balance sheet items. For ratios that use numbers from both statements—for example, rate of return on assets—the current rate method does not maintain perfect proportionality. However, the difference between the "mixed-statement ratio" expressed in foreign currency and the translated ratio expressed in U.S. dollars is usually very small.

If *all* accounts in a statement are translated at the *same* rate—which is what happens under the current rate method—then the translated statements have the same proportionality as the untranslated statements expressed in foreign currency units. In other words, the quick ratio of the Swiss subsidiary derived from its pretranslated Swiss franc statements will be identical to the quick ratio once the statements are translated into dollars using the current rate method. The current rate method provides a practical way to get from foreign currency units to dollars while still maintaining or very closely approximating the subsidiary's financial ratios. *Furthermore, by denying income statement recognition to the balancing debit or credit that arises from translation, the uncertain ultimate effect of exchange rate changes is explicitly carried forward.* Figure 16.3 is a diagram of the *SFAS No. 52* translation approach.

Figure 16.3

TRANSLATION APPROACH USED IN *SFAS NO. 52*

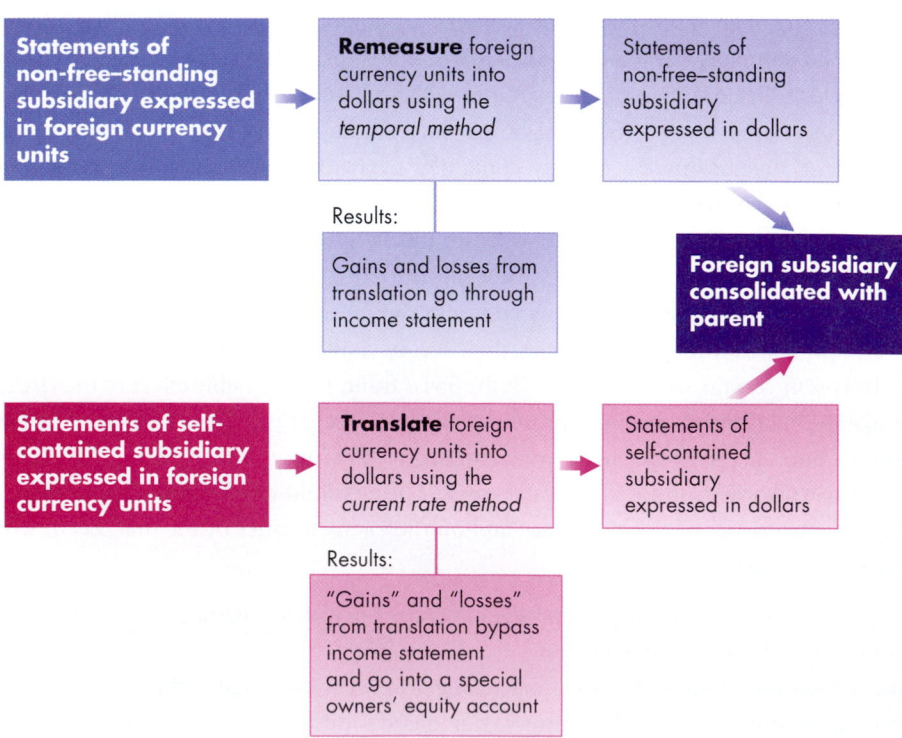

The figure shows that *SFAS No. 52* requires firms to categorize their foreign subsidiaries into one of two groups: (1) *non-freestanding subsidiaries,* whose activities are so closely integrated with the parent that they are considered to be engaging in foreign currency transactions on behalf of the parent; or (2) *self-contained subsidiaries* with an independent or virtually independent operating existence of their own. For subsidiaries in the first group, exchange rate movements have an immediately determinable effect on dollar cash flows; for this reason, translation gains or losses are run through the income statement. By contrast, subsidiaries in the second group are put into an income "holding pattern," because exchange rate movements have an indeterminate impact on the parent's ultimate dollar cash flows. Consequently, a *neutral* translation mechanism—the current rate method—is used for these subsidiaries, and the resulting equity debits or credits are simply treated as balancing items rather than as elements of income.

Illustrative Disclosure Exhibit 16.8 contains excerpts from the Pfizer Inc. 2002 annual report. Exhibit 16.8(a) shows a portion of the footnote disclosure regarding foreign subsidiaries. Most of Pfizer's foreign subsidiaries are translated using the current rate method, which means that translation adjustments go to a currency translation adjustment account in the "Shareholders' equity" section of the balance sheet. This section is reproduced in Exhibit 16.8(b).

Note that the highlighted currency translation adjustment loss is shown as part of Comprehensive income in the "Shareholders' equity" section of the balance sheet in Exhibit 16.8(b). Here we learn that the translation adjustment gain was $85 million (net of tax) in 2002, compared to a $37 million loss in 2001. Several factors may have contributed to this increase—rising exchange rates, operating profits at foreign subsidiaries, or a real increase in the company's net foreign investment. Analysts would have to dig deeper to understand exactly why the translation gains occurred and what they mean.

EXHIBIT 16.8	Pfizer Inc.

Panel (a)

Excerpts from 2002 Annual Report

For most international operations, local currencies have been determined to be their functional currencies. We translate assets and liabilities to their U.S. dollar equivalents at rates in effect at the balance sheet date and record translation adjustments in Shareholders' equity. We translate statement of income accounts at average rates for the period and record these adjustments in Other (income)/deductions—net.

For operations in highly inflationary economies, we translate the balance sheet items as follows:

- Monetary items (that is, assets and liabilities that will be settled for cash) at rates in effect at the balance sheet date, with translation adjustments recorded in Other (income)/deductions—net

- Nonmonetary items at historical rates (that is, those rates in effect when the items were first recorded)

(continued on next page)

EXHIBIT 16.8   Pfizer Inc. (*continued*)

Panel (b)

Consolidated Statement of Shareholders' Equity
Year Ended December 31

($ in millions)	Common Stock Shares	Common Stock Par Value	Additional Paid-In Capital	Employee Benefit Trusts Shares	Employee Benefit Trusts Fair Value	Treasury Stock Shares	Treasury Stock Cost	Retained Earnings	Accum. Other Comprehensive Income/(Exp.)	Total
Balance December 31, 2000	6,749	$337	$8,895	(74)	$(3,382)	(435)	$ (7,858)	$19,599	$(1,515)	$16,076
Comprehensive income:										
Net income								7,788		7,788
Other comprehensive expense—net of tax										
Currency translation adjustment									(37)	(37)
Net unrealized loss on available-for-sale securities									(91)	(91)
Minimum pension liability									(106)	(106)
Total other comprehensive expense									(234)	(234)
Total comprehensive income										7,554
Cash dividends declared								(2,869)		(2,869)
Stock option transactions	40	2	981	8	337	6	104			1,424
Purchases of common stock						(89)	(3,665)			(3,665)
Employee benefit trust transactions—net			(724)	(1)	395	2	25			(304)
Other	3	1	148	—	—	1	16	(88)	—	77
Balance December 31, 2001	6,792	340	9,300	(67)	(2,650)	(515)	(11,378)	24,430	(1,749)	18,293
Comprehensive income:										
Net income								9,126		9,126
Other comprehensive expense—net of tax										—
Currency translation adjustment									85	85
Net unrealized loss on available-for-sale securities									(32)	(32)
Minimum pension liability									(179)	(179)
Total other comprehensive expense									(126)	(126)
Total comprehensive income										9,000
Cash dividends declared								(3,313)		(3,313)
Stock options transactions	34	1	789	9	366	—	(8)			1,148
Purchases of common stock						(153)	(4,996)			(4,996)
Employee benefit trusts transactions—net			(863)	—	498	1	28			(337)
Other	3	—	142	—	—	—	13	—	—	155
Balance December 31, 2002	6,829	$341	$9,368	(58)	$(1,786)	(667)	$(16,341)	$30,243	$(1,875)	$19,950

SUMMARY

- Financial reporting for intercorporate equity investments depends on the size of the parent company's ownership share. Proportionate share size is used to infer the purpose of the investment.
- When the ownership share is less than 20%, it is presumed that the investor cannot exert influence on the decisions of the investee. These *minority passive investments* are shown at market value on the balance sheet. Unrealized gains or losses on the trading portfolio are recorded on the income statement, while unrealized gains and losses on the available-for-sale portfolio are recorded in a special owners' equity account as part of comprehensive income.

- *Minority active investments* involve between 20% and 50% ownership and are presumed to give the investor the ability to influence operating decisions of the investee. The equity method is used to account for such investments whereby the investor records its proportionate share of the investee's profits and losses each period with a corresponding adjustment to the investment account.

- Full consolidation is required when ownership exceeds 50%. Beginning in 2002, the purchase method of accounting is used to account for all business combinations. Under purchase accounting, the identifiable net assets of the subsidiary are recorded at fair market value at date of acquisition. The excess of the price paid to acquire the subsidiary's stock over the fair value of the identifiable net assets of the subsidiary is recorded as goodwill.

- Goodwill is no longer amortized, but is subject to an annual impairment test. If goodwill is determined to be impaired, it is written down with an offsetting charge to earnings.

- Prior to July 2001, certain business combinations accomplished by stock-for-stock exchanges were accounted for using the pooling-of-interests method. Under pooling, the subsidiary's net assets are recorded on the consolidated financial statements at book value on the acquisition date and no goodwill is recorded. Although pooling is no longer allowed, it continues to affect the financial statements of mergers consummated before July 2001 when *SFAS No. 141* became effective.

- The collapse of Enron brought about a demand for increased disclosure and transparency regarding companies' interests in *special purpose entities (SPE)* or *variable interest entities (VIE)*. A VIE is a corporation, partnership, trust, or any other legal structure used for business purposes that either (a) does not have equity investors with voting rights, or (b) has equity investors that do not provide sufficient financial resources for the entity to support its own activities. *FASB Interpretation No. 46* requires a company to consolidate a VIE if that company is subject to a majority of the risk of loss from the VIE's activities, and is entitled to receive a majority of the entity's residual returns or both. A company that consolidates a VIE is called the *primary beneficiary* of that entity.

- Majority-owned foreign subsidiaries also must be consolidated. This requires foreign currency amounts to be re-expressed in dollars. Foreign subsidiaries that are mere extensions of the U.S. parent and have no self-sufficiency are remeasured using the *temporal method*. The temporal method treats the subsidiaries' business transactions as if they had been undertaken by the parent— but in the foreign currency.

- Foreign subsidiaries that are freestanding economic units are remeasured using the *current rate method*. This method provides an easy way to re-express foreign currency amounts in dollars while still maintaining the subsidiary's financial ratios.

APPENDIX

POOLING-OF-INTERESTS ACCOUNTING

To see how pooling works and its financial statement effects relative to the purchase method, let's return to the Alphonse and Gaston example from earlier in the chapter. Instead of acquiring a 100% ownership in Gaston with cash, assume that Alphonse exchanges 8,000,000 shares of its own stock with a fair market value of $10,000,000 for all of the outstanding stock of Gaston.

In a stock-for-stock exchange, the owners of *both* Alphonse and Gaston continue as equity investors in the newly merged corporation. This continuation of ownership interests in poolings contrasts sharply with what happens in a cash buyout. After a cash buyout, the acquired company's former shareholders have no further equity interest in the combined enterprise.

Pooling-of-interests reporting rules treat the two formerly independent companies as though they have decided to join resources and "keep house together." Since both original ownership interests survive, **no buyout is considered to have taken place.** In the consolidation of Alphonse's and Gaston's financial statements, the *book values* of the two entities are combined. As in purchase accounting, however, intercompany transactions and double-counted items must be eliminated, as shown in Exhibit 16.9 on the next page.

> The entry to record the acquisition on Alphonse's books would use the *book value* of Gaston's net assets ($2,000,000 + $6,500,000 − $500,000) as the carrying amount in the investment account—that is,
>
> | | | |
> |---|---|---|
> | **DR** Investment in Gaston | $8,000,000 | |
> | **CR** Common Stock | | $8,000,000 |

EXHIBIT 16.9	Alphonse and Gaston

Preparation of Consolidated Balance Sheet (Pooling-of-Interest Method—100% acquistion)

	After the Acquisition		Adjustments and Eliminations		Consolidated
	Alphonse	Gaston	Dr.	Cr.	Balance Sheet
Assets					
Current assets	$ 5,000,000	$2,000,000			$ 7,000,000
Fixed assets, net	20,000,000	6,500,000			26,500,000
Investment in Gaston	8,000,000	—		$8,000,000	—
	$33,000,000	$8,500,000			$33,500,000
Liabilities and Equity					
Current Liabilities	$ 1,000,000	$ 500,000			$ 1,500,000
Common Stock	32,000,000	8,000,000	$8,000,000		32,000,000
	$33,000,000	$8,500,000	$8,000,000	$8,000,000	$33,500,000

The only adjustment needed here is the elimination of the potential double-counting of Gaston's net assets and equity. This entry is identical to the purchase accounting (or cash buyout) adjustment illustrated in Exhibit 16.2 (see notations "A," "B," and "C"). No other adjustments or reclassifications are needed, since Alphonse's "Investment in Gaston" account equals the net book value shown on Gaston's books. This means that under a pooling of interests there will never be a write-up of assets to a new, higher carrying value. Similarly, there will never be any goodwill recognized.

Purchase, Pooling, and Financial Analysis

The pooling-of-interests method has been widely criticized. To help understand why, consider Exhibit 16.10, which highlights the differences in consolidated balance sheets that would result for Alphonse & Gaston Company, the combined organization, under purchase versus pooling-of-interests accounting.

EXHIBIT 16.10	Alphonse and Gaston

Purchase versus Pooling-of-Interests Method: Comparative Consolidated Balance Sheets

	Purchase Method	Pooling-of-Interests Method	Difference
Assets			
Current assets	$ 7,000,000	$ 7,000,000	—
Fixed assets minus accumulated depreciation	28,000,000	26,500,000	$1,500,000
Goodwill	500,000	—	500,000
	$35,500,000	$33,500,000	$2,000,000
Liabilities and Equity			
Current liabilities	$ 1,500,000	$ 1,500,000	—
Common stock	32,000,000	32,000,000	—
Capital in excess of par	2,000,000	—	$2,000,000
	$35,500,000	$33,500,000	$2,000,000

This comparison makes the financial statement differences under purchase versus pooling-of-interests accounting easy to see. Prior to the acquisition, Gaston had a fair value of $10,000,000—the amount of cash Alphonse was willing to pay to gain control. Purchase accounting brings Gaston into the consolidated statement at its fair value of $10,000,000; under pooling-of-interests accounting, Gaston is shown in the consolidated statement at its net book value of $8,000,000. The $2,000,000 difference is shown in the "Difference" column in Exhibit 16.10.

Critics argue that pooling permits acquiring companies to record acquisitions at artificially low amounts. In our example Gaston is *worth* $10,000,000, and this is presumably the value that the sellers demanded. Therefore, the value of Alphonse stock that Gaston's shareholders received must have been close to $10,000,000. ***Despite this economic reality, the transaction is booked at $8,000,000 under the pooling-of-interests method.*** Critics charge that this understatement distorts the balance sheet as well as subsequent income statements. The income in future years is affected since fixed assets are $1,500,000 lower—the unrecorded difference between fair value and book value—under pooling than under purchase accounting, thereby lowering future depreciation expense. Similarly, since there is no goodwill under pooling, there is no goodwill write-off to reduce future earnings. Both of these effects make income under pooling higher.

> By contrast, under purchase accounting, goodwill is subject to an annual impairment test. If impaired, goodwill is written down with an offsetting charge to earnings of the consolidated entity.

Critics further charge that the lower pooling balance sheet numbers for gross assets and equity make rate-of-return ratios appear higher. That's because, under pooling, the denominator of both the return-on-assets and return-on-equity ratios is lower. Some critics suggest that these distortions are not accidental. They argue that the *cosmetic* statement effects of pooling explain its popularity among takeover-minded executives prior to 2002, when *SFAS No. 141* went into effect. Pooling provided an opportunity to buy companies and then record the acquisition on the books at artificially low numbers, thereby improving the appearance of subsequent financial statements.

Figure 16.4 demonstrates that companies clearly preferred to use pooling rather than the purchase method for large deals before pooling was banned. For deals larger than $100 million, both the dollar value (panel [a]) and the number of deals (panel [b]) were much greater for transactions accounted for as poolings rather than purchases throughout most of the 1990–2000 period. The

Panel a

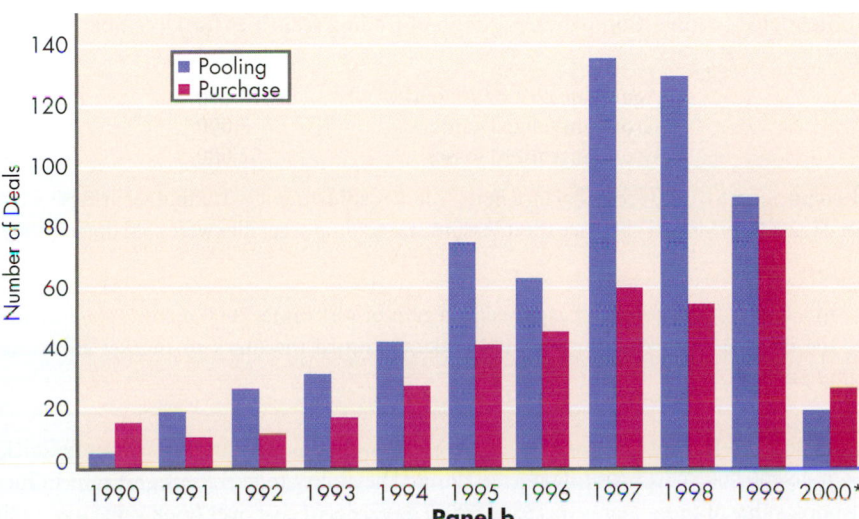

Panel b

* 2000 data through November 1, 2000 only
Source: Securities Data Corporation.

Figure 16.4

LARGE U.S. ACQUISITIONS ACCOUNTED FOR AS PURCHASE VERSUS POOLING OF INTERESTS

(a) Dollar value of Large U.S. Acquisitions (Deal Size > $100 million) Using Purchase versus Pooling-of-Interest Accounting (b) Number of Large U.S. Acquisitions (Deal Size > $100 Million) Using Purchase versus Pooling-of-Interest Accounting reason that pooling was so popular for high dollar-value deals is obvious—pooling avoids the drain on the post-combination earnings that would otherwise result under purchase accounting. But as noted previously, many believe pooling artificially inflates the post-combination earnings of the combined entity and understates the asset base used to generate those earnings. As a statement user, you need to be aware of these potential distortions because financial statements continue to be impacted by poolings consummated prior to July 2001, when *SFAS No. 141* went into effect.

EXERCISES

E16 – 1

Mark-to-market for trading and available-for-sale securities

The following data pertain to Tyne Company's investments in marketable equity securities. (Assume all securities were held throughout 2005 and 2006.)

		Market Value	
	Cost	12/31/06	12/31/05
Trading	$150,000	$155,000	$100,000
Available for sale	150,000	130,000	120,000

Required:

1. What amount should Tyne report as unrealized holding gain (loss) in its 2006 income statement?
2. What amount should Tyne report as net unrealized gain (loss) on available-for-sale securities at December 31, 2006 in its statement of stockholders' equity? Ignore tax effects.

E16 – 2

Mark-to-market for available-for-sale securities

During 2005 Rex Company purchased marketable equity securities as a short-term investment. These securities are classified as available-for-sale. The cost and market values at December 31, 2005 were as follows:

Security	Cost	Market Value
Company A— 100 shares	$ 2,800	$ 3,400
Company B—1,000 shares	17,000	15,300
Company C—2,000 shares	31,500	29,500
	$51,300	$48,200

Rex sold 1,000 shares of Company B stock on January 31, 2006 for $15 per share, incurring $1,500 in brokerage commission and taxes.

Required:

1. Ignoring taxes, how much should Rex report as unrealized gain or loss on its available-for-sale securities at December 31, 2005 in the statement of stockholders' equity?
2. On the sale, Rex should report a realized loss of how much?

E16 – 3

Mark-to-market for trading securities

Information related to Jones Company's portfolio of trading securities for December 31, 2006 is provided next:

Aggregate cost of securities	$340,000
Gross unrealized gains	8,000
Gross unrealized losses	52,000

Jones reported a $10,000 credit balance in its "Market adjustment—Trading securities" account in its December 31, 2005 (prior year) balance sheet. Assume no trading securities were sold during 2005 or 2006.

Required:

1. How much should Jones report as unrealized gain or loss on its 2006 income statement?
2. Give the journal entry that Jones would make to record the mark-to-market adjustment to its trading portfolio.

E16 – 4

Equity method

In January 2005 the Harold Corporation acquired 20% of the outstanding common stock of Otis Company for $400,000. This investment gave Harold the ability to exercise significant influence over Otis. The book value of these shares was $300,000. The excess of cost over book value was attributed to an identifiable intangible asset, patent, which was undervalued on Otis' balance sheet and which had a remaining useful life of 10 years.

For the year ended December 31, 2005 Otis reported net income of $90,000 and paid cash dividends of $20,000 on its common stock.

Required:

1. How much would Harold Corporation's income increase in 2005 as a result of its investment in Otis?
2. What is the carrying value of Harold's investment in Otis Company at December 31, 2005?

Sage, Inc. bought 40% of Adams Corporation's outstanding common stock on January 2, 2005 for $400,000. The carrying amount of Adams' net assets at the purchase date totaled $900,000. Fair values and carrying amounts were the same for all items except for plant and inventory, for which fair values exceeded the carrying amounts by $90,000 and $10,000, respectively. The plant has an 18-year life. All inventory was sold during 2005. Goodwill, if any, is to be amortized over 40 years. During 2005 Adams reported net income of $120,000 and paid a $20,000 cash dividend.

E16 – 5

Equity method

AICPA
ADAPTED

Required:

1. What amount should Sage report in its income statement from its investment in Adams for the year ended December 31, 2005?
2. What would be the December 31, 2005 balance in the "Investment in Adams" account?

On January 1, 2005 Boggs, Inc. paid $700,000 for 100,000 shares of Mattly Corporation, which represented 30% of Mattly's outstanding common stock. The following computation was made by Boggs:

Purchase price	$700,000
30% equity in book value of Mattly's net assets	500,000
Excess of cost over book value	$200,000

E16 – 6

Equity versus cost method for long-term investments

ADAPTED

The excess cost over book value was attributed to undervalued depreciable assets with a remaining life of 20 years (zero salvage). Mattly reported net income for the year ended December 31, 2005 of $300,000. Mattly Corporation paid cash dividends of $100,000 on July 1, 2005.

Required:

1. If Boggs, Inc. exercised significant influence over Mattly Corporation and properly accounted for the long-term investment under the equity method, the amount of net investment revenue Boggs should report from its investment in Mattly would be how much?
2. If Boggs, Inc. did not exercise significant influence over Mattly Corporation and properly accounted for the long-term investment under the cost method, the amount of net investment revenue Boggs should report from its investment in Mattly would be how much?

On April 30, 2005, Pound Corp. purchased for cash all 200,000 shares of the outstanding common stock of Shake Corp. for $20 per share. At April 30, 2005, Shake's balance sheet showed net assets with a book value of $3,000,000. On that date, the fair value of Shake's property, plant and equipment exceeded book value by $300,000.

E16 – 7

Determining the value of goodwill

Required:

What amount should Pound report as goodwill on its April 30, 2005 consolidated balance sheet?

On April 1, 2005 Dart Company paid $620,000 for all the issued and outstanding common stock of Wall Corporation in a transaction properly accounted for as a purchase. The recorded assets and liabilities of Wall Corporation on April 1, 2005 follow:

E16 – 8

Goodwill—purchase method

AICPA
ADAPTED

Cash	$ 60,000
Inventory	180,000
Property and equipment (net of accumulated depreciation of $220,000)	320,000
Goodwill (net of accumulated write-downs of $50,000)	100,000
Liabilities	(120,000)
Net assets	$540,000

On April 1, 2005 Wall's inventory had a fair value of $150,000, and its property and equipment (net) had a fair value of $380,000.

Required:

What is the amount of goodwill resulting from the business combination?

E16 – 9

Consolidated financial statements

AICPA
ADAPTED

On January 1, 2005 Pitt Company purchased an 80% investment in Saxe Company. The acquisition cost was equal to Pitt's equity in Saxe's net assets at that date. On January 1, 2005 Pitt and Saxe had retained earnings of $500,000 and $100,000, respectively. During 2005 (1) Pitt had net income of $200,000, which included its equity in Saxe's earnings, and declared dividends of $50,000; (2) Saxe had net income of $40,000 and declared dividends of $20,000; and (3) there were no other intercompany transactions between the parent and subsidiary.

Required:

What should the consolidated retained earnings be on December 31, 2005?

E16 – 10

Determining consolidated retained earnings

On January 1, 2005 Pack Corp. purchased all of Slam Corp.'s common stock for $500,000. On that date the fair values of Slam's net assets equaled their book values of $400,000. During 2005, Slam paid cash dividends of $8,000. The following balance sheet and income statement accounts are reported on Pack and Slam's separate financial statements at December 31, 2005:

	Pack	Slam
Balance sheet accounts:		
Investment in Slam	$552,000	$ 0
Retained earnings	780,000	250,000
Income statement accounts:		
Equity in earnings of Slam	60,000	0
Net income	150,000	60,000

Required

What amount of retained earnings will be reported in Pack's December 31, 2005 consolidated balance sheet?

E16 – 11

Consolidated balance sheet

CMA
ADAPTED

Immediately after the purchase of 60% ownership of the Island Company by the Sea Company, the separate condensed balance sheets of the two companies are as follows:

	Sea Company	Island Company
Other assets	$750,000	$320,000
Investment in Island Company	187,500	—
	$937,500	$320,000
Liabilities	$250,000	$ 70,000
Common stock	450,000	200,000
Retained earnings	237,500	50,000
	$937,500	$320,000

Required:

What would be the dollar amount of the total assets in the consolidated balance sheet immediately after the acquisition?

E16 – 12

Transaction foreign exchange gain/loss

AICPA
ADAPTED

On September 1, 2005 Cano & Company, a U.S. corporation, sold merchandise to a foreign firm for 250,000 francs. Terms of the sale require payment in francs on February 1, 2006. On September 1, 2005 the spot exchange rate was $0.20 per franc. At Cano's year-end on December 31, 2005, the spot rate was $0.19, but the rate increased to $0.22 by February 1, 2006, when payment was received.

Required:

1. What would be the foreign currency transaction gain or loss recorded in 2005?
2. What would be the foreign currency transaction gain or loss recorded in 2006?

Stone has provided the following information on its available-for-sale securities:

Aggregate cost as of 12/31/05	$170,000
Unrealized gain as of 12/31/05	4,000
Unrealized losses as of 12/31/05	26,000
Net realized gains during 2005	30,000

Stone reported $1,500 in the contra-asset valuation account to reduce these securities to their market value at December 31, 2004.

Required:

What amount should be debited as an unrealized loss to the stockholders' equity section of Stone's December 31, 2005 balance sheet as a result of 2005 market value changes related to Stone's available-for-sale securities? (Ignore taxes.)

E16 – 13

Mark-to-market for available-for-sale securities

ADAPTED

Gehl Company founded on January 1, 2005 had the following short-term investments in securities at the end of 2005 and 2006 (all were held in the "trading" portfolio):

Equity Security	Cost	2006 Market Value
A	$ 96,000	$ 94,000
B	184,000	162,000
C	126,000	136,000

Required:

If the company recorded a $4,000 debit to its "Market adjustment—trading securities" account at the end of 2006 as its mark-to-market adjustment, what must have been the unrealized gain or loss recorded at the end of 2005?

E16 – 14

Mark-to-market for trading securities

Required:

1. An entity is generally considered to be a VIE subject to consolidation by the sponsoring entity if outside third-party equity is less than what percentage of the market value of the VIE's assets?
2. When two or more corporations establish an entity that is deemed to be a VIE subject to consolidation, what is the guiding principle used to determine which corporation should consolidate the SPE?

E16 – 15

Consolidation of variable interest entities

Scale Inc. is 100% owned by Pinto, Inc. The following information is from the 2005 income statements of Pinto and Scale:

	Pinto	Scale
Sales	$1,000,000	$600,000
Cost of goods sold	600,000	540,000
Gross profit	400,000	60,000
Depreciation expense	60,000	15,000
Other expenses	130,000	30,000
Income from operations	210,000	15,000
Gain on sale of equipment to Scale	16,000	0
Income before income taxes	$ 226,000	$ 15,000

E16 – 16

Elimination of intercompany profit

Additional Information:

1. Sales revenue reported by Pinto includes $200,000 of intercompany sales to Scale. Three-fourths of this inventory was sold by Scale to outside customers by the end of 2005. Pinto sells to Scale on terms similar to its outside customers.
2. Scale purchased equipment from Pinto for $60,000 on January 1, 2005. The equipment is depreciated using the straight-line method over eight years and no residual value is assumed.

Required:

1. How much intercompany profit should be eliminated from Scale's inventory when preparing 2005 consolidated financial statements?
2. What amount of depreciation expense should be reported in the 2005 consolidated income statement?

E16 – 17

Elimination of intercompany inventory transactions

Crest Corp. recorded the following transactions with its investees during 2005:

1. Sold inventory to Drape Inc. for $75,000. The inventory had originally cost Crest $65,000. Drape had one-fourth of this inventory on hand at year-end. Crest owns 15% of Drape's common stock and does not exert significant influence over Drape's operations.
2. Purchased $200,000 of inventory from Stream Corp., a wholly owned subsidiary. Stream's gross profit on the sale was $40,000. Crest had $20,000 of this inventory remaining on December 31, 2005.

Required:

What amount of inventory will be eliminated when preparing Crest's December 31, 2005 consolidated balance sheet?

E16 – 18

Consolidated sales and cost of goods sold with intercompany transactions

Pate Corp. owns 80% of Strange Inc.'s common stock. During 2005, Pate sold Strange inventory for $600,000 on the same terms as sales made to outside customers. Strange sold the entire inventory purchased from Pate by the end of 2005. Pate and Strange report the following for 2005:

	Pate	Strange
Sales	$2,700,000	$1,600,000
Cost of sales	1,800,000	900,000
Gross profit	$ 900,000	$ 700,000

Required:

1. What amount should Pate report as sales revenue in its 2005 consolidated income statement?
2. What amount should Pate report as cost of sales in its 2005 consolidated income statement?

E16 – 19

Elimination of intercompany sales and profits

The following information is derived from the separate and consolidated financial statements of Pyle Inc. and its subsidiary, Stek Corp., at December 31, 2005:

	Pyle	Stek	Consolidated (after eliminations)
Balance sheet accounts:			
Accounts receivable	$ 26,000	$ 17,000	$ 32,000
Inventory	45,000	15,000	55,000
Income statement accounts:			
Revenues	$330,000	$170,000	$460,000
Cost of goods sold	190,000	100,000	255,000
Gross profit	$140,000	$ 70,000	$205,000

Additional Information:

There were intercompany inventory sales from Pyle to Stek during 2005. Stek had not paid Pyle for all of these sales by the end of 2005.

Required:

1. What amount of unrealized intercompany profit was eliminated when preparing consolidated financial statements?
2. What was the total amount of intercompany inventory sales made from Pyle to Stek during 2005?
3. What amount did Stek owe to Pyle at December 31, 2005?

E16 – 20

Purchase versus pooling

CMA
ADAPTED

On July 1, 2000 Pushway Corporation issued 200,000 shares of $5 par value common stock in exchange for all of Stroker Company's common stock. This stock had a fair market value that was $200,000 in excess of the stockholders' equity of Stroker Company on the date of exchange. This difference was attributed to the fact that the fair value of Stroker Company's equipment was higher than book value. The equipment has an estimated remaining life of 10 years. Pushway Corporation and Stroker Company reported depreciation expense in 2000 of $400,000 and $100,000, respectively, before consolidation and before any adjustment for the exchange. For financial reporting purposes, both companies use a calendar year and the straight-line depreciation method, with depreciation calculated on a monthly basis beginning with the month of acquisition.

Required:

1. Assume the business combination is appropriately accounted for as a purchase. Consolidated depreciation expense reported in 2000 would be how much?
2. Assume the business combination is appropriately accounted for as a pooling of interests. Consolidated depreciation expense reported in 2000 would be how much?

A wholly owned subsidiary of Ward, Inc. has certain expense accounts for the year ended December 31, 2005, stated in local currency units (LCU) as follows:

	LCU
Depreciation of equipment (related assets were purchased January 1, 2003)	120,000
Provision for doubtful accounts	80,000
Rent	200,000

The exchange rates at various dates are as follows:

	Dollar Equivalent of LCU
12/31/05	$0.40
Average for year ended 12/31/05	0.44
1/1/03	0.50

Assume that the LCU is the subsidiary's functional currency and that the charges to the expense accounts occurred approximately evenly during the year.

Required:

What total dollar amount should be included in Ward's 2005 consolidated income statement to reflect these expenses?

E16 – 21

Foreign currency translation

Lindy, a calendar-year U.S. corporation, bought inventory items from a supplier in Germany on November 5, 2005 for 100,000 marks, when the spot rate was $0.4295. At Lindy's December 31, 2005 year-end, the spot rate was $0.4245. On January 15, 2006 Lindy bought 100,000 marks at the spot rate of $0.4345 and paid the invoice.

Required:

How much foreign exchange gain or (loss) should Lindy report in its income statements for 2005 and 2006?

E16 – 22

Transaction foreign exchange gain/loss

AICPA
ADAPTED

Scroll, Inc., a wholly owned subsidiary of Pirn, Inc., began operations on January 1, 2002. The following information is from the condensed 2005 income statements of Pirn and Scroll:

	Pirn	Scroll
Sales to Scroll	$100,000	$ —
Sales to others	400,000	300,000
	500,000	300,000
Cost of goods sold		
Acquired from Pirn	—	(80,000)
Acquired from others	(350,000)	(190,000)
Gross profit	150,000	30,000
Depreciation	(40,000)	(10,000)
Other expenses	(60,000)	(15,000)
Income from operations	50,000	5,000
Gain on sale of equipment to Scroll	12,000	—
Income before income taxes	$ 62,000	$ 5,000

E16 – 23

Intercompany eliminations on consolidated statements

Additional Information:

- Sales by Pirn to Scroll are made on the same terms as those made to third parties.
- Equipment purchased by Scroll from Pirn for $36,000 on January 1, 2005 is depreciated using the straight-line method over four years.

Required:

1. In Pirn's December 31, 2005 consolidated worksheet, how much intercompany profit should be eliminated from Scroll's inventory?
2. What amount should be reported as depreciation expense in Pirn's 2005 consolidated income statement?

PROBLEMS/DISCUSSION QUESTIONS

P16 – 1

Intercorporate investments— Balance sheet

The balance sheets of Herb Corporation and Aside Chemical Company at December 31, 2004 were as follows:

($ in thousands)	Herb	Aside
Assets	$850	$400
Liabilities	$275	$100
Common stock (par value, $1)	200	100
Other equity (paid-in capital plus retained earnings)	375	200
	$850	$400

Required:

1. Assume that on January 1, 2005 Herb Corporation sold an additional 100,000 shares of its stock to its existing shareholders for $425,000. The entire proceeds of the stock issue were then used to buy all the shares of Aside. Prepare a consolidated balance sheet after the acquisition.
2. Assume the preceding facts except that Herb acquired only 80% of the stock for a cash payment of $425,000. How would the consolidated balance sheet differ from that in requirement 1?
3. Now assume a slightly altered set of initial conditions. While the respective December 31, 2004 balance sheets for the two companies were identical to those shown above, the 100,000 shares of Herb stock were not sold to existing Herb Corporation shareholders. Instead, assume that these 100,000 shares (which had a January 1, 2005 market value of $425,000) were issued to Aside's shareholders in exchange for all 100,000 shares of Aside's stock. Prepare a consolidated balance sheet after the acquisition.

P16 – 2

Equity method

On January 1, 2005 the Figland Company purchased for cash 40% of the 300,000 shares of voting common stock of the Irene Company for $1,800,000. At the time, 40% of the book value of the underlying equity in the net assets of Irene was $1,400,000; $50,000 of the excess was attributed to the excess of fair market value over book value of inventory, which Irene accounts for using the first-in, first-out (FIFO) inventory method; and $150,000 is attributed to undervaluation of depreciable assets with an average remaining life of 10 years. The remainder is attributed to implicit goodwill.

As a result of this transaction, Figland has the ability to exercise significant influence over the operating and financial policies of Irene. Irene's net income for the year ended December 31, 2005 was $600,000. During 2005 Irene paid $325,000 in dividends to its stockholders.

Required:

1. How much income would Figland report on its 2005 income statement for its investment in Irene?
2. What would be the balance in the "Investment in Irene Company" account on December 31, 2005?

P16 – 3

Mark-to-market accounting

Consider the following information:

1. Giant Motors purchases 5% of Crane Tire Company's common stock (one of its suppliers) for $30 million on January 1, 2005.
2. Crane Tire Company earned $25 million in net income for 2005.
3. Crane Tire Company pays total dividends of $15 million during 2005.
4. The market value of Giant Motors' 5% investment in Crane Tire is $25 million on December 31, 2005.

Required:

1. Assume the investment in Crane Tire is considered a trading security by Giant Motors management. At what amount should Giant Motors report its investment in Crane Tire Company in its 2005 balance sheet?

2. How would Giant Motors' investment in Crane Tire Company affect its 2005 income statement?
3. In contrast to requirement 1, assume that the investment in Crane Tire is considered as an available-for-sale security by Giant Motors' management. At what amount should Giant Motors report its investment in Crane Tire Company in its 2005 balance sheet?
4. Using the facts presented in requirement 3, determine how, if at all, Giant Motors' investment in Crane Tire Company would affect its 2005 income statement.

Second National Insurance Company provided the information shown below for its trading securities portfolio:

P16 – 4

Mark-to-market for trading securities

Security	Date	Acquisition Cost	Market Values 12/31/04	12/31/05	12/31/06
Company A Common	1/15/04	$50,000	$60,000	$55,000	$58,000
Company B Common	6/30/04	30,000	25,000	13,000[1]	10,000
Company C Preferred	2/1/05	20,000	—	25,000	18,000
Company D Warrants	5/1/06	10,000	—	—	12,000

[1] Second National sold 50% of the Company B common shares for $14,000 on July 1, 2005. Market values for December 31, 2005 and December 31, 2006 are for the Company B shares remaining in the trading portfolio.

Required:

1. Provide the journal entries to record the mark-to-market adjustment on December 31, 2004. Assume Second National uses an account entitled "Market adjustment—trading securities" to adjust the cost of the trading portfolio to year-end market values. Show supporting calculations in good form.
2. Provide the entry to record the sale of Company B common shares on July 1, 2005. Assume the last market adjustment for these shares was on December 31, 2004.
3. Provide the journal entry and supporting calculations for the mark-to-market adjustment on December 31, 2005.
4. Provide the journal entry and mark-to-market adjustment on December 31, 2006.
5. What would the entry to record the sale of Company B common shares on July 1, 2005 have been if this security had been considered an available-for-sale security? Ignore tax effects.

At December 31, 2004 Poe Corporation properly reported the following available-for-sale securities. All these securities were acquired in 2004.

P16 – 5

Comprehensive intercorporate investments problem

	Cost	Fair Value
Axe Corporation, 1,000 shares, $2.40 convertible preferred stock	$ 40,000	$ 42,000
Purl, Inc., 6,000 shares of common stock	60,000	66,000
Day Company, 2,000 shares of common stock	55,000	40,000
Total available-for-sale securities	$155,000	$148,000

On January 2, 2005 Poe purchased 100,000 shares of Scott Corporation common stock for $1,700,000, representing 30% of Scott's outstanding common stock and an underlying equity of $1,400,000 in Scott's net assets on that date. The excess of cost over Poe's equity in the book value of Scott's net assets at acquisition is attributed to depreciable assets to be depreciated over a 40-year period with zero salvage value. As a result of Poe's 30% ownership of Scott, Poe has the ability to exercise significant influence over Scott's financial and operating policies.

During 2005 Poe disposed of the following securities:

- January 18—sold 2,500 shares of Purl for $13 per share.
- June 1—sold 500 shares of Day for $21 per share.

The following 2005 dividend information pertains to stock owned by Poe:

- April 5 and October 5—Axe paid dividends of $1.20 per share on its $2.40 preferred stock to stockholders of record on March 9 and September 9, respectively.
- June 30—Purl paid a $1.00 per share dividend on its common stock.
- March 1, June 1, September 1, and December 1—Scott paid quarterly dividends of $0.50 per share on each of these dates. Scott's net income for the year ended December 31, 2005 was $1,200,000.

At December 31, 2005 Poe's management intended to hold Scott's stock on a long-term basis, with the remaining investments considered available-for-sale securities. Market prices per share of these securities were as follows:

	Market Value at December 31, 2005
Axe Corporation—preferred	$56
Purl, Inc.—common	11
Day Company—common	22
Scott Corporation—common	16

Required:

1. Determine the unrealized gain or loss on Poe's available-for-sale securities for 2004, and provide the journal entry to record the mark-to-market adjustment on December 31, 2004. Ignore tax effects.
2. Prepare the journal entries to record the realized gains or losses on Poe's sales of securities for 2005.
3. Prepare the entries to record Poe's receipt of dividends on all securities in 2005 and all entries related to Poe's equity investment in Scott Corporation.
4. Determine the unrealized gain or loss on Poe's available-for-sale securities for 2005 and provide the journal entry to record the mark-to-market adjustment on December 31, 2005. Ignore tax effects.

P16 – 6

Intercorporate investments— Equity method

Consider the following sequence of events:

- On January 1, 2005 Big Time Motors purchases 25% of Cooper Tire Company's common stock (one of its suppliers) for $150 million. The book value of Cooper Tire Company's net assets on this date was $400 million.*
- Cooper Tire Company earned $25 million in net income for 2005.
- Cooper Tire Company declares and pays total dividends of $15 million during 2005.
- On January 1, 2006 Big Time Motors purchases an additional 15% of Cooper Tire Company common stock for $100 million.*
- Cooper Tire Company had a net loss of $40 million for 2006.
- Cooper Tire Company pays total dividends of $18 million during 2006.

*Assume cost in excess of book value is attributable to goodwill.

Required:

1. What amount of investment income should Big Time Motors report on its 2005 income statement as a result of its investment in Cooper Tire? At what amount would Big Time Motors report its investment in Cooper Tire Company in its December 31, 2005 balance sheet?
2. At what amount should Big Time Motors report its investment in Cooper Tire Company in its December 31, 2006 balance sheet?

P16 – 7

Purchase method with goodwill

On January 1, 2005 Delta Inc. acquired all the outstanding stock of Sigma Company for $80,000 cash. Following are the balance sheets for Delta and Sigma immediately before the acquisition, as well as fair market value information regarding Sigma Company:

	Delta Inc.	Sigma Company Book Value	Sigma Company Fair Value
Assets			
Cash	$ 91,000	$ 8,000	$ 8,000
Accounts receivable	19,000	15,000	9,000
Inventory	47,000	31,000	43,000
Land	12,000	5,000	12,000
Plant and equipment, net	66,000	35,000	51,000
Total	$235,000	$94,000	$123,000
Liabilities and shareholders' equity			
Accounts payable	$ 52,000	$35,000	$ 35,000
Long-term debt	66,000	15,000	15,000
Common stock			
Delta—5,000 shares, $1.00 par	5,000	—	
Sigma—4,000 shares, $0.50 par	—	2,000	
Additional paid-in capital	30,000	12,000	
Retained earnings	82,000	30,000	
Total	$235,000	$94,000	

Required:

1. Give the journal entry Delta would make to record the acquisition of Sigma.
2. Calculate the amount of goodwill that Delta will record as a result of acquiring Sigma.
3. Provide the elimination entry Delta would make to prepare the consolidated balance sheet immediately after the acquisition.
4. Prepare Delta Inc.'s balance sheet immediately after its acquisition of Sigma Company.

On January 1, 2000 DGA, Inc. acquired all the outstanding stock of CLH Systems in exchange for DGA's common stock, which had a market value of $100,000. The acquisition is accounted for as a purchase. Below are the balance sheets for DGA and CLH Systems immediately before the acquisition, as well as fair market value information regarding CLH Systems:

P16 – 8

Purchase method versus pooling and effect on ratios

	DGA Inc.	CLH Systems Book Value	CLH Systems Fair Value
Assets			
Cash	$166,000	$ —	$ —
Accounts receivable	25,000	15,000	15,000
Inventory	49,500	13,000	13,000
Land	12,000	7,000	7,000
Plant and equipment, net	76,000	25,000	36,000
Patents	2,500	6,500	10,500
Total	$331,000	$66,500	$81,500
Liabilities and shareholders' equity			
Accounts payable	$ 64,000	$29,000	$29,000
Other liabilities	35,000	—	
Common stock, no par	80,000	5,000	
Retained earnings	152,000	32,500	
Total	$331,000	$66,500	

Required:

Student Note: This problem was set in 2000 when goodwill was still amortized under APB Opinion 17 and pooling-of-interest accounting was still permitted.

1. Give the journal entry DGA, Inc. would make to record the acquisition of CLH Systems.
2. Calculate the amount of goodwill that DGA, Inc. will record as a result of acquiring CLH Systems.
3. Provide the elimination entry DGA, Inc. would make to prepare the consolidated balance sheet immediately after the acquisition.
4. Prepare DGA, Inc.'s balance sheet immediately after its acquisition of CLH Systems.
5. Assume that DGA and CLH reported net income of $145,000 (before equity in CLH earnings) and $25,000, respectively in 2000. Also, consolidated total assets (before adjustments for goodwill amortization and stepped-up-basis depreciation) at December 31, 2000 were identical to the consolidated total assets at acquisition (determined in requirement 4).

   Goodwill is being amortized over 40 years in accordance with APB 17. Assume the remaining useful life for the Plant and Equipment and the Patents is five (5) years. Determine the following (ignore income taxes):
   - Consolidated net income for the year ended December 31, 2000.
   - ROA at December 31, 2000 (Net Income/Total assets).
6. Under *SFAS No. 142*, purchased goodwill is no longer amortized, but is carried on the balance sheet at its historical value unless impaired. How would your answer to requirement 5 change under the following conditions:
   - No impairment of goodwill.
   - 90% of the goodwill was impaired.
7. Repeat requirements 1, 2, 3, 4, and 5 assuming all of the same facts above except that DGA, Inc. acquired CLH Systems by issuing 2,000 shares of its no par common stock and accounted for the transaction as a pooling of interests. At that time DGA's shares were trading for $50.00 per share.

P16 – 9

Consolidation at acquisition

Prince Corp. and Sprite Corp. reported the following balance sheets at January 1, 2005:

	Prince	Sprite
Current assets	$30,000	$15,000
Noncurrent assets	55,000	25,000
Total assets	$85,000	$40,000
Current liabilities	$20,000	$10,000
Long-term debt	20,000	5,000
Stockholders' equity	45,000	25,000
Total liabilities and stockholders' equity	$85,000	$40,000

On January 2, 2005, Prince issued $30,000 in debt and used the proceeds to purchase 95% of Sprite's common stock. The excess of the purchase price over Sprite's book value of net assets was allocated 60% to inventory and 40% to goodwill.

Required:

What will Prince report on its January 2, 2005 consolidated balance sheet for the following items?
1. Current assets
2. Noncurrent assets
3. Current liabilities
4. Noncurrent liabilities (include minority interests)
5. Stockholders' equity

P16 – 10

Consolidated account balances with intercompany transactions

The following information is reported in the separate and consolidated balance sheets and income statements of Palace Corp. and its subsidiary, Show Corp., at December 31, 2005:

	Palace	Show	Consolidated (after eliminations)
Balance sheet accounts:			
Accounts receivable	$ 58,000	$ 36,000	$ 80,000
Inventory	52,000	40,000	80,000
Investment in Show	120,000	—	—
Goodwill	—	—	30,000
Minority interest	—	—	5,000
Stockholders' equity	308,000	100,000	308,000
Income statement accounts:			
Revenues	$350,000	$240,000	$510,000
Cost of goods sold	245,000	200,000	377,000
Gross profit	105,000	40,000	133,000
Equity in earnings of Show	16,000	—	—
Net income	70,000	20,000	80,000

Additional Information:

During 2005, Palace sold goods to Show at the same markup on cost that Palace uses for all sales. At December 31, 2005, Show had not paid for all of these goods and still held 50% of them in inventory.

Required:

1. What was the amount of intercompany sales from Palace to Show during 2005?
2. What was the carrying amount of the inventory that Show purchased from Palace on the December 31, 2005 consolidated balance sheet?
3. How much did Show owe to Palace for intercompany sales at December 31, 2005?
4. What percent of Show's stock is owned by Palace?

P16 – 11

Consolidation with intercompany sales

On October 1, 2005, Pacer Corp. acquired all of Sunny Corp.'s outstanding stock for cash. The fair value of Sunny's net assets was less than the purchase price but greater than the net carrying amount. During October 2005, Pacer sold goods to Sunny at a profit. At December 31, 2005, 40% of these goods remained in Sunny's inventory.

Required:

1. Specify reasons for preparing consolidated financial statements that present operating results, cash flows, and financial position as if a parent company and its subsidiaries were a single entity.
2. How will the acquisition affect Pacer's consolidated balance sheet at October 1, 2005?
3. What eliminations are required for the intercompany sales when preparing consolidated financial statements at December 31, 2005?
4. What is the effect on Pacer's separate balance sheet immediately after the October 1, 2005 acquisition?

The following are the balance sheets for Plate and Salad immediately prior to Plate's September 1, 2005 acquisition of Salad:

P16 – 12

Elimination entries and consolidated balance sheet

	Plate	Salad
Assets		
Cash	$500,000	$100,000
Accounts receivable	50,000	20,000
Inventory	100,000	30,000
Land	50,000	10,000
Bldg. & equip., net	200,000	100,000
Total	$900,000	$260,000
Liabilities & equity		
Accounts payable	$ 40,000	$ 80,000
Bonds payable	200,000	0
Common stock & PIC	300,000	100,000
Retained earnings	360,000	80,000
Total	$900,000	$260,000

Consider the following cases:

Case 1:
Plate buys 100% of Salad's common stock for $180,000 cash. The fair value of Salad's assets and liabilities equal their book value.

Case 2:
Plate buys 100% of Salad's common stock for $210,000 cash. The fair value of Salad's land is $20,000, the fair value of Salad's buildings and equipment is $110,000 and all other fair values equal book values.

Required:

1. Prepare the September 1, 2005 journal entry on Plate's books to record the acquisition of Salad.
2. Prepare the elimination entries needed to prepare a consolidated balance sheet immediately after the acquisition.
3. Prepare the consolidated balance sheet immediately after the acquisition.

On January 1, 2005, Pluto Company purchased all of Saturn Company's common stock for $1,000,000 cash. On that date Saturn Company had retained earnings of $200,000 and common stock of $600,000. The book values of Saturn's assets and liabilities were equal to fair values except for the following:

P16 – 13

Elimination entries and accounting for goodwill

	Book Value	Fair Value
Equipment (net)	$200,000	$220,000
Land	250,000	300,000

Additional Information:

1. The equipment had an estimated remaining useful life of 5 years at acquisition.
2. Goodwill was not impaired in 2005, but was impaired by $25,000 in 2006.
3. Reported income for Pluto (excluding equity income from Saturn's earnings) and Saturn are:

	Pluto	Saturn
Year 2005	$500,000	$200,000
Year 2006	$350,000	$100,000

Required:

1. Prepare the January 1, 2005 journal entry on Pluto's books to record the acquisition of Saturn.
2. Prepare the elimination entries needed to prepare a consolidated balance sheet immediately after acquisition.
3. Calculate consolidated income for 2005 and 2006.
4. How would your answers to requirement 3 change under pre-*SFAS No. 142* amortization rules for goodwill?

   (Assume a 40-year amortization period.)

P16 – 14

Business acquisitions
and ratio analysis

Company B, an auto parts company, has made several acquisitions with newly issued stock over the past five years, using the purchase method of accounting. In each case the purchase price exceeded the fair value of the net assets of the acquired company. AutoParts Heaven, a competitor, has made no acquisitions. Wholesale prices of auto parts have been rising over the last five years. Both Company B and AutoParts Heaven account for inventories using the FIFO method.

Required:

1. Briefly explain why Company B's acquisition history makes it difficult to analyze the *trend* of Company B's financial data and ratios.
2. Briefly explain why Company B's acquisition history makes it difficult to compare the *ratios* of Company B with those for AutoParts Heaven.
3. For each of the following financial measures, compare the effect (higher, lower, or no effect) of the purchase method on the financial measure of Company B to the effect of the pooling-of-interests method. Briefly explain why each effect occurs:

   a. Gross profit margin percentage
   b. Long-term debt-to-equity ratio
   c. Pre-tax earnings

P16 – 15

Translation effect on ratios

AutoParts Heaven is a U.S. company whose operations include a large, 100% owned foreign subsidiary. The subsidiary's functional currency is the dollar. The local currency in the country where the foreign subsidiary operates is appreciating against the U.S. dollar. The subsidiary accounts for inventories using the FIFO method.

Required:

Compare each of the following ratios for the foreign subsidiary *in its functional currency after translation* to the same ratios *in the local currency before translation*. Briefly explain why each ratio differs.

1. Gross profit margin percentage
2. Operating profit margin
3. Net profit margin

P16 – 16

Business acquisitions
and ratio analysis

The balance sheets of ABD, Inc. and C Corporation on December 31, 2005 are given next. (Unless otherwise noted, all amounts are in millions.)

	ABD, Inc.	C Corporation
Assets		
Cash	$200	$ —
Accounts receivable	—	600
Inventory	300	—
Current assets	500	600
Plant and equipment, net	—	800
Total	$500	$1,400
Liabilities and shareholders' equity		
Accounts payable	$250	$ —
Long-term debt	—	1,050
Total liabilities	$250	$1,050
Common stock ($1 par per share)	100	200
Additional paid-in capital	50	—
Retained earnings	100	150
Total	$500	$1,400

1. Immediately following the preparation of the preceding balance sheets, ABD issues 250 shares of common stock and receives $350 in cash proceeds. ABD immediately uses these cash proceeds to purchase 100% of the common stock of C Corporation. Provide the balance sheet for ABD, Inc. after these two transactions. (*Note:* On its own financial statements, ABD accounts for its investment in C Corporation using the equity method.)

2. Provide the *consolidated* balance sheet that ABD, Inc. would report immediately following the investment in C Corporation. How do these two methods of reporting the acquisition, in requirements 1 and 2, differ in their description of what ABD bought? What are some key ratios that are affected by the accounting method?

3. For this question only, suppose that C Corporation's "Plant and equipment, net" account had been $5,800 and its "Long-term debt" account had been $6,050. How would your answers to requirements 1 and 2 have changed? (A qualitative answer, rather than a whole balance sheet, will do here.)

4. For this question only, suppose that at the time of the acquisition, ABD owed $20 to C Corporation for services it had provided in the preceding year. How would your answer to requirement 2 change? (Again, a qualitative answer will do.)

5. For this question, suppose that ABD, Inc. issued 250 shares of common stock, received $400 in proceeds, and used the entire proceeds to purchase 100% of the outstanding common shares of C Corporation. Provide the *consolidated* balance sheet that ABD, Inc. would report immediately following the investment in C Corporation.

6. Start with the information in requirement 5. Now suppose that ABD only acquired 80% of the outstanding common stock of C Corporation. Provide the *consolidated* balance sheet that ABD, Inc. would report immediately following the investment in C Corporation.

7. Start with the information in requirement 5. Now suppose that ABD *exchanged* its 250 common shares (which had a market value of $400) for the 200 outstanding common shares of C Corporation. What method would ABD use to account for the acquisition? Provide the *consolidated* balance sheet that ABD, Inc. would report immediately following the investment in C Corporation. Why might the management of ABD prefer to structure the acquisition and consolidation in this fashion?

CASES

C16 – 1

AOL Time Warner: Goodwill Impairment

On January 11, 2001, America Online Inc. acquired Time Warner Inc. for approximately $147 billion. The merged company was named AOL Time Warner Inc. Subsequent to acquisition, the recorded goodwill became significantly impaired and required adjustment in the 2002 fiscal year. AOL Time Warner's condensed income statements and balance sheets are presented, along with footnote disclosures related to the acquisition and goodwill impairment.

AOL Time Warner Inc.

Consolidated Statement of Operations Years Ended December 31,

($ in millions)	2002	2001	2000
Revenues	$40,961	$37,166	$7,605
Cost of revenues	(24,315)	(20,533)	(3,866)
Selling, general, and administrative	(9,916)	(9,079)	(1,864)
Amortization of goodwill and other intangibles	(732)	(7,186)	(99)
Impairment of goodwill and other intangibles	(45,538)	—	—
Merger and restructuring costs	(335)	(250)	(10)
Operating income (loss)	(39,875)	118	1,766
Other income (expense)	(4,559)	(4,874)	67
Income tax expense	(140)	(139)	(712)
Income before discontinued operations and cumulative effect of accounting change	(44,574)	(4,895)	1,121
Discontinued operation	113	(39)	—
Cumulative effect of accounting change	(54,235)	—	—
Net income (loss)	$(98,696)	$(4,934)	$1,121

(*continued on next page*)

AOL Time Warner Inc. (*continued*)

Consolidated Balance Sheet December 31,

($ in millions)	2002	2001
Assets		
Total current assets	$ 11,155	$ 10,251
Noncurrent inventories and film costs	3,351	3,490
Investments, including available-for-sale securities	5,138	6,886
Property, plant and equipment	12,150	12,669
Intangible assets subject to amortization	7,061	7,289
Intangible assets not subject to amortization	37,145	37,708
Goodwill	36,986	127,420
Other assets	2,464	2,791
Total assets	$115,450	$208,504
Liabilities and Shareholders' Equity		
Total current liabilities	$ 13,395	$ 12,976
Total long-term liabilities	49,238	43,501
Total liabilities	62,633	56,477
Contributed capital	155,179	155,216
Accumulated other comprehensive income (loss)	(428)	49
Retained earnings (loss)	(101,934)	(3,238)
Total shareholders' equity	52,817	152,027
Total liabilities and shareholders' equity	$115,450	$208,504

NOTE 1. SUMMARY OF SIGNIFICANT ACCOUNTING POLICIES

The Merger was accounted for by AOL Time Warner as an acquisition of Time Warner under the purchase method of accounting for business combinations. The financial results for Time Warner have been included in AOL Time Warner's results since January 1, 2001, as permitted under generally accepted accounting principles. Under the purchase method of accounting, the cost of approximately $147 billion to acquire Time Warner, including transaction costs, was allocated to its underlying net assets, based on their respective estimated fair values. The excess of the purchase price over the estimated fair values of the net assets acquired was recorded as goodwill. This allocation includes intangible assets, such as film and television libraries, music catalogues and copyrights, cable television and sports franchises, and brands and trademarks.

NOTE 2. GOODWILL AND INTANGIBLE ASSETS

As discussed in Note 1, in January 2002, AOL Time Warner adopted FAS 142, which requires companies to stop amortizing goodwill and certain intangible assets with an indefinite useful life. Instead, FAS 142 requires that goodwill and intangible assets deemed to have an indefinite useful life be reviewed for impairment upon adoption of FAS 142 (January 1, 2002) and annually thereafter.

Under FAS 142, goodwill impairment is deemed to exist if the net book value of a reporting unit exceeds its estimated fair value. The Company's reporting units are generally consistent with the operating segments underlying the segments identified in Note 16 Segment Information. This methodology differs from AOL Time Warner's previous policy, as provided under accounting standards existing at that time, of using undiscounted cash flows on an enterprise-wide basis to determine if goodwill was recoverable.

Upon adoption of FAS 142 in the first quarter of 2002, AOL Time Warner recorded a noncash charge of $54.199 billion to reduce the carrying value of goodwill. Such charge is nonoperational in nature and is reflected as a cumulative effect of accounting change in the accompanying consolidated statement of operations. In calculating the impairment charge, the fair value of the impaired reporting units underlying the segments were estimated using either a discounted cash flow methodology, market comparisons, recent comparable transactions or a combination thereof.

The $54.199 billion goodwill impairment is associated entirely with goodwill resulting from the Merger. The amount of the impairment primarily reflects the decline in the Company's stock price since the Merger was announced and valued for accounting purposes in January of 2000. Prior to performing the review for impairment, FAS 142 required that all goodwill deemed to be related to the entity as a whole be assigned to all of the Company's reporting units, including the reporting units of the acquirer. This differs from the previous accounting rules where goodwill was assigned only to the businesses of the company acquired. As a result, a portion of the goodwill generated in the Merger has been reallocated to the AOL segment.

During the fourth quarter of 2002, the Company performed its annual impairment review for goodwill and other intangible assets and recorded an additional charge of $45.538 billion, which is recorded as a component of operating income in the accompanying consolidated statement of operations. The $45.538 billion is reflective of the overall decline in market values and includes charges to reduce the carrying value of goodwill at the AOL segment ($33.489 billion), Cable segment ($10.550 billion) and Music segment ($646 million), as well as a charge to reduce the carrying value of brands and trademarks at the Music segment ($853 million).

The $33.489 billion charge at the AOL segment reflects the AOL segment's lower than expected performance, including the continued decline in the online advertising market. The $10.550 billion charge at the Cable segment reflects current market conditions in the cable television industry, as evidenced by the decline in the stock prices of comparable cable television companies. The $1.499 billion charge at the Music segment reflects declining valuations in the music industry, including the negative effect of piracy.

A summary of changes in the Company's goodwill during the year ended December 31, 2002, and total assets at December 31, 2002, by business segment is as follows (millions):

Business Segment	January 1, 2002 Balance	Acquisitions & Adjustments	Cumulative Effect of Accounting Change	4th Quarter Impairment	December 31, 2002 Balance
AOL	$ 27,729	$8,536	$ —	$(33,489)	$ 2,776
Cable	33,259	267	(22,976)	(10,550)	—
Filmed Entertainment	9,110	(71)	(4,091)	—	4,948
Networks	33,562	(4)	(13,077)	—	20,481
Music	5,477	(35)	(4,796)	(646)	—
Publishing	18,283	(243)	(9,259)	—	8,781
Corporate	—	—	—	—	—
Total	$127,420	$8,450	$(54,199)	$(44,685)	$36,986

The impairment charges are non-cash in nature and do not affect the Company's liquidity or result in the non-compliance with respect to any debt covenants, including the covenant to maintain at least $50 billion of GAAP net worth contained in the Company's main revolving credit agreements.

Required:

1. Based on the information provided, what total amount of goodwill impairment was recorded in 2002? How is the impairment presented in the income statement, and why is it reported in this manner?
2. According to the footnote disclosure, goodwill impairments were recorded for each of the operating segments. Why does AOL Time Warner conduct impairment tests at the segment level? Explain the importance to financial statement users of reporting goodwill impairments by operating segments.
3. What does AOL Time Warner disclose about the effect of this goodwill impairment on compliance with its debt covenants? Does this disclosure raise any questions about the amount of the goodwill impairment recorded in 2002?

C16 – 2

Shopko: Business acquisitions and analysis of sales growth

The disclosure rules for business combinations complicate financial analysis. Trend analysis becomes difficult because comparative financial statements are not retroactively adjusted to include data for the acquired company for periods prior to the acquisition.

For example, consider Shopko's acquisition of Pamida on July 6, 1999. Excerpts from Shopko's 1999 Annual Report highlight the revenue and earnings growth achieved in that year. In the president's letter, William Podany noted the following:

"For more than ten consecutive years we have achieved new records for revenues and this year we are pleased to report another year of record earnings."

The Management's Discussion and Analysis (MD&A) section began with the following statement:

"Consolidated net sales for fiscal 1999 (52 weeks) increased $939.5 million or 31.8% over fiscal 1998 weeks (52 weeks) to $3,898.1 million."

The details of the acquisition were disclosed in the following note in Shopko's 1999 Annual Report:

On July 6, 1999, the Company acquired all of the outstanding voting and nonvoting common stock of Pamida for $94.0 million in cash, $285.8 million in assumed debt and $138.6 million in assumed trade and other accrued liabilities. Pamida is a retail chain headquartered in Omaha, Nebraska, operating Pamida retail stores in 15 Midwest, North Central and Rocky Mountain states. In connection with the Pamida acquisition, the Company incurred special charges of $8.1 million for employee retention programs, elimination of administrative functions and various integration initiatives. The allocation of the purchase price of Pamida was based on estimated fair values at the date of acquisition.

This acquisition was accounted for under the purchase method of accounting and the allocation of the purchase price was based on fair values at the date of acquisition. Goodwill associated with the Pamida acquisition of approximately $186.6 million is being amortized on a straight-line basis over 40 years. The results of operations since the dates of acquisition have been included in the consolidated statements of earnings.

The following presents selected unaudited pro forma consolidated statement of earnings information that has been prepared assuming the Pamida acquisition occurred on January 31, 1999 and February 1, 1998, respectively:

	Fiscal Years Ended	
($ in thousands, except per share data—unaudited)	January 29 2000	January 30 1999
Net sales	$4,181,567	$3,630,951
Earnings before extraordinary item	101,190	56,678
Diluted earnings per share before extraordinary item	3.54	2.14

Shopko's consolidated statements of earnings for the years ended January 29, 2000 and January 30, 1999 follow:

Consolidated Statement of Earnings

	Fiscal Years Ended	
($ in thousands)	January 29 2000	January 30 1999
Revenues:		
Net sales	$3,898,090	$2,958,557
Licensed department rentals and other income	13,856	12,325
	3,911,946	2,970,882

($ in thousands)	Fiscal Years Ended	
	January 29 2000	January 30 1999
Costs and Expenses:		
Cost of sales	3,047,930	2,296,085
Selling, general and administrative expenses	601,157	471,546
Special charges	8,068	5,723
Depreciation and amortization expenses	84,438	67,590
	3,741,593	2,840,944
Income from operations	170,353	129,938
Interest expense—net	(46,894)	(38,311)
Gain on sale of ProVantage stock	56,760	—
Earnings before income taxes, minority interest and extraordinary item	180,219	91,627
Provision for income taxes	71,800	35,991
Earnings before minority interest and extraordinary item	108,419	55,636
Minority interest	(2,463)	—
Earnings before extraordinary item	105,956	55,636
Extraordinary (loss) on retirement of debt, net of income taxes of $2,443	(3,776)	—
Net earnings	$ 102,180	$ 55,636

Required:

1. How should a financial statement user interpret the reference to 31.8% sales growth in the MD&A section?

2. Suppose you are asked to prepare a sales forecast for the year ended February 3, 2001. Based on the information shown above, what is the best estimate of Shopko's sustainable growth in sales between the years ended January 30, 1999 and January 29, 2000? Explain your answer.

City Holding Company is a multi-bank holding company headquartered in West Virginia. The Company is comprised of multiple facilities located in West Virginia, Ohio, and California. The banking subsidiaries provide a full range of banking services and make investments in debt and equity securities under limitations and restrictions imposed by regulations of the Comptroller of the Currency.

Appearing on the following pages are the consolidated balance sheet and cash flow statement of City Holding Company, as well as selected footnote information pertaining to the available-for-sale securities for 2002 and 2001.

Using the information provided, determine responses to the questions that follow. Provide detailed support where appropriate.

Note: Unrealized gains (losses) on available-for-sale securities are not recognized for tax purposes until the securities are sold. Accordingly the tax effects of these unrealized gains (losses) are recognized as adjustments to the deferred tax liability (asset) accounts. Unrealized gains (losses) on available-for-sale securities are shown net of related tax effects as an adjustment to stockholders' equity. Assume the realized gains and losses reported in the footnote on page 940 all relate to available-for-sale securities. Transfers of securities from the held-to-maturity to available-for-sale category are recorded at market with the unrealized gain (loss) recorded in stockholders' equity.

C16 – 3

City Holding Company: Mark-to-market accounting for available-for-sale securities

STRETCH

Required:

1. Determine the net before-tax unrealized holding gain (loss) on available-for-sale securities that City Holding recognized in 2002. Assume no adjustments are made to the unrealized holding gain (loss) account when securities are sold.

2. Assuming a 35% tax rate, determine the deferred tax amounts related to the net unrealized holding gains (losses) that were recorded in 2002. Indicate whether the deferred tax amounts were a liability or an asset.

3. Give the entry that City Holding made at December 31, 2002 to record the unrealized gain (loss) on available-for-sale securities and to adjust the related stockholders' equity account.

4. Give the entry that City Holding made to record sales and calls on available-for-sale securities in 2002.

5. To the extent possible, explain the year-to-year change in the cost basis of the available-for-sale securities (from $377,013,000 on December 31, 2001 to $436,070,000 on December 31, 2002).

City Holding Company and Subsidiaries

Consolidated Balance Sheets

	December 31	
($ in thousands)	2002	2001
Assets		
Cash and due from banks	$ 109,318	$ 81,827
Federal funds sold	20,000	88,500
Cash and cash equivalents	129,318	170,327
Investment securities available for sale, at fair value	445,384	383,552
Investment securities held-to-maturity, at amortized cost		
(approximate fair value at December 31, 2002 – $74,415)	72,410	—
Total investment securities	517,794	383,552
Securities purchased under agreement to resell	27,202	—
Loans		
Gross loans	1,204,391	1,390,255
Allowance for loan losses	(28,504)	(48,635)
Net loans	1,175,887	1,341,620
Retained interests	80,923	71,271
Premises and equipment	37,802	43,178
Accrued interest receivable	11,265	12,422
Net deferred tax assets	35,895	47,443
Other assets	31,825	46,482
Total assets	$2,047,911	$2,116,295
Liabilities		
Deposits		
Noninterest-bearing	$ 281,290	$ 284,649
Interest-bearing	1,283,290	1,406,646
Total deposits	1,564,580	1,691,295
Federal funds purchased and securities sold under		
agreement to repurchase	146,937	127,204
Securities sold, not yet purchased	26,284	—
Long-term debt	25,000	29,328
Corporation-obligated mandatorily redeemable capital		
securities of subsidiary trusts holding solely subordinated		
debentures of City Holding Company	87,500	87,500
Other liabilities	32,217	34,619
Total liabilities	1,882,518	1,969,946
Preferred stock, par value $25 per share: 500,000 shares		
authorized; none issued	—	—
Common stock, par value $2.50 per share: authorized—		
50,000,000 shares authorized; 16,919,248 and 16,892,913 shares		
issued and outstanding at December 31, 2002 and 2001,		
respectively, including 261,563 and 4,979 shares in treasury	42,298	42,232
Capital surplus	59,029	59,174
Retained earnings	66,076	41,152
Cost of common stock in treasury	(6,426)	(136)
Accumulated other comprehensive income	4,416	3,927
Total stockholders' equity	165,393	146,349
Total liabilities and stockholders' equity	$2,047,911	$2,116,295

City Holding Company and Subsidiaries

Consolidated Statements of Cash Flows

	Years Ended December 31		
($ in thousands)	2002	2001	2000
Operating Activities			
Net income	$ 32,459	$(26,000)	$(38,373)
Cumulative effect of accounting change, net of tax	—	17,985	—
Net income (loss) before cumulative effect	32,459	(8,015)	(38,373)
Adjustments to reconcile net income (loss) to net cash provided by operating activities:			
Amortization and accretion, including write-off of goodwill	1,621	1,014	40,837
Loss on fixed asset disposals	—	3,951	4,805
Provision for depreciation	5,749	8,777	12,291
Provision for loan losses	1,800	32,178	25,480
Deferred income tax expense (benefit)	11,214	(8,463)	(22,802)
Net periodic pension benefit	(322)	(273)	(285)
Loans originated for sale	—	(93,875)	(219,748)
Purchases of loans held for sale	—	—	(16,065)
Proceeds from loans sold	2,929	112,146	324,354
Realized (gains) losses on loans sold	(445)	(3,039)	1,596
(Increase) decrease in retained interests	(9,652)	2,435	—
Realized investment securities (gains) losses	(1,459)	(2,382)	5,015
Decrease (increase) in accrued interest receivable	1,157	4,821	(93)
Decrease in other assets	4,111	5,785	25,572
Increase (decrease) in other liabilities	2,901	(12,661)	5,045
Net cash provided by (used in) operating activities	52,063	42,399	147,629
Investing Activities			
Proceeds from maturities and calls of securities held-to-maturity	4,994	—	—
Purchases of securities held-to-maturity	(40,783)	—	—
Proceeds from sales of securities available-for-sale	348,052	262,241	51,606
Proceeds from maturities and calls of securities available for sale	165,014	171,546	32,417
Purchases of securities available for sale	(608,709)	(431,113)	(80,640)
Net decrease (increase) in loans	147,121	400,832	(64,191)
Net cash paid in sales of subsidiaries, divisions, and branches	—	(37,869)	—
Realized gain on sales of subsidiaries, divisions, and branches	—	(8,036)	—
Purchases of premises and equipment	(373)	(3,511)	(97)
Net cash provided by (used in) investing activities	15,316	354,090	(60,905)
Financing Activities			
Net (decrease) increase in noninterest-bearing deposits	(3,359)	16,280	24,803
Net (decrease) increase in interest-bearing deposits	(123,356)	(234,508)	103,368
Net increase in short-term borrowings	19,733	(98,562)	(153,953)
Proceeds from long-term debt	10,000	—	—
Repayment of long-term debt	—	—	(85,000)
Purchases of treasury stock	(7,473)	—	—
Exercise of stock options	1,104	—	—
Cash dividends paid	(5,037)	—	(7,426)
Net cash provided by financing activities	(108,388)	(316,790)	(118,208)
Increase (decrease) in cash and cash equivalents	(41,009)	79,699	(31,484)
Cash and cash equivalents at beginning of year	170,327	90,628	122,112
Cash and cash equivalents at end of year	$129,318	$170,327	$ 90,628

NOTES TO CONSOLIDATED FINANCIAL STATEMENTS
CITY HOLDING COMPANY AND SUBSIDIARIES

Note Four: Investments

During 2002, the Company initiated an investment strategy to invest in trust preferred securities issued by other financial institutions. Only those securities issued by financial institutions that satisfy various asset size, profitability, equity-to-asset ratio, and certain other criteria, as pre-established by management, are evaluated for potential investment. Securities acquired were predominantly investment grade or were reviewed and approved for investment by the Company's executive loan committee. As of December 31, 2002, the Company had invested $40.75 million, classified as held-to-maturity, and $17.43 million, classified as available-for-sale, pursuant to this strategy.

Also during 2002, the Company transferred debt securities with an estimated fair value of $37.14 million and an amortized cost basis of $36.03 million from the available-for-sale classification to the held-to-maturity category. Transfers of debt securities into the held-to-maturity category from the available-for-sale classification are made at fair value at the date of transfer. The unrealized holding gain of $1.11 million at the date of transfer is retained in the other comprehensive income section of stockholders' equity and in the carrying value of the held-to-maturity securities. Such amounts are amortized over the remaining life of the security.

The aggregate carrying and approximate market values of securities follow. Fair values are based on quoted market prices, where available. If quoted market prices are not available, fair values are based on quoted market prices of comparable financial instruments.

Available-for-Sale Securities

	December 31, 2002			
($ in thousands)	Cost	Gross Unrealized Gains	Gross Unrealized Losses	Estimated Fair Value
U.S. Treasury securities and obligations of U.S. government corporations and agencies	$107,108	$5,607	$—	$112,715
Obligations of states and political subdivisions	22,687	804	—	23,491
Mortgage-backed securities	130,739	2,819	—	133,558
Other debt securities	51,591	101	(76)	51,616
Total debt securities	312,125	9,331	(76)	321,380
Equity securities	123,945	59	—	124,004
	$436,070	$9,390	$(76)	$445,384

Available-for-Sale Securities

	December 31, 2001			
($ in thousands)	Cost	Gross Unrealized Gains	Gross Unrealized Losses	Estimated Fair Value
U.S. Treasury securities and obligations of U.S. government corporations and agencies	$202,422	$6,751	$ (318)	$208,855
Obligations of states and political subdivisions	64,609	1,426	(135)	65,900
Mortgage-backed securities	90,969	90	(1,519)	89,540
Other debt securities	6,089	161	—	6,250
Total debt securities	364,089	8,428	(1,972)	370,545
Equity securities	12,924	83	—	13,007
	$377,013	$8,511	$(1,972)	$383,552

Gross gains of $1.46 million were realized during 2002 on sales and calls of securities. There were no gross losses realized during 2002. Gross gains of $2.67 million and $105,000 and gross losses of $290,000 and $5.12 million were realized on sales and calls of securities during 2001 and 2000, respectively. Of the gross gains reported in 2002, $1.35 million was directly attributable to two interest rate risk management processes utilized during the year. First, the Company reported $0.62 million in gains realized from the Company's investment in a mutual fund that generates capital gains, as opposed to interest income. Second, as further discussed in Note Five, the Company reported $0.73 million in gains realized from an investment transaction that entailed the short-sale of a high-coupon U.S. Treasury bond. Gross gains of $2.67 million in 2001 include $1.62 million of gains realized from the Company's investment in a mutual fund during 2001. The Company maintained an average balance of $46.25 million invested in the mutual fund during 2001. This mutual fund generated capital gains, as opposed to interest income, which utilized capital loss carryforwards available to the Company for income tax purposes. The capital loss carryforwards were primarily generated by the gross securities losses recognized in 2000 and 1999. Gross losses of $5.12 million in 2000 are comprised of losses the Company recognized on its investments in small business investment corporations.

The book value of securities pledged to secure public deposits and for other purposes as required or permitted by law approximated $158.11 million and $260 million at December 31, 2002 and 2001, respectively.

On June 17, 2002, Sears, Roebuck, and Company acquired Lands' End. Sears' income statements and balance sheets have been condensed from the 2002 Annual Report. Sears disclosed the acquisition in Note 2, and disclosed the effect of implementing *SFAS No. 142* in Note 17.

C16 – 4

Sears' Acquisition of Lands' End

Sears, Roebuck and Co.

Consolidated Statements of Income

(millions, except per common share data)	2002	2001	2000
Revenues			
Total revenues	$41,366	$40,990	$40,848
Costs and Expenses			
Cost of sales, buying and occupancy	25,646	26,234	26,632
Selling and administrative	9,249	8,892	8,807
Provision for uncollectible accounts	2,261	1,866	884
Depreciation and amortization	875	863	839
Interest	1,143	1,415	1,248
Special charges and impairments	111	542	251
Total costs and expenses	39,285	39,812	38,661
Operating income	2,081	1,178	2,187
Other income, net	372	45	36
Income before income taxes, minority interest, and cumulative effect of change in accounting principle	2,453	1,223	2,223
Income taxes	858	467	831
Minority interest	11	21	49
Income before cumulative effect of change in accounting principle	1,584	735	1,343
Cumulative effect of a change in accounting for goodwill	(208)	—	—
Net Income	$ 1,376	$ 735	$ 1,343

Sears, Roebuck and Co.

Consolidated Balance Sheets
(millions, except per share data)

	2002	2001
Assets		
Total current assets	$39,983	$36,105
Total property and equipment, net	6,910	6,824
Goodwill	944	294
Tradenames and other intangible assets	704	—
Other assets	1,868	1,094
Total Assets	$50,409	$44,317
Liabilities		
Total current liabilities	18,597	15,584
Long-term debt and capitalized lease obligations	21,304	18,921
Pension and postretirement benefits	2,491	2,417
Minority interest and other liabilities	1,264	1,276
Total Liabilities	43,656	38,198
Total Shareholders' Equity	6,753	6,119
Total Liabilities and Shareholders' Equity	$50,409	$44,317

NOTE 2—ACQUISITION

On June 17, 2002, the Company acquired 100 percent of the outstanding common shares of Lands' End. The results of Lands' End's operations have been included in the consolidated financial statements since that date. Headquartered in Dodgeville, Wisconsin, Lands' End is a leading direct merchant of traditionally styled, casual clothing for men, women and children, accessories, footwear, home products and soft luggage.

The Company acquired Lands' End for $1.8 billion in cash. The acquisition has been accounted for using the purchase method in accordance with *SFAS No. 141*, "Business Combinations." Accordingly, the total purchase price has preliminarily been allocated to the assets acquired and liabilities assumed based on their estimated fair values at acquisition as follows (amounts in millions):

Merchandise inventories	$ 238
Property and equipment	185
Intangible assets (primarily indefinite lived tradenames)	704
Goodwill	834
Other assets	48
Accounts payable and other liabilities	(169)
Total	$1,840

Of the $704 million acquired intangibles, $700 million was assigned to registered tradenames that are not subject to amortization and $4 million was assigned to customer lists with an estimated useful life of three years.

The amount allocated to goodwill is reflective of the benefit the Company expects to realize from leveraging the Lands' End brand name across its retail business. The goodwill related to the Lands' End acquisition is not deductible for tax purposes.

NOTE 17—IMPLEMENTATION OF NEW ACCOUNTING STANDARD

Effective at the beginning of 2002, the Company adopted *SFAS No. 142*, "Goodwill and Other Intangible Assets". Upon adoption of *SFAS No. 142*, goodwill amortization ceased. Goodwill is now subject to fair-value based impairment tests performed, at a minimum, on an annual basis. In addition, a transitional goodwill impairment test is required as of the adoption date. These impairment tests are conducted on each business of the Company where goodwill is recorded, and may require two steps. The initial step is designed to identify potential goodwill impairment by comparing an estimate of fair value for each applicable business to its respective carrying value. For those businesses where the carrying value exceeds fair value, a second step is performed to measure the amount of goodwill impairment in existence, if any.

The Company had approximately $371 million in positive goodwill and $77 million in negative goodwill recorded in its consolidated balance sheet at the beginning of 2002 as well as approximately $104 million in positive goodwill related to an equity method investment which is not subject to *SFAS No. 142* impairment tests. The $77 million in negative goodwill was required to be recognized into income upon adoption of the Statement. The Company completed the required transitional goodwill impairment test in the first quarter of 2002 and determined that $261 million of goodwill recorded within the Company's Retail and Related Services segment, primarily related to NTB and Orchard Supply Hardware, was impaired under the fair value impairment test approach required by *SFAS No. 142*.

The fair value of these reporting units was estimated using the expected present value of associated future cash flows and market values of comparable businesses where available. Upon adoption of the Statement, a $208 million charge, net of tax and minority interest, was recognized in the first quarter of 2002 to record this impairment as well as the recognition of negative goodwill and was classified as a cumulative effect of a change in accounting principle.

The following table presents the pro forma effect of the adoption of *SFAS No. 142* on recent fiscal periods as if the change was applied at the beginning of the respective fiscal year:

(millions, except earnings (loss) per common share)	2001	2000
Reported net income	$735	$1,343
Add back:		
Negative goodwill amortization	(14)	(15)
Positive goodwill amortization	20	24
Pro forma net income	$741	$1,352

The Company's policy is to test the realizability of goodwill as of the end of the fiscal year. The Company tested the realizability of the $944 million of goodwill as of December 28, 2002 resulting in no additional impairment being recorded.

Required:

1. What amount did Sears allocate to goodwill in the Lands' End acquisition? Provide possible reasons for Sears paying this premium to purchase Lands' End.
2. How does Sears account for this goodwill under *SFAS No. 142*? How would Sears have accounted for this goodwill under pre-*SFAS No. 142* rules?
3. How will the change in goodwill accounting affect Sears' income in future years?
4. Based on the disclosures, explain the change in Sears' reported goodwill on its balance sheet from 2001 and 2002.
5. Footnote 2 states that the acquired tradenames are not subject to amortization but the acquired customer lists are amortized over three years. Provide an explanation for the different accounting treatments for these two acquired intangible assets.

Excerpts from the 2002 annual report of Air Products and Chemicals, Inc. are shown next. The income statement and balance sheet are condensed but the footnote entitled "Summarized Financial Information of Equity Affiliates" is shown in its entirety.

The footnote provides information on several joint ventures that Air Products has entered into—primarily to incinerate municipal solid waste and generate electricity.

C16 – 5

Air Products: Joint ventures and off-balance sheet effects

Required:

1. What are some of the reasons companies give to justify entering into joint ventures?
2. Using the information provided, estimate what the effect on Air Products' return-on-assets ratio and debt-to-equity ratio would have been if its proportionate share of the joint ventures had been included as individual assets and liabilities on the consolidated balance sheet. For this purpose use a tax rate of 35% and assume that Air Product's proportionate ownership in these equity affiliates averaged 37%.

Air Products and Chemicals, Inc. and Subsidiaries

Consolidated Income Statement (Modified)

($ in millions)	Years Ended September 30	
	2002	**2001**
Sales and other income	$5,401.2	$5,857.8
Costs and expenses		
Cost of sales	3,827.7	4,243.3
Selling and administrative	715.1	752.1
Research and development	120.6	122.5
Other (income) expense, net	(37.1)	(5.5)
Operating income	774.9	745.4
Income from equity affiliates, net of related expenses	76.2	81.2
Gain on sale of U.S. packaged gas business	55.7	—
Gain on divestiture of interest in cogeneration facilities	—	101.6
Loss on early retirement of debt	—	(75.8)
Interest expense	122.3	191.2
Income before taxes and minority interest	784.5	661.2
Income taxes provision (benefit)	240.8	190.5
Minority interest in earnings of subsidiary companies	18.3	5.1
Net income	$ 525.4	$ 465.6

Air Products and Chemicals, Inc. and Subsidiaries

Consolidated Balance Sheets (Modified)

($ in millions)	September 30	
	2002	**2001**
Assets		
Total current assets	$ 1,909.3	$ 1,684.8
Investment in net assets of and advances to equity affiliates	484.2	499.5
Plant and equipment, at cost	10,879.8	10,226.5
Less accumulated depreciation	(5,502.0)	(5,108.0)
Plant and equipment, net	5,377.8	5,118.5
Goodwill	431.1	384.7
Other noncurrent assets	292.6	396.6
Total assets	$ 8,495.0	$ 8,084.1
Liabilities and shareholder's equity		
Total current liabilities	$ 1,256.2	$ 1,352.4
Long-term debt	2,041.0	2,027.5
Deferred income and other noncurrent liabilities	827.4	702.0
Deferred income taxes	725.6	778.4
Total liabilities	4,850.2	4,860.3
Minority interest in subsidiary companies	184.4	118.0
Total shareholder's equity	3,460.4	3,105.8
Total liabilities and shareholder's equity	$ 8,495.0	$ 8,084.1

SUMMARIZED FINANCIAL INFORMATION OF EQUITY AFFILIATES

The following table presents summarized financial information on a combined 100% basis of the principal companies accounted for by the equity method. Amounts presented include the accounts of the following equity affiliates: Stockton CoGen Company (50%); Pure Air on the Lake, L.P. (50%); Bangkok Cogeneration Company Limited (48.8%); Daido Air Products Electronics, Inc. (49%); Sapio Produzione Idrogeno Ossigeno S.r.L. (49%); INFRA Group (40%); Air Products South Africa (50%); Bangkok Industrial Gases Company Ltd. (50.6%); INOX Air Products Limited (INOX) (49.4%); APP GmbH in WPS GmbH & CoKG (20%); DuPont Air Products Nanomaterials, LLC (50%); Island Pipeline Gas (33%); Tyczka Industrie-Gases GmbH (50%); and principally other industrial gas producers. In the fourth quarter of 2002, the company obtained control of San Fu after increasing its ownership interest from 48% to 70%. In the fourth quarter of 2001, the company sold its 50% interest in Cambria CoGen Company and Orlando CoGen Limited. Amounts presented reflect the accounts of these companies for the periods during which the equity method was applied.

($ in millions)	2002	2001
Current assets	$ 732.6	$ 833.9
Noncurrent assets	1,148.7	1,391.0
Current liabilities	572.5	605.1
Noncurrent liabilities	452.2	620.3
Net sales	1,608.8	1,690.2
Sales less cost of sales	543.0	611.5
Net income	196.3	219.4

The company's share of income of all equity affiliates for 2002, 2001 and 2000 was $88.7, $91.1 and $99.6, respectively. These amounts exclude $12.5, $9.9 and $12.0 of related net expenses incurred by the company. Dividends received from equity affiliates were $42.0, $44.9 and $49.7 in 2002, 2001 and 2000, respectively.

The investment in net assets of and advances to equity affiliates at 30 September 2002 and 2001 included investment in foreign affiliates of $449.5 and $465.9, respectively.

As of 30 September 2002 and 2001, the amount of investment in companies accounted for by the equity method included goodwill in the amount of $69.6 and $77.2, respectively. Goodwill is no longer amortized, as discussed in Note 1.

The oil industry in the early 1980s was undergoing significant change. In the late 1970s international crude oil prices were predominately determined by Organization of Petroleum Exporting Countries (OPEC) posted prices that were stated in U.S. dollars. While OPEC prices continued to exert a powerful influence on market prices in the early 1980s, a combination of factors led to excess crude oil supply. These factors included a widespread recession that began in late 1981, an increase in non-OPEC oil output, and a sustained rise in European oil prices attributable to the strength of the U.S. dollar.

As a consequence of these factors, after peaking in 1981 at an average of $34.50 per barrel, official OPEC sales prices in U.S. dollars began a slow but steady decline. (The real extent of the decline is difficult to assess since "unofficial" price cutting was widely practiced by 1985 and may have been practiced by some countries even earlier.) The trade-weighted value of the U.S. dollar, however, rose consistently over the 1980–83 period. This latter effect more than offset the OPEC price decline, which explains why oil prices in most European currencies continued to rise even after 1981. Summary data regarding these effects are provided in Exhibit 1.

Earnings for 1982 were generally depressed throughout the oil industry as a consequence of the severe recession. Exxon's 1982 income decreased slightly despite $1.9 billion of inventory profits attributable to depletion of old LIFO layers. The pattern of oil price declines that began in late 1981 was widely expected by analysts at the time to continue into 1983 and beyond. As a consequence, oil industry profit forecasts were generally pessimistic.

Both Texaco and Exxon adopted the FASB's *SFAS No. 52* on Foreign Currency Translation in 1982. Selected excerpts from Texaco's 1982 annual report are shown in Exhibit 2; corresponding excerpts from Exxon's 1982 annual report are reproduced in Exhibit 3. Notice that Texaco chose the dollar as the functional currency for *all* of its foreign subsidiaries, while Exxon chose the local currency as the functional currency for most of its foreign subsidiaries.

A majority of the other multinational oil companies followed Texaco's approach and chose the U.S. dollar as the functional currency for virtually all foreign subsidiaries. (However, many of these firms did use the Canadian dollar as the functional currency for their Canadian oil subsidiaries.) While the U.S. dollar actually strengthened against most foreign currencies well into 1985, in early 1983 (when Texaco and Exxon were finalizing their 1982 reporting choices), the general consensus among economic experts was that the U.S. dollar was "overvalued" and therefore due for a substantial fall.

C16 – 6

Texaco and Exxon: Functional currency choices

EXHIBIT 1	Summary Data Regarding Oil Prices and Exchange Rates

Crude Oil Official Sales Price (U.S. $ per Barrel)

	1978	1979	1980	1981	1982	1983
OPEC average	$12.93	$18.67	$30.87	$34.50	$33.63	$29.31

Trade-Weighted Value of the U.S. Dollar

	1980	1981	1982	1983
	90.7	99.5	109.8	114.2

Index numbers, 1980–82 average = 100. Each number shows the U.S. dollar's trade-weighted appreciation or depreciation measured against 15 other major currencies,* using averages of daily noon spot exchange rates in New York and bilateral trade weights based on 1980 trade in manufactured goods. Figures are calendar-year averages.

*Canada, Japan, Australia, France, Germany, Italy, the United Kingdom, Austria, Belgium, the Netherlands, Spain, Switzerland, Denmark, Norway, and Sweden.

Source: World Financial Markets, Morgan Guaranty Trust Company of New York.

EXHIBIT 2	Condensed, Selected Excerpts from Texaco's 1982 Annual Report

Statements of Consolidated Income, Balance Sheet, and Retained Earnings

Income Statement

	For the Years Ended December 31	
($ in millions)	1982	1981
Revenues	$48,019	$59,297
Deductions		
Costs and operating expenses	(39,890)	(49,334)
All other deductions	(5,492)	(5,798)
	(45,382)	(55,132)
Provision for income taxes	(1,356)	(1,855)
Net income	$ 1,281	$ 2,310

Balance Sheet

Assets

Total current assets	$ 9,343	$11,947
Investments and advances	2,162	2,193
Net properties, plant and equipment	14,086	12,753
Deferred charges	1,523	596
Total assets	$27,114	$27,489

Liabilities and stockholders' equity

Total current liabilities	$ 6,243	$ 7,025
Long-term debt	1,731	2,112
Capital lease obligations	696	748
Deferred credits—Income taxes	2,205	2,159
Other deferred credits and noncurrent liabilities	1,845	1,540
Minority interest in subsidiary companies	168	153
Total stockholders' equity	14,226	13,752
Total liabilities and stockholders' equity	$27,114	$27,489

Retained earnings

Balance at beginning of year	$11,915	$10,345
Add: Net income for the year	1,281	2,310
Deduct: Cash dividends	780	740
Balance at end of year	$12,416	$11,915

EXHIBIT 2	Condensed, Selected Excerpts from Texaco's 1982 Annual Report (*continued*)

Notes to Consolidated Financial Statements

Note 1. Revision in Accounting Policy

In accordance with Financial Accounting Standards Board Statement No. 52, Texaco revised its accounting policy for the translation of amounts recorded in foreign currencies into U.S. dollars effective January 1, 1982.

The Company determined that the U.S. dollar is the functional currency for its foreign operations, which resulted in a minor revision in its previous accounting procedures. Under this revised policy, deferred income tax accounts are translated at current exchange rates rather than the combination of current and historic rates. The cumulative effect of this accounting change was recorded in the fourth quarter of 1982, and prior periods were not restated because the effect of this change was immaterial.

Under the provisions of Statement No. 52, the functional currency for each company operating abroad is either the U.S. dollar or the local currency. In the judgment of Texaco's management, the U.S. dollar represents the functional currency for all operations abroad because: (1) international pricing in the petroleum business is dominated by OPEC crude prices based on U.S. dollars, and (2) there exists an extensive interrelationship between the operations of the Company's foreign entities and the parent company because of the high level of intercompany transactions, which are generally denominated in U.S. dollars.

Note 11. Foreign Currency Translation

Currency gains and losses resulted in gains of $38 million in 1982, losses of $36 million in 1981, and gains of $4 million in 1980, before applicable income taxes. The effects after applicable income taxes were gains of $62 million and $57 million in 1982 and 1981, respectively, and losses of $69 million in 1980. These amounts include Texaco's equity in such gains and losses of the Japanese and South Korean affiliates of the Caltex group of companies, which are accounted for by Caltex on the equity method.

EXHIBIT 3	Condensed Excerpts from Exxon's 1982 Annual Report

Consolidated Statement of Income and Earnings Reinvested

Income Statement

($ in thousands)	1982	1981
Revenue	$103,558,545	$114,922,561
Costs and other deductions		
Purchases, operating, and other deductions	(77,929,543)	(86,753,601)
Income, excise, and other taxes	(21,443,070)	(23,342,745)
Net income	$ 4,185,932	$ 4,826,215
Earnings reinvested		
Balance at beginning of year	$ 25,629,781	$ 23,397,835
Net income	4,185,932	4,826,215
Dividends	(2,604,456)	(2,594,269)
Balance at end of year	$ 27,211,257	$ 25,629,781

(*continued on next page*)

EXHIBIT 3	Condensed Excerpts from Exxon's 1982 Annual Report (*continued*)

Balance Sheet

	December 31	
($ in thousands)	1982	1981
Assets		
Total current assets	$19,792,686	$23,242,248
Investments and advances	1,714,484	1,643,229
Property, plant and equipment, net	38,981,829	35,285,519
Other assets, including intangibles	1,799,551	1,403,961
Total assets	$62,288,550	$61,574,957
Liabilities		
Total current liabilities	$16,464,740	$17,741,855
Long-term debt	4,555,580	5,153,444
Annuity reserves and accrued liabilities	2,697,771	2,041,182
Deferred income tax credits	8,676,170	7,490,551
Deferred income	268,170	178,694
Equity of minority shareholders in affiliated companies	1,185,928	1,226,365
Total liabilities	33,848,359	33,832,091
Shareholders' equity		
Capital stock	1,760,554	1,826,023
Earnings reinvested	27,211,257	25,629,781
Cumulative foreign exchange translation adjustments	(531,620)	287,062
Total shareholders' equity	28,440,191	27,742,866
Total liabilities and shareholders' equity	$62,288,550	$61,574,957

Analysis of Change in Cumulative Foreign Exchange Translation Adjustments	December 31	
	1982	1981
Balance at beginning of year	$ 287,062	$ 1,534,582
Adjustments for the year	(818,682)	(1,247,520)
Balance at end of year	$ (531,620)	$ 287,062

2. Accounting change

The method of accounting for foreign currency translation was changed in 1982 by implementation of Financial Accounting Standards Board Standard No. 52—Foreign Currency Translation. The statement was given initial application as of January 1, 1980; all 1980 and 1981 financial data have been restated for comparability.

FAS-52 was implemented by using the local currency of the country of operation as the "functional currency" for translating the accounts of the majority of foreign operations. These operations include essentially all foreign petroleum refining and marketing as well as chemical operations, except for those located in highly inflationary economies; also included are exploration and production operations where the production is consumed locally, such as in Australia, Canada, the United Kingdom, and continental Europe. For other foreign operations, principally exploration and production operations in Norway, Malaysia, and the Middle East, together with operations in highly inflationary economies, the U.S. dollar is used as the functional currency.

FAS-52 provides that asset and liability accounts which are fixed in terms of currencies other than the functional currency be remeasured and stated in the functional currency using the applicable exchange rate at the balance sheet date. Adjustments arising from such remeasurement are included in current net income.

For those operations for which the local currency was adopted as the functional currency, translation of all asset and liability accounts is required to convert the functional currency amounts into U.S. dollars, using exchange rates at the balance sheet date. Adjustments resulting

EXHIBIT 3	Condensed Excerpts from Exxon's 1982 Annual Report (*continued*)

from this translation process are accumulated in a separate component of shareholders' equity entitled "Cumulative foreign exchange translation adjustments," and are not included in determining net income. The initial cumulative adjustment, effective as of January 1, 1980, was an increase in shareholders' equity of $1,752 million.

The effect of implementing these procedures was to decrease net income for 1980, 1981, and 1982 by $300 million ($0.34 per share), $741 million ($0.86 per share), and $130 million ($0.15 per share), respectively. Earnings reinvested at January 1, 1980, December 31, 1980, and December 31, 1981 were reduced from amounts previously reported by $20 million, $320 million, and $1,061 million, respectively.

Required:

1. *SFAS No. 8*—which was replaced by *SFAS No. 52*—required companies to use the temporal method exclusively. Using the disclosures in the case, one can infer that Exxon had a relatively higher exposed net liability position under the *SFAS No. 8* temporal method than its liability exposure under the current rate method, which it dominantly adopted for *SFAS No. 52*. Demonstrate this point using the data reported in the case.
2. Given that most other multinational oil firms did not concur with Exxon's functional currency choice in adopting *SFAS No. 52*, try to construct a "story" that could explain Exxon's selection.

COLLABORATIVE LEARNING CASE

The Tribune Company is engaged in the businesses of publishing and entertainment. Operations include newspapers such as the *Chicago Tribune*, television and radio stations, and the Chicago Cubs National League baseball team. In February 1993 a previously wholly owned, consolidated newsprint subsidiary, QUNO Corporation, issued shares to outsiders in an initial public offering. After the stock offering, the Tribune Company owned 49% of outstanding *voting* common shares and 59% of total common shares. Beginning with the 1993 annual report, the Tribune Company accounted for QUNO using the equity method of accounting. Prior years' financial statements in which QUNO was consolidated were not restated.

Exhibit 1 contains a note from the 1992 Tribune annual report, which describes the QUNO initial public offering and provides pro forma data. (These pro forma data were not repeated in the 1993 annual report.) Exhibit 2 contains condensed financial statements from the 1993 Tribune Company annual report. Exhibit 3 shows selected excerpts from the notes to the 1993 financial statements relating to the QUNO deconsolidation as well as a small section taken from the management discussion and analysis portion of the annual report relating to QUNO.

C16 – 7

The Tribune Company— Financial statement effects of consolidating versus not consolidating a subsidiary

COLLABORATIVE

EXHIBIT 1	1992 Annual Report Disclosure of Subsequent Event

QUNO Initial Public Offering

QUNO INITIAL PUBLIC OFFERING On February 17, 1993 the Company's newsprint subsidiary, QUNO Corporation, sold 9 million shares of common stock in an initial public offering. At the conclusion of the offering, the Company holds 8.8 million, or 49%, of the voting common shares and 4.2 million nonvoting common shares for a combined total of 59% of QUNO's total 22 million outstanding common shares. The Company also holds a $138.8 million subordinated debenture, convertible into 11.7 million voting common shares of QUNO. As the Company's voting interest is now less than 50%, the Company will account for its investment in QUNO using the equity method of accounting beginning in 1993.

(continued on next page)

EXHIBIT 1	1992 Annual Report Disclosure of Subsequent Event (continued)

At closing, QUNO used the net proceeds of approximately $100 million from the stock offering plus proceeds of approximately $80 million from QUNO's new bank financing agreement to repay a portion of its intercompany borrowings owed the Company. The net price per share realized from the offering was approximately the same as the Company's carrying value per share of its investment in QUNO. In April 1993 QUNO plans to use additional proceeds of approximately $80 million from its new bank financing agreement to repay its New Zealand dollar notes which are guaranteed by the Company.

The following unaudited pro forma consolidated financial position data assumes [that] the QUNO common share offering had occurred on December 27, 1992 and that the proceeds of the share offering and related debt transactions had been used to reduce debt:

| | December 27, 1992 | |
($ in thousands)	As Reported	Pro Forma (Unaudited)
Assets		
Investment in QUNO	$ —	$ 277,466
Net properties	1,073,943	606,061
All other assets	1,677,627	1,532,985
Total assets	$2,751,570	$2,416,512
Liabilities and stockholders' investment		
Total debt	$ 840,971	$ 580,971
All other liabilities	998,710	923,652
Stockholders' investment	911,889	911,889
Total liabilities and stockholders' investment	$2,751,570	$2,416,512

EXHIBIT 2	Tribune Company and Subsidiaries

1993 Financial Statements
Condensed Consolidated Statements of Income

| | | | Years Ended | |
($ in thousands)		December 26, 1993	December 27, 1992	December 29, 1991
Operating Revenues	Publishing	$1,229,402	$1,176,180	$1,150,882
	Broadcasting and entertainment	727,213	684,051	617,514
	Newsprint operations (Canada)	—	366,269	422,128
	Intercompany	(4,105)	(121,556)	(146,551)
	Total operating revenues	1,952,510	2,104,944	2,043,973
Operating Expenses	Cost of sales (exclusive of items shown below)	998,345	1,150,956	1,121,334
	Selling, general, and administrative	495,000	546,046	497,616
	Depreciation and amortization of intangible assets	102,762	139,579	137,048
	Total operating expenses	1,596,107	1,836,581	1,755,998
Operating Profit		356,403	268,363	287,975
Equity in QUNO net loss		(18,355)	—	—
Interest expense (net of interest income)		(5,621)	(35,472)	(46,100)
Income Before Income Taxes		332,427	232,891	241,875
Income taxes		(143,821)	(96,266)	(99,894)

EXHIBIT 2	Tribune Company and Subsidiaries (*continued*)

	Years Ended		
(*$ in thousands*)	December 26, 1993	December 27, 1992	December 29, 1991
Income Before Cumulative Effects of Changes in Accounting Principles	188,606	136,625	141,981
Cumulative effects of changes in accounting principles, net of tax	—	(16,800)	—
Net Income	$ 188,606	$ 119,825	$ 141,981

1993 Financial Statements
Condensed Consolidated Statements of Financial Position
(*$ in thousands*)

Assets	Dec. 26, 1993	Dec. 27, 1992
Total current assets	$ 491,259	$ 574,338
Investment in and advances to QUNO	250,923	—
Properties (net of accumulated depreciation of $599,552 and $913,522)	601,615	1,073,943
Other assets	1,192,613	1,103,289
Total assets	$2,536,410	$2,751,570

Liabilities and Stockholders' Investment		
Total current liabilities	505,027	632,999
Long term debt (less portions due within one year)	510,838	740,979
Other noncurrent liabilities	424,918	465,703
Total stockholders' investment	1,095,627	911,889
Total liabilities and stockholders' investment	$2,536,410	$2,751,570

EXHIBIT 3	Tribune Company and Subsidiaries

Excerpts from Notes to 1993 Financial Statements and Management Discussion and Analysis
Note 2: Investment in QUNO Corporation

On February 17, 1993 the Company's previously wholly owned newsprint subsidiary, QUNO Corporation ("QUNO"), completed an initial public offering of 9 million shares of common stock. The Company now holds 8.8 million, or 49%, of the voting common shares and 4.2 million nonvoting common shares for a combined total of 59% of QUNO's total 22 million outstanding common shares. The Company also holds a $138.8 million subordinated debenture, convertible at the option of the company into 11.7 million voting common shares of QUNO. The debenture is callable by QUNO after December 27, 1997, matures in 2002 and bears interest at an effective rate of 2.77%. As the Company's voting interest is less than 50%, the Company is using the equity method of accounting for its investment in QUNO beginning in 1993. Prior year financial statements have not been restated. At closing, QUNO used the net proceeds of approximately $100 million from the stock offering plus proceeds of approximately $80 million from QUNO's new stand-alone bank financing agreement to repay a portion of its intercompany borrowings owed the Company. The net price per share realized from the offering was approximately the same as the Company's carrying value per share of its investment in QUNO. Summarized 1993 financial information for QUNO was as follows:

(*$ in thousands*)

Revenues	$386,646	Current assets	$130,989
Operating loss	(31,110)	Noncurrent assets	458,649
Net loss	(28,881)	Current liabilities	82,213
		Noncurrent liabilities	309,346

. . . (data from original report omitted)   (*continued on next page*)

EXHIBIT 3	Tribune Company and Subsidiaries (*continued*)

QUNO manufactures newsprint for sale to the Company's newspapers and other North American and overseas customers. The Company is party to a contract with QUNO expiring in 2007 to supply newsprint based on market prices. Under the contract, the Company has agreed to purchase specified minimum amounts of newsprint each year subject to certain limitations. The specified minimum annual volume is 250,000 metric tons in years 1994 to 1999, 225,000, 200,000, and 175,000 metric tons in years 2000 to 2002, respectively, and 150,000 metric tons in each of years 2003 to 2007. In 1993, 33% of QUNO's sales, or $127.2 million, were to the Company's newspapers, which represented 74% of their consumption.

. . . (data from original report omitted)

Note 6: Long-Term Debt

Long-Term Debt Consists of ($ in thousands)	December 26 1993	December 27 1992
Promissory notes, weighted-average interest rate of 3.3%	$ 41,829	$200,387
Medium-term notes, weighted-average interest rates of 7.3% and 8.7%, due 1993–2003	163,200	107,900
New Zealand dollar notes, U.S. dollar interest rate of 8.6%, paid 1993	—	77,427
8.0% notes, paid 1993	—	100,000
8.40% guaranteed ESOP notes, due 1993–2003	280,999	300,913
8.19% guaranteed ESOP notes, due 1993–98	17,970	20,777
Other notes and obligations	32,657	33,567
Total debt	536,655	840,971
Less portions due within one year	(25,817)	(99,992)
Long-term debt	$510,838	$740,979

In 1990 the Company began offering up to $200.0 million of its Series B medium-term notes, which have maturities from two to ten years and may not be redeemed by the Company prior to maturity. The proceeds from the sale of the notes have been used for general corporate purposes. The final $78 million of these notes were issued during 1993. The Company redeemed its $100 million 8% notes prior to their scheduled maturity. These notes, which were originally due in 1996, were redeemed in July 1993 at par. The Company financed this redemption with commercial paper. QUNO's New Zealand dollar notes were repaid by QUNO in April 1993 with proceeds from its new stand-alone bank financing agreement.

(Excerpt From Management Discussion and Analysis)
Equity in QUNO Net Loss

The Company's 1993 equity in QUNO's net loss, after interest expense and taxes, was $18.4 million. This amount represents 100% of QUNO's net loss prior to February 17, 1993, the date of QUNO's stock offering, and 59% of QUNO's net loss thereafter. QUNO reported an operating loss of $31 million in 1993, $23 million less than the $54 million operating loss incurred in 1992. This was the result of higher average newsprint selling prices and lower operating expenses, partially offset by a 4% decrease in newsprint shipments. Though average newsprint selling prices began to soften in the second half of 1993, they averaged 5% higher in 1993 than in 1992 due to the implementation of transaction price increases in August 1992 and March 1993.

Required:

1. Do you agree with the Tribune Company's decision not to consolidate QUNO Corporation in 1993?
2. What factors do you think prompted the decision?
3. Suggest some reasons that might explain why the Tribune Company decided not to deconsolidate QUNO in the 1992 comparative financial statements. Is this decision consistent with GAAP?

CHAPTER 17

Statement of Cash Flows

Ode to Cash Flow
Though my bottom line is black, I am flat upon my back,
My cash flows out and my customers pay slow,
The growth of my receivables is almost unbelievable;
The result is certain—unremitting woe!
And I hear the banker utter an ominous low mutter,
"Watch cash flow!"[1]

Learning Objectives

After studying this chapter, you will understand:

1. The major sources and uses of cash reported in the operating, investing, and financing sections of the statement of cash flows.

2. Why accrual net income and operating cash flow differ and the factors that explain this difference.

3. The difference between the direct and indirect method of determining cash flow from operations.

4. How to prepare a statement of cash flows from comparative balance sheet data, an income statement, and other financial information.

5. Why changes in balance sheet accounts over a year may not reconcile to the corresponding account changes included in the statement of cash flows.

6. What "cash burn rates" are and how they can be used to evaluate the financial viability of Internet and start-up companies.

As this poem suggests, accrual earnings may not always provide a reliable measure of enterprise performance and financial health. There are several reasons for this. Accrual accounting is often based upon subjective judgments that can introduce measurement error and uncertainty into reported earnings. Examples include estimates of uncollectible receivables, useful lives of assets, and future pension and healthcare benefits. One-time write-offs and restructuring charges require subjective judgments that can adversely affect the quality of the reported earnings number as a reliable indicator of the long-run performance of a company. Moreover, managers can readily manipulate accrual income by postponing discretionary expenditures for research and development or advertising or by purposeful last-in, first-out (LIFO) dipping.

For these reasons, analysts must scrutinize a firm's cash flows—not just its accrual earnings—to evaluate its performance and creditworthiness. A significant difference between accrual earnings and operating cash flow may be a "red flag" that signals distortions of reported profits or impending financial difficulties.

Equity analysts are interested in operating cash flows because a firm's value ultimately depends upon the discounted present value of its expected future cash flows. Recent operating cash flows are sometimes used in conjunction with current earnings as a jumping-off point for generating forecasts of expected future

---

[1] H. S. Bailey, Jr., cited in R. Green, "Are More Chryslers in the Offing?" *Forbes* (February 2, 1981), p. 69.

operating cash flows. Thus, cash flows can provide useful information for assessing equity values.[2]

Commercial lenders monitor a firm's operating cash flows because such cash flows provide the resources for periodic interest payments and the eventual repayment of principal. Low or negative operating cash flows signal poor credit risks.

Investment bankers scrutinize operating cash flows before deciding whether to underwrite a debt or equity issue. They know that the ultimate purchasers of the securities will assess the attractiveness of the securities based, in part, upon the firms' expected operating cash flows.

Statement Format

Some form of **funds flow statement** has been required under GAAP since the early 1970s.[3] The purpose of this statement is to provide users with a clear explanation of what caused the liquid assets of the company to increase or decrease during the reporting period. The format of this statement was originally designed to explain changes in **working capital**—current assets minus current liabilities. But since 1988, the Financial Accounting Standards Board (FASB) has mandated that firms provide a **cash flow statement** that explains the sources and uses of cash.[4] Firms are required to disclose cash flows generated (or used) from three distinct types of activities:

> "Funds" is a generic term used to describe liquid assets—those readily convertible into cash or cash equivalents. The two most common definitions of funds are *working capital* and *cash*. A funds flow statement shows the inflows and outflows of funds as defined for that statement.

1. **Operating cash flows** result from events or transactions that enter into the determination of net income—that is, transactions related to the production and delivery of goods and services to customers. In effect, operating cash flows are the cash-basis revenues and expenses of a company.

2. **Investing cash flows** result from the purchase or sale of productive assets like plant and equipment, from the purchase or sale of marketable securities (government bonds or stocks and bonds issued by other companies), and from the acquisitions of other companies or divestitures.

3. **Financing cash flows** result when a company sells its own stocks or bonds, pays dividends or buys back its own shares (treasury stock), or borrows money and repays the amounts borrowed.

The International Accounting Standard (IAS) format for cash flow statements is similar to the U.S. GAAP format. See "Cash Flow Statements," *IAS No. 7* (revised 1992, London: International Accounting Standards Committee, 1992). Cash flows are classified by operating, investing, and financing activities. Operating cash flows can be reported using either the direct method or the indirect method, but the direct method is preferred (paras. 18–20). One difference in the IAS approach is that firms have latitude in classifying cash flows from interest and dividends received or paid. Interest paid can be classified either as operating or financing cash flows; interest and dividends received can be classified either as operating or investing cash flows (para. 33).

SFAS No. 95 allows firms the option of choosing between two alternative formats for presenting cash flows from *operating* activities: (1) the **direct approach**, and (2) the **indirect approach**. Each of these alternative formats is illustrated on the following pages.

International

---

[2] Research evidence that supports this assertion includes J. Rayburn, "The Association of Operating Cash Flow and Accruals with Security Returns," *Journal of Accounting Research* (Supplement, 1986), pp. 112–33; P. Wilson, "The Relative Information Content of Accruals and Cash Flows: Combined Evidence at the Earnings Announcement and Annual Report Release Date," *Journal of Accounting Research* (Supplement, 1986), pp. 165–200; P. Wilson, "The Relative Information Content of Accrual and Funds Components of Earnings After Controlling for Earnings," *The Accounting Review* (April 1987), pp. 293–322; M. Johnson and D. Lee, "Financing Constraints and the Role of Cash Flow from Operations in the Prediction of Future Profitability," *Journal of Accounting, Auditing and Finance* (Fall 1994), pp. 619–52.

[3] "Reporting Changes in Financial Position," *Accounting Principles Board (APB) Opinion No. 19* (New York: American Institute of Certified Public Accountants [AICPA], 1971).

[4] "Statement of Cash Flows," *Statement of Financial Accounting Standards (SFAS) No. 95* (Stamford, CT: Financial Accounting Standards Board [FASB], 1987).

The Direct Approach

Exhibit 17.1 presents the 2002 statement of cash flows for ABM Industries broken down into operating, investing, and financing activities. Operating activities generated a positive cash flow of $110.919 million. Investing activities resulted in a net cash outflow of $59.318 million, and most of this total was due to capital expenditures for property and equipment and purchases of other businesses. The company paid out $35.226 million of cash for financing activities, principally for stock repurchases, dividend distributions, and debt repayment, while raising funds from stock issuance and long-term borrowing. Thus, ABM's overall cash position increased by $16.375 million in 2002 ($110.919 − $59.318 − $35.226), highlighted in Exhibit 17.1.

> ABM is the largest facility services contractor listed on the New York Stock Exchange, performing mechanical and engineering services for commercial and industrial facilities throughout North America.

ABM follows the direct approach to presenting cash flows from operations. The direct approach requires that firms report major classes of gross cash receipts (cash revenues) and gross cash payments (cash expenses). Note that "Interest paid" and "Interest received" are shown as components of cash flows from operating activities. This treatment is in accordance with *SFAS No. 95*. However, many financial

> The specific categories included by the FASB in para. 27 of *SFAS No. 95* are:
> (a) cash collected from customers (including lessees and licensees)
> (b) interest and dividends received
> (c) other operating cash receipts
> (d) cash paid to employees and other suppliers of goods and services
> (e) interest paid
> (f) income taxes paid
> (g) other operating cash payments

EXHIBIT 17.1 ABM Industries Incorporated

Statement of Cash Flows "Direct" Approach

($ in millions)	2002	2001
Cash flows from operating activities		
Cash received from customers	$2,212.269	$2,117.691
Other operating cash receipts	16.149	5.523
Interest received	1.602	0.859
Cash paid to suppliers and employees	(2,094.597)	(2,021.762)
Interest paid	(1.156)	(2.991)
Income taxes paid	(23.348)	(33.524)
Net cash provided by operating activities	110.919	65.796
Cash flows from investing activities		
Additions to property, plant and equipment	(7.491)	(16.922)
Proceeds from sale of assets	1.702	1.253
(Increase) decrease in investments and long-term receivables	(1.081)	0.049
Purchase of businesses	(52.448)	(23.401)
Proceeds from sale of business	—	12.000
Net cash used in investing activities	(59.318)	(27.021)
Cash flows from financing activities		
Common stock issued	17.955	26.688
Common stock purchases	(23.632)	—
Preferred stock redemption	—	(6.400)
Dividends paid	(17.730)	(16.202)
(Decrease) increase in bank overdraft	—	(15.952)
Long-term borrowings	—	108.000
Repayments of long-term borrowings	(11.819)	(133.857)
Net cash provided by (used in) financing activities	(35.226)	(37.723)
Net increase (decrease) in cash and cash equivalents	16.375	1.052
Cash and cash equivalents beginning of year	3.052	2.000
Cash and cash equivalents end of year	$ 19.427	$ 3.052

Years Ended October 31

analysts and other statement users believe that interest paid should be included as part of cash flows from financing activities while interest received should be included with cash flows from investing activities. Nevertheless, the FASB classifies these two items as elements of cash flows from operating activities because "in general, cash flows from operating activities should reflect the cash effects of transactions and other events that enter into the determination of net income."[5]

ABM discloses "Cash received from customers" of $2,212.269 million on its 2002 cash flow statement. This number differs from the accrual accounting revenue number of $2,191.957 million, which is reported on ABM's 2002 income statement and shown in Exhibit 17.2. There are several reasons for this difference:

1. Some 2002 credit sales made late in the year had not been collected in cash by year-end.
2. Some 2002 credit sales were made to customers who ultimately were unable to pay their balance due.
3. During 2002, cash was received for payment on accounts receivable generated from sales in prior years.

EXHIBIT 17.2	ABM Industries Incorporated	

Income Statement

	Years Ended October 31	
($ in millions, except per share amounts)	2002	2001
Revenues and other income	$2,191.957	$2,149.171
Expenses		
Operating expenses and cost of goods sold	1,946.750	1,919.054
Selling, general and administrative	174.827	162.313
Interest	1.052	2.602
Goodwill amortization	—	12.257
	2,122.629	2,096.226
Income before income taxes	69.328	52.945
Income taxes	22.600	20.119
Net income	$ 46.728	$ 32.826
Net income per common share		
Basic	$ 0.95	$ 0.68
Diluted	0.92	0.65
Average common and common equivalent shares		
Basic	49.116	47.598
Diluted	51.015	50.020

Likewise, the "Cash paid to suppliers and employees" of $2,094.597 million on ABM's 2002 cash flow statement (Exhibit 17.1) differs from the "Operating expenses and cost of goods sold" ($1,946.750 million) and from "Selling, general and administrative" expenses ($174.827 million), which total $2,121.577 million and are reported on ABM's accrual-basis income statement (Exhibit 17.2). Similarly, "Income taxes paid" ($23.348 million) and "Interest paid" ($1.156 million) from the cash flow statement differ from the "Income taxes" ($22.600 million) and "Interest" ($1.052 million) reported on ABM's income statement (Exhibit 17.2).

Overall, Exhibits 17.1 and 17.2 show that ABM generated positive operating cash flows of $110.919 million in 2002, while its accrual-basis net income was only $46.728 million. Why is there such a large discrepancy between ABM's net income and operating cash flows? The answer is found in the reconciliation of net income to cash from operations, the alternative indirect

---

[5] *SFAS No. 95*, para. 88.

approach allowed by *SFAS No. 95* for presenting cash flows from operating activities. This other statement format from ABM's 2002 cash flow statement is shown in Exhibit 17.3.[6]

EXHIBIT 17.3	ABM Industries Incorporated

Reconciliation of Net Income to Cash from Operating Activities Excerpts from Statement of Cash Flows

($ in millions)	Years Ended October 31 2002	2001
Net income	$ 46.728	$ 32.826
Adjustments:		
① Depreciation and intangible amortization	15.182	14.071
Goodwill amortization	—	12.257
② Provision for bad debts	11.910	6.134
③ Gain on sale of assets	(0.236)	(0.041)
Gain on sale of business	—	(0.718)
④ Increase in deferred income taxes	(1.338)	(12.138)
⑤ Decrease (increase) in trade accounts receivable	38.299	(24.340)
⑥ Increase in inventories	(4.081)	(3.223)
⑦ Decrease (increase) in prepaid expenses and other current assets	3.093	(3.045)
⑧ (Increase) decrease in other assets	(3.410)	0.040
⑨ Increase (decrease) in income taxes payable	0.590	(1.267)
⑩ Increase (decrease) in retirement plans accrual	2.308	(0.903)
⑪ Increase in insurance claims liability	6.665	18.872
⑫ (Decrease) increase in trade accounts payable and other accrued liabilities	(4.791)	27.271
Total adjustments to net income	64.191	32.970
Net cash provided by operating activities	$110.919	$ 65.796

The Indirect Approach

The indirect approach begins with the accrual-basis net income (before extraordinary items) and adjusts for the following:

- Items *included* in accrual-basis net income that *did not* affect cash in the current period, such as
    1. noncash revenues or gains (like revenues earned but not received in cash, and gains on the disposal of fixed assets);
    2. noncash expenses or losses (like depreciation and amortization, provision for bad debt expense, and expenses accrued but not paid in cash).
- Items *excluded* from accrual-basis income that *did* affect operating cash flows in the current period, such as
    3. cash inflows (revenues) received but not recognized as earned in the current period (like rent received in advance and collections on account);
    4. cash outflows (expenses) paid but not recognized for accrual purposes in the current period (like prepaid insurance and payments on account).

The indirect approach is used by the overwhelming majority of public companies. Of the 600 companies included in the AICPA's annual financial reporting survey, 592—or 98.7%—used the indirect approach for reporting cash generated by operating activities.[7] There are two reasons why firms favor the indirect approach:

---

[6] This reconciliation schedule is required of all firms that use the direct method of presenting operating cash flows. "Statement of Cash Flows," *SFAS No. 95* (Stamford, CT: FASB, 1987), para. 28.

[7] Y. Lofe and A. Mrakovcic (ed.), *Accounting Trends and Techniques* (New York: AICPA, 2002).

1. The indirect approach is easier for firms to implement because it relies exclusively on data already available in the accrual accounts.
2. The indirect approach is more familiar to many accountants because this format was widely used in the changes in working capital statement that preceded *SFAS No. 95*.

We'll use Exhibit 17.3 to show how the indirect approach reconciles accrual accounting net income ($46.728 million in Exhibit 17.2) with cash flow from operations ($110.919 million in Exhibit 17.1). Each one of the reconciling items is discussed individually.

Items ① through ③ in Exhibit 17.3 represent amounts included in the $46.728 million net income figure *that did not have a cash flow effect*—that is, they did not cause cash to increase or decrease during the year. Since they did not have a cash flow effect, the accrual-basis net income must be adjusted for these items to arrive at cash flows from operations.

① **Depreciation and Amortization** This is the most common example of an indirect method adjustment. During 2002, ABM made the following entry for depreciation and amortization expense ($ in millions):

DR	Depreciation and amortization	$15.182	
CR	Accumulated depreciation and amortization		$15.182

While the debit reduced income, the credit did not represent a cash outflow. Hence, this typical noncash expense causes "Net income" to diverge from "Cash provided by operating activities." That's why depreciation expense must be added back to net income as a reconciling item under the indirect method.

② **Provision for Bad Debt Expense** ABM uses the "allowance method" to record bad debt expense (Chapter 8). During 2002, ABM made the following entry ($ in millions):

DR	Bad debt expense	$11.910	
CR	Allowance for doubtful accounts		$11.910

Although this entry reduced accrual-basis net income, it did not cause a corresponding decrease in cash. Therefore, this amount must be added to accrual income to arrive at cash flows from operations.

③ **Gain on Sale of Assets** This represents the difference between the selling price and book value of assets sold during the period. For 2002, ABM sold assets for a gain of $0.236 million. The proceeds from the asset sales shown in the "Investing activities" section of ABM's cash flow statement totaled $1.702 million. Thus, the gain of $0.236 million that increased accrual income does *not* reflect the $1.702 million increase in cash related to this transaction. Since the gain is a non-cash addition to accrual income, it must be subtracted from this amount to arrive at cash flows from operations.

Items ④ through ⑫ represent amounts that were included in the $46.728 million net income for which the income effect either exceeds or falls below the cash flow effect. Because the income effect and the cash flow effect differ, the following adjustments must appear in the reconciliation.

> We can infer that the assets sold had a net book value of $1.466 million by subtracting the gain of $0.236 million from the cash proceeds received from the sale of $1.702. So the entry to record the sale of assets was ($ in millions):
>
> | | | | |
> |---|---|---|---|
> | **DR** | Cash | $1.702 | |
> | **CR** | Assets (net of accumulated depreciation) | | $1.466 |
> | **CR** | Gain on sale | | 0.236 |

④ **Increase in Deferred Income Taxes (Asset)** ABM showed an increase in its net deferred tax assets (or a decrease in deferred tax liabilities) for 2002 of $1.338 million. Thus, ABM's taxable income exceeded its book income in 2002 due to a variety of temporary differences we discussed in Chapter 13. When this happens, the debit to income tax expense falls below the taxes owed and paid in the current period. This increase in net deferred tax assets must be subtracted from accrual-basis net income because the tax expense *understates* the cash outflow for taxes.

⑤ **Decrease in Accounts Receivable** During 2002, ABM's accounts receivable decreased by $38.299 million. This means sales on account (accrual-basis revenue) fell below cash collections on account (cash-basis revenue) in 2002. Accordingly, an addition must be made to accrual-basis income to arrive at cash provided by operating activities.

> The entry to record ABM's taxes for 2002 is shown below ($ in millions). Adjustment ⑨ below corrects for the current portion of tax expense not paid in cash and for previous years' taxes paid in the current year.
>
> | | | | |
> |---|---|---|---|
> | **DR** | Tax expense | $22.600 | |
> | **DR** | Deferred tax asset | 1.338 | |
> | | **CR** Cash or taxes payable | | $23.938 |

⑥ **Increase in Inventories** During 2002 ABM's inventories increased by $4.081 million. So ending inventory was higher than beginning inventory, which means that inventory purchased was greater than the cost of inventory sold during the year. Let's temporarily assume that all inventory purchases were paid for in cash. (Adjustment ⑫ discussed below for changes in accounts payable and other accrued liabilities corrects for non-cash inventory purchases.) The inventory buildup means the cash outflow for inventory exceeded accrual-basis cost of goods sold. Thus, the increase in inventories must be subtracted from accrual-basis income to obtain cash flows from operations because the cash outflow for inventory exceeded the amount charged to expense under accrual accounting.

⑦ **Decrease in Prepaid Expenses and Other Current Assets** This decrease of $3.093 million represents amounts that were expensed during the year in excess of amounts paid out in cash. Therefore, this amount caused a decrease in accrual-basis earnings without a corresponding decrease in cash. ABM adds this decrease to accrual earnings to obtain cash flows from operations.

⑧ **Increase in Other Assets** This increase of $3.410 million represents cash outflows that were charged to asset accounts rather than expense accounts. Accordingly, these amounts represent a decrease in cash, but they don't cause a decrease in accrual earnings. ABM subtracts this increase from accrual earnings to obtain cash flows from operations because this asset increase represents an operating cash outflow for the period.

⑨ **through** ⑪ **Increase in Taxes Payable, Retirement Plans Accrual, and Insurance Claims Liability** Because all of these liability accounts increased, we discuss their effect on the cash flow statement together. In each case, the off-setting debits to these increases in accrued liability accounts were to various expense accounts that decreased accrual earnings. But because these expenses did not result in cash outflows, the increases in these liability accounts are added to accrual earnings to obtain operating cash flows.

⑫ **Decrease in Trade Accounts Payable and Other Accrued Liabilities** When Accounts payable and Other accrued liabilities decrease, this implies that cash paid out to satisfy these obligations exceeds the amounts accrued as expenses on the income statement. As a consequence, the decreases in these liability accounts are subtracted from accrual earnings to obtain operating cash flows.

Both the direct and indirect approaches for computing net cash provided by operating activities will obviously report the same number—$110.919 million in ABM's 2002 annual report. Those who prefer the direct approach justify their preference by claiming that this method discloses operating cash flows by category—inflows from customers, outflows to suppliers, etc. They contend that this categorization facilitates cash flow predictions. For example, assume that an analyst expects product selling prices to increase by 6% in the ensuing year. The direct method's disclosure of cash received from customers could then be multiplied by 106% to construct next year's cash forecast. (There is no similarly easy way to incorporate the expectation of a 6% price increase in the indirect method approach.)

Analysts who prefer the indirect approach do so because the size and direction of the items reconciling income to operating cash flow provide a rough yardstick for evaluating the quality of earnings. When a company reports high accounting income but simultaneously has low or negative cash flow from operations, this situation is considered a sign of low-quality earnings that are not sustainable. For example, if the excess of income over cash flow is accompanied by a large buildup in accounts receivable, this increase could indicate that the company is aggressively recognizing revenue (see Chapters 3 and 8). The receivables buildup may have occurred, for example, if a company shipped unwanted merchandise to distributors in an effort to inflate sales. Or the buildup could result from sales to customers with marginal creditworthiness that may never be collected.

Although the FASB allowed a choice between the direct and indirect approaches when it formulated *SFAS No. 95*, it anticipated that the vast majority of firms would use the indirect approach. Since few firms were expected to use the direct approach, the FASB feared that users might find it difficult to compare the operating cash flows of firms using the direct approach to firms using the indirect approach. To address this comparability concern, the FASB requires firms using the direct approach to *also* provide a reconciliation between accrual earnings and operating cash flows like the one that is presented by those firms using the indirect approach. Since ABM chose the direct approach, this explains why we have operating cash flow information for them under both methods.

> *SFAS No. 95* also requires firms using the indirect approach to separately disclose income taxes paid.

Additionally, firms using the indirect approach are required to separately disclose the amount of interest paid. Consequently, those who believe interest expense represents a cash flow from financing activities will always have sufficient information available to reclassify this item out of cash flows from operating activities for firms using the indirect approach. However, the FASB does *not* require a separate disclosure of dividends and interest income *received*. Therefore, analysts who believe that these items should be classified as cash flows from investing activities will not have sufficient information to make this reclassification for firms who opt for the indirect approach.

One additional difficulty confronting analysts using *SFAS No. 95* disclosures relates to the treatment of income taxes. Recall from Chapter 2 that intraperiod income tax allocation is followed in constructing the income statement—that is, the income tax expense associated with income from continuing operations is separately disclosed. Items not included in the computation of income from continuing operations (such as extraordinary items and the cumulative effects of changes in accounting principles) are reflected *net* of their associated income tax effects. This is done to facilitate predictions by statement users. The tax expense associated with the presumably recurring income from continuing operations is reported separately from the tax expense associated with items appearing below income from continuing operations. Regrettably, *SFAS No. 95* does not treat *cash* outflows for income taxes in the same way. The entire amount of taxes paid in cash is included in the "Cash flows from operating activities" computation even though some of the taxes relate, for example, to gains on sales of assets whose gross cash flows are included in the "Cash flows from investing activities" section of the statement. The failure to differentiate tax cash flows by type (those pertaining to income from continuing operations versus other items) complicates forecasts of future cash flows. The FASB justifies this treatment as follows:

> The Board decided that allocation of income taxes paid to operating, investing, and financing activities would be so complex and arbitrary that the benefits, if any, would not justify the costs involved. (*SFAS No. 95*, para. 92.)

While this cost-benefit justification may be correct, *SFAS No. 95* provides no evidence to support this assertion.

RECAP

The statement of cash flows provides a summary of a firm's operating, investing, and financing activities that explain its change in cash position for the period. Operating cash flows can be presented using either the direct or indirect approach. The direct approach details major sources of cash receipts and major categories of cash expenditures. The indirect approach begins with accrual earnings and adjusts for (1) items included in accrual-basis income that did not affect cash, and (2) items excluded from accrual earnings that did affect operating cash flows.

Other Elements of the Cash Flow Statement

Let's return to Exhibit 17.1. ABM's cash flow statement illustrates the typical range of items included in the "Investing activities" and "Financing activities" sections of the statement. The items included are relatively straightforward, and there should be no difficulties in interpreting these disclosures. For example, ABM shows investing cash outflows in 2002 for purchases of property and equipment ($7.491 million), purchase of investments and long-term receivables ($1.081 million), and acquisition of other businesses ($52.448 million). Direct cash inflows from investing activities resulted from the sale of assets ($1.702 million).

Financing cash inflows resulted from the issuance of common stock ($17.955 million). Major financing cash outflows occurred for purchase of treasury stock ($23.632 million), dividends paid ($17.730 million), and repayment of long-term borrowings ($11.819 million).

The net result of ABM's operating, investing, and financing activities for the year was an increase in cash and cash equivalents of $16.375 million.

Preparing the Cash Flow Statement

This section illustrates the procedures used to prepare a cash flow statement. Exhibits 17.4(a) and (b) provide comparative 2004–2005 balance sheet data, a 2005 income statement, and selected additional information for Burris Products Corporation.

Reviewing the comparative balance sheets in Exhibit 17.4(a) shows that the cash balance decreased by $8,000 during 2005. The purpose of a cash flow statement is to explain the underlying *causes* for this $8,000 change in the cash balance. Recall that the causes for change arise from operating, investing, and financing activities.

Constructing a cash flow statement requires the preparer to gather information like that in Exhibit 17.4. The three-step process that follows is then used to build the components of the statement.

Step 1: Identify the journal entry or entries that led to the reported change in each balance sheet account.

Step 2: Determine the net cash flow effect of the journal entry (or entries) identified in Step 1.

Step 3: Compare the financial statement effect of the entry (Step 1) with its cash flow effect (Step 2) to determine what cash flow statement treatment is necessary for each item.

This three-step approach is used to develop Burris' cash flow statement in Exhibit 17.5 on page 963 using the indirect method of determining cash flow from operations.

EXHIBIT 17.4	Burris Products Corporation

Comparative Balance Sheets, 2005 Income Statement and Additional Information

Panel (a)

	December 31		Increase or
Comparative Balance Sheets	2005	2004	Decrease
Cash	$ 25,000	$ 33,000	$ 8,000 Decrease
Accounts receivable	171,000	180,000	9,000 Decrease
Inventory	307,000	295,000	12,000 Increase
Land	336,000	250,000	86,000 Increase
Buildings and equipment	1,628,000	1,430,000	198,000 Increase
Accumulated depreciation	(653,000)	(518,000)	135,000 Increase
	$1,814,000	$1,670,000	
Accounts payable	$ 163,000	$ 160,000	$ 3,000 Increase
Customer advance deposits	99,000	110,000	11,000 Decrease
Bonds payable	500,000	500,000	–0– —
Discount on bonds payable	(66,000)	(70,000)	4,000 Decrease
Deferred income tax payable	100,000	94,000	6,000 Increase
Common stock	850,000	800,000	50,000 Increase
Retained earnings	168,000	76,000	92,000 Increase
	$1,814,000	$1,670,000	

Panel (b)

2005 Income Statement

Sales revenues	$3,030,000
Cost of goods sold	(2,526,625)
Depreciation expense	(158,000)
Sales commissions (all cash)	(34,000)
Interest expense	(44,000)
Gain on sale of equipment	17,000
Income before taxes	284,375
Income tax expense	(102,375)
Net income	$ 182,000

Additional information

1. Equipment with a cost of $63,000 and a book value of $40,000 was sold for $57,000.
2. Cash dividends of $90,000 were paid in 2005.

Cash Flows from Operations

The operating cash flow section of the statement in Exhibit 17.5 begins with net income of $182,000. Under the indirect approach, net income represents an initial rough approximation of the cash generated by operations. Starting the statement with net income presumes that revenues are ultimately collected in cash and that expenses represent cash outflows. In the long run this approximation is basically correct. However, in any single period accrual accounting net income will not equal that same period's cash flow from operations. The reason is that cash flows for some revenue and expense items occur either before or after accrual accounting revenue and expenses are recognized. The adjustment for these differences between the timing of revenue and expense recognition and cash flow impact appear as the eight numbered items below the net income figure in Exhibit 17.5. We now explain each of these items.

EXHIBIT 17.5	Burris Products Corporation

2005 Statement of Cash Flows

Operating Activities

Net income			$182,000
Adjustments to reconcile net income to cash			
provided by operating activities			
① Depreciation		$158,000	
② Gain on equipment sale		(17,000)	
③ Amortization of bond discount		4,000	
④ Deferred income taxes increase		6,000	
⑤ Accounts receivable decrease		9,000	
⑥ Customer advance deposits decrease		(11,000)	
⑦ Inventory increase		(12,000)	
⑧ Accounts payable increase		3,000	
			140,000
Cash provided by operating activities			322,000
Investing Activities			
② Equipment sale			$ 57,000
⑨ Land purchase			(86,000)
⑩ Buildings and equipment purchase			(261,000)
Cash used for investing activities			(290,000)
Financing Activities			
⑪ Common stock issued			$ 50,000
⑫ Dividend paid			(90,000)
Cash used for financing activities			(40,000)
Net decrease in cash during 2001			$ (8,000)

① **Depreciation** The income statement in Exhibit 17.4(b) indicates that depreciation expense recognized during 2005 was $158,000. We use the three-step analytic approach, as follows:

Step 1: The journal entry that generated the account change was:

DR Depreciation expense	$158,000	
CR Accumulated depreciation		$158,000

Step 2: Neither of the two accounts that appear in the Step 1 journal entry involve cash. Indeed, depreciation is unlike most other expenses, since the cash outflow often occurs *before* the expense recognition—that is, when the asset is initially purchased.

Step 3: Depreciation expense was included as an element in the determination of net income (Step 1) as if it were a cash outflow. But depreciation expense does not represent a cash outflow (Step 2). Consequently, depreciation expense must be added back to net income.

In short, depreciation expense is added back to accrual-basis income to obtain operating cash flows because it was included in the determination of net income even though—unlike most other expenses—it does not represent a cash outflow of the current period.

② **Gain on Equipment Sale** The net income number includes a gain on equipment sale of $17,000, as shown in Exhibit 17.4(b). Using the same three-step approach, we arrive at the following:

Step 1: With the additional information disclosed beneath the income statement in Exhibit 17.4(b), we can develop the following journal entry for the gain:

DR Accumulated depreciation	$23,000	
DR Cash	57,000	
CR Equipment		$63,000
CR Gain on sale		17,000

> Notice that if the equipment originally cost $63,000 and its book value was $40,000, the accumulated depreciation must have been $23,000.

Step 2: Scrutiny of the journal entry reveals that the sale resulted in a cash inflow of $57,000. This cash inflow is the result of investment activities.

Step 3: Comparing the accrual accounting effect (Step 1) to the cash flow effect (Step 2) reveals three problems: (1) the recognized accrual gain ($17,000) does not correspond to the cash inflow ($57,000); (2) the $17,000 gain is included in income, and thus would be categorized as an operating cash inflow unless adjustments are made; and (3) the $57,000 cash inflow from investing activities must be separately reflected in the statement.

The cash flow statement in Exhibit 17.5 reflects the information uncovered in Step 3. The gain of $17,000 is subtracted from net income to arrive at cash flow from operations, and the total cash received of $57,000 is correctly categorized and shown as a cash inflow from investing activities.

③ **Amortization of Bond Discount** Exhibit 17.4(a) discloses that the discount on bonds payable account decreased by $4,000 during 2005. The three-step approach shows the following:

Step 1: Since the income statement reports interest expense as $44,000, the journal entry that led to the balance sheet change for discount on bonds payable was:

DR Interest expense	$44,000	
CR Discount on bonds payable		$ 4,000
CR Cash		40,000

Step 2: An examination of the journal entry reveals that interest expense of $44,000 was deducted in computing net income, although the cash outflow for the payment of interest in 2005 was only $40,000.

Step 3: Since the accrual accounting income statement charge for interest expense ($44,000) exceeds the cash outflow ($40,000), the difference of $4,000 must be added back to net income in the operating section of the cash flow statement.

④ **Deferred Income Taxes Increase** Deferred income taxes payable increased by $6,000, as shown in Exhibit 17.4(a). The three-step approach shows the following:

Step 1: Since income tax expense for 2005 was $102,375, the journal entry for taxes in 2005 was:

DR Income tax expense	$102,375	
CR Deferred income payable		$ 6,000
CR Cash		96,375

Step 2: Again, there is a disparity between the amount of the expense included in the determination of net income ($102,375) and the cash outflow to pay taxes ($96,375).

Step 3: Because the income statement expense charge is larger than the cash outflow by $6,000, this $6,000 must be added back in the operating activities section of the cash flow statement in Exhibit 17.5.

⑤ **Accounts Receivable Decrease** During 2005, Exhibit 17.4(a) shows that accounts receivable decreased by $9,000. Following the three-step approach we obtain:

Step 1: If we assume that all 2005 sales were initially credit sales, the aggregate entry to record these sales would be:

DR Accounts receivable	$3,030,000	
CR Sales revenue		$3,030,000

If we assume the only transaction causing a decrease in accounts receivable is collections on account, then the $9,000 decrease during 2005 implies the following entry for cash collections:

DR Cash	$3,039,000	
CR Accounts receivable		$3,039,000

Step 2: Examination of the entries in Step 1 reveals that when the total in accounts receivable decreased, the amount of cash collections during the year ($3,039,000) exceeded the amount of accrual revenues included in income ($3,030,000).

Step 3: The $9,000 excess of cash collections over accrual revenues must be added back to net income in Exhibit 17.5 in order to obtain cash from operations.

⑥ **Customer Advance Deposits Decrease** Burris Products Corporation requires cash payments from customers prior to the sale of special-order custom merchandise. This advance payment represents a liability on the balance sheet. As the custom products are delivered to customers, the liability is reduced and revenue is recognized. During 2005, the amount of the liability decreased by $11,000, as shown in Exhibit 17.4(a).

Step 1: The accounting entry that reflects the reduction in the advance payment liability during 2005 was:

DR Customer advance deposits	$11,000	
CR Sales revenues		$11,000

Step 2: Scrutinizing the entry in Step 1 indicates that accrual-basis sales revenues increased by $11,000. However, there was no corresponding cash flow effect this year since the cash flow originated in 2004 when the special products were ordered and paid for and the liability was initially recorded.

Step 3: Because revenues included in the computation of 2005 net income exceeded 2005 cash inflows by $11,000, this amount must be deducted in the operating section of the cash flow statement.

⑦ **Increase in Inventory** When inventory increases during a period, the dollar amount of new inventory purchases exceeds the cost of goods that were sold.

Step 1: If we initially assume that all inventory is purchased for cash (we will relax this assumption in adjustment ⑧ discussed next), then the two accounting entries giving rise to a $12,000 increase in inventory (see Exhibit 17.4[a]) are:

DR Inventory	$2,538,625	
CR Cash		$2,538,625

($2,526,625 Cost of goods sold + $307,000 Ending inventory − $295,000 Beginning inventory)

and

DR Cost of goods sold	$2,526,625	
CR Inventory		$2,526,625

Notice that the combined result of these two entries increases inventory by $12,000.

Step 2: Comparing the two journal entries in Step 1 indicates that the cost-of-goods-sold number that is deducted in the computation of net income ($2,526,625) is $12,000 *lower* than the cash outflow to buy inventory.

Step 3: Since net income understates the cash outflow to acquire inventory, $12,000 must be deducted from income in Exhibit 17.5.

⑧ **Increase in Accounts Payable** Adjustment ⑦ for the increase in inventory was computed under the assumption that all inventory was purchased for cash. We assumed this because it makes it easier to see why an increase in inventory must be adjusted for when preparing a cash flow statement. We now relax this assumption since scrutiny of Exhibit 17.4(a) shows that accounts payable increased by $3,000 during 2005. A $3,000 increase in accounts payable means that $3,000 of the $12,000 inventory increase during the year was not paid for in cash. Therefore, $3,000 is added to net income in the cash flow statement.

There is another way to look at adjustments ⑦ and ⑧ that may make it easier for you to understand the accrual-to-cash adjustment. Together, adjustments ⑦ and ⑧ are designed to isolate the difference between accrual accounting's cost-of-goods-sold measure and cash inventory purchases. Specifically:

Accrual accounting cost-of-goods-sold deduction included in determining income	$2,526,625
Add: Adjustment ⑦ (inventory increase)	12,000
Equals: 2005 *total* inventory purchases	$2,538,625
Subtract: Adjustment ⑧ (payables increase)	(3,000)
Equals: 2005 *cash* inventory purchases	$2,535,625

In combination, adjustments ⑦ and ⑧ subtract $9,000 from income, an amount equal to the difference between cost of goods sold ($2,526,625) and cash inventory purchases ($2,535,625).

Cash Flows from Investing Activities

Turning to the investing activities section of Burris's cash flow statement (Exhibit 17.5), we see there are three transactions that affected cash—one that resulted in a cash inflow and two that reduced cash.

② **Equipment Sale** This transaction was analyzed earlier when we adjusted accrual net income for the gain on sale of equipment. The $57,000 cash received when this equipment was sold represents an investing source of cash.

⑨ **Land** Exhibit 17.4(a) indicates that the land account increased by $86,000. The analysis here is straightforward.

Step 1: The journal entry that reflects this increase is

DR Land	$86,000	
CR Cash		$86,000

Step 2: This transaction represents an outflow of cash of $86,000.

Step 3: The cash outflow is categorized as a $86,000 investment outflow.

⑩ **Buildings and Equipment Purchase** The "Buildings and equipment" account increased by $198,000 during 2005 (see Exhibit 17.4[a]). However, in computing the cash outflow that was incurred to acquire these fixed assets, we cannot simply use the $198,000 net account change. The reason is that some equipment was also sold during 2005 (see preceding Item ②). It is therefore necessary to adjust the change in the buildings and equipment account for the cost of the equipment sold in order to deduce the amount of buildings and equipment purchased.

Step 1: When several items affect a particular account, it is useful to begin by reconstructing the account over the period being analyzed.

Buildings and Equipment

12/31/04 balance	$1,430,000		
"Plug" figure necessary to balance the account	261,000	Reduction in account arising from sale of equipment (see discussion of Item ②)	$63,000
12/31/05 balance	$1,628,000		

The analysis reveals that the gross increase in buildings and equipment was $261,000 and resulted in the following journal entry:

DR Buildings and equipment	$261,000	
CR Cash		$261,000

Step 2: This transaction represents a cash outflow of $261,000.

Step 3: The outflow is categorized as a $261,000 investment cash outflow.

This adjustment illustrates that when constructing a cash flow statement, the analyst must be careful to look beyond just the net change in the account—he or she must also consider other known items that were added to or subtracted from the account during the period.

Cash Flows from Financing Activities

The financing section of Burris' cash flow statement in Exhibit 17.5 shows two other account changes during the period that had cash flow implications.

⑪ **and** ⑫ **Stock Sale and Dividend Paid** The increase in the common stock account indicates that additional capital was raised when new shares were sold. Furthermore, the additional information lists a cash dividend of $90,000 (see Exhibit 17.5). The analysis of these items is straightforward:

Step 1:   The stock sale journal entry was:

DR Cash		$50,000	
CR Common stock			$50,000

The dividend generated the following entry:

DR Retained earnings		$90,000	
CR Cash			$90,000

Step 2:   The cash effects of these items are unambiguously indicated in the entries—that is, a $50,000 inflow for the new financing and a $90,000 dividend outflow.

Step 3:   Both the cash inflow of $50,000 as well as the cash outflow of $90,000 should be categorized as cash flows from financing activities.

RE CAP   **To prepare a cash flow statement: (1) Re-create the accounting entries that explain the changes in all noncash balance sheet accounts, (2) determine the net cash flow effect of the entry and the type of activity that generated or used the cash, and (3) compare the accrual accounting effect of the entry with the cash flow effect to determine what adjustments, if any, are needed to convert accrual earnings to cash flow from operations.**

Reconciling Between Statements: Some Complexities

Users of financial statements will frequently encounter situations in which changes in balance sheet accounts over the year will *not* reconcile to the corresponding account changes in the statement of cash flows. We'll demonstrate this discrepancy and explain why it happens using data from the H.J. Heinz Company's 2002 annual report. The fundamental point of our analysis is this: *while all accruals cause changes in balance sheet accounts, not all changes in operating balance sheet accounts (for example, receivables, inventory, and payables) result in accruals that are recognized on the income statement.* Therefore, trying to infer accruals that affect income from analyzing changes in balance sheet accounts can be, and often is, misleading.

Exhibit 17.6 shows Heinz's statement of cash flows for the fiscal year ended May 1, 2002 and the previous fiscal year. Exhibit 17.7 shows data from Heinz's 2002 comparative balance sheet for two selected accounts—Inventory and Property, plant and equipment. The operating section of Heinz's cash flow statement is prepared using the indirect approach, and starts with fiscal 2002 accrual-basis net income of $883,889,000. Adjustments to reconcile net income to cash provided by operations are presented next. Notice that on the cash flow statement, the change in inventory of $89,918,000 is *subtracted* from accrual-basis income, implying that inventory *increased* by this amount. However, the change in "Inventory" on Heinz's comparative balance sheet (Exhibit 17.7) shows an increase of $119,593,000—a discrepancy of nearly $30 million.

> The term "accruals" is used in a generic sense to include not only accrued revenues and accrued expenses, but also deferred revenues and deferred expenses. So "accrual adjustments" include situations where the revenue or expense recognition under accrual accounting occurs both before and after the cash flow.

> To understand why, review discussion on p. 966 for Item ⑦ in Exhibit 17.5 for Burris Products.

EXHIBIT 17.6	H.J. Heinz Company and Subsidiaries

Consolidated Statement of Cash Flows

	Fiscal Years Ended	
($ in thousands)	May 1, 2002 (52 weeks)	May 2, 2001 (52 weeks)
Operating Activities:		
Net income	$ 833,889	$ 478,012
Adjustments to reconcile net income to cash provided by operating activities:		
Depreciation	207,131	213,968
Amortization	94,566	85,198
Deferred tax provision	120,296	67,468
① Loss on sale of The All American Gourmet business	—	94,600
Cumulative effect of changes in accounting principle	—	16,906
Benefit from tax planning and new tax legislation in Italy	—	(93,150)
② Provision for restructuring	17,886	587,234
Other items, net	(126,977)	(79,415)
Changes in current assets and liabilities, excluding effects of acquisitions and divestitures:		
Receivables	(94,995)	(119,433)
③ Inventories	(89,918)	209,428
Prepaid expenses and other current assets	(23,158)	(11,017)
Accounts payable	(34,368)	(69,754)
Accrued liabilities	(99,703)	(553,268)
Income taxes	86,773	(320,432)
Net accrual adjustments*	57,553	28,333
Cash provided by operating activities	891,422	506,345
Investing Activities:		
④ Capital expenditures	(213,387)	(411,299)
Proceeds from disposals of property, plant and equipment	18,966	257,049
⑤ Acquisitions, net of cash acquired	(834,838)	(672,958)
⑥ Proceeds from divestitures	32,859	151,112
Purchases of short-term investments	—	(1,484,201)
Sales and maturities of short-term investments	17,314	1,493,091
Investment in The Hain Celestial Group, Inc.	—	(79,743)
Other items, net	(15,209)	(27,210)
Cash used for investing activities	(994,295)	(774,159)
Financing Activities:		
Proceeds from long-term debt	2,009,111	1,536,744
Payments on long-term debt	(329,178)	(48,321)
(Payments on) proceeds from commercial paper and short-term borrowings, net	(1,270,984)	(680,858)
Proceeds from issuance of preferred stock of subsidiary	325,000	—
Dividends	(562,567)	(537,312)
Purchase of treasury stock	(45,363)	(90,134)
Exercise of stock options	63,731	93,901
Other items, net	(8,491)	9,077
Cash provided by (used for) financing activities	181,259	283,097
Effect of exchange rate changes on cash	(10,314)	(14,051)
Net increase in cash and cash equivalents	68,072	1,232
Cash and cash equivalents at beginning of year	138,849	137,617
Cash and cash equivalents at end of year	$ 206,921	$ 138,849

* This line added by authors for clarity.

EXHIBIT 17.7	H.J. Heinz Company and Subsidiaries

Selected Accounts from Comparative Balance Sheets

($ in thousands)	May 1, 2002	May 2, 2001	Changes in Account Balances*
Inventories:			
Finished goods and work-in-process	$ 1,193,989	$ 1,095,954	
Packaging material and ingredients	333,565	312,007	
Total inventories	1,527,554	1,407,961	$ 119,593
Property, Plant and Equipment Accounts:			
Land	63,075	54,774	8,301
Buildings and leasehold improvements	880,490	878,028	2,462
Equipment, furniture, and other	2,929,082	2,947,978	(18,896)
	3,872,647	3,880,780	(8,133)
Less: Accumulated depreciation	−1,622,573	−1,712,400	−(89,827)
Total property, plant and equipment, net	$ 2,250,074	$ 2,168,380	$ 81,694

*Amounts without parentheses represent increases in accounts from 2001 to 2002, while amounts with parentheses represent decreases in accounts.

A similar discrepancy exists when trying to reconcile changes in Heinz's "Property, plant and equipment" balance sheet account with information presented on its cash flow statement. Heinz's comparative balance sheets show a year-to-year *decrease* in the Property, plant and equipment account (before accumulated depreciation) of $8,133,000 (Exhibit 17.7). However, the "Investing activities" section of Heinz's statement of cash flows (Exhibit 17.6) shows fiscal year 2002 capital expenditures (implying an *increase* in Property, plant and equipment) of $213,387,000—a difference of $221,520,000.

Why don't the changes in working capital accounts like Inventory and fixed asset accounts like Property, plant and equipment shown on Heinz's balance sheet correspond with the changes in these accounts shown on its statement of cash flows? There are at least four reasons for these differences:

1. Asset write-offs due to impairment, corporate restructuring, or retirement,
2. Translation adjustments on assets and liabilities held by foreign subsidiaries,
3. Acquisitions and divestitures of other companies, and
4. Simultaneous investing and financing activities not directly affecting cash.

Discrepancies in Current Accruals

We'll use Heinz's inventory account to illustrate reasons for the discrepancy between working capital components of net accrual adjustments on the cash flow statement and changes in these accounts on the balance sheet. From Exhibit 17.7, the change in inventories from Heinz's comparative balance sheet is an increase of $119,593,000 while the inventory increase implied by the accrual adjustment on Heinz's cash flow statement (Exhibit 17.6) is $89,918,000. Although a precise reconciliation is not possible, the primary factors causing the $29,675,000 difference arise for the reasons explained next.

Write-offs Due to Restructuring The following excerpt from Heinz's footnote 4 "Restructuring Charges" describing its "Streamline" reorganization and restructuring program reveals that a portion of the restructuring charge shown on its 2002 cash flow statement (Item ② in Exhibit 17.6) relates to inventory and property, plant and equipment write-downs:

In the fourth quarter of Fiscal 2001, the company announced a restructuring initiative named "Streamline" which included:

- A worldwide organizational restructuring aimed at reducing overhead costs;
- The closure of the company's tuna operations in Puerto Rico;
- The consolidation of the company's North American canned pet food production to Bloomberg, Pennsylvania; and
- The divestiture of the company's U.S. fleet of fishing boats and related equipment.

During the first quarter of Fiscal 2002, the company recognized restructuring charges and implementation costs totaling $16.1 million pretax ($0.04 per share). In the fourth quarter of Fiscal 2002, the company recorded a net charge of $1.7 million pretax to reflect revisions in original cost estimates. . . . Non-cash asset write-downs . . . related to property, plant and equipment and current assets . . . Current asset write-downs included inventory and packaging material, prepaids and other current assets and were determined based on management's estimate of net realizable value.

This write-off resulted in a decrease of an undisclosed amount to the inventory accounts unrelated to the sales of merchandise. It is part of the $17,886,000 million "Provision for restructuring" adjustment that is added back to accrual-basis net income shown in the "Operating activities" section of Heinz's 2002 statement of cash flows (Item ② in Exhibit 17.6). So this write-down in inventory on the balance sheet is not part of the $89,918,000 inventory accrual adjustment shown in the cash flow statement (Item ③ in Exhibit 17.6).

Translation Adjustments Heinz has numerous foreign subsidiaries whose statements are translated using the current rate approach described in Chapter 16. This method of measuring the increase or decrease in inventories of foreign subsidiaries generates a potential discrepancy between the balance sheet inventory change figure and the statement of cash flows inventory change figure. Here's why. On the cash flow statement, inventory change is computed by comparing purchases with cost of goods sold. If purchases exceed cost of goods sold, an inventory increase is indicated. To determine the direction of the inventory change for *foreign* subsidiaries, *translated* purchases and cost of goods sold are compared. Inventory purchases and cost of goods sold are translated into dollars using the exchange rate in effect at the time of the transaction. In contrast, the inventory change on the balance sheet is computed differently. Foreign subsidiaries' beginning inventories are translated at the beginning-of-period rate of exchange while ending inventories are translated at the end-of-period rate of exchange. The difference corresponds to the different nature of the two statements: The balance sheet reflects an *instant in time* (and thus uses the *exchange rate at that instant*); the cash flow statement uses a *series of exchange rates*. It should not be surprising therefore that the measures of inventory change on the two statements will differ.

> For simplicity, the translation may also be done using the weighted-average rate of exchange in effect over the period.

Acquisitions and Divestitures Another reason why the inventory change on the two statements differs is because of acquisitions and divestitures. Companies bought and sold usually possess inventories. The ending inventory number reported on the consolidated balance sheet includes the inventory of subsidiary companies purchased and excludes the inventories

> This difference will usually not arise when *all* foreign subsidiaries are accounted for using the temporal method (Chapter 16). The reason is that the method for computing inventory change for temporal method subsidiaries on the cash flow statement translates both beginning and ending inventory at the *historical* rate of exchange. The historical rate is also used on the balance sheet. For firms whose subsidiaries all utilize the temporal approach, inventory change differences between the two statements will usually not arise.

of subsidiaries or divisions sold during the year. But on the statement of cash flows, the inventory of companies acquired is reported as a component of "Acquisitions, net of cash acquired" and the inventory of companies sold is part of the "Proceeds from divestitures" reported in the "Investing activities" section of Exhibit 17.6. *Therefore, the inventory change figure on the cash flow statement is limited to inventory changes for those segments of the firm that were owned at both the start and end of the reporting period.*

> Changes in inventories due to acquisitions or divestitures do not create a corresponding accrual adjustment to cost of goods sold on the income statement. Therefore, changes due to these events would *not* be included as part of the inventory adjustment to accrual-basis income (Item ⑤ in Exhibit 17.6) to arrive at operating cash flows.

The same factors will explain discrepancies between changes in other working capital accounts on the balance sheet and accrual adjustments shown on the statement of cash flows.

Discrepancies Related to Property, Plant and Equipment

A portion of the discrepancy between the change in Property, plant and equipment on the balance sheet and Capital expenditures on the cash flow statement can be explained by asset write-downs taken in conjunction with Heinz's "Streamline" reorganization and restructuring program described earlier. As shown above in the excerpt from footnote 4 in Heinz's 2002 10-K report, a portion of the $17.8 million restructuring charge shown on the cash flow statement is for asset write-downs related to property, plant and equipment, which explains some of the change in this account on the balance sheet.

Three additional events are likely to have contributed to the reported balance sheet change:

Retirements During the year, Heinz may have retired fixed assets (not related to the restructuring) that were not fully depreciated. Recall from Chapter 10 that the entry to record the retirement would take the following form:

DR Accumulated depreciation—plant and equipment	XXX	
DR Loss on retirement	XXX	
CR Plant and equipment (for cost of assets retired)		XXX

Prior to 1995 it was possible to determine the cost of assets retired from Schedule V, Property, Plant and Equipment—a required schedule in firms' 10-K reports filed with the SEC—that reconciled the beginning and ending balances of the property, plant and equipment account reported in firms' balance sheets. Unfortunately, this schedule is no longer required. Therefore, it is generally not possible for external users to determine the exact dollar amount of the year-to-year change in fixed asset accounts due to retirements.

Foreign Currency Translation Adjustment As noted already, Heinz translates the accounts of most of its foreign subsidiaries using the current rate approach. Accordingly, the Property, plant and equipment accounts of these subsidiaries are translated using the current rate of exchange—at the balance sheet date—between the dollar and the foreign currency. If the dollar falls (rises) in relation to the functional currencies of these subsidiaries, this would result in an increase (decrease) in the balance of the Property, plant and equipment account that would not be reflected on the cash flow statement. Again, these adjustments were recorded in Schedule V of the 10-K report prior to 1995 but are no longer disclosed, making it difficult to ascertain the impact of translation adjustments on individual changes in balance sheet accounts.

Acquisitions and Divestitures Heinz acquired and sold companies during the year. These companies all owned property, plant and equipment. This immediately raises a classification dilemma on Heinz's statement of cash flows: Should that portion of cash flow related to the cost of properties acquired be classified as "Capital expenditures" or should it be included as a part of

"Acquisitions, net of cash acquired"? Under the *SFAS No. 95* classification criteria, "Capital expenditures" contain only cash outflows made to acquire property directly. Cash outflows for property acquired as part of a business acquisition are classified under "Acquisitions," following *SFAS No. 95* guidelines. You can see from examining the "Investing activities" section of the statement of cash flow in Exhibit 17.6 that Heinz paid $834,838,000 for acquisitions, net of cash acquired (Item ⑤). Part of this purchase price would contribute to an increase in property, plant and equipment because the acquired firms' assets are included in Heinz's consolidated reports if Heinz's ownership exceeds 50%.

The "Investing activities" section of Exhibit 17.6 also shows cash proceeds from divestitures of $32,859,000 (Item ⑥). When business units included as part of a consolidated entity are sold, the Property, plant and equipment account is reduced by the book value—cost minus accumulated depreciation—of the fixed assets in the business unit sold. Before it was eliminated by the SEC, Schedule V of the 10-K report provided detailed information on increases and decreases in the Property, plant and equipment account due to acquisitions and divestitures. Now that this schedule is no longer required, analysts and other statement users must rely on fragmented and somewhat incomplete information provided elsewhere in the statements to deduce the book value of assets sold.

To illustrate how this is done, recall from Chapter 10 that the gain or loss on asset disposal is the difference between the sales price and the book value of the assets sold. Unfortunately, Heinz does not separately disclose any gain or loss on asset sales in fiscal year 2002. However, for fiscal year 2001, Heinz discloses a "Loss on sale of the All American Gourmet business" of $94,600,000 (Item ① in Exhibit 17.6) along with "Proceeds from divestitures" of $151,112,000 (Item ⑥ in Exhibit 17.6). So we'll use information from fiscal 2001 to show you how the calculation is made. Combining these two pieces of information, we can deduce the book value of assets sold or divested in 2001 as follows:

	($ in 000)
Proceeds from divestiture	$151,112
Add: Loss on assets sold	94,600
Book value of assets sold	$245,712

Unfortunately, it is not possible to determine from the information given what portion of this $245,712,000 book value relates to property, plant and equipment versus current assets like inventory or receivables held by the business units that were sold.

This calculation assumes that the cash proceeds from divestiture represents the entire sales price of the assets sold. If non-cash consideration was received (for example, a promissory note), then the sales price and the cash proceeds would differ and the amount of the note would need to be considered in calculating the book value of assets sold.

Simultaneous Non-Cash Financing and Investing Activities

Occasionally firms will engage in investing and financing activities that cause changes in balance sheet asset and liability accounts even though they do not affect cash receipts or cash payments. Examples include (1) purchasing a building by incurring a mortgage to the seller; (2) acquiring an asset by entering into a capital lease; or (3) issuing stock for non-cash assets in connection with a business acquisition. *SFAS No. 95* requires firms to disclose these non-cash simultaneous financing and investing activities either in a narrative or in a schedule, which is sometimes included as a separate section of the statement of cash flows. Although there is no evidence in Heinz's 2002 annual report that any of the balance sheet changes in property, plant and equipment were acquired with non-cash consideration, this is fairly common, especially for Internet and start-up companies that are typically short on cash.

Exhibit 17.8 shows Amazon.com's 2001 cash flow statement. Note the supplemental schedule (at the bottom of this statement) summarizing each of the three types of simultaneous financing and investing activities we just discussed. Each of these transactions resulted in increases in fixed asset accounts on Amazon's balance sheet but did not have a direct effect on cash flows. Also note that Amazon received non-cash revenues in the form of equity securities of other companies for advertising and promotional services. The latter is a common form of transaction among Internet companies.

| EXHIBIT 17.8 | Amazon.com Inc. |

Consolidated Statement of Cash Flows (Condensed)

($ in thousands)	Years Ended December 31 2001	Years Ended December 31 2000
Operating Activities:		
Net loss	$(567,277)	$(1,411,273)
Adjustments to reconcile net loss to net cash used in operating activities:		
Depreciation of fixed assets and other amortization	84,709	84,460
Stock-based compensation	4,637	24,797
Equity in losses of equity-method investees, net	30,327	304,596
Amortization of goodwill and other intangibles	181,033	321,772
Non-cash restructuring-related and other	73,293	200,311
Loss (gain) on sale of marketable securities, net	(1,335)	(280)
Other losses (gains), net	2,141	142,639
Non-cash interest expense and other	26,629	24,766
Cumulative effect of change in accounting principle	10,523	—
Changes in operating assets and liabilities:		
Inventories	30,628	46,083
Prepaid expenses and other current assets	20,732	(8,585)
Accounts payable	(44,438)	22,357
Accrued expenses and other current liabilities	50,031	93,967
Unearned revenue	114,738	97,818
Amortization of previously unearned revenue	(135,808)	(108,211)
Interest payable	(345)	34,341
Net cash used in operating activities	(119,782)	(130,442)
Investing Activities:		
Sales and maturities of marketable securities	370,377	545,724
Purchases of marketable securities	(567,152)	(184,455)
Purchases of fixed assets, including internal-use software and Web-site development	(50,321)	(134,758)
Investments in equity-method investees and other investments	(6,198)	(62,533)
Net cash provided by (used in) investing activities	(253,294)	163,978
Financing Activities:		
Proceeds from exercise of stock options and other	16,625	44,697
Proceeds from issuance of common stock, net of issuance costs	99,831	—
Proceeds from long-term debt and other	10,000	681,499
Repayment of long-term debt and other	(19,575)	(16,927)
Financing costs	—	(16,122)
Net cash provided by financing activities	106,881	693,147
Effect of exchange-rate changes on cash and cash equivalents	(15,958)	(37,557)
Net increase (decrease) in cash and cash equivalents	(282,153)	689,126
Cash and cash equivalents at beginning of period	822,435	133,309
Cash and cash equivalents at end of period	$ 540,282	$ 822,435
Supplemental Cash Flow Information:		
Fixed assets acquired under capital leases	$ 4,597	$ 4,459
Fixed assets acquired under financing agreements	1,000	4,844
Equity securities received for commercial agreements	331	106,848
Stock issued in connection with business acquisitions and minority investments	5,000	32,130

The year-to-year changes in comparative balance sheet accounts may not coincide with the changes implied from amounts reported on the statement of cash flows. The factors contributing to these differences include (1) asset write-downs due to impairment or restructuring, (2) the translation of foreign subsidiary accounts using the year-end current exchange rate between the dollar and the foreign currency, (3) acquisitions and divestitures of other companies, and (4) simultaneous non-cash financing and investing transactions. Footnote disclosures, along with information in the income statement and in the operating section of the cash flow statement, are often helpful in reconciling some of these differences.

Analytical Insights: Cash Burn Rates of Start-up and Internet Companies

The ability to generate positive operating cash flows is critical to the survival and success of any company. This is particularly true for start-up companies and Internet companies. Expenditures for managerial talent, employees with technical expertise, computer hardware, physical plant, research and development, and advertising create heavy cash flow demands on start-up or Internet companies while they await cash inflows from new products or services they are developing. As a result, such companies generate negative operating cash flows while at the same time investing large amounts of cash in business infrastructure and operating assets.

The **"cash burn rate"** has become a popular metric for assessing how quickly start-up or Internet firms are using up their cash reserves.[8] The related measure of **"months to burnout"** provides an estimate of how much longer a company can survive without an infusion of external capital (via debt or equity financing).

> A recent survey conducted by Pegasus Research International, an Internet stock evaluation firm, reports that 74% of the 371 publicly traded Internet companies in the United States had negative operating cash flows as of the fourth quarter of 1999. See J. Willoughby, "Burning Up," *Barron's* (March 20, 2000), p. 29.

The "cash burn rate" is typically calculated in one of two ways:

Method (1): Cash used for operations plus cash used for capital expenditures and purchases of ongoing businesses (net of cash received) divided by the number of months covered by the cash flow statement (that is, 12 for annual and 3 for quarterly statements).

Method (2): Earnings before interest, taxes, depreciation and amortization (EBITDA) excluding nonrecurring gains and losses divided by number of months covered by the income statement.

The "months to burnout" is calculated as:

$$\frac{\text{Cash} + \text{Cash equivalents} + \text{Short-term marketable securities}}{\text{Cash burn rate}}$$

> These amounts are taken from the balance sheet at the end of the quarter or year.

We'll illustrate these measures using data from Amazon.com's 2001 annual cash flow statement given in Exhibit 17.8 along with earnings and other balance sheet information (not shown). In Exhibit 17.8, Amazon's net cash used in operations was $119,782,000. In the "Investing activities"

---

[8] Ibid.; J. Willoughby, "Up in Smoke," *Barron's* (June 19, 2000), p. 31; J. Willoughby, "Smoldering," *Barron's* (October 2, 2000), p. 38; M. Krantz, "E-retailers Run Low on Fuel," *USA Today* (April 26, 2000), p. 1B; S. Pulliam and P. Beckett, "Goldman's E-Commerce List Reduces Nonclients to Low Tiers," *Wall Street Journal* (June 20, 2000).

section, Amazon used additional cash of $50,321,000 to buy fixed assets and another $6,198,000 to make investments in equity method investees. Thus, the cash burn rate computed using Method (1) is −($119,782,000 + $50,321,000 + $6,198,000)/12 months = −$176,301,000/12 months = −$14,691,750 per month. Amazon's cash, cash equivalents, and short-term marketable securities from its December 31, 2001 balance sheet (not shown) totaled $996,585,000. Dividing this number by the cash burn rate yields 67.8 "months to burnout."

The EBITDA cash burn rate [Method (2)] is computed from data reported in Amazon's 2001 10-K as follows:

	($ in thousands)
Loss from operations before interest and other income	$(412,257)
Add back—	
Depreciation and amortization of fixed assets	84,709
Amortization of deferred stock-based compensation	4,637
Amortization of goodwill and other intangibles	181,033
Gain on sale of marketable securities	(1,335)
Adjusted EBITDA for 2001	$(143,213)

Dividing this number by 12 months yields an EBITDA cash burn rate of −$11,934,417 per month. Dividing this amount into the cash, cash equivalents and marketable securities amount of $996,585,000 yields 83.5 "months to burnout."

Using EBITDA generally yields a lower cash burn rate and longer time to burnout because it ignores working capital cash flows and cash used to acquire fixed assets (capital expenditures) and cash used to acquire other businesses. These expenditures are often necessary to carry out a firm's business plan and to continue to build market share. Therefore, some suggest that cash burn rate Method (1) is a better metric for evaluating the financial viability of Internet stocks.[9]

Exhibit 17.9 presents cash burn rates and months to burnout based on data for the second quarter 2000 for a selected group of Internet stocks. As can be seen, many of these companies were perilously close to running out of funds to support their operations without a significant infusion of additional debt or equity financing. The last column of Exhibit 17.9 reveals that roughly three years after these cash burn rates were computed, only nine of the twenty-five firms (36%) listed were still in operation. Thus, it appears that cash burn rates are reasonably good predictors of non-survival.

---

[9] Recall from Chapter 5 that EBITDA is a "flawed" measure of operating cash flow, although some analysts mistakenly use it for that purpose. The same point could be made here—if you want to measure the *cash* burn rate, look to cash flows [Method (1)], not EBITDA [Method (2)].

| **EXHIBIT 17.9** | **Estimated Cash Burn Rates for Selected Internet Companies** |

($ in millions) Company	Revenues	Burn Rate (1)[1] (CFO + Capital Expenditures)[3]	Ending Cash Balance[2] as of 6/30/00	Months Until Burnout (1)	Burn Rate (2)[1] (EBITDA)*	Months Until Burnout (2)	Date Ceased Operation[6]
GenesisIntermedia.com	$ 7.6	−$10.20	$0.4	0.12	−$4.97	0.24	04/30/02
Onemain.com	40.9	−24.90	1.4	0.17	−3.58	1.17	08/09/00
drkoop.com	2.5	−23.50	2.0	0.26	−22.65	0.26	12/17/01
Choice One	10.4	−55.40	8.1	0.44	−13.89	1.75	—
Streamline.com	8.9	−12.80	4.8	1.13	−8.90	1.62	11/22/00
Medium4.com	0.1	−2.50	1.4	1.68	−1.70	2.47	—
Bluefly	4.3	−6.00	3.9	1.95	−4.99	2.34	—
Medinex Systems	1.6	−5.70	3.8	2.00	−5.54	2.06	11/27/02
LendingTree	7.7	−27.90	19.0	2.04	−18.76	3.04	08/08/03
Audiohighway.com	0.6	−4.90	3.5	2.14	−4.81	2.18	01/10/01
Streamedia Comm	0.1	−2.50	1.8	2.16	−1.91	2.83	04/11/01
Pacific Softworks	0.5	−0.90	0.7	2.33	−0.98	2.14	—
Cavion Tech	0.4	−2.50	2.0	2.40	−2.28	2.63	02/23/01
Quokka Sports	12.6	−24.00	19.6	2.45	−15.43	3.81	04/27/01
RMI.net	11.8	−3.00	2.5	2.50	−3.65	2.05	10/30/01
BiznessOnline.com	7.1	−2.60	2.7	3.12	−2.08	3.89	11/07/02
TriZetto Group	17.8	−7.70	8.4	3.27	−5.27	4.78	—
Pets.com	8.8	−31.30	37.2	3.57	−21.91	5.09	09/13/02
ZipLink	6.9	−5.10	6.6	3.88	−3.96	5.00	12/04/00
Claimsnet.com	0.3	−2.50	3.4	4.08	−2.73	3.74	—
eGain Comms[4]	6.3	−18.30	30.2	4.95	−18.00	5.03	—
Netzee	4.3	−2.90	5.4	5.59	−3.18	5.09	01/03/03
Intraware[5]	41.5	−8.50	18.1	6.39	−8.81	6.16	—
US SearchCorp.com	5.9	−2.90	9.0	9.31	−8.84	3.05	—
RoweCom	38.9	34.70	10.1	—	−11.34	2.67	11/06/01

[1]Calculated from data for second quarter 2000. Numbers in these columns are divided by 3 before calculating months to burnout.
[2]Includes cash, cash equivalents and short term marketable securities at end of second quarter 2000.
[3]Cash from operations + capital expenditures + purchases of going businesses.
[4]Calculated from data for year ended June 30, 2000.
[5]Calculated for second quarter ended August 31, 2000.
[6]Determination made August 2003.

*Source: Pegasus Research International as reported in *Barron's*, October 2, 2000 and company quarterly reports filed with SEC.

SUMMARY

- The statement of cash flows provides information for assessing the ability of a firm to generate sufficient cash to pay for operating expenses, capital improvements, and currently maturing obligations.
- Firms able to generate consistently strong positive cash flows from operations are considered better credit risks and benefit from a lower cost of capital.
- The two alternative methods for presenting the operating section of a cash flow statement are the direct and indirect approach.
- Most firms use the indirect approach that begins with accrual-basis earnings and adjusts for depreciation, amortization, non-cash gains and losses, and changes in non-cash working capital accounts—for example, inventories, receivables, and payables—that cause earnings to differ from operating cash flows for the period.
- Frequently, you will encounter situations where the changes in non-cash accounts shown on comparative balance sheets will not reconcile with the adjustments shown on the cash flow statement. These discrepancies are due to one or more of the following causes: (1) Asset write-offs due

to impairment, corporate restructuring, or retirement; (2) Translation adjustments on assets and liabilities held by foreign subsidiaries; (3) Acquisitions and divestitures of other companies or operating units; and (4) Simultaneous investing and financing activities not directly affecting cash. Failure to understand how these events cause balance sheet account changes to differ from changes in account balances shown on the cash flow statement can lead to incorrect interpretation of both statements.

- Knowing how to prepare and interpret cash flow statements is critical to conducting sound credit analysis and making informed investment and lending decisions. This is particularly true for start-up and Internet companies that often have negative operating cash flows. Cash burn rates and months to burnout are measures that can be helpful in evaluating the financial viability of these companies.

EXERCISES

E17 – 1
Determining cash flow from operations

Information for ABC Company is as follows ($ in thousands):

Net income	$280
Equity in investee loss	20
Decrease in prepaid expenses	7
Cash paid for new plant equipment	30
Amortization of premium on bonds payable	10
Decrease in accounts payable	2
Increase in inventory	21
Depreciation expense	13
Increase in salaries payable	8
Increase in accounts receivable	15
Dividends paid to stockholders	5

Required:
What is the net cash provided by operating activities?

E17 – 2
Determining cash flow from operations

AICPA
ADAPTED

Lino Company's worksheet for the preparation of its 2005 statement of cash flows included the following information:

	December 31	January 1
Accounts receivable	$29,000	$23,000
Allowance for uncollectible accounts	1,000	800
Prepaid rent expense	8,200	12,400
Accounts payable	22,400	19,400

Lino's 2005 net income is $150,000.

Required:
What amount should Lino include as net cash that is provided by operating activities in the statement of cash flows?

E17 – 3
Cash flow from operations

AICPA
ADAPTED

Patsy Corporation has estimated its activity for December 2005. Selected data from these estimated amounts are as follows:

Sales	$350,000
Gross profit (based on sales)	30%
Increase in gross trade accounts receivable during month	10,500
Change in accounts payable during month	–0–
Increase in inventory during month	5,000
Variable selling, general, and administrative (SG&A) expenses include a charge for uncollectible accounts of 1% of sales; Accounts receivable write-offs were $3,000	
Total SG&A expenses are $35,000 per month plus 15% of sales	
Depreciation expense of $20,000 per month is included in fixed SG&A	

Required:

1. Calculate accrual-basis net income for December.
2. On the basis of the preceding data, what is the net cash flow provided from operating activities for December?

Roe Company is preparing a statement of cash flows for the year ended December 31, 2005. It has the following account balances:

E17 – 4

Analysis of changes in balance sheet accounts

AICPA
ADAPTED

	December 31	
	2004	**2005**
Machinery	$250,000	$320,000
Accumulated depreciation—machinery	102,000	120,000
Loss on sale of machinery		4,000

During 2005, Roe sold for $26,000 a machine that cost $40,000, and purchased several other items of machinery.

Required:

1. How much depreciation expense was recorded on machinery for 2005?
2. What was the amount of machinery purchased in 2005?

Karr, Inc. reported net income of $300,000 for 2005. Changes occurred in several balance sheet accounts as follows:

E17 – 5

Cash flows from investing and operating activities

AICPA
ADAPTED

Equipment	$25,000 increase
Accumulated depreciation	40,000 increase
Note payable	30,000 increase

Additional Information:

1. During 2005 Karr sold equipment that cost $25,000 and had accumulated depreciation of $12,000, for a gain of $5,000.
2. In December 2005 Karr purchased equipment costing $50,000 with $20,000 cash and a 12% note payable of $30,000.
3. Depreciation expense for the year was $52,000.

Required:

1. In Karr's 2005 statement of cash flows, what should be the net cash from operating activities?
2. In Karr's 2005 statement of cash flows, what should be the net cash used in investing activities?

In preparing its cash flow statement for the year ended December 31, 2005, Reve Company collected the following data:

E17 – 6

Cash flows from investing and financing activities

AICPA
ADAPTED

Gain on sale of equipment	$ 6,000
Proceeds from sale of equipment	10,000
Purchase of A.S., Inc. bonds (par value $200,000)	180,000
Amortization of bond discount	2,000
Dividends declared	45,000
Dividends paid	38,000
Proceeds from the sale of treasury stock (carrying amount $65,000)	75,000

Required:

Determine the following amounts that should be reported in Reve's 2005 statement of cash flows.

1. What amount should Reve report as net cash used in investing activities?
2. What amount should Reve report as net cash provided by financing activities?

Alp, Inc. had the following activities during 2005:

E17 – 7

Cash flow from investing activities

AICPA
ADAPTED

- Acquired 2,000 shares of stock in Maybel, Inc. for $26,000.
- Sold an investment in Rate Motors for $35,000 when the carrying value was $33,000.
- Acquired a $50,000, four-year certificate of deposit from a bank. (During the year, interest of $3,750 was paid to Alp.)
- Collected dividends of $1,200 on stock investments.

Required:

In Alp's 2005 statement of cash flows, what amount would be shown for net cash used in investing activities?

E17 – 8

Cash flows from investing and financing activities

AICPA
ADAPTED

Kollar Corporation's transactions for the year ended December 31, 2005 included the following:
1. Purchased real estate for $550,000 using cash borrowed from a bank.
2. Sold investment securities for $500,000.
3. Paid dividends of $600,000.
4. Issued 500 shares of common stock for $250,000.
5. Purchased machinery and equipment for $125,000 cash.
6. Paid $450,000 toward a bank loan.
7. Reduced accounts receivable by $100,000.
8. Increased accounts payable by $200,000.

Required:

1. Determine Kollar's net cash used in investing activities for 2005.
2. Determine Kollar's net cash used in financing activities for 2005.

E17 – 9

Determining operating cash flow

AICPA
ADAPTED

Metro, Inc. reported net income of $150,000 for 2005. Changes occurred in several balance sheet accounts during 2005 as follows:

Investment in Videogold, Inc. stock, carried on the equity basis	$5,500 increase
Accumulated depreciation, caused by major repair to projection equipment	2,100 decrease
Premium on bonds payable	1,400 decrease
Deferred income tax liability (long term)	1,800 increase

Required:

Determine the reported net cash provided by operating activities for Metro in 2005.

E17 – 10

Determining operating, investing, and financing cash flows

AICPA
ADAPTED

The differences in Beal Inc.'s balance sheet accounts at December 31, 2005 and 2004 are presented next:

	Increase (Decrease)
Assets	
Cash and cash equivalents	$ 120,000
Short-term investments	300,000
Accounts receivable, net	–0–
Inventory	80,000
Long-term investments	(100,000)
Plant assets	700,000
Accumulated depreciation	–0–
	$1,100,000
Liabilities and Stockholders' Equity	
Accounts payable and accrued liabilities	$ (5,000)
Dividends payable	160,000
Short-term bank debt	325,000
Long-term debt	110,000
Common stock, $10 par	100,000
Additional paid-in capital	120,000
Retained earnings	290,000
	$1,100,000

The following information is related to 2005:

- Net income was $790,000.
- Cash dividends of $500,000 were declared.
- A building costing $600,000 and having a carrying amount of $350,000 was sold for $350,000.
- Equipment costing $110,000 was acquired through the issuance of long-term debt.
- A long-term investment was sold for $135,000. There were no other transactions affecting long-term investments.
- Ten thousand shares of common stock were issued for $22 a share.

Required:

In Beal's 2005 statement of cash flows, determine:
1. Net cash provided by operating activities.
2. Net cash used in investing activities.
3. Net cash provided by financing activities.

Metro, Inc. reported net income of $150,000 for 2005. Changes occurred in several balance sheet accounts during 2005 as follows:

Investment in Videogold, Inc. stock, carried on the equity basis	$5,500 increase
Accumulated depreciation, caused by major repair to projection equipment	$2,100 decrease
Premium on bonds payable	$1,400 decrease
Deferred income tax liability (long-term)	$1,800 increase

E17 – 11

Determining cash provided by operations

AICPA
ADAPTED

Required:

In Metro's 2005 cash flow statement, the reported net cash provided by operating activities should be how much?

During 2005, Xan, Inc. had the following activities related to its financial operations:

Payment for the early retirement of long-term bonds payable (carrying value $370,000)	$375,000
Distribution in 2005 of cash dividend declared in 2004 to preferred shareholders	$ 31,000
Carrying value of convertible preferred stock in Xan, converted into common shares	$ 60,000
Proceeds from sale of treasury stock (carrying value at cost, $43,000)	$ 50,000

E17 – 12

Determining cash used in financing activities

AICPA
ADAPTED

Required:

In Xan's 2005 statement of cash flows, net cash used in financing activities should be how much?

Kollar Corp's transactions for the year ended December 31, 2005 include the following:

- Purchased real estate for $550,000 cash borrowed from a bank.
- Sold available-for-sale securities for $500,000.
- Paid dividends of $600,000.
- Issued 500 shares of common stock for $250,000.
- Purchased machinery and equipment for $125,000 cash.
- Paid $450,000 toward a bank loan.
- Reduced accounts receivable by $100,000.
- Increased accounts payable by $200,000.

E17 – 13

Determining cash used in investing and financing activities

AICPA
ADAPTED

Required:

1. Kollar's net cash used in investing activities for 2005 was how much?
2. Kollar's net cash used in financing activities for 2005 was how much?

In preparing its cash flow statement for the year ended December 31, 2005, Reve Co. collected the following data:

Gain on sales of equipment	$ (6,000)
Proceeds from sale of equipment	10,000
Purchase of A.S., Inc. bonds (par value $200,000, classified as held-to-maturity)	(180,000)
Amortization of bond discount	2,000
Dividends declared	(45,000)
Dividends paid	(38,000)
Proceeds from sale of treasury stock (carrying amount $65,000)	75,000

E17 – 14

Determining cash used (provided) by investing and financing activities

AICPA
ADAPTED

Required:

1. In its December 31, 2005 statement of cash flows, what amount should Reve report as net cash used in investing activities?
2. In its December 31, 2005 statement of cash flows, what amount should Reve report as net cash provided by financing activities?

PROBLEMS/DISCUSSION QUESTIONS

P17 – 1

Indirect approach, classification of cash flows, and disclosure

The following condensed trial balance of Probe Co., a publicly held company, has been adjusted except for income tax expense.

Probe Co.

Condensed Trial Balance

	12/31/05 Balance Dr. (Cr.)	12/31/04 Balance Dr. (Cr.)	Net Change Dr. (Cr.)
Cash	$ 473,000	$ 817,000	$(344,000)
Accounts receivable, net	670,000	610,000	60,000
Property, plant and equipment	1,070,000	995,000	75,000
Accumulated depreciation	(345,000)	(280,000)	(65,000)
Dividends payable	(25,000)	(10,000)	(15,000)
Income tax payable	35,000	(150,000)	185,000
Deferred income tax liability	(42,000)	(42,000)	—
Bonds payable	(500,000)	(1,000,000)	500,000
Unamortized premium on bonds	(71,000)	(150,000)	79,000
Common stock	(350,000)	(150,000)	(200,000)
Additional paid-in-capital	(430,000)	(375,000)	(55,000)
Retained earnings	(185,000)	(265,000)	80,000
Sales	(2,420,000)		
Cost of goods sold	1,863,000		
Selling and administrative expenses	220,000		
Interest income	(14,000)		
Interest expense	46,000		
Depreciation	88,000		
Loss on sale of equipment	7,000		
Gain on extinguishment of bonds	(90,000)		
	$ 0	$ 0	$ 300,000

Additional Information:

- During 2005, equipment with an original cost of $50,000 was sold for cash, and equipment costing $125,000 was purchased.
- On January 1, 2005, bonds with a par value of $500,000 and related premium of $75,000 were redeemed. The $1,000 face value, 10% par bonds had been issued on January 1, 1995, to yield 8%. Interest is payable annually every December 31 through 2014.
- Probe's tax payments during 2005 were debited to income taxes payable. Probe recorded a deferred income tax liability of $42,000 based on temporary differences of $120,000 and an enacted tax rate of 35%. Probe's 2005 financial statement before income taxes was greater than its 2005 taxable income, due entirely to temporary differences, by $60,000. Probe's cumulative net taxable temporary differences at December 31, 2005 were $180,000. Probe's enacted tax rate for the current and future years is 30%.
- 60,000 shares of common stock, $2.50 par value, were outstanding on December 31, 2004. Probe issued an additional 80,000 shares on April 1, 2005.
- There were no changes in retained earnings other than dividends declared.

Required:

For each transaction in items 1 through 6 below, choose where to report those activities from list A and dollar amount from list B.

1. Cash paid for income taxes
2. Cash paid for interest
3. Redemption of bonds payable
4. Issuance of common stock
5. Cash dividends paid
6. Proceeds from sale of equipment

   - List A

     a. Operating activities on Probe's statement of cash flows
     b. Investing activities on Probe's statement of cash flows
     c. Financing activities on Probe's statement of cash flows
     d. Supplementary information to Probe's statement of cash flows
     e. Not reported on Probe's statement of cash flows

   - List B

     f. $20,000
     g. $23,000
     h. $42,000
     i. $46,000
     j. $50,000
     k. $55,000
     l. $65,000
     m. $80,000
     n. $185,000
     o. $200,000
     p. $255,000
     q. $265,000
     r. $410,000
     s. $485,000
     t. $575,000

Dice Corporation's balance sheet accounts as of December 31, 2005 and 2004 and information relating to 2001 activities are presented next.

P17 – 2

Determining cash provided (used) by operating, investing, and financing activities

ADAPTED

Dice Corporation

Balance Sheet

	2005	2004
Assets		
Cash	$ 230,000	$ 100,000
Short-term investments	300,000	–0–
Accounts receivable—net	510,000	510,000
Inventory	680,000	600,000
Long-term investments	200,000	300,000
Plant assets	1,700,000	1,000,000
Accumulated depreciation	(450,000)	(450,000)
Goodwill	90,000	100,000
Total assets	$3,260,000	$2,160,000
Liabilities and Stockholders' Equity		
Accounts payable and accrued liabilities	$ 825,000	$ 720,000
Short-term debt	325,000	–0–
Common stock ($10 par)	800,000	700,000
Additional paid-in capital	370,000	250,000
Retained earnings	940,000	490,000
Total liabilities and stockholders' equity	$3,260,000	$2,160,000

Information relating to 2005 activities follows:

- Net income for 2005 was $690,000.
- Cash dividends of $240,000 were declared and paid in 2005.
- Equipment costing $400,000 and having a carrying value of $150,000 was sold in 2005 for $150,000.
- A long-term investment was sold in 2005 for $135,000. There were no other transactions affecting long-term investments in that year.
- Ten thousand shares of common stock were issued in 2005 for $22 per share.
- Short-term investments consist of Treasury bills maturing on June 30, 2006.

Required:

1. What was the amount of net cash provided by Dice's 2005 operating activities?
2. What was the amount of net cash used in Dice's 2005 investing activities?
3. What was the amount of net cash provided by Dice's 2005 financing activities?

P17 – 3

Comparing direct and indirect methods of determining cash flows from operations

CMA
ADAPTED

The Spoke Company, a major retailer of bicycles and accessories, operates several stores and is a publicly traded company. The comparative statement of financial position and income statement for Spoke as of May 31, 2005 follows. The company is preparing its statement of cash flows to comply with *SFAS No. 95.*

Spoke Company

Comparative Statement of Financial Position as of May 31, 2005 and May 31, 2004

	May 31 2005	May 31 2004
Assets		
Cash	$ 43,250	$ 20,000
Accounts receivable	70,000	50,000
Merchandise inventory	210,000	250,000
Prepaid expenses	9,000	7,000
Total current assets	332,250	327,000
Plant assets	600,000	510,000
Less: Accumulated depreciation	(150,000)	(125,000)
Net plant assets	450,000	385,000
Total assets	$782,250	$712,000
Liabilities and Shareholders' Equity		
Accounts payable	$123,000	$115,000
Salaries payable	47,250	72,000
Interest payable	27,000	25,000
Total current liabilities	197,250	212,000
Long-term debt		
Bonds payable	70,000	100,000
Total liabilities	267,250	312,000
Shareholders' Equity		
Common stock, $10 par	370,000	280,000
Retained earnings	145,000	120,000
Total shareholders' equity	515,000	400,000
Total liabilities and shareholders' equity	$782,250	$712,000

Spoke Company

Income Statement for the Year Ended May 31, 2005

Sales	$1,255,250
Cost of merchandise sold	712,000
Gross margin	543,250
Expenses	
Salary expense	252,100
Interest expense	75,000
Other expenses	8,150
Depreciation expense	25,000
Total expenses	360,250
Operating income	183,000
Income tax expense	43,000
Net income	$ 140,000

The following is additional information concerning Spoke's transactions during the year ended May 31, 2005:

- All sales during the year were made on account.
- All merchandise was purchased on account, comprising the total accounts payable account.
- Plant assets costing $90,000 were purchased by paying $40,000 in cash and by issuing 5,000 shares of stock.
- The "Other expenses" are related to prepaid items.
- All income taxes incurred during the year were paid during the year.
- In order to supplement its cash, Spoke issued 4,000 shares of common stock at par value.
- There were no penalties assessed for the retirement of bonds.
- Cash dividends of $115,000 were declared and paid at the end of the fiscal year.

Required:

1. Prepare a statement of cash flows for Spoke Company for the year ended May 31, 2005 using the direct method. Be sure to support the statement with appropriate calculations. (A reconciliation of net income to net cash is not required.)
2. Using the indirect method, calculate only the net cash flow from operating activities for Spoke Company for the year ended May 31, 2005.
3. Compare and contrast the direct method and the indirect method for reporting cash flows from operating activities, as prescribed by *SFAS No. 95*. What are the advantages and limitations of each approach?

The following are selected balance sheet accounts of Zach Corporation at December 31, 2005 and 2004, as well as the increases or decreases in each account from 2004 to 2005. Also presented is selected income statement information for the year ended December 31, 2005, as well as additional information.

P17–4

Determining amounts reported on statement of cash flows

Selected Balance Sheet Accounts

	2005	2004	Increase (Decrease)
Assets			
Accounts receivable	$ 34,000	$ 24,000	$10,000
Property, plant and equipment	277,000	247,000	30,000
Accumulated depreciation	(178,000)	(167,000)	11,000
Liabilities and Stockholders' Equity			
Bonds payable	49,000	46,000	3,000
Dividends payable	8,000	5,000	3,000
Common stock, $1 par	22,000	19,000	3,000
Additional paid-in capital	9,000	3,000	6,000
Retained earnings	104,000	91,000	13,000

Selected Income Statement Information for the Year Ended December 31, 2005

Sales revenue	$155,000
Depreciation	33,000
Gain on sale of equipment	13,000
Net income	28,000

Additional Information:

- Accounts receivable relate to sales of merchandise.
- During 2005 equipment that cost $40,000 was sold for cash.
- During 2005 $20,000 of bonds payable were issued in exchange for property, plant and equipment. There was no amortization of bond discount or premium.

Required:

Items 1 through 5, which follow, represent activities that will be reported in Zach's statement of cash flows for the year ended December 31, 2005. For each item, determine both the amount that should be reported in Zach's 2005 statement of cash flows and the section (operating, investing, or financing) in which the item should appear.

1. Cash collections from customers (direct method)
2. Payments for the purchase of property, plant and equipment
3. Proceeds from the sale of equipment
4. Cash dividends paid
5. Redemption of bonds payable

P17 – 5

Determining amounts reported on statement of cash flows

The Flax Corporation uses the direct method to prepare its statement of cash flows. Flax's trial balances at December 31, 2005 and 2004 are as follows:

	December 31	
	2005	2004
Debits		
Cash	$ 35,000	$ 32,000
Accounts receivable	33,000	30,000
Inventory	31,000	47,000
Property, plant and equipment	100,000	95,000
Unamortized bond discount	4,500	5,000
Cost of goods sold	250,000	380,000
Selling expenses	141,500	172,000
General and administrative expenses	137,000	151,300
Interest expense	4,300	2,600
Income tax expense	20,400	61,200
	$756,700	$976,100
Credits		
Allowance for uncollectible accounts	$ 1,300	$ 1,100
Accumulated depreciation	16,500	15,000
Trade accounts payable	25,000	17,500
Income taxes payable	21,000	27,100
Deferred income taxes	5,300	4,600
8% callable bonds payable	45,000	20,000
Common stock	50,000	40,000
Additional paid-in capital	9,100	7,500
Retained earnings	44,700	64,600
Sales	538,800	778,700
	$756,700	$976,100

Additional Information:

- Flax purchased $5,000 in equipment during 2005.
- Flax allocated one third of its depreciation expense to selling expenses and the remainder to general and administrative expenses.

Show your work for all answers to the following questions:

Required:

What amount should Flax report in its statement of cash flows for the year ended December 31, 2005 for the following:

1. Cash collected from customers?
2. Cash paid for goods sold?
3. Cash paid for interest?
4. Cash paid for income taxes?
5. Cash paid for selling expenses?

The balance sheets of Global Trading Company follow:

P17 – 6

Preparation and analysis of cash flow statement

Global Trading Company

Balance Sheets as of December 31

	2005	2004
Assets		
Cash	$120,000	$108,000
Accounts receivable	50,000	300,000
Less: Allowance for doubtful accounts	(20,000)	(30,000)
Inventory	80,000	250,000
Prepaid insurance	–0–	20,000
Property, plant and equipment	500,000	500,000
Less: Accumulated depreciation	(450,000)	(400,000)
Goodwill	–0–	70,000
Total assets	$280,000	$818,000
Liabilities and Owners' Equity		
Accounts payable	$100,000	$ 22,000
Salaries payable	17,000	11,000
Bank loan	82,500	390,000
Capital stock	75,000	75,000
Retained earnings	5,500	320,000
Total liabilities and owners' equity	$280,000	$818,000

The following additional information is also provided: (1) The company reported a net loss of $279,500 during the year 2005, (2) there are no income taxes, (3) goodwill as of December 31, 2004 was part of an acquisition made during 2004, and (4) the company's bank provides a working capital loan to a maximum of 75% of net accounts receivable and inventory.

Required:

1. Prepare a statement of cash flows using the indirect method for the year ended December 31, 2005.
2. On the basis of available information, provide an assessment of the financial performance of the company during 2005. In answering this part, consider both the net income and cash flows of the company. Also evaluate the future prospects of the company.
3. Assuming that the bad debt expense during 2005 was $55,000, calculate the bad debts written off during the year. Further assume that the company collected $1,250,000 cash from its customers during 2005 and then compute the sales revenue for the year. You may assume that all sales are credit sales.
4. In answering this part, assume that Global uses the first-in, first-out (FIFO) inventory method. On December 31, 2005 the company purchased $35,000 worth of inventory on credit from a supplier. The transaction was inadvertently not recorded since physical possession was not obtained as of December 31, 2005. Discuss the effect of this omission on the financial statements of Global Trading Company.

P17 – 7

Preparation of the cash flow statement and balance sheet

The following is the cash account of JKI Advertising Agencies for the year ended December 31, 2005:

Cash Account

	DR	CR
Beginning balance as of 1/1/05	$ 30,000	
Cash collected from clients	215,000	
Cash received from sale of land at book value	150,000	
Rent collected	50,000	
Capital contributions	35,000	
Line of credit borrowing from Town Bank	50,000	
Salaries paid		$130,000
Purchase of office equipment		20,000
Cash paid for insurance		12,000
Building loan repaid		85,000
Cash paid for interest		9,000
Dividends declared and paid		18,000
Cash paid for customer lawsuit		32,000
Cash paid for taxes		31,000
	$530,000	$337,000
Ending balance as of 12/31/05	$193,000	

Provided next are the income statement for the year ended December 31, 2005 and the balance sheet as of December 31, 2005 for JKI Advertising Agencies.

Assume there are no bad debts and no deferred taxes.

JKI Advertising Agencies

Income Statement for the Year Ended December 31, 2005

Advertising revenue	$250,000
Rent revenue	36,000
Salaries expense	(126,000)
Employee incentive bonus	(25,200)
Depreciation expense—building	(20,000)
Depreciation expense—office equipment	(8,000)
Insurance expense	(12,000)
Interest expense	(10,000)
Income before taxes	84,800
Income tax expense	(33,920)
Net income	$ 50,880

JKI Advertising Agencies

Balance Sheet as of December 31, 2005

Cash	$193,000
Accounts receivable	80,000
Prepaid insurance	3,000
Building	600,000
Less: Accumulated depreciation	(380,000)
Office equipment	80,000
Less: Accumulated depreciation	(39,000)
Total assets	$537,000
Salaries payable	$ 7,000
Interest payable	3,500
Rent received in advance	14,000
Bonus payable	25,200
Taxes payable	2,920
Borrowing from Town Bank	50,000
Building loan	35,000
Capital stock	135,000
Retained earnings	264,380
Total of liabilities and equities	$537,000

Required:

1. Based on the cash account, prepare a statement of cash flows using the direct approach.
2. Prepare the balance sheet as of December 31, 2004.
3. Prepare the operating section of the cash flow statement for the year ended December 31, 2005 under the indirect approach.
4. Evaluate the following statements:

   a. "Since depreciation is added to net income when calculating cash flow from operations, depreciation is a direct source of operating cash flow."
   b. "Over the entire life of a company, its cash flow from operations will equal its net income."

5. JKI has a policy of accruing an employee's incentive bonus at 20% of salary. Instead, if JKI had calculated the bonus at 25% of salary, what would be the revised figure for cash flow from operations under the indirect approach?

Excerpts from the financial statements of Briggs & Stratton Corporation and Ramsay Health Care, Inc. are provided next. (**Note:** Year 1 is previous year and Year 2 is current year.)

P17 – 8

Reconciliation of changes in balance sheet accounts with amounts reported in the cash flow statement

Briggs and Stratton Corporation

Excerpts from Consolidated Balance Sheets as of July 3, Year 2 and June 27, Year 1

	Year 2	Year 1
Assets		
Current assets		
Cash and cash equivalents	$221,101,000	$ 39,501,000
Short-term investments	–0–	70,422,000
Receivables, less reserves of $1,678,000		
and $754,000, respectively	122,597,000	124,981,000

Briggs and Stratton Corporation

Consolidated Statements of Cash Flows for the Years Ended July 3, Year 2 and June 27, Year 1

	Year 2	Year 1
Cash Flows from Operating Activities		
Net income	$ 69,923,000	$ 70,345,000
Adjustments to reconcile net income to net cash provided by operating activities:		
Cumulative effect of accounting changes, net of income taxes	32,558,000	–0–
Depreciation	42,950,000	47,222,000
(Gain) loss on disposition of plant and equipment	(96,000)	4,027,000
Loss on foreign subsidiary	–0–	3,500,000
Change in operating assets and liabilities:		
(Increase) decrease in receivables	2,384,000	(21,366,000)
(Increase) in inventories	(11,605,000)	(1,576,000)
(Increase) in other current assets	(10,593,000)	(1,893,000)
Increase in accounts payable, accrued liabilities and income taxes	38,132,000	13,731,000
Other, net	1,420,000	(3,699,000)
Net cash provided by operating activities	$165,073,000	$110,291,000

Ramsay Health Care, Inc. and Subsidiaries

Consolidated Statements of Cash Flows Year Ended June 30

	Year 2	Year 1
Cash Flows from Operating Activities		
Net income (loss)	$ 1,322,000	$(1,560,000)
Adjustments to reconcile net income (loss) to net cash provided by operating activities:		
Cumulative effect of change in accounting for income taxes	–0–	(2,353,000)
Depreciation and amortization	7,638,000	7,173,000
Loss on early extinguishment of debt	258,000	1,580,000
Write-off of development and other costs	–0–	1,367,000
(Gain) loss on disposal of assets	722,000	(121,000)
Provision for deferred income taxes	(1,188,000)	(696,000)
Provision for doubtful accounts	5,846,000	8,148,000
Provision for loss on sales and closure of facilities	–0–	6,415,000
Minority interests	4,824,000	1,126,000
Adjustments for (increase) decrease in operating assets:		
Patient accounts receivable	(2,169,000)	(8,833,000)
Other current assets	(2,071,000)	1,233,000
Other noncurrent assets	(554,000)	164,000
Adjustments for increase (decrease) in operating liabilities:		
Accounts payable	(2,484,000)	940,000
Accrued salaries, wages and other liabilities	3,150,000	(674,000)
Unpaid self-insurance claims	(1,078,000)	(456,000)
Amounts due to third-party contractual agencies	(1,385,000)	724,000
Total adjustments	11,509,000	15,737,000
Net cash provided by operating activities	$12,831,000	$14,177,000

Ramsay Health Care, Inc. and Subsidiaries

Excerpts from Consolidated Balance Sheets

	June 30	
	Year 2	Year 1
Current Assets		
Patient accounts receivable, less allowances for doubtful accounts of $3,925,000 and $4,955,000 at June 30, Year 2 and Year 1, respectively	$23,019,000	$26,696,000

Required:

1. Reconcile the difference, if any, between the change in accounts receivable as reported in the statement of cash flows and the change in receivables based on the balance sheet values for each company.
2. Explain the different reporting practices adopted by the two companies with respect to adjustments made in the statement of cash flows for changes in accounts receivable.

Presented next are the balance sheet accounts of Bergen Corporation as of December 31, 2005 and 2004.

P17 – 9

Preparation of cash flow
statement—Indirect method

ADAPTED

	2005	2004	Increase (Decrease)
Assets			
Current Assets:			
Cash	$ 541,000	$ 308,000	$233,000
Accounts receivable, net	585,000	495,000	90,000
Inventories	895,000	780,000	115,000
Total current assets	2,021,000	1,583,000	438,000
Land	350,000	250,000	100,000
Plant and equipment	1,060,000	720,000	340,000
Accumulated depreciation	(295,000)	(170,000)	(125,000)
Leased equipment under capital lease	158,000	–0–	158,000
Marketable investment securities, at cost	–0–	75,000	(75,000)
Investment in Mason, Inc. at cost	180,000	180,000	–0–
Total assets	$3,474,000	$2,638,000	$836,000
Liabilities and Stockholders' Equity			
Current liabilities:			
Current portion of long-term debt	$ 159,000	$ –0–	$159,000
Accounts payable and accrued expenses	760,000	823,000	(63,000)
Total current liabilities	919,000	823,000	96,000
Note payable, long-term	300,000	–0–	300,000
Liability under capital lease	124,000	–0–	124,000
Bonds payable	500,000	500,000	–0–
Unamortized bond premium	16,000	18,000	(2,000)
Deferred income taxes	60,000	45,000	15,000
Common stock, par-value $20	640,000	600,000	40,000
Additional paid-in capital	304,000	244,000	60,000
Retained earnings	611,000	408,000	203,000
Total liabilities and stockholders' equity	$3,474,000	$2,638,000	$836,000

Additional Information:

- On January 2, 2005 Bergen sold all of its marketable investment securities for $95,000 cash.
- On March 10, 2005 Bergen paid a cash dividend of $30,000 on its common stock. No other dividends were paid or declared during 2005.
- On April 15, 2005 Bergen issued 2,000 shares of its common stock for land having a fair value of $100,000.
- On May 25, 2005 Bergen borrowed $450,000 from an insurance company. The underlying promissory note bears interest at 15% and is payable in three equal annual installments of $150,000. The first payment is due on May 25, 2006.
- On June 15, 2005 Bergen purchased equipment for $392,000 cash.
- On July 1, 2005 Bergen sold equipment costing $52,000, with a book value of $28,000 for $33,000 cash.
- On September 1, 2005 Bergen paid a $20,000 additional tax assessment for 2004 due to an error in tax calculation discovered by the Internal Revenue Service. This payment was appropriately recorded by Bergen as a prior period adjustment.
- On December 31, 2005 Bergen leased equipment from Tilden Company for a ten-year period. Equal payments under the lease are $25,000 and are due on December 31 each year. The first payment was made on December 31, 2005. The present value at December 31, 2005 of the ten lease payments is $158,000. Bergen appropriately recorded the lease as a capital lease. The $25,000 lease payment due on December 31, 2006 will consist of $9,000 principal and $16,000 interest.

- Bergen's net income for 2005 is $253,000.
- Bergen owns a 10% interest in the voting common stock of Mason, Inc. Mason reported net income of $120,000 for the year ended December 31, 2005 and paid a common stock dividend of $55,000 during 2005.

Required:

Prepare a cash flow statement for Bergen using the indirect method for 2005.

P17 – 10

Preparing an income statement from statement of cash flows and comparative balance sheets

The following are balance sheets of Kang-Iyer Financial Consultants:

Kang-Iyer Financial Consultants

Balance Sheet December 31, 2005

	December 31	
	2005	**2004**
Cash	$ 30,000	$ 70,000
Accounts receivable	80,000	15,000
Less: Allowance for doubtful accounts	(8,000)	(1,500)
Prepaid rent	–0–	30,000
Land	600,000	400,000
Building	500,000	–0–
Less: Accumulated depreciation	(10,000)	–0–
Total assets	$1,192,000	$513,500
Salaries payable	100,000	20,000
Interest payable	20,000	5,000
Loan from Village Bank	700,000	200,000
Contributed capital	75,000	30,000
Retained earnings	297,000	258,500
Total liabilities and owners' equity	$1,192,000	$513,500

The bad debts total written off during the year 2005 totaled $41,500.

Kang-Iyer Financial Consultants

Statement of Cash Flows for the Year Ended December 31, 2005

Cash Flow from Operating Activities	
Cash collected from customers	$250,000
Cash paid to employees	(70,000)
Cash paid for interest	(50,000)
Cash flow from operations	130,000
Cash Flow from Investing Activities	?
Cash Flow from Financing Activities	
Dividends paid	(15,000)
Change in cash	(40,000)
Beginning cash balance	70,000
Ending cash balance	$ 30,000

Required:

Complete the following cash flow statement and prepare an income statement for the year ended December 31, 2005. *Hint:* To prepare the income statement, use the information in the balance sheets and the cash flow statement to "solve" for the income statement items. For example, by preparing a T-account for salaries payable and then incorporating in this account the information on cash paid to employees, you can solve for salaries expense.

Best Corporation's financial statements for 2004 and 2005 and additional information for 2005 are presented next.

Best Corporation

Balance Sheets

	2005	2004
Assets		
Current assets:		
Cash	$ 480,000	$ 220,000
Accounts receivable—net	840,000	560,000
Merchandise inventory	760,000	470,000
Total current assets	2,080,000	1,250,000
Land, buildings, and fixtures	1,330,000	800,000
Less: Accumulated depreciation	210,000	150,000
Total noncurrent assets	1,120,000	650,000
Total assets	$3,200,000	$1,900,000
Liabilities and Stockholders' Equity		
Current liabilities:		
Accounts payable	$ 830,000	$ 440,000
Accrued expenses	300,000	130,000
Dividends payable	40,000	—
Total current liabilities	1,170,000	570,000
Stockholders' equity:		
Common stock ($10 par value)	1,200,000	900,000
Additional paid-in capital	200,000	100,000
Retained earnings	630,000	330,000
Total stockholders' equity	2,030,000	1,330,000
Total liabilities and stockholders' equity	$3,200,000	$1,900,000

Best Corporation

Income Statements Years Ended December 31

	2005	2004
Credit sales	$6,300,000	$4,000,000
Cost of goods sold	4,900,000	3,200,000
Gross profit	1,400,000	800,000
Expenses (including income taxes)	700,000	630,000
Net income	$ 700,000	$ 170,000

Best Corporation

Changes in Stockholders' Equity Years Ended December 31

	2005	2004
Common Stock		
Balance 1/1/05	$ 900,000	$900,000
Additional shares sold 4/1/05	100,000	–0–
20% stock dividend 6/1/05	200,000	–0–
Balance 12/31/05	$1,200,000	$900,000
Additional Paid-in Capital		
Balance 1/1/05	$ 100,000	$100,000
Additional shares sold 4/1/05	25,000	–0–
20% stock dividend 6/1/05	75,000	–0–
Balance 12/31/05	$ 200,000	$100,000
Retained Earnings		
Balance 1/1/05	$ 330,000	$250,000
Net income	700,000	170,000
Cash dividends	(125,000)	(90,000)
Stock dividends	(275,000)	–0–
Balance 12/31/05	$ 630,000	$330,000

Additional Information:

- During 2005 Best sold fixtures with a book value of $30,000 ($100,000 cost minus $70,000 accumulated depreciation) at a $10,000 loss. This loss was included in the income statement. Depreciation expense for 2005 was $130,000. Best purchased $630,000 of new fixtures during 2005.
- Common stock issued during 2005 was as follows:

Date	Number of Shares
4/1/05	10,000
6/1/05	20,000

Required:

1. How much cash from operations should be reported in the statement of cash flows for 2005?
2. How much cash was provided by financing activities?
3. How much cash was used by investing activities?

P17 – 12

Analysis of statement of cash flows

The financial statements of Cavalier Toy Stores (a fictitious merchandising company) follow:

Cavalier Toy Stores

Income Statements for the Year Ended December 31, 2005

Sales revenue		$1,500,000
Cost of goods sold		(1,200,000)
Gross margin		300,000
Other expenses:		
Salaries expense	$200,000	
Bad debt expense	100,000	
Insurance expense	30,000	
Office supplies expense	55,000	
Depreciation expense—office building	30,000	
Depreciation expense—office equipment	45,000	
Interest expense	90,000	550,000
Net loss		$ (250,000)

Cavalier Toy Stores

Statement of Retained Earnings for the Year Ended December 31, 2005

Retained earnings 1/1/05	$600,000
Net loss for the year	(250,000)
Dividends paid	(300,000)
Retained earnings 12/31/05	$ 50,000

Cavalier Toy Stores

Balance Sheets

	December 31	
	2005	**2004**
Assets		
Current assets:		
Cash	$ 30,000	$ 180,000
Accounts receivable	100,000	525,000
Less: Allowance for doubtful accounts	(10,000)	(30,000)
Prepaid insurance	5,000	35,000
Inventory	50,000	550,000

	December 31	
	2005	**2004**
Noncurrent assets:		
Office building	900,000	–0–
Less: Accumulated depreciation	(30,000)	–0–
Office equipment	200,000	200,000
Less: Accumulated depreciation	(85,000)	(40,000)
Total assets	**$1,160,000**	**$1,420,000**
Liabilities and Owners' Equity		
Current liabilities:		
Salaries payable	$ 100,000	$ 80,000
Interest payable	8,000	16,000
Accounts payable for inventory purchases	252,000	64,000
Dividends payable	–0–	50,000
Noncurrent liabilities:		
Loan from Thrifty Bank	700,000	560,000
Owners' Equity:		
Contributed capital	50,000	50,000
Retained earnings	50,000	600,000
Total liabilities and owners' equity	**$1,160,000**	**$1,420,000**

Required:

1. Prepare a statement of cash flows using the indirect method.
2. Compute the following for the year ended December 31, 2005:

   a. Bad debts written off during the year
   b. Cash collected from customers
   c. Purchases of inventory made during the year
   d. Cash paid to suppliers for inventory purchases
   e. Cash paid for insurance.

3. The following is an excerpt from the chief executive officer's letter to the stockholders that was included in the annual report of Cavalier Toy Stores:

   It feels real good to finish 2005 and be thankful that your company achieved its best year ever. I am sure that you are all puzzled by my statement given the net loss we have reported in the income statement. Let me explain. Although our gross margin has declined from last year's because of competitive pressures, we have set a company record in terms of sales revenue. You know quite well how accounting income can be manipulated. We don't play that game. We let cash flows tell our success story. Also, we have very efficiently managed our receivables and inventory, and at the same time, taken advantage of all available credit from our suppliers. More importantly, I am sure all of you are very pleased with the dividends that you have received this year. Let me end this letter by proudly inviting you to visit our new executive office building. While touring the luxurious executive suites, please remember that your top management team did not burden you with one dollar of debt to buy this building.

   Assume you are a commercial lending officer at Thrifty Bank. The working capital loan given to Cavalier Toy Stores has a balance outstanding as of December 31, 2005 of $700,000 and is repayable by April 1, 2006. The CEO has sent a loan proposal to Thrifty Bank requesting renewal of the loan for one more year and an increase in the credit limit to $1,000,000. Your job is to write a report to your boss with a specific recommendation on whether to accept or reject the proposal. Base your recommendation on the information available to you. In your report, please consider all the claims made by the CEO in the letter to stockholders.

P17 – 13

Preparation of the cash flow statement

AICPA
ADAPTED

Presented next are the balance sheets of Farrell Corporation as of December 31, 2005 and 2004, as well as the statement of income and retained earnings for the year ended December 31, 2005.

Farrell Corporation

Balance Sheets December 31, 2005 and 2004

	2005	2004	Increase (Decrease)
Assets			
Cash	$ 275,000	$ 180,000	$ 95,000
Accounts receivable, net	295,000	305,000	(10,000)
Inventories	549,000	431,000	118,000
Investment in Hall, Inc. (equity method)	73,000	60,000	13,000
Land	350,000	200,000	150,000
Plant and equipment	624,000	606,000	18,000
Less: Accumulated depreciation	(139,000)	(107,000)	(32,000)*
Goodwill	16,000	20,000	(4,000)
Total assets	$2,043,000	$1,695,000	$348,000
Liabilities and Stockholders' Equity			
Accounts payable and accrued expenses	$ 604,000	$ 563,000	$ 41,000
Note payable, long-term	150,000	–0–	150,000
Bonds payable	160,000	210,000	(50,000)
Deferred income taxes	41,000	30,000	11,000
Common stock, par value $10	430,000	400,000	30,000
Additional paid-in capital	226,000	175,000	51,000
Retained earnings	432,000	334,000	98,000
Treasury stock, at cost	–0–	(17,000)	17,000
Total liabilities and stockholders' equity	$2,043,000	$1,695,000	$348,000

*This is an increase, but because Accumulated depreciation is shown as a deduction from Plant and equipment, it is shown with parentheses.

Farrell Corporation

Statement of Income and Retained Earnings for the Year Ended December 31, 2005

Net sales		$1,950,000
Operating expenses		
Cost of sales	$1,150,000	
Selling and administrative expenses	505,000	
Depreciation	53,000	
		1,708,000
Operating income		242,000
Other (income) expense		
Interest expense	15,000	
Equity in net income of Hall, Inc.	(13,000)	
Loss on sale of equipment	5,000	
Amortization of goodwill	4,000	11,000
Income before income taxes		231,000
Income taxes		
Current	79,000	
Deferred	11,000	
Provision for income taxes		90,000
Net income		141,000
Retained earnings 1/1/05		334,000
		475,000
Cash dividends, paid 8/14/05		43,000
Retained earnings 12/31/05		$ 432,000

Additional Information:

- On January 2, 2005 Farrell sold equipment that cost $45,000 with a $24,000 book value for $19,000 cash.
- On April 1, 2005 Farrell issued 1,000 shares of common stock for $23,000 cash.
- On May 15, 2005 Farrell sold all of its treasury stock for $25,000 cash.
- On June 1, 2005 individuals holding $50,000 face value of Farrell's bonds exercised their conversion privilege. Each of the 50 bonds was converted into 40 shares of Farrell's common stock.
- On July 1, 2005 Farrell purchased equipment with $63,000 cash.
- On December 31, 2005 land with a fair market value of $150,000 was purchased through the issuance of a long-term note in the amount of $150,000. The note bears interest at the rate of 15% and is due on December 31, 2010.
- Deferred income taxes represent temporary differences relating to the use of accelerated depreciation methods for income tax reporting and the straight-line method for financial statement reporting.

Required:

Prepare a statement of cash flows (indirect approach) and all necessary related schedules of Farrell Corporation for the year ended December 31, 2005.

Omega Corporation's comparative balance sheet accounts worksheet at December 31, 2005 and 2004 follow, with a column showing the increase (decrease) from 2004 to 2005.

P17 – 14

Statement of cash flows—
Indirect approach

AICPA
ADAPTED

Comparative Balance Sheet Worksheet

	2005	2004	Increase (Decrease)
Cash	$ 800,000	$ 700,000	$100,000
Accounts receivable	1,128,000	1,168,000	(40,000)
Inventories	1,850,000	1,715,000	135,000
Property, plant and equipment	3,307,000	2,967,000	340,000
Accumulated depreciation	(1,165,000)	(1,040,000)	(125,000)
Investment in Belle Company	305,000	275,000	30,000
Loan receivable	270,000	–0–	270,000
Total assets	$6,495,000	$5,785,000	$710,000
Accounts payable	$1,015,000	$ 955,000	$ 60,000
Income taxes payable	30,000	50,000	(20,000)
Dividends payable	80,000	90,000	(10,000)
Capital lease obligation	400,000	–0–	400,000
Capital stock, common, $1 par	500,000	500,000	–0–
Additional paid-in capital	1,500,000	1,500,000	–0–
Retained earnings	2,970,000	2,690,000	280,000
Total liabilities and stockholders' equity	$6,495,000	$5,785,000	$710,000

Additional Information:

- On December 31, 2004 Omega acquired 25% of Belle Company's common stock for $275,000. On that date, the carrying value of Belle's assets and liabilities, which approximated their fair values, was $1,100,000. Belle reported income of $120,000 for the year ended December 31, 2005. No dividend was paid on Belle's common stock during the year.
- During 2005 Omega loaned $300,000 to Chase Company, an unrelated company. Chase made the first semiannual principal repayment of $30,000, plus interest at 10%, on October 1, 2005.
- On January 2, 2005 Omega sold equipment for $40,000 cash that cost $60,000 and had a carrying amount of $35,000.
- On December 31, 2005 Omega entered into a capital lease for an office building. The present value of the annual rental payments is $400,000, which equals the fair value of the building. Omega made the first rental payment of $60,000, when due, on January 2, 2006.
- Net income for 2005 was $360,000.
- Omega declared and paid cash dividends for 2005 and 2004 as follows:

	2005	2004
Declared	12/15/05	12/15/04
Paid	2/28/06	2/28/05
Amount	$80,000	$90,000

Required:

Prepare a statement of cash flows for Omega Corporation for the year ended December 31, 2005 using the indirect approach.

CASES

C17 – 1

Q-Mart Retail Stores, Inc. (KR): Analysis of statement of cash flows

The income statement and comparative balance sheet of Q-Mart Retail Stores, Inc. follow.

Q-Mart Retail Stores, Inc.

Income Statement for the Year Ended December 31, 2005

Sales revenue	$1,500,000
Cost of goods sold	(1,050,000)
Gross profit	450,000
Operating expenses:	
Salaries expense	(80,000)
Insurance expense	(60,000)
Bad debt expense	(50,000)
Depreciation expense—building	(25,000)
Depreciation expense—computer equipment	(35,000)
Interest expense	(55,000)
Other expenses	(20,000)
Net income before income taxes	125,000
Provision for income taxes	(43,750)
Net income	$ 81,250

Note: There are no deferred income taxes for this company.

Q-Mart Retail Stores, Inc.

Comparative Balance Sheet

	December 31	
	2005	**2004**
Current Assets		
Cash	$ 120,000	$ 504,750
Accounts receivable	500,000	100,000
Less: Allowance for doubtful accounts	(50,000)	(11,000)
Inventory	350,000	75,000
Prepaid insurance	20,000	–0–
Noncurrent Assets		
Building	1,000,000	750,000
Less: Accumulated depreciation—building	(125,000)	(100,000)
Computer equipment	140,000	–0–
Less: Accumulated depreciation—computer	(35,000)	–0–
Total assets	$1,920,000	$1,318,750
Current Liabilities		
Salaries payable	$ 10,000	$ 42,000
Accounts payable due to suppliers	12,000	17,000
Income tax currently payable	15,000	8,000
Noncurrent Liabilities		
Loan from Upstate Bank	500,000	300,000
Stockholders' Equity		
Common stock	1,000,000	610,000
Retained earnings	383,000	341,750
Total liabilities and stockholders' equity	$1,920,000	$1,318,750

The CEO of Q-Mart, Mr. Peddler, is quite anxious about the dramatic decline in his company's cash position. He would like your help in understanding the sources and uses of Q-Mart's cash flows.

Required:

1. Prepare a statement of cash flows for the year ended December 31, 2005 using the indirect method. (*Hint:* In answering this part, just focus on the change in net accounts receivable when converting from net income to cash flow from operations.)
2. Compute the bad debts written off during 2005.
3. Compute the cash collected from customers during 2005. (Assume all sales are credit sales.)
4. Compute the amount of inventory purchases during 2005.
5. Compute the cash paid to suppliers during 2005. (Assume all purchases are credit purchases.)
6. Prepare a short memo to Mr. Peddler identifying the major reasons for the decline in the cash position. Evaluate whether this decline is an indication of future profitability or impending troubles. What additional information do you need to complete this evaluation?

Mr. Peddler skimmed through your cash flow statement. He is still quite puzzled about the change in his firm's cash position. He needs answers for the following questions.

7. "I see that our buildup in accounts receivable is a major drain on our cash flows. If I had known this, I would have stopped all sales to customers during the end of the year to boost our cash flows. What do you think of this strategy?"
8. "I see that depreciation is a source of cash flows. I think I have found the golden goose. Next year, I will increase the depreciation expense twofold to further boost our cash flows. What do you think of this idea?"
9. "I have heard people say that cash flow is king and earnings don't matter. Aren't investors likely to be concerned about our cash flow performance? Tell me what an investor might gain from jointly examining both the income statement and statement of cash flows."

Vulcan Corporation (a real company whose name has been disguised) is a leading worldwide manufacturer and distributor of uncoated and coated rubber-like fiberboard products. Vulcan's products are marketed to various industries, including companies in the following businesses: footwear, headwear, luggage, leather goods, belt backing, furniture, electronic integrated component packaging, and automotive supplies.

Information developed using Vulcan Corporation's financial statements for the year ended October 31, 2005 appears below.

C17 – 2

Vulcan Corporation: Understanding cash flow statements

Vulcan Corporation

Cash Flow from Operating Activities

($ in thousands)	Year Ended October 31, 2005
Cash received from customers	$37,378
Cash paid to suppliers	(26,884)
Cash paid for general and administrative expenses	(8,002)
Cash paid for interest	(810)
Cash paid for income taxes	(74)
Net cash provided by operating activities	$ 1,608

Vulcan Corporation

Selected Balance Sheet Information

	October 31	
($ in thousands)	2005	2004
Accounts receivable, net	$14,120	$11,043
Inventories	5,465	5,798
Property, plant and equipment, net	10,707	11,523
Accounts payable	7,756	6,375
Accrued general and administrative expenses	2,559	1,871
Interest payable	130	52
Deferred taxes payable	936	675

Additional Information:

- Total comprehensive income for the year ended October 31, 2005 was $336,000.
- Other comprehensive loss (net of applicable income taxes) consisted of unrealized loss on investments classified as available-for-sale securities of $286,000.
- Equipment purchased during the year totaled $854,000.
- The book value of equipment retired during the year totaled $348,000.

Required:

1. Compute Vulcan Corporation's net income loss for the year ended October 31, 2005. (*Hint:* All components of other comprehensive income or loss have been provided.)
2. Prepare Vulcan Corporation's combined Statement of Income (Loss) and Comprehensive Income (Loss) for the year ended October 31, 2005.
3. Determine Vulcan Corporation's net cash provided by operating activities using the indirect method.

C17 – 3

Fillio Corporation (KR): Comprehensive statement of cash flows

This problem is based on the financial statements and selected footnotes of Fillio Corporation presented on the next few pages. Fillio is a Delaware corporation that is engaged in the contract manufacturing and testing of products and assemblies for use in the computer, communications, medical, instrumentation, and peripherals industries. The company has two operating facilities in Parma, Ohio, one in Columbus, Ohio, and one in Youngstown, Ohio. This is a real company whose name has been disguised.

Required:

1. Using the indirect method, prepare the statement of cash flows for the year ended December 31, 2005 in as much detail as possible. For example, borrowing and repayment should be shown separately as financing inflow and outflow, respectively. Similarly, to the extent information is available, separately disclose and explain the changes to each asset and each liability account that affected Fillio Corporation's cash flows in 2005.
2. Redo the operating section of the statement of cash flows using the direct method. *Assumptions:* In preparing the statement of cash flows using the direct method, you may assume that (a) the entire depreciation expense relates to manufacturing operations, (b) prepaid expenses as well as accrued payroll and related expenses relate to marketing, general and administrative expenses, (c) other payables and accruals relate to other expenses, and (d) accrued settlement and restructuring costs as well as accrued settlement costs pertain to litigation settlements and restructuring charges expensed in prior accounting periods.

Fillio Corporation

Balance Sheet

	December 31	
($ in thousands)	2005	2004
Assets		
Current assets		
Cash	$ 897	$ 48
Trade accounts receivable	19,021	32,803
Less: Allowance for doubtful accounts	(531)	(608)
Income tax refund receivable	229	6,960
Inventories	28,410	50,869
Prepaid expenses	1,195	360
Total current assets	49,221	90,432
Property, plant and equipment		
Land	295	295
Buildings and improvements	9,850	9,386
Building construction in progress	178	371
Machinery and equipment	45,476	45,522
Less: Accumulated depreciation	(26,327)	(18,630)
Deferred financing costs and other, net	2,230	1,817
Total assets	$80,923	$129,193

($ in thousands)	December 31	
	2005	**2004**
Liabilities		
Current liabilities		
Current maturities of long-term debt	$ 2,322	$ 7,451
Trade accounts payable	7,592	30,317
Accrued payroll and related expenses	1,162	2,421
Accrued interest	1,087	1,054
Other payables and accruals	2,254	2,273
Accrued settlement and restructuring costs	1,500	3,932
Total current liabilities	15,917	47,448
Long-term liabilities		
Accrued settlement costs	–0–	1,500
Long-term debt	30,017	36,316
Subordinated convertible debentures	34,500	34,500
Total long-term liabilities	64,517	72,316
Stockholders' Equity		
6% Redeemable convertible preferred stock—no par value; authorized 5,000,000 shares; issued and outstanding 1,243,700 shares in 2005 and 1,050,000 in 2004 stated value is $10.00 per share	12,437	10,500
Common stock—par-value $0.01 per share; authorized 50,000,000 shares; issued and outstanding 11,012,373 and 10,872,024 shares in 2005 and 2004, respectively	110	109
Additional paid-in capital	29,544	29,019
Accumulated deficit	(41,602)	(30,199)
Total stockholders' equity	489	9,429
Total liabilities and stockholders' equity	$80,923	$129,193

Fillio Corporation

Income Statement for the Year Ended December 31, 2005
($ in thousands)

Sales	$184,137
Cost of sales	(181,010)
Gross profit	3,127
Marketing, general, and administrative expenses (including bad debt expense of $238)	(7,227)
Interest expense	(5,417)
Interest income (on income tax refund)	1,048
Settlement with Sitco	(1,837)
Other expense (including amortization of deferred financing costs and loss on write-off of equipment)	(935)
Total expenses (net of interest income)	(14,368)
Net loss	$(11,241)
Dividend in kind on preferred stock	(162)
Net loss applicable to common shares	$(11,403)

Additional Information

- *Dividend in kind on preferred stock:* The company has the option of paying a dividend in kind to the preferred shareholders. In 2005 the company exercised this option and issued 16,200 additional preferred shares in lieu of cash dividends (that is, one share per $10.00 of dividend).
- *Settlement with Sitco:* During the second quarter of 2005, the Company recognized a one-time nonrecurring charge of $1,837,000 related to an agreement with Sitco for the satisfaction of certain payments owing from the Company to Sitco. Under the terms of the agreement, the Company agreed to pay Sitco an aggregate $62,000 in cash and $1,775,000 in Series A Preferred Stock (valued at $10.00 per share). The preferred stock was distributed to Sitco during 2005.
- *Property, plant and equipment:* Depreciation expense for the year 2005 was $8,330,000. Machinery and equipment with a net book value of $227,000 was written off as worthless during 2005. Furthermore, the Company purchased some new machinery and equipment and invested additional money on buildings during 2005.
- *Long-term debt:* A summary of long-term debt follows.

	Balance as of December 31	
	2005	**2004**
Industrial development revenue bonds	$ 1,280	$ 1,600
Revolving line of credit, retired in 2005	–0–	19,973
Revolving equipment line of credit, retired in 2005	–0–	15,762
2005 Revolving line of credit	21,006	–0–
2005 Equipment term loan	6,000	–0–
Senior notes secured by equipment	2,450	6,432
2005 Bank loan secured by real property at prime plus 2% (The original term loan was for $3,000, which was reduced to 1,500 in December 2005 after payment to the lenders of $1,500 from the income tax refund proceeds.)	1,500	–0–
2005 Equipment loan at 9% (original amount borrowed $200)	103	–0–
Total debt	$32,339	$43,767
Less: Current maturities of long-term debt	(2,322)	(7,451)
Long-term debt	$30,017	$36,316

- *Deferred financing costs:* As part of its credit agreement restructuring costs in March 2005, the Company issued an aggregate of 50,000 shares of common stock to its former bank lenders and 50,000 shares of common stock to its term lenders. These shares were issued as compensation for the financing costs of $400,000 due to the lenders. These financing costs are included in "Deferred financing costs" and are being amortized over the life of the credit agreements. In addition, the company paid $601,000 cash for other loan initiation/structuring costs, which are also included in "Deferred financing costs."
- *Common stock:* In addition to the common shares issued to compensate for the financing costs, the Company issued additional shares to its employees under its Employee Incentive Stock Option Plans for $126,000 cash. No other common shares were issued during the year.

C17 – 4

Lucky Lady, Inc.:
Comprehensive statement
of cash flows

The income statement for the year ended December 31, 2005 as well as the balance sheets as of December 31, 2005 and December 31, 2004 for Lucky Lady, Inc. follow. This information is taken from the financial statements of a real company whose name has been disguised.

Lucky Lady, Inc.

Income Statement

($ in thousands)	For the Year Ended December 31, 2005
Revenues	
Casino	$ 26,702
Rooms	2,897
Food and beverage	2,351
Other hotel/casino	5,066
Airline	20,784
Total revenues	57,800
Operating Expenses	
Casino	9,341
Rooms	1,016
Food and beverage	2,529
Other hotel/casino	5,777
Airline	20,599
Selling, general, and administrative (including bad debt expense of $3,855)	19,679
Depreciation expense	8,018
Hotel preopening expenses	45,130
Aircraft carrying value adjustment	68,948
Total operating expenses	181,037
Operating income	(123,237)

($ in thousands)	For the Year Ended December 31, 2005
Nonoperating items:	
Interest income	12,231
Interest expense	(6,596)
Other, net	16
Income before taxes	(117,586)
Provision for income taxes	–0–
Net income (loss)	$(117,586)

Lucky Lady, Inc.

Balance Sheets

($ in thousands)	December 31 2005	December 31 2004
Assets		
Cash	$ 211,305	$ 579,963
Gross accounts receivable	35,249	2,178
Less: Allowance for doubtful accounts	(4,733)	(1,531)
Prepaid expenses	11,755	1,219
Inventories	12,662	154
Total current assets	266,238	581,983
Gross property, plant and equipment	953,796	471,506
Less: Accumulated depreciation	(86,512)	(21,796)
Pre-opening expenses	–0–	10,677
Other operating assets	26,601	21,116
Total assets	$1,160,123	$1,063,486
Liabilities and Stockholders' Equity		
Accounts payable	$ 14,181	$ 4,322
Accrued salaries and wages	8,194	945
Accrued interest on long-term debt	9,472	9,429
Other accrued liabilities	33,502	9,744
Construction payables	96,844	32,296
Current maturities, capital leases	1,830	289
Current maturities, long-term debt	1,573	–0–
Total current liabilities	165,596	57,025
Deferred revenues	10,784	–0–
Deferred income taxes	6,517	6,517
Long-term obligation, capital leases	14,044	162
Long-term debt	481,427	473,000
Total liabilities	678,368	536,704
Common stock	506	485
Capital in excess of par value	662,365	589,827
Common stock in treasury	(29,490)	(29,490)
Retained earnings (deficit)	(151,626)	(34,040)
Total stockholders' equity	481,755	526,782
Total liabilities and equity	$1,160,123	$1,063,486

Additional Information and Author-Supplied Explanations:

- *Aircraft valuation adjustment:* The company reduced the book value of its aircraft and related equipment to their expected recoverable values, and recognized an aircraft carrying value adjustment in the 2005 income statement. [*Author Note:* You may treat this item as "extra" depreciation recorded during the year due to abnormal decline in the asset value.]

- *Property, plant and equipment:* Includes land, buildings, aircraft equipment, furniture and fixtures, equipment under capital lease, etc. During 2005, the company acquired equipment under capital leases for $16,987,000. The company also sold equipment with a net book value of $2,501,000 for $684,000 cash. [*Author Note:* The gain or loss on this sale is combined with some other item in the income statement. Any other change in the gross book value of Property, plant and equipment may be attributed to outright purchase of other equipment and building construction costs.]

- *Capital lease and long-term liabilities:* [*Author Note:* When preparing the cash flow statement, you may find it convenient to combine the current and long-term portions of each of these liabilities.]
- *Pre-opening expenses:* Pre-opening expenses include direct project salaries, advertising, and other pre-opening services incurred during the pre-opening period of the Lucky Lady Hotel. Such expenses were expensed upon opening of the facility.
- *Stock offering:* The increases in common stock and capital in excess of par accounts are due to a common stock offering completed on August 17, 2005.
- *Laundry loan:* On June 16, 2005 the company obtained a $10,000,000 loan from a financial institution for a laundry facility in North Las Vegas, Nevada. As of December 31, 2005, $10,000,000 has been drawn down under the loan. Construction of the facility was completed in December 2005. The laundry provides the laundry and dry-cleaning services for the Lucky Lady Hotel.

Required:

1. Using the indirect method, prepare the statement of cash flows for the year ended December 31, 2005 in as much detail as possible. For example, borrowing and repayment, if any, should be shown separately as financing inflow and outflow, respectively. Similarly, to the extent information is available, separately disclose and explain the changes to each asset and each liability account that affected Lucky Lady's cash flows during 2005.
2. Redo the operating section of the cash flow statement using the direct method.

C17 – 5

Opus One, Inc. (KR):
Preparation and analysis of the cash flow statement

The following information is based on the 2005 annual report of Opus One, Inc. (a real company whose name has been disguised). Opus One operates in a single business segment, the retailing and servicing of home audio, car audio, and video equipment. Its operations are conducted in Texas through 20 stores and two service centers. The information provided in the annual report has been combined and abbreviated.

The following additional information is provided with respect to the year ended June 30, 2005:

- The company did not declare or pay any cash or stock dividends during the year.
- The company reported a loss of $7,377 from scrapping equipment with a book value of the same amount.
- The depreciation expense for the year was $2,265,735.
- The following breakdown is provided for the long-term debt:

	June 30	
($ in thousands)	**2005**	**2004**
Long-Term Debt		
Term loan	$3,420,000	$ –0–
Mortgage note	534,475	555,455
Total	3,954,475	555,455
Less: Current installments	(681,716)	(21,348)
Long-term debt—current installments	$3,272,759	$534,107

Opus One, Inc.

Balance Sheet June 30, 2005 and 2004

	June 30	
($ in thousands)	**2005**	**2004**
Current Assets		
Cash	$ 50,885	$ 19,481
Receivables	4,625,920	6,963,195
Less: Allowance for bad debts	(403,000)	(1,200,000)
Inventories	25,986,364	26,801,526
Prepaid expenses	455,875	710,058
Income taxes receivable	1,573,055	3,073,537

($ in thousands)	June 30	
	2005	**2004**
Noncurrent Assets		
Property and equipment	22,182,371	20,637,912
Less: Accumulated depreciation	(9,031,181)	(6,822,553)
Deferred tax asset, net	1,043,403	531,803
Pre-opening costs	370,458	877,179
Goodwill	366,750	366,750
Less: Accumulated amortization	(122,509)	(98,059)
Total assets	$47,098,391	$51,860,829
Current Liabilities		
Revolving credit agreements	$ 4,810,398	$18,743,407
Accounts payable	11,054,418	7,951,545
Accrued liabilities	4,025,816	3,257,672
Current installments of long-term debt	681,716	21,348
Long-Term Liabilities		
Long-term debt minus current installments	3,272,759	534,107
Other liabilities and deferred credits	4,072,586	3,308,714
Total liabilities	27,917,693	33,816,793
Shareholders' Equity		
Common stock and additional paid-in capital	10,126,944	10,117,946
Retained earnings	9,053,754	7,926,090
Total shareholders' equity	19,180,698	18,044,036
Total liabilities and shareholders' equity	$47,098,391	$51,860,829

On February 26, 2005 the company obtained a term loan of $3,600,000 from a bank, due February 28, 2009.

Required:

1. Prepare a statement of cash flows for the year ended June 30, 2005 using the indirect approach.
2. On the basis of the cash flow statement, analyze the financial performance of Opus One during the fiscal year 2005.

COLLABORATIVE LEARNING CASE

What follows are the consolidated statements of cash flows of Best Buy Company, Inc. The information provided in the annual report has been combined and abbreviated.

C17 – 6

Best Buy Company, Inc.: Analysis of financial performance from the cash flow statement and other information

Best Buy Company, Inc.

Consolidated Statements of Cash Flows

($ in thousands)	For the Fiscal Years Ended		
	February 26 Year 3	**February 27 Year 2**	**February 28 Year 1**
Operating Activities			
Net earnings	$347,070	$216,282	$ 81,938
Depreciation, amortization and other non-cash charges	109,541	78,367	71,584
	456,611	294,649	153,522
Changes in operating assets and liabilities:			
Receivables	(56,900)	(36,699)	(16,121)
Merchandise inventories	(137,315)	14,422	71,271
Other assets	(11,005)	(4,251)	(3,278)
Accounts payable	302,194	249,094	147,340
Other liabilities	108,829	82,544	63,950
Accrued income taxes	97,814	62,672	33,759
Total cash provided by operating activities	760,228	662,431	450,443

(*continued on next page*)

Best Buy Company, Inc. (continued)

($ in thousands)	For the Fiscal Years Ended		
	February 26 Year 3	February 27 Year 2	February 28 Year 1
Investing Activities			
Additions to property and equipment	(361,024)	(165,698)	(72,063)
(Increase) decrease in recoverable costs from developed properties	(21,009)	(65,741)	45,270
(Increase) decrease in other assets	(18,081)	(18,128)	4,494
Total cash used in investing activities	(400,114)	(249,567)	(22,299)
Financing Activities			
Long-term debt payments	(29,946)	(165,396)	(22,694)
Long-term debt borrowings	–0–	–0–	10,000
Issuance of common stock	32,229	20,644	14,869
Repurchase of common stock	(397,451)	(2,462)	–0–
Total cash (used in) provided by financing activities	(395,168)	(147,214)	2,175
Increase (Decrease) in Cash and Cash Equivalents	$ (35,054)	$265,650	$430,319

The following data is based on information provided by the company in its SEC filings:

Best Buy Co., Inc. is the nation's largest volume specialty retailer of name-brand consumer electronics, home office equipment, entertainment software and appliances. Part of the Company's strategy is to provide a selection of brand name products comparable to retailers that specialize in the Company's principal product categories and seeks to ensure a high level of product availability for customers. The number of stores operated by the company increased from 272 at the end of Year 0, to 284, 311 and 357 at the end of Year 1, Year 2 and Year 3, respectively. When entering a major metropolitan market, the Company establishes a district office, service center and major appliance warehouse. Each new store requires working capital of approximately $4 million for merchandise inventory (net of vendor financing), leasehold improvements, fixtures and equipment. Pre-opening costs of approximately $600,000 per store are incurred through hiring, relocating and training new employees, and in merchandising the store. These costs are expensed as incurred.

Required:

1. Using information provided in the cash flow statement, compare Best Buy's earnings and cash flows from operations for the last three years and provide an explanation for the differences between these two numbers within each year and from year-to-year. Does earnings or operating cash flows provide a better indication of Best Buy's performance? Explain.
2. How have new store openings affected Best Buy's working capital needs over the last three years? Compare the company's actual changes in working capital to the working capital needed to support new store openings and comment on any differences.
3. Comment on the year-to-year changes in inventories for the last three years and how these changes have been financed.
4. Comment on any insights gained from an analysis of the Investing and Financing section of Best Buy's cash flow statement.

Remember to check the book's Companion Website for additional problem and case material.

www.prenhall.com/revsine

CHAPTER 18

Overview of International Financial Reporting Differences and Inflation

Learning Objectives

After studying this chapter, you will understand:

1. Why financial reporting philosophies and detailed GAAP procedures differed across countries in the past.

2. How globalization has relaxed cross-border barriers and prompted convergence of reporting standards across countries.

3. The reasons for the increased importance of the International Accounting Standards Board (IASB).

4. Efforts by the FASB and IASB to converge their respective standards and facilitate cross-border financial transactions.

5. Mechanisms for coping with reporting differences that persist.

6. Factors that will help determine whether the SEC will ease rules that require foreign companies that wish to have securities traded on U.S. exchanges to reconcile their reporting methods to U.S. GAAP.

7. Whether compliance with GAAP is carefully monitored in different countries.

8. That companies in foreign countries with high inflation rates depart from the historical cost reporting model.

9. The two major approaches for adjusting financial reports for changing prices—current cost accounting and general price-level accounting.

International investment in equity and debt securities has grown exponentially in the last decade. Exhibit 18.1 shows the remarkable growth in cross-border transactions in bonds and equities.

You can see from Exhibit 18.1 that during the 1980s, gross purchases and sales of U.S. securities by non-U.S. traders averaged $1,734 billion per year. But by 2001 these transactions by foreign traders totaled $20,188 billion annually—that's more than eleven times larger than what they had been in the 1980s. Exhibit 18.1 also shows that purchases and sales of foreign securities by U.S. traders experienced an even larger rate of increase. In the 1980s these transactions averaged $299 billion per year; in 2001 they totaled $5,789 billion—more than nineteen times their level in the 1980s.

It is also evident from Exhibit 18.1 that these remarkable growth rates occurred for both debt and equity securities across both foreign and domestic traders.

There is other evidence of this growth in international investment. Stock exchanges across the world now list significant numbers of foreign companies. For example, Exhibit 18.2 shows that foreign firms comprise 19.2% of the listings on the New York Stock Exchange (461 ÷ 2,400) and 17.5% of the listings on the London exchange (409 ÷ 2,332). And the numbers of these foreign listings continue to grow.

This unprecedented access to global capital as well as to global consumer markets has allowed companies from many countries to grow large. Exhibit 18.3 shows the home country of the five largest firms in eight selected industries for 2002. Clearly, investors who choose to concentrate on a specific industrial or commercial sector are compelled to think globally these days.

The growth of global investing has been fueled by several factors. For example, many major industrial countries have relaxed their security market regulatory rules, thus making it easier for foreign firms to meet listing requirements. Another factor relates to improvements in telecommunications and computer technology. Finally, investors understand that portfolios based on a global investment strategy are less risky than portfolios composed exclusively of domestic securities. That's because foreign issuers of securities are often subject to economic conditions that differ from those of domestic companies, thereby creating greater portfolio diversification.

EXHIBIT 18.1	**Market Value of U.S. Cross-Border Transactions in Long-Term Securities by Type of Security**				
Type of Security (Billions of dollars, annual rate)	**1980–89**	**1990–94**	**1995–99**	**2000**	**2001**
Gross foreign purchases and sales of U.S. securities	$1,734	$5,414	$11,715	$16,917	$20,188
Debt	1,515	4,906	9,339	9,881	13,810
Treasury	1,408	4,524	8,271	7,803	10,531
Agency	45	198	561	1,305	1,979
Corporate	62	184	507	773	1,300
Equity	219	508	2,376	7,036	6,378
Gross U.S. purchases and sales of foreign securities	299	1,577	3,756	5,537	5,789
Debt	216	1,130	2,267	1,923	2,542
Equity	83	447	1,489	3,614	3,247

Note: Figures for 2001 are based on data through June.

Source: *Federal Reserve Bulletin*, October 2001, p. 640.

EXHIBIT 18.2	**Foreign Listings on Selected Stock Exchanges**		
Stock Exchange	**Total Number of Companies Listed**	**Number of Domestic Companies Listed**	**Number of Foreign Companies Listed**
New York Stock Exchange	2,400	1,939	461
NASDAQ	4,063	3,618	445
Toronto Stock Exchange	1,299	1,261	38
Deutsche Börse*	983	748	235
London	2,332	1,923	409
Tokyo	2,141	2,103	38
Singapore	492	424	68

*Floor trading, including the market segment "Freiverkehr" (unofficial regulated market).

Source: World Federation of Exchanges website, www.world-exchanges.org. Data as of 2001.

International Financial Reporting

Earlier Impediments to Foreign Securities Transactions

This reporting approach originated and evolved in both the United Kingdom and the United States. In turn, this Anglo-American accounting perspective had an important influence on financial reporting in most British Commonwealth countries and numerous others. In the United Kingdom, the audit must ascertain whether the financial statements give a **true and fair view** of the company's state of affairs and profit or loss. The phrase "true and fair view" is central to financial reporting in the United Kingdom because it expresses the notion that financial statements must reflect the underlying economic conditions experienced by the reporting firm.

Before the early 1990s—that is, before cross-border investment started to soar—global investment decisions were complicated by the diversity of financial reporting measurement and disclosure rules used in different countries. Even the philosophy and objective of financial reporting differed considerably between nations. Two widely divergent financial reporting approaches existed. First, there was a group of countries whose financial statements were intended (at least in principle) to capture and reflect the underlying economic performance of the reporting entity. Financial reporting rules in those countries were designed and selected to achieve this objective and thereby help external users make informed investment decisions. We'll call this reporting philosophy the **economic performance approach**.

EXHIBIT 18.3 | Largest Companies in Eight Selected Industries, Ranked by 2002 Revenues

($ in millions)	2002 Revenues		2002 Revenues
Airlines		**Food and Drug Stores**	
1. AMR, United States	$ 17,299	1. Carrefour, France	$ 64,979
2. Japan Airlines, Japan	17,099	2. Royal Ahold, Netherlands	59,455
3. Lufthansa Group, Germany	16,045	3. Kroger, United States	51,760
4. UAL, United States	14,286	4. Metro Holding, Switzerland	48,715
5. Delta Air Lines, United States	13,305	5. Tesco, Britain	40,387
Banks: Commercial and Savings		**Insurance: Property Casualty (Stock)**	
1. Citigroup, United States	$100,789	1. Allianz, Germany	$101,930
2. Deutsche Bank, Germany	52,133	2. American International Group, U.S.	67,482
3. Credit Suisse, Switzerland	52,122	3. Munich Re Group, Germany	51,980
4. BNP Paribas, France	51,127	4. Berkshire Hathaway, United States	42,353
5. Bank of America Corp., United States	45,732	5. Zurich Financial Services, Switzerland	40,638
Electronics, Electrical Equipment		**Petroleum Refining**	
1. Siemens, Germany	$ 77,205	1. Exxon/Mobil, United States	$182,466
2. Hitachi, Japan	67,228	2. Royal Dutch/Shell Group, Brit./Netherl.	179,431
3. Sony, Japan	61,335	3. BP, Britain	178,721
4. Matsushita Electric, Japan	60,744	4. Total Fina Elf, France	96,945
5. Samsung Electronics, S. Korea	47,606	5. ChevronTexaco, United States	92,043
Food Consumer Products		**Telecommunications**	
1. Nestlé, Switzerland	$ 57,279	1. Nippon Telegraph & Telephone, Japan	$ 89,644
2. Unilever, Britain/Netherlands	45,636	2. Verizon Communications, United States	67,625
3. Conagra, United States	27,630	3. Deutsche Telekom, Germany	50,760
4. PepsiCo, United States	25,112	4. Vodafone, Britain	46,987
5. Sara Lee, United States	17,628	5. AT&T, United States	46,727

Source: Fortune 2003 Global 500, www.fortune.com/fortune/global500. Reprinted with permission of *Fortune*.

Second, there was a large group of countries whose financial rules did not necessarily try to capture "economic reality." Instead, accounting reports in these countries simply conformed to mandated laws or detailed tax rules designed to achieve purposes like raising tax revenues to fund government activities or stimulating capital investment. We'll call this financial reporting grouping the **commercial and tax law approach**. Since this latter approach was widespread, investors reading foreign financial statements were frequently confronted with unfamiliar reporting rules, unique tax-driven financial statement items, and country-specific nuances. Happily, this confusing array of cross-border financial reporting options has been greatly simplified in recent years. Indeed, this simplification continues at a rapid rate as the economic performance approach becomes widespread. In the next section, we outline this important transformation and explain why it happened.

Growing Predominance of the Economic Performance Approach

The difference in financial reporting standards between various foreign countries has been greatly reduced in recent years. This is remarkable since the growing complexity of societal and scientific advances often leads in the exact opposite direction—more complicated, not less complicated, decision models. So it is important to understand the factors driving the convergence of international reporting standards and the resulting

> Examples include France, Italy, and Belgium, where financial statements prepared for domestic distribution are heavily influenced by national tax laws. In Germany, Japan, and Switzerland, these statements are influenced by both commercial and tax laws. For example, to qualify for tax benefits in many countries, a company that claims expense deductions on its tax return must also include these same expenses in their published financial statements. Specifically to obtain the extra depreciation allowed by the German tax law, companies' financial statement depreciation expense must reflect the same depreciation charges shown on the tax return. This effectively requires conformity between tax and book amounts and greatly restricts the ability of financial statements to reflect economic performance.

decrease in financial reporting differences across countries. To understand this convergence, it is first necessary to understand the causes for the diversity that previously prevailed in worldwide financial reporting.

Why Do Reporting Philosophies Differ Across Countries?

What factors give rise to differences among countries' financial reporting concepts and rules? Why do certain countries' statements adopt an economic performance approach while the statements in other countries merely conform to arbitrary legal formats using a commercial or tax law approach?

A country's financial reporting philosophy does not exist in a vacuum. Instead, it is designed to achieve certain goals. The objective of financial reporting evolves from the specific legal, political, and financial institutions within a country, as well as from its social customs and systems. As one example, German workers have been entitled to representation on governing boards of German firms since the early 1950s. Understandably, these labor representatives championed accounting practices that would insure firm continuity—and thus future employment opportunities. Partially as a consequence of labor's active board participation, Germany developed ultraconservative accounting rules and dividend guidelines designed to protect companies' survival prospects and workers' jobs. So financial reporting differences across countries often mirror societal differences.

One critically important reason for cross-country differences in financial reporting arises from differences in how companies obtain financing. In countries where the bulk of the investment capital is attracted from a broad base of external investors, these investors understandably want comprehensive data to help them select appropriate securities. So external investors who provide capital demand a reporting system that clearly reflects the past economic performance and future prospects of potential investment opportunities. The United States, United Kingdom, and Canada provide examples of this type of broad-based ownership since an exceedingly large portion of firms' capital requirements in these countries are provided by individual debt and equity investors—either through direct investments in companies or indirectly through pension plans and mutual funds. *The financial reporting environment in these countries has evolved to meet this demand for information.* The economic performance approach flourished and guided policymakers like the SEC and FASB as they resolved new reporting issues.

By contrast, in countries like Japan and Germany, only a small amount of firms' financing was historically provided by individual investors. The primary capital providers in Germany were several large banks—and the government itself. The German stock market was small. Similarly, six or eight large banks provide much of the financing in Japan; in addition, firms there also raise capital from members of their associated corporate group. As a consequence, external equity financing from individual investors was also relatively unimportant in Japan. In countries like Japan and Germany, historically there were just a few important capital providers who had great power—such as the ability to acquire information directly from the firm seeking capital. *Because of this concentrated power and because of the insignificance of the public market, the demand for economically realistic reporting standards was low.* Instead, financial reporting standards conformed to income tax rules or other commercial laws.

> These loosely interconnected corporate associations are called **keiretsu**. Members of the keiretsu typically own shares of other members of the keiretsu; this arrangement provides a source of financing and further aligns the group's incentives toward mutual benefits. Cross-ownerships in the 20% to 30% range are not unusual in these situations.

> "Traditionally, Japanese companies have been managed on behalf of their employees, not shareholders. The majority of a company's shares are likely to be held by banks and other companies for the purpose of maintaining a relationship, so there was little concern about shareholder returns and little fear of hostile takeovers. . . . [A]ccounting rules now under consideration would compel greater disclosure, making it harder for companies to sweep problems under the rug." (A. Pollack, "Japan Considers Opening the Veiled Corporate Ledger," *New York Times* [August 5, 1997].)

But sources of financing do shift over time. When this happens in a country, changes in the financial reporting environment will occur as well, as we discuss in the next section.

The Convergence of Reporting Standards Across Countries At the start of this chapter, Exhibits 18.1 and 18.2 presented data showing the surge in certain cross-border financial transactions. This represents one facet of a phenomenon called globalization. "The term globalization describes the increased mobility of goods, services, labor, technology and capital throughout the world."[1] Globalization is an ongoing process that accelerated over the 1990s as telecommunications and distribution facilities grew increasingly sophisticated.

This "relaxation" of cross-border barriers in markets for goods, labor, and capital has increased international competitiveness—that is, globalization. Many firms throughout the world have accordingly sought to maintain or strengthen their market position by expanding and investing in new facilities and technologies. This expansion has made it necessary for them to access new and ever larger sources of capital to finance these initiatives. But firms in countries that used the commercial and tax law approach to financial reporting like France, Germany, and Japan faced a severe disadvantage in raising capital as globalization progressed in the mid-1990s. Foreign investors and other potential capital providers demanded transparent financial reports prepared using familiar reporting standards that reflected underlying firm economic performance. Statements based on narrow, national tax rules, which firms in these countries normally used, were deemed unsuitable. Consequently, many firms in countries whose financial reporting used the commercial and tax law approach felt compelled to provide foreign investors with *supplemental* financial statements prepared using either U.S. GAAP or standards issued by the International Accounting Standards Board, called **International Financial Reporting Standards**, or **IFRS**. The hope was that by preparing their financial reports using procedures required by the home countries of potential investors, their statements would be more understandable to these foreign investors. Examples include Daimler-Benz that began issuing U.S. GAAP reports in 1996 and Hoechst that began using International Accounting Standards for financial reporting beginning in 1995. These foreign firms apparently felt that the greater transparency and familiarity of either U.S. GAAP or IFRS financial reports would help attract more capital from investors outside their home country.

> IFRS—like U.K. and U.S. GAAP—also incorporate the economic performance approach to financial reporting. Statements prepared using IFRS are also designed to provide a "true and fair view" of the underlying economic conditions experienced by the reporting firm.

As this trend accelerated, a two-tiered financial reporting system has emerged in many countries that had previously used the commercial and tax law approach to financial reporting. In the first financial reporting tier, rigid book/tax conformity is maintained in **parent company** financial statements. The parent is an amalgamation that corresponds to the tax-paying and statutory entities comprising the firm—often (but not always) in the form of a holding company. Because the parent company statements conform to the tax law, national legal rules are satisfied. In the second financial reporting tier, separate statements directed to potential external investors are prepared. They are called **consolidated financial statements** (also called **group statements** in overseas accounting terminology). The group statements include all of the various operating subsidiaries of the firm. *These statements use either U.S. GAAP or IFRS to report performance. Firms hoped that these group statements—prepared using more investor-friendly and familiar rules—would facilitate access to foreign capital.*

> Consolidated financial statements were described in Chapter 16.

So during the late 1990s both U.S. GAAP and IFRS were widely used in an effort to make financial reports more understandable to foreign investors using this two-tiered approach.

The Rise of International Financial Reporting Standards In 2001 and 2002, accounting scandals at companies like Enron, WorldCom, HealthSouth, and Global Crossing tarnished U.S. financial reporting and consequently lowered the appeal of U.S. GAAP for some foreign firms. Many believe this tipped the scales in favor of IFRS as the way firms began to cope with the financial reporting demands of globalization. In June 2002 the Council of the European Union

---

[1] Government of Canada website: www.gc.ca.

adopted an "IAS Regulation" requiring all publicly traded EU companies to adopt IFRS for financial reporting in consolidated statements by January 1, 2005. EU member states can, if they wish, extend this requirement to all companies, including those that are not publicly traded. In the words of the European Commission:

> The Regulation will help eliminate barriers to cross-border trading in securities by ensuring that company accounts throughout the EU are more reliable and transparent and that they can be more easily compared.[2]

The Regulation affects approximately 7000 companies in the EU and will dramatically enhance the visibility of IFRS—the standards issued by IASB. For this reason, we digress and describe the IASB in more detail in the next section.

The International Accounting Standards Board (IASB)

The International Accounting Standards Board (IASB) was called the International Accounting Standards Committee (IASC) prior to its restructuring in 2001. It began operating on July 1, 1973, following an agreement by professional accounting organizations in Australia, Canada, France, Germany, Japan, Mexico, the Netherlands, Ireland, the United Kingdom, and the United States. The objectives of the IASB are as follows:

> The Board is committed to developing, in the public interest, a single set of high quality, understandable and enforceable global accounting standards that require transparent and comparable information in general purpose financial statements. In addition, the Board cooperates with national accounting standard setters to achieve convergence in accounting standards around the world.[3]

IASB representation includes more than 112 countries and approximately 150 professional organizations. By 2003, the IASB had 41 International Financial Reporting Standards in effect. Issuing a new standard requires approval by eight of the Board's fourteen members. While these standards are not binding on participating countries, one of the goals of the IASB is to "persuade governments and standard-setting bodies that published financial statements should comply with International Accounting Standards in all material respects."[4] The EU's vote to implement IFRS for publicly traded companies by 2005 is an important step towards broad-based acceptance of the IASB.

Guidelines for selecting IASB members state that the Board should not be dominated by any particular constituency or regional interest. As of March 2004, nine different countries were represented on the board. Compared to U.S. GAAP, existing IASB standards allow firms much more latitude. IFRS often permit different accounting treatments for similar economic events. One of these treatments is termed the **benchmark treatment** while other reporting approaches are called the **allowed alternative**

The adoption of new IFRS in the European Union is not automatic, however. The European Commission has established a screening mechanism whereby each new IFRS will be reviewed for suitability by an Accounting Regulatory Commission (ARC) comprised of representatives from all EU member states. It is too soon to know whether the ARC will prove to be an impediment to quick adoption of newly proposed IFRS. (See S. A. Zeff, "'Political' Lobbying on Proposed Standards: A Challenge to the IASB," *Accounting Horizons* (March 2002), pp. 43–54). However, an IASB board member—and current U.S. liaison to the IASB—responded as follows to questions about what he believes to be the greatest challenge to the IASB:

> I think it's the resistance to having an independent standard setter in Europe. Europeans don't seem to want one or appreciate what is meant by independent standard setting. They tend to see it as a process of negotiation rather than contemplation and analysis. . . . I'm not confident that the IASB will be left alone to be a standard setter. That depends upon the behavior of the politicians, particularly in Europe, and if, in fact, they interfere with the process of providing international accounting standards.

Source: Interview with James J. Leisenring, as quoted in "The FASB Report," *Financial Accounting Series* (Norwalk, CT: FASB, September 30, 2003), p. 3.

---

2 European Commission Press Release, June 7, 2002.
3 International Accounting Standards Board website: www.iasb.org.uk.
4 "Preface to International Financial Reporting Standards," *International Accounting Standards* 2000 (London: IASB, 2000), p. 32.

treatment. Use of *either* treatment complies with IFRS. Some critics contend that this latitude is a natural result of the diversity of IASB's board members and constituencies. Specifically, unique business practices in particular countries may cause IASB board members from these countries to resist a proposed benchmark treatment. This resistance gives rise to the allowed alternative treatment(s). In this manner, national financial reporting differences survive in IFRS through the allowed range of acceptable practices. To be approved, a standard must meet a "lowest common denominator" criterion—that is, it must be broadly acceptable across the entire spectrum of countries represented. And to achieve this broad acceptance, the standard may have to encompass many alternatives and latitude in application. Critics contend that the resulting "compromise" standards are sometimes so innocuous as to be uninformative.

International Financial Reporting Standards differ from U.S. GAAP in another important way—the level of detail they encompass. IFRS frequently follow a more "broad-brush," generalized overview approach than do U.S. GAAP counterpart standards. This difference in the level of standard setting detail has generated a strong debate about which of the two approaches is preferable. Critics of the IASB approach contend that IFRS standards are so general and their guidance is so ambiguous that firm managers have excessive latitude in choosing reporting methods. This latitude makes it easier for them to evade covenant restrictions, realize bonus targets, reach earnings goals, or achieve other contracting incentives. They contend that since U.S. GAAP contains more detailed rules and implementation guidance, similar transactions tend to result in more similar accounting treatments under the FASB's approach.

Supporters of IFRS counter that IASB standards are built upon broad principles, not narrowly defined, detailed rules like those of U.S. GAAP. They further assert that under a broad principles approach, the financial reporting objective of the standard is made clear. This leads to closer conformity between financial statement numbers and underlying economic performance. By contrast, they argue that narrow U.S. GAAP rules allow managers to invent "loopholes" that conform to the letter of the standard but simultaneously violate its spirit. These critics point to examples like Enron's use of off-balance sheet special purpose entities (SPEs) to hide corporate liabilities. (Provided certain narrow guidelines were satisfied, U.S. GAAP did not require consolidation of SPEs, thereby allowing Enron to keep real corporate liabilities off the consolidated balance sheet.[5]) The numerous other financial reporting irregularities and abuses in the United States during 2001–2002 added credibility to this argument. As a consequence, the FASB has added an item to its agenda, which will examine the desirability of moving U.S. GAAP to a principles-based reporting approach.[6] This will determine whether U.S. GAAP standards will continue to be written using detailed rules or will, instead, move toward the broad principles approach utilized by IASB.

In addition, the FASB has undertaken a series of activities designed to "further the goal of convergence of U.S. GAAP with International Financial Reporting Standards."[7] These initiatives include joint projects conducted with IASB addressing complicated issues such as revenue recognition and business combinations. Also, in December 2003 the FASB issued four exposure drafts that propose convergence in financial reporting for several detailed issues.[8] So it is reasonable to

Contracting

> Special purpose entities—now also called variable interest entities—are discussed in Chapters 8 and 16.

> An IASB interpretation succinctly outlines conditions that identify when SPEs are controlled by the parent and thus require consolidation. Following this IASB guideline would have precluded Enron from keeping these liabilities off-balance sheet under IFRS. See Standing Interpretations Committee, Interpretation SIC-12, "Consolidation—Special Purpose Entities" (IASB, June 1998).

---

[5] This loophole is now mostly closed in U.S. GAAP. See "Consolidation of Variable Interest Entities," *FASB Interpretation No. 46* (FASB, December 2003).

[6] Financial Accounting Standards Board, "Proposal: Principles-Based Approach to U.S. Standard Setting," October 21, 2002.

[7] Financial Accounting Standards Board website: www.fasb.org.

[8] These exposure drafts are: "Accounting Changes and Error Corrections—a replacement of *APB Opinion No. 20* and *FASB Statement No. 3*"; "Exchanges of Productive Assets—an amendment of *APB Opinion No. 29*"; "Earnings per Share—an amendment of *FASB Statement No. 128*"; and "Inventory Costs—an amendment of *ARB No. 43, Chapter 4*," (FASB, December 2003).

expect that this process will continue, and existing differences between U.S. GAAP and IFRS will be narrowed in the future.

Some Differences Between U.S. GAAP and IFRS

As indicated in the previous section, both the FASB and IASB are engaged in efforts to converge U.S. GAAP and IFRS. But as this book goes to press, there are numerous differences that remain that are not yet slated for review. Here are several noteworthy examples.

- *Long-lived asset revaluations.* U.S. GAAP specifies that long-lived assets be measured at original cost minus both accumulated depreciation and impairment loss (if any). Under IFRS, an allowed alternative treatment permits firms to revalue property, plant, and equipment upward if its replacement cost has increased above original cost.[9]
- *Reversal of impairment losses.* Under U.S. GAAP, once an impairment loss has been recognized on either long-lived tangible assets, intangible assets, or goodwill, subsequent reversal of the previously recognized impairment loss is prohibited, as discussed in Chapters 10 and 16. Under IFRS, reversals of impairment losses are permitted.[10]
- *Joint ventures.* Under U.S. GAAP, if a joint venturer does not own more than 50% of a venture, it accounts for its investment using the equity method, as discussed in Chapters 11 and 16. Under IFRS, the benchmark treatment requires a venturer to report its interest in a jointly controlled entity using proportionate consolidation.[11] This means that if the venturer owns a 50% interest in the entity, the venturer's balance sheet and income statement should include 50% of the entity's assets, liabilities, revenues, and expenses. But an allowed alternative treatment under *IAS 31* is to use the equity method—as in U.S. GAAP.[12]
- *Research and development.* Under U.S. GAAP, R&D expenditures are charged to expense in the period they are made. Under IFRS, separate rules apply to the "research phase" and the "development phase." *IAS 38* expenses research as incurred, just as U.S. GAAP does. However, development phase expenditures can be capitalized if technical feasibility and other criteria demonstrating value creation are attained.[13]
- *Capitalized interest.* U.S. GAAP requires capitalization of interest incurred on borrowed funds during construction of assets for a firm's own use or during construction of assets intended for sale or lease, as described in Chapter 10. Under IFRS, the benchmark treatment is to recognize all interest costs as an expense in the period they are incurred. However, interest capitalization is an allowed alternative treatment for "qualifying assets," similar to the U.S. GAAP rules.[14]

The continuing existence of differences like these complicate comparisons between companies using U.S. GAAP and competitors using IFRS.

Coping with Reporting Differences That Persist

How should regulators like the Securities and Exchange Commission respond to the remaining diversity in financial reporting requirements that persists across countries? What information requirements should be imposed by the securities regulatory commission in Country A if a firm from Country B wishes to sell securities in Country A?

---

[9] "Property, Plant and Equipment," *International Accounting Standard (IAS) 16* (revised 1998) (London: IASB, 1998), paras. 29–40.

[10] "Impairment of Assets," *IAS 36* (London: IASB, 1998), paras. 94–112. However, reversals of impairment losses for goodwill are allowed only under exceptional circumstances (para. 109).

[11] "Financial Reporting of Interests in Joint Ventures," *IAS 31* (revised 2000) (London: IASB, 2000), paras. 25–31.

[12] Ibid., paras. 32–33.

[13] "Intangible Assets," *IAS 38* (London: IASB, 1998), paras. 39–52.

[14] "Borrowing Costs," *IAS 23* (revised 1993) (London: IASB, 1993), paras. 7–18.

There are at least four different approaches that regulatory commissions in a country can use to deal with foreign issuers of securities. They can:

1. Compel foreign issuers to use the host country's reporting rules.
2. Create a bilateral arrangement between a particular host country and a particular foreign country that allows the host country's regulators to accept financial statements prepared using that foreign country's financial reporting principles.
3. Allow every foreign issuer to use the foreign issuer's own financial reporting rules in a host country without a requirement to reconcile to host country GAAP.
4. Require foreign issuers to use International Financial Reporting Standards.

We next examine each of these alternatives.

Foreign Issuers Use Host Country Financial Reporting Rules The United States Securities and Exchange Commission requires foreign companies that wish to have securities traded on U.S. exchanges to reconcile their own reporting methods to U.S. GAAP. This reconciliation is mandated by the SEC on Form 20-F. Cadbury Schweppes—a large British-headquartered producer of beverages and confectionery products—provided the reconciliation illustrated in Exhibit 18.4. The disclosure is designed for the convenience of U.S. financial statement readers since it reconciles Cadbury Schweppes' financial results under U.K. GAAP to what those numbers would have been under U.S. GAAP. Form 20-F provides U.S. investors with income statement, balance sheet, and other numbers computed using familiar U.S. rules. This allows investors to evaluate the performance of foreign issuers relative to U.S. companies using a common reporting basis—U.S. GAAP. However, this reconciliation is controversial from two perspectives.

EXHIBIT 18.4	Cadbury Schweppes

Edited Excerpts from the 2002 Form 20-F Reconciliation to U.S. GAAP
Summary of Differences between U.K. and U.S. Generally Accepted Accounting Principles
Effects on profit of differences between U.K. and U.S. generally accepted accounting principles

(£ in millions)	2002	2001
Profit for the financial year from continuing operations, net of tax (per U.K. GAAP)	£548	£542
U.S. GAAP adjustments:		
Amortization of goodwill and intangibles	53	(109)
Restructuring costs	(1)	(1)
Interest capitalised	6	7
Depreciation of capitalised interest	(2)	(2)
Pension costs	10	9
Disposal gain adjustments	7	—
Derivatives—Impact of transition adjustment	1	41
Derivatives	(9)	(12)
SAYE/LTIP	4	(4)
Other Items	—	3
Taxation on above adjustments	(4)	(11)
Deferred taxation	(48)	15
Profit for the financial year from continuing operations, net of tax, before cumulative effect of a change in accounting principle	565	478
Cumulative effect on prior years (to 31 December 2000) of implementation of SFAS 133, net of tax	—	15
Profit for the financial year from continuing operations, net of tax (per U.S. GAAP)	£565	£493

One controversy involves competitive disadvantages that reconciliation may impose on U.S. markets; the second concerns whether the reconciliation really overcomes differences between U.S. and foreign GAAP.

U.S. stock exchanges contend that the Form 20-F reconciliation creates competitive disadvantages because it is costly for foreign firms to reconcile their statements to U.S. GAAP. The result, the exchanges contend, is that burdensome disclosure requirements make foreign issuers reluctant to list their securities on U.S. exchanges. To avoid this burden, some firms simply forgo selling their securities in the United States, the exchanges assert. As a consequence, there's a dual loss—U.S. exchanges lose the business of listing foreign issues, and the cost of buying foreign securities is higher for U.S. investors since they must buy them abroad.

There is some evidence to support the exchanges' position. Prior to October 1983, foreign firms could trade their shares on the National Association of Securities Dealers Automated Quotations (NASDAQ) system without registering with the SEC, and they did not have to reconcile their accounting to U.S. GAAP. After this date, registration became mandatory, and the number of foreign securities traded on NASDAQ declined from 294 to 213 over the ensuing eight years.[15] This decline occurred despite the tremendous *increase* in U.S. investors' purchases of foreign securities over these years.

The second problem with the Form 20-F reconciliation is that even after a foreign company reconciles its numbers to U.S. GAAP, the information it provides may still not be truly comparable to the information provided by U.S. firms. The reason is that SEC rules do not require foreign firms to prepare complete financial statements on a U.S. GAAP basis. All that is required is that Form 20-F contain a *reconciliation* between the firm's home-country financial statements and U.S. GAAP. This is easily seen in Exhibit 18.4 where Cadbury Schweppes discloses its income statement adjustments necessary to arrive at U.S. GAAP income. Since no "finalized" statement in U.S. GAAP format is provided, it is not straightforward for U.S. investors to reconstruct a multi-step income statement that identifies categories such as gross margin that may be useful for financial analysis. Additional footnotes (not shown) are provided, but the burden of reconstructing U.S. GAAP format statements falls on the analyst.

Making Bilateral Multijurisdictional Agreements Another method for dealing with international financial reporting diversity is "multijurisdictional disclosure," a procedure that is followed to an extent between Canada and the United States. Under this procedure, the U.S. SEC will accept for registration purposes the Canadian GAAP statements of a Canadian firm seeking to issue debt or preferred stock. The agreement does not cover other equity issues like common stock.

The firm issuing financial statements benefits because it avoids the cost of reformulating its statements into another country's GAAP, but statement users must be knowledgeable about the financial reporting standards of *both* Canada and the United States. This cost is tempered by the fact that reporting methods in Canada and the United States are somewhat similar. Indeed, the multijurisdictional disclosure approach seems feasible only between countries with broadly similar accounting measurement and disclosure standards.

Allowing Foreign Issuer's Reporting Standards to Be Used The third approach for coping with international reporting diversity is for a host country to allow foreign firms to use their own country's financial reporting rules. The host country could allow French firms to report their results using French accounting principles, Indian firms could report their results using Indian accounting principles, and so on. This approach imposes no costs on the reporting

---

[15] F. R. Edwards, "Listing of Foreign Securities on U.S. Exchanges," *Journal of Applied Corporate Finance* (Winter 1993), pp. 28–36.

firm; however, it does place tremendous burdens on analysts in the host country who need to be knowledgeable about a wide range of foreign financial reporting practices. While this approach imposes high costs on statement users, it is the practice on the London Stock Exchange. There, foreign listed companies from other EU countries may use their own national GAAP, or IFRS, or U.S. GAAP—all without a requirement to reconcile to U.K. GAAP. However, U.K. companies must use U.K. GAAP.

Using International Financial Reporting Standards The International Organization of Securities Commissions (IOSCO) is an association of 181 national securities regulators from throughout the world based in Madrid, Spain. One of the organization's objectives is "to promote high standards of regulation in order to maintain just, efficient and sound markets."[16] In the 1990s IOSCO stated that it would consider recognizing IASB standards for cross-border registrations if IASB developed a set of acceptable fundamental, or core, financial reporting standards. These core standards were completed in 1998. IOSCO then evaluated their suitability and issued a press release on May 17, 2000. The release recommended that IOSCO members permit use of the core standards "as supplemented by reconciliation, disclosure and interpretation where necessary. . . . " This qualified acceptance gives individual countries' securities commissions the following choices in cross-border registrations:

1. The statements prepared using IASB standards can be accepted without adjustment.
2. The IASB standards must be reconciled to local GAAP (an example is the current SEC Form 20-F reconciliation).
3. Supplemental disclosures that contain more information than the IASB standards must be provided.
4. Certain accounting treatments may be disallowed.

While the IOSCO endorsement of IASB standards left considerable discretion regarding their utilization in cross-country filings, it did stimulate further efforts toward international convergence of financial reporting standards.

As a member of IOSCO, the U.S. SEC promised to review IASB core standards. If the SEC determines that these standards meet its criteria and are acceptable, it will consider allowing foreign issuers of securities in the United States to use IASB standards in lieu of U.S. GAAP. This review is still in process. In 2000, the SEC solicited feedback about the suitability of IASB standards by issuing a "concept release."[17] The release posed 26 specific questions about the likely impact of allowing foreign registrants to use IASB standards in SEC filings.

The most recent SEC statement on this issue was made in a speech by former SEC Chairman Harvey L. Pitt. Noting that publicly listed EU firms will be required to use IFRS beginning in 2005, Pitt stated:

The SEC's Statement on International Standards April 1, 1996—The SEC is pleased the IAS[B] has undertaken a plan to accelerate its developmental efforts to complete the requisite core set of standards by March 1998. The commission supports the IAS[B]'s objective to develop, as expeditiously as possible, accounting standards that could be used for preparing financial statements used in cross-border offerings. From the commission's perspective, there are three key elements to this program and the commission's acceptance of its results:
- The standards must include pronouncements that constitute a comprehensive, generally accepted basis of accounting.
- The standards must be of high quality—they must result in comparability and transparency, and they must provide for full disclosure.
- The standards must be rigorously interpreted and applied.

The commission is committed to working with its securities regulatory colleagues, through IOSCO, and with the IAS[B] to provide the necessary input to achieve the goal of establishing a comprehensive set of international accounting standards. As soon as the IAS[B] completes its project, accomplishing each of the noted key elements, it is the commission's intention to consider allowing the utilization of the resulting standards by foreign issuers offering securities in the United States.

---

[16] IOSCO website, www.iosco.org.

[17] Securities and Exchange Commission, "International Accounting Standards," Release Nos. 33-7801, 34-42430; International Series No. 1215, February 16, 2000.

If, by 2005, there has been sufficient progress in the improvement and short-term convergence of accounting standards, in the development of a process and structure for consistent interpretation and application of [IFRS], and in the enhancement of financial reporting infrastructure, *then I believe that 2005 could become the target date on which it may be appropriate for the SEC to determine whether foreign private issuers from EU member countries should be required to reconcile from [IFRS] to U.S. GAAP*[18] (Emphasis added).

In this statement, Mr. Pitt noted that an enhancement of the financial reporting infrastructure—not just improvement in the standards themselves—is also necessary for the SEC to accept IFRS. The 2000 SEC Concept Release outlined what is meant by enhancement of the financial reporting infrastructure:

Accordingly, while the accounting standards used must be high quality, they also must be supported by an infrastructure that ensures that the standards are rigorously interpreted and applied, and that issues and problematic practices are identified and resolved in a timely fashion. Elements of this infrastructure include:

- effective, independent and high quality accounting and auditing standards setters;
- high quality auditing standards;
- audit firms with effective quality controls worldwide;
- profession-wide quality assurance; and
- active regulatory oversight.[19]

So the SEC appears willing to consider dropping the Form 20-F reconciliation procedure for firms using improved IFRS supported by an enhanced reporting infrastructure. That is, these foreign firms would be allowed to satisfy SEC filing requirements using IFRS rather than U.S. GAAP provided substantial progress in consistent interpretation and application is achieved.

RECAP

Several methods exist for coping with diverse international financial reporting standards. Existing U.S. rules require foreign registrants to reconcile their accounting to U.S. GAAP. But the emerging "front-runner" approach for overcoming reporting differences is a movement to an internationally consistent set of reporting principles developed by the IASB. Whether the IASB rules will ultimately be permitted by the SEC for foreign issuers offering securities in the United States depends on the SEC's assessment of the quality of the rules and reporting infrastructure that are developed.

Monitoring Compliance

As indicated in the previous section, one of the SEC's requirements for accepting IFRS is improvements in regulatory oversight. Not only do financial reporting rules differ across countries, but so do the mechanisms for monitoring compliance with these rules. Different countries have different structures for determining whether the stated principles are actually being followed by firms. Of course, most industrialized countries require publicly traded firms to have audited financial statements. The independent auditor provides one mechanism for monitoring compliance with reporting rules. However, there have been instances in which auditors' independence and even adherence to professional standards were challenged. This is why a backup mechanism for monitoring financial reports—in addition to the audit function—is needed as an additional safeguard for statement readers.

---

[18] Remarks at the *Financial Times'* Conference on Regulation & Integration of the International Capital Markets, by Chairman Harvey L. Pitt, U.S. Securities and Exchange Commission, London, U.K., October 8, 2002.
[19] Securities and Exchange Commission, op. cit.

In the United States, the SEC has the authority to challenge financial reports it believes do not conform to GAAP. There have been many cases in which the SEC has objected to the accounting principles used in statements filed with the commission. The reporting firms were then compelled to alter their financial statements to bring them into compliance with the commission's interpretation of GAAP.

However, the SEC's staff is not very large in relation to the number of statements filed with it. It would be wrong to conclude that each firm's numbers are carefully scrutinized every year. In the early 1980s in a well-publicized case, *Fortune* magazine contended that Aetna Insurance was violating GAAP in its treatment of income tax loss carryforwards. The SEC acknowledged that due to staffing shortages, it had never read the Aetna filing and was unaware of the issues raised in the *Fortune* article.[20] This understaffing continues. During the 1990s, the number of corporate filings increased by 60% while the size of the review staff increased by only 29%. A recent study stated that as a consequence "certain filings were subject to less frequent and less complete reviews as workloads increased."[21] Currently, the SEC scrutinizes the financial statements for all new registrants—called initial public offerings (IPOs)—that are filed with the commission. What little staff time remains is then used to review—on a sampling basis—the statements of longer-established registrants. As you can see, the SEC compliance "safety net" is not exhaustive.

It can be worse in other countries.[22] For years in Australia, New Zealand, and the United Kingdom, the independent auditor represented the *only* monitoring and compliance force. This situation persists in New Zealand. In Australia the Australian Securities and Investments Commission (formerly called the Australian Securities Commission) was established in 1991 to expand monitoring. Similarly, in the United Kingdom a private-sector agency called the Financial Reporting Review Panel (FRRP) was formed in 1991. The U.K. Parliament has delegated authority to this group to bring actions in civil court for perceived breaches of "true and fair view" reporting. More recently, FRRP began formulating explicit enforcement review procedures to (1) monitor firms' compliance with U.K. reporting rules and (2) initiate remedial actions when violations are detected.

In the Netherlands a type of "accounting court," which is called the Enterprise Chamber, was created by Parliament in 1970. Interested parties can bring alleged violations of Dutch financial reporting laws to this group. However, the cost and inconvenience of this process has led to a decline in the number of actions initiated in recent years. The current effectiveness of the Dutch Enterprise Chamber as a compliance enforcement mechanism is unclear.

So in many countries, important elements of a high-quality financial reporting infrastructure are absent. Regulatory oversight may not exist or may lack enforcement powers. Auditing standards to verify compliance with IFRS may be rudimentary and/or haphazardly applied. And local audit firms themselves may not have effective quality controls. For all of these reasons, to achieve ultimate acceptability of IFRS for filings with the SEC, deficiencies in enforcement mechanisms in other countries must continue to be rectified. Once this is accomplished, the SEC will review these mechanisms and determine their adequacy as a means for protecting U.S. investors.

RE**CAP**

Users of foreign financial statements need to be cognizant of the mechanisms in place to monitor compliance with reporting rules. Understanding that reporting rules differ across countries is only one part of the story. It is also important to understand that there might be country-by-country differences in the degree of adherence to the reporting rules that are supposed to be in effect.

---

[20] C. J. Loomis, "Behind the Profits Glow at Aetna," *Fortune* (November 15, 1982), pp. 54–58.

[21] United States General Accounting Office, "Report to Congressional Requesters: SEC Operations—Increased Workload Creates Challenges," GAO-02-302, March 2002, p. 12.

[22] See S. A. Zeff, "International Accounting Principles and Auditing Standards," *The European Accounting Review* (September 1993), pp. 403–10.

Inflation Accounting

Inflation—a decline in the purchasing power of a country's currency—complicates analysis of international financial reports. When inflation is high, historical cost-based financial statements are misleading or totally irrelevant. Financial reporting standards in countries with high rates of inflation mandate some form of **inflation accounting** for both tax and financial statement reporting. Mexico is an example. Two forms of inflation accounting are required by Mexican GAAP: (1) specific price-change adjustments, and (2) general price-level adjustments. Each of these inflation accounting approaches is explained and illustrated in this section.

Introduction: General Versus Specific Price Changes All prices do not change at the same rate. During periods of inflation it is not unusual for the prices of some goods and services to actually fall and move in the opposite direction of prices in general. Let's illustrate using U.S. data. Between 1998 and 2002 the general level of prices as measured by the gross national product (GNP) Implicit Price Deflator *increased* by 7.3%. Over this same period, the average price level for electronic components and accessories *fell* by 7.6%. This illustrates that the *direction* of price change will sometimes differ among economic sectors. Furthermore, the *rate* of price change can also differ across items. For example, the Producer Price Index (PPI) for commodities rose from a 1998 level of 130.7 to 138.9 in December 2002, an increase of 6.27%; over the same period, the PPI for natural gas went from 83.9 to 122.5, an increase of 46%. Thus, the rate of increase for the natural gas sector was more than seven times the rate of increase for all commodities.

These examples illustrate that significant differences are likely to arise between *average* rates of inflation for the economy as a whole and *specific* rates of price change for a given firm. Diversity in rates of price changes generates controversy regarding the appropriate method for reflecting economic activity in these circumstances. Some believe that adjustments for changing prices should be based on the specific level of costs and prices experienced by each individual firm. This approach is called **current cost accounting**. The rationale for the current cost approach is that since each firm is unique, its own unique level of costs and prices should be reflected in its accounts.

Others believe that adjustments for changing prices should be based upon the general rate of inflation experienced in the economy as a whole. According to those that hold this view, inflation adjustments would be derived from broad indices of overall price changes, such as the Consumer Price Index (CPI). This method of adjusting for inflation is called **general price-level accounting**.

We'll first explain and illustrate current cost accounting and then do the same for general price-level accounting.

Current Cost Accounting

Current cost refers to the market price that an individual firm would have to pay in order to replace the specific assets it owns. Current cost accounting (discussed briefly in Chapter 9 where last-in, first-out [LIFO] and first-in, first-out [FIFO] were contrasted) is designed to accomplish the following two objectives: (1) to reflect all nonmonetary assets like inventory, buildings, and equipment at their current replacement cost as of the balance sheet date; and (2) to differentiate between (a) current cost income from continuing operations and (b) increases or decreases in current cost amounts (also called "holding gains" or "inventory profits").

> Remember, current cost accounting for inventories and long-lived assets is a departure from historical costing and is not allowed under U.S. GAAP.

These objectives are accomplished by first periodically increasing or decreasing the balance sheet asset carrying amount as current cost changes. Then, as the asset is sold or used up, this current cost carrying amount is written off the books and matched against the revenues from sales. These steps are illustrated in simplified form by the following example.

> A firm purchases a unit of inventory for $100 at the beginning of 2005. The asset's current cost increases by $15 in 2005, and it is sold for $180 on January 1, 2006.

Exhibit 18.5 illustrates income statements and inventory carrying amounts for this example.

EXHIBIT 18.5	Current Cost Versus Historical Cost		

Income Statements and Inventory Carrying Amounts

	2005	2006	Total
Current Cost			
Sales revenues	—	$180	$180
Current cost of goods sold	—	115*	115
Current cost income from continuing operations	—	65	65
Unrealized increase in current cost amount (or holding gain)	$ 15	—	15
Change in owners' equity	$ 15	$ 65	$ 80
Inventory carrying amount (end of year)	$115*	—	

*($100 + $15)

	2005	2006	Total
Historical Cost			
Sales revenues	—	$180	$180
Historical cost of goods sold	—	100	100
Total historical cost income	—	$ 80	$ 80
Inventory carrying amount (end of year)	$100	—	

There is controversy about how to treat increases in current cost like the $15. Are the increases to be included in net income? Alternatively, are they a direct (nonincome) equity increase?

If the firm wishes to maintain start-of-period equity capital expressed in nominal dollars, then the increase is included in net income. However, if the firm wants to maintain start-of-period equity expressed in dollars of physical productive capacity, then the $15 increase in current cost is not income—that is, it is a direct credit to owners' equity.[23]

Regardless of whether increases in current cost are treated as income or as a (non-income) direct credit to owners' equity, the cumulative change in owners' equity under the current cost approach for the two years combined—$80 in this case—is equal to the *cumulative* equity change under the historical cost approach. However, although the total equity change is the same, the *timing* of equity-change recognition and the *classification* of the equity change by causes differ between the current and historical cost approaches.

Current cost income differentiates between operating profits and holding gains. In the example, $15 of the total $80 change in equity is attributable to increases in current cost amounts; these increases are recognized as they occur by increasing the inventory carrying amount. Assuming the increase is considered to be a direct credit to owners' equity, the accounting entry to recognize the inventory carrying amount change is:

In its 2002 annual report, Teléfonos de México S.A. describes its current cost adjustment process for domestic origin nonmonetary assets as follows:

> The appraised value of land, buildings and other fixed assets of domestic origin at December 31, 1996, and the cost of subsequent additions to such assets were restated based on the NCPI.

Prior to 1997, Mexican accounting required appraisals of nonmonetary assets. But since January 1, 1997, the previous appraised values can be updated by applying the Mexican National Consumer Price Index (NCPI) to the December 31, 1996 appraisal amounts. *In accordance with Mexican GAAP, the restatement debit or credit offset is not included in income but is taken directly to owners' equity.* So Mexican GAAP illustrates the direct owners' equity (other comprehensive income) treatment of adjustments for all nonmonetary assets (including inventory) in a real-world setting.

---

[23] For a simple overview of different capital maintenance concepts, see L. Revsine, "A Capital Maintenance Approach to Income Measurement," *The Accounting Review* (April 1981), pp. 383–89. Current cost is not GAAP in the United States. If it were, the direct credit to owners' equity would be a part of other comprehensive income, which was discussed in Chapter 2.

DR Inventory	$15	
CR Owners' equity—Unrealized increase		
in current cost amount		$15

When the sale is made in 2006, the new inventory carrying amount ($115) is matched against the selling price of $180 to yield the $65 current cost income from continuing operations shown in Exhibit 18.5. By contrast, historical cost procedures recognize no equity change as input costs increase. Instead, equity increases are deferred until the sale occurs in 2006. At that time, historical cost accounting reports the equity change as one lump-sum number ($80) and does not break this number into separate operating profit and holding gain components.

Analysis

The failure of historical cost accounting to differentiate between operating profits and holding gains is a serious limitation of traditional accounting. Proponents of current cost accounting argue that the $80 profit number reported under historical cost accounting provides a misleading picture of current operating efficiency because it seems to imply that the spread between sales price and cost is $80. Statement readers might infer that each *future* sale would also generate a margin of $80. But this is incorrect. Because the current spread between selling price and replacement cost is only $65 ($180 − $115), current cost advocates contend that the $65 figure provides the better measure of existing *operating* efficiency and is also the proper starting point for analysts to use in developing estimates of future per-unit net operating cash inflows. Furthermore, the $15 difference between the current cost operating profit of $65 and total historical cost income of $80 is attributable to cost increases over the period that the inventory was held. These holding gains, it is argued, may or may not be sustainable, so they should be disclosed as a separate item to avoid unwarranted inferences. *Since historical cost does not separately disclose operating profits and holding gains, critics claim that it obscures different elements of total profitability that may have different patterns of sustainability.*

LIFO inventory accounting represents an attempt to separate operating profits from holding gains within the framework of the historical cost model. As discussed in Chapter 9, this separation is not achieved when LIFO dipping occurs because reported LIFO profit includes both current cost operating profits *and* realized holding gains. Furthermore, during periods of rising input costs, the LIFO inventory carrying amount can be far below the current economic cost of the assets that are tied up in inventory. Consequently, traditionally computed ratios (like return on assets) will tend to be overstated because of the understatement of the denominator. A further distortion of return ratios exists when LIFO dipping occurs because the numerator—income—is inflated by the realized holding gains. So, in summary, LIFO doesn't reliably approximate current cost accounting numbers.

Over the 1979–1985 period, U.S. companies with inventories plus property, plant, and equipment totalling more than $125 million were required to disclose certain supplementary information prepared on a current cost basis.[24] Exhibit 18.6 presents a representative current cost disclosure for Union Carbide that was taken from its 1985 annual report. For most companies, 1985 represents the latest disclosure, since these disclosures were made voluntary in 1986.[25]

---

[24] "Financial Reporting and Changing Prices," *Statement of Financial Accounting Standards (SFAS) No. 33* (Stamford, CT: FASB, 1979).

[25] See "Financial Reporting and Changing Prices," *SFAS No. 89* (Stamford, CT: FASB, 1986). The ostensible reason for altering the disclosure requirement was that because inflation rates had abated, the disclosures were no longer essential. An unexpressed—but more plausible—explanation was that managers of capital-intensive firms opposed the disclosures, since they generated adverse reactions directed against managers by shareholders. For example, it is difficult to justify managerial bonuses tied to reported income when the supplemental disclosure indicated losses were being incurred on a current cost basis. The simplest financial reporting remedy for avoiding this conflict is to dispense with the disclosure altogether. Managers of firms aggressively lobbied the FASB to rescind *SFAS No. 33*. One explanation for why the FASB acquiesces to such efforts is developed in L. Revsine, "The Selective Financial Misrepresentation Hypothesis," *Accounting Horizons* (December 1991), pp. 16–27.

EXHIBIT 18.6	Union Carbide Corporation (UCC)

1985 Annual Report Supplemental Disclosure
Year Ended December 31, 1985
Data on Changing Prices

($ in millions)	At Historical Cost—Nominal Dollars	Adjusted for Changes in Specific Prices Current Cost—Nominal Dollars
Summary statement of income adjusted for changing prices		
Net sales	$9,003	$9,003
Cost of sales	6,252	6,281
Depreciation	596	711
Other operating expense—net	1,708	1,708
Interest expense	292	292
Provision for income taxes	53	53
Minority share of income	27	29
Net income before unusual charges and extraordinary item	$ 75	$ (71)
Per share	$ 0.36	$(0.34)
Summary balance sheet data adjusted for changing prices		
Inventories	$1,422	$2,259
Property, plant, and equipment, net of accumulated depreciation	5,780	7,453
UCC stockholders' equity	4,019	6,529

Under the *Statement of Financial Accounting Standards (SFAS) No. 33* current cost rules, the only balance sheet accounts adjusted were nonmonetary assets such as inventory, buildings, and equipment. (Monetary and nonmonetary items are defined in more detail later in this chapter on p. 1029.) Actual market replacement costs were used wherever such data were available. When actual market replacement costs were not available, indices that reflected cost changes for the specific asset category being measured were employed. All monetary assets and liabilities (such as cash, receivables, and accounts payable) were reported at their face value without adjustment. As shown in Exhibit 18.6, Union Carbide Corporation (UCC) displayed the current cost amounts for these balance sheet categories as well as their income statement effects on cost of sales and depreciation side-by-side with the historical cost amounts. UCC's historical cost income ($75 million) became a current cost loss ($71 million).

The UCC stockholders' equity number in Exhibit 18.6 was increased as a balancing item that resulted after the inventory and other assets were written up. Specifically,

DR Inventories ($2,259 – $1,422)	$ 837	
DR Property, etc. ($7,453 – $5,780)	1,673	
CR Stockholders' equity ($6,529 – $4,019)		$2,510

In countries like Mexico, where inflation is a continuing problem, current cost data for inventories can be determined from invoices received near the balance sheet date, from suppliers' end-of-period price lists, or from recently updated standard cost amounts. In all cases the objective is to estimate the current cost that would be incurred to *replace* the actual asset in use. ***Input costs that would be paid by the firm are used, not selling prices that would be charged to customers.***

To illustrate the procedure, let us assume that a building constructed in 1990 has the following book value at December 31, 2005:

Historical cost of building	$100,000,000
Accumulated depreciation	30,000,000
Net book value	$ 70,000,000

Further assume that a construction cost index (base period 1980 = 100.0) for this type of building is available and has the following index values:*

Average index value for 1990	246
Index value for December 31, 2005	396

The estimated replacement cost of the building at December 31, 2005 would be:

	Historical Cost Amounts		Index Adjustment		Estimated Current Cost Amounts
Cost of building	$100,000,000	×	$\dfrac{396}{246}$	=	$160,975,600
Accumulated depreciation	30,000,000	×	$\dfrac{396}{246}$	=	48,292,680
Net book value	$ 70,000,000				$112,682,920

*The measurement and use of price indices is discussed on pp. 1027–1029.

Since inventories are purchased virtually continuously, actual market prices will usually be available at any date, making index adjustments rarely necessary for inventory. Land, buildings, and equipment are purchased sporadically, so actual current market costs will not always be available for these items. When fixed asset market costs *are* available—for example, from used equipment dealers' price lists—these market costs would be used to determine current cost balance sheet amounts. For custom designed buildings and special purpose equipment, actual market replacement costs will seldom be determinable. In these cases, **market value estimation techniques** must be used.

Market value estimation techniques may take several forms. For example, construction cost price indices by geographical area are widely available. The construction cost index value would be applied to the historical book value of buildings to yield an estimated replacement cost. Special purpose price indices for equipment are also available. These price indices are reported on both an industry basis (for example, an index specific to equipment used in the automotive industry) and by type of equipment (for example, an index for general purpose electronics equipment). Again, the index value would be multiplied by the historical book value of the equipment in order to obtain an estimated replacement cost. Market value estimation techniques can also be used to estimate land values. For example, real estate tax assessment data can form the basis for estimating the current cost of land.

Under *SFAS No. 33*, current cost adjustments on the income statement were usually limited to cost of goods sold and to depreciation expense. The current cost expense on the income statement was defined as the cost that prevailed at the time an asset was sold or used up in operations. *If current costs changed after assets were sold or used up, no retroactive adjustment was made to reflect end-of-year current costs in the income statement.*

Here's an example. Sallas Company had the following sales transactions and associated costs during 2005:

Sales during the year	$3,300,000
Current cost of inventory sold using current cost *at the time of sale*	2,700,000
Current cost of inventory sold using current cost *at year-end*	2,950,000

The reported gross margin using current cost accounting would be:

Sales revenues	$3,300,000
Current cost of goods sold	2,700,000
Current cost gross margin	$ 600,000

The $2,950,000 *year-end* current cost of inventory sold is ignored, since the objective of current costing is to reflect the margin that existed using costs and selling prices that prevailed *at the time of each sale.* Items like sales revenues, salaries, and miscellaneous expenses are presumed to be stated at or near prevailing prices at the time that they appear on the income statement, and therefore they do not require adjustment. ***Thus, the current cost income statement results in a matching of actual sales revenues with the current costs that were in effect at the time of each sale.***

By capturing the margin that was in effect at the time of each sale, current costing provides a basis for forecasting future margins and therefore future cash flows. The reasoning is based on the premise that today's *real* margin provides the best basis for estimating tomorrow's margin. The desire to capture the contemporaneous margin—or spread—between selling price and replacement cost explains why the cost of goods sold account is not adjusted "after-the-fact" to year-end replacement cost. If an "after-the-fact" adjustment were made, actual sales prices would be "matched" with subsequent costs that were not even known when sales prices were set.

Exhibit 18.6 shows a $146 million difference ($75 million − [− $71 million]) between historical and current cost net income in 1985 for UCC. Recall that conventional historical cost income is comprised of two components: (1) current cost income from continuing operations, and (2) realized holding gains. So the $71 million current cost loss means that much more than 100% of UCC's 1985 historical cost income ($75 million) consisted of realized holding gains. Examining the Exhibit 18.6 income statement disclosure reveals that UCC's realized holding gains arose from three sources:

This is easily seen by returning to Exhibit 18.5. Conventional historical cost income ($80) can be decomposed as follows:

Current cost income from continuing operations	$65
Plus: Realized holding gains	15
Equals: Historical cost income	$80

Cost of goods sold difference	$ 29	($6,281 − $6,252)
Depreciation difference	115	($711 − $596)
Minority share difference[26]	2	($29 − $27)
Realized holding gains in 1985	$146	

Computing realized holding gains allows us to see the various components of UCC's historical cost income number:

Reported current cost loss from continuing operations	$(71)	(Given)
Realized holding gains	146	(*Computed above*)
Historical cost income	$ 75	(Given)

Over the period that the *SFAS No. 33* disclosures were required, it was not unusual for capital intensive companies like UCC to report historical cost income while simultaneously revealing losses on a current cost basis. The frequency of these disparities fueled the criticisms directed against the traditional income determination approach of historical costing. To give some idea about the relative size of adjusted current cost earnings in relation to reported historical cost earnings, consider the Exhibit 18.7 data from the 1983 *SFAS No. 33* disclosures.

We deliberately focus on 1983 because this was a year of relatively low inflation—3.2% as measured by the CPI. Nevertheless, as shown in Exhibit 18.7, the ratio of current cost profit as a percentage of historical cost profit was only 43% across all industries. That meant that for every dollar of historical cost profit reported during 1983, 57% (1.00 − .43) was attributable to realized holding gains. The eight "worst off" industries (airlines, etc.) had results comparable to UCC's since they reported *losses* on a current cost basis. Consequently, no meaningful ratio value could be computed for these firms in Exhibit 18.7 since the numerator was negative.

---

[26] The minority share difference arises because the current cost income from those subsidiaries with minority shareholders was apparently *higher* than the historical cost income.

EXHIBIT 18.7	Summary of *SFAS No. 33* Disclosures for 1983			

Ratio of Current Cost to Historical Cost Income

The Best Off	Current-cost profits as percentage of historical cost	The Worst Off	Current-cost profits as percentage of historical cost
1. Publishing/TV	86%	1. Airline	Loss
2. Office equipment	85	2. General machinery	Loss
3. Aerospace	84	3. Metal and mining	Loss
4. Drugs	84	4. Paper	Loss
5. Retailing (nonfood)	80	5. Rails and trucking	Loss
6. Tobacco	77	6. Special machinery	Loss
7. Services	76	7. Steel	Loss
8. Instruments	76	8. Tire and rubber	Loss
9. Electrical	75	9. Natural resources	38%
10. Textiles	72	10. Building materials	42
11. Appliances	72	11. Real estate	47
All-industry average	**43%**		

Source: Reprinted from April 30, 1984 issue of *Business Week* by special permission, Copyright © 1984 by The McGraw-Hill Companies, Inc.

Even modest rates of increase in input cost can lead to significant differences between historical cost financial statement numbers and their inflation-adjusted equivalents. The reason is that the effect of changing prices on balance sheet numbers is cumulative. An example is plant and equipment. If equipment prices are increasing at a rate of 6% per year, a piece of equipment purchased six years ago for $100,000 would have a replacement cost today of $141,852. Furthermore, this cumulative balance sheet effect ultimately affects the income statement because the "misstated" assets are depreciated or charged to cost of goods sold at their original historical cost. The following excerpt from the 2002 20-F filing of Teléfonos de México S.A. illustrates the materiality of cumulative price-change adjustments:

The Company's consolidated financial statements are prepared in accordance with Mexican GAAP, which differ in certain significant respects from generally accepted accounting principles in the United States ("U.S. GAAP").

The reconciliation to U.S. GAAP does *not* include the reversal of the adjustments to the financial statements for the effects of inflation required under Mexican GAAP (Bulletin B-10), because the *application of Bulletin B-10 represents a comprehensive measure of the effects of price level changes in the Mexican economy and, as such, is considered a more meaningful presentation than historical cost-based financial reporting for both Mexican and U.S. accounting purposes.* (Emphasis added.)

Teléfonos de México states that their 20-F reconciliation between Mexican and U.S. GAAP does not reverse the inflation adjustments required by Mexican GAAP. The reason is that the inflation-adjusted numbers are deemed to be "more meaningful" than the non-adjusted numbers required by U.S. GAAP. The Mexican inflation rate for 2002 was only 5.7%, close to the 2001 rate. So even relatively modest input cost increases can—in the opinion of Teléfonos de México's management—lead to significant statement effects.

Current Cost Disclosures and Monetary Items During the 1970s and 1980s current cost disclosures centered on nonmonetary assets like inventory and equipment. When the rate of inflation abated in the 1980s, the perceived importance of the effort to adjust nonmonetary assets diminished. With the collapse of the U.S. savings and loan industry in the mid-1980s and the difficulties experienced by many commercial banks, the focus of market value disclosures began to shift to certain types of monetary assets and liabilities. The reason for this shift is that financial institutions are regulated using accounting numbers, particularly owners' equity. These institutions are required to have a certain minimum proportion of equity, which is called **regulatory capital**. Financial assets and liabilities—loans to borrowers, customer deposits, etc.—comprise the bulk of these financial intermediaries' balance sheet amounts. Because savings and loans (S&Ls) and banks used historical cost accounting, the measure of capital used for regulatory purposes was insensitive to changes in the underlying value of these financial institutions' assets and liabilities. Consequently, it was widely believed that inadequate accounting rules were a factor in many of the S&L and bank failures.

In an effort to provide more complete information to the financial community and regulators, the FASB has required footnote disclosure of the current value of financial institutions' items like loans and deposits.[27] The FASB also introduced disclosure requirements for financial instruments like long-term investments and long-term debt obligations.[28] These fair value disclosures are in the footnotes rather than in the body of the financial statements themselves. In addition, current value data for certain investments in debt and equity securities now appear on the balance sheet itself, as illustrated in Chapter 16.[29] The FASB has also issued three statements that require current value measurements on the balance sheet for derivative instruments, as discussed in Chapter 11.[30] So there is a clear trend towards including more current cost data in U.S. GAAP financial statements.

General Price-Level Accounting

A currency unit such as the U.S. dollar possesses value because of the goods and services that it will buy. The real amount of goods and services that can be acquired at any moment is what determines the **purchasing power** of a currency.

Current costing, as we just discussed, is one way to measure purchasing power. It measures changes in the prices of the specific assets and liabilities of the firm. Current costing thus captures changes in *specific purchasing power*.

General price-level accounting, another way to measure purchasing power, makes no attempt to measure changes in specific prices. Instead, it focuses on changes in *general purchasing power*.

The general purchasing power approach uses a **price index**. All indices are intended to price a market basket of goods and services at various points of time to determine how the price of the market basket has changed.

Overview of Adjustment Mechanics U.S. GAAP financial statements record the dollar amount expended or incurred at the date of the original transaction. However, because the purchasing power of these dollars changes over time, the amounts stated in original (or "nominal") dollars are not comparable. In other words, historical cost statements ignore changes in the purchasing power of the currency. *The objective of general price-level accounting is to adjust all historical amounts into common purchasing power units using a broad purchasing power index.* Here's an example. Adess Corporation owns two assets. One was acquired on January 1, 1988 and the other on January 1, 2003:

---

[27] "Disclosures about Fair Value of Financial Instruments," *SFAS No. 107* (Norwalk, CT: FASB, 1991).

[28] "Disclosure of Information about Financial Instruments with Off-Balance Sheet Risk and Financial Instruments with Concentrations of Credit Risk," *SFAS No. 105* (Norwalk, CT: FASB, 1990); and "Disclosure about Derivative Financial Instruments and Fair Value of Financial Instruments," *SFAS No. 119* (Norwalk, CT: FASB, 1994).

[29] "Accounting for Certain Investments in Debt and Equity Securities," *SFAS No. 115* (Norwalk, CT: FASB, 1993).

[30] "Accounting for Derivative Instruments and Hedging Activities," *SFAS No. 133*; "Accounting for Certain Derivative Instruments and Certain Hedging Activities," *SFAS No. 138*; and "Amendment of Statement 133 on Derivative Instruments and Hedging Activities," *SFAS No. 149* (Norwalk, CT: FASB, 1998, 2000, and 2003).

Date	Original Transaction Amount	General Purchasing Power Index as of January 1
1988 (Asset 1)	$200,000	76
2003 (Asset 2)	200,000	193
2005	—	207
	$400,000	

The gross book value of $200,000 for each asset using historical cost does not reflect the difference in the purchasing power of the *nominal* dollars invested in each asset. That is, the $200,000 of 1988 dollars that were expended on Asset 1 did not have the same purchasing power as the $200,000 of 2003 dollars that were expended on Asset 2; nor does the sum of these amounts have the same purchasing power as $400,000 of January 1, 2005 dollars. *In order to reflect changes in the purchasing power of the measuring unit between 1988 and 2005, all amounts must be restated into dollars of uniform purchasing power.* If all amounts were restated to reflect the purchasing power of the January 1, 2005 dollar, the adjustment would be:

Asset Acquired in	Amount		Restatement Factor		Restated into 2005 Dollars
1988	$200,000	×	$\dfrac{207}{76}$	=	$544,737
2003	200,000	×	$\dfrac{207}{193}$	=	214,508
					$759,245

To understand these restated numbers, let's consider the $544,737 amount in 2005 dollars for the asset acquired in 1988. This number indicates that it would take $544,737 dollars on January 1, 2005 to have the same purchasing power that $200,000 had on January 1, 1988. Similarly, the $200,000 invested on January 1, 2003 has a purchasing power equivalent in January 1, 2005 dollars of $214,508.

Generalizing from the example, to restate historical amounts into current purchasing power units, the nominal dollar amount is multiplied by a **restatement factor**, which is a ratio of price indices. The numerator of the ratio is the price index level of the current period, and the denominator of the ratio is the price index relating to the period of the original transaction amount. To restate 1988 dollars into what those dollars are equivalent to in 2005 purchasing power, we calculate:

$$\text{1988 transaction amount to be restated} \times \frac{\text{2005 General purchasing power index}}{\text{1988 General purchasing power index}} = \text{2005 purchasing power equivalent}$$

In our example, the 2005 index value is 207 and the 1988 index value is 76, so the restatement factor is 207/76, as shown above.

General price-level accounting is not intended to reflect current market values of assets and liabilities. This is not surprising, since the restatement factor relates to overall average purchasing power changes rather than to changes in the prices of the specific items being adjusted. The intent of general price-level accounting is simply to make historical currency amounts that are expended in different time periods comparable by adjusting all amounts to current purchasing power dollar equivalents. In this sense, general price-level accounting does not abandon the historical cost principle. Instead, nominal dollar historical costs are simply restated into dollars of constant purchasing power.

To apply constant dollar accounting in practice, *SFAS No. 33* required firms to measure purchasing power changes by using the CPI for all urban consumers.[31] This index was selected because it is published monthly, and, unlike most other broad purchasing power indices, it is not retroactively adjusted after initial publication. This meant that the "final" CPI value was always available promptly for use in the preparation of annual constant dollar financial statements. Some critics argued, however, that this practical advantage of using the CPI was negated by the fact that a price index like the CPI, which is based only on consumer purchases, doesn't necessarily measure the purchasing power changes experienced by industrial firms.

> After restating financial statements to a current cost basis, Teléfonos de México S.A. then applies a general price level (constant peso) adjustment described as follows:
>
> > The Company recognizes the effects of inflation on financial information as required by Mexican Accounting Principles Bulletin B-10, "Accounting Recognition of the Effects of Inflation on Financial Information," issued by the Mexican Institute of Public Accountants (MIPA). Consequently, the amounts shown in the accompanying financial statements and in these notes are expressed in thousands of constant Mexican pesos as of December 31, 2002. The December 31, 2002 restatement factor applied to the financial statements at December 31, 2001 and 2000 was 1.057% and 1.1035%, which represent the rate of inflation from December 31, 2001 and December 31, 2000 up to December 31, 2002, respectively, based on the Mexican National Consumer Price Index (NCPI) published by Banco de México (the Central Bank).
>
> This puts all years' comparative statements in pesos of constant purchasing power. Year-to-year comparisons devoid of inflation illusion can then be made.

Overview of the Concepts General price-level accounting requires a clear delineation between monetary items and nonmonetary items, because purchasing power changes affect each category differently. A **monetary item** is money, or a claim to receive or to pay a sum of money, which is fixed in amount. Examples include cash, accounts receivable, accounts payable, and bonds payable. What you should understand about these items is that they are stated in monetary units and that the claim or amount remains fixed even if the price level changes. By contrast, a **nonmonetary item** is not fixed in amount, and its price will likely change as the general level of prices changes. Examples of nonmonetary items include inventories, buildings, manufacturing equipment, and obligations under product warranties.

To illustrate the general concepts of constant dollar accounting, let's consider a firm that is financed entirely with equity. Suppose its only asset is land (a nonmonetary asset), which was purchased for $1,000 on January 1, 2005. Using the basic accounting equation, the firm would appear as follows on this date:

A	=	L	+	E
Land $1,000				Owners' equity $1,000

If we assume that the general level of prices rose by 4% during 2005 and that no transactions occurred during the year, the constant dollar basic accounting equation at the end of 2005 would reflect:

A	=	L	+	E
Land $1,040				Owners' equity $1,040

Notice that both amounts have been restated by the ratio 104/100 to reflect December 31, 2005 general purchasing power. This means that it takes $1,040 on December 31, 2005 to have the same general purchasing power that $1,000 had on January 1, 2005. All other nonmonetary items would be adjusted similarly in preparing general price-level financial statements.

Under constant dollar accounting, the upward restatement of owners' equity is *not* considered to be income. An analogy makes it easy to understand why. Whether you express a temperature at

---

[31] *SFAS No. 33*, para. 39.

12° Celsius or at its equivalent of 54° Fahrenheit does not change the underlying real level of the temperature. So too with the purchasing power adjustment from $1,000 January 1, 2005 dollars to $1,040 December 31, 2005 dollars. All that has happened is that the measurement unit has been changed. There is no income or loss.

By contrast, when the assets held are monetary, rather than nonmonetary, a gain or loss *does* occur. Let's illustrate this by assuming that the asset held on January 1, 2005 was cash rather than land. Cash, of course, is a monetary item. Since prices, on average, rose by 4% during 2005, to be in the same general purchasing power position at the end of 2005 as it was at the beginning of 2005, the firm would have to possess a cash balance of $1,040. The reasoning is simple—it takes $1,040 end-of-year dollars to buy what $1,000 bought at the start of the year. If, however, there were no transactions during 2005 and if the ending cash balance is still $1,000, then the firm has suffered a real loss of $40 during 2005 because the purchasing power of its cash has declined. This would be reflected in the end-of-period general price-level accounting equation as:

> Net monetary assets are the difference between gross monetary assets and gross monetary liabilities. So, if a firm's only monetary items are cash of $35,000 and accounts payable of $15,000, its net monetary assets balance is $20,000. Notice that monetary liabilities generate a *gain* when price levels rise. The reason is that, by definition, the dollar amount of the liability is fixed and can be paid off with dollars possessing diminished purchasing power. So it is the *net* monetary asset or liability position of the firm that determines whether purchasing power changes result in a loss or a gain. That is, firms with a net monetary liability position (that is, an excess of gross monetary liabilities over gross monetary assets) experience purchasing power gains from inflation.

A	=	L	+	E	
Cash $1,000				Owners' equity	1,040
				Purchasing	
				power loss	(40)

When a firm holds *net* monetary assets during a period of inflation, a loss occurs since the purchasing power of the net monetary assets declines. Put somewhat differently, since monetary items are automatically expressed in end-of-period dollars, no adjustment of these items is necessary in constant dollar balance sheets; however, the implicit gain or loss that results from holding monetary items during a period of general inflation must be recognized. The purchasing power gain or loss account appears on the income statement and is ultimately closed to owners' equity.[32]

> Teléfonos de México S.A. described the gain or loss from holding monetary items as follows in its 2002 annual report:
>
> > The net monetary gain represents the impact of inflation on monetary assets and liabilities. The net monetary gain of each year is included in the statements of income as a part of the comprehensive financing cost.

---

[32] A loss on monetary items that is recognized while the asset carrying value is not changed might cause you to question how the balance sheet can still balance under such circumstances. The issue is best understood by considering the gain or loss on monetary items as a two-step computational process. First, when 4% inflation occurs during 2005 for the all-cash firm in the example, the following entry might be made to put all amounts into end-of-period dollars:

DR Cash	$40	
CR Owners' equity		$40

After this entry is made, the end-of-period general price-level accounting equation is:

A	=	L	+	E
Cash $1,040				Owners' equity $1,040

Cash is now shown as $1,040 when, in reality, the December 31, 2005 balance is only $1,000. The difference, of course, is the purchasing power loss. To adjust cash to the proper year-end balance, the following entry must be made:

DR Owners' equity (purchasing power loss)	$40	
CR Cash		$40

After this entry is made, the basic accounting equation shows:

A	=	L	+	E
Cash $1,040				Owners' equity $1,040
				Purchasing
				power loss (40)

Although formal journal entries are seldom employed when historical cost statements are adjusted to a general price-level basis, an understanding of the hypothetical journal entries described here makes it easier to grasp the mechanics of the purchasing power gain or loss on monetary items.

SUMMARY

- Cross-border investing in debt and equity securities grew at a phenomenal rate in the last decade.
- Initially, the ease of engaging in international securities transactions was impeded by the diversity of financial reporting measurement and disclosure rules required in various countries.
- Reporting rules in some countries like the United States, Canada, and the United Kingdom strived to reflect firms' underlying economic performance.
- But reporting rules in many other countries—Germany, France, and Japan were examples—merely complied with taxation or other statutory requirements.
- Investors in countries like the United States were uneasy about providing capital to foreign firms whose financial statements were often difficult for them to understand.
- Globalization forced many firms in countries using a commercial or tax law approach to financial reporting to seek foreign capital. In turn, this led many countries—particularly in the European Union—to allow domestic financial reporting rules to reflect economic performance better, making it easier for firms in their country to raise investment capital from abroad. Consequently, international reporting differences have narrowed considerably. But differences still exist.
- Various mechanisms for coping with cross-country reporting diversity have evolved. In the United States, foreign issuers are required to reconcile their home country reporting rules to U.S. GAAP. Another approach that is gaining significant support is one in which companies are urged to use rules written by the IASB. These standards would then become a type of international accounting language. This approach gained considerable support when the European Commission voted to require all publicly traded EU companies to use International Financial Reporting Standards in their consolidated statements by January 1, 2005.
- Mechanisms for monitoring compliance with GAAP also differ significantly from country to country—both in the form of the monitoring and its effectiveness.
- Inflation is a serious problem in certain countries. Where this is the case, historical cost reporting becomes less meaningful and inflation accounting is often used.
- Two methods for reflecting changing prices are current cost accounting and general price-level accounting.
- Current cost accounting measures changes in the specific purchasing power of the company for which the financial statements are being prepared.
- By contrast, general price-level accounting strives to reflect overall, average changes in purchasing power.

EXERCISES

Allocating resources in the most efficient manner maximizes the wealth of any country. It is generally acknowledged that financial information plays an important role in efficient resource allocation.

Required:

Given that both of the preceding statements are correct, why are the financial reporting rules in some countries designed to be very helpful to external individual investors (for example, in the United States and Canada) whereas in other countries (for example, in Japan and Germany), they are less helpful?

E18 – 1

Why do financial reporting rules differ?

Some analysts contend that a single, standardized set of uniform financial reporting rules that would be required for all companies in all countries would improve interfirm comparisons and enhance financial analysis.

Required:

Do you agree that uniform reporting across many countries will always enhance the comparability of financial data and analyses? Why or why not?

E18 – 2

Overcoming reporting diversity

E18 – 3

Overriding GAAP rules

Slough Estates is a U.K.-based property developer that prepares its profit and loss statement and balance sheet using current cost accounting. The most important asset class subject to revaluation is the company's portfolio of investment properties, which accounted for 86% of total assets in 2002.

In the footnotes to its 2002 annual report, the company discloses that it provides for no depreciation on investment properties. It justifies this departure from U.K. GAAP in the following passage from the Accounting Policies footnote:

> This treatment may be a departure from the requirements of the Companies Act concerning depreciation of fixed assets. However, these properties are not held for consumption but for investment and the directors consider that systematic annual depreciation would be inappropriate.
>
> The accounting policy adopted is therefore necessary for the financial statements to give a true and fair view. Depreciation or amortization is only one of the many factors reflected in the annual valuation and the amount which might otherwise have been shown cannot reasonably be separately identified or quantified.

Required:

Slough Estates is here exercising a well-established right within U.K. accounting to "override" the specific provisions of GAAP in order to allow the financial statements to give a "true and fair view" of the business's performance. Would U.S. accountants allow a similar departure from U.S. GAAP? Explain.

E18 – 4

Current cost accounting

Highrate Company's 2005 historical cost income statement is as follows:

Sales	$20,000
Cost of sales	8,000
Gross margin	12,000
Depreciation	2,000
Other operating expenses	8,000
Net income	$ 2,000

Highrate's management is concerned about the increase in inventory costs as well as the increasing costs of property, plant, and equipment. Management believes that the current cost of inventory sold is 25% higher than its historical cost at the time of sale. In addition, if property, plant, and equipment were valued at current costs, an additional $1,000 of depreciation would be recorded.

Required:

1. Prepare a current cost income statement for Highrate Company.
2. Assume you are a shareholder of Highrate Company. Which net income figure do you think is more useful? Why?

E18 – 5

General price-level accounting

The following schedule shows the average general purchasing power index of the indicated years:

2003	100
2004	125
2005	150

Carl Corporation's plant and equipment consisted of the following totals at December 31, 2005:

Date Acquired	Percentage Depreciated	Historical Cost
2003	30%	$30,000
2004	20	20,000
2005	10	10,000
		$60,000

Depreciation is calculated at 10% per annum on a straight-line basis. A full year's depreciation is charged in the year of acquisition. There were no disposals in 2005.

Required:

What amount of depreciation expense should be included in a general price-level accounting income statement?

When computing purchasing power gain or loss on net monetary items, which of the following accounts are classified as nonmonetary?

1. Receivables under capitalized leases
2. Obligations under capitalized leases
3. Minority interest
4. Unamortized discount on bonds payable
5. Long-term receivables
6. Equity investment in unconsolidated subsidiaries
7. Obligations under warranties
8. Accumulated depreciation of equipment
9. Advances to unconsolidated subsidiaries
10. Allowance for uncollectible accounts
11. Unamortized premium on bonds payable

E18 – 6

Distinguishing between monetary and nonmonetary items

AICPA
ADAPTED

Lewis Company was formed on January 1, 2004. Selected balances from the historical cost balance sheet at December 31, 2004 were as follows:

Land (purchased in 2004)	$120,000
Investment in nonconvertible bonds (purchased in 2004 and expected to be held to maturity)	60,000
Long-term debt	80,000

The general purchasing power index was 100 when the debt was issued and the land and bonds were purchased; it was 110 at December 31, 2005.

Required:

In a general price-level accounting balance sheet at December 31, 2005, at what amounts should the land, investment, and long-term debt be shown?

E18 – 7

General price-level accounting

AICPA
ADAPTED

As described in the text, IASB standards allow firms to exercise more latitude than exists in U.S. GAAP.

Required:

1. Taking this latitude difference into account, consider what would happen if the SEC were to allow foreign issuers of securities in the United States to use IASB standards in lieu of U.S. GAAP. What problems would you anticipate? Would there be a "level playing field" for both foreign and U.S. companies when they seek investment capital?
2. In light of your answer in requirement 1, what is your conjecture about how top management of U.S. companies would react to an SEC decision that allows foreign issuers to use IASB standards?

E18 – 8

Attitude of U.S. companies toward IASB standards

PROBLEMS/DISCUSSION QUESTIONS

Accounting standards vary across national boundaries. As stated in the chapter, a specific country's financial reporting standards are a function of its legal environment, customs, and social objectives. In addition, the primary source of capital for companies within a country influences the country's financial reporting standards.

Required:

Assume there are two countries in the world. In the first country, Equityland, companies acquire capital through individual investors, who purchase equity shares on public stock exchanges. Companies in the second country, Debtland, acquire their capital from a few large banks. Answer the following questions on the basis of your understanding of the differences in the financial reporting incentives of firms domiciled in Equityland versus Debtland.

1. Who are the primary users of companies' financial reports?
2. What are the users concerned about when assessing companies' financial reports?
3. What financial ratios might financial statement users in the two countries employ when examining companies' economic performances?
4. How are the disclosure demands of financial statement users in Equityland different from those of users in Debtland?

P18 – 1

Capital sources and disclosure differences

P18 – 2

Overcoming reporting
diversity: Extraordinary
items

Portugal Telecom's 2002 income statement was prepared in accordance with Portuguese GAAP and reported the following amounts for extraordinary items and net income:

(€ in thousands)	2002	2001	2000
Extraordinary items	€(15,620)	€218,916	€496,406
Net income	316,435	(35,259)	498,058

During this three-year period, some of the extraordinary items included above were the following:

Provisions to adjust the assets and liabilities of TMN subsidiary (2002)	€ (50,915)
Gains on disposals of Telefónica shares (2000, 2001, 2002)	185,840
Gain on disposal of PT Multimedia shares (2000)	483,063
Gains on disposal of PTM.com shares (2000, 2001)	375,979
Issuance of additional common stock by subsidiaries (2000, 2001)	(171,303)
Loss on transfer of the investment in Zip.net between two subsidiaries of Portugal Telecom (2000)	(336,097)

Required:

1. Discuss whether each of the following would be reported as extraordinary under U.S. GAAP:

   a. Provisions to adjust the assets and liabilities of a subsidiary.
   b. Gains on disposal of shares of an investee.
   c. Gains or losses resulting from the issuance of additional common stock by an investee.

2. Assume you subscribe to a global data service that provides only summary financial information limited to net income, total assets, and total stockholders' equity. How does this limit your analysis of international companies?

3. The loss resulting from the transfer of one subsidiary's investment in Zip.net to another would not have been recognized under U.S. GAAP because both subsidiaries are under the common control of Portugal Telecom. However, U.S. GAAP would have required the recognition of an impairment charge of similar magnitude because the fair value of Zip.net had declined. Would this impairment loss have been extraordinary? Explain.

P18 – 3

Extraordinary items

Schoeller-Bleckmann Oilfield Equipment AG is an Austrian manufacturer of drilling equipment. The company is listed on NASDAQ Europe and the Vienna Stock Exchange, and it prepares its consolidated financial statements using IFRS.

Schoeller-Bleckmann's income statement for the year ending 31 December 2002 included the following:

(€ in thousands)	
Income on ordinary activities before taxation	€19,759
Extraordinary expenses	(1,696)
Income taxes on ordinary activities	(6,188)
Income taxes on extraordinary expenses	577
Income after taxation	€12,452

The company described the extraordinary expense in greater detail in the notes to its financial statements.

> In 2001 an employee of Knust-SBO [a Houston-based subsidiary] who was driving a company owned vehicle became involved in a motor vehicle collision with another vehicle. The driver of the other vehicle suffered injuries from the accident.
>
> This individual alleged that her injuries from the accident served to significantly impair her ability to live her life in the manner that she was accustomed to before the accident and sued Knust-SBO. . . . During the course of the lawsuit's legal proceedings in the year 2002, the Company began to fear the unpredictable nature of a jury trial. Accordingly, to avoid a jury trial and protracted legal costs, Knust-SBO negotiated for a litigation settlement and paid directly to the plaintiff an uninsured amount of €1,696 thousand. All settlement monies were disbursed by December 31, 2002.

Required:

1. As discussed in Chapter 2, U.S. GAAP applies very stringent criteria to the classification of extraordinary items. IFRS rules for what constitute extraordinary items, although substantially similar, are slightly less prescriptive and therefore potentially more open to interpretation. On the basis of your knowledge of U.S. GAAP, discuss how Schoeller-Bleckmann's extraordinary expense would have been reported if the company had followed U.S. GAAP.
2. Identify reasons for and against applying restrictive categorization criteria to determine whether particular gains or losses are extraordinary.

China Petroleum and Chemical Corporation (Sinopec) is a large integrated Chinese petroleum and petrochemical company. Its shares are listed on the Shanghai Stock Exchange, as well as in Hong Kong, New York, and London. The company prepares two full sets of financial statements using People's Republic of China accounting rules and IFRS, as well as a reconciliation of its IFRS accounts to U.S. GAAP.

P18 – 4

Fixed asset revaluations

A summary of the reconciliation between IFRS and U.S. GAAP is provided below.

(RMB in millions)	2002	2001
Shareholders' equity under IFRS	154,485	147,669
Revaluation of property, plant and equipment*	(12,699)	(16,528)
Reversal of impairment of long-lived assets	(608)	(667)
Other	(349)	(103)
Shareholders' equity under U.S. GAAP	140,829	130,371
Net income under IFRS	16,080	
Revaluation of property, plant and equipment**	3,236	
Reversal of impairment of long-lived assets	59	
Other	140	
Net income under U.S. GAAP	19,515	

*The revaluation amount was credited directly to shareholders' equity, not included in income.

**Adjusted for approximated tax effects.

Required:

1. Identify various approaches that companies can use to make their financial statements more understandable to foreign investors. What approaches has Sinopec used?
2. IFRS permits the revaluation of property, plant, and equipment and reversals of impairment charges on long-lived fixed assets. These accounting differences cause IFRS shareholders' equity to be overstated relative to U.S. GAAP. However, as indicated in the income reconciliation, they also cause IFRS net income to be *understated* relative to U.S. GAAP. Explain why IFRS standards in this case cause opposite directional adjustments to the balance sheet (decreasing U.S. GAAP equity) and the income statement (increasing U.S. GAAP income).
3. What is Sinopec's ROE when it reports under IFRS? What is the company's ROE under U.S. GAAP? Which measure do you prefer? Explain.

Slough Estates is a U.K.-based property developer with holdings of investment properties in the U.K., France, Germany, the U.S.A., and Canada. The company prepares its financial statements based on annual revaluations of its property portfolio, which are allowed under both U.K. GAAP and IFRS.

P18 – 5

Revaluations and ratio effects

Information from Slough Estates' balance sheets for 2002 and 2001 include the following data:

(£ in millions)	2002	2001
Investment properties (at valuation)	£3,632.6	£3,514.2
Other assets (at cost or valuation)	598.5	651.2
Total assets	4,231.1	4,165.4
Liabilities	1,986.0	1,928.8
Unrealized revaluation reserves	1,481.6	1,502.0
Other shareholders' equity	763.5	734.6
Total liabilities and shareholders' equity	£4,231.1	£4,165.4

Net income plus after-tax interest was approximately £136.7 million in 2002. The company also disclosed that the historical cost basis of the investment properties portfolio was £2,141.6 million and £1,999.5 million in 2002 and 2001, respectively. Despite this large difference, historical cost net income would have been essentially the same as the amount reported above, which was computed on a current cost basis.

Required:

1. Calculate Slough Estates' 2002 ROA based on the company's published profit and loss statement and balance sheets.
2. Recalculate this ratio assuming Slough Estates had used historical cost accounting. Which ratio would you prefer to use when analyzing the company?
3. Real estate companies commonly use revaluation accounting for their property portfolios when accounting standards permit this treatment. Speculate on reasons for this behavior.

P18 – 6

Revaluations and executive compensation

As noted in P18–5, Slough Estates is a U.K.-based property developer that prepares its profit and loss statement and balance sheet using current cost accounting. At Slough Estates, senior executive compensation is governed by the remuneration committee, made up of non-executive directors of the company. This committee is charged with establishing performance criteria under which executives are awarded bonuses and stock options. The annual report discloses that the two performance criteria selected by committee are diluted earnings per share and net assets per share.

Required:

1. Describe the role property revaluations play in setting executive compensation at Slough Estates.
2. Assume you have been assigned by your company's compensation committee to design an executive bonus scheme based on asset revaluations. What factors would you consider in setting your policy? (*Hint:* You should certainly consider who would perform the revaluations, what assets would be included, and who would control the timing of such revaluations.)

P18 – 7

Overcoming reporting diversity

Stork N.V., domiciled in Amsterdam, The Netherlands, is an industrial company with operations worldwide. In a footnote to its Year 2 financial report, Stork disclosed the following current value information (in thousands of guilders):

	Year 2	Year 1
Fixed assets	858,000	825,000
Additional depreciation to be recorded under current value accounting	12,106	12,066

Information from Stork's profit and loss statement and balance sheet includes the following data:

Net income	81,257	55,906
Fixed assets	692,913	657,315
Shareholders' equity	778,364	749,093

Required:

1. Using the data reported on Stork's profit and loss statement and balance sheet, what is Stork's Year 2 ROE?
2. If Stork N.V. were to book the revaluation of its fixed assets, what is its Year 2 ROE?
3. Which ROE is more relevant when comparing Stork's performance to the performance of an industrial firm domiciled in the United States? Explain.
4. Australian GAAP allows firms the option of revaluing their fixed assets. Which ROE measure is more relevant when comparing Stork's performance to the performance of an industrial firm domiciled in Australia? Explain.

P18 – 8

Overcoming reporting diversity

A recent income statement of Electrolux, a Swedish company that owns the U.S.-based appliance company Frigidaire, reports the following (in millions of Swedish kronor):

Sales	100,121
Operating expense	(92,594)
Share of income in associated companies	(10)
Operating income before depreciation	7,517

A footnote discloses that operating expense included the following items:

Capital gains on sales of real estate	114
Losses on sales of operations	(325)
Capital gains on sale of shares in Email Ltd.	204
Total included in operating expense	(7)

Required:

Describe how each of the items disclosed in the footnote would be reported if Electrolux prepared its financial statements in accordance with U.S. GAAP.

Both Canadian GAAP and IFRS allow companies the choice of either expensing or capitalizing interest incurred on construction-related borrowings. Canadian Pacific Railway expenses all such interest, choosing to follow what IFRS classifies as the benchmark treatment. As discussed in Chapter 10, U.S. GAAP requires companies to capitalize "avoidable" construction-related borrowing costs.

P18 – 9

Capitalization of interest

Required:

1. Assume that Canadian Pacific's construction-related spending and borrowings are smoothly increasing over time. How would you expect the company's policy of expensing all construction-related interest to affect the time series of the company's reported income and owners' equity?
2. Assume Canadian Pacific undertakes a very large bridge and tunnel construction project and incurs substantial borrowing costs during 2005. What effect would the company's policy of expensing rather than capitalizing borrowing costs have on the following for 2005?

   a. Net income
   b. Fixed asset turnover (that is, sales divided by fixed assets)
   c. Operating cash flow
   d. Return on assets

SABMiller was formed in 2002 when South African Breweries acquired the Miller Brewing Company thereby creating one of the world's largest brewers. The company's shares are listed in London and Johannesburg, and it prepares its accounts using U.K. GAAP.

P18 – 10

Reversal of impairment losses

SABMiller's accounting policy on fixed asset impairment conforms to IFRS. It states,

> When the [historical cost] carrying values of fixed assets are written down by any impairment amount, the loss is recognized in the profit and loss account in the period in which incurred. Should circumstances or events change and give rise to a reversal of the previous impairment loss, the reversal is recognized in the profit and loss account in the period in which it occurs and the carrying value of the asset is increased. The increase in the carrying value of the asset will only be up to the amount that it would have been had the original impairment not occurred.

In conformity with this policy, SABMiller's 2002 income statement contained the following items (in millions of U.S. dollars):

Brewery closure costs in Pitesti, Romania	$ 9
Asset impairment provision in Ursus, Romania	10
Reversal of asset impairment provision in Velke Popovice, Czech Republic	(11)

Required:

1. How does SABMiller's accounting for fixed asset impairment differ from that prescribed by U.S. GAAP?
2. Should investors be concerned that a company's management might time the reversal of impairment provisions to smooth income or achieve other financial reporting goals? What factors would a company's auditors consider when scrutinizing such reversals?

As described in this chapter, IAS 38 permits firms to capitalize "development phase" costs incurred on internal projects once technical feasibility and other criteria demonstrating the existence of an asset are met.

Nokia, the Finnish telecommunications giant, prepares its financial statements using IFRS and, consistent with the IAS 38 standard, capitalizes a range of product development costs.

Nokia lists its shares on the New York Stock Exchange and discloses the impact of capitalizing its various product development costs in the following U.S. GAAP reconciliation included with its Form 20-F filing. The reconciling item includes only non-software development costs. Software development costs are capitalized under both Nokia's application of IFRS and U.S. GAAP.

(€ in millions)	2002	2001	2000
Net income reported under IFRS	€3,381	€2,200	€3,938
Development costs	(66)	(104)	(65)
Other adjustments	288	(193)	(26)
Net income under U.S. GAAP	€3,603	€1,903	€3,847

	2002	2001
Shareholders' equity reported under IFRS	€14,281	€12,205
Development costs	(421)	(355)
Other adjustments	290	171
Shareholders' equity under U.S. GAAP	€14,150	€12,021

Required:

1. Did Nokia's capitalization of development costs increase or decrease IFRS net income relative to U.S. GAAP income during 2000 to 2002? Explain. Can you expect this relationship to always hold?
2. Did Nokia's capitalization of development costs increase or decrease IFRS shareholders' equity relative to U.S. GAAP equity during 2001 and 2002? Explain. Can you expect this relationship to always hold?
3. List some reasons why a company's management might capitalize development costs.

LM Ericsson is one of the world's largest suppliers of mobile and fixed-line telecommunications products. The company is headquartered in Stockholm, with shares listed in Sweden and other European exchanges, as well as ADRs (American Depository Receipts) listed on the NASDAQ market in the U.S. Until 2002, the company expensed all software development expenditures, in conformity with Swedish GAAP. In 2002, Ericsson adopted *SFAS No. 86*, the U.S. accounting standard under which software development expenditures are capitalized when technical feasibility for that product is established. The company now amortizes software development assets over three to five years in addition to testing them for impairment annually.

In the notes to its 2002 Annual Report, Ericsson disclosed that its expenditures on software development totaled 3,442, 8,084, and 11,339 in 2002, 2001, and 2000, respectively. (All data in this problem are stated in millions of Swedish kronor—SEK.) The notes also disclosed that intangible assets on the balance sheet contained the newly created software development asset. This asset's value was 3,200 million, which was net of accumulated amortization and impairment write-downs of 242 million.

The company's 20-F filing with the U.S. SEC contained the following reconciliation to U.S. GAAP shareholders' equity and net income:

(SEK in millions)	2002	2001	2000
Shareholders' equity under Swedish GAAP	73,607	68,587	91,686
Capitalization of software development costs	11,562	16,502	18,637
Other	(1,966)	(7,288)	(1,106)
Shareholders' equity under U.S. GAAP	83,203	77,801	109,217
Net income (loss) under Swedish GAAP	(19,013)	(21,264)	21,018
Capitalization of software development costs	(4,940)	(2,135)	4,133
Other	4,035	(1,004)	(1,758)
Net income (loss) under U.S. GAAP	(19,918)	(24,403)	23,393

Required:

1. Would Ericsson's net income have been higher or lower than that actually reported in 2000, 2001, and 2002 had the company always capitalized its software development expenditures? Explain.
2. Assuming the company had always capitalized its software development expenditures, what would the value of the software development asset have been in the 2000, 2001, and 2002 balance sheets?
3. What was the impact of the company's accounting change on the reported pre-tax loss for 2002?

In its 2002 Annual Report, Alcatel, the French telecom company, described its goodwill accounting policy as follows.

P18 – 13

Goodwill amortization

> Goodwill is amortized using the straight-line method over a period, determined for each transaction, which does not exceed twenty years.

This policy conforms to French accounting standards and IFRS. Goodwill amortization is a significant expense for Alcatel, which the company clearly breaks out on its income statement:

(€ in millions)	2002	2001	2000
Amortization of goodwill	(589)	(1,933)	(576)
Net income (loss)	(4,745)	(4,963)	1,324

Required:

1. How does Alcatel's goodwill accounting policy differ from that required under U.S. GAAP? Explain.
2. In 2002, Alcatel acquired a controlling interest in Alcatel Shanghai Bell. Alcatel reported that goodwill from the acquisition amounted to €205 million and that the amortization horizon for this intangible asset would be 20 years. How would accounting for the acquisition under U.S. GAAP have affected the company's net income and shareholders' equity? Explain. (Assume that the acquisition was made at the beginning of the year and the goodwill resulting from the Alcatel Shanghai Bell acquisition was not impaired as of the end of the year.)
3. As noted above, Alcatel clearly identifies the amortization of goodwill in its income statement. This is a common practice among companies with substantial goodwill amortization expenses. Why might companies find it advantageous to adopt this disclosure practice?

In its 2002 Annual Report, Nokia provides consolidated financial statements for the Nokia Group prepared under IFRS. These statements combine the annual report of the Nokia parent company, based in Finland, with those of its many subsidiaries around the world. Nokia also provides parent-level statements prepared under Finnish Accounting Standards. The 2002 group and parent-level balance sheets are summarized below.

P18 – 14

Group and parent-level financial statements

(€ in millions)	Group	Parent-Level
Property, plant and equipment	€ 1,874	€ 0
Investments in subsidiaries	0	3,519
Loans to group companies (including receivables)	0	10,023
Deferred tax assets	731	0
Other assets	20,722	4,715
Total assets	€23,327	€18,257
Liabilities from group companies	€ 0	€ 3,738
Other liabilities	9,046	2,649
Shareholders' equity	14,281	11,870
Total liabilities and shareholders' equity	€23,327	€18,257

Required:

1. Why might a parent company report no holdings of property, plant and equipment on its balance sheet?
2. Why might a parent company report no significant deferred tax items?
3. Why does the Nokia Group report no loans to or liabilities from group companies?

Cemex is one of the world's largest cement companies. Based in Monterrey, Mexico, the company has significant operations in such diverse economies as those of the United States, Spain, Venezuela, Colombia, Thailand, and Egypt. Some of these countries have recently experienced substantial inflation.

The following table summarizes the consolidated income statements presented in Cemex's 2002 annual report. As discussed in the chapter, Mexican GAAP requires companies to make various adjustments for the effects of inflation. One adjustment is to present comparative income statements and balance sheets in units of constant purchasing power. Another is to recognize a gain or loss from holding monetary items. Cemex refers to its net gain from holding monetary items as its "monetary position result."

(in millions of constant Mexican pesos as of December 31, 2002)	2000	2001	2002
Operating income	17,193.5	16,549.9	13,602.0
Comprehensive financing result:			
Financial expense	(4,853.6)	(4,121.6)	(3,451.6)
Financial income	255.7	407.7	463.0
Results from valuation and liquidation of financial instruments	(80.0)	1,999.2	(3,285.1)
Foreign exchange result	(312.9)	1,539.6	(800.3)
Monetary position result	3,183.9	2,824.5	3,655.2
Net comprehensive financing result	(1,806.9)	2,649.4	(3,418.8)
Other (including taxes)	(4,187.0)	(5,874.8)	(4,398.1)
Consolidated net income	11,199.6	13,324.5	5,785.1

In its 2002 report, Cemex disclosed that domestic Mexican inflation rates were 9.03%, 4.56%, and 5.53% in 2000, 2001, and 2002, respectively. These rates were substantially below those that generally prevailed in the 1990s. Cemex also provided a weighted-average inflation rate computed across all the economies in which the company operates. In 2002, this multi-country rate grew from comparatively low levels to 9.16%, substantially above the domestic Mexican rate of inflation. Cemex specifically cited hyperinflation in Venezuela of 31.2% as having affected its performance in 2002.

Required:

1. Does holding a monetary asset exposed to the effects of inflation result in a monetary gain or monetary loss? What about a monetary liability? Explain.
2. Cemex consistently reports gains classified as "monetary position results." Is the company in a net monetary asset or liability position; that is, does the company have a larger amount of monetary assets or liabilities? Explain.
3. Why might the monetary position result for 2002 be larger than for 2000 despite the fact that Mexican inflation was substantially lower?
4. Cemex's 2001 annual report calculates consolidated net income for 2000 and 2001 as 10,259.8 and 12,206.4 million pesos, respectively. These figures differ from the numbers for 2000 and 2001 consolidated net income presented above. Can you explain the discrepancy?

At the end of 2002, Portugal Telecom and Telefónica, the Spanish telecom company, formed Brasilcel, a 50:50 joint venture that provides mobile phone service to the Brazilian market. Under Portuguese GAAP, Portugal Telecom must account for this joint venture using the proportional consolidation method. Proportional consolidation, which is also the benchmark method under IFRS, requires Portugal Telecom to include 50% of Brasilcel's assets and liabilities in its balance sheet. Under U.S. GAAP, Portugal Telecom would have accounted for its investment in Brasilcel using the equity method.

Portugal Telecom is listed on the New York Stock Exchange, so the company files a Form 20-F with the U.S. SEC. The 2002 20-F provided a comparison of Portugal Telecom's actual balance sheet, showing the Brasilcel joint venture under the proportional consolidation method, with a pro-forma balance sheet accounting for Brasilcel using the equity method. Both balance sheets, which follow, were prepared using identical accounting principles apart from the treatment of the joint venture.

(€ in millions) December 31, 2002	Proportional Consolidation	Equity Method
Other assets	€13,350	€10,646
Investments	376	2,277
Total assets	€13,726	€12,923
Liabilities	€10,615	€ 9,812
Shareholders' equity	3,111	3,111
Total liabilities and shareholders' equity	€13,726	€12,923

Required:

1. Why is shareholders' equity equal under the two methods while assets and liabilities are larger under the proportional consolidation method?
2. Using Portugal Telecom as an example, discuss how the application of proportional consolidation might affect an investor's perceptions of a company's financial leverage and return on assets. For simplicity, assume that Portugal Telecom's net income plus after-tax interest was €695 in 2002 under both methods.

Infosys, an Indian software company, prepares its Indian GAAP financial statements primarily using the historical cost convention. However, the company also provides supplemental balance sheets in which it books and annually revalues two self-developed intangible assets, brand equity and human resources. The disparity between these balance sheets can be seen in the following table:

P18 – 17

Recording self-developed intangible assets

Balance Sheets as of March 31, 2003

(in millions of Indian rupees)	Indian GAAP Balance Sheet	Supplemental Balance Sheet
Brand equity	—	74,880.0
Human resources	—	104,170.3
Other assets	36,143.0	35,638.8
Total assets	36,143.0	214,689.1
Liabilities	7,078.1	7,032.3
Shareholders' equity	29,064.9	207,656.8
Total liabilities and shareholders' equity	36,143.0	214,689.1

The pro forma entry that Infosys uses to construct its supplemental balance sheet is approximately as follows:

DR	Brand equity	74.9	
DR	Human resources	104.2	
	CR Other assets		.5
	CR Shareholders' equity		178.6

Required:

1. How does Infosys's supplemental balance sheet depart from standard accounting practices used in the U.S.?
2. Infosys justifies recording intangibles in supplemental disclosures by noting that "intangible assets have a significant role in defining the growth of a hi-tech company." What arguments might Infosys use to support this statement?
3. The supplemental balance sheet reports that the company's largest economic asset is "human resources." What factors would an appraiser consider when assigning a valuation to this asset?

CASES

(This is a continuation of C16–9 that is available on our website at www.prenhall.com/revsine.)

In its 1979 annual report, Tyler Corporation repeatedly emphasized a 33% increase in sales between 1978 and 1979. In addition to acquiring Thurston on April 6, Tyler confronted double-digit inflation during 1979. Since Tyler's gross property, plant, and equipment exceeded $150 million, it was required to disclose supplementary inflation adjusted data under *SFAS No. 33*, as described in the chapter. A portion of that (unaudited) disclosure is shown next.

C18 – 1

Tyler Corporation (2): Adjusting reported trend data

Statement of Income Adjusted for Effects of Changing Prices

Year Ended December 31, 1979

	Historical Financial Statements	Adjusted for General Inflation (Constant Dollar)	Adjusted for Changes in Specific Prices (Current Cost/ Constant Dollar)
Net sales	$519,242,000	$546,992,000	$546,992,000
Costs and expenses			
Cost of sales	411,515,000	435,254,000	435,254,000
Selling, administrative, and general expenses	39,178,000	41,360,000	41,360,000
Depreciation	15,007,000	19,206,000	22,146,000
Interest expense	11,212,000	11,779,000	11,779,000
	476,912,000	507,599,000	510,539,000
Income before income tax and gain from decline in purchasing power of net amounts owed	42,330,000	39,393,000	36,453,000
Income tax	18,873,000	19,879,000	19,879,000
Net income before gain from decline in purchasing power of net amounts owed	23,457,000	19,514,000	16,574,000
Gain from decline in purchasing power of net amounts owed	–0–	8,569,000	8,569,000
Net income including gain from decline in purchasing power of net amounts owed	$ 23,457,000	$ 28,083,000	$ 25,143,000
Per common share			
Net income before gain from decline in purchasing power of net amounts owed	$ 2.34	$ 1.94	$ 1.65
Gain from decline in purchasing power of net amounts owed	–0–	.85	.85
Net income, including gain from decline in purchasing power of net amounts owed	$ 2.34	$ 2.79	$ 2.50
Shareholders' equity at December 31, 1979	$115,535,000	$205,825,000	$240,151,000
Average shares outstanding	10,040,000	10,040,000	10,040,000

Five-Year Summary of Financial Data Adjusted for Effects of Changing Prices

	Years Ended December 31				
	1975	1976	1977	1978	1979
Net sales	$383,302,000	$412,794,000	$447,722,000	$458,952,000	$546,992,000
Cash dividends per common share	0.21	0.32	0.38	0.44	0.48
Market price per common share at year-end	7.08	15.00	15.60	18.41	15.38
Year-end consumer price index	166.3	174.3	186.1	202.9	229.9

Required:

1. Explain the methodology that Tyler Corporation used to adjust "Net sales" from the historical cost amount of $519,242,000 to the inflation adjusted figure of $546,992,000.
2. There is a "five-year summary" at the bottom of the footnote disclosure. The net sales number for 1978 is $458,952,000. Explain the methodology Tyler used to derive this number.
3. After adjusting for inflation, what was the sales growth between 1978 and 1979?
4. The growth rate that you computed in requirement 3 adjusts the sales growth rate for inflation but not for the acquisition of Thurston (described in C16–9). How can a statement reader

simultaneously adjust for *both* the acquisition and inflation? Taking both factors into account, what was the "real" sales growth between the two years? (*Hint:* Utilize the pro forma sales information from C16–9 in conjunction with the inflation information from this case to answer this part.)

In its *SFAS No. 33* footnote disclosure, Tyler described how it managed operations and capital in an inflationary environment. Regarding Tyler's capital management, the footnote stated:

> The Company has also prudently used long-term debt to leverage its capital structure. Long-term debt has been the primary vehicle for financing the acquisition of each of the four operating units. Strong cash flow from the operating units has been used to repay long-term debt with dollars having less purchasing power.
>
> During 1978 and 1979 the capital structure of the Company has changed substantially. At December 31, 1979 the debt-to-equity ratio was 48/52 as compared to the 37/63 ratio at December 31, 1978 and 28/72 at December 31, 1977.

During 1979 Tyler acquired Thurston Motor Lines for approximately $45.5 million in cash. Tyler's annual report contained a footnote entitled Credit Commitments from Banks, which is excerpted next:

C18 – 2

Tyler Corporation (3): Borrowing strategies under inflationary conditions

CREDIT COMMITMENTS FROM BANKS

Under commitments from banks, the Company may borrow at the then effective prime rate of interest up to $25,000,000 on an unsecured short-term basis. The Company is required to be free from borrowings under the commitments for at least 60 consecutive days during the preceding twelve months. There were no borrowings outstanding under these commitments at December 31, 1978 and 1979.

Long-Term Debt	1978	1979
Parent		
8 ¾ % unsecured note due in annual installments of $2,500,000 through 1979, $3,000,000 thereafter	$32,500,000	$30,000,000
Unsecured $50,000,000 revolving line of credit, interest at 106% of prime rate through March 1981, thereafter ½ of 1% above prime rate	–0–	43,000,000
Subsidiaries		
Unsecured $6,000,000 revolving line of credit, interest at prime rate	–0–	4,150,000
5 ¾ % to 8% secured notes	428,000	1,411,000
	32,928,000	78,561,000
Less current maturities	2,636,000	4,366,000
	$30,292,000	$74,195,000

Scheduled repayments of long-term debt during the five years following December 31, 1979 are as follows: 1980—$4,366,000; 1981—$10,679,000; 1982—$12,447,000; 1983—$12,445,000; 1984—$12,445,000.

Required:

Consider the financing methods Tyler used to acquire companies like Thurston; then evaluate the effectiveness of Tyler's strategy for using debt as a means for protecting shareholders in an inflationary environment.

C18 – 3

Tyler Corporation (4): Inflation's effect on GAAP ratios

Tyler Corporation sometimes placed ads in the *Wall Street Journal* in order to highlight its financial performance. The following advertisement appeared in the September 22, 1982 edition of the *Wall Street Journal*:

RETURN ON EQUITY

	Tyler Corporation	Median of Fortune 500	Top 10% (50th) of Fortune 500
1981	19.1%*	13.8%	21.3%
1980	19.8*	14.4	22.2
1979	20.3	15.9	22.3
1978	21.4	14.3	21.0
1977	20.9	13.5	19.8
1976	19.8	13.2	19.5
1975	20.7	11.5	18.6
1974	21.4	13.3	19.8
1973	18.5	12.4	18.9
1972	19.7	10.4	16.6
1971	15.9	9.1	16.4

For most of its history, Tyler's return on shareholders' equity has generally been in or close to the top 10% of the Fortune 500 companies. To learn more, contact us for a copy of our annual report.

*Before extraordinary item.

Tyler Corporation
3100 Southland Center
Dallas, Texas 75201

The gross domestic product (GDP) implicit price deflator is a price index that is designed to capture price changes for all items that enter into the computation of GDP. Overall inflation as measured by the year-to-year change in GDP implicit price deflators for the period covered in the ad was:

1981	10.0%
1980	9.5
1979	8.6
1978	7.9
1977	6.9
1976	6.3
1975	9.6
1974	8.7
1973	6.4
1972	4.6
1971	5.4

Required:

1. Carefully explain how continuing, pervasive price increases would affect ROE as computed under GAAP. (*Hint:* How does inflation affect the ROE numerator—income, and the denominator—assets minus liabilities?)
2. Tyler Corporation had a somewhat large proportion of long-lived assets. Specifically, net property, plant, and equipment comprised approximately 30% of total assets. How, if at all, does this capital intensity affect the comparison made between Tyler and other *Fortune 500* companies in the *Wall Street Journal* ad?

The Robinson Company's statement of financial position on January 1, 2005, appeared as follows:

Robinson Company

Statement of Financial Position
January 1, 2005

Assets			Equities	
Cash		$ 5,000		
Inventory		8,000		
Fixed asset—cost	$10,000			
Less: Accumulated depreciation	5,000			
		5,000	Common stock	$18,000
		$18,000		$18,000

The inventory consisted of 10 units acquired at an original cost of $800 per unit on November 1, 2004. Robinson Company owns only a single fixed asset that was purchased new on January 1, 2000 for $10,000. The asset has a ten-year life, no salvage value, and experiences a straight-line decline in service potential.

On June 30, 2005, five of the 10 inventory units were sold for $8,600 cash. Robinson Company's pricing strategy was based upon a target return of 20% on the original cost of the assets sold and/or utilized in operations. Dividends equal to total reported historical cost income were also declared and paid on June 30. No other transactions occurred during 2005. Assume, for simplicity, that the only costs incurred were depreciation and cost of goods sold. Historical cost financial results for 2005 were as follows:

Robinson Company

Statement of Income and Retained Earnings
Year Ended December 31, 2005

Sales revenues		$8,600
Cost of goods sold	$4,000	
Depreciation	1,000	
		5,000
Operating income		3,600
Plus: Retained earnings, 1/1/05		–0–
Less: Dividend		3,600
Retained earnings, 12/31/05		–0–

Balance Sheet
December 31, 2005

Assets			Equities	
Cash		$10,000		
Inventory		4,000		
Fixed asset—cost	$10,000			
Less: Accumulated depreciation	6,000			
		4,000	Common stock	$18,000
		$18,000		$18,000

Overall inflation as measured by the Consumer Price Index was:

Index value on	1/1/00	100
Index value on	11/1/04	178
Index value on	1/1/05	180
Index value on	6/30/05	190
Index value on	12/31/05	200

At January 1, 2005 the replacement cost of a five-year-old fixed asset that was identical in all respects to the asset owned by Robinson Company was $7,000. A newer, more efficient model of this machine was introduced in early February 2000; the estimated replacement cost of the improved model in a condition equivalent to that of Robinson Company's asset was $8,000 on January 1, 2005. Both used asset prices remained in effect throughout 2005.

The replacement cost of the inventory on January 1, 2005 was $810 per unit. The replacement cost at the date of sale (June 30) was $875. At year-end, the per-unit inventory replacement cost was $890.

Required:

1. Using the preceding data, compute Robinson Company's historical cost/constant dollar income for 2005 (in year-end dollars) and the December 31, 2005 historical cost/constant dollar balance sheet.

To answer this part, you must compute the gain or loss on net monetary items for 2005. This computation was not illustrated in the chapter but is straightforward. First, the net change in monetary items *in nominal dollars* as well as the causes for the change must be computed. These are:

Net monetary assets, 1/1/05	$ 5,000
Increase in net monetary assets:	
From sales revenues	8,600
Decrease in net monetary assets:	
To pay dividends	(3,600)
Net monetary assets in historical dollars, 12/31/05	$10,000

Next, the timing of the increases and decreases must be established. Here, each took place on June 30. The beginning balance as well as the increases or decreases must be restated to their December 31, 2005 purchasing power equivalent. For example, the January 1 balance would be adjusted by a ratio of 200/180, while sales and dividends would be adjusted by a factor of 200/190. The sum of these three adjusted figures indicates what the net monetary asset balance would have been had all monetary flows been "indexed." Comparing this number to the actual $10,000 amount in nominal dollars results in the gain or loss on monetary items.

Adjusting the income statement also requires you to carefully assess the timing of the income statement flow and to apply the appropriate index adjustment factor.

2. Based upon these data, determine current cost income on a physical capital maintenance basis for 2005—that is, treat holdings gains as a direct owners' equity adjustment (other comprehensive income) rather than as an element of net income. Also prepare the December 31, 2005 current cost balance sheet. Does the current cost income number you derive provide a valid measure of the dividend that can be paid without endangering future productive capacity? Discuss.

C18 – 5

Differences in reporting philosophies

The excerpt below is from a newspaper article:[33]

TOKYO, WEDNESDAY, AUGUST 19, 1992

With another steep drop in share prices deepening the sense of crisis in Japan's financial system, the Finance Minister announced a series of measures Tuesday aimed at halting the two-and-a-half-year stock market slide. . . .

In his package . . . the Finance Minister, Tsutomu Hata, sought to put pressure on big investors not to sell shares and said financial institutions would be permitted to withhold negative financial data from the public in the hope of easing worries about the system's fundamental health. He also said steps would be taken to encourage Japanese banks to make more loans. . . .

"This was perhaps the first real admission from the Finance Minister that the situation is severe and that they have to do something," said Richard Koo, a senior economist at the Nomura Research Institute. "But as far as the content goes, I'm not impressed. . . . "

---

[33] J. Sterngold, "Japan Announces Series of Steps to Try to Halt Stock Market Slide," *New York Times* (August 19, 1992).

Required:

1. Evaluate the financial reporting philosophy inherent in the Finance Ministry announcement and compare it to what you understand to be the objective of financial reporting that is designed to enhance efficient investment decisions. What are the differences? What do you think motivated the announcement?
2. What is your conjecture about the nature of the *specific* "negative financial data" that financial institutions would be permitted to withhold?
3. Do you think that the announcement achieved its intended objective?

COLLABORATIVE LEARNING CASE

The comparative income statements, balance sheets, and cash flow statements of BP p.l.c. follow. The chapter stressed the similarities between the financial reporting approaches in the United Kingdom and the United States. However, significant differences do exist. The purpose of this case is to provide you with an opportunity to utilize your understanding of U.S. GAAP along with logic and intuition to familiarize yourself with some of the differences between the two countries' financial reporting procedures.

C18 – 6

BP: Understanding non-U.S. financial statements

Required:

1. Some of BP's terminology and account titles differ from U.S. usage. Explain the following using U.S. financial reporting terms:

   a. The income and cash flow statements, as well as the left columns of the balance sheet, are labeled *Group* statements. What is the U.S. financial reporting equivalent of the term "group"?
   b. Under U.S. GAAP, what would the following BP balance sheet accounts be called?

   - Stocks
   - Debtors
   - Creditors
   - Capital and reserves
   - Called up share capital
   - Share premium account
   - Reserves

   c. Under U.S. GAAP, what would the following income and cash flow statement accounts be called?

   - Turnover
   - Exceptional items
   - Investments in associated undertakings

2. The *format* (or *structure*) of the BP financial statements also differs from that of U.S. statements. Discuss the following differences:

   a. The income statement includes an item termed "stock holding gains (losses)."

   - What are they?
   - Does their inclusion in the statement mean that the "bottom-line" profit number is not measured on an historical cost basis? Explain.
   - Why do you think BP makes this disclosure?

   b. The income statement includes items labeled "Profit (loss) on sale of businesses" and "Profit (loss) on sale of fixed assets." How, if at all, do the income statement location and treatment of these items differ from U.S. GAAP?
   c. At first glance, the BP balance sheet appears unfamiliar.

   - What are the primary differences between their format and a "typical" U.S. GAAP balance sheet format?
   - What items "balance" in BP's balance sheet? Explain the difference in balance sheet format using the basic accounting equation (A = L + E).
   - What balance sheet relationship does the BP format highlight that must be computed in U.S. statements?

   d. What are the differences in cash flow format between BP's presentation and U.S. GAAP? Comment on any differences between the U.K. and U.S. treatment of interest received (and paid) as well as dividends received (and paid).

BP Annual Report and Accounts 2002

Group Income Statement	For the Years Ended 31 December	
($ in millions)	2002	2001
Turnover	$180,186	$175,389
Less: Joint ventures	1,465	1,171
Group turnover	178,721	174,218
Replacement cost of sales	155,528	147,001
Production taxes	1,274	1,689
Gross profit	21,919	25,528
Distribution and administration expenses	12,632	10,918
Exploration expense	644	480
	8,643	14,130
Other income	641	694
Group replacement cost operating profit	9,284	14,824
Share of profits of joint ventures	346	443
Share of profits of associated undertakings	616	760
Total replacement cost operating profit	10,246	16,027
Profit (loss) on sale of businesses	(33)	(68)
Profit (loss) on sale of fixed assets	1,201	603
Replacement cost profit before interest and tax	11,414	16,562
Stock holding gains (losses)	1,129	(1,900)
Historical cost profit before interest and tax	12,543	14,662
Interest expense	1,279	1,670
Profit before taxation	11,264	12,992
Taxation	4,342	6,375
Profit after taxation	6,922	6,617
Minority shareholders' interest (MSI)	77	61
Profit for the year	6,845	6,556
Distribution to shareholders	5,375	4,935
Retained profit for the year	$ 1,470	$ 1,621
Earnings per ordinary share—cents		
Basic	30.55	29.21
Diluted	30.41	29.04
REPLACEMENT COST RESULTS:		
Historical cost profit for the year	$ 6,845	$ 6,556
Stock holding (gains) losses (net of MSI)	(1,104)	1,900
Replacement cost profit for the year	5,741	8,456
Exceptional items, net of tax	(1,043)	(165)
Replacement cost profit before exceptional items	$ 4,698	$ 8,291
Earnings per ordinary share—cents		
On replacement cost profit before exceptional items	20.97	36.95

Balance Sheets
At 31 December
($ in millions)

	Group 2002	Group 2001	Parent 2002	Parent 2001
Fixed assets				
Intangible assets	$ 15,566	$ 16,489	$ –0–	$ –0–
Tangible assets	87,682	77,410	–0–	–0–
Investments				
Joint ventures—Gross assets	4,829	4,661		
—Gross liabilities	798	800		
Net investment	4,031	3,861	–0–	–0–
Associated undertakings	4,626	5,433	3	3
Other	2,154	2,669	51,944	46,703
	10,811	11,963	51,947	46,706
Total fixed assets	114,059	105,862	51,947	46,706
Current assets				
Stocks	10,181	7,631	–0–	–0–
Debtors—amounts falling due:				
Within one year	26,905	21,988	1,892	713
After more than one year	6,245	4,681	11,689	20,560
Investments	215	450	–0–	–0–
Cash at bank and in hand	1,520	1,358	1	3
	45,066	36,108	13,582	21,276
Creditors—amounts falling due within one year				
Finance debt	10,086	9,090	–0–	–0–
Other creditors	36,215	28,524	9,906	7,642
Net current assets (liabilities)	(1,235)	(1,506)	3,676	13,634
Total assets less current liabilities	112,824	104,356	55,623	60,340
Creditors—amounts falling due after more than one year				
Finance debt	11,922	12,327	–0–	–0–
Other creditors	3,455	3,086	98	191
Provisions for liabilities and charges				
Deferred taxation	13,514	11,702	–0–	–0–
Other provisions	13,886	11,482	142	216
Net assets	70,047	65,759	55,383	59,933
Minority shareholders' interest—equity	638	598	–0–	–0–
BP shareholders' interest	$69,409	$65,161	$55,383	$59,933
Represented by:				
Capital and reserves				
Called up share capital	5,616	5,629	5,616	5,629
Share premium account	3,794	3,590	3,794	3,590
Capital redemption reserve	449	424	449	424
Merger reserve	27,033	26,983	26,336	26,286
Other reserves	173	223	173	223
Profit and loss account	32,344	28,312	19,015	23,781
	$69,409	$65,161	$55,383	$59,933

Group Cash Flow Statement

($ in millions)	For the Years Ended 31 December	
	2002	2001
Net cash inflow from operating activities	$19,342	$22,409
Dividends from joint ventures	198	104
Dividends from associated undertakings	368	528
Servicing of finance and returns on investments		
Interest received	231	256
Interest paid	(1,204)	(1,282)
Dividends received	102	132
Dividends paid to minority shareholders	(40)	(54)
Net cash outflow from servicing of finance and returns on investments	(911)	(948)
Taxation		
UK corporation tax	(979)	(1,058)
Overseas tax	(2,115)	(3,602)
Tax paid	(3,094)	(4,660)
Capital expenditure and financial investment		
Payments for tangible and intangible fixed assets	(12,049)	(12,142)
Payment for fixed assets—investments	(67)	(72)
Proceeds from the sale of fixed assets	2,470	2,365
Net cash outflow for capital expenditure and financial investment	(9,646)	(9,849)
Acquisitions and disposals		
Investments in associated undertakings	(971)	(586)
Proceeds from sale of investment in Ruhrgas	2,338	–0–
Acquisitions, net of cash acquired	(4,324)	(1,210)
Net investment in joint ventures	(354)	(497)
Proceeds from the sale of businesses	1,974	538
Net cash outflow for acquisitions and disposals	(1,337)	(1,755)
Equity dividends paid	(5,264)	(4,827)
Net cash (outflow) inflow	$ (344)	$ 1,002
Financing	(181)	972
Management of liquid resources	(220)	(211)
Increase in cash	57	241
	$ (344)	$ 1,002

Statement of Total Recognized Gains and Losses

($ in millions)	For the Years Ended 31 December	
	2002	2001
Profit for the year	$6,845	$6,556
Currency translation differences (net of tax)	3,333	(828)
Total recognized gains and losses relating to the year	10,178	5,728
Prior year adjustment—change in accounting policy	(9,206)	
Total recognized gains and losses since last annual accounts	972	

Appendix I

Please visit our internet site (www.prenhall.com/revsine) for a spreadsheet template that can be used to find present value factors for interest rates not shown in this appendix.

| Table 1 | | | | | | | PRESENT VALUE OF $1 | | | | | | | | |

$$p = \frac{1}{(1 + r)^n} = (1 + r)^{-n}$$

(n) Periods	2%	3%	4%	5%	6%	7%	8%	9%	10%	11%	12%	15%	16%	17%
1	0.98039	0.97087	0.96154	0.95238	0.94340	0.93458	0.92593	0.91743	0.90909	0.90090	0.89286	0.86957	0.86207	0.85470
2	0.96117	0.94260	0.92456	0.90703	0.89000	0.87344	0.85734	0.84168	0.82645	0.81162	0.79719	0.75614	0.74316	0.73051
3	0.94232	0.91514	0.88900	0.86384	0.83962	0.81630	0.79383	0.77218	0.75132	0.73119	0.71178	0.65752	0.64066	0.62437
4	0.92385	0.88849	0.85480	0.82270	0.79209	0.76290	0.73503	0.70843	0.68301	0.65873	0.63552	0.57175	0.55229	0.53365
5	0.90573	0.86261	0.82193	0.78353	0.74726	0.71299	0.68058	0.64993	0.62092	0.59345	0.56743	0.49718	0.47611	0.45611
6	0.88797	0.83748	0.79031	0.74622	0.70496	0.66634	0.63017	0.59627	0.56447	0.53464	0.50663	0.43233	0.41044	0.38984
7	0.87056	0.81309	0.75992	0.71068	0.66506	0.62275	0.58349	0.54703	0.51316	0.48166	0.45235	0.37594	0.35383	0.33320
8	0.85349	0.78941	0.73069	0.67684	0.62741	0.58201	0.54027	0.50187	0.46651	0.43393	0.40388	0.32690	0.30503	0.28478
9	0.83676	0.76642	0.70259	0.64461	0.59190	0.54393	0.50025	0.46043	0.42410	0.39092	0.36061	0.28426	0.26295	0.24340
10	0.82035	0.74409	0.67556	0.61391	0.55839	0.50835	0.46319	0.42241	0.38554	0.35218	0.32197	0.24718	0.22668	0.20804
11	0.80426	0.72242	0.64958	0.58468	0.52679	0.47509	0.42888	0.38753	0.35049	0.31728	0.28748	0.21494	0.19542	0.17781
12	0.78849	0.70138	0.62460	0.55684	0.49697	0.44401	0.39711	0.35553	0.31863	0.28584	0.25668	0.18691	0.16846	0.15197
13	0.77303	0.68095	0.60057	0.53032	0.46884	0.41496	0.36770	0.32618	0.28966	0.25751	0.22917	0.16253	0.14523	0.12989
14	0.75788	0.66112	0.57748	0.50507	0.44230	0.38782	0.34046	0.29925	0.26333	0.23199	0.20462	0.14133	0.12520	0.11102
15	0.74301	0.64186	0.55526	0.48102	0.41727	0.36245	0.31524	0.27454	0.23939	0.20900	0.18270	0.12289	0.10793	0.09489
16	0.72845	0.62317	0.53391	0.45811	0.39365	0.33873	0.29189	0.25187	0.21763	0.18829	0.16312	0.10686	0.09304	0.08110
17	0.71416	0.60502	0.51337	0.43630	0.37136	0.31657	0.27027	0.23107	0.19784	0.16963	0.14564	0.09293	0.08021	0.06932
18	0.70016	0.58739	0.49363	0.41552	0.35034	0.29586	0.25025	0.21199	0.17986	0.15282	0.13004	0.08081	0.06914	0.05925
19	0.68643	0.57029	0.47464	0.39573	0.33051	0.27651	0.23171	0.19449	0.16351	0.13768	0.11611	0.07027	0.05961	0.05064
20	0.67297	0.55368	0.45639	0.37689	0.31180	0.25842	0.21455	0.17843	0.14864	0.12403	0.10367	0.06110	0.05139	0.04328
25	0.60953	0.47761	0.37512	0.29530	0.23300	0.18425	0.14602	0.11597	0.09230	0.07361	0.05882	0.03038	0.02447	0.01974
30	0.55207	0.41199	0.30832	0.23138	0.17411	0.13137	0.09938	0.07537	0.05731	0.04368	0.03338	0.01510	0.01165	0.00900
35	0.50003	0.35538	0.25342	0.18129	0.13011	0.09366	0.06763	0.04899	0.03558	0.02592	0.01894	0.00751	0.00555	0.00411
40	0.45289	0.30656	0.20829	0.14205	0.09722	0.06678	0.04603	0.03184	0.02209	0.01538	0.01075	0.00373	0.00264	0.00187

Table 2   PRESENT VALUE OF AN ORDINARY ANNUITY OF $1

$$POA = \left(1 - \frac{1}{(1 + r)^n}\right) / r$$

(n) Periods	2%	3%	4%	5%	6%	7%	8%	9%	10%	11%	12%	15%	16%	17%
1	0.98039	0.97087	0.96154	0.95238	0.94340	0.93458	0.92593	0.91743	0.90909	0.90090	0.89286	0.86957	0.86207	0.85470
2	1.94156	1.91347	1.88609	1.85941	1.83339	1.80802	1.78326	1.75911	1.73554	1.71252	1.69005	1.62571	1.60523	1.58521
3	2.88388	2.82861	2.77509	2.72325	2.67301	2.62432	2.57710	2.53129	2.48685	2.44371	2.40183	2.28323	2.24589	2.20958
4	3.80773	3.71710	3.62990	3.54595	3.46511	3.38721	3.31213	3.23972	3.16987	3.10245	3.03735	2.85498	2.79818	2.74324
5	4.71346	4.57971	4.45182	4.32948	4.21236	4.10020	3.99271	3.88965	3.79079	3.69590	3.60478	3.35216	3.27429	3.19935
6	5.60143	5.41719	5.24214	5.07569	4.91732	4.76654	4.62288	4.48592	4.35526	4.23054	4.11141	3.78448	3.68474	3.58918
7	6.47199	6.23028	6.00205	5.78637	5.58238	5.38929	5.20637	5.03295	4.86842	4.71220	4.56376	4.16042	4.03857	3.92238
8	7.32548	7.01969	6.73274	6.46321	6.20979	5.97130	5.74664	5.53482	5.33493	5.14612	4.96764	4.48732	4.34359	4.20716
9	8.16224	7.78611	7.43533	7.10782	6.80169	6.51523	6.24689	5.99525	5.75902	5.53705	5.32825	4.77158	4.60654	4.45057
10	8.98259	8.53020	8.11090	7.72173	7.36009	7.02358	6.71008	6.41766	6.14457	5.88923	5.65022	5.01877	4.83323	4.65860
11	9.78685	9.25262	8.76048	8.30641	7.88687	7.49867	7.13896	6.80519	6.49506	6.20652	5.93770	5.23371	5.02864	4.83641
12	10.57534	9.95400	9.38507	8.86325	8.38384	7.94269	7.53608	7.16073	6.81369	6.49236	6.19437	5.42062	5.19711	4.98839
13	11.34837	10.63496	9.98565	9.39357	8.85268	8.35765	7.90378	7.48690	7.10336	6.74987	6.42355	5.58315	5.34233	5.11828
14	12.10625	11.29607	10.56312	9.89864	9.29498	8.74547	8.24424	7.78615	7.36669	6.98187	6.62817	5.72448	5.46753	5.22930
15	12.84926	11.93794	11.11839	10.37966	9.71225	9.10791	8.55948	8.06069	7.60608	7.19087	6.81086	5.84737	5.57546	5.32419
16	13.57771	12.56110	11.65230	10.83777	10.10590	9.44665	8.85137	8.31256	7.82371	7.37916	6.97399	5.95423	5.66850	5.40529
17	14.29187	13.16612	12.16567	11.27407	10.47726	9.76322	9.12164	8.54363	8.02155	7.54879	7.11963	6.04716	5.74870	5.47461
18	14.99203	13.75351	12.65930	11.68959	10.82760	10.05909	9.37189	8.75563	8.20141	7.70162	7.24967	6.12797	5.81785	5.53385
19	15.67846	14.32380	13.13394	12.08532	11.15812	10.33560	9.60360	8.95011	8.36492	7.83929	7.36578	6.19823	5.87746	5.58449
20	16.35143	14.87747	13.59033	12.46221	11.46992	10.59401	9.81815	9.12855	8.51356	7.96333	7.46944	6.25933	5.92884	5.62777
25	19.52346	17.41315	15.62208	14.09394	12.78336	11.65358	10.67478	9.82258	9.07704	8.42174	7.84314	6.46415	6.09709	5.76623
30	22.39646	19.60044	17.29203	15.37245	13.76483	12.40904	11.25778	10.27365	9.42691	8.69379	8.05518	6.56598	6.17720	5.82939
35	24.99862	21.48722	18.66461	16.37419	14.49825	12.94767	11.65457	10.56682	9.64416	8.85524	8.17550	6.61661	6.21534	5.85820
40	27.35548	23.11477	19.79277	17.15909	15.04630	13.33171	11.92461	10.75736	9.77905	8.95105	8.24378	6.64178	6.23350	5.87133

| Table 3 | | PRESENT VALUE OF AN ANNUITY DUE OF $1 | | | | | | | | | | | | |

$$P_{AD} = 1 + \left(1 - \frac{1}{(1+r)^{n-1}}\right) / r$$

(n) Periods	2%	3%	4%	5%	6%	7%	8%	9%	10%	11%	12%	15%	16%	17%
1	1.00000	1.00000	1.00000	1.00000	1.00000	1.00000	1.00000	1.00000	1.00000	1.00000	1.00000	1.00000	1.00000	1.00000
2	1.98039	1.97087	1.96154	1.95238	1.94340	1.93458	1.92593	1.91743	1.90909	1.90090	1.89286	1.86957	1.86207	1.85470
3	2.94156	2.91347	2.88609	2.85941	2.83339	2.80802	2.78326	2.75911	2.73554	2.71252	2.69005	2.62571	2.60523	2.58521
4	3.88388	3.82861	3.77509	3.72325	3.67301	3.62432	3.57710	3.53129	3.48685	3.44371	3.40183	3.28323	3.24589	3.20958
5	4.80773	4.71710	4.62990	4.54595	4.46511	4.38721	4.31213	4.23972	4.16987	4.10245	4.03735	3.85498	3.79818	3.74324
6	5.71346	5.57971	5.45182	5.32948	5.21236	5.10020	4.99271	4.88965	4.79079	4.69590	4.60478	4.35216	4.27429	4.19935
7	6.60143	6.41719	6.24214	6.07569	5.91732	5.76654	5.62288	5.48592	5.35526	5.23054	5.11141	4.78448	4.68474	4.58918
8	7.47199	7.23028	7.00205	6.78637	6.58238	6.38929	6.20637	6.03295	5.86842	5.71220	5.56376	5.16042	5.03857	4.92238
9	8.32548	8.01969	7.73274	7.46321	7.20979	6.97130	6.74664	6.53482	6.33493	6.14612	5.96764	5.48732	5.34359	5.20716
10	9.16224	8.78611	8.43533	8.10782	7.80169	7.51523	7.24689	6.99525	6.75902	6.53705	6.32825	5.77158	5.60654	5.45057
11	9.98259	9.53020	9.11090	8.72173	8.36009	8.02358	7.71008	7.41766	7.14457	6.88923	6.65022	6.01877	5.83323	5.65860
12	10.78685	10.25262	9.76048	9.30641	8.88687	8.49867	8.13896	7.80519	7.49506	7.20652	6.93770	6.23371	6.02864	5.83641
13	11.57534	10.95400	10.38507	9.86325	9.38384	8.94269	8.53608	8.16073	7.81369	7.49236	7.19437	6.42062	6.19711	5.98839
14	12.34837	11.63496	10.98565	10.39357	9.85268	9.35765	8.90378	8.48690	8.10336	7.74987	7.42355	6.58315	6.34233	6.11828
15	13.10625	12.29607	11.56312	10.89864	10.29498	9.74547	9.24424	8.78615	8.36669	7.98187	7.62817	6.72448	6.46753	6.22930
16	13.84926	12.93794	12.11839	11.37966	10.71225	10.10791	9.55948	9.06069	8.60608	8.19087	7.81086	6.84737	6.57546	6.32419
17	14.57771	13.56110	12.65230	11.83777	11.10590	10.44665	9.85137	9.31256	8.82371	8.37916	7.97399	6.95423	6.66850	6.40529
18	15.29187	14.16612	13.16567	12.27407	11.47726	10.76322	10.12164	9.54363	9.02155	8.54879	8.11963	7.04716	6.74870	6.47461
19	15.99203	14.75351	13.65930	12.68959	11.82760	11.05909	10.37189	9.75563	9.20141	8.70162	8.24967	7.12797	6.81785	6.53385
20	16.67846	15.32380	14.13394	13.08532	12.15812	11.33560	10.60360	9.95011	9.36492	8.83929	8.36578	7.19823	6.87746	6.58449
25	19.91393	17.93554	16.24696	14.79864	13.55036	12.46933	11.52876	10.70661	9.98474	9.34814	8.78432	7.43377	7.07263	6.74649
30	22.84438	20.18845	17.98371	16.14107	14.59072	13.27767	12.15841	11.19828	10.36961	9.65011	9.02181	7.55088	7.16555	6.82039
35	25.49859	22.13184	19.41120	17.19290	15.36814	13.85401	12.58693	11.51784	10.60857	9.82932	9.15656	7.60910	7.20979	6.85409
40	27.90259	23.80822	20.58448	18.01704	15.94907	14.26493	12.87858	11.72552	10.75696	9.93567	9.23303	7.63805	7.23086	6.86946

Appendix II

WWW/Electronic Resources for Financial Information

This appendix describes some of the many www/electronic resources currently available for gathering industry-level and company specific financial information to support the text and your on-going financial information needs. Some of these resources are free, others are only available on a "subscription" basis, and still others charge a fee per unit of time or information.

Internet Resources www.prenhall.com/revsine

For students, www.prenhall.com/revsine provides homework problem aids, an online study guide tied chapter-by-chapter to the text, In the News items, Internet Exercises, and more.

For faculty, Instructor's Resource Center located at www.prenhall.com/revsine provides access to all faculty supplements—all in one place.

Accounting Organizations

American Institute of Certified Public Accountants: The AICPA is the national, professional organization for all U.S. Certified Public Accountants. This site describes the organization and answers frequently asked questions about becoming a CPA. Member resources and information about the profession are also provided. **www.aicpa.org**

Financial Accounting Standards Board: The FASB sets the standards for financial accounting and reporting in the U.S. Its Internet site provides information about the structure and workings of the organization, current standards, and emerging issues. **www.fasb.org**

International Accounting Standards Board: The IASB sets global financial accounting and reporting standards, promotes rigorous use of those standards, and works toward the convergence of national accounting standards and International Accounting Standards. This site will help you stay abreast of financial accounting and reporting practices worldwide. **www.iasb.org**

Public Companies Accounting Oversight Board. The PCAOB is a private sector, non-profit corporation, created by the Sanbanes-Oxley Act of 2002, to oversee the audits of public companies. The PCAOB has broad authority to investigate and discipline public accounting firms and auditors. **www.pcaobus.org**

Government Agencies

Department of Commerce: This site provides links to other sites, many of which have important information for business people. **www.doc.gov**

Federal Trade Commission: This site contains a large amount of information about the commission itself as well as the laws and regulations it administers. It also contains good links to other business-oriented sites. **www.ftc.gov**

Internal Revenue Service: This is a surprisingly flashy site, full of free information about the IRS and tax-related issues. **www.irs.ustreas.gov**

Securities and Exchange Commission: This site can be helpful for researching specific industries and companies (see next site). **www.sec.gov**

SEC EDGAR Database: This site contains electronic copies of SEC filings by publicly traded companies. The EDGAR project was launched several years ago on a voluntary basis, so not all public companies have been participating since inception. It is an invaluable source for full text 10-K (annual), 10-Q (quarterly) financial information, and corporate proxy statements. **www.edgar-online.com** and **www.tenkwizard.com**

Securities Exchanges

American Stock Exchange: As the nation's second largest floor-based exchange, the AMEX has a significant presence in common stocks, index shares, and equity derivative securities. **www.amex.com**

Chicago Board of Trade: One of Chicago's two major futures and options exchanges, the Board of Trade deals in agricultural products like corn and soybeans and in financial instruments like U.S. Treasury bonds. **www.cbot.com**

Chicago Mercantile Exchange: Chicago's other futures and options exchange, the Merc has plenty of information about futures and options investing, including online courses. There's also information on prices and the products that are traded, from pork bellies to Eurodollars. **www.cme.com**

NASDAQ: The National Association of Securities Dealers Automated Quotation (NASDAQ) exchange Web site has tools that help you track the market, search for stock quotes, research company information, and keep abreast of financial news. **www.nasdaq.com**

New York Stock Exchange: The world's most famous stock exchange. This site provides a history of the exchange and details on the companies that are added each week. You can track the movement of the entire market and there are links to every listed company that has a Web site. **www.nyse.com**

General Business News

Newspapers: For up-to-the-minute business news from around the world and a wealth of information about the economy and specific companies and industries, try the *Financial Times* (**www.news.ft.com**), *Investors Business Daily* (**www.investors.com**) the *New York Times* (**www.nyt.com**), or the *Wall Street Journal* (**www.wsj.com**).

Financial Magazines: *Business Week* (**www.businessweek.com**), the *Economist* (**www. economist.com**), and *Fortune* (**www.fortune.com**) are just three of the many financial magazines that provide business news and analysis on the Internet.

Financial portals: These sites have financial news, stock quotes, earnings projections, and information about companies and industries, plus links to other useful sites. Try Microsoft's MoneyCentral (**www.moneycentral.msn.com**), The Street.com (**www.thestreet.com**), SmartMoney's Map of the Market (**www.smartmoney.com**), or the granddaddy of financial portals, Yahoo! (**finance.yahoo.com**).

Industry and Company Information

BestCalls.com: Listen in via phone or Webcast to the CEO of your favorite company explaining recent performance of the business and its future prospects. The site has live broadcasts and recordings of quarterly earnings announcements and management interviews for nearly 2,600 companies. **www.bestcalls.com**

Bloomberg Personal Online: This is the most recent addition to the Bloomberg Media Family. It provides the interactive investor with data and analysis previously available only on the Bloomberg Terminal, as well as industry and company data (some at a fee) with links to other sources. **www.bloomberg.com**

Businesswire: This site contains information, primarily in the form of press releases, about U.S. companies both large and small. **www.businesswire.com**

Dun & Bradstreet: This site has tips about a variety of business-related topics, as well as marketplace information. You can purchase D&B services here, too. **www.dnb.com**

Hoover's Online: This massive site provides information, some of which you must pay for, about thousands of companies. **www.hoovers.com**

Multex Investor: A great source for brokerage research online. Search the site by company, industry, research provider, or specific analyst. Registration is free but the research isn't. **www.multexinvestor.com**

PR Newswire: This is an excellent source of current news about companies. Hundreds of companies post their press releases here. **www.prnewswire.com**

Commercial Vendors and Databases

Factiva: A joint venture between Dow Jones and Reuters, this service provides current and archival information about companies, industries, and important business events worldwide. The service is available by subscription and provides electronic access to business news wires, financial and trade publications, and company financial reports.

Global Access: This subscription service of Disclosure Incorporated offers a comprehensive searchable financial database of U.S. and international companies. It includes real-time and historical SEC filings, scanned images of annual reports, full-text articles and summaries from the financial and business press, earnings estimates and stock quotes, insider information, and investment research reports. Financial reports are downloadable to Excel or other spreadsheet formats.

Lexis-Nexis: This service is available by subscription. The Accounting Information Library (NAARS) includes the complete financial statement portion of annual reports for more than 4,000 publicly traded companies, plus a vast collection of professional accounting literature.

Standard & Poor's: This service is available by subscription. The COMPUSTAT database consists of fundamental financial and market information on U.S. traded companies with hundreds of financial data items collected from a wide variety of sources including news wire services, news releases, shareholder reports, direct company contacts, and quarterly and annual documents filed with the SEC. The GLOBAL Vantage database contains detailed information on 11,000 companies from 70 countries.

Index